American Casebook Series
Hornbook Series and Basic Legal Texts
Nutshell Series

of

WEST PUBLISHING COMPANY
P.O. Box 64526
St. Paul, Minnesota 55164–0526

ACCOUNTING

Faris' Accounting and Law in a Nutshell, 377 pages, 1984 (Text)

Fiflis, Kripke and Foster's Teaching Materials on Accounting for Business Lawyers, 3rd Ed., 838 pages, 1984 (Casebook)

Siegel and Siegel's Accounting and Financial Disclosure: A Guide to Basic Concepts, 259 pages, 1983 (Text)

ADMINISTRATIVE LAW

Davis' Cases, Text and Problems on Administrative Law, 6th Ed., 683 pages, 1977 (Casebook)

Davis' Basic Text on Administrative Law, 3rd Ed., 617 pages, 1972 (Text)

Davis' Police Discretion, 176 pages, 1975 (Text)

Gellhorn and Boyer's Administrative Law and Process in a Nutshell, 2nd Ed., 445 pages, 1981 (Text)

Mashaw and Merrill's Cases and Materials on Administrative Law–The American Public Law System, 2nd Ed., 976 pages, 1985 (Casebook)

Robinson, Gellhorn and Bruff's The Administrative Process, 2nd Ed., 959 pages, 1980, with 1983 Supplement (Casebook)

ADMIRALTY

Healy and Sharpe's Cases and Materials on Admiralty, 2nd Ed., approximately 900 pages, February 1986 (Casebook)

Maraist's Admiralty in a Nutshell, 390 pages, 1983 (Text)

Sohn and Gustafson's Law of the Sea in a Nutshell, 264 pages, 1984 (Text)

AGENCY—PARTNERSHIP

Fessler's Alternatives to Incorporation for Persons in Quest of Profit, 258 pages, 1980 (Casebook)

AGENCY—PARTNERSHIP—Continued

Henn's Cases and Materials on Agency, Partnership and Other Unincorporated Business Enterprises, 2nd Ed., 733 pages, 1985 (Casebook)

Reuschlein and Gregory's Hornbook on the Law of Agency and Partnership, 625 pages, 1979, with 1981 pocket part (Text)

Seavey, Reuschlein and Hall's Cases on Agency and Partnership, 599 pages, 1962 (Casebook)

Selected Corporation and Partnership Statutes and Forms, 555 pages, 1985

Steffen and Kerr's Cases and Materials on Agency-Partnership, 4th Ed., 859 pages, 1980 (Casebook)

Steffen's Agency-Partnership in a Nutshell, 364 pages, 1977 (Text)

AGRICULTURAL LAW

Meyer, Pedersen, Thorson and Davidson's Agricultural Law: Cases and Materials, 931 pages, 1985 (Casebook)

ALTERNATIVE DISPUTE RESOLUTION

Kanowitz' Cases and Materials on Alternative Dispute Resolution, approximately 1000 pages, 1985 (Casebook)

AMERICAN INDIAN LAW

Canby's American Indian Law in a Nutshell, 288 pages, 1981 (Text)

Getches, Rosenfelt and Wilkinson's Cases on Federal Indian Law, 660 pages, 1979, with 1983 Supplement (Casebook)

ANTITRUST LAW

Gellhorn's Antitrust Law and Economics in a Nutshell, 2nd Ed., 425 pages, 1981 (Text)

Gifford and Raskind's Cases and Materials on Antitrust, 694 pages, 1983 with 1985 Supplement (Casebook)

List current as of September, 1985

T7202—1g

I

LAW SCHOOL PUBLICATIONS—Continued

ANTITRUST LAW—Continued

Hovenkamp's Economics and Federal Antitrust Law, Student Ed., 414 pages, 1985 (Text)

Oppenheim, Weston and McCarthy's Cases and Comments on Federal Antitrust Laws, 4th Ed., 1168 pages, 1981 with 1985 Supplement (Casebook)

Posner and Easterbrook's Cases and Economic Notes on Antitrust, 2nd Ed., 1077 pages, 1981, with 1984-85 Supplement (Casebook)

Sullivan's Hornbook of the Law of Antitrust, 886 pages, 1977 (Text)

See also Regulated Industries, Trade Regulation

ART LAW

DuBoff's Art Law in a Nutshell, 335 pages, 1984 (Text)

BANKING LAW

Lovett's Banking and Financial Institutions in a Nutshell, 409 pages, 1984 (Text)

Symons and White's Teaching Materials on Banking Law, 2nd Ed., 993 pages, 1984 (Casebook)

BUSINESS PLANNING

Epstein and Scheinfeld's Teaching Materials on Business Reorganization Under the Bankruptcy Code, 216 pages, 1980 (Casebook)

Painter's Problems and Materials in Business Planning, 2nd Ed., 1008 pages, 1984 (Casebook)

Selected Securities and Business Planning Statutes, Rules and Forms, 470 pages, 1985

CIVIL PROCEDURE

Casad's Res Judicata in a Nutshell, 310 pages, 1976 (text)

Cound, Friedenthal, Miller and Sexton's Cases and Materials on Civil Procedure, 4th Ed., 1202 pages, 1985 with 1985 Supplement (Casebook)

Ehrenzweig, Louisell and Hazard's Jurisdiction in a Nutshell, 4th Ed., 232 pages, 1980 (Text)

Federal Rules of Civil-Appellate-Criminal Procedure—West Law School Edition, 852 pages, 1985

Friedenthal, Kane and Miller's Hornbook on Civil Procedure, Student Edition, 876 pages, 1985 (Text)

Hodges, Jones and Elliott's Cases and Materials on Texas Trial and Appellate Procedure, 2nd Ed., 745 pages, 1974 (Casebook)

Hodges, Jones and Elliott's Cases and Materials on the Judicial Process Prior to Trial in Texas, 2nd Ed., 871 pages, 1977 (Casebook)

CIVIL PROCEDURE—Continued

Kane's Civil Procedure in a Nutshell, 2nd Ed., approximately 260 pages, 1986 (Text)

Karlen's Procedure Before Trial in a Nutshell, 258 pages, 1972 (Text)

Karlen, Meisenholder, Stevens and Vestal's Cases on Civil Procedure, 923 pages, 1975 (Casebook)

Koffler and Reppy's Hornbook on Common Law Pleading, 663 pages, 1969 (Text)

Marcus and Sherman's Complex Litigation—Cases and Materials on Advanced Civil Procedure, 846 pages, 1985 (Casebook)

Park's Computer-Aided Exercises on Civil Procedure, 2nd Ed., 167 pages, 1983 (Coursebook)

Siegel's Hornbook on New York Practice, 1011 pages, 1978 with 1985 Pocket Part (Text)

See also Federal Jurisdiction and Procedure

CIVIL RIGHTS

Abernathy's Cases and Materials on Civil Rights, 660 pages, 1980 (Casebook)

Cohen's Cases on the Law of Deprivation of Liberty: A Study in Social Control, 755 pages, 1980 (Casebook)

Lockhart, Kamisar and Choper's Cases on Constitutional Rights and Liberties, 5th Ed., 1298 pages plus Appendix, 1981, with 1985 Supplement (Casebook)—reprint from Lockhart, et al. Cases on Constitutional Law, 5th Ed., 1980

Vieira's Civil Rights in a Nutshell, 279 pages, 1978 (Text)

COMMERCIAL LAW

Bailey's Secured Transactions in a Nutshell, 2nd Ed., 391 pages, 1981 (Text)

Epstein and Martin's Basic Uniform Commercial Code Teaching Materials, 2nd Ed., 667 pages, 1983 (Casebook)

Henson's Hornbook on Secured Transactions Under the U.C.C., 2nd Ed., 504 pages, 1979 with 1979 P.P. (Text)

Murray's Commercial Law, Problems and Materials, 366 pages, 1975 (Coursebook)

Nordstrom and Clovis' Problems and Materials on Commercial Paper, 458 pages, 1972 (Casebook)

Nordstrom and Lattin's Problems and Materials on Sales and Secured Transactions, 809 pages, 1968 (Casebook)

Nordstrom, Murray and Clovis' Problems and Materials on Sales, 515 pages, 1982 (Casebook)

Selected Commercial Statutes, 1389 pages, 1985

Speidel, Summers and White's Teaching Materials on Commercial and Consumer Law, 3rd Ed., 1490 pages, 1981 (Casebook)

LAW SCHOOL PUBLICATIONS—Continued

COMMERCIAL LAW—Continued

Stockton's Sales in a Nutshell, 2nd Ed., 370 pages, 1981 (Text)

Stone's Uniform Commercial Code in a Nutshell, 2nd Ed., 516 pages, 1984 (Text)

Uniform Commercial Code, Official Text with Comments, 994 pages, 1978

UCC Article 9, Reprint from 1962 Code, 128 pages, 1976

UCC Article 9, 1972 Amendments, 304 pages, 1978

Weber and Speidel's Commercial Paper in a Nutshell, 3rd Ed., 404 pages, 1982 (Text)

White and Summers' Hornbook on the Uniform Commercial Code, 2nd Ed., 1250 pages, 1980 (Text)

COMMUNITY PROPERTY

Mennell's Community Property in a Nutshell, 447 pages, 1982 (Text)

Verrall and Bird's Cases and Materials on California Community Property, 4th Ed., 549 pages, 1983 (Casebook)

COMPARATIVE LAW

Barton, Gibbs, Li and Merryman's Law in Radically Different Cultures, 960 pages, 1983 (Casebook)

Glendon, Gordon and Osakive's Comparative Legal Traditions: Text, Materials and Cases on the Civil Law, Common Law, and Socialist Law Traditions, 1091 pages, 1985 (Casebook)

Glendon, Gordon, and Osakwe's Comparative Legal Traditions in a Nutshell, 402 pages, 1982 (Text)

Langbein's Comparative Criminal Procedure: Germany, 172 pages, 1977 (Casebook)

COMPUTERS AND LAW

Mason's An Introduction to the Use of Computers in Law, 223 pages, 1984 (Text)

CONFLICT OF LAWS

Cramton, Currie and Kay's Cases-Comments-Questions on Conflict of Laws, 3rd Ed., 1026 pages, 1981 (Casebook)

Scoles and Hay's Hornbook on Conflict of Laws, Student Ed., 1085 pages, 1982 (Text)

Scoles and Weintraub's Cases and Materials on Conflict of Laws, 2nd Ed., 966 pages, 1972, with 1978 Supplement (Casebook)

Siegel's Conflicts in a Nutshell, 469 pages, 1982 (Text)

CONSTITUTIONAL LAW

Engdahl's Constitutional Power in a Nutshell: Federal and State, 411 pages, 1974 (Text)

CONSTITUTIONAL LAW—Continued

Lockhart, Kamisar and Choper's Cases-Comments-Questions on Constitutional Law, 5th Ed., 1705 pages plus Appendix, 1980, with 1985 Supplement (Casebook)

Lockhart, Kamisar and Choper's Cases-Comments-Questions on the American Constitution, 5th Ed., 1185 pages plus Appendix, 1981, with 1985 Supplement (Casebook)—abridgment of Lockhart, et al. Cases on Constitutional Law, 5th Ed., 1980

Manning's The Law of Church-State Relations in a Nutshell, 305 pages, 1981 (Text)

Miller's Presidential Power in a Nutshell, 328 pages, 1977 (Text)

Nowak, Rotunda and Young's Hornbook on Constitutional Law, 2nd Ed., Student Ed., 1172 pages, 1983 (Text)

Rotunda's Modern Constitutional Law: Cases and Notes, 2nd Ed., 1004 pages, 1985, with 1985 Supplement (Casebook)

Williams' Constitutional Analysis in a Nutshell, 388 pages, 1979 (Text)

See also Civil Rights

CONSUMER LAW

Epstein and Nickles' Consumer Law in a Nutshell, 2nd Ed., 418 pages, 1981 (Text)

McCall's Consumer Protection, Cases, Notes and Materials, 594 pages, 1977, with 1977 Statutory Supplement (Casebook)

Selected Commercial Statutes, 1389 pages, 1985

Spanogle and Rohner's Cases and Materials on Consumer Law, 693 pages, 1979, with 1982 Supplement (Casebook)

See also Commercial Law

CONTRACTS

Calamari & Perillo's Cases and Problems on Contracts, 1061 pages, 1978 (Casebook)

Calamari and Perillo's Hornbook on Contracts, 2nd Ed., 878 pages, 1977 (Text)

Corbin's Text on Contracts, One Volume Student Edition, 1224 pages, 1952 (Text)

Fessler and Loiseaux's Cases and Materials on Contracts, 837 pages, 1982 (Casebook)

Freedman's Cases and Materials on Contracts, 658 pages, 1973 (Casebook)

Friedman's Contract Remedies in a Nutshell, 323 pages, 1981 (Text)

Fuller and Eisenberg's Cases on Basic Contract Law, 4th Ed., 1203 pages, 1981 (Casebook)

Hamilton, Rau and Weintraub's Cases and Materials on Contracts, 830 pages, 1984 (Casebook)

Jackson and Bollinger's Cases on Contract Law in Modern Society, 2nd Ed., 1329 pages, 1980 (Casebook)

LAW SCHOOL PUBLICATIONS—Continued

CONTRACTS—Continued

Keyes' Government Contracts in a Nutshell, 423 pages, 1979 (Text)

Reitz's Cases on Contracts as Basic Commercial Law, 763 pages, 1975 (Casebook)

Schaber and Rohwer's Contracts in a Nutshell, 2nd Ed., 425 pages, 1984 (Text)

COPYRIGHT

See Patent and Copyright Law

CORPORATIONS

Hamilton's Cases on Corporations—Including Partnerships and Limited Partnerships, 2nd Ed., 1108 pages, 1981, with 1981 Statutory Supplement and 1985 Supplement (Casebook)

Hamilton's Law of Corporations in a Nutshell, 379 pages, 1980 (Text)

Henn's Cases on Corporations, 1279 pages, 1974, with 1980 Supplement (Casebook)

Henn and Alexander's Hornbook on Corporations, 3rd Ed., Student Ed., 1371 pages, 1983 (Text)

Jennings and Buxbaum's Cases and Materials on Corporations, 5th Ed., 1180 pages, 1979 (Casebook)

Selected Corporation and Partnership Statutes, Regulations and Forms, 555 pages, 1985

Solomon, Stevenson and Schwartz' Materials and Problems on Corporations: Law and Policy, 1172 pages, 1982 with 1984 Supplement (Casebook)

CORPORATE FINANCE

Hamilton's Cases and Materials on Corporate Finance, 895 pages, 1984 (Casebook)

CORRECTIONS

Krantz's Cases and Materials on the Law of Corrections and Prisoners' Rights, 2nd Ed., 735 pages, 1981, with 1982 Supplement (Casebook)

Krantz's Law of Corrections and Prisoners' Rights in a Nutshell, 2nd Ed., 384 pages, 1983 (Text)

Popper's Post-Conviction Remedies in a Nutshell, 360 pages, 1978 (Text)

Robbins' Cases and Materials on Post Conviction Remedies, 506 pages, 1982 (Casebook)

Rubin's Law of Criminal Corrections, 2nd Ed., 873 pages, 1973, with 1978 Supplement (Text)

CREDITOR'S RIGHTS

Bankruptcy Code, Rules and Forms, Law School and C.L.E. Ed., 602 pages, 1984

Epstein's Debtor-Creditor Law in a Nutshell, 3rd Ed., approximately 385 pages, 1986 (Text)

CREDITOR'S RIGHTS—Continued

Epstein and Landers' Debtors and Creditors: Cases and Materials, 2nd Ed., 689 pages, 1982 (Casebook)

Epstein and Sheinfeld's Teaching Materials on Business Reorganization Under the Bankruptcy Code, 216 pages, 1980 (Casebook)

LoPucki's Player's Manual for the Debtor-Creditor Game, 123 pages, 1985 (Coursebook)

Riesenfeld's Cases and Materials on Creditors' Remedies and Debtors' Protection, 3rd Ed., 810 pages, 1979 with 1979 Statutory Supplement and 1981 Case Supplement (Casebook)

White's Bankruptcy and Creditor's Rights: Cases and Materials, 812 pages, 1985 (Casebook)

CRIMINAL LAW AND CRIMINAL PROCEDURE

Cohen and Gobert's Problems in Criminal Law, 297 pages, 1976 (Problem book)

Davis' Police Discretion, 176 pages, 1975 (Text)

Dix and Sharlot's Cases and Materials on Criminal Law, 2nd Ed., 771 pages, 1979 (Casebook)

Federal Rules of Civil-Appellate-Criminal Procedure—West Law School Edition, 852 pages, 1985

Grano's Problems in Criminal Procedure, 2nd Ed., 176 pages, 1981 (Problem book)

Israel and LaFave's Criminal Procedure in a Nutshell, 3rd Ed., 438 pages, 1980 (Text)

Johnson's Cases, Materials and Text on Criminal Law, 3rd Ed., 783 pages, 1985 (Casebook)

Kamisar, LaFave and Israel's Cases, Comments and Questions on Modern Criminal Procedure, 5th ed., 1635 pages plus Appendix, 1980 with 1985 Supplement (Casebook)

Kamisar, LaFave and Israel's Cases, Comments and Questions on Basic Criminal Procedure, 5th Ed., 869 pages, 1980 with 1985 Supplement (Casebook)—reprint from Kamisar, et al. Modern Criminal Procedure, 5th ed., 1980

LaFave's Modern Criminal Law: Cases, Comments and Questions, 789 pages, 1978 (Casebook)

LaFave and Israel's Hornbook on Criminal Procedure, Student Ed., 1142 pages, 1985 with 1985 P.P. (Text)

LaFave and Scott's Hornbook on Criminal Law, 763 pages, 1972 (Text)

Langbein's Comparative Criminal Procedure: Germany, 172 pages, 1977 (Casebook)

Loewy's Criminal Law in a Nutshell, 302 pages, 1975 (Text)

LAW SCHOOL PUBLICATIONS—Continued

CRIMINAL LAW AND CRIMINAL PROCEDURE—Continued

Saltzburg's American Criminal Procedure, Cases and Commentary, 2nd Ed., 1193 pages, 1985 with 1985 Supplement (Casebook)

Uviller's The Processes of Criminal Justice: Investigation and Adjudication, 2nd Ed., 1384 pages, 1979 with 1979 Statutory Supplement and 1983 Update (Casebook)

Uviller's The Processes of Criminal Justice: Adjudication, 2nd Ed., 730 pages, 1979. Soft-cover reprint from Uviller's The Processes of Criminal Justice: Investigation and Adjudication, 2nd Ed. (Casebook)

Uviller's The Processes of Criminal Justice: Investigation, 2nd Ed., 655 pages, 1979. Soft-cover reprint from Uviller's The Processes of Criminal Justice: Investigation and Adjudication, 2nd Ed. (Casebook)

Vorenberg's Cases on Criminal Law and Procedure, 2nd Ed., 1088 pages, 1981 with 1985 Supplement (Casebook)

See also Corrections, Juvenile Justice

DECEDENTS ESTATES

See Trusts and Estates

DOMESTIC RELATIONS

Clark's Cases and Problems on Domestic Relations, 3rd Ed., 1153 pages, 1980 (Casebook)

Clark's Hornbook on Domestic Relations, 754 pages, 1968 (Text)

Krause's Cases and Materials on Family Law, 2nd Ed., 1221 pages, 1983 (Casebook)

Krause's Family Law in a Nutshell, 2nd Ed., approximately 420 pages, 1986 (Text)

Krauskopf's Cases on Property Division at Marriage Dissolution, 250 pages, 1984 (Casebook)

ECONOMICS, LAW AND

Goetz' Cases and Materials on Law and Economics, 547 pages, 1984 (Casebook)

Manne's The Economics of Legal Relationships—Readings in the Theory of Property Rights, 660 pages, 1975 (Text)

See also Antitrust, Regulated Industries

EDUCATION LAW

Alexander and Alexander's The Law of Schools, Students and Teachers in a Nutshell, 409 pages, 1984 (Text)

Morris' The Constitution and American Education, 2nd Ed., 992 pages, 1980 (Casebook)

EMPLOYMENT DISCRIMINATION

Player's Cases and Materials on Employment Discrimination Law, 2nd Ed., 782 pages, 1984 (Casebook)

Player's Federal Law of Employment Discrimination in a Nutshell, 2nd Ed., 402 pages, 1981 (Text)

See also Women and the Law

ENERGY LAW

Rodgers' Cases and Materials on Energy and Natural Resources Law, 2nd Ed., 877 pages, 1983 (Casebook)

Selected Environmental Law Statutes, 786 pages, 1985

Tomain's Energy Law in a Nutshell, 338 pages, 1981 (Text)

See also Natural Resources Law, Environmental Law, Oil and Gas, Water Law

ENVIRONMENTAL LAW

Bonine and McGarity's Cases and Materials on the Law of Environment and Pollution, 1076 pages, 1984 (Casebook)

Findley and Farber's Cases and Materials on Environmental Law, 2nd Ed., 813 pages, 1985 (Casebook)

Findley and Farber's Environmental Law in a Nutshell, 343 pages, 1983 (Text)

Rodgers' Hornbook on Environmental Law, 956 pages, 1977 with 1984 pocket part (Text)

Selected Environmental Law Statutes, 786 pages, 1985

See also Energy Law, Natural Resources Law, Water Law

EQUITY

See Remedies

ESTATES

See Trusts and Estates

ESTATE PLANNING

Kurtz' Cases, Materials and Problems on Family Estate Planning, 853 pages, 1983 (Casebook)

Lynn's Introduction to Estate Planning, in a Nutshell, 3rd Ed., 370 pages, 1983 (Text)

See also Taxation

EVIDENCE

Broun and Meisenholder's Problems in Evidence, 2nd Ed., 304 pages, 1981 (Problem book)

Cleary and Strong's Cases, Materials and Problems on Evidence, 3rd Ed., 1143 pages, 1981 (Casebook)

Federal Rules of Evidence for United States Courts and Magistrates, 337 pages, 1984

Graham's Federal Rules of Evidence in a Nutshell, 429 pages, 1981 (Text)

LAW SCHOOL PUBLICATIONS—Continued

EVIDENCE—Continued

Kimball's Programmed Materials on Problems in Evidence, 380 pages, 1978 (Problem book)

Lempert and Saltzburg's A Modern Approach to Evidence: Text, Problems, Transcripts and Cases, 2nd Ed., 1296 pages, 1983 (Casebook)

Lilly's Introduction to the Law of Evidence, 486 pages, 1978 (Text)

McCormick, Elliott and Sutton's Cases and Materials on Evidence, 5th Ed., 1212 pages, 1981 (Casebook)

McCormick's Hornbook on Evidence, 3rd Ed., Student Ed., 1155 pages, 1984 (Text)

Rothstein's Evidence, State and Federal Rules in a Nutshell, 2nd Ed., 514 pages, 1981 (Text)

Saltzburg's Evidence Supplement: Rules, Statutes, Commentary, 245 pages, 1980 (Casebook Supplement)

FEDERAL JURISDICTION AND PROCEDURE

Currie's Cases and Materials on Federal Courts, 3rd Ed., 1042 pages, 1982 with 1985 Supplement (Casebook)

Currie's Federal Jurisdiction in a Nutshell, 2nd Ed., 258 pages, 1981 (Text)

Federal Rules of Civil-Appellate-Criminal Procedure—West Law School Edition, 852 pages, 1985

Forrester and Moye's Cases and Materials on Federal Jurisdiction and Procedure, 3rd Ed., 917 pages, 1977 with 1985 Supplement (Casebook)

Redish's Cases, Comments and Questions on Federal Courts, 878 pages, 1983 with 1986 Supplement (Casebook)

Vetri and Merrill's Federal Courts, Problems and Materials, 2nd Ed., 232 pages, 1984 (Problem Book)

Wright's Hornbook on Federal Courts, 4th Ed., Student Ed., 870 pages, 1983 (Text)

FUTURE INTERESTS

See Trusts and Estates

IMMIGRATION LAW

Aleinikoff and Martin's Immigration Process and Policy, 1042 pages, 1985 (Casebook)

Weissbrodt's Immigration Law and Procedure in a Nutshell, 345 pages, 1984 (Text)

INDIAN LAW

See American Indian Law

INSURANCE

Dobbyn's Insurance Law in a Nutshell, 281 pages, 1981 (Text)

Keeton's Cases on Basic Insurance Law, 2nd Ed., 1086 pages, 1977

INSURANCE—Continued

Keeton's Basic Text on Insurance Law, 712 pages, 1971 (Text)

Keeton's Case Supplement to Keeton's Basic Text on Insurance Law, 334 pages, 1978 (Casebook)

Keeton's Programmed Problems in Insurance Law, 243 pages, 1972 (Text Supplement)

York and Whelan's Cases, Materials and Problems on Insurance Law, 715 pages, 1982, with 1985 Supplement (Casebook)

INTERNATIONAL LAW

Buergenthal and Maier's Public International Law in a Nutshell, approximately 250 pages, 1985 (Text)

Folsom, Gordon and Spanogle's International Business Transactions – a Problem-Oriented Coursebook, approximately 1150 pages, 1985 (Casebook)

Henkin, Pugh, Schachter and Smit's Cases and Materials on International Law, 2nd Ed., 1152 pages, 1980, with Documents Supplement (Casebook)

Jackson's Legal Problems of International Economic Relations, 1097 pages, 1977, with Documents Supplement (Casebook)

Kirgis' International Organizations in Their Legal Setting, 1016 pages, 1977, with 1981 Supplement (Casebook)

Weston, Falk and D'Amato's International Law and World Order—A Problem Oriented Coursebook, 1195 pages, 1980, with Documents Supplement (Casebook)

Wilson's International Business Transactions in a Nutshell, 2nd Ed., 476 pages, 1984 (Text)

INTERVIEWING AND COUNSELING

Binder and Price's Interviewing and Counseling, 232 pages, 1977 (Text)

Shaffer's Interviewing and Counseling in a Nutshell, 353 pages, 1976 (Text)

INTRODUCTION TO LAW

Dobbyn's So You Want to go to Law School, Revised First Edition, 206 pages, 1976 (Text)

Hegland's Introduction to the Study and Practice of Law in a Nutshell, 418 pages, 1983 (Text)

Kinyon's Introduction to Law Study and Law Examinations in a Nutshell, 389 pages, 1971 (Text)

See also Legal Method and Legal System

JUDICIAL ADMINISTRATION

Carrington, Meador and Rosenberg's Justice on Appeal, 263 pages, 1976 (Casebook)

Nelson's Cases and Materials on Judicial Administration and the Administration of Justice, 1032 pages, 1974 (Casebook)

LAW SCHOOL PUBLICATIONS—Continued

JURISPRUDENCE

Christie's Text and Readings on Jurisprudence—The Philosophy of Law, 1056 pages, 1973 (Casebook)

JUVENILE JUSTICE

Fox's Cases and Materials on Modern Juvenile Justice, 2nd Ed., 960 pages, 1981 (Casebook)

Fox's Juvenile Courts in a Nutshell, 3rd Ed., 291 pages, 1984 (Text)

LABOR LAW

Gorman's Basic Text on Labor Law—Unionization and Collective Bargaining, 914 pages, 1976 (Text)

Leslie's Labor Law in a Nutshell, 2nd Ed., approximately 400 pages, 1986 (Text)

Nolan's Labor Arbitration Law and Practice in a Nutshell, 358 pages, 1979 (Text)

Oberer, Hanslowe and Andersen's Cases and Materials on Labor Law—Collective Bargaining in a Free Society, 2nd Ed., 1168 pages, 1979, with 1979 Statutory Supplement and 1982 Case Supplement (Casebook)

See also Employment Discrimination, Social Legislation

LAND FINANCE

See Real Estate Transactions

LAND USE

Hagman's Cases on Public Planning and Control of Urban and Land Development, 2nd Ed., 1301 pages, 1980 (Casebook)

Hagman's Hornbook on Urban Planning and Land Development Control Law, 706 pages, 1971 (Text)

Wright and Gitelman's Cases and Materials on Land Use, 3rd Ed., 1300 pages, 1982 (Casebook)

Wright and Wright's Land Use in a Nutshell, 2nd Ed., 356 pages (Text)

LEGAL HISTORY

Presser and Zainaldin's Cases on Law and American History, 855 pages, 1980 (Casebook)

See also Legal Method and Legal System

LEGAL METHOD AND LEGAL SYSTEM

Aldisert's Readings, Materials and Cases in the Judicial Process, 948 pages, 1976 (Casebook)

Berch and Berch's Introduction to Legal Method and Process, 550 pages, 1985 (Casebook)

Bodenheimer, Oakley and Love's Readings and Cases on an Introduction to the Anglo-American Legal System, 161 pages, 1980 (Casebook)

LEGAL METHOD AND LEGAL SYSTEM—Continued

Davies and Lawry's Institutions and Methods of the Law—Introductory Teaching Materials, 547 pages, 1982 (Casebook)

Dvorkin, Himmelstein and Lesnick's Becoming a Lawyer: A Humanistic Perspective on Legal Education and Professionalism, 211 pages, 1981 (Text)

Fryer and Orentlicher's Cases and Materials on Legal Method and Legal System, 1043 pages, 1967 (Casebook)

Kelso and Kelso's Studying Law: An Introduction, 587 pages, 1984 (Coursebook)

Kempin's Historical Introduction to Anglo-American Law in a Nutshell, 2nd Ed., 280 pages, 1973 (Text)

Kimball's Historical Introduction to the Legal System, 610 pages, 1966 (Casebook)

Murphy's Cases and Materials on Introduction to Law—Legal Process and Procedure, 772 pages, 1977 (Casebook)

Reynolds' Judicial Process in a Nutshell, 292 pages, 1980 (Text)

See also Legal Research and Writing

LEGAL PROFESSION

Aronson, Devine and Fisch's Problems, Cases and Materials on Professional Responsibility, 745 pages, 1985 (Casebook)

Aronson and Weckstein's Professional Responsibility in a Nutshell, 399 pages, 1980 (Text)

Mellinkoff's The Conscience of a Lawyer, 304 pages, 1973 (Text)

Mellinkoff's Lawyers and the System of Justice, 983 pages, 1976 (Casebook)

Pirsig and Kirwin's Cases and Materials on Professional Responsibility, 4th Ed., 603 pages, 1984 (Casebook)

Schwartz and Wydick's Problems in Legal Ethics, 285 pages, 1983 (Casebook)

Selected Statutes, Rules and Standards on the Legal Profession, 276 pages, Revised 1984

Smith's Preventing Legal Malpractice, 142 pages, 1981 (Text)

Wolfram's Hornbook on Professional Responsibility, Student Edition, approximately 950 pages (Text)

LEGAL RESEARCH AND WRITING

Cohen's Legal Research in a Nutshell, 4th Ed., 450 pages, 1985 (Text)

Cohen and Berring's How to Find the Law, 8th Ed., 790 pages, 1983. Problem book by Foster and Kelly available (Casebook)

Cohen and Berring's Finding the Law, 8th Ed., Abridged Ed., 556 pages, 1984 (Casebook)

Dickerson's Materials on Legal Drafting, 425 pages, 1981 (Casebook)

Felsenfeld and Siegel's Writing Contracts in Plain English, 290 pages, 1981 (Text)

LAW SCHOOL PUBLICATIONS—Continued

LEGAL RESEARCH AND WRITING—
Continued

Gopen's Writing From a Legal Perspective, 225 pages, 1981 (Text)

Mellinkoff's Legal Writing—Sense and Nonsense, 242 pages, 1982 (Text)

Rombauer's Legal Problem Solving—Analysis, Research and Writing, 4th Ed., 424 pages, 1983 (Coursebook)

Squires and Rombauer's Legal Writing in a Nutshell, 294 pages, 1982 (Text)

Statsky's Legal Research, Writing and Analysis, 2nd Ed., 167 pages, 1982 (Coursebook)

Statsky's Legislative Analysis: How to Use Statutes and Regulations, 2nd Ed., 217 pages, 1984 (Text)

Statsky and Wernet's Case Analysis and Fundamentals of Legal Writing, 2nd Ed., 441 pages, 1984 (Text)

Teply's Programmed Materials on Legal Research and Citation, 334 pages, 1982. Student Library Exercises available (Coursebook)

Weihofen's Legal Writing Style, 2nd Ed., 332 pages, 1980 (Text)

LEGISLATION

Davies' Legislative Law and Process in a Nutshell, 279 pages, 1975 (Text)

Nutting and Dickerson's Cases and Materials on Legislation, 5th Ed., 744 pages, 1978 (Casebook)

Statsky's Legislative Analysis: How to Use Statutes and Regulations, 2nd Ed., 217 pages, 1984 (Text)

LOCAL GOVERNMENT

McCarthy's Local Government Law in a Nutshell, 2nd Ed., 404 pages, 1983 (Text)

Michelman and Sandalow's Cases-Comments-Questions on Government in Urban Areas, 1216 pages, 1970, with 1972 Supplement (Casebook)

Reynolds' Hornbook on Local Government Law, 860 pages, 1982 (Text)

Valente's Cases and Materials on Local Government Law, 2nd Ed., 980 pages, 1980 with 1982 Supplement (Casebook)

MASS COMMUNICATION LAW

Gillmor and Barron's Cases and Comment on Mass Communication Law, 4th Ed., 1076 pages, 1984 (Casebook)

Ginsburg's Regulation of Broadcasting: Law and Policy Towards Radio, Television and Cable Communications, 741 pages, 1979, with 1983 Supplement (Casebook)

Zuckman and Gayne's Mass Communications Law in a Nutshell, 2nd Ed., 473 pages, 1983 (Text)

MEDICINE, LAW AND

King's The Law of Medical Malpractice in a Nutshell, 340 pages, 1977 (Text)

Shapiro and Spece's Problems, Cases and Materials on Bioethics and Law, 892 pages, 1981 (Casebook)

Sharpe, Fiscina and Head's Cases on Law and Medicine, 882 pages, 1978 (Casebook)

MILITARY LAW

Shanor and Terrell's Military Law in a Nutshell, 378 pages, 1980 (Text)

MORTGAGES

See Real Estate Transactions

NATURAL RESOURCES LAW

Laitos' Cases and Materials on Natural Resources Law, 938 pages, 1985 (Casebook)

See also Energy Law, Environmental Law, Oil and Gas, Water Law

NEGOTIATION

Edwards and White's Problems, Readings and Materials on the Lawyer as a Negotiator, 484 pages, 1977 (Casebook)

Williams' Legal Negotiation and Settlement, 207 pages, 1983 (Coursebook)

OFFICE PRACTICE

Hegland's Trial and Practice Skills in a Nutshell, 346 pages, 1978 (Text)

Strong and Clark's Law Office Management, 424 pages, 1974 (Casebook)

See also Computers and Law, Interviewing and Counseling, Negotiation

OIL AND GAS

Hemingway's Hornbook on Oil and Gas, 2nd Ed., Student Ed., 543 pages, 1983 (Text)

Huie, Woodward and Smith's Cases and Materials on Oil and Gas, 2nd Ed., 955 pages, 1972 (Casebook)

Lowe's Oil and Gas Law in a Nutshell, 443 pages, 1983 (Text)

See also Energy and Natural Resources Law

PARTNERSHIP

See Agency—Partnership

PATENT AND COPYRIGHT LAW

Choate and Francis' Cases and Materials on Patent Law, 2nd Ed., 1110 pages, 1981 (Casebook)

Miller and Davis' Intellectual Property—Patents, Trademarks and Copyright in a Nutshell, 428 pages, 1983 (Text)

Nimmer's Cases on Copyright and Other Aspects of Entertainment Litigation, 3rd Ed., 1025 pages, 1985 (Casebook)

LAW SCHOOL PUBLICATIONS—Continued

POVERTY LAW

Brudno's Poverty, Inequality, and the Law: Cases-Commentary-Analysis, 934 pages, 1976 (Casebook)

LaFrance, Schroeder, Bennett and Boyd's Hornbook on Law of the Poor, 558 pages, 1973 (Text)

See also Social Legislation

PRODUCTS LIABILITY

Noel and Phillips' Cases on Products Liability, 2nd Ed., 821 pages, 1982 (Casebook)

Noel and Phillips' Products Liability in a Nutshell, 2nd Ed., 341 pages, 1981 (Text)

PROPERTY

Aigler, Smith and Tefft's Cases on Property, 2 volumes, 1339 pages, 1960 (Casebook)

Bernhardt's Real Property in a Nutshell, 2nd Ed., 448 pages, 1981 (Text)

Boyer's Survey of the Law of Property, 766 pages, 1981 (Text)

Browder, Cunningham and Smith's Cases on Basic Property Law, 4th Ed., 1431 pages, 1984 (Casebook)

Bruce, Ely and Bostick's Cases and Materials on Modern Property Law, 1004 pages, 1984 (Casebook)

Burby's Hornbook on Real Property, 3rd Ed., 490 pages, 1965 (Text)

Burke's Personal Property in a Nutshell, 322 pages, 1983 (Text)

Chused's A Modern Approach to Property: Cases-Notes-Materials, 1069 pages, 1978 with 1980 Supplement (Casebook)

Cohen's Materials for a Basic Course in Property, 526 pages, 1978 (Casebook)

Cunningham, Stoebuck and Whitman's Hornbook on the Law of Property, Student Ed., 916 pages, 1984 (Text)

Donahue, Kauper and Martin's Cases on Property, 2nd Ed., 1362 pages, 1983 (Casebook)

Hill's Landlord and Tenant Law in a Nutshell, 2nd Ed., approximately 353 pages, 1986 (Text)

Moynihan's Introduction to Real Property, 254 pages, 1962 (Text)

Uniform Land Transactions Act, Uniform Simplification of Land Transfers Act, Uniform Condominium Act, 1977 Official Text with Comments, 462 pages, 1978

See also Real Estate Transactions, Land Use

PSYCHIATRY, LAW AND

Reisner's Law and the Mental Health System, Civil and Criminal Aspects, 696 pages, 1985 (Casebooks)

REAL ESTATE TRANSACTIONS

Bruce's Real Estate Finance in a Nutshell, 2nd Ed., 262 pages, 1985 (Text)

REAL ESTATE TRANSACTIONS—Continued

Maxwell, Riesenfeld, Hetland and Warren's Cases on California Security Transactions in Land, 3rd Ed., 728 pages, 1984 (Casebook)

Nelson and Whitman's Cases on Real Estate Transfer, Finance and Development, 2nd Ed., 1114 pages, 1981, with 1986 Supplement (Casebook)

Nelson and Whitman's Hornbook on Real Estate Finance Law, 2nd Ed., Student Ed., approximately 900 pages, 1985 (Text)

Osborne's Cases and Materials on Secured Transactions, 559 pages, 1967 (Casebook)

REGULATED INDUSTRIES

Gellhorn and Pierce's Regulated Industries in a Nutshell, 394 pages, 1982 (Text)

Morgan, Harrison and Verkuil's Cases and Materials on Economic Regulation of Business, 2nd Ed., 670 pages, 1985 (Casebook)

Pozen's Financial Institutions: Cases, Materials and Problems on Investment Management, 844 pages, 1978 (Casebook)

See also Mass Communication Law, Banking Law

REMEDIES

Dobbs' Hornbook on Remedies, 1067 pages, 1973 (Text)

Dobbs' Problems in Remedies, 137 pages, 1974 (Problem book)

Dobbyn's Injunctions in a Nutshell, 264 pages, 1974 (Text)

Friedman's Contract Remedies in a Nutshell, 323 pages, 1981 (Text)

Leavell, Love and Nelson's Cases and Materials on Equitable Remedies and Restitution, 3rd Ed., 704 pages, 1980 (Casebook)

McCormick's Hornbook on Damages, 811 pages, 1935 (Text)

O'Connell's Remedies in a Nutshell, 2nd Ed., 325 pages, 1985 (Text)

York, Bauman and Rendleman's Cases and Materials on Remedies, 4th Ed., 1029 pages, 1985 (Casebook)

REVIEW MATERIALS

Ballantine's Problems

Black Letter Series

Smith's Review Series

West's Review Covering Multistate Subjects

SECURITIES REGULATION

Hazen's Hornbook on The Law of Securities Regulation, Student Ed., 739 pages, 1985 (Text)

Ratner's Securities Regulation: Materials for a Basic Course, 3rd Ed., approximately 1000 pages, 1986 (Casebook)

LAW SCHOOL PUBLICATIONS—Continued

SECURITIES REGULATION—Continued

Ratner's Securities Regulation in a Nutshell, 2nd Ed., 322 pages, 1982 (Text)

Selected Securities and Business Planning Statutes, Rules and Forms, 470 pages, 1985

SOCIAL LEGISLATION

Hood and Hardy's Workers' Compensation and Employee Protection Laws in a Nutshell, 274 pages, 1984 (Text)

LaFrance's Welfare Law: Structure and Entitlement in a Nutshell, 455 pages, 1979 (Text)

Malone, Plant and Little's Cases on Workers' Compensation and Employment Rights, 2nd Ed., 951 pages, 1980 (Casebook)

See also Poverty Law

TAXATION

Dodge's Cases and Materials on Federal Income Taxation, 820 pages, 1985 (Casebook)

Dodge's Federal Taxation of Estates, Trusts and Gifts: Principles and Planning, 771 pages, 1981 with 1982 Supplement (Casebook)

Garbis and Struntz' Cases and Materials on Tax Procedure and Tax Fraud, 829 pages, 1982 with 1984 Supplement (Casebook)

Gelfand and Salsich's State and Local Taxation and Finance in a Nutshell, approximately 240 pages, 1985 (Text)

Gunn's Cases and Materials on Federal Income Taxation of Individuals, 785 pages, 1981 with 1985 Supplement (Casebook)

Hellerstein and Hellerstein's Cases on State and Local Taxation, 4th Ed., 1041 pages, 1978 with 1982 Supplement (Casebook)

Kahn and Gann's Corporate Taxation and Taxation of Partnerships and Partners, 2nd Ed., 1204 pages, 1985 (Casebook)

Kragen and McNulty's Cases and Materials on Federal Income Taxation: Individuals, Corporations, Partnerships, 4th Ed., 1287 pages, 1985 (Casebook)

McNulty's Federal Estate and Gift Taxation in a Nutshell, 3rd Ed., 509 pages, 1983 (Text)

McNulty's Federal Income Taxation of Individuals in a Nutshell, 3rd Ed., 487 pages, 1983 (Text)

Posin's Hornbook on Federal Income Taxation of Individuals, Student Ed., 491 pages, 1983 with 1985 pocket part (Text)

Rice and Solomon's Problems and Materials in Federal Income Taxation, 3rd Ed., 670 pages, 1979 (Casebook)

Rose and Raskind's Advanced Federal Income Taxation: Corporate Transactions—Cases, Materials and Problems, 955 pages, 1978 (Casebook)

Selected Federal Taxation Statutes and Regulations, 1402 pages, 1985

TAXATION—Continued

Soboloff and Weidenbruch's Federal Income Taxation of Corporations and Stockholders in a Nutshell, 362 pages, 1981 (Text)

TORTS

Christie's Cases and Materials on the Law of Torts, 1264 pages, 1983 (Casebook)

Dobbs' Torts and Compensation—Personal Accountability and Social Responsibility for Injury, 955 pages, 1985 (Casebook)

Green, Pedrick, Rahl, Thode, Hawkins, Smith and Treece's Cases and Materials on Torts, 2nd Ed., 1360 pages, 1977 (Casebook)

Green, Pedrick, Rahl, Thode, Hawkins, Smith, and Treece's Advanced Torts: Injuries to Business, Political and Family Interests, 2nd Ed., 544 pages, 1977 (Casebook)—reprint from Green, et al. Cases and Materials on Torts, 2nd Ed., 1977

Keeton, Keeton, Sargentich and Steiner's Cases and Materials on Torts, and Accident Law, 1360 pages, 1983 (Casebook)

Kionka's Torts in a Nutshell: Injuries to Persons and Property, 434 pages, 1977 (Text)

Malone's Torts in a Nutshell: Injuries to Family, Social and Trade Relations, 358 pages, 1979 (Text)

Prosser and Keeton's Hornbook on Torts, 5th Ed., Student Ed., 1286 pages, 1984 (Text)

Shapo's Cases on Tort and Compensation Law, 1244 pages, 1976 (Casebook)

See also Products Liability

TRADE REGULATION

McManis' Unfair Trade Practices in a Nutshell, 444 pages, 1982 (Text)

Oppenheim, Weston, Maggs and Schechter's Cases and Materials on Unfair Trade Practices and Consumer Protection, 4th Ed., 1038 pages, 1983 (Casebook)

See also Antitrust, Regulated Industries

TRIAL AND APPELLATE ADVOCACY

Appellate Advocacy, Handbook of, 249 pages, 1980 (Text)

Bergman's Trial Advocacy in a Nutshell, 402 pages, 1979 (Text)

Binder and Bergman's Fact Investigation: From Hypothesis to Proof, 354 pages, 1984 (Coursebook)

Goldberg's The First Trial (Where Do I Sit?, What Do I Say?) in a Nutshell, 396 pages, 1982 (Text)

Haydock, Herr and Stempel's, Fundamentals of Pre-Trial Litigation, 768 pages, 1985 (Casebook)

Hegland's Trial and Practice Skills in a Nutshell, 346 pages, 1978 (Text)

Hornstein's Appellate Advocacy in a Nutshell, 325 pages, 1984 (Text)

LAW SCHOOL PUBLICATIONS—Continued

TRIAL AND APPELLATE ADVOCACY— Continued

Jeans' Handbook on Trial Advocacy, Student Ed., 473 pages, 1975 (Text)

McElhaney's Effective Litigation, 457 pages, 1974 (Casebook)

Nolan's Cases and Materials on Trial Practice, 518 pages, 1981 (Casebook)

Parnell and Shellhaas' Cases, Exercises and Problems for Trial Advocacy, 171 pages, 1982 (Coursebook)

Sonsteng, Haydock and Boyd's The Trialbook: A Total System for Preparation and Presentation of a Case, Student Ed., 404 pages, 1984 (Coursebook)

TRUSTS AND ESTATES

Atkinson's Hornbook on Wills, 2nd Ed., 975 pages, 1953 (Text)

Averill's Uniform Probate Code in a Nutshell, 425 pages, 1978 (Text)

Bogert's Hornbook on Trusts, 5th Ed., 726 pages, 1973 (Text)

Clark, Lusky and Murphy's Cases and Materials on Gratuitous Transfers, 3rd Ed., 970 pages, 1985 (Casebook)

Gulliver's Cases and Materials on Future Interests, 624 pages, 1959 (Casebook)

Gulliver's Introduction to the Law of Future Interests, 87 pages, 1959 (Casebook)— reprint from Gulliver's Cases and Materials on Future Interests, 1959

McGovern's Cases and Materials on Wills, Trusts and Future Interests: An Introduction to Estate Planning, 750 pages, 1983 (Casebook)

Mennell's Cases and Materials on California Decedent's Estates, 566 pages, 1973 (Casebook)

TRUSTS AND ESTATES—Continued

Mennell's Wills and Trusts in a Nutshell, 392 pages, 1979 (Text)

Powell's The Law of Future Interests in California, 91 pages, 1980 (Text)

Simes' Hornbook on Future Interests, 2nd Ed., 355 pages, 1966 (Text)

Uniform Probate Code, 5th Ed., Official Text With Comments, 384 pages, 1977

Waggoner's Future Interests in a Nutshell, 361 pages, 1981 (Text)

WATER LAW

Getches' Water Law in a Nutshell, 439 pages, 1984 (Text)

Sax and Abram's Cases and Materials on Legal Control of Water Resources in the United States, approximately 980 pages, 1986 (Casebook)

Trelease's Cases and Materials on Water Law, 3rd Ed., 833 pages, 1979, with 1984 Supplement (Casebook)

See also Energy Law, Natural Resources Law, Environmental Law

WILLS

See Trusts and Estates

WOMEN AND THE LAW

Kay's Text, Cases and Materials on Sex-Based Discrimination, 2nd Ed., 1045 pages, 1981, with 1986 Supplement (Casebook)

Thomas' Sex Discrimination in a Nutshell, 399 pages, 1982 (Text)

See also Employment Discrimination

WORKERS' COMPENSATION

See Social Legislation

CORPORATIONS

LAW AND POLICY

MATERIALS AND PROBLEMS

By

LEWIS D. SOLOMON

George Washington University

RUSSELL B. STEVENSON, Jr.

George Washington University

DONALD E. SCHWARTZ

Georgetown University

AMERICAN CASEBOOK SERIES

ST. PAUL, MINN.

WEST PUBLISHING CO.

1982

Library of Congress Cataloging in Publication Data

Solomon, Lewis D.

 Materials and problems on the law and policies on corporations.

 (American casebook series)

 Includes index.

  1. Corporation law—United States—Cases. I. Stevenson, Russell B. II. Schwartz, Donald E., 1930– . III. Title. IV. Series.

KF1413.S63 1982 346.73′066 82–11128
         347.30666

ISBN 0–314–65583–2

S., S. & S. Law & Pol.Corps. ACB

2nd Reprint—1985

PREFACE

Our principal reason for adding yet another casebook to an already well-populated field is that, in the course of a combined experience of several decades of teaching corporations, we have become firmly convinced that the most effective pedagogical approach to the course (as well as to a number of other traditional law school subjects) is some variant of the so-called "problem method." And, although it is possible to employ that approach through the vehicle of a conventional casebook, we have found that solution considerably less than ideal. We have therefore set out to create from scratch a set of materials specifically designed to facilitate the use of the problem method.

While the problem method has been both the reason for undertaking this project and its theme, we have on occasion departed from this approach in favor of more traditional techniques, when to do so seemed appropriate. We are aware, moreover, that not all teachers will want to use the materials in the same way (we do not ourselves) and have therefore arranged them in such a way as to allow the maximum flexibility in the use, or nonuse, of the problems. It should, in fact, be possible to use the book in a quite conventional manner, making little or no reference to the problems.

We believe there are advantages to the problem method in a course such as corporations. First, by the second year students are convinced (although not always correctly) that they have learned all there is to know about reading cases; they tend, accordingly, to be bored by a pedagogical approach that emphasizes analyzing cases and extracting the law from them.

Second, during the first year of the typical law school curriculum, students learn to "make the arguments" on both sides of every issue, but are all too seldom given much explicit exercise in developing the all-important qualities of judgment that distinguish the good lawyer from the merely adequate. The problems in the book are consciously designed to make the student confront the hard task of deciding what course of action to recommend in the face of a legal situation that is often unclear. In dealing with the problems, then, the student is called on to go beyond the abstract exercise of reading cases and extracting holdings. Instead he or she is encouraged to use the cases, statutes, and other materials as a practicing lawyer would: as tools to assist in resolving a concrete problem. Indeed, that is how lawyers, and surely how business lawyers, spend most of their time.

PREFACE

Third, the conventional law school course often gives too little attention to developing legal skills other than case analysis. This is particularly unfortunate in a course such as corporations in which the great bulk of the practice is planning and counselling rather than litigation. We have, therefore, attempted to design the problems to afford the teacher convenient opportunities to give the students exercise in planning, counselling, interviewing, negotiating, drafting, advocacy, litigation, statutory construction, and policymaking.

While the bulk of the material covered by the book will be familiar to the experienced teacher of corporation law, we have endeavored also to present material in several areas that are ignored or only touched lightly by most casebooks in the field. The treatment of the ethical problems that most often confront the corporate lawyer is, for example, quite specific. We have also included in a substantial amount of material on corporate accountability and corporate governance, topics that are not only important of themselves but have assumed increasing practical importance to corporate counsel over the last few years. Presenting this material in the form of carefully focussed problems helps, we have found, to avoid the fuzzy open-endedness that too often characterizes class discussion in these areas.

Most teachers of corporation law have found that the majority of second-year law students lack even a rudimentary understanding of what a corporation is and how it functions. We try to deal with this problem at the beginning of the book. Chapters 2 and 3 of the book introduce the student early on to some of the basic concepts that will be explored in greater detail in the rest of the course. The study of *First National Bank of Boston v. Bellotti* gives the teacher the opportunity to discuss the role of corporations in the society, some of the legal differences between corporate and natural persons, and the use of the law to regulate the behavior of large economic institutions. The case is also sufficiently topical and the policy issues it confronts sufficiently interesting that it should help to seize the students' attention at the outset and convince them that preconceptions they may have harbored about the dryness of corporation law are not well-founded.

The Chespeake Marine Services problem in the third chapter is intended to introduce some of the fundamental concepts of the law of corporations, including the duty of care and the duty of loyalty; to illustrate judicial attitudes toward the interaction of the common law with a corporation statute; and perhaps most important, to provide the student with a basic understanding of the structure of the corporation and the interaction of its various elements. In short, the teacher should be able to use these two chapters to provide an overview of the entire course, an undertaking which we believe to be extremely useful to the teaching of a subject matter that is normally completely outside the experience of the students. We strongly urge the teacher to overcome the urge to skip over these chapters "to save time;" we believe that the investment of three or four class hours to provide an overview of the course at the beginning will be well repaid later on.

We also believe that it helps the comprehension of a student, without a substantial background in business, to begin grappling with the legal problems of the corporation in the context of small business. In Chapters 5 and 6 we use an elementary problem of acquiring a small enterprise and devising a corporate form for it.

Most students also come to the course totally without any feeling for the basic business and accounting concepts that underlie the law of corporations. We have attempted, therefore, to furnish material in Chapter 5 to provide the student enough familiarity with these concepts to be able to grapple with their more complex application to the cases and materials that follow.

We have placed a great deal of emphasis throughout the book on the construction and use of statutes and regulations, wherever possible referring the student to the particular sections that appear relevant to a given problem. In light of its widespread influence we have used the Model Business Corporation Act as the basic text, although we have tried to point out the differing approaches taken by Delaware, New York, California and other jurisdictions wherever appropriate. It should be possible with only modest effort to adapt the book to a focus on some other state statute if that is preferable.

The book is designed to be supplemented by the West Publishing Company's Selected Corporation and Partnership Statutes, Regulations and Forms which contains in convenient form the Model Business Corporation Act, the Delaware General Corporation Law, various other relevant statutes, applicable portions of the federal securities laws and rules, and sample articles of incorporation, by-laws, and other forms.

As to editorial details, citations in the texts of cases and other material, as well as the footnotes of courts and commentators, have been omitted without so specifying. The footnotes of decisions and excerpts from books and articles bear the original number; those of the authors are indicated by asterisks and similar symbols.

A teacher's manual is available from the publisher. It contains further details and suggestions as to how the book and the problems might be used.

We wish to express our gratitude to the numerous typists and student research assistants who labored with us as the book metamorphasized through numerous drafts. We are particularly indebted to Professor Jeffrey D. Bauman of Georgetown Law School who had the courage, if not the wisdom, to teach his own course from an earlier version of the book and from whose many useful suggestions we profited enormously. We are grateful to Professor William Klein of U.C.L.A. Law School for several helpful suggestions. Last, but far from least, we wish to thank our students—both those the teaching of whom taught us much of what we know of the law of corporations and inspired us to undertake the writing of this book, and those who served as patient guinea pigs on whom we tried out three draft editions and whose reactions and constructive criticism added much to the final product.

ACKNOWLEDGEMENTS

The following copyright holders have graciously consented to the reprinting of excerpts from their published works:

American Bar Association, Code of Professional Responsibility EC 4-1, 4-2, DR 4-101, EC 5-14, 5-15, 5-18, 5-19, DR 5-105, EC 6-1, EC 7-5, 7-8, DR 7-101, 7-102;

A. Berle and G. Means, The Modern Corporation and Private Property (rev. ed. 1968), Copyright © 1968 by Adolf A. Berle;

Berle, The Price of Power: Sale of Corporate Control, 50 Corn.L.Q. 628 (1965);

Berle, The Theory of Enterprise Liability, 47 Colum.L.Rev. 343 (1947);

Brudney and Chirelstein, A Restatement of Corporate Freezeouts, 87 Yale L.J. 1354 (1977); Reprinted by permission of The Yale Law Journal Company and Fred B. Rothman & Company, from The Yale Law Journal, Vol. 87, 1356-57, n. 9;

Buxbaum, Preferred Stock-Law and Draftsmanship, 42 Calif.L.Rev. 243, 244-47, 253-54, 257-62, 263-66, 290-93 (1954); Copyright © 1954, California Law Review, Inc., Reprinted by permission;

Coffee, Beyond the Shut-Eyed Sentry: Toward a Theoretical View of Corporate Misconduct and an Effective Legal Response, 63 Va.L.Rev. 1099, 1131-39, 1148-49 (1977);

Coffee, Corporate Crime and Punishment: A Non-Chicago View of the Economics of Criminal Sanctions, 17 Am.Crim.L.Rev. 419, 459-61 (1980);

Coffee and Schwartz, The Survival of the Derivative Suit: An Evaluation and a Proposal for Legislative Reform, 81 Colum.L.Rev. 261 (1981);

Comment, Corporate Opportunity, 74 Harv.L.Rev. 765, 770-71 (1961); Copyright © (1961) by The Harvard Law Review Association;

A. Conard, Corporations in Perspective 11-12 (1976);

Conard, A Behavioral Analysis of Directors' Liability for Negligence, 1972 Duke L.J. 895, 899-903, 907-909, 912-916; Copyright © (1972), Duke University School of Law;

Conard, Reflections on Public Interest Directors, 75 Mich.L.Rev. 941, 959-960 (1977);

Conference on Codification of the Federal Securities Laws, 22 Bus. Law. 793, 922 (1967); Copyright (1967) by the American Bar Association. All rights reserved. Reproduction with the permission of the American

ACKNOWLEDGEMENTS

Bar Association and its Section of Corporation, Banking and Business Law.

Cutler, Remarks in Commentaries on Corporate Structure and Governance 374 (D. Schwartz ed. 1979); Copyright 1979 by the American Law Institute. Reprinted with the permission of the American Law Institute—American Bar Association Committee on Continuing Professional Education;

Developments in the Law—Conflicts of Interest in the Legal Profession, 94 Harv.L.Rev. 1244, 1339–1342 (1981); Copyright © (1981) by the Harvard Law Review Association;

Dooley, Enforcement of Insider Trading Restrictions, 66 Va.L.Rev. 1, 24–5 (1980);

M. Eisenberg, The Structure of the Corporation, 56–62, 77–84, 113–22 (1976);

Folk, De Facto Mergers in Delaware: Hariton v. Arco Electronics, Inc., 49 Va.L.Rev. 1261, 1280–81 (1963);

M. Friedman, Capitalism & Freedom 133–34 (1962); Reprinted from Capitalism and Freedom by Milton Friedman by permission of the University of Chicago Press; Copyright © (1962) University of Chicago Press;

Friend, Discussion and Questions from the Floor, in Economic Policy and the Regulation of Corporate Securities 115–117 (H. Manne ed. 1969);

Haudek, The Settlement and Dismissal of Stockholder Action-Part I, 22 Sw.L.J. 767 (1968); Copyright © 1968, Southern Methodist University;

Hetherington and Dooley, Illiquidity and Exploitation: A Proposed Statutory Solution to the Remaining Close Corporation Problem, 63 Va.L. Rev. 1, 26–7 (1977);

Hutson, 12 C.P.S. (BNA) the Annual Stockholders' Meeting (1980);

J. W. Hurst, The Legitimacy of the Business Corporation in the Law of the United States 4 (1970);

L. Kelso and P. Hetter, Two Factor Theory 262–63 (Vintage Book ed. 1967);

L. Loss, Securities Regulation 34, 124–26 (2d ed. 1961);

Manne, Mergers and the Market for Corporate Control, Reprinted from 110 Journal of Political Economy 112–14 by Henry L. Manne by permission of the University of Chicago Press. Copyright 1965 by the University of Chicago;

Manne, Shareholder Social Proposals Viewed by an Opponent, 24 Stan.L.Rev. 481, 492–3 (1972);

ACKNOWLEDGEMENTS

Manne, What Kind of Controls on Insider Trading Do We Need?, in the Attack on Corporate America 121–24 (M. Johnson ed. 1978); Copyright © Law and Economic Center, University of Miami;

Manning, A Concise Textbook on Legal Capital 1–35 (2d ed. 1981);

Manning, The Shareholder's Appraisal Remedy: An Essay for Frank Coker, 72 Yale L.J. 223, 246–47 (1962); Reprinted by permission of The Yale Law Journal Company and Fred B. Rothman & Company from The Yale Law Journal, Vol. 72, pp. 223, 246–47;

B. Manning, A Taxonomy of Corporate Law Reform, in Commentaries on Corporate Structure and Governance 120–122, 124, 128–129 (D. Schwartz ed. 1979); Copyright 1979 by The American Law Institute. Reprinted with the permission of The American Law Institute—American Bar Association Committee on Continuing Professional Education;

Marsh, Are Directors Trustees? Conflict of Interest and Corporate Morality, 22 Bus.Law. 35, 36–44, 48–49 (1966); Copyright (1966) by the American Bar Association. All rights reserved. Reproduced with the permission of the American Bar Association and its Section of Corporation, Banking and Business Law;

Merrill, Lynch, Pierce, Fenner & Smith Inc., How to Read a Financial Report, adapted and reprinted by permission;

Model Rules of Professional Conduct, Excerpted from Model Rules of Professional Conduct, May 30, 1981, Copyright American Bar Association;

R. Nader, M. Green, J. Seligman, Taming the Giant Corporation 108 (1976);

A. Nevins & F. Hill Ford: Expansion and Challenge 1915–1933, 97, 99–100, 105 (1957);

L. Nizer, My Life in Court 247, 448–49 (1961); Copyright © (1961), by Louis Nizer, Reprinted by permission of Doubleday & Company, Inc.;

Note, Authority of a Corporation President to Bind the Corporation by Virtue of His Office, 50 Yale L.J. 348 (1940); Reprinted by permission of The Yale Law Journal Company and Fred B. Rothman & Company from The Yale Law Journal Vol. 50, pp. 348, 350–53;

Palmieri, Lawyers Are the Key to Corporate Governance, in Commentaries on Corporate Structure and Governance 365, 367–68 (D. Schwartz ed. 1979); Copyright 1979 by The American Law Institute. Reprinted with the permission of The American Law Institute—American Bar Association Committee on Continuing Professional Education;

R. Posner, Antitrust Law: An Economic Perspective 225–26 (1976); Reprinted from Antitrust Law, An Economic Perspective by Richard Posner, by permission of the University of Chicago Press; Copyright © (1976), University of Chicago Press;

ACKNOWLEDGEMENTS

R. Posner, Economic Analysis of Law 124–126, 292–295 (2d ed. 1977);

Ratner, Rule 10b–5 libretto;

Redlich, Lawyers, the Temple, and the Market Place, 30 Bus.Law. 65 (March, 1975); Copyright 1975 by the American Bar Association. All rights reserved. Reproduced with the permission of the American Bar Association and its Section of Corporation, Banking and Business Law;

Schneider and Manko, Going Public—Practice, Procedure and Consequences, 15 Vill.L.Rev. 283, 290–294, 296–300 (1970), Reprinted with permission from Villanova Law Review, Volume 15 No. 2, pp. 283–312; Copyright © 1970 by Villanova University;

Schotland, Unsafe At Any Price: A Reply to Manne, Insider Trading and the Stock Market, 53 Va.L.Rev. 1425, 1440–43, 1447–51 (1967);

Schwartz, The Public-Interest Proxy Contest: Reflections on Campaign GM, 69 Mich.L.Rev. 419 (1971);

T. Shaffer, Legal Interviewing and Counseling 39–45 (1976);

J. Sobeloff, Tax and Business Organization Aspects of Small Business 3–27 (1974); Copyright 1974 by The American Law Institute. Reprinted with the permission of The American Law Institute—American Bar Association Committee on Continuing Professional Education;

Solomon, Restructuring the Corporate Board of Directors: Fond Hope-Faint Promise? 76 Mich.L.Rev. 581, 594–97 (1978);

Sommer, Should Corporate Laws Function to Restrain Antisocial and Illegal Conduct?, in Commentaries on Corporate Structure and Governance 257 (D. Schwartz ed. 1979); Copyright 1979 by The American Law Institute. Reprinted with the permission of The American Law Institute—American Bar Association Committee on Continuing Professional Education;

R. Stevenson, Corporations and Information: Secrecy, Access and Disclosure 80–82 (1980); published by the Johns Hopkins University Press;

Stevenson, Corporation and Social Responsibility: In Search of the Corporate Soul, 42 Geo.Wash.L.Rev. 709, 718–720 (1974);

Stevenson, The Corporation as a Political Institution, 8 Hofstra L. Rev. 39, 40–1, 45, 50–1 (1979);

Stewart, Professional Ethics for the Business Lawyer: The Morals of the Market Place, 31 Bus.Law. 463, 463–464, 466–468 (1975); Copyright (1975) by the American Bar Association. All rights reserved. Reproduced with the permission of the American Bar Association and its Section of Corporation, Banking and Business Law;

Stigler, Public Regulation of the Securities Markets 19 Bus.Law. 721, 724–30 (1964); Copyright (1964) by the American Bar Association. All

ACKNOWLEDGEMENTS

rights reserved. Reproduced with the permission of the American Bar Association and its Section of Corporation, Banking and Business Law;

Weiss, Foreign Corrupt Practices Act of 1977: The Anti-Bribery Provisions in Practising Law Institute, Tenth Annual Institute on Securities Regulation 71, 81–82 (A. Fleischer, M. Lipton, & R. Stevenson eds. 1979);

Winter, State Law, Shareholder Protection, and the Theory of the Corporation, 6 J.Legal Stud. 251 (1977).

*

SUMMARY OF CONTENTS

*

TABLE OF CONTENTS

TABLE OF CONTENTS

TABLE OF CONTENTS

TABLE OF CONTENTS

TABLE OF CONTENTS

TABLE OF CONTENTS

TABLE OF CONTENTS

TABLE OF CASES

The principal cases are in italic type. Cases cited or discussed are in roman type. References are to pages.

TABLE OF CASES

TABLE OF CASES

TABLE OF CASES

TABLE OF CASES

TABLE OF CASES

TABLE OF CASES

CORPORATIONS

LAW AND POLICY

MATERIALS AND PROBLEMS

Chapter 1

INTRODUCTION

A. AN HISTORICAL SKETCH OF THE CORPORATION

We tend to view the business corporation today as an association of individuals, organized to further a common purpose, and possessing a combination of attributes (*e.g.*, continuity of existence, limited liability, separate legal entity, centralized management and transferability of interests) which distinguishes the corporation from other forms of association. Much of the history of corporations is a chronology of the evolution of those attributes.

At the outset, it must be noted that there is no such thing as a definitive history of corporate development; there is a great deal of disagreement among legal scholars as to the significance of various historical antecedents to the evolution of the modern business corporation. What seems most likely is that there is no single line of descent (A. Conard, Corporations in Perspective 126 (1976)) and that the evolution of the corporation was (and continues to be) an eclectic process, in which those characteristics and practices that reflected current policies and needs were synthesized into the emerging corporate concept, while those that were less adaptable to the current actualities were gradually discarded.

1. DEVELOPMENT IN ENGLAND

The development of corporations in England has been variously traced back to Greece at the time of Solon, to the trading practices of the Assyrians, to practices on the continent, and to the transmission by the Church of the Roman Empire's recognition of the concepts of juristic personality and collective entity.* Other writers argue that practices and concepts recognized in ancient law merely present analogies to later developments, and that English corporations are *sui generis*, having developed in response to English experience. *See, e. g.*, J.W. Hurst, The Legitimacy of the Business Corporation in the Law of the United States 2 (1970).

Early English law of corporations was concerned with ecclesiastical, municipal and charitable bodies, and only later focused on commercial associations. The early ecclesiastical corporation emerged at

* In fact, the concept of collective entity may have predated a concept of individual entity. Primitive law viewed society as an aggregation of families rather than as a collection of individuals. *See*, Fletcher, Cyclopedia Corporations § 1 n. 1, citing Maine, Ancient Law. In Rome, members of a family were subject to parental power, and any rights acquired by a member belonged not to the individual member but to the father, the *paterfamilias*. For a desciption of the Roman family, *see* R. Sohm, Institutes of Roman Law 177–81 (3d ed. 1907).

1

least in part as a device for holding property by the church so that parishes and religious chapters could succeed to property upon the deaths of priests and priors. And it was to these ecclesiastical, municipal and charitable bodies that the concession theory of corporate existence was first applied, *i.e.*, that corporate existence could only be conferred by a grant of the sovereign.

The principal medieval commercial associations were the merchant guilds. Many of these guilds obtained royal charters as a means of obtaining special privileges, especially monopolies of trade. While the royal charter thus conferred privileges, it also served an important function to the sovereign. "The major impetus derived from the need of the national authority to assert itself and to establish its superiority in law over otherwise devisive local governments or interest groups." *Id.* at 3. *See also*, Stevens on Corporations 2 (2d ed. 1949).

To a large extent, the merchant guilds served different purposes than modern corporations and lacked many of the characteristics that we commonly think of as being essential to business corporations. They did develop forms of management and governance similar to the governors and assistants of later English regulated companies. But each member of a guild continued to trade on his own account, subject to the regulations of the guild, and remained individually liable for his own acts. The guilds functioned primarily to regulate trade by their members and to protect the monopoly against the intrusion of nonmembers.

During the period in which the guilds remained active, the Company of the Staple and the Company of the Merchant Adventurers were organized for trading overseas, the former handling the raw commodities of a town and the latter handling the export of manufactured products. The earliest companies were virtually extensions of the guild principle to foreign trade. The members remained individually liable and traded on their own accounts, subject to the regulations of the company, as enforced by a governor and assistants elected by the members. While royal charters for these early regulated companies have been found as early as the fourteenth century (*see* Gower's Principles of Modern Company Law 24 (4th ed. 1979)), they did not become common until the sixteenth century, with the expansion of foreign trade and settlement. Charters were obtained "largely because of the need to acquire a monopoly of trade for members of the company and governmental power over the territory for the company itself." *Id.*

In the sixteenth and early seventeenth centuries the principle of trading on joint stock previously confined to partnerships, was introduced into the regulated companies, which became joint commercial enterprises rather than trade protection associations. The transition was gradual. Probably the company which best typifies the transition to joint stock is the East India Company.

When the East India Company was first chartered in 1600, members could subscribe to joint stock or could carry on trade privately. Initially, each voyage was separately funded, and the proceeds were divided at the end of each voyage. But beginning in 1614, subscriptions to joint stock were taken not for each voyage but for a period of years, and in the 1650's permanent joint stock was introduced. The shares were freely transferable and individual liability was limited to the amount of shares owned. The Company kept a stock transfer book. The capital stock grew to an enormous size, and in 1709 the Company made a large loan to the English government. It appears that the Company was the first corporation engaged in large state operations with a perpetual charter and, most significantly, a permanent capital.

By 1692, England had three large joint stock companies, the East India Company, the Royal African Company, and the Hudson Bay Company. They were treated as extensions of the state and expected to perform important public functions, notably trade. They were given a monopoly in carrying on a particular trade and the right to make regulations with regard to it. In 1692, private trading was finally forbidden to members of joint stock companies.

The transition from the early trading companies to the permanent joint stock company also involved a shift in the function served by incorporation. According to a noted legal historian (J. W. Hurst, The Legitimacy of the Business Corporation in the Law of the United States 4 (1970)):

> From the late sixteenth century royal chartering of companies to develop foreign trade and colonies was a prominent feature of national policy. A royal charter was essential to such ventures. In times of political uncertainty merchants who combined for a foreign venture without explicit royal sanction risked prosecution for criminal conspiracy against the national interest. Moreover, the royal charter legitimized a range of public functions performed by such trading organizations in organizing terms of trade, setting up local governments, controlling customs, and, in effect, making foreign policy in their areas of operation. Thus, in this early phase such corporate privileges as served private profit seeking were an incidental return for the public jobs the corporation undertook. But throughout the late seventeenth century trade began to bulk larger than public functions in the activities of such companies. By the eighteenth century English lawmakers and businessmen alike had come to regard the corporation mainly as a structure useful to private trading operations; public responsibilities receded so far into the background as to become of secondary account.

Trading on joint stock became increasingly frequent throughout the seventeenth century and was extended to companies for domestic operation. The practice of conducting business on a joint stock basis was not confined to incorporated companies. Unincorporated joint stock companies were able to obtain many of the advantages commonly associated with incorporation through use of complex deeds of settlement. The deeds of settlement could provide for transferability of shares, for continuity of life, and for central management. Some writers have suggested that these unincorporated associations, rather than the monopolistic trading companies, were the real forerunners of the modern business corporation. *See, e.g.*, H. W. Ballantine, Corporations 33 (rev. ed. 1946). It seems likely that each form of association borrowed from the other as the two developed side by side. E. Dodd & R. Baker, Corporations 14 (2d ed. 1951).

The beginning of the eighteenth century was characterized by a boom of promotion and speculation in both incorporated and unincorporated companies. The grandiose scheme of the South Sea Company to acquire virtually the entire English National Debt by buying out the debt holders or exchanging their holdings for the Company's stock gave impetus to this boom. When the flood of speculative enterprises was at its height in 1720, Parliament enacted the famous "Bubble Act," "An Act to Restrain the Extravagant and Unwarranted Practice of Raising Money by Voluntary Subscriptions for Carrying on Projects Dangerous to the Trade and Subjects of this Kingdom." The Bubble Act was aimed at the operation of unincorporated joint stock companies with transferable shares and forbade individuals to act as a corporation without a charter. Its actual effect, however, was to restrain the growth of corporations. While the Act permitted incorporation, and some companies succeeded in obtaining charters, the Act reflected a general distrust of corporations and both the Crown and Parliament were hesitant to grant charters. Because the terms of the Bubble Act were vague, and because of the difficulties in obtaining charters, the Act served to encourage the very associations it was designed to destroy. Entrepreneurs sought ways to circumvent the restrictions of the Act and turned increasingly to the use of deeds of settlement as a means of organizing capital and effort. This device "pooled resources in the control of trustees to manage them for designated business purposes. Equity would recognize the transferability of shares in such a pool. By the early nineteenth century such an arrangement might even include limited liability for debts * * *." J. W. Hurst, *supra* at 3. It seems clear that, by the time of its repeal in 1825, the Bubble Act was essentially a dead letter.

2. DEVELOPMENTS OF CORPORATE LAW IN THE UNITED STATES

The principles of the Bubble Act were extended to the American colonies, precluding the formation of unincorporated joint stock companies. Although the Act did not preclude the formation of duly chartered corporations, the population of colonial America was distrustful of such entities as instruments of royal prerogative and antithetical to the ideals of economic equality. It did not take long, however, for the corporation to become acclimated to the American environment. Initially the way was forged by non-business entities such as charities, churches, cities and boroughs, but these were followed shortly by the incorporation of banks, stage and navigation companies, turnpikes and canals and other financial and transportation businesses. During this period charters were granted by special acts of the legislatures, which, although the matter was not free of doubt, were tacitly understood to have acceded to the power of the Crown in the granting of corporate status.

By 1800 there were about 335 incorporated businesses, all of which had been created by special acts of the legislature. For this reason corporate policy during this period was shaped for the most part by legislative practice. But the number of corporations formed in the early 1800's grew geometrically, and to cope with the burden this imposed on the legislatures, charters became increasingly standardized. A corporate charter was also considered a valuable privilege, and the legislative monopoly on the conferral of this privilege created certain obvious temptations, to which some legislators and entrepreneurs inevitably yielded, to their mutual profit. Criticism of the resulting corruption resonated with a growing feeling on the part of the business community that incorporation was a right rather than a privilege, and that there should be equality of opportunity to acquire corporate status, rather than reserving it for a select few. Finally, incorporation was becoming a matter of economic necessity. As industrial and manufacturing concerns grew, individual fortunes were no longer adequate to finance such enterprises. The combination of these factors eventually led ultimately to the passage of general corporation laws allowing any group of persons to organize themselves into a corporation by complying with the prescribed conditions. New York was the pioneer in the enactment of such legislation; the statute passed in that state in 1811 gave the privilege of self-incorporation to the organizers of certain manufacturing companies with capital not in excess of $100,000 and an existence limited to a twenty-year period.

This is not to say that the rapid growth of corporations in size and number went without opposition. Throughout the historical development of the corporation in America there have been those who feared the aggregations of capital and the growing power the corporations seemed to be acquiring in American society, and this period was no exception. But this opposition did little to stem the tide of corporate growth, and other states soon followed New York's lead in encouraging incorporation by enacting general incorporation statutes. Many of the earlier restrictions on size and duration which the special charters had imposed were iifted; a state had little incentive to enact stringent laws as it would only encourage would-be corporations to seek their charters in some other state.

It was not uncommon in the early nineteenth century for the states themselves to become partners in corporate enterprises. One of the reasons for this was that many of the early corporations were involved in transportation and other business that had traditionally been conducted by the state. In addition, it was a good way to give financial support to an enterprise while providing some public accountability (and perhaps enriching the state as well). L. Friedman, A History of American Law 448 (1973). State involvement fell off in the 1830's and '40's however; many of the states' investments went bad in the Panic of 1837, in addition to which there was some public feeling that the states had no business meddling in what was properly the sphere of private capital. Eventually, direct state investment was prohibited altogether.

Thus the period from 1800 to 1850 saw substantial changes in the law of corporations. From its early form as an *ad hoc* organization that was as much a vehicle for conferring monopoly privileges on a small group of investors as it was a legal form for conducting business, the corporation evolved into a distinctive entity legally available to all, in which one was free to shape the organization of one's own business with few restrictions on entry, duration or management. *See id.* at 170.

Having been thus unleashed from the constraints imposed by special charters, the corporation continued to flourish during the latter half of the nineteenth century. The burgeoning of the railroad industry did much to shape the growth of corporations during this period. The management of railway companies necessitated a larger corporate organization, and the capital requirements were so immense that the fortunes of single individuals (especially after the withdrawal of state investment) were inadequate. A variety of financial instruments, for which the corporate form proved convenient, were devised to meet these large capital requirements. Corporations gradually became more dependent on the availability of an open market for corporate securities. And, this was the era when such men as Cornelius Vanderbilt, Jay Gould and James Fisk became known for their "tawdry battles" in the stock exchange.

But once again the rapid growth of corporate power and the unchecked abuses which seemed to follow were disturbing to many. These abuses eventually brought about pressures to reform the internal corporate mechanism and to impose limits on corporate power vis-a-vis society as a whole. By the 1850's and 1860's the device of the shareholders' suit was available to correct corporate fraud, and other doctrines were emerging which were aimed at imposing greater control over corporate management. Railway regulation was a leading public issue in the 1870's, and in the 1880's the Interstate Commerce Commission was created primarily for the purpose of controlling the railroads. In 1890 the Sherman Act was passed to combat the trusts. Thus, while this period by and large was one in which businessmen had a free hand in adapting the corporated instrument to their will, there were nevertheless initial regulatory efforts being imposed to circumscribe some of the power and impact of large corporations.

Two further points. The liberalization of state corporation laws to their enabling mold, starting with New Jersey and culminating with Delaware is considered in Chapter 7, Part B: 4. Federal regulation of securities is discussed in Chapters 12, 13, 19, and 22.

B.   THE MODERN CORPORATION: A QUANTITATIVE OVERVIEW

When we speak of the corporation in modern society we generally have in mind the huge, multibillion-dollar, multimillion shareholder enterprises—those corporate giants whose decisions seem to dominate our day-to-day lives. While it is doubtless true that these organizational behemoths have substantial power in the marketplace, quantitative data reveal that they are far from typical of the American corporation.

The number of active corporations in 1976 has been estimated to be 2,105,000. Statistical Abstract of the United States 563 (1979). In terms of dollar assets, the spectrum of corporate size in the same year has been broken down in the table below.

Assets	Total Assets (Billions)	% Distribution	Number of Active Corps (Thousands)	% Distribution
under $100,000	$38.	.8	1,215.7	57.8
$100,000 – $1 mil.	$230.	4.8	735.1	34.9
$1 mil. – $10 mil.	$335.	7.1	127.0	6
$10 mil. – $25 mil.	$209.	4.4	13.2	.6
$25 mil. – $50 mil.	$218.	4.6	6.2	.3
$50 mil. – $100 mil.	$230.	4.8	3.3	.2
$100 mil. – $250 mil.	$359.	7.6	2.3	.1
$250 mil. and over	$3,124	65.9	2.0	.1

As the table illustrates, over 90 percent of U. S. corporations had assets of under a million, or, stated another way, the proportion of corporate millionaires to the total number of corporations was less than one in ten. Breaking this down even further, the biggest block of corporations have assets between $10,000 and $1,000,000, and the median corporation has assets of slightly under $100,000. A. Conard, Corporations in Perspective 100, 101 (1976). Thus it would appear that in terms of size, corporations are spread along an unbroken spectrum, with the greatest concentration in numbers at the lower end.

It is also apparent from the table that, though corporations with assets of over ten million make up about 1.3 percent of the total number of corporations, they also control 87 percent of the total assets.

In addition, it has been estimated that corporate business owns about 28 percent of the tangible wealth in the United States and that, while this figure has not changed much in the last 50 years, in the period from 1950 to 1969 corporate profits formed a shrinking proportion of the national income. N. Jacoby, Corporate Power and Social Responsibility 35 (1973).

By and large the number of employees of corporations are distributed in much the same way as the dollar value of assets (although this varies dramatically from industry to industry), with a slightly lower ratio of employees to assets in the 100 largest companies. It has been estimated that slightly under half of the total labor force was employed in the corporate sector in 1969, and that less than a quarter worked for companies employing more than two hundred people.

Another important consideration is the number of investors. Though there is less information with regard to this than to other aspects of corporate size, the available data on shareholders appear to fit the general pattern of corporate statistics. In 1971, General Motors, which ranked first in sales, had about 1,360,000 shareholders; Standard Oil of New Jersey, ranked second, had 808,000. But over 90 percent of the total corporations have ten or fewer shareholders, 1 percent have more than one hundred, and fewer than one hundred corporations have more than one hundred thousand. Conard, *supra* at 119.

In summary, it is evident that since the greatest concentration of numbers is found in corporations with assets between $10,000 and $1,000,000 and with less than ten shareholders, if there were such a thing as the typical American corporation it certainly would not be the corporate giant. While an emphasis on the multibillion-dollar enterprise is doubtless valuable to the macroeconomist as an indicator of U. S. production, for the lawyer to have the same focus is misleading. For in the development of a body of corporate law appropriate to govern such diverse entities, it is important that rules of law be considered in light of their applicability to corporations of widely different dimensions.

Chapter 2

INTRODUCTION TO THE LAW OF
CORPORATIONS: PART ONE

For many years the role played by the large corporation in society has been the subject of controversy although the controversy has ebbed and flowed. As independent concentrations of economic—and many would say, social and political—power, corporations have been attacked as lacking in "legitimacy." The exercise of their power has been characterized by some as not "responsible," and by others as not "accountable." Since the shareholders, who are the "owners" of the corporation, do not exercise any effective control over the day-to-day operations of large publicly-held corporations, corporate managers have come to constitute a sort of economic oligarchy who make decisions affecting in important ways the lives of the numerous members of the corporation's various "constituencies" who relate to it as employees, consumers, suppliers, and just ordinary citizens.

The questions raised by this controversy can be divided into two broad classes. First, to what extent can it be said that the corporation does wield "too much" power, that is, power that is not subject to the legitimation of effective mechanisms of social control? Second, by what mechanisms is corporate behavior harnessed to the service of social goals, or, at the least, in the pursuit of private goals, prevented from trammeling the public welfare? The market mechanism—combined with some measure of government regulation—is surely one such mechanism. There are also the internal mechanisms of corporate goverance—and the respective roles played by shareholders and management—to be considered.

Later in these materials we will have the opportunity to discuss these questions in greater detail. We merely raise them here to ask that you keep them in mind as we proceed. Ultimately, in some form, these questions underlie every one of the principles of corporation law we will be confronting.

In the end, the fundamental question, to which all of these others are tied, is, What is the corporation? What is—or should be—the relationship of this juridical "person" to the state, to its shareholders, to its management, and to the rest of society? Those are the questions you should be considering in approaching the first problem and the case that follows.

PROBLEM

CORPORATIONS IN POLITICS

You have recently gone to work in the general counsel's office of a large, publicly-held manufacturing corporation. As one of your first assignments, the general counsel has asked you to assist him in preparing for his participation in a program on the role of corporations in politics. The topic on which he is to speak is independent expenditures by corporations in campaigns for federal office.

The Federal Corrupt Practices Act prohibits corporations and labor unions from making any "contribution or expenditure in connection with any election" for federal office. 2 U.S.C.A. § 441b. While it is clear that this prohibition extends to *direct* campaign contributions to a candidate, the language can be interpreted to allow corporations or labor unions to make *independent* expenditures in support of a particular candidate so long as they are not solicited by or coordinated with the candidate. The Federal Election Commission has, however, issued regulations that take the contrary view, interpreting the Act to bar independent expenditures as well as direct contributions. 11 C.F.R. § 114. That regulation is the subject of some controversy. Your boss is to discuss whether it should be changed so as to permit corporations to expend corporate funds in indirect support of candidates for federal office. He has been asked to confine his remarks to the policy issues associated with the political role of corporations; another panelist will address the First Amendment questions.

In preparing to discuss the matter with your boss you should consider the following questions:

1. Is there a sound basis for believing that the integrity of the political process is more likely to be impaired by political contributions from corporations than by those from individuals?

2. Would the political process suffer if corporations were totally prohibited from making political contributions? In what way?

3. If there are valid reasons for concern about corporate political activities, do they arise simply from the characteristics of a corporation? Is there something about corporate status alone that makes corporate political activities suspect?

4. Is there reason for particular concern about the political activities of *large* corporations? If there are to be prohibitions on corporate political contributions, should there be a distinction based on the size of the corporation? The number of shareholders?

5. How are the interests of shareholders affected by political expenditures made by their corporations? Is the impact of a political expenditure any different from that of any other expenditure of cor-

porate funds? By what mechanisms can shareholders protect their interests? Are they sufficient?

6. By what process does a corporation decide what political candidates or causes it will support? What criteria are relevant to the decision?

FIRST NATIONAL BANK OF BOSTON v. BELLOTTI

435 U.S. 765, 98 S.Ct. 1407, 55 L.Ed.2d 707 (1978),
reh. den. 438 U.S. 907, 98 S.Ct. 3126, 57 L.Ed.2d 1150.

[A Massachusetts statute prohibited a corporation incorporated under the laws of Massachusetts or doing business in the State of Massachusetts from giving or expending anything of value

For the purpose of aiding, promoting or preventing the nomination or election of any person to public office, or aiding, promoting or antagonizing the interests of any political party, or influencing or affecting the vote of any question submitted to the voters, other than one materially affecting any of the property, business or assets of the corporation.

The statute created the irrebuttable presumption that "[n]o question submitted to the voters solely concerning the taxation of income, property or transactions of individuals shall be deemed materially to affect the property, business or assets of the corporation." No similar prohibitions were contained in the statute on the expenditures by individuals conducting similar businesses.

In upholding the constitutionality of the statute, the Massachusetts Supreme Judicial Court stated "that only when a general political issue materially affects a corporation's business property or assets may that corporation claim First Amendment protection for its speech or other activities entitling it to communicate its position on that issue to the general public." 359 N.E.2d 1262, 1290. The appellants, two national banking associations and three business corporations, believe that the adoption of a graduated personal income tax would materially affect their business specifically in the words of the Massachusetts Supreme Judicial Court, by "discouraging highly qualified executives and highly skilled professional personnel from settling, working or remaining in Massachusetts; promoting a tax climate which would be considered unfavorable by business corporations, thereby discouraging them from settling in Massachusetts with "resultant adverse effects" on the plaintiff banks' loans, deposits, and other services; and tending to shrink the disposable income of individuals available for the purchase of the consumer products manufactured by at least one of the plaintiff corporations." 359 N.E.2d at 1266.

The United States Supreme Court held in a five to four decision that the statute constituted an unconstitutional abridgement of speech protected under the First Amendment. The majority noted that the protection of political expression was a major reason for adopting the First Amendment as indispensable in a democracy and "this is no less time because the speech comes from a corporation rather than an individual." 98 S.Ct. at 1416. Adopting the line of reasoning of commercial speech cases, the Court indicated "The inherent worth of the speech in terms of its capacity for informing the public does not depend upon the identity of its source, whether corporation, association, union or individual." 98 S.Ct. at 1416. Mr. Justice Powell writing for the majority then continued:]

III

* * *

In the realm of protected speech, the legislature is constitutionally disqualified from dictating the subjects about which persons may speak and the speakers who may address a public issue. Police Dept. of Chicago v. Mosley, 408 U.S. 92, 96, 92 S.Ct. 2286, 2290, 33 L.Ed.2d 212 (1972). If a legislature may direct business corporations to "stick to business," it also may limit other corporations—religious, charitable, or civic—to their respective "business" when addressing the public. Such power in government to channel the expression of views is unacceptable under the First Amendment. Especially where, as here, the legislature's suppression of speech suggests an attempt to give one side of a debatable public question an advantage in expressing its views to the people,[22] the First Amendment is plainly offended. Yet the State contends that its action is necessitated by governmental interests of the highest order. We next consider these asserted interests.

IV

The constitutionality of § 8's prohibition of the "exposition of ideas" by corporations turns on whether it can survive the exacting scrutiny necessitated by a state-imposed restriction of freedom of speech. Especially where, as here, a prohibition is directed at speech itself, and the speech is intimately related to the process of governing, "the State may prevail only upon showing a subordinating interest which is compelling," Bates v. City of Little Rock, 361 U.S. 516,

---

22. *Cf.* City of Madison, Joint School Dist. No. 8 v. Wisconsin Employment Relations Comm'n, 429 U.S. 167, 175–176, 97 S.Ct. 421, 426–427, 50 L.Ed.2d 376 (1976).

Our observation about the apparent purpose of the Massachusetts Legislature is not an endorsement of the legislature's factual assumptions about the views of corporations. We know of no documentation of the notion that corporations are likely to share a monolithic view on an issue such as the adoption of a graduated personal income tax. Corporations, like individuals or groups, are not homogeneous. They range from great multi-national enterprises whose stock is publicly held and traded to medium-size public companies and to those that are closely held and controlled by an individual or family. It is arguable that small or medium-size corporations might welcome imposition of a graduated personal income tax that might shift a greater share of the tax burden onto wealthy individuals. * * *

524, 80 S.Ct. 412, 417, 4 L.Ed.2d 480 (1960); "and the burden is on the Government to show the existence of such an interest." Elrod v. Burns, 427 U.S. 347, 362, 96 S.Ct. 2673, 49 L.Ed.2d 547 (1976).

* * * [The] [a]ppellee nevertheless advances two principal justifications for the prohibition of corporate speech. The first is the State's interest in sustaining the active role of the individual citizen in the electoral process and thereby preventing diminution of the citizen's confidence in government. The second is the interest in protecting the rights of shareholders whose views differ from those expressed by management on behalf of the corporation. However weighty these interests may be in the context of partisan candidate elections,[26] they either are not implicated in this case or are not served at all, or in other than a random manner, by the prohibition in § 8.

A

Preserving the integrity of the electoral process, preventing corruption, and "sustain[ing] the active, alert responsibility of the individual citizen in a democracy for the wise conduct of government"[27] are interests of the highest importance. Preservation of the individual citizen's confidence in government is equally important.

26. In addition to prohibiting corporate contributions and expenditures for the purpose of influencing the vote on a ballot question submitted to the voters, § 8 also proscribes corporate contributions or expenditures "for the purpose of aiding, promoting or preventing the nomination or election of any person to public office, or aiding, promoting, or antagonizing the interests of any political party." * * * In this respect, the statute is not unlike many other state and federal laws regulating corporate participation in partisan candidate elections. Appellants do not challenge the constitutionality of laws prohibiting or limiting corporate contributions to political candidates or committees, or other means of influencing candidate elections. *Cf.* Pipefitters Local Union No. 562 v. United States, 407 U.S. 385, 92 S.Ct. 2247, 33 L.Ed.2d 11 (1972); United States v. United Automobile Workers, 352 U.S. 567, 77 S.Ct. 529, 1 L.Ed.2d 563 (1957); United States v. CIO, 335 U.S. 106, 68 S. Ct. 1349, 92 L.Ed. 1849 (1948). About half of these laws, including the federal law, 2 U.S.C.A. § 441b (1976 ed.) (originally enacted as the Federal Corrupt Practices Act, 34 Stat. 864), by their terms do not apply to referendum votes. Several of the others proscribe or limit spending for "political" purposes, which may or may not cover referenda. See Schwartz v. Romnes, 495 F.2d 844 (CA2 1974).

The overriding concern behind the enactment of statutes such as the Federal Corrupt Practices Act was the problem of corruption of elected representatives through the creation of political debts. See United States v. United Automobile Workers, *supra*, 352 U.S., at 570–575, 77 S.Ct., at 530–533; Schwartz v. Romnes, *supra*, at 849–851. The importance of the governmental interest in preventing this occurrence has never been doubted. The case before us presents no comparable problem, and our consideration of a corporation's right to speak on issues of general public interest implies no comparable right in the quite different context of participation in a political campaign for election to public office. Congress might well be able to demonstrate the existence of a danger of real or apparent corruption in independent expenditures by corporations to influence candidate elections. *Cf.* Buckley v. Valeo, *supra*, 424 U.S., at 46, 96 S.Ct., at 647; Comment, The Regulation of Union Political Activity: Majority and Minority Rights and Remedies, 126 U.Pa.L.Rev. 386, 408–410 (1977).

27. United States v. United Automobile Workers, *supra*, 352 U.S., at 575, 77 S.Ct., at 533.

* * * According to appellee, corporations are wealthy and powerful and their views may drown out other points of view. If appellee's arguments were supported by record or legislative findings that corporate advocacy threatened imminently to undermine democratic processes, thereby denigrating rather than serving First Amendment interests, these arguments would merit our consideration. *Cf.* Red Lion Broadcasting Co. v. FCC, 395 U.S. 367, 89 S.Ct. 1794, 23 L.Ed.2d 371 (1969). But there has been no showing that the relative voice of corporations has been overwhelming or even significant in influencing referenda in Massachusetts,[28] or that there has been any threat to the confidence of the citizenry in government.

* * * Nor are appellee's arguments inherently persuasive or supported by the precedents of this Court. Referenda are held on issues, not candidates for public office. The risk of corruption perceived in cases involving candidate elections, simply is not present in a popular vote on a public issue. To be sure, corporate advertising may influence the outcome of the vote; this would be its purpose. But the fact that advocacy may persuade the electorate is hardly a reason to suppress it: The Constitution "protects expression which is eloquent no less than that which is unconvincing." Kingsley Int'l Pictures Corp. v. Regents, 360 U.S., at 689, 79 S.Ct., at 1365. We noted only recently that "the concept that government may restrict the speech of some elements of our society in order to enhance the relative voice of others is wholly foreign to the First Amendment * * *." *Buckley*, 424 U.S., at 48–49, 96 S.Ct., at 649.[30] * * *

---

28. In his dissenting opinion, Mr. Justice WHITE relies on incomplete facts with respect to expenditures in the 1972 referendum election, in support of his perception as to the "domination of the electoral process by corporate wealth." The record shows only the extent of corporate and individual contributions to the two committees that were organized to support and oppose, respectively, the constitutional amendment. It does show that three of the appellants each contributed $3,000 to the "opposition" committee. The dissenting opinion makes no reference to the fact that amounts of money expended independently of organized committees need not be reported under Massachusetts law, and therefore remain unknown.

Even if viewed as material, any inference that corporate contributions "dominated" the electoral process on this issue is refuted by the 1976 election. There the voters again rejected the proposed constitutional amendment even in the absence of any corporate spending, which had been forbidden by the decision below.

30. Mr. Justice WHITE argues, without support in the record, that because corporations are given certain privileges by law they are able to "amass wealth" and then to "dominate" debate on an issue. He concludes from this generalization that the State has a subordinating interest in denying corporations access to debate and, correspondingly, in denying the public access to corporate views. The potential impact of this argument, especially on the news media, is unsettling. One might argue with comparable logic that the State may control the volume of expression by the wealthier, more powerful corporate members of the press in order to "enhance the relative voices" of smaller and less influential members.

Except in the special context of limited access to the channels of communication, *see* Red Lion Broadcasting Co. v. FCC, 395 U.S. 367, 89 S.Ct. 1794, 23 L.Ed.2d 371 (1969), this concept contradicts basic tenets of First Amendment jurisprudence. * * *

B

Finally, appellee argues that § 8 protects corporate shareholders, an interest that is both legitimate and traditionally within the province of state law. Cort v. Ash, 422 U.S. 66, 82–84, 95 S.Ct. 2080, 2089–2091, 45 L.Ed.2d 26 (1975). The statute is said to serve this interest by preventing the use of corporate resources in furtherance of views with which some shareholders may disagree. This purpose is belied, however, by the provisions of the statute, which are both underinclusive and overinclusive.

The underinclusiveness of the statute is self-evident. Corporate expenditures with respect to a referendum are prohibited, while corporate activity with respect to the passage or defeat of legislation is permitted, *see* n. 31, *supra*, even though corporations may engage in lobbying more often than they take positions on ballot questions submitted to the voters. Nor does § 8 prohibit a corporation from expressing its views, by the expenditure of corporate funds, on any public issue until it becomes the subject of a referendum, though the displeasure of disapproving shareholders is unlikely to be any less.

The fact that a particular kind of ballot question has been singled out for special treatment undermines the likelihood of a genuine state interest in protecting shareholders. It suggests instead that the legislature may have been concerned with silencing corporations on a particular subject. Indeed, appellee has conceded that "the legislative and judicial history of the statute indicates * * * that the second crime was 'tailor-made' to prohibit corporate campaign contributions to oppose a graduated income tax amendment." Brief for Appellee 6.

Nor is the fact that § 8 is limited to banks and business corporations without relevance. Excluded from its provisions and criminal sanctions are entities or organized groups in which numbers of persons may hold an interest or membership, and which often have resources comparable to those of large corporations. Minorities in such groups or entities may have interests with respect to institutional speech quite comparable to those of minority shareholders in a corporation. Thus the exclusion of Massachusetts business trusts, real estate investment trusts, labor unions, and other associations undermines the plausibility of the State's purported concern for the persons who happen to be shareholders in the banks and corporations covered by § 8.

The overinclusiveness of the statute is demonstrated by the fact that § 8 would prohibit a corporation from supporting or opposing a referendum proposal even if its shareholders unanimously authorized the contribution or expenditure. Ultimately shareholders may decide, through the procedures of corporate democracy, whether their corporation should engage in debate on public issues.[34] Acting through their power to elect the board of directors or to insist upon protective provisions in the corporation's charter, shareholders normally are presumed competent to protect their own interests. In addition to intra-corporate remedies, minority shareholders generally have access to the judicial remedy of a derivative suit to challenge corporate disbursements alleged to have been made for improper corporate purposes or merely to further the personal interests of management.

Assuming, *arguendo*, that protection of shareholders is a "compelling" interest under the circumstances of this case, we find "no substantially relevant correlation between the governmental interest asserted and the State's effort" to prohibit appellants from speaking. Shelton v. Tucker, 364 U.S., at 485, 81 S.Ct., at 250.

V

Because that portion of § 8 challenged by appellants prohibits protected speech in a manner unjustified by a compelling state interest, it must be invalidated. The judgment of the Supreme Judicial Court is *Reversed.*

Mr. Justice WHITE, with whom Mr. Justice BENNAN and Mr. Justice MARSHALL join, dissenting.

* * * [A]s this case comes to us, the issue is whether a State may prevent corporate management from using the corporate treasury to propagate views having no connection with the corporate business. * * * I do not suggest for a moment that the First Amendment requires a State to forbid such use of corporate funds, but I do strongly disagree that the First Amendment forbids state interference with managerial decisions of this kind.

By holding that Massachusetts may not prohibit corporate expenditures or contributions made in connection with referenda involving issues having no material connection with the corporate business, the Court not only invalidates a statute which has been on the books in one form or another for many years, but also casts considerable doubt upon the constitutionality of legislation passed by some 31

---

34. Appellee does not explain why the dissenting shareholder's wishes are entitled to such greater solicitude in this context than in many others where equally important and controversial corporate decisions are made by management or by a predetermined percentage of the shareholders. Mr. Justice WHITE's repeatedly expressed concern for corporate shareholders who may be "coerced" into supporting "causes with which they disagree" apparently is not shared by appellants' shareholders. Not a single shareholder has joined appellee in defending the Massachusetts statute or, so far as the record shows, has interposed any objection to the right asserted by the corporations to make the proscribed expenditures.

* * *

The critical distinction here is that no shareholder has been "compelled" to contribute anything. Apart from the fact, noted by the dissent, that compulsion by the State is wholly absent, the [shareholder] invests in a corporation of his own volition and is [free to withdraw his investment at any time and for any reason.] * * *

States restricting corporate political activity, as well as upon the Federal Corrupt Practices Act, 2 U.S.C.A. § 441b (1976 ed.). The Court's fundamental error is its failure to realize that the state regulatory interests in terms of which the alleged curtailment of First Amendment rights accomplished by the statute must be evaluated are themselves derived from the First Amendment. The question posed by this case, as approached by the Court, is whether the State has struck the best possible balance, *i.e.*, the one which it would have chosen, between competing First Amendment interests. Although in my view the choice made by the State would survive even the most exacting scrutiny, perhaps a rational argument might be made to the contrary. What is inexplicable, is for the Court to substitute its judgment as to the proper balance for that of Massachusetts where the State has passed legislation reasonably designed to further First Amendment interests in the context of the political arena where the expertise of legislators is at its peak and that of judges is at its very lowest. Moreover, the result reached today in critical respects marks a drastic departure from the Court's prior decisions which have protected against governmental infringement the very First Amendment interests which the Court now deems inadequate to justify the Massachusetts statute.

I

There is now little doubt that corporate communications come within the scope of the First Amendment. This, however, is merely the starting point of analysis, because an examination of the First Amendment values that corporate expression furthers and the threat to the functioning of a free society it is capable of posing reveals that it is not fungible with communications emanating from individuals and is subject to restrictions which individual expression is not. Indeed, what some have considered to be the principal function of the First Amendment, the use of communication as a means of self-expression, self-realization, and self-fulfillment, is not at all furthered by corporate speech. It is clear that the communications of profitmaking corporations are not "an integral part of the development of ideas, of mental exploration and of the affirmation of self." They do not represent a manifestation of individual freedom or choice. Undoubtedly, as this Court has recognized, *see* NAACP v. Button, 371 U.S. 415, 83 S.Ct. 328, 9 L.Ed.2d 405 (1963), there are some corporations formed for the express purpose of advancing certain ideological causes shared by all their members, or, as in the case of the press, of disseminating information and ideas. Under such circumstances, association in a corporate form may be viewed as merely a means of achieving effective self-expression. But this is hardly the case generally with corporations operated for the purpose of making profits. Shareholders in such entities do not share a common set of political or social views, and they certainly have not invested their money for the purpose of advancing political or social causes or in an enterprise engaged in the business of disseminating news and opinion. In fact, as discussed *infra*, the government has a strong interest in assuring that investment decisions are not predicated upon agreement or disagreement with the activities of corporations in the political arena.

Of course, it may be assumed that corporate investors are united by a desire to make money, for the value of their investment to increase. Since even communications which have no purpose other than that of enriching the communicator have some First Amendment protection, activities such as advertising and other communications integrally related to the operation of the corporation's business may be viewed as a means of furthering the desires of individual shareholders. This unanimity of purpose breaks down, however, when corporations make expenditures or undertake activities designed to influence the opinion or votes of the general public on political and social issues that have no material connection with or effect upon their business, property, or assets. Although it is arguable that corporations make such expenditures because their managers believe that it is in the corporations' economic interest to do so, there is no basis whatsoever for concluding that these views are expressive of the heterogeneous beliefs of their shareholders whose convictions on many political issues are undoubtedly shaped by considerations other than a desire to endorse any electoral or ideological cause which would tend to increase the value of a particular corporate investment.   *   *   *

*   *   *

It bears emphasis here that the Massachusetts statute forbids the expenditure of corporate funds in connection with referenda but in no way forbids the board of directors of a corporation from formulating and making public what it represents as the views of the corporation even though the subject addressed has no material effect whatsoever on the business of the corporation. These views could be publicized at the individual expense of the officers, directors, stockholders, or anyone else interested in circulating the corporate view on matters irrelevant to its business.

The governmental interest in regulating corporate political communications, especially those relating to electoral matters, also raises considerations which differ significantly from those governing the regulation of individual speech. Corporations are artificial entities created by law for the purpose of furthering certain economic goals. In order to facilitate the achievement of such ends, special rules relating to such matters as limited liability, perpetual life, and the accumulation, distribution, and taxation of assets are normally applied to them. States have provided corporations with such attributes in order to increase their economic viability and thus strengthen the economy generally. It has long been recognized however, that the special status of corporations has placed them in a position to control vast amounts of economic power which may, if not regulated, dominate not only the economy but also the very heart of our democracy, the electoral process. Although Buckley v. Valeo, 424 U.S. 1, 96 S.Ct. 612, 46 L.Ed.2d 659 (1976), provides support for the position that the desire to equalize the financial resources available to candidates does not justify the limitation upon the expression of support which a restriction upon individual contributions entails, the interest of Massachusetts and the many other States which have restricted corporate political activity is quite different. It is not one of equalizing the resources of opposing candidates or opposing positions, but rather of preventing institutions which have been permitted to amass wealth as a result of special advantages extended by the State for certain economic purposes from using that wealth to acquire an unfair advantage in the political process, especially where, as here, the issue involved has no material connection with the business of the corporation. The State need not permit its own creation to consume it. Massachusetts could permissibly conclude that not to impose limits upon the political activities of corporations would have placed it in a position of departing from neutrality and indirectly assisting the propagation of corporate views because of the advantages its laws give to the corporate acquisition of funds to finance such activities. Such expenditures may be viewed as seriously threatening the role of the First Amendment as a guarantor of a free marketplace of ideas. Ordinarily, the expenditure of funds to promote political causes may be assumed to bear some relation to the fervency with which they are held. Corporate political expression, however, is not only divorced from the convictions of individual corporate shareholders, but also, because of the ease with which corporations are permitted to accumulate capital, bears no relation to the conviction with which the ideas expressed are held by the communicator.

* * *

This Nation has for many years recognized the need for measures designed to prevent corporate domination of the political process. The Corrupt Practices Act, first enacted in 1907, has consistently barred corporate contributions in connection with federal elections. This Court has repeatedly recognized that one of the principal purposes of this prohibition is "to avoid the deleterious influences on federal elections resulting from the use of money by those who exercise control over large aggregations of capital." United States v. International Union United Automobile Workers, 352 U.S. 567, 585, 77 S.Ct. 529, 538, 1 L.Ed.2d 563 (1957). Although this Court has never adjudicated the constitutionality of the Act, there is no suggestion in its cases construing it, that this purpose is in any sense illegitimate or deserving of other than the utmost respect; indeed, the thrust of its opinions, until today, has been to the contrary. See *Automobile Workers, supra,* 352 U.S., at 585, 77 S.Ct., at 538.

II

There is an additional overriding interest related to the prevention of corporate domination which is substantially advanced by Massachusetts' restrictions upon corporate contributions: assuring that shareholders are not compelled to support and financially further beliefs with which they disagree where, as is the case here, the issue involved does not materially affect the business, property, or other affairs of the corporation. The State has not interfered with the prerogatives of corporate management to communicate about matters that have material impact on the business affairs entrusted to them, however much individual stockholders may disagree on economic or ideological grounds. Nor has the State forbidden management from formulating and circulating its views at its own expense or at the expense of others, even where the subject at issue is irrelevant to corporate business affairs. But Massachusetts *has* chosen to forbid corporate management from spending corporate funds in referenda elections absent some demonstrable effect of the issue on the economic life of the company. In short, corporate management may not use corporate monies to promote what does not further corporate affairs but what in the last analysis are the purely personal views of the management, individually or as a group.

This is not only a policy which a State may adopt consistent with the First Amendment but one which protects the very freedoms that this Court has held to be guaranteed by the First Amendment. * * *

The Court assumes that the interest in preventing the use of corporate resources in furtherance of views which are irrelevant to the corporate business and with which some shareholders may disagree is a compelling one, but concludes that the Massachusetts statute is nevertheless invalid because the State has failed to adopt the means best suited, in its opinion, for achieving this end. It proposes that the aggrieved shareholder assert his interest in preventing the expenditure of funds for nonbusiness causes he finds unconscionable through the channels provided by "corporate democracy" and purports to be mystified as to "why the dissenting shareholder's wishes are entitled to such greater solicitude in this context than in many others where equally important and controversial corporate decisions are made by management or by a predetermined percentage of the shareholders." * * * The interest which the State wishes to protect here is identical to that which the Court has previously held to be protected by the First Amendment: the right to adhere to one's own beliefs and to refuse to support the dissemination of the personal and political views of others, regardless of how large a majority they may compose. In most contexts, of course, the views of the dissenting shareholder have little, if any, First Amendment significance. By purchasing interests in corporations shareholders accept the fact that corporations are going to make decisions concerning matters such as advertising integrally related to their business operations according to the procedures set forth in their charters and bylaws. Otherwise, corporations could not function. First Amendment concerns of stockholders are directly implicated, however, when a corporation chooses to use its privileged status to finance ideological crusades which are unconnected with the corporate business or property and which some shareholders might not wish to support. * * * There is no apparent way of segregating one shareholder's ownership interest in a corporation from another's. It is no answer to respond, as the Court does, that the dissenting "shareholder * * * is free to withdraw his investment at any time and for any reason." * * * Clearly the State has a strong interest in assuring that its citizens are not forced to choose between supporting the propagation of views with which they disagree and passing up investment opportunities.

Finally, even if corporations developed an effective mechanism for rebating to shareholders that portion of their investment used to finance political activities with which they disagreed, a State may still choose to restrict corporate political activity irrelevant to business functions on the grounds that many investors would be deterred from investing in corporations because of a wish not to associate with corporations propagating certain views. The State has an interest not only in enabling individuals to exercise freedom of conscience without penalty but also in eliminating the danger that investment decisions will be significantly influenced by the ideological views of corporations. While the latter concern may not be of the same constitutional magnitude as the former, it is far from trivial. Corporations, as previously noted, are created by the State as a means of furthering the public welfare. One of their functions is to determine, by their success in obtaining funds, the uses to which society's resources are to be put. A State may legitimately conclude that corporations would not serve as economically efficient vehicles for such decisions if the investment preferences of the public were significantly affected by their ideological or political activities. It has long been recognized that such pursuits are not the proper business of corporations. The common law was generally interpreted as prohibiting corporate political participation. * * *

* * *

I would affirm the judgment of the Supreme Judicial Court for the Commonwealth of Massachusetts.

Mr. Justice REHNQUIST, dissenting.

This Court decided at an early date, with neither argument nor discussion, that a business corporation is a "person" entitled to the protection of the Equal Protection Clause of the Fourteenth Amendment. Santa Clara County v. Southern Pacific R. Co., 118 U.S. 394, 396, 6 S.Ct. 1132, 30 L.Ed. 118 (1886). Likewise, it soon became accepted that the property of a corporation was protected under the

Due Process Clause of that same Amendment. *See, e.g.,* Smyth v. Ames, 169 U.S. 466, 522, 18 S.Ct. 418, 424, 42 L.Ed. 819 (1898). Nevertheless, we concluded soon thereafter that the liberty protected by that Amendment "is the liberty of natural, not artificial persons." Northwestern Nat. Life Ins. Co. v. Riggs, 203 U.S. 243, 255, 27 S.Ct. 126, 129, 51 L.Ed. 168 (1906). Before today, our only considered and explicit departures from that holding have been that a corporation engaged in the business of publishing or broadcasting enjoys the same liberty of the press as is enjoyed by natural persons, Grosjean v. American Press Co., 297 U.S. 233, 244, 56 S.Ct. 444, 446, 80 L.Ed. 660 (1936), and that a nonprofit membership corporation organized for the purpose of "achieving * * * equality of treatment by all government, federal, state and local, for the members of the Negro community" enjoys certain liberties of political expression. NAACP v. Button, 371 U.S. 415, 429, 83 S.Ct. 328, 336, 9 L.Ed.2d 405 (1963).

The question presented today, whether business corporations have a constitutionally protected liberty to engage in political activities, has never been squarely addressed by any previous decision of this Court.[1] However, the General Court of the Commonwealth of Massachusetts, the Congress of the United States, and the legislatures of 30 other States of this Republic have considered the matter, and have concluded that restrictions upon the political activity of business corporations are both politically desirable and constitutionally permissible. The judgment of such a broad consensus of governmental bodies expressed over a period of many decades is entitled to considerable deference from this Court. I think it quite probable that their judgment may properly be reconciled with our controlling precedents, but I am certain that under my views of the limited application of the First Amendment to the States, which I share with the two immediately preceding occupants of my seat on the Court, but not with my present colleagues, the judgment of the Supreme Judicial Court of Massachusetts should be affirmed.

Early in our history, Mr. Chief Justice Marshall described the status of a corporation in the eyes of federal law:

"A corporation is an artificial being, invisible, intangible, and existing only in contemplation of law. Being the mere creature of law, it possesses only those properties which the charter of creation confers upon it, either expressly, or as incidental to its very existence. These are such as are supposed best calculated to ef-

---

1. Our prior cases, mostly of recent vintage, have discussed the boundaries of protected speech without distinguishing between artificial and natural persons. *See, e.g.,* Linmark Associates, Inc. v. Township of Willingboro, 431 U.S. 85, 97 S.Ct. 1614, 52 L.Ed.2d 155 (1977); Buckley v. Valeo, 424 U.S. 1, 96 S.Ct. 612, 46 L.Ed.2d 659 (1976). Nevertheless, the Court today affirms that the failure of those cases to draw distinctions between artificial and natural persons does not mean that no such distinctions may be drawn. The Court explicitly states that corporations may not enjoy all the political liberties of natural persons, although it fails to articulate the basis of its suggested distinction.

fect the object for which it was created." Dartmouth College v.
Woodward, 4 Wheat. 518, 636, 4 L.Ed. 629 (1819).

The appellants herein either were created by the Commonwealth or
were admitted into the Commonwealth only for the limited purposes
described in their charters and regulated by state law. Since it cannot be disputed that the mere creation of a corporation does not invest it with all the liberties enjoyed by natural persons, United States
v. White, 322 U.S. 694, 698–701, 64 S.Ct. 1248, 1251–1252, 88 L.Ed.
1542 (1944) (corporations to not enjoy the privilege against self-incrimination), our inquiry must seek to determine which constitutional
protections are "incidental to its very existence." *Dartmouth College, supra,* 4 Wheat. at 636.

There can be little doubt that when a State creates a corporation
with the power to acquire and utilize property, it necessarily and implicitly guarantees that the corporation will not be deprived of that
property absent due process of law. Likewise, when a State charters
a corporation for the purpose of publishing a newspaper, it necessarily assumes that the corporation is entitled to the liberty of the press
essential to the conduct of its business. *Grosjean* so held, and our
subsequent cases have so assumed. Until recently, it was not
thought that any persons, natural or artificial, had any protected
right to engage in commercial speech. *See* Virginia State Board of
Pharmacy v. Virginia Citizens Consumer Council, 425 U.S. 748,
761–770, 96 S.Ct. 1817, 1825–1829, 48 L.Ed.2d 346 (1976). Although
the Court has never explicitly recognized a corporation's right of commercial speech, such a right might be considered necessarily incidental to the business of a commercial corporation.

It cannot be so readily concluded that the right of political expression is equally necessary to carry out the functions of a corporation
organized for commercial purposes. A State grants to a business
corporation the blessings of potentially perpetual life and limited liability to enhance its efficiency as an economic entity. It might reasonably be concluded that those properties, so beneficial in the economic sphere, pose special dangers in the political sphere.
Furthermore, it might be argued that liberties of political expression
are not at all necessary to effectuate the purposes for which States
permit commercial corporations to exist. So long as the Judicial
Branches of the State and Federal Governments remain open to protect the corporation's interest in its property, it has no need, though it
may have the desire, to petition the political branches for similar protection. Indeed, the States might reasonably fear that the corporation would use its economic power to obtain further benefits beyond
those already bestowed. I would think that any particular form of
organization upon which the State confers special privileges or immunities different from those of natural persons would be subject to like
regulation, whether the organization is a labor union, a partnership, a
trade association, or a corporation.

One need not adopt such a restrictive view of the political liberties of business corporations to affirm the judgment of the Supreme Judicial Court in this case. That court reasoned that this Court's decisions entitling the property of a corporation to constitutional protection should be construed as recognizing the liberty of a corporation to express itself on political matters concerning that property. Thus, the Court construed the statute in question not to forbid political expression by a corporation "when a general political issue materially affects a corporation's business, property or assets." 371 Mass. 773, 785, 359 N.E.2d 1262, 1270 (1977).

I can see no basis for concluding that the liberty of a corporation to engage in political activity with regard to matters having no material effect on its business is necessarily incidental to the purposes for which the Commonwealth permitted these corporations to be organized or admitted within its boundaries. Nor can I disagree with the Supreme Judicial Court's factual finding that no such effect has been shown by these appellants. Because the statute as construed provides at least as much protection as the Fourteenth Amendment requires, I believe it is constitutionally valid.

It is true, as the Court points out that recent decisions of this Court have emphasized the interest of the public in receiving the information offered by the speaker seeking protection. The free flow of information is in no way diminished by the Commonwealth's decision to permit the operation of business corporations with limited rights of political expression. All natural persons, who owe their existence to a higher sovereign than the Commonwealth, remain as free as before to engage in political activity. *Cf.* Maher v. Roe, 432 U.S. 464, 474, 97 S.Ct. 2376, 2382, 53 L.Ed.2d 484 (1977).

I would affirm the judgment of the Supreme Judicial Court.

Chapter 3

AN INTRODUCTION TO THE LAW OF
CORPORATIONS: PART TWO

A. INTRODUCTION

As the principal function of the preceding chapter was to set the stage for later discussion of the problems surrounding the role of the corporation in society, the purpose of this chapter is to introduce you to some of the basic terms and concepts of the traditional law of corporations.

In approaching the problems and the following materials, you should be particularly conscious that they intentionally cast you in the role of planner and counsellor to your client, a role to which the usual first-year law school course does not expose students more than casually. That is, however, the role played by the corporate lawyer most of the time. The emphasis of these materials is, therefore, on the use of corporate law by the lawyer as planner.

You will probably find yourself somewhat uncomfortable in the planning role at first. A real client wishes his or her counsellor to assist in structuring a transaction to provide the maximum in benefits with the least legal and business risk. We live in a world of uncertainty. It is the nature of business that undertakings that hold unusual potential for profit often involve doing things that have not been done before. Such transactions, in turn, often present novel and difficult legal questions. It is not enough in such circumstances to give your client the arguments that can be made on both sides. The client is paying (often at very high rates) for the benefit of your legal training, your experience, and, most of all, your judgment. It is to begin to develop those intangible qualities that make up sound judgment, that you will be asked throughout this course what action you would advise your client to take.

Creativity is another ability of the first-rate lawyer. The capacity to generate alternative approaches to surmount some legal or business obstacle marks the difference between an average counsellor and a good one. Rarely does the answer, "That is illegal," or "You cannot do it" suffice. The client's inevitable response is, "Well, then tell me how I *can* do it." The lawyer who cannot, most of the time, find an acceptable alternative to accomplish the client's objective, is likely to find himself or herself looking for another client.

B. SOME BASIC TERMS AND CONCEPTS

The following, rather simplistic, discussion of some terms and concepts and their place in the standard corporate framework will help you understand the problems and the materials that follow.

1. ORGANIC DOCUMENTS

There are three documentary sources of the formal structure of the corporation. The first, in descending hierarchical order, is the state *corporation statute,** the law which permits incorporation and which imposes certain requirements on the organization and operation of corporations. *The articles of incorporation* (also known in some states as the *charter* or the *certificate* of *incorporation*) furnish in a sense the constitution of the corporation. They contain certain minimum provisions dictated by the statute and also a variety of other provisions governing the internal affairs of the corporation. The by-laws, have for their principal purpose, the establishment of the detailed mechanics of the governance of the corporation. They are generally lengthier than the articles and are somewhat easier to amend.

2. THE CORPORATE ACTORS

The traditional governance model of a corporation is pyramidal.** At the base are the *stockholders* (or *shareholders*) who are the owners of the corporation (subject, of course, to the claims of creditors and holders of certain corporate securities having various prior interests).

The stockholders' power of ultimate control over the corporation is embodied in their right to elect the *board of directors* and also to approve or disapprove certain fundamental changes in the corporate structure such as the amendment of the articles of incorporation. The board is normally composed of at least three, and in large corporations often as many as twenty or more, individuals charged with overseeing the management of the corporation's affairs. In firms

---

* The statute to which we will most often refer in these materials is the Model Business Corporation Act (MBCA). The Model Act, drafted by the Committee on the Corporate Laws of the Section of Corporation, Banking and Business Law of the American Bar Association, was first published in 1950. Originally patterned after the Illinois Business Corporation Act of 1933, it has been revised periodically by the ABA committee.

The Model Business Corporation Act is, of course, only a model and is not in effect in its pure form anywhere. Nevertheless it has exerted a strong influence on the laws of some 35 states. An excellent reference tool that provides a de-

tailed discussion of the Act, its background, and its interpretation as well as a useful general gloss on many questions of corporation law is the Model Business Corporation Act Annotated (2d ed. 1971), a three-volume work that is periodically supplemented to reflect revisions to the Act and recent cases bearing on its interpretation.

** It should be noted that this pyramidal structure is not by any means always pyramidal in practice. There are many corporations, for example, with only one shareholder and three directors, in which the officerships are filled by only two or three persons.

with a small number of shareholders (often referred to as "close corporations") the directors usually include—and are sometimes limited to—the principal shareholders, who are often employees of the corporation as well. In firms with more widely dispersed share ownership, a substantial proportion of the directors, increasingly a majority, is composed of outsiders, *i.e.*, individuals not employed by the firm.* Directors are not, qua directors, considered employees of the corporation, but act as representatives of the shareholders.

At the top of the metaphorical pyramid are the *officers* of the corporation, usually including a president, one or more vice-presidents, a secretary, and a treasurer. Their specific formal duties, imposed by the corporation statute and the by-laws, are generally rather limited. Beyond that, however, they constitute the top management of the corporation and are thus responsible for running its day-to-day affairs.

3. CORPORATE SECURITIES

The ownership interest in a corporation is represented by shares of *stock*, which represent the *equity* or ownership interest. There is always *common stock*. There may be one or more classes of *preferred stock*, which represents an ownership interest that is given certain priorities over the common stock. The amount of *authorized stock* that a corporation may issue and its terms are determined by the articles of incorporation. The portion of the authorized stock that has been sold and remains in the hands of the shareholders is the stock *outstanding*. The remainder is designated *authorized but unissued* stock, if it has never been issued, or *treasury stock* if it has been issued and later repurchased by the corporation. The distinction between authorized but unissued stock and *treasury stock* is rather technical and will be discussed at a later point.

Stock, common or preferred, is considered an *equity security*, a term that derives from the "equity of redemption" of a mortgagor and relates to the fact that stockholders stand at the end of the line when it comes to distributions of corporate funds. The other principal class of corporate financial instruments consists of *debt securities*, which include *bonds*, *debentures*, and *notes*. We will discuss the characteristics of various types of corporate securities in more detail in a later chapter.

4. FIDUCIARY PRINCIPLES

The relationships among the various corporate actors are governed in large measure by *fiduciary* principles drawn originally from the law of trusts. The basic fiduciary duty that officers and directors

---

* It is also common to find on boards, lawyers, accountants, and bankers, who are not employees of the corporation, but who have a substantial relationship with it.

are said to owe to their corporation is traditionally divided into a *duty of care* and a *duty of loyalty*.

PROBLEM

CHESAPEAKE MARINE SERVICES—PART I

The Chesapeake Marine Services Company, Inc., ("Chesapeake") is incorporated in the state of Columbia.* Its business consists principally of the provision of barge and towing services. It also maintains a small shipyard in which it services its own vessels and does some work for others. Its articles of incorporation and by-laws are essentially the same as those in the book, *Selected Corporation and Partnership Statutes, Regulations and Forms*, except that the articles contain the following provisions:

> Wherever a vote of the shareholders is required by statute for the approval of an amendment to these Articles or a merger or sale of all or substantially all of the corporation's assets, such approval shall be by the holders of two-thirds of the outstanding shares.

Chesapeake's largest shareholder is John Apple, who owns 350 shares, slightly over one-third of the 1,000 shares of common stock. He is a director of the corporation, being guaranteed a seat on the board by the size of his holdings. Apple also owns a half interest in United Harbor Services, Inc. ("United") a somewhat smaller firm that is a competitor of Chesapeake's. He acquired that interest about three years ago after a dispute with Chesapeake over the continuation of leases on two tugboats he owned and had leased to the company for several years. When Chesapeake's board of directors refused to renew the leases for the vessels, he conveyed them to United in exchange for half of its stock.

Apple, who has been in the marine transport business for many years, acquired his stock in a series of purchases over the last few years. His more recent acquisitions have been resisted by members of the Lambert family, the other principal shareholders of Chesapeake, who have told Apple directly that they would be strongly opposed to his trying to gain control over the business. Shortly after the board refused to renew its leases on Apple's boats, it also voted to dismiss him from the post of Vice-President of the corporation, which he had held since his initial purchase of Chesapeake stock.

Chesapeake currently has fifteen shareholders none of whom, with the exception of Apple, own more than 200 shares. The board consists of Apple, James Lambert (the president of the company), two other members of the Lambert family, and Nancy Carter, another major shareholder.

---

* Here, as in all the problems in this book, you may assume, unless some variation is indicated, that the applicable statutory provisions are the relevant sections of the Model Business Corporation Act.

For the past two or three years, Chesapeake's management has been concerned about what is perceived as a shortage of capital. The firm's business has been growing, and it needs to expand the facilities of the shipyard. It could also make profitable use of one or two more vessels. Within the last year, moreover, working capital has been uncomfortably tight, to the point at which payments to suppliers have had to be delayed occasionally, resulting in the loss of some of the usual discounts for prompt payment. A year ago James Lambert asked Chesapeake's bank about borrowing additional money. He was turned down because bank officials felt the company had already borrowed as much as was prudent and because they had doubts about the future growth of its business.

Under these circumstances, Lambert decided it was necessary to raise new equity capital. At the last board meeting, he moved to recommend an amendment to the articles of incorporation to double the number of authorized shares of common stock. Apple declared that he was opposed to such an amendment because he did not believe that there was any need for new capital. He indicated that he would do everything he could to block the proposal. Although the other members of the board all favored the amendment of the articles of incorporation, the motion was withdrawn.

1. How would a company in Chesapeake's situation normally raise new capital? What alternatives are there?

2. Why should the articles of incorporation (Article Fourth) contain a limit on the number of shares of common stock that can be issued? See MBCA §§ 15 and 54.

3. Because of the provision of the articles of incorporation, quoted above, Apple's ownership of more than one-third of the common stock puts him in a position to block any amendment to the articles. What is the purpose of that article? Is it consistent with MBCA §§ 54, 58, and 59?

4. Until 1969, the MBCA required the approval of amendments to the articles, as well as mergers and sales of substantially all of the assets (see Sections 73 and 79), by a two-thirds majority of the shares; and many state statutes still require an extraordinary majority for such "fundamental changes" in the corporate structure. How are such provisions to be rationalized with Section 35 of the MBCA and its equivalents to be found in virtually every corporation statute?

5. Is there any impropriety in the fact that Apple, a director, is opposing a step that appears to be good for the corporation when he has a conflicting interest in a competing business?

Does it matter whether Apple's opposition to raising new capital is motivated by a good faith belief that it would not be in the corporation's best interest to do so or whether he simply wishes to impede Chesapeake's ability to compete with United?

6.   Would your answers to the questions in number 5 be different if Apple had resigned his seat on the board prior to seeking to block the proposed amendment and was thus neither an officer nor a director?

Consider the following cases:

The following well-known excerpt from Pepper v. Litton, 308 U.S. 295, 60 S.Ct. 238, 84 L.Ed. 281 (1939), will set the stage for some of the issues concerning fiduciary duties:

> * * *   A director is a fiduciary. So is a dominant or controlling stockholder or group of stockholders. Their powers are in trust. Their dealings with the corporation are subjected to rigorous scrutiny and where any of their contracts or engagements with the corporation is challenged the burden is on the director or stockholder not only to prove the good faith of the transaction but also to show its inherent fairness from the viewpoint of the corporation and those interested therein. The essence of the test is whether or not under all the circumstances the transaction carries the earmarks of an arm's length bargain. If it does not, equity will set it aside.
>
> * * *
>
> * * *   [A fiduciary] cannot serve himself and his *cestuis* second. He cannot manipulate the affairs of his corporation to their detriment and in disregard of the standards of common decency and honesty. He cannot by the intervention of a corporate entity violate the ancient precept against serving two masters. He cannot by the use of the corporate device avail himself of privileges normally permitted outsiders in a race of creditors. He cannot utilize his inside information and his strategic position for his own preferment. He cannot violate rules of fair play by doing indirectly through the corporation what he could not do directly. He cannot use his power for his personal advantage and to the detriment of the stockholders and creditors no matter how absolute in terms that power may be and no matter how meticulous he is to satisfy technical requirements. For that power is at all times subject to the equitable limitation that it may not be exercised for the aggrandizement, preference, or advantage of the fiduciary to the exclusion or detriment of the *cestuis*. Where there is a violation of those principles, equity will undo the wrong or intervene to prevent its consummation.

BAYER v. BERAN

49 N.Y.S.2d 2 (Sup.Ct.1944)

SHIENTAG, Justice.

These derivative stockholders' suits present for review two transactions upon which plaintiffs seek to charge the individual defendants, who are directors, with liability in favor of the corporate defendant, the Celanese Corporation of America. There are two causes of action alleging breach of fiduciary duty by the directors, one in connection with a program of radio advertising embarked upon by the corporation towards the end of 1941, and the other relating to certain payments of $30,000 a year made to Henri Dreyfus, one of its vice-presidents and a director, pursuant to a contract of employment entered into with him by the corporation. Before taking up the specific transactions complained of, I shall consider generally certain pertinent rules to be applied in determining the liability of directors of a business corporation such as is here involved.

Despite abuses that have developed in connection with the derivative stockholders' suit, abuses which should be dealt with promptly and effectively, it must be remembered that such an action is, at present, the only civil remedy that stockholders have for breach of fiduciary duty on the part of those entrusted with the management and direction of their corporations. We cannot therefore allow the prevailing mood of justifiable dissatisfaction with some of the temporary incidents of such suits to cause us to lose sight of certain deep-rooted, traditional concepts of the obligations of directors to their corporation and its stockholders.

* * *

The concept of loyalty, of constant, unqualified fidelity, has a definite and precise meaning. The fiduciary must subordinate his individual and private interests to his duty to the corporation whenever the two conflict. Winter v. Anderson, 242 App.Div. 430, 275 N.Y.S. 373. In an address delivered in 1934, Mr. Justice, now Chief Justice, Stone declared that the fiduciary principle of undivided loyalty was, in effect, "the precept as old as Holy Writ, that 'a man cannot serve two masters'. More than a century ago equity gave a hospitable reception to that principle and the common law was not slow to follow in giving it recognition. No thinking man can believe that an economy built upon a business foundation can long endure without loyalty to that principle". He went on to say that "The separation of ownership from management, the development of the corporate structure so as to vest in small groups control of resources of great numbers of small and uninformed investors, make imperative a fresh and active devotion to that principle if the modern world of business is to perform its proper function". Stone, The Public Influence of the Bar, 48 Harvard Law Review 1, 8.

A director is not an insurer. On the one hand, he is not called upon to use an extraordinary degree of care and prudence; and on the other hand it is established by the cases that it is not enough for a director to be honest, that fraud is not the orbit of his liability. The director may not act as a dummy or a figurehead. He is called upon to use care, to exercise judgment, the decree of care, the kind of judgment that one would give in similar situations to the conduct of his own affairs.

The director of a business corporation is given a wide latitude of action. The law does not seek to deprive him of initiative and daring and vision. Business has its adventures, its bold adventures; and those who in good faith, and in the interests of the corporation they serve, embark upon them, are not to be penalized if failure, rather than success, results from their efforts. The law will not permit a course of conduct by directors, which would be applauded if it succeeded, to be condemned with a riot of adjectives simply because it failed. Directors of a commercial corporation may take chances, the same kind of chances that a man would take in his own business. Because they are given this wide latitude, the law will not hold directors liable for honest errors, for mistakes of judgment. The law will not interfere with the internal affairs of a corporation so long as it is managed by its directors pursuant to a free, honest exercise of judgment uninfluenced by personal, or by any considerations other than the welfare of the corporation.

To encourage freedom of action on the part of directors, or to put it another way, to discourage interference with the exercise of their free and independent judgment, there has grown up what is known as the "business judgment rule". "Questions of policy of management, expediency of contracts or action, adequacy of consideration, lawful appropriation of corporate funds to advance corporate interests, are left solely to their honest and unselfish decision, for their powers therein are without limitation and free from restraint, and the exercise of them for the common and general interests of the corporation may not be questioned, although the results show that what they did was unwise or inexpedient." Pollitz v. Wabash R. Co., 207 N.Y. 113, 124, 100 N.E. 721, 724. Indeed, although the concept of "responsibility" is firmly fixed in the law, it is only in a most unusual and extraordinary case that directors are held liable for negligence in the absence of fraud, or improper motive, or personal interest.

The "business judgment rule", however, yields to the rule of undivided loyalty. This great rule of law is designed "to avoid the possibility of fraud and to avoid the temptation of self-interest." Conway, J., in Matter of Ryan's Will, 291 N.Y. 376, 406, 52 N.E.2d 909, 923. It is "designed to obliterate all divided loyalties which may creep into a fiduciary relation * * *." Thacher, J., in City Bank Farmers Trust Co. v. Cannon, 291 N.Y. 125, 132, 51 N.E.2d 674, 676. "Included within its scope is every situation in which a trustee chooses to deal with another in such close relation with the trustee that possible advantage to such other person might influence, consciously or unconsciously, the judgment of the trustee * * *." Lehman, Ch. J., in Albright v. Jefferson County National Bank, 292 N.Y. 31, 39, 53 N.E.2d 753, 756. The dealings of a director with the corporation for which he is the fiduciary are therefore viewed "with jealousy by the courts." Globe Woolen Co. v. Utica Gas & Electric Co., 224 N.Y. 483, 121 N.E. 378, 380. Such personal transactions of directors with their corporations, such transactions as may tend to produce a conflict between self-interest and fiduciary obligation, are, when challenged, examined with the most scrupulous care, and if there is any evidence of improvidence or oppression, any indication of unfairness or undue advantage, the transactions will be voided. "Their dealings with the corporation are subjected to rigorous scrutiny and where any of their contracts or engagements with the corporation are challenged the burden is on the director not only to prove the good faith of the transaction but also to show its inherent fairness from the viewpoint of the corporation and those interested therein." Pepper v. Litton, 308 U.S. 295, 306, 60 S.Ct. 238, 245, 84 L.Ed. 281.

While there is a high moral purpose implicit in this transcendent fiduciary principle of undivided loyalty, it has back of it a profound understanding of human nature and of its frailties. It actually accomplishes a practical, beneficent purpose. It tends to prevent a clouded conception of fidelity that blurs the vision. It preserves the free exercise of judgment uncontaminated by the dross of divided allegiance or self-interest. It prevents the operation of an influence that may be indirect but that is all the more potent for that reason. The law has set its face firmly against undermining "the rule of undivided loyalty by the 'disintegrating erosion' of particular exceptions." Meinhard v. Salmon, 249 N.Y. 458, 464, 164 N.E. 545, 546.

The first, or "advertising", cause of action charges the directors with negligence, waste and improvidence in embarking the corporation upon a radio advertising program beginning in 1942 and costing about $1,000,000 a year. It is further charged that they were negligent in selecting the type of program and in renewing the radio contract for 1943. More serious than these allegations is the charge that the directors were motivated by a noncorporate purpose in causing the radio program to be undertaken and in expending large sums of money therefor. It is claimed that this radio advertising was for the benefit of Miss Jean Tennyson, one of the singers on the program, who in private life is Mrs. Camille Dreyfus, the wife of the president of the company and one of its directors; that it was undertaken to "further, foster and subsidize her career"; to "furnish a vehicle" for her talents.

Eliminating for the moment the part played by Miss Tennyson in the radio advertising campaign, it is clear that the character of the advertising, the amount to be expended therefor, and the manner in which it should be used, are all matters of business judgment and rest peculiarly within the discretion of the board of directors. Under the authorities previously cited, it is not, generally speaking, the function of a court of equity to review these matters or even to consider them. Had the wife of the president of the company not been involved, the advertising cause of action could have been disposed of summarily. Her connection with the program, however, makes it necessary to go into the facts in some detail.

[The court here reviews the history of the decision to launch on a program of radio advertising, stating that the format finally chosen "was not adopted on the spur of the moment or at the whim of the directors," but was the result of careful deliberation and was calculated to support the image of the product that the corporation desired to project.]

So far, there is nothing on which to base any claim of breach of fiduciary duty. Some care, diligence and prudence were exercised by these directors before they committed the company to the radio program. It was for the directors to determine whether they would resort to radio advertising; it was for them to conclude how much to spend; it was for them to decide the kind of program they would use. It would be an unwarranted act of interference for any court to attempt to substitute its judgment on these points for that of the directors, honestly arrived at. The expenditure was not reckless or unconscionable. Indeed, it bore a fair relationship to the total amount of net sales and to the earnings of the company. The fact that the company had offers of more business than it could handle did not, in law, preclude advertising. Many corporations not now doing any business in their products because of emergency conditions advertise those products extensively in order to preserve the good will, the public interest, during the war period. The fact that the company's product may not now be identifiable did not bar advertising calculated to induce consumer demand for such identification. That a program of classical and semiclassical music was selected, rather than a variety program, or a news commentator program, furnishes no ground for legal complaint. True, variety programs have a wider popular appeal than do musicals, but it would be a very sad thing if the former were the only kind of radio programs to be used. Some of the largest industrial concerns in the country have recognized this and have maintained fine musical programs on the radio for many years.

Now we have to take up an unfortunate incident, one which cannot be viewed with the complacency displayed by some of the directors of the company. This is not a closely held family corporation. The Doctors Dreyfus and their families own about 135,000 shares of common stock, the other directors about 10,000 shares out of a total outstanding issue of 1,376,500 shares. Some of these other directors were originally employed by Dr. Camille Dreyfus, the president of the company. His wife, to whom he has been married for about twelve years, is known professionally as Miss Jean Tennyson and is a singer of wide experience.

Dr. Dreyfus, as was natural, consulted his wife about the proposed radio program; he also asked the advertising agency, that had been retained, to confer with her about it. She suggested the names of the artists, all stars of the Metropolitan Opera Company, and the name of the conductor, prominent in his field. She also offered her own services as a paid artist. All of her suggestions as to personnel were adopted by the advertising agency. While the record shows Miss Tennyson to be a competent singer, there is nothing to indicate that she was indispensable or essential to the success of the program. She received $500 an evening. It would be far-fetched to suggest that the directors caused the company to incur large expenditures for radio advertising to enable the president's wife to make $24,000 in 1942 and $20,500 in 1943.

Of course it is not improper to appoint relatives of officers or directors to responsible positions in a company. But where a close relative of the chief executive officer of a corporation, and one of its dominant directors, takes a position closely associated with a new and expensive field of activity, the motives of the directors are likely to be questioned. The board would be placed in a position where selfish, personal interests might be in conflict with the duty it owed to the corporation. That being so, the entire transaction, if challenged in the courts, must be subjected to the most rigorous scrutiny to determine whether the action of the directors was intended or calculated "to subserve some outside purpose, regardless of the consequences to the company, and in a manner inconsistent with its interests." Gamble v. Queens County Water Co., 123 N.Y. 91, 99, 25 N.E. 201, 202.

After such careful scrutiny I have concluded that, up to the present, there has been no breach of fiduciary duty on the part of the directors. The president undoubtedly knew that his wife might be one of the paid artists on the program. The other directors did not know this until they had approved the campaign of radio advertising and the general type of radio program. The evidence fails to show that the program was designed to foster or subsidize "the career of Miss Tennyson as an artist" or to "furnish a vehicle for her talents". That her participation in the program may have enhanced her prestige as a singer is no ground for subjecting the directors to liability, as long as the advertising served a legitimate and a useful corporate purpose and the company received the full benefit thereof.

The musical quality of "Celanese Hour" has not been challenged, nor does the record contain anything reflecting on Miss Tennyson's competence as an artist. There is nothing in the testimony to show that some other soprano would have enhanced the artistic quality of the program or its advertising appeal. There is no suggestion that the present program is inefficient or that its cost is disproportionate to what a program of that character reasonably entails. Miss Tennyson's contract with the advertising agency retained by the directors was on a standard form, negotiated through her professional agent. Her compensation, as well as that of the other artists, was in conformity with that paid for comparable work. She received less than any of the other artists on the program. Although she appeared with greater regularity than any other singer, she received no undue prominence, no special build-up. Indeed, all of the artists were subordinated to the advertisement of the company and of its products. The company was featured. It appears also that the popularity of the program has increased since it was inaugurated.

It is clear, therefore, that the directors have not been guilty of any breach of fiduciary duty, in embarking upon the program of radio advertising and in renewing it. It is unfortunate that they have allowed themselves to be placed in a position where their motives concerning future decisions on radio advertising may be impugned. The free mind should be ever jealous of its freedom. "Power of control carries with it a trust or duty to exercise that power faithfully to promote the corporate interests, and the courts of this State will insist upon scrupulous performance of that duty." Lehman, Ch. J., in Everett v. Phillips, 288 N.Y. 227, 232, 43 N.E.2d 18, 19. Thus far, that duty has been performed and with noteworthy success. The corporation has not, up the present time, been wronged by the radio advertising attacked in the complaints.

[With respect to the second cause of action, the court concluded that the re-employment as a chemist of one of the organizers of the corporation, although he did not devote his entire time and effort to the corporation, did not constitute negligence or the waste of corporate assets where there was full and adequate consideration for the remuneration provided.]

GAMBLE v. QUEENS COUNTY WATER CO.

123 N.Y. 91, 25 N.E. 201 (1890).

[Mullins, a stockholder in the Queens County Water Co., had contracted to sell the "Rockaway Beach Extension" to the corporation in exchange for $60,000 in face amount of its bonds and $50,000 in face amount of its stock. The transaction had been approved by a vote of the shareholders in which Mullins had participated. The court held that the actual cost of building the extension was just over $69,000.]

PECKHAM, J.

* * * The so-called "Rockaway Beach Extension" was not built by defendant Mullins under any contract with the defendant corporation. * * * Upon its completion, Mullins was the sole and absolute owner thereof, with power to operate it himself, or to sell it to others, or, in brief, to exercise such acts of ownership over the property as any other owner might have exercised. This is not the case of a trustee entering into a contract with himself, or purchasing from himself, where the contract is liable to be repudiated at the mere will, or even whim, of the *cestui que trust*. Having the rights of an absolute owner of this extension, Mullins was at liberty to make such contract in regard to its disposal as he should see fit, so long of course as he did not, while acting in his own interest on the one side, also act on the other in the capacity of trustee or representative, so

that his interest and his duty might conflict. In this case, Mullins did not so act. He bases his right to the stock and bonds of the company defendant upon the vote of the majority of its shareholders taken at a regularly convened meeting, to purchase the property at the price named in the resolution adopted at such meeting, the price being $60,000 in bonds, and $50,000 in the stock of such company. At this meeting, 479 out of a total of 500 shares, into which the capital stock of the company was divided, were represented, and 467 shares were voted upon in favor of the adoption of such resolution, while the 30 of the plaintiff were voted upon by him in opposition thereto, and 3 shares were not voted upon. There were a majority of shareholders, and a majority of shares voted upon, in favor of such resolution, without counting the defendant Mullins or his shares, although he voted upon them in favor of such resolution. In so doing, he committed no legal wrong. A shareholder has a legal right at a meeting of the shareholders to vote upon a measure, even though he has a personal interest therein separate from other shareholders. In such a meeting, each shareholder represents himself and his own interests solely, and he in no sense acts as a trustee or representative of others. The law of self-interest has at such time very great and proper sway. There can be little doubt, too, that at such meetings those who do vote upon their own stock vote upon it in the light solely of their own interest, or at least in what they conceive to be their own interest. Their action resulting from such votes must not be so detrimental to the interests of the corporation itself as to lead to the necessary inference that the interests of the majority of the shareholders lie wholly outside of and in opposition to the interests of the corporation, and of the minority of the shareholders, and that their action is a wanton or a fraudulent destruction of the rights of such minority. In such cases it may be stated that the action of the majority of the shareholders may be subjected to the scrutiny of a court of equity at the suit of the minority shareholders. * * *

I think that where the action of the majority is plainly a fraud upon, or, in other words, is really oppressive to the minority shareholders, and the directors or trustees have acted with and formed part of the majority, an action may be sustained by one of the minority shareholders suing in his own behalf, and in that of all others coming in, etc., to enjoin the action contemplated, and in which action the corporation should be made a party defendant. It is not, however, every question of mere administration or of policy in which there is a difference of opinion among the shareholders that enables the minority to claim that the action of the majority is oppressive, and which justifies the minority in coming to a court of equity to obtain relief. Generally the rule must be that in such cases the will of the majority shall govern. The court would not be justified in interfering, even in doubtful cases, where the action of the majority might be susceptible of different constructions. To warrant the interposition of the court in favor of the minority shareholders in a corporation or joint stock association, as against the contemplated action of the majority, where such action is within the corporate powers, a case must be made out which plainly shows that such action is so far opposed to the true interests of the corporation itself as to lead to the clear inference that no one thus acting could have been influenced by any honest desire to secure such interests, but that he must have acted with an intent to subserve some outside purpose, regardless of the consequences to the company and in a manner inconsistent with its interests.   Otherwise the court might be called upon to balance probabilities of profitable results to arise from the carrying out of the one or the other of different plans proposed by or on behalf of different shareholders in a corporation, and to decree the adoption of that line of policy which seemed to it to promise the best results, or at least to enjoin the carrying out of the opposite policy.   This is no business for any court to follow.   *   *   *

From these views it results that the judgment in this action must be reversed, and a new trial ordered, costs to abide event.

All concur.

PROBLEM

CHESAPEAKE MARINE SERVICES—PART II

Prevented by Apple's opposition from increasing Chesapeake's stock, Lambert has come to your firm for advice as to some other way of raising additional equity capital.   After discussing the matter with you, the partner for whom you work has asked you to investigate the legal implications of the following plan: Chesapeake would organize a subsidiary, CMS Shipyard, Inc., and transfer to the subsidiary, in exchange for 2,000 of its 10,000 authorized shares of common stock, all the assets of Chesapeake's shipyard division plus $10,000 in cash.   The new subsidiary would then issue another 1,500 shares of common stock at a price of $100 per share.   Half of the new stock would be purchased by members of the Lambert family and the balance by two or three outside investors.   None would be offered to Apple.   Part of the cash thus raised would be used to expand the facilities of the shipyard and the balance would be loaned to the parent corporation to purchase the desired new vessels and for general corporate purposes.

The cash and the book value * of the assets transferred to the new subsidiary would be about $200,000 or ten percent of Chesapeake's total assets of $2 million.   To replace those assets would,

---

* "Book value" of an asset is the value at which it is carried on the accounts of a business.   According to standard accounting practice, book value is generally equal to the cost of the asset or, in the case of a depreciable asset, cost less an allowance for depreciation arrived at by a more-or-less arbitrary formula.   As a result of this practice, the "real" value of an asset may depart significantly from its book value.   The book value of a corporation is the aggregate of the book value of its assets less its liabilities.

however, cost substantially more than $200,000. The shipyard division has been responsible for about 15 percent of Chesapeake's overall profits for the last several years.

The partner has asked you to consider the following questions:

1. Is the transaction authorized by the applicable provisions of the statute, the articles, and the by-laws? What formal steps would be required to accomplish it? Consider particularly MBCA §§ 4, 19, 41, and 79.

2. What rights does Apple have in Chesapeake that are diminished with respect to the new subsidiary?

3. If Apple brings a proceeding to rescind or enjoin the transaction, which, if any, of the following theories might succeed? The establishment of the subsidiary and the planned financial arrangements are:

(a) in violation of some specific provision of the MCBA;

(b) unwise;

(c) a breach of the duty of loyalty of the directors;

(d) unlawful because the majority shareholders are "doing indirectly what they could not do directly."

Are there other theories that might be successful? You should attempt to work out those theories that seem to have some merit as specifically as possible and develop the most effective counter-arguments that are available to the corporation and the board.

4. Should the motives of Lambert or Apple make any difference to any of the possible claims?

In answering these questions, reconsider Bayer v. Beran and consider the following:

C. EQUITABLE LIMITATIONS ON LEGAL POSSIBILITIES

SCHNELL v. CHRIS–CRAFT INDUSTRIES, INC.

285 A.2d 437 (Del.Sup.1971).

[The controversy arose out of a proxy contest for control of Chris-Craft between the incumbent management and a dissident group of shareholders who were dissatisfied with the company's economic performance. Both sides sought to solicit enough proxies (*i.e.*, agency powers entitling them to vote the stock of other shareholders—*see* Chapter 12, *infra*) to control a majority of the stockholder vote for the election of directors at the next annual meeting of shareholders. The insurgent group (the plaintiffs in this case) made a public filing with the Securities and Exchange Commission announcing its intention to wage a control fight on October 16, 1971. On October 18, the board of Chris-Craft met and amended the corporation's by-laws, which had previously fixed the date of the annual meeting as January

11, to authorize the board to set an annual meeting date at any time in December or January. The board then proceeded to schedule the date of the upcoming meeting for December 8, thereby reducing the time available to the insurgents to mount their campaign by over a month. It also set the place of the meeting as Cortland, New York. The management justified the change in the meeting date on the grounds that weather conditions made it difficult to get to Cortland in January and that holding the meeting well before the Christmas holiday would reduce problems with delays of notices in the mail. Meanwhile, however, the defendants had taken a number of other actions to impede the insurgents including resisting providing them with the list of stockholders they were entitled to have under Delaware law. Although the trial court found that the defendant's actions, including the change in the date of the annual meeting, were designed to obstruct the plaintiffs' proxy solicitation, it refused to order that the meeting be rescheduled for its original date, on the ground that the plaintiffs had delayed too long in seeking judicial relief. On appeal, the Supreme Court reversed.]

HERRMANN, Justice (for the majority of the Court):

* * *

It will be seen that the Chancery Court considered all of the reasons stated by management as business reasons for changing the date of the meeting; but that those reasons were rejected by the Court below in making the following findings:

"I am satisfied, however, in a situation in which present management has disingenuously resisted the production of a list of its stockholders to plaintiffs or their confederates and has otherwise turned a deaf ear to plaintiffs' demands about a change in management designed to lift defendant from its present business doldrums, management has seized on a relatively new section of the Delaware Corporation Law for the purpose of cutting down on the amount of time which would otherwise have been available to plaintiffs and others for the waging of a proxy battle. Management thus enlarged the scope of its scheduled October 18 directors' meeting to include the by-law amendment in controversy after the stockholders commitee had filed with the S.E.C. its intention to wage a proxy fight on October 16.

"Thus plaintiffs reasonably contend that because of the tactics employed by management (which involve the hiring of two established proxy solicitors as well as a refusal to produce a list of its stockholders, coupled with its use of an amendment to the Delaware Corporation Law to limit the time for contest), they are given little chance, because of the exigencies of time, including that required to clear material at the S.E.C., to wage a successful proxy fight between now and December 8. * * *."

In our view, those conclusions amount to a finding that management has attempted to utilize the corporate machinery and the Delaware Law for the purpose of perpetuating itself in office; and, to that end, for the purpose of obstructing the legitimate efforts of dissident stockholders in the exercise of their rights to undertake a proxy contest against management. These are inequitable purposes, contrary to established principles of corporate democracy. The advancement by directors of the by-law date of a stockholders' meeting, for such purposes, may not be permitted to stand. Compare Condec Corporation v. Lunkenheimer Company, Del.Ch., 230 A.2d 769 (1967).

When the by-laws of a corporation designate the date of the annual meeting of stockholders, it is to be expected that those who intend to contest the reelection of incumbent management will gear their campaign to the by-law date. It is not to be expected that management will attempt to advance that date in order to obtain an inequitable advantage in the contest.

Management contends that it has complied strictly with the provisions of the new Delaware Corporation Law in changing the by-law date. The answer to that contention, of course, is that inequitable action does not become permissible simply because it is legally possible.

* * *

Accordingly, the judgment below must be reversed and the cause remanded, with instructions to nullify the December 8 date as a meeting date for stockholders; to reinstate January 11, 1972 as the sole date of the next annual meeting of the stockholders of the corporation; and to take such other proceedings and action as may be consistent herewith regarding the stock record closing date and any other related matters.

NOTE—INDEPENDENT LEGAL SIGNIFICANCE

A number of other cases, most of them involving mergers * or recapitalizations,** have taken what seems, on the surface at least, to be a rather different view of the effect of a statutory provision. The crux of the plaintiff's argument in these cases was in each case that the defendants were making use of a mechanism provided in one section of the statute to accomplish by a roundabout means a transac-

* A merger is one of several statutory techniques for combining two or more corporations into one. In the course of the merger the surviving corporation acquires all of the assets and assumes all of the liabilities of the merging corporations. The shareholders of the surviving corporation normally simply continue to hold their stock. The shareholders of the other corporation or corporations exchange their shares for securities of the surviving corporation or, in some cases, other consideration, including cash.

** A recapitalization involves a change in the capital structure of a corporation, usually accomplished by an amendment to the articles, in the course of which some or all of the corporation's securities are converted into securities of different characteristics.

tion that would have been foreclosed to them had they sought to make use of a different, and often more "normal" statutory procedure. In *Bove v. Community Hotel Corp. of Newport, R.I.*, 105 R.I. 36, 249 A.2d 89 (1969), for example, the management wished to effect a change in the capital structure of the corporation that would have the effect of eliminating the requirement that it pay substantial dividend arrearages to the holders of preferred stock before any dividends were paid on the common stock. Under Rhode Island law, a "recapitalization" by amendment of the charter of the corporation would have required the unanimous approval of the preferred shareholders, an approval that would not have been forthcoming. Blocked from using that alternative, the corporation instead set up a new shell corporation and sought to merge the old corporation into it, with the result that the preferred stock of the old corporation would be converted into common stock of the new one and the dividend arrearages would disappear. Some of the preferred shareholders sought to enjoin this transaction. In denying the requested relief, the Rhode Island Supreme Court stated:

> It is true, of course, that to accomplish the proposed recapitalization by amending [the corporation's] articles of association under relevant provisions of the general corporation law would require the unanimous vote of the preferred shareholders, whereas under the merger statute, only a two-third vote of those stockholders will be needed. Concededly, unanimity of the preferred stockholders is unobtainable in this case, and plaintiffs argue, therefore, that to permit the less restrictive provisions of the merger statute to accomplish indirectly what otherwise would be incapable of being accomplished directly by the more stringent amendment procedures of the general corporation law is tantamount to sanctioning a circumvention or perversion of that law.

> The question, however, is not whether recapitalization by the merger route is a subterfuge, but whether a merger which is designated for the sole purpose of cancelling the rights of preferred stockholders with the consent of less than all has been authorized by the legislature. The controlling statute is § 7–5–2. Its language is clear, all-embracing and unqualified. It authorizes any two or more business corporations *which were or might have been organized* under the general corporation law to merge into a single corporation; and it provides that the merger agreement shall prescribe "* * * the terms and conditions of consolidation or merger, the mode of carrying the same into effect * * * *as well as the manner of converting the shares of each of the constituent corporations into shares or other securities of the corporation resulting from or surviving such consolidation or merger*, with such other details and provisions as are deemed necessary." (emphasis ours) Nothing in that language even suggests that the legislature intended to make *underlying purpose* a standard for determining permissibility. Indeed, the

contrary is apparent since the very breadth of the language selected presupposes a complete lack of concern with whether the merger is designed to further the mutual interests of two existing and nonaffiliated corporations or whether alternatively it is purposed solely upon effecting a substantial change in an existing corporation's capital structure.

Moreover, that a possible effect of corporate action under the merger statute is not possible, or is even forbidden, under another section of the general corporation law is of no import, it being settled that the several sections of that law may have independent legal significance, and that the validity of corporate action taken pursuant to one section is not necessarily dependent upon its being valid under another. Hariton v. Arco Electronics, Inc., 40 Del. Ch. 326, 182 A.2d 22, aff'd, 41 Del.Ch. 74, 188 A.2d 123.

We hold, therefore, that nothing within the purview of our statute forbids a merger between a parent and a subsidiary corporation even under circumstances where the merger device has been resorted to solely for the purpose of obviating the necessity for the unanimous vote which would otherwise be required in order to cancel the priorities of preferred shareholders.

QUESTIONS

1. There is no doubt that the by-law change in *Schnell* was in technical compliance with the applicable statute. Indeed, although the trial court's opinion, quoted by the Supreme Court, stated that "management has seized on a relatively new section of the Delaware Corporation Law," the change would also have complied with the old provision. What, then, is the source of the law that the Supreme Court found the defendants to have violated?

2. In both *Schnell* and *Bove* the plaintiffs argued that a transaction that was in compliance with the corporate statute should be enjoined because the transaction was improperly motivated. In the former case, the allegedly improper purpose was to obstruct a valid takeover effort. In the latter, the motive was allegedly to circumvent a provision of the statute designed to protect the plaintiffs' interests. Why should the court grant relief in one case and not in the other?

3. Would *Schnell* have come out the same way had the management made the by-law change before learning of the insurgents' efforts (and therefore could not have been motivated by the desire to block those efforts). In other words, is the detrimental effect on the plaintiffs enough to justify judicial relief, or is an improper purpose required as well?

Chapter 4

THE CONSEQUENCES OF CORPORATENESS

A. INTRODUCTION

The idea that a collectivity, such as the corporation, possesses the legal attributes of a natural person is largely taken for granted today. For example, a corporation may own property, enter into contracts, sue and be sued in its own name. Similarly, as a separate legal entity, the corporation serves, in Mr. Justice Holmes' phrase, as a "nonconductor" of liability * whose independent existence protects its officers, directors, and shareholders from individual liability for obligations of the corporation. Behind these commonplace notions, however, lies one of the most powerful ideas in the history of the law of commerce. Without it the modern corporation as we know it would be an impossibility.

Although it is an enormous conceptual step to say that the corporation will be treated as a juridical "person" for many purposes, it is clear that legal distinctions must be drawn between corporate and natural persons. While corporations can hardly be imprisoned or executed, they have been held capable of holding the intent requisite for the commission of certain crimes and intentional torts.

In sum, the statement that a corporation is a "person" is a metaphor—as one author has put it, a "pun" **—a useful metaphor, to be sure, but one that serves as a weak reed on which to base semantic arguments of the character: The law imposes X obligation (or grants X right) to "persons"; the corporation is a "person"; it is therefore subject to (or the beneficiary of) X. Thus, while saying that corporations are persons serves as a useful shorthand for the fact that the law recognizes them as distinct legal entities endowed with separate legal characteristics that are often identical to those of natural persons, it must constantly be borne in mind that this is not always or necessarily the case.

On the "Existence" of Corporations. The idea that a group of natural persons associated for the purpose of carrying on some business may be treated as a separate legal entity is hardly a new one. Given the practical demands of commerce, that is hardly surprising. Although its ultimate source has been the subject of some debate among historians, the concept dates back at least as far as the ancient Romans, who may have borrowed it from the Greeks.

---

* Donnell v. Herring-Hall-Marvin Safe Co., 208 U.S. 267, 28 S.Ct. 288, 52 L.Ed. 481 (1908).

** Graham, An Innocent Abroad: The Constitutional Corporate "Person", 2 U. C.L.A.L.Rev. 155, 161 (1955).

The nature of the corporate "person" has provided a fertile ground for controversy among legal scholars, philosophers, and even theologians. What is a corporation? Is it merely a "fiction", a creation of the intellect, and thus, according to the most important corollary of that position, dependent for its recognition by the law on some act by the state (normally the grant of a charter)? Or do collectivities such as the corporation have, as Otto Von Gierke argued in a four-volume treatise, a "real" existence quite independent of governmental concession with the consequences that they must be recognized by the law as distinct entities with legal capacity whether or not the state has affirmatively granted them that status?

During the latter half of the last century and well into this one, these questions and related ones were the subject of an enormous volume of scholarly and judicial discussion both in Anglo-American circles and on the Continent. By the middle of this century, however, the debate seemed largely to have died out, pushed aside as metaphysical theorizing by the legal realists who argued that what was important was not whether the corporation was "real" or "fictional" but what legal consequences should flow in specific contexts from corporate status. Later writers have largely agreed with the view expressed in an article written by the pragmatist philosopher, John Dewey, in 1926 that conceptual approaches to the problem of corporate personality were useless in dealing with practical problems and should be abandoned.*

In recent years, however, the debate has been revived in connection with various proposals to use the incorporating (or chartering) mechanism as a vehicle to make private corporations more "accountable" to society at large (proposals to which we will return in a later chapter). Proponents of this means of rectifying what is seen as corporate misfeasance and malfeasance insist on the "fiction-concession" theory of corporate existence, arguing that, as the state alone can create business corporations and endow them with the capacity to act as legal entities, the state can condition its grant of the corporate "privilege" in whatever manner best serves the interests of all. The counterargument made by opponents of this device is that corporations are merely private arrangements among individuals with whose structure the state has no business interfering.**

The predominant Anglo-American judicial view has traditionally been that the corporation is, indeed a "fiction." In the well-known Suttons' Hospital Case, Lord Coke wrote, " * * * the corporation itself is only in abstract to, and rests only in intendment and consider-

* Dewey, The Historic Background of Corporate Legal Personality, 35 Yale L.J. 655 (1926). See Radin, The Endless Problem of Corporate Personality, 32 Colum.L.Rev. 643 (1932); Latty, The Corporate Entity as a Solvent of Legal Problems, 34 Mich.L.Rev. 597 (1936).

** See, R. Hessen, A New Concept of Corporations: A Contractual and Private Property Model, 30 Hastings L.J. 1327 (1979).

ation of the law.* Chief Justice Marshall's opinion in the *Dartmouth College* case ** is worth setting out in full:

A corporation is an artificial being, invisible, intangible, and existing only in contemplation of law. Being the mere creature of law, it possesses only those properties which the charter of its creation confers upon it, either expressly or as incidental to its very existence. These are such as are supposed best calculated to effect the object for which it was created. Among the most important are immortality, and, if the expression may be allowed, individuality; properties by which a perpetual succession of many persons are considered as the same, and may act as a single individual. They enable a corporation to manage its own affairs, and to hold property without the perplexing intricacies, the hazardous and endless necessity, of perpetual conveyances for the purpose of transmitting it from hand to hand. It is chiefly for the purpose of clothing bodies of men, in succession, with these qualities and capacities, that corporations were invented, and are in use. By these means, a perpetual succession of individuals are capable of acting for the promotion of the particular object, like one immortal being.

B.   LITIGATION BY SHAREHOLDERS

The most significant consequence of what Chief Justice Marshall called "individuality" is the legal distinction it creates between the corporation and its shareholders who are by virtue of this distinction not responsible for any of its obligations and, conversely, may not exercise directly any of its rights.

This is not to say, however, that shareholders may never sue to rectify some invasion of their interests. Where some right belonging to the corporation, as a separate entity, is at stake, shareholders are entitled (under circumstances that we will explore in greater detail in Chapter 15) to bring what is called a *derivative suit*. Originally a derivative suit was conceived of as a suit against the corporation in equity to compel it to bring an action against some third party, most often the officers and directors themselves. The shareholder's right grew out of the alleged wrongfulness of the failure of the managers of the corporation to institute the action. The corporation was joined as a reluctant party to the suit, whose prosecution was controlled by the plaintiff shareholders. This combination of actions in an equity court has today been replaced by statutory provisions that establish the right of shareholders to bring derivative suits and regulate the manner in which they are prosecuted. *E.g.*, MBCA § 49.

Where a transaction affects some right of the shareholders directly, that is, to say not merely as a consequence of a diminution of the

* *Sutton's Hospital Case*, 10 Co. Rep. 23 a (1613).

** Trustees of Dartmouth College v. Woodward, 17 U.S. (4 Wheat.) 518, 634, 4 L.Ed. 629, 659 (1819).

value of their shares by reason of an injury to the corporation, they retain their right to sue the wrongdoer (sometimes the corporation itself) in a *direct* action. In large corporations such actions are, for obvious reasons, often brought as class actions.

The distinction between a derivative suit and a direct action, although relatively straightforward in concept, is not always an easy one to draw.* In some situations, courts have even held that an action could be maintained as either (or both).** A classic example of the problem is a shareholder action to compel the declaration of the directors, it is open to the shareholders to claim in a lawsuit that the directors had abused that discretion and to seek an injunction ordering that a dividend be paid. Courts have differed on whether the essence of such a suit is that the directors have breached their fiduciary duty to manage the corporation wisely or whether it is founded on a breach of the shareholders' contract with the corporation arising out of their ownership of its stock.***

The characterization of a particular lawsuit as either direct or derivative is not merely semantic. Important practical consequences, which we will explore in Chapter 15, often turn on it.

PROBLEM

CHESAPEAKE MARINE SERVICES—PART III

In Part II of the Chesapeake Marine Services problem, should Apple bring his suit for rescission of the transaction that created and capitalized the subsidiary as a direct or a derivative suit? Or is it both?

GREEN v. VICTOR TALKING MACHINE CO.

24 F.2d 378 (2d Cir. 1928), cert. denied 278 U.S. 602, 49 S.Ct. 9, 73 L.Ed. 530.

[The plaintiff, Mrs. Green, had acquired all of the stock of the Pearsall Company under the will of her late husband. She sued the Victor Talking Machine Co., basing federal jurisdiction on diversity of citizenship. The complaint alleged that the Pearsall Company had been in the business of purchasing and reselling the products of the defendant, that the defendant had agreed to continue to sell its products to the Pearsall Company to induce Mr. Green to purchase the shares of a former minority shareholder, and that after Mr. Green's

---

* *See* Comment, Distinguishing Between Direct and Derivative Shareholder Suits, 110 U.Pa.L.Rev. 1147 (1962); Note, Protection of Shareholder's Rights: Derivative v. Representative Suits, 46 Ill.L. Rev. 937 (1952); Note, Corporations: Individual Recovery in Derivative Actions, Derivative Actions: Policy Considerations Leading to Choice of Derivative Form: 40 Calif.L.Rev. 127 (1952).

** *E.g.,* J. I. Case Co. v. Borak, 377 U. S. 426, 84 S.Ct. 1555, 12 L.Ed.2d 423 (1964).

*** In Gordon v. Elliman, 306 N.Y. 456, 119 N.E.2d 331 (1954), for example, the New York Court of Appeals held, 4–3, that a suit to compel dividends was a derivative action. The specific result of the case was subsequently reversed by a change in the New York statute involved.

death the defendant had engaged in a tortious scheme to force Mrs. Green to sell her stock. When she refused to do so, the defendant ceased to sell its products to the Pearsall Company, thereby destroying the Pearsall Company's value as a going concern and reducing the plaintiff's stock to worthlessness. Judge SWAN held that the allegations of fraud and intimidation directed to forcing Mrs. Green to sell her stock did not state a cause of action as they were unsuccessful. He then went on to discuss the allegations of wrongful interference with the business of the Pearsall Company.]

The essence of her complaint is that defendant, after inducing her testator to purchase certain shares in the Pearsall Company, impaired the value of them (1) by affirmative interference with its business; and (2) by refusing to continue to deal with it; and did these things with the purpose of inducing her to sell her stock to the defendant's nominee, and, failing in that, with the purpose of destroying the value of her shares.

Considering first the affirmative interference with the corporation's business: The attempt to induce employees to leave the Pearsall Company, not only is nowhere alleged to have been successful, but, if so, would have given rise to a cause of action to the corporation, rather than to its shareholders. The allegations of disclosure of confidential information, damage to credit, and unfair interference with business are mere conclusions of the pleader; but, even if they were treated as adequately pleaded, they would be subject to the same objection that they charge a breach of duty owing to the corporation rather than to its shareholders. The shareholders' rights are derivative, and, except through the corporation, the shareholders have no relation with one who commits a tort against the corporation's rights.

When there are numerous shareholders, it is apparent that each suffers relatively, depending upon the number of shares he owns, the same damage as all the others, and that each will be made whole if the corporation obtains restitution or compensation from the wrongdoer. Obviously it is sound policy to require a single action to be brought by the corporation, rather than to permit separate suits by each shareholder. In logic the result is justified, because the only right of the shareholder which has been infringed is what may be called his derivative or corporate right. Having elected to conduct their business in a corporate form, the men behind the corporation have, in the phrase of Justice Holmes, "interposed a nonconductor" between themselves and those who deal with them in their corporate enterprise. Donnell v. Herring-Hall-Marvin Safe Co., 208 U.S. 267, 273, 28 S.Ct. 288, 52 L.Ed. 481. Even when all the stock is owned by a sole shareholder, there seems no adequate reason to depart from the general rule that the corporation and its shareholders are to be treated as distinct legal persons. Therefore even a sole shareholder has no independent right which is violated by trespass upon or conversion of the corporation's property. Only his "corporate rights" have been invaded, and consequently he cannot sue the tort-feasor in an action at law.

Admitting this to be the general rule, the appellant contends that the result is different when a tort-feasor is animated by malice toward a particular shareholder, and that in such circumstances the principle that intentional harm without justification is actionable gives the shareholder a personal right of action, whether he is a sole shareholder or one of many. With this contention we cannot agree. Assuming that the allegations of the complaint are adequate to charge that the defendant's motive in doing the above-mentioned affirmative acts to the injury of the corporation's credit and business was a malicious desire to damage plaintiff as a shareholder, the cause of action is still the corporation's. The intention of the defendant is to invade the "corporate rights" of the shareholders; that is, the corporation's rights, whether this end is desired as a means of satisfying a grudge against some particular shareholder or all of them, or for some other motive. A defendant's motive in interfering with the corporation's business may be material in determining whether his interference is tortious or privileged, as in the case of fair competition; but his motive will not of itself create an independent cause of action in favor of shareholders, because only their derivative or corporate rights have been infringed. The policy of having their remedy lie in a suit by the corporation is not affected by the wrongdoer's malice toward an individual shareholder.

For a shareholder to obtain a personal right of action there must be relations between him and the tort-feasor independent of those which the shareholder derives through his interest in the corporate assets and business. Thus, in Ritchie v. McMullen, 79 F. 522, 533 (C. C.A.6), where the shareholder had pledged his stock with defendants who were directors of the corporation, it was held that the pledge created a duty in defendants not to use their power as directors for the purpose of impairing the value of the pledgor's stock. Judge Taft, who wrote the opinion, cited in support of the decision Walsham v. Stainton, 1 De Gex, J. & S. 678. There the plaintiff sold her stock to defendants at less than its real value, as a result of a conspiracy by them to use their powers as controlling shareholders and officers of the corporation, so as to deceive plaintiff as to the value of her shares. The suit was to compel them to account for the actual value of the shares, and the court held there was a direct liability to the plaintiff because they thus acquired her shares. If she had not parted with them, we think her remedy for any impairment of their value due to defendants' conduct would have had to be through a suit by the corporation.

In the instant case defendant is charged with having induced plaintiff's testator to purchase one-third of the shares the plaintiff now owns. Did that fact create a duty to plaintiff's testator, to which plaintiff has succeeded, that the defendant should not thereafter commit torts against the corporation which would impair the value of those shares? There is no allegation of any fraud or deception by defendant at the time it induced the purchase. No tort was committed against the testator which has survived to his [executor]. Therefore the defendant owed no duty to the plaintiff, any greater than it would owe to any other transferee of Mr. Green's shares. We cannot think that one who in good faith induces another to buy shares in a corporation owes to him and to all successive owners of those shares a duty, independent of that owed to the corporation, not to do a wrong to the corporation which will impair the value of those shares. The damage to them is the same as to all other shares, the rights of the shareholder which have been injured are derivative rights, and the remedy should lie in a suit by the corporation.

* * *

Nor does the allegation of a contractual duty to plaintiff's testator aid her. If it be assumed that the allegations of the complaint are sufficient to charge a contractual duty owing by defendant to the Pearsall Company, despite the indefiniteness of the terms of such a contract, and despite the fact that it was made with a shareholder, not with the corporation, nevertheless a breach of that duty would give a right of action to the corporation, not to its shareholders. Nor can it be maintained that one who breaks a contract with a corporation commits a tort upon its shareholders. If it be assumed that the defendant's contract was with plaintiff's testator, a breach by defendant of this contract would not be a tort against plaintiff, individually or as [executor]. And the allegation that this defendant's conduct was pursuant to a conspiracy between defendant and its own directors adds nothing. It is but a reiteration in another form of the allegation of nonfeasance by the defendant corporation, which can act only through its officers or agents.

We are satisfied that the complaint states no cause of action in tort in the plaintiff. The judgment is affirmed.

C. THE CORPORATION AS A CONSTITUTIONAL PERSON

1. DUE PROCESS AND EQUAL PROTECTION

As we have already seen in *Bellotti*, there has been, to put it mildly, some controversy over the extent to which corporations are to be treated as "persons" enjoying the various rights and liberties granted by the Constitution. Perhaps the Supreme Court's most important decisions in that regard are its holding in Santa Clara County v. Southern Pacific Railroad Co., 118 U.S. 394, 6 S.Ct. 1132, 30 L.Ed. 118 (1886), that corporations are "persons" within the equal protection clause of the Fourteenth Amendment and in the *Minneapolis & St. Louis Railway Co.* v. *Beckwith*, 129 U.S. 26, 9 S.Ct. 207, 32 L.Ed. 585

(1888), that they are protected by the due process clause. The history of those decisions is debated in the following unusual colloquy.

WHEELING STEEL CORP. v. GLANDER

337 U.S. 562, 69 S.Ct. 1291, 93 L.Ed. 1544 (1949).

[The State of Ohio levied an *ad valorem* tax on the accounts receivable derived from sales of goods manufactured within Ohio and applied the tax to foreign corporations that were incorporated and had their principal places of business in states other than Ohio. The Court, in an opinion by Mr. Justice JACKSON, held that the Ohio scheme discriminated against nonresidents in a way that denied the petitioners equal protection. Mr. Justice DOUGLAS filed a dissent based on the proposition that a corporation is not a "person" entitled to equal protection under the Fourteenth Amendment. This called forth a further opinion by Mr. Justice JACKSON addressing that point. Excerpts from this opinion and from the dissent follow.]

By Mr. Justice JACKSON.

The writer of the Court's opinion deems it necessary to complete the record by pointing out why, in writing by assignment for the Court, he assumed without discussion that the protections of the Fourteenth Amendment are available to a corporation. It was not questioned by the State in this case, nor was it considered by the courts below. It has consistently been held by this Court that the Fourteenth Amendment assures corporations equal protection of the laws, at least since 1886, Santa Clara Co. v. Southern Pacific R. Co., 118 U.S. 394, 396, 6 S.Ct. 1132, 30 L.Ed. 118, and that it entitles them to due process of law, at least since 1889, Minneapolis R. Co. v. Beckwith, 129 U.S. 26, 28, 9 S.Ct. 207, 32 L.Ed. 585.

It is true that this proposition was once challenged by one Justice. Connecticut General Co. v. Johnson, 303 U.S. 77, 83, 58 S.Ct. 436, 439, 82 L.Ed. 673 (dissenting opinion). But the challenge did not commend itself, even to such consistent liberals as Mr. Justice Brandeis and Mr. Justice Stone, and I had supposed it was no longer pressed.
* * *

Without pretending to a complete analysis, I find that in at least two cases during this current term the same question was appropriate for consideration, as here. In Railway Express v. New York, 336 U.S. 106, 69 S.Ct. 463, a corporation claimed to be deprived of both due process and equal protection of the law, and in Ott v. Mississippi Barge Line, 336 U.S. 169, 69 S.Ct. 432, a corporation claimed to be denied due process of law. At prior terms, in many cases the question was also inherent, for corporations made similar claims under the Fourteenth Amendment. * * * Although the author of the present dissent was the writer of each of the cited Court's opinions, it was not intimated therein that there was even doubt whether the corporations had standing to raise the questions or were entitled to protection of the Amendment. Instead, in each case the author, as I have done in this case, proceeded to discuss and dispose of the corporation's contentions on their merits, a quite improper procedure, I should think, if the corporation had no standing to raise the constitutional questions. Indeed, if the corporation had no such right, it is difficult to see how this Court would have jurisdiction to consider the case at all.

*   *   *

In view of this record I did not, and still do not, consider it necessary for the Court opinion to review the considerations which justify the assumption that these corporations have standing to raise the issues decided.

Mr. Justice DOUGLAS, with whom Mr. Justice BLACK concurs, dissenting.

It has been implicit in all of our decisions since 1886 that a corporation is a "person" within the meaning of the Equal Protection Clause of the Fourteenth Amendment. Santa Clara Co. v. South. Pacific R. Co., 118 U.S. 394, 396, 6 S.Ct. 1132, 30 L.Ed. 118, so held. The Court was cryptic in its decision. It was so sure of its ground that it wrote no opinion on the point, Chief Justice Waite announcing from the bench:

> The court does not wish to hear argument on the question whether the provision in the Fourteenth Amendment to the Constitution, which forbids a State to deny to any person within its jurisdiction the equal protection of the laws, applies to these corporations. We are all of opinion that it does.

There was no hisotry, logic, or reason given to support that view. Nor was the result so obvious that exposition was unnecessary.

The Fourteenth Amendment became a part of the Constitution in 1868. In 1871 a corporation claimed that Louisiana had imposed on it a tax that violated the Equal Protection Clause of the new Amendment. Mr. Justice Woods (then Circuit Judge) held that "person" as there used did not include a corporation and added, "This construction of the section is strengthened by the history of the submission by congress, and the adoption by the states of the 14th amendment so fresh in all minds as to need no rehearsal." Insurance Co. v. New Orleans, Fed.Cas.No.7,052, 1 Woods 85, 88.

What was obvious to Mr. Justice Woods in 1871 was still plain to the Court in 1873. Mr. Justice Miller in the Slaughter House Cases, 16 Wall. 36, 71, 21 L.Ed. 394, adverted to events "almost too recent to be called history" to show that the purpose of the Amendment was to protect human rights—primarily the rights of a race which had just won its freedom. And as respects the Equal Protection Clause he stated, "The existence of laws in the States where the newly emancipated negroes resided, which discriminated with gross injustice and hardship against them as a class, was the evil to be remedied by this clause, and by it such laws are forbidden." 16 Wall. at page 81, 21 L. Ed. 394.

Moreover what was clear to these earlier judges was apparently plain to the people who voted to make the Fourteenth Amendment a part of our Constitution. For as Mr. Justice Black pointed out in his dissent in Connecticut General Co. v. Johnson, 303 U.S. 77, 87, 58 S. Ct. 436, 441, 82 L.Ed. 873, the submission of the Amendment to the people was on the basis that it protected human beings. There was no suggestion in its submission that it was designed to put negroes and corporations into one class and so dilute the police power of the States over corporate affairs. Arthur Twining Hadley once wrote that "The Fourteenth Amendment was framed to protect the negroes from oppression by the whites, not to protect corporations from oppression by the legislature. It is doubtful whether a single one of the members of Congress who voted for it had any idea that it would touch the question of corporate regulation at all."[1]

Both Mr. Justice Woods in Insurance Co. v. New Orleans, supra, Fed.Cas.No.7,052, 1 Woods page 88, and Mr. Justice Black in his dissent in Connecticut General Co. v. Johnson, supra, 303 U.S. at pages 88–89, 58 S.Ct. at pages 441–442, 82 L.Ed. 673, have shown how strained a construction it is of the Fourteenth Amendment so to hold. Section 1 of the Amendment provides:

> All *persons* born or naturalized in the United States, and subject to the jurisdiction thereof, are *citizens* of the United States and of the State wherein they reside. No State shall make or enforce any law which shall abridge the privileges or immunities of *citizens* of the United States; nor shall any State deprive any *person* of life, liberty, or property, without due process of law; nor deny to any *person* within its jurisdiction the equal protection of the laws. (Italics added.)

"Persons" in the first sentence plainly include only human beings, for corporations are not "born or naturalized."

Corporations are not "citizens" within the meaning of the first clause of the second sentence.

It has never been held that they are persons whom a State may not deprive of "life" within the meaning of the second clause of the second sentence.

---

1. The Constitutional Position of Property in America, 64 Independent 834, 836 (1908). He went on to say that the Dartmouth College case, 4 Wheat. 518, 4 L.Ed. 629, and the construction given the Fourteenth Amendment in the Santa Clara case "have had the effect of placing the modern industrial corporation in an almost impregnable constitutional position." *Id.*, p. 836.

As to whether the framers of the Amendment may have had such an undisclosed purpose see Graham, The "Conspiracy Theory" of the Fourteenth Amendment, 47 Yale L.J. 371.

"Liberty" in that clause is "the liberty of natural, not artificial, persons." Western Turf Ass'n v. Greenberg, 204 U.S. 359, 363, 27 S. Ct. 384, 385, 386, 51 L.Ed. 520.

But "property" as used in that clause has been held to include that of a corporation since 1889 when Minneapolis R. Co. v. Beckwith, 129 U.S. 26, 9 S.Ct. 207, 32 L.Ed. 585, was decided.

It requires distortion to read "person" as meaning one thing, then another within the same clause and from clause to clause. It means, in my opinion, a substantial revision of the Fourteenth Amendment. As to the matter of construction, the sense seems to me to be with Mr. Justice Woods in Insurance Co. v. New Orleans, supra, Fed.Cas. No.7,052, 1 Woods at page 88, where he said, "The plain and evident meaning of the section is, that the persons to whom the equal protection of the law is secured are persons born or naturalized or endowed with life and liberty, and consequently natural and not artificial persons."

History has gone the other way. Since 1886 the Court has repeatedly struck down state legislation as applied to corporations on the ground that it violated the Equal Protection Clause. Every one of our decisions upholding legislation as applied to corporations over the objection that it violated the Equal Protection Clause has assumed that they are entitled to the constitutional protection. But in those cases it was not necessary to meet the issue since the state law was not found to contain the elements of discrimination which the Equal Protection Clause condemns. But now that the question is squarely presented I can only conclude that the Santa Clara case was wrong and should be overruled.

One hesitates to overrule cases even in the constitutional field that are of an old vintage. But that has never been a deterrent heretofore and should not be now.

We are dealing with a question of vital concern to the people of the nation. It may be most desirable to give corporations this protection from the operation of the legislative process. But that question is not for us. It is for the people. If they want corporations to be treated as humans are treated, if they want to grant corporations this large degree of emancipation from state regulation, they should say so. The Constitution provides a method by which they may do so. We should not do it for them through the guise of interpretation.

QUESTIONS

1. What would Justices Douglas and Black do about a corporation whose property was taken by eminent domain without compensation (or with clearly inadequate compensation)? Would they leave it (and its shareholders) without any redress under the Constitution, or would they allow the corporation to sue to protect the rights of its

shareholders? *Cf. N.A.A.C.P.* v. *Alabama ex rel. Patterson*, 357 U. S. 449, 458–60, 78 S.Ct. 1163, 2 L.Ed.2d 1488 (1958).

2.   Is it relevant to this dispute that the Court held early on that a corporation was not a "citizen" entitled to the protection of the privileges and immunities clause of the Fourteen Amendment? *Paul* v. *Virginia*, 75 U.S. (8 Wall.) 168, 19 L.Ed. 357 (1868).

2. THE FOURTH AND FIFTH AMENDMENTS

We have seen that a corporation is a "person entitled to the equal protection of the laws, *Santa Clara County*, with a right not to be deprived of its property (presumably it is not capable of being deprived of life or liberty) without due process of law, *Minneapolis R. Co.* v. *Beckwith*, and with standing to assert the rights of freedom of speech and the press protected by the First Amendment, *First National Bank of Boston* v. *Bellotti*, 435 U.S. 765, 98 S.Ct. 1407, 55 L. Ed.2d 707 (1978). It is not, however, a "citizen" entitled to be accorded the privileges and immunities of citizens. What of other constitutional rights?

One area of more than passing interest in a day of comprehensive governmental regulation of corporate activity is the extent to which the state can obtain access to corporate records or premises owned by a corporation for the purposes of law enforcement. The Supreme Court held in *Hale* v. *Henkel*, 201 U.S. 43, 26 S.Ct. 370, 50 L.Ed. 652 (1906), a case involving a federal antitrust investigation, that corporations cannot claim the Fifth Amendment's privilege against self-incrimination. The Court ruled that although an officer or employee of a corporation could refuse to produce documents of the corporation on the grounds that they might tend to incriminate him, he could not assert any similar right on behalf of the corporation, itself. The Court's opinion went on:

> Upon the other hand, the corporation is a creature of the State. It is presumed to be incorporated for the benefit of the public. It receives certain special privileges and franchises, and holds them subject to the laws of the State and the limitations of its charter. Its powers are limited by law. It can make no contract not authorized by its charter. Its rights to act as a corporation are only preserved to it so long as it obeys the laws of its creation. There is a reserved right in the legislature to investigate its contracts and find out whether it has exceeded its powers. It would be a strange anomaly to hold that a State, having chartered a corporation to make use of certain franchises, could not in the exercise of its sovereignty inquire how these franchises had been employed, and whether they had been abused, and demand the production of the corporate books and papers for that purpose. The defense amounts to this: That an officer of a corporation, which is charged with a criminal violation of the statute, may plead the criminality of such corporation as a refusal to produce its books.

To state this proposition is to answer it. While an individual may lawfully refuse to answer incriminating questions unless protected by an immunity statute, it does not follow that a corporation, vested with special privileges and franchises, may refuse to show its hand when charged with an abuse of such privileges.

It is true that the corporation in this case was chartered under the laws of New Jersey, and that it receives its franchise from the legislature of that State; but such franchises, so far as they involve questions of interstate commerce, must also be exercised in subordination to the power of Congress to regulate such commerce, and in respect to this the General Government may also assert a sovereign authority to ascertain whether such franchises have been exercised in a lawful manner, with a due regard to its own laws. Being subject to this dual sovereignty, the General Government possesses the same right to see that its own laws are respected as the State would have with respect to the special franchises vested in it by the laws of the State. The powers of the General Government in this particular in the vindication of its own laws, are the same as if the corporation had been created by an act of Congress. It is not intended to intimate, however, that it has a general visitatorial power over state corporations.

Although the Supreme Court has squarely held that corporations have at least "some Fourth Amendment rights", G.M. Leasing Corp. v. United States, 429 U.S. 338, 353; 97 S.Ct. 619, 629, 50 L.Ed.2d 530 (1977), it has indicated that those rights are somewhat less than those enjoyed by individuals. Oklahoma Press Publishing Co. v. Walling, 327 U.S. 186, 202–208, 66 S.Ct. 494, 90 L.Ed. 614 (1946).

Both the Fifth Amendment privilege against self-incrimintion and the Fourth Amendment protection against unreasonable search and seizure have been considered part of Mr. Justice Brandeis' famous "right to be let alone." See Olmstead v. United States, 277 U.S. 438, 478, 48 S.Ct. 564, 572, 72 L.Ed. 944, 956 (1928) (dissenting opinion). It is clear, however, that to the extent that corporations are entitled to some constitutional protection of their "privacy", it is at best an attenuated protection. In United States v. Morton Salt Co., 338 U.S. 632, 70 S.Ct. 357, 94 L.Ed. 401 (1950), the corporation objected to an order of the Federal Trade Commission directing the making of certain reports. In rejecting the claim that the order infringed upon the corporation's Fourth Amendment rights the Court said:

> While they may and should have protection from unlawful demands made in the name of public investigation, corporations can claim no equality with individuals in the enjoyment of a right to privacy. They are endowed with public attributes. They have a collective impact upon society, from which they derive the privilege of acting as artificial entities. The Federal Government allows them the privilege of engaging in interstate commerce. Favors from government often carry with them an enhanced

measure of regulation. Even if one were to regard the request for information in this case as caused by nothing more than official curiosity, nevertheless law-enforcing agencies have a legitimate right to satisfy themselves that corporate behavior is consistent with the law and the public interest.

In arguing in favor of a right of privacy Brandeis wrote in his dissent in *Olmstead*,

> The makers of our Constitution undertook to secure conditions favorable to the pursuit of happiness. They recognized the significance of man's spiritual nature, of his feelings and his intellect. They know that only a part of the pain, pleasure and satisfactions of life are to be found in material things. They sought to protect Americans in their beliefs, their thoughts, their emotions and their sensations. They conferred, as against the government, the right to be let alone—the most comprehensive right and the right most valued by civilized men.

It is obviously not these interests that the Supreme Court had in mind when it held that corporations may assert some rights under the Fourth Amendment. What, then, are the interests at stake? Of the rationales given in Hale v. Henkel and United States v. Morton Salt Co. for placing limits on corporate "privacy", which do you prefer? Or are they the same?

D. CORPORATE PURPOSES AND CORPORATE POWERS: THE DOCTRINE OF ULTRA VIRES

1. INTRODUCTION

The statutory charter that created early corporations included as one of its principal provisions a statement of the purposes for which the corporation was to be formed. Modern general incorporation statutes adopt the same principle in a requirement that the articles of incorporation state the purpose for which the corporation is to be formed. *Cf.* MBCA § 54(c). According to the common law doctrine of *ultra vires* (literally, "beyond the power"), a corporation may not engage in activities outside the scope of the purposes thus defined. In a famous English case, for example, the House of Lords held that a corporation whose charter authorized it to "sell or lend all kinds of railway plant, to carry on the business of mechanical engineers and general contractors, etc." exceeded its powers in purchasing a concession to construct and operate a railway line in Belgium. The corporation contracted with one Riche to do the construction, but after Riche had done some of the work, the corporation repudiated the contract. Riche's suit on the contract was rejected by the House of Lords on the ground that the corporation lacked the power to build a railroad and thus to bind itself to a contract for the purpose. Ashbury Railway Carriage & Iron Co. v. Riche, 33 N.S. Law Times Rep. 450 (1875).

The doctrine of *ultra vires* found its roots principally in a suspicion of concentrations of economic power. The historical origins of the doctrine are discussed in the well-known excerpt from Justice Brandeis' dissenting opinion in Liggett v. Lee, 288 U.S. 517, 53 S.Ct. 481, 77 L.Ed. 929 (1933) which is set forth on pp. 128–130. A second reason for giving effect to the limitations on a corporation's power that might be written into its charter is to enable investors in such a corporation to limit their economic exposure to the risks of a defined business undertaking.

The legal mechanisms available to challenge an allegedly *ultra vires* act took the form of either a "quo warranto" (literally, "by what authority") proceeding instituted by the state for the forfeiture of the corporate charter or the assertion of the corporate incapacity in various forms in the context of private lawsuits. That a corporate act was unauthorized and therefore void was often asserted as a defense to an action against the corporation on a corporate obligation, as in the *Ashbury Railway Carriage* case. Early thinking even went so far as to argue that a corporation lacked the authority to commit a tort; that since tortious acts committed by its agents were *ultra vires*, a corporation could not be liable in tort. As might easily be understood, although a rare case or two seemed to accept this argument, it was ultimately resoundingly rejected.

The *ultra vires* doctrine could also be asserted affirmatively in a shareholder action against a corporation's managers who caused the corporation to suffer a loss by engaging in activity outside its authority. In at least one relatively modern case the shareholders of a corporation were held personally liable as partners on a contract found to be outside the purposes specified in the articles of incorporation (although there were other factors that contributed to the result). Lurie v. Arizona Fertilizer & Chemical Co., 101 Ariz. 482, 421 P.2d 330 (1966).

In the nineteenth century a large portion of the law of corporations was devoted to the resolution of disputes arising under the *ultra vires* doctrine; nowadays the issue is rarely seen in the courts. Clearly, the original purpose of the doctrine, the curbing of the powers of the large corporation, was a failure. That it was may be partially attributable to the harshness with which older courts, as exemplified by the *Ashbury Railway Carriage* case, applied the doctrine.

2. THE MODERN DOCTRINE

Once states began to enact general incorporation statutes in lieu of granting corporate charters one at a time it also became a simple matter to circumvent the limitations of the *ultra vires* doctrine by drafting the articles of incorporation in as broad terms as the draftsman could imagine. Purposes clauses often went on for pages, listing—or at least attempting to list—every conceivable activity in which a corporation might engage, when in fact the immediate intention of the promoters was to undertake only the first activity on the list. Today, corporate statutes often provide, as does Delaware in § 102(a)(3), "It shall be sufficient to state, either alone or with other businesses or purposes, that the purpose of the corporation is to engage in any lawful act or activity for which corporations may be organized under the General Corporation Law of Delaware, and by such statement all lawful acts and activities shall be within the purpose of the corporation, except for express limitations, if any." Since the same statute, in § 101(b) provides that "[a] corporation may be incorporated or organized under this chapter to conduct or promote any lawful business or purposes, except as may otherwise be provided by the constitution or other law of this State" the organic documents of the corporation provide no limitation on corporate purposes.

Although it was, and still is, frequently ignored by corporate draftsmen, there is a conceptual distinction to be drawn between corporate *purposes* and corporate *powers*. It would be *ultra vires* for a corporation either to engage in business not included within the statement of purposes found in its charter or to seek to exercise, in carrying on business within its purposes, a power denied it by the charter or the statute. It was formerly the practice for articles of incorporation to elaborate at great length a list of "powers" as well as one of "purposes." In practice, however, it is often difficult to distinguish between the two, and out of an excess of caution, draftsmen often listed among the "purposes" of a corporation what were, properly conceived, merely powers. For example the "purposes" clauses found in many form books include acquiring or dealing in real property. For most corporations this would not be a purpose but simply the "power" to acquire real estate in the normal course of affairs. But (to illustrate the difficulty of the distinction) dealing in real property would clearly be a "purpose" of a corporation organized to go into the real estate business. Today most of this learning has been made largely irrelevant by modern statutory treatment such as that of MBCA § 4, which grants to business corporations every power they might conceivably wish to exercise, and throws in for good measure, "all powers necessary or convenient to effect [the corporation's] purposes."

In addition to adopting a permissive approach both to the definition of corporate purposes and to the statutory grant of powers, modern corporate statutes also often impose limits on uses to which the doctrine of *ultra vires* can be put, most importantly largely eliminating the use of the defense of *ultra vires* by a corporation against an otherwise valid corporate obligation. *See, e.g.,* MBCA § 7. As a result, the doctrine is now nearly defunct.

There are, however, three areas in which there is some life left in the old learning, particularly in those few states whose statutes are more sparing than the Model Act in their grants of express corporate powers. First, at common law a corporation was prohibited from becoming a member of a partership, on the theory that to do so exposed the assets of the corporation to risks created by decisions of the other partners and thus not within the control of the board of directors. *See* Whittenton Mills v. Upton, 76 Mass. (10 Gray) 852 (1858). Most statutes today contain express authorization for corporations to become partners, and even where this is not the case, it is generally possible for the corporation to acquire the power by an appropriate provision in its articles of incorporation.

Corporations were also once generally not authorized to guarantee the obligations of others, this on the theory that such guarantees could not be in the interest of the shareholders. *See* Brinson v. Mill Supply Co., Inc., 219 N.C. 498, 14 S.E.2d 505 (1941). This limitation has also largely disappeared, both as a result of the evolution of the case law and modern statutory provisions (although the latter are sometimes subject to qualification).

The third, and most significant, area in which the *ultra vires* doctrine is of continuing concern relates to the "waste" of corporate assets by their use for other than corporate purposes. Although shareholders have sought to show that their corporations have "given away" or "wasted" assets in a variety of different ways, the most common charge has been that a corporate charitable donation was *ultra vires*.

It is interesting to observe that while some conduct may be lawful under the law in general it may be improper under the strictures of corporate law. In First National Bank of Boston v. Bellotti, 435 U.S. 765, 98 S.Ct. 1407, 55 L.Ed.2d 707 (1978) the Court struck down a legislative attempt to control corporate political activities but observed that "minority shareholders generally have access to the judicial remedy of a derivative suit to challenge corporate disbursements alleged to have been made for improper corporate purposes or merely to further the personal interests of management." 435 U.S. at 795, 98 S.Ct. at 1426.

The next section is devoted to the questions of law and policy raised by claims of "waste" and "improper corporate purpose."

3. ULTRA VIRES AND CORPORATE CHARITABLE GIVING

PROBLEM

UNION AIRLINES

You are general counsel for Union Airlines, Inc., a major U.S. domestic air carrier headquartered in Georgetown, Columbia. The company has $1 billion in assets and generates $700 million in annual revenues. Due to increased competition and higher fuel prices, Union's profits have declined steadily for the last several years, and it has posted large losses for the last three.

Wright, the company's chief executive officer just called you to tell you that he would like to make a corporate donation of $500,000 to the Georgetown Opera Company to help bail it out of a financial crisis that threatens to prevent the Opera from opening the current season.

1. He would like your opinion on the legality of the gift before he presents the matter to the board of directors for its approval. What should you tell him?

2. You are also a member of the board. Assuming that you have found no legal obstacles to the proposed donation, in your capacity as board member, what considerations should you weigh before voting? How would you vote?

NOTE—CORPORATIONS AND CHARITABLE CONTRIBUTIONS

In absolute terms, corporations are large contributors to charities. In 1979, for example, they donated $2.2 billion. Statistical Abstract of the United States 363 (1980). But relative to individual giving, corporate philanthropy is quite small. In the same year, individuals gave $36.5 billion. *Id.* Moreover, while individuals tend to contribute between 2 and 3 percent of their income to charities, the average corporate gift is more on the order of 1 percent of pretax income.

The reasons for corporate largess are not exclusively altruistic. The Internal Revenue Code allows corporations, like individuals, to deduct charitable contributions from income in calculating the amount of income tax due. The allowable deduction for corporations, however, is 10 percent of taxable income, whereas individuals may deduct contributions up to 50 percent of their income.

Advocates of at least moderate amounts of corporate philanthropy, including the managements of most major corporations, typically argue that charitable giving is in the best long-run interest of the corporation. That view is not universal, however. Critics, including many shareholders, protest that such giving deprives shareholders of money they might otherwise receive as dividends. They urge that it is not for the management of a corporation to give away money properly belonging to the shareholders. If the shareholders wish to make such gifts, they should make that decision themselves.

Modern statutory provisions, such as MBCA § 4(m), together with a number of cases similar to those set forth below have gone a long way toward eliminating any doubts there may have been about the power of corporations to make *some* charitable contributions. The establishment of the basic principle that corporations may use their assets for ends that are unrelated—or at least not *directly* related—to the financial well-being of the shareholders, does not put an end to the legal issues, however. If corporate managers overdo "their" largess, they may be guilty of wasting corporate assets. A simple illustration of the concept of waste in another context is that, while it is of course legal for a corporation to pay salaries to its officers, if those salaries become too high, they may become "wasteful" and therefore *ultra vires*. *See, e.g.*, Rogers v. Hill, 289 U.S. 582, 53 S.Ct. 731, 77 L.Ed. 1385 (1933), reproduced *infra*, Chapter 14. Likewise the proportionality of charitable contributions bears on their validity. It is clear that at some point, a gift that is valid in principle, can become so large as to constitute a waste of corporate assets. Drawing that line, however, is another matter.

THEODORA HOLDING CORP. v. HENDERSON

257 A.2d 398 (Del.Ch.1969).

[For many years, Girard Henderson dominated the affairs of Alexander Dawson, Inc., through his controlling interest in that corporation. In 1955, he transferred shares to his then wife, Theodora Henderson, as part of a separation agreement. In 1967, Mrs. Henderson formed the Theodora Holding Corporation and transferred to it 27 percent of the outstanding stock of Alexander Dawson, Inc. During that year, the combined dividends paid by Alexander Dawson, Inc. to Mrs. Henderson and her corporation totalled $286,240.

From 1960 to 1966, Girard Henderson had caused Alexander Dawson, Inc. to make annual corporate contributions ranging from $60,000 to $70,000 or higher to the Alexander Dawson Foundation ("the Foundation"), which Henderson had formed in 1957. All contributions were unanimously approved by the shareholders. In 1966, Alexander Dawson, Inc. donated to the Foundation a large tract of land valued at $467,750 for the purpose of establishing a camp for under-privileged boys. In April 1967, Mr. Henderson proposed that the board approve a $528,000 gift of company stock to Theodora Ives, who suggested that the gift be made instead to a charitable corporation supported by her mother and herself. In December 1967, Girard Henderson caused a reduction in the size of the board of directors of Alexander Dawson, Inc. from eight to three members. The gift of stock to the Foundation was thereafter approved.

This gift was challenged in a suit by the Theodora Holding Corporation against certain individuals, including Gerard Henderson, seeking an accounting and the appointment of a liquidating receiver for Alexander Dawson, Inc.]

MARVEL, Vice Chancellor.

* * *

Title 8 Del.C. § 122 provides as follows:

Every corporation created under this chapter shall have power to—

* * *

(9) Make donations for the public welfare or for charitable, scientific or educational purposes, and in time of war or other national emergency in aid thereof.

There is no doubt but that the Alexander Dawson Foundation is recognized as a legitimate charitable trust by the Department of Internal Revenue. It is also clear that it is authorized to operate exclusively in the fields of " * * * religious, charitable, scientific, literary, or educational purposes, or for the prevention of cruelty to children or animals * * * ". Furthermore, contemporary courts recognize that unless corporations carry an increasing share of the burden of supporting charitable and educational causes that the business advantages now reposed in corporations by law may well prove to be unacceptable to the representatives of an aroused public. The recognized obligation of corporations towards philanthropic, educational and artistic causes is reflected in the statutory law of all of the states, other than the states of Arizona and Idaho.

In A. P. Smith Mfg. Co. v. Barlow, 13 N.J. 145, 98 A.2d [581], appeal dismissed, 346 U.S. 861, 74 S.Ct. 107, 98 L.Ed. 373, a case in which the corporate donor had been organized long before the adoption of a statute authorizing corporate gifts to charitable or educational institutions, the Supreme Court of New Jersey upheld a gift of $1500 by the plaintiff corporation to Princeton University, being of the opinion that the trend towards the transfer of wealth from private industrial entrepreneurs to corporate institutions, the increase of taxes on individual income, coupled with steadily increasing philanthropic needs, necessitate corporate giving for educational needs even were there no statute permitting such gifts, and this was held to be the case apart from the question of the reserved power of the state to amend corporate charters. The court also noted that the gift tended to bolster the free enterprise system and the general social climate in which plaintiff was nurtured. And while the court pointed out that there was no showing that the gift in question was made indiscriminately or to a pet charity in furtherance of personal rather than corporate ends, the actual holding of the opinion appears to be that a corporate charitable or educational gift to be valid must merely be within reasonable limits both as to amount and purpose.

* * *

I conclude that the test to be applied in passing on the validity of a gift such as the one here in issue is that of reasonableness, a test in which the provisions of the Internal Revenue Code pertaining to charitable gifts by corporations furnish a helpful guide. The gift here under attack was made from gross income and had a value as of the time of giving of $528,000 in a year in which Alexander Dawson, Inc.'s total income was $19,144,229.06, or well within the federal tax deduction limitation of 5% of such income. The contribution under attack can be said to have "cost" all of the stockholders of Alexander Dawson, Inc. including plaintiff, less than $80,000, or some fifteen cents per dollar of contribution, taking into consideration the federal tax provisions applicable to holding companies as well as the provisions for compulsory distribution of dividends received by such a corporation. In addition, the gift, by reducing Alexander Dawson, Inc.'s reserve for unrealized capital gains taxes by some $130,000, increased the balance sheet net worth of stockholders of the corporate defendant by such amount. It is accordingly obvious, in my opinion, that the relatively small loss of immediate income otherwise payable to plaintiff and the corporate defendant's other stockholders had it not been for the gift in question, is far out-weighed by the overall benefits flowing from the placing of such gift in channels where it serves to benefit those in need of philanthropic or educational support, thus providing justification for large private holdings, thereby benefiting plaintiff in the long run. Finally, the fact that the interests of the Alexander Dawson Foundation appear to be increasingly directed towards the rehabilitation and education of deprived but deserving young people is peculiarly appropriate in an age when a large segment of youth is alienated even from parents who are not entirely satisfied with our present social and economic system.

* * *

UNION PACIFIC RAILROAD CO. v. TRUSTEES, INC.

8 Utah 2d 101, 329 P.2d 398 (1958).

[Union Pacific Railroad Company sought declaratory judgment that a contribution of $5,000 to a nonprofit organization for charitable, scientific, religious, or educational purposes was valid. The lower court had held that the gift was ultra vires. Neither the company's charter nor legislation gave the corporation the express power to make the contribution.]

HENRIOD, Justice.

* * *

Directors of the plaintiff testified with singular unanimity that such new concept conceived in a shifting socio-economic atmosphere was born of new corporate business policy. It seems to be nurtured by legislative, corporate and judicial thinking. A reasonable percentage of corporate income, they urge, should be earmarked for worthy causes, as a necessary and proper item of business expense, just as funds are tagged for advertising, public relations and the like.

Mr. E. Roland Harriman, Chairman of plaintiff's Board, said "I think it is good business to do so; in the long run beneficial to our stockholders * * * I think the public has come to expect that we will support worthwhile local and national causes, and, in effect, we agree with this viewpoint." Mr. John S. Sinclair, director, said: "We have come to expect corporations to behave in the field of social consciousness as individuals would behave,—that is, with a prudent eye to its financial capacity and selectivity as to the objects of its generosity   *   *   *   Corporate donations create good will in the community." Mr. William C. Mullendore, director, said "The basis of our policy of making contributions in aid of   *   *   *   educational and charitable institutions is, first of all, as a citizen of the community dependent upon the good will of the customers   *   *   *. We have included in our regular operating expenses the provision for those donations, as necessarily included in a much larger   *   *   *   budget for maintenance of our physical equipment."

*   *   *

It strikes us as being rather inconceivable, in what seems to be a visible, substantial national trend, that men heretofore known for their administrative and executive experience and ability, suddenly and deliberately would espouse a program on behalf of a corporation in which they are interested, and to whose shareholders they are amenable and accountable, if they were not confident that their company presently and directly, or within the foreseeable future, would receive a quid pro quo as the resultant of good will engendered by contributions.   *   *   *

The iconoclast may discount the suggestion that corporations have been endowed with a new kind of altruistic conscience, as being mythical and hardly a reason to support corporate action based on implied power, but aside from any desire to assist others without hope of reward, when a contribution to a laudable cause has been made, a real, important and serious question is posed: Why was the contribution made? We believe that if it were made with the studied and not unreasonable conviction that it would benefit the corporation, it should be the type of thing that should rest in the sound discretion of management and within the ambit of a legitimate exercise of implied authority in the ordinary course of the company's business. It is not too much unlike the sponsoring of a baseball team, subsidizing promising scholars with a view toward possibly employing them later on, giving to the local community chest, paying the salary of a public relations expert, sponsoring a concert or television program, or conducting a newspaper or radio advertising program. Such actions seldom produce any immediate and direct corporate benefits, but all involve use of corporate funds that otherwise could have gone to shareholders had such funds remained unspent. Few would venture that the company could not do all these things without express, specific authority in the charter. We think that a power once denied today may be implied under changed conditions and philosophies, and that in the light of present day industrial and business exigencies, common sense dictates that included in the implied powers of a corporation, an authority should be numbered that allows contributions of reasonable amounts to selected charitable, scientific, religious or educational institutions, if they appear reasonably designed to assure a present or foreseeable future benefit to the corporation; that management's decisions in such matters should not be rendered impotent unless arbitrary and unreasonably indefensible, or unless countermanded or eliminated by action of the shareholders at a proper meeting.

The contribution in the instant case appears to fall within implied corporate powers under such principles.

WORTHEN, Justice (dissenting).

I dissent.

*   *   *

The entire argument of the majority opinion is devoted to the claimed need of the recipients of the charity and scant attention is given to the question of the legality of the gift. It adopts that questionable philosophy that the end justifies the means. But we are bound by the Constitution, statutes and prior decisions of this court holding that the gift in question is entirely outside the present powers of the corporation.

I cannot say that I am in disagreement with the lofty purposes announced by certain directors of appellant corporation, but what I do say is this: That the worthwhileness of the end and the aim envisioned by the directors is no proper substitute for stockholder authority to act as proposed.

The entire argument of the court's opinion is devoted to the crying need of the recipients of the charity. We are satisfied that great need exists for private contributions in increasing amounts in order that private educational institutions of the country may continue operating in the style to which they have become accustomed or better. Only among the inhabitants of Sherwood Forest has need been accepted as justifying the end.   *   *   *

*   *   *

The directors who testified are men of national reputation, men of vast business experience and men whose motives are not in question; still the backbone of every corporation is the army of less prominent persons, who invested the funds that were essential to the growth and success of the company—the stockholders.

*   *   *

I am not yet ready to acknowledge that it is good public policy to permit exploitation by each monopolistic corporations, in permitting them to put their corporate hands into the pockets of their patrons, in order to take more than they need for a reasonable return on their investment by a rate structure established and permitted by a public agency. Such practices are dangerous, against public policy and constitute a method of indirect taxation for such private charitable institutions.

* * *

Chapter 5

VALUING THE CORPORATION
(AND AN INTRODUCTION TO
FINANCIAL ACCOUNTING)

PROBLEM

EAST WIND BOATS—PART I

Jack Hardy, 32 years of age, is a successful real estate broker. His friend, Judy Luff, 30, recently received her MBA and has begun work as a stock broker. Jack has become tired of the real estate business, and he and Judy have recently began talking about establishing their own business. They are ardent sailors, and they became acquainted a few years ago with Harry Stern and John Star, who have for 20 years been in partnership in East Wind Boats, a small firm that builds custom sailboats, and performs repairs. The firm enjoys an excellent reputation. Harry and John, together with three employees, build about four large sailboats a year, which sell in the range of $75,000 apiece. They regularly have all the work they can handle.

Harry and John are both getting along in years and have recently decided to retire and to sell their business. They like Jim and Judy, have agreed, in principle, to sell the boatyard to them if satisfactory terms can be worked out.

Jack and Judy plan both to be actively involved on a full time basis in the management of the business. They would like to expand it by adding a line of smaller, less expensive sailboats, which they believe would do well in the current market. They estimate the cost of additional equipment, increased working capital, and an expanded sales effort would require an additional investment on top of the sales price of the going business. Judy's wealthy client, Edward Teach, who is himself an enthusiastic sailor, has indicated that he would be willing to put up the capital needed for the expansion if Judy and Jack purchase the business.

As of the end of its last fiscal year, East Wind's balance sheet was as follows:

EAST WIND BOATS

Balance Sheet

Assets		Liabilities and Partners' Capital	
Current Assets		Current Liabilities	
Cash	$10,000	Accounts Payable	$30,000
Accounts Receivable (net)	20,000		
Inventory	70,000	Accrued Expenses Payable	15,000
Total Current Assets	$100,000	Total Current Liabilities	$45,000
Fixed Assets		Long-Term Liabilities	
Land and Buildings	95,000	First Mortgage Note	50,000
Machinery and Equipment	100,000	Notes Payable	60,000
Furniture and Fixtures	5,000	Total Liabilities	155,000
Less Accumulated			
Depreciation	(80,000)		
		Partners' Capital	
Net Fixed Assets	120,000	Stern	35,000
Other Assets		Star	35,000
Prepaid Items	5,000	Total Partner's Capital	70,000
Total Assets	$225,000		
		Total Liabilities and Partners' Capital	$225,000

Notes: 1. The machinery and equipment was purchased at the price shown on the balance sheet and is in good repair. Depreciation is on a level (straight line) basis over the estimated life of the equipment.

2. The land is a large waterfront lot purchased for $10,000 fifteen years ago. Comparable nearby property recently sold for $20,000. There are two buildings, an office building built five years ago for $35,000 and a fifteen-year old shed that originally cost $50,000 to build. The cost of replacing the buildings would be about $200,000 today.

3. The inventory is shown at the lower of cost or market, on a consistent basis for each year.

East Wind's profit-and-loss statements for the last three fiscal years were as follows:

EAST WIND BOATS

Income Statement

	19×3	19×2	19×1
Net Sales	$320,000	$300,000	$280,000
Cost of sales and operating expenses			
Labor and materials	177,000	165,000	164,000
Depreciation	25,000	23,000	23,000
Selling and administrative	15,000	14,000	10,000
Cost of sales	217,000	202,000	197,000
Operating Profit	103,000	98,000	83,000
Interest Expense	13,000	13,000	13,000
Net Profit	$90,000	$85,000	$70,000

Stern and Star each withdrew from the business, $40,000, $37,500, and $35,000 for the three years shown above. The net profit shown above is *before* these withdrawls.

Judy and Jack have asked you to take a close look at East Wind to see what kind of shape the company is in, and whether there are any particular problems. At your request they have given you the financial statements. At least at this time, you are the only professional person advising them.

Although you are neither an accountant nor a financial analyst, your examination of the financial statements includes some standard tests of the soundness of East Wind that those professionals would make in order to meet the needs of your clients. You must develop a feel for their business situation because they will look to you for advice on whether to go ahead with the purchase and, if so for recommendations on how to proceed with the transaction.

Examine the statements and answer the following questions:

1. What is East Wind's

    a. Working capital? Current assets – current liabilities

    b. Current ratio? Current assets ÷ Current liabilities

    c. Liquidity ratio? Current assets – inventories ÷ Current liabilities

    d. Book value? 225,000 –155000 = 70,000

2. Has the operating profit margin improved in the most recent year over the previous years?

3. What was the inventory turnover for the most recent year?

4. What were the partners' share of the partnership earnings, computed as a percentage of their investment, in the most recent year?

Part A of this chapter deals with these matters.

A. INTRODUCTION TO FINANCIAL ACCOUNTING

1. IN GENERAL

The language and concepts of accounting are essential tools of lawyers, in many contexts. Financial accounting is of particular concern to those who seek to understand business organizations.

This brief note will introduce you to the two principal financial statements employed by business enterprises—the balance sheet and the income statement.*

The balance sheet represents the financial picture of a business organization as it stands on one particular day, in contrast to the income statement, which presents the results of the operation of the

---

* Adapted from "How to Read a Financial Report" by permission of the copy-   right owner Merrill Lynch, Pierce, Fenner & Smith Incorporated.

business over a specified period. A firm customarily presents the balance sheet and income statement figures for two or more years in order to show how the situation of the firm has changed over time.

2.   THE BALANCE SHEET

YOUR COMPANY, INC.

Balance Sheet—December 31, 198X

ASSETS

Current Assets

Cash	$450,000
Marketable securities at cost (Market value: $890,000)	850,000
Accounts receivable	
Less: allowance for bad debts: $100,000;	2,000,000
Inventories	2,700,000
TOTAL CURRENT ASSETS	$6,000,000

Fixed Assets
(property, plant, and equipment)

Land	$ 450,000
Building	3,800,000
Machinery	950,000
Office equipment	100,000
	$5,300,000
Less: accumulated depreciation	(1,800,000)
NET FIXED ASSETS	$3,500,000

Other Assets

Prepayments and deferred charges	100,000
Intangibles (goodwill, patent, trademarks)	100,000
TOTAL ASSETS	$9,700,000

LIABILITIES

Current Liabilities

Accounts payable	$1,000,000
Notes payable	850,000
Accrued expenses payable	330,000
Federal income taxes payable	320,000
TOTAL CURRENT LIABILITIES	$2,500,000

Long-Term Liabilities

First mortgage bonds; 5% interest, due in 10 years	2,700,000
TOTAL LIABILITIES	$5,200,000

STOCKHOLDERS' EQUITY

Stated Capital

Common stock, $1 par value each authorized, issued and outstanding 300,000 shares	$ 300,000
Capital Surplus	2,500,000
Earned Surplus	1,700,000
TOTAL STOCKHOLDERS' EQUITY	$4,500,000
TOTAL LIABILITIES AND STOCKHOLDERS' EQUITY	$9,700,000

The Accounting Equation. The balance sheet for a corporation is divided into two sides: on the left are shown *assets*; on the right are shown *liabilities* which represent the debts of business and *stockholders' equity* (or partners' capital). Both sides are always in balance. In the assets column are listed all the goods and property owned by a business as well as claims against others yet to be collected. Under liabilities are listed all debts of a business payable to others. Under stockholders' equity are listed the amount the stockholders would split up if Your Company, Inc. had gone out of business on the date of the balance sheet assuming (what is probably never so) that the assets were sold for exactly the amount shown on the balance sheet. If that were to occur, the shareholders of Your Company, Inc. would receive $4,400,000 as their portion of the business, that is, total assets (less intangibles) of $9,600,000 less the amount required to pay the corporation's total liabilities of $5,200,000.

The rights of the owners of a business may, more generally, be called "owners' equity." The type of business ownership may make the use of a different term more appropriate. Stockholders' equity will often be used to indicate owners' equity in a corporation; the term "proprietorship" would frequently be associated with a sole proprietorship. For a partnership, the ownership rights of the partners is reflected on a balance sheet as "partners' capital" or "partners' interest."

Regardless of the form of business organization, the accounting equation can always be stated as follows: assets less liabilities equals owners' equity. This equation serves as the basis for the balance sheet.

The Balance Sheet: A Detailed Analysis. Let us systematically examine each of the main sections of a corporation's balance sheet, namely, assets, liabilities, and stockholders' equity. As we discuss each item, consider the balance sheet for Your Company, Inc. set out above. We begin with assets, which are subdivided into current assets fixed assets, and other assets.

a. **Assets**

1. *Current assets,* in general, include cash and other assets which in the normal course of business will be turned into cash in the

reasonably near future, generally within a year from the date of the balance sheet. More specifically current assets may be broken into:

a. *Cash* is just what you would expect—bills and silver in the till (petty cash fund) and money on deposit in the bank.

b. *Marketable securities* represent temporary investment of excess or idle cash which is not needed immediately. It is usually invested in commercial paper and government securities. Because these funds may be needed on short notice, it is essential that the securities be readily marketable and subject to a minimum of price fluctuation. The general practice is to show marketable securities at the lower of their original cost or the current market value. If securities are shown at cost, the current aggregate market value should be shown parenthetically.

c. *Accounts receivable* is the amount not yet collected from customers to whom goods were shipped prior to payment. Customers are usually given 30, 60, or 90 days in which to pay. The amount due from customers as shown in the balance sheet is $2,000,000. However, experience shows that some customers fail to pay their bills either because of financial difficulties or by reason of some catastrophic event befalling their business. Therefore, in order to show the accounts receivable item at a figure representing reality, the total shown includes a deduction to provide for bad debts, usually calculated as a percentage of the total accounts outstanding. This year that reserve was $100,000.

d. *Inventories*. The inventory of a manufacturer is composed of three groups: raw materials to be used in the product, partially finished goods in process of manufacture, and finished goods ready for shipment to customers. The generally accepted method of valuation of the inventory is *cost or market, whichever is lower*, which gives a conservative figure. Where this method is used, the value of an item for balance sheet purposes will be its original cost unless, as a result of deterioration, obsolescence, decline in prices, or other factors, its market price is less than that, in which case it is carried at the latter figure. Cost for purposes of valuing work-in-process and finished-goods inventory includes an allocation of production and other expenses as well as the cost of materials.

Once it has been decided that costs are included in the inventory account, there are two major methods of valuing numerous items of inventory:

(i) First in, first out (FIFO) assumes *for accounting purposes* (whatever the fact) that the first units purchased or produced are the first units sold. Thus those still in inventory are carried at the cost of the last ones purchased or produced.

(ii) Last in, first out (LIFO), assumes the opposite, namely that the last goods purchased or produced are the first ones sold. The inventory is thus generally valued at the cost of the first units purchased or produced. In inflationary times this means that the true value of inventory carried on a LIFO basis may be far greater than that shown on the books. At first glance, this seems unrealistic and unnecessary.

However, the real importance of the inventory figure is how it affects the calculation of profits and taxes. Operating profits are determined by subtracting from revenues the cost of goods sold plus selling and administrative costs. Cost of goods sold is figured by adding to the opening inventory the amount of purchases during the year and then subtracting the closing inventory. The lower the closing inventory, the higher the cost of goods sold. The higher the cost of goods sold, the lower the profits. In other words, the lower the inventory, the lower the profit (and the lower the taxes). Therefore, a conservative method for pricing the inventory offsets the inflationary impact of spiraling inventory costs and tends to eliminate that inflationary contribution to profits.

By contrast, FIFO inventory accounting may yield a more realistic picture of the actual worth of inventory, but by the same measure it may show unrealistic, or illusory profits.

e. *Summary.* Current assets include primarily cash, marketable securities, accounts receivable, and inventories. These are "working" assets in the sense that they are in a constant cycle of being converted into cash. Inventories when sold become accounts receivable; receivables upon collection become cash; cash is used to pay debts and operating expenses.

2. *Fixed assets* are sometimes referred to as "property, plant and equipment." They represent those assets not intended for sale which are used over and over again in order to manufacture the product, display it, warehouse it, and transport it. Accordingly, this category includes land, buildings, machinery, equipment, furniture, and vehicles.

The figures given on the balance sheet for fixed asset items represent the "value" of those items in only the crudest way. According to generally accepted accounting principles ("GAAP"), fixed assets are listed at their original cost less an allowance for depreciation. It is widely recognized that, particularly in times of inflation, the resulting figure may be substantially different from either the actual market value of the asset or its replacement cost, which are often much higher. In balance sheet terms, however, this tends to result in a "conservative" estimate of the asset value of the firm, which has traditionally been considered preferable to permitting assets to be valued according to some less objective method that might be thought to produce a more accurate measure of the true value of the asset.

Depreciation can be thought of in theoretical terms as an attempt to recognize, again in a very crude way, the decline in value of assets over time. This decline may be the result of the wear and tear of normal use, the action of the elements, or technological obsolescence. Depreciation is calculated by spreading the cost of acquiring an asset over its expected useful life according to one of a number of formulas. The annual depreciation charge is treated like an expense, and reduces profits (and taxes). Depreciation serves another function. Each year the results of operations are made to include a proportionate share of the cost of assets necessary for production. The cost is thus "recovered" over time. If a delivery truck costs $10,000, for example, and it is expected to be used for five years, using the "straight-line" method of calculating depreciation, its balance sheet value will be reduced by $2,000 each year, and the income statement will be "charged" with that amount. You will recognize, of course, that this may be an insufficient deduction in inflationary times because the "real" cost might be taken to mean the cost of replacing the truck, not the cost of the old truck. However, the income statement will match the historic cost against present revenues. The balance sheet at the end of the first year would show:

Truck (cost)	$10,000
Less: accumulated depreciation	2,000
Net depreciated value	$8,000

The balance sheet at the end of the second year would show:

Truck (cost)	$10,000
Less: accumulated depreciation	4,000
Net depreciated value	$6,000

In the balance sheet for Your Company, Inc., there is shown a figure for accumulated depreciation. This amount is the total of accumulated depreciation for all fixed assets other than land. Land is not subject to depreciation, and its listed value remains unchanged from year to year. The item net fixed assets, therefore, is the valuation for balance sheet purposes of the investment in property, plant, and equipment. As explained before, it generally consists of the costs of the various assets in this classification, diminished by the depreciation accumulated to the date of the balance sheet.

3. *Other Assets*.

a. *Prepayments and Deferred Charges*. Prepaid items represent expenses already incurred for benefits to be realized in the future. For example if during the year the company paid fire insurance premiums covering a three-year period, and leased a computer, paying rental for two years in advance, the balance sheet date would reflect these prepayments as assets.

Deferred charges represent a type of asset similar to prepayments. For example, a manufacturer may have spent a large sum of money for introducing a new product, or for moving its plant to a new location, or for research and development. Since the benefits from these expenditures will be reaped over future years, management may think it not reasonable to charge off the full expenditure in the year when payment was made. Instead, the cost incurred may, in accordance with approved accounting principles, be gradually written off over several years.

b. *Intangibles* may be defined as assets having no physical existence, yet having substantial value to the company; for example a franchise granted by a city to a cable TV company allowing exclusive service in certain areas, or a patent granted by law for exclusive manufacture of a specific article. Another intangible asset sometimes found in corporate balance sheets is goodwill. A goodwill account appears only when one company acquires another. The difference between the price paid and the value of the assets acquired, if any, may be treated as "goodwill." Although accounting practices for treating goodwill vary, it must, as a rule, be written off over a period of not more than 40 years.

b. Liabilities

Liabilities are usually divided into current liabilities and long-term liabilities.

1. *Current liabilities* include all debts that fall due within the coming year. In a sense the current assets item is a companion to current liabilities because current assets are the source from which payments are made on current debts. The relationship between these two items reveals a great deal about the financial well-being of a firm, as we shall see later on. For now we need to define the subgroups within the current liabilities item.

a. *Accounts payable* represents the amounts that the company owes to its regular business creditors from which it has bought goods on open account. The company usually has 30, 60, or 90 days in which to pay.

b. *Notes payable* represents money owed to a bank or other lenders and evidenced by a written promissory note due in one year or less. Longer-term borrowing is listed under long-term liabilities.

c. *Accrued Expenses Payable.* On any given day a business has accumulated obligations that have not yet matured such as salaries and wages, interest on funds borrowed from banks and from bondholders, fees to attorneys, insurance premiums, rent, payments for utilities, pensions, and similar items. To the extent that the amounts accrued are unpaid at the date of the balance sheet, they are grouped as a total under *accrued expenses payable.*

d. *Federal Income Tax Payable.* The debt due to the Internal Revenue Service is the same type as any other item under accrued expenses payable. However, by reason of the amount and the importance of the tax factor, it is generally stated separately as *federal income tax payable.*

2. *Long-term Liabilities*. In discussing current liabilities, we included debts due within one year from the balance sheet date. Under the heading of long-term liabilities are listed debts due after one year from the date of the balance sheet. In our sample balance sheet, the only long-term liability is the 5% first mortgage bond due in 10 years. The money was received by the company as a loan from the bondholders, who in turn were given a certificate called a bond as evidence of the loan. The bond is really a formal promissory note issued by the company, which in this case agreed to repay the debt at maturity and agreed also to pay interest at the rate of 5% per year. Furthermore, in addition to the written promise of the company to repay the loan at maturity, the bondholders have an added safeguard indicated by the words first mortgage. This means that if the company is unable to pay off the bonds in cash when they are due, bondholders have a claim or lien before other creditors on the mortgaged assets which may be sold and the proceeds used to satisfy the debt.

c. Stockholders' Equity

Stockholders' equity is the total ownership interest that all stockholders have in this corporation. In other words, the equity represents the corporation's net worth, which is the amount by which the assets exceed the liabilities. The equity is separated for legal and accounting reasons into three categories: stated capital, capital surplus, and earned surplus.

1. *Stated capital* is also known as capital stock or shareholders' investment. This item represents all or a portion of the value that shareholders transferred to the corporation in the past in exchange for shares, represented by stock certificates, which the corporation issued to the shareholders. The amount of stated capital, expressed in dollars, is usually simply the product of the par value * of the stock multiplied by the number of issued and outstanding shares. If the stock is sold for more than its par value the excess is ordinarily regarded as capital surplus but the board of directors may choose to call it stated capital if they want. In our example, we have assumed that all of the difference was allocated to capital surplus which, as we will see later, allows the corporation slightly more financial flexibility than if some or all of the difference had been allocated to stated capital. Thus, in Your Company, Inc., the stated capital of $300,000 is derived by multiplying the one dollar par value of each share by the 300,000 issued and outstanding shares of common stock.

2. *Capital surplus* is also known as capital in excess of par value of stock, or paid-in surplus. It is the amount paid in by shareholders in payment for their shares that was in excess of the par value. If Your Company, Inc. sold for $10 share of stock with a par

---

* The par value of a stock is an arbitrary dollar amount stated in the articles of incorporated and on the stock certificate. It bears no relationship to the stock's value. For a more extended discussion of the significance of par value and stated capital see Chapter 8, *infra*.

value of $1, stated capital would be increased by $1, and capital surplus by $9. According to its balance sheet Your Company, Inc., has sold 300,000 shares of $1 par value stock for $10 per share. Thus the balance sheet shows $300,000 allocated to stated capital and $2,700,000 to capital surplus.

3. *Earned surplus* is sometimes known as accumulated or retained earnings. It is the difference between the sum of all profits earned by a firm since it was organized minus the sum of all dividends it has paid. Thus, if at the end of its first year, a firm's profits are $80,000 and no dividends are declared on the stock, then the balance sheet will show an earned surplus of $80,000. If, in the second year, the profits are $140,000 and dividends equal to $40,000 are paid on the stock, the aggregate earned surplus will be $180,000, that is, $80,000 from the first year's profits and $100,000 from the second year's profits.

d. What Does the Balance Sheet Show?

Before we undertake to analyze the figures on the balance sheet, a word is in order about the auditing of financial statements. A company's financial statements may be examined by an auditor who is an independent public accountant or a firm of accountants. The auditor then expresses its opinion, based on the application of certain auditing procedures designed to test the accuracy of the items in the financial statements, that the financial statements have been prepared in accordance with generally accepted accounting principles, and they fairly present the financial condition of the company. Or, the auditor may refuse to say that, or may qualify its opinion, for example, by stating that the assets are fairly stated provided the inventory can be sold, as to which there may be doubt. The opinion is commonly referred to (except by auditors) as a certificate.

A balance sheet affords an analyst a number of keys to the overall worth and the financial health of a company. Among the more important of these are working capital, the current ratio, the liquidity ratio, and various capitalization ratios.

Working capital is also called net current assets or net working capital. It is the difference between current assets and current liabilities. For Your Company, Inc., it is equal to $3,500,000 ($6,000,000 – $2,500,000). Since current assets provide the source from which current liabilities are paid, a business should maintain a comfortable margin between the two. Adequate working capital is also essential for a company to expand its volume and take advantage of business opportunities.

The current ratio is an indicator of the adequacy of a company's working capital position. It is simply current assets divided by current liabilities. For Your Company, Inc., it is 2.4 to 1 ($6,000,000 divided by $2,500,000). As a rule of thumb, analysts say that, in general, current assets should be at least twice as large as current liabilities. This is just a generalization, however. Firms having a small inventory and easily collectible accounts receivable can operate safely with a lower current ratio than companies having a greater proportion of their current assets in inventory and selling their products on credit. A gradual increase in the current ratio, based on a comparison of last year's balance sheet with those of previous years, is a sign of financial strength. Too large a ratio, however, 4 or 5 to 1, may be a sign of business contraction or the underutilization of liquid assets.

The *liquidity ratio*, also known as the "acid test," is the ratio of "quick assets" to current liabilities. Quick assets are cash, marketable securities, and other assets readily reducible to cash (generally current assets less inventory). The liquidity ratio for Your Company, Inc. is 1.3 to 1 ($3,300,000 divided by $2,500,000). This ratio provides a more sophisticated evaluation of the current ratio, as a corporation with a high current ratio may still not be in a good position to meet its current liabilities if a large portion of its current assets is in the form of inventory.

The *book value* or net asset value of a share of common stock represents the amount of corporate assets backing or protecting the common stock. In other words it is the amount of money each share would receive on the liquidation of the corporation if (and this would almost never be the case) the assets would be sold at exactly their balance sheet values. The book value of a share of common stock of Your Company, Inc. is $14.67. This figure is the result of subtracting from the corporation's total tangible assets of $9,600,000 (*i.e.*, total assets of $9,700,000 less intangible assets of $100,000) the total liabilities of $5,200,000 (*i.e.* current liabilities of $2,500,000 plus long-term liabilities of $2,700,000) which results in $4,400,000 available for the common stock. The $4,400,000 figure is divided by the number of issued and outstanding shares (300,000) to yield a net book value per share of common stock of $14.67. It follows from the balance sheet equation (assets equals liabilities plus stockholders' equity) that book value is also equal to total stockholders' equity less intangible assets.

There are a number of possible *capitalization or debt-equity ratios*, which depend on the amount of different securities issued by a corporation. They represent the proportional claims of each class of outstanding security on the assets of the corporation remaining after the current liabilities have been paid. Your Company, Inc., has a relatively simple capital structure, with only mortgage bonds and common stock to be considered. The ratio of common stock to debt, or the equity to debt ratio for Your Company is approximately 1.67 to 1 ($4,500,000 divided by $2,700,000). If a company, in addition to common stock, also has issued preferred stock (about which more will be said later), it is possible to show a three-part proportion: common stock to preferred stock to debt. Or the common and preferred stock, both being considered "equity securities," may be lumped to-gether and an equity to debt ratio may be calculated.

Another way to approach these ratios is to calculate the percent-age that each outstanding class of security represents of the compa-ny's total capitalization. The total capitalization of Your Company, Inc. is $7,200,000 ($4,500,000 divided by $2,700,000). Thus the com-mon stock ratio is 62.5% and the bond ratio is 37.5%.

In general too great a proportion of debt to equity may be danger-ous, as the interest on the debt must be paid in bad times as well as good, whereas a dividend on stock may be omitted if a company's fortunes so require.

As with all the ratios, there is no absolute golden rule which reveals the correct number. To determine the health of a company, an analyst would need to know a lot about the business and its re-quirements and would want to compare from year to year and from company to company within the industry.

3. THE INCOME STATEMENT

YOUR COMPANY, INC.

The Income Statement

INCOME STATEMENT FOR YEAR ENDING DECEMBER 31

CONSOLIDATED INCOME STATEMENT	198X	Previous Year
Net Sales	$11,000,000	$10,200,000
Cost of sales and operating expenses		
Cost of goods sold	8,200,000	7,684,000
Depreciation	300,000	275,000
Selling and administration expenses	1,400,000	1,325,000
Operating profit	$ 1,100,000	$ 916,000
Other income		
Dividends and interest	50,000	27,000
TOTAL INCOME	$ 1,150,000	$ 943,000
Less: interest on bonds	135,000	135,000
Income before provision for federal income tax	$ 1,015,000	$ 808,000
Provision for federal income tax	447,600	352,430
NET PROFIT FOR YEAR	$ 567,400	$ 455,570
COMMON SHARES OUTSTANDING	300,000	300,000
NET EARNINGS PER SHARE	$1.89	$1.52

While the balance sheet portrays a picture of the basic financial soundness of a company at a particular time, it provides little or no information about how profitable that company is, the characteristic that is ultimately of the greatest interest to both investors and man-agement. For that we have to turn to the income statement, also called the profit-and-loss statement or the statement of the results of operations. The income statement shows how the company has fared over a period of time. Of course it is a historical record and is thus of interest to an investor chiefly insofar as it can form the basis for a projection of future earnings. Projecting, however, is a perilous business. For that reason, an income statement often shows the results for two or more consecutive periods in order to facilitate the identification of trends that may indicate what is likely to happen in the next period. You will note that the income statement for Your Company, Inc., shows the results of operations for two years.

For most larger companies an income statement represents an effort to match the revenues from sales during a given period against the costs incurred by the company in producing and selling the product or services sold during that period, regardless of when actual cash payment was made.*   The amount of detail found in income statements varies considerably, but they all end with the "bottom line" which shows how much the company earned (or lost) during the period.

Net sales is the most important source of revenue and always is presented first on the income statement. If the company is a railroad or a utility, this item would normally be called *operating revenues*. The word "net" is used to indicate that the amount given is net of returns, discounts, or other allowances.

For a manufacturing company the *cost of sales and operating expenses* is usually divided into several major items. The *cost of goods sold* includes the cost of materials and labor directly attributable to the production of the product. *Depreciation*, as we have already seen, is a more or less artificial means of allocating the costs arising from the decline in value of fixed assets, or which charge to the period in question the cost of the asset. *Selling and administrative expenses*, in addition to advertising expenditures, sales commissions and the like, includes the salaries of managers and clerical personnel as well as other costs not directly attributable to the manufacture of particular items of product.

When these costs are deducted from net sales the result is the *operating profit*. This is given before *other income* (in the case of Your Company, Inc., made up of dividends and interest on money it had invested in bank accounts and securities during the year) is added to produce *total income*. From this must be deducted *interest expense*, which is stated separately because it gives an indication of the cost of capital borrowed by the firm and must be paid to the bondholders year after year. The almost-final result is the pre-tax income, from which federal income taxes must be deducted to arrive at the *net profit*.

---

* This is known as the "accrual basis" of accounting. Some smaller companies operate on the "cash basis" according to which cash outlays during a period are matched against cash receipts during that period without any effort made to allocate costs so that they match with the sales to which they are properly attributable.

4. ACCUMULATED RETAINED EARNINGS STATEMENT

In addition to the balance sheet and income statement, many corporations also use an Accumulated Retained Earnings Statement (also known as a Statement of Retained Earnings or a Surplus Statement). This statement indicates the amount of earned surplus at the beginning of the accounting period, the net income (or loss) for the period, any dividends paid, and the earned surplus at the end of the period. Therefore, the statement serves to reconcile the earned surplus item shown on the balance sheet with the net income (or loss) during an accounting period.

YOUR COMPANY, INC.

	198X	Previous Year
ACCUMULATED RETAINED EARNINGS STATEMENT		
Balance January 1	$ 1,332,650	$ 1,027,080
NET PROFIT FOR YEAR	567,350	455,570
TOTAL	$ 1,900,000	$ 1,482,650
Less: dividends paid on common stock	200,000	150,000
BALANCE DECEMBER 31	$ 1,700,000	$ 1,332,650

5. ANALYZING THE INCOME STATEMENT AND THE INTER-RELATIONSHIP BETWEEN THE INCOME STATEMENT AND THE BALANCE SHEET

The income statement, like the balance sheet, will, by itself, tell us considerably more if we make a few detailed comparisons.

The *operating profit margin* is the operating profit (profit before interest and taxes) expressed as a percentage of net sales. It is a basic indicator of the efficiency of the corporation's operations. Your Company, Inc., in its most recent accounting year, had an operating profit of $1,100,000 and net sales of $11,000,000 or a 10% operating profit margin. In other words each dollar of sales produced 10 cents of gross profit from operations.

The operating profit margin for the year just completed compares with the 9% operating profit margin in the previous year ($916,000 operating profit on $10,000,000 sales). The improvement from 9% to 10% may reflect an increase in the efficiency of operations or changes in products manufactured or types of customers served.

The *net profit ratio* provides another guide to indicate how satisfactory the year's activities have been. In Your Company, Inc., the most recent year's net profit was $567,000 on $11,000,000 of sales or 5.2%. Last year, Your Company's net profit ratio was 4.5% ($455,000 net profit on net sales of $10,200,000).

There are also a number of useful analytic tools built from ratios between items from both the income statement and the balance sheet.

Inventory turnover is one of the more important. How large an
⌐uld a company carry? The answer to this question de-
⌐f many factors, including, the type of busi-
e way to measure the adequacy of
ze at the balance sheet date with
r Company, Inc., inventory was
0,000. Thus the inventory turnover

⌐y measure of how effectively a com-
money. It is determined by calculat-
e as a percentage of stockholder's eq-
earned net profits of $567,350 on
,000, or a return on equity of approxi-
higher this ratio is, the more productive
al is being put.

⌐ is given particular attention by inves-
simply the net profits after taxes divided
hares outstanding.* For Your Company,
e were $1.89 ($567,350 divided by 300,000
share are one part of the "price-earnings
at interest to the stock market (the other
ice of the common stock). If the stock of
ing at 15¹⁄₈ its price-earnings ratio would be
9).

B.   VALUING THE ENTERPRISE

PROBLEM

EAST WIND BOATS—PART II

Now that you have studied the financial statements, and some other documents as well, Hardy, Luff and Teach want your assistance in
negotiating the purchase of East Wind Boats. Their first concern is
to determine the value of the business.

Stern and Star have offered to sell the business for $100,000. Our
clients think that is a lot of cash, but they think that terms can be
worked out as well as other necessary contract provisions. They
want counsel's reaction to whether the price seems fair and, in general, what conditions are necessary to make the price fair. How do you
advise?

1. THE OLD MAN AND THE TREE: A PARABLE OF VALUA-
TION

Once there was a good, wise man who owned an apple tree. The
tree was a fine tree, and with little care it produced a crop of apples

---

* If the corporation also had an issue   be necessary first to deduct the preferred
of preferred stock outstanding, it would   dividends before calculating this ratio.

each year which he sold for $100. The man was getting old, wanted to retire to a different climate and decided to sell the tree. He enjoyed teaching a good lesson, and he placed an advertisement in the Business Opportunities section of the Wall Street Journal in which he said he wanted to sell the tree for "the best offer."

The first person to respond to the ad offered to pay the $50 which, the offeror said, was what he would be able to get for selling the apple tree for firewood after he had cut it down. "You are a very foolish person," said the old man. "You are offering to pay only the salvage value of this tree. That might be a good price for a pine tree or perhaps even this tree if it had stopped bearing fruit or if the price of apple wood had gotten so high that the tree was more valuable as a source of wood than as a source of fruit. But my tree is worth much more than $50."

The next person to come to see the old man offered to pay $100 for the tree. "For that," said she, "is what I would be able to get for selling this year's crop of fruit which is about to mature."

"You are not quite so foolish as the first one," responded the old man. "At least you see that this tree has more value as a producer of apples than it would as a source of fire wood. But $100 is not the right price. You are not considering the value of next year's crop of apples, nor that of the years after. Please take your $100 and go elsewhere."

The next person to come along was a young man who had just started business school. "I am going to major in marketing," he said. "I figure that the tree should live for at least another fifteen years. If I sell the apples for $100 a year, that will total $1,500. I offer you $1,500 for your tree."

"You, too, are foolish," said the man. Surely the $100 you would earn by selling the apples from the tree fifteen years from now cannot be worth $100 to you today. In fact, if you placed $41.73 today in a bank account paying only 6% interest, compounded annually, that small sum would grow to $100 at the end of fifteen years. Therefore the present value of $100 worth of apples fifteen years from now, assuming an interest rate of 6%, is only $41.73, not $100. "Pray," said the old man, "take your $1,500 and invest it safely in high-grade corporate bonds until you have graduated from business school and know more about finance."

Before long, there came a wealthy physician, who said, "I don't know much about apple trees, but I know what I like. I'll pay the market price for it. The last fellow was willing to pay you $1,500 for the tree, and so it must be worth that."

"Doctor," advised the old man, "you should get yourself a knowledgeable investment adviser. If there were truly a market in which apple trees were traded with some regularity, the prices at which they were sold would be a good indication of their value. But there is no such market. And the isolated offer I just received tells very little about how much my tree is really worth—as you would surely realize if you had heard the other foolish offers I have heard today. Please take your money and put it in a good tax shelter."

The next prospective purchaser to come along was an accounting student. When the old man asked "What price are you willing to give me?" the student first demanded to see the old man's books. The old man had kept careful records and gladly brought them out. After examining them the accounting student said, "Your books show that you paid $75 for this tree ten years ago. Furthermore, you have made no deductions for depreciation. I do not know if that conforms with generally accepted accounting principles, but assuming that it does, the book value of your tree is $75. I will pay that."

"Ah, you students know so much and yet so little," chided the old man. "It is true that the book value of my tree is $75, but any fool can see that it is worth far more than that. You had best go back to school and see if you can find some books that will show you how to use your numbers to better effect."

The next prospective purchaser was a young stock broker who had recently graduated from business school. Eager to test her new skills she, too, asked to examine the books. After several hours she came back to the old man and said she was now prepared to make an offer that valued the tree on the basis of the capitalization of its earnings.

For the first time the old man's interest was piqued and he asked her to go on.

The young woman explained that while the apples were sold for $100 last year, that figure did not represent profits realized from the tree. There were expenses attendant to the tree, such as the cost of fertilizer, the expense of pruning the tree, the cost of the tools, expenses in connection with picking the apples, carting them into town and selling them. Somebody had to do these things, and a portion of the salaries paid to those persons ought to be charged against the revenues from the tree. Moreover, the purchase price, or cost, of the tree was an expense. A portion of the cost is taken into account each year of the tree's useful life. Finally, there were taxes. She concluded that the profit from the tree was $40 last year.

"Wow!" exclaimed the old man. "I thought I made $100 off that tree."

"That's because you failed to match expenses with revenues, in accordance with generally accepted accounting principles," she explained. "You don't actually have to write a check to be charged with what accountants consider to be your expenses. For example, you bought a station wagon some time ago and you used it part of the time to cart apples to market. The wagon will last a while and each year some of the original cost has to be matched against revenues. A portion of the amount has to be deducted each year even though you expended it all at one time. Accountants call that depreciation. I'll bet you never figured that in your calculation of profits."

"I'll bet you're right," he replied. "Tell me more."

"I also went back into the books for a few years and I saw that in some years the tree produced less apples than in other years, the prices varied and the costs were not exactly the same each year. Taking an average of only the last three years, I came up with a figure of $35 as a fair sample of the tree's earnings. But that is only half of what we have to do so as to figure the value."

"What's the other half?" he asked.

"The tricky part," she told him. "We now have to figure what percentage of the value of the tree is represented by its fair average earnings for a single year. If I believed that the tree was a one year wonder, I would say 100% of its value—as a going business—was represented by one year's earnings. But if I believe, as both you and I do, that the earnings from a single year are but a fraction of what the tree will produce, then the key is to figure out that fraction. In other words, the tree is capital, and to compute its value we must capitalize the earnings. We must divide them by the right fraction."

"Do you have something in mind?" he asked.

"I'm getting there. If this tree could produce steady, and predictable earnings each year, it would be like a U.S. Treasury bond. But its earnings are not guaranteed. So we have to take into account risk and uncertainty. If the risk of its ruin is high, I will insist that a single year's earnings represent a higher percentage of the value of the tree. After all, apples could become a glut on the market one day and you would have to cut the price and increase the costs of selling them. Or some doctor could discover a link between eating an apple a day and heart disease. A drought could cut the yield of the tree. Or, heaven forbid, the tree could become diseased and die. These are all risks. And of course we do not know what will happen to costs that we know we have to bear."

"You are a gloomy one," reflected the old man. "There are treatments, you know, that could be applied to increase the yield of the tree. This tree could help spawn a whole orchard."

"I am aware of that," she assured him. "We will include that in the calculus. The fact is, we are talking about risk, and investment analysis is a cold business. We don't know with certainty what's going to happen. You want your money now and I'm supposed to live with the risk. That's fine with me, but then I have to look through a cloudy crystal ball, and not with 20/20 hindsight. And my resources are limited. I have to choose between your tree and the strawberry patch down the road. I cannot do both and the purchase of your tree will deprive me of alternative investments. That means I have to compare the opportunities and the risks. To determine the proper rate at which we should capitalize earnings, I have looked at investment opportunities that are comparable to the apple tree, particularly in the agribusiness industry, where these factors have been taken into account. I have concluded that it is appropriate to use a capitalization rate of 20%. In other words, average earnings over the last three years (which seems to be a representative period) represent 20% of the value of the tree. And that is the risk I am willing to take. I am not willing to take any greater risk, because I don't have to since I can buy the strawberry patch instead. Now, to figure the price, we simply divide 35 by .20."

"Long division was never my long suit. Is there a simpler way of doing the figuring?" he asked hopefully.

"There is," she assured him. "The reciprocal of .20 is 5. If you don't want to divide by the capitalization rate, you can multiply by its reciprocal, which we Wall Street types prefer. We call that reciprocal the price-earnings (or P–E) ratio. Any way you do the math, the answer is $175. That's my offer."

The old man sat back and said he greatly appreciated the lesson. He would have to think about her offer, and he asked if she could come by the next day.

When the young woman returned she found the old man emerging from a sea of work sheets, small print columns of numbers and a calculator. "Glad to see you," he said. "I think we can do some business."

"It's easy to see how you Wall Street smartees make so much money, buying people's property for a fraction of the value. I think my tree is worth more than you figured, and I think I can get you to agree to that."

"I'm open minded," she assured him.

"The number you worked so hard over my books to come up with was something you called profits, or earnings. I'm not so sure it tells you anything that important."

"Of course it does," she protested. "It measures efficiency and economic utility."

"Maybe," he mused, "but it sure doesn't tell you how much money you've got. I looked in my safe yesterday after you left and I saw I had some stocks that hadn't ever paid much of a dividend to me. And I kept getting reports each year telling me how great the earnings were, but I sure couldn't spend them. It's just the opposite with the tree. You figured the earnings were lower because of some amounts I'll never have to spend. It seems to me these earnings are an idea worked up by the accountants. Now I'll grant you that ideas, or concepts as you call them, are important and give you lots of useful information, but you can't fold them up, and put them in your pocket."

Surprised, she asked, "What is important, then?"

"Cash flow," he answered. "I'm talking about dollars you can spend, or save or give to your children. This tree will go on for years yielding revenues after costs."

"Don't forget the risks," she reminded him. "And the uncertainties."

"Quite right," he observed. "I think we can deal with that. Chances are that you and I could agree, after a lot of thought, on the possible range of revenues and costs. I suspect we would estimate that for the next five years, there is a 25% chance that the cash flow will be $40, a 50% chance it will be $50 and a 25% chance it will be $60. That makes $50 our best guess, if you average it out. Then let us figure that for ten years after that the average will be $40. And that's it. The tree doctor tells me it can't last any longer than that. Now all we have to do is figure out what you pay today to get $50 a year from now, two years from now, and so on for the first five years until we figure what you would pay to get $40 a year for each of the ten years after that."

"Simple," she said. "You want to discount to the present value of future receipts. Of course you need to determine the rate at which you discount."

"Precisely," he noted. "That's what all these charts and the calculator are doing." She nodded knowingly as he showed her discount tables that revealed what a dollar received at a later time is worth today, under different assumptions of the discount rate. It showed, for example, that at a 12% discount rate, a dollar delivered a year from now is worth $.89 today, simply because $.89 today, invested at 12%, will produce $1 a year from now.

"You could put your money in a savings bank or a savings and loan association and receive 5% interest, insured. But you could also put your money into obligations of the United States Government and earn 12% interest. That looks like the risk free rate of interest to me. Anywhere else you put your money deprives you of the opportunity to earn 12% risk free. Discounting by 12% will only compensate you for the time value of the money you invest in the tree rather than in government securities. But the cash flow from the apple tree is not riskless, sad to say, so we need to use a higher discount rate to compensate you for the risk in your investment. Let us agree that we discount the receipt of $50 a year from now by 20%, and so on with the other deferred receipts. That is about the rate that is applied to investments with this magnitude of risk. You can check that out with my cousin who just sold his strawberry patch yesterday. According to my figures, the present value of the anticipated net revenues is $219.50. You can see how much I'm allowing for risk because if I discounted the stream at 12%, it would come to $318.20."

After a few minutes reflection, the young woman said to the old man, "It was a bit foxy of you yesterday to let me appear to be teaching you something. Where did you learn so much about finance as an apple grower?"

"Don't be foolish, my young friend," he counseled her. "Wisdom comes from experience in many fields. Socrates taught us how to learn. I'll tell you a little secret; I spent a year in law school."

The young woman smiled at this last confession. "I have enjoyed this little exercise but let me tell you something that some of the financial whiz kids have told me. Whether we figure value on the basis of the discounted cash flow method or the capitalization of earnings, so long as we apply both methods perfectly we should come out at exactly the same point."

"Of course!" the old man exclaimed. "Some of the wunderkinds are catching on. The question is, however, which method is more likely to be misused. I prefer to calculate by my method because I don't have to monkey around with depreciation. You have to make these arbitrary assumptions about useful life and how fast you're going to depreciate. Obviously that's where you went wrong in your figuring."

"You are a crafty old devil," she rejoined. "There are plenty of places for your calculations to go off. It's easy to discount cash flows when they are nice and steady, but that doesn't help you when you've got some lumpy expenses that do not recur. For example, several years from now that tree will require some extensive pruning and spraying operations that simply do not show up in your flow. The labor and chemicals for that once only occasion throw off the evenness of your calculations. But I'll tell you what," "I'll offer you $200. My cold analysis tells me I'm overpaying, but I really like that tree. I think the psychic rewards of sitting in its shade must be worth something."

"It's a deal," said the old man. "I never said I was looking for the *perfect* offer, but only the *best* offer. There is much good sense in your analysis."

"I have one final observation," she said. "People in the stock market have been figuring value on the capitalization of earnings method for many years. I'm not so sure that your method is any better than mine."

"Neither am I," mused the old man.

MORAL: There are several. Methods are useful as tools, but good judgment comes not from methods alone, but from experience. And experience comes from bad judgment.

Listen closely to the experts, and hear those things they don't tell you. Behind all the sweet sounds of their conclusory notes, there is a great deal of discordant uncertainty. One wrong assumption can carry you pretty far from the truth.

Finally, you are never too young to learn.

2. NOTE: CONTEXT AND OTHER CONSIDERATIONS

1. In response to the question, "How much is a business worth?", one must ask "Who wants to know?" Valuation of a business is best viewed as a process directed to a particular end. The nature of that process, and the result it achieves, may vary according to the purpose for which a value is sought. It is one thing to negotiate the selling of a going business (or a flowering apple tree); it is quite another to appraise the business for estate tax purposes and still another matter to determine the value of a business when the owner of 80% of the business wants to buy out the other 20%.

2. Predictions are an important but difficult aspect of valuation. One cannot predict sales by simply applying prior percentage increases to future years. Even if sales can be satisfactorily forecast, what about the problem of forecasting costs and expenses? A profit prediction might be valuable information but is a sales forecast useful? Is it worthwhile guessing at forecasts which are so uncertain? Shouldn't one confine himself to the historical information at hand, and gauge capitalization rates accordingly?

3. We cannot lose sight of the qualitative difference between profits and money. In The Money Game (1967) by "Adam Smith" the story is told about another "Mr. Smith" who was astute enough to invest $20,000 in a company called International Tabulator, which became IBM. Of course he became a millionaire, and he never sold a share. Since IBM's dividends were meagre, Mr. Smith was forced to work hard at his own business to provide for his family. And he always counseled his family, "If anything happens to me, whatever you do, don't sell IBM." The children listened, and when he died, they sold only enough to pay estate taxes, and they each grew as rich as their father. However, they too had to work hard to provide for their growing families, because all their money was in IBM, which paid meagre dividends. The third generation is now telling their children, "Whatever you do, don't sell IBM."

The author concludes: "In short, for three generations the Smiths have worked as hard as their friends who had no money at all, *and they have lived just as if they had no money at all*, even though the various branches of the Smith family all put together are very wealthy indeed. And the IBM is there, nursed and watered and fed, the Genii of the House, growing away in the early hours of the morning when everyone is asleep. IBM has been so good to them that even after divisions among children and rounds of estate taxes they are all millionaires or nearly so. Presumably the Smiths will go on, paying off their mortgages, and watching their IBM grow with joy, always blossom, never fruit. It is a parable of pure capitalism, never jam today and a case of jam tomorrow; but as any of the Smiths will tell you, anyone who has sold IBM has regretted it."

4. Many factors contribute to the determination of the proper capitalization rate.

In Arthur Dewing's Financial Policy of Corporations (5th ed. 1953), the following categories of capitalization rates are suggested:

1. Old established businesses, with large capital assets and excellent goodwill—10%, a value ten times the net earnings. Very few industrial enterprises would come within this category.

2. Businesses, well established, but requiring considerable managerial care. To this category would belong the greater number of old, successuly industrial businesses, large and small—12½%, a value eight times the net earnings.

3. Businesses, well established, but involving possible loss in consequence of shifts of general economic conditions. They are strong, well established businesses, but they produce a type of commodity which makes them vulnerable to depressions. They require considerable managerial ability, but little special knowledge on the part of the executives—15%, a value approximately seven times the net earnings.

4. Businesses requiring average executive ability—and at the same time comparatively small capital investment. These businesses are highly competitive, but established goodwill is of distinct importance. This class includes the rank and file of medium-size, highly competitive industrial enterprise—20%, a value approximately five times the net earnings.

5. Small industrial businesses, highly competitive, and requiring a relatively small capital outlay. They are businesses which anyone, even with little capital, may enter—25%, a value approximately four times the net earnings.

6. Industrial businesses, large and small, which depend on the special, often unusual skill of one, or of a small group of managers. They involve only a small amount of capital; they are highly competitive and the mortality is high among those who enter the competitive struggle—50%, a value approximately twice the net earnings.

7. Personal service businesses. They require no capital or at the most a desk, some envelopes and a few sheets of paper. The manager must have a special skill coupled with an intensive and thorough knowledge of his subjects. The earnings of the enterprise are the objective reflection of this skill; and he is not likely to be able to create "an organization" which can successfully "carry on" after he is gone. He can sell the business, including the reputation and the "plan of business," but he cannot sell himself, the only truly valuable part of the enterprise—100%, a value equal, approximately, to the earnings of a single year.

Events soon overtook the Dewing table, which was a standard work for years, and in the late 1960's many stocks (known as glamour stocks because of the allure they held for investors, *e.g.*, IBM, Xerox, Polaroid, Eastman Kodak) sold for multipliers of 50 or better.

Eventually a sharp reaction set in, and prices receded to numbers even lower than the Dewing table. Often times the stock sold at a price below the liquidating value of its assets, suggesting that the company was worth more dead than alive!

Obviously, no magic wand can produce the "right number" and the valuation exercise is a matter of judgment. Uncertainty is the enemy of optimism, and the glow of an earlier time when no end to growth was in sight has probably faded. The fundamentals Dewing described no longer look naively conservative, but may again be close to the mark.

Economists, who prefer to calculate value on the theory of discounting to the present value of expected cash flows, encounter the same degree of imprecision in determining the discount rate. Minus risk, the selection of a number to reflect the time value of money is fairly simple. But the risk factor is an imponderable, carrying with it different aspects of risk. Fixing the right amount by which which one must be compensated to incur such risk may be analytically more satisfying than determining capitalization rates, but it is subject to the same frailities of judgment.

An excellent analysis is found in Business Organization and Finance (1980) by Professor William Klein.

Chapter 6

THE CHOICE OF ORGANIZATIONAL FORM

PROBLEM

EAST WIND BOATS — PART III

You have turned your attention to the legal problems that must be resolved in the planned acquisition of East Wind Boats. Initially, the clients (with counsel) need to determine the legal form in which they will operate the business. In your interviews with them you have learned a number of additional facts that may be relevant to this decision.

Teach is now 62 years old. His insurance brokerage business is a partnership with two other individuals who are about his age. He is thinking of retiring from that business in a few years. He is married and has a son, Bill, who is presently a college junior. Bill is not sure what he wants to do when he graduates except that he has made it clear that he does not want to be an insurance broker. He also loves sailing, however, and is very enthusiastic about his father's involvement in the East Wind Boats venture. Ed Teach is equally excited about the project, but he says he is too busy with other affairs to spend much time in helping with its day-to-day management. He would, however, like to make his substantial business experience available where it can be helpful.

Hardy and Luff, on the other hand, plan to spend full time on East Wind Boats. Hardy is from a modest background and he has little in the way of assets besides the money he plans to invest in the business. In addition to the money she plans to invest, Luff has a stock portfolio worth about $50,000. Her retired father is relatively well-to-do, and she stands to inherit several hundred thousand dollars.

You have also discussed briefly the financial prospects of the business. Since they are purchasing a going concern, Hardy, Luff, and Teach are more optimistic about profitability during the first few years than they might be if they were starting from scratch. However, because of their plans for expansion which requires substantial borrowing at high interest rates, there is a real possibility that they will show losses for at least the first few years.

When Hardy first came to you about this transaction, one of the things he told you was, "We want you to incorporate the business for us." After reflecting on the matter, how should you respond?

A. INTRODUCTION

Clients who are about to start or acquire a business are likely to ask a lawyer to form a corporation for this purpose. There is a mystique associated with the corporate form of doing business that often leads people to believe, if only subliminally, that using a corporation is important for their success. In fact, however, the use of a corporation may be counter productive to success. It was perhaps out of desire to counter the durable myth about the virtues of the corporate form that motivated the authors of one of the leading texts on corporate practice to write, as the first sentence in Chapter I of their book, "When in doubt, don't incorporate." G. Seward & W. Nauss, Basic Corporate Practice § 1.01 (2d. ed. 1977). The point is simply that the choice of business form requires considerable analysis of tax and other aspects, and while there are often good reasons to incorporate, the decision is hardly automatic.

B. THE ECONOMICS OF THE CHOICE

R. POSNER, ECONOMIC ANALYSIS OF
LAW 289–292 (2d ed. 1977).

The Nature of the Firm. Transaction costs—the costs involved in ordering economic activity through voluntary exchange—are a recurrent theme in this book. Here we use it to explain why so much economic activity is carried on by firms rather than by individuals.

Contrast two methods of organizing production. In one, the entrepreneur contracts with one person to supply the component parts, with another to assemble them, and with a third to sell the finished product. In the second method, he hires them to perform these tasks as his employees under his direction. The first method of organizing production is the traditional domain of contract law, the second of master-servant law. The essence of the first method is that the entrepreneur negotiates with each of the three contractors an agreement specifying the price, quantity, quality, due date, credit terms, etc., of the contractor's performance. The essence of the second method is that the entrepreneur pays them wages, not for a specific performance, but for the right to direct their performance.

Neither method of organizing economic activity is costless. The first method, contract, usually requires that the details of the supplier's performance be spelled out at the time of the signing of the contract. This may require protracted and costly negotiations, elaborate bidding procedures, etc. And should changed circumstances require modification of any term of the agreed-upon performance, the agreement must be renegotiated. The second method, the firm, involves incentive, information, and communication costs. Since the supplier is not paid directly for his output, he has less incentive than before to minimize his costs. And information about costs and value is ob-

scured in the firm since the employees do not bid for the various resources that they use in production, a process that would indicate
where those resources could be employed most valuably. Furthermore, since performance in the firm is directed by the employer's orders, machinery for minimizing failures of communication up and
down the chain of command is necessary—machinery both costly and
imperfect. In sum, the contract method of organizing economic activity encounters the problem of high transaction costs, the method of
organizing economic activity through the firm, the problem of loss of
control. It is the control problem rather than the law of diminishing
returns that places an upper limit on the efficient size of firms. Diminishing returns limit the amount of any single product that a firm
can efficiently produce. The limit on the number of products is a
function of the costs of directing performance in very large organizations.

Problems in Financing Business Ventures. The theory of the
firm tells us why so much economic activity is organized in firms but
not why most of those firms are corporations. A clue is that firms in
which the inputs are primarily labor rather than capital are frequently organized as partnerships or individual proprietorships. The corporation is primarily a method of solving problems encountered in
raising substantial amounts of capital for a venture.

How does the impecunious entrepreneur who has a promising idea
for a new venture go about raising the capital necessary to launch
the venture? Borrowing *all* the money is probably out of the question. If the riskless interest rate is 6 percent but the venture has a
50 percent chance of failing (and of having no assets out of which to
repay the loan), the lender, if risk neutral, will charge an interest rate
of 112 percent. The high interest, plus amortization, will impose
heavy fixed costs on the venture from the outset and this will increase the danger of failure, and in turn the interest rate. And, if
the venture's prospects cannot be predicted with reasonable confidence, it will be very difficult even to calculate an appropriate interest rate.

These difficulties could in principle be overcome by careful and
imaginative drafting of the loan agreement, but the transaction costs
might be very high. An alternative is for the entrepreneur to admit a
partner to the business who is entitled to receive a portion of the
profits of the venture, if any, in exchange for contributing the necessary capital to it. The partner's compensation is determined automatically by the fortunes of the business. There is no need to compute
an interest rate although this is implicit in the determination of the
fraction of any future profits that he is to receive in exchange for his
contribution. And there are no fixed costs of debt. The partner receives his profits only if and as earned.

But there are still problems. A partnership can be dissolved by,
and is automatically dissolved on the death of, any partner. The im-

permanance of the arrangement may deter the commitment of large amounts of money to an enterprise in which it may be frozen for many years. Again, the partners may be able to negotiate around this hurdle but not without incurring transaction costs that may be high. Moreover, to the extent that they agree to limit the investing partner's right to dissolve the partnership and withdraw his money, the liquidity of his investment is reduced and he may be placed at the mercy of the active partner.

Further, since each partner is personally liable for the debts of the partnership, a prospective investor will want to ascertain the likely extent of the enterprise's potential liability, or even to participate in the actual management of the firm in order to assure that it does not run up huge debts. And still a risk of indefinite liability would remain. In principle, the enterprise could include in all of its contracts with customers and suppliers a clause limiting its liability to the assets of the enterprise (some business trusts do this). But the negotiation of such waivers would be costly. And it would be utterly impracticable to limit most tort liability in this way. Nor, as we shall see, is insurance a complete answer.

Advantages of Corporations

The corporate form is the normal solution that the law and business practice have evolved to meet the problems discussed in the preceding section. The corporation's perpetual existence obviates the need for a special agreement limiting withdrawal or dissolution. The shareholder's liability for corporate debts is limited to the value of his shares. Passive investment is further encouraged by (1) a complex of legal rights vis-a-vis management and any controlling group of shareholders, and (2) the fact that equity interests in a corporation are broken up into shares of relatively small value that can be, and in the case of most of the larger corporations are, traded in organized markets. The corporate form enables an investor to make small equity investments, to reduce risk through diversification, and to liquidate his investment quickly and cheaply.

C. NON–TAX ASPECTS

The three basic forms of business organization are the sole proprietorship, the partnership, and the corporation. Two less frequently used forms are the joint stock company and the Massachusetts Trust.*

* The joint stock company is a profit-seeking association of individuals rather than a distinct legal entity, whose capital is contributed by members in exchange for freely transferable shares. Members have limited control over the company's managers, yet their personal liability will extend beyond the amount of their investment.

The business, or Massachusetts Trust, is also not recognized as a legal "person" but is created by a written declaration of trust. Property is transferred to trustees to be managed and controlled for the benefit of beneficiaries, who possess freely transferable interests. Generally, beneficiaries will not incur personal liability for the trust's obligations unless they also act as trustees, hold title to trust property or retain the right to control the trustee's management of the business.

Each of the above-described forms has certain attributes that render it more adaptable to one particular set of circumstances. Furthermore, unless the sole proprietorship is to be used, the choice will ordinarily be partnership or incorporation, and it must be remembered that there can exist an overlapping of attributes among these forms. This is particularly true with close corporations.* Several states have statutes relieving close corporations from many of the requirements present in their regular corporate statutes, thus allowing them to assume several noncorporate attributes. In addition, courts have often created the same effect by leniently applying regular corporate statutes to close corporations.

J. SOBELOFF, TAX AND BUSINESS ORGANIZATION ASPECTS OF SMALL BUSINESS 3–26 (1974).
(Footnotes omitted.)

Expenses and Manner of Organization

In a few instances, the cost of organizing a business may be a factor. An individual trading in his own name may operate as a sole proprietor without any expense or formality or organization whatsoever. If the business is conducted under an assumed or fictitious name, the cost of filing fees and advertising is usually small.

If more than one person is involved in the business, a general partnership may be organized with little or no expense or formality. Written articles of agreement, though advisable, are not required by the Uniform Partnership Act. Generally, no registration or filing fee is required unless the partnership is conducted under an assumed or fictitious name. In the latter event, the cost of compliance with statutory requirements, as in the case of a sole proprietorship, is nominal. Furthermore, a partnership doing business in a foreign state will generally be free from statutory requirements of qualification applicable to foreign corporations.**

The formation of a limited partnership, however, necessitates strict compliance with statutory requirements. This will entail a written agreement and a filing of a certificate setting forth the rights and duties of the partners among themselves and indicating the general and limited partners. [ULPA § 2]. Advertising may be required. Because of this, the legal expense in the formation of a limit-

---

Neither of these forms is used with any frequency today, and we will not consider them further.—Eds.

* The subject of close corporations is considered in detail in Chapter 11.—Eds.

** The partnership, as an aggregation of individuals, may be guaranteed, under the privileges and immunities clause of the Constitution, the right to do business in a foreign jurisdiction without having additional conditions, such as a registration requirement, imposed upon it. The question has not been definitively resolved. *See* A. Bromberg, Crane and Bromberg on Partnership 108–109 (1968). —Eds.

ed partnership will usually exceed that incurred in the formation of a general partnership of similar size and scope.*

* * *

A business corporation requires formal articles of incorporation, compliance with statutory procedures, and the payment of filing fees and organization expenses, usually based on the capital structure. If one intends to do business in a single jurisdiction only, usually it is best to incorporate there since the corporation would generally be subject to only one set of state procedures and expenses, taxes, and laws. Furthermore, the advising attorney would be more familiar with the laws of that state and with the procedures and personnel of the courts having jurisdiction over the corporation.

Doing business in a state other than that of incorporation will require a certificate of authority from the state as well as the designation and maintenance in that state of a registered agent of the foreign corporation. Failure to obtain the proper authorization will carry penalties. The foreign corporation will also be subject to suit in the nondomiciliary jurisdiction. Although the corporate law of the state of incorporation will generally govern the foreign corporation, in certain instances it may find itself subject to a conflicting law of the foreign state. Furthermore, a corporation doing business other than in its state of incorporation may find itself subject to a second income tax unless its activities are within the minimal categories of the Federal Interstate Income Act.

* * *

When the expense of organization is a primary consideration a sole proprietorship or a general partnership would afford the most economical vehicle for transacting business. At the other extreme, the formation of a business corporation will usually entail the greatest expense and the greatest degree of formality in initial organization.

Liability

Unlimited personal liability is the general rule for individual owners, general partners, and members of joint stock companies. This is a distinct disadvantage as compared with the limited liability enjoyed by shareholders of corporations, limited partners, and, for the most part, beneficiaries of a business trust.

In a sense, all forms, except the sole proprietorship, enjoy a form of restricted liability. The business and personal assets of a sole proprietor are subject to the claims of all creditors without limitation by the amount of actual capital contribution to the business. His existing liabilities continue upon dissolution or sale of the business.

---

* The ULPA does not contain any provisions for the recognition of limited partnerships organized under the law of another state. Courts may, nevertheless, treat them as distinct legal entities under the applicable choice-of-law rules.—Eds.

General partners, either in a general or limited partnership, are liable for firm obligations and the wrongful acts of their copartners in the partnership business. Liability to existing business creditors also continues after dissolution of the firm. However, under the rule of marshalling assets, firm assets must first be applied to partnership creditors and individual assets to the claims of individual creditors. [UPA § 40(h).] * Partnership property as such is not subject to levy and sale on execution by the creditor of a partner, but the creditor can look only to a charging order upon the interest of the partner in the profits of the firm to satisfy that partner's personal debts.

* * *

The limited liability of the shareholders of a corporation, properly organized in accordance with the statute of the state of incorporation, is probably its greatest source of popular appeal as a form of business organization. * * *

The corporation, however, is not the only form of enterprise that carries with it limited liability for its members. The limited partnership and the business trust also insulate the members or limited partners against liability for firm obligations. Assuming compliance with the statutory formalities, the limited partner is not subject to the liabilities of a general partner so long as he does not participate in the management and control of the enterprise or in the conduct of its business by rendering services.** The limited partner's estate is free from firm obligations; the assets of the business, except for a charging order against his interest in the profits, are exempt from personal creditors. His liability for existing firm obligations cease upon transfer of his interest, although he remains liable for existing firm creditors to the extent that he may have withdrawn capital from the partnership. * * *

Business Entity

* * *

The right to sue or be sued and to hold, deal in, and dispose of property in a common or firm name is an advantageous business attribute. A corporation is the only organization which completely possesses this attribute. At common law a partnership was not capable of suing or being sued, and of acquiring or disposing of property in its firm name. By express provisions of statutes in a number of jurisdictions, however, suits may now be brought by or against a partnership in the firm name alone. However, in suits against the part-

---

* Any surplus in either the partnership or individual assets category may be applied to the claims of the creditors in the other category.—Eds.

** There is uncertainty with respect to whether a right of review or veto by limited partners constitutes intervention in management under UPA § 7 which provides: "A limited partner shall not become liable as a general partner unless, in addition to the exercise of his rights and powers as a limited partner, he takes part in the control of the business."—Eds.

nership, personal liability of the partners can normally be obtained only through service of process to obtain personal jurisdiction of the partners as individual parties defendant.* Further, the Uniform Partnership Act permits the acquisition and conveyance of real estate in the partnership name, and partnerships may also convey and mortgage real estate without the necessity of joining a spouse of a partner, even though such joinder is normally required for the conveyance of real estate.

* * *

A sole proprietorship has no entity apart from the individual owner. Although a sole proprietorship may be conducted under an assumed or fictitious name, the addition of the name under which the proprietor is trading is purely descriptive. A sole proprietorship, of course, will require the joinder of a spouse in any conveyance of real estate, whether or not it is considered a part of the business.

A corporation is regarded in all jurisdictions as a separate entity that may sue and be sued, convey and receive property, and enter into contracts in its own name. Furthermore, for the purpose of diversity of citizenship jurisdiction in the federal courts, the corporation is recognized as a citizen of the state in which it is incorporated and also the state in which it has its principal place of business.

Continuity of Existence

* * *

With a sole proprietorship, death terminates the business. If the business is dependent on the proprietor's personal attention and supervision, provision can be made in the proprietor's will for the temporary operation of the business by his personal representative pending its sale or liquidation. To limit the risk of loss to business assets, authority to incorporate the business, unless provided specifically by statute, should be included in the will. This is primarily a matter of probate law rather than of business law. If the nature of the business is that franchises necessary to continue the business would terminate with the proprietor's death, thought should be given to another form of organization that would preserve the legal entity, despite the proprietor's death, and would avoid the need to transfer or to lose valuable franchise rights.

One of the disadvantages of a general partnership is the dissolution of the firm [with the active partnership relation coming to an end under UPA § 29], absent any agreement, caused by either the death or the withdrawal of a partner [UPA §§ 31 and 32. A partner, even in violation of the partnership agreement, may quit and dissolve the firm. UPA § 31(2)]. If no definite term or particular undertaking is

---

* The joint debtor acts or common name statutes provide, in essence, that a judgment based on the service of one partner may be collected from (1) the partner served and (2) the partnership, but not from the individual assets of the partners who were not served.—Eds.

agreed upon, any partner may withdraw. If there is an agreement, withdrawal contrary to its term gives the remaining partners the right to buy out the interest of the withdrawing partner, but liquidation [that is, the disposition of the partnership assets, the payment of its debts, and the termination * of its business] may still occur if they do not have the funds to do so. In either case, the necessity of liquidation of the business could mean a substantial loss to all the partners. When a death occurs, the personal representative of the deceased partner ordinarily cannot join as a partner in continuing the business. The surviving partners in winding up the partnership affairs are forbidden, as a practical matter, from purchasing the interest of the deceased partner without the consent of the personal representative. The continuation of the business can be assured only through effective provisions in the partnership agreement.

Some measure of continuity of existence can be assured in a limited partnership. The partnership agreement may provide that a limited partner's capital contribution shall not be withdrawn until an agreed date. However, if no time is fixed for withdrawal, the limited partner can rightfully withdraw his capital contribution after six-months notice to the other members of the partnership. The death of a limited partner does not cause a dissolution of the partnership, and the articles can expressly empower a limited partner to substitute a new limited partner in his place, in which case his estate becomes a member of the firm. While a limited partnership is terminated by the death of the sole general partner or all of the general partners, * * * death or withdrawal of fewer than all general partners does not necessarily mean dissolution. The limited partnership is dissolved at the expiration of the term stated in the certificate. Although this can be almost any length of time, the limited partnership theoretically lacks the perpetual existence of a corporation.

* * *

The perpetual existence of a corporation is not interrupted by the death or withdrawal of the shareholders from the enterprise. The business continues to exist as a separate entity unaffected, in legal contemplation, by the life span or whims of the participants. However, the practical effect of death should not go unnoticed. Stock ownership in the closely held corporation may have no ready market. The estate of the deceased stockholder may be left with no means of recouping the capital investment. To counter such a situation, provision should be made for the liquidation of the interest of a deceased shareholder either by redemption of his stock by the corporation or through a buy and sell agreement with the remaining stockholders.

---

* Liquidation does not inexorably follow dissolution. The business of a dissolved partnership may, and indeed usually is, taken up by a new partnership without liquidation. This, in fact, follows automatically if the remaining partners simply continue to run the business, even if they take no formal action to solemnize the creation of a new partnership.—Eds.

The funding of stock purchase or redemption plan with life insurance should be considered.

Transferability of Interest

* * *

Obviously, the sole proprietor has complete freedom to sell or transfer all or part of his business interest. He is subject only to the general restrictions on transfers of property or business interests imposed by law, such as the requirements of the Bulk Sales Act, and joinder is required by the law of the jurisdiction.

General partners in either a general or a limited partnership are of necessity in close personal relationship with each other. They require the consent of all partners to [the admission of a new partner UPA § 18(g). The transfer of a partnership interest without consent gives the transferee very limited rights. UPA § 27.] Thus a general partner has the advantage of not having an unwanted partner thrust upon him without his consent. On the other hand, the general partner is subject to the disadvantage that liquidation of his interest in the business may be the only means of disposing of his interest.

In contrast, the limited partner may assign his interest, but the assignee will only have the right to receive his assignor's share of the profits. The assignee can become a substitute limited partner with all the additional rights of the limited partner if all members consent, or if the assignor, under the provisions of the certificate makes him so. Since limited partners cannot participate actively in the management and control of the firm, the limited partnership serves to combine the advantage of restricting management to a small group of general partners without fear of interference from undesirable outsiders, while giving the investors (limited partners) the unrestricted right to dispose of their capital investments by sale rather than through liquidation.

One of the most favorable attributes of a corporation is the flexibility it affords to transfer [an] interest in the business. The ownership of corporate property, unlike the partnership interest, may be divided into any desired number and types of shares, each representing different rights to the assets and the income of the business. The shareholder can sell or give away all or any portion of his holdings. Moreover, he may transfer only certain rights while retaining others. For example, where the corporate structure includes nonvoting or preferred stock, an interest in the income or assets may be transferred while control is retained or vice versa. Thus ownership of an interest in a corporation is divisible in many ways not available to a partner or a member of another entity. However, these attributes may not apply to close corporations under certain close corporation statutes that impose restrictions absent any shareholder agreement, on the issuance of transfer of stock. With no statutory restriction or restrictive agreement, a shareholder may dispose of his stock by gift or sale without the consent and even over the objection of other shareholders. Since share ownership usually includes the right to elect directors, and thus to have a voice in management, the sale of any sizable portion of the capital stock may result in new, unwanted corporate management.

* * *

In general, therefore, if transferability of interest is a paramount consideration, the corporation will be the most effective and certainly the most flexible business organization. The general partnership is at its greatest disadvantage when transferability of interest is a requisite.

Management and Control

* * *

A most important different among the various business organizations lies in the method and manner of conducting the everyday affairs of the enterprise. A sole proprietorship has no formalities of management. The owner makes his own decisions. * * * He is free to engage in business in his own state and any foreign states without registration or qualification, subject to compliance only with general statutes if trading under an assumed or fictitious name or if engaged in a business requiring a license. His business is subject to a minimum of control and supervision by federal, state and local authorities, and then only the extent that they are imposed against all individuals.

The general partnership is also free of most governmental regulations and restrictions and may be operated with little formality. The partners make their decisions in accordance with the provisions of the partnership agreement. However, continuity in management may be difficult, since, ordinarily, unanimity of agreement is needed from all the partners, which may not be easily obtained if there are several partners. Each member of the firm has an equal right to participate actively in the management and control of the enterprise. Even though the majority of partners' rule routine affairs [UPA § 18(h)] * in the absence of anything in the articles of agreement to the contrary, majority rule refers to one vote for each partner and not to a majority of interest in the partnership. Personal conflicts may be difficult to resolve. In addition each partner is a general agent of the firm for firm business. [UPA § 9, but note the exceptions listed in UPA § 9(3).]

* * *

Countervailing this is the ability of each partner to voice objections effectively by the threat of dissolution if action is taken contrary to his individual wishes. Though this tends to obstruct continuity

---

* UPA § 18(h) provides that action contrary to the terms of the partnership agreement may only be taken by the approval of all of the partners.—Eds.

of management, it prevents arbitrary control by the numerical majority. The partnership possesses a distinct advantage over the corporation in that it is generally subject to few governmental restrictions and regulations. Ordinarily a partnership is not required to publish financial statements. It is free to trade anywhere individuals may, relatively free from regulation.

The management and control of a limited partnership is vested in the general partners in much the same manner as in a general partnership. If the limited partners participate in the control of the business or perform services, they lose their limitation of liability and become liable as though a general partner. The limited partnership is thus an advantageous business device in which at least one partner is willing to assume the risk of a general partner by managing the business, while the other members are content to invest as limited partners, sharing in profits but relieved from both personal liability and obligations of management or the performance of services. The limited partners, without losing that status, may exercise [rights in certain circumstances] enumerated in section 10 in the Uniform Limited Partnership Act. There is some uncertainty, however, of the immunity of the limited partner when he attempts to intervene in the conduct of the business to protect his investment. * * * The general partner or partners conduct the business with the same minimum formalities required of a general partnership. The limited partnership has been the most frequent choice of * * * syndicates for real estate or other "tax shelter" investment. General partners provide the necessary management and services while the limited partners contribute capital and thus share in profits with a limitation on personal liability like that of a shareholder in a corporation and without the obligation to perform services expected of a general partner. At the same time, the limited partner may enjoy some tax advantages that would not be available to him in all circumstances if the business were incorporated.

Management and control of a corporation is centralized in a board of directors. The directors act in a representative capacity and are responsive only to indirect control by the shareholders, thus assuring continuity of corporate policy. The majority shareholders control the corporate policy through their power to elect a majority to the board of directors. Voting rights are ordinarily allocated—one vote for each share, not each person. This makes it difficult for the minority shareholders to voice any effective opposition, and subjects them to the will of the majority. Management and control are thus separated from ownership by the intermediate board of directors, which, in turn, acts only through the corporate officers and agents. Shareholders are under no obligation or duty to perform services for the enterprise. Their direct control is limited to a few specific actions outside the usual course of the corporate business. For example, a sale of substantially all the assets of the corporation or the amendment of the articles of incorporation will usually require shareholders approval. The shareholder agreements of close corporations, however, may be permitted to regulate many of the corporate affairs traditionally considered within the domain of the board. In fact, a board may not be required.

Operation of a corporation requires many formalities not encountered in the operation of other forms of business organizations. It is necessary that a corporation act in accordance with its charter and by-laws, hold meetings of stockholders and directors, keep accurate books of account and minutes of meetings, register in states other than in which it is incorporated before transacting business there, and file both information and tax reports beyond those required of unincorporated businesses. The authority of officers through whom the corporation must act requires substantiation by certified copies of resolutions and occasionally by production of a certified copy of the by-laws.

* * *

Capital and Credit Requirements

* * *

There is no statutory amount of capital required for a sole proprietor or either a general or a limited partnership to begin business. In [some] states corporations, however, are required to have a minimum amount of capital, usually $1,000, paid in as a condition to the commencement of business * * *. But the statutory minimum generally is so small that it is little more than a nominal requirement. The acquisition of capital and credit is actually more of a practical problem than a legal one.

The capital and credit of a sole proprietorship and a general partnership are limited by the individual resources of the owner or members. Each is individually and personally liable for money borrowed. As a general rule, these business organizations do not desire or attract capital which is provided by the sole proprietor or general partners. The sole proprietor or general partner usually combines his own service with his own capital and participation in management to promote the success of the enterprise. Credit is of course important, but credit generally depends upon considerations other than the form of business organization.

The limited partnership, on the other hand, is a device by which capital is obtained from investors who do not wish to perform services or participate in management, but are attracted by the possibility of larger returns on their investment through participation in profits. The limitation of liability is another feature that appeals to the investor as is demonstrated by the use of limited partnerships to raise capital for real estate ventures. Private investors seeking participation in large real estate ventures are willing to entrust a limited cash investment to a manager or operator in return for a share of the anticipated profit. The investor will contribute capital only, and not services, and wants no voice in the operation of the business except in the selection of the investment (which is usually made before the limited partner joins the partnership) and the time for termination and liquidation when the profit has been realized. The disadvantage of the limited partnership as a means of raising capital is the practical difficulty of disposing of the share of the limited partner. Although a limited partner may assign his share or, if the articles permit, sell his share and substitute another as limited partner in his stead, there are practical limitations on his ability to find a purchaser. The disposition of the investment of a limited partner does not possess the flexibility inherent in a stockholder's investment in a corporation.

The corporation is the traditional form of raising capital from outside investors. The stockholder possesses the advantage of limited liability while participating in the profits of the enterprise in proportion to his share of the total capital investment. In addition, the stockholder, in general, may transfer his shares of stock freely by sale or gift or by pledge, with complete flexibility. Thus he may split his shares into as many fractional parts as suit his interest in an almost unlimited manner. In small corporations the possibility of raising capital through the sale of stock may prove more illusory than real. The position of a minority stockholder has many disadvantages, resulting from the inability of the minority interest to actually control or influence the corporate policy or even to compel distribution of dividends. The market for the sale of stock in small corporations may be negligible. Ordinarily only larger businesses enjoy an actual market for their stock. Thus, as has been well said, incorporation is no guarantee of outside capital.

D. THE TAX CONSEQUENCES OF BUSINESS ORGANIZATIONS: A BRIEF EXAMINATION

Because different forms of doing business present different tax consequences, the decision of choosing the form of enterprise often turns on that factor. The major tax implications of that choice are summarized below, hopefully in a form which is useful for students who have not yet studied tax. Some of the more troublesome or complicated points are touched on only lightly, or omitted altogether and this survey should not be regarded as a comprehensive statement of the law.

1. SOLE PROPRIETORSHIPS

The simplest form of doing business, operating as a sole proprietor, is also the simplest from a tax standpoint. No new business enterprise has been created. There is no shift of property from one owner to another. Instead, an individual has segregated some assets for their dedication to the business. This necessitates the maintenance of records by the individual so that it is possible to determine the income and expenses relating to that activity. This is done main-ly for business reasons. In addition, however, business income is re-ported by the taxpayer on a separate Schedule C attached to the individual's tax return on Form 1040. The Internal Revenue Code permits the taxpayer to deduct from his gross income, the "ordinary and necessary expenses paid or incurred during the taxable year in carrying on any trade or business * * *." (Sec. 162.)

In paying taxes, the individual owner of a business reports both business income and income from other sources. If the business loses money, as is common in its early years, those losses will offset income from other sources (if any) and reduce total tax liability. For tax years beginning after 1983, individual tax rates vary from 11% to 50%. Corporate tax rates start higher, but have a lower maximum. The rate is 15% on the first $25,000 of taxable income, 18% on $25,000 to $50,000 of taxable income, 30% on $50,000 to $75,000 of taxable income, 40% on $75,000 to $100,000 of taxable income and 46% on taxable income above $100,000. (Sec. 11(b).) On the first $100,000 of corporate income, the tax at the corporate level will normally be less than individual rates that would apply to sole proprietorships or partnerships.

The fluctuation in rates and the varying courses of individual affairs point to the futility of generalizing about the advisability, from a tax standpoint, of choosing one form of business over another. Too much depends upon the individual circumstances. The circumstances will include the extent of outside income, the extent of outside deductions, the number of dependents, the possibility of early business losses, the possibilities of ultimate success, the individual's need for cash from the operations of the business, and the nature of the business itself.

2. PARTNERSHIP v. CORPORATION

The most common alternative facing an entrepreneur is the choice between a partnership and a corporation. We will therefore concentrate on the differences in tax treatment of doing business in these two forms.

a. Classification for Tax Purposes

The initial difficulty may be in determining whether a business organization is to be treated as a corporation from a tax standpoint. Limited partnerships offer limited liability to some investors, as does a corporation, and may also provide a tax shelter by passing through losses and deductions to the partners. Corporations deduct their own losses; they afford no tax benefit to stockholders (unless an election under Subchapter S has been made, as we discuss below). Therefore, it is important to know how the organization will be regarded. The classification of an organization as a corporation or as a partnership is made under the Internal Revenue Code; it does not depend on how the organization is classified under state law. However, the presence or absence of some of the key characteristics, in turn, depends on applicable state law, principally the Uniform Partnership Act and the Uniform Limited Partnership Act.

The relevant Income Tax Regulations state that the characteristics of a corporation are: (1) associates, (2) an objective to carry on a business and divide the profits, (3) continuity of life, (4) centralized management, (5) limited liability, and (6) free transferability of interests.

The first two characteristics are equally applicable to corporations or partnerships, but they are often the only characteristics which distinguish a corporation from a trust. The other four items will distinguish an organization which is taxed as a corporation from one which is treated as a partnership.

According to the Regulations, a partnership has no continuity of life if, under local law, death or withdrawal of a partner dissolves the organization, as Sections 29 and 32 of the Uniform Partnership Act so provide. The fact that most partnership agreements provide for continuation of the business does not alter the conclusion.

Centralized management is found in corporations which conventionally centralize authority in the board of directors. General partners, on the other hand, are each agents for each other partner according to Section 9 of the Uniform Partnership Act, and this is contradictory to centralized management. The Regulations conclude that a general partnership cannot achieve centralized management vis-a-vis third parties. A limited partnership, on the other hand, can accomplish this if "substantially all" of the interests are owned by limited partners. An example of the latter is a real estate venture with a few general partners which sells limited partnership interests to the public at large in order to raise practically all of the capital. Management is then effectively centralized in the few general partners.

Limited liability is, of course, the key corporate characteristic. General partners have no such limitation on their liability, but limited partners do. If the general partners are mere dummies for the limited partners and if they have no substantial assets apart from their partnership interests, the practical equivalent of limited liability is accomplished. Business trusts will ordinarily possess this characteristic, as well.

Free transferability of interest allows corporate stockholders to sell their shares. Sometimes this is contractually restricted. The Regulations recognize this as a "modified" free transferability. But partnerships never reach this equivalence since the Uniform Partnership Act permits only the assignment of a partner's right to profits and not his status as partner.

Thus, Professors Bittker and Eustice observe, "The regulations also make it plain that partnerships governed by the Uniform Partnership Act and the Uniform Limited Partnership Act, or their local equivalents, can rarely, if ever, be treated as associations." B. Bittker and J. Eustice, Federal Income Taxation of Corporation and Shareholders 2–12 (4th ed. 1979). The same may not be true for joint ventures. Business trusts and joint stock association, moreover, will usually be classified as associations for tax purposes by application of the Regulations.

It is common to see an association with some, but not all, of the enumerated characteristics. If the organization possesses three of the corporate characteristics, the Regulations, in the examples set forth, hold that the organization will be taxed as a corporation, even if there is no limited liability. No one characteristic will be determinative.

b. Tax Significance of the Corporate or Partnership Form

An important generality to be noted in the difference between tax treatment is that corporations, apart from the persons who own the stock, pay taxes. A corporation is a legal entity. A partnership, by contrast, is considered an aggregate of individuals and although certain rights are created in the aggregation, from a tax standpoint, the partnership is not an entity and hence, it is not a taxpayer. It files an information return, but the purpose is essentially to determine how much tax the individual partners will pay on the income derived from the operation of the business.

This difference has focused on what has somewhat loosely been called "double taxation." The corporation pays a tax on the income it receives and when that income is distributed to shareholders, in the form of dividends, it is again taxed in the hands of the shareholders. Since the partnership itself pays no tax, the income from the business is taxed only to the partners, but the tax is paid whether or not the income is distributed.

The inclination of the tax advisor is therefore to seek means of avoiding double taxation. Often this means the formation of a business as a partnership, but it could also mean the retention of earnings in a corporation. In large business, of course, it is usually impossible to operate as a general partnership because of the other limitations of that form, such as lack of free transferability of interests and the need for limited liability and centralized management. (Note that a limited partnership can achieve these results.) But in small business, the general partnership form is often feasible.

Alternatively, the tax advisor seeks to structure the corporation to minimize the effect of double taxation. Note that we have said that the income is taxed both to the corporation and the shareholder when the income is distributed to the shareholder *as a dividend*. If it is distributed to the shareholder in the form of a salary, it is taxed to the shareholder, but it is not taxed to the corporation since it constitutes a deductible expense. The same is true of interest on a loan or rent on a building or for equipment. So, if the shareholder is an employee, he will have no need for dividends if the amount which would otherwise be paid to him as a salary. Similarly, if his investment in the corporation is, in part, in the form of a bond or a note, the interest paid to him will be an acceptable substitute for dividends. Or if he owns the corporation's plant or equipment, rent paid to him will be deductible by the corporation. There are important caveats to these comments, which are discussed below.

There is a further tax measure which can be adopted which we will discuss in more detail later but which we merely mention at this point—the Subchapter S corporation. In essence, this is a corporation which has elected to be taxed under the provisions of Subchapter S of the Internal Revenue Code and which (with rare exceptions) pays no tax itself, but instead has its income taxed to the shareholders, whether or not it is actually distributed to those shareholders. While this bears resemblance to partnership taxation, there are sufficient differences to make it unwise to say that such corporation is taxed as a partnership; it is taxed as a Subchapter S corporation.

3. COMPARISON OF TAX TREATMENT: PARTNERSHIP v. CORPORATION

The comparison of tax treatment between various forms of business organization can best be analyzed if we examine the tax treatment upon (1) the organization of the business, (2) the operation of the business and (3) the disposition of interests in the business.

a. Organization of the Business

The Internal Revenue Code permits the organizers of a business to transfer property to the partnership or the corporation, without payment of tax at that time even though the property has appreciated in value. (No loss is allowed, either.) Suppose, for example, Hardy and Luff desire to form a company to repair boats on premises owned by Hardy, which he will sell to the corporation for stock. The cost of acquiring the property was $5,000, but today it is worth $50,000. Luff will contribute stocks and bonds which cost her $25,000 but which also have a value of $50,000. Hardy and Luff will each own one-half of the business to be formed. If the transfer to the partnership or corporation, whichever they chose to form, resulted in payment of a tax, the tax on the increases in the value of the contributed properties might be so substantial it would discourage the formation of the business. The Internal Revenue Code provides, in Section 721, that no gain or loss is to be recognized for an interest in the partnership. Similarly, Section 351 of the Internal Revenue Code provides that no gain shall be recognized if property is transferred to a corporation solely in exchange for its stock or securities, if immediately following that exchange, the person or persons who contributed property own (as a group) at least 80% of the voting stock and 80% of each other class of stock of the corporation. Nor can the organizers deduct the amount of any loss which they might realize upon the formation of the partnership or corporation. Suppose Luff's securities which were worth $50,000 had cost her $100,000. She now has a one-half interest in a business whose total assets are $100,000. The organization of the partnership or the corporation is not viewed as an event which would permit her to give effect to the capital loss of $50,000 which she had realized when she exchanged those stocks and bonds.

It is important at this time to consider the concept of "tax basis." The basis of an asset is usually the cost of that asset, minus the depreciation which the owner was allowed to deduct. The difference between *basis* and the *amount realized* (another concept requiring special definition, but not here) when the asset is exchanged measures the amount of the gain on which a tax may be payable. Basis is important to the owner not only for purposes of measuring gain or loss upon exchange, but because it determines the amount which may be deducted as depreciation. The higher the basis the greater the depreciation (which is keyed to the taxpayer's basis) and hence the larger the deduction which may be taken to determine taxable income.

It is also important to be aware that the Internal Revenue Code imposes a lower rate of tax on "capital gains" as compared to ordinary income. Thus, income from a salary is taxed at ordinary income tax rates while the gain realized from the sale of stock or other capital assets is taxed at capital gains rates. Ordinary tax rates on earned income begin at 11% and climb to 50% in the case of individuals and corporate tax rates vary from 15% to 46%. Capital gains rates, on the other hand, in the case of an individual are generally 40% of the rate on ordinary income and in no event more than 20% (except in unusual instances where the alternative minimum tax of § 55 applies). The capital gains rate for a corporation is 28% (with minor exceptions).

The significance of basis when applied to the formation of a business entity is that any asset which the organizers transfer to the partnership or the corporation in a "tax free" transaction retains the same basis as it had in the hands of the former owner. Luff's securities, worth $50,000, have a tax basis in the hands of the corporation or partnership of $25,000. If the securities were immediately sold, the corporation or partnership would realize a taxable gain of $25,000 although the securities had not appreciated at all since acquired by the business organization. Consequently, the tax which would otherwise have been paid when the asset was acquired is merely postponed until the new owner sells the asset.

The most important point from this quick survey is that the incident of formation of either a partnership or corporation generally results in no tax to either the former owner of the property or to the partnership or the corporation. No initial tax advantage is gained by choosing one form over the other.

b. Operation of a Partnership

Let us pursue Hardy and Luff through the operation of the partnership and their disposition of their partnership interest or their ultimate transformation into a larger business operated in corporate form. At the end of each, the partnership will compute its net income and accordingly file an information return. The partnership may pay "salaries" to Hardy and Luff and at the end of the year it will retain some of its profits in the business and distribute the remaining portion to Hardy and Luff. (There is an incongruity which must be recognized in a partnership payment of salary to an owner, but the Internal Revenue Code permits this payment to be deducted just as if it were paid to an employee who is not an owner.) The partnership, as noted earlier will pay no tax on its net income. Hardy and Luff will pay taxes, at their respective individual rates, on the "salaries" which they received as well as on the amounts distributed to them. As to the remainder of the net income, which was not distributed to them they will nonetheless pay a tax on their proportionate share, in this case one-half each. Subsequent distributions of the amount on which they were taxed but which was not distributed to them will be received by Hardy and Luff without the imposition of a further tax.

The partnership will compute its net income in much the same manner as will an individual. There are exceptions to this; they are not important in this overview. To determine how much of the profit or how much of the loss is to be attributed to each of the partners, reference is initially made to the partnership agreement existing between the parties. In the absence of a formal partnership agreement, or in the event it is incomplete with reference to the particular point in question, the tax law makes certain assumptions. For example, if the partners neglect to state how much of the profits each is entitled to receive, then the law presumes that they are all equal partners. The difference in the personal circumstances of the partners suggest some interesting thoughts for planning a business enterprise. For example, let us assume that Luff, in addition to being a partner in this business, also receives income as the beneficiary of a family trust in the amount of $25,000 a year. Hardy, on the other hand, receives no income from any other source. The partners decide that each of them is to have a salary of $7,500 per annum during the first two years of the partnership during which time the business is expected to operate at a deficit, which is the common experience for new businesses. Let us also assume that the deficit in the first two years amounts to $50,000 each year, including the deduction for the salaries paid to Hardy and Luff. Luff, in our example, has income of $25,000 from the trust plus $7,500 received as salary for a total of $32,500 and she may take as a deduction the $25,000 loss which constitutes her share of the partnership's loss. Thus, the total income she will report is $7,500. Hardy has income of only $7,500 from which he may deduct $25,000, and hence he will pay no tax. This leaves him with $17,500 of undeducted loss which he may carry back against income reported in earlier years and obtain a refund, and if some loss still remains undeducted, he may carry that forward and apply it against income received in subsequent years. Whether he has such prior income or subsequent income will depend upon his personal circumstances. By contrast, Luff receives immediate benefit or relief from the fact that the partnership initially operates at a loss and she can enjoy a substantial income at a low tax cost. The ability to directly offset personal income with losses from a business is one of the attractive tax features of a partnership form of doing business. The business, in this form, functions as a tax shelter. If the business subsequently becomes so profitable that the partners are put in a very high tax bracket (even though much of the income is retained in the business) they may find that this is the appropriate occasion to change to a corporate form.

c. Disposition of Partnership Interest

When Hardy and Luff formed the partnership, they each received a 50% interest in the partnership. This partnership interest constitutes an asset and it, too, has a tax basis. The basis is the same as the basis of the property which they contributed in order to obtain their interests. Thus, Hardy's basis is $5,000 (the cost of his property) and Luff's basis is $25,000 (the cost of the securities she contributed). That basis will fluctuate during the life of the partnership. For example, each partner's basis will be increased by his share of partnership income on which he pays a tax but which is retained by the partnership for use in the business. Every distribution of property to a partner will result in a decrease in the basis of his partnership interest.

Suppose after several years of operation Hardy and Luff decide to terminate their business and to sell all the partnership property and distribute the proceeds to the partners with the result that each receives $50,000. Each partner will subtract from the $50,000 distribution his or her basis in the partnership. The basis will first reflect the partnership's operations in its last year (during which it sold its assets) and the partner's share of any gain will increase the basis. Hardy would have realized a gain of $45,000 and Luff's gain would amount to $25,000, providing the basis in their partnership interests were still the same as their original basis, namely, $5,000 and $25,000. Hardy and Luff, respectively, will be taxed on these amounts and they will pay a tax at capital gains rates at this time. This description is subject to important but extremely complex qualifications which cannot be examined here.

Suppose instead of liquidating the business, Hardy decides that he wants to continue the business but Luff prefers to retire. Because the business has done well assume Luff sells her one-half partnership interest to White for $75,000. Luff has realized a profit of $50,000 on this disposition, (assuming her basis equals $25,000) and she pays a tax at capital gains rates on this amount. White, the new owner of one-half of the business, has a basis in that interest amounting to $75,000, the amount he paid for it.

After several years of operating in the partnership form the partners may now wish to operate the business as a corporation. Nothing will change except the form of business enterprise. The partners consider it essential that this transformation not result in the imposition of any tax on the partners or on the corporation which is to be newly formed. If the assets of the partnership are exchanged for the stock or stock and securities of a corporation of which the partners, taken in the aggregate own 80% of each class of stock, then, as discussed earlier in connection with the formation of corporation, generally no gain will be recognized to the former partners. If the partners are selling out their business to a corporation which they do not control, then there will be a tax imposed on the sale of their partnership interests.

d. Operation of a Corporation

If Hardy and Luff choose to operate their business in the form of a corporation, they need to decide whether stock or other securities of the corporation should be issued in exchange for the property acquired. The corporation may issue various amounts of common stock or common stock together with either preferred stock or debt securities of the corporation. To the owners of a small business such as the one hypothesized, the tax significance of the choice stems from the single fact that when a corporation distributes dividends to its shareholders, the corporation receives no deduction for the amount distributed to its shareholder. By contrast, when the corporation pays interest on indebtedness even if the creditor is a shareholder, a deduction is allowed to the corporation for the payment of the interest. Hence, there will be a great temptation to label the securities of the corporation debt rather than stock in order that payments will be deducted by the corporation, thereby reducing its taxable income and reducing or perhaps even eliminating so-called double taxation. However, the debt must be genuine, and not merely stock disguised and labeled as debt. Detailed regulations under § 385 have tried to chart the course between debt and stock. Individual shareholders treat dividends and interest as practically the same; corporate holders of stock may prefer dividends because of a special deduction. (§ 243.) The stockholders of the corporation may seek to capitalize the company "thinly," *i.e.*, a small amount of stock and a large amount of debt.* There have been many battles between the Internal Revenue Service and corporations regarding the characterization of the security which has been issued. The Service, obviously, is not bound to accept the corporation's own characterization.

This last point serves to illustrate what may be the most important point about the tax aspects of doing business through a corporation; namely that individuals by forming a corporation have created a tax-paying entity. If the business earned as much money as it did when operated in partnership form and there is no reason to think otherwise, then the owners of the business will be worse off financially if they distribute the profits to themselves as dividends, than if they had operated as a partnership. They may, of course, reduce the corporation's profits by taking personal salaries, and if their salaries were equal to the entire amount of the company's profits, the corporation ordinarily would have no profits. Under these circumstances the consequences of operating in either partnership or corporate form would produce no tax differences. The Internal Revenue Code as noted above, permits the deduction of "ordinary and necessary" business expenses. The amount allowed as a deduction for salaries is limited to a reasonable amount. The salaries paid to owner-employees are carefully scrutinized. If a business grows to substantial proportions it will be difficult to deduct as "reasonable salaries" sums which fully equal the profits of the company. Thus, if the business grows, the likelihood is that the corporation will be taxed on at least some of its income, and if that income is then distributed to the shareholders, it will be taxed again.

Just as in the case of a partnership, the corporation computes its net income in much the same manner as does an individual. The essential difference is in the rate paid. If a business is likely to produce a substantial amount of profits and will require accumulations of capital for use in the business, the difference in rates may be one of the more compelling reasons to form a corporation. If the owners of the business are persons of substantial means with substantial unearned income from dividends and interest, it is entirely possible that their tax brackets would exceed 46% although not by much. Certainly if their share of the income from a successful company were to be taxed to them, the rate might exceed 46%. If a partnership retains the use of funds, the partners are nonetheless taxed on their full share of the amount earned by the partnership, whether or not anything is distributed to them. Thus, they will be taxed on income which is accumulated by the business at a rate which may be as high as 50%. On the other hand, the corporation may, subject to certain restrictions, accumulate its earnings at a tax cost not exceeding 46%. Earnings accumulation may be considered important for the

* The subject of thinly capitalized corporations is discussed in greater detail in Chapters 9 and 13.—Eds.

success of the business, and the tax costs of accumulation are important to estimate.   \

However, the real advantage to the corporate form stems from
the opportunity to reduce the effective rate well below 46%. Corporations (and not individuals) are permitted significant relief through
several special provisions. The principal tax reducing provision is the
investment tax credit, under § 46. Corporations do not have to make
large expenditures to obtain large tax benefits. Mere paperwork can
confer the tax benefits upon corporations with otherwise taxable income by arranging leasing transactions with companies that report
losses. The key point: real corporate rates are well below the stated
rates.

Losses resulting from the operation of the business are deductible
only by the corporation and not directly by the owners, as distinguished from the tax treatment of losses from the operation of a
partnership. Corporate losses may be applied, within limits, as deductions against the later income otherwise taxable to the corporation. They will not be of direct benefit to the shareholders, however.

Shareholders, if employed in the business, on the other hand, have
an opportunity not available to partners to defer certain of their income until later years when presumably their tax brackets will be
lower. Pension plans, profit sharing plans and stock options are all
available to corporate employees to a greater extent than is available
to partners. The favorable tax treatment of such "fringe benefits" is
one of the most important tax advantages of a corporation over a
partnership.

There are many unique aspects of the operation of a corporation
from a tax standpoint, but these can await a course in federal taxation of corporations and are not necessary for our overall view of the
tax aspects of a corporation.

e. Disposition of Corporate Interests

Securities in a corporation, just as a partnership interest, are capital assets, and when a shareholder disposes of his interest in a corporation he may normally expect that a tax paid will be at capital gains
rates.

But if a corporation is acquired by another corporation in a merger or some other kind of reorganization, the stockholders of the acquired corporation will not recognize any (gain or loss) if they exchange their stock only for stock of the acquiring corporation. There
are important rules which must be observed in order to assure this
tax-free (really tax deferral) reorganization treatment, some of these
are briefly considered in Chapter 20. A complete discussion must
await a subsequent course.

4. SUBCHAPTER S CORPORATIONS

Finally, a word about Subchapter S. If a corporation has fewer than twenty-five individual stockholders, and if it meets certain other qualifications, it may make an election under Subchapter S of the Code whereby the corporation will pay no tax (with some exceptions) and all the income will be taxed to the shareholders, whether or not distributed, in a matter similar to a partnership. Other corporate features will be retained, such as the taxation of certain dividends, dispositions of an interest in the corporation, and deferred compensation. This provision was designed for the benefit of small businesses so that tax consequences could be eliminated as a factor in choice of business organization. It contains many technical intricacies and sometimes entraps shareholders into unintended tax results. Used wisely, and carefully, it may be used well.

5. CONCLUSION

The corporation is the only business association which possesses its own tax individuality, although business conducted in other forms gives rise to special tax rules. The corporation has its own tax rates and is itself a taxpayer. There are sometimes advantages and disadvantages to operating as a corporation, and each situation must be carefully analyzed and planned. Adjustments, such as salaries or Subchapter S elections, can make the corporate choice the wise one but it is not invariably so. Often the result will turn on more complex questions which are not even suggested in this survey.

Chapter 7

THE INCORPORATION PROCESS

PROBLEM

EAST WIND BOATS—PART IV

Hardy, Luff, and Teach have decided to operate East Wing Boats as a corporation and have asked you to handle the incorporation. You are now confronted with the following questions:

1. You have represented Hardy in past business dealings, and it was his suggestion that the three of them call upon you. All three have now asked you to handle the legal work in forming the corporation. Is there any reason why you should not proceed with this representation?

2. Should the business be incorporated in Columbia, in Delaware, or in some other jurisdiction?

3. Assuming that you have selected Columbia as the place of incorporation, what are the formalities with which you must comply? (Consider MBCA §§ 53–57.) How long would you expect the process to take?

4. What are the consequences if some formality is neglected but your clients commence doing business in the belief that East Wind Boats has been validly incorporated?

5. As you are working on the incorporation papers, you receive a call from Hardy. He tells you that he has just talked to a local contractor about the new building that he, Luff, and Teach have decided to add to the boatyard. The contractor has no work for the next few weeks and is willing to construct the building at a very favorable price if he can have a signed contract and begin work on Monday. Your clients want to go ahead. Your experience tells you that it will be impossible to complete the incorporation of East Wind Boats by that time, because some details need to be resolved. How should the contract be handled?

A. LAWYERS' CONFLICTS OF INTEREST

Excerpts from the American Bar Association
Code of Professional Responsibility

CANON 5

A Lawyer Should Exercise Independent Professional Judgment on Behalf of a Client

Interests of Multiple Clients

EC 5–14 Maintaining the independence of professional judgment required of a lawyer precludes his acceptance or continuation of employment that will adversely affect his judgment on behalf of or dilute his loyalty to a client. This problem arises whenever a lawyer is asked to represent two or more clients who may have differing interests, whether such interests be conflicting, inconsistent, diverse, or otherwise discordant.

EC 5–15 If a lawyer is requested to undertake or to continue representation of multiple clients having potentially differing interests, he must weigh carefully the possibility that his judgment may be impaired or his loyalty divided if he accepts or continues the employment. He should resolve all doubts against the propriety of the representation. A lawyer should never represent in litigation multiple clients with differing interests; and there are few situations in which he would be justified in representing in litigation multiple clients with potentially differing interests. If a lawyer accepted such employment and the interests did become actually differing, he would have to withdraw from employment with likelihood of resulting hardship on the clients; and for this reason it is preferable that he refuse the employment initially. On the other hand, there are many instances in which a lawyer may properly serve multiple clients having potentially differing interests in matters not involving litigation. If the interests vary only slightly, it is generally likely that the lawyer will not be subjected to an adverse influence and that he can retain his independent judgment on behalf of each client; and if the interests become differing, withdrawal is less likely to have a disruptive effect upon the causes of his clients.

EC 5–16 In those instances in which a lawyer is justified in representing two or more clients having differing interests, it is nevertheless essential that each client be given the opportunity to evaluate his need for representation free of any potential conflict and to obtain other counsel if he so desires. Thus before a lawyer may represent multiple clients, he should explain fully to each client the implications of the common representation and should accept or continue employment only if the clients consent. If there are present other circumstances that might cause any of the multiple clients to question the undivided loyalty of the lawyer, he should also advise all of the clients of those circumstances.

* * *

EC 5–18 A lawyer employed or retained by a corporation or similar entity owes his allegiance to the entity and not to a stockholder, director, officer, employee, representative, or other person connected with the entity. In advising the entity, a lawyer should keep paramount its interests and his professional judgment should not be influenced by the personal desires of any persons or organization. Occasionally a lawyer for an entity is requested by a stockholder, director, officer, employee, representative, or other person connected with the entity to represent him in an individual capacity; in such case the lawyer may serve the individual only if the lawyer is convinced that differing interests are not present.

EC 5–19 A lawyer may represent several clients whose interests are not actually or potentially differing. Nevertheless, he should explain any circumstances that might cause a client to question his undivided loyalty. Regardless of the belief of a lawyer that he may properly represent multiple clients, he must defer to a client who holds the contrary belief and withdraw from representation of that client.

DR 5–105 Refusing to Accept or Continue Employment if the Interests of Another Client May Impair the Independent Professional Judgment of the Lawyer.

(A) A lawyer shall decline proffered employment if the exercise of his independent professional judgment in behalf of a client will be or is likely to be adversely affected by the acceptance of the proffered employment, except to the extent permitted under DR 5–105(C).

(B) A lawyer shall not continue multiple employment if the exercise of his independent professional judgment in behalf of a client will be or is likely to be adversely affected by his representation of another client, except to the extent permitted under DR 5–105(C).

(C) In the situations covered by DR 5–105(A) and (B), a lawyer may represent multiple clients if it is obvious that he can adequately represent the interest of each and if each consents to the representation after full disclosure of the possible effect of such representation on the exercise of his independent professional judgment on behalf of each.

(D) If a lawyer is required to decline employment or to withdraw from employment under DR 5–105, no partner or associate of his or his firm may accept or continue such employment.

A Proposed Final Draft of the Model Rules of Professional Conduct was proposed to the American Bar Association by a special study group on May 30, 1981, to replace the existing Code. While these proposed rules have not been adopted (and may *not* be adopted) and are in the process of revision, they are worth examining.

Rule 1.7 Conflict of Interest: General Rule

(a) A lawyer shall not represent a client if the lawyer's ability to consider, recommend, or carry out a course of action on behalf of the client is adversely affected by the lawyer's responsibilities to another client or a third person or by the lawyer's own interests.

(b) When a lawyer has responsibilities or interests that might adversely affect the representation of a client, the lawyer shall not represent the client unless:

(1) The lawyer reasonably believes that the representation is compatible with the best interest of the client; and

(2) the client consents after disclosure. When representation of multiple clients in a single matter is undertaken, the disclosure shall include explanation of the implications of the common representation and the advantages and risks involved.

Comment:

Loyalty to a Client

Loyalty is an essential element in the lawyer's relationship to a client. An improper conflict of interest may exist before representation is undertaken, in which event the representation should be declined. If such a conflict arises after representation has been undertaken and cannot be remedied by disclosure to and consent by the client, the lawyer must withdraw from the representation. See Rule 1.16. Where more than one client is involved and a conflict arises after representation, whether the lawyer may continue to represent any of the clients is determined by Rule 1.9.

Other Conflict Situations

Conflicts of interest in contexts other than litigation sometimes may be difficult to assess. Relevant factors in determining whether there is potential for adverse effect include the duration and intimacy of the lawyer's relationship with the client or clients involved, the functions being performed by the lawyer, the likelihood that actual conflict will arise and the likely prejudice to the client from the conflict if it does arise.

The question is often one of proximity and degree. A lawyer may not represent multiple parties to a negotiation whose interests are fundamentally antagonistic to each other, but common representation is permissible where the clients are generally aligned in interest even though there is some difference of interest among them.

A lawyer for a corporation or other organization who is also a member of its board of directors should determine whether the responsibilities of the two roles may conflict. The lawyer may be called on to advise the corporation in matters involving actions of the directors. Consideration should be given to the frequency with which such situations may arise, the potential intensity of the conflict, the effect of the lawyer's removing himself from the board and the possibility of the corporation's obtaining legal advice from another lawyer in such situations. If there is material risk that the dual role will compromise the lawyer's independence of professional judgment, the lawyer should not serve as a director.

B.   CHOICE OF THE STATE OF INCORPORATION

1. INTRODUCTION: THE LAW APPLICABLE TO CORPORATIONS

What turns on the decision of where to incorporate? Until you know the answer to that question, you cannot intelligently choose the state of incorporation.

As we have already seen * a corporation is a legal person, and has certain constitutional entitlements, including equal protection of the law. Under early doctrine, a state could exclude out-of-state corporations altogether from engaging in intrastate business within its borders; Bank of Augusta v. Earle, 38 U.S. (13 Pet.) 519, 10 L.Ed. 274 (1839); Paul v. Virginia, 75 U.S. (8 Wall.) 168, 19 L.Ed. 357 (1868); Railway Express Agency v. Virginia, 282 U.S. 440, 51 S.Ct. 201, 75 L. Ed. 450 (1931); and thus may subject foreign corporations to conditions on doing business within the state. The Court recently concluded that it is "now established that whatever the extent of a state's authority to exclude foreign corporations from doing business within its boundaries, that authority does not justify imposition of more onerous taxes or other burdens on foreign corporations than those imposed on domestic corporations, unless the discrimination between foreign and domestic corporations bears a rational relation to a legitimate state purpose." Western & Southern Life Insurance Co. v. State Board of Equalization of California, 451 U.S. 648, 101 S.Ct. 2070, 68 L.Ed.2d 514 (1981). See Watson v. Employers Liability Assurance Corp., Ltd., 348 U.S. 66, 75 S.Ct. 166, 171, 99 L.Ed. 74, 83 (1954) (concurring opinion of Frankfurter, J., reviewing precedents). In practice states do not exclude foreign corporations, but they do seek to assert some control, mainly for revenue raising purposes. Thus, if a company is to engage in "local" business ** in a foreign state, it must register within the state and thereby qualify to do business there as a foreign corporation. But if the corporation's intrastate activities are an inseparable part of an interstate transaction, it

---

* Chapter 4, part C.

** What constitutes "doing business" has generated countless court opinions but remains, nevertheless, an unusually unrefined area of the law of corporations. It should be noted that "doing business" for the purpose of requiring a corporation to register as a foreign corporation is not necessarily "doing business" for the purposes of jurisdiction of the courts or amenability to service of process, and that both are different from "doing business" for the purpose of imposing state taxes. See H. Henn, Handbook of the Law of Corporations and Other Business Enterprises, 149–166 (2d ed. 1970).

may not be required to qualify as a foreign corporation. Eli Lilly & Co. v. Sav-on-Drugs, 366 U.S. 276, 81 S.Ct. 1316, 6 L.Ed.2d 288 (1961); Allenberg Cotton Co. v. Pittman, 419 U.S. 20, 95 S.Ct. 260, 42 L.Ed. 2d 249 (1974).

Originally, the main purpose of the registration requirement was to assure that foreign corporations would be subject to the jurisdiction of the courts of the state and amenable to service of process in the state, objectives that have been largely achieved by the expansion of long-arm jurisdiction. Today, sanctions for a failure to qualify to do business are relatively mild; they generally entail little more than a temporary bar to access to local courts. This may be embarrassing when the corporation is sued and is unable to file an answer or a counterclaim; but under most statutes, registration even after the suit is filed removes this bar.

The principles embodied in the full faith and credit clause of the Constitution and the idea of comity require a state which hosts a foreign corporation to respect the legislative enactments and judicial decisions of the home state of the foreign corporation. When a corporation incorporated in one state does business in another it carries with it whatever rights were conferred by the act of incorporation and the applicable law of its home state.

The law of the state of incorporation also ordinarily determines the rules that govern the "internal affairs" of a corporation. Restatement, Second, Conflicts of Laws §§ 296–310 (1971). Although the term has no clear definition, "internal affairs" are in general those matters bearing on the relationships among the participants in the corporation. For the most part, this means the relationship between owners (shareholders) and managers (officers and directors). The internal affairs rule also applies to the relationships between different classes of shareholders, the relationship between shareholders and creditors, and between shareholders and employees. For example, the law of the state of incorporation governs the right of stockholders to vote, to receive distributions of corporate property, to receive information from the management about the affairs of the corporation, to limit the powers of the corporation to specifically chosen fields of activity, and to bring suit on behalf of the corporation when the managers refuse to do so. It also determines the procedures by which the board of directors will act, the managers' right to be indemnified by the corporation when they are sued for their conduct, and the corporation's right to issue stock and to merge with other companies. Perhaps most importantly, the internal affairs rule governs the law that implements the idea that the managers of a corporation are managing other people's property and thus owe a fiduciary duty to the corporation.

This, by no means exhaustive, list suggests the impossibility of administering any other rule, at least if the corporation is a multi-state venture. How could it be decided, for example, which stockholders were entitled to vote at an annual meeting if it were necessary to refer to the potentially conflicting law of every state in which the corporation did business? Obviously with respect to such questions a choice must be made; the internal affairs rule makes it by deciding them according to the law of the state of incorporation.

Of course, the "external affairs" of a corporation are generally governed by the law of the place where the activities occur rather than by the place of incorporation. For example, a state's labor laws govern conditions of employment and minimum wages of the operations of all businesses within the state, wherever the businesses might be incorporated. State tax laws generally apply to activities of any corporation within the state, especially those that are imposed on corporate real estate and income. (Franchise taxes, which are collected by the state of incorporation from companies incorporated there, do not depend on the situs of a corporation's activities or property.)

Some activities are governed by both internal and external rules. For example, state corporation law controls the right to merge and the procedure to be followed, but mergers are also independently subject to anti-trust laws and securities laws.

The internal affairs doctrine is merely a choice-of-law rule and, like other such rules is amenable to change by a particular jurisdiction (subject always to the requirement of the federal Constitution). Thus in an effort to protect its citizens a state is, in principle at least, free to apply some or all of its own corporate law rules to corporations that have substantial contacts with the state even though they are incorporated elsewhere. New York and California have chosen to exercise this power over what have been called "pseudo-foreign" corporations, meaning corporations that carry on most of their activities or have a majority of their shareholders in the state but are incorporated in another state. West's Ann. Calif. Code, § 2115, McKinney's N.Y. BCL §§ 1317–20.

The California statute makes certain provisions of California law governing corporate affairs applicable to foreign corporation if (1) more than 50 percent of its property, payroll, and sales are within California and (2) more than 50 percent of its voting securities are held of record by persons with California addresses. A corporation falling within this class becomes subject to, among others, the California provisions on dividends and other distributions of corporate property, election and removal of directors, directors' standard of care, indemnification of officers and directors, and the regulation of mergers and sales of assets. One of the provisions made applicable by the statute is a requirement that "cumulative" voting (a procedure discussed in greater detail in Chapter 10) be used in the election of directors rather than "straight" voting, which is at least optional in most other states. Suppose a corporation is incorporated in a state that allows "straight" voting for directors but it meets the California tests for pseudo-foreign corporations. How are directors elected? That question arose in litigation involving the Arden-Mayfair Corporation, which is incorporated in Delaware but has most of its assets and shareholders in California. Louart Corporation, a major shareholder of Arden-Mayfair, brought an action in a California court seeking to compel Arden-Mayfair to comply with the California cumulative voting rule. Louart Corp. v. Arden-Mayfair Corp. Civ. No. C–193–091 (Super.Ct. of L.A. County, May 1, 1978). While that suit was pending, Arden-Mayfair sued Louart in Delaware seeking a declaratory judgment that the California rule did not apply. Arden-Mayfair Corp. v. Louart Corp., 34 Del. Ch. 221, 385 A.2d 3 (1978). The California court held § 2115 to be invalid as to Arden-Mayfair on the grounds that applying the statute would unduly burden interstate commerce. The Delaware action was dismissed for lack of jurisdiction over Louart. Subsequently the chairman of Arden-Mayfair's board obtained an order from the Delaware Chancery court declaring that Delaware, and not California law, would be applicable to the proceedings. Palmer v. Arden-Mayfair, Inc. No. 5549 (Del.Ch., July 6, 1978). See Note, 16 San Diego L.Rev. 943 (1979). This litigation does not furnish final, or perhaps even satisfying answers to the interesting and complex problems it raises, and they will no doubt arise again.

2. PRACTICAL CONSIDERATIONS

Before it is possible to make an intelligent judgment as to the place of incorporation, it is first necessary to understand the nature and scope of the business that is to be incorporated. The lawyer must know where the company intends to operate and what kinds of activity it intends to conduct in particular locations. For most businesses, particularly smaller ones, there is a strong presumption in favor of incorporating where the principal operations are to be conducted. This is particularly so when operations are confined to a single state. Incorporating there will reduce filing, reporting and tax burdens. But if a company intends to operate in more than one state (which is often the case), it may be required to qualify to do business as a foreign corporation in other jurisdictions. (However, not every excursion into another jurisdiction constitutes "doing business" for the purposes of that state's registration requirement.)

If the lawyer concludes that the corporation is not required to qualify as a foreign corporation in any state because all of its activities are local, the recommendation will ordinarily be to incorporate locally. Only if particular provisions of the corporation law of the jurisdiction of incorporation are especially burdensome to the owners or managers of the corporation, will counsel recommend foreign incorporation. Such a situation would be unusual for most small businesses.

Some of the relevant factors to be considered in deciding where to incorporate are:

1. The organization tax rates and the franchise tax rates.

2. The simplicity of operation of the corporation. For example, some jurisdictions, but not all, permit: (1) a corporation's board of directors to act by unanimous consent without a meeting or by means of a conference telephone call, and (2) a corporation to dispense with stockholder meetings and shareholders to act by the consent of the holders of a sufficient number of shares.

3. Restrictions on dividends and other distributions. These may be important for a number of reasons, and the directors may be personally liable for dividends or other distributions that are not permitted under state law.

4. Shareholder rights. Some jurisdictions severely limit the participatory rights of shareholders. It should be noted that this does not necessarily reflect an anti-shareholder attitude; simplicity in operation and restriction on the opportunity for dissidents to obstruct may be in the best interests of the majority of the shareholders.

5. Indemnification. Officers and directors are entitled to be indemnified for their expenses at the conclusion of a law suit, provided that they have not been found to have acted improperly. The scope and the procedure of indemnification provisions vary among the states. Ordinarily, this is a consideration more relevant to a publicly held company than to a privately held one.

6. Provisions for close corporations. A number of states provide easier operational arrangements and a stretching of the corporate norms to accommodate the private bargain that participants in a close corporation might want to strike, which in some cases deviates from the statutory pattern. Some states permit this more freely than others.

7. Liability for wages. Obviously counsel would prefer not to incorporate where a jurisdiction's corporation laws threaten the availability of limited liability for shareholders. For the most part, states provide limited liability for shareholders. However, in a significant departure from the norm of limited liability, New York and Wisconsin impose some personal liability on the shareholders for unpaid wages to employees. In New York, § 630 of the Business Corporation Law provides that the ten largest shareholders of a company are jointly and severally liable for all "debts, wages or salaries due or owing to any of its laborers, servants or employees other than contractors, for services performed by them for such corporation." The statute does not apply to corporations for whose securities there is a public market.

Wisconsin imposes a more limited personal liability on shareholders in Wis.Stat.Ann. § 180.40(6) by making the shareholders of every corporation, other than railroad corporations, personally liable for all debts (not to exceed six months' service in any case) owing to employees, up to the amount equal to the par value of their shares, or the consideration paid for their no par shares. As we shall soon see, this may be only a token amount. Unlike the New York provision, however, the Wisconsin provision applies to shareholders of foreign corporations. Joncas v. Krueger, 61 Wis.2d 529, 213 N.W.2d 1 (1973).

3. POLICY CONSIDERATIONS

The issue of public policy that grows out of the selection of the state of incorporation is whether there should be any choice at all. The internal affairs of corporations may be the only area of law where the parties are allowed freely to select the body of law that will govern their responsibilities to non-consenting persons. Of course, there is a choice-of-law problem present in the case of companies whose activities cut across state lines, just as there is with respect to commercial agreements involving interstate shipment of goods or payment of alimony where the place of marriage and the domicile are different. But in most areas of the law, a state must have some significant relationship to the parties or interest in their dispute before its law is applied or its courts are used. This is not true of corporation law, however. Although it struck down a Delaware statute that gave Delaware courts quasi in rem jurisdiction over shareholders of Delaware corporations by means of sequestration of their shares (whose situs was deemed to be in Delaware), the Supreme Court acknowledged in Shaffer v. Heitner, 433 U.S. 186, 97 S. Ct. 2569, 53 L.Ed.2d 683 (1977), that when the case was heard in some appropriate forum, Delaware substantive law would apply.*   See Ratner and Schwartz, The Impact of Shaffer v. Heitner on the Substantive Law of Corporations, 45 Brooklyn L.Rev. 641 (1979).

Some states have sought to attract incorporation in their states in order to generate franchise tax revenues. This is especially important to smaller states because the franchise tax can make a noticeable difference in state revenues. Consequently, state statutes have often been designed to appeal to those who make the decision where to incorporate, namely, managers and their lawyers.

One state's corporation laws, in order to be competitive with the corporation laws of other states, abjures any regulatory purpose and instead seeks to provide a minimal framework for businesses to operate free of operational restrictions. The policy of modern statutes has been described as "enablingism." Latty, Why Are Corporation Laws Largely "Enabling?" 50 Cor.L.Q. 599 (1965); Garrett, The Limited Role of Corporation Statutes in Commentaries on Corporate

* Delaware promptly amended its statute to provide a different means of obtaining jurisdiction over nonresident directors. Under the new rule, 10 Del. Code §§ 311–14, all directors of a Delaware corporation are deemed to consent to the appointment of the Secretary of State as their agent for service of process. The constitutionality of this provision was affirmed in Armstrong v. Pomerance, 423 A.2d 174 (Del.Super. 1980).

Structure and Governance 95 (D. Schwartz ed. 1979). Things were not always so. The following excerpt from Mr. Justice Brandeis' famous dissenting opinion in Liggett Co. v. Lee recounts some of the historical development.

LIGGETT v. LEE

288 U.S. 517, 53 S.Ct. 481, 77 L.Ed. 929 (1933).

Mr. Justice BRANDEIS (dissenting in part).

* * *

[The case, itself, was a challenge to the constitutionality of a tax imposed by Florida on chain stores. The Court struck down the tax. Brandeis' dissenting view was that "Whether the corporate privilege shall be granted or withheld is always a matter of state policy * * *. If a state believes that adequate protection * * * can be secured, without revoking the corporate privilege, by imposing * * * upon corporations the handicap of higher, discriminatory license fees as compensation for the privilege, I know of nothing in the Fourteenth Amendment to prevent it from making the experiment."]

Second. The prevalence of the corporation in America has led men of this generation to act, at times, as if the privilege of doing business in corporate form were inherent in the citizen; and has led them to accept the evils attendant upon the free and unrestricted use of the corporate mechanism as if these evils were the inescapable price of civilized life, and, hence, to be borne with resignation. Throughout the greater part of our history a different view prevailed. Although the value of this instrumentality in commerce and industry was fully recognized, incorporation for business was commonly denied long after it had been freely granted for religious, educational, and charitable purposes. It was denied because of fear. Fear of encroachment upon the liberties and opportunities of the individual. Fear of the subjection of labor to capital. Fear of monopoly. Fear that the absorption of capital by corporations, and their perpetual life, might bring evils similar to those which attended mortmain. There was a sense of some insidious menace inherent in large aggregations of capital, particularly when held by corporations. So at first the corporate privilege was granted sparingly; and only when the grant seemed necessary in order to procure for the community some specific benefit otherwise unattainable. The later enactment of general incorporation laws does not signify that the apprehension of corporate domination had been overcome. The desire for business expansion created an irresistible demand for more charters; and it was believed that under general laws embodying safeguards of universal application the scandals and favoritism incident to special incorporation could be avoided. The general laws, which long embodied severe restrictions upon size and upon the scope of corporate activity, were, in part, an expression of the desire for equality of opportunity.

(a) Limitation upon the amount of the authorized capital of business corporations was long universal. The maximum limit frequently varied with the kinds of business to be carried on, being dependent apparently upon the supposed requirements of the efficient unit. Although the statutory limits were changed from time to time, this principle of limitation was long retained. Thus in New York the limit was at first $100,000 for some businesses and as little as $50,000 for others. Until 1881 the maximum for business corporations in New York was $2,000,000; and until 1890, $5,000,000. In Massachusetts the limit was at first $200,000 for some businesses and as little as $5,000 for others. Until 1871 the maximum for mechanical and manufacturing corporations was $500,000; and until 1899 $1,000,000. The limit of $1,000,000 was retained for some businesses until 1903.

In many other states, including the leading ones in some industries, the removal of the limitations upon size was more recent. Pennsylvania did not remove the limits until 1905. Its first general act not having contained a maximum limit, that of $500,000 was soon imposed. Later, it was raised to $1,000,000; and, for iron and steel companies, to $5,000,000. Vermont limited the maximum to $1,000,000 until 1911, when no amount over $10,000,000 was authorized if, in the opinion of a judge of the Supreme Court, such a capitalization would tend "to create a monopoly or result in restraining competition in trade." Maryland limited until 1918 the capital of mining companies to $3,000,000; and prohibited them from holding more than 500 acres of land (except in Allegany county, where 1,000 acres was allowed). New Hampshire did not remove the maximum limit until 1919. It had been $1,000,000 until 1907, when it was increased to $5,000,000. Michigan did not remove the maximum limit until 1921. The maximum, at first $100,000, had been gradually increased until in 1903 it became $10,000,000 for some corporations and $25,000,000 for others; and in 1917 became $50,000,000. Indiana did not remove until 1921 the maximum limit of $2,000,000 for petroleum and natural gas corporations.

(b) Limitations upon the scope of a business corporation's powers and activity were also long universal. At first, corporations could be formed under the general laws only for a limited number of purposes—usually those which required a relatively large fixed capital, like transportation, banking, and insurance, and mechanical, mining, and manufacturing enterprises. Permission to incorporate for "any lawful purpose" was not common until 1875; and until that time the duration of corporate franchises was generally limited to a period of 20, 30, or 50 years. All, or a majority, of the incorporators or directors, or both, were required to be residents of the incorporating state. The powers which the corporation might exercise in carrying out its purposes were sparingly conferred and strictly construed. Severe limitations were imposed on the amount of indebtedness, bonded or otherwise. The power to hold stock in other corporations was not conferred or implied. The holding company was impossible.

(c) The removal by the leading industrial states of the limitations upon the size and powers of business corporations appears to have been due, not to their conviction that maintenance of the restrictions was undesirable in itself, but to the conviction that it was futile to insist upon them; because local restriction would be circumvented by foreign incorporation. Indeed, local restriction seemed worse than futile. Lesser states, eager for the revenue derived from the traffic in charters, had removed safeguards from their own incorporation laws. Companies were early formed to provide charters for corporations in states where the cost was lowest and the laws least restrictive. The states joined in advertising their wares. The race was one not of diligence but of laxity. Incorporation under such laws was possible; and the great industrial States yielded in order not to lose wholly the prospect of the revenue and the control incident to domestic incorporation.

The history of the changes made by New York is illustrative. The New York revision of 1890, which eliminated the maximum limitation on authorized capital, and permitted intercorporate stockholding in a limited class of cases, was passed after a migration of incorporation from New York, attracted by the more liberal incorporation laws of New Jersey. But the changes mady by New York in 1890 were not sufficient to stem the tide. In 1892, the Governor of New York approved a special charter for the General Electric Company, modelled upon the New Jersey act, on the ground that otherwise the enterprise would secure a New Jersey charter. Later in the same year the New York corporation law was again revised, allowing the holding of stock in other corporations. But the New Jersey law still continued to be more attractive to incorporators. By specifically providing that corporations might be formed in New Jersey to do all their business elsewhere, the state made its policy unmistakably clear. Of the seven largest trusts existing in 1904, with an aggregate capitalization of over two and a half billion dollars, all were organized under New Jersey law; and three of these were formed in 1899. During the first seven months of that year, 1336 corporations were organized under the laws of New Jersey, with an aggregate authorized capital of over two billion dollars. The Comptroller of New York, in his annual report for 1899, complained that "our tax list reflects little of the great wave of organization that has swept over the country during the past year and to which this state contributed more capital than any other state in the Union." "It is time," he declared, "that great corporations having their actual headquarters in this State and a nominal office elsewhere, doing nearly all of their business within our borders, should be brought within the jurisdiction of this State not only as to matters of taxation but in respect to other and equally important affairs." In 1901 the New York corporation law was again revised.

New Jersey was the first state to depart from the early philosophy of strict limitations on corporations beginning with its 1888 incorporation statute, which was followed by a revision in 1896. With its 1899 statute Delaware entered the competition, and eventually succeeded in becoming the leading state for the incorporation of large businesses.* Charles Beard, the noted historian, described how this came about in testimony before a Senate Committee considering federal corporate legislation in 1937:

> Under the leadership of Woodrow Wilson, after he was challenged by Theodore Roosevelt to reform his own state, the legislature of New Jersey passed a series of laws doing away with corporate abuses and applying high standards to corporations. What was the result? The revenues of the State from taxes on corporations fell. Malefactors moved over into other states. In time the New Jersey Legislature repealed its strict and prudent legislation, and went back, not quite, but almost to old ways.   * * *   Hearings on S. 10 Before a Subcommittee of the Senate Committee on the Judiciary, 75th Cong., 1st Sess. 326 (1937).

It has been observed that:

> The sovereign state of Delaware is in the business of selling its corporation law. This is profitable business, for a corporation law is a good commodity to sell. The market is large, and relatively few producers compete on a national scale. The consumers of this commodity are corporations.   * * *   Delaware, like any other good businessman, tries to give the consumer what he wants. In fact, those who will buy the product are not only consulted about their preferences, but are also allowed to design the product and run the factory. Comment, Law for Sale: A Study of the Delaware Corporation Law of 1967, 117 U.Pa.L.Rev. 861 (1969).

Critics such as Professor William Cary have decried this phenomenon, criticizing Delaware as leading a "race for the bottom." Cary, Federalism and Corporate Law: Reflections Upon Delaware, 83 Yale L.J. 663, 705 (1974). They argue that as a result of a sort of Gresham's law of corporate statutes, states that might want to tighten up their controls on corporations, using the vehicle of corporation law, are not free to do so since any such effort would merely cause corporations to abandon that state in favor of a more hospitable jurisdiction such as Delaware or Nevada. The problem is not perhaps as grave as all that, however, as the following excerpt suggests.

---

* New York is leading home for corporations, with Delaware in tenth place. However, Delaware is the corporate home of more than half the Fortune 500 companies and is clearly first among corporations listed on the New York Stock Exchange.

A.   CONARD, CORPORATIONS IN PERSPECTIVE
(1976) pp. 11–12.

*   *   *   [W]e should guard ourselves against imagining that each state's legislature is conspiring each year to make its corporation code a little more alluringly permissive than any other.   A very few states have been flaunting more fun at lower prices for traveling enterprises;   the rest have been grudgingly granting the minimum concessions deemed necessary to keep most of their breadwinners at home.   The performance might better be called a "chase" than a "race," since it is characterized by one or two starting off in the lead, and the others striving only to stay within hailing distance.   Most legislatures retain a few provisions that are stricter than Delaware's but most of their companies will tolerate these rather than suffer the expense and inconvenience of a Delaware incorporation.   The attitude of contemporary corporation law makers was expressed with unusual candor by the Law Reform Commission of New Jersey when it said,

> It is clear that the major protections to investors, creditors, employees, customers and the general public have come, and must continue to come, from Federal legislation and not from state corporation acts   *   *   *.   Any attempt to provide such regulations in the public interest through state incorporation acts and similar legislation would only drive corporations out of the state to more hospitable jurisdictions.*   We should guard ourselves also against assuming that all of the liberality engendered by the "race of laxity" entails social or economic evils.   One of the first relaxations that shocked public opinion was the grant of power to corporations to hold shares in other corporations.   Nearly everyone will concede today that this power ought to exist.   *   *   *

In evaluating the effect of the competition among states to become corporate homes, it is necessary to consider the radically contrasting view of another group of scholars who analogize this competition to competition in the marketplace for goods and services and conclude that the the "race" led by Delaware is not only not headed "to the bottom," but will inevitably *improve* corporate law.   Consider the following argument by one of the ablest proponents of that view.

WINTER, STATE LAW, SHAREHOLDER PROTECTION, AND THE THEORY OF THE CORPORATION,
6 J. Legal Stud. 251 (1977).

[Professor Cary's] claim, it is absolutely critical to note, is not that an overriding social goal is sacrificed by state law, but simply that

----

* Corporation Law Reform Commission of New Jersey, Report, in N.J.Stat.Ann. 14A: ix, xi (1969).

Delaware is preventing *private* parties from optimizing their *private* arrangements. With all due respect both to Professor Cary and to the almost universal academic support for his position, it is implausible on its face. The plausible argument runs in the opposite direction: (1) If Delaware permits corporate management to profit at the expense of shareholders and other states do not, then earnings of Delaware corporations must be less than earnings of comparable corporations chartered in other states and shares in the Delaware corporations must trade at lower prices. (2) Corporations with lower earnings will be at a disadvantage in raising debt or equity capital. (3) Corporations at a disadvantage in the capital market will be at a disadvantage in the product market and their share price will decline, thereby creating a threat of a takeover which may replace management. To avoid this result, corporations must seek out legal systems more attractive to capital. (4) States seeking corporate charters will thus try to provide legal systems which optimize the shareholder-corporation relationship.

The conclusion that Delaware shares sell for less is implicit in Professor Cary's analysis, for if a "higher" legal standard for management conduct will increase investor confidence, investor confidence in Delaware stock must have been less than in stocks of other states for more than a generation. This lack of confidence would have long been reflected in the price of Delaware shares. Moreover, a reduction in the earnings of a corporation will affect its ability to raise debt capital, as well as equity, since the risk of a lender is thereby increased and a higher interest rate will be charged. Delaware corporations, therefore, not only face a lower share price but also must pay higher interest rates.

* * *

Intervention in private transactions which impose no social cost can be justified only as a means of reducing the costs to the private parties. Thus, a prime function of state corporation codes is to supply standard terms which reduce the transaction costs, and thereby increase the benefits, of investing by eliminating costly bargaining which might otherwise accompany many routine corporate dealings. But substituting a mandatory legal rule for bargaining also may impose a cost in the form of the elimination of alternatives which the parties might prefer.

Much of the legal literature calling for further federal regulation either assumes that no costs will fall upon shareholders or merely undertakes a cursory "eyeballing" of the potential costs. To be sure, self-dealing and fraud exist in corporate affairs and their elimination is desirable. But at some point the exercise of control by general rules of law may impose costs on investors which damage them in both quantity and quality quite as much as self-dealing or fraud. A paradox thus results: maximizing the yield to investors generally may, indeed almost surely will, result in a number of cases of fraud or self-dealing; and eliminating all fraud or self-dealing may decrease the yield to shareholders generally.

*   *   *

A state which rigs its corporation code so as to reduce the yield to shareholders will spawn corporations which are less attractive as investment opportunities than comparable corporations chartered in other states or countries, as well as bonds, savings accounts, land, etc. Investors must be attracted before they can be cheated, and except for those seeking a "one shot," "take the money and run," opportunity to raid a corporation, management has no reason to seek out such a code.   *   *   *   The chartering decision, therefore, so far as the capital market is concerned, will favor those states which offer the optimal yield to both shareholders and management.

*   *   *

So far as the capital market is concerned, it is not in the interest of management to seek out a corporate legal system which fails to protect investors, and the competition between states for charters is generally a competition as to which legal system provides an optimal return to both interests. Only when that competition between legal systems exists can we perceive which legal rules are most appropriate for the capital market. Once a single legal system governs that market, we can no longer compare investor reaction. Ironically, in view of the conventional wisdom, the greater danger is not that states will compete for charters but that they will not.

C.   THE PROCESS OF INCORPORATION

The process of forming a corporation is simple and quick. Although the procedure differs slightly from state to state, provisions of MBCA §§ 53–57 illustrate the procedure generally required.

The organization is accomplished by people known as "incorporators." Until fairly recently, all states required three incorporators who signed the necessary documents and then faded from the scene. Because they played no role of any consequence, the requirement of three incorporators has largely disappeared, and a single incorporator may now sign the necessary documents in most states. Indeed, under many statutes the incorporator need not be a natural person; a corporation may serve as the incorporator.

The incorporator signs and files the articles of incorporation with the Secretary of State or another designated official, and in some cases also files with a county official in the county where the principal place of business of the corporation in that state will be located. Sometimes the corporation will not have a place of business in the state, in which case the "registered" address will function merely as a mail drop and constitute the office where service of process or other official notice is sent.

The drafting of the articles of incorporation may be a relatively complex undertaking because the promoters wish to embody some or all of the terms of a complex arrangement in the articles. On the other hand, it is possible and probably more common, to create a corporation with a simple, one page document. The filing of the articles of incorporation is accompanied by the payment of a fee, part of which is usually calculated on the basis of the number of authorized shares or the aggregate legal capital of the company, as is more specifically described in Chapter 8.

In Model Act jurisdictions, formal corporate existence commences with the issuance of the certificate of incorporation by state officials. MBCA § 56. In some other states, the corporation's existence commences with the filing of the articles of incorporation.

After the corporation has come into full legal existence, the statute requires that an organizational meeting be held, either by the incorporators, who select the first members of the board of directors, or, where the initial board is named in the articles of incorporation, by the board members so named. At its first meeting, the board typically accomplishes a number of standard tasks, including the election of additional members, if any, to the board, the adoption of by-laws, the appointment of officers, the adoption of a corporate seal, the designation of a bank as depository for corporate funds, and often the sale of stock to the initial shareholders. You should review the sample by-laws and sample minutes of an organization meeting of the board of directors that are included in West Selected Corporation and Partnership Statutes, Regulations and Forms.

In many cases, the routine legal work associated with the incorporation process is not performed directly by the attorney but, under the attorney's instruction, by a corporation service company, which performs the clerical work for a relatively modest fee. The result is a standard form of corporation, not a handcrafted one, but one that is often sufficient for ordinary situations. In addition to providing "boilerplate" articles of incorporation, by-laws, and forms of stock certificate and handling the filing of the necessary documents with the state, service companies perform a variety of other routine tasks such as handling the qualification of the corporation to do business in other jurisdictions, acting as "registered agent" for the corporation, and assisting in the filing of annual and other reports required by the jurisdiction of incorporation and the states in which the corporation is registered as a foreign corporation. On the doors of the Wilmington, Delaware offices of the major service companies there can be found a veritable "who's who" of American industry.

D. DEFECTIVE INCORPORATION

1. AT COMMON LAW

Although the process of forming a corporation is not a difficult one, there is room for error, and occasionally a slip occurs and the intended corporation does not come into legal existence—at least not when the parties expected. Because a corporation does not have a common law existence, but only a statutory one, any defect in the incorporation process has the effect of denying corporateness. A partnership, on the other hand, can come into existence without any formalties and does not require the execution of a written partnership agreement or filing with the state.*   In fact, a partnership may exist in the eyes of the law even though it does not exist in the minds or hearts of the "partners." Since the Uniform Partnership Act defines a partnership as "an association of two or more persons to carry on as co-owners a business for profit," it follows that a business organization that intends to function as a corporation but fails to comply with the statutory requirements is in fact a partnership (unless, of course, there is only one stockholder, in which case the enterprise will be a sole proprietorship). The principal consequence of this fact is that the owners of the business will not enjoy the limited liability that was probably the principal reason for their attempt to incorporate.

All this may seem a bit harsh. Defects can arise from a wide variety of circumstances. The incorporators may have neglected to make any filing at all, which is the most serious omission, or they may have filed but made a relatively small error, *e.g.*, improper notarization, shortfall on the filing fee, a neglected signature or the like. They may have failed to make a required second filing, *e.g.*, to file with both the state and county where the principal office is to be located. Most of these defects are technical in the most Pickwickian sense; they go to the heart of nothing. Does not "justice" demand that third parties be denied access to the personal resources of the shareholders should the business become unable to pay its debts, if: (1) the investors of the would-be corporation believed that they had taken all the steps necessary to create a corporation and had instructed their lawyer to file the necessary papers; (2) the lawyer thought he had filed all the necessary papers; and (3) the persons with whom the organization dealt believed they were doing business with a corporation and expected to look only to that organization for payment of any debt? Of course, there is some state interest in having parties comply with the formalities required for incorporation, but the threat to that interest seems remote when the failure of the parties to comply with some technical requirement was inadvertent. Acting on this perception, courts of equity developed the concept that the business

* The creation of a limited partnership does require the filing of a partnership instrument.

association could, in a proper case, be a *"de facto"* corporation, even if it was not a corporation *"de jure."* Courts also developed the concept of *corporation by estoppel* to achieve results deemed "just" where the de facto corporation doctrine could not be used. Ballantine, Manual of Corporation Law and Practice 92 (1930) states:

> The so-called estoppel that arises to deny corporate capacity does not depend on the presence of the technical elements of the equitable estoppel, viz, misrepresentations and change of position in reliance thereon, but on the nature of the relations contemplated, that one who has recognized the organization as a corporation in business dealings should not be allowed to quibble or raise immaterial issues on matters which do not concern him in the slightest degree or affect his substantial rights.

CRANSON v. INTERNATIONAL BUSINESS MACHINES CORP.

234 Md. 477, 200 A.2d 33 (1964).

HORNEY, Judge.

On the theory that the Real Estate Service Bureau was neither a *de jure* nor a *de facto* corporation and that Albion C. Cranson, Jr., was a partner in the business conducted by the Bureau and as such was personally liable for its debts, the International Business Machines Corporation brought this action against Cranson for the balance due on electric typewriters purchased by the Bureau. At the same time it moved for summary judgment and supported the motion by affidavit. In due course, Cranson filed a general issue plea and an affidavit in opposition to summary judgment in which he asserted in effect that the Bureau was a *de facto* corporation and that he was not personally liable for its debts.

The agreed statement of facts shows that in April 1961, Cranson was asked to invest in a new business corporation which was about to be created. Towards this purpose he met with other interested individuals and an attorney and agreed to purchase stock and become an officer and director. Thereafter, upon being advised by the attorney that the corporation had been formed under the laws of Maryland, he paid for and received a stock certificate evidencing ownership of shares in the corporation, and was shown the corporate seal and minute book. The business of the new venture was conducted as if it were a corporation, through corporate bank accounts, with auditors maintaining corporate books and records, and under a lease entered into by the corporation for the office from which it operated its business. Cranson was elected president and all transactions conducted by him for the corporation, including the dealings with I.B.M., were made as an officer of the corporation. At no time did he assume any personal obligation or pledge his individual credit to I.B.M. Due to an oversight on the part of the attorney, of which Cranson was not aware, the certificate of incorporation, which had been signed and acknowledged prior to May 1, 1961, was not filed until November 24, 1961. Between May 17 and November 8, the Bureau purchased eight typewriters from I.B.M., on account of which partial payments were made, leaving a balance due of $4,333.40, for which this suit was brought.

Although a question is raised as to the propriety of making use of a motion for summary judgment as the means of determining the issues presented by the pleadings, we think the motion was appropriate. Since there was no genuine dispute as to the material facts, the only question was whether I.B.M. was entitled to judgment as a matter of law. The trial court found that it was, but we disagree.

The fundamental question presented by the appeal is whether an officer of a defectively incorporated association may be subjected to personal liability under the circumstances of this case. We think not.

Traditionally, two doctrines have been used by the courts to clothe an officer of a defectively incorporated association with the corporate attribute of limited liability. The first, often referred to as the doctrine of *de facto* corporations, has been applied in those cases where there are elements showing: (1) the existence of law authorizing incorporation; (2) an effort in good faith to incorporate under the existing law; and (3) actual user or exercise of corporate powers. The second, the doctrine of estoppel to deny the corporate existence, is generally employed where the person seeking to hold the officer personally liable has contracted or otherwise dealt with the association in such a manner as to recognize and in effect admit its existence as a corporate body.

* * *

I.B.M. contends that the failure of the Bureau to file its certificate of incorporation debarred *all* corporate existence. But, in spite of the fact that the omission might have prevented the Bureau from being either a corporation *de jure* or *de facto*, we think that I.B.M. having dealt with the Bureau as if it were a corporation and relied on its credit rather than that of Cranson, is estopped to assert that the Bureau was not incorporated at the time the typewriters were purchased. In 1 Clark and Marshall, Private Corporations, § 89, it is stated:

> The doctrine in relation to estoppel is based upon the ground that it would generally be inequitable to permit the corporate existence of an association to be denied by persons who have represented it to be a corporation, or held it out as a corporation, or by any persons who have recognized it as a corporation by dealing with it as such; and by the overwhelming weight of authority, therefore, a person may be estopped to deny the legal incorporation of an association which is not even a corporation *de facto*.

In cases similar to the one at bar, involving a failure to file articles of incorporation, the courts of other jurisdictions have held that where one has recognized the corporate existence of an association, he is estopped to assert the contrary with respect to a claim arising out of such dealings.

Since I.B.M. is estopped to deny the corporate existence of the Bureau, we hold that Cranson was not liable for the balance due on account of the typewriters.

Judgment reversed; the appellee to pay the costs.

———

Suppose Cranson's lawyer prepared the incorporation papers and gave them to Cranson who had agreed to file them and then Cranson neglected to do so. Should the case be decided the same way?

2. THE IMPACT OF THE MODEL BUSINESS CORPORATION ACT

The de facto corporation and corporation by estoppel doctrines created, in the eyes of some commentators at least, "uncertainties" about corporate existence, although it is by no means certain what harm these uncertainties did to anyone. In the typical situation, of which *Cranson* is a good example, the plaintiff must be pleasantly surprised to find that what he thought was a corporation was never validly incorporated. The de facto corporation doctrine only restores the plaintiff to the position which he originally anticipated. But the desire for predictability is strongly felt by those who plan business transactions. MBCA 56 and 146 reflect the legislative attempt to provide this certainty. They were interpreted in Robertson v. Levy, 197 A.2d 443 (D.C.App.1964) to have abolished the de facto corporation and corporation by estoppel doctrines. Levy and Robertson had entered into a contract under which Levy was to form a corporation to purchase Robertson's business. Levy filed articles of incorporation and six days later Robertson transferred his business to the "corporation" which gave its note in exchange. In the meantime, however, the articles of incorporation had been returned as defective, and refiled, but the certificate, denoting official corporateness, was not issued until nine days after the delivery of the note. The company later failed, and Robertson sued Levy on the note, which he had signed as "president" of the "corporation."

After reviewing the historical development of de facto corporation and corporation by estoppel doctrines, the court concluded that the previously-cited sections of the Model Act, which had been adopted in the District of Columbia, were intended "to eliminate problems inherent in the de jure, de facto and, estoppel concepts." Courts were thus no longer to inquire into equities but were to recognize corporate existence only when the appropriate authorities have issued a certificate of incorporation; individuals who presume to act as a corporation are jointly and severally liable for "its" acts. That Robertson intended to look only to the "corporation" for payment of the note, and had accepted a note from the "corporation," did not, therefore, estop him from recovering from Levy personally.

The comment to the 1969 version of the Model Act agrees with Robertson v. Levy on the abolition of the de facto corporation doctrine, stating:

> Under the unequivocal provisions of the Model Act, any steps short of securing a certificate of incorporation would not constitute apparent compliance. Therefore a de facto corporation cannot exist under the Model Act.

The comments to the MBCA §§ 56 and 146 do not however rule out the continued existence of the estoppel concept. Yet, in Cahoon v. Ward, 231 Ga. 871, 875, 204 S.E.2d 622, 625 (1974), the court expressed the view, in dicta, that the estoppel concept, too, had been laid to rest, absent a specific statute reserving the doctrine. Although the court in Robertson v. Levy purportedly eliminated both the de facto corporation and the estoppel concept, the same panel later expressly upheld a corporation by estoppel in Namerdy v. Generalcar, 217 A.2d 109 (D.C.App.1966). The Oregon Supreme Court, interpreting substantially similar versions of MBCA §§ 56 and 146, followed Robertson v. Levy in abolishing de facto incorporation, but did not reach the issue of the validity of the estoppel concept. Timberline Equipment Co., Inc. v. Davenport, 267 Or. 64, 514 P.2d 1109 (1973).

There are difficulties in applying the de facto corporation doctrine, it is true, and it may be those difficulties that led the draftsmen of the Model Act to decide to eliminate it. But the doctrine (together with the doctrine of estoppel) did have the benefit of enabling courts to alleviate the harsh results that often flow from too rigid an application of the formal requirements for corporate existence. See Comment, Defective Incorporation: De Facto Corporations, Corporations by Estoppel, and Section 21–2054, 58 Neb.L.Rev. 763, 766 (1979). Assuming that the de facto doctrine has been abolished in states that follow the Model Act approach, courts could still leave themselves free to apply the equitable doctrine of estoppel on a case by case basis. The question is whether the demands of "certainty" dictate that this doctrine, too, should go.

One final question that you might wish to ponder, albeit with some fear in your heart, is the liability of the lawyer who fails to achieve corporateness and who fails to constrain the business dealings of his clients until full compliance with statutory requirements had been achieved.

E.   PRE–INCORPORATION ACTIVITIES OF PROMOTERS

There may be occasions when it is necessary for the promoters of a corporation to execute contracts on behalf of the corporation before the formalities of incorporation are completed and the corporation has come into legal existence. This is less of a problem than it once was as the formalities of incorporation have been simplified over the years and can now generally be completed in a few days. Nevertheless there are still times when it is necessary to execute a contract with a third party before incorporation is completed. Since at the time of such a transaction there is no corporation capable of being a party to the contract, the application of traditional principles of contract and agency law presents certain conceptual questions: Can the corporation subsequently become bound by the contract, and if so, under what theory? Is the promoter who executes the contract liable on the contract if the corporation never comes into existence? Or if it fails? If the corporation does come into existence and adopts the contract as its own, can the corporation sue on the contract?

The leading English case held that a pre-incorporation contract executed by the promoters bound only the promoters and that the corporation could not subsequently become a party after it came into existence. Kelner v. Baxter, L.R. 2 P.C. 174 (1866). The underlying theory was that under traditional rules of agency law a contract could be ratified by a principal only if the principal was in existence at the time the contract was executed. The result is that, although the corporation might become liable for benefits received by it under the contract, it does not, by accepting benefits, ratify the contract and so become liable on it. Neither, in fact, can the corporation adopt the contract, even by explicit vote of its board of directors. Although a few early American decisions accepted this doctrine, *e.g.*, Abbott v. Hapgood, 150 Mass. 248, 22 N.E. 907, 908 (1889), it has by now been almost completely repudiated in this country. It is generally accepted that a corporation may, once it comes into existence, adopt and so become liable *on the contract*. In McArthur v. Times Printing Co., 48 Minn. 319, 51 N.W. 216 (1892), a contract was enforced against a corporation although execution occurred prior to corporate existence. The contract sprung into being upon the formation of the corporation and adoption by the board. Ratification was impossible, since the contract could not relate back to the time prior to corporate existence, at least insofar as the corporation was affected.

Against the background of the theoretical hurdles suggested by Kelner v. Baxter, the American courts had some difficulties finding a rational basis to justify a conclusion that the corporation can become bound by a contract executed before the corporation had any life of its own. There have been at least four different conceptual bases advanced to support this result: (1) ratification, (2) adoption, (3) the acceptance of a continuing offer, and (4) novation or the creation of a new contract based upon mutual agreement of the parties. *See,* H. Ballantine, Ballantine on Corporations 108 (Rev. ed. 1946). Perhaps the best explanation is that pre-incorporation agreements are *sui generis* and need not be strait-jacketed by the traditional common law principles of agency and contracts.

The intention of the contracting parties is the principal focus of judicial opinions on the question. The promoter may claim that it was "intended" that once the contemplated corporation was brought into existence his own liability would fall by the wayside and the corporation would substitute for him. This is clear enough if the contract contains a novation provision stating that the promoter's liability terminates if the corporation is formed and manifests a willingness to become a party to the contract. Even without a specific novation provision, the promoter may argue that he fulfilled his promise by creating the corporation which is able to step in to his shoes and giving it the opportunity to pay its debt. It has been held, however, that this is not enough, and that the corporation must adopt the contract by some affirmative act before it becomes bound and the promoter is released. RKO-Stanley Warner Theatres, Inc. v. Graziano, 467 Pa. 220, 355 A.2d 830 (1976); Herbert v. Boardman, 134 Vt. 78, 340 A.2d 710 (1975).

How is adoption accomplished? More than the creation of the corporation is needed, even though its promoter possesses knowledge of the contract. Where that promoter becomes a member of the board of directors of the corporation, at least, it is fair to impute his knowledge of the contract to the corporation, and subsequent acts by the corporation—with such knowledge—may constitute adoption. See Peters Grazing Association v. Legerski, 544 P.2d 449 (Wyo.1975). The corporation may also, of course, adopt the contract by express action of its directors.

When the corporation never comes into existence or comes into existence and subsequently becomes unable to perform its obligations under the contract, the third party may sue the individuals who signed the contract on its behalf. If the promoters do not disclose to the third party that the corporation does not exist at the time of the execution of the contract, they may be liable on a theory of breach of an implied warranty that the corporate principal exists and that the promoter has the authority to act for the corporation. When the third party relies on this implied representation to his detriment, he can sue to hold the promoter individually liable on the contract.

But what if the third party knows of the nonexistence of the corporation? How should a court construe a contract signed, to take a well known example, "D. J. Geary, for a bridge company to be organized and incorporated"? O'Rorke v. Geary, 207 Pa. 240, 56 A. 541 (1903). There are several possible interpretations: (1) The parties intend that Geary is to use his best efforts to bring a corporation into existence and to have it adopt the contract as its own. There is no intention that Geary will ever be bound personally. (2) The parties intend that Geary will be liable on the contract until such time as he successfully incorporates the corporation and has it adopt the contract. (3) The parties intend that Geary will be bound on the contract and will remain bound even if the corporation comes into existence and adopts the contract.

The rule stated in § 326 of the Restatement of Agency, Second, provides: "Unless otherwise agreed, a person who, in dealing with another purports to act as agent for a principal whom both know to be non-existent or wholly incompetent, becomes a party to such contract." Under this rule, of course, Geary would be bound on the contract and would remain bound even if the corporation were ultimately to adopt it.

Considerations of fairness, however, may support a different result. In Quaker Hill, Inc. v. Parr, 148 Colo. 45, 363 P.2d 1056 (1961), for example, the plaintiff sold nursery stock to the defendants. At the suggestion of the plaintiff, the contract of sale named as purchaser a corporation that did not yet exist. The defendants did ultimately organize a corporation (using a different name than that in the contract because the original name was already in use in the state). The corporation, however, never functioned as a going concern, and the nursery stock (all of which died) remained unpaid for. The court held the defendants were not liable for the purchase price as the evidence suggested that the plaintiffs had intended to look only to the corporation and not to the individual defendants for payment.

The third party may also argue, often successfully based on the precedents, that partial performance by the promoter during the pre-incorporation period gives rise to an inference that the promoter intended to be personally bound. That was, in fact, the holding of O'Rorke v. Geary. See also White & Bollard, Inc. v. Goddeman, 58 Wn.2d 180, 361 P.2d 571 (1961).

Ultimately, the problem is one of adequate draftsmanship, there being no reason why any one of these interpretations should not be spelled out explicitly in the contract and given effect by the courts. The parties can choose to arrange their affairs in a different manner, to avoid problems. For example, the promoter may take an option, which can be assigned to the corporation after its formation. In this manner, the promoter never becomes an obligee. However, there will inevitably be cases in which the parties do not or are unable to arrange their affairs neatly, and the courts are left to struggle with the resulting problems.

STANLEY J. HOW & ASSOCIATES, INC. v. BOSS

222 F.Supp. 936 (S.D. Iowa 1963).

[Boss, the defendant, contracted to have the plaintiff, an architecture firm, design a motor hotel and restaurant in Edina, Minnesota. How delivered detailed plans and specifications in accordance with the contract, but was paid only $14,500 of its $38,250 fee.

The execution of the contract took place at a meeting between How, Boss, and one Hunter, a business associate of Boss. The plaintiff had filled out a blank of the standard form agreement, the first page of which provided that the contract was between Boss Hotels Co., Inc. and the plaintiff. The signature lines contained the same indication. Boss and Hunter then "took the prepared contract to a back room out of the hearing of the plaintiff and discussed it between themselves." They erased the words "Boss Hotels Co., Inc." and replaced them by the words:

"Owner: /s/ Edw. A. Boss
By: Edwin A. Boss, Agent for
a Minnesota Corporation to be
formed who will be the obligor."

They then took the contract back to How, showed it to him, and asked him whether the revision was acceptable. How answered in the affirmative.

The defendant and his associates subsequently organized an Iowa corporation, 75% of the stock of which was taken by the Boss Hotels Co. It was with checks of the Iowa corporation that How was given partial payment for his services. At the time of suit, the Iowa corporation had no assets.]

HANSON, District Judge.

* * *

Comment b under Section 326 of the R.S. of Agency sets out the three possible understandings that the parties may have when the agreement is made on behalf of a corporation to be formed by one of the parties. These are as follows:

(One) An offer or option to the corporation to be formed which will result in a contract if it is accepted when the corporation is formed. The correlative promise for the continuing offer or option is the promoter's promise to organize the corporation and give it the opportunity to pay the debt. Cases on this type of understanding are cited in 41 A.L.R.2d p. 517. This type of situation was in the Restatement treated as two different types of situations, but for purposes of this case can be treated as one type of situation.

The second type of situation is where the parties agree to a present contract by which the promoter is bound, but with an agreement that his liability terminates if the corporation is formed and manifests its willingness to become a party. * * *

This second possible interpretation is not very important in this case because a novation was not pleaded or argued. * * *

The third type of understanding is where the parties have agreed to a present contract upon which, even though the corporation later becomes a party, the promoter remains liable either primarily or as surety for the performance of the corporation's obligation. * * *

In the present case, the contract was signed: "Edwin A. Boss, agent for a Minnesota corporation to be formed who will be the obligor." The defendant argues that this is an agreement that the new corporation is solely liable. The problem here is what is the import of the words "who will be the obligor." It says nothing about the present obligor. The words "will be" connote something which will take place in the future.   *   *   *

*   *   *   To resolve this ambiguity, it is helpful to resort to the usual rules of interpretation of ambiguous contracts.

One rule of interpretation is to give meaning to all parts of the contract unless there are parts of the writing so inconsistent that it is impossible. The contract states that three-fourths of the contract price was to have been paid by the time the drawings and specifications were completed, and that this was to have been paid in monthly payments. If this part of the contract is given effect, it clearly tends to show that the parties intended that there was to be a present obligor on the contract. The plaintiff's interpretation of the way the contract was signed is consistent with all parts of the contract. The defendant's interpretation is inconsistent with the payment provisions of the contract. The court must try to give effect to all parts of the agreement if they can be found consistent. Another rule is that the writing must be strictly construed against the party who drafted the writing in question.   *   *   *

Also, and perhaps most important, there are a number of cases which say that in the promoter contract cases where the contract called for performance, at least in part, before the corporation is organized, this indicates that the promoter is intended to be personally liable on the contract. This was the type of case where the work was to begin by Mr. How before the corporation was organized and certainly to be completed before the corporation was in business.

The R.S. of Agency Section 326 is exactly the same rule of law as has been used by the Iowa court in King Features Syndicate, Dept. of Hearst Corp. International News Service Division v. Courrier [241 Iowa 870, 43 N.W.2d 718, 41 A.L.R.2d 467,] [*supra*]. Comment a of this Section of the Restatement explains the rule. It says:

> If, therefore, the other party knows that there is no principal capable of entering into such a contract, there is a rebuttable inference that, although the contract is nominally in the name of the nonexistent person, the parties intend that the person signing as agent should be a party, unless there is some indication to the contrary.

In the present case, there are not sufficient words to show an indication to the contrary to offset this inference.

Mr. How's testimony and his business record, Exhibit K, show that he did not intend that the new corporation was the sole obligor on the contract. He stated that he believed Boss Hotel Co., Inc. or Boss Hotels was liable on the contract. This is not inconsistent with thinking Mr. Boss was liable on the contract but it is inconsistent with intending that the new corporation was to be solely liable on the contract. Promoters other than the one signing the contract may be liable on the contract also. In this case, Boss Hotel Co., Inc. was not made a party but this does show a reason why Mr. How might state that he felt Boss Hotel Co., Inc. was liable on the contract. The oral testimony on this point was only generally to the effect that the parties agreed that the contract was all right as written, but it did tend to support the conclusion that Mr. Boss was intended to be the present obligor on the contract.

Even if this rule in Section 326 of the R.S. of Agency means that any words to the contrary destroy the inference, the words which were used, the rules of interpretation of contracts, and the extrinsic evidence offered by the parties show conclusively that the reasonable interpretation put on the contract by Mr. How, that is, that Mr. Boss was a present obligor on the contract, must be taken as the proper interpretation of the contract.

* * *

The defendant in his brief argues that there was an adoption of the contract by the new corporation. * * * Adoption of the contract by the corporation is not sufficient to relieve the promoter of his liability. There must be a novation or agreement to that effect. The defendant does not really argue the contrary. The defendant did not plead a novation nor argue that one existed. The defendant argues that the plaintiff agreed to look solely to the new corporation, and it is in this regard that the defendant says the plaintiff's hopes were fulfilled when the corporation, so the defendant claims, did adopt the contract.

While in Decker v. Juzwik, [121 N.W.2d 652 (1963)] [*supra*] the court in sustaining the novation relied in part upon the fact that payments had been made by the new corporation, there are a number of cases saying that the mere fact that payments were made by a third party and accepted by the plaintiff is not sufficient to establish a novation. * * *

The defendant argues that a practical construction has been put on the contract to the effect the plaintiff agreed to look solely to the credit of the new corporation. For this construction, the defendant relies upon the fact that the two checks which were given to Mr. Boss carried the letterhead of the new corporation and were signed by Edwin Hunter. As already explained, this is not sufficient especially where a novation was not pleaded or argued. This would be an attempt to penalize the plaintiff for being patient and not demanding strict compliance. The court feels there was no waiver of rights and none was pleaded.

* * *

In this case, the defendant was the principal promoter, acting for himself personally and as President of Boss Hotels, Inc. The promoters abandoned their purpose of forming the corporation. This would make the promoter liable to the plaintiff unless the contract be construed to mean: (1) that the plaintiff agreed to look solely to the new corporation for payment, and (2) that the promoter did not have any duty toward the plaintiff to form the corporation and give the corporation the opportunity to assume and pay the liability.

* * *

* * * In all situations wherein the promoter is not personally bound, the contracting party is agreeing that the new corporation should assume the liability. The phrase "content to take the risk of the ultimate incorporation and assumption of his claim" is the key to the distinction. In some cases, the promoters do not agree that this assumption will take place.

Applying this law to the present case, the court would have to hold that even if the plaintiff had agreed to look to the credit of the new corporation, the defendant would be liable. The defendant was the key promoter and as such would be a primary factor in abandoning the project. This would make the defendant liable.

* * *

Accordingly the court concludes that the plaintiff, Stanley J. How & Associates, Inc., should have and recover judgment against the defendant, Edwin A. Boss, in the sum of $23,750.00, with interest and costs and, accordingly, a judgment will be entered.

* * *

Chapter 8

FINANCIAL STRUCTURE OF THE CORPORATION

A. CORPORATE SECURITIES

PROBLEM

EAST WIND BOATS—PART V

Judy Luff, Jack Hardy, and Ed Teach have agreed to purchase East Wind Boats from Stern and Star on the following terms: The sellers will transfer all their assets, tangible and intangible, to East Wind Boats Corporation, a Columbia corporation, which will be owned entirely by Judy, Jack and Ed. The Corporation will pay Stern and Star $50,000 in cash now and issue to them a written promise to pay $50,000 in ten years. Stern and Star will receive annual payments of $6,000. If the corporation fails to make the annual payment when due, then the entire $50,000 will be due immediately. Stern and Star will have no vote in the affairs of the company, and no right to receive any payments except as just described.

Ed will invest $60,000 in cash in the new company. He will have 20% of the voting power on all matters. He will be entitled to receive $7,500 a year before anything (other than salaries) is paid to Jack or Judy in any year, and, in addition, he will be entitled to a 20% share in any amounts (other than salaries) that are paid out in each year. In the event the company liquidates, he will be entitled to receive $50,000 before Jack or Judy receive anything, and 20% of any additional amount that is paid out thereafter.

Jack and Judy will each invest $20,000. They will each be entitled to 40% of the vote on all matters, to receive 40% each of all amounts that may be paid each year after all priority amounts have been paid, and to receive 40% of any amounts paid out to the owners if the company liquidates after all prior claims have been paid. One of the pieces of paper they would like to receive from the company, in return for their investment, is a promise to pay $10,000 upon demand of the holder. They will not be entitled to any assured or preferred annual payments.

1. What capital structure do you recommend for the corporation: what securities, with what terms, and in what amounts should the corporation issue to each investor?

2. What should you advise your clients about the business and legal risks your capital structure entails for the corporation and the investors?

1. INTRODUCTION

The ownership of a corporation, or any economic enterprise for that matter, can be thought of as comprised of three distinct features: the power to exercise control over the management of the enterprise, the right to receive income from its operations, and a share in the assets.   In a partnership, the relative interests in these attributes are determined by contract—the partnership agreement.   However, in a corporation the investors express their relative interests through the ownership of securities.   Corporate securities can divide up and package these different interests any way the investors choose.

Corporate planners have great flexibility in designing the securities that express different preferences as to risk and income because statutory and case law impose few limitations.   Corporate securities are largely features of contract—which includes the articles of incorporation—whose terms can be modified at the will of the draftsman. Within the contours of a given corporation, there is great latitude to allocate control, income and risk by using different types and amounts of securities that best suit the needs of the corporation and its investors.   But unlike the partnership where the contract spells out the interests, corporate interests are expressed through symbols—securities.   This gives corporate investors greater flexibility since the securities are personal property that can be sold in whole or in part, as compared with partners who cannot sell their partnership status at all.

The various types of corporate securities can be thought of as arrayed on a spectrum in accordance with the degree of risk associated with the security.   At one end is the common stock, a security that carries the highest degree of risk, but, concomitantly, enjoys the greatest possibility of gain if the business is successful.   Common stockholders usually have all the voting power of the corporation.   At the other end of the spectrum is the bond, which carries with it a right to receive fixed interest payments (and no more) at stated intervals and the repayment of the principal (and no more) at a date certain.   To provide additional assurance that the debt represented by the bonds will be repaid, they are often secured by a mortgage on some or even all of the assets of the corporation, thus placing the bondholders first in line upon the liquidation of the corporation. Bondholders do not have an ownership interest in the corporation at all; they are creditors.   They have no voice in management.

In between these polar extremes the planner has the possibility of devising a virtually unlimited number of securities which share to a greater or lesser extent in one or more of the three basic characteristics of ownership discussed above.   Traditionally these securities are divided into two classes, debt and equity.   Debt securities, as their name implies, represent a fixed obligation to repay the principal amount of the security at a future date and, in the meantime, to make

[handwritten margin note: Features of ownership]

interest payments. The term "equity" derives originally from the law of real estate according to which the owner of a mortgage property is said to have "an equity of redemption." In other words, the rights of the owner of the property are subject to the mortgage and consist essentially of the entitlement to the residual left after the payment of the interest and principal owing to the mortgagee. By analogy, the rights of the holder of an equity security are to the residual income and assets left after the principal and interest payments due on any corporate indebtedness are satisfied.

Although as a practical matter the spectrum between common stock and bonds can really be thought of as a continuum, the intermediate securities are traditionally treated as falling into three separate classes: common stock, preferred stock, and debt, which in turn, may be classified as debentures and bonds. In what follows, we will discuss each of these types of security briefly. A more extended discussion may be found in W. Klein, Business Organizations and Finance 158–195 (1980).

2. COMMON STOCK

Common stock is the most basic of the corporate securities; all corporations must have common stock, and most small corporations issue no other kind of security. The common stock is usually entitled to the exclusive power to elect the directors of the corporation, although in some corporations the common stockholders share some of their voting power with the preferred stockholders. Common stock may be divided into classes with varying rights, and it is possible to have non-voting common stock, although there must be at least one class entitled to vote.

The common stock's participation in income takes the form of dividends, which may be paid only after the rights of the more senior securities (debt and preferred stock) have been satisfied. The income that is left "belongs" entirely to the common stockholders, although they are entitled actually to receive distributions from this income only upon the declaration of a dividend by the board of directors, a decision that is within the board's discretion. Most corporations of any size do not distribute all of the funds that would be available for dividends, but retain at least some for reinvestment in the business. Where this is the case, part of the "income" received by common stockholders takes the form, not of the dividends, but of increases in the value of their stock due to the growth of the corporation. Indeed, for tax reasons, many shareholders would prefer that a substantial portion of the earnings available for dividends be plowed back into the business rather than distributed.

The common stock's interest in the assets of the corporation is limited to the right to receive what is left of those assets on liquidation after all of the creditors and senior security holders of the corporation have been paid. In economic terms this means that the common stock bears the greatest risk of loss. Conversely, should the corporation be successful, the common stockholder's residual interest may become quite valuable on liquidation. As a practical matter, however, corporations are seldom liquidated except when they are in financial difficulty, in which case it is unlikely that the common stockholders will receive anything at all. They may realize the increase in value by selling their stock to another investor at a price that reflects the enhancement in value. Corporations in difficulty do, however, occasionally rearrange the capital structure in what is known as a "recapitalization," in which case, the relative interests of the common stockholders and the more senior security holders do become important.

3. PREFERRED STOCK

All of the securities other than common stock, including preferred stock and debt securities, are classes of "senior securities" because their rights are superior to the common stockholders. Of course, seniority is relative, and preferred stock is the least senior of the senior securities. Preferred stock, like common stock, generally represents a permanent investment in the corporation, by contrast to debt securities which mature and are repaid at the end of a defined time. On the other hand, preferred stock is often "redeemable" by the corporation, that is to say the corporation is entitled to repurchase the stock at a defined price.

The terms governing preferred stock, like those governing common stock, are set forth in the articles of incorporation. The general presumption at common law is that "stock is stock;" therefore unless the articles of incorporation provide otherwise, preferred is entitled to the same voting rights as common stock. Nevertheless, the normal practice is to state in the articles that preferred stock has no voting rights. This is often, however, subject to the exception that the preferred stockholders will be entitled to vote and elect some or all of the board of directors if the holders fail to receive a certain number of dividends. In addition, the corporation statute usually affords the preferred stockholders the right to vote on changes in the corporate structure that affect their rights and preferences as stockholders.

Like the common stockholders, preferred stockholders are not absolutely entitled to receive dividend distributions. The decision to pay dividends is left entirely to the discretion of the board of directors. This allows more flexibility than is the case with respect to a debt security, on which interest *must* be paid at regular intervals. The seniority of preferred stock arises out of the standard provision that no dividends will be paid on the common stock until the preferred stockholders have received their dividends. This dividend preference is stated either as a dollar amount or as a percentage of the par value of the stock. The preferred dividends are usually cumulative; that is, if a dividend for any year is not paid currently, it accumulates, and the accumulated dividend arrearages must be paid as well as current dividends before any dividends may be paid on the common stock. While the preferred shareholders' participation in income is normally limited to the payment of the preferred dividends, preferred stock may be made "participating," in which case, in addition to receiving the preferred dividends, it shares in parity with the common stock on any dividends paid to the common. Indeed, on the principle that "stock is stock" some courts have interpreted preferred stock clauses to require such participation unless a contrary intent is clearly spelled out in the articles.

In addition to the dividend preference, preferred stock normally benefits from a liquidation preference which entitles it to receive a specified amount on liquidation before any distributions are made to the common stockholders. This amount is usually the price originally paid for the stock plus any accumulated dividends, and, in some circumstances, a small "liquidation premium."

The standard features of preferred stock described above may be supplemented by a variety of others, including the right to convert the preferred stock at the option of the shareholder to common stock at a specified ratio, and perhaps the right of the corporation to redeem the preferred stock. Redemption means the corporation can compel the holder to sell his shares back to the corporation, a right that is likely to be exercised when the corporation can obtain the funds at a cheaper cost. Thus, the preferred stock can take on the features of a debt security both from the standpoint of the holder and the corporation.

4. AUTHORIZATION AND ISSUANCE OF EQUITY SECURITIES

First some terminology. "Authorized" shares are those shares of stock created by an appropriate clause in the articles of incorporation. When these shares are first sold to stockholders, they are "issued." Shares are always "authorized" and something else. The "something else" may be "and outstanding" or "and issued, but not outstanding" or "but unissued."

If authorized shares are "authorized and outstanding" it means that they have been issued and are still owned by a shareholder. If they are "authorized and issued but not outstanding," it means that they were previously issued to someone, but have since been repurchased by the company itself. These shares are commonly referred to as "treasury shares." If the shares are "authorized but unissued" it means that they have never been issued, or, if they were, a procedure has been followed to restore them to their virginal state.

Corporation statutes do not dictate how many of what kind of shares are authorized; the source of that information is always the articles of incorporation. The corporation statute of every jurisdiction requires the articles of incorporation to state the number of shares that a corporation is authorized to issue and to describe certain characteristics of those shares. (Read MBCA § 54(d) and Articles Four of the Model Articles of Incorporation.)

When the corporation has issued all of the stock authorized by its articles of incorporation it is then unable to issue any more shares without amending its articles of incorporation. That amendment is accomplished by vote of both the Board of Directors and stockholders. (MBCA § 59.) You will recall that in the Chesapeake Marine Services Problem the majority shareholders were forced to resort to indirect methods to try to obtain new capital because the company had exhausted its supply of authorized shares of stock.

How many shares should the organizers of a corporation authorize? A corporation may want to issue additional shares at a later date to raise new money, to use for employee benefit plans, or to acquire other companies. On the practical level, it is tempting to authorize a very large number of shares so that the corporation will be able to issue additional shares in the future without having to first amend the articles. It will save time, and probably money, to plan for these contingencies at the beginning; amendments to the articles of incorporation take time and require the payment of additional fees to the lawyer who prepares the amendment and to the state in the form of filing fees and other charges.

However, the decision as to how many shares should be authorized may involve more than a question of convenience or a simple calculation of fees. The power to *issue* shares normally resides in the board of directors as a part of its general power of management. Therefore, once the shareholders have "authorized" the issuance of shares under the conventional corporation model, they have yielded their direct control over the issuance of those shares.* In large corporations, individual shareholders have little influence over the management of the corporation anyway and yielding the power to issue shares does not constitute the surrender of any real power. Convenience usually decides the question in favor of an initial authorization of a large number of shares. In close corporations the analysis is different. The shareholders may wish to retain control over the issuance of new shares by limiting the original authorization to the number of shares contemplated to be issued immediately. The issuance of any new shares would then require an amendment of the articles and thus a vote of the shareholders. You will recall that it was just such a requirement that gave Apple the power to veto the increase in capitalization in the Chesapeake Marine Services problem.

---

* State law sometimes requires shareholder approval for the issuance of large number of shares. 15 Ohio Rev.Code Ann. § 1701.83(A). The New York Stock Exchange rules, applicable to companies whose stock trades on that exchange, requires shareholder approval if an issuance results in a 20% increase in shares. *See* N.Y.S.E. Company Manual, p. A 283–4.

5. DEBT SECURITIES

The holders of debt securities—usually denominated as "bonds" or "debentures"—are creditors of a corporation, but they should not be confused with trade creditors, who sell goods and services with the expectation of being paid in 30 (or sometimes 60 to 90) days. Nor do they occupy the same position as a financial institution that lends money on a short-term basis. The holders of debt securities furnish a part of the permanent capital structure of a corporation and in so doing partake of an ongoing interest in its fortunes. Customarily, however, they have no voting rights in the company's affairs.

As a matter of more precise terminology, bonds are secured by a mortgage on corporate assets, whereas debentures are backed only by the general credit of the corporation. Bonds also generally have longer maturities (20 years or more) than debentures (usually 10–20 years), although there is no rigid rule in this regard. The use of bonds secured by collateral, rather than unsecured debentures is more traditional in some industries than others. Where money is borrowed to make heavy capital investment, the collateral often consists of the asset that was acquired or produced. Railroad bonds, public utility bonds, and land financing are several examples. Corporate borrowing today, however, is more likely to take the form of debentures. As is often done we will ignore the distinction and use the term "bond" to speak generically of both bonds and debentures.

The terms of a debt security are fixed by a complex contract, often known as an "indenture." If the bonds are sold to the public, the contract takes the form of a trust agreement between the corporation, the bondholders, and the indenture trustee, which is usually a large bank. The role of the trustee is to oversee compliance by the corporation with the terms of the indenture and generally to protect the interests of the security holders.

In whatever form the terms are fixed, it is fundamental that the debt instrument set forth a fixed obligation to repay the sum loaned to the corporation by a particular date. The instrument will also provide that interest in a fixed amount will be paid at periodic intervals. The interest obligation is not dependent on the corporation's having earned a profit, but is instead a firm requirement; if the company fails to pay the amount when due, the company is then in default on the loan, the entire principal is due, and the creditors can pursue whatever legal remedies they are entitled to, usually including the right to begin bankruptcy proceedings.

If the loan is collateralized, then the terms of the security or mortgage must also be fixed. The contract may also commit the company to do certain things or to refrain from doing certain things that might jeopardize the position of the debt holders, provisions known as covenants or negative covenants. The company may agree, for example, not to pay any dividends or repurchase any of its own shares unless it meets certain conditions of solvency. These restrictions, in fact, are usually more important to a large corporation's ability to pay dividends than the restrictions imposed by law.

The indenture will also contain a number of other important provisions. Frequently, it requires the company to make a payment to a "sinking fund" so as not to face the requirement of making the entire payment at one time on the maturity date. A sinking fund is a periodic appropriation of cash paid by the corporation to a trustee to provide for the orderly retirement of a debt. Payments are a fixed charge to the corporation, but, subject to agreement between the corporation and the trustee, the amount of payment may be pegged to the corporation's earnings.

The securities may be redeemable, or "callable" at the option of the company at a fixed price. This is an important right of the corporation which it is likely to avail itself when interest rates decline and high interest loans can be replaced with low interest borrowing. The "call" price is usually fixed above the face amount that would be paid if the security were allowed to mature to compensate the holder of the security for the loss of the balance of the stream of interest payments. Sometimes the bonds are convertible into the corporation's common stock so that the holder can shift from a creditor to an equity investor. Convertible debt securities may also help the corporation raise capital; they enable a corporation to raise funds today on the basis of tomorrow's earnings. Since the purchase of the debt security becomes another way of buying common stock, the debt holder's right to convert often pegs the market value of the debt obligation to the market value of the corporation's common stock.

Because the terms and conditions of debt securities are entirely fixed by contract and are often the result of extensive negotiations, the parties may produce a hybrid instrument that has elements of both debt and equity securities. The convertible debenture, referred to above is one example of this. Other variations are possible. For example, the parties might provide that the interest rate called for in the contract will be paid only to the extent the company has actually earned that amount. This instrument is known as an "income bond." State law in several jurisdictions even permits the parties to provide that debt security holders can vote in exactly the same manner as equity security holders. Such provisions are not frequently used because they cause a debt security so to resemble an equity security that the advantages of using debt, particularly tax advantages, discussed below, would be threatened.

Debt securities may be issued in the name of the particular owner, in which case they are "registered," or they may be issued to "the bearer." In order to transfer registered bonds, some notation must be made on the records of the company, which maintains a registry of owners. Interest payments are sent through the mail to the registered owner. Bearer bonds are transferred merely by delivery of the instrument. Interest is paid by detaching a coupon affixed to the bearer security and presenting it to the company, or to a bank acting as agent; hence the reference to bond holders as "coupon clippers." The interest rate is still sometimes referred to as the "coupon" of the bond, regardless of the form in which it is issued. In the United States, registered bonds are the norm, but in Europe and South America bearer instruments are more common.

Bonds may be sold by the holder to other investors, and not necessarily at the same price represented on the face of the instrument. Ordinarily, bonds are issued in denominations of $1,000. Suppose the bonds of A Corp. contain a promise to pay $1,000 in 20 years with annual interest payments of $100. That means the bond pays annual interest at 10% of its face amount. If investors have available to them other alternatives that pay interest at 15% and that carry the same degree of risk as the bonds of A Corp., they will not pay $1,000 for the bonds of A Corp.; instead they will pay approximately $666 for that bond. Why? Because at that price, the $100 annual interest payment represents a 15% interest rate on the amount invested. Conversely, if interest rates fall to 8%, the price of the bonds of A Corp. on the market will rise to approximately $1,250. The 15% or 8% figures are known as "yields" of a bond, that is, they represent the return as a percentage of the actual investment of an investor who pays $666 or $1,250 for the bond.

6. THE ISSUANCE OF DEBT SECURITIES

As we have noted, debt securities are simply a matter of contract; the manner of issuing them is, in many respects no different from that of entering into any other corporate contract. Corporation law generally imposes no limitation on how much debt a corporation may incur. Some corporations which are subject to special regulatory regimes (public utilities, for example) may need approval from a regulatory body before issuing additional debt. Agreements with other creditors may often impose limits on the creation of new debt. Thus bond indentures may contain clauses restricting further borrowing in some manner.

The issuance of long-term debt is a sufficiently important transaction that it requires approval by the board of directors. This is consistent, of course, with the requirement that the board must approve the issuance of stock. Incurring short-term debt, on the other hand, is less significant and may be undertaken on the authority of senior officers without action by the board.

7. THE ADVANTAGES OF DEBT SECURITIES

a. In General

We have observed that the corporate capital structure may include senior securities which entitle the holder to priority over the common stockholders in receiving periodic distributions (either in the form of dividends or interest) and a similar prior claim to the assets of the company in the event of liquidation. These senior securities may be either preferred stock or debt. We noted that the payment of preferred stock dividends rests in the discretion of the board of directors, who may choose to omit a dividend if the company is experiencing hard times. By contrast, the holder of a debt security is a creditor and is entitled to periodic payments and the return of his investment whether the company prospers or not. On the face of it, therefore, it would seem that corporations would favor the use of preferred stock over debt because of the greater risks. Failure to pay interest or to pay the loan constitutes a default which has serious consequences. However, the theoretical advantage of preferred stock, is often more apparent than real. The company generally feels compelled to pay preferred stock dividends on a regular basis, just as it would pay interest on a debt, in order to attract investors. Management does not look upon these dividends as optional. Of course, the consequences of a missed dividend takes a heavy enough toll on a company that passes its preferred dividends.

b. Tax Aspects

Perhaps the most important reason for favoring debt over preferred stock is found in the Internal Revenue Code. Despite the economic similarity of the two securities, the tax law draws a very important distinction between them. Interest paid on a corporate debt is a deductible business expense under section 163 of the Internal Revenue Code, but dividends on preferred or common stock are not. For example, if a company has earnings of $50,000 and pays a $10,000 dividend to the preferred stockholders, it is taxed on the entire $50,000. However, if the preferred stock were replaced by bonds and the $10,000 were paid as interest, the taxable income of the corporation would be reduced to $40,000. Both interest and dividends are taxed at ordinary income rates but § 128(b) provides an exclusion for 15% of interest with a maximum of $3,000 ($6,000 on a joint return), commencing in 1985. Moreover, the repayment of the principal of a debt instrument generally constitutes for the recipient of a tax-free return of capital. The redemption of preferred stock, on the other hand, often results in a taxable gain to the stockholder, and sometimes it is taxed at ordinary income rates. While there are a variety of tax wrinkles affecting the use of preferred stock and debt, making it advantageous to use preferred stock in some situations, the generalization about the advantage of debt holds. The tax advantage of debt often results in disputes between taxpayers and the Internal Revenue Service as to whether the security is in reality stock although it is labelled debt. More on this later.

c. The Leverage Effect

Another aspect of the use of debt is the leverage effect. Corporations borrow money because they hope to obtain a larger return from the use of that money than the interest cost incurred. Since anything earned in excess of the cost of borrowed money belongs to the common stockholders, the corporation is, in effect, using other people's money as a lever to increase the return enjoyed by the common stockholders. The expression sometimes used to describe this is "trading on the equity"—offering safety to debt holders in exchange for a possible higher return to the common holders.

The problem is that leverage works both ways: just as the shareholder's return is increased if the corporation does well, so are their losses magnified if it does poorly. This follows from the requirement that the borrowed funds must be repaid and interest payments made regularly even if the new investment is unprofitable. Put another way, borrowing increases the risks of the equity owners, but also amplifies their profits if they are successful.

To illustrate, assume that a corporation has 100,000 shares of common stock issued and outstanding, and that earnings before taxes are $1,000,000. If we further assume an effective tax rate of 50%, the net earnings of the company are $500,000 or $5 per share. The market price of the shares is $50. The company needs an additional $1,000,000 to finance a new project. To raise the money the company could sell 20,000 additional shares of common stock at $50 per share, or it could borrow $1,000,000 at the prevailing interest rate of 10%. What would be the most profitable course of action for the current owners of common stock?

While there is no "right" answer, it is instructive to examine the alternatives under various possibilities. Suppose the following four alternatives: (1) The company earns a 20% return from the new investment, i.e., the $1,000,000 invested produces additional operating profits of $200,000; (2) the company earns a 10% return, or $100,000 from the new investment, i.e., the profits earned are equal to the interest that would be paid if borrowed funds were used; (3) the company breaks even on the new investment, i.e., it still earns the same $1,000,000 before taxes that it earned before; (4) the company incurs a loss of $900,000 from the new investment, i.e., its total earnings before taxes are reduced to $100,000. The following table shows how each of these possible outcomes would affect the common shareholders under the alternative assumptions that the $1,000,000 is raised by borrowing and that it is raised by selling stock.

(1) Company earns 20% from the new investment

	Borrowed Money	New Stock
Earnings before interest	$1,200,000	$1,200,000
Interest on debt	(100,000)	—
Income before taxes	1,100,000	1,200,000
Income taxes	(500,000)	(600,000)
Balance available to common	550,000	600,000
Earnings per share	$5.50	$5.00

(2) Company earns 10% from the new investment

	Borrowed Money	New Stock
Earnings before interest	$1,100,000	$1,100,000
Interest on debt	(100,000)	—
Income before taxes	1,000,000	1,100,000
Balance available to common	500,000	550,000
Earnings per share	$5.00	$4.58

(3) Company derives nothing from the new investment

	Borrowed Money	New Stock
Earnings before interest	$1,000,000	$1,000,000
Interest on debt	(100,000)	—
Income before taxes	900,000	1,000,000
Income taxes	(450,000)	(500,000)
Balance available to common	450,000	500,000
Earnings per share	$4.50	$4.17

(4) Company loses $900,000 on the new investment

	Borrowed Money	New Stock
Earnings before interest	$ 100,000	$ 100,000
Interest on debt	(100,000)	—
Income before taxes	0	100,000
Income taxes	0	(50,000)
Balance available to common	0	50,000
Earnings per share	0	$.42

The table demonstrates the leverage effect from the use of debt. Since borrowed funds provide a fixed, but assured return to the creditors, the common stockholders have traded on their equity to retain for themselves all the earnings above the amount promised to the creditors. The larger the return from the borrowed funds, the more the common stockholders magnified their own earnings, because they did not share anything with the creditors above the interest payments on the debt.

At the same time, the common stockholders increased the risk to themselves and the corporation by borrowing and promising to pay creditors under any and all circumstances. If the enterprise suffered losses from its new venture, the common stockholders absorbed the entire burden, while the creditors received the same amount they would have received if profits were generated. The more debt—or the more leverage the common stockholders seek—the more they increase their risk because of the increase in the fixed obligations.

Although conventional wisdom dictates that a certain amount of borrowing increases the value of the common stock, this point of view may overlook the opposing tendency of the market to downgrade the value of the stock due to the higher risk created by borrowing.

8. THE LEGAL PERILS OF EXCESSIVE DEBT

We have already seen that the debt portion of a corporation's capital structure increases the business risks borne by the corporation and its common stockholders. A corporation that is too "thinly" capitalized—that is, one with too little equity and too much debt—may face a number of legal perils as well.

First, the Internal Revenue Service is keenly aware of the tax temptations to the use of debt, particularly the deductibility of interest payments, and is alert to the potential that those tax advantages may be abused, particularly by closely-held corporations. If, in an effort to benefit from large interest corporations, the shareholders of a corporation attempt to treat too great a portion of their investment as "debt," the Service will seek to recharacterize the entire amount of the debt as equity. The result is that no interest deduction at all will be allowed, the payments made on the "debt" being treated as dividends. The corporation may also be disqualified from electing Subchapter S status, since it will no longer meet the requirement that it have only a single class of stock. One of the principal considerations in this determination is the debt-equity ratio. Regulation § 1.385–6(f) provides a safe harbor if the ratio does not exceed 10:1 and if the inside ratio (excluding the amounts owed to outside creditors) is 3:1. Other factors include:

— Whether the instrument in question fixes the time of repayment and the interest rate;

— Whether the instrument is subordinate to or preferred to any indebtedness or the corporation;

— Whether the security is convertible into stock;

— What relationship exists between stock holdings in the corporation and debt holdings in question.

The second peril of "thin incorporation" is that it increases the risk that the corporate veil might be pierced and the shareholders made liable for obligations of the corporation, a problem we will consider in the next chapter.

The final peril of a top heavy capital structure is that the courts may treat putative debt as equity in bankruptcy proceedings. The bankruptcy courts have exercised their equity function to develop a doctrine that subordinates the claims of shareholder-creditors to those of other creditors (the usual result being that the shareholders receive nothing) when the corporation is inadequately capitalized. This approach is known as the "Deep Rock Doctrine," after the name of a bankrupt company involved in one of the leading cases. Taylor v. Standard Gas & Electric Co., 306 U.S. 307, 59 S.Ct. 543, 83 L.Ed. 669 (1939). *See also* Pepper v. Litton, 308 U.S. 295, 60 S.Ct. 283, 84 L.Ed. 281 (1939) and Comstock v. Group of Institutional Investors, 335 U.S. 211, 68 S.Ct. 1454, 92 L.Ed. 1911 (1948).

IN RE FETT ROOFING & SHEET METAL CO., INC.

438 F.Supp. 726 (E.D.Va.1977), aff'd without opinion 605 F.2d 1201.

CLARKE, District Judge.

This matter comes before the Court on the appeal by plaintiff from an order of United States Bankruptcy Judge Hal J. Bonney, Jr., which dismissed plaintiffs' complaint, subordinated the note claims of the plaintiff to the claims of all other creditors and set aside deeds of trust which purported to secure the note claims. Appellant contends that the Bankrputcy Judge's findings of fact and conclusions of law were completely erroneous and that appellant's claims against the bankrupt should be reinstated. Jurisdiction of this Court is based on 28 U.S.C.A. § 1334; Bankruptcy Act §§ 38, 39(c), 11 U.S.C.A. §§ 66, 67(c); and Bankruptcy Rule 801.

The Facts

The record below discloses that the bankrupt, Fett Roofing and Sheet Metal Co., Inc., was owned and run prior to 1965 by plaintiff herein, Donald M. Fett, Sr., as a sole proprietorship. During 1965, Mr. Fett incorporated his business, transferring to the new corporation assets worth $4,914,85 for which he received 25 shares of stock. The stated capital of the corporation was never increased during the course of the corporation's existence. Mr. Fett was the sole stockholder and also the president of the corporation. The roofing business continued to be run completely by Mr. Fett much as it had been prior to its incorporation. In short, Fett Roofing was a classic "one-man" corporation. Over the years, plaintiff advanced money to his business as the need arose. Three of these transactions made in 1974, 1975 and 1976 involved the transfer to the corporation of $7,500, $40,000 and $30,000, respectively. In each instance plaintiff borrowed from the American National Bank, made the funds available to his business and took back demand promissory notes. On April 6, 1976, at a time his business had become insolvent, plaintiff recorded three deeds of trust intended to secure these notes with the realty, inventory, equipment and receivables of Fett Roofing and Sheet Metal Co., Inc. The deeds were backdated to indicate the dates on which the money had actually been borrowed. On November 8, 1976, an involuntary petition in bankruptcy was filed.

After a trial in which both sides presented considerable evidence and the plaintiff personally testified regarding his claim, Judge Bonney made the following findings of fact.

1. The bankrupt was undercapitalized at its inception in 1965, and remained undercapitalized throughout its existence. The capital necessary for the operation and continuation of its business was provided by the complainant in the form of so-called loans on an "as-needed" basis. Promissory notes, including the three involved herein, were given to the complainant in the course of such transactions.

2. The three deeds of trust which purport to secure the said notes were all back-dated to create the impression that they were executed contemporaneously with the advance of funds and the giving of the notes; all three were in fact executed and recorded during the first week of April 1976, when the notes were, by their terms, past due.

3. The purpose of the deeds of trust was to delay, hinder, and defraud the creditors of the bankrupt, and to give the complainant a

preference over them, in the event a liquidation of assets became necessary.

4. Complainant was in sole control of the affairs of the bankrupt, and was its sole stockholder. His interests were at all times identical to and indistinguishable from that of the bankrupt; he was the *alter ego* of the bankrupt.

5. At the time these three deeds of trust were executed and recorded, the bankrupt was, and for several months had been, unable to meet its obligations as they came due in the ordinary course of business. Many of the debts listed in the schedules filed by the bankrupt were incurred and delinquent prior to April 1976.

6. Complainant knew that his corporation was insolvent no later than February 1976.

Based on these findings, Judge Bonney concluded that the advances made by plaintiff to his corporation were actually contributions to capital, not loans, and that claims based on them therefore should be subordinated to those of all the other creditors of the bankrupt. The Judge further found that even if the transfers had been *bona fide* loans, the deeds of trust intended to secure them would have been null and void as having been given with actual intent to delay, hinder and defraud creditors in violation of § 67d(2)(d) of the Bankruptcy Act, 11 U.S.C.A. § 107(d)(2)(d). In addition, Judge Bonney determined that such loans were given in fraud of creditors under state law and therefore were voidable under § 70(e) of the Bankruptcy Act, 11 U.S.C.A. § 110(e).

Because we have concluded that the Bankruptcy Judge was correct in his determination that the plaintiff's transfers of money to his corporation were capital contributions and not loans we do not consider the soundness of the last two legal findings.

The Law

* * *

A director, officer, majority shareholder, relatives thereof or any other person in a fiduciary relation with a corporation can lawfully make a secured loan to the corporate beneficiary. Faucette v. Van Dolson, 397 F.2d 287 (4th Cir.), cert. denied, 393 U.S. 938, 89 S.Ct. 301, 21 L.Ed.2d 274 (1968). However, when challenged in court a fiduciary's transaction with the corporation will be subjected to "rigorous scrutiny" and the burden will be on him " * * * not only to prove the good faith of the transaction but also to show its inherent fairness from the viewpoint of the corporation and those interested therein." Pepper v. Litton, 308 U.S. 295, 60 S.Ct. 238, 84 L.Ed. 281 (1939); Geddes v. Anaconda Copper Mining Co., 254 U.S. 590, 599, 41 S.Ct. 209, 65 L.Ed. 425 (1921).

Where a director or majority shareholder asserts a claim against his own corporation, a bankruptcy court, sitting as a court of equity, will disregard the outward appearances of the transaction and determine its actual character and effect.

> Similar results have properly been reached in ordinary bankruptcy proceedings. Thus, salary claims of officers, directors and stockholders in the bankruptcy of "one-man" or family corporations have been disallowed or subordinated where the courts have been satisfied that allowance of the claims would not be fair or equitable to other creditors. And that result may be reached　*　*　* where on the facts the bankrupt has been used merely as a corporate pocket of the dominant stockholder, who, with disregard of the substance or form of corporate management, has treated its affairs as his own. And so-called loans or advances by the dominant or controlling stockholder will be subordinated to claims of other creditors and thus treated in effect as capital contributions by the stockholder not only in the foregoing types of situations but also where the paid-in capital is purely nominal, the capital necessary for the scope and magnitude of the operation of the company being furnished by the stockholder as a loan.

Pepper v. Litton, *supra*, 308 U.S. at 308–310, 60 S.Ct. at 246.

The record on this appeal reveals the bankrupt to have been a large construction contractor requiring ample amounts of capital. As indicated above, the corporation was capitalized at slightly under $5,000 when it was created in 1965. No increment to this initial amount was ever formally made. According to the schedule filed with the Bankruptcy Judge, the bankrupt's debt to secured creditors alone stood at $413,000. This is a debt-to-equity ratio of over 80 to 1. While this fact by itself will not serve to convert what is otherwise a *bona fide* loan into a contribution to capital, it does cast serious doubt on the advances by a person in plaintiff's special situation being considered debt rather than equity. The fact that no evidence was adduced by plaintiff to show that the "borrowings" in question were formally authorized by the corporation or that interest was ever paid on them, coupled with the undisputed day-in-and-day-out control over corporate affairs wielded by plaintiff, as president and sole stockholder leave little doubt that plaintiff, ignoring corporate formalities, was infusing new capital into his business and avoiding such necessities as charter amendment or the issuance of new stock. The record discloses that the funds transferred to the corporations were used to finance the acquisition of equipment and material necessary to the functioning of the business. Although one of the advances was used to pay a *bona fide* tax liability, this does not affect its character as a capital contribution under the particular circumstances of this case. In re Trimble Co., 479 F.2d 103, 115 (3d Cir. 1973). The fact that plaintiff at various times characterized these advances as "recapitalization" can only reinforce a conclusion which consideration of the entire record makes inevitable.

The Courts of this circuit have had no reluctance to pierce through surface appearances in these matters and distinguish contributions to capital from genuine loans. In Braddy v. Randolph, 352 F.2d 80 (4th Cir. 1965), a case with some striking similarities to the present dispute, the plaintiff, president, director and a principal stockholder of a bankrupt corporation, filed four claims based on four notes secured by deeds of trust. In affirming the rejection of these claims, the Court of Appeals stated:

> To finance this volume and to keep the business going even though operating at a loss, the Bankrupt borrowed heavily and constantly from the four officers and the North Carolina National Bank (hereinafter Bank). The money which officers, Braddy, Zeliff, Craft and Foster, "loaned" the Bankrupt was normally acquired from the Bank by use of their personal credit and personal assets. Based on the volume of business and the fact that the Bankrupt began borrowing from the officers and the Bank at the outset of operations, we think the referee and court could reasonably conclude that these "loans" were necessitated by the initial insufficiency of the Bankrupt's equity capital and that the "loans" made by the officers were, in effect, contributions to capital. Rather than invest more capital the officers and stockholders, by the use of the borrowed funds, substantially shifted and evaded the ordinary financial risks connected with this type of business enterprise and, at the same time, permitted the corporation to remain in a constant state of or in imminent danger of insolvency.

> * * *

> Although the advances contested here were made well after the corporation was created, there is evidence in the record that plaintiff had "loaned" the bankrupt money over the years and that the transfers here in issue were only the latest in a series of contributions made necessary by the corporation's grossly inadequate capitalization. Since these three transactions were "part of a plan of permanent personal financing," the fact that they did not occur at the outset of corporate existence is not crucial and the claims based on them are properly subordinated to those of other creditors.

> Since the transfers made by plaintiff to the bankrupt were, in contemplation of law, capital contributions the deeds of trust purporting to secure these advances were properly set aside since there was in fact "no debt to be secured." Arnold v. Phillips, 117 F.2d 497, 501 (5th Cir. 1941).

> As the cases make clear, no one fact will result in the determination that putative loans are actually contributions to capital. The Court is guided by equitable principles that look to the result of the transaction as well as to the formal indicia of its character. A person in the special position of the plaintiff " * * * cannot by the use of the corporate device avail himself of the privileges normally permitted outsiders in a race of creditors." Pepper v. Litton, *supra*, 308 U.

S. at 311, 60 S.Ct. at 247. It is not necessary that fraud, deceit or calculated breach of trust be shown. Where, as here, a corporate insider, indeed the corporate alter ego has so arranged his dealings with his corporate principal that he achieves as unfair advantage over outside creditors dealing at arms length, the Court will subordinate his claim to theirs.

For the foregoing reasons, the Order appealed from is affirmed.

NOTE—"THIN" CORPORATIONS

How does a lawyer assisting in planning a capital structure presently (and a court retrospectively) decide what is an adequate initial capitalization? In In re Mobile Steel Co., 563 F.2d 692 (5th Cir. 1977) the corporation was formed to purchase assets of an existing steel fabricating enterprise. The shareholder-creditors contributed $250,000 in the form of equity capital and another $250,000 in the form of debentures. The corporation obtained an initial bank loan of $650,000 secured by a pledge of realty and over $800,000 from a factor secured by a pledge of accounts receivable. The court stated:

> The concept of undercapitalization has never been rigorously defined. Absolute measures of capital inadequacy, such as the amount of stockholder equity or other figures and ratios drawn from the cold pages of the corporation's balance sheets and financial statements, are of little utility, for the significance of this data depends in large part upon the nature of the business and other circumstances. Nor is the fact of eventual failure an appropriate test. Cf. Automotriz Del Golfo de California S.A. (de) C. V. v. Reswick, 47 Cal.2d 792, 799, 306 P.2d 1, 6 (1957) (Carter J. dissenting) (disregard of corporate entity). This would be tantamount to ruling that an investor who takes an active role in corporate affairs must advance to his corporation all of the funds, which hindsight discloses it needed to survive. Instead, we think that for the purposes of determining whether claims against the bankrupt estate held by organizers or shareholders should be subordinated on the ground of undercapitalization, the amount of capitalization that is adequate is

> > what reasonably prudent men with a general background knowledge of the particular type of business and its hazards would determine was reasonable capitalization in the light of any special circumstances which existed at the time of incorporation of the now defunct enterprise.

N. Lattin, The Law of Corporations §§ 15, 77 (2d ed. 1971); cf. H. Ballantine, Corporations 302–03 (rev. ed. 1946) (disregard of corporate entity); see generally E. Latty, Subsidiaries and Affiliated Corporations, 119–28 & 133–38 (1936). This general definition is helpful because it focuses on the culpability of the organizer-stockholders and pegs the assessment to more specific standards which do not involve open-ended quantitative questions. Foremost among the standards which the general statement suggests are the following:

(1) Capitalization is inadequate if, in the opinion of a skilled financial analyst, it would definitely be insufficient to support a business of the size and nature of the bankrupt in light of the circumstances existing at the time the bankrupt was capitalized;

(2) Capitalization is inadequate if, at the time when the advances were made the bankrupt could not have borrowed a similar amount of money from an informed outside source.

563 F.2d at 702–3.

What if the corporation has adequate initial capitalization, but suffers a later drain of capital? The court in In re Trimble Co., 479 F.2d 103, 116 (3d Cir. 1973) stated:

In the instant case, the corporation was adequately capitalized to begin with, but suffered overwhelming losses during the years 1958 through 1961. In such a situation, a test which may be used to decide whether a contribution by a proprietary interest is a loan or an additional injection of capital is whether the advance was made at a time when a bank or other ordinary commercial agency would be willing to lend it funds. [Footnote omitted.]

In re Branding Iron Steak House, 536 F.2d 299, 301–2 (9th Cir. 1976) stated:

A creditor's claim cannot be subordinated to the claims of other creditors simply because the claimant is an officer, director, or controlling shareholder in a bankrupt corporation. * * * However, when it would be inequitable to permit such a creditor to share equally with other creditors, the Bankruptcy Judge may subordinate his claim. Costello v. Fazio, 256 F.2d 903 (9th Cir. 1958); Anno. 51 A.L.R.2d 989, 993.

In *Costello, supra,* three individuals engaged in a partnership for the operation of a plumbing company. The partnership capital consisted of $51,620.78, of which each of the three partners had invested unequal amounts. After four years of operation the business was undergoing serious financial difficulties, and the decision was made to incorporate. In the year preceding incorporation net losses totalled $22,521.34. In anticipation of incorporation, all of the partnership capital except $6,000 was withdrawn and converted into debt evidenced by promissory notes issued to two of the partners. An expert testified that there was little hope of financial success at that time in view of the recent business reverses. The business was incorporated, and the partnership debts, including the two promissory notes issued to the former partners, were assumed by the corporation. Two years later, when the corporation filed a voluntary petition in bankruptcy, the two former partners made claims on their promissory notes. The

Bankruptcy Referee refused to subordinate their claims, finding that the corporation was adequately capitalized and that the claimants had not acted for their own personal or private benefit to the detriment of the corporation. The District Court affirmed, but our Court reversed, holding that both of the critical findings of the Bankrputcy Referee were clearly erroneous.

Here, the Bankrputcy Judge concluded that the present case is controlled by *Costello*. Because of the result we reach we can assume without deciding that the Bankruptcy Judge was correct in concluding that the restaurant was undercapitalized. Nevertheless, given this assumption, undercapitalization is the only significant fact common to both our present case and *Costello*.

In *Costello*, the claimants argued that mere undercapitalization should not, in and of itself, be sufficient to require subordination of their claims. We responded that "much more" than mere undercapitalization had been shown. 256 F.2d at 910. It seems virtually undeniable that the facts in *Costello* reflect a calculated maneuver by the investors, met with consistent business reverses, to attempt to reduce their risk to the detriment of other creditors. The *Costello* court found it significant and the partners "stripped the business of 88% of its stated capital at a time when it had a minus working capital and had suffered substantial business losses." 256 F.2d at 910.

In contrast, here the bankrupt did not begin to suffer business losses until several years after its incorporation. There was thus no clear intention by Richmond and Alexander to shift their risk to other creditors in the face of business reverses. Indeed, there was no stripping away of the restaurant's capitalization at all. Richmond held promissory notes for money loaned to the restaurant from the outset. At no time was existing capital withdrawn and converted into debt.

Moreover, it is not disputed that Richmond was not at all active in the operation of the enterprise. Before the legitimate claim of an officer, director, or shareholder of a bankrupt corporation may be subordinated to the claims of other creditors, not only must that person have the ability and intent to control the corporation, but he must in fact exercise that control to the detriment of other creditors. In re Brunner Air Compressor Corp., 287 F.Supp. 256, 265 (N.D.N.Y.1968). The record is devoid of any evidence whatsoever that Richmond exercised such control.

In our view, mere undercapitalization, standing alone, is not enough to justify the subordination of the legitimate claims of officers, directors, and shareholders of a bankrupt corporation to those of other creditors. We acknowledge that a claim may be subordinated even in the absence of fraud or mismanagement, * * * Nevertheless, a Bankruptcy Court is a court of equity, and subordination requires some showing of suspicious, inequitable conduct beyond mere initial undercapitalization of the enterprise.   *   *   *

B.   DRAFTING PREFERRED STOCK PROVISIONS

PROBLEM

EAST WIND BOATS—PART VI

After discussion with you and among themselves, your clients have decided to have part of Ed Teach's investment in East Wind take the form of preferred stock. In preparing the articles of incorporation, you have come to the section setting forth the terms of the preferred stock. You have found the following form in a book of forms. Revise it to correct any inadequacies and to fit it to the needs of your clients.

The corporation shall be authorized to issue ___ shares of preferred stock. All or any part of the aforesaid shares of the preferred stock may be issued by the corporation from time to time and for such consideration as may be determined upon and fixed by the board of directors, as provided by law, with due regard to the interest of the existing shareholders; and when such consideration has been received by the corporation, such shares are deemed fully paid.

The nature and extent of the preferences, rights, privileges, and restrictions granted to or imposed upon the holders of the respective classes of stock are as follows:

(a) The holders of the preferred stock shall be entitled to receive from the surplus or net profits arising from the business of the corporation a fixed yearly dividend of ten Dollars ($10) per share, in priority to the payment of any dividend on the common stock. All remaining profits which may be applied to the payment of dividends shall be distributed to the common shareholders.

(b) In the event of liquidation or dissolution or winding up (whether voluntary or involuntary) or sale of all of the assets of the corporation, the holders of the preferred stock shall be entitled to be paid one hundred five Dollars ($105) per share and the unpaid dividends accrued thereon out of net assets before any amount shall be paid to holders of the common stock; and after the payment to the preferred stock the remaining assets and funds shall be divided and paid to the holders of the common stock pro rata according to their respective shares.

(c) On or after _____, the corporation shall have the right from time to time to purchase, redeem, retire, and cancel any and all, of the outstanding preferred stock of the corporation, on any dividend date or upon ten days' written notice to the holder or holders of the preferred stock to be purchased, redeemed, retired or canceled, in such manner and amounts as the board of directors may determine, by paying to the respective holders of the stock so retired, or by depositing to their order in the office of the corporation, a sum equal to one hundred five Dollars ($105) per share of the stock so retired and canceled, together with all unpaid accumulated dividends thereon, if any.   In case of such deposit written notice shall forthwith be given to the respective holders of the stock so retired or canceled, by mailing such notice to such holders at their last known address as shown by the corporate records.

BUXBAUM, PREFERRED STOCK—LAW AND DRAFTSMANSHIP

42 Calif.L.Rev. 243, 244–47, 253–54, 257–62, 263–66, 290–93 (1954).

THE DIVIDEND RIGHT

The Cumulative Feature

Dividend rights of shareholders are contractual.   Usually the corporate articles explicitly grant the cumulative feature of dividends ("cumulative" is enough) or deny it in as certain terms.   [That is, the amount the dividends accumulates each year, and the accumulation must be paid in full before the common is entitled to receive dividends.   Example: Preferred is cumulative, $5.   No dividend is paid in year 1.   In year 2, $10 must be paid to the preferred before dividends can be paid to the common.]   Deficient phrasing may lead to conflicting decisions as to the existence of a contract.   The construction, however, may be influenced by the court's understanding of the "normal rights" of a preferred share of stock.   The majority of courts hold that "in the abstract" dividends on preferred stocks are cumulative.   * * *

If the articles specify that dividends shall be noncumulative, several problems remain.   Basically they are contractual problems, but interpretation here seems influenced by judicial notions as to the "rights" of such stock labelled "noncumulative" with no further gloss.   To the majority of courts these noncumulative dividends are discretionary [Ed., once passed they are lost.] but it has been held that a noncumulative stock may nevertheless be "cumulative if earned."   If specifically so expressed, the result will follow in all jurisdictions.   In New Jersey this "dividend credit" doctrine has been extended to noncumulative stock independently of contractual provision and is based partly on statute and partly on judicial opinion as to "rights" of noncumulative stock.   Though it may be that these cases have not interpreted the bare term "noncumulative" as meaning cumulative if earned, they have construed as "cumulative if earned," provisions which other courts would call "noncumulative and discretionary."

Right to Participate in Dividends Beyond a Stated Preference

Since shareholders' dividend rights are contractual, an express statement that the stock does not participate in dividend payments beyond a set rate of return will govern any rules of construction of law otherwise applicable. This and the statement that the preferred stock is entitled to dividends at the rate of ___% annually "and no more" are today's usual provisions. Disputes can only arise over share contracts creating a set return or a permissive (or maximum) return: "6% annually" or "up to (not exceeding) 6% annually," in each case "before any dividends shall be paid the common." The majority of courts find a limit on all these statements. The maxim that a share of stock is a share of stock unless further rights and limitations are expressed is either ignored or deemed overcome by the contract's terms. The phrasing found in articles to justify this construction seems ambiguous. A minority would hold such stock participating and merely require a "primary" dividend to preferred before payment to common. When that has been paid, however, the force of "not exceeding ___%" has been dissipated and further payments are unrestricted.

The articles should specify the extent of participation. After the "primary" dividend, preferred may participate at once in any payments to common or may only participate after an equivalent amount has been paid the common. Articles specifying "preferred shall receive dividends of 7% before any are paid the common, and then are entitled to dividends equal to those paid the common," leave this choice open. The better phrasing would provide for payment of a specific amount to the common (usually equivalent per share to that paid the preferred) before admitting the participation. Another problem is the size of the dividend. It should be set per share, not as an aggregate per class, and the certificate should specify participation "share for share" or "at the same rate" as payments to the common, and not "equally with the common."

* * *

Discretion

Occasionally a corporation desires to limit the discretion of its board of directors in the declaration of dividends. Appropriate language to that effect will be honored by the courts as a contractual stipulation to pay dividends upon certain conditions. However, the ordinary provision that dividends shall be paid "when, as and if declared by the board of directors" with or without "in their discretion" will prevent shareholder attack except on "abuse of discretion." "Abuse of discretion" embodies a vague area of fraud and bad faith and, while occasionally proven, is a difficult action to sustain. Whatever this area, it cannot be limited further by the articles, which can do no more than leave the declaration of dividends to the board of directors' discretion; complaints based on an abuse of that discretion cannot prospectively be foreclosed.

Discretion is more frequently and successfully questioned upon construction of the articles. The phrasing must usually differ substantially from that quoted above, for courts are reluctant to find an intent to deprive the board of directors of this discretion. In a few cases, these questions of construction merge into questions of law. It has been said, for instance, that discretion is somewhat limited when the stock involved is noncumulative; such stock may be of the "mandatory dividend" type though its language is not appreciably different from that used for cumulative stock. The mere statement that the stock was to receive noncumulative dividends at a rate interpreted as mandatory if earnings exist. Cumulative stock is apparently treated more strictly and mere statements of the source of dividend payments do not make such stock mandatory. This or any contract diverting profits to a specific corporate purpose is valid; but the language of these articles is sufficiently ambiguous to provoke litigation. The difficulty apparently arises from an attempt to retain discretionary power in the board of directors while nevertheless setting policy guides for the exercise of their discretion.

* * *

THE LIQUIDATION PREFERENCE

Preferred shares do not participate before common stock in distributions upon liquidation, dissolution or winding-up unless the share-contract or a statute so specify. Statutes may provide for preferential participation to a varied extent and modern corporate articles specifically grant the preference. Some statutes have specifically denied the preference unless granted by the article, thus restating the common law rule. [MBCA § 15.] If the statute requires that the certificate of incorporation express the preference, a by law attempting to do so is ineffective.

* * *

Participation beyond the preferential distribution is doubtful. If the articles are silent the majority of courts find no participation preference and require pro rata distribution—to preferred and common—of all assets. Where the contract specifies that payment to the preferred of par and arrears is payment in full there is no excess participation. There is no American case authority concerning excess participation beyond a stated preference. The bare statement of rights of preferred stock in liquidation is not helpful. Similar problems arise from the varied types of participation possible, as in participation in dividends beyond a stated preference. Preferred may participate equally (or in stated ratio) with common at once after the fixed preferential payment, or after common has received, exclusively, a similar (or stated) amount. The participation may be equal per class, or equal per share. Any arrangement desired, whether because of peculiar capital contributions involved, prior dividend or asset distributions or any other reason will be honored by the courts if expressed.

* * *

The most important issue in drafting or construing the articles' liqidation clause is its scope. What is a liquidation dissolution or winding-up (the common phrase)? Against what corporate action does even a seemingly all-inclusive clause fail to provide protection? In the absence of contractual provision a transfer of one company's assets to another has been held not a liquidation, but depending on the exact transaction the opposite result may be reached. A merger or consolidation is not a liquidation or dissolution. A mere suspension of business, because of physical plant or equipment destruction, for example, is no dissolution. But a reduction of capital preparatory to an increase for a new issue has been held a partial liquidation, *i.e.*, its burden must fall on the common.

Many of these results are obviated by, or written into, corporate articles. The liquidation preference by its terms covers liquidation, dissolution and winding-up, whether voluntary or not. Usually merger, consolidation and sale, and lease or any conveyance of assets are expressly excepted from the preference. These contractual terms control. * * *

* * *

THE REDEMPTION PRIVILEGE

The power of a corporation to purchase its own stock, once the subject of some doubt, is today recognized by the majority of jurisdictions. Many statutes grant it, some, at least by implication, forbidding its exercise in certain instances. * * *

Courts today seldom void a contract to purchase shares. But the contract is subject to avoidance if at the time of payment or performance the company is insolvent, the payment would harm creditors or capital would be impaired, depending on the substantive rules of purchase applicable locally. If at that time one of these limitations is violated, the contract is unenforceable. These doctrines apply to contracts to redeem as well as to contracts of purchase. The former are but a form of the latter, except where statutory treatment purposely differs. * * *

Most articles give the corporation power to repurchase and redeem stock at its option. Specific features of redemption of a particular class of stock are usually detailed by the board of directors in the certificate of preferences (under delegation of authority from articles and statute). The company is usually given the right to redeem all or part of the particular stock at its option. Compulsory redemption clauses are seldom used today except for sinking fund purposes. Some statutes forbid such clauses since they make possible a potential fraud on creditors and other shareholders. Compulsory redemption in any event is somewhat anomalous to the nature of preferred stock. * * *

Rarely does a corporation fail to express in its articles that redemption shall be in the board of directors' discretion. The contract may, however, fail to specify how redemption is to be accomplished, simply calling certain stock "redeemable." If so, redemption is probably at the company's option. Again, today's articles require redemption at a given figure plus accrued dividends. Though there is type of inchoate right to the latter by virtue of corporate membership, a contractual provision denying accruals at liquidation or at redemption is apparently valid. Most articles, too, permit total or partial redemption. The latter is obviously open to abuse, for the company, by redeeming insiders' stock before any decline, can enable these persons to pull out of the company before a storm, leaving less favored shareholders in a relatively worse position. To avoid this, most articles provide that selection of shares for a partial redemption be made "by lot, or pro rata." Certainly this provision is desirable; yet some articles say "by lot, by pro rata *or* as the board of directors decides," or simply the latter. These are nothing more than loopholes. In the latter case a court might hold that the intent of the total redemption provision called for an objective selection; in the first instance discrimination would seem to result. In any event, the possibility of judicial leniency does not justify such phrasing.

Redemption with Dividends Accrued

The redemption price, as stated, customarily includes accrued dividends. Thus compulsory redemption would not deprive a shareholder of his accrual, but would leave him in a position similar to that found upon liquidation. If there is no surplus then redemption at a price including arrearages permits partial liquidation of some of a single class of stock. In states that permit this practice, and everywhere if a surplus exists, shareholders must depend on the contractual phrasing for complete protection if that is desired, or for an exact statement of the practices permitted. * * *

The Sinking Fund

A sinking fund provides for the periodic retirement of preferred stock, as distinguished from stock that merely may be repurchased.

The benefits of a sinking fund are of a twofold nature. The continuous reduction of the size of the issue makes for increasing safety and the easier repayment of the balance at maturity. Also important is the support given to the market for the issue through the repeated appearance of a substantial buying demand.[2]

2. Graham & Dodd, Security Analysis 308 (2d ed. 1951).

This continuous reduction is not a certainty; as will be seen, the shares are not always retired. But if reduced, the progressively fewer remaining shareholders are somewhat more sure of dividend payments. Under the usual sinking fund contract, the corporation regularly reduces its dividend obligations and thus gains flexibility for planning future financing. Conflicting rights will thus arise which require strict compliance with sinking funds' terms and which indirectly encourage exact phrasing of each provision.

* * *

DIRECT AND PROTECTIVE VOTING RIGHTS

Voting is the theoretical means of shareholder control over corporate actions. Electing the board of directors is ideally the indirect means of expressing opinions and desires concerning corporate policies. Voting blanket approval of management's activities over the preceding period has a similar purpose. The voting requirements for a particular action—a merger of an issue of new preferred stock—are the more direct means of expressing consent. These are important transactions, final in their effect on the shareholder-company relation. The effect justifies and requires the prior consent of each shareholder.

Modern preferred stock by its own contract is usually nonvoting. The typical articles deny any vote to the preferred, "except as hereinafter provided." They then specify the actions—usually those set out in the statute—upon which preferred may vote. Apart from this vote on certain transactions nearly all articles today disinter the voting right—to some extent—upon default in payment of dividends. The typical clause creates the voting right, in the preferred stock as a class, when three or four of six *nonconsecutive* dividend payments (i. e., on the specific dividend dates) have been missed. When nonconsecutive, the corporation cannot avoid the shift in control by paying a dividend just often enough—as on one quarterly dividend date annually—to keep the provision suspended. The purpose of the clause would be vitiated if more dividends could be passed than are needed to activate the voting right just as long as they are not passed consecutively. A provision that the control shifts "whenever four dividend payments are missed" is ambiguous and should be avoided as provoking dispute. It is certainly construable as "consecutive," but if that result is desired it should be expressed. Such phrasing is a source of potential abuse by creating a stock seeming to differ from what it in fact is.

The vote given is usually the right to elect a given number of directors. This number may range widely: one, three, the greatest minority, the least majority of all.   *   *   *

Assuming a default occurs when four nonconsecutive dividends are missed, the voting right then created continues until the default is cured. "Cure" may be by full payment of the total arrearage of it may be by payment of sufficient dividends to reduce the arrearage to one less dividend than the least amount originally activating the voting right. Many articles allow retention of the voting control by the preferred until the arrearage is completely paid. The futility of constant voting shifts if payment of only the excess accumulation beyond the default level cured the default right might lead a court to require full payment even though the articles speak merely of "revesting upon curing of the default." In any event, the right of "return" is subject to revesting in the preferred when another arrearage of "default size" develops. This undoubtedly results though the contract be silent as to revesting upon later default.   *   *   *

8/2

C.   THE PROBLEM OF LEGAL CAPITAL

PROBLEM

EAST WIND BOATS—PART VII

Suppose the acquisition took the following form:

Hardy, Luff and Teach purchase the assets and business of East Wind Boats for $50,000 in cash and the delivery of a note for $50,000, payable in ten years, bearing interest at 12% per annum. Soon thereafter, they form East Wind Boats Corporation. The corporation acquires all the property they purchased from Stern and Star, in exchange for 500 shares of common stock and 500 shares of preferred stock and the assumption of all liabilities. Stern and Star consent to a novation of their note. (Corporation takes over their note)

1. If the corporation is formed under Delaware law, and all the stock has par value of $100, will the shares be fully paid, validly issued and non-assessable? What is the risk of liability of the shareholders, with respect to this transaction, to creditors in the event the corporation fails?

2. What is the answer to the above questions if the stock had par value of $10?

3. What is the answer to the questions if the corporation were formed in a jurisdiction that followed the Model Business Corporation Act?

The following drill of balance sheet fundamentals is intended to assist you with the problem in this part.

DRILL EXERCISE

Balance Sheet Transactions

A

How would you account for the following transactions on the balance sheet of a corporation organized under Delaware law? (See §§ 152–154 of the General Corporation Law of Delaware.)

1. Assume 100 shares of common stock, $100 par value per share, are authorized and 10 shares each are issued to Janet Entrepreneur and Peter Promoter for $100 per share, for cash. Complete the entries for the assets and the shareholders' equity accounts on the corporation's balance sheet.

Assets	Liabilities and Shareholder's Equity	
Cash $ 2000	Stated Capital (100 shares common stock, $100 par value, authorized; 20 shares issued and outstanding)	$ 2000
	Total Liabilities and Shareholders' Equity	$ 2000
Total Assets $ 2000		

a. What does it mean that 100 shares are "authorized" but only 20 are "issued and outstanding"? Reread Section 4, Part 4 of this chapter.

b. What is the meaning of a $100 par value?

c. What does the stated capital item represent? Is it a fund for the benefit of creditors?   *par value & outstanding shares*

2. Assume the same facts as in 1 except the stock has a $10 par value. Complete the entries for the assets and shareholders' equity accounts on the corporation's balance sheet.

Assets	Liabilities and Shareholder's Equity	
Cash $ 2000	Stated Capital (100 shares common stock, $10 par value, authorized; 20 shares issued and outstanding)	$ 200
	Capital Surplus	$ 1800
	Total Liabilities and Shareholder's Equity	$ 2000
Total Assets $ 2000		

a. What does the capital surplus item represent? Is it a fund for the benefit of creditors? *- more for shareholders*

b. What if the $10 par value stock is sold for $5 per share? Consider Del.GCL §§ 162 (a) and 163.

3. Assume the same facts as in 1, except the stock has no par value. Complete the entries for the assets and shareholders' equity accounts on the corporation's balance sheet.

Assets	Liabilities and Shareholder's Equity	
Cash $ 2000	Stated Capital (100 shares common stock, no par value, authorized; 20 shares issued and outstanding)	$ ____
	Capital Surplus	$ ____
	Total Liabilities and Shareholder's Equity	$ ____
Total Assets $ 2000		

4. Assume the same facts as in 1, except that in consideration for her stock Janet transfers land worth $1,000. Complete the entries

for the assets and shareholders' equity accounts for the corporation's balance sheet.

Assets	Liabilities and Shareholder's Equity
Cash $ 1000	
Land $ 1000	Stated Capital (100 shares common stock; $100 par value, authorized; 20 shares issued and outstanding) $ 2000
	Total Liabilities and Shareholder's Equity $ 2000
Total Assets $ 2000	

5. Assume that Janet transfers land "worth" $5000 *[$ 500]* which the board values at $1,000.

ie. 1000 worth of shares for 500

a. Assume that 10 shares of $100 par value are issued to Janet. Is the stock validly issued? Is Janet liable to anyone for anything? Consider Del. GCL §§ 152, 162, 163.

b. Assume that 10 shares of $10 par value are issued to Janet. Is the stock validly issued? Is Janet liable to anyone for anything?

B

6. Assume the same facts as in 1 except that the corporation is incorporated in a jurisdiction which has provisions to MBCA §§ 18 and 19.

a. How is the stock described on the balance sheet?

b. Instead of cash consideration for her stock, Janet transfers a note for $1,000 guaranteed by a reputable bank. Is the stock validly issued?

c. Instead of cash consideration for her stock, Janet enters into an agreement to serve as general manager of the business for the next year. Is the stock validly issued?

1. PRELIMINARY NOTE

Much of the elaborate scheme you are about to confront is on its way to the storehouse of antiquated legal curiosities. It was designed by the 19th century architects of corporation law as a structure to protect corporate creditors by requiring corporations to provide a cushion known as "legal capital." It was a highly conceptual framework which does not work, and probably never did. You are condemned to learn it, however, because at the present time, and for some time to come, it is the law and must be mastered if you are to save your clients from liability and yourself from malpractice. Moreover, it is often necessary to go back to the past to understand the present. Beginning with the revision of the California Corporation Law in 1975 and then followed by the adoption by the Committee on Corporate Laws of the American Bar Association of amendments to the Model Business Corporation Act in 1980, the foundation for a new model has been laid.

We will pursue both the old and the new learning in this section, using the Model Act (as revised) to represent the new and Delaware Law as representative of the old and, for the most part, the present law.

Dean Manning's debunking of the effectiveness of the hoary principles of legal capital which follows must not obscure the need for the lawyer to understand these requirements. Undoubtedly this is not the first time students will have studied a legal construct that is based on fiction and which does not work, nor will it be the last. Some of these we study because the process affords good training. Others we study simply because they are there and we have to live with them. The field of legal capital belongs to the latter category.

One of the reasons why this subject has importance is because lawyers are often required to express opinions about the legality of the capital structure of a corporation. A good discussion is found is Israels, Problems of Par and No-Par Shares: A Reappraisal, 47 Colum.L.Rev. 1279 (1947). The lawyer must express an opinion in a variety of contexts that the shares of the corporation are "validly issued, fully paid and non-assessable." To render such an opinion he must examine the particulars of the issuance of the corporate stock and see whether the consideration paid for the shares was acceptable and sufficient within the meaning of the statute. One context for the rendering of such an opinion is the occasion of a corporation selling shares to public stockholders. At that time the corporation will be required to comply with the federal securities laws, which we discuss in Chapter 12. Compliance requires the company to file an opinion of counsel with the Securities and Exchange Commission in which the attorney opines as to the validity of the shares. It is likely that a carelessly rendered opinion, that turns out to be incorrect, would cause the lawyer to be liable in a malpractice suit to those investors who suffered as a result of their erroneous belief, even though those persons were not a client of the attorney rendering the opinion. Perhaps the law has not yet gone that far; nonetheless, the serious possibility that it might is enough to alarm and alert every attorney who has to render an opinion about the legal capital of a corporation.

The revision of the financial provisions of the Model Act eliminates many of the legal fictions, as we shall see, and makes life easier for the lawyer.

2. THE REGIME OF LEGAL CAPITAL AND PAR VALUE

B. MANNING, A CONCISE TEXTBOOK ON LEGAL CAPITAL, (2d ed. 1981) pp. 1–35.

The interests of creditors of a corporation and the interests of shareholders of a corporation are likely to conflict whenever assets of shareholders are to be committed to the corporation's treasury and whenever assets are to be distributed to shareholders from the corporate treasury. The legal apparatus built by common law and statute around the concept of "legal capital" is fundamentally aimed at striking a partial accommodation of that conflict of interests. * * *

In the usual case * * * it will be a matter of major concern to the creditor of the corporation to seek four objectives—precisely as in the case of the lender to an individual debtor.

(1) The creditor will be happier if his corporate debtor has substantial assets in the corporate till at the time he extends credit and thereafter;

(2) The creditor will want to prevent the corporation from incurring debts to other general creditors with whom he may have to share the corporation's limited assets;

(3) The creditor will want the corporate assets to remain free and unencumbered of any lien interests by a prior (secured) creditor; and

(4) The creditor will want to preserve a cushion of protective assets, and will want to see to it that no claimants who rank junior to him (usually shareholders, but sometimes subordinated debt holders) make off with assets of the corporation while the creditor's claim is still outstanding and unpaid. * * *

The legal doctrines revolving around the concept of "legal capital" developed as a partial response to, and was mainly attributable to, this perspective of the creditors of corporations. Before the accommodation reached by the legal capital system can be appreciated, however, it is necessary to take a look at the shareholder's perspective of the matter. * * *

The ideal world as conceived by the creditor of the corporation is a world that is normally wholly unacceptable to the shareholder. The investor who buys shares of stock in the incorporated enterprise and the investor who lends money to the incorporated enterprise, are, as a matter of economics, engaged in the same kind of activity and are motivated by the same basic objectives. They are both making capital investment; they both expect or hope to get their money back in the long run, either by liquidating pay-out or by sale of the security; and they both expect and hope to receive income from their investment in the interim before their capital is returned to them in full. In the stereotypic model transaction, the investor who chose to take a shareholder's position rather than a creditor's position in a transaction, simply made a calculated economic judgment that he could make more money by relinquishing to creditor investors a "prior" claim for interest and a fixed principal payment on maturity, and, in the hope of a larger income or large ultimate capital gain, by opting for uncertain "dividends" and the residual claim to the assets of the enterprise that would remain after all the creditors, with their fixed claims, had been paid off.*   The shareholder's willingness to admit the "priori-ty" of the creditor's interest claim and claim for principal payment on maturity, does *not* imply, however, that the shareholder is willing to stand by chronologically until such time as the creditors have been paid in full. The shareholder will insist, in general, that if, as he hopes, the enterprise makes money (and perhaps even if it does not), the shareholders will receive some return on (or of) their investment from time to time, regardless of the fact that there are creditor claims outstanding. Such periodic payments to shareholders are characterized as "dividends;" and, in the usual and normal case of the healthy incorporated enterprise, it is assumed that some assets will be regularly paid out from the corporate treasury to the share-holder investors in dividend form.

Simple as this observation may be, its implications are far-reach-ing. If all creditors had to be paid off before *any* payment could be made to shareholder investors, and if shareholders received nothing until ultimate liquidation of the enterprise when they would divide the residuum left after payment of all creditors—if, in other words, the terms "prior" and "before" were chronological as well as hierar-chical—the creditor would not have to worry about assets being drained away into the hands of junior claimants and he would sleep better at night. But once it is conceded that *during the life* of the creditor's claims, assets may be passed out to an investing group that hierarchically ranks below the creditors, the question becomes una-voidable: How much of the assets in the treasury of the incorporated enterprise may be distributed to shareholders, when, and under what circumstances? * * *

Accepting the model as given, how should corporate law, statuto-ry or judge made, regulate the activities of businessmen and lawyers so as to deal with the combination of the corporate creditor's perspec-tive and the shareholder's perspective—namely:

(1) The creditor of the corporation desires that the enterprise have large quantities of assets against which the only other claimants are those who rank junior to him, *i.e.*, the shareholders. Shareholders, by contrast, would like to have as little as possible of their own assets

* This stereotypic model, like the other illustrative models used here, is grossly oversimplified.

In the first place, it groups together as a unitary interest all of those character-ized as "shareholders." Even as credi-tors may be arrayed along a spectrum of claim from secured to subordinated, shareholders are often divided among themselves into subclassifications of hier-archical claim by the creation of different classes of stock, each class having a dif-ferentiated claim to dividends, liquidation payments, voting rights, etc. In usual parlance these classes are spoken of as either "preferred" or "common," but the usage is misleading since the various classes (or series) may be almost infinite-ly varied in their terms and still remain "stock" so long as their claim to liquida-tion payment falls hierarchically below the lowest ranking creditor's claim in liq-uidation. As a result, clashes of interest *among* shareholder classes may in some circumstances be as intense as, or even more intense than, the more generalized clash of interest between shareholders as a whole and creditors as a whole. * * *

tied up in the enterprise and exposed to the jeopardy of creditors' claims.

(2) The creditor does not ordinarily welcome the creation of additional creditors' claims against the limited assets of the enterprise. The shareholder investor will often (not always) be willing for the incorporated enterprise to incur further debt in order to benefit from leverage, especially when his own equity investment position is small.

(3) The creditor would prefer would that the junior investment claimant, the shareholder, receive nothing as return on his investment for so long a time as the creditor's claim has not been paid. The shareholder, on the other hand, insists upon a concurrent return paid out to him as the enterprise earns profits.

(4) The creditor wants protection against all manner of asset distributions to shareholders. The shareholder wants maximum freedom to receive such distributions.

(5) Each shareholder wants assurance that each other shareholder has contributed to the corporate pot a proprietorship investment proportionate to his shareholdings.

The provisions of state corporation codes dealing with legal capital are addressed to resolving, or at least accommodating, these conflicts.   *   *   *

Consider a newly formed corporate enterprise at the stage of its initial financing by the issue of shares; the only assets in the corporate treasury area those which the stockholders have just put in for their stock, and the enterprise has done no business. If, at that time, a prospective lender asks the question, "How much assets does the corporation have free and clear after claims of creditors" the answer will be the same as the answer to the question, "How much did the shareholders put in?" Similarly, if a loan is then made to the corporation, the question, "How much assets did the corporation have at the time of the loan" has the same answer as the question, "How much assets have the shareholders put in over all time?" On this simplistic model, the statutory stated capital scheme is based. The scheme assumes that the key to protection of the creditor lies in the answer to these two questions which, taken together, become, "How much assets have shareholders put into the corporate treasury since the formation of the corporation?" Whether or not that question is one that really interests a creditor, it is the elemental question to which the statutory legal capital scheme is addressed.

The nineteenth century pattern of corporate financing provided a ready suggestion to judges and statutory draftsmen for a way to gauge the quantity of assets that shareholders had, at some time or another, put into the corporate treasury. According to that pattern of corporate practice, an enterpreneurial organizer, the "promoter" who had conceived of an idea for a new business would make the rounds of people who had money to invest ("capitalists" all, whether little grey widows or sturdy yeomen), and seek to persuade them to invest in stock of the proposed enterprise. If the idea had appeal, and if the promoter was persuasive, he would succeed in obtaining commitments from them to buy stock. Such commitments called subscription agreements, had a number of features about them that were jarring to nineteenth century concepts of contract law and their assimilation into contractual jurisprudence proved very awkward. But its essence was simple enough: the subscriber agreed that if enough other subscribers were found, and if a corporation was formed for the purpose of the enterprise envisioned by the promoter, he, the subscriber, would, on call of the future board of directors of the corporation when organized, put in a set amount of money, or other assets, and would receive a set number of shares of the newly formed corporation. Given this practice, it was to be expected, and was perhaps inevitable, that in drawing up the subscription agreements for any single enterprise, a fixed mathematical relationship would be set between the amount of dollars to be invested by subscriber and the number of shares to be issued. That relationship produced the concept of the "par value" of the stock to be issued. In the normal situation, no equity investor could expect to obtain a share of stock for less than the par value of it, since presumably all other purchasers were paying that amount. Similarly, no share subscriber could be persuaded to agree to pay more than the par value for a share since other investors were receiving a similar share by paying in the par value. * * *

The stock certificates were formal and elaborate, and, in analogy to paper currency or banknotes, bore upon their face as the most dominant feature, the share's "par value" stated as a fixed number of dollars, typically $100. This number represented the amount the shareholders had agreed to pay for each share according to the subscription agreements. In time, by statute, the par value of the stock was required to be stated as a provision in the corporate charter.

The essentially arbitrary character of this number must be understood. If, for example, each of three investors agreed to invest $10,000 in stock of a new company, the number of shares to be issued, N, and the par value $P, could be anything—could be any number that the promoters might set so long as $N \times \$P = \$30,000$. Further, so far as the shareholders in this case were concerned, it was immaterial what "par" was so long as each one received the same number of shares for his $10,000 investment.

Against this familiar background of practice, however, it was easy for the courts—and legislatures—to take a next assumption, and it early became a matter of common understanding, that the "par value" was what the shareholder *ought* to have paid for his stock. Stock which was issued without a corresponding pay-in of assets valued at an amount equal to par was called "watered stock"—stock issued not against assets but against water. (The term also echoed an

Investor paid less than par value

ancient sharp practice in another field, the aquatizing of livestock before weighing them in for sale.) The term "bonus shares" was reserved to describe shares that were issued to someone who had paid in nothing for them. Bonus shares and watered stock obviously gave the recipient shareholder a free, or cut-rate, ride, to the disadvantage of the other shareholders who had put more assets per share into the corporate pot. * * *

It will be clear to the reader that the development of the "par" concept just described arose as a response to the problems of assuring equitable contribution among shareholders. But development of the shareholder's par payment obligation served, in a somewhat fortuitous and naive way, to further the corporate creditor's interest in seeing shareholder assets committed to the enterprise. One can spin at least a hypothetical argument as to why this should be and how it came to be.

If a creditor extends credit immediately after the incorporation of the new enterprise and if he has been informed that the par value of the shares is P and the number of shares that have been issued is N, it is not unreasonable for him to assume that the shareholders have collectively contributed into the corporate treasury an amount of dollars equal to the par value of the shares issued multiplied by the number of shares that were issued, or $PN. In a kind of rough and ready way, assuming that there have been no other transactions, the creditor might infer that the number $PN is an approximation of the total assets of the corporation, and on that basis might conclude that he could safely lend a certain amount of funds to the enterprise.

Did any rational creditor ever in fact act that way or extend credit on such a naive basis? The answer has to be "no." But two things did occur.

First, the number $PN came in time to be called in legal discourse the corporation's "capital."

Second, if the enterprise ultimately went broke, and the creditor did not get paid, and he found out at that later time that some shareholder had *not* in fact paid into the corporate treasury an amount of assets equal to the par value of the shares he had received, the creditor's lawyer would certainly *argue* in a suit against the shareholder that: (i) Everyone knows that shareholders should pay into the corporate treasury assets equal to the par value of the shares issued to them; (ii) the defendant shareholder did not pay in that amount; (iii) the corporation is insolvent, creditors are unpaid, and the shareholders are not liable for the corporation's debts; (iv) therefore the court should require the defendant shareholder to pay over to this energetic suing creditor, to the extent of his claim against the corporation, the amount by which the defendant shareholder failed to pay in to the corporation assets equal to the aggregate par value of the stock he received; and (v) if (iv) does not appeal to the court as the appropriate remedy, then the defendant shareholder should be required to pay into *the corporate treasury* now for the benefit of all corporate creditors, the full amount by which he failed earlier to pay into the corporate treasury assets of a value equal to the aggregate par value of the shares he received.   *   *   *

[I]n time, this much became clear:

(i) The courts came to recognize that shareholders have some obligation to invest in the corporate enterprise;

(ii) It came to be understood (perhaps "assumed" is a better word) that the measure of the shareholder's liability was the number of shares issued to him times the par value of the shares; and

(iii) It came to be recognized that at least some creditors could in at least some circumstances enforce this obligation of the shareholder in some way.   *   *   *

In the nineteenth century pattern of corporate financing, it was simply assumed that good companies—respectable companies—solid investments—would have stock with a high par value. It is a tribute, indeed, to the power of mythology and folklore, that the buying market, the investment bankers who feed it, corporate managements, and their legal counsel all continue today to feel considerably more comfortable with a $50 par stock and cannot say "penny stock" without a sneer. And it remains true today that most "preferred" stocks continue to carry a high par value. Nonetheless, eventually the practical argument prevailed and the invariable practice of using high par value common stock gradually gave way to the use of low par common stock.   *   *   *

With this shift made, a typical transaction might see a promoter (*i.e.*, his lawyer) set a par of $10 per share and a *higher* subscription agreement, say $50 per share. What difference does it make to any shareholder that the par is lower than the purchase price, so long as each initial equity investor pays in the same amount per share? With this development, however, the prototype corporate model outlined earlier is reduced to splinters. If the subscription agreement calls for $50 per share for the $10 par stock, but the subscriber-shareholder pays in only $5 per share, should a subsequent unpaid corporate creditor be able at a later time to force an additional payment of $5— to bring the shareholder's contribution up to the par value of $10—or should he be able to enforce a liability of $45—the balance the shareholder had agreed to pay under the subscription agreement? At this point it becomes conceptually critical whether the creditor is suing on a theory of statutory obligation of the shareholder to pay par, or on a conceptual theory of enforcement of the shareholder's obligation to pay the corporation in accordance with the terms of the subscription. More important for present analytical purposes, the separation of par and purchase price has the effect of opening a chasm between the lawyer's perspective and economist's concept of the enterpreneur's capital investment. If there are ten subscribers in a newly incorporated enterprise each of whom buys 10 shares of stock at a price of $50 per share, the economist, or the businessman would say that the company's beginning "capital" is $5,000.   But the lawyer (and later the accountant) will tell the economist or the businessman that the "capital" is determined by par, and in this case is the number of issued shares, 100, multiplied by the par value of each share, $10, for a total of $1,000; the other $4,000 is something else about which we will hear more later.   With the evolution of low par stock, came the evolution of that strange lawyer's convention, "legal capital"—the $1,000 in the example just given.

* * *

It was not until 1912 that analysis of the matter had reached a sufficiently wide circle to produce statutory authorization of no par stock.   The advent of no par stock did not, however, have the effect of eliminating the concept of legal capital.   It was, and still is, statutorily necessary to designate some dollar number on the corporate balance sheet as "capital."   Since, with no-par stock, it is no longer possible to calculate what the "capital" is by multiplying the number of shares issued times the par value, a "capital" number can be arrived at for this purpose only by fiat—by declaration—by stating it. The responsibility for making that statement, and the power to make it, is placed by corporation statutes with the board of directors, and the dollar number declared by them made in the customary form of a board resolution, is the "stated capital" of the corporation.   It remains so until such time as it is changed to something else by means set forth in the corporation act.   The accountants accept this designation of "stated capital" and it appears on the right hand side of the corporate balance sheet as the corporate "capital."

Although no-par stock is common in the world of contemporary corporate finance, it is interesting that it has not preempted the field, and par stock continues to be in majority use.   This is true for several reasons.   For a long time, the computational method of the federal stamp act on stock issuance favored par against no par stock and some state franchise tax provisions still do.   Additionally, for a careful lawyer concerned about such things, it is appealing that a low par value on a share of stock sets the outer limit of liability of a subscriber-shareholder as against a creditor's claims, whereas in the case of no par stock the subscriber's liability would appear inevitably—for want of any other criterion—to be measured by the full amount that he agreed to pay for each share of the stock.   More important than either of these factors, however, are the two points referred to in the discussion of par stock.   To the market's ear, no par stock does not quite have the same ring of virtue as par stock (though it sounds better than "penny stock").   At the same time, the use of lower par values, and the ease of shareholder amendment to reduce par in situations where the par proved not to have been low enough, combined to make par stock a usable tool in the hands of the experienced corporate practitioner.

* * *

What does the law do to prevent shareholders of a distressed company from pulling assets out of the corporate treasury just when the creditor needs them? * * *

Two basic propositions slowly emerged: (1) The measuring rod for judging the propriety or impropriety of the distributions to equity holders is the corporation's "capital"; and (2) "capital" refers not to assets but to that abstract number that is obtained by multiplying the number of shares of stock outstanding by the par value assigned to each share. Following the emergence of low par and no par stock, the next step was, of course, to expand the second of these propositions to read that "capital" means "stated capital," or "legal capital."
* * *

The general concept of the legal capital scheme is that no distribution may be made to shareholders unless there is a "surplus"—that is, sufficient assets in the corporation to pay off the creditors *plus* an additional amount of assets greater than the "stated capital." If the accounting entries representing the enterprise's assets do not total to a figure equal to the indebtedness of the enterprise plus the "capital", the capital is said to be "impaired" and the stock is said to be "under water". In such a condition (if one assumes that the figures on the assets side of the corporation's balance sheet are equal to their sell-off value), if all the assets were to be sold off for cash, and if all creditors were to be paid off, the money that would be left for the equity investors, the shareholders, would be less than the "capital" they put into the enterprise in the first place. Where that is the condition, the statutory scheme forbids the distribution of assets to shareholders by dividend or otherwise. * * *

The following statements may now be made about "legal capital".

a. Legal capital is a number expressed in dollars.

b. That number is initially the product of par value—itself an arbitrary dollar amount printed on the stock certificate and recited in the certificate of incorporation—multiplied by the number of shares "outstanding."

c. Legal capital is a number that appears on the *right-hand,* or claimant's side of the balance sheet, *not* on the left hand asset side. "Legal capital" is *not* an asset, a fund, or a collection of assets. And it does not refer to an asset, a fund, or a collection of assets. (The same is true of "surplus.")

d. Legal capital is a number that can at best be read to convey a message by implication—a message about an historical event. It can be read to imply that a valuation of at least that amount was placed upon some indeterminate assets that were transferred to the corporation at some indeterminate past time in exchange for shares then issued.

Legal capital is entirely a legal invention, highly particularized in its meaning, historical in reference, *and not relatable in any way to the ongoing economic condition of the enterprise.* For most purposes, it is best thought of simply as a dollar number—a number having certain consequences and derived by specified statutory procedures, but just a number.

The law makes use of the concept of "legal capital" in two ways:

a.   It is the maximum number of dollars up to which someone might in certain circumstances be able sometime to hold some shareholders liable if the implied statement in [a–d] above could be proved to be false.

b.   It is a datum line, or water table, or bench mark, or nock on a measuring stick laid along side the total number on the asset side of the balance sheet, on the basis of which lawyers will—or will not—sign an opinion that a proposed distribution of corporate assets to shareholders is valid, legal, and generates no liabilities either for the board of directors that declares it or the shareholders who receive it.

And here is the real bite.   In the world of corporate finance, transactions are utterly dependent upon opinions of legal counsel.   If the financial lawyers are unwilling to opine favorably upon the legality of a corporate transaction, or a subcomponent of it, the transaction will usually not go through.   Whenever a corporate financial transaction requires the lawyers to inquire into a company's legal capital position, the impact of the statutory schemes of legal capital is enormously magnified by the Go/No-go function performed by opinions of counsel.   The lawyers, in turn, are compelled to develop an understanding of the statutory scheme and of its application.   From that state of affairs "legal capital" draws its vitality, and this small book draws its functional relevance.

3.   THE ISSUANCE OF STOCK AND SHAREHOLDERS' LIABILITIES

a.   Quantity of consideration

Under a regime of legal capital marked by the use of par value, corporation law was much consumed, as Dean Manning notes, with the question of "watered stock."   It was common practice for corporate promoters to issue stock to themselves for assets valued at more than their true worth.   This practice inflated the left hand side of the company's balance sheet with overvalued assets.   Of perhaps greater concern to the law, the legal capital that appeared on the right-hand-side of the ledger was higher than it should properly have been.   The excess over the true value of assets consisted of nothing more substantial than "water," providing no benefit or cushion to creditors should the company get in difficulty. Such a company was, from the outset, "under water."

The response of the law to this situation, to require payment for stock equal to par value, was difficult to enforce. Where the promoters consciously watered their stock in an effort to deceive other investors by representing to them that the corporation's assets were more valuable than was in fact the case, there was other, more straight forward, remedies, such as an action for fraud, but which required different kind of proof.

The difficulties of enforcing liability for watered stock are illustrated by the leading case of Hospes v. Northwestern Manufacturing Co., 48 Minn. 174, 50 N.W. 1117 (1892). Assets with a value of $2,265,000 were transferred to a company in exchange for preferred stock with an aggregate par value of the same amount. With this there was no problem. But the promoters also issued themselves common stock with a par value of $1,500,000. A judgment creditor later sought to recover from the shareholders the par value of this bonus stock. The plaintiff did not allege that it was ignorant of the bonus shares or that it had been deceived or injured in any way by the issuance; instead, the plaintiff argued that the capital of the corporation—the aggregate par value of the outstanding shares—constituted a "trust fund" for the benefit of the creditors, a theory supported by earlier authority. Rejecting this theory, the court held that the right of a creditor to compel holders of bonus stock to pay in its par value (even though they had not contracted to do so) must rest on a finding that creditors had somehow been defrauded. The court said:

> The phrase that "the capital of a corporation constitutes a trust fund for the benefit of creditors" is misleading. Corporate property is not held in trust, in any proper sense of the term. The trust implies two estates of interests—one equitable and one legal; one person, as trustee, holding the legal title while another, as the *cestui que trust* has the beneficial interest. Absolute control and power of this position are inconsistent with the idea of a trust. The capital of a corporation is its property. It has the whole beneficial interest in it, as well as the legal title. It may use the income and profits of it, and sell and dispose of it, the same as a natural person. It is a trustee for its creditors in the same sense and to the same extent as a natural person, but no further.

50 N.W. at 1119.

The court reasoned that the right of the creditor to recover must rest on grounds "that the acts of the stockholders with reference to the corporate capital constitutes a fraud on their rights." *Id.* at 1120. But an action in fraud demands a showing that the defrauded party relied on the deceit. Any person who was a creditor prior to the issuance of the bonus shares obviously did not rely on the capital contributed by those shareholders and was unaffected by the fact that the shares were issued without consideration. Such a person would have no action for watered stock. Were creditors who extended credit after the issuance of the bonus stock defrauded? Starting from (as Dean Manning has demonstrated) the probably incorrect premise that the stated capital is the basis on which people deal with the corporation and extend it credit, the court reasoned that creditors have the right to assume that the stated capital has been paid. The fraud on subsequent creditors consists in the misrepresentation of the amount of the stated capital. Subsequent creditors (not the corporation or creditors asserting a corporate cause of action) who were deceived to their detriment by the misrepresentation of stated capital may sue the shareholders for the unpaid consideration. The court dispensed with any requirement that a creditor allege and prove actual reliance, although it did say that the shareholders could attempt to show that the creditors knew of the failure to pay the par value of their stock by way of an affirmative defense.

Professor Ballantine, after criticizing the fictitious nature of the "holding out" theory as a rationale for imposing liability on shareholders to subsequent creditors for watered or bonus stock, suggested as follows:*

> The capital stock of a corporation is the basis of its credit, not because of actual reliance by creditors on the precise amount of stock issued, but because the contributions of the stockholders are the substitute for their personal liability. It is not any misrepresentation of fact as to the amount of paid-in capital which is the basis of liability, but the obligation imposed by law on the stockholder to contribute capital as an incident of membership in a limited liability corporation. This obligation is in the nature of an asset of the corporation and should be available to prior creditors and to subsequent creditors with notice as well as to those whose debts were contracted after the subscription without notice.
> * * *

The liability of shareholders with respect to their acquisition of stock from the company is codified by such provisions as Section 162 of the Delaware statute. The extent of the liability is stated to be "the sum necessary to complete the amount of the unpaid balance of the consideration for which shares were issued or to be issued by the corporation." The present language of the statute replaced a former version which provided liability up to the par value of par value stock and the unpaid balance of the consideration for no-par stock.

Some nagging interpretative questions remain. Suppose the company issues $5 par value stock to the public at a price of $10 per share, but sells to the promoter for $7. Does the "consideration for which shares were issued" mean the general price of $10 or the particular $7 price? The reporter for the present revision of the statute

* Ballantine, Stockholders' Liability in Minnesota, 7 Minn.L.Rev. 79, 90 (1922).

says that it means $10 because otherwise the sale "would thwart the statutory purpose of protecting creditors of the insolvent corporation." *See* E. Folk, The Delaware Corporation Law 163 (1972). Surely that is correct if the promoter purchased the shares for $3, because issuance of shares for less than par value is prohibited by Section 153. However, when the price paid exceeds par value, is it so clear that the statutory purpose has been frustrated?

Suppose the promoter (or any shareholder) transfers non-cash consideration for stock, and the identified property is stated to be the "consideration payable for the shares." If the stock has an aggregate par value of $10,000 but the property is later determined to be worth $5,000, is there liability under Section 162? The promoter has, in fact, paid the consideration that was to be paid for the issuance of the stock. But the corporation is required to translate the consideration into dollars to test whether par value has been paid. Arguably, there is liability for fraud if there was a misrepresentation on the balance sheet, but that is a different case, requiring different proof from that required to recover under Section 162. Reading the statute as a whole, the requirement to pay at least par would seem to control the obligation.

If the promoter promises to pay $10 for $5 par value stock, but then pays only $5, has the stock been validly issued? The standards of Section 153 have been met. However, is the stock fully paid and non-assessable? In other words, is there liability under Section 162 when the whole of the promised consideration has not been paid?

The issue is simplified under Section 25 of the Model Act because notions of par value do not figure in the issuance of stock. However, the question remains as to whether the promoter who buys for less than the general price must lose his bargain.

b. Valuation Revisited

In determining whether a corporation has issued watered stock, valuation of the assets transferred to the corporation by the shareholders becomes critical. For example, if stock is issued in consideration for the transfer of a business, a determination must be made as to the value of that business. Under any legal regime, whether or not par value and legal capital are part of it, it will be necessary sooner or later for the directors to approve a balance sheet which translates the assets of the business into dollars—for financial reporting practices or for corporate law purposes or for both. When they do so should they record the value of the business as worth only the sum of the values of its separate assets, or should they use the usually higher going-concern value of the business? Reconsider Part I of the East Wind Boats problem.

The manner in which the valuation issue was handled under the traditional par value statutes is illustrated in another leading case, See v. Heppenheimer, 69 N.J. Equity 36, 61 A. 843 (1905). In that case, a group of promoters tried to monopolize the straw paper industry by buying 39 mills for the manufacture of straw paper and putting them together in one company. They paid $2,250,000 for the mills and then transferred them to the Columbia Straw Company for consideration consisting of one million dollars in bonds, one million dollars of preferred stock (at par value) and three million dollars (at par value) of common stock. Placing this total of $5 million of assets for which they had paid only $2,250,000 was not based purely on fancy. By creating a monopoly, the promoters projected that they could increase the profitability of the mills so greatly that $5 million would be a conservative estimate of their worth, calculated on a capitalization-of-earnings basis. Unfortunately for their scheme, it coincided with technological developments in the paper industry that made straw paper largely obsolete, and their would-be monopoly failed miserably. The creditors of the corporation subsequently sued the promoters for the unpaid consideration for their stock. The issue in the case was whether five million dollars was the proper valuation for the assets transferred to Columbia.

The court held that the promoters' approach to valuation was improper. Their good faith belief that they were embarking on a highly profitable venture was irrelevant. The prospective and contingent profits of the business were too speculative. They were held to have transferred only the value of the separate assets, which the court measured at their reproduction cost. There was no "good will" in this new business. According to the court, "It has made no business friends, nor any business reputation." 61 A. at 847.

However, it should be noted that in the later decision of Railway Review v. Groff Drill & Machine Tools Co., 84 N.J.Eq. 321, 91 A. 1021 (1914), the same court held that capitalizing the present earnings of an ongoing business, rather than relying on the book value of the assets, was not an overvaluation of the assets. The court distinguished See v. Heppenheimer by noting that there was a big difference between ascribing value to "prospective profits, arising from new conditions created by the fact of transfer," 91 A. at 1021, from basing value on established past and present earning capacity.

The modern approach to valuation in the context of watered stock liability, substantially lessens the possibility that shareholders who have transferred property to a corporation in exchange for their stock will be held liable to pay in additional consideration. The shareholder's liability, as we have observed, is determined under provisions like § 25 of the Model Act and § 162 of Delaware law. Even assuming that shareholders must pay no less than the minimum for which shares may lawfully be issued, it is commonly provided that the board's judgment as to the value of property exchanged for stock is conclusive, absent fraud, or, as in § 152 of Delaware law, in the absence of "actual fraud." The effect may be to make the good faith determination of the board of directors of the value of the property determinative. Interpretative questions still lurk, however: Does the "fraud" necessary to establish liability require that the directors have overvalued the assets with a specific intent to defraud creditors, or will something less do? And what does "good faith" mean? Must the directors take some affirmative action to justify value or is a "clean heart, empty head" sufficient? How does "actual fraud" differ from plain old "fraud"?

c. Quality of Consideration

A question closely related to the quantity of consideration is the quality or type of consideration for which stock may validly be issued. Even in times of rampant inflation cash is acceptable consideration for new stock. But what other forms of "property" may be acceptable may, at times, be unclear. State statutory requirements vary in their language and in the way the courts interpret them.

A good example is the service rendered by a promoter on behalf of the corporation during the pre-incorporation period. Such services may at times be denied the label of "labor or services actually performed for the corporation" (MBCA § 19) and may be treated as invalid past consideration because the corporation did not have the capacity to contract with the individual at the time of performance. Can the promoter, nonetheless, claim that he has contributed "property" and take back stock? While it may be difficult to avoid the conceptual muddle (except by such clear statutory provisions as New York Bus.Corp.L. § 504(a) or California Corp. Code § 409(a)(1)) which make clear that shares may be issued for "services actually rendered * * * for the corporation for its benefit in its formation of reorganization") courts have generally recognized the good sense in allowing individuals to be paid for pre-incorporation services. *E.g.,* Shore v. Union Drug Co., 18 Del.Ch. 74, 156 A. 204 (1931).

How can an individual possessing skills that are valuable to a corporation and in exchange for which the corporation may well want to issue stock for that stock contribute valuable consideration for that stock? Under MBCA § 19 an executory contract to render future services would be invalid consideration. Could the individual's special skills be treated as a form of intangible property such as good will? The accounting definition of the term, *i.e.,* the excess of consideration paid for a *going concern* over the value of the tangible assets, suggests a negative answer. Of course, if the value of the individual's knowledge was included as part of the purchase price of his or her sole proprietorship, then his or her "contribution" might be treated as valid property in a jurisdiction recognizing good will as consideration.

According to Professor Herwitz,*

The traditional concern about future services as consideration for stock lies chiefly in the fact that such services can prove valuable to a business only as a going concern and are totally devoid of realizable value for creditors or stockholders in the event of a liquidation of the enterprise. While of course other intangible items, notably goodwill, may prove worthless upon the failure of an enterprise, promised future services are subject to the special objection that they have no realizable value from the outset. Moreover, future services do not lend themselves readily to any objective standards for measuring the quantity of value involved. This difficulty is aggravated by the fact that such items are commonly transferred by the very people in control of the corporation, who thereby become judges of the amount of their own contributions. And in any event it has been common experience that corporate promoters are more likely to be extravagant when making payments in stock than when laying out hard cash. * * *

But a corporation can certainly make an advance payment of salary to an employee, probably in a fairly substantial amount, if it is necessary to induce someone with a particular skill to come to work for the enterprise. And it can probably also pay a bonus to such an employee if it is necessary to acquire his or her services. If such an advance payment or bonus could be then used by the employee to purchase stock, why not just short-circuit the process and allow the corporation to issue the stock directly in exchange for the promise of future services? That was, in fact the analogy used by the court in Petrishen v. Westmoreland Finance Corp., 394 Pa. 552, 147 A.2d 392 (1959), one of the few cases that approved the practice.

What about other related forms of "property?" Would a "business plan," for example, constitute valid consideration? *See* Scully v. Automobile Finance Co., 11 Del.Ch. 355, 101 A. 908, 909 (Ch. 1917) (holding that it was not, on grounds that it "was not salable or transferable, and had no commercial value, and was not property in any sense."). How about secret processes or formulas in the possession of the employee? It has been held that as long as the benefits to the corporation do not derive exclusively from the employee's services trade secrets can support the valid issuance of stock. *E.g.*, Durand v. Brown, 236 F. 609 (6th Cir. 1916); Kunkle v. Soule, 68 Colo. 524, 190 P. 536 (1920). But there are cases that hold the converse on the theory that the value of such items is too speculative. *E.g.*, O'Bear-Nester Glass Co. v. Antiexplo Co., 101 Tex. 431, 108 S.W. 967 (1908).

If the stock is issued and the employee performs the services or transfers a trade secret with real value, it may become difficult for the corporation to challenge the initial issuance. *Cf.* Vineland Grape Juice Co. v. Chandler, 80 N.J.Eq. 437, 85 A. 213 (1912) (in order to

---

* Herwitz, Allocation of Stock Between Services and Capital in the Organization of a Close Corporation, 75 Harv.L.Rev. 1098, 1105–6 (1962) (footnotes omitted).

attack issuance of stock corporation must at least tender value of work done for its benefit). By the same token, if the services are not performed or the "trade secret" turns out to be valueless, the corporation's remedies for breach of contract may include cancellation of the stock. Therm-O-Proof Insulation Mfg. Co. v. Hoffman, 329 Ill. App. 645, 69 N.E.2d 725 (1946); Trotta v. Metalmold Corp., 139 Conn. 668, 96 A.2d 798 (1953).

Promissory notes present another common problem in this area, and many states prohibit their use as consideration for stock, especially unsecured notes signed by a purchaser-shareholder. Suppose the note is secured? Calif.Corp.Code § 409(a)(1) provides that a promissory note "adequately secured by collateral other than the shares acquired * * *" is good consideration for the purchase of shares. Suppose the note is unsecured, but guaranteed? The court in Eastern Oklahoma Television Co. Inc. v. Ameco, Inc., 437 F. 2d 138 (10th Cir. 1971) held a personal guarantee of an obligation of the corporation was, in part, adequate consideration for the issuance of stock. *See also* Citizens Bank of Windsor v. Landers, 570 S.W.2d 756 (Mo.Ct.App.1978).

d. Liability for the Issuance of Stock for Inadequate or Invalid Consideration

Most jurisdictions impose statutory liability on the recipient of shares for which the full legal consideration has not been paid. Read MBCA § 25 and Del. GCL § 162. Unlike the common law principles relating to watered stock liability (exemplified by the approach of the *Hospes* case), these statutory provisions benefit *all* creditors, not just those who have extended credit subsequent to the issuance of the stock (and therefore might arguably have relied on the payment of full consideration). Note that under the Model Act, the obligation to pay the full amount agreed to be paid (presumably no less than the minimum allowed under law), runs to the corporation. However, if the corporation is insolvent this remedy is for the benefit of the creditors. If the corporation is healthy, cancellation of the shares may be the more appropriate remedy. But if all other shareholders acquiesce in the issuance of stock for invalid consideration and accept the benefits of the transaction, the corporation may be estopped from seeking the cancellation of these shares. Herwitz, Allocation of Stock Between Services and Capital in the Organization of a Close Corporation, 75 Harv.L.Rev. 1098, 1108 n. 37 (1962).

e. Avoiding Liability Under the Regime of Par Value

The problems of watered stock liability arose initially from the business fact that when stock was issued (at least on the organization of a company) it was almost always issued at par value of $100. The difficulties posed by the threat of liability made it inevitable that lawyers would devise a way around them. One approach was to issue stock *without* par value. The suspicion that this practice, calculated as it was to avoid what was at least nominally a set of rules designed to protect creditors, might not be entirely cricket was overcome by amendments to corporation statutes to authorize no-par stock. (*See, e. g.,* Del. GCL § 153.)

A second practice, that did not require statutory amendments, was to use of "low-par" stock. The particular par value was an arbitrary choice in the first place, and it was necessary only to change habits of thought and legal custom to set a different arbitrary but low figure. Thus, if the plan was to issue stock at $100 a share, the articles of incorporation might set its par at $1 per share. Subscribers could then exchange property valued at $100 per share for their stock with scant fear that a court might subsequently find they had paid too little for their stock (and impose on them the obligation to make up the difference) so long as the property was worth at least $1 per share.

Either of these techniques also avoided the embarrassing situation that confronted a corporation that had initially sold $100 par value stock at par. For example, a corporation which had not been successful, might be faced with the need to raise new capital. Since the new stock to be issued would probably not be salable at $100 per share, how would it be possible to raise the necessary capital without selling "watered" or "discount" stock? One answer was given by the leading case of Handley v. Stutz, 139 U.S. 417, 11 S.Ct. 530, 35 L.Ed. 227 (1891), which allowed a corporation so situated to issue the new stock at less than par. But unless courts of the jurisdiction in which the business was incorporated had clearly announced that they would follow that rule, the only safe course was probably to reduce the par value of the shares by amending the articles of incorporation, a technique that was not only awkward from a practical standpoint, but might pose different legal problems. The use of low-par or no-par stock resolved the problem nicely, although it admittedly did little to further the avowed policy of watered-stock liability.

The standard practice of well-informed corporate draftsmen today is to use either low-par or no-par stock, the choice often depending on the manner in which the relevant jurisdiction calculates the tax or "franchise fee" payable on incorporation, which is frequently calculated on the basis of the aggregate authorized capital of the corporation (with no-par stock "deemed" to have some arbitrary par for the purpose).

One realizes that since these devices have become commonplace the jig is up,—the regime of par value and legal capital is dead.

f. Legal Capital Under the Revised Model Act

MBCA § 18(a) abolishes par value stock, and MBCA § 54 omits any provision that the articles must specify whether the stock is par or no par.* Shares may be issued for such consideration as authorized by the board, at a fixed price, a minimum price, based on a formula or other method of price determination. According to the comment of the Corporate Laws Committee of the American Bar Association, the drafting group of the Model Act, to MBCA § 18, "The provision for a minimum price or a formula or other method for determining the price is included in order to give greater flexibility in issuing the shares in accordance with the limitations set forth by the board and to allow such variations in the price as may be necessary or appropriate to reflect the changing market conditions." 34 Bus. Lawyer 1867, 1879 (1979). In other words, business conditions—and not the artificial notion of par value—are to determine the price for which shares may be issued. The issuance of shares still requires valid consideration which must be expressed in dollars. But whatever the method of fixing the price chosen by the board, the amount of consideration paid for the shares need no longer fit the Procrustean bed of par value in order for the stock to be legally issued. There is thus no incentive, at least none under corporate law, to exaggerate the value of the consideration paid for the shares. The revision did not alter the liability provisions of § 25. How would See v. Heppenheimer, *supra*, be decided under the revised Model Act?

g. Note: Preemptive Rights and Other Duties in the Issuance of Shares

The precise number of shares that a stockholder owns in a corporation at a particular time determines his position relative to others. What is important, however, is not so much the *number* of shares, as the *percentage* of shares.

Therefore, a shareholder's interest in the corporation will be diminished and adversely affected if additional shares are sold to other investors. We refer to this as the "dilution" of his interest.

On closer analysis, we can see that the statements made above, at one time accepted almost as gospel, may not hold true. If the additional shares are sold at a price that reflects the fair value of those shares, and if the proceeds received for their sale is used by the corporation to produce income at least equal to the rate of return on the existing capital, the shareholder's economic interest will not be diluted but may even be increased. For example, if the company has 100 shares of common stock issued and outstanding, and if the excess of

---

* MBCA § 54(d) formerly provided that articles must specify:

d. [T]he aggregate number of shares which the corporation shall have authority to issue; if such shares are to consist of one class only, the par value of each such shares, or a statement that all the shares are without par value. * * *

assets over liabilities equals $10,000, then each share has a book value of $100. The sale of another 50 shares at $100 per share would not dilute the economic value of anyone's shares, provided the company can profitably employ the new $5,000. Sale at a price above $100 would increase the value of all the outstanding shares. Of course, the holder of 25 shares, who once was able to cast 25% of the voting power of the corporation will now only be about to cast one-sixth of the voting power. His voting power has been diluted. In a small corporation this dilution may have real economic consequences. However, if the corporation had 10 million shares outstanding the stockholders' 100 shares gave him a voting interest of 1,000th of 1%, and to talk of a 50% dilution of that interest is not very useful. Further, if there is a public trading market for the shares, a shareholder who wants to maintain his position can go into the market and buy more shares. The dilution the shareholder fears is a sale of shares well below the market price or the book value of the shares.

This suggests that the doctrine of preemptive rights has importance in some situations, but not in others. The state statutes, by and large, tend to be either like Section 26 or 26A of the Model Act. An exception is the New York Business Corporation Act, Section 622, which spells out the meaning of preemptive rights. In any event, what to do about the subject is largely a matter that must be focused on by the draftsmen of the articles of incorporation.

Few large companies continue to utilize preemptive rights as a means of financing, because of delays that it causes. To carry out a "rights offering," the corporation distributes to its shareholders a document, known as a warrant, entitling the holder to buy shares. The right might be to allow each 10 shares to purchase one new share, at a price *below* its current market value prior to a particular date. A holder of 105 shares will then receive 105 warrants, enabling him to buy 10½ shares. But franctional shares are not issued. What to do? If he can buy five more warrants he will then have enough to buy 11 shares. The warrants, then, have a value because each one represents 10% of the bargain—the difference between market price for the stock and the bargain price offered to shareholders. Conversely, our shareholder can sell five of his warrants before they expire. He should have no trouble finding buyers because the warrants offer an opportunity to buy the shares at a bargain price. Thus, a market develops for the warrants during their brief existence.

The availability of preemptive rights presents a number of technical issues that courts have dealt with over the years. The issuance of previously authorized but heretofore unissued shares has been thought not to be subject to preemptive rights, on the theory that this was the fulfillment of an anticipated dilution. Dunlay v. Avenue M. Garage & Repair Co., Inc., 253 N.Y. 274, 170 N.E. 917 (1930). However, it is not uncommon for corporations to authorize more shares than they intend to issue initially, and preemptive rights are sometimes applied to the issuance of those shares, especially if they have been unissued for many years. *See* N. Lattin, Corporations 495 (2d ed. 1971).

When shares are issued for property, as distinct from cash, the existing shareholders are unable to match the purchase price. The corporation may be prejudiced if preemptive rights apply, and some courts have declined to allow that. Thom v. Baltimore Trust Co., 158 Md. 352, 148 A. 234 (1930).

An exception is also found for shares issued to employees in connection with compensation plans. *See* N.Y.Bus.Corp.Law § 622(e)(2). Although payment is made in cash, the issuance of these shares is related to the unique services contributed. In practical fact, application of preemptive rights could kill employee stock plans.

More important for the protection of stockholders are equitable principles that govern the issuance of stock.

Hyman v. Velsicol Corp., 342 Ill.App. 489, 97 N.E.2d 122 (1951), concerned a closely held corporation organized by an inventor and his financial backers. The inventor (plaintiff in this suit) acquired 20% of the stock for his patents; the financiers each bought 40% of the stock. The company enjoyed great success. The inventor sought a larger stock interest, and refused to assign to the company certain new patents until this was done. Failing in that effort, the inventor resigned from Velsicol and formed a new company to manufacture his new product, but Velsicol Corp. succeeded in a suit to compel assignment of the new product.

Velsicol's board then adopted a plan of recapitalization. The 200 shares outstanding were "split" into 2000 shares (that merely increased by 10 times the shares each person owned), par value was decreased from $100 to $10 (keeping the aggregate par value unchanged). The board voted to authorize 100,000 new shares and to issue 68,000 new shares at $10 per share.

Preemptive rights applied to the new shares, and the financiers exercised their rights. They did so by surrendering notes evidencing prior loans they had made to their corporation plus a relatively small amount of cash. Capitalization of the notes (*i.e.*, changing debt into equity) had been urged by the company's banks to improve its financial position.

Plaintiff objected to the plan, and rather than pay $136,000 in cash for the shares he was entitled to buy to maintain his relative position (which he was required to do within 12 days), he brought suit to enjoin the transaction. The lower court agreed since it found the plan was inequitable and motivated only by a desire to "oppress and defraud" plaintiff.

The appellate court reversed and denied the relief. It found that the plan "was legal and not unfair." Among other things, the court found there was no merit in plaintiff's contention that the par value was insignificant compared to the true value. "The directors were not required to recommend the stock at a price equivalent to the 'true value.'" The court also noted that "if the plan was legal and fair, the questions of defendants' state of mind with respect to plaintiff and as to the effect of the plan on his interests are immaterial."

The court concluded as follows:

We think that the right which plaintiff had to a proportionate share of the new stock issued at the new par value was respected in this case by the issuance to him of the additional stock, arising from the stock split, and the issuance to him of subscription warrants * * * By the issuance of the additional stock and the preemptive rights to plaintiff he was given the opportunity to protect his pro-rata interest in the corporation. The defendants were not to blame for his failure to obtain the money necessary for him to avail himself of his preemptive rights * * *.

97 N.W.2d at 125.

Does this case load too much freight on the slender shoulders of preemptive rights? Apparently Velsicol's maximum earnings in any one year after 1940 was just over $350,000. It is not unreasonable to assume that this figure gives at least a crude indication of the magnitude of earnings during the last few years. Capitalized at 25%, the stock outstanding at the time of the transaction had a value of approximately $1,500,000. Since, after the recapitalization, there were 2,000 shares outstanding, this means that each share stock had a value of about $700. If the calculation is even close to correct, the controlling stockholders were purchasing stock at a small fraction of its fair value. Of course, Hyman *was* given an opportunity to protect his interests by purchasing at the same price as the other shareholders, but this would have required him to come forth with the sum of $136,000 within a relatively short period of time. It is significant that the court holds that it was enough that he was afforded his preemptive rights and that it need not inquire otherwise into the fairness of the transaction. Perhaps the court was reacting to Hyman's own not entirely honorable behavior.

On the question of fairness of price, Katzowitz v. Sidler, 24 N.Y. 2d 512, 301 N.Y.S.2d 470, 249 N.E.2d 359 (1969), held that the issuance of stock at less than fair value can injure shareholders by forcing them to invest additional sums to avoid dilution of their interest.

Of course investors can sell their warrants, which theoretically have large value. But in a close corporation, where there is no market for the stock, that right is an illusion.

In *Katzowitz* the stock was offered at its par value of $100 when its economic value was $1,300. The purpose was to eliminate plaintiff's interest. The court commented, "The price was not so much a bargain as it was a tactic, conscious or unconscious on the part of the directors, to place Katzowitz in a compromising situation." 249 N.W. 2d at 365.

In Schwartz v. Marien, 37 N.Y.2d 487, 373 N.Y.S.2d 122, 335 N.E. 2d 334 (1975), preemptive rights did not apply at all because the corporation issued treasury shares. *See* Section 622(e)(4) of the New York Bus.Corp.Act. The board issued three shares to members of the family group which had been a 50% owner and two shares to long term employees. The plaintiff, a member of the other 50% family group, demanded the right to buy five additional shares, but she was refused by the board.

The court found that there was a fiduciary obligation that protects shareholders in the issuance of shares even when its articles of incorporation have abolished preemptive rights. A bona fide business purpose could justify unequal treatment of shareholders, but the burden of planning such justification rested with the directors. This is particularly so in a close corporation; "not only must it be shown that it was sought to achieve a bona fide independent business objective, but as well that such objective could not have been accomplished substantially as effectively by other means which would not have disturbed proportionate stock of ownership." 335 N.E.2d at 338.

Proof of fraud of conspiracy was not required. "Rather, plaintiff's rights of recovery depends on proof of breach of its fiduciary duty owed by the directors to plaintiff-appellant stockholder." *Id.*

Does it appear that the legal device of preemptive rights does not always serve to protect the interests of those in need, and that the absence of preemptive rights will not deter the courts from achieving fairness?

D.   DIVIDENDS AND OTHER DISTRIBUTIONS

PROBLEM

EAST WIND BOATS—PART VIII

At the end of its first year after the sale, East Wind Boats, Inc.'s balance sheet, prior to the payment of any dividend, is as appears on page 201.

Assume that Hardy, Luff and Teach invested $100,000 in the company and received 1,000 shares of common stock, the only stock that was issued. The company has also issued a ten year note in the amount of $50,000 to Stern and Star that appears on the balance sheet as a long term liability. The company made a profit from its operations of $5,000.

For purposes of this problem, note that there are no shares of preferred stock.

	Assets		Liabilities and Shareholders' Equity	
Assets			**Liabilities**	
Current Assets			Current Liabilities	
Cash		$ 40,000	Accounts Payable	$ 50,000
Accounts Receivable		35,000	Notes Payable (current portion)	10,000
Inventory		100,000	Accrued Expenses Payable	15,000
Total Current Assets		$175,000	Total Current Liabilities	$75,000
Fixed Assets			Long-Term Liabilities	
Land and Building		95,000	First Mortgage	50,000
Machinery and Equipment		130,000	Notes Payable	100,000
Furniture and Fixtures		10,000		
Less: Accumulated Depreciation		(90,000)		
Net Fixed Assets		145,000	Total Long-Term Liabilities	150,000
Other Assets			Shareholders' Equity	
			Common stock (1000 shs.)	100,000
Prepaid Items		10,000	Earned Surplus	5,000
Total Assets		$330,000	Total Liabilities and Shareholders' Equity	$330,000

1.   Can East Wind Boats, Inc., pay a dividend to its shareholders in the amount of $10,000 at this time?

2.   A dispute has arisen between Teach and the other shareholders. The parties have decided to resolve it by having the company repurchase Teach's 200 shares for $110,000. Assuming that the corporation can borrow sufficient money on a long term basis, can it make the purchase?

(3) Suppose the balance sheet shown above is for a date three years later. The company has paid no dividends and has not repurchased any shares. The company now wants to repurchase Teach's 200 shares for $75,000. The accountants have informed management that under generally accepted accounting principles the company must write down its assets by an amount of $50,000. Can it make the purchase?

4.   Suppose the balance sheet shown above is for a date three years after the corporation was formed, and no dividends have been paid and no stock has been repurchased. Hardy and Luff draw salaries from the business, but Teach does not. Management has been talking with one of its suppliers for two years about buying the supplier's business, but they have been constantly rebuffed. Teach has been demanding a dividend be paid in the amount of $30,000, but the other directors have opposed it. What is the likelihood that Teach would succeed in a suit to compel the payment of the dividend he seeks?

Answer the above questions on the following alternate assumptions:

(a) The corporation is incorporated in Delaware and the par value of the common stock is $100.

(b) The corporation is incorporated in Delaware and the stock is $10 par value.

(c) The corporation is incorporated under the MBCA.

Consider Del.Gen.Corp.Law §§ 160, 170, 244 and MBCA 6 and 45.

1. LEGAL SOURCES OF DIVIDENDS

a. Business Aspects

The payment—or at least the substantial possibility—of periodic dividends is a crucial attribute of corporate stock and its value. The gains that shareholders hope to reap from their investment may take the form of capital appreciation realized on the eventual sale of the stock, dividends received while it is held, or a combination of the two. (In theory shareholders might also wait to realize their gains upon the dissolution of the corporation, but profitable enterprises are seldom liquidated, and the promise of an indefinite return at an indefinite future time is not often likely to provide sufficient incentive for an investor to purchase stock.) For various reasons (most having something to do with federal income taxation) shareholders may be willing, or even eager to take most of their return in the form of capital appreciation and to forego the more immediate reward of a dividend. This is particularly true of a closely held corporation in which the shareholders are all employees and can take money out of the business in the form of salaries and other compensation. In the market for the shares of publicly-held corporations, however, it is the rare investor that is satisfied with relying entirely on capital gains; changes in the fortunes of a particular company, in business conditions generally, and the stock market make that too risky. Many investors, moreover, depend on the regular receipt of dividends as part of their income, especially when they invest in companies where stability, rather than growth, is the pattern. AT&T and public utilities are prime examples.

In raising capital by selling stock, corporations must compete with alternative uses of the funds of prospective investors, including consumption, the purchase of gold bars or diamonds, savings accounts, money market funds, government debt obligations, real estate, and the race track, just to mention a few. Consequently, corporations pay careful attention to gearing their dividend policy to maximize the value of their stock, thereby enabling them to raise capital at the lowest possible cost.

b. Legal Protection for Senior Interests

Decisions concerning the payment of dividends are not left entirely to the workings of the market place and the discretion of corporate managers. As Dean Manning demonstrated in the excerpt of Part C (2), *supra*, the interests of common shareholders in the size and frequency of dividend payments conflicts sharply with those of creditors. As the directors are elected by the stockholders and are principally accountable to them, the law has traditionally taken the view that trade creditors and the holders of debt instruments require some legal protection against the possibility that the board might adopt an overly-generous dividend policy.

Preferred stockholders are also in need of some protection from the payment of excessive dividends on the common stock. They normally are limited to the receipt of their preferred dividends, with the remaining profits being at the disposal of the common. Unless provision is made for some cushion to absorb the shock of a bad year, the preferred stockholders take nearly the same risks as the common without the potential of sharing in the benefits of a good year. The market price of preferred stock tends to reflect the size of that cushion. A less obvious concern of preferred stockholders, to which the law has paid little attention, is that a management policy of stingy dividends denies preferred stockholders the fruits of their investment.

The bulwark erected by the law to protect senior interests from the payment of excessive dividends takes two general forms, with many state statutes using both. First, virtually every corporation statute prohibits the payment of a dividend or other distribution of corporate assets to stockholders if the corporation is "insolvent" or would be rendered insolvent by the payment. There are two possible measures of insolvency, both of which are found in the Model Business Corporation Act. Section 45, as revised, prohibits dividends or stock repurchases when the corporation is unable to pay its debts as they come due in the usual course of business (the "equity sense" of insolvency) or when total assets are less than total liabilities plus any sum that would be paid to preferred shareholders in the event of liquidation (a strict interpretation of the "bankruptcy sense" of insolvency). The California statute uses a similar approach.

The second general approach to restricting corporate distributions uses the concept of legal capital and the associated notion of "surplus." One form of this approach permits dividends to be paid only to the extent that the corporation has "earned surplus." *   This term

---

* MBCA § 45(a) formerly provided:

Dividends may be declared and paid in cash or property only out of unre-served and unrestricted earned surplus of the corporation, except as otherwise provided in this section.

is generally defined** to mean a surplus which arises from the accumulation of profits during the life of the enterprise. While there are difficult interpretative questions involved in the meaning of the operative terms, the policy is plain enough. Dividends are supposed to be the fruit of the tree, and unless fruit has been borne, nothing can be picked. A more permissive version of this approach allows dividends to be paid out of "surplus," without regard to whether it is "earned" or some other kind of surplus.*** The theory underlying such provisions is that the cushion for creditors need be no more than the amount of the stated capital. The rest of the shareholders' equity account is "surplus," either "earned" or "capital," and is at the disposition of the shareholders.

In addition to the payments that might be made under one of the foregoing provisions, some states also permit the payment of dividends whenever the corporation has current earnings.† The statutes define current earnings in various ways, sometimes looking only to the most recent fiscal year, and sometimes looking to the preceding year, either alone or in combination with the current year. Such so-called "nimble dividend" provisions in effect allow the payment of dividends by currently profitable corporations even though the lack of available surplus requires the impairment of stated capital.

c. "Excessive" Dividends and the Failure of the Traditional Devices

The elaborate legal restrictions against payment of "excessive" dividends to common shareholders that have been built around the legal capital regime are another example of the failure of that concept. In plain fact, these limitations have proven insignificant in restricting pay-outs of cash. First, restricting dividends to a corporation's accumulated profits, shown by the earned surplus account on the balance sheet, is subject to a number of interpretative difficulties. While it is reasonable to believe that accounting conventions—notably the accounting profession's so-called generally accepted accounting principles—will determine the meaning of the key statutory terms, except in California that result is not mandated by the statute. Moreover, accounting conventions are not necessarily designed to serve the conceptual objectives of the legal regime as embodied in the cor-

---

** MBCA § 2(1) formerly provided:

"Earned surplus" means the portion of the surplus of a corporation equal to the balance of its net profits, income, gains, and losses from the date of incorporation * * *.

*** See e.g., Del. GCL § 170 N.Y.Bus. Corp.Law § 510. Before its revision, MBCA § 46 permitted "distributions" from capital surplus, and many states currently have such a rule. What is a "distribution?" Simply a cash payment not labeled a dividend that could be paid under § 45 if (1) there was surplus available, and (2) the articles of incorporation or a shareholder resolution authorized the payment. It is true that there might be some disadvantage in making a distribution that cannot be labeled a dividend, but that is a restriction imposed more by the market place than by the law.

† E.g., Del. GCL § 170. The former version of MBCA § 45 also included such a provision.

porate statute. In any case, many states have vitiated almost entirely the limitation on the payment of dividends only out of earned surplus by adopting the former version of MBCA § 46, which permits "distributions" out of *any* kind of surplus, including capital surplus.

The Delaware and New York restrictions, which adopt the policy of limiting the protection for senior security holders to legal capital, are subject to the manipulations that we have examined earlier. That is, the amount of legal capital consists of aggregate par value, and that figure can be set as low as management or the promoters elect to make it. An amount paid for the stock in excess of the par value constitutes capital surplus under the Delaware and New York statutes. That amount can be distributed to the shareholders if the corporation is neither insolvent nor would be rendered insolvent. We do not think of this as a dividend, and it may not be proper to label the payment a dividend, but it surely is a distribution with respect to stock that reduces the cash available to pay creditors. Thus, in effect part of the consideration paid for the stock can be paid out to the investor so long as the company can continue to pay its bills on time. That represents impairment or invasion of capital in the economic sense of the word. A creditor would be foolish to think legal restriction on dividends protects his interest under such circumstances.

The liberality of restrictions on dividend payment from stated capital may go even further, however. What else can surplus consist of? Suppose the corporation's real estate increases in value, as we know to be the general trend, due largely to the shrinking value of the dollar. Can the corporation now elect to restate the value of its real estate at the higher market price? If the corporation chooses to reflect the higher value, it will make an entry on the left side of the balance sheet (assets) which it will have to match by an equivalent increase on the right side of the balance sheet. The only account on the right side that could be increased is the shareholders' equity, more specifically, "surplus." It would probably not be earned surplus but some form of capital surplus, perhaps called "revaluation surplus." Thus, surplus, and dividend paying power, is increased simply by inflation and not by business operations. In the celebrated case of Randall v. Bailey, 23 N.Y.S.2d 173 (Sup.Ct.1940), aff'd 288 N. Y. 280, 43 N.E.2d 43 (1942), the court sustained the payment of a dividend that was based on the existence of a revaluation surplus created in this manner. The issue has been faced by few other courts, and Randall v. Bailey has not explicitly been followed anywhere else, although a decision in New York is by itself significant.

The standards of the accounting profession frown on this conduct as generally accepted accounting principles adhere to presentation of assets at historical cost. Thus, in any financial statement prepared or examined by accountants, the assets ordinarily cannot be written up to present values, regardless of what corporate law provides. At the same time, corporate managers are not beholden to accounting rules (although they may be influenced by them) and on a separate, but completely proper, set of books they can compute the amount available for distribution to shareholders.

In addition to the use of revaluation surplus (or where Randall v. Bailey is not accepted, *see e.g.*, Woodson v. Lee, 73 N.M. 425, 389 P.2d 196 (1963)) there are other legal techniques that can be used. Suppose the corporation decides to reduce the par value of each share of stock from $10 to $1. This procedure requires an amendment to the certificate of incorporation, which necessitates shareholder approval. *See, e.g.*, Del. GCL § 242. The stated capital account consists of the aggregate par value of the issued and outstanding shares, and that figure will be reduced by the reduction of par. Because the reduction of par value does not affect the left side of the balance sheet, the diminution of the stated capital account will have to be matched by an increase in some other account on the right side of the balance sheet, namely, surplus. Thus, lowering par value creates surplus (so-called "reduction surplus") out of which dividends may be paid under the Delaware or New York statutes.*

d. Protection Against Excessive Dividends Under the Model Act

The revisions to the Model Business Corporation Act abandon restrictions based on legal capital or surplus tests altogether. Instead, MBCA § 45 simply prohibits "distributions," as defined in § 2(i), if after the distribution (1) the corporation would be unable to pay its debts as they come "due in the usual course of its business," or (2) the corporation's total assets are less than its total liabilities plus any sum that would be paid to the preferred stock in the event of liquidation. Stated differently, after the payment of a dividend, the corporation must be able to pass both the equity and the bankruptcy tests of insolvency. Neither of these tests can be applied with mechanical precision; both require the exercise of judgment. Under the Act, the judgment is that of the directors. So long as they have acted in good faith and "with a reasonable basis for believing that the distribution authorized was permitted by statute, after due consideration of what they believed to be the relevant factors," * their judgment should be determinative. More specifically, the directors should determine whether the corporation can pay its debts by making a cash flow analysis "based on a business forecast and budget for a sufficient period of time to permit a conclusion that known obligations of the

---

* Stated capital may occasionally exceed the aggregate par value of the outstanding shares because the board of directors has chosen to allocate or convert all or part of the earned or capital surplus to stated capital. *See, e.g.*, Del. GCL § 154; N.Y.Bus.Corp.Law § 506. Statutes usually also authorize the reversal of this process by a reduction of capital by simple resolution of the board of directors (so long, of course, as it is not reduced below aggregate par value). *See, e.g.*, Del. GCL § 244; N.Y. BCL §§ 516, 517. This too, would increase the amount legally available to pay dividends. However, in the example in the text, § 244 would not be applicable because a reduction in stated capital is required.

* Comments to § 45, 34 Bus.Law. 1867, 1882 (1979).

corporation can reasonably be expected to be satisfied over the period of time that they will mature rather than a simple measurement of current assets against current liabilities * * *. * * * [T]he primary focus of the directors' decision to make a distribution should normally be on the corporation's prospects and obligations in the shorter term, unless special factors concerning the corporation's prospects require the taking of a longer term perspective." **

MBCA § 45(b) contains what Dean Manning calls "the big bomb."† The statute excises all the old tests of legal capital and surplus and instead authorizes the necessary asset and liability determinations to be made on the basis of (1) specified financial statements or (2) fair valuation or other reasonable method. Instead of adopting professional accounting concepts as the foundation of the balance sheet, as is followed in California (Compare Calif.Corp.Code § 114 and § 500 (b)), the Model Act leaves the issue to the judgment of the board.

The Comments of the Corporate Laws Committee explain:

> The determination of a corporation's assets and liabilities and the choice of the permissible basis on which to do so are left to the judgment of its board of directors. This is consistent with other authority granted a corporation's board of directors. In making a judgment under new section 45(b), the board may rely under section 35 upon opinions, reports or statements including financial statements and other financial data prepared or presented by public accountants or others, as provided in section 35 * * *.

> *Financial Statement Basis.* Incorporating technical accounting terminology and specific accounting concepts into new section 45 was rejected, principally because such terminology and concepts are constantly under review and subject to revision by the Financial Accounting Standards Board, the American Institute of Certified Public Accountants, the Securities and Exchange Commission and others. The Committee concluded that the Model Act should leave such determinations and resolutions of accounting matters to the judgment of the board of directors, taking into account its obligation to be reasonably informed as to pertinent standards of importance that bear upon the subject at issue.

> *   *   *

> While the directors will normally be entitled to use generally accepted accounting principles and to give presumptive weight to the advice of professional accountants with respect thereto, it is important to recognize that the new Section requires the use of accounting practices and principles that are reasonable in the circumstances, and does not constitute a statutory enactment of generally accepted accounting principles. In the view of the Committee, the widespread controversy concerning various accounting

** B. Manning, A Concise Textbook on   † *Id.*
Legal Capital, 171 (2d ed. 1981).

principles, and their constant reevaluation, requires a statutory standard of reasonableness, as a matter of law, recognizing that there may be equally acceptable alternative solutions to specific issues as well as areas requiring judgment in interpreting such principles. This does not mean that the statute is intended to reject the use and reliance upon generally accepted accounting principles; on the contrary, it is expected that their use would be the basic rule in most cases. The statutory language does, however, require informed business judgment in the entire circumstances in applying particular accounting principles to the circumstances that exist at the time, for purposes of the ultimate legal measurement of the validity of distributions.

If a corporation's financial statements are not presented in accordance with generally accepted accounting principles, however, a board of directors should normally carefully consider the extent to which the assets may not be fairly stated or the liabilities may be understated, to determine the fairness of the aggregate amount of assets and the aggregate amount of liabilities.

Fair Valuation Basis. New section 45 also gives specific authority for determinations on the basis of a fair valuation or other method that is reasonable in the circumstances. The statute accordingly specifically authorizes departures from historical cost accounting and sanctions the utilization of appraisal methods for the purpose of determining the fund available for distributions. In the view of the Committee, the prescription in the statute of a particular method or methods of valuation would be inadvisable, since different methods may have equal validity depending upon the circumstances, including the type of enterprise and the purpose for which the determination is made * * *. In most cases, a fair valuation method on a going concern basis would likely be appropriate, if expectations are that the enterprise will continue as a viable going concern. In determining the value of assets, all of the assets of a corporation, whether or not reflected in the financial statements (*e.g.*, a valuable executory contract), should be considered. Ordinarily a corporation should not selectively revalue assets. Likewise, all of a corporation's obligations and commitments should be considered and quantified to the extent appropriate and possible. In any event, new section 45(b) imposes upon the board of directors the responsibility of applying a method of determining the aggregate amounts of assets and liabilities that is reasonable in the circumstances.*

e. Stock Dividends

Not all dividends involve the distribution of cash to stockholders. Corporations occasionally distribute what are known as "stock divi-

---

* Comments, 34 Bus. Law at 1883–5 (1979).

dends" in which not cash, but additional shares of stock are distributed to the shareholders. In a pure economic sense, such a dividend results in no meaningful change in the financial state of the corporation at all. Its only consequence is that the shareholders' ownership in the corporation is divided among a greater number of shares. Indeed, often the principal reason for making such a "dividend" is to give the appearance of distributing something to the shareholders when the corporation is not in a position to pay a more meaningful dividend in cash. (Another, more substantial, reason may be to reduce the market price of the shares in order to make them more easily salable.)

Since a stock dividend does not result in the distribution of any of the corporation's assets, there is no need to place limitations on it for the protection of creditors. Indeed, because the par value (if any) of the shares distributed must be added to stated capital (*see, e. g.*, Del. GCL § 173) a stock dividend can actually benefit creditors. Consequently the law is generally less restrictive of the payment of stock dividends. MBCA § 18(b) requires only that the dividend be permitted in the articles of incorporation or by shareholder vote. Some states that still have a surplus test for dividends expressly permit the use of revaluation surplus for stock dividends.

f. Repurchase of Shares

There are variety of reasons why a corporation might want to repurchase some of its outstanding stock. It may have liquid assets that it finds itself unable to put to productive use. Such a corporation is said to be "over-capitalized," and it can increase the earnings of its remaining shareholders by repurchasing some of its stock. A close corporation may wish to repurchase shares pursuant to stock transfer restriction agreement of the sort discussed in Chapter 11. It may be necessary for a corporation that is party to a merger or sale of assets to purchase the shares of shareholders who exercise their appraisal rights. See Chapter 20, Part C(2). Repurchase of stock is occasionally used as a tactic in fighting off a takeover attempt. (See Chapter 22, *infra.*). A repurchase on a pro rata basis has almost exactly the same effect as a dividend, the only difference being that the number of shares outstanding is also reduced pro rata.

Whatever the business motive for the repurchase, and whether it is pro rata or all from one shareholder, the effect is to take assets from the corporation and put them in the hands of the shareholders. The impact on creditors is the same as if the corporation had paid a dividend. Consequently, corporation statutes generally impose restraints on the repurchase of stock similar to those imposed on dividends. New York, for example, generally permits repurchases only out of surplus (of any kind), although it allows repurchase or redemption of redeemable shares out of capital (N.Y. BCL § 513). Delaware prohibits the repurchase of common stock if it would impair capital

(Del. GCL § 160), which amounts to essentially the same thing. The former version of MBCA § 6 allowed repurchase only out of "unrestricted and unreserved * earned surplus" unless the articles of incorporation of a shareholder resolution gave authority for a repurchase out of capital surplus. The revised version of the Model Act handles the repurchase of shares by defining it as a "distribution" in § 2(i), thus subjecting it to the limitations contained in § 45. 6.40

Once reacquired, shares are treated by most statutes as "treasury stock." They remain technically "issued," but are, of course, not "outstanding." If treasury shares are resold (technically they are "sold" and not "issued" although there seems to be little or no practical distinction), the restriction imposed on surplus when they were purchased is eliminated.

Treasury shares may generally not be voted by the corporation. (*E.g.*, Del. GCL § 160(c).)

The revised version of the Model Act has eliminated the concept of treasury shares altogether. MBCA § 6 now provides that reacquired shares automatically revert to the status of authorized but unissued stock, thereby avoiding the unnecessary complexity of the prior law.

2. LIABILITY FOR UNLAWFUL DISTRIBUTIONS

We have already examined one form of liability growing out of the regime of legal capital: the right of a creditor to sue the recipients of watered stock for the difference between what they paid in and the par value of the stock they received or the consideration promised, if greater than par. An unlawful distribution to the stockholders has much the same effect on creditors as a sale of watered stock—the reduction of the assets of a corporation below the amount of stated capital—but the remedy is somewhat different. MBCA § 48, which is fairly typical, makes the directors who voted for a dividend, distribution, or repurchase of stock that violates the restrictions of the Act liable to the corporation. *See also* Del. GCL § 174; and N. Y.Bus.Corp.Law § 719.* A director held liable under this section has an action for contribution against shareholders who received a distribution knowing that it was improper. MBCA § 48, Del. GCL § 174(c).

8.33

---

* Surplus became "restricted" under the former version of the Act when shares were repurchased and not canceled. An amount equal to the aggregate par value of the shares repurchased was required by § 6 to be restricted and thus no longer available for distribution or repurchase of additional shares. The board of directors could "reserve" a portion of a corporation's surplus for a particular purpose (such as to provide a fund for the purchase of capital facilities) by resolution, thereby imposing limitations on its distribution.

* New York also makes the violation of the restrictions on distributions a criminal offense under some circumstances. See N.Y. Penal Law § 190.35.

3. JUDICIAL CONTROL OF THE PAYMENT OF DIVIDENDS

DODGE v. FORD MOTOR CO.

204 Mich. 459, 170 N.W. 668, 3 A.L.R. 413 (1919).

[This famous action was brought by the Dodge brothers, two minority shareholders, against the Ford Motor Company, Henry Ford, and other members of the board of directors, to compel the payment of a dividend and other relief. The lower court held for the plaintiffs and the defendants appealed.

The company was begun in 1903 with an initial capital of $150,000. Henry Ford took 225 of the 1,500 shares authorized, the Dodge brothers took 50 shares each, and several others subscribed to a few shares each. At the time the suit was brought, the plaintiffs owned ten percent of the outstanding stock, and Ford owned 58% and completely dominated the company. During the initial years the business of the company, as the court put it, rather mildly "continued to expand" until 1916 its total assets were $132 million, its working capital exceeded $48 million and its surplus was almost $112 million.

The corporation paid regular quarterly dividends amounting to $1,200,000 per year and in addition had paid, during the years 1911 through 1915 a total of $41 million in "special dividends." The plaintiffs alleged that Ford had "declared it to be the settled policy of the company not to pay in the future any special dividends, but to put back into the business for the future all of the earnings of the company other than the regular dividend   *   *   *."

The defendants appealed from a lower court order directing the corporation to pay a dividend of $10 million, enjoining it from building a smelter at the River Rouge plant and restraining it from "increasing of the fixed capital assets," or "holding of liquid assets   *   *   * in excess of such as may be reasonably required in the proper conduct and carrying on of the business and operations" of the corporation.]

OSTRANDER, C. J.

*   *   *

To develop the points now discussed, and to a considerable extent they may be developed together as a single point, it is necessary to refer with some particularity to the facts.

When plaintiffs made their complaint and demand for further dividends, the Ford Motor Company had concluded its most prosperous year of business. The demand for its cars at the price of the preceding year continued. It could make and could market in the year beginning August 1, 1916, more than 500,000 cars. Sales of parts and repairs would necessarily increase. The cost of materials was likely to advance, and perhaps the price of labor; but it reasonably might have expected a profit for the year of upwards of $60,000,000.

* * * It had declared no special dividend during the business year except the October, 1915, dividend. It had been the practice, under similar circumstances, to declare larger dividends. Considering only these facts, a refusal to declare and pay further dividends appears to be not an exercise of discretion on the part of the directors, but an arbitrary refusal to do what the circumstances required to be done. These facts and others call upon the directors to justify their action, or failure or refusal to act. In justification, the defendants have offered testimony tending to prove, and which does prove, the following facts: It had been the policy of the corporation for a considerable time to annually reduce the selling price of cars, while keeping up, or improving, their quality. As early as in June, 1915, a general plan for the expansion of the productive capacity of the concern by a practical duplication of its plant had been talked over by the executive officers and directors and agreed upon; not all of the details having been settled, and no formal action of directors having been taken. The erection of a smelter was considered, and engineering and other data in connection therewith secured. In consequence, it was determined not to reduce the selling price of cars for the year beginning August 1, 1915, but to maintain the price and to accumulate a large surplus to pay for the proposed expansion of plant and equipment, and perhaps to build a plant for smelting ore. It is hoped, by Mr. Ford, that eventually 1,000,000 cars will be annually produced. The contemplated changes will permit the increased output.

The plan, as affecting the profits of the business for the year beginning August 1, 1916, and thereafter, calls for a reduction in the selling price of the cars. It is true that this price might be at any time increased, but the plan called for the reduction in price of $80 a car. The capacity of the plant, without the additions thereto voted to be made (without a part of them at least), would produce more than 600,000 cars annually. This number, and more, could have been sold for $440 instead of $360, a difference in the return for capital, labor, and materials employed of at least $48,000,000. In short, the plan does not call for and is not intended to produce immediately a more profitable business, but a less profitable one; not only less profitable than formerly, but less profitable than it is admitted it might be made. The apparent immediate effect will be to diminish the value of shares and the returns to shareholders.

[The court here discussed the allegedly "eleemosynary" motives behind the failure to pay a larger dividend, a matter taken up in chapter 17, *infra.*]

*   *   *

There is committed to the discretion of directors, a discretion to be exercised in good faith, the infinite details of business, including the wages which shall be paid to employés, the number of hours they shall work, the conditions under which labor shall be carried on, and the price for which products shall be offered to the public.

It is said by appellants that the motives of the board members are not material and will not be inquired into by the court so long as their acts are within their lawful powers. As we have pointed out, and the proposition does not require argument to sustain it, it is not within the lawful powers of a board of directors to shape and conduct the affairs of a corporation for the merely incidental benefit of shareholders and for the primary purpose of benefiting others, and no one will contend that, if the avowed purpose of the defendant directors was to sacrifice the interests of shareholders, it would not be the duty of the courts to interfere.

We are not, however, persuaded that we should interfere with the proposed expansion of the business of the Ford Motor Company. In view of the fact that the selling price of products may be increased at any time, the ultimate results of the larger business cannot be certainly estimated. The judges are not business experts. It is recognized that plans must often be made for a long future, for expected competition, for a continuing as well as an immediately profitable venture. The experience of the Ford Motor Company is evidence of capable management of its affairs. It may be noticed, incidentally, that it took from the public the money required for the execution of its plan, and that the very considerable salaries paid to Mr. Ford and to certain executive officers and employés were not diminished. We are not satisfied that the alleged motives of the directors, in so far as they are reflected in the conduct of the business, menace the interests of shareholders. It is enough to say, perhaps, that the court of equity is at all times open to complaining shareholders having a just grievance.

Assuming the general plan and policy of expansion and the details of it to have been sufficiently, formally approved at the October and November, 1917, meetings of directors, and assuming further that the plan and policy and the details agreed upon were for the best ultimate interest of the company and therefore of its shareholders, what does it amount to in justification of a refusal to declare and pay a special dividend or dividends? The Ford Motor Company was able to estimate with nicety its income and profit. It could sell more cars than it could make. Having ascertained what it would cost to produce a car and to sell it, the profit upon each car depended upon the selling price. That being fixed, the yearly income and profit was determinable, and, within slight variations, was certain.

* * *

The decree of the court below fixing and determining the specific amount to be distributed to stockholders is affirmed. * * *

NOTES

Dodge v. Ford is the most illustrious case on the right of a shareholder to compel the payment of a dividend, although it is most often recalled for its philosophical discussion of the role of a corporation in society, an aspect of the case that we will consider in Chapter 17. The litigation was the product of a struggle between two powerful economic forces, Henry Ford and the Dodge brothers. At the time the Ford Motor Company was mainly an assembler of automobiles from parts it purchased from others. The Dodges were among the Ford's principal suppliers as well as owners of 22 percent of the Ford stock. With the profits of their own operations, considerably augmented by dividends from Ford, they had commenced manufacturing their own competing automobiles. The lawsuit was precipitated by Ford's decision to use much of its enormous surplus to expand its operations by the construction of the River Rouge facility and the iron smelting operations, a decision that deprived the Dodge brothers of funds they wished to use in their own expansion program.

The ultimate resolution of the controversy was the purchase by Ford for $105 million of all of the $41\frac{1}{2}$ percent of the outstanding stock in the hands of others, thus giving him complete ownership of one of the largest industrial enterprises in the world, a degree of control exceeding anything that Rockefeller, Morgan, and Carnegie, his peers of the day, ever exercised over their own business empires. It was more than ten years after Ford's death before the Ford Motor Company had a stockholder voting rights who was not a member of the Ford family.

Notwithstanding the outcome in *Dodge v. Ford*, stockholders face an uphill battle when bringing an action to compel the corporation's board of directors to declare a dividend. In the absence of "bad faith" or "an abuse of discretion" by the board, a court will not interfere with the board's exercise of its business judgment. An example of judicial attitudes on this question is found in Gottfried v. Gottfried, 73 N.Y.S.2d 692 (Sup.Ct.1947). The plaintiff-shareholders of a closely held corporation unsuccessfully alleged a battery of claims, including (1) there was bitter animosity between the directors (who were the majority shareholders) and the plaintiffs (the minority shareholders); (2) the majority shareholders desired to coerce the minority shareholders to sell their stock to the majority at a grossly inadequate price; (3) the majority shareholders desired to avoid heavy personal income taxes on any dividends that might be declared; (4) the majority shareholders, who were on the corporation's payroll, paid themselves excessive salaries and bonuses and borrowed money from the corporation, and the nonpayment of dividends was designed to compel the minority shareholders, who were not on the corporation's payroll, to sell their stock to the majority shareholders.

Although the court expressed sympathy for the minority shareholders, who had been discharged from the corporate payroll, it did not find the hostility and dissension among stockholders as a sufficient justification for judicial intervention to compel the payment of a dividend based on the directors' "bad faith." According to the court "The essential test of bad faith is to determine whether the policy of the directors is dictated by their personal interests rather than corporate welfare. Directors are fiduciaries. Their [beneficiaries] are the corporation and the stockholders as a body. Circumstances appraised in the light of the financial condition and requirements of the corporation, will determine the conclusion as to whether the directors have or have not been animated by personal, as distinct from corporate considerations." (73 N.Y.S.2d at 695.) The court found that bonuses and corporate loans to the majority shareholders were a long-standing company practice. In addition, the remuneration to one defendant could not be considered excessive when the defendant had played an important role in the "tremendous expansion" of the company's subsidiary, Hanscom Baking Corporation, between 1933 and 1946. In dismissing the complaint and directing judgment for the defendants, the court concluded:

> The testimony discloses that many general considerations affected the policy of the Board of Directors in connection with dividend payments. Some of the major factors were as follows: The recognition that earnings during the war years might be abnormal and not representative of normal earning capacity; the pressing need for heavy expenditures for new equipment and machinery, replacement of which had been impossible during the war years; heavy expenditures required to finance the acquisition and equipment of new Hanscom stores in harmony with the steady growth of the business; the increased initial cost of opening new stores because, under present conditions, it has become difficult to lease appropriate sites necessitating actual acquisition by ownership of locations; the erection of a new bakery for Hanscom at a cost of approximately $1,000,000 inasmuch as the existing plant is incapable of producing the requirements of Hanscom sales which are running at the rate of approximately $6,000,000 per annum; unstable labor conditions with actual and threatened strikes; several pending actions involving large sums of money under the Federal Fair Labor Standards Act; a general policy of financing expansion through earnings requiring long-term debt.

> The plaintiffs oppose many of these policies of expansion. There is no evidence of any weight to the effect that these policies of the Board of Directors are actuated by any motives other than their best business judgment. If they are mistaken, their own stock holdings will suffer proportionately to those of the plaintiffs. With the wisdom of that policy the court has no concern. It is this court's conclusion that these policies and the expenditures which they entail are undertaken in good faith and without relation to any conspiracy, scheme and plan to withhold dividends for the purpose of compelling the plaintiffs to sell their stock or pursuant to any other sinister design. (72 N.Y.S.2d at 700–01.)

While the court's dismissal of the shareholders' complaint in *Gottfried* represents the usual disposition of dividend cases, shareholders have received a favorable hearing in a few cases. The Michigan Court of Appeals took a fresh look at the facts supporting an outside shareholders' claim for a declaration of dividends. In Miller v. Magline, Inc., 76 Mich.App. 284, 256 N.W.2d 761 (1977), the corporation's board of directors had adopted a management compensation scheme providing for a low base salary plus a generous incentive bonus program, with any remaining profits to be retained by the corporation as a working capital. The court upheld the chancellor's decision in favor of the plaintiffs on the basis of the defendant's breach of their fiduciary duty:

> It is our opinion that under all of the circumstances of the case, that the directors of the management group were placed in the impossible situation of trying to give an impartial answer to the determination as to whether dividends should be granted. They already were taking a profit distribution via a percentile of profits before taxes. Therefore, we deem it an untenable position to argue that nonpayment of dividends is justified on the basis that such a concept of profit distribution would imperil the continued well being of the corporation. If such retention of profits were indicated they should have been more diligent in seeing that distributions based upon percentage of profits also should be curtailed.

256 N.W.2d at 770.

KAMIN v. AMERICAN EXPRESS CO.

86 Misc.2d 809, 383 N.Y.S.2d 807 (Sup.Ct.1976), aff'd on opinion below, 54 A.D. 654, 387 N.Y.S.2d 993 (1st Dept.1976).

EDWARD J. GREENFIELD, Justice.

In this stockholders' derivative action, the individual defendants, who are the directors of the American Express Company, move for an order dismissing the complaint for failure to state a cause of action pursuant and alternatively, for summary judgment.

The complaint is brought derivatively by two minority stockholders of the American Express Company, asking for a declaration that a certain dividend in kind is a waste of corporate assets, directing the defendants not to proceed with the distribution, or, in the alternative, for monetary damages. The motion to dismiss the complaint requires the Court to presuppose the truth of the allegations. It is the defendants' contention that, conceding everything in the complaint, no viable cause of action is made out.

After establishing the identity of the parties, the complaint alleges that in 1972 American Express acquired for investment 1,954,418 shares of common stock of Donaldson, Lufken and Jenrette, Inc. (hereafter DLJ), a publicly traded corporation, at a cost of $29.9 million. It is further alleged that the current market value of those shares is approximately $4.0 million. On July 28, 1975, it is alleged, the Board of Directors of American Express declared a special dividend to all stockholders of record pursuant to which the shares of DLJ would be distributed in kind. Plaintiffs contend further that if American Express were to sell the DLJ shares on the market, it would sustain a capital loss of $25 million, which could be offset against taxable capital gains on other investments. Such a sale, they allege, would result in tax savings to the company of approximately $8 million, which would not be available in the case of the distribution of DLJ shares to stockholders. It is alleged that on October 8, 1975 and October 16, 1975, plaintiffs demanded that the directors rescind the previously declared dividend in DLJ shares and take steps to preserve the capital loss which would result from selling the shares. This demand was rejected by the Board of Directors on October 17, 1975.

It is apparent that all the previously-mentioned allegations of the complaint go to the question of the exercise by the Board of Directors of business judgment in deciding how to deal with the DLJ shares.
*   *   *

*   *   *

Examination of the complaint reveals that there is no claim of fraud or self-dealing, and no contention that there was any bad faith or oppressive conduct. The law is quite clear as to what is necessary to ground a claim for actionable wrongdoing.   *   *   *

More specifically, the question of whether or not a dividend is to be declared or a distribution of some kind should be made is exclusively a matter of business judgment for the Board of Directors.

*   *   * Courts will not interfere with such discretion unless it be first made to appear that the directors have acted or are about to act in bad faith and for a dishonest purpose. It is for the directors to say, acting in good faith of course, when and to what extent dividends shall be declared   *   *   * The statute confers upon the directors this power, and the minority stockholders are not in a position to question this right, so long as the directors are acting in good faith   *   *   *.

Thus, a complaint must be dismissed if all that is presented is a decision to pay dividends rather than pursuing some other course of conduct. Weinberger v. Quinn, 264 App.Div. 405, 35 N.Y.S.2d 567, affd. 290 N.Y. 635, 49 N.E.2d 131. A complaint which alleges merely that some course of action other than that pursued by the Board of Directors would have been more advantageous gives rise to no cognizable cause of action. Courts have more than enough to do in adjudicating legal rights and devising remedies for wrongs. The directors' room rather than the courtroom is the appropriate forum for thrashing out purely business questions which will have an impact on profits, market prices, competitive situations, or tax advantages.
*   *   *

It is not enough to allege, as plaintiffs do here, that the directors made an imprudent decision, which did not capitalize on the possibility of using a potential capital loss to offset capital gains. More than imprudence or mistaken judgment must be shown.

> Questions of policy of management, expediency of contracts or action, adequacy of consideration, lawful appropriation of corporate funds to advance corporate interests, are left solely to their honest and unselfish decision, for their powers therein are without limitation and free from restraint, and the exercise of them for the common and general interests of the corporation may not be questioned, although the results show that what they did was unwise or inexpedient. Pollitz v. Wabash Railroad Co., 207 N.Y. 113, 124, 100 N.E. 721, 724.

Section 720(a)(1)(A) of the Business Corporation Law permits an action against directors for "the neglect of, or failure to perform, or other violation of his duties in the management and disposition of corporate assets committed to his charge." This does not mean that a director is chargeable with ordinary negligence for having made an improper decision, or having acted imprudently. The "neglect" referred to in the statute is neglect of duties (i.e., malfeasance or nonfeasance) and not misjudgment. To allege that a director "negligently permitted the declaration and payment" of a dividend without alleging fraud, dishonesty or nonfeasance, is to state merely that a decision was taken with which one disagrees.

    * * * The affidavits of the defendants and the exhibits annexed thereto demonstrate that the objections raised by the plaintiffs to the proposed dividend action were carefully considered and unanimously rejected by the Board at a special meeting called precisely for that purpose at the plaintiffs' request. The minutes of the special meeting indicate that the defendants were fully aware that a sale rather than a distribution of the DLJ shares might result in the realization of a substantial income tax saving. Nevertheless, they concluded that there were countervailing considerations primarily with respect to the adverse effect such a sale, realizing a loss of $25 million, would have on the net income figures in the American Express financial statement. Such a reduction of net income would have a serious effect on the market value of the publicly traded American Express stock. This was not a situation in which the defendant directors totally overlooked facts called to their attention. They gave them consideration, and attempted to view the total picture in arriving at their decision. While plaintiffs contend that according to their accounting consultants the loss on the DLJ stock would still have to be charged against current earnings even if the stock were distributed, the defendants' accounting experts assert that the loss would be a charge against earnings only in the event of a sale, whereas in the event of distribution of the stock as a dividend, the proper accounting treatment would be to charge the loss only against surplus. While

the chief accountant for the SEC raised some question as to the appropriate accounting treatment of this transaction, there was no basis for any action to be taken by the SEC with respect to the American Express financial statement.

The only hint of self-interest which is raised, not in the complaint but in the papers on the motion, is that four of the twenty directors were officers and employees of American Express and members of its Executive Incentive Compensation Plan. Hence, it is suggested, by virtue of the action taken earnings may have been overstated and their compensation affected thereby. Such a claim is highly speculative and standing alone can hardly be regarded as sufficient to support an inference of self-dealing. There is no claim or showing that the four company directors dominated and controlled the sixteen outside members of the Board. * * *

* * *

QUESTION

What is the rational basis for the directors' refusal to provide the identical economic benefit to the shareholders and achieve a tax savings of $8,000,000 for a corporation? Should the court second guess the directors?

4. PLANNING CONSIDERATIONS

As we will consider in greater detail in Chapter 11, the shareholders of close corporations will sometimes enter into an agreement to make the payment of dividends mandatory, at least under certain circumstances. The courts tend to uphold these agreements. Unlike the publicly traded corporation, where the dynamics of the stock market will produce a dividend policy that satisfies most stockholders, the management of a close corporation does not look to the stock market for fresh capital. If the stockholders of a public company are discontent with the company's dividend policy, they can sell their shares in the market place and invest elsewhere. If shareholders in a close corporation do not receive dividends, they are likely to derive no economic value from their shares. This is particularly true of a shareholder who is not employed by the corporation and does not receive regular salary payments from the corporation. Thus, for shareholders in a closely-held corporation who do not receive a salary and dividend payments and who lack a public market for their shares, the liquidity of these shareholders' investments becomes illusory.

5. POLICY ASPECTS

It should be recognized that, from a societal point of view, important consequences flow from the decision to leave the payment of dividends to the board's discretion. If corporations were required to pay out their entire profits each year to their shareholders, corporate managers would have dominion over far fewer assets. Thus, corporations needing more capital would be required, each year, to compete with alternative investment opportunities. At the same time, shareholders would receive a greater flow of cash each year. The law has not imposed such a requirement on corporations. But it might be asked whether it would be advantageous from a policy perspective to do so. Louis Kelso, an attorney-economist who is the proponent of increased employee ownership of the stock of their corporate-employers, advocates requiring corporations to pay out as a dividend all the profits for each year, allowing only the retention of a small amount of essential cash. In the book Two Factor Theory by Kelso and Patricia Hetter, the authors comment as follows:

[W]e propose that each mature corporate (defined as a corporation that has effective access to market sources of capital funds, including funds available under Second Income Plan proposals to finance new capital formation), must gradually be compelled, by tax guidance, amendment of relevant corporation laws, otherwise, to pay out all of its net earnings, after depreciation and operating reserves only, to its stockholders. The right of the owner—the stockholder—to receive all the net income produced by what is owed is the essence of private property. To withhold the wages of capital is no more justifiable than to withhold the wages of labor. Stated affirmatively, the flow of purchasing power to those who engaged in producing wealth is just as disrupted by corporate management's withholding the wages of capital (corporate net earnings) as it would be were the wages of labor withheld.

Like the corporate income tax, the practice of corporate boards of directors to withhold from stockholders the income their capital produces (retained earnings) does not hurt primarily the concentrated wealthholder. It hurts the small capitalist, who needs his dividends to live on, and it hurts the individual who owns no capital at all, but who could become an owner under the techniques of the Second Income Plan. If non-capital-owning households and individuals are to be enabled to buy and pay for capital out of its earnings—and this, let us repeat, is their only hope of ever acquiring capital ownership means—it is crucial that they receive those earnings in full. Pages 77–8.

Chapter 9

LIMITATIONS ON LIMITED LIABILITY

PROBLEM

EAST WIND BOATS—PART IX

East Wind Boats, Inc. has operated successfully for several years. About three years ago, Hardy, Luff, and Teach, believing that the boat construction operation was well-launched, decided to branch out into the booming field of boat chartering. Accordingly they organized East Wind Charters, Inc., ("Charters") as a wholly-owned subsidiary of East Wind Boats, Inc. ("Boats"). Boats invested $25,000 cash and received 1,000 shares of common stock and a demand note for $20,000. Charters used the cash to acquire a fleet of four sailboats, borrowing the remaining $75,000 of the purchase money from a bank. The loan was secured by a mortgage on the boats.

Hardy, Luff, and Teach are the officers and directors of Charters but draw no compensation for their service in those capacities. They have held only three formal board meetings in three years, each one when some major transaction was to be considered. Formal shareholders' meetings (there is only one shareholder) were held each year at the time of the shareholders' meeting of Boats. The only business transacted at these meetings has been the reelection of the board of directors and the passage of a resolution ratifying all acts of the corporation engaged in by the officers and the board during the preceding year.

Charters' only office is located in Boats' offices at the boatyard. There is one employee, a bookkeeper/administrator, who works half-time for Charters and half-time for Boats. Individual charter transactions are handled by this employee or by Hardy or Luff. Teach has been inactive in the business of both corporations. Charters pays Boats $300 a month for rent and "administrative services." Charters' letterheads, billheads, advertising brochures, and other printed forms all carry the words, "East Wind Charters, Inc., a subsidiary of East Wind Boats, Inc." It maintains a separate bank account at the same bank used by Boats.

Charters was very successful. It earned $7,000 during its first year of operation and $15,000 during its second. The amounts of these profits remaining after taxes were distributed to Boats as a dividend at the close of each year. Charters and Boats used the same accountant and filed a consolidated tax return.

Six months ago one of Charters' boats went down in a severe storm, and four of the people aboard drowned. The families of the victims instituted a wrongful death action against Charters, its insurance carrier, Boats, Hardy, Luff, and Teach, alleging that the boat was improperly equipped and that the defendants negligently failed to warn the decedents that a storm had been forecast. The complaint seeks damages substantially in excess of the amount of insurance carried by Charters.

Charters has been unable to repay the loan to the banks which financed the purchase of the vessels, and suit has been brought against Charters, Boats, Hardy, Luff and Teach for the balance due.

You have been approached by counsel for the estates of the victims and counsel for the banks about settlement of the claims. Plaintiffs' counsel say that they are confident that the court will disregard the corporate veil and hold all of the defendants liable for the conduct of Charters.

Your clients need guidance in reacting to the settlement discussions. Advise them as to the likelihood that a court will impose liability on them for each of the claims against Charters.

Boats has also asked you to advise it on its legal position as to the $20,000 note issued by Charters in connection with the purchase of stock.

A PLANNING PROBLEM

MASON AND BILDER

Your clients, Melissa Mason and Don Bilder were classmates in architecture school. Melissa now has her own small architecture practice. Don recently left a large firm to become a contractor specializing in remodelling urban residential real estate. They have decided to go into the real estate development business together. They want to begin by purchasing and rehabilitating six contiguous townhouses on a block on the fringes of an area that had previously been run down but is in the process of renovation. The houses were acquired by the city for back taxes several years ago and are all vacant and in various states of disrepair. Melissa and Don believe they can purchase the shells for an average of about $25,000 each. They estimate that the renovation work will cost between $50,000 and $80,000 for each house assuming that there are no serious structural defects. Melissa and Don's capital contribution will consist of another $5,000 per house representing the difference between what a bank will lend for construction and the expected cost of the renovation. They will thus each invest $30,000 in the venture.

Don presently has the assets of his contracting business, worth about $20,000 net, in a corporation, Don's, Inc., of which he is the sole shareholder. He is presently working on three other jobs, but as soon as they are finished he plans to devote full time to the project with Melissa. If this first project is successful, both expect to devote all their energies to similar development undertakings.

Melissa and Don have come to you for advice on how best to structure their undertaking. They have discussed several possible alternatives including:

1. Create a new corporation in which they will invest equal amounts, that will buy the houses.

2. Set up six separate corporations, in which they will each invest $5,000, that will own one house apiece.

3. Have the stock of the six corporations owned by a single corporation (a holding company), all of whose stock will be owned by Don and Melissa.

They would like you to advise them not only as to the corporate structure but also as to the form in which their investment should be made. Your clients would like to minimize the risks for the overall venture, and protect their own investment to the extent possible. Which one of these alternatives would you recommend? Do you have any better suggestions?

A. INTRODUCTION

As we have seen, one of the principal advantages of the corporate form of business is that it limits the potential loss of a shareholder to the amount invested in the enterprise. This general principle holds whether the shareholder is a natural person or another corporation. Of course the corporation itself remains liable for its own obligations. But a creditor of the corporation may look only to the corporate assets for recovery.

Like most other rules, however, this one has its exceptions. Where justice requires it, courts occasionally disregard the corporate entity and allow the plaintiffs to reach the assets of the shareholders. The expression frequently used to describe this result is "piercing the corporate veil." Particularly where the corporation is a wholly owned subsidiary of another corporation, courts use less colorful phrases to justify disregarding the corporate fiction. They do so when they find the subsidiary to be the "agent," "alias," "alter ego," "corporate double," "dummy," or "instrumentality" of the parent. None of these terms is particularly helpful in describing those situations in which a court will "pierce the corporate veil." As Justice Cardozo observed, "the whole problem of the relation between parent and subsidiary is one that is still enveloped in a mist of metaphor. Metaphors in law are to be narrowly watched, for starting as devices to liberate thought, they end often by enslaving it." Berkey v. Third Avenue Railway Co., 244 N.Y. 84, 94, 155 N.E. 58, 61 (1926).

As the following materials indicate, there are a variety of factors that may lead a court to impose liability on a shareholder for the obligations of the corporation. They fall generally into two classes: (1) insufficient attention to corporate formalities and (2) "abuse" of the corporate entity by pushing its advantages to extremes. A useful perspective on the problem is to see it as a matter of allocation of losses. The ultimate question posed to a court is: when the assets of a corporate are inadequate to fulfill its obligations to the plaintiff, under what circumstances should the court shift the burden of those losses from the plaintiff to the shareholders of the corporation? The answer to that question may depend on the behavior of the shareholders as well as on whether the claim sounds in tort or in contract. A planner often faces the problem of seeking maximum advantage of the limitation of liability afforded by the corporate form without crossing the line beyond which a court is likely to pierce the corporate veil and eliminate *all* of the protection it affords.

Forms of business organization that provide for limited liability appear in virtually every developed legal system. We have become so accustomed to them that we tend to ignore the significant public policy issues they present: What public purpose is served by allowing a few individuals, perhaps even one person, to create an enterprise and cast it in a structure which limits their liabilities growing out of the business to the amount invested in it? If there is some public advantage to such a structure, is it appropriate to impose some conditions or qualifications on the privilege? Is everyone entitled to make use of the limited liability form? Can it be used for any kind of business? Must there be at least some minimum amount of investment? Should all creditors—lenders, suppliers of goods and services, employees, tort victims—be treated alike?

A familiar view of the problem is summed up in a well-known quotation from United States v. Milwaukee Refrigerator Transit Co., 142 F. 247, 255 (E.D.Wis.1905): "[W]hen the notion of legal entity is to defeat public convenience, justify wrong, protect fraud, or defend crime, the law will regard the corporation as an association of persons." As you read the following materials, ask yourself whether they suggest a more precise standard or whether the best that one can say is that the corporate veil will be pierced when it appears just and equitable to do so.

B. DISREGARDING THE CORPORATE ENTITY: THE LEGAL STANDARDS

BRUNSWICK CORP. v. WAXMAN

459 F.Supp. 1222 (E.D.N.Y.1978), aff'd 599 F.2d 34 (2d Cir. 1979).

[The following statement of facts is based on the opinion by the Court of Appeals.

Brunswick Corporation (Brunswick) brought this diversity action against the individual defendants seeking over a million dollars in damages. This amount represented the deficiency due under conditional sales contracts between Brunswick and the Waxman Construction Corporation (Construction Corp.) whereby the latter entity purchased bowling lanes and pinsetters. The individual defendants,

Harry Waxman and the late Sydney Waxman, signed the contracts as president and secretary of the Construction Corp. Plaintiff urged that the Waxmans should be held personally liable for the deficiency.

In August 1960, the Waxmans' formed Construction Corp. as a no-asset New York corporation to act as signatory and obligor on a series of conditional sales agreements for the purchase of bowling equipment to be operated in five new bowling alleys. The five alleys and the Brunswick equipment were operated by the Waxmans' through five separate partnerships, which owned or leased the real property on which the bowling alleys were located, but charged Construction Corp. no rent for the use of the premises. Nor did the Waxmans' pay rent to Construction Corp. for the use of the bowling equipment. In addition, the Waxmans' owned in their individual or partnership capacities all the licenses and permits necessary to operate the alleys. Proceeds from the daily operation of the businesses were deposited in individual bowling alley accounts and later transferred into a central Waxman enterprises bank account from which funds were withdrawn to meet the necessary operating expenses of the alleys. It was from this central bank account that amounts due on the sales contracts with Brunswick were withdrawn and deposited in Construction Corp. account. The court below found that Construction Corp.'s sole corporate activity was the transfer of funds into and out of its bank account for the purpose of meeting the installment payments under the Brunswick contracts. Construction Corp. held no stockholders' or directors' meetings, adopted no bylaws, and issued no stock. While it filed federal and New York State income tax returns, none of these returns showed any income, nor did they report the Brunswick equipment as corporate assets.

Due to a general decline in the bowling industry, Construction Corp. was unable to meet its payment obligations under the sales contracts. Pursuant to a 1963 extension agreement, title to the Brunswick equipment was transferred from Construction Corp. to five new corporations, which were also to receive from the Waxmans' an additional $375,000 in non-Brunswick assets. However, the Waxmans' never transferred the additional assets to the five corporations. In addition, these newly formed corporations were as inactive as the Construction Corp. had been. By late 1965, two of the five corporations, Bruckner Lanes, Inc. and Pike Lanes, Inc., were in default. In 1966, Brunswick repossessed its equipment held by Bruckner Lanes and sold it at a substantial deficiency. Although an extension agreement was reached with Pike Lanes in 1966, that corporation continued in substantial default and its equipment was also repossessed and sold by Brunswick at a substantial deficiency.]

BARTELS, District Judge.

DISCUSSION

Brunswick's basic claim in this action is that the Waxmans operated Brunswick's equipment in their individual capacities and in complete disregard of the corporations they had formed. Accordingly, Brunswick contends, the Waxmans have abandoned the protection of limited liability those corporations would have otherwise provided, and have, as a matter of law, rendered themselves personally liable for their corporations' obligations.

Historically the corporate form has for centuries been used for various diverse governmental and private purposes, and today it has become a key institution in the American free enterprise system. *See* H. Henn, Law of Corporations, 11–25 (2d ed. 1970). This concept has, among others, three basic objectives, to provide (1) limited liability, (2) perpetual existence, and (3) transferability of shares. As stated in Bartle v. Home Owners Co-operative, Inc., 309 N.Y. 103, 127 N.E.2d 832 (1955), "the law permits the incorporation of a business for the very purpose of escaping personal liability." However, when the privilege of incorporation has been abused, it is necessary to "pierce the corporate veil" to "prevent fraud or to achieve equity." International Aircraft Trading Co. v. Manufacturers Trust Co., 297 N.Y. 285, 79 N.E.2d 249 (1948). As early as 1905 Judge Sanborn in United States v. Milwaukee Refrigerator Transit Co., 142 F. 247, 255 (C.C.E. D.Wis.1905), observed: "when the notion of legal entity is used to defeat public convenience, justify wrong, protect fraud, or defend crime, the law will regard the corporation as an association of persons."

The circumstances under which the court should disregard the corporate fiction are not always clear and it is difficult, if not impossible, to formulate a precise and categorical definition applicable to all situations, *see* Berkey v. Third Ave. Ry. Co., 244 N.Y. 84, 155 N.E. 58, 61 (1926), each case being *sui generis*. The burden, however, in each case rests upon the plaintiff to establish that there is a basis which serves for disregard of the corporate form.

The Instrumentality Rule

New York courts, whose rules we must follow, have advanced a variety of theories to define the particular circumstances and factors which justify disregard of the corporate entity. Some have applied the theory of agency, holding that a corporation may be so dominated and controlled by its stockholders as to become a mere agent, acting for the stockholders as principals. *See* e. g. Berkey v. Third Ave. Ry. Co., *supra*; Majestic Factors Corp. v. Latino, 15 Misc.2d 329, 184 N. Y.S.2d 658 (1959). "No conceptual problems are involved where liability is imposed upon shareholders under conventional theories of agency or tort law—independently of any theory of corporation law or of the corporate entity." 2 G. Hornstein, Corporation Law and Practice, 263 (1959). But the agency theory is not always available and as Mr. Justice Dore explained in Lowendahl v. Baltimore & O. R. Co., 247 App.Div. 144, 287 N.Y.S. 62, aff'd, 272 N.Y. 360, 6 N.E.2d 56 (1936), "any severely logical application of agency rules would destroy the protection afforded stockholders by incorporation." For if all systems of control exercised over a corporation by those who own it are illegal, then "the rule of the separate entity and responsibility of corporations for their own acts and contracts is swallowed up in the exception." *Id.* This is particularly true when the corporation is owned and controlled by one or two persons. Thus, except in case of express agency, estoppel, or tort, *Lowendahl* advanced the so-called "instrumentality" rule as a practical and effective "theory for breaking down corporate immunity when equity so requires." 287 N.Y.S. at 75.

Under the "instrumentality" rule, the factors which determine whether the corporate veil should be withdrawn are (1) domination and control over the corporation by those who are to be held liable which is so complete that the corporation has no separate mind, will, or existence of its own; (2) the use of this domination and control to commit fraud or wrong or any other dishonest or unjust act; and (3) injury or unjust loss resulting to the plaintiff from said control and wrong. 287 N.Y.S. at 76. While this rule emerged in the parent-subsidiary context, some of the same criteria have been carried over in determining whether to pierce the corporate veil in other contexts. For instance, in this case the Waxmans disregarded their corporations after the signing of the contracts so that thereafter they did not function as active corporations. The corporations were acting for themselves and not as agents for the Waxmans in acquiring title to the property and in incurring liability for the purchase price. Subsequently, the corporations did receive moneys from the Waxmans in order to meet their payments to Brunswick. Since, however, we find that there was no misappropriation of corporate assets or profits, and consequently no fraud or wrong to Brunswick, we do not find that all the criteria of the instrumentality rule for imposing personal liability are present. We must therefore invoke some different criteria if we are to disregard the corporate form. Under such circumstances, the overwhelming weight of authority requires at least some type of abuse of the corporate concept which is the cause of the injury to third parties.

Personal Conduct of Corporate Business

Absent special circumstances, limited personal liability cannot be effectuated simply by the act of incorporation. The protection extends only to those transactions which are engaged in by a corporation, for its own purposes, in fact as well as in name. If, as Judge Fuld observed in Walkovszky v. Carlton, 18 N.Y.2d 414, 418, 276 N.Y. S.2d 585, 588, 223 N.E.2d 6, 8 (1966), "the corporation is a 'dummy' for its individual stockholders who are in reality carrying on the business in their personal capacities for purely personal rather than corporate ends" then stockholders must be personally liable and financially responsible as well. *See,* African Metals Corp. v. Bullowa, 288 N.Y. 78, 41 N.E.2d 466 (1942). Fraud or other wrongful purpose is not a necessary element. For example, a failure to observe corporate formalities coupled with inadequate capitalization has frequently been cited as a basis for disregarding the corporate entity and imposing individual liability where such facts are causally connected with the injury. *See, e. g.* Anderson v. Abbott, 321 U.S. 349, 64 S.Ct. 531, 88 L.Ed. 793 (1944); DeWitt Truck Brokers v. W. Ray Flemming Fruit Co., 540 F.2d 681 (4th Cir. 1976); Francis O. Day v. Shapiro, 105 U.S.App.D.C. 392, 267 F.2d 669 (1959).

Some courts have held that unjust enrichment alone may justify imposition of personal liability on those who have conducted ostensibly corporate business in their individual capacities. However, we have been unable to find any New York authority to this effect. *But cf.* Bartle v. Home Owners Co-operative, Inc., *supra.* Another example of disregarding corporate formalities is where stockholders have represented that they would be liable for their corporations' obligations, and are therefore estopped from denying liability. *See, e. g.* Weisser v. Mursam Shoe Corp., 127 F.2d 344 (2d Cir. 1942). Likewise stockholders will be liable if they deprived their corporation of the income and profits required to meet its obligations. As the Court of Appeals observed in Natelson v. A. B. L. Holding Co., *supra,* 260 N. Y. at 238, 183 N.E. at 375, the business of a corporation must be carried on by the corporation "and its profits must be available to meet liabilities, before the individuals may share." It is not merely the disregard of corporate formalities which justifies piercing, but the fact that the stockholders' conduct has caused the creditors' losses which justifies the imposition of personal liability.

Parties' Contentions

Brunswick asserts that the Waxmans are liable personally and that the language of *Walkovszky, supra,* and *African Metals, supra,* in effect, establishes a *per se* rule which imposes liability simply on the basis of a failure to observe the corporate formalities. We find no support for this broad assertion. Actually, *Walkovszky* is not applicable. There the plaintiff was injured when he was run down by a taxicab owned by the defendant-corporation which in turn was wholly owned by the individual defendant as a stockholder. The complaint alleged fraud and that the corporation did not have a separate existence, and charged that its assets were insufficient. The complaint was dismissed because, as Judge Fuld observed, the plaintiff had failed to make any

"sufficiently particularized statements" * * * that the defendant * * * and his associates are actually doing business in their individual capacities, shuttling their personal funds in and out of the corporations "without regard to formality and to suit their immediate convenience."

18 N.Y.2d 420, 276 N.Y.S.2d 590, 223 N.E.2d 10.

African Metals, supra, is also inapposite because there the action was for rescission predicated upon fraud. To accomplish the fraud, the individual defendants organized a corporation with very limited assets and no credit facilities. A sale of nickel cathodes was negotiated in the name of the corporation by the defendants who individually and fraudulently manipulated the sale and retained the purchase money. The court observed that where there is fraud

Incorporation does not exempt the individuals from liability for an enterprise which they themselves choose to carry on as individuals independently of the corporation. It cannot be said, as a matter of law, upon this record, that there is no evidence or inferences from evidence that these defendants were not joint venturers dealing personally in this enterprise.

288 N.Y. at 85, 41 N.E.2d at 470.

The Waxmans in defending their actions, insist that they are exempt from personal liability because they do not satisfy all the criteria of the instrumentality rule. We do not believe that this rule is completely applicable to the present circumstances. Although we conclude that the Waxmans' corporations had no separate mind or existence, we also find that these corporations were never sufficiently functional to justify describing them as an instrumentality which committed wrongs causing plaintiff's injury.

No-Asset Corporations

The transactions between Brunswick and the Waxmans' corporations were much like a common form of real estate transaction in which a "dummy" corporation is established for the sole purpose of taking title and assuming mortgage obligations and thus exempting the sole stockholder from liability. There is no question that the Waxmans employed a no-asset or "straw" corporation to purchase the bowling alleys from Brunswick. Straw corporations have been used for many purposes, such as compliance with state usury or investment laws and insulation of principals from liability.

When Brunswick made its initial sale to the Waxman Construction Corp. for the Bruckner and Turnpike Lanes it knew that the land and buildings upon which the lanes and pinsetters were to be erected, were owned by the Waxmans and that the Construction Corp. was a no-asset corporation. Brunswick was under no illusion that the Construction Corp. was an agent for the Waxmans.[4] Although under-

---

4. In fact, P. L. Fulvio, Brunswick's major accounts manager, stated in a memorandum to Brunswick's credit committee dated December 2, 1964 that "I reminded Barell [the Waxmans' attorney] and [Sydney] Waxman that I was not do-

capitalization of the bowling operation might under other circumstances indicate that the corporate form was being used to mislead creditors and should be pierced, Brunswick had full knowledge of the lack of capitalization, and consented to it. Brunswick was not misled into doing business with a no-asset corporation and is hardly in a position now to complain that in the absence of any additional assets in that corporation its liability should be shifted to the Waxmans. As the court said in Hanson v. Bradley, 298 Mass. 371, 10 N.E.2d 259, 264 (S.J.C.1937):

> The plaintiff was not wronged by the fact that the corporation was organized with a trifling capital and could not live except upon borrowed money; nor by the fact that the lenders insited upon security. He knew the essential facts and accepted the situation.

* * *

The result is that the complaint should be and hereby is dismissed and judgment entered for the defendants.

So ordered.

NOTE

In affirming the judgment of the district court, the appellate court, in Brunswick Corp. v. Waxman, 599 F.2d 34 (2d Cir. 1979) commented:

> Although we are persuaded that the district judge reached the proper result here in dismissing the complaint, we cannot subscribe entirely to his views on the law of New York in the field of piercing the corporate veil and the disregard of the corporate fiction. New York law in this area is hardly as clear as a mountain lake in springtime. Since Professor Wormser's initial discussion of the topic in Piercing the Veil of Corporate Entity, 12 Colum.L. Rev. 496 (1912), there have been scores of articles and hundreds of cases discussing the problem, advancing and espousing various theories. *See* Cary, Corporations 109–49 (4th ed. 1969) [hereinafter cited as Cary]. In particular we are dubious that, as suggested by the district court, the plaintiff need establish that the Waxmans committed a fraud on Brunswick and that there be a causal connection between the fact that the Waxmans conducted business individually and the contract losses suffered by Brunswick. * * * We are rather inclined to agree with Professor Cary that "[n]o concept of separate corporate personality will suffice to solve an actual problem." Cary, *supra*, at 110. "What the formula comes down to, once shorn of verbiage about control, instrumentality, agency and corporate entity, is that liability is im-

ing business with Waxman but with his corporation. * * * "

posed to reach an equitable result." Latty, Subsidiaries and Affiliated Corporations 191 (1936).

599 F.2d at 35–6.

Walkovszky v. Carlton, 18 N.Y.2d 414, 270 N.Y.S.2d 585, 223 N.E. 2d 6 (1966) involved the common practice of organizing a taxicab business into different corporations, each to own one or two cabs, and having the stock of each corporation owned by the same individual. Each corporation would own only its own cab. The minimum liability insurance allowed by law was carried on each taxi. The plaintiff, seriously injured by a cab owned by a corporation whose stock was owned by Carlton, sued all the companies and Carlton. The latter moved to dismiss on grounds that no cause of action was stated against him. The Court of Appeals agreed with the defendant.

FULD, J.: This is not to say that it is impossible for the plaintiff to state a valid cause of action against the defendant Carlton. However, the simple fact is that the plaintiff has just not done so here. While the complaint alleges that the separate corporations were undercapitalized and that their assets have been intermingled, it is barren of any "sufficiently particular[ized] statements" * * * that the defendant Carlton and his associates are actually doing business in their individual capacities, shuttling their personal funds in and out of the corporations "without regard to formality and to suit their immediate convenience." * * * Such a "perversion of the privilege to do business in a corporate form" * * * would justify imposing personal liability on the individual stockholders. * * * Nothing of the sort has in fact been charged, and it cannot reasonably or logically be inferred from the happenstance that the business of Seon Cab Corporation may actually be carried on by a larger corporate entity composed of many corporations which, under general principles of agency, would be liable to each other's creditors in contract and in tort.

Either the stockholder is conducting the business in his individual capacity or he is not. If he is, he will be liable; if he is not, then, it does not matter—insofar as his personal liability is concerned—that the enterprise is actually being carried on by a larger "enterprise entity".

* * *

The individual defendant is charged with having "organized, managed, dominated and controlled" a fragmented corporate entity but there are no allegations that he was conducting business in his individual capacity. Had the taxicab fleet been owned by a single corporation, it would be readily apparent that the plaintiff would face formidable barriers in attempting to establish personal liability on the part of the corporation's stockholders. The fact that the fleet ownership has been deliberately split up among many corporations does not ease the plaintiff's burden in that respect. The corporate form may not be disregarded merely because the assets of the corporation, together with the mandatory insurance coverage of the vehicle which struck the plaintiff, are insufficient to assure him the recovery sought. If Carlton were to be held individually liable on those facts alone, the decision would apply equally to the thousands of cabs which are owned by their individual drivers who conduct their businesses through corporations organized pursuant to section 401 of the Business Corporation Law, * * * and carry the minimum insurance required by [the Vehicle and Traffic Law.]

223 N.E.2d at 9.

* * *

In point of fact, the principle relied upon in the complaint to sustain the imposition of personal liability is not agency but fraud. Such a cause of action cannot withstand analysis. If it is not fraudulent for the owner-operator of a single cab corporation to take out only the minimum required liability insurance, the enterprise does not become either illicit or fraudulent merely because it consists of many such corporations. The plaintiff's injuries are the same regardless of whether the cab which strikes him is owned by a single corporation or part of a fleet with ownership fragmented among many corporations. Whatever rights he may be able to assert against parties other than the registered owner of the vehicle come into being not because he has been defrauded but because, under the principle of *respondeat superior*, he is entitled to hold the whole enterprise responsible for the acts of its agents.

223 N.E.2d at 10.

* * *

Judge KEATING dissented:

From their inception these corporations were intentionally undercapitalized for the purpose of avoiding responsibility for acts which were bound to arise as a result of the operation of a large taxi fleet having cars out on the street 24 hours a day and engaged in public transportation. And during the course of the corporations' existence all income was continuously drained out of the corporation for the same purpose.

The issue presented by this action is whether the policy of this State, which affords those desiring to engaged in a business enterprise the privilege of limited liability through the use of the corporate device, is so strong that it will permit that privilege to continue no matter how much it is abused, no matter how irresponsibly the corporation is operated, no matter what the cost to the public. I do not believe that it is.

223 N.E.2d at 11.

* * *

The Legislature in requiring minimum liability insurance of $10,000, no doubt, intended to provide at least some small fund for recovery against those individuals and corporations who just did not have and were not able to raise or accumulate assets sufficient to satisfy the claims of those who were injured as a result of their negligence. It certainly could not have intended to shield those individuals who organized corporations, with the specific intent of avoiding responsibility to the public, where the operation of the corporate enterprise yielded profits sufficient to purchase additional insurance. Moreover, it is reasonable to assume that the Legislature believed that those individuals and corporations having substantial assets would take out insurance far in excess of the minimum in order to protect those assets from depletion. Given the costs of hospital care and treatment and the nature of injuries sustained in auto collisions, it would be unreasonable to assume that the Legislature believed that the minimum provided in the statute would in and of itself be sufficient to recompense innocent victims of motor vehicle accidents   * * *   for the injury and financial loss inflicted upon them.

* * *

What I would merely hold is that a participating shareholder of a corporation vested with a public interest, organized with capital insufficient to meet liabilities which are certain to arise in the ordinary course of the corporation's business, may be held personally responsible for such liabilities. Where corporate income is not sufficient to cover the cost of insurance premiums above the statutory minimum or where initially adequate finances dwindle under the pressure of competition, bad times or extraordinary and unexpected liability, obviously the shareholder will not be held liable.

The only types of corporate enterprises that will be discouraged as a result of a decision allowing the individual shareholder to be sued will be those such as the one in question, designed solely to abuse the corporate privilege at the expense of the public interest.

223 N.E.2d at 13–14.

MINTON v. CAVANEY

56 Cal.2d 576, 15 Cal.Rptr. 641, 364 P.2d 473 (1961).

TRAYNOR, Justice.

The Seminole Hot Springs Corporation, hereinafter referred to as Seminole, was duly incorporated in California on March 8, 1954. It conducted a public swimming pool that it leased from its owner. On

June 24, 1954 plaintiffs' daughter drowned in the pool, and plaintiffs recovered a judgment for $10,000 against Seminole for her wrongful death. The judgment remains unsatisfied.

On January 30, 1957, plaintiffs brought the present action to hold defendant Cavaney personally liable for the judgment against Seminole. Cavaney died on May 28, 1958 and his widow, the executrix of his estate, was substituted as defendant. The trial court entered judgment for plaintiffs for $10,000. Defendant appeals.

Plaintiffs introduced evidence that Cavaney was a director and secretary and treasurer of Seminole and that on November 15, 1954, about five months after the drowning, Cavaney as secretary of Seminole and Edwin A. Kraft as president of Seminole applied for permission to issue three shares of Seminole stock, one share to be issued to Kraft, another to F. J. Wettrick and the third to Cavaney. The commissioner of corporations refused permission to issue these shares unless additional information was furnished. The application was then abandoned and no shares were ever issued. There was also evidence that for a time Seminole used Cavaney's office to keep records and to receive mail. Before his death Cavaney answered certain interrogatories. He was asked if Seminole "ever had any assets?" He stated that "insofar as my own personal knowledge and belief is concerned said corporation did not have any assets." Cavaney also stated in the return to an attempted execution that "[I]nsofar as I know, this corporation had no assets of any kind or character. The corporation was duly organized but never functioned as a corporation."

Defendant introduced evidence that Cavaney was an attorney at law, that he was approached by Kraft and Wettrick to form Seminole, and that he was the attorney for Seminole. Plaintiffs introduced Cavaney's answer to several interrogatories that he held the post of secretary and treasurer and director in a temporary capacity and as an accommodation to his client.

Defendant contends that the evidence does not support the court's determination that Cavaney is personally liable for Seminole's debts and that the "alter ego" doctrine is inapplicable because plaintiffs failed to show that there was " '(1) * * * such unity of interest and ownership that the separate personalities of the corporation and the individual no longer exist and (2) that, if the acts are treated as those of the corporation alone, an inequitable result will follow.' " Riddle v. Leuschner, 51 Cal.2d 574, 580, 335 P.2d 107, 110.

The figurative terminology "alter ego" and "disregard of the corporate entity" is generally used to refer to the various situations that are an abuse of the corporate privilege. The equitable owners of a corporation, for example, are personally liable when they treat the assets of the corporation as their own and add or withdraw capital from the corporation at will (see Riddle v. Leuschner, 51 Cal.2d 574, 577–581, 335 P.2d 107); when they hold themselves out as being personally liable for the debts of the corporation (Stark v. Coker, 20 Cal.

2d 839, 847, 129 P.2d 390); or when they provide inadequate capitalization and actively participate in the conduct of corporate affairs.

In the instant case the evidence is undisputed that there was no attempt to provide adequate capitalization. Seminole never had any substantial assets. It leased the pool that it operated, and the lease was forfeited for failure to pay the rent. Its capital was "'trifling compared with the business to be done and the risks of loss * * *.'" Automotriz Del Golfo De California S. A. De C. V. v. Resnick, supra, 47 Cal.2d 792, 797, 306 P.2d 1, 4. The evidence is also undisputed that Cavaney was not only the secretary and treasurer of the corporation but was also a director. The evidence that Cavaney was to receive one-third of the shares to be issued supports an inference that he was an equitable owner, and the evidence that for a time the records of the corporation were kept in Cavaney's office supports an inference that he actively participated in the conduct of the business. The trial court was not required to believe his statement that he was only a "temporary" director and officer "for accommodation." In any event it merely raised a conflict in the evidence that was resolved adversely to defendant. Moreover, section 800 of the Corporations Code provides that "* * * the business and affairs of every corporation shall be controlled by, a board of not less than three directors." Defendant does not claim that Cavaney was a director with specialized duties. It is immaterial whether or not he accepted the office of director as an "accommodation" with the understanding that he would not exercise any of the duties of a director. A person may not in this manner divorce the responsibilities of a director from the statutory duties and powers of that office.

There is no merit in defendant's contentions that the "alter ego" doctrine applies only to contractual debts and not to tort claims or that the judgment in the action against the corporation bars plaintiffs from bringing the present action.

In this action to hold defendant personally liable upon the judgment against Seminole plaintiffs did not allege or present any evidence on the issue of Seminole's negligence or on the amount of damages sustained by plaintiffs. They relied solely on the judgment against Seminole. Defendant correctly contends that Cavaney or his estate cannot be held liable for the debts of Seminole without an opportunity to relitigate these issues. Cavaney was not a party to the action against the corporation, and the judgment in that action is therefore not binding upon him unless he controlled the litigation leading to the judgment.

The judgment is reversed. Held for Cavaney

C.   INTRA–ENTERPRISE LIABILITY

1. INTRODUCTION

It is often desirable, for business reasons, to divide up an enterprise into two or more separate corporations. These may be related to each other as parent and subsidiary or as "brother and sister" corporations owned by the same parent or by the same group of individual stockholders. It may be argued that this artificial division of one economic enterprise into separate corporations should not be permitted to defeat recovery by a plaintiff with a meritorious cause simply because the particular corporation with which the plaintiff dealt happened to have an insufficient share of the assets of the enterprise to satisfy the judgment. Professor Berle pointed out in The Theory of Enterprise Liability, 47 Colum.L.Rev. 343, 348 (1947) that courts have, under certain circumstances, accepted that argument:

> Another illustration of judicial erection of a new entity occurs in situations where the corporate personality (as embodied in its charter, books, and so forth) does not correspond to the actual enterprise, but merely to a fragment of it. The result is to construct a new aggregate of assets and liabilities. Typical cases appear where a partnership or a central corporation owns the controlling interest in one or more other corporations, but has so handled them that they have ceased to represent a separate enterprise and have become, as a business matter, more or less indistinguishable parts of a larger enterprise. The decisions disregard the paper corporate personalities and base liability on the assets of the enterprise. The reasoning by which courts reach this result varies: it is sometimes said that one corporation has become a mere "agency" of another; or that its operations have become so intermingled that it has lost its identity; or that the business arrangements indicate that it has become a "mere instrumentality".

See also Landers, A Unified Approach to Parent, Subsidiary and Affiliate Questions in Bankruptcy, 42 U.Chi.L.Rev. 589, 639 (1975), suggesting that consolidation of intra-enterprise corporate entities should be the presumptive approach, rebutted only "where the usual incentives to operate separate businesses as a single enterprise are absent or where creditors have actually relied on the credit of one of the separate companies."

2. PARENT AND SUBSIDIARY CORPORATIONS

The division of a business enterprise into multiple corporations is done for the convenience and profit maximization of the owners. Sometimes one corporation owns the stock of another, and the relationship is that of parent and subsidiary. Sometimes one corporation (a holding company) owns the stock of many corporations, all of whom are subsidiaries of the parent, and siblings, or affiliates, as to each other. While it may be appropriate to respect the limited liability of the shareholders of the *parent* corporation, it can be argued that all the related corporations should be treated as a single entity. See Berle, The Theory of Enterprise Liability, 47 Colum.L.Rev. 343 (1947); Landers, A Unified Approach to Parent, Subsidiary and Affiliate Questions in Bankruptcy, 42 U.Chi.L.Rev. 589 (1975). The courts, however, have not adopted such a universal rule.

Many cases have dealt with assertions of responsibility of the parent for the activity of the subsidiary. The different contexts of the claims provide guidance as to the result.

American Trading & Production Corp. v. Fischback & Moore, Inc., 311 F.Supp. 412 (N.D.Ill.1970) involved liability resulting from a fire that destroyed McCormick Place, an exposition hall, in Chicago. Plaintiff's exhibit was destroyed and it sued Fischback and Moore Electrical Contracting, Inc., a subsidiary of Fischback & Moore, Inc., the electrical contractors allegedly at fault for the fire. The parent was also sued although it was not directly involved, and it moved for summary judgment in its favor.

The salient aspects of the relationship between the two corporations were described as follows:

At the time of the fire, all four of the Subsidiary's directors were also directors of the Parent, and four of the Subsidiary's eight officers were also officers of the Parent. However, the corporations maintain separate offices and conduct separate directors' meetings. The financial books and records of the Subsidiary are maintained by its employees in Chicago, and contains only entries related to its own operations. The Subsidiary has its own bank accounts and negotiates its own loans from third parties; however, these loans are reviewed and guaranteed by the Parent. On occasion, the Subsidiary has borrowed money from the Parent; these loans are evidenced by notes and call for interest at the prime rate.

The Subsidiary and Parent file separate tax returns. However, financial statements of the Parent and all subsidiaries are consolidated. The payroll of the Subsidiary is paid by the Subsidiary rather than the Parent, and salary levels are determined by the Subsidiary subject to review by the Parent. The Subsidiary has never purchased goods or services from the Parent, nor has the Parent purchased goods and services from the Subsidiary. Purchasing is independently handled by each corporation, as are labor union relations.

The Subsidiary notifies the Parent of bids made on contracting jobs and of contracts awarded. However, neither bids nor contracts are reviewed by the Parent, nor are matters relating to the manner of performance and the materials to be used subject to review. On contracts exceeding $5,000,000 the profit "mark up" to be charged may be determined after consultation with the Par-

ent. The Subsidiary forwards schedules to the Parent regarding
new jobs acquired and contracts on hand for each three month period, and submits reports on material purchases, estimates, salary
changes and financial data on a more frequent basis.

On one occasion the Subsidiary sought review by the Parent of
a lease it had negotiated for additional yard space for its equipment. On other occasions, the Parent has determined which of its
subsidiaries should bid on a particular project. There is evidence
that the Parent's management considered it and the subsidiaries
to be one "family." This is reflected in some annual reports and
in advertising in Fortune magazine, wherein the Parent claimed
the credit in its own name for projects (including McCormick
Place) in fact performed by the Subsidiary.

Financial data of record reveals that the Subsidiary's net worth
was $511,503 in 1966 and $684,574 in 1967. It paid dividends of
$100,000 in 1966 and $369,000 in 1967, which amounts represented
substantially all of its after tax earnings. The corresponding
gross income figures for those years, $6,128,000 and $12,798,000
represent 4.42% and 8.07%, respectively, of the consolidated gross
income of the Parent and its subsidiaries. The Parent's gross income, apart from the income from subsidiaries, approximated
$77,000,000 in each of these two years.

The Parent and all subsidiaries are participants in a group liability insurance policy. The subsidiary pays its own share of the
premium, and has $15,000,000 worth of coverage applicable to lia-
bility arising out of the McCormick Place fire.

311 F.Supp. at 414–45.

The court analyzed these facts as follows:

1. Exercise of a degree of supervision by a 100% parent is not
sufficient to render the subsidiary an "instrumentality." *Id.* at 415.

2. Observance of corporate formalities, which were scrupulously
maintained, is significant. *Id.*

3. The fact that Parent considers its subsidiaries to be members
of a family "does not destroy the separate existence of each member." *Id.* at 416.

4. No elements of injustice existed. Nobody who contracted
with subsidiary believed they were dealing with parent. *Id.*

NOTE—"REVERSE VEIL–PIERCING"

The unusual prospect of "veil piercing in reverse" arises in workmen's compensation cases. While traditionally, a court will not disregard the corporate form in the absence of some form of fraud, these
cases differ radically in their approach. An example is Boggs v. Blue
Diamond Co., 590 F.2d 655 (6th Cir. 1979), cert. denied, 444 U.S. 836,
100 S.Ct. 71, 62 L.Ed.2d 47 (1979). Blue Diamond, which operated a

number of mines through separate subsidiaries, sought to be treated as one with its subsidiaries so that it could claim immunity from tort liability under Kentucky's Workmen's Compensation Act. The thrust of the parent company's arguments was that it qualified as an immune "employer" or "contractor" under the Act. The court responded by noting that the immunity provisions have been construed narrowly while " 'every presumption should be on the side of preserving' common law rights." 590 F.2d at 660. The court declined to disregard the corporate entities at the request of a parent corporation and held that for purposes of the Act the parent corporation was not an "employer" or a "contractor". Thus, the parent could be liable in tort for injuries to its subsidiary's employees arising out of the parent's negligence.

Boggs raises mainly an issue of statutory interpretation, in which the equities implicit in the specific legislation play a major role in the outcome. Nonetheless, even without consideration of specific legislation a court might still decline to pierce the veil in behalf of a parent. In Mingin v. Continental Can Co., 171 N.J.Super. 148, 408 A.2d 146 (1979), a factory worker in a container operation sustained injuries because of defective machine part. His immediate employer and the manufacturer of the defective part were both subsidiaries of a holding company, Continental Can. All three entities were covered under a common insurance policy. Continental argued that no common law action lay against it because of its unity with the container company. The court disagreed on the ground that the adoption of Continental's theory would prevent a significant portion of the population from recovering on products liability claim because of the presence of business conglomerates in American life.

3. "SIBLING" CORPORATIONS

MANGAN v. TERMINAL TRANSPORTATION SYSTEM, INC.

157 Misc. 627, 284 N.Y.S. 183 (Sup.Ct.1935), aff'd, per curiam
247 App.Div. 853, 286 N.Y.S. 666 (3d Dept.1936).

[The plaintiffs sued for injuries sustained in an accident caused by the negligence of the driver of a taxicab owned and operated by an affiliate of the defendant. After holding that the driver had been negligent, the court discussed the defendant's liability. The facts relating to the defendant's relationship with its affiliate are set out in the following passage.]

Were not the operating companies mere agents and instrumentalities of the defendant in carrying out its business?

The defendant says the operating companies hired, disciplined, and discharged their own drivers, received and banked their own cash, and performed other acts which it says labels them as separate corporate entities.

Just how did these companies operate? We have pointed out that each was owned or controlled by the same holding company, that each had two of its three directors in common, and that each operating company had the same contract with the defendant. The directors of all the contracting parties were chosen by the same holding company.

The defendant gave directions as to what terminals the respective operating companies should serve from day to day. The defendant provided inspectors and starters at each terminal, and supervisors who at times at least were on the streets "controlling drivers, regulating them, seeing that they observed the rules of the City of New York and rules of the company." The defendant at its office in the General Motors Building kept the books of the operating companies. The daily receipts were reported to the defendant which did the accounting for the operating companies and drew the checks for their payroll at least. The defendant maintained a claim department for the operating companies and furnished legal services. It sold the operating companies all parts, gasoline, oil, grease, and tires. The defendant hired all mechanics and maintained a central repair garage. The defendant examined and investigated all persons applying for positions as drivers. If acceptable, the applicant received a certificate which authorized the operating company to hire him. If a driver was hired without such certificate, he was required within a limited period to obtain it. While the defendant denies that it ever gave instructions to, hired, or discharged a driver, it maintained a traffic department from which notices were sent to the operating companies relative to complaints, and directions to drivers. One read in part: "Drivers who become disgruntled when getting a short call will do well to seek employment with some other company as in the future any complaint (in this respect) will be reason for instant dismissal." In other words, the operating companies did not hire a driver without the defendant's approval, and, it may be fairly implied, disciplined or discharged a driver if the defendant said so. Suppose by contract the defendant expressly reserved the right to hire, discharge, and control drivers, could it escape liability because the title to the *equity* in the cabs was in the operating company?

* * *

We think the corporate entity of the four so-called operating companies should be disregarded and the defendant held liable.

* * *

In the present case, control over the four operating companies is exercised both by the contracts between them and the defendant, and by the holding company's ownership of all the stock of the defendant and a controlling interest in the stock of the operating companies.

The directors of both parties to each of these contracts are elected by the same holding company.

* * *

We hold that the four operating companies were the agents and instrumentalities through which the defendant carried on its business, that their operation was controlled by the defendant, and that it is liable for the negligence of the driver of the cab involved.

D.   TORT VS. CONTRACT LIABILITY

In considering efforts to pierce the corporate veil in actions arising in contract, courts generally follow an analysis similar to that employed in the tort cases considered above. Is there any reason why the courts should treat the two differently? One answer to that question is suggested by Judge Frank in Weisser v. Mursam Shoe Corp., 127 F.2d 344, 347 n. 6 (2d Cir. 1942): "The only real differences between tort and contract cases in this field are (1) the defense of the Statute of Frauds and the sealed instrument rule, which should not be important, and (2) the possibility that, in contract cases, the plaintiff chose to deal with the subsidiary." There may also be reason to weigh certain factors less heavily in contract than in tort actions. It has been argued, for example, that a potential creditor has the opportunity to investigate the corporation's assets and to demand cash or adequate security before doing business with the firm if its assets are inadequate. This is a means of self-protection not available to the tort plaintiff, however. It follows, therefore, that undercapitalization should be given less weight in deciding whether to pierce the corporate veil in contract actions than in suits in tort. *See* Hamilton, The Corporate Entity, 49 Tex.L.Rev. 979, 984–89 (1971); Comment, Disregard of the Corporate Entity: Contract Claims, 28 Ohio St.L.J. 441, 442, 468 (1968); Clark, The Duties of the Corporate Debtor to its Creditors, 90 Harv.L.Rev. 505, 543 (1977). *But see* Note, Limited Liability: A Definitive Judicial Standard for the Inadequate Capitalization Problem, 47 Temple L.Q. 321, 343–45 (1974).

One commentator favors a more radical distinction between tort and contract liability. Observing that "Corporations owned by affluent shareholders, yet too impoverished to meet their tort liabilities, are the inevitable product of present-day incorporation laws," the author suggests that the corporate entity should afford no shield for the shareholders against tort liability. Note, Should Shareholder Be Personally Liable for the Torts of Their Corporations? 76 Yale L.J. 1190 (1967).

E. POLICY ASPECTS

PROBLEM

LIMITED LIABILITY: POLICY ASPECTS

You have been retained as a consultant to your jurisdiction's law revision commission. You have been asked to prepare a report commenting on proposed statute:

§ 1. A close corporation * is an incorporated enterprise whose common stock is held by or for not more than twenty-five persons, not counting those who own stock representing neither one per cent or more of the outstanding common stock nor more than a total book value of $10,000.

§ 2. If an enterprise was a close corporation on any day of the first nine months of the preceding calendar year, it shall be conclusively presumed to be a close corporation throughout the present calendar year. If a corporation did not exist during such nine month period, it shall be conclusively presumed to be a close corporation if it was such at any time during the three months preceding the tort for which shareholder liability is sought. In all other cases, an enterprise shall be conclusively presumed not to be a close operation.

§ 3. Any person who holds stock or securities in a close corporation for other than investment purposes shall be personally liable for torts the corporation commits while he owns such stock or securities. Any person who actively participates in the management of an enterprise, as an officer or director, or who owns more than ten percent of the corporation's outstanding stock shall be presumed to hold his stock or securities for other than investment purposes.

In thinking about your report, you have isolated the following questions you believe should be addressed:

1. Is the general thrust of the statute desirable? What are the reasons for and against holding shareholders of a close corporation liable for its torts?

2. Why should the proposed statute be limited to close corporations as defined? Is the definition of close corporations adequate?

3. Should exposure to personal liability be limited to common stockholders?

4. Why should the proposed statute be limited to tort claimants?

5. Is compulsory insurance a preferable alternative to personal liability?

---

* The concept of a close corporation is discussed in Chapter 11, *infra*.

6. As an alternative (or additional) approach, should all of the corporations in an enterprise composed of a parent and one or more subsidiaries or chains of subsidiaries be held liable for the obligations of one of the corporations within the enterprise so that claimants are able to satisfy their claims from the assets of the enterprise as a whole? Should it matter whether the obligations arise out of tort or contract? If some such scheme were adopted, how would the "enterprise" be defined? Among other considerations, what percentage of stock ownership should be required before an affiliated corporation is held liable?

In your assessment, consider the following:

R. POSNER, AN ECONOMIC ANALYSIS
OF LAW (2d ed. 1977).

§ 14.4 Piercing the Corporate Veil

In two situations, disregarding limited liability ("piercing the corporate veil," in the jargon of corporation law) may arguably promote efficiency. The first is illustrated by the taxi company in which each taxicab is incorporated separately in order to limit tort liability to accident victims. The separate incorporation of the taxicabs increases the risk that the taxi company will default on its tort obligations. If this were a negotiated obligation, the creditor-victim would charge a higher interest rate to reflect the increased risk, but it is not, negotiations between the taxi company and the accident victims before the accident being infeasible. The result of separate incorporation is therefore to externalize a cost of taxi service.

It does not follow, however, that veil piercing would be optimal, even in this situation. Permitting tort victims to reach the shareholders' assets would be a source of additional risk to the shareholder—and an increase in risk is a real cost to people who are risk averse. To be sure, the company could insure itself against its torts. But this would not be a completely satisfactory alternative to limited liability. The managers might fail to take out adequate insurance; the insurance company might for a variety of reasons refuse or be unable to pay a tort judgment against the insured (the insurance company might, for example, become insolvent); the particular tort might be excluded from the coverage of the insurance policy. An alternative would be to require any company engaged in dangerous activity to post a bond equal to the highest reasonable estimate of the probable extent of its tort liability. Shareholders would be protected (in what sense?) and accident costs internalized. Another alternative would be to treat the assets of all of the affiliated taxicab corporations as a single pool for purposes of meeting tort victims' claims against any of the corporations. But there would be a problem in defining the appropriate boundaries of the pool. Would it include the assets of affiliated corporations in a different business, or of an affiliated corporation engaged in the taxi business but in another state?

The other and more important case in which piercing the corporate veil may be warranted is where separate incorporation is misleading to creditors. If corporations are permitted to represent that they have greater assets to pay creditors than they actually have, the result will be to increase the costs that creditors must incur to ascertain the true creditworthiness of the corporations with which they deal. Misrepresentation is a way of increasing a creditor's information costs, and the added costs are wasted from a social standpoint to the extent that the misrepresentation could be prevented at lower cost by an appropriate sanction against it.

Misrepresentation is in fact the dominant approach used by the courts in deciding whether to pierce the corporate veil. True, they often describe the criterion for piercing as whether the debtor corporation is merely an "agent," "alter ego," or "instrumentality" of the shareholder, a confusing test. But a careful reading of these decisions suggests that in applying the agent-alter ego-instrumentality test the courts commonly ask whether the shareholder engaged in conduct or made representations likely to deceive the creditor into thinking that the debtor had more assets than it really had or that the shareholder was the real debtor. And some courts have explicitly adopted a misrepresentation rationale for determining whether to pierce the corporate veil.

Often a shareholder is a corporation rather than an individual, and it may seem that the policy of risk shifting that underlies the principle of limited liability would not apply in that case. If a parent corporation is made liable for its subsidiary's debts, the exposure of the parent's shareholders to liability, although greater than if the subsidiary enjoyed limited liability, is limited to their investment in the parent and can be further reduced by their holding a diversified portfolio of equities. However, it may be necessary to distinguish between the "publicly held" corporation (many shareholders, regularly traded stock) and the "close" corporation (few shareholders, no market in the stock). While the investor in the publicly held corporation can minimize the risk transmitted to him from the ventures undertaken and liabilities incurred by a corporation in which he owns stock, simply by holding a diversified portfolio for corporate securities, the investor in a close corporation frequently does not enjoy the same opportunities for diversification and therefore might not be able to protect himself effectively against the consequences of unlimited liability of corporate shareholders. Suppose, for example, that Mr. A. Smith wants to invest in a mining venture but the entire Smith fortune (other than that which Smith plans to commit to the mining venture) is invested in a radio station owned by a corporation of which Smith is the sole stockholder. If he forms a new corporation to conduct the mining venture, and if the assets of affiliated corporations may be pooled to satisfy the claims of creditors of one of the affiliates, Smith has hazarded his entire fortune on the outcome of the mining venture. In this case there is no difference between piercing the corporate veil to reach the assets of an affiliated corporation and piercing it to reach an individual shareholder's assets. The case is extreme, but approximations to it are common in the world of small business.

It has been argued that the case for limited liability is weaker for corporate than for personal shareholders because affiliated corporations, even if engaged in totally unrelated lines of business, will be managed differently from independent firms, since the owners will seek to maximize the profits of the enterprise as a whole rather than the profits of any individual corporation. Normally, however, the profits of the group will be maximized by maximizing the profits of each constituent corporation. Indeed, if the corporations are engaged in truly unrelated lines of business, the profits of each will be completely independent.

The common owner could take measures that concealed or distorted the relative profitability of his different enterprises, as by allocating capital among them at arbitrary interest rates. But it is not true that owners invariably or typically adopt such measures. Such measures are costly because they reduce the information available to the common owner about the efficiency with which his various corporations are being managed. The costs rise rapidly with the size of the overall enterprise. That is why large corporations typically treat their major divisions and subsidiaries as "profit centers," which are expected to conduct themselves as if they were independent firms. For similar reasons, divisional managers are compensated on the basis of the profitability of the subsidiary or division rather than of the enterprise as a whole.

Even when the activities of affiliated corporations are closely related—when they produce substitute or complementary goods—each corporation normally will be operated as a separate profit center in order to assure that the profits of the group will be maximized. It is only in the exceptional case that maximizing the profits of a group of related corporations will involve different behavior from what could be expected of separately owned corporations. To be sure, where there are genuine costs savings from common ownership, as in some cases where the affiliated corporations operate at successive stages in the production of a good, the two corporations will be managed differently from separately owned corporations in the same line of business in the sense that their operations will be integrated in a way independent corporations are not. But it would not follow that either corporation was, in any sense relevant to the reasonable expectations of creditors, something other than a bona fide profit-maximizing firm. Rather, each corporation would simply be more profitable than its nonintegrated competitors because its costs were lower. It would be perverse to penalize such a corporation for its superior efficiency by withdrawing the privilege of limited liability enjoyed by its nonintegrated competitors. Moreover, in this case as well, the common owner has a strong incentive to avoid intercorporate transfers that, by distorting the profitability of each corporation, make it more difficult for the common owner to evaluate their performance. That is why the price at which one division of a vertically integrated firm will "sell" its output to another division is normally the market price for the good in question (less any savings in cost attributable to making an intrafirm transfer compared to a market transaction) rather than an arbitrary transfer price designed artificially to enhance the profits of one division at the expense of the other.

The important difference between a group of affiliates engaged in related businesses and one engaged in a number of unrelated businesses is not that the conduct of corporations in the first group will differ from that of nonaffiliated corporations in the same businesses, but that the creditor dealing with a group of affiliates in related businesses is more likely to be misled into thinking that he is dealing with a single corporation. The misrepresentation principle seems adequate to deal with these cases.

Even if the law's only conern were creditor protection, a rule abrogating the limited liability of affiliated corporations would be difficult to justify, for it is not clear that it would reduce the risks of any class of creditors. True, the creditor of A Corporation would know that if A defaulted, he could reach the assets of its affiliate B—but he would also know that if B defaulted, B's creditors might have a claim on the assets of A that might cause A to default on his claim. Similarly, creditors of individuals would confront a greater risk of default if the liability of individuals as shareholders were not limited to their shares. Creditors' risks might not be smaller and their information costs would be higher.

———

The Posner view is disputed by Professor Jonathan Landers in Another Word on Parents, Subsidiaries and Affiliates in Bankruptcy, 43 U.Chi.L.Rev. 527 (1976). Professor Landers points out that the formation of a complex business enterprise into several corporations is undertaken for the convenience of the organizers who believe that such a structure will maximize their returns from the enterprise as a whole. It is irrelevant to them from which segment of the business the profits derive. Commingling of funds and loose organization is of no consequence to the people who form and operate the business in this manner. He favors a policy of allowing persons who do business with the corporate structure to be able to satisfy their claims from the enterprise as a whole and not to be limited to a single segment of it. In particular, he believes that the Posner consent and contract analysis neglects the plight of the tort claimant who is conscripted into doing business with the company. See id. at 529.

Chapter 10

CONTROL IN THE CORPORATION

A. THE CORPORATE ACTORS: SHAREHOLDERS, DIRECTORS, AND OFFICERS

Corporate law provides for a corporate governance model consisting of three sets of actors: shareholders, directors, and officers. The basic statutory model has traditionally been the same for all corporations regardless of the number of shareholders or the amount of sales or profits. As we shall see in a later chapter, the model has been adapted in recent years to accommodate the needs of the closely held corporation.

The statutory model defines the nature and functions of the corporate managers in only the most general fashion. Most statutes require little more than that a corporation have, as the MBCA puts it, "a president, one or more vice presidents * * *, a secretary, and a treasurer." MBCA § 50. These offices, except those of the president and secretary, may usually all be vested in the same individual. Although it requires that a corporation have these officers, the typical statute has little or nothing to say about their duties and powers. *See, e. g.*, MBCA § 50. ("All officers * * * shall have such authority and perform such duties * * * as may be provided in the by-laws, or as may be determined by resolution of the board of directors * * *.") The statutes generally make no mention of the chairman of the board, who, in practice as well as in popular lore, is frequently the most important corporate official.*

Indeed, a more important title than any of these is "chief executive officer," "general manager," or some similar indicator of a manager's actual position in the corporate hierarchy that is not mentioned at all in the statute. In any event, however vaguely defined the duties of a corporation's officers are by law, it is understood in practice that it is they who manage the corporation's affairs on a day-to-day basis.

Although management makes the routine decisions (and many major ones) regarding a corporation's operations, the ultimate responsibility for authority over the conduct of its affairs rests with the board of directors, which, according to the traditional model, is elected by the shareholder-owner of the company to oversee "their" business.

---

* This is by no means always so. In some companies the chairmanship of the board is largely an honorific title given to a retired or semi-retired former chief executive or other distinguished member of the board whose role consists of little more than actually presiding over board meetings. In others the same individual is both president and board chairman (and is usually also the chief executive officer).

Corporation statutes are quite explicit in placing that power and responsibility. Thus the MBCA (§ 35) provides that, "All corporate powers shall be exercised by or under authority of, and the business and affairs of a corporation shall be managed under the direction of, a board of directors * * *."* The role actually played by a board of directors varies widely from one corporation to another, depending on the size of the company, the number and composition of the board, whether the company is publicly or privately owned, the style of the chief executive officer, and, a cynical observer might note, how recently the members of the board have been sued. (We will consider some of these at greater length in a later chapter. The important thing to note at this point is that, with a very few exceptions, the board is the ultimate decisionmaking authority in the corporation at least in form.)

Aside from their general powers to oversee the conduct of the corporation's business, the directors are also given by the statute authority to make certain specific decisions. These include declaration of dividends (MBCA § 45), the selection, supervision, and removal of officers (MBCA § 50), and the initiation of fundamental changes such as amendment of the articles of incorporation (MBCA § 59(a)), merger or consolidation (MBCA §§ 71, 72, 73), sale of assets other than in the regular course of business (MBCA § 79), and voluntary dissolution (MBCA § 84). These decisions cannot be made on the authority of an officer.

The body for which, in an important sense, the rest of the structure exists is the shareholders. Although they "own" the corporation, by organizing their enterprise in corporate form they are required to delegate most of the discretion of an owner to manage his property to the board and through it to the management. (In a closely held corporation, of course, the principal shareholders are usually also directors, and thus the "delegation" of power by the shareholders to the board is only formal.) The shareholders do retain, however, certain authority superior to the board. First, of course, they elect and, in some situations, may remove the directors. MBCA §§ 36, 39. They are also given by statute the power to approve or disapprove—but not generally to initiate, which is reserved to the board—certain fundamental corporate changes, including amendments to the articles of incorporation (MBCA § 59), merger or consolidation (MBCA § 73), sale of all or substantially all of the assets (MBCA § 79), and voluntary dissolution (MBCA § 84). Finally, the shareholders have traditionally had the power, either by statute or as a result of case law, to amend the by-laws. (MBCA § 27 now provides that directors adopt and have the "power to alter, amend or repeal the by-laws or adopt new by-laws, subject to repeal or change by action of the shareholders * * *." There is some question as to the effect of

---

* Until recently this section read, "The business and affairs of a corporation shall be managed *by* a board of directors * * *." (Emphasis supplied.) What do you suppose was the reason for the change?

this statute on the right of shareholders to initiate amendments to the by-laws.)

B. ACTION BY EXECUTIVES: AGENCY PRINCIPLES AND THE AUTHORITY OF CORPORATE OFFICERS

1. INTRODUCTION TO SOME BASIC AGENCY CONCEPTS

The corporation, an incorporeal entity, can only act through the agency of flesh and blood human beings. An understanding of the law of corporations, therefore, requires some knowledge of the law of agency. If you have not already had a formal course in agency law, you have by now at least had some exposure to its principles in other basic courses. But since as, Oliver Wendell Holmes put it, "common sense is opposed to the fundamental theory of agency," * a review of those principles here is in order before we go on to examine their operation in a corporate context.

An agency is a consensual relationship between two parties in which one, the *agent*, agrees to act for the benefit of the other, the *principal*, in accordance with his instructions. The relationship between principal and agent is of a *fiduciary* character, which is to say, oversimplifying a bit, that the agent owes to the principal a duty of loyalty and obedience. The agent is bound not to act contrary to a reasonable order of the principal given within the scope of the agent's employment; and, also within the scope of the employment, the agent must always put the interests of the principal above his own. Perhaps of greatest relevance to the material in this chapter, the existence of an agency relationship confers on the agent a legal *power* to create rights in the principal's favor and, correlatively, to subject the principal to liability to third parties.

An agent may derive the power to bind his principal in a legal relationship with a third party from a number of theoretical sources. First, the agent may have been granted *authority* to bind the principal. According to the Restatement, Second Agency, § 7, this authority "is the power of the agent to affect the legal relations of the principal by acts done in accordance with the principal's manifestations of consent to him." It may either be *express* authority, growing out of explicit words or conduct granting the power to do the act; or it may be *implied* from words or conduct taken in the context of the relations between the principal and the agent. In either case, the authority rests on the dealings between the two and "can be created by written or spoken words or other conduct of the principal which, reasonably interpreted, causes the agent to believe that the principal desires him so to act on the principal's account." Restatement, Second, Agency § 26.

* Holmes, Agency, 5 Harv.L.Rev. 1, 14 (1891).

Although it sounds paradoxical to put it thus, an agent may also bind his principal even though he lacks the authority to do so.* (Perhaps Holmes was right.) The principal may, for example, create *apparent authority* "by written or spoken words or any other conduct * * * which, reasonably interpreted, causes the third person to believe that the principal consents to have the act done on his behalf by the person purporting to act for him." Restatement, Second, Agency § 27. Note that the existence of *actual* authority depends upon communications between the principal and the agent, whereas the existence of apparent authority depends on communications between the principal and the third party.** An agent may also bind his principal by what the Restatement calls *"inherent agency power."* (Restatement, Second, Agency § 8A). The easiest example of such power (which is, within the terminology of the Restatement, not "authority") is the rule that a principal is liable for the *torts* of his servant under the doctrine *respondeat superior.* Since a principal would normally not authorize an agent to commit a tort, it is clear that this rule cannot be based on any theory of delegation of power. It is based instead simply on considerations of public policy. It is thought to be fair that the principal be held responsible to someone injured by a tort committed by a servant acting within the scope of his employment.

Although the rule is less well-understood, an agent may, without express or implied authority—and even acting contrary to instructions—bind his principal in contract when the transaction is closely related to his general mandate. This is true even though the communication between the principal and the third party necessary for the creation of apparent authority is lacking. The rule, like the doctrine of *respondeat superior*, is in part founded on considerations of fairness. As the Restatement, Second, Agency puts it, "because agents are fiduciaries acting generally in the principal's interests, and are trusted and controlled by him, it is fairer that the risk of loss caused by disobedience of agents should fall upon the principal rather than upon third persons." (§ 8A, Comment b.) The rule is also designed to foster convenient and efficient modes of doing business. A well-known statement of the policy is found in Kidd v. Thomas A. Edison, Inc., 239 F. 405 (S.D.N.Y.1917). The defendant's agent had hired the

---

* This paradox prompted Professor Seavey to urge that the term "authority" be limited to cases of actual authority, that is, where the principal has expressly or implicitly granted the agent a power. Seavey, The Rationale of Agency, 29 Yale L.J. 859, 860–61 (1920). This sound recommendation was swamped in the sea of long usage, and Professor Seavey apparently ultimately abandoned it. *See* W. Seavey, Handbook of the Law Agency 13 (1964); Seavey, Agency Powers, 1 Okl. L.Rev. 3, 3–4 (1948).

** The principle of *estoppel* is often used to impose liability on the principal in situations in which apparent authority might have been used. The technical distinction is that for the principal to be estopped from denying the agent's authority, the third party must have changed position in reliance on some representation by the principal. *See* Restatement, Second, Agency § 31.

plaintiff to engage in a series of recitals designed to show the fidelity with which her voice could be reproduced by the defendant's records. The defendant claimed that the agent's authority was explicitly limited to contracting only for such recitals as he could later persuade record dealers to sponsor. Judge Learned Hand held that the defendant was liable for the fees for the unconditional recital tour the jury had found the agent to have agreed to. He reasoned:

> The responsibility of a master for his servant's act is not at bottom a matter of consent to the express act, or of an estoppel to deny that consent, but it is a survival from ideas of status, and the imputed responsibility congenial to earlier times, preserved now from motives of policy. While we have substituted for the archaic status a test based upon consent, i. e., the general scope of the business, within that sphere the master is held by principles quite independent of his actual consent, and indeed in the face of his own instructions. * * *.

> The considerations which have made the rule survive are apparent. If a man selects another to act for him with some discretion, he has by that fact vouched to some extent for his reliability * * *. The very purpose of delegated authority is to avoid constant recourse by third persons to the principal, which would be a corollary of denying the agent any latitude beyond his exact instructions. [239 F. at 407, 408.]

The term inherent agency power did not develop from the case law, but was used for the first time in the Restatement to describe the result in a class of cases for which there was thought to be no other satisfactory explanation in terms of the traditional categories of agency law. It has since appeared in only a few judicial opinions.* Perhaps its principal difficulty is that the concept, while appealing, has no clearly defined limits. Although perhaps preferable analytically to such terms as implied authority or apparent authority, which are often inaccurately used to explain a particular holding, "public policy" or "business convenience" (see Seavey, The Rationale of Agency, 29 Yale L.J. 859, 885 (1920)) provide only the crudest indication of when inherent power exists. As some of the materials that follow suggest, the concept presents particular problems in a corporate context, especially with regard to the extent which corporate officers would be deemed to have inherent powers by virtue of their offices.

Finally, someone may become obligated to a third party by the *ratification* of the act of another who, at the time of the act, lacked the power to bind the ratifier. Ratification is defined by the Restatement, Second, Agency § 8 as "the affirmance by a person of a prior act which did not bind him but which was done or professedly done on his account, whereby the act, as to some or all persons, is given effect

---

* Professor Seavey, writing in 1964, reports that he had found only two such cases. W. Seavey, Handbook of the Law of Agency 16 (1964).

as if originally authorized by him." When someone ratifies an authorized act done by another in his name, it is said that the ratification "relates back" so as to leave the resulting state of affairs precisely as it would have been had the authority been conferred before
the act. There need be no agency relationship at the time of the act.
The ratification is what creates it.

Ratification is simply the unilateral consent of the ratifier, which
may be inferred from "any act, words or conduct which reasonably
tend to show intention to ratify." Meyers v. Cook, 87 W.Va. 265, 104
S.E. 593 (1920). It is probably enough in many instances that the
incipient principal acquiesces in the transaction without raising objection to it. It comes as a surprise to many students that the ratifier's
decision to accept the act need not be communicated. According to
Professor Seavey, "Affirmance does not require a manifestation of
consent to the agent, to the other party or any one." W. Seavey,
Handbook of the Law of Agency 67 (1964).

A simple hypothetical may help to illustrate some of these concepts. Suppose that Priscilla Principal, a horse breeder, says to her
employee, Andrew Agent, "Andy, please go down to the stables, put
up a sign, "HORSES FOR SALE," and sell all of my horses for $500
apiece." Andrew has *express authority* to sell the horses. He also
probably has *implied authority* to accept an apparently valid check
in payment since, as long as Priscilla had not previously demanded
cash in such transactions, it is reasonable to assume that she intended that Andrew accept checks. He may or may not have implied authority to accept a used car or a hogshead of tobacco worth $500,
depending on what would be reasonably understood from the circumstances (such as the normal practices in the trade or in the locality)
and from the prior dealings between him and Priscilla.

Suppose, now, that Priscilla gives him the same instructions but
adds, "except Native Dancer. Whatever you do, don't sell Native
Dancer." She also sends out letters to prospective buyers saying, "I
am selling off my horses. If you are interested, please see Andrew
Agent at the stables. He is authorized to act for me." If Andrew
sells Native Dancer to a recipient of the letter, Priscilla may not recover the horse. By communicating what would appear to a reasonable person to be an intention to give Andrew the authority to sell
Native Dancer, she has clothed him with *apparent authority* and is
bound by his act, even though it was directly contrary to her instructions.

Now suppose that Priscilla has delegated the management of her
horse farm to Andrew, who regularly buys and sells horses according
to his own judgment. Under these circumstances, if he sells Native
Dancer to a stranger who has not received Priscilla's letter (and who
thus has no basis for believing in Andrew's apparent authority), the
sale is binding on Priscilla by virtue of Andrew's *inherent agency
power.*

Finally, suppose that Andrew has never before sold any horses for Priscilla (and thus has no inherent power), but he nevertheless purports to sell Native Dancer to the stranger. When Priscilla learns of the sale, she declares, "Well I guess that's okay. Five hundred dollars is a pretty good price for that nag anyway." She has *ratified* the transaction and becomes bound as if Andrew had been authorized to accomplish it in the first place. Indeed, she ratifies the transaction even if she says nothing but takes no steps to rescind it.

PROBLEM

AGENCY RELATIONS—PART I

In order to test your understanding of basic agency concepts, consider whether the principal would be bound, and on what theory, in each of the following circumstances assuming the parties executed a contract:

1. The board of directors of East Wind Boats, Inc., passes a resolution directing Jack Hardy, the president of the corporation, to contract for the construction of a new building at the boatyard.

2. Judy Luff, the vice president of the corporation, purchases $1000 worth of plastic resin. She frequently purchases materials used in East Winds operations, but the board has never explicitly authorized her to do so.

3. Will Wright is a foreman in the boatyard. He has been instructed not to purchase any materials without first asking Hardy or Luff, and he has never done so. One day while Hardy and Luff are away at a business conference, however, a representative of a wholesale lumber dealer visits the boatyard and tells Wright that he has a temporary oversupply of teak which he is willing to sell at a substantial discount. Wright signs a purchase order for $1000 worth.

4. Wright goes to an auto dealer (who has never seen him before) and signs a contract to purchase a new pickup truck for East Wind. He signs, "East Wind Boats, Inc., by Will Wright." When he tells Hardy and Luff what he has done, Luff responds, "You shouldn't really have done that without asking us Will. But I guess you're right; we do need the truck." They accept delivery without protest.

PROBLEM

AGENCY RELATIONS—PART II

Harold Hawks entered into a contract a little over a year ago with Acoustics Incorporated, a small manufacturer of high fidelity speakers, under the terms of which he was to become the exclusive regional distributor for Acoustics' products for a period of three years. The contract provided that Hawks was to purchase speakers from the corporation at its listed wholesale prices and resell them to his customers at a 15% markup. It also contained the somewhat unusual provision that, if Hawks' purchases in any given year exceed $500,000, he would be paid a "commission" at the end of the year of 2% of *all* his purchases.

Hawks negotiated the contract with Acoustics' president, James Huston, whose signature appeared at the bottom of the document thus:

> Acoustics, Incorporated
>
> By /s/ James Huston
>
> James Huston, President

A few months after the contract was signed there was a management shakeup at Acoustics and Huston was dismissed.

During the first year of the contract, Hawks purchased $650,000 worth of speakers from the firm. He wrote the new president, Margo Pickford, asking for his 2% commission. Her letter of response said that she knew nothing of the contract and denied any liability under it. Furthermore, she said, while Acoustics would be happy to continue with Hawks as a distributor, it did not consider the arrangement exclusive, and was in fact in the process of working out an arrangement with another distributor in the same region.

There was a second exchange of correspondence, in which Hawks sent Pickford a copy of the contract and she wrote back that even if Huston had signed it, he had not been authorized to do so.

1.   You have been retained to advise him as to his legal rights. You are considering whether to file a breach of contract action. On what theories might you proceed? What additional information would you like to have? How would you get it?

2.   You represent the corporation in an action brought by Hawks. Would you advise settling the claim?

PROBLEM

AGENCY RELATIONS—PART III

You represent the Third National Bank and Trust Company which is about to loan a substantial amount of money to Universal Widgets, Inc., a wholly owned subsidiary of Universal Inc. The loan is to be secured by a mortgage on the Universal Widget's plant, and, because Universal is a relatively new company with a short operating history, the bank has also insisted on a guarantee executed by the parent corporation. You have been asked by the bank to handle the closing of the deal, at which you will be asked to provide an opinion that the mortgage, note, and guarantees are "valid, binding, and enforceable in accordance with their terms."

What documents should you require that the other side present at the closing in order to assure the validity of the mortgage, note and guarantee and to allow you to give the opinion of counsel requested by the bank? Are there any other legal questions that you should check? What remedial legal doctrines are available on which you might fall back should some defect in the formalities of the transaction go undetected?

2. SPECIAL PROBLEMS OF AGENCY IN A CORPORATE CONTEXT: THE INHERENT AUTHORITY OF OFFICERS

There is much confusion over the nature and extent of the authority possessed by corporate officers, in particular the president, merely because of their position. The confusion extends to the most fundamental theoretical level. Such authority as an officer possesses could be thought to result expressly from the intention of the board of directors in appointing someone to the office. It could find its source in apparent authority, *i.e.*, the power that a reasonable person dealing with the corporation would believe the officer to possess. It may arise from implication from prior dealings in which the officer has been allowed to exercise powers without challenge by the board. Or, finally, it could be considered to be a power akin to the Restatement's "inherent agency power," a view supported by cases such as Moyse Real Estate Co. v. First National Bank of Commerce, 110 Miss. 620, 70 So. 821 (1916), in which the court said:

> Nearly all of the big business and a large part of the small business is now conducted by corporations, and if it be the law that persons dealing with the president of a corporation about matters of business clearly within the powers of the corporation to transact must deal at arm's length, and demand that the president exhibit his credentials before entering into contracts with him, it seems to us that not only the corporation, but also those dealing with corporations, will be seriously hampered.

* * *

> If it be true that the president did not possess the authority assumed by him in the present case, the proof of his lack of authority was in the possession of the corporation, and there would have been no difficulty in the way of its production. On the other hand, it might be very difficult and expensive for the plaintiff to have secured the evidence to show his authority.

Courts have not been meticulous in choosing among the alternate agency theories in holding corporations bound by the acts of their officers. This may be just as well, for those theories were developed to describe the legal relations created when one individual appoints another to act as his agent and are not well suited to a corporate context. A part of the problem grows out of the dual role occupied by corporate officers. Their offices carry with them certain responsibilities related to the organizational structure of the corporation. (See, *e. g.*, the description of the duties of the officers in the Model

By-Laws contained in the book, Selected Corporations and Partnership Statutes, Regulations and Forms.) In this capacity they are concerned principally with the internal management of the corporation and do not deal with persons outside it. On the other hand, some corporate employees must act for the corporation in its relations to the outside world, and it is often the officers who do so, particularly in major transactions. The failure to distinguish between these two functions has contributed to the confusion over the sources of officers' authority as agents for the corporation. *See* Kempin, The Corporate Officer and the Law of Agency, 44 Va.L.Rev. 1273 (1958). See also Note, Inherent Power as a Basis of a Corporate Officer's Authority to Contract, 57 Colum.L.Rev. 868 (1957).

NOTE, AUTHORITY OF A CORPORATION PRESIDENT TO BIND THE CORPORATION BY VIRTUE OF HIS OFFICE

50 Yale L.J. 348, 350–53 (1940).

[I]t has become increasingly difficult to piece together a composite picture of the corporation's liability for the acts of its president. It is evident, however, that the tremendous growth of corporate business, both in size and in compass, in the past fifty years, coupled with emergence of dominating personalities at the head of many corporations, has resulted in an inevitable concentration of executive power in the corporate president. A corollary of this has been the decline in importance, until recent legislation checked the trend, of the board of directors in the active management of corporate affairs. Judicial recognition of this shift of power has resulted in most states in the sanctioning, as within the president's authority by virtue of his office, of such actions as issuance and endorsement of negotiable paper, borrowing funds, and making short term employment contracts.

The general increase in the scope of the president's authority as it is commonly exercised in business practice has resulted in one significant procedural change. In many jurisdictions the burden of proving authority, or want thereof, has been shifted from the third person to the corporation. This is important not only because the burden of proving authority was often difficult for a party not having access to the internal records of the corporation, but also because it has led to closer judicial analysis of authority, particularly of that authority resulting by virtue of office. That this change of view may have some effect upon the substantive law of what is to be included in the scope of the president's authority by virtue of his office seems possible. The Delaware court in [Halo-Petroleum Corp. of America v. Hannigan, 14 A.2d 401 (Del.Sup.Ct.1940)] spoke of the "reasonable and practical view" that the president be "presumed to have, by virtue of his office, certain more or less limited powers in the transaction of the usual and ordinary business of the corporation." Other cases show some indication that a rule of procedure as to who shall have the burden of proof might well develop into an absolute grant of authority to the president by virtue of his office.

*   *   *

Many jurisdictions, primarily those in which corporate enterprise has been less prevalent, have clung to the older view that there is no authority in the president by virtue of his office to bind the corporation. Those that do allow the presumption have generally adopted one of two views: either that there is a rebuttable presumption of authority to perform any act within the scope of the company's ordinary business or, more broadly, to do anything that the directors could authorize. The basis of the latter view is protection to third parties dealing with the president whenever he could conceivably be acting with authority, while the purpose of the former limitation is to protect third persons only in ordinary situations where they would be likely to expect him to be acting with authority, *i.e.*, when he is carrying on the ordinary business of the company.

LEE v. JENKINS BROTHERS

268 F.2d 357 (2d Cir. 1959), cert. denied,
361 U.S. 913, 80 S.Ct. 257, 4 L.Ed.2d 183.

[Lee sued Jenkins Brothers, a corporation, to recover pension payments allegedly due him under an oral contract made in 1920 on behalf of the corporation by Yardley. The Court of Appeals affirmed the District Court's dismissal of the case, ruling that the evidence of the alleged agreement was insufficient to present a jury question. The court went on, however, to say that there was sufficient evidence in the record to present a jury question as to the extent of Yardley's authority to make the alleged agreement for the corporation. On the law governing this question, Medina, J., said:]

Our question on this phase of the case then boils itself down to the following: can it be said as a matter of law that Yardley as president, chairman of the board, substantial stockholder and trustee and son-in-law of the estate of the major stockholder, had no power in the presence of the company's most interested vice president to secure for a "reasonable" length of time badly needed key personnel by promising an experienced local executive a life pension to commence in 30 years at the age of 60, even if Lee were not then working for the corporation, when the maximum liability to Jenkins under such a pension was $1500 per year.

A survey of the law on the authority of corporate officers does not reveal a completely consistent pattern. For the most part the courts perhaps have taken a rather restrictive view on the extent of powers of corporate officials, but the dissatisfaction with such an approach has been manifested in a variety of exceptions such as ratification, estoppel, and promissory estoppel. See Note, 57 Colum.L. Rev. 868 (1957). For the most part also there has been limited discussion of the problem of apparent authority, perhaps on the assumption that if authority could not be implied from a continuing course of action between the corporation and the officer, it could not have been apparent to third parties either.

Such an assumption is ill-founded. The circumstances and facts known to exist between officer and corporation, from which actual authority may be implied, may be entirely different from those circumstances known to exist as between the third party and the corporation. The two concepts are separate and distinct even though the state of the proofs in a given case may cause considerable overlap.

The rule most widely cited is that the president only has authority to bind his company by acts arising in the usual and regular course of business but not for contracts of an "extraordinary" nature. The substance of such a rule lies in the content of the term "extraordinary" which is subject to a broad range of interpretation.

The growth and development of this rule occurred during the late nineteenth and early twentieth centuries when the potentialities of the corporate form of enterprise were just being realized. As the corporation became a more common vehicle for the conduct of business it became increasingly evident that many corporations, particularly small closely held ones, did not normally function in the formal ritualistic manner hitherto envisaged. While the boards of directors still nominally controlled corporate affairs, in reality officers and managers frequently ran the business with little, if any, board supervision. The natural consequence of such a development was that third parties commonly relied on the authority of such officials in almost all the multifarious transactions in which corporations engaged. The pace of modern business life was too swift to insist on the approval by the board of directors of every transaction that was in any way "unusual."

The judicial recognition given to these developments has varied considerably. Whether termed "apparent authority" or an "estoppel" to deny authority, many courts have noted the injustice caused by the practice of permitting corporations to act commonly through their executives and then allowing them to disclaim an agreement as beyond the authority of the contracting officer, when the contract no longer suited its convenience. Other courts, however, continued to cling to the past with little attempt to discuss the unconscionable results obtained or the doctrine of apparent authority. Such restrictive views have been generally condemned by the commentators.

The summary of holdings pro and con in general on the subject of what are and what are not "extraordinary" agreements is inconclusive at best   *   *   *.   But the pattern becomes more distinct when we turn to the more limited area of employment contracts.

It is generally settled that the president as part of the regular course of business has authority to hire and discharge employees and fix their compensation. In so doing he may agree to hire them for a specific number of years if the term selected is deemed reasonable. But employment contracts for life or on a "permanent" basis are generally regarded as "extraordinary" and beyond the authority of any corporate executive if the only consideration for the promise is the employee's promise to work for that period. Jenkins would have us analogize the pension agreement involved herein to these generally condemned lifetime employment contracts because it extends over a long period of time, is of indefinite duration, and involves an indefinite liability on the part of the corporation.

It is not surprising that lifetime employment contracts have met with substantial hostility in the courts, for these contracts are often oral, uncorroborated, vague in important details and highly improbable. * * *

However, at times such contracts have been enforced where the circumstances tended to support the plausibility of plaintiff's testimony. Thus when the plaintiff was injured in the course of employment and he agreed to settle his claim of negligence against the company for a lifetime job, authority has been generally found and the barrage of other objections adequately disposed of. And where additional consideration was given such as quitting other employment, giving up a competing business, or where the services were "peculiarly necessary" to the corporation, the courts have divided on the enforceability of the contract.

What makes the point now under discussion particularly interesting is the failure of the courts denying authority to make lifetime contracts to evolve any guiding principle. More often than not we find a mere statement that the contract is "extraordinary" with a citation of cases which say the same thing, without giving reasons. * * *

Where reasons have been given to support the conclusion that lifetime employments are "extraordinary," and hence made without authority, a scrutiny of these reasons may be helpful for their bearing on the analogous field of pension agreements. It is said that: they unduly restrict the power of the shareholders and future boards of directors on questions of managerial policy; they subject the corporation to an inordinately substantial amount of liability; they run for long and indefinite periods of time. Of these reasons the only one applicable to pension agreements is that they run for long and indefinite periods of time. There the likeness stops. Future director or shareholder control is in no way impeded; the amount of liability is not disproportionate; the agreement was not only not unreasonable but beneficial and necessary to the corporation; and pension contracts are commonly used fringe benefits in employment contracts. Moreover, unlike the case with life employment contracts, courts have often gone out of their way to find pension promises binding and definite even when labeled gratuitous by the employer. The consideration given to the employee involved is not at all dependent on profits or sales, nor does it involve some other variable suggesting director discretion.

Apparent authority is essentially a question of fact. It depends not only on the nature of the contract involved, but the officer negotiating it, the corporation's usual manner of conducting business, the size of the corporation and the number of its stockholders, the circumstances that give rise to the contract, the reasonableness of the contract, the amounts involved, and who the contracting third party is, to list a few but not all of the relevant factors. In certain instances a given contract may be so important to the welfare of the corporation that outsiders would naturally suppose that only the board of directors (or even the shareholders) could properly handle it. It is in this light that the "ordinary course of business" rule should be given its content. Beyond such "extraordinary" acts, whether or not apparent authority exists is simply a matter of fact.

Accordingly, we hold that, assuming there was sufficient proof of the making of the pension agreement, Connecticut, in the particular circumstances of this case, would probably take the view that reasonable men could differ on the subject of whether or not Yardley had apparent authority to make the contract, and that the trial court erred in deciding the question as a matter of law. We do not think Connecticut would adopt any hard and fast rule against apparent authority to make pension agreements generally, on the theory that they were in the same category as lifetime employment contracts.

* * *

SCIENTIFIC HOLDING CO., LTD. v. PLESSEY INC.

510 F.2d 15 (2d Cir. 1974).

[Scientific Holding Company, Ltd. (Scientific), an Illinois corporation, was the successor to International Scientific, Ltd. (ISL), a Barbados company engaged in the manufacture of computer components. ISL was experiencing severe financial difficulties and on February 4, 1970 contracted to sell all of its assets and business to Plessey Inc. (Plessey), a Delaware subsidiary of The Plessey Company, Ltd., a large English company. The contract included a clause conditioning Plessey's obligation to close the transaction on the truth of ISL's representation that operating losses subsequent to December 31, 1969, did not exceed $20,000 per month. A portion of the purchase price was contingent on ISL's assets generating a profit during a "measuring year" to commence on the first day of the month following the closing. During that year ISL's management was to continue to operate its business, subject to the provision that if ISL's profits commencing with the third calendar month of the measuring year averaged less than $15,000 per month, Plessey would have the right to assume control.

On that date of the scheduled closing it appeared that ISL's losses for January and February 1970, were in excess of $20,000 per month. Plessey refused to close unless the agreement was modified to allow Plessey to take over management of the business if profits averaged less than $15,000 per month beginning with the second calendar month after the closing.

ISL was represented at the closing by Kovar, its president and chief operating officer. The ISL board resolution approving the sale stated that "the proper officers of this Corporation are authorized and directed to make such changes in that agreement as in the opinion of the directors shall be necessary or appropriate * * *." Kovar expressed doubts at the closing that he had the authority to agree to the modification sought by Plessey. Nevertheless, he finally did sign the amended agreement.

ISL did not meet the $15,000 profit level by May 1970, and Plessey notified ISL by letter of June 9, 1970, that it was assuming management control. The transferred assets eventually failed to generate any profits during the measuring year and Plessey accordingly made no contingent payment. Scientific, as successor to ISL, sued Plessey in part on the theory that the amendment at the closing was invalid because Kovar lacked authority to accede to it and that Plessey's takeover was therefore premature and had prevented performance by ISL of the profit condition that would have entitled it to the additional payment.]

FRIENDLY, Circuit Judge.

C.

* * * In two early opinions, the New York Court of Appeals stated that the president or other general officer of a corporation engaged in business activities had, by virtue of his office, prima facie power to make any contract for the corporation that the board of directors could have authorized or ratified, and that the burden of proving any lack of authorization was on those seeking to impeach the contract. *See* Patterson v. Robinson, 116 N.Y. 193, 22 N.E. 372 (1889) (president); Hastings v. Brooklyn Life Ins. Co., 138 N.Y. 473, 34 N.E. 289 (1893) (secretary who was one of corporation's general managing agents). However, a number of subsequent New York cases indicated adherence to the narrower proposition that the presumption of the president's authority extends only to transactions in the ordinary course of the company's business. * * *

In 1934, Judge L. Hand, speaking for this court in Schwartz v. United Merchant & Manufacturers, Inc., 72 F.2d 256 (2 Cir. 1934), attempted to discern the precise content of the New York "rule." After briefly summarizing most of the applicable New York decisions, Judge Hand concluded that "there is no absolute rule in New York that any contract which the president of a company may make, however out of the ordinary, throws upon the company the duty of showing that he was unauthorized. It is true that whatever powers are usual in the business may be assumed to have been granted; but the presumption stops there   *   *   *." *Id.* 72 F.2d at 258. Although certain commentators have found this holding to be inconsistent with the *Patterson-Hastings* rule, *see* Note, Inherent Power As a Basis of a Corporate Officer's Authority To Contract, 57 Colum.L. Rev. 868, 873 (1957), most subsequent New York cases, as well as federal cases applying New York law, have adopted the "ordinary business rule"   *   *   *.

[U]nder New York Business Corporations Law § 909(a)(3), McKinney's Consol.Laws, c. 4, and apparently under the stockholders' resolution authorizing the liquidation and sale of assets, the directors could have authorized the changes contained in the March 2 amendment. If the *Patterson-Hastings* rule were indeed the law of New York, this might end the matter since it would not be unreasonable to say that when a corporation dispatches its president to close an authorized contract, it endows him with actual and not merely apparent authority to agree to changes, material but not going to the heart of the contract, for which developments at the closing may call. However, the case becomes closer if, as we believe, the law of New York is what Judge Hand stated in *Schwartz*. And it becomes closer still in view of the statements allegedly made by Kovar to Plessey's representatives at the closing questioning his authority to authorize the amendments since these expressed doubts might preclude reliance on his apparent authority as ISL's president, chief operating officer, and principal negotiator of the agreement. It is an accepted principle of the law of agency that a person with notice of a limitation which has been placed on an agent's authority cannot subject the principal to liability upon a transaction with the agent if he knows or should know that it is outside the scope of the agent's authority. Knowledge of Kovar's statements alone would hardly constitute express "knowledge" of his lack of authority, such as was present in [Ernst Iron Works, Inc. v. Duralith Corp., 270 N.Y. 165, 200 N.E. 683 (1936),] since his expression of "doubts" might reasonably have been interpreted by Plessey's representatives under the circumstances as a calculated bluff designed to gain additional time both to consider their demands and possibly to negotiate more favorable terms. However, depending upon the authority typically accorded presidents of corporations to approve at the closing modifications of agreements which are outside the ordinary course of business, Kovar's expression of doubt may have been sufficient to place a duty on Plessey to inquire with ISL's board as to the actual scope of his authority, which if not satisfied would prevent it from relying on his apparent authority,—an issue to which counsel have not addressed themselves.   *   *   *

The decisive point is that even assuming *arguendo* the March 2 amendment to be invalid as unauthorized, at least if the jury had accepted the testimony of Kovar and Lewis [the attorney who represented ISL at the closing], direction of a verdict was nevertheless proper on the ground that Scientific's failure to repudiate the amendment for lack of authorization until mid-July estopped it from doing so later.   *   *   *

If Kovar and Lewis had "serious doubts" with respect to the former's authority to agree to the amendments, it is almost beyond belief that they did not recognize an imperative obligation to inform their principal which they must fulfill as soon as practicable. If, as they aver, they did not discharge that duty, their knowledge of the amendment is nevertheless imputed to the corporation. In Hurley v. John Hancock Mutual Life Ins. Co., 247 App.Div. 547, 288 N.Y.S. 199, 202 (4th Dept. 1936), the court stated:

> It is a well-settled principle of agency that as a general rule, the principal is bound by notice to or knowledge of his agent in all matters within the scope of the agency, although in fact the information may never have actually been communicated.

Even if Kovar had no authority to amend the contract, attendance at the closing was surely "within the scope of his agency" as the term is used in this context, namely, to exclude attribution of facts which came to the knowledge of the agent when acting in a purely private capacity or adversely to the principal, and all knowledge acquired by him at the closing thus is imputed to the corporation. Moreover, as said in Restatement of Agency 2d § 272, "the liability of a principal is affected by the knowledge of an agent concerning a matter as to which he acts within his power to bind the principal *or* upon which it is his duty to give the principal information." (Emphasis added.)
*   *   *

Judgment affirmed.

Joseph Greenspon's Sons Iron & Steel Co. v. Pecos Valley Gas Co., 34 Del. 567, 156 A. 350 (1931) involved the liability of a gas company on a contract made by its president to purchase 45 miles of gas pipe for approximately $145,000 without express authority from the board of directors. The court charged the jury as follows:

> I have been asked specifically to charge you that if you should find that Albert T. Woods, President of the defendant corporation, signed the contract in question, that then the corporation would necessarily be conclusively bound by such contract, for I am requested to state that the power of a President of a corporation is as complete and effective as is the power of a Board of Directors acting pursuant to a vote of the Board.

> This I decline to do as I deem it an extreme and incorrect view of the powers of a President of a corporation.

> The powers of a President of a corporation, *i. e.*, the powers over its business and property, are, of course, merely the powers of an agent, for a corporation can speak in no other manner. The

control over the company's business and property is vested in the Board of Directors, but subject to this control certain powers are delegated by implication to certain officers. Corporations have assumed and acquired such a position in the business world that the office of President carries with it certain implied powers of an agency. He is usually either expressly or by implied consent made the chief executive officer, without special authority or explicitly delegated power he may perform all acts of an ordinary nature which by usage or necessity are incidents to his office and by virtue of his office he may enter into a contract and bind his corporation in matters arising from and concerning the usual course of the corporation's business. These are the implied powers of the President of the corporation and they inhere in him by virtue of the position itself. Beyond these powers—beyond the carrying out of the usual and proper functions of the corporation necessary for the proper and convenient management of the business of the corporation, the President remains as any other Director of the company, and other and further powers must be specifically conferred.

The plaintiff contends that the action of the President in ordering the pipe was an ordinary and usual duty and within the powers impliedly placed by the law in a President who is also managing executive of a corporation. Whether or not this is true in any given case depends upon all the facts of the case, including the character of the goods ordered, the amount thereof in relation to the size and condition of the company, the nature of the company, its purposes and aims, and upon many other facts and circumstances. Whether or not a specific action of a President is within his usual duties is, therefore, a question of fact for the determination of the jury.

The powers of a President of a corporation in excess of those hereinbefore suggested, that is, in excess of power over the ordinary and usual business of the corporation, must be specifically given, and the following are the usual sources of this grant of power:

1. Some provision of statutory law;

2. Corporate charter;

3. Some by-law of the company;

4. Resolution of the Board of Directors.

A fifth and perhaps the most usual source of the grant of the unusual or extraordinary powers of a President arises by implication of law from a course of conduct on the part of both the President and the corporation showing that he had been in the habit of acting in similar matters on behalf of the company and that the company had authorized him so to act and had recognized, approved and ratified his former and similar actions.

3. THE CREATION OF EXPRESS AUTHORITY

Given the uncertainties in the extent of the authority of a corporate officer, even of the president, careful counsel representing a party in dealings with a corporation will usually insist, at least in major transactions, on adequate evidence that the individuals who purport to act for the corporation have the power to do so.

What is sufficient to constitute such evidence? The basic source of nearly all authority in the corporation is the statutory provision conferring power to manage its affairs on the board of directors. *See, e. g.,* MBCA § 35. The board's power of management is not absolute, as the approval of the shareholders is required by statute for a few transactions that are so significant as to bring about a fundamental change in a corporation's business or structure. But for most ordinary transactions, even those of great magnitude, the board is the ultimate authority.

The best written evidence of a decision taken by the board is the resolution by which the decision is formalized, perhaps together with the minutes of the meeting at which it was passed, of which the resolution usually forms a part. It is customary for the board, in approving a major transaction, to designate some official, often the president, to execute the documents and do the other acts necessary to consummate it. For less weighty affairs the board may make a broader delegation of authority; for example, it may empower the president to bind the corporation to all contracts of a certain type or below a certain value. The other party to such a transaction, if in doubt as to the authority of the official with whom he or she is dealing, will normally request to be furnished with a copy of the resolution that confers the authority and the minutes of the board meeting at which the resolution was adopted.

But how is the third party to know that the resolution is genuine? The customary practice is to have the resolution certified by the secretary of the corporation, who usually also affixes the corporate seal. The affixing of a seal is normally not necessary, but in some jurisdictions it may lend weight to the certification. *See* H. Henn, Handbook of the Law of Corporations and Other Business Enterprises 231 n. 9, 446 (2d ed. 1970). And, since the inquiry into authority must presumably stop somewhere short of requiring a majority of the directors to be present in person to swear that, yes, they did vote for the resolution, it has been held that the corporation is bound by the certification of the secretary. In the Matter of Drive-In Development Corp., 371 F.2d 215 (7th Cir. 1966), cert. denied 387 U.S. 909, 87 S.Ct. 1691, 18 L. Ed.2d 626. In the closing of a major transaction, careful counsel may also want to examine the articles and by-laws of the corporate party on the other side in order to be certain that no quirk in one of those documents requires some unusual formality or otherwise casts doubt on the board's approval of the authority of the representatives of the corporation to do the acts necessary to consummate the transaction.

C. FORMALITIES OF ACTION BY THE BOARD
OF DIRECTORS

PROBLEM

THE WIDGET CORPORATION

You are counsel to the Widget Corporation, which is incorporated in a jurisdiction which has adopted the Model Business Corporation Act, and which has articles and by-laws similar to the Model Articles of Incorporation and Model By-laws in the book, Selected Corporation and Partnership Statutes, Regulations and Forms. The by-laws (Article III, Section 2) provide for an eight-member board of directors. The president of the corporation advises you that she has just negotiated a sale of one of the corporation's plants on advantageous terms that will provide desperately needed working capital for the corporation. The sale agreement requires board authorization within 36 hours. One of the directors is in a local hospital for minor surgery, one is in London on business, one is mountain climbing in Nepal, and another is sailing in the Caribbean.

1. Would a unanimous vote by the four available directors at a special meeting of the board be effective? Consider MBCA §§ 40, 43, 144 and Article III of the Model By-laws.

2. Suppose the president visits the ailing board member in the hospital, explains the merger fully, and has him execute a proxy authorizing the president to cast the director's vote in favor of the sale at the board meeting. The transaction subsequently receives the unanimous vote of the four available directors at a special meeting. Is this valid board action?

3. What other alternatives are available for the board to authorize the merger? Consider MBCA §§ 43, 44, and Article III of the Model By-laws.

4. How could the by-laws be modified to meet some future sudden crisis when it is not possible to assemble a quorum of directors at a board meeting?

1. ACTION BY THE BOARD AT A MEETING

The board of directors traditionally takes formal action by vote at a meeting. Each director has one vote; and a director may not vote by proxy. Lippman v. Kehoe Stenograph Co., 11 Del.Ch. 80, 95 A. 895 (1915). Unless the articles or by-laws provide otherwise, the vote of a majority of the directors present at a board meeting at which there is a quorum is necessary to pass a resolution. See MBCA § 40. See also MBCA § 43.

The reason for the usual requirement that the board come together at a meeting to act is found in the maxim, "Two heads are better than one." By consulting together the board members may draw on each director's knowledge and experience, and more ideas and points of view are likely to be considered in the formulation of a final decision, leading to a better conclusion, it is thought, than if the directors were to act separately.

Also, on a less pragmatic level, the directors derive their authority and power from the corporation and the shareholders and this delegation is made to the board, as a body. In a century-old decision, Baldwin v. Canfield, 26 Minn. 43, 1 N.W. 261 (1879), A, the sole shareholder of a corporation, pledged his shares to B. A then sold all of the corporation's property, giving a deed executed by all the directors acting separately. B sued to cancel the deed. In holding for B, the court stated:

> As we have already seen, the court below finds that, by its articles of incorporation, the government of the [corporation], and the management of its affairs, was vested in the board of directors. The legal effect of this was to invest the directors with such government and management *as a board*, and not otherwise. This is in accordance with the general rule that the governing body of a corporation, as such, are agents of the corporation only as a board, and not individually. Hence it follows that they have no authority to act, save when assembled at a board meeting. The separate action, individually, of the persons comprising such governing body, is not the action of the constituted body of men clothed with the corporate powers.

Courts have frequently refused to uphold informal action by directors without a meeting when the board's alleged authority to bind the corporation was challenged by the corporation (Peirce v. Morse-Oliver Bldg. Co., 94 Me. 406, 47 A. 914 (1900)), the directors of the corporation (Schuckman v. Rubenstein, 164 F.2d 952 (6th Cir. 1947) cert. denied 333 U.S. 875, 68 S.Ct. 905, 92 L.Ed. 1151 (1948)), the corporation's trustee in bankruptcy (Hurley v. Ornsteen, 311 Mass. 477, 42 N.E.2d 273 (1942)), or pledgees of the corporation's stock (Baldwin v. Canfield, 26 Minn. 43, 1 N.W. 261 (1879)). Although they frequently fail to articulate their reasons for requiring formal board action, "underlying most all of the decisions   *   *   *   is a single policy: to protect shareholders and their investment from arbitrary, irresponsible or unwise acts on the part of the directors. When presented with informal director action, the courts will decline to apply the general rule when the shareholders, by their actions, indicate that they do not wish the protection or when such application will not afford them any greater protection." Note, Corporations: When Informal Action by Corporate Directors Will Be Permitted to Bind the Corporation, 53 Boston U.L.Rev. 101 (1973).

Notwithstanding the traditional rule that a board cannot act except at a meeting, the courts are not blind to the fact that informal board action, particularly in close corporations, is extremely common. The press of urgent business, laziness, inadequate legal counsel, and a general disdain for what many executives consider "meaningless" technicalities may all contribute to failures to adhere to the conventional formalities. Consequently, perhaps out of concern that strict application of the rule would work injustices and might expose innocent third parties to an unacceptable risk that a corporation might be free to renounce its obligations when it became convenient to do so, courts have found numerous justifications to hold corporations liable on agreements undertaken without a formal board meeting. Among those justifications are the following: *

a. *Unanimous Informal Agreement by the Directors.* The court in Gerard v. Empire Square Realty Co., 195 App.Div. 244, 249, 187 N.Y.S. 306, 310 (1921) noted, "if all the directors are of one mind * * * discussion is futile * * *." In all probability there will be no discussion at all; the directors, being in agreement, will simply act, and, as a result, there will be no opportunity to further the corporate purpose.

b. *Emergency.* Situations arise where the board must make very quick decisions to prevent great harm or to take advantage of great opportunity. In such a situation, it may be impossible to assemble the board at a meeting. The corporation must proceed on the opinions of those directors who can be contacted in whatever manner contact may be made.

c. *Representation of the Interests of All Shareholders.* A conclusion reached at a meeting at which all the shareholders of the corporation are present will likely bind the corporation. *See e. g.,* Brainard v. De La Montanya, 18 Cal.2d 502, 116 P.2d 66 (1941); In re Kartub, 7 Misc.2d 72, 152 N.Y.S.2d 34 (Sup.Ct.1956), aff'd, 3 A.D.2d 896, 163 N.Y.S.2d 938 (1957). Courts have also held the corporation bound if the directors who participate in the informal action constitute a majority of the board and own a majority of the corporation's issued and outstanding shares. *See e. g.,* Air Technical Development Co. v. Arizona Bank, 101 Ariz. 70, 416 P.2d 183 (1966); Phillips Petroleum Co. v. Rock Creek Mining Co., 449 F.2d 664 (9th Cir. 1971).

To buttress these common law exceptions to the general rule, a majority of states have enacted statutory provisions allowing informal director action under some conditions. MBCA § 44, for example, allows action to be taken without a meeting on the unanimous written consent of the directors. MBCA § 43 (third paragraph) permits board action to be taken by a conference telephone call.

The next case considers the interplay of judicially fashioned exceptions upholding informal board action and the modern statutory exceptions. Do you agree with the court's conclusion?

---

* See generally Note, Corporations: When Informal Action by Corporate Directors Will Be Permitted to Bind the Corporation, 53 Boston U.L.Rev. 101 (1973).

VILLAGE OF BROWN DEER v. CITY OF MILWAUKEE

16 Wis.2d 206, 114 N.W.2d 493 (1962) cert. denied
371 U.S. 902, 83 S.Ct. 205, 9 L.Ed.2d 164 (1962).

[The president of the corporation, who was also its majority share-holder and one of its eleven directors, had customarily resolved corporate problems with only infrequent meetings of the board. The court held that the president lacked authority to sign a petition for municipal annexation of land on behalf of the corporation where he had failed to obtain the written consent of all of the directors required under a Wisconsin statute permitting action by the board of directors without a meeting. The court distinguished the challenged action from usual corporate decisions, calling it a "political act" rather than a business decision. Justice GORDON reasoned as follows:]

* * *

Sec. 180.91, Stats.1955, provides as follows:

Any action required by the articles of incorporation or by-laws of any corporation or any provision of law to be taken at a meeting or any other action which may be taken at a meeting, may be taken without a meeting if a consent in writing setting forth the action so taken shall be signed by all of the shareholders, subscribers, directors or members of a committee thereof entitled to vote with respect to the subject matter thereof. Such consent shall have the same force and effect as a unanimous vote, and may be stated as such in any articles or document filed with the secretary of state under this chapter.

Sec. 180.91 was adopted in order to permit informal action by the board of directors. Corporations owe their existence to the statutes. Those who would enjoy the benefits that attend the corporate form of operation are obliged to conduct their affairs in accordance with the laws which authorized them. In 2 Fletcher, Cyclopedia Corporations, sec. 392, p. 227, it is stated:

By the overwhelming weight of authority, when the power to do particular acts, or general authority to manage the affairs of the corporation, is vested in the directors or trustees, it is vested in them, not individually, but as a board, and, as a general rule, they can act so as to bind the corporation only when they act as a board and at a legal meeting.

The legislature having specified the means whereby corporations could function informally, it becomes incumbent upon the courts to enforce such legislative pronouncements. The legislature has said that the corporation could act informally, without a meeting, by obtaining the consent in writing of all of the Directors. In our opinion, this pronouncement has preempted the field and prohibits corporations from acting informally without complying with sec. 180.91, Stats.

One of those who helped draft the Wisconsin Business Corporation Law, Dean George Young, has discussed this section in 1952 Wis. L.Rev. 5, and he says, at p. 19:

> In addition, informal action may be taken without any meeting under section 180.91 by either directors or shareholders upon the unanimous written consent of all entitled to vote upon the subject of the action taken. Permitting corporate action based solely upon written assent, of course, sacrifices whatever wisdom there may be in requiring that decisions be made only after face to face discussion, but the advantage of flexibility probably outweighs any disadvantage. In any event, we all know that in fact many corporate meetings are held without the requisite formalities and the waivers and minutes are later prepared *ex post facto* to show compliance with the law. Such subterfuges should no longer be excusable under the new provision.

* * *

2. NOTICE AND QUORUM

Another formality required for action by the board to be effective is that all of the members of the board receive advance notice of the time and place of the meeting. The practical purpose of the notice requirement is to make personal attendance at a meeting reasonably possible. The notice requirements for regularly scheduled meetings of a board are typically less stringent than for special meetings. MBCA § 43 relegates the need for notice of a special meeting and the notice requirements to the corporate by-laws. Under MBCA § 43 notice of the business to be transacted or the purpose of a meeting need not be provided unless required by the by-laws. If a meeting of a board is held without the required notice, any action taken at the meeting is invalid.

Since the notice requirement is for the benefit of the directors, it may be waived by any director who did not receive it either by a signed waiver (given either before or after the meeting) (MBCA § 144) or by attendance at the meeting without protest. MBCA § 43; Article III § 5 of the Model By-laws. The Model Act does permit a director to attend a meeting for the express purpose of protesting the manner in which it was convened without waiving objections to notice. MBCA § 43.

A quorum requirement exists to prevent secret and unrepresentative meetings. Traditionally, the quorum necessary to hold a valid board meeting which is legally competent to transact business consists of a majority of the total number of the board of directors. MBCA § 40. Model By-laws, Article III § 6. A corporation's articles of incorporation or by-laws may increase the quorum requirement. MBCA § 40.

3.　COMMITTEES OF THE BOARD

In many corporations, particularly larger ones, it is difficult, if not impossible, for the board, acting as a whole, effectively to discharge all of its responsibilities. This problem has been amplified by the trend of the last few years toward increasing numbers of "outside" directors—*i. e.*, directors who are not employees of the corporation— on the boards of large, publicly-held companies. One response to this difficulty has been the delegation of various functions of the board to committees, which are usually empowered to exercise, within limits, the authority of the board in the areas for which the committees are charged with responsibility. *See generally* McMullen, Committees of the Board of Directors, 29 Bus.Law. 755 (1974).

Board committees are not a new phenomenon. Although there was at one time some doubt as to the ability of boards to delegate their functions, cases as early as the end of the last century upheld the practice. *See, e. g.*, Sheridan Electric Light Co. v. Chatham National Bank, 127 N.Y. 517, 522, 28 N.E. 467, 468 (1891). Today the practice has been explicitly authorized by statute in nearly every state. *See* MBCA § 42.

Probably the most common board committee is the executive committee. According to a 1966 study, some 97 percent of manufacturing companies with more than 25,000 employees used executive committees. The Executive Committee of the Board of Directors; Duties, Membership, Compensation, 3 Conference Board Record 16 (July 1966). Such a committee may be empowered to perform all but the most extraordinary board functions. They can furnish flexibility and expedition when the meetings of the regular board are infrequent, when the board is large, when it is confronted with a steady stream of important matters for which it would be impossible to convene the full board, and in dealing with less important matters of corporate housekeeping which, for technical reasons, must be acted on at the board level. *See* J. Juran & J. Louden, The Corporate Director 249 (1966).

Another committee of substantial importance in publicly-held corporations is the audit committee. Its functions usually include the selection of the company's auditors, the specification of the scope of the audit, the review of audit results, and the oversight of internal accounting procedures. The audit committee was given increased visibility by the "improper payments" scandals of the mid-70s. As a result of the outcry generated by the events uncovered during investigations of those problems and of pressure by the Securities and Exchange Commission, the New York Stock Exchange now requires that all corporations listed on the Exchange have audit committees. To nudge publicly-traded non-Big Board companies to adopt audit committees, the SEC now requires that they disclose to their stockholders each year whether they have a standing audit committee. Schedule 14A, Item 6(d)(1). The theory underlying this thrust is that an audit committee composed of independent directors will function as watchdogs whose presence will help insure the integrity of the management.

Other relatively common committees include finance (usually responsible for giving advice on financial structure, the issuance of new securities, and the management of the corporation's investments), nomination (responsible for nominating new directors and officers), and compensation * (responsible for fixing the salaries and other compensation of executives). Audit committees are also common, and indeed, required by the New York Stock Exchange, but this is usually a monitoring rather than an action committee. This by no means exhausts the range of specialized committees available to a creative board of directors.

A committee can be created to serve a permanent or temporary function. Its role may be active, as where the committee is empowered to make decisions on behalf of the board, or passive, where the committee researches and presents background material for the board but itself makes no decisions. Increasingly, case law and the statutes have begun to reflect the view that committees serve a desirable function of allowing greater control and supervision by the board. When responsibility is parcelled out among subgroups of directors, each subgroup develops expertise in an aspect of the business. The board as a whole is better informed as a result of the knowledge of its members in particular areas. Under MBCA § 35 a director is therefore permitted to rely upon a committee on which he does not serve, to the extent that he reasonably believes the committee merits confidence.

D.   ACTION BY SHAREHOLDERS

PROBLEM

CUMULATIVE VOTING

X Corporation has an 8 member board of directors and 1500 shares of voting stock issued and outstanding. At the upcoming shareholder meeting to elect a board of directors, it is expected that 900 shares will be voted. Assume that George, a shareholder, wants

* The SEC rule cited above also requires the corporations to which it applies to tell their shareholders whether the company has audit, nomination and compensation committees. The idea of this requirement is that audit committees will review, produce, and enhance accountability of management and more accurate disclosure; that nominating committees will select directors that are more independent and that compensation committees will fix salaries that are more in line with the value of the services performed by management than might otherwise be the case.

to evaluate the possibility of i) getting himself elected to the board, or ii) winning control of a majority of the board (5 positions).

1. How many shares must George assemble to achieve his two plans under a straight voting system? How many shares are necessary under a cumulative voting system?

2. Assume cumulative voting is mandated by statute.

a. You represent the management of X Corporation, which wishes to frustrate cumulative voting. Consider the possibility of classification of the board of directors. MBCA § 37. What action do you recommend?

b. Assume the corporation already has several representatives of minority shareholders on its board of directors. How can management minimize the impact of these directors on operations?

1. INTRODUCTION

Shareholders act by vote, either at an annual meeting or at a special meeting convened for a particular purpose at a time other than the regularly-scheduled meeting. The typical statutory pattern gives one vote to each share, not one vote to each stockholder.* This pattern may be varied by special provisions in the articles of incorporation. A fairly common variation, for example, is a provision that holders of preferred stock have no vote unless the corporation fails to pay dividends for a certain number of periods, at which point the preferred stock becomes entitled to elect a specified number of directors.

The most important item of business at an annual meeting is the election of directors. *See* Model By-laws, Article II § 1. The annual meeting is also often used to take other actions, such as the appointment of auditors and the approval of management compensation plans.

To facilitate the conduct of a shareholders' meeting, only shareholders "of record" as of a specified date shortly before the meeting are entitled to vote. The "record date" is usually fixed by the board subject to the provisions of the by-laws and the statute. *See* MBCA § 30; Model By-laws, Article II § 5.

In light of the informality characteristic of most closely held corporations modern corporation statutes also generally provide for the taking of action by shareholders without a formal vote. *See* MBCA § 145; Model By-laws, Article II § 11.

Just as is the case for action by the directors, action by the shareholders requires the observance of certain formalities in order to be valid.

---

* For an interesting discussion of the development of this rule see Ratner, The Government of Business Corporations: Critical Reflections on the Rule of "One Share, One Vote," 56 Cornell L.Rev. 1 (1970).

2. THE CALL

The by-laws usually fix the date of the annual meeting. *See* Model By-laws, Article II § 1. *See also* MBCA § 28. A special meeting may be called in accordance with the provisions of the by-laws. Model By-laws, Article II § 2. Most corporation statutes provide that shareholders owning a specified percentage of the stock may call a special meeting on their own initiative. *See* MBCA § 28.

3. NOTICE

Written notice of an annual or special meeting must be given to shareholders prior to the meeting. *See* MBCA § 29; Model By-laws, Article II § 4. *See* MBCA § 144.

4. QUORUM

A quorum must be represented at a shareholders meeting, either in person or by proxy, for an action taken at the meeting to be effective. The Model Act pattern provides for a quorum of a majority of the shares issued and outstanding, but allows the articles to reduce that to as little as one-third of the issued and outstanding shares. MBCA § 32; Model By-laws, Article II § 7.

5. VOTING

The standard general principal governing shareholder voting is that action is taken by the "affirmative vote of a majority of the shares represented at the meeting and entitled to vote on the subject matter." MBCA § 32. This rule is occasionally varied by statute or according to provisions of the articles or by-laws so that a greater number of shares must be voted for particular actions to be taken by the shareholders. Where shares of stock are divided into classes, there may also be a requirement for separate approval by a majority of the shares of each class. *See, e. g.,* MBCA § 60.

Shareholders need not be present at a meeting in order to cast their vote, but may vote by proxy, a device without which the conduct of a shareholders meeting for a large, publicly held corporation would be a practical impossibility. A proxy is simply a limited form of agency power by which a shareholder authorizes another, who will be present at the meeting, to exercise the shareholder's voting rights. In the typical annual meeting of a public corporation, the management of the company solicits from shareholders proxies authorizing one or more members of the management to vote stock held by the shareholders at the meeting. The proxy may either give the proxy holder discretion to vote as he pleases or may direct him to vote in a particular way. The proxy solicitation process is closely regulated by the federal securities laws, a subject we shall consider in greater detail in Chapter 13.

There are two principal methods for conducting an election of directors. In "straight voting" each share is entitled to one vote for each director to be elected, but a shareholder is limited in the number of votes he may cast for any given director to the number of shares he owns. This means that any shareholder or group of shareholders controlling 51% of the shares may elect all of the members of the board.

"Cumulative voting," the alternative method, is designed to allow shareholder groups to elect directors in rough proportion to the shares held by each group and thus to guarantee minority representation on the board. Under cumulative voting, each share again carries a number of votes equal to the number of directors to be elected, but a shareholder may "cumulate" his or her votes by casting them all for one candidate or allocating them in any manner among a number of candidates.

The number of shares required to elect a given number of directors under a cumulative voting regime may be calculated by the following formula:

$$x = \frac{s \times d}{D + 1} + 1$$

Where:

x = Number of shares required to elect directors;

s = Number of shares represented at the meeting;

d = Number of directors it is desired to elect; and

D = Total number of directors to be elected.

To understand this formula, it is helpful to work through a simple example. Suppose that four directors are to be elected at a meeting at which 1000 shares are represented. In order to elect one director a minority group would have to control 201 shares. With that number, the minority group would have 804 votes, which would all be cast for one candidate. The majority would have 799 × 4 or 3196 votes. If the majority distributed these equally among four candidates, each would receive 799 votes, and the one candidate receiving the minority's 804 votes would be guaranteed a seat. In other words, just over 20% of the shares guarantees the election of one of four directors. If only three directors were to be elected, it would require just over 25% to elect one director. What percentage is necessary to elect one member to a five member board? (Note that the reason for the "+ 1" at the end of the formula is the avoidance of the tie that would occur if, in this example, the minority controlled only 200 votes. Then it would be possible for five candidates each to receive 800 votes.) A little further consideration will easily show how the formula would work if it were desired to elect more than one director.

Some state corporation statutes make cumulative voting mandatory, in implementation of a policy favoring minority representation.

In most, however, cumulative voting is optional, depending on an election made in the articles of incorporation. The statute may provide that, unless articles provide to the contrary cumulative voting applies, or it may adopt the reverse presumption. *See* MBCA § 33.

Incumbent management has occasionally sought to undermine the effectiveness of cumulative voting in order to prevent the election of what management usually characterizes as "disruptive," or "divisive" representatives of minority interests. One technique for doing so was illustrated by Coalition to Advance Public Utility Responsibility, Inc. v. Engels, 364 F.Supp. 1202 (D.Minn.1973). The by-laws of Northern States Power Company provided for a board elected by cumulative voting for a term of one year. The plaintiff (CAPUR), a coalition representing several public interest organizations, had been critical of some of Northern State's policies, particularly with respect to environmental and consumer affairs. At the 1972 annual meeting, CAPUR had succeeded in getting 9 percent of the vote on a stockholder resolution. It sought, at the 1973 annual meeting to elect Mrs. Alpha Smaby to the fourteen-member board, which would have required only 6.7 percent of the stockholder vote. The management was not pleased by this effort. According to a letter to stockholders signed by Engels, the chairman and chief executive officer, "It is my opinion that, if these organizations should succeed in imposing their social and economic views upon the operating practices of the Company, management could not continue to administer the affairs of the Company effectively." The board's tactical response to this perceived threat was to vote to reduce the number of directors to 12, to increase their term of office to three years, and to classify the board members and stagger their terms so that only four would be elected each year. The immediate effect of these changes was to increase the amount of votes necessary to elect a director to just over 20 percent. Management sought shareholder approval of the amendments as the first order of business at the annual meeting, but did not say that the purpose was to prevent the election of Mrs. Smaby.

CAPUR sued to block the amendments. Relying on Schnell v. Chris-Craft Industries, Inc., 285 A.2d 437 (Del.1971) and Condec Corp. v. Lunkenheimer Co., 230 A.2d 769 (Del.Ch.1967), the court enjoined the defendants from classifying the board for the 1973 annual meeting. The court found that the management actions were "certainly questionable in light of their fiduciary obligation." Not only had management sought to "change the rules in the middle of the game, but they failed to make adequate disclosure in the proxy statement."

When the election—according to the old rules—was finally held, however, Mrs. Smaby failed to receive the votes necessary to elect her. Pursuant to a settlement worked out by the litigants the company did amend its articles and by-laws effective for the 1974 annual meeting. Since then, according to a letter from the secretary of the corporation, "Except for the repeated comment by a single shareholder at some subsequent shareholder meetings, the subject has had little attention   *   *   *."

E. CONFLICTS BETWEEN THE BOARD AND THE SHAREHOLDERS

PROBLEM

LAFRANCE COSMETICS

LaFrance Cosmetics, Inc. a Columbia corporation, manufactures a line of cosmetics and perfumes. Its stock is held 20 percent by Mimi LaFrance, widow of the founder; 13 percent by her son Pierre; 13 percent by her daughter Margaret; 20 percent by the Third National Bank & Trust Company as trustee for the Columbia Museum of Modern Art; and 34 percent by public shareholders. The board of directors consists of Mimi, Pierre, Margaret, Margaret's husband George, and Victor Gaugin, a retired private investor. Mimi is the president of the company and the only one of the LaFrance family actively involved in its management other than as a director.

Shortly before the late Mr. LaFrance died, he guided the corporation into a major expansion of its activities from cosmetics alone to a line of perfumes for which he had great hope. It was to finance that expansion that the company went public. Today the perfume division, which is housed in a separate plant, accounts for nearly two-thirds of the company's assets. Unfortunately this division has not been very successful. In the seven years it has been in operation, it has shown a small profit in only the last two.

LaBelle, S.A., a large French perfume manufacturer has just approached LaFrance with an offer to buy its perfume facilities for $5 million in cash, a figure slightly greater than LaFrance's original investment in the operation. Mimi and Pierre are anxious to accept the offer. Margaret and George believe that the perfume business is on the verge of becoming successful and are against the sale. Gaugin is undecided.

You have been asked by Mimi for advice on the procedures that would have to be followed under Columbia law for LaFrance to sell the perfume division. LaFrance intends to furnish a copy of your opinion to M. Daumier, LaBelle's French counsel, so that LaBelle may be assured that the sale is properly authorized.

1. Mimi would like to know what procedures would be required if Gaugin votes in favor of the sale. The community in which the business is located is a conservative one, and she is concerned that the bank may oppose selling the perfume factory to foreigners. She wants to know, therefore, if shareholder approval is necessary. Consider MBCA §§ 78 and 79 and the *Gimbel* case.

2. Mimi has asked you to consider whether, if Gaugin sides with Margaret and George, there is any way that the shareholders can

force the sale over the opposition of a majority of the board. In this latter connection, there are several possibilities, which require you to answer the following questions:

a.   Can the shareholders simply pass a resolution directing the sale of the perfume division? Consider Auer v. Dressel.

b.   (i) Could the shareholders remove one or more of the directors who oppose the sale and replace them with others who favor the sale? Consider MBCA §§ 28, 29, 38, 39, and 145, and Model By-laws, Article III § 9 and Article II §§ 2, 4, 7, and 11.

(ii) Consider the tactics that might be used by the directors who oppose the sale.

(iii) Would your response to (i) be different if the by-laws contained the following provision? "A director may be removed for cause by the vote of the shareholders holding a majority of the shares present or represented at an annual or special shareholders meeting." Consider *Auer v. Dressel* and *Campbell v. Loew's.*

c.   (i) Could the board be "packed" by amending the by-laws and adding new directors who would vote in favor of the sale? Assume that by-laws of LaFrance are similar to the Model By-laws but that they provide for a board of directors numbering five. The articles of incorporation of LaFrance provide for a five-member board. Consider MBCA §§ 27, 36, and 58, and Model By-laws, Article III §§ 2 and 9, and Article XI. Reconsider *Auer v. Dressel* and *Campbell v. Loew's.*

(ii) Consider the tactics that might be used by the directors who oppose the sale. Reconsider the *Gamble* and *Schnell* cases.

d.   Are there any other techniques the shareholders might use to force their will on a reluctant board?

e.   What is counsel's role if you are advised (or believe) that the shareholders and majority of the board are at odds?

GIMBEL v. SIGNAL COMPANIES, INC.

316 A.2d 599 (Del.Ch.1974), aff'd per curiam, 316 A.2d 619 (Del.Sup.).

Here—sale okay—because not "all or substantially all" of corporations assets

[On December 21, 1973, at a special meeting, the board of directors of Signal Companies, Inc. ("Signal") approved a proposal to sell its wholly owned subsidiary Signal Gas & Oil Co. ("Signal Oil") to Burmah Oil Inc. ("Burmah") for a price of $480 million. Based on Signal's books, Signal Oil represented 26% of Signal's total assets, 41% of its net worth, and produced 15% of Signal's revenues and earnings. The contract provided that the sale would take place on January 15, 1974 or upon obtaining the necessary governmental consents, whichever was later, but, in no event, after February 15, 1974, unless mutually agreed.

On December 24, 1973, plaintiff, a Signal shareholder, sued for a preliminary injunction to prevent consummation of the sale. The plaintiff, among other contentions, alleged that approval only by Signal's board was insufficient and that a favorable vote from a majority of the outstanding shares of Signal was necessary to authorize the sale].

QUILLEN, Chancellor.

* * *

I turn first to the question of 8 Del.C. § 271(a)[3] which requires majority stockholder approval for the sale of "all or substantially all" of the assets of a Delaware corporation. A sale of less than all or substantially all assets is not covered by negative implication from the statute. Folk, The Delaware General Corporation Law, Section 271, p. 400, ftnt. 3; 8 Del.C. § 141(a).

It is important to note in the first instance that the statute does not speak of a requirement of shareholder approval simply because an independent, important branch of a corporate business is being sold. The plaintiff cites several non-Delaware cases for the proposition that shareholder approval of such a sale is required. But that is not the language of our statute. Similarly, it is not our law that shareholder approval is required upon every "major" restructuring of the corporation. Again, it is not necessary to go beyond the statute. The statute requires shareholder approval upon the sale of "all or substantially all" of the corporation's assets. That is the sole test to be applied. While it is true that test does not lend itself to a strict mathematical standard to be applied in every case, the qualitative factor can be defined to some degree notwithstanding the limited Delaware authority. But the definition must begin with and ultimately necessarily relate to our statutory language.

In interpreting the statute the plaintiff relies on Philadelphia National Bank v. B.S.F. Co., 41 Del.Ch. 509, 199 A.2d 557 (Ch.1964), rev'd on other grounds, 42 Del.Ch. 106, 204 A.2d 746 (Supr.Ct.1964).

3. "Every corporation may at any meeting of its board of directors sell, lease, or exchange all or substantially all of its property and assets, including its good will and its corporate franchises, upon such terms and conditions and for such consideration, which may consist in whole or in part of money or other property, including shares of stock in, and/or other securities of, any other corporation or corporations, as its board of directors deems expedient and for the best interests of the corporation, when and as authorized by a resolution adopted by a majority of the outstanding stock of the corporation entitled to vote thereon at a meeting duly called upon at least 20 days notice. The notice of the meeting shall state that such a resolution will be considered."

The predecessor statute was evidently originally enacted in 1916 in response to Chancellor Curtis' statement of the common law rule in Butler v. New Keystone Copper Co., 10 Del.Ch. 371, 377, 93 A. 380, 383 (Ch.1915):

The general rule as to commercial corporations seems to be settled that neither the directors nor the stockholders of a prosperous, going concern have the power to sell all, or substantially all, the property of the company if the holder of a single share dissent.

In that case, B.S.F. Company owned stock in two corporations. It sold its stock in one of the corporations, and retained the stock in the other corporation. The Court found that the stock sold was the principal asset B.S.F. Company had available for sale and that the value of the stock retained was declining. The Court rejected the defendant's contention that the stock sold represented only 47.4% of consolidated assets, and looked to the actual value of the stock sold. On this basis, the Court held that the stock constituted at least 75% of the total assets and the sale of the stock was a sale of substantially all assets.

But two things must be noted about the *Philadelphia National Bank* case. First, even though shareholder approval was obtained under § 271, the case did not arise under § 271 but under an Indenture limiting the activities of B.S.F. for creditor financial security purposes. On appeal, Chief Justice Wolcott was careful to state the following:

> We are of the opinion that this question is not necessarily to be answered by references to the general law concerning the sale of assets by a corporation. The question before us is the narrow one of what particular language of a contract means and is to be answered in terms of what the parties were intending to guard against or to insure.

42 Del.Ch. at 111–112, 204 A.2d at 750.

Secondly, the *Philadelphia National Bank* case dealt with the sale of the company's only substantial income producing asset.

The key language in the Court of Chancery opinion in *Philadelphia National Bank* is the suggestion that "the critical factor in determining the character of a sale of assets is generally considered not the amount of property sold but whether the sale is in fact an unusual transaction or one made in the regular course of business of the seller." (41 Del.Ch. at 515, 199 A.2d at 561). Professor Folk suggests from the opinion that "the statute would be inapplicable if the assets sale is 'one made in furtherance of express corporate objects in the ordinary and regular course of the business'" (referring to language in 41 Del.Ch. at 516, 199 A.2d at 561). Folk, *supra*, Section 271, p. 401.

But any "ordinary and regular course of the business" test in this context obviously is not intended to limit the directors to customary daily business activities. Indeed, a question concerning the statute would not arise unless the transaction was somewhat out of the ordinary. While it is true that a transaction in the ordinary course of business does not require shareholder approval, the converse is not true. Every transaction out of normal routine does not necessarily require shareholder approval. The unusual nature of the transaction must strike at the heart of the corporate existence and purpose. As it is written at 6A Fletcher, Cyclopedia Corporations (Perm.Ed. 1968 Rev.) § 2949.2, p. 648:

> The purpose of the consent statutes is to protect the shareholders from fundamental change, or more specifically to protect the shareholder from the destruction of the means to accomplish the purposes or objects for which the corporation was incorporated and actually performs.

It is in this sense that the "unusual transaction" judgment is to be made and the statute's applicability determined. If the sale is of assets quantitatively vital to the operation of the corporation and is out of the ordinary and substantially affects the existence and purpose of the corporation, then it is beyond the power of the Board of Directors. With these guidelines, I turn to Signal and the transaction in this case.

Signal or its predecessor was incorporated in the oil business in 1922. But, beginning in 1952 Signal diversified its interests. In 1952, Signal acquired a substantial stock interest in American President lines. From 1957 to 1962 Signal was the sole owner of Laura Scudders, a nationwide snack food business. In 1964, Signal acquired Garrett Corporation which is engaged in the aircraft, aerospace, and uranium enrichment business. In 1967, Signal acquired Mack Trucks, Inc., which is engaged in the manufacture and sale of trucks and related equipment. Also in 1968, the oil and gas business was transferred to a separate division and later in 1970 to the Signal Oil subsidiary. Since 1967, Signal has made acquisition of or formed substantial companies none of which are involved or related with the oil and gas industry. As indicated previously, the oil and gas production development of Signal's business is now carried on by Signal Oil, the sale of the stock of which is an issue in this lawsuit.

According to figures published in Signal's last annual report (1972) and the latest quarterly report (September 30, 1973) and certain other internal financial information, the following tables can be constructed.

SIGNAL'S REVENUES (in millions)

	9 Mos. Ended September 30,	December 31,	
	1973	1972	1971
Truck manufacturing	$655.9	$712.7	$552.5
Aerospace and industrial	407.1	478.2	448.0
Oil and gas	185.8	267.2	314.1
Other	16.4	14.4	14.0

SIGNAL'S PRE–TAX EARNINGS (in millions)

	9 Mos. Ended September 30,	December 31,	
	1973	1972	1971
Truck manufacturing	$ 55.8	$ 65.5	$ 36.4
Aerospace and industrial	20.7	21.5	19.5
Oil and gas	10.1	12.8	9.9

SIGNAL'S ASSETS (in millions)

	9 Mos. Ended September 30,	December 31,	
	1973	1972	1971
Truck manufacturing	$581.4	$506.5	$450.4
Aerospace and industrial	365.2	351.1	331.5
Oil and gas	376.2	368.3	369.9
Other	113.1	102.0	121.6

SIGNAL'S NET WORTH (in millions)

	9 Mos. Ended September 30,	December 31,	
	1973	1972	1971
Truck manufacturing	$295.0	$269.7	$234.6
Aerospace and industrial	163.5	152.2	139.6
Oil and gas	280.5	273.2	254.4
Other	(55.7)	(42.1)	(2.0)

Based on the company's figures, Signal Oil represents only about 26% of the total assets of Signal. While Signal Oil represents 41% of the Signal's total net worth, it produces only about 15% of Signal's revenues and earnings. * * *

While it is true, based on the experience of the Signal-Burmah transaction and the record in this lawsuit, that Signal Oil is more valuable than shown by the company's books, even if, as plaintiff suggests in his brief, the $761,000,000 value attached to Signal Oil's properties by the plaintiff's expert Paul V. Keyser, Jr., were substituted as the asset figure, the oil and gas properties would still constitute less than half the value of Signal's total assets. Thus, from a straight quantitative approach, I agree with Signal's position that the sale to Burmah does not constitute a sale of "all or substantially all" of Signal's assets.

In addition, if the character of the transaction is examined, the plaintiff's position is also weak. While it is true that Signal's original purpose was oil and gas and while oil and gas is still listed first in the certificate of incorporation, the simple fact is that Signal is now a conglomerate engaged in the aircraft and aerospace business, the manufacture and sale of trucks and related equipment, and other businesses besides oil and gas. The very nature of its business, as it now in fact exists, contemplates the acquisition and disposal of independent branches of its corporate business. Indeed, given the operations since 1952, it can be said that such acquisitions and dispositions have become part of the ordinary course of business. The facts that the oil and gas business was historically first and that authorization for such operations are listed first in the certificate do not prohibit disposal of such interest. As Director Harold M. Williams testified, business history is not "compelling" and "many companies go down the drain because they try to be historic."

It is perhaps true, as plaintiff has argued, that the advent of multi-business corporations has in one sense emasculated § 271 since one business may be sold without shareholder approval when other substantial businesses are retained. But it is one thing for a corporation to evolve over a period of years into a multi-business corporation, the operations of which include the purchase and sale of whole businesses, and another for a single business corporation by a one transaction revolution to sell the entire means of operating its business in exchange for money or a separate business. In the former situation, the processes of corporate democracy customarily have had the opportunity to restrain or otherwise control over a period of years. Thus, there is a chance for some shareholder participation. The Signal development illustrates the difference. For example, when Signal, itself formerly called Signal Oil and Gas Company, changed its name in 1968, it was for the announced "need for a new name appropriate to the broadly diversified activies of Signal's multi-industry complex."

* * *

I conclude that measured quantatively and qualitatively, the sale of the stock of Signal Oil by Signal to Burmah does not constitute a sale of "all or substantially all" of Signal's assets. This conclusion is supported by the closest case involving Delaware law which was been cited to the Court. Wingate v. Bercut, 146 F.2d 725 (9th Cir. 1944). Accordingly, insofar as the complaint rests on 8 Del.C. § 271(a), in my judgment, it has no reasonable probability of ultimate success.

* * *

———

In connection with the right of shareholders to vote in a transaction involving a sale of substantially all the corporation's assets, *see also* Katz v. Bregman, 431 A.2d 1274 (Del.Ch.1981).

AUER v. DRESSEL

306 N.Y. 427, 118 N.E.2d 590 (1954).

[The plaintiffs, who owned a majority of the Class A stock of R. Hoe & Co., Inc., brought an action for an order to compel the president of the corporation to call a special shareholders' meeting pursuant to a by-law provision requiring such a meeting when requested by holders of a majority of the stock. The articles of incorporation provided for an eleven-member board, nine of whom were to be elected by the Class A stockholders and two of whom by the Common stockholders. The purposes of the special meeting were:

A.   to vote on a resolution indorsing the administration of Joseph L. Auer, the former President and demanding his reinstatement;

B.   to amend the articles of incorporation and by-laws to provide that vacancies on the board of directors arising from the removal of a director by the shareholders be filled only by the shareholders;

C.   to consider and vote on charges to remove four Class A directors for cause and to elect their successors;

D.   to amend the by-laws to reduce the quorum requirement for board action.

The president refused to call the meeting on the ground, among others, that the foregoing purposes were not proper subjects for a Class A shareholder meeting.]

DESMOND, Judge.

* * *

* * * The obvious purpose of the meeting here sought to be called (aside from the indorsement and reinstatement of former president Auer) is to hear charges against four of the class A directors, to remove them if the charges be proven, to amend the by-laws so that the successor directors be elected by the class A stockholders, and further to amend the by-laws so that an effective quorum of directors will be made up of no fewer than half of the directors in office and no fewer than one third of the whole authorized number of directors. No reason appears why the class A stockholders should not be allowed to vote on any or all of those proposals.

The stockholders, by expressing their approval of Mr. Auer's conduct as president and their demand that he be put back in that office, will not be able, directly, to effect that change in officers, but there is nothing invalid in their so expressing themselves and thus putting on notice the directors who will stand for election at the annual meeting. As to purpose (B), that is, amending the charter and by-laws to authorize the stockholders to fill vacancies as to class A directors who have been removed on charges or who have resigned, it seems to be settled law that the stockholders who are empowered to elect directors have the inherent power to remove them for cause, In re Koch, 257 N.Y. 318, 321, 322, 178 N.E. 545, 546 * * *. Of course, as the Koch case points out, there must be the service of specific charges, adequate notice and full opportunity of meeting the accusations, but there is no present showing of any lack of any of those in this instance. Since these particular stockholders have the right to elect nine directors and to remove them on proven charges, it is not inappropriate that they should use their further power to amend the by-laws to elect the successors of such directors as shall be removed after hearing, or who shall resign pending hearing. Quite pertinent at this point is Rogers v. Hill, 289 U.S. 582, 589, 53 S.Ct. 731, 734, 77 L.Ed. 1385, which made light of an argument that stockholders, by giving power to the directors to make by-laws, had lost their own power to make them; quoting a New Jersey case, In re Griffing Iron Co., 63 N.J.L. 168, 41 A. 931, the United States Supreme Court said: " 'It would be preposterous to leave the real owners of the corporate property at the mercy of their agents, and the law has not done so' ". Such a change in the by-laws, dealing with the class A directors only, has no effect on the voting rights of the common stockholders, which rights have to do with the selection of the remaining two directors only. True, the certificate of incorporation authorizes the board of directors to remove any director on charges, but we do not consider that provision as an abdication by the stockholders of their own traditional, inherent power to remove their own directors. Rather, it provides an additional method. Were that not so, the stockholders might find themselves without effective remedy in a case where a majority of the directors were accused of wrongdoing and, obviously, would be unwilling to remove themselves from office.

We fail to see, in the proposal to allow class A stockholders to fill vacancies as to class A directors, any impairment or any violation of paragraph (h) of article Third of the certificate of incorporation, which says that class A stock has exclusive voting rights with respect to all matters "other than the election of directors". That negative language should not be taken to mean that class A stockholders, who have an absolute right to elect nine of these eleven directors, cannot amend their by-laws to guarantee a similar right, in the class A stockholders and to the exclusion of common stockholders, to fill vacancies in the class A group of directors.

 * * * Any director illegally removed can have his remedy in the courts, see People ex rel. Manice v. Powell, 201 N.Y. 194, 94 N.E. 634.

The order should be affirmed, with costs, and the Special Term directed forthwith to make an order in the same form as the Appellate Division order with appropriate changes of dates.

VAN VOORHIS, J., dissented on the grounds that none of the cited purposes were appropriate subjects for action by shareholders at the requested meeting. Proposal A, the indorsement of Auer's tenure as president, was only "an idle gesture." The dissent argued that the second proposal was improper because the articles of incorporation authorized the directors to fill vacancies on the board, and the change sought would have denied the common stockholders their rights to a say in the replacement of directors through their two representatives on the board. Such a change, it was argued could be made only through special voting procedures. Proposal C, the removal of directors, was improper because a shareholders meeting was "altogether unsuited to the performance of duties which partake of the nature of the judicial function." Since most shareholders would vote by proxy, their decision would have to be made before the meeting at which the charges against the directors would be made and discussed. The fourth proposal was treated as irrelevant without action on the other three.]

CAMPBELL v. LOEW'S, INC.

36 Del.Ch. 563, 134 A.2d 852 (1957).

[This case involved a battle for control of Loew's Inc., by two factions, one headed by its President, Vogel, and the other by Tomlinson. At the February, 1957 shareholders' meeting the two factions effected a compromise; each faction was to have 6 directors and a neutral director would complete the 13 member board. In July, 1957, two of the Vogel directors, one Tomlinson director and the neutral director resigned. On July 30, 1957 there was a board meeting attended only by the five Tomlinson directors, who attempted to fill two vacancies. These elections were ruled invalid for lack of a quorum. Tomlinson v. Loew's Inc., 36 Del.Ch. 516, 134 A.2d 518 (1957) aff'd, 37 Del.Ch. 8, 135 A.2d 136 (Del.Supr.1957). Meanwhile, on July 29, 1957, Vogel, as president, sent out a notice calling a special shareholders' meeting for September 12, 1957 for the following purposes:

    1. to fill director vacancies;

    2. to amend the by-laws to increase the number of board members from 13 to 19; to increase the quorum from 7 to 10; and to elect six additional directors;

    3. to remove Tomlinson and Stanley Meyer as directors and to fill the vacancies thus created.

The plaintiff brought an action to enjoin this special shareholder's meeting and for other relief.]

SEITZ, Chancellor.

*   *   *

I believe it is appropriate first to consider those contentions made by plaintiff which concern the legality of the call of the stockholders' meeting for the purposes stated.

Plaintiff contends that the president had no authority in fact to call a special meeting of stockholders to act upon policy matters which have not been defined by the board of directors. Defendant says that the by-laws specifically authorize the action taken.

It is helpful to have in mind the pertinent by-law provisions:

Section 7 of Article I provides:

> Special meetings of the stockholders for any purpose or purposes, other than those regulated by statute, may be called by the President * * *.

Section 2 of Article IV reads:

> The President * * * shall have power to call special meetings of the stockholders * * * for any purpose or purposes * * *.

It is true that Section 8(11) of Article II also provides that the board of directors may call a special meeting of stockholders for any purpose. But, in view of the explicit language of the by-laws above quoted, can this Court say that the president was without authority to call this meeting for the purposes stated? I think not. I agree that the purposes for which the president called the meeting were not in furtherance of the routine business of the corporation. Nevertheless, I think the stockholders, by permitting the quoted by-laws to stand, have given the president the power to state these broad purposes in his call. Moreover, it may be noted that at least one other by-law (Article V, § 2) makes certain action of the president subject to board approval. The absence of such language in connection with the call provision, while not conclusive, is some evidence that it was intended that the call provision should not be so circumscribed.

The plaintiff argues that if this by-law purports to give the president the power to call special stockholders' meetings for the purposes here stated, then it is contrary to 8 Del.C. § 141(a), which provides:

> The business of every corporation organized under the provisions of this chapter shall be managed by a board of directors, except as hereinafter or in its certificate of incorporation otherwise provided.

I do not believe the call of a stockholders' meeting for the purposes mentioned is action of the character which would impinge upon the power given the directors by the statute. I say this because I believe a by-law giving the president the power to submit matters for stockholder action presumably only embraces matters which are appropriate for stockholder action. So construed the by-laws do not impinge upon the statutory right and duty of the board to manage the business of the corporation. Plaintiff does not suggest that the matters noticed are inappropriate for stockholder consideration. And, of course, the Court is not concerned with the wisdom of the grant of such power to the president.

Plaintiff's next argument is that the president has no authority, without board approval, to propose an amendment of the by-laws to enlarge the board of directors. Admittedly this would be a most radical change in this corporate management. Indeed, it may well involve the determination of control. However, as I have already indicated, I believe the wording of the by-laws authorizes such action.

Plaintiff next argues that the president had no power to call a stockholders' meeting to fill vacancies on the board. As I understand plaintiff's argument it is that the existence of Article V, § 2 of the by-laws, which provides that the stockholders or the remaining directors may fill vacancies, by implication, precludes the president from calling a stockholders' meeting for that purpose; that provision being intended for stockholder use only at the initiative of the stockholders. First of all, the by-laws permit the president to call a meeting for any purpose. This is broad and all-embracing language and I think it must include the power to call a meeting to fill vacancies. The fact that the stockholders may on their initiative have the right to call a meeting for that purpose does not seem to be a sufficient reason for implying that the president is thereby deprived of such power.

Plaintiff points to the "extraordinary state of affairs" which the recognition of such power in the president would create. Obviously it gives the president power which may place him in conflict with the members of the board. But such consequences inhere in a situation where those adopting the by-laws grant such broad and concurrent power to the board and to the president. The validity but not the wisdom of the grant of power is before the Court. I conclude that under the by-laws the president has the power to call a meeting to fill vacancies on the board.

*   *   *

I therefore conclude that the president had the power to call the meeting for the purposes noticed. I need not consider the effect of the fact that the executive committee recommended that a special stockholders' meeting be called.

Plaintiff next argues that the stockholders have no power between annual meetings to elect directors to fill newly created directorships.

Plaintiff argues in effect that since the Loew's by-laws provide that the stockholders may fill "vacancies", and since our Courts have construed "vacancy" not to embrace "newly created directorships" (Automatic Steel Products v. Johnston, 31 Del.Ch. 469, 64 A.2d 416, 6 A.L.R.2d 170), the attempted call by the president for the purpose of filling newly created directorships was invalid.

Conceding that "vacancy" as used in the by-laws does not embrace "newly created directorships", that does not resolve this problem. I say this because in Moon v. Moon Motor Car Co., 17 Del.Ch. 176, 151 A. 298, it was held that the stockholders had the inherent right between annual meetings to fill newly created directorships. See also Automatic Steel Products v. Johnston, above. There is no basis to distinguish the Moon case unless it be because the statute has since been amended to provide that not only vacancies but newly created directorships "may be filled by a majority of the directors then in office * * * unless it is otherwise provided in the certificate of incorporation or the by-laws * * *". 8 Del.C. § 223. Obviously, the amendment to include new directors is not worded so as to make the statute exclusive. It does not prevent the stockholders from filling the new directorships.

* * *

I therefore conclude that the stockholders of Loew's do have the right between annual meetings to elect directors to fill newly created directorships.

Plaintiff next argues that the shareholders of a Delaware corporation have no power to remove directors from office even for cause and thus the call for that purpose is invalid. The defendant naturally takes a contrary position.

While there are some cases suggesting the contrary, I believe that the stockholders have the power to remove a director for cause. This power must be implied when we consider that otherwise a director who is guilty of the worst sort of violation of his duty could nevertheless remain on the board. It is hardly to be believed that a director who is disclosing the corporation's trade secrets to a competitor would be immune from removal by the stockholders. Other examples, such as embezzlement of corporate funds, etc., come readily to mind.

But plaintiff correctly states that there is no provision in our statutory law providing for the removal of directors by stockholder action. In contrast he calls attention to § 142 of 8 Del.C., dealing with officers, which specifically refers to the possibility of a vacancy in an office by removal. He also notes that the Loew's by-laws provide for the removal of officers and employees but not directors. From these facts he argues that it was intended that directors not be removed even for cause. I believe the statute and by-law are of course some evidence to support plaintiff's contention. But when we seek to exclude the existence of a power by implication, I think it is pertinent to consider whether the absence of the power can be said to subject the corporation to the possibility of real damage. I say this because we seek intention and such a factor would be relevant to that issue. Considering the damage a director might be able to inflict upon his corporation, I believe the doubt must be resolved by construing the statutes and by-laws as leaving untouched the question of director removal for cause. This being so, the Court is free to conclude on reason that the stockholders have such inherent power.

I therefore conclude that as a matter of Delaware corporation law the stockholders do have the power to remove directors for cause. I need not and do not decide whether the stockholders can by appropriate charter or by-law provision deprive themselves of this right.

* * *

I turn next to plaintiff's charges relating to procedural defects and to irregularities in proxy solicitation by the Vogel group.

Plaintiff's first point is that the stockholders can vote to remove a director for cause only after such director has been given adequate notice of charges of grave impropriety and afforded an opportunity to be heard.

* * *

I am inclined to agree that if the proceedings preliminary to submitting the matter of removal for cause to the stockholders appear to be legal and if the charges are legally sufficient on their face, the Court should ordinarily not intervene. The sufficiency of the evidence would be a matter for evaluation in later proceedings. But where the procedure adopted to remove a director for cause is invalid on its face, a stockholder can attack such matters before the meeting. This conclusion is dictated both by the desirability of avoiding unnecessary and expensive action and by the importance of settling internal disputes, where reasonably possible, at the earliest moment. Compare Empire Southern Gas Co. v. Gray, 29 Del.Ch. 95, 46 A.2d 741. Otherwise a director could be removed and his successor could be appointed and participate in important board action before the illegality of the removal was judicially established. This seems undesirable where the illegality is clear on the face of the proceedings.

* * *

Turning now to plaintiff's contentions, it is certainly true that when the shareholders attempt to remove a director for cause, "* * * there must be the service of specific charges, adequate notice and full opportunity of meeting the accusation * * *". See Auer v. Dressel [306 N.Y. 427, 118 N.E.2d 593], above. While it involved an invalid attempt by directors to remove a fellow director for cause, nevertheless, this same general standard was recognized in Bruch v. National Guarantee Credit Corp. [13 Del.Ch. 180, 116 A. 741], above. The Chancellor said that the power of removal could not "be exercised in an arbitrary manner. The accused director would be entitled to be heard in his own defense".

Plaintiff asserts that no specific charges have been served upon the two directors sought to be ousted; that the notice of the special meeting fails to contain a specific statement of the charges; that the proxy statement which accompanied the notice also failed to notify the stockholders of the specific charges; and that it does not inform the stockholders that the accused must be afforded an opportunity to meet the accusations before a vote is taken.

Matters for stockholder consideration need not be conducted with the same formality as judicial proceedings. The proxy statement specifically recites that the two directors are sought to be removed for the reasons stated in the president's accompanying letter. Both directors involved received copies of the letter. Under the circumstances I think it must be said that the two directors involved were served with notice of the charges against them.   *   *   *

*   *   *

I next consider plaintiff's contention that the charges against the two directors do not constitute "cause" as a matter of law. It would take too much space to narrate in detail the contents of the president's letter. I must therefore give my summary of its charges. First of all, it charges that the two directors (Tomlinson and Meyer) failed to cooperate with Vogel in his announced program for rebuilding the company; that their purpose has been to put themselves in control; that they made baseless accusations against him and other management personnel and attempted to divert him from his normal duties as president by bombarding him with correspondence containing unfounded charges and other similar acts; that they moved into the company's building, accompanied by lawyers and accountants, and immediately proceeded upon a planned scheme of harassment. They called for many records, some going back twenty years, and were rude to the personnel. Tomlinson sent daily letters to the directors making serious charges directly and by means of innuendos and misinterpretations.

Are the foregoing charges, if proved, legally sufficient to justify the ouster of the two directors by the stockholders? I am satisfied that a charge that the directors desired to take over control of the corporation is not a reason for their ouster. Standing alone, it is a perfectly legitimate objective which is a part of the very fabric of corporate existence. Nor is a charge of lack of cooperation a legally sufficient basis for removal for cause.

The next charge is that these directors, in effect, engaged in a calculated plan of harassment to the detriment of the corporation. Certainly a director may examine books, ask questions, etc., in the discharge of his duty, but a point can be reached when his actions exceed the call of duty and become deliberately obstructive. In such a situation, if his actions constitute a real burden on the corporation then the stockholders are entitled to relief. The charges in this area made by the Vogel letter are legally sufficient to justify the stockholders in voting to remove such directors. In so concluding I of course express no opinion as to the truth of the charges.

I therefore conclude that the charge of "a planned scheme of harassment" as detailed in the letter constitutes a justifiable legal basis for removing a director.

I next consider whether the directors sought to be removed have been given a reasonable opportunity to be heard by the stockholders on the charges made.

* * *

There seems to be an absence of cases detailing the appropriate procedure for submitting a question of director removal for cause for stockholder consideration. I am satisfied, however, that to the extent the matter is to be voted upon by the use of proxies, such proxies may be solicited only after the accused directors are afforded an opportunity to present their case to the stockholders. This means, in my opinion, that an opportunity must be provided such directors to present their defense to the stockholders by a statement which must accompany or precede the initial solicitation of proxies seeking authority to vote for the removal of such director for cause. If not provided then such proxies may not be voted for removal. And the corporation has a duty to see that this opportunity is given the directors at its expense. Admittedly, no such opportunity was given the two directors involved. * * *

I therefore conclude that the procedural sequence here adopted for soliciting proxies seeking authority to vote on the removal of the two directors is contrary to law. The result is that the proxy solicited by the Vogel group, which is based upon unilateral presentation of the facts by those in control of the corporate facilities, must be declared invalid insofar as they purport to give authority to vote for the removal of the directors for cause.

A preliminary injunction will issue restraining the corporation from recognizing or counting any proxies held by the Vogel group and others insofar as such proxies purport to grant authority to vote for the removal of Tomlinson and Meyer as directors of the corporation.

* * *

[Chancellor Seitz went on to deal with a number of other questions relating to the use by the Vogel faction of corporate funds and facilities in the solicitation of proxies. He ruled, among other things, that the Vogel faction, which stood for existing policy, was justified in using corporate funds for the solicitation of proxies. He did not rule on whether the Tomlinson faction would also have access to the corporate treasury for that purpose. Finally, the Chancellor declined

to issue an injunction ordering the four Vogel directors to attend
board meetings so as to constitute a quorum. He held that, under
the circumstances, at least, it was not a breach of their fiduciary duty
to engage in a concerted plan to prevent the board from acting by
refusing to attend meetings.]

Note—More on Campbell v. Loew's

The controversy described in Campbell v. Loew's, Inc., reflects
just one phase of a lengthy and bitter struggle for control of the company that not only owned the Metro-Goldwyn-Mayer film studio, but
was a quarter of a billion dollar industrial empire, which held a wide
variety of tangible and intangible assets. The battle was a personal
as well as a business contest; it represented a bid for power and re-
venge by Louis B. Mayer, one of the founders of MGM, who had been
forced to resign as head of the MGM studio after several years in
which the studio had suffered heavy losses. Mayer apparently saw
his opportunity to make his bid for control when the President of
Loew's resigned in mid-term and was replaced by Joseph Vogel, who
had worked his way up from usher to head of the Loew's theater
chain.

Because Mayer had resigned from MGM under decidedly inauspi-
cious circumstances, he chose not to seek control of Loews openly.
Instead, using Stanley Meyer (one of the directors whose removal
was at issue in Campbell v. Loew's, Inc.) as an intermediary, he approached Joseph Tomlinson, Loew's largest stockholder, to spearhead
the challenge. Prior to the February 1957 annual meeting Tomlinson
called for Vogel's resignation as President, for Mayer's return to the
MGM studio and for a drastic restructuring of the Board of Directors. Vogel, fearing that Tomlinson's efforts might gain support
from two banking houses that held substantial blocks of Loew's
stock, agreed to a compromise to avert a proxy fight. At the meeting, the thirteen-member Board of Directors was reconstituted to include six members each from the Tomlinson and Vogel factions, and a
thirteenth "neutral" member, who was selected by the banks.

At the first meeting of the new board, held on the afternoon of
the shareholders' meeting, Tomlinson proposed that Vogel be removed as President and replaced by Stanley Meyer. Though the proposal was defeated, so were Vogel's hopes for conciliation with the
Tomlinson faction.

Tomlinson demanded that the corporation provide him with an office, and he moved in with attorneys and accountants. He began to
make demands for immediate delivery of voluminous corporate
records including contracts, expense accounts, interoffice correspondence, and cost data, some of which dated back twenty years. Some
of the documents were in warehouses, others were needed for daily
use, while still others were highly confidential. The requests were
sometimes rude or insulting.

The demand for records was followed by a campaign of daily letters to Vogel, with copies to the other directors. According to Louis Nizer, who served as Vogel's counsel,

> On the face of them these letters had a sincere businesslike ring. Seemingly, they were conservatively stated and solidly based on fact. They gave every appearance of being written in good faith to stave off some disastrous conduct upon which Vogel seemed intent. Their chief purpose was to create a state of alarm over the incompetence, if not, indeed, the bad motives, of the management, and to give fair warning before the corporate assets were dissipated by stupidity and malfeasance. They also put enormous pressures on the directors.   *   *   *   But when we [the Vogel faction, in investigating the charges in the letters] called for explanation from our executives and accountants, we found that we had a perfect answer.*

The letter campaign ended as abruptly as it had started. Meanwhile, rumors continued to circulate about Vogel's mismanagement, board meetings were disrupted for caucuses by the separate factions, and potentially lucrative deals which Vogel had arranged were destroyed when word of negotiations was apparently "leaked" by members of the Tomlinson faction.

The next major skirmish in the battle took place on July 12, 1957, in what Fortune magazine described as the "ambush at Culver City." ** A special meeting of the board had been scheduled in California to give the members an introduction to the MGM studio. Two of the Vogel directors were unable to attend. At the meeting a management-consulting firm that had been hired to undertake an efficiency study of Loew's management and personnel presented a report that recommended that Vogel be removed as President. The Tomlinson directors immediately moved to vote upon the recommendation. Vogel successfully parried the attack by refusing to entertain the motion, noting that at a special directors' meeting only items listed on the agenda could be discussed.

After the abortive directors' meeting, Vogel determined to inform the shareholders of the Tomlinson faction's obstructionist activities and to seek the removal of Tomlinson and Stanley Meyer for cause at a special shareholders' meeting which he called for September 12, 1957. He also sought to have the board expanded to nineteen members, and to have his candidates fill the newly-created seats. The consulting firm withdrew its recommendations, indicating that it would support Vogel if he could win shareholder support. In the face of what promised to be a bitter proxy fight, two Vogel directors,

---

* L. Nizer, My Life in Court, 427, 448–49 (1961).

** Sheehan, The Cliff-Hanger at MGM, 56 Fortune 134 (October 1957). *See also*

Hughes, MGM: War Among the Lion Tamers, 56 Fortune 98 (August 1957).

one Tomlinson director and the "neutral" director resigned, leaving the Tomlinson faction with a five to four majority.

The Tomlinson faction called a special meeting of the Board for July 30, which the Vogel faction refused to attend. Though less than a quorum, the directors present voted to fill two of the vacancies with Louis B. Mayer and a friend. This newly-constituted "quorum" then voted to call off the special shareholders' meeting and to limit Vogel's authority to enter into contracts without prior Board approval. The actions of this rump board meeting were held invalid for lack of a quorum in Tomlinson v. Loew's, Inc., 36 Del.Ch. 516, 134 A.2d 518 (1957) aff'd, 37 Del.Ch. 8, 135 A.2d 136 (Del.Supr.1957). It was against this background that the action was instituted challenging Vogel's authority to call the special shareholders' meeting and seeking to enjoin Vogel from voting the proxies he had obtained.

Vogel was victorious at the meeting. The enlargement of the board was approved and all but one of the new directors elected to fill vacancies were his nominees. Vogel consolidated his position at the next annual meeting, at which four of the remaining members of the Tomlinson faction were replaced. Tomlinson was able to protect his own seat as a result of cumulative voting. When one of the new directors defected to join Tomlinson in threatening a renewed proxy contest, Vogel responded by asking the shareholders to abolish cumulative voting. When they agreed, Vogel was able at last to elect a board that gave him unanimous support.

The MGM saga did not end there. Much the same script was replayed twice in the 1960's with new actors. The principal reason for all this corporate politics was old movies, of which MGM owned over 1000. Television's voracious appetite for them was making them "become more valuable every minute." (Forbes, June 15, 1966, at 15.)

F.   THE SHAREHOLDERS' RIGHT OF INSPECTION

Full exercise of a shareholder's right to vote, to oppose management's proposed slate in election of directors, or to initiate (and maintain) a lawsuit may depend on a shareholder's access to the corporation's records. At common law, the right of a shareholder to inspect corporate books and records was considered to stem from the shareholder's equitable ownership of the assets of the corporation. The right was not confined to formal minutes of official action, but was "held to include the documents, contracts, and papers of the corporation." Otis-Hidden Co. v. Scheirich, 187 Ky. 423, 219 S.W. 191, 194 (1920). Despite the broad access afforded shareholders, the right of inspection was not absolute. In order to avoid disruption of the business of the corporation, inspection could only be had at reasonable times and places and, more importantly, only for a "proper purpose." See, e. g., In re Steinway, 159 N.Y. 250, 53 N.E. 1103 (1899); State ex rel. Rogers v. Sherman Oil Co., 31 Del. 570, 117 A. 122 (Del.Supr. 1922).

Provisions affording shareholders a right of inspection are now part of the statutory law of every state. Some of these provisions have been construed as merely codifying the common law right, *see, e. g.,* State ex rel. O'Hara v. National Biscuit Co., 69 N.J.L. 198, 54 A. 241 (1903); Dines v. Harris, 88 Colo. 22, 291 P. 1024 (1930), while others have been held to enlarge it. Many inspection statutes impose limitations on the right of inspection, especially as to persons eligible to assert the right and as to specific records subject to inspection. MBCA, § 52, for example, limits access to "relevant books and records of accounts, minutes, and record of shareholders" thus, according to the drafters, "protecting against the possibility of expensive and vexatious fishing expeditions." 2 Model Bus.Corp.Act Ann. § 52, ¶ 2 (1971). The Delaware statute limits the right of inspection to stockholders of record, thus denying the right to holders of voting trust certificates or those who hold their shares in "street name." Del. GCL § 220. Many other states limit the right to inspect to persons who hold a certain percentage of outstanding shares or voting trust certificates, or who have held their shares for minimum lengths of time. *See, e. g.,* MBCA § 52; N.Y. BCL § 624(b). Nevertheless, either by specific statutory provision or by judicial interpretation, the common law right of a shareholder to inspect the books and records at proper times and for a proper purpose is usually preserved, and a shareholder not meeting the statutory requirements may be able to obtain inspection upon demonstrating a proper purpose.

The shareholder's traditional remedy to enforce the right of inspection was a writ of mandamus. Some statutes also provide for the assessment of penalties against corporate employees who improperly refuse to permit inspection. *See, e. g.,* MBCA § 52. The drafters of the MBCA noted that the primary purpose of the inspection legislation was to prescribe penalties to prevent unreasonable refusals since "[w]ith no penalties imposed, the corporation or its officers could, by refusing access, delay inspection until the right was actually litigated, and if inspection were granted additional delay and expense arose before adequate information could be obtained." 2 Model Bus.Corp.Act Ann. § 52, ¶ 2 (1971). The sanctions tend to be relatively mild, however, and may in practice be largely ineffectual. Moreover, it is possible that the corporate officials may be indemnified, either directly by the corporation or through insurance policies carried for them by the company, from any penalties imposed on them by statute. Interestingly, New York law, which formerly provided for a penalty for wrongful refusal, has deleted the penalty provision since it was seldom enforced and was of little satisfaction to the shareholder. *See* N.Y. BCL § 624.

It is interesting to note that, despite the clear existence of both common law and statutory rights of inspection, many corporate charters or by-laws purport to limit access to corporate records.* Where the effect of such provisions would be to abridge either the common law or statutory right of inspection, they have been routinely declared invalid. *See, e. g.,* State ex rel. Cochran v. Penn-Beaver Oil Co., 34 Del. 81, 143 A. 257 (1926); Hodgens v. United Copper Co., 67 A. 756 (N.J.1907). *See* Koenigsburg, Provisions in Corporate Charters and Bylaws Governing the Inspection of Books by Stockholders, 30 Geo.L.J. 227, 247–48 (1942).

Probably the most difficult hurdle faced by a shareholder seeking inspection of corporate books and records is the establishment of a proper purpose. Most statutes contain no definition of proper purpose or define it in such vague terms as "a purpose reasonably related to such person's interest as a stockholder." *See, e. g.,* Del. GCL § 220(b). A shareholder has no right to inspection "if his purpose be to satisfy his curiosity, to annoy or harass the corporation, or to accomplish some object hostile to the corporation or detrimental to its interests." Albee v. Lamson & Hubbard Corp., 320 Mass. 421, 69 N.E.2d 811, 813 (1946). Thus, access to shareholder lists will be denied where the object is to sell the list for personal profit, *see, e. g.,* State ex rel. Theile v. Cities Service Co., 31 Del. 514, 115 A. 773 (1922), or to aid a competing business, *see, e. g.,* Slay v. Polonia Publishing Co., 249 Mich. 609, 229 N.W. 434 (1930). Conversely, proper purposes have been held to include determination of the value of shares, *see, e. g.,* Bankers Trust Co. v. H. Rosenhirsch Co., 20 Misc.2d 792, 190 N.Y. S.2d 957 (Sup.Ct.1959), communication with other shareholders (including solicitation of proxies, solicitation of shareholders to join in a derivative suit, offers to purchase stock), *see, e. g.,* Weber v. Continental Motors Corp., 305 F.Supp. 404 (S.D.N.Y.1969), and ascertainment of possible corporate mismanagement, *see, e.g.,* Briskin v. Briskin Manufacturing Co., 6 Ill.App.3d 740, 286 N.E.2d 571 (1972). Once a proper purpose has been established, the fact that a shareholder may have other, improper purposes for seeking inspection will generally not be considered a valid defense to a corporation's refusal to allow inspection. *See, e. g.,* General Time Corp. v. Talley Industries, Inc., 43 Del.Ch. 531, 240 A.2d 755 (Del.Supr.1968).

Allocation of the burden of proof on the question of proper purpose may be crucial to the shareholder's success in obtaining the records sought. Many cases construing the common law right of inspection have placed the burden of proving proper purpose on the

---

* A typical provision is found in the Amended Certificate of Incorporation of the United States Steel Corporation: "The Board of Directors from time to time shall determine whether and to what extent, and at what times and places, and under what conditions and regulations, the accounts and books of the Corporation, or any of them, shall be open to the inspection of the stockholders, and no stockholder shall have any right to inspect any account or book or document of the Corporation, except as conferred by law or authorized by the Board of Directors, or by the stockholders."

shareholder. *See, e. g.*, Albee v. Lamson & Hubbard Corp., 320 Mass. 421, 69 N.E.2d 811 (1946). However, where a shareholder alleges a proper purpose, statutes incorporating the right of inspection have generally been construed as shifting the burden of showing improper purpose to the corporation. 5 Fletcher Cyclopedia Corporations § 2253.1 (Perm. ed. 1976).

In determining whether the shareholder has alleged or proved a proper purpose for inspection, courts have focused on whether the asserted purpose is germane to the requesting party's status as a shareholder. Traditionally, the inquiry has centered around the shareholder's legitimate interest in obtaining information related to his economic interest in the corporation. *See* 2 Model Bus.Corp.Act Ann. § 52, ¶ 2 (1971). But is the shareholder's interest in a corporation limited solely to economic matters? Given the ever-increasing controversy about corporate accountability, might not a shareholder be properly interested in corporate social and political policies?

STATE ex rel. PILLSBURY v. HONEYWELL, INC.

291 Minn. 322, 191 N.W.2d 406 (1971).

[Petitioner, determined to stop Honeywell Inc.'s (Honeywell) production of anti-personnel fragmentating bombs used in Vietnam, purchased 100 shares for the "sole purpose" of gaining a voice in the company's affairs. His requests for a shareholders' list was refused. He then filed for a writ of mandamus, and, after depositions, relief was denied. Honeywell is a Delaware corporation, but the court held that the same result obtained whether Delaware or Minnesota law applied.]

KELLY, Justice.

* * *

The trial court ordered judgment for Honeywell, ruling that petitioner had not demonstrated a proper purpose germane to his interest as a stockholder. Petitioner contends that a stockholder who disagrees with management has an absolute right to inspect corporate records for purposes of soliciting proxies. He would have this court rule that such solicitation is per se a "proper purpose." Honeywell argues that a "proper purpose" contemplates concern with investment return. We agree with Honeywell.

This court has had several occasions to rule on the propriety of shareholders' demands for inspection of corporate books and records. Minn.St. 300.32, not applicable here, has been held to be declaratory of the common-law principle that a stockholder is entitled to inspection for a proper purpose germane to his business interests. While inspection will not be permitted for purposes of curiosity, speculation, or vexation, adverseness to management and a desire to gain control of the corporation for economic benefit does not indicate an improper purpose.

Several courts agree with petitioner's contention that a mere desire to communicate with other shareholders is, per se, a proper purpose. This would seem to confer an almost absolute right to inspection. We believe that a better rule would allow inspections only if the shareholder has a proper purpose for such communication.   *   *   *

The act of inspecting a corporation's shareholder ledger and business records must be viewed in its proper perspective. In terms of the corporate norm, inspection is merely the act of the concerned owner checking on what is in part his property. In the context of the large firm, inspection can be more akin to a weapon in corporate warfare.   *   *   *   Because the power to inspect may be the power to destroy, it is important that only those with a bona fide interest in the corporation enjoy that power.

That one must have proper standing to demand inspection has been recognized by statutes in several jurisdictions. Courts have also balked at compelling inspection by a shareholder holding an insignificant amount of stock in the corporation.

Petitioner's standing as a shareholder is quite tenuous. He only owns one share in his own name, bought for the purposes of this suit. He had previously ordered his agent to buy 100 shares, but there is no showing of investment intent. While his agent had a cash balance in the $400,000 portfolio, petitioner made no attempt to determine whether Honeywell was a good investment or whether more profitable shares would have to be sold to finance the Honeywell purchase. Furthermore, peitioner's agent had the power to sell the Honeywell shares without his consent. Petitioner also had a contingent beneficial interest in 242 shares. Courts are split on the question of whether an equitable interest entitles one to inspection. See 5 Fletcher, Private Corporations, § 2230 at 862 (Perm. ed. rev. vol. 1967). Indicative of petitioner's concern regarding his equitable holdings is the fact that he was unaware of them until he had decided to bring this suit.

Petitioner had utterly no interest in the affairs of Honeywell before he learned of Honeywell's production of fragmentation bombs. Immediately after obtaining this knowledge, he purchased stock in Honeywell for the sole purpose of asserting ownership privileges in an effort to force Honeywell to cease such production.   *   *   *
But for his opposition to Honeywell's policy, petitioner probably would not have bought Honeywell stock, would not be interested in Honeywell's profits and would not desire to communicate with Honeywell's shareholders. His avowed purpose in buying Honeywell stock was to place himself in a position to try to impress his opinions favoring a reordering of priorities upon Honeywell management and

its other shareholders. Such a motivation can hardly be deemed a proper purpose germane to his economic interest as a shareholder.[5]

*   *   * From the deposition, the trial court concluded that petitioner had already formed strong opinions on the immorality and the social and economic wastefulness of war long before he bought stock in Honeywell. His sole motivation was to change Honeywell's course of business because that course was incompatible with his political views. If unsuccessful, petitioner indicated that he would sell the Honeywell stock.

We do not mean to imply that a shareholder with a bona fide investment interest could not bring this suit if motivated by concern with the long- or short-term economic effects on Honeywell resulting from the production of war munitions. Similarly, this suit might be appropriate when a shareholder has a bona fide concern about the adverse effects of abstention from profitable war contracts on his investment in Honeywell.

In the instant case, however, the trial court, in effect, has found from all the facts that petitioner was not interested in even the long-term well-being of Honeywell or the enhancement of the value of his shares. His sole purpose was to persuade the company to adopt his social and political concerns, irrespective of any economic benefit to himself or Honeywell. This purpose on the part of one buying into the corporation does not entitle the petitioner to inspect Honeywell's books and records.

Petitioner argues that he wishes to inspect the stockholder ledger in order that he may correspond with other shareholders with the hope of electing to the board one or more directors who represent his particular viewpoint. *   *   * While a plan to elect one or more directors is specific and the election of directors normally would be a proper purpose, here the purpose was not germane to petitioner's or Honeywell's economic interest. Instead, the plan was designed to further petitioner's political and social beliefs. Since the requisite propriety of purpose germane to his or Honeywell's economic interest is not present, the allegation that petitioner seeks to elect a new board of directors is insufficient to compel inspection.

5. We do not question petitioner's good faith incident to his political and social philosophy; nor did the trial court. In a well-prepared memorandum, the lower court stated: "By enumerating the foregoing this Court does not mean to belittle or to be derisive of Petitioner's motivations and intentions because this Court cannot but draw the conclusion that the Petitioner is sincere in his political and social philosophy, but this Court does not feel that this is a proper forum for the advancement of these political-social views by way of direct contact with the stockholders of Honeywell Company or any other company. If the courts were to grant these rights on the basis of the foregoing, anyone who has a political-social philosophy which differs with that of a company in which he becomes a shareholder can secure a writ and any company can be faced with a rash and multitude of these types of actions which are not bona fide efforts to engage in a proxy fight for the purpose of taking over the company or electing directors, which the courts have recognized as being perfectly legitimate and acceptable."

*   *   *

The order of the trial court denying the writ of mandamus is affirmed.

————

Pillsbury probably marks the low tide in the stockholder's right to inspect. It appears that Delaware courts do not believe it is a proper interpretation of Delaware law. Credit Bureau Reports, Inc. v. Credit Bureau of St. Paul, Inc. 290 A.2d 689 (Del.Ch.1972) aff'd., 290 A.2d 691 (Del.Supr.). *See* Note, Shareholder's Right to Inspection of Corporate Stock Ledger, 4 Conn.L.Rev. 707 (1972).

Chapter 11

CONTROL PROBLEMS IN THE CLOSELY
HELD CORPORATION

A. INTRODUCTION

One of the difficulties of the American law of corporations is that
it attempts to shoehorn small, closely held, or "close," corporations,
which often have relatively few assets and a handful of shareholders,
into the same legal structure as publicly held giants of the size and
character of General Motors and AT&T. Although the corporation
statutes of some other industrialized countries make special provision
for the close corporation, often treating it in an entirely separate statute and endowing it with a name distinct from that applied to its larger cousin,* American statutes generally treat all corporations the
same regardless of size or the dispersion of ownership of stock.

The principal difficulty with American law's failure (in general) to
differentiate between the close and the public corporation grows out
of the fact that the shareholders of a close corporation are likely to
think themselves more as partners whose enterprise happens to be
incorporated only because of the legal and tax advantages (such as
they are) that incorporation confers. In the management of their
business they usually seek to behave as an "incorporated partnership," and in so doing they often find their behavior in conflict with
legal norms developed for an entirely different organizational model.
The officers and directors of a close corporation must, for example,
think it strange that, in carrying out their corporate duties, they are
held by the law to act as fiduciaries for the shareholders when, as is
often the case, they are the only shareholders. This tension between
the legally-sanctioned model and ordinary human inclinations creates
a challenge for the attorney. It is a challenge, however, that can
usually be met by careful planning and drafting. In this chapter we
will examine the devices, some within the corporate framework and
some extrinsic to it, that are available to the corporate planner.

---

* France, for example, distinguishes
between a *societé anonyme* ("S.A."),
which is public and generally large, and a
societé a responsabilité limité ("S.A.R.
L."), a small to medium size company
with 50 or fewer shareholders. In Germany the equivalent distinction is drawn
between the Aktiengesellschaft ("A.G.")
and the Gesellschaft mit beschrankte
Haftung ("G.m.b.H."). In England there
is separate statutory treatment of the
private company and the public company.
Scholars in the Continental countries
draw a conceptual distinction between
"associations of persons," which encompass their equivalents of our partnerships, and "associations of capital," the
S.A. and the A.G. The S.A.R.L. and the
G.m.b.H. are considered hybrids that fall
in between the two extremes. As you
read the following materials you might
ask yourself whether a similar conceptual distinction could play a useful role in
American law. *See* Manne, Our Two
Corporate Systems: Law and Economics,
53 Va.L.Rev. 259 (1967).

302

For many years the major hurdle faced by the planner of the close corporation was the reluctance of the courts to give effect to arrangements—whether embodied in the articles, by-laws, or a separate instrument—that departed too far from the traditional model. Two parallel developments of the last ten or twenty years have substantially loosened the bonds of this judicial straitjacket. First, the courts, taking a more realistic view of the practical demands of operating a business as a close corporation, have become far more tolerant of departures from the norm.

Second, and perhaps more importantly, legislatures, too, have recognized the unnecessary rigidity of a structure developed for a different sort of enterprise, and the inequities that regularly grew out of the strict application of this structure to corporations with few shareholders. A growing number of states have amended various provisions of their corporation statutes in such a way as to allow more flexibility to close corporation planners. For example, the current version of MBCA § 35 provides that "[T]he business and affairs of a corporation shall be managed under the direction of, a board of directors *except as may be otherwise provided in* this Act or *the articles of incorporation*. If any such provision is made in the articles of incorporation, the powers and duties conferred or imposed upon the board of directors by this Act shall be exercised or performed to such extent and by such persons as shall be provided in the articles of incorporation." (Emphasis added.)

This "unified" approach, which treats all corporations alike, regardless of whether they are closely or publicly held, but provides greater flexibility by expressly permitting variations from the conventional mold, is by far the most common. *See* 1 F. O'Neal, Close Corporations: Law and Practice § 1.13a (2d ed.1971).

A second approach is the "comprehensive" close corporation statute, which allows the planner to elect treatment under a special statutory regime applicable only to those corporations that choose to be governed by it. The provisions of Del. G C L §§ 341–356 are a good example. They apply only to corporations that meet certain tests and that elect close corporation status. The provisions of the California statute are similar, although they are scattered through various sections rather than being collected in one place. *See, e.g.,* Cal.Corp. Code §§ 158, 202(a), and 300. The approach of Maryland, one of the pioneers in developing close corporation legislation, is to group in Md. Corp.Code §§ 110–111 a set of provisions that apply to any corporation that elects them (without requiring that it meet standards for qualification as a "close corporation") unless the organizers have made other provisions.

The latest development in this field has been the preparation by the Committee on Corporate Laws of the Section of Corporation, Banking, and Business Law, of the ABA of a "Statutory Close Corporation Supplement," which seeks to add to the flexibility of the "uni-

fied" approach discussed above by adding an integrated package of
provisions that may be elected by a qualifying corporation. As this
"Supplement" is likely to be influential in the development of legislation in other states, you should become generally familiar with its
structure.

Although it is today probably possible to accomplish under even
the most traditional statute much of what a close corporation might
wish by way of special arrangements, the case law in many jurisdictions will often leave some doubt as to the validity of particular provisions, and more extreme departures from the traditional model—such
as the management of a corporation by its shareholders without the
intervention of a board of directors—may be altogether unavailable.
Under these circumstances, counsel organizing a close corporation in
a jurisdiction that has not adopted one or the other of the schemes
described above may wish to consider the advisability of incorporating in a jurisdiction that has taken a more solicitous view of the small
enterprise, even though doing so will entail the additional expense
and inconvenience of foreign incorporation discussed in Chapter 7.

Notwithstanding the availability of flexible statutory provisions
and the increasing willingness of the courts to accept departures
from the norm, it remains essential for the student to be familiar
with the older rules, not only because they are still operative in many
jurisdictions, but because such a familiarity is indispensable to a full
understanding of the more "modern" statutory and judicial approaches. Many of the cases that follow, therefore, are drawn from the
traditional current of judicial thinking. You should remain aware, as
you read them, that at least some of the rules they enunciate have
given way in many jurisdictions to a more relaxed approach. Most of
the questions of policy raised by these cases, however, remain very
much of continuing concern.

One final matter needs attention before we proceed to introduce
the problem: What, exactly, is a "close corporation?" There is, in
fact, no generally agreed-upon definition of the term. A recent attempt at a formulation of a definition is found in Donahue v. Rodd
Electrotype Co. of New England, Inc., 367 Mass. 578, 328 N.E.2d 505
(1975). The plaintiff-shareholder was the widow and heir of former
employee of the corporation who had worked his way up to vice president, in the process acquiring a substantial minority interest in its
stock. The balance was held by Harry Rodd or members of his family. When Rodd decided to withdraw from the business, he caused the
corporation to buy a large block of his stock for $36,000. Upon learn-
ing of the purchase, the plaintiff and her husband (before his death)
objected, then offered to sell their shares to the corporation on the
same terms. When that offer was refused, they brought suit. In
reversing the trial court's dismissal of the action, the Supreme Judicial Court of Massachusetts explained its holding in terms of an anal-

ysis of the characteristics of close corporations, which it defined as follows:

There is no single, generally accepted definition. Some commentators emphasize an "integration of ownership and management," in which the stockholders occupy most management positions. Others focus on the number of stockholders and the nature of the market for the stock. In this view, close corporations have few stockholders; there is little market for corporate stock. The Supreme Court of Illinois adopted this latter view in Galler v. Galler, 32 Ill.2d 16, 203 N.E.2d 577 (1965): "For our purposes, a close corporation is one in which the stock is held in a few hands, or in a few families, and wherein it is not at all, or only rarely, dealt in by buying or selling." We accept aspects of both definitions. We deem a close corporation to be typified by: (1) a small number of stockholders; (2) no ready market for the corporate stock; and (3) substantial majority stockholder participation in the management, direction and operations of the corporation.

[handwritten: closed corp.]

As thus defined, the close corporation bears striking resemblance to a partnership. Commentators and courts have noted that the close corporation is often little more than an "incorporated" or "chartered" partnership. The stockholders "clothe" their partnership "with the benefits peculiar to a corporation, limited liability, perpetuity and the like." In the Matter of Surchin v. Approved Business Machine Co., Inc., 55 Misc.2d 888, 889, 286 N.Y.S. 2d 580, 581 (Sup.Ct.1967). In essence, though, the enterprise remains one in which ownership is limited to the original parties or transferees of their stock to whom the other stockholders have agreed, in which ownership and management are in the same hands, and in which the owners are quite dependent on one another for the success of the enterprise. Many close corporations are "really partnerships, between two or three people who contribute their capital, skills, experience and labor." Kruger v. Gerth, 16 N. Y.2d 802, 805, 263 N.Y.S.2d 1, 3, 210 N.E.2d 355, 356 (1965) (Desmond, C.J., dissenting).

———

However defined, it is clear that close corporations are extremely numerous and that thousands are created or go out of business each year, with all of the legal problems entailed.

NOTE ON PREINCORPORATION AGREEMENTS

It is possible to organize a closely held corporation without drafting more than the articles, by-laws, and minutes of the organization meeting; indeed, that manner of proceeding is probably the rule. Where it is followed, the control and financial arrangements are informally agreed upon often prior to incorporating the business and become concrete after the completion of the formalities of organization.

There are, however, a number of advantages to working out these arrangements more formally in advance of the organizing process and memorializing them in a preincorporation agreement.* It may be desirable to bind the promoters in advance of securing financial commitments from investors. Moreover, as we shall see presently, several of the more useful control devices cannot, by their nature, be set forth within the articles and by-laws, but must be included in a separate agreement among some or all of the shareholders. If there is need for such an agreement, it makes sense to write it at the beginning. From a practical point of view, the discipline of spelling out the details of financial and control arrangements often proves useful for all parties and their lawyers. By consolidating all of the parties' arrangements in one place, later misunderstandings and gaps in the structure are more easily avoided than where just casual attention is given to such matters.

PROBLEM

PISCES TACKLE CO.—INTRODUCTION

You have known Phil Flyer and Les Leader since high school. Ardent fishermen both, they went to work after college for a local sporting goods manufacturer, Flyer as a production engineer and Leader in the sales and marketing department. They have been talking for some time about going into business for themselves in the manufacture of fishing rods. Flyer has developed a good deal of expertise in a new graphite technology that is becoming increasingly popular, and Leader believes that there is room in the market for a small line of high quality graphite rods. They have mentioned their idea to you, solicited your (free) opinion on some of the details—with a promise, of course, that they would come to you as paying clients should they ever attempt to make their plans a reality. Having both recently turned thirty, they have decided that this is the time to strike out on their own by forming a new company to be called Pisces Tackle Company, Inc.

They do not have much capital themselves; each has saved about $20,000 he could put into their enterprise. Leader has discussed their idea with his cousin, Harriet Hooks, a young stockbroker and investor who, having recently inherited a good deal of money from her father, has been looking for investment possibilities. Hooks is also a

---

* Dean O'Neal distinguishes between a "promoters' contract," which merely binds the parties to proceeding with the organization of a corporation with a defined configuration, and a "shareholders' agreement," which consists of arrangements intended to bind the shareholders in various ways (to be discussed below) that will survive long after the corporation has been formally organized. He suggests that where both ends are sought, it may be best to use two different documents. 1 F. O'Neal, Close Corporations: Law and Practice § 2.23 (2d ed.1971).

dedicated angler and is attracted by the rod company idea on both aesthetic and economic grounds. She is willing to invest $50,000 in the undertaking in return for a one-half interest. She does not want to participate actively in the day-to-day management of the business, but she does insist on "full representation" on the board, which appears to mean that she wants to be able to elect half of the directors. Flyer and Leader believe that with their $40,000 and Hooks' $50,000 they would have sufficient equity capital to get their new enterprise off the ground. Flyer and Leader would each get 25 percent and Hooks, 50 percent of the equity.

The three have come to your office to ask your help in organizing the business. After preliminary discussions, they have agreed to incorporate. They have settled on an all common stock capital structure. Flyer is to be president, Leader, vice president and treasurer, and Hooks, secretary. The parties intend that Flyer will have control over engineering and production matters and Leader will run the financial and sales end of the business. As neither Flyer nor Leader will have any outside source of income, each is to draw, initially, a salary of $20,000. Hooks will not be paid a salary for her more limited participation, at least at this time. They have tentatively agreed on a four-member board of directors consisting of the three of them and an additional director chosen by Hooks.

B.   SOME ETHICAL CONSIDERATIONS

PROBLEM

PISCES TACKLE CO.—PART I

Flyer and Leader stay in your office for a few minutes after Hooks has left. They tell you that they have discussed, in Hooks' absence, the problems that might arise in the relations among the three of them, and that Flyer is a bit concerned that, as close as he is to Leader, blood might ultimately prove thicker than water and that Leader and Hooks might gang up against him. Moreover, Flyer and Leader feel strongly that initially they should produce only very fine—and expensive—rods in order to build up a reputation for high quality. They are afraid that Hooks may become impatient with this strategy and start demanding a higher-volume, lower-price operation that might produce greater returns in the short run. Consequently, they are considering entering into some agreement between themselves to vote together at shareholders' meetings on the election of directors. They ask you whether such an agreement would be valid.

Should you become involved in drafting a side agreement between Flyer and Leader? Whether or not you do, have you any obligation to tell Hooks about their intentions in that regard?

In dealing with these questions consider the materials in Chapter 7, part A.

C.   RESTRICTING SHAREHOLDERS' VOTING DISCRETION

PROBLEM

PISCES TACKLE CO.—PART II

Pisces intends to incorporate under Columbia law, where it will conduct its business and where its shareholders live. There are few judicial decisions dealing with close corporations.

Assume that, on your advice, Flyer and Leader have told Hooks of their concerns and that Hooks has said she has no objection to their entering into some arrangement whereby they agree always to vote together at shareholders' meetings. Assume also that Hooks has no objection to your drafting this agreement and that you are satisfied that her consent overcomes the ethical problems * that would otherwise be presented. What would be the best way of accomplishing Flyer and Leader's desire? Answer the following questions assuming that the applicable law is (a) common law; (b) the MBCA (especially § 34), and (c) either N.Y. BCL §§ 609(f), 609(g), and 620(a); Del. GCL §§ 218; Calif. §§ 300, 706, Md. Corp. and Assoc. § 4–401 or § 11 of the MBCA Close Corporation Supplement.

1.   Can you construct a legally valid means of accomplishing Flyer and Leader's aims using these devices?

2.   What practical problem do you see for the arrangements you devised?

3.   Consider, for each device, how it will be enforced if Flyer and Leader were to have a falling out.

4.   Would you recommend an agreement similar to that used in *Ringling Brothers*? Were you to be asked to revise that agreement, what changes would you make?

1. AN INTRODUCTION TO THE LEGAL OBSTACLES

LEHRMAN v. COHEN

42 Del. 222, 222 A.2d 800 (1966).

HERRMANN, Justice.

The primary problem presented on this appeal involves the applicability of the Delaware Voting Trust Statute. Other questions involve the legality of stock having voting power but no dividend or liquidation rights except repayment of par value, and an alleged unlawful delegation of directorial duties and powers.

---

* That you are asked to make this assumption should not necessarily be taken as implying approval of this manner of proceeding, which would, notwithstanding Hooks' consent, still pose important ethical and practical problems for the attorney.

[Giant Food, Inc., a Delaware corporation that runs a chain of su-
permarkets, was organized in 1935 by N. M. Cohen and Samuel Lehrman. Initially its voting stock consisted of Class AC shares, all of
which were owned by members of the Cohen family, and Class AL
shares, all of which were owned by members of the Lehrman family.
Each class was entitled to elect two members of a four member
board. A settlement of a family dispute that arose after Samuel
Lehrman's death in 1949 left his son, Jacob, owning all of the AL
shares, a number equal to the number of AC shares held by the Cohen family. In order to prevent a deadlock, one share of a third class
of stock, AD, was created, which was entitled to elect a fifth director.
This share had no right to dividends or distributions in liquidation beyond its $10 value. It was immediately issued to Joseph B. Danzan-
sky, who has served as the company's counsel since 1944. Danzansky voted to elect himself the fifth director, and remained in that post
until the events that gave rise to the suit. The court's statement of
the facts continues:]

From the outset and until October 1, 1964, the defendant N. M.
Cohen was president of the Company. On that date, a resolution was
adopted at the Company's annual stockholders' meeting to give
Danzansky a fifteen year executive employment contract at an annual salary of $67,600., and options for 25,000 shares of the non-voting
common stock of the Company. The AC and AD stock were voted in
favor and the AL stock was voted against the resolution. At a directors meeting held the same day, Danzansky was elected president of
the Company by a 3–2 vote, the two AL directors voting in opposition.
On December 11, 1964, Danzansky resigned as director and voted his
share of AD stock to elect as the fifth director, Millard F. West, Jr., a
former AL director and investment banker whose firm was one of the
underwriters of the public issue of the Company's stock. The newly
constituted board ratified the election of Danzansky as president;
and, on January 27, 1965, after the commencement of this action and
after a review and report by a committee consisting of the new AD
director and one AL director, Danzansky's employment contract was
approved and adopted with certain modifications.

The plaintiff brought this action on December 11, 1964, basing it
upon two claims: The First Claim charges that the creation, issuance,
and voting of the one share of Class AD stock resulted in an arrangement illegal under the law of this State for the reasons hereinafter
set forth. The Second Claim, addressed to the events of October 1,
1964, charges that the election of Danzansky as president of the Company and his employment contract violated the terms of the [1949]
deadlock-breaking arrangement, as made between the holders of the
AC and AL stock, and constituted breaches of contract and fiduciary
duty. The plaintiff and the defendants filed cross-motions for summary judgment as to the First Claim. The Court of Chancery, after
considering the contentions now before us and discussed *infra*, grant-

ed summary judgment in favor of the defendants and denied the plaintiff's motion for summary judgment. The plaintiff appeals.

I.

The plaintiff's primary contention is that the Class AD stock arrangement is, in substance and effect, a voting trust; that, as such, it is illegal because not limited to a ten year period as required by the Voting Trust Statute. The defendants deny that the AD stock arrangement constitutes a disguised voting trust; but they concede that if it is, the arrangement is illegal for violation of the Statute. Thus, issue is clearly joined on the point.

The criteria of a voting trust under our decisions have been summarized by this Court in Abercrombie v. Davies, 36 Del.Ch. 371, 130 A.2d 338 (1957). The tests there set forth, accepted by both sides of this cause as being applicable, are as follows: (1) the voting rights of the stock are separated from the other attributes of ownership; (2) the voting rights granted are intended to be irrevocable for a definite period of time; and (3) the principal purpose of the grant of voting rights is to acquire voting control of the corporation.

Adopting and applying these tests, the plaintiff says, as to the first element, that the AD arrangement provides for a divorcement of voting rights from beneficial ownership of the AC and AL stock; that the creation and issuance of the share of AD stock is tantamount to a pooling by the AC and AL stockholders of a portion of their voting stock and giving it to a trustee, in the person of the AD stockholder, to vote for the election of the fifth director; that after the creation of the AD stock, the AC and AL stockholders each hold but 40% of the voting power, and the AD stockholder holds the controlling balance of 20%; that the AD stock has no property rights except the right to a return of the $10. paid as the par value; and that, therefore, there has been a transfer of the voting rights devoid of any participating property rights. So runs the argument of the plaintiff in support of his contention that the first of the *Abercrombie* criteria for a voting trust is met.

The contention is unacceptable. The AD arrangement did not separate the voting rights of the AC or the AL stock from the other attributes of ownership of those classes of stock. Each AC and AL stockholder retains complete control over the voting of his stock; each can vote his stock directly; no AL or AC stockholder is divested of his right to vote his stock as he sees fit; no AL or AC stock can be voted against the shareholder's wishes; and the AL and AC stock continue to elect two directors each.

The AD stock arrangement, as we view it, became a part of the capitalization of the Company. The fact that there is but a single share, or that the par value is nominal, is of no legal significance; the one share and the $10. par value might have been multiplied many times over, with the same consequence. It is true that the creation of the separate class of AD stock may have diluted the voting *power* which had previously existed in the AC and AL stock—the usual consequence when additional voting stock is created—but the creation of the new class did not divest and separate the voting *rights* which remain vested in each AC and AL shareholder, together with the other attributes of the ownership of that stock. The fallacy of the plaintiff's position lies in his premise that since the voting power of the AC and AL stock was reduced by the creation of the AD stock, the percentage of reduction became the *res* of a voting trust. In any recapitalization involving the creation of additional voting stock, the voting power of the previously existing stock is diminished; but a voting trust is not necessarily the result.

Since the holders of the Class AC and Class AL stock of the Company did not separate the voting rights from the other attributes of ownership of those classes when they created the Class AD stock, the first *Abercrombie* test of a voting trust is not met.

This conclusion disposes of the second and third *Abercrombie* tests, i.e., that the voting rights granted are irrevocable for a definite period of time, and that the principal object of the grant of voting rights is voting control of the corporation. Having held that the AC and AL stockholders have not divested themselves of their voting rights, although they may have diluted their voting powers, we do not reach the remaining *Abercrombie* tests, both of which assume the divestiture of voting rights.

In the final analysis, the essence of the question raised by the plaintiff in this connection is this: Is the substance and purpose of the AD stock arrangement sufficiently close to the substance and purpose of § 218 to warrant its being subjected to the restrictions and conditions imposed by that Statute? The answer is negative not only for the reasons above stated, but also because § 218 regulates trusts and pooling agreements amounting to trusts, not other and different types of arrangements and undertakings possible among stockholders. The AD stock arrangement is neither a trust nor a pooling agreement.

We hold, therefore, that the Class AD stock arrangement is not controlled by the Voting Trust Statute.

II.

The plaintiff's second point is that even if the Class AD stock arrangement is not a voting trust in substance and effect, the AD stock is illegal, nevertheless, because the creation of a class of stock having voting rights only, and lacking any substantial participating proprietary interest in the corporation, violates the public policy of this State as declared in § 218.

The fallacy of this argument is twofold: First, it is more accurate to say that what the law has disfavored, and what the public policy underlying the Voting Trust Statute means to control, is the separation of the vote from the stock—not from the stock ownership. 5 Fletcher Cyclopedia Corporations, § 2080, pp. 363–369; compare Abercrombie v. Davies, supra. Clearly, the AD stock arrangement is not violative of that public policy. Secondly, there is nothing in § 218, either expressed or implied, which requires that all stock of a Delaware corporation must have both voting rights and proprietary interests. Indeed, public policy to the contrary seems clearly expressed by 8 Del.C. § 151(a) which authorizes, in very broad terms, such voting powers and participating rights as may be stated in the certificate of incorporation. Non-voting stock is specifically authorized by § 151(a); and in the light thereof, consistency does not permit the conclusion, urged by the plaintiff, that the present public policy of this State condemns the separation of voting rights from beneficial stock ownership.

We conclude that the plaintiff's contention in this regard cannot withstand the force and effect of § 151(a). In our view, that Statute permits the creation of stock having voting rights only, as well as stock having property rights only. The voting powers and the participating rights of the Class AD stock being specified in the Company's certificate of incorporation, we are of the opinion that the Class AD stock is legal by virtue of § 151(a).

*   *   *

We are told that if the AD stock arrangement is allowed thus to stand, our Voting Trust Statute will become a "dead letter" because it will be possible to evade and circumvent its purpose simply by issuing a class of non-participating voting stock, as was done here. We have three negative reactions to this argument:

First, it presupposes a divestiture of the voting rights of the AC and AL stock—an untenable supposition as has been stated. Secondly, it fails to take into account the main purpose of a Voting Trust Statute: to avoid secret, uncontrolled combinations of stockholders formed to acquire voting control of the corporation to the possible detriment of non-participating shareholders. It may not be said that the AD stock arrangement contravenes that purpose. Finally on this point, if we misconceive the legislative intent, and if the AD stock arrangement in this case reveals a loophole in § 218 which should be plugged, it is for the General Assembly to accomplish—not for us to attempt by interstitial judicial legislation.

III.

The plaintiff advances yet another reason for invalidating the AD stock. The essence of this argument is that the only function of that class of stock is to break directorial deadlocks; that the issuance of the AD stock is merely a technical device to permit that result; that, as such, it is illegal because it permits the AC and AL directors of the

Company to delegate their statutory duties to the AD director as an arbitrator.

* * *

As to the means adopted for the accomplishment of that purpose, we find the AD stock arrangement valid by virtue of § 141(a) of the Delaware Corporation Law which provides:

> The business of every corporation organized under the provisions of this chapter shall be managed by a board of directors, except as hereinafter or in its certificate of incorporation otherwise provided.

The AD stock arrangement was created by the unanimous action of the stockholders of the Company by amendment to the certificate of incorporation. The stockholders thereby provided how the business of the corporation is to be managed, as is their privilege and right under § 141(a). It was this stockholder action which delegated to the AD director whatever powers and duties he possesses; they were not delegated to him by his fellow directors, either out of their own powers and duties, or otherwise.

It is settled, of course, as a general principle, that directors may not delegate their duty to manage the corporate enterprise. But there is no conflict with that principle where, as here, the delegation of duty, if any, is made not by the directors but by stockholder action under § 141(a), via the certificate of incorporation.

* * *

Finding no error in the judgment below, it is affirmed.

2. DEVICES OUTSIDE THE CORPORATE MACHINERY

Although one can find a number of variants, the devices available to shareholders to limit in some fashion the way in which they vote their stock can be divided into three principal classes: (1) voting trusts, (2) irrevocable proxies, and (3) vote pooling agreements. A *voting trust* is created by the conveyance by the participating shareholders of legal title to their shares to a voting trustee or a group of trustees pursuant to the terms of a trust agreement. This transfer is normally registered on the corporation's stock transfer ledger, which shows the trustees as legal owners of the shares. The former shareholders—now beneficiaries of the trust—receive in exchange for their shares trust certificates which evidence their equitable ownership of the stock. These certificates are usually transferable, and entitle the owner to receive whatever dividends are paid on the underlying stock. They are, in effect, shares of stock shorn of their voting power and perhaps certain other rights normally appurtenant to the ownership of stock, such as the right to inspect the corporate books or to institute a derivative suit.

Since the terms of the trust agreement are a matter of contract, the trustees may be given full discretion to vote the shares in the trust for the election of directors and for any other matter to come before the shareholders, or their exercise of the franchise may be limited in some respects.

At an earlier stage in the development of the law of corporations courts tended to view voting trusts with suspicion, in many cases holding them void as against public policy. State legislatures responded by passing statutes permitting voting trusts but subjecting them to certain regulations: principally a limitation on their effective life and the requirement that their terms be made a matter of public record so that they could not be hidden from other shareholders not party to the arrangement. *See* MBCA § 34. Today virtually all jurisdictions have such legislation.

Limiting legislation on voting trusts

Some of the judicial dislike for the voting trust has survived, however, in the doctrine that an arrangement that amounts to a voting trust in operation but does not comply with the terms of a voting trust statute is invalid. The application, or attempted application, of this doctrine is illustrated in the *Lehrman* case and the *Ringling Brothers* case below.

Many of the same concerns that led to judicial invalidation of voting trusts are equally applicable to the *irrevocable proxy*. It is, as we have seen,* quite common for a shareholder to give a proxy to vote his shares to someone else, and even to give that person entire discretion to decide how they should be voted. But the ordinary proxy, like any agency power, may generally be revoked at the will of the principal, and the proxy holder remains subject to the control of the shareholder. *See* Restatement, Second, Agency § 118.

It is sometimes desired, however, that the shareholder make the grant of the proxy irrevocable, subject perhaps to some contingency or the passage of a specified time. In such a case, the shareholder loses control of the exercise of the franchise for the period of the proxy, and it can be said that "the vote is separated from the stock," the very problem that lies at the heart of the objections to voting trusts. Thus, whether because they find them to violate basic principles of agency law, or to be against public policy, the courts tend to be reluctant to enforce irrevocable proxies against a shareholder.

Agency law does recognize as valid an agency power "coupled with an interest." *See* Restatement, Second, Agency §§ 138–139. The modern trend is to recognize this principle in the corporate context and to uphold irrevocable proxies that are "coupled with an interest." The difficulty is to determine what sort of "interest" will support an irrevocable proxy. The older, more conservative view is that the interest must be in the stock, itself, such as that created by a pledge of the equitable interest by one who has contracted or who

* *See* Chapter 10, Section D.

has an option to purchase the shares. In re Chilson, 19 Del.Ch. 398, 168 A. 82 (Ch.1933). The more recent tendency, however, has been to reject a formalistic application of agency principles and approach the problem with greater appreciation of the practical realities of arranging the affairs of a close corporation. Irrevocable proxies have been upheld, for example, where the proxy has been given as an inducement to the holder to furnish money to the corporation. Hey v. Dolphin, 92 Hun. 230, 36 N.Y.S. 627 (Sup.Ct.1895); Chapman v. Bates, 61 N.J.Eq. 658, 47 A. 638 (Ct.Err. & App.1900).

As the problem presents itself most often to the close corporation planner, the putative proxy holder seldom has a direct interest in the stock. Commonly, two or more shareholders seek to enter into a contractual arrangement involving the grant of irrevocable proxies, the consideration for which is merely the mutual promises of the parties to the agreement. In this situation it is hard to find an "interest" sufficient to support the proxy. Faced with this problem some courts have found that where the proxy holder was induced to purchase stock in reliance on the agreement, his interest in the corporation as shareholder is enough. A few other courts have been willing to go even farther than this already strained interpretation and, though nominally adhering to the doctrine, have broadened it "to such an extent that it is hardly recognizable." 1 F. O'Neal, Close Corporations § 5.36 (2d ed.1971). Although not always admitting to it, these courts have enforced irrevocable proxies supported by only the mutual promises contained in a shareholders' agreement simply because the business realities of the close corporation seemed to demand it. As one court put it, "The power to vote the stock was necessary in order to make * * * control of the corporation secure." State ex rel. Everett Trust & Savings Bank v. Pacific Waxed Paper Co., 22 Wash. 2d 844, 852, 157 P.2d 707, 711 (1945).

Recognizing that the artificial requirement of the common law rule—that a proxy must be coupled with an interest in order to be irrevocable—makes little sense in the close corporation context, some state legislatures have effectively eliminated it by statute.* (Query: What is the effect of MBCA § 34 on such arrangements?) Absent such a statute or a clear holding by the state courts upholding irrevo-

---

* See, e.g., N.Y. BCL §§ 609(f) and (g), 620(a). Rather than a separate statute dealing with special problems of the closely-held corporation, the New York Business Corporation Law attempts in a single statute to meet the needs of both the close corporation and the public corporation. The Business Corporation Law contains a number of provisions relevant mainly to the close corporation. These provisions, which are scattered throughout the statute rather than being placed in a separate section, provide increased flexibility to the corporation which enables an attorney to mold the corporate form to meet special needs of clients. Although the New York Business Corporation Law never comprehensively defines the term "close corporation," note that under N.Y. BCL § 620(c), the provisions of § 620(b), which allows for restrictions to be placed on the Board's discretion, are applicable where the corporation's shares are not publicly traded. See also the definition of a close corporation under N.Y. BCL § 630, which makes such a corporation's ten largest shareholders liable for debts, wages and salaries owing to its laborers, servants, or employees.

cable proxies in shareholder agreements, the planner is probably well-advised not to rely too heavily on an irrevocable proxy, simpliciter. If the use of the device is unavoidable, it is probably desirable at least to support it with cross options to purchase the shares involved. *See* W. Painter, Corporate and Tax Aspects of Closely Held Corporations 121 (1971). *See* generally, Comment, Irrevocable Proxies, 43 Tex.L. Rev. 733 (1965).

The third technique often found in close corporation control arrangements is the so-called *vote pooling agreement*. As is the case with voting trusts and irrevocable proxies, the basic purpose of such an agreement is to bind some (or occasionally all) of the shareholders to vote together—either in a particular way or pursuant to some specified procedure—on designated questions or on all questions that come before the shareholders. As the famous *Ringling Brothers* case excerpted below indicates, it is generally accepted that such agreements are valid. The difficulty they pose is the manner in which they are to be enforced.

———

RINGLING v. RINGLING BROS.—BARNUM & BAILEY COMBINED SHOWS, INC.

29 Del.Ch. 318, 49 A.2d 603 (1946).

[The 1000 issued and outstanding shares of common stock of Ringling Brothers—Barnum & Bailey Combined Shows, Inc. were owned or controlled as follows: 315 by plaintiff Edith Ringling, 315 by defendant Aubrey Haley, and 370 by defendant Jonn Ringling North. To best use their majority holdings and the corporation's cumulative voting structure, in 1941, plaintiff and Mrs. Haley executed a ten year "Memorandum of Agreement." In addition to giving either party the right of first refusal in the event the other party wanted to sell her stock, the instrument set forth the following two provisions:

2. In exercising any voting rights to which either party may be entitled by virtue of ownership of stock or voting trust certificates held by them in either of said corporations each party will consult and confer with the other and the parties will act jointly in exercising such voting rights in accordance with such agreement as they may reach with respect to any matter calling for the exercise of such voting rights.

3. In the event the parties fail to agree with respect to any matter covered by paragraph 2 above, the question in disagreement shall be submitted for arbitration to Karl D. Loos, of Washington, D.C., as arbitrator and his decision thereon shall be binding upon the parties thereto. Such arbitration shall be exercised to the end of assuring for the respective corporations good management and such participation therein by the members of the

Ringling family as the experience, capacity and ability of each may warrant. The parties may at any time by written agreement designate any other individual to act as arbitrator in lieu of said Loos.

Prior to the annual meeting of shareholders in 1946, the parties to the agreement had successfully elected five of the seven directors: Edith Ringling; her son Robert Ringling; Aubrey Haley; her husband James Haley; and William Dunn, Jr., who had served for some years on the board as representative of the interests of a bank that had loaned a substantial sum of money to the circus. The other two directors were John Ringling North and his nominee, a Mr. Woods. By 1946 relations between the Ringlings and the Haleys had broken down and the Haleys had formed an alliance with North. Thus was the stage set for the 1946 annual shareholders meeting. The new Haley-North faction sought to elect five of the seven directors, but to do so, Aubrey Haley would have to violate the terms of the agreement with Edith Ringling.

Haley violates agreement w/ Ringling

There were eight nominations for director—the seven incumbents and a Mr. Griffin, who was nominated by North. The tactical situation for the voting was described by the Delaware Supreme Court in its opinion on appeal (Ringling Bros.—Barnum & Bailey Combined Shows v. Ringling, 29 Del.Ch. 610, 53 A.2d 441 (1947)): "Each lady was entitled to cast 2205 votes (since each had the cumulative voting rights of 315 shares, and there were seven vacancies in the directorate). The sum of the votes of both is 4410, which is sufficient to allow 882 votes for each of five persons. Mr. North, holding 370 shares, was entitled to cast 2590 votes, which obviously cannot be divided so as to give to more than two candidates as many as 882 votes each. It will be observed that in order for Mrs. Ringling and Mrs. Haley to be sure to elect five directors (regardless of how Mr. North might vote) they must act together in the sense that their combined votes must be divided among five different candidates and at least one of the five must be voted for by both Mrs. Ringling and Mr. Haley." (53 A.2d at 444 n. 1) When it came time to vote, Mr. Haley (his wife was ill and did not attend the meeting) refused to cooperate with Edith Ringling. When called upon to resolve the dispute, Loos directed that the stock of the parties to the agreement be voted so that, taken with the way North actually voted, the following results would be obtained:

Candidates for Election

	Edith	Robert	Dunn	Mrs. Haley	Mr. Haley	North	Woods	Griffin
Haley votes			441	882	882			
Ringling votes	882	882	441					
North votes						863	864	863
Totals	882	882	882	882	882	863	864	863

Refusing to follow Loos' instructions, Mr. Haley voted all his wife's shares for her and for himself. Edith, however, voted as directed by Loos. This produced the following tally:

Candidates for Election

	Edith	Robert	Dunn	Mrs. Haley	Mr. Haley	North	Woods	Griffin
Haley votes				1103	1102			
Ringling votes	882	882	441					
North votes						863	864	863
Totals	882	882	441	1103	1102	863	864	863

The chairman of the meeting ruled that the votes should be counted as if Haley had voted in accordance with the arbitrator's instructions and that, therefore, the directors elected were the first seven of the eight candidates (Griffin, who had tied with North, apparently having gracefully deferred to him). The Haleys, however, insisted that the voting agreement was invalid and that Griffin had been elected instead of Dunn. There followed a rather chaotic directors meeting at which Mrs. Ringling participated under protest, claiming that the stockholders meeting had been adjourned without an effective election of directors and at which both Dunn and Griffin attempted to participate as directors in voting for different slates of officers. Shortly after that meeting, Mrs. Ringling brought this suit. After stating the facts, the lower court, Vice Chancellor SEITZ, continued:]

Having concluded that the Delaware law must be applied to test the validity of this Agreement, it is next pertinent to examine defendants' contentions that the Agreement is unenforceable under Delaware law because it is only "an agreement to agree", or because it involves an attempted delegation of irrevocable control over voting rights in a manner which is against the public policy of this state.

Do we have here only "an agreement to agree", by which defendants mean that there exists no legally enforceable obligation?

Preliminarily, I think it clear that the mutual promises contained in the Agreement constitute sufficient consideration to support it. The mutual restraints on the actions of the parties with respect to the sale and voting of their stock comply with the consideration requirements of contract law.

Did the parties only agree to agree? Certainly the parties agreed to agree as to how they would vote their stock, but they also provided that they would be bound by the decision of a named person in the event they were unable to agree. Thus, an explicitly stated consequence follows their inability to agree. This consequence is conditioned upon the existence of a fact which is objectively ascertainable by the so-called arbitrator as well as a court of equity, namely, that the parties are in disagreement as to how their stock should be voted. The Agreement to agree has, therefore, provisions which are capable of being enforced with respect to particular facts. Moreover, the very nature and object of the Agreement render it impossible for the parties to do more than agree to agree, and to provide an enforceable alternative in the event no agreement is reached.

Defendants urge that no standard is provided in the Agreement for the guidance of the parties in reaching an agreement and that the purposes and policies which should guide them are not set forth and cannot be foretold. The Agreement does perhaps leave something to be desired in the way of explicitly setting forth the function and purpose of the Agreement for the guidance of the parties. However, I think it clear that the same language which is expressed as the standard by which the arbitrator should act must necessarily be read as the governing standard for the parties. This language provides: "* * * Such arbitration shall be exercised to the end of assuring for the respective corporations good management and such participation therein by the members of the Ringling family as the experience, capacity and ability of each may warrant. The parties may at any time by written agreement designate any other individual to act as arbitrator in lieu of said Loos."

It is quite evident that no agreement could set forth explicit guides to govern the parties because it is impossible in the nature of things to anticipate all the various subjects on which the vote of the stockholders might be required. Moreover, there is no reason to believe that the arbitrator would be expected to apply a different guiding principle in arriving at a decision than that which would guide the stockholders who agreed to submit to such arbitration.

I conclude that the Agreement is sufficiently definite in terms of the duties and obligations imposed on the parties to be legally enforceable on the state of facts here presented.

Turning to defendants' second objection, is the Agreement invalid as an attempted delegation of irrevocable control and voting rights in a manner which is against the public policy of this state? The answer to the question must depend upon the answer to two questions of a more explicit character, namely:

(1) Is the Agreement a voting trust agreement in which event it would admittedly be invalid for failure to comply with the statutory requirements of this state governing voting trusts?

(2) If not a voting trust agreement, is it, nevertheless, invalid as being against public policy because of the provision that the parties shall be bound by the instructions of the arbitrator as to how they shall vote in the event of a disagreement?

Section 18 of our General Corporation Law, provides the exclusive method for creating voting trusts of stock of a Delaware corporation, Appon et al. v. Belle Isle Corporation et al., Del.Ch., 46 A.2d 749, affirmed by Supreme Court of Delaware, September 13, 1946. Does the present Agreement create a voting trust as that term is employed in Section 18? This court in Peyton v. William C. Peyton Corporation et al., 22 Del.Ch. 187, 199, 194 A. 106, 111 (reversed on other grounds 23 Del.Ch. 321, 7 A.2d 737, 123 A.L.R. 1482), has thus described a voting trust: "A voting trust as commonly understood is a device whereby two or more persons owning stock with voting powers, divorce the voting rights thereof from the ownership, retaining to all intents and purposes the latter in themselves and transferring the former to trustees in whom the voting rights of all the depositors in the trust are pooled."

Does the present Agreement fall within the limitations of the quoted definition? I think not. The stockholders under the present Agreement vote their own stock at all times which is the antithesis of a voting trust because the latter has for its chief characteristic the severance of the voting rights from the other attributes of ownership. See in re Chilson, 19 Del.Ch. 398, 168 A. 82. In the cases where the parties to the present Agreement cannot reach an accord as to how they will vote, and are directed by the arbitrator as to how they shall vote their shares, the substance of the matter may be said not to differ in effect from a voting trust situation. However, considering the whole Agreement, there is this substantial distinction. Voting trustees have continuous voting control for the period of time stipulated in the agreement of trust. While here, the right of the arbitrator to direct the vote is limited to those particular cases where a stockholder's vote is called for and the parties cannot agree. True, the arbitration provision gives teeth to the Agreement but the parties desired that they should have the initial choice to determine policy in so far as it was determined by the vote of their shares and that a third party identified as an arbitrator should only resolve a conflict. In a voting trust as generally understood, the trustees in the very first instance determine policy and implement it by their votes.

This Agreement is actually a variation of the well-known stock pooling agreement and as such is to be distinguished from a voting trust. As is stated in 5 Fletcher Cyc. Corp. (Perm.Ed.) § 2064, at page 199, "Such agreements are distinct from voting trusts, and are not controlled by the same principles." It is my conclusion that the present Agreement is not a voting trust within the meaning of that term as used in Section 18 of our General Corporation Law and as a consequence, is not invalid for failure to comply with the provisions thereof.

Does the provision for arbitration constitute such a severance of voting control from ownership as to violate some public policy of this state with respect thereto?

The law with respect to agreements of the general type with which we are here concerned is fairly stated as follows in 5 Fletcher Cyc. Corp. (Perm.Ed.) § 2064, at page 194: "Generally, agreements and combinations to vote stock or control corporate action and policy are valid, if they seek without fraud to accomplish only what the parties might do as stockholders and do not attempt it by illegal proxies, trusts, or other means in contravention of statutes or law."

The principle of law stated seems to be sound and I think it is applicable here with respect to the legality of the Agreement under consideration. In the first place, there is no constitutional or statutory objection to the Agreement and defendants do not seriously challenge the legality of its objects. Indeed, in my opinion the objects and purposes of the Agreement as they are recited in the Agreement are lawful in principle and no evidence was introduced which tended to show that they were unlawful in operation.

The only serious question presented under this point arises from the defendants' contention that the arbitration provision has the effect of providing for an irrevocable separation of voting power from stock ownership and that such a provision is contrary to the public policy of this state. Perhaps in no field of the law are the precedents more varied and irreconcilable than those dealing with this phase of the case.

By adhering to strict literalism, it can be said that the present Agreement does not separate voting rights from ownership because the arbitrator only directs the parties as to how they shall vote in case of disagreement. However, recognizing substance rather than form, it is apparent that the arbitrator has voting control of the shares in the instances when he directs the parties as to how they shall vote since, if the Agreement is to be binding, they are also bound by his direction. When so considered, it is perhaps at variance with many, but not all of the precedents in other jurisdictions dealing with agreements of this general nature.

* * *

Directing attention to the present Agreement, what vice exists in having an arbitrator agreed upon by the parties decide how their stock shall be voted in the event they are unable to agree? The parties obviously decided to contract with respect to this very situation and to appoint as arbitrator one in whom both had confidence. The cases which strike down agreements on the ground that some public policy prohibits the severance of ownership and voting control argue that there is something very wrong about a person "who has no beneficial interest or title in or to the stock" directing how it shall be voted. Such a person, according to these cases, has "no interest in the general prosperity of the corporation" and moreover, the stockholder himself has a duty to vote. See Bostwick et al. v. Chapman et al. (Shepaug Voting Trust Cases), 60 Conn. 553, 24 A. 32. Such reasons ignore the realities because obviously the person designated to determine how the shares shall be voted has the confidence of such shareholders. Quite naturally they would not want to place such power over their investment in the hands of one whom they felt would not be concerned with the welfare of the corporation. The objection based on the so-called duty of the stockholders to vote, presumably in person, is ludicrous when considered in the light of present day corporate practice. Thus, precedents from other jurisdictions which are based on reasons which have, in my opinion, lost their substance under present day conditions cannot be accorded favorable recognition. No public policy of this state requires a different conclusion.

Once it be concluded that no constitutional or statutory objection to the validity of the present Agreement exists, as I have found, then I think the objection to its legality must be based not on some abstract public policy but on fraud or illegality of purpose. Since no such fraud or illegality has been shown, defendants' objections must fall.

Defendants say that even if the Agreement is valid under the statutes and public policy of this state, it is, nevertheless, to be governed by "principles applicable to proxy delegations and, hence, would be revocable." Defendants go on to show how, in their opinion, the alleged proxy was revoked and conclude therefrom that the Agreement was not violated. It is perfectly obvious that the construction of the Agreement contended for by defendants, if accepted, would in effect render it meaningless. The answer to this contention of the defendants must be that we are not here concerned with a proxy situation as between the parties to the Agreement on one hand, and the arbitrator Loos on the other. The Agreement does not contemplate such a proxy either in form or in substance.

* * *

I conclude that the stock held under the Agreement should have been voted pursuant to the direction of the arbitrator Loos to the parties or their representatives. When a party or her representative refuses to comply with the direction of the arbitrator, while he is properly acting under its provisions (as did Aubrey B. Haley's proxy here), then I believe the Agreement consitutes the willing party to the Agreement an implied agent possessing the irrevocable proxy of the recalcitrant party for the purpose of casting the particular vote. Here an implied agency based on an irrevocable proxy is fully justified to implement the Agreement without doing violence to its terms. Moreover, the provisions of the Agreement make it clear that the proxy may be treated as one coupled with an interest so as to render it irrevocable under the circumstances. * * *

It is the opinion of the court that the nature of the Agreement does not preclude the granting of specific performance, e.g., see Clark v. Dodge, 269 N.Y. 410, 199 N.E. 641. Indeed, the granting of such relief here is well within the spirit of certain principles laid down by our courts in cases granting specific performance of contracts to sell stock which would give the vendee voting control. Obviously, to deny specific performance here would be tantamount to declaring the Agreement invalid. Since petitioner's rights in this respect were properly preserved at the stockholders' meeting, the meeting was a nullity to the extent that it failed to give effect to the provisions of the Agreement here involved. However, I believe it preferable to hold a new election rather than attempt to reconstruct the contested meeting. In this way the parties will be acting with explicit knowledge of their rights.

A meeting of the stockholders should be held before a master to be appointed by this court pursuant to the provisions of Section 31 of the General Corporation Law. It is conceivable that prior to such meeting the parties to the Agreement will be able to agree as to how they will vote their stock, since such a possibility was lost prior to the meeting here reviewed through certain unfortunate happenings having nothing to do with the merits of the policy disagreement. It is obviously to the advantage of both parties to avoid the necessity for calling upon the arbitrator to act, and he will only act if the parties are unable to agree and action by him is requested. It must and should be assumed that the so-called arbitrator, if called upon to act, will bring to bear that sense of duty and impartiality which doubtless motivated the parties in selecting him for such an important role. In any event, the master in conducting the election will be bound to recognize and to give effect to the Agreement here involved, if its terms are properly invoked.

A decree accordingly will be advised.

Chancellor Seitz' decree left the board composed of the two Ringlings and Dunn (who was presumably aligned with them, at least up to a point) in one camp and the two Haleys, North, and Woods in the other. Thus, although Edith Ringling had "won" the lawsuit, the Haley-North faction was nevertheless in control. But the latter was not happy at having lost in the trial court, and Mrs. Haley took an appeal.* Excerpts from the Supreme Court's opinion follow.

RINGLING BROS.—BARNUM & BAILEY COMBINED SHOWS v. RINGLING

29 Del.Ch. 610, 53 A.2d 411 (Del.1947).

[PEARSON, J., after stating the terms of the voting agreement continued as follows:]

* * *

Before taking up defendants' objections to the agreement, let us analyze particularly what it attempts to provide with respect to vot-

---

* One might properly ask, with respect to this judicial circus:

(1) why did Edith sue in the first place, since the result of her "victory" left her on the short end of a 4–3 split on the board? and (2) why did Aubrey Haley, on the long end of that split, appeal? The question becomes particularly keen in light of the Supreme Court's disposition of the appeal, which left the Haley-North faction worse off than had no appeal been taken.

ing, including what functions and powers it attempts to repose in Mr. Loos, the "arbitrator". The agreement recites that the parties desired "to continue to act jointly in all matters relating to their stock ownership or interest in" the corporation. The parties agreed to consult and confer with each other in exercising their voting rights and to act jointly—that is, concertedly; unitedly; towards unified courses of action—in accordance with such agreement as they might reach. Thus, so long as the parties agree for whom or for what their shares shall be voted, the agreement provides no function for the arbitrator. His role is limited to situations where the parties fail to agree upon a course of action. In such cases, the agreement directs that "the question in disagreement shall be submitted for arbitration" to Mr. Loos "as arbitrator and his decision thereon shall be binding upon the parties". These provisions are designed to operate in aid of what appears to be a primary purpose of the parties, "to act jointly" in exercising their voting rights, by providing a means for fixing a course of action whenever they themselves might reach a stalemate.

Should the agreement be interpreted as attempting to empower the arbitrator to carry his directions into effect? Certainly there is no express delegation or grant of power to do so, either by authorizing him to vote the shares or to compel either party to vote them in accordance with his directions. The agreement expresses no other function of the arbitrator than that of deciding questions in disagreement which prevent the effectuation of the purpose "to act jointly". The power to enforce a decision does not seem a necessary or usual incident of such a function. Mr. Loos is not a party to the agreement. It does not contemplate the transfer of any shares or interest in shares to him, or that he should undertake any duties which the parties might compel him to perform. They provided that they might designate any other individual to act instead of Mr. Loos. The agreement does not attempt to make the arbitrator a trustee of an express trust. What the arbitrator is to do is for the benefit of the parties, not for his own benefit. Whether the parties accept or reject his decision is no concern of his, so far as the agreement or the surrounding circumstances reveal. We think the parties sought to bind each other, but to be bound only to each other, and not to empower the arbitrator to enforce decisions he might make.

From this conclusion, it follows necessarily that no decision of the arbitrator could ever be enforced if both parties to the agreement were unwilling that it be enforced, for the obvious reason that there would be no one to enforce it. Under the agreement, something more is required after the arbitrator has given his decision in order that it should become compulsory: at least one of the parties must determine that such decision shall be carried into effect. Thus, any "control" of the voting of the shares, which is reposed in the arbitrator, is substantially limited in action under the agreement in that it is subject to the overriding power of the parties themselves.

The agreement does not describe the undertaking of each party with respect to a decision of the arbitrator other than to provide that it "shall be binding upon the parties". It seems to us that this language, considered with relation to its context and the situations to which it is applicable, means that each party promised the other to exercise her own voting rights in accordance with the arbitrator's decision. The agreement is silent about any exercise of the voting rights of one party by the other. The language with reference to situations where the parties arrive at an understanding as to voting plainly suggests "action" by each, and "exercising" voting rights by each, rather than by one for the other. There is no intimation that this method should be different where the arbitrator's decision is to be carried into effect. Assuming that a power in each party to exercise the voting rights of the other might be a relatively more effective or convenient means of enforcing a decision of the arbitrator than would be available without the power, this would not justify implying a delegation of the power in the absence of some indication that the parties bargained for that means. The method of voting actually employed by the parties tends to show that they did not construe the agreement as creating powers to vote each other's shares; for at meetings prior to 1946 each party apparently exercised her own voting rights, and at the 1946 meeting, Mrs. Ringling, who wished to enforce the agreement, did not attempt to cast a ballot in exercise of any voting rights of Mrs. Haley. We do not find enough in the agreement or in the circumstances to justify a construction that either party was empowered to exercise voting rights of the other.

* * *

Legal consideration for the promises of each party is supplied by the mutual promises of the other party. The undertaking to vote in accordance with the arbitrator's decision is a valid contract. The good faith of the arbitrator's action has not been challenged and, indeed, the record indicates that no such challenge could be supported. Accordingly, the failure of Mrs. Haley to exercise her voting rights in accordance with his decision was a breach of her contract. It is no extenuation of the breach that her votes were cast for two of the three candidates directed by the arbitrator. His directions to her were part of a single plan or course of action for the voting of the shares of both parties to the agreement, calculated to utilize an advantage of joint action by them which would bring about the election of an additional director. The actual voting of Mrs. Haley's shares frustrates that plan to such an extent that it should not be treated as a partial performance of her contract.

Throughout their argument, defendants make much of the fact that all votes cast at the meeting were by the registered shareholders. The Court of Chancery may, in a review of an election, reject votes of a registered shareholder where his voting of them is found to be in violation of rights of another person. It seems to us that upon the application of Mrs. Ringling, the injured party, the votes representing Mrs. Haley's shares should not be counted. Since no infirmity in Mr. North's voting has been demonstrated, his right to recognition of what he did at the meeting should be considered in granting any relief to Mrs. Ringling; for her rights arose under a contract to which Mr. North was not a party. With this in mind, we have concluded that the election should not be declared invalid, but that effect should be given to a rejection of the votes representing Mrs. Haley's shares. No other relief seems appropriate in this proceeding. Mr. North's vote against the motion for adjournment was sufficient to defeat it. With respect to the election of directors, the return of the inspectors should be corrected to show a rejection of Mrs. Haley's votes, and to declare the election of the six persons for whom Mr. North and Mrs. Ringling voted.

This leaves one vacancy in the directorate. The question of what to do about such a vacancy was not considered by the court below and has not been argued here. For this reason, and because an election of directors at the 1947 annual meeting (which presumably will be held in the near future) may make a determination of the question unimportant, we shall not decide it on this appeal. If a decision of the point appears important to the parties, any of them may apply to raise it in the Court of Chancery, after the mandate of this court is received there.

An order should be entered directing a modification of the order of the Court of Chancery in accordance with this opinion.

NOTE—MORE ON RINGLING BROS.

The enterprise that eventually became known as "The Greatest Show on Earth" had its modest beginnings back in 1882 as a small family entertainment show in Mazomanie, Wisconsin, staged by John Ringling and four of his talented brothers. Sons of August Rungeling, an immigrant German harnessmaker, the brothers, with the help of a hyena, were the whole performance: John did a dance in wooden shoes, Al juggled plates, and Charlie and Alf T. provided the musical entertainment. The show gradually grew and prospered, and before long it had moved into the P.T. Barnum territory of New England. In 1906, Bailey died, the Ringling brothers were able to buy a majority interest in Barnum & Bailey stock, and eventually combined the two shows, establishing themselves "supremely uppermost" in the circus world.

This era was a fairly peaceful one in the circus' history—about the only time during which the enterprise was not divided by bitter feuding among family factions. At the head of the circus was John Ringling, an extraordinary individual at one time listed as one of the ten richest men in the world, who in addition to running the circus amassed an enormous art collection and had interests in railroads, oil wells, banks, and numerous other risk-laden ventures. By the early 1930's however, John Ringling had fallen into serious financial difficulties. Between his numerous creditors and a tempestuous second wife, he became embroiled in over one hundred lawsuits. He also lost control of the circus. In 1929, when he neglected to renew his lease for the circus' traditional April opening in New York's Madison Square Garden, he found that a competitor had taken his place. Ringling's reaction was characteristic. He promptly bought out the competitor, borrowing $1,700,000 from a New York loan company. Hard times in 1932 forced Ringling to default on his loan and allowed creditors to take control of the circus.

When John Ringling died in 1936, he left a will that seemed calculated to confuse as well as annoy everyone mentioned in it. (For example, a codicil to the will disinherited his sister Ida North and her two sons, but neglected to remove them as executors.) But despite its confused state and the lawsuits that it attracted like flies, the estate was valued at $23,500,000.

Ringling's death left the stock of the circus under the control of three factions within the family and this is where the trouble began. John's brother, Charlie, had left a one-third interest in the corporation to his wife, Edith, and her son, Robert; brother Alf's daughter-in-law, Aubrey Ringling owned a third; and the remaining third was controlled by John's sister, Ida North and her two sons, Henry and John, as executors of the estate.

John Ringling North was the shrewdest member of the clan, even surpassing his Uncle John in ambition and ingenuity. In the financial crisis and confusion that followed the death of John Ringling, North took hold of the reins. His first task was to rid the circus of the debt that had left it under control of creditors. Toward that end he bought himself a new $200 suit, strolled into the Manufacturer's Trust Company, and calmly requested a loan of $1,000,000. With the help of this money and the purchase of a crowd-attracting gorilla, Gargantua, the circus was back on the road with North, as president, temporarily in control.

The Manufacturer's Trust loan was secured in part by the voting trust agreement which provided that John would nominate three of the seven directors of the circus, Edith and Aubrey would nominate three, and the bank would nominate the seventh. The state of affairs was anything but satisfactory to the other two corners of the family triangle, represented by Edith and Aubrey. In anticipation of the expiration of this voting trust, they formed an alliance and consulted Karl D. Loos, a Washington, D.C. attorney who had been involved in the effort to untangle John Ringling's estate. They requested that he draw up an agreement that would enable them to wrest control of the circus from North after the voting trust expired in 1943. Loos first suggested another voting trust, but this suggestion was rejected out of hand by his clients who had already had enough of voting trusts.   Deprived of that simple alternative, the attorney drew up what came to be known as "The Ladies Agreement," the one at issue in the case. According to Loos, he was not sure at the time whether, or how, the agreement would be enforced; he merely did the best he could to carry out his clients' wishes.

Upon the lapsing of the voting trust agreement in 1943, Aubrey and Edith took control of the circus from North.   Edith's son Robert replaced him as president, and Haley (an accountant who had come to help untangle John Ringling's estate and stayed on to become Aubrey Ringling's second husband) became vice president.   With an admonition that the canvas of the Big Top needed fireproofing, John Ringling North took (what turned out to be temporary) leave of the circus.

On July 6, 1944, in Hartford, Connecticut, the Big Top caught fire. It burned for eight to ten minutes and then collapsed on a panic-stricken audience.   It was the worst circus disaster in history.   One hundred sixty-eight people died and another 487 were injured.   Although the resulting millions of dollars of negligence claims vastly exceeded the circus' insurance coverage, the Ringling family never considered bankruptcy.   They finally made arrangements under which the circus could continue operations under the terms of a "Hartford Arbitration Agreement," according to which they agreed not to contest liability and to pay all damage claims approved by an arbitration committee.

Meanwhile, Connecticut brought criminal manslaughter charges against James Haley, who was the senior circus executive on the lot at the time of the fire, and several other circus managers.   Robert Ringling had had the good fortune to be out of town on the day of the fire and escaped liability.   Haley and five others received jail sentences.   At a subsequent hearing on the "indispensibility" of the convicted men to the operation of the circus, Robert Ringling was less than enthusiastic in his testimony on the value of James Haley. Perhaps because of that incident, perhaps because of his bitterness that it was he, and not Robert who had taken the fall, and perhaps because Robert neither visited nor wrote him while he was imprisoned—whereas John Ringling North had done both—upon Haley's release on December 24, 1945, he was ready to change sides.   It was at the annual meeting in April 1946 that Haley, representing his bedridden wife, cast his vote in a manner that gave rise to the lawsuit above.

3. DEVICES WITHIN THE CORPORATE MACHINERY

Perhaps the most convenient means of allocating seats on the board in a relatively uncomplicated close corporation is cumulative voting, the mechanics of which we have already examined.* You may want to review that discussion in deciding whether cumulative voting would work here.

Another technique that is almost as simple and somewhat more flexible is class voting for directors. This entails dividing the voting stock into two or more classes, each of which is entitled to elect one or more of the total number of directors. In the simple case of a corporation with three shareholders, each of whom wishes to be assured of electing one of the three board members, three classes of shares would be created (usually denominated, somewhat prosaically, classes "A", "B", and "C") and each would be given the right to elect one director. Since it is not necessary that the same number of shares be issued (or authorized) for each class, it is possible to use this arrangement to guarantee a seat on the board to a shareholder who owns too small a number of shares to be assured of electing a director by cumulative voting. The rights of the different classes may be manipulated in other ways as well. The separate approval of each class of stock might be required, for example, wherever a shareholder vote is called for; or for certain specified transactions. Although there may be statutory limitations, it is possible in some jurisdictions to make one or more classes of non-voting stock, or stock with a right to vote only on certain matters. It should be evident that the number and variety of changes that can be rung on this basic device are limited only by the imagination of the draftsman and, as always, the possibility that a court might find that some particular variation works such a hardship on a stockholder, or departs so far from conventional patterns, that it should be disallowed.

It is obvious that a device inserted in the articles or by-laws for the purpose of assuring minority shareholders the ability to be represented on the board will be frustrated if the majority have the power to remove directors. In the absence of some provision in the statute or the articles authorizing removal, shareholders have only their common-law right to remove directors for "cause." *People ex rel. Manice v. Powell*, 201 N.Y. 194, 94 N.E. 634 (1911). *See Auer v. Dressel*, 306 N.Y. 247, 118 N.E.2d 590 (1954). *See generally* Travers, Removal of the Corporate Director During His Term of Office, 53 Iowa L.Rev. 389 (1967). Many more "modern" corporation statutes now authorize removal without cause, usually subject to the restriction that, where either the statute or articles require cumulative voting, a director may not be removed if the number of shares voted against removal would have been enough to elect him. *See, e.g.*, MBCA § 39. It is also generally held that a provision in the articles or by-laws authorizing the shareholders to remove a director without cause is valid. *See*

* See Chapter 10, Section D.

1 F. O'Neal, Close Corporations: Law and Practice, § 3.59 (2d ed. 1971).

The close corporation planner should devote attention to the removal problem. Where one or more members of the board are not shareholders but sit as an accommodation to shareholders, it may be desirable to assure the shareholders' control over their nominees by authorizing removal without cause in the articles and by-laws. On the other hand, if the statute allows removal without cause, it may be necessary to restrict that power in some fashion in order to protect the minority.

D.   RESTRICTIONS ON THE DISCRETION OF THE BOARD

PROBLEM

PISCES TACKLE CO.—PART III

Flyer and Leader would like to guarantee their officerships: Flyer as president and Leader as vice-president and treasurer; and they are concerned that future events may permit the board to remove them. They would also like to nail down the salaries they are to draw from the corporation for the first three or four years. Hooks understands their concern and is willing to enter into some arrangement that would fulfill these objectives, provided that, since she will not draw money in the form of a salary, she has some assurance that their salaries will not be increased above what is agreed and that she will receive dividends should the corporation show a profit. Hooks also wants to be secretary of the corporation. The three have asked you about the validity of a shareholders' agreement by which they would bind themselves "to their best efforts" to elect each other to their respective officerships, to have Flyer and Leader each paid salaries of $20,000 per year, and to have the corporation pay annually a dividend equal to one-half of its net profits, Flyer and Leader would also like to limit the company's operations for the first few years to the production of high quality rods.

1.   Would a unanimous shareholder's agreement designed to achieve these ends be valid under the case law? Under MBCA § 35 (second sentence)? Under either N.Y. § 620, Cal.Corp.Code § 300, Del. GCL § 350, or § 11 of the MBCA Close Corporation Supplement?

2.   Would a shareholders' agreement between Flyer and Leader designed to achieve these ends be valid under the case law? Under MBCA § 35 (second sentence)? Under either N.Y. BCL § 620, Cal. Corp.Code § 300, Del. GCL § 350 or § 11 of the MBCA Close Corporation Supplement?

3.   In addition, or as an alternative to a shareholders' agreement, should any of these provisions be put in the corporation's articles of incorporation, or the by-laws, or both? Consider the validity of the technique under the case law, under MBCA § 35 (second sentence),

under N.Y. BCL §§ 601(c), 620 and 715(b), Cal.Corp.Code § 204; or Del. GCL § 351.

4. Would you recommend that the articles of incorporation, or the by-laws, or both contain high vote and/or high quorum requirements (*e.g.*, a requirement that 80% of the outstanding shares must approve any change in the articles dealing with dividends)? Consider the validity of this technique under the case law, under MBCA §§ 54, 32 and 40, under either N.Y. BCL §§ 616 and 709; or Cal.Corp.Code § 204. Reconsider the Chesapeake Marine Services Problem.

5. In addition to using a shareholders' agreement or provisions in the articles of incorporation or by-laws, would you recommend the Flyer and Leader execute employment contracts with the corporation? What are the benefits for them and the corporation? Consider N.Y. BCL § 715(b).

6. Finally, to what extent could you work out a simpler means to accomplish your clients' goals by using an integrated close corporation statute? Consider either Del. GCL §§ 341–356; Md.Corp. and Assoc. §§ 4–101–4–603; or the MBCA Close Corp.Supp. Would you advise incorporating in one of these jurisdictions in order to take advantage of its close corporation provisions?

1. RESTRICTIONS IN SHAREHOLDER VOTING AGREEMENTS

The New York common law governing shareholder voting agreements, which purport to restrict the discretion of the board of directors, was summarized in Haenel v. Epstein, N.Y.L.J., June 10, 1980 (Sup.Ct.) at 13:

A. "The Big Four"

The New York Court of Appeals, prior to the enactment of Business Corporation Law section 620(a) and 620(b) set forth, in four cases, dubbed "the big four" the law with regard to shareholder agreements.

Manson v. Curtis (223 N.Y 313, 119 N.E. 559 [1918]) involved an agreement between the holders of a majority, but not all, of the shares of a corporation. The agreement provided that each party was to name three directors, with a seventh director to be elected as mutually agreed upon. One of the parties, the plaintiff, was to be continued in his position of General Manager for a year and, as such, was to manage the business of the corporation and shape its policy. The court, finding, in effect, the provision concerning election of directors, to be, standing alone, innocent and legal, determined that the agreement as a whole was invalid as its fundamental and dominant purpose was to vest management authority solely in plaintiff. So construed, the latter provisions were found to deprive the directors of their statutory duty to manage the corporation. The agreement was found totally illegal and not capable of "severability."

Stated simply, the Court of Appeals in Manson decided that while it was not illegal for two or more stockholders owning the majority of stock to agree upon the directors whom they would elect, the powers delegated to the non-directors were too broad. (See 50 Columbia Law Review No. 1, January, 1950, "The Corporate Director: Can his hands be tied in advance," Edmund T. Delaney).

Manson recited the law as to the interaction of majority stockholders; dominant managers; and the statutory authority of a board of directors. Employing the often used terminology "a sterilized board of directors," the case set forth the law as follows:

The affairs of every corporation shall be managed by its board of directors * * *.

The corporation is the owner of the property but the directors in the performance of their duty possess it, and act in every way as if they owned it.

Directors are the exclusive executive representatives of the corporation and are charged with the administration of its internal affairs and the management and use of its assets * * *. Clearly the law does not permit the stockholders to create a sterilized board of directors * * *. We conclude that the agreement here is illegal and void and its violation is not a basis for a cause of action. (223 N.Y. at pp. 319–324) (Compare Business Corporation Law section 701)

Manson, significant not only for its holding, but for its dictum on the permissible scope of shareholder agreements, stated in that regard as follows:

An ordinary agreement, among a minority in number, but a majority in shares, for the purpose of obtaining control of the corporation by the election of particular persons as directors is not illegal. Shareholders have the right to combine their interests and voting powers to secure such control of the corporation and the adoption of an adhesion by it to a specific policy and course of business. Agreements upon a sufficient consideration between them, of such intendment and effect, are valid and binding, if they do not contravene any express charter or statutory provision or contemplate any fraud, oppression or wrong against other stockholders or other illegal object.

This concept, expressed in dictum, later formed the basis of the legislature's enactment of Business Corporation Law 620(a).

Finally, the court in Manson indicated that if all stockholders agreed, they "may do as they choose with the corporate concerns and assets, provided the interests of creditors are not affected, because they are the complete owners of the corporation."

*   *   *

In McQuade v. Stoneham (263 N.Y. 323, 189 N.E. 234 [1934]), the agreement was not between all shareholders, but between the holder of the majority of the shares and two other shareholders. But the agreement's terms, the parties were to use their best efforts to keep one another in office as directors and officers; and salaries, amount of capital, number of shares, by-laws and policy were not to be changed except by unanimous consent. Holding the agreement invalid, the court stated:

> Stockholders may, of course, combine to elect directors. That rule is well settled. As Holmes, Ch.J., pointedly said (Brightman v. Bates, 175 Mass. 105, 111): "If stockholders want to make their power felt, they must unite. There is no reason why a majority should not agree to keep together." The power to unite is, however, limited to the election of directors and is not extended to contracts whereby limitations are placed on the power of directors to manage the business of the corporation by the selection of agents at defined salaries.

The agreement restricted the powers of the board of directors. It did not condition such intrusion by use of such terms as "subject to the discretion of the Board of Directors" or "so long as they remain faithful, efficient and competent." As such, there was an impermissible usurpation of function.

Clark v. Dodge (269 N.Y 410, 199 N.E. 641 [1936]) followed. It represented an apparent change in the thinking of the court. Here, the agreement was signed by all shareholders. Dodge was to vote for Clark as director and General Manager so long as Clark proved faithful, efficient and competent. The court sustained a cause of action for specific enforcement of the agreement. In distinguishing McQuade, the court held that here the impairment of the directors' powers was slight. The court held as follows:

> There was no attempt to sterilize the board of directors, as in the Manson and McQuade cases. The only restrictions on Dodge were (a) that as a stockholder he should vote for Clark as a director—a perfectly legal contract; (b) that as a director he should continue Clark as general manager, so long as he proved faithful, efficient and competent—an agreement which could harm nobody; (c) that Clark should always receive as salary or dividends one-fourth of the "net income." For the purposes of this motion, it is only just to construe that phrase as meaning whatever was left for distribution after the directors had in good faith set aside whatever they deemed wise; (d) that no salaries to other officers should be paid, unreasable

in amount or incommensurate with services rendered—a beneficial and not a harmful agreement.

The court's thinking in Clark was influenced by the fact that all stockholders signed the agreement. This is evidenced as follows:

> As the parties to the action are the complete owners of the corporation, there is no reason why the exercise of the power and discretion of the directors cannot be controlled by valid agreement between themselves, provided that the interest of creditors is not affected (269 N.Y. at p. 410).

Thus, following Clark, the state of the law was and is that all stockholders can agree to infringe "slightly" upon the statutory authority of the board of directors. So, too, it was and still is the law that a majority, but less than all the stockholders, can agree to vote for certain persons as directors (see also "Shareholder Agreements and the Statutory Norm," 43 Cornell L.Q. 68, 72–73 [1957]) * * *.

Long Park, Inc. v. Trenton-New Brunswick Theaters Co. (297 N.Y. 174, 77 N.E.2d 633 [1948]) is the fourth in the line of the "big four." As in Clark, the agreement involved all shareholders. By its terms, one of the shareholders was to be "manager," and was to be given full authority to supervise the operation of the corporation. The court held the agreement sterilized the board of directors, was a complete surrender of the directors' powers, and, therefore, was invalid as a violation of the statute giving management powers to the directors. Apparently, the court determined that the agreement had exceeded the permissible limits of infringement construed in Clark.

TRIGGS v. TRIGGS

46 N.Y.2d 305, 413 N.Y.S.2d 325, 385 N.E.2d 1254 (1978).

[The following statement of facts is taken from the dissenting opinion of GABRIELLI, J.]

The bone of contention in this case is control of Triggs Color Printing Corporation, a small firm founded by decedent in 1925. The firm appears to have prospered for some years and, with the passage of time, decedent's three sons became involved in the business to varying degrees. As of 1963, the corporation had issued some 254 shares of voting stock. Of these, decedent personally owned 149 shares and the remainder were distributed equally between his three sons, with each son owning 35 shares. At that time, decedent apparently selected his son Ransford, the plaintiff in this action, as the one he deemed best suited to control the business following decedent's death. To that end, decedent transferred 36 of his shares to plaintiff. Thus, out of the 254 voting shares, decedent owned 113 shares, plaintiff owned 71 shares, and each of the other two sons owned 35 shares.

Shortly thereafter, plaintiff and decedent entered into the written agreement at issue in this case. The two agreed to vote their shares together so as not only to elect both of them as directors, but also to elect decedent chairman of the board at a guaranteed annual salary, and to appoint plaintiff president of the corporation at a guaranteed annual salary. Additionally, the agreement contained the following provision: "It is the present contemplation of Frederick Triggs, Sr. to execute an agreement with the Corporation for the Corporation to re-purchase his stock in the event of his death. In the event for any reason that such agreement has not been executed between the said Frederick Triggs, Sr. and the Corporation, then, in that event, the re-maining Stockholder, to wit: Ransford D. Triggs, shall have the right and option to purchase the said stock of Frederick Triggs, Sr. for a period of sixty (60) days following the death of Frederick Triggs, Sr."

A few months later, decedent did enter into a repurchase agree-ment with the corporation. One year later, in 1964, the repurchase agreement with the corporation was canceled by consent of both de-cedent and the corporation. During the next few years, plaintiff gradually assumed an ever greater role in corporate affairs, and de-cedent's influence waned. Eventually the two had a falling out, and decedent appears to have begun to regret his choice of plaintiff as his successor. The corporation experienced some financial difficulties under plaintiff's management, and the salary paid to decedent was decreased, at first with his consent and later over his objections. Fi-nally, in February, 1970, decedent executed a codicil to his will by which he bequeathed his 113 shares of voting stock to his other two sons, and declared the 1963 agreement with plaintiff to be null and void. In April, 1970, decedent died.

Following decedent's death, plaintiff sought to exercise the option to purchase the 113 shares from the estate, but the estate refused to transfer the stock. Some four years later, in September, 1974, plain-tiff commenced this action seeking to compel the estate to honor the option. * * * Following service of an answer, but some time prior to trial, defendant moved to dismiss the complaint for failure to state a cause of action, alleging for the first time that the agreement was illegal.

OPINION OF THE COURT

JONES, Judge.

* * *

After a trial without a jury the court granted respondent specific performance of the stock purchase option. A majority at the Appel-

late Division agreed, and we now affirm.   The pertinent facts are recited in the dissenting opinion.

* * *

Appellant contends that because the March 19, 1963 agreement
was not executed or approved by all of the corporate shareholders, its
provisions requiring the election of respondent and his father as officers and fixing their compensation constituted an impermissible restriction of the rights and obligations of the board of directors to
manage the business of the corporation under the doctrine of Manson
v. Curtis, 223 N.Y. 313, 119 N.E. 559 and related cases (see 3 White,
New York Corporations [13th ed.], par. 620.03, subd. [2]).   No argument is made that the stock purchase option, standing alone would be
invalid; the assertion is that the agreement must be read as a whole
and that it must be invalidated in its entirety.   The critical issue is
whether, because of the initial inclusion of provisions which could
have been said to fetter the authority of the board to select corporate
officers and to fix their compensation, the stock purchase provision is
now unenforceable.

The uncontroverted evidence is that in the years following the
signing of the agreement, the assertedly illegal provisions of the
agreement were ignored; no attempt was made to observe or enforce
them and the management of corporate affairs was in no way restricted in consequence of the 1963 agreement.   The evil to which the
cited rule of law is addressed was never sought to be achieved nor
was it realized.   Although Triggs, Sr., and Ransford continued to
serve as directors, the record discloses there were also three or four
other, independent directors.   That Triggs, Sr., continued to be elected chairman of the board (he was also elected corporate treasurer)
and Ransford, corporate president and that for several years their
salaries were fixed by the board at the figures stated in the March
19, 1963 agreement was in consequence of action freely taken by the
entire board of directors and cannot be attributed to the sanction of
the March 19, 1963 agreement of which the other directors, constituting a majority of the board, were wholly unaware.   Indeed Triggs,
Sr., took no exception when, on May 11, 1965, the board reduced his
salary from $20,000 (the agreement figure) to $10,800, and when the
board later entirely eliminated his salary his complaint in April of
1969 was predicated on the departure from the board's action of May
11, 1965 rather than on any asserted violation of the provisions of the
March 19, 1963 agreement.

The legal issue here, too, depends on what is now an affirmed factual determination.   The claim of illegality, raised for the first time
some 13 years after the agreement had been signed, must fail because, as the trial court concluded, the March 19, 1963 agreement
"did not in any way sufficiently stultify the Board of Directors in the

operations of this business" within the doctrine on which appellant would rely.

Analytically we are presented with an agreement which in a single document deals with two different sets of obligations. On the one hand, the agreement contains the stock purchase option exercisable on the death of the father as to which, standing alone, there is no claim of illegality. On the other, there are the provisions with respect to the election of corporate officers and the fixation of their salaries, which are of questionable legality. Any illegality exists, however, only to the extent that the agreement operated to restrict the freedom of the board of directors to manage corporate affairs. * * * The fact is that the courts below have enforced only the stock option provisions of the March 19, 1963 agreement.

* * *

Accordingly, the order of the Appellate Division should be affirmed, with costs.

GABRIELLI, Judge (dissenting).

Dissent says yes

I respectfully dissent. Defendant executor appeals from an order of the Appellate Division which affirmed a judgment of Supreme Court, following a nonjury trial, which granted plaintiff specific performance of an option to purchase certain stock from the estate of his deceased father. The order appealed from should be reversed since the underlying agreement is unenforceable in that it improperly sought to limit the powers of the board of directors to manage the corporation. Moreover, even were the agreement itself valid, the option was terminated in accord with its own provisions some time prior to decedent's death.

* * *

It has long been the law in this State that a corporation must be managed by the board of directors (Business Corporation Law, § 701) who serve as trustees for the benefit of the corporation and all its shareholders. To prevent control of the corporation from being diverted into the hands of individuals or groups who in some cases might not be subject to quite the same fiduciary obligations as are imposed upon directors as a matter of course, the courts have always looked unfavorably towards attempts to circumvent the discretionary authority given the board of directors by law. Such matters normally arise in the context of an agreement between shareholders to utilize their shares so as to force the board of directors to take certain actions. Unless in accord with some statutorily approved mechanism for shifting power from the board of directors to other parties (e.g., Business Corporation Law, § 620, subd. [b]), such agreements have been found valid only where the proponent of the agreement can prove that the violation of the statutory mandate is minimal and, more importantly that there is no danger of harm either to the general public or to other shareholders (see Clark v. Dodge, 269 N.Y. 410, 199 N.E. 641).

It is, of course, proper for shareholders to combine in order to elect directors whom they believe will manage the corporation in accord with what those shareholders perceive to be the best interests of the corporation. Thus, an agreement between two shareholders to vote for a particular director or directors is not illegal and may be enforceable in an appropriate case (Business Corporation Law, § 620, subd. [a]). If some shareholders seek to go beyond this, however, if they agree to vote their shares so as to impose their decisions upon the board of directors, such an agreement will normally be unenforceable. The agreement sought to be enforced in this case is just such an agreement.

In essence, the agreement between decedent and plaintiff consisted of three fundamental provisions: first, decedent promised to vote his shares so as to ensure the election of plaintiff as a director and his appointment as president for a 10-year period at a given salary; second, plaintiff promised to vote his shares so as to ensure the continuation of decedent as chairman of the board at a given salary for at least 10 years; and, third, decedent gave plaintiff a conditional option to purchase decedent's voting shares after his death. It is beyond dispute that the promises to secure the appointment of each party at a specific position other than director at a guaranteed annual salary are illegal. Plaintiff contends that the agreement is nonetheless enforceable by analogy to our decision in Clark v. Dodge, 269 N. Y. 410, 199 N.E. 641, *supra*, in which we sustained an agreement between two shareholders who together owned all of the shares in the corporation. This argument is based on a fundamental misinterpretation of the significance of our decision in that case. Rather than illustrating any divergence from the great body of other cases which have found such agreements to be illegal and unenforceable, the *Clark* decision reflects a reasoned and flexible application of the principles which are in fact common to all such cases.

The dispositive consideration must always be the possibility of harm to either the other shareholders or to the general public either prospectively at the time the agreement was entered into or at the time it is sought to be enforced. In those cases in which the agreement is made by less than all the shareholders, almost any attempt to reduce the authority granted to the board by law will create a significant potential for harm to other shareholders even if the potential for harm to the general public is minimal. This is so because the effect of such an agreement is to deprive the other shareholders of the benefits and protections which the law perceives to exist when the corporation is managed by an independent board of directors, free to use its own business judgment in the best interest of the corporation.

In *Clark*, the possibility of harm to other shareholders was nonexistent, for in fact there were no other shareholders. In the instant case, in contradistinction, there were and are two other shareholders, not privy to the agreement between plaintiff and decedent. Moreover, the instant agreement for the continuation of plaintiff and decedent in their respective positions is in no way dependent on their performances in those positions, whereas the agreement in *Clark* provided that Clark was to be continued as manager "so long as he proved faithful, efficient and competent" (Clark v. Dodge, 269 N.Y. 410, 417, 199 N.E. 641, 643, *supra*).

It has been suggested that even if the agreement is indeed illegal on its face, the defendant, in order to successfully assert the defense of illegality, must prove that the other shareholders did not know of and acquiesce in the agreement. This contention is illogical, and is at any rate inapplicable to the instant case. In this as in all actions the burden of proof is in the first instance always on the plaintiff who must prove his cause of action. * * * [E]ven were the burden with respect to this issue to be improperly placed upon defendant, that burden has been met.

It has also been suggested that the option should be severed from the other provisions of the agreement and separately enforced since it alone would not be illegal. The flaw in this argument is that it improperly assumes that decedent would have given plaintiff this option by itself, without the other parts of their agreement. This assumption is one in which we may not indulge. Indeed, it appears that the illegal parts of the agreement were an intrinsic part of the covenant between these parties. * * *

In sum, law and logic both compel the conclusion that the option which plaintiff seeks to enforce was an inseverable part of a basically illegal agreement. As such, it may not be enforced.

* * *

Accordingly, I vote to reverse the order appealed from and to dismiss the complaint.

FUCHSBERG, Judge (dissenting).

My vote too is for reversal. However, the decisional path that I would take differs appreciably not only from that of the majority but from that of my fellow dissenters as well.

Specifically, unlike the other dissenters, I am of the opinion that the parties entered into an enforceable agreement. But, for the reasons well stated both in Judge Gabrielli's alternative rationale and in Mr. Justice Lupiano's dissenting memorandum at the Appellate Division (61 A.D.2d 911, 402 N.Y.S.2d 820), I conclude that we are required to find that the agreement was not ambiguous and that, as a matter of law, it terminated in accordance with its terms during the father's lifetime.

I also take issue with the majority's reasoning that the option was enforceable only because it was separable from an otherwise illegal contract. In my view, the entire agreement is lawful qua agreement, and since it is one entered into between the controlling stockholders of a small, nonpublic corporation, it is not to be scrutinized by a rigid, hypertechnical reading of section 27 of the General Corporation Law, now part of section 701 of the Business Corporation Law.

Small, closely held corporations whose operation is dominated, as its stockholders and creditors usually are aware, by a particular individual or small group of individuals, must be distinguished, legally and pragmatically, from large corporations whose stock is traded on a public securities exchange and where the normal stockholders' relationship to those managing the corporation is bound to be impersonal and remote. Obviously, the latter's operations are rarely, if ever, covered by stockholders' agreements, and the Business Corporation Law itself is the sole restriction on their management.

In the close corporation, investors who themselves are not part of the dominant group commonly rely on the identities of the individuals who run the business and on the likelihood of their continuance in power. As a practical matter, these individuals will be expected to exercise a broad discretion and considerable informality in carrying out their management functions; this flexibility may be regarded as one of the strengths of a smaller organization. Indeed, faith in the integrity and ability of the managers is what usually motivates the investment. Looked at realistically, such corporations, often organized solely to obtain the advantage of limited personal liability for their principals, to qualify for a particular tax classification, or for some similar reason, are frequently "little more * * * than charter partnerships" (Ripin v. United States Woven Label Co., 205 N.Y. 442, 447, 98 N.E. 855, 856). Control of such matters as choice of officers and directors, amounts of executive salaries, and options to buy or sell each other's stock—exactly the sort of things with which the agreement before us dealt—is usually mapped out by agreements among stockholders.

In short, so long as an agreement between stockholders relating to the management of the corporation bears no evidence of an intent to defraud other stockholders or creditors, deviations from precise formalities should not automatically call for a slavish enforcement of the statute. For this is the "governing criteri[on]" by which to test "the validity of a stockholders' agreement" (Delaney, The Corporate Director: Can His Hands Be Tied in Advance, 50 Colum.L.Rev. 52, 61; see, also, 1 O'Neal, Close Corporations, § 5.08). This would not leave without remedy those minority stockholders in close corporations whose interests may be abused. Available to them and at least equally effective are the equitable remedies by which officers and directors can be made to respond for violations of their trust obligations (Meinhard v. Salmon, 249 N.Y. 458, 164 N.E. 545).

Analysis of the agreement and its surrounding circumstances here illustrates the wisdom of this approach. The corporation had for a long time been a one-man business in every sense, the man being Triggs, the father. Until he gave a minority interest to each of his sons, he was the owner of all the voting stock; afterwards, it was all owned by the father and his sons, who were preparing to succeed him. At the time of the agreement, the father, together with the son who was the other party to the disputed writing, held the majority of this stock. Given their service in the business, their stockholding, and their relationship to each other and to the history of the corporation, it was to be expected—and not at all extraordinary—that an arrangement for their continuance in office and their compensation would be executed. There is not the slightest indication that, had the parties gone through the routine of presenting the contract to duly called stockholders' and directors' meetings, it would not have been rubber-stamped as a matter of course. It is significant that no other stockholder challenged the agreement during the father's lifetime and that the dispute since then has gravitated only around the son's insistence that the option to purchase his father's shares had not expired, a term which in any event, though it found its way into the stockholders' agreement, related to an essentially personal matter distinct from any corporate management obligations as such.

In sum, given that no other shareholder or member of the general public has been harmed, there is no good reason to measure the agreement by the less sophisticated standards of yesteryear. Tellingly, the often conflicting and unpatterned holdings that characterized our varied decisions on this point in the past have been overshadowed by the enactment of subdivision (b) of section 620 of the Business Corporation Law. At that time, the Legislature expressly indicated that it intended to overrule, at least in part, many of those decisions that struck down shareholders' agreements. In doing so, it made clear its purpose to approve and expand the ruling in Clark v. Dodge, 269 N.Y. 410, 199 N.E. 641, *supra*, which upheld a controverted stockholders' agreement in a close corporation context.

––––––

In Zion v. Kurtz, 50 N.Y.2d 92, 428 N.Y.S.2d 199, 405 N.E.2d 681 (1980), the court interpreted an agreement between the two stockholders of a Delaware corporation which specified that no "business or activities" shall be conducted without the consent of the minority shareholders. The court found that, since the agreement was not incorporated in the articles, it did not comply fully with § 351 of the Delaware close corporation statute. The court nevertheless gave effect to the agreement in a 4 to 3 decision.

The majority observed that it was "[c]lear from those provisions [of the close corporation statute] that the public policy of Delaware does not proscribe a provision such as that contained in the shareholders' agreement here in issue even though it takes all management functions away from the directors." Moreover, referring to § 620(b) of the New York statute, the court stated that it was also "clear that no New York public policy stands in the way of our application of the Delaware statute and decisional law above referred to."

Gabrielli, J., dissented, arguing that the effect of the agreement was to "sterilize" the board of directors, and that the courts of neither Delaware nor New York had shown such tolerance for arrangements in close corporations that deviated from the statutory norm as to accept such an extreme. Although he admitted that the agreement might have been enforced in Delaware had it been made part of the articles, he viewed its inclusion there as a mandatory requirement of the statute, and disagreed with the majority's view that "Since there are no intervening rights of third persons, the agreement requires nothing that is not permitted by statute, and all of the stockholders of the corporation assented to it, the certificate of incorporation may be ordered reformed, by requiring Kurtz to file the appropriate amendments, or more directly he may be held estopped to rely upon the absence of those amendments from the corporate charter."

2. HIGH VOTING OR QUORUM REQUIREMENTS

A control device carefully designed to protect minority interests and implemented by well-drafted clauses of the articles and by-laws is worth very little if a majority stockholder, or minority stockholders who can combine to form a majority, have the power to amend the articles or by-laws. Consequently, it may be desirable for the planner to make some provision for giving minority interests a veto over any such changes. A similar veto power may also be useful with respect to significant decisions, such as the appointment or removal of officers, the establishment of salaries, the fixing of dividends, or the issuance of new stock. (Recall the discussion in the Chesapeake Marine Services problem.)

The most straightforward method of providing a veto is the use of extraordinary majority voting requirements for action by the board or the shareholders on specified questions. One alternative is simply to require a unanimous vote on these questions. It may, however, be safer to require something less than unanimous vote on these questions. The best approach may be to require something less than unanimity yet sufficiently high that the vote of one shareholder or one director would be sufficient to block the transaction. A requirement that board action cannot be taken without the approval of three-quarters of the members, for example, would be sufficient to give an effective power of veto to each member of a three-person board.

The reason for the caution in this area is that a few courts have struck down extraordinary majority voting requirements for one reason or another. The New York Court of Appeals, for example, held in Benintendi v. Kenton Hotel, 294 N.Y. 112, 60 N.E.2d 829 (1945), that by-law provisions requiring unanimity for any action by either the board or the shareholders were invalid as against public policy because they made it difficult for the corporation to conduct its business and created a substantial risk of deadlock.* Although this ruling was subsequently reversed by the legislature (N.Y. BCL §§ 616 and 709), similar cases in other jurisdictions together with a number of decisions invalidating extraordinary majority requirements on statutory grounds ** created the small, but ever-nagging possibility that the courts might invalidate such provisions. That possiblity seems, however, to be fading. Courts have come more and more to accept the fact that departures by close corporations from the traditional corporate model do not inevitably entail untoward results. Moreover, a great many legislatures have enacted statutory provisions that authorize, specifically or by implication, high vote requirements in the articles or by-laws. *See, e.g.,* MBCA §§ 32, 40, 54 and N.Y. BCL §§ 616 and 709.

A high quorum requirement, for either shareholder meetings or board meetings, can serve many of the same functions as a high voting requirement. At least one court has held, however, that where directors deliberately stay away from board meetings in order to prevent some action from being taken, thus cannot, as shareholders, "complain of an irregularity which they themselves have caused." ***

Query: If the draftsman has already included in the articles a high vote requirement for action by the board and shareholders, is anything to be gained by adding a high quorum requirement as well? *Compare* 1 F. O'Neal, Close Corporations: Law and Practice, § 4.22 (2d ed. 1971) with Dykstra, Molding the Utah Corporation: Survey and Commentary, 7 Utah L.Rev. 1, 6 (1960).

3. RESTRICTIONS BY CONTRACT WITH THE CORPORATION

KENNERSON v. BURBANK AMUSEMENT CO.

120 Cal.App.2d 157, 260 P.2d 823 (1953).

PETERS, J. Plaintiff brought this action against defendants for damages for the claimed breach of an employment contract * * * [which] contains the following clauses:

"1. The First Party [Burbank] does hereby hire and/or employ the Second Party to act as General Manager of the Manor Theatre in each and all of its business operations * * * for a period of five (5) years * * * for the agreed salary of $125.00 per week * * * plus

---

* *See also* Kaplan v. Block, 183 Va. 327, 31 S.E.2d 893 (1944).

** *See, e.g.,* Wells v. Beekman Terrace, Inc., 23 Misc.2d 22, 197 N.Y.S.2d 79 (Sup. Ct.1960); Model, Roland & Co. v. Industrial Acoustics Co., 16 N.Y.2d 703, 209 N. E.2d 553, 261 N.Y.S.2d 896 (1965).

*** Gearing v. Kelly, 11 N.Y.2d 201, 203, 182 N.E.2d 391, 227 N.Y.S.2d 897 (1962). *But see* Campbell v. Loew's, Inc., 36 Del.Ch. 563, 587, 134 A.2d 852, 866 (1957).

five (5%) per cent of the gross amount of sales from all concessions such as candy, popcorn, beverages, etc., payable weekly, and Second Party agrees   *   *   *   to pay for all inventory shortages.

"2.   The Second Party shall have the sole authority and jurisdiction in purchasing and booking all motion pictures, stage attractions and other forms of entertainment to be used at the Manor Theatre.

"3.   The Second Party shall have the exclusive right to fix and establish all policies to be followed in the operation of the Manor Theatre, and to determine all charges for admission and to hire and discharge all necessary help to operate and maintain said theatre and fix all salaries and wages to be paid such help.

*   *   *

"5.   The Second Party shall have the right to carry on any other business for his benefit, or engage in other work during the term of this contract, it being understood, however, that he will at all times manage the business of the First Party in a first-class manner.   Second Party undertakes that the operation of said theatre will show a revenue in excess of operating costs, excluding depreciation and rent," and excluding certain catastrophes or acts of the Board of Directors of Burbank.

*   *   *   Clause 7 confers on certain shareholders of Burank the power of cancellation   *   *   *   It reads as follows: "7.   This contract may be cancelled by First Party at any time within one (1) year from the date hereof by giving sixty (60) days written notice to Second Party, and upon written consent of more than eighty (80%) per cent of those persons to whom the stock of First Party was originally issued, regardless of the number of shares of stock originally issued to them and regardless of whether or not they continue to be shareholders, and together with approval of a majority of the Board of Directors."

*   *   *

*   *   *   Section 800 of the Corporations Code provides that "all corporate powers shall be exercised by or under authority of" the board of directors.   Section 820, in its very first sentence, requires that "Directors and officers shall exercise their powers in good faith, and with a view to the interests of the corporation."   In addition, it is the law that "Even though the requirements of section 820 are technically met, transactions that are unfair and unreasonable to the corporation may be avoided."   Remillard Brick Co. v. Remillard-Dandini Co., 109 Cal.App.2d 405, 418, 241 P.2d 66, 74.

*   *   *

Inasmuch as the directors must exercise and maintain control over corporate affairs in good faith, they are prohibited from delegating such control and management to others, and any contract so providing is void. By this contract with Kennerson the board has attempted to confer upon him the practical control and management of substantially all corporate powers. The sole asset of this corporation was the management of, and the fixtures in, the Manor Theatre building. By the contract the board has attempted to transfer all control over bookings, personnel, admission prices, salaries, contracts, expenses and even fiscal policies to Kennerson. While the contract provides that moneys are to be banked in the name of Burbank, Kennerson is granted full power to withdraw the same, subject to paying expenses. Kennerson is authorized to book "other forms of entertainment," so that he could, without restraint, change the very nature of the enterprise, and could even assign his powers to others. The fact that Kennerson is under a duty to make periodic reports to the board does not constitute a sufficient retention of control over discretionary corporate policies to comply with the rule.

Kennerson admits that it is the law that a board cannot divest itself of its fundamental powers by contract, but contends that the requirement that Kennerson must report and account saves this contract from violating this rule.

California has recognized the rule that the board cannot delegate its function to govern. As long as the corporation exists, its affairs must be managed by the duly elected board. The board may grant authority to act, but it cannot delegate its function to govern. If it does so, the contract so providing is void.

This also seems to be the general rule in this country. A case quite similar to the instant one is Long Park v. Trenton-New Brunswick Theatres Co., 297 N.Y. 174, 77 N.E.2d 633. There the New York Court of Appeals in a six-to-one decision held invalid, as a matter of law, a contract to manage a theatre business, which contract was somewhat similar to the one here involved. There the board attempted to delegate to another corporation the right to manage all the theatres leased or to be leased by the granting corporation. As in the instant case, full and uncontrolled authority over bookings, policies, admission prices and personnel was granted. The court held 77 N.E.2d at page 634 that by such a contract "the powers of the directors over the management of its theatres, the principal business of the corporation, were completely sterilized. Such restrictions and limitations upon the powers of the directors are clearly in violation of section 27 of the General Corporation Law of this State and the New Jersey statute."

* * * The problem is, of course, one of degree. If the contract, as in the instant case, attempts to delegate substantially all corporate powers to an agent, then it has gone too far. Such a contract must be held to be void and unenforceable. The judgment enforcing such a contract must be reversed.

The judgment appealed from is reversed.   Contract void

NOTE—EMPLOYMENT CONTRACTS FOR EXECUTIVES

Contracts of employment are normally not specifically enforceable, a principle not generally considered to be affected by the fact that one of the parties is a corporation. There have been exceptions, however. In Jones v. Williams, 139 Mo. 1, 39 S.W. 486 (1897), for example, the court granted specific performance of a contract employing the plaintiff as editor of a newspaper for five years. It relied in part on the fact that editorial control of a newspaper is a unique sort of power whose loss could not easily be compensated in damages and in part on the fact that the plaintiff had been induced by the contract to leave another position and to invest a substantial sum of money in the stock of the paper.

Specific performance may have much to recommend it in the circumstances that often surround internecine disputes in close corporations. *See, e.g.,* Collins v. Collins Fruit Co., 189 So.2d 262 (Fla.App. 1966). Nevertheless, most courts seem unwilling to depart from the standard rule, allowing only an action for damages for breach of contract when an officer is fired before the expiration of his contract. *See* 1 F. O'Neal, Close Corporations: Law and Practice § 6.05 (2d ed. 1971).

Where the contract is for the employment of an officer of a corporation, there is a more troublesome problem for the draftsman. Courts have occasionally held such contracts not only not simply specifically enforceable but invalid altogether where the term of the contract extended beyond that of the board of directors. The theory of most of such holdings is that it would be against public policy for one board to bind its successors in a matter as important as the exercise of their responsibility, often imposed by statute (*see, e.g.,* MBCA § 50), to appoint the officers. *E.g.,* Edwards v. Keller, 133 S.W.2d 823 (Tex.Civ.App.1939) (Texas subsequently altered its corporation statute to change the result). In other cases, whose results are perhaps more defensible, courts have held merely that contracts of employment for an unusually long duration, particularly for the lifetime of the person employed, are invalid. *See* 1 F. O'Neal, Close Corporations: Law and Practice § 6.06 (2d ed. 1971).

A partial answer to the difficulties this may pose for the planner of a close corporation is to have the agreement read that the party is to be employed not as an officer but in some non-elected capacity, such as general manager, sales manager, or operations supervisor. As artificial as this device may appear, it seems to have overcome the reluctance of some courts to uphold long-term contracts for the employment of officers. *E.g.,* Streett v. Laclede-Christy Co., 409 S.W.2d 691 (Mo.1966). *See* O'Neal, *supra,* § 6.10. *See generally* Washington and Rothschild, Compensating the Corporate Executive, 108–117 (3d ed. 1962).

E.   RESTRICTIONS ON THE TRANSFER OF SHARES

PROBLEM

PISCES TACKLE CO.—PART IV

In the course of your discussions with Flyer, Leader and Hooks, they have expressed concern about what would happen to their interests in the corporation should one of them die or decide to withdraw. You advised them that it is standard practice for shareholders in close corporations to enter into an agreement by which they restrict the transfer of their stock. They have asked you to draft such an agreement for them.

Flyer is married and has two small children. He has little in the way of assets outside of what he plans to invest in the business. Leader is a bachelor; his only close relative is a brother who, having failed out of college twice is now "getting himself together" in Aspen, Colorado, where he supports himself working as a waiter and at various odd jobs. Hooks recently married a somewhat older man who is an executive with IBM. They have no children.

1. Since there are so many approaches to a stock transfer agreement, you have decided to prepare an outline of the major features you would recommend to your clients, given their personal and financial situations. Draft the outline, considering the following questions:

a. How will the price at which any transfers take place be determined? Will it vary according to whether the occasion for the transfer is the death of one of the parties or his or her decision to withdraw from the business? What if one of the three decides to give his or her stock away? To pledge it for a loan?

b. How will any purchase options be funded?

c. In what instrument or instruments should the transfer restriction be included?

2. Assuming that your clients have accepted your recommendations, draft the full agreement. Assume that either Del. GCL § 202, the MBCA Close Corp.Supp. §§ 6 and 14, or Md.Corp. and Assoc. § 4–503 is applicable. How would your draft be affected?

1.   INTRODUCTION

Were the closely held enterprise operated as a partnership, the partners would have the right of *delectus personae*, the power of each partner to veto the admission into the partnership of a new member.[*]

The underlying reasons that led to the development of this principle in the law of partnership do not disappear simply because the

---

[*] Uniform Partnership Act, § 18(g).

owners of a small business have chosen to incorporate. It is appropriate, therefore, that in most closely-held corporations the shareholders include some arrangement in their organizational scheme which approximates the right of *delectus personae*. Such arrangements usually take the form of transfer restriction agreements whereby the ability of the shareholders to alienate their stock is limited in some fashion.

In planning the affairs of the close corporation there is a practical problem that complicates the drafting, as well as the interpretation, of transfer restriction agreements. It is evident that however carefully the owners of a close corporation and their counsel design machinery to insure the desired balance of control, that machinery can run amok or cease functioning altogether should one of the shareholders sell, give, or bequeath his stock. The second aim of a transfer restriction agreement then is to provide for the continuation of a workable control scheme when, as is inevitable, one of the shareholders dies or decides to sell or give away his interest.

Stock transfer agreements are also extremely important in planning the estates of the shareholders. Any sound estate plan provides some measure of liquidity to the estate in order to pay the decedent's personal debts, the expenses of administering the estate, and federal and state estate taxes. Where the estate consists in significant part of stock in a closely held corporation, for which shares there is by definition no ready market, the desired liquidity can often be furnished by some sort of stock purchase agreement combined with adequate planning for its funding. In addition, the operation of a buy-sell agreement at the time of death of a stockholder assists in establishing a value for the stock at that time. This is important for the purpose of determining the amount of estate taxes that are due; it reduces the risk that the taxing authorities will claim that the stock is worth substantially more than its value as established by the agreement. Finally, a buy-out provision may meet the desire of shareholders to diversify the assets of their estates to be passed on to their heirs. This is particularly desirable in a close corporation whose success may depend in large measure on the abilities and efforts of one or two shareholders, whose deaths may make the investment of all or nearly all of the assets of the estate in the stock of the corporation imprudent.

Also it is well to keep in mind that there are a variety of ways in which a shareholder may dispose of stock. The most common ones are by sale and bequest. But the planner should also consider the prospect of inter vivos transfers by way of gifts, creation of trusts, pledges, or other means by which the right to vote the stock and receive dividends might pass to hands of someone other than the original, and perhaps key, shareholder.

Given the sound reasons underlying transfer restrictions, it may strike the noninitiate as somewhat odd that their validity and enforceability have been the subject of a great deal of controversy and uncertainty. Much of the litigation over transfer restriction agreements has been the product of poor draftsmanship. In addition to practical concerns, the draftsman must reckon with the American rule that unreasonable restraints on the alienation of personal property are void. It is interesting to contrast this position with that of British law, which views transfer restrictions as merely voluntary agreements among the shareholders and as such should be treated like any other contract. *See* Gower, Some Contrasts Between British and American Corporation Law, 69 Harv.L.Rev. 1369, 1377–78 (1956).

Whatever the law ought to be—and it seems clear that is evolving in the direction of greater tolerance for transfer restrictions (*see, e.g.*, Allen v. Biltmore Tissue Corp., 2 N.Y.2d 534, 161 N.Y.S.2d 418, 141 N.E.2d 812 (1957))—the validity of particular agreements has occasioned considerable litigation; perhaps in part because poorly drafted agreements so often end in a result that is unsatisfactory to one of the parties. In many of these cases however, the lawsuit could have been avoided—and the parties' original desires satisfied—had closer attention been paid to the drafting of the provisions at the outset.

There are two basic approaches to drafting buy-sell agreements. The designated purchaser may be the corporation that issues the stock, a technique known as an "entity purchase" agreement or "redemption agreement." Alternatively, the purchase option (or occasionally obligation) may be given to the other shareholders, in which case the agreement is known as a "cross-purchase" arrangement. Fairly frequently the two approaches are combined.

2. TYPES OF TRANSFER RESTRICTIONS

Transfer restrictions may take three basic forms, two or more of which are often found combined in the same agreement. First, the restriction may impose limitations on the freedom of a shareholder to transfer stock. Second, the corporation or the remaining shareholders may be given an option to purchase the shares of another shareholder upon the occurrence of certain events, such as the death of a shareholder or the termination of his or her employment with the corporation. Third, what is often called a "buy-sell agreement" may require the corporation or the remaining shareholders to purchase the stock of another shareholder upon the occurrence of similar triggering events. This requirement may or may not be coupled with a coordinate obligation of the shareholder or his estate to sell the stock.

Although transfer restriction agreements are generally a matter of contract and may therefore be cast in whatever form is appropriate for the circumstances of the particular corporation and its shareholders, restrictions on the freedom of shareholder to transfer his or her shares commonly take one of three forms:

(1) Under a "right of first refusal," before a shareholder is free to sell his or her stock to a third person it must first be offered to the

Right of first Refusal

corporation or to the remaining shareholders (or both) at the same price and on the same terms and conditions offered by the outsider. Typically the right, if extended to the other shareholders, is given in proportion to their respective holdings. If any shareholder is unable to purchase or declines to do so, his or her allocation may be taken up proportionately by the remaining shareholders.

First option provision

(2) Another common form of restriction is the first option provision. The principal distinction between a first option provision and a right of first refusal is that the offer to the corporation or the remaining shareholders is made at a price and on terms fixed by the arrangement rather than by an offer made by an outside purchaser. Even if the basic restriction is cast in the form of a right of first refusal, it may be desirable to include a first option provision to deal with transfers of stock other than by sale to third parties. Obviously, a right of first refusal would not serve to deal with transfers by gift or devise.

(3) Finally, a shareholder's disposition of stock may be conditioned upon the consent of the corporation's board of directors or of the other shareholders. The validity of such a restriction is in substantial doubt, however. In Rafe v. Hindin, 29 A.D.2d 481, 288 N.Y.S.2d 662 (2d Dept. 1968), for example, a New York court held that an agreement between two fifty percent shareholders of a corporation, which prohibited either from selling his shares to a third party without the consent of the other, was invalid. The court said:

> It is further noted that, because the individual defendant is given by the legend on the stock certificate the arbitrary right to refuse for any reason or for no reason to consent to the transfer of the plaintiff's stock to a prospective purchaser, and since no price is stated at which the plaintiff must sell to the individual defendant and which the latter is required to pay to the plaintiff for the plaintiff's stock, the legend may be construed as rendering the sale of the plaintiff's stock impossible to anyone except to the individual defendant at whatever price he wishes to pay. This construction makes the restriction illegal.

Since one of the major purposes of transfer restriction agreements is to give shareholders some degree of control over the identity of co-owners of the business, such agreements often entitle the corporation or its remaining shareholders to purchase the stock of any shareholders who withdraw from the business. Such options may be activated upon the death of a shareholder, the termination of his or her employment, the pledging of his or her shares to another, or any other action that threatens to replace the shareholder by another. These options typically confer an absolute right to purchase the stock even though the shareholder or his or her estate may wish to retain the shares.

Where a right of first refusal gives the corporation or the remaining shareholders the option to purchase the shares of a deceased or withdrawing stockholder, a "buy-sell agreement" imposes an obligation to purchase. Usually used to provide liquidity to the estate of a deceased stockholder, these agreements are frequently funded by insurance policies taken out on the lives of the principal stockholders.

Transfer restrictions are most commonly adopted at the time a close corporation is formed; the restriction being a matter of negotiation among the initial shareholders. What is the status though of a shareholder who purchases stock, either from the corporation or from one of the initial shareholders, after the transfer restriction becomes effective? The applicability of the agreement to a newcomer may depend on the document in which the agreement is inserted in the first instance. It may be included in the articles of incorporation in a by-law provision, or in a separate contract among the shareholders. A shareholder who acquires stock subject to a private agreement embodied in a separate contract entered into by the other shareholders, to which contract the acquiring stockholder is not a party, may not be bound by the terms of the agreement. It is customary therefore to make transfer restrictions a part of the by-laws or the articles. As between these two instruments, should there be any difference with respect to the enforceability of the restriction? Consider carefully the language of MBCA § 54. *See* 2 F. O'Neal, Close Corporations: Law and Practice § 7.14 (2d ed. 1971).

In order to be valid against a purchaser of the stock without notice, a transfer restriction must be "noted conspicuously" on the stock certificate itself. Uniform Commercial Code § 8–204. The term "conspicuous" is defined in U.C.C. § 1–201(10). For a judicial interpretation of what is "conspicuous" *see* Ling & Co. v. Trinity Savings & Loan Ass'n, 482 S.W.2d 841 (Tex.Sup.Ct.1972).

A related question is whether the shareholders of the corporation may adopt a by-law containing transfer restrictions that is valid against a shareholder who does not consent to the by-law. In Tu-Vu Drive-In Corp. v. Ashkins, 61 Cal.2d 283, 38 Cal.Rptr. 348, 391 P.2d 828 (1964), the court gave an affirmative answer to that question. Three years after the corporation in *Tu-Vu* was organized, the board of directors adopted a by-law provision giving a right of first refusal to the other shareholders and then to the corporation, before any shareholder could sell to an outsider. The by-law was approved by the plaintiff, who owned 54% of the stock. Subsequently, one of the minority shareholders granted to an outsider an option to purchase her stock, although it was never exercised. The plaintiff brought an action for a declaratory judgment that the by-law was enforceable over the minority stockholder's asserted right to choose to whom she wished to sell her stock. The question, according to the court, was whether the restriction was an unreasonable restraint on alienation. Holding that it was not, the court said, "In the light of the legitimate interests to be furthered by the by-law [the defendant's] asserted right becomes 'innocuous and insubstantial.' The by-law merely proscribes [the defendant's] choice of transferees while insuring to her the price and terms equal to those offered by the outsider."

3. THE VALUATION PROCESS

JONES v. HARRIS

63 Wash.2d 559, 388 P.2d 539 (1964).

FINLEY, Judge.

This is an action by a minority shareholder in two close corporations to determine the price at which he is contractually bound to sell his shares to the remaining shareholders, and for an accounting by the corporations as to sums allegedly due him.

The parties formed the corporations in question in 1953 to purchase Radio Station KXLY and Television Station KXLY–TV, situated in Spokane, Washington. Joseph Harris and Norman Eisenstein (defendants-appellants) contributed the greater part of the financial backing for the venture and subscribed to ninety per cent of the capital stock of both corporations. Richard E. Jones, (Plaintiff-respondent) agreed to manage the stations and took the remaining ten per cent of the capital stock. At the time the corporations were formed, the parties entered into a written contract respecting the ownership and control of the stations. Among other things, it provided that Jones was to manage the stations until such time as notice of termination was given by either party, sixty days prior to the expiration of any calendar year. In the event that Jones was so terminated, the following sections controlled the disposition of his interest in the corporations:

> * * * the parties agree that Jones shall be obligated to sell and Eisenstein and Harris shall be obligated to buy jointly, at book value, the stock of Jones in the Radio Corp. and in the Television Corp. In determining book value *solely for the purposes hereof,* it is agreed that the depreciable assets shall be computed at cost, less eighty (80) percent of the depreciation as the same appears on the books * * *. (Italics ours.)

and

> (e) If any part of the purchase price to be paid for either KXLY or KXLY–TV is required to be allocated to good-will, then it is agreed that in arriving at the book value * * * effect shall be given to the original amount required to be allocated to such good-will without any charge-off or depreciation, even though such charge-off or depreciation may be reflected in the books of said corporations.

* * *

There can be no doubt that a ten per cent interest in the two corporations is worth, in terms of market value, far more than the net worth figure on the corporate balance sheets of December 31, 1958, would indicate. Ten per cent of the December 31, 1958, net worth figure, plus twenty per cent of the depreciation and amortization accounts, totals only $25,936.33. It may be noted that experts set the market value of the corporations at upwards of $2,500,000 at the time of trial, and that by the time of this appeal appellants had sold these same corporations for $3,225,000, cash. It seems quite probable that *at the time the contract was drawn*, considering the way it was drawn, the parties contemplated the price of the shares resulting from "book value," plus twenty per cent of taken depreciation would continue to represent some reasonable approximation of the fair value. Had the corporations enjoyed a lesser degree of success, the formula might have accomplished the purpose very well, without any problem arising such as that herein involved.

But whether the parties reasonably should have anticipated that book value would not approximate the true value of the corporations, nevertheless, book value was the basic ingredient of the formula they chose to determine the "buy-out" price. Conceding that the term "book value" can vary from its basic or generally accepted meaning—*i.e.*, according to the purpose for which it is used—the parties here explicitly attempted to limit its meaning and to define book value "solely for the purposes" of the buy-out contract. Because they anticipated a rapid tax write-off in the form of depreciation, they arranged to use only eighty per cent of the amount in calculating the respondent's interest. The contract cannot be said to have been unfair or inequitable *when it was made*, and now is too clear to admit of interpretation to include and emphasize equities, nonexistent at the inception of the contract, but which have evolved and now seem persuasive. Many close corporations have similar buy-out provisions, and the courts would do a disservice to business practice by substituting an "appraisal" or "market value" formula when hindsight shows that "book value," as originally conceived, has become unrealistic with the passing of time.

The courts, of course, are not bound irrevocably to a single definition of "book value." But, when a term that has a generally accepted meaning is used, the parties are hard pressed afterwards to claim their intent was otherwise. "Book value" normally means the value of the corporation as shown on the books of account of that corporation, after subtracting liabilities. In such cases courts should accept the book accounts, when they are kept in accord with accepted accounting practice and not with an eye to the advantageous exercise of the "buy-out" option. If arbitrary valuations appear in the accounts, the court can then substitute amounts determined through correct accounting procedures. Aron v. Gillman (1955), 309 N.Y. 157, 128 N.E. 2d 284, 51 A.L.R.2d 598.

In the present case the only accounts which the respondent attacks as inconsistent with proper accounting procedure were set up exactly as the organization contract anticipated. Whatever the effect of this might be as to third parties, it is binding on the respondent. He cannot complain that the depreciation accounts were unduly swollen to obtain a rapid tax write-off; the contract anticipated this and provided that he would benefit by twenty per cent of the amount so taken being added in evaluating his shares. Nor can he complain that the absence of a good-will account led to an overevaluation of depreciable assets. Section (e) of the contract specified that good will would be considered in pricing his shares *only if* the Internal Revenue Service later required a re-allocation of part of the purchase price to good will. As he suggests no other discrepancy in the accounts, the respondent is bound by the balance sheets of the corporations as of December 31, 1958, the date his obligation to sell his stock interest matured. Respondent's ten per cent interest in the corporations, at book value adjusted in accord with the contract, is as the appellant contends: $25,936.33.

The findings of the trial court concerning the accounting are affirmed. The judgment on the price to be paid for the shares belonging to Jones is reversed. The parties shall bear their own costs, and the case is remanded for entry of judgment in accord with the foregoing views and determinations.

NOTE—VALUATION

The valuation provisions of a share transfer restriction agreement are among the most important—and difficult—to draft. There are a variety of techniques available, of which it is only possible here to suggest a few of the more important. See generally, O'Neal, Restrictions on Transfer of Stock in Closely Held Corporations: Planning and Drafting, 65 Harv.L.Rev. 773 (1952). They include:

1. *Book Value.* This is a popular method but one that, as Jones v. Harris suggests, may lead to inequitable results. The book value of a company may bear little relationship to its value as an ongoing concern. Moreover, despite its apparent simplicity, book value turns out in application often to be remarkably ambiguous. Does it, for example, include intangible assets, especially "goodwill"? What about income taxes that are accrued but unpaid, and may not appear on the books? If the corporation carries insurance on life of the shareholder whose death is the occasion for the exercise of a buy-sell provision, are the proceeds of the insurance to be included? Should assets that have appreciated substantially be written up before book value is calculated? If this technique is used, it is desirable that these and other questions be anticipated and dealt with in the agreement; and doing so turns what starts out to be a simple approach into one full of complexity.

2. *Capitalized Earnings.* An agreement may attempt to reach an objective appraisal of the fair value of the stock which is more sophisticated than that provided by book value by establishing a

formula according to which the earnings of the business may be capitalized. Like book value, however, this technique presents certain difficulties of drafting. It is especially critical that the earnings of the business be carefully defined.

3. *Mutual Agreement.* Another relatively popular technique is for the parties to the agreement to set a value for the shares and to revise it at stated intervals, usually annually. While this may lead to a fairer price, it is subject to the significant drawback that for psychological reasons the parties often neglect to conduct the revaluations, as focussing implicitly on the possibility that one of them might soon die or that they may have a falling out is not a particularly pleasant undertaking.

4. *Right of First Refusal.* Where the principal concern is that one of the parties may sell his interest to an outsider, providing that a shareholder must, before selling, offer his shares to the corporation (or the other shareholders) at the same price, and on the same terms and conditions offered by the outsider, has great appeal. This approach may, however, substantially increase the already great difficulties a shareholder in a close corporation faces in selling his stock, as a prospective buyer may well be put off by the prospect of spending considerable effort in negotiating a sale only to have the shares bought out from under him pursuant to a right of first refusal. Moreover, this approach is obviously useful only for prospective sales to third parties and is of no utility in providing against the transfer of shares by gift, devise, or inheritance.

5. *Appraisal.* It is possible to avoid some of the pitfalls of the preceding methods by simply leaving the evaluation of the shares to appraisal by a neutral third party according to some predetermined procedure. One of the most convenient techniques of doing so is to provide for arbitration according to the rules of the American Arbitration Association or some other recognized arbitral organization.

4. ADDITIONAL DRAFTING PROBLEMS

VOGEL v. MELISH

46 Ill.App.2d 465, 196 N.E.2d 402 (1964).

DRUCKER, Justice.

This is an appeal from a declaratory judgment finding that a stock share agreement terminated on the death of one of the two parties.

Plaintiff in his action sought a determination of the status of an agreement between himself and Frank Koster concerning their rights and privileges of selling, transferring, conveying or otherwise disposing of their shares of stock in the Vogel Tool and Dye Corporation. Each owned 455 of a total of 1150 outstanding shares. The agreement made in 1954 provided in part (1) that each party thereto should have personal custody of each other's stock and each would assume

(handwritten margin note: never mentions death)

all liability for the safekeeping of the certificates; (2) that if either party desired to sell, transfer, assign or convey or otherwise dispose of any shares, an offer must be transmitted to the other party who then had the right to accept such offer in full or in part in the manner set forth within said contract.

Koster died and in his will bequeathed his stock to a trustee for the benefit of his widow for life and then to his sons. In 1960 the widow, as executor, sought to have transferred to herself individually some of the shares in payment of her widow's award.

(handwritten margin note: award π=partner)

The prayer of the Complaint was that the contract be declared terminated at the death of Koster and in the alternative, that, if the court determined the contract to be in force, plaintiff be given the option to purchase some or all of the decedent's shares, and further that the executor be directed to turn over to plaintiff the shares standing in his name and that plaintiff be directed to deliver to the executor the shares standing in Koster's name.

The trial court found that the death of Koster and the transfer of his shares to the executor did not give plaintiff the option to purchase Koster's shares; that the agreement terminated upon the death of Koster; that all shares of stock were free of restraint; and that plaintiff's shares should be delivered to him and Koster's shares to the executor.

* * *

The contract before us contained no specific declaration of rights with respect to the shares in the event of the death of one of the parties.

Defendants contend that under paragraph 6 of the contract the agreement did not terminate at the death of Koster but inures to the benefit of the executor and the heirs and that transfers of the shares to the executor, from her to the trustee and from the trustee to the sons, should not constitute a disposition entitling plaintiff to purchase the shares.

Paragraph 6 of the contract states: "The parties hereto further agree that the provisions of this agreement shall be binding upon and inuring to the benefit of the parties hereto and their respective administrators, executors, heirs and personal representatives."

In determining the meaning of this provision, we must consider not only its language but its relation to the entire agreement.

The purpose of the contract is declared therein to be that the parties "are desirous of entering into a mutual agreement with each other respecting rights and privileges of selling, transferring, conveying or otherwise disposing of said shares of said corporation." In effectuating this purpose the agreement goes on to provide in paragraph 3:

> If any one of the parties hereto desire to sell, transfer, assign, convey or otherwise dispose of all or part of the shares owned by said party in the aforesaid corporation, an offer to sell said shares shall first be made by said party to the other party, said offer shall be in writing stating the number of shares offered for sale and transmitted by registered United States mail.

This clearly refers to a disposition during the lifetimes of the parties since otherwise a notification of a desire to bequeath the shares could not have been held to be operative.

* * *

The provisions of the agreement dealing with the sale of stock which allow the offeree to accept "in full or in part" and fix a "maximum consideration" to be paid based on "total assets" (rather than net worth which would be the usual basis), evince an intention to reach a result based on a close, personal, working relationship and not to deal with strangers.

Some significance must also be read into such clauses as "personal custody" (of stock certificates) and "assume all liability for the safekeeping of said certificates."

Applying the rule of strict construction to the entire contract before us, we are convinced that it should be construed to have terminated the restriction on alienation at the death of one of the parties.

With further reference to Paragraph 6, providing that the agreement shall inure to the benefit of the "parties hereto and their respective administrators, executors, heirs and personal representatives," we believe a reasonable interpretation of this clause to be that it would apply should one party die during the pendency of a tendered offer or a time payment sale made pursuant to the conditions set out in Paragraph 5.

* * *

We agree with the court's finding (1) that the contract terminated at the death of Koster; (2) that the transfer of his shares to the executor did not give plaintiff the option to purchase Koster's stock; (3) that all shares are free of restraint; and (4) that plaintiff's shares should be delivered to him and Koster's shares to the executor.

The judgment of the Circuit Court is affirmed.

Affirmed.

NOTE—SOME ADDITIONAL CONSIDERATIONS

Vogel v. Melish should provide a lesson to the draftsman. Perhaps because transfer restrictions are restraints on alienation and therefore disfavored at common law, many courts tend to ignore the intent of the parties and find such restrictions unenforceable.

As we have seen, the parties, in formulating transfer restrictions, may be motivated by a variety of considerations, including the desire to exercise something like the right of *delectus personae*, the maintenance of a control balance within the corporate structure so that no one shareholder becomes dominant, and the provision of liquidity for the estate of a deceased stockholder. Unfortunately, these aims may occasionally conflict. Helmly v. Schultz, 219 Ga. 201, 131 S.E.2d 924 (1963) provides an interesting illustration. The transfer restriction agreement there was included in a by-law which provided as follows:

> No stockholder shall sell or give away his stock in the corporation without first offering to sell the same to the remaining stockholders substantially in proportion to the stock already owned by them. Such remaining stockholders shall have fifteen (15) days from the date such offer is made to them in which to purchase said stock before the same may be given or sold to any other person. The price to be paid by such remaining stockholders for such stock shall be the book value of the stock on the first day of the month in which said offer is made. A reference to this bylaw shall appear on each stock certificate issued by the corporation.

When Mrs. Schultz decided to sell her shares, to comply with the by-law, she offered them first to the stockholders adding the condition that all her stock be purchased at the same time and paid for in cash. Only one of the shareholders sought to accept the offer. When Mrs. Schultz refused to sell to him alone, he brought an action for specific performance of the contract he alleged had been formed by his acceptance. The court refused to grant relief, holding that the offer, made "according to the by-laws," was "to *all the stockholders*—each in his proportionate share * * *." Thus the court found that the purpose of the by-law was "to keep the stock ownership in equal proportion among the original stockholders." Had their principal intention been to prevent outsiders from acquiring stock, they could have provided in the transfer restriction for a disproportionate purchase by one or more shareholders.

5. FUNDING

A buy-sell arrangement is of little practical utility unless the person or persons who have the option (or obligation) to purchase have the financial ability to do so. Unless some means of funding is planned for, both the shareholders and the corporation may find themselves without the wherewithal to purchase the shares, and the corporation may even be prevented by statutory restrictions from making the purchase if it lacks the necessary surplus. Reconsider Chapter 8, Section D(f).

Where the putative purchaser is the corporation, one means of funding the purchase is the establishment of a sinking fund in which the corporation regularly sets aside money to be saved for that purpose. A second and perhaps the most common technique is for the corporation to purchase and maintain life insurance on the lives of the shareholders in an amount adequate to fund all or a substantial part of any repurchase for which the corporation may become obligated on their death. Where this is the case it is important that the effect of the receipt of insurance proceeds on the value of the corporation be taken into account when drafting the valuation section of the agreement. A third method of funding is to defer payment by the use of promissory notes or installment obligations.

F. OPPRESSION OF MINORITY SHAREHOLDERS: DISSENSION, DEADLOCK, AND DISSOLUTION

PROBLEM

PISCES TACKLE CO.—PART V

1. Flyer has told you that he is concerned about being "frozen out" by Leader and Hooks. Specifically, he is fearful of losing his officership and his right to compensation.

a. How realistic are his concerns in light of the *Wilkes* case?

b. What additional protection, *e.g.*, shareholder agreement, provisions in the articles and/or by-laws, or employment contract, should you recommend to him? How are the other stockholders likely to react to your suggestions?

c. How realistic are Flyer's concerns that Leader and Hooks may issue additional shares thereby diminishing his interest in the corporation and possibly even "freezing" him out? What protections are available with respect to the issuance of new shares in the absence of preemptive rights? Do you regard them as satisfactory? Assume you have decided to provide for preemptive rights and MBCA § 26A is in force. How should preemptive rights be handled? Cf. Del. GCL § 102(b)(3). Reconsider Chapter 8, Section C(g) and the Chesapeake Marine Services Problem in the light of these concerns.

2. Suppose that the parties have decided on a four-member board.

a. Is some type of deadlock-breaking arrangement desirable? What would you recommend?

b. Some states have adopted special provisions to assist in breaking deadlocks of close corporations. Suppose that Columbia had enacted the equivalent of Del. GCL §§ 226, 352, and 353. What effect would this have on your answers to question 2a? If Columbia had no such provision, would you recommend incorporation in Delaware in order to take advantage of those sections, even if Pisces Tackle would be doing business only in Columbia? Suppose the MBCA

Close Corp. Supp. §§ 15 and 16 are in force in Columbia, do they solve the problem adequately?

1. INTRODUCTION

Perhaps the most difficult problem facing the close corporation planner, a problem that lurks in the background of virtually all of the preceding material, is how to provide against that day, which comes all too frequently in small businesses, when the owners cease to get along with each other. Conflict may manifest itself in a variety of ways. There are recorded cases in which shareholders have ceased speaking to each other, yet have managed to continue their business for years. In at least a few instances intracorporate disputes have ended in violence.* One of the principal difficulties is that differences over matters of business policy or practice are frequently aggravated by differences of a more personal nature. The managers of large corporations, too, occasionally have their personality clashes, but, taking place within the structure of a larger and more resilient organization the consequences seldom have so disastrous an effect on the overall fortunes of the enterprise.

When, for whatever reasons, relations between a minority shareholder and the controlling interests of a corporation break down, the result is often an effort by the majority to "freeze out" the weaker party. The techniques by which this has been accomplished are numerous, and new ones continue to be created by enterprising controlling shareholders and their attorneys. The *Wilkes* opinion that follows this introduction contains a good listing of those that are more common. Of course, the possibility that the parties may one day come to a parting of ways is seldom entirely absent from the thoughts of individuals embarking on a corporate venture, and competent counsel should bring that possibility gently to the fore. The result is usually some effort by the parties and their counsel to provide adequate protection for minority interests. The difficulty for the planner in these situations is to walk the narrow line between protecting minority shareholders against oppression by the majority and designing a control mechanism that is so cumbersome that it impedes the functioning of the corporation or, at the extreme, leads to a situation in which the parties are so badly deadlocked that the corporation cannot carry on its affairs. That situation occasionally leads to the ultimate remedy for internecine dissension: judicial dissolution of the corporation.

Since the planner cannot possibly provide against every eventuality or protect minority interests against every possible scheme to freeze them out, a useful beginning point for the discussion is to examine the attitude of the courts when confronted with an allegation

---

* *E.g.*, Nashville Packet Co. v. Neville, 144 Tenn. 698, 235 S.W. 64 (1921).

that the majority is treating the minority unfairly. We have selected a case representative of progressive judicial thinking in this area.

2. JUDICIAL PROTECTION OF MINORITY INTERESTS IN THE CLOSE CORPORATION

WILKES v. SPRINGSIDE NURSING HOME, INC.

370 Mass. 842, 353 N.E.2d 657 (1976).

HENNESSEY, Chief Justice.

On August 5, 1971, the plaintiff (Wilkes) filed a bill in equity for declaratory judgment in the Probate Court for Berkshire County, naming as defendants T. Edward Quinn (Quinn), Leon L. Riche (Riche), the First Agricultural National Bank of Berkshire County and Frank Sutherland MacShane as executors under the will of Lawrence R. Connor (Connor), and the Springside Nursing Home, Inc. (Springside or the corporation). Wilkes alleged that he, Quinn, Riche and Dr. Hubert A. Pipkin (Pipkin) entered into a partnership agreement in 1951, prior to the incorporation of Springside, which agreement was breached in 1967 when Wilkes's salary was terminated and he was voted out as an officer and director of the corporation. Wilkes sought, among other forms of relief, damages in the amount of the salary he would have received had he continued as a director and officer of Springside subsequent to March, 1967.

* * * A judgment was entered dismissing Wilkes's action on the merits. We granted direct appellate review. On appeal, Wilkes argued in the alternative that (1) he should recover damages for breach of the alleged partnership agreement; and (2) he should recover damages because the defendants, as majority stockholders in Springside, breached their fiduciary duty to him as a minority stockholder by their action in February and March, 1967.

* * * [W]e reverse so much of the judgment as dismisses Wilkes's complaint and order the entry of a judgment substantially granting the relief sought by Wilkes under the second alternative set forth above.

* * *

[In 1951, Wilkes, Riche, Quinn, and Pipkin purchased a building lot to use as a nursing home.]

* * * [O]wnership of the property was vested in Springside, a corporation organized under Massachusetts law.

Each of the four men invested $1,000 and subscribed to ten shares of $100 par value stock in Springside.[6] At the time of incorporation, it was understood by all of the parties that each would be a director

6. On May 2, 1955, and again on December 23, 1958, each of the four original investors paid for and was issued additional shares of $100 par value stock, eventually bringing the total number of shares owned by each to 115.

of Springside and each would participate actively in the management and decision making involved in operating the corporation.[7] It was, further, the understanding and intention of all the parties that, corporate resources permitting, each would receive money from the corporation in equal amounts as long as each assumed an active and ongoing responsibility for carrying a portion of the burdens necessary to operate the business.

The work involved in establishing and operating a nursing home was roughly apportioned, and each of the four men undertook his respective tasks. * * *

At some time in 1952, it became apparent that the operational income and cash flow from the business were sufficient to permit the four stockholders to draw money from the corporation on a regular basis. Each of the four original parties initially received $35 a week from the corporation. As time went on the weekly return to each was increased until, in 1955, it totalled $100.

In 1959, after a long illness, Pipkin sold his shares in the corporation to Connor, who was known to Wilkes, Riche and Quinn through past transactions with Springside in his capacity as president of the First Agricultural National Bank of Berkshire County. Connor received a weekly stipend from the corporation equal to that received by Wilkes, Riche and Quinn. He was elected a director of the corporation but never held any other office. He was assigned no specific area of responsibility in the operation of the nursing home but did participate in business discussions and decisions as a director and served additionally as financial adviser to the corporation.

* * *

[Beginning in 1965, personal relationships between Wilkes and the other shareholders began to deteriorate.] As a consequence of the strained relations among the parties, Wilkes, in January of 1967, gave notice of his intention to sell his shares for an amount based on an appraisal of their value. In February of 1967 a directors' meeting was held and the board exercised its right to establish the salaries of its officers and employees.[10] A schedule of payments was established whereby Quinn was to receive a substantial weekly increase

---

7. Wilkes testified before the master that, when the corporate officers were elected, all four men "were * * * guaranteed directorships." Riche's understanding of the parties' intentions was that they all wanted to play a part in the management of the corporation and wanted to have some "say" in the risks involved; that, to this end, they all would be directors; and that "unless you [were] a director and officer you could not participate in the decisions of [the] enterprise."

10. The by-laws of the corporation provided that the directors, subject to the approval of the stockholders, had the power to fix the salaries of all officers and employees. This power, however, up until February, 1967, had not been exercised formally; all payments made to the four participants in the venture had resulted from the informal but unanimous approval of all the parties concerned.

and Riche and Connor were to continue receiving $100 a week. Wilkes, however, was left off the list of those to whom a salary was to be paid. The directors also set the annual meeting of the stockholders for March, 1967.

At the annual meeting in March, Wilkes was not reelected as a director, nor was he reelected as an officer of the corporation. He was further informed that neither his services nor his presence at the nursing home was wanted by his associates.

The meetings of the directors and stockholders in early 1967, the master found, were used as a vehicle to force Wilkes out of active participation in the management and operation of the corporation and to cut off all corporate payments to him. Though the board of directors had the power to dismiss any officers or employees for misconduct or neglect of duties, there was no indication in the minutes of the board of directors' meeting of February, 1967, that the failure to establish a salary for Wilkes was based on either ground. The severance of Wilkes from the payroll resulted not from misconduct or neglect of duties, but because of the personal desire of Quinn, Riche and Connor to prevent him from continuing to receive money from the corporation. Despite a continuing deterioration in his personal relationship with his associates, Wilkes had consistently endeavored to carry on his responsibilities to the corporation in the same satisfactory manner and with the same degree of competence he had previously shown. Wilkes was at all times willing to carry on his responsibilities and participation if permitted so to do and provided that he receive his weekly stipend.

1. We turn to Wilkes's claim for damages based on a breach of the fiduciary duty owed to him by the other participants in this venture. In light of the theory underlying this claim, we do not consider it vital to our approach to this case whether the claim is governed by partnership law or the law applicable to business corporations. This is so because, as all the parties agree, Springside was at all times relevant to this action, a close corporation as we have recently defined such an entity in Donahue v. Rodd Electrotype Co. of New England, Inc. [367 Mass. 578], 328 N.E.2d 505 (1975).

In *Donahue*, we held that "stockholders in the close corporation owe one another substantially the same fiduciary duty in the operation of the enterprise that partners owe to one another." [*Id.* at 593 (footnotes omitted)], 328 N.E.2d at 515. As determined in previous decisions of this court, the standard of duty owed by partners to one another is one of "utmost good faith and loyalty." Cardullo v. Landau, 329 Mass. 5, 8, 105 N.E.2d 843 (1952). Thus, we concluded in *Donahue*, with regard to "their actions relative to the operations of the enterprise and the effects of that operation on the rights and investments of other stockholders," "[s]tockholders in close corporations must discharge their management and stockholder responsibilities in conformity with this strict good faith standard. They may not act out of avarice, expediency or self-interest in derogation of their duty of loyalty to the other stockholders and to the corporation." [367 Mass. at 593 n. 18], 328 N.E.2d at 515.

In the *Donahue* case we recognized that one peculiar aspect of close corporations was the opportunity afforded to majority stockholders to oppress, disadvantage or "freeze out" minority stockholders. In *Donahue* itself, for example, the majority refused the minority an equal opportunity to sell a ratable number of shares to the corporation at the same price available to the majority. The net result of this refusal, we said, was that the minority could be forced to "sell out at less than fair value," [367 Mass. at 592], 328 N.E.2d at 515, since there is by definition no ready market for minority stock in a close corporation.

"Freeze outs," however, may be accomplished by the use of other devices. One such device which has proved to be particularly effective in accomplishing the purpose of the majority is to deprive minority stockholders of corporate offices and of employment with the corporation. F. H. O'Neal, "Squeeze-Outs" of Minority Shareholders 59, 78–79 (1975). See [367 Mass. 589], 328 N.E.2d 505. This "freeze-out" technique has been successful because courts fairly consistently have been disinclined to interfere in those facets of internal corporate operations, such as the selection and retention or dismissal of officers, directors and employees, which essentially involve management decisions subject to the principle of majority control. As one authoritative source has said, "[M]any courts apparently feel that there is a legitimate sphere in which the controlling [directors or] shareholders can act in their own interest even if the minority suffers." F. H. O'Neal, *supra* at 59 (footnote omitted).

The denial of employment to the minority at the hands of the majority is especially pernicious in some instances. A guaranty of employment with the corporation may have been one of the "basic reason[s] why a minority owner has invested capital in the firm." Symposium—The Close Corporation, 52 Nw.U.L.Rev. 345, 392 (1957). See F. H. O'Neal, *supra* at 78–79. The minority stockholder typically depends on his salary as the principal return on his investment, since the "earnings of a close corporation * * * are distributed in major part in salaries, bonuses and retirement benefits." 1 F. H. O'Neal, Close Corporations § 1.07 (1971).[13] Other noneconomic interests of the minority stockholder are likewise injuriously affected by barring him from corporate office. See F. H. O'Neal, "Squeeze-Outs" of Minority Shareholders 79 (1975). Such action severely restricts his participation in the management of the enterprise, and he is relegated to enjoying those benefits incident to his status as a stockholder. See Symposium—The Close Corporation, 52 Nw.U.L.

13. We note here that the master found that Springside never declared or paid a dividend to its stockholders.

Rev. 345, 386 (1957). In sum, by terminating a minority stockholder's employment or by severing him from a position as an officer or director, the majority effectively frustrate the minority stockholder's purposes in entering on the corporate venture and also deny him an equal return on his investment.

 * * * The distinction between the majority action in *Donahue* and the majority action in this case is more one of form than of substance. Nevertheless, we are concerned that untempered application of the strict good faith standard enunciated in *Donahue* to cases such as the one before us will result in the imposition of limitations on legitimate action by the controlling group in a close corporation which will unduly hamper its effectiveness in managing the corporation in the best interests of all concerned. The majority, concededly, have certain rights to what has been termed "selfish ownership" in the corporation which should be balanced against the concept of their fiduciary obligation to the minority.

Therefore, when minority stockholders in a close corporation bring suit against the majority alleging a breach of the strict good faith duty owed to them by the majority, we must carefully analyze the action taken by the controlling stockholders in the individual case. It must be asked whether the controlling group can demonstrate a legitimate business purpose for its action. See Bryan v. Brock & Blevins Co., 343 F.Supp. 1062, 1068 (N.D.Ga.1972), aff'd, 490 F.2d 563, 570–571 (5th Cir. 1974); Schwartz v. Marien, 37 N.Y.2d 487, 492, 373 N.Y.S.2d 122, 335 N.E.2d 334 (1975). In asking this question, we acknowledge the fact that the controlling group in a close corporation must have some room to maneuver in establishing the business policy of the corporation. It must have a large measure of discretion, for example, in declaring or withholding dividends, deciding whether to merge or consolidate, establishing the salaries of corporate officers, dismissing directors with or without cause, and hiring and firing corporate employees.

When an asserted business purpose for their action is advanced by the majority, however, we think it is open to minority stockholders to demonstrate that the same legitimate objective could have been achieved through an alternative course of action less harmful to the minority's interest. See Schwartz v. Marien, *supra*. If called on to settle a dispute, our courts must weigh the legitimate business purpose, if any, against the practicability of a less harmful alternative.

Applying this approach to the instant case it is apparent that the majority stockholders in Springside have not shown a legitimate business purpose for severing Wilkes from the payroll of the corporation or for refusing to reëlect him as a salaried officer and director. The master's subsidiary findings relating to the purpose of the meetings of the directors and stockholders in February and March, 1967, are supported by the evidence. There was no showing of misconduct on Wilkes's part as a director, officer or employee of the corporation which would lead us to approve the majority action as a legitimate response to the disruptive nature of an undesirable individual bent on injuring or destroying the corporation. On the contrary, it appears that Wilkes had always accomplished his assigned share of the duties competently, and that he had never indicated an unwillingness to continue to do so.

It is an inescapable conclusion from all the evidence that the action of the majority stockholders here was a designed "freeze out" for which no legitimate business purpose has been suggested. Furthermore, we may infer that a design to pressure Wilkes into selling his shares to the corporation at a price below their value well may have been at the heart of the majority's plan.[14]

In the context of this case, several factors bear directly on the duty owed to Wilkes by his associates. At a minimum, the duty of utmost good faith and loyalty would demand that the majority consider that their action was in disregard of a long-standing policy of the stockholders that each would be a director of the corporation and that employment with the corporation would go hand in hand with stock ownership; that Wilkes was one of the four originators of the nursing home venture; and that Wilkes, like the others, had invested his capital and time for more than fifteen years with the expectation that he would continue to participate in corporate decisions. Most important is the plain fact that the cutting off of Wilkes's salary, together with the fact that the corporation never declared a dividend, assured that Wilkes would receive no return at all from the corporation.

2. The question of Wilkes's damages at the hands of the majority has not been thoroughly explored on the record before us. Wilkes, in his original complaint, sought damages in the amount of the $100 a week he believed he was entitled to from the time his salary was terminated up until the time this action was commenced. However, the record shows that, after Wilkes was severed from the corporate payroll, the schedule of salaries and payments made to the other stockholders varied from time to time. In addition, the duties assumed by the other stockholders after Wilkes was deprived of his share of the corporate earnings appear to have changed in significant respects. Any resolution of this question must take into account whether the corporation was dissolved during the pendency of this litigation.

Therefore our order is as follows: So much of the judgment as dismisses Wilkes's complaint and awards costs to the defendants is reversed. * * *

---

14. This inference arises from the fact that Connor, acting on behalf of the three controlling stockholders, offered to purchase Wilkes's shares for a price Connor admittedly would not have accepted for his own shares.

NOTE—MORE ON WILKES v. SPRINGSIDE NURSING HOME

The background, and denouement, of the *Wilkes* case, which is also a tale of effective advocacy, is eloquently described in the following excerpt from a letter from David Martel, Esq.:

Stanley J. Wilkes is my uncle (my mother's brother) and was one of ten children of Polish immigrants who grew up on a farm in nearby Hatfield, Massachusetts. Although his formal education was minimal, in his later years, after settling in Pittsfield, Massachusetts, he was very successful in real estate investments. It was this reputation that led to the formation of the enterprise that fostered this litigation. * * *

I recall hearing talk in the family about how he had been victimized by his "partners" and I remember seeing him at a family gathering around 1971 when he was in a distressed state. He had hired a Pittsfield lawyer who had unsuccessfully brought suit in the Superior Court against the other corporate officers and the corporation alleging unlawful, fraudulent and arbitrary actions on the part of the stockholders. The Pittsfield lawyer was not equal to the test and the suit was dismissed without a determination. I should add that, for reasons which are still a mystery to us, no *res judicata* argument was ever raised by the opposition in the subsequent litigation.

At any rate, when I saw Mr. Wilkes in 1971, he was convinced more than ever that he had been wronged, but fearful that he could never have this wrong redressed. He asked me if I knew any lawyer in Massachusetts he might turn to. I was then only in law school myself, but I had been close friends in college with a son of James F. Egan, who I knew was one of the most resourceful and effective trial lawyers in Springfield.

* * * [T]he trial before the Master began late in 1972. Mr. Egan knew of an old but undeveloped line of cases in Massachusetts which said that an enterprise in corporate form could nonetheless be treated as a partnership. His approach at the trial was to develop facts to show that, over sixteen years of corporate existence (up to Wilkes' ouster), the parties had all been equals and that this was in fact a partnership. The trial testimony provided an excellent record for an appellate court to define shareholder responsibilities in this context. As it turned out, after the Master's hearing but before confirmation of the Master's report in the Probate Court, the Supreme Court decided Donohue v. Rodd Electrotype, 328 N.E.2d 505, where the close corporation duty of "utmost good faith and loyalty" was first enunciated. * * *

* * * On remand to the Probate Court, the judge referred the matter to a Master for a hearing on damages. On the morning the hearing was to begin, the case was settled.

* * * We * * * agreed to settle for an amount of the sale proceeds after distribution of the dividend to Mr. Wilkes. * * *

After his ouster, Mr. Wilkes continued to visit the nursing home since he was well liked by the staff there. After a short time, however, these visits stopped when he was told by counsel for the majority shareholders that his presence was no longer desired.

———

Wilkes might be said to be a classic example of a "freeze-out" in a close corporation. As in most litigation arising out of dissension in close corporations, it presents the court with the difficult task of choosing sides in a struggle in which the usual rules often are not functioning. The *Wilkes* court sought to resolve that dilemma by asking whether there was a "business purpose" for the transaction being challenged. Is that a sound approach? Consider the following:

In close corporations, freezeouts generally arise in the context of a dispute over the disentanglement of what are essentially partnership arrangements among more or less active participants for whose securities there is no market. The parties are visibly at loggerheads over division of the business's prosperity or over the conduct of its business; their disagreements are of a continuing kind, likely both not to be resolved until the business terminates and to plague the parties as they remain unable to disentangle satisfactorily. There is, therefore, reason to facilitate or encourage the departure of one group or the other from the enterprise—both in terms of the personal well-being of the participants, and because of the impact of continuing disagreements on their conduct of the enterprise. It does not follow that corporate law should permit the controlling group to have an advantage in bargaining over the terms of the break-up. Still, the difficulty with flatly forbidding freezeouts is that, if the majority does not have the power to force the minority out, the majority may be forced to accede to the demands of the minority because of the threat of deadlock. Moreover, unlike the investors in a public corporation, the parties in a close corporation can contract in advance about their arrangements; any skew in the corporate law that permits majority power to displace the minority can thus be offset by contract. Modern statutes purport to offer special solutions for the problem of disentangling the essentially personal relationships of parties in conflict in close corporations. *See, e.g.,* Del.Code tit. 8, §§ 352, 355 (1975); N.Y.Bus.Corp.Law, § 1104 (McKinney 1963); *id.* § 1111(b)(3), (c). If, notwithstanding such legislation, freezeouts are permitted by statute, any judicially imposed solution will require compliance with some conception of "fairness," however crude it may be. But it is hard to see any role for "business purpose" as a doctrine in filtering permissible from impermissible freezeouts in close corporations, even as that conception is rigorously confined in cases like Schwartz v. Marien, 37 N.Y.2d 487, 492, 373 N.Y.S.2d 122, 127, 335 N.E.2d 334, 338 (1975), or Wilkes v. Springside Nursing Home, Inc., 353 N.E.2d 657, 663 (Mass.1976).

(Brudney & Chirelstein, A Restatement of Corporate Freezeouts, 87 Yale L.J. 1354, 1356–57 n. 9 (1977).

3. PLANNING FOR DEADLOCK (HEREIN OF ARBITRATION AND OTHER DEVICES)

Students occasionally misunderstand the meaning of the term, "deadlock." It does not signify merely that the directors or shareholders are evenly divided on a particular vote. In such cases the motion simply fails to carry for want of a majority. If this happens only on occasion, there is no reason that the corporation cannot continue to function normally.

A true deadlock occurs when relations among the shareholders or directors have deteriorated to the point that whenever one faction says something is white, the other says it is black, with the result that virtually no resolution can muster a majority. At this point the corporation may become nearly paralyzed. Although most seem to manage to continue to operate after a fashion, trying to do business in such circumstances can be neither comfortable nor convenient.

The close corporation planner must, then, be aware of the possibility of deadlock and to the extent possible make advance provision for it. The solution may be as simple as providing for an uneven number of directors on the board, although where the stock is equally divided, the selection of the "neutral" director itself poses a problem. And it has happened that the "neutral" director has died or resigned (sometimes in disgust) and the shareholders have been unable to fill the vacancy, leaving the board deadlocked.

You have already been introduced to a technique that was used to deal with the potential of deadlock in *Ringling Brothers*, in which the parties sought to rely on someone trusted by both sides to resolve matters on which they were unable to agree. You should also reconsider here the deadlock-breaking mechanism used in Lehrman v. Cohen.

The arrangements in both Lehrman v. Cohen and *Ringling* partook of many of the characteristics of a simple arbitration agreement. But it is significant that in neither case had the parties characterized the arrangement as a conventional arbitration scheme (although Loos was designated as "arbitrator" in *Ringling*). It is apparent from the opinions, moreover, that the Delaware courts were reluctant to say straightforwardly that they were enforcing an arbitration agreement. Underlying this apparent aversion to applying the law of arbitration to the sort of dispute that often arises in close corporations is a long-standing judicial reservation about the enforceability of arbitration awards in such cases, which in part is founded on the practical limitations of the use of arbitration to resolve disputes over the management of corporations.

It is obvious, to begin with, that the directors or shareholders cannot run to an arbitrator (or, worse yet, a panel of arbitrators) every time they disagree over some business decision. Moreover, following a pattern consecrated by long historical precedent, the courts have tended to be jealous of incursions by arbitration into their jurisdiction, and have managed to establish a variety of obstacles to the enforcement of arbitration agreements.

While in most jurisdictions nearly all of those obstacles have been removed by legislation providing that agreements to arbitrate future disputes are to be given specific performance, the use of arbitration in the corporate context continues to raise special problems related to some of the same doctrines you have come across in the previous material on the validity of other control arrangements.

In Application of Vogel, 25 A.D.2d 212, 268 N.Y.S.2d 237 (1965), aff'd 19 N.Y.2d 589, 278 N.Y.S.2d 236, 224 N.E.2d 738, for example, the two parties had each purchased 50 percent of the stock of a corporation that operated a moving and storage business. At the same time they had entered a shareholders' agreement that provided for arbitration "in the event of a dispute, or difference, arising between them in the course of their transaction with each other." When they took over corporation, they obtained a five year lease on the warehouse that had been used for the business. When the lease expired, one of the shareholders sought to have the corporation exercise an option to purchase the warehouse, but the other refused, admittedly because of an agreement he had with the owners of the warehouse. The former shareholder then sought arbitration of the question whether the corporation should purchase the warehouse. Rejecting the argument that arbitration would take the management of the corporation out of the hands of the board of directors, to which it is committed by statute, the court ordered that arbitration proceed. A dissenting opinion objected that, "It is obvious that [if the agreement were enforced] either of these parties could destroy the business of the corporation by insisting on arbitrating any of the numberless questions which may develop in the operation of the business."

4. DISSOLUTION

PROBLEM

PISCES TACKLE CO.—PART VI

Because of Flyer's concern about being "frozen out," he, Leader, and Hooks are considering using a four-member board, two of whom would be nominated by Flyer. They have heard that one remedy for dissension within a corporation is forced dissolution, and they have asked you for a further explanation. If Pisces Tackle is incorporated in Columbia.

1.   Under what circumstances might a court, on the application of Flyer, compel dissolution of the corporation pursuant to MBCA § 97 (a)(2)? What would be the practical and legal consequences of a dissolution decree? Does Del. GCL § 226 offer a preferable alternative? What about Del. GCL §§ 352, 353 and 355?

2.   What role, if any, should the possiblity of dissolution play in planning the control structure of the corporation? Would you recommend that the shareholders' agreement contain a clause requiring the parties to dissolve the corporation under some circumstances? What would those circumstances be?

––––––––––

Dissolution of a corporation is the ultimate remedy for dissension among shareholders, but it is seldom a satisfactory one. For this reason it is usually not automatically available, but depends on the discretion of the court.

Dissolution, which is technically the extinguishment of the legal existence of the corporate entity, is to be distinguished from two related terms, "liquidation" and "winding up." The liquidation of an enterprise is, as the word implies, the reduction of its assets to cash or some other "liquid" form. While it usually implies the cessation of a corporation's normal business operation, it does not necessarily involve dissolution; the corporation may remain a "shell" whose sole function is to own the now liquid assets. The winding up of a corporation consists of the orderly termination of its affairs by liquidating its assets, paying off its creditors, and distributing what remains to its shareholders.

State statutes generally allow for voluntary dissolution by act of the corporation or its shareholders (see MBCA §§ 83–93) and also provide for involuntary dissolution by a court upon petition by a state official (see MBCA §§ 94–96) or a shareholder or creditor (see MBCA §§ 97–105).

While at first glance dissolution may appear an eminently sensible solution for the paralysis of a close corporation stemming from shareholder dissension or an attempt to freeze out one of the shareholders, on closer examination it becomes evident that the problem is more complex. First, there is the question of whether dissolution will be in the best interest of the community of interests known as "the corporation." Are the difficulties so severe that attempts at continued operation would lead only to deterioration of the business and a wasting of assets, or could the corporation continue to operate profitably? Second, there is the problem of finding an equitable resolution among the shareholders. If involuntary dissolution is sought, there must be at least one shareholder who finds that alternative worse for his interests than an attempt to continue the battle. In many instances, the result of dissolution would be that one shareholder or group of shareholders would be able to take over the business for themselves, perhaps at a price unfair to the others. Although the facts of every case vary, the court with which a petition for dissolution is filed almost inevitably finds itself caught in the middle, and faced with the task of finding the most equitable solution for all concerned without much in the way of useful statutory guidance.

MASINTER v. WEBCO CO.

262 S.E.2d 433 (W.Va.1980).

MILLER, Justice.

[In 1949 Masinter, Cohen, and Webb formed a corporation, which later became WEBCO Company, to operate a pawnshop in Huntington, West Virginia. The three contributed the same amount of capital and received the same number of shares. The business was subsequently broaded into a retail merchandise store. The business was operated by Cohen and Webb. Masinter, who owned a retail business in Charleston, acted as a corporate secretary and met regularly with the other two to make the business decisions that arose. The corporation paid no dividends, but all three shareholders received salaries. Until 1973 the corporation "from the standpoint of corporate meetings and the keeping of minutes, operated in a relatively informal fashion."

In 1970 an urban renewal project required the relocation of the business. To finance the move the corporation borrowed $1.2 million. All of its assets, and the shares of the three stockholders, were pledged as security for the loan. Cohen and Webb also guaranteed the note personally. When Masinter refused to do so, relations between him and the two stockholders began to deteriorate. At a formal board meeting in 1973 Cohen and Webb voted to remove Masinter from the board and to terminate him as secretary. The corporation subsequently borrowed another $700,000, apparently without formal notice to Masinter. The terms of this loan prohibited the payment of dividends, bonuses, or advances to the shareholders without approval of the lender. Masinter filed suit, and the trial court gave summary judgment for the defendants.]

*   *   *   [T]he complaint requested two forms of relief: a dissolution of the corporation under W.Va.Code, 31–1–81 [1931], and damages as a result of the alleged oppressive conduct on the part of the defendants.

After the parties had undertaken some discovery, the defendants moved for summary judgment. The Circuit Court referred the matter to a special commissioner, who concluded that there was insufficient evidence to warrant any relief to the plaintiff. The court confirmed the commissioner's written findings and granted summary judgment to the defendants.

Both the trial court and the commissioner apparently conceived that the plaintiff's claim for statutory dissolution encompassed the damage claim for oppressive conduct, and that in order to recover the plaintiff would have to show facts which would warrant a dissolution.

It is clear under our law that an aggrieved minority shareholder is not confined solely to the remedy of dissolution. A fundamental proposition is that the majority stockholders in a corporation owe a fiduciary duty to the minority, as do the officers and directors * * *.

While the existence of the fiduciary duty rule is widely acknowledged, it does not mean that the officers and directors are not accorded a rather broad latitude in the conduct of corporate affairs. We adhered to much the same test in Meadows v. Bradshaw-Diehl Co., [139 W.Va. 569, 81 S.E.2d 63 (1954)] which involved the failure to pay dividends:

> It is a rule of general application that if there is no fraud or bad faith by the directors, that it is within their discretion whether they declare dividends or otherwise and courts have no right to interfere with such discretion. * * * [139 W.Va. at 578, 81 S.E.2d at 68]

It is implicit in our statutory dissolution cases that dissolution is a severe remedy, since, if granted, it will terminate the corporate life. In Hall v. McLuckey, 134 W.Va. 595, 604, 60 S.E.2d 280, 286 (1950), we characterized dissolution as "drastic in nature" and stated that it was to be reserved for "plain cases." Indeed, most courts have concluded that because of the drastic consequences of dissolution, less drastic alternatives should be fashioned if possible. A leading commentator on corporate law, advocating this approach, has stated:

> Winding-up a corporation is so drastic a remedy that it is not ordered if the wrong may be adequately repaired by milder relief. Unless the wrongs are being conducted systematically or continuously, it may be possible to redress past derelictions by ordering an accounting, or by the setting aside and cancellation of wrongful acts, or to prevent future wrongs by injunction or mandamus, or to effect relief by some combination of these and other remedies. [Hornstein, A Remedy for Corporate Abuse—Judicial Power to Wind Up a Corporation at the Suit of a Minority Stockholder, 40 Col.L.Rev. 220, 236 (1940)]

In a number of cases, this Court has recognized the right of a shareholder to bring an action against the corporation or its majority shareholders to obtain relief other than dissolution. * * *

* * *

Most states have adopted the view that a dissolution statute does not provide the exclusive remedy for injured shareholders and that the courts have equitable powers to fashion appropriate remedies where the majority shareholders have breached their fiduciary duty to the minority by engaging in oppressive conduct. In Baker v. Commercial Body Builders, Inc., 264 Or. 614, 628–29, 507 P.2d 387, 393–94 (1973), this definition of oppressive conduct was given:

> While general definitions of "oppressive" conduct are of little value for application in a specific case, perhaps the most widely quoted definitions are that "oppressive conduct" for the purposes of such a statute is:
>
> > burdensome, harsh and wrongful conduct; a lack of probity and fair dealing in the affairs of a company to the prejudice of some of its members; or a visual departure from the standards of fair dealing, and a violation of fair play on which every shareholder who entrusts his money to a company is entitled to rely.
>
> We agree, however, that the question of what is "oppressive" conduct by those in control of a "close" corporation as its majority stockholders is closely related to what we agree to be the fiduciary duty of a good faith and fair dealing owed by them to its minority stockholders.
>
> Our cases recite substantially the same standards under our fiduciary rule. * * * Thus, we conclude that our cases involving the fiduciary duty owed by majority shareholders, officers and directors of a corporation embrace the same standard which other courts have evolved under the term "oppressive conduct."

In the present case, the summary judgment was not an appropriate method to dispose of the case. Significant factual issues existed. Specifically, the court treated the plaintiff's claims by the dissolution standard. No attempt was made to analyze the case from the standpoint that the action of the majority shareholders toward Masinter might constitute oppressive conduct. Because the summary judgment improperly foreclosed further factual inquiry, we are unable to state whether sufficient facts can be developed to warrant a finding of oppressive conduct.

The particular type of oppressive conduct suggested from Masinter's allegations is the attempt to "freeze or squeeze out" a minority shareholder by depriving him, without any legitimate business purpose, of any benefit from his ownership and investment in a corporation. Two broad factual patterns appear to exist under this category of oppressive conduct. The first is where the minority shareholder has made a parity of capital investment with the other shareholders with the expectation of full-time remunerative employment with the corporation, and this expectation has been realized. Characteristically, the minority shareholder has worked for the corporation over a period of time, only to find that through no fault of his own and not as a result of any legitimate business purpose, his services and all remuneration are terminated.

The second pattern is where the minority holder has originally been involved in the formation of the corporation, or induced to invest in it, with the expectation of some return on his investment. Further, he has received some return, either by salary or dividend, but finds that this return has been severed for no legitimate business purpose and not as a result of any dereliction on his part.

These factual patterns do not constitute the only occurrences that may demonstrate oppressive conduct by a majority shareholder against the minority in a squeeze or freeze-out situation, but these seem to be the most applicable to the present case.

Since this case will be returned for further factual development, it is inappropriate to discuss the possible relief that may be available if oppressive conduct is found. In Baker v. Commercial Body Builders, Inc., 264 Or. 614, 632–33, 507 P.2d 387, 395–96 (1973), the court listed ten possible forms of relief against oppressive conduct short of outright dissolution.[12]

* * *

The trial court was * * * in error in granting summary judgment for the individual defendants, Cohen and Webb. Therefore, the

12. "(a) The entry of an order requiring dissolution of the corporation at a specified future date, to become effective only in the event that the stockholders fail to resolve their differences prior to that date."

"(b) The appointment of a receiver, not for the purposes of dissolution, but to continue the operation of the corporation for the benefit of all of the stockholders, both majority and minority, until differences are resolved or 'oppressive' conduct ceases."

"(c) The appointment of a 'special fiscal agent' to report to the court relating to the continued operation of the corporation, as a protection to its minority stockholders, and the retention of jurisdiction of the case by the court for that purpose."

"(d) The retention of jurisdiction of the case by the court for the protection of the minority stockholders without appointment of a receiver or 'special fiscal agent.'"

"(e) The ordering of an accounting by the majority in control of the corporation for funds alleged to have been misappropriated."

"(f) The issuance of an injunction to prohibit continuing acts of 'oppressive' conduct and which may include the reduction of salaries or bonus payments found to be unjustified or excessive."

"(g) The ordering of affirmative relief by the required declaration of a dividend or a reduction and distribution of capital."

"(h) The ordering of affirmative relief by the entry of an order requiring the corporation or a majority of its stockholders to purchase the stock of the minority stockholders at a price to be determined according to a specified formula or at a price determined by the court to be a fair and reasonable price."

"(i) The ordering of affirmative relief by the entry of an order permitting minority stockholders to purchase additional stock under conditions specified by the court."

"(j) An award of damages to minority stockholders as compensation for any injury suffered by them as the result of 'oppressive' conduct by the majority in control of the corporation."

order of the trial court is * * * reversed * * * with respect to the defendants Cohen and Webb, and the case is remanded for further proceedings.

Affirmed in part; reversed in part; remanded.

NOTE—DISSOLUTION AND THE COURTS

Close corporations, as we have seen, normally function more like partnerships than like the abstract entity described in the usual corporation statute. Involuntary dissolution, or the threat thereof, usually enters the picture only when the "partners" have ceased to get along with one another. At that point, one of the dominant characteristics of the corporation, the illiquidity of the interests of the shareholders, becomes cumbrously evident. When one of the shareholders wants to extricate himself by selling his interest, typically the only purchasers on the horizon are the other shareholders. But, particularly if they are on the outs with the would-be seller, the other shareholders are seldom in the mood to offer a generous price. In these circumstances the former is likely to turn to an action for dissolution as a tool to be used in the negotiations. See generally, Hetherington and Dooley, Illiquidity and Exploitation: A Proposed Statutory Solution to the Remaining Close Corporation Problem, 63 Va.L.Rev. 1 (1977).

The courts, however, seldom appear to perceive the problem that they find thus dumped in their laps in quite those terms. They "traditionally have regarded dissolution as a drastic remedy to be invoked only as a last resort." Id. at 26. Solicitous of the welfare of "the corporation" (presumably including employees, creditors, and the community as well as stockholders) they have characterized dissolution as "judicially imposed death." In re Radom & Niedorff, Inc., 307 N.Y. 1, 7, 119 N.E.2d 563, 565 (1954). Their principal concern has been to determine whether dissolution will be beneficial to the shareholders.

The academic commentators, on the other hand, have tended to be less concerned about the continued existence of the corporation. See, e.g., Israels, The Sacred Cow of Corporate Existence: Problems of Deadlock and Dissolution, 19 U.Chi.L.Rev. 778 (1952). As Professors Hetherington and Dooley point out,

> * * * [A] partnership is "dissolved" whenever one of the general partners withdraws from the firm, and dissolution requires only such a settling of accounts as will be sufficient to allow the departing partner to withdraw his interest. It does not mean the end of the business. The remaining partners are free to continue the enterprise, and only if they choose not to do so will the firm's assets be liquidated.

In corporate involuntary dissolution cases, the courts appear to assume that a decree will result in the termination of the business.

Perceiving a public interest in the continuation of profitable firms, courts understandably grant dissolution reluctantly and only after considering competing interests in preserving the firm. The concern is misplaced in this instance, and both the courts and the legislatures have misperceived the effect of a dissolution decree. In practical effect a decree is no different than the dissolution of a partnership. The entry of a decree results in the termination of the business only if both the majority and the minority shareholders desire that result. Each faction has the ability at any stage of the proceeding to insure the continued existence of the firm by buying out, or selling out to, the other faction. The business will cease only if continuing it is not in the interest of any of its shareholders.

The point becomes clearer if one focuses on the motives for bringing a dissolution proceeding. Except for the rare case where the petition is prompted by pique, a shareholder suing for dissolution is trying to accomplish one of three things: (1) to withdraw his investment from the firm; (2) to induce the other shareholders to sell out to him; or (3) to use the threat of dissolution to induce the other shareholders to agree to a change in the balance of power or in the policies of the firm. All of these objectives can be accomplished without dissolution. If the petitioner wants to sell out, he is interested in receiving the highest possible price and is indifferent whether the purchase funds are raised by the other shareholders individually or by a sale of the firm's assets. If the second or third objectives motivate the suit, it is plain that the petitioner does not want dissolution at all. In all three situations, a dissolution petition is a means to another end.

Since the petitioner can always achieve his purposes without dissolution, and since the defendant will always oppose it, the dispute is very likely to be settled without liquidating the firm's assets and terminating its business. The court's decision to grant or to deny dissolution is significant only as it affects the relative bargaining strength of the parties; negotiations will go forward in any event.

(Hetherington and Dooley, Illiquidity and Exploitation: A Proposed Statutory Solution to the Remaining Close Corporation Problem, 63 Va.L.Rev. 1, 26–27 (1977)).

In a survey of reported cases in which dissolution was sought since 1960, Professors Hetherington and Dooley found that in only a small portion did the court award the relief sought. Even more striking, where a decree of dissolution was entered most of the disputes were subsequently settled before the firm was actually liquidated. In the few instances in which the decree was ultimately carried out, either the corporation was in marginal financial condition or the business was continued in some other form. *Id.* at 32–33.

Chapter 12

THE REGULATION OF SECURITIES ISSUANCE

A. INTRODUCTION

1. WHY SECURITIES REGULATION?

The purchasers of securities—from the largest banks, insurance companies, and other "institutional investors" to the most modest householder looking for a more profitable place than a savings account to invest a small nest egg—are, in a sense, consumers. In that sense the securities laws, state and federal, constitute an enormously complex and comprehensive consumer protection scheme—one of the earliest such schemes to find its way into the American legal scene. Why, it might be asked, was it that laws designed to protect purchasers of securities came so long before any similar effort was made to protect purchasers of automobiles, or radios, or toothpaste; and why do those laws remain, for the most part, more far-reaching and often better enforced?

There is, to be sure, more than one reason. But certainly the most important is to be found in the central role played by the market for securities in a capitalist economy. We can survive with automobiles that do not run well, with radios that do not play, or with toothpaste that fails to fight cavities. We could probably survive as well with a securities market in which the public had little trust, which misallocated capital resources, and which made it difficult for entrepreneurs to raise money, but it is quite clear that we would do so with a far less productive and innovative economy. Since the early part of the century it has been the perception of lawmakers (a perception with which some critics now take exception) that without the kind of protection furnished investors by the securities laws, the capital markets and ultimately the economy—would be far less healthy. It is hardly any surprise that the two most important federal statutes, the Securities Act of 1933 and the Securities Exchange Act of 1934, were passed in the depths of the Great Depression.

In addition to the '33 Act and the '34 Act, there are four other principal pieces of securities legislation: the Public Utilities Holding Company Act of 1935, the Trust Indenture Act of 1939, the Investment Company Act of 1940, and the Investment Advisers Act of 1940. None of these four, however, is as significant to the average corporate practitioner as the '33 and the '34 Acts, and we will not consider them further in these materials.

Throughout all of these statutes, as Professor Louis Loss put it in the leading treatise on securities law, "there is the recurrent theme * * * of disclosure, again disclosure, and still more disclosure." 1

L. Loss, Securities Regulation 21 (2d ed. 1961). In none of them is this as true as it is in the Securities Act of 1933. Taking its cue from Justice Brandeis's famous dictum that "sunlight is the best disinfectant,"[*] the Congress responded to the crisis of confidence that then beset the securities markets with a statute that depends almost exclusively on disclosure. Its central instrument is the registration statement that must be filed with the Securities and Exchange Commission prior to the offer or sale of any security sold through the use of the mails or the facilities of interstate commerce unless one of the numerous rather complex exemptions to this basic requirement is available.

2. THE UNDERWRITING PROCESS

In order to understand the manner in which the '33 Act functions, it is first necessary to understand a little of the manner in which new securities are typically sold in this country.[**] The entire process is usually called "underwriting," a term that stems from the "old-fashioned," or "strict," or "stand-by" system of underwriting that originated in England. Underwriting of this sort amounts to an insurance scheme, by which an investment banker (or "underwriter" in securities jargon) assists the company that issues the securities (the "issuer") in selling its securities to the public and agrees, for a fee, to insure the success of the offering from the issuer's point of view by purchasing any part of the new issue not taken up by the public within a certain time. This method is seldom used today in the United States except for certain types of offerings to existing shareholders by means of warrants or rights.

"Firm commitment" underwriting is the form taken by most ordinary securities offerings. It can be analogized to the merchandising of radios, or writing paper, or any consumer good sold at retail. There is a "manufacturer," the issuer; there are "wholesalers," the underwriters; and there are "retailers," the securities dealers who sell to members of the public who become the ultimate investors. In a firm commitment underwriting the members of the underwriting group do not insure the offering in the usual sense, but actually purchase the securities, reselling them at a markup (the "spread") to a larger group of firms that compose the "selling group" of dealers. They in turn resell, again at a differential, to the investing public.

A third type of underwriting, most prevalent in relatively small offerings by companies "going public" for the first time, is known as "best efforts" underwriting. It is not an underwriting at all in the sense that it guarantees the success of the offering, but rather entails a commitment by the underwriters only to use their best efforts to market the securities, which they undertake only as agent for the issuer and not as purchasers of the securities themselves. Ironically,

---

[*] L. Brandeis, Other People's Money and How the Bankers Use It 92 (1914).

[**] The following discussion is largely drawn from Loss, op.cit., at 106–117.

this sort of underwriting is also used with some frequency by large, well-established issuers that wish to save that portion of the underwriters' compensation attributable to the assumption of the risk of a failure to sell out the entire offering. The underwriters, and the selling group where the size of the offering calls for one, still play an important role in this variety of offering; without their contacts with potential investors and their selling effort, few issuers would be able to place any substantial amount of securities with the public. In this as in other types of underwriting, moreover, the investment banking houses that act as "lead underwriters" often perform a valuable financial consulting service—advising the issuer on the form of the offering, its timing, the amount of securities that can be expected to be sold, and the price. (With respect to this last item, of course, the underwriter occupies a role in all but best-efforts underwritings that is at least partially adversarial to the issuer; the lower the price at which the offering is made, the lower the risk assumed by the underwriter.)

3. THE SECURITIES ACT OF 1933

The dominant feature of the '33 Act is Section 5, which, to oversimplify a bit, makes it unlawful, unless there is an exemption, to sell any security by use of the mails or the facilities of interstate commerce unless a registration statement regarding the security is in effect. In order to get the desired information about the security into the hands of investors without requiring them to go to the SEC to read the registration statement, Congress also requires that a "statutory prospectus" (in the jargon of the profession), including the most important portions of the registration statement, be delivered to the buyer prior to or at the same time as the security.*

The information that must be included in the registration statement is set forth in "Schedule A" to the Act ** as amplified and interpreted by SEC regulations.

---

* The form of this requirement gave rise to the criticism that the purchaser received in most cases only a "retrospectus," the effective decision to purchase having been made prior to the receipt of any form of prospectus. Congress responded to this objection in 1954 by amending the Act to permit the delivery of a "preliminary prospectus"--also called a "red herring" because of the legend announcing its preliminary character required to be printed on its cover—which is in effect the final draft of the prospectus as it is first filed by the issuer with the SEC for its review. It is permitted to omit certain pieces of information that will be eventually added to the final prospectus, including the price of the securities, which has typically not been firmly settled between the issuer and the

underwriters at the time the preliminary prospectus is filed.

The Commission has taken further steps by regulation to encourage the dissemination of preliminary prospectuses to potential purchasers of the security prior to the time the registration statement becomes effective and final sales may take place.

** The following is a summary listing of the 32 items included in the schedule. (Only Items 1–27 must be included in "Part I" of the registration statement, which is the prospectus.):

1 Business name of issuer

2 State of incorporation of organization

3 Business address

By this time, you may have been struck by the broad sweep of Section 5, which, without any exemptions from its operation, would encompass virtually every sale of a security anywhere within the United States (the courts having given an extremely broad reading to what constitutes the use of the facilities of interstate commerce). This apparent breadth is the consequence of the approach of the draftsmen of the statute to defining the area of applicability of Section 5, which was to lay down an all-encompassing prohibition and then to exclude by various exemptions virtually all transactions other than a new public offering of securities. As a consequence, the true scope of the statute cannot be understood without at least a general idea of the nature of the exemptions from its registration requirements.

4. THE SECURITIES EXCHANGE ACT OF 1934

Before we proceed to examine the exemptions from registration under the '33 Act an overview on the Securities Exchange Act of 1934 is in order. Unlike the '33 Act, which is a relatively narrow statute focused almost entirely on the offer and sale of new issues of securities to the public by a company or a controlling person, the '34 Act has a much broader range. The '34 Act is an amalgamation of provisions touching nearly every aspect of securities trading and the regulation of securities exchanges and securities professionals.

The '34 Act requires that issuers having a class of security traded on a national securities exchange, and those having assets of $3 million or more and a class of equity security held of record by five hundred or more persons, must register the security with the SEC. This registration is to be distinguished from registration under the '33

4 Names and addresses of officers, directors, and promoters

5 Underwriters' names and addresses

6 Owners of securities

7 Amount of securities held or subscribed for

8 Description of issuer's business

9 Issuer's capitalization

10 Options in connection with securities to be offered

11 Amount of stock issued or to be offered

12 Amount and nature of funded debt

13 Use of proceeds from securities

14 Executive salaries

15 Estimated amount of proceeds from securities

16 Offering price to public

17 Underwriters' commissions

18 Offering expenses of issuer

19 Information concerning prior offerings

20 Payments to promoters

21 Information concerning property acquired or to be acquired with proceeds from securities

22 Officers', stockholders', or directors' interests in the property acquired

23 Names and addresses of counsel passing on legality of issue

24 Information concerning material contracts

25 Balance sheets

26 Profit and loss statements

27 Profit and loss statements for acquired business

28 Copies of underwriting contracts

29 Copies of opinions of counsel

30 Copies of contracts

31 Copies of organization papers

32 Copies of underlying securities agreements or indentures

Act, although the registration form calls for much of the same information contained in a '33 Act registration statement.

Companies that have so registered ("reporting companies") are required to file various periodic and other reports with the Commission designed to keep the information in its files reasonably current. The most important of these is the annual report filed on Form 10–K. This is supplemented by a quarterly report (on Form 10–Q) and occasional reports that must be filed upon the occurrence of significant events in a company's business (Form 8–K). These reports are publicly available either from the Commission itself or from one of a large number of libraries and information services that maintain copies, or digest and reproduce the information contained in the reports. They are an important source of information for investment analysts and investors that follow the securities of reporting companies closely. Together with the annual report to shareholders (which is somewhat different from the 10–K report) and the material usually included in management proxy solicitations, these reports put a good deal of information in the hands of shareholders, investors, and investment analysts that contributes, in theory at least, substantially to the efficient functioning of the securities markets and the effective performance of their role as allocators of capital resources.

Additionally, certain kinds of transactions require special disclosure. Thus, the solicitation of proxies may be made only subject to the rules, and specified information must be provided (Section 14(a)). If a bidder seeks to buy a large number of shares in a special transaction, and invites shareholders to "tender" their shares, that "tender offer" is also subject to special rules (Section 14(d)).

The proxy rules, in particular, supplement the periodic reporting requirements. Proxy solicitations occur at regular intervals, on the occasion of annual meetings. The Commission has prescribed rules designed to produce meaningful disclosure to investors as well as to facilitate the conduct of the meeting. Not only must the proxy statement contain pertinent information about directors who are candidates for election, but the company must also send an annual report with detailed financial and other information to its shareholders.

Officers and directors and 10% shareholders of companies that are subject to the reporting requirements must report their stock holdings to the SEC, and any changes in their ownership (Section 16(a)). More than that, if they derive any profit from purchases and sales occurring within six months of each other ("short swing profits") they must surrender those profits on demand to their company (Section 16(b)). The idea behind this seemingly Draconian provision is to prevent so called "insider trading" based on undisclosed information.

The '34 Act creates both civil liabilities that may be privately enforced and various enforcement tools that the SEC may use. Thus, there may be civil recovery if false or misleading information is filed with the Commission (subject to numerous technical limits) (Section

18) or if defined insiders derive short swing profits. Any contractual provisions made in violation of the statute is void as between the parties (Section 29). This provision, and the anti-fraud rules adopted by the SEC, have given rise to implied private rights of action in favor of the persons they were intended to benefit.

After first creating the SEC, and endowing it with power to define improper conduct, prescribe disclosure requirements, and go to court and function quasi-judicially, the '34 Act also regulates the trading markets. The securities exchanges (such as the New York Stock Exchange, the American Stock Exchange and about a dozen others) must register with the SEC and adopt satisfactory rules designed to promote just and equitable principles of trade and to prevent manipulation and fraud. The stock exchanges limit trading on their "floors" to companies whose securities are listed, and each exchange has its own standards for listing securities, based on size of the company, performance and number of shareholders. Some brokerage firms are members of exchanges; it is said they own "seats" on an exchange. The SEC has supervisory power over the exchanges and the administration of their rules.

However, not all trading occurs on stock exchanges; indeed most of it takes place in the "over the counter" market. An organization known as the National Association of Securities Dealers, Inc. ("NASD") functions as a self-regulatory rulemaking body for activity in that arena, and its existence and functions are recognized in the statute. Most stockbrokers belong to the NASD, and find it commercially necessary to maintain their membership in good order. Again, the SEC has supervisory power over this private regulatory body. The Commission also has power to regulate extensions of credit (so-called "margin") in the securities business; it can suspend trading of securities; and it may define manipulation and deception. The most famous rule ever adopted by the SEC is Rule 10b–5, which was adopted in 1942 pursuant to the Commission's power under Section 10(b) to define conduct which constitutes manipulation or deception.

In addition to regulation of the market place, the '34 Act requires brokers and dealers who engage in the interstate commerce of securities (a defined term) to register with the SEC, and comply with rules governing their conduct, or else face suspension or revocation of their licenses. The NASD and the stock exchanges may discipline their members under the statutory scheme of self regulation. There are other self-regulatory groups, dealing with municipal securities and clearing agencies as well, but these are more specialized activities.

B. EXEMPTIONS FROM THE '33 ACT REGISTRATION REQUIREMENTS

PROBLEM

PISCES TACKLE—PART VII

The Pisces Tackle Company has now been in business for five years and has firmly established its reputation as a quality rod manufacturer. Flyer, Leader, and Hooks, its principals, would now like to expand into the production of a line of less expensive rods and also to begin to manufacture a new type of reel that Flyer has developed. To accomplish both of these ends they need to raise about $1,000,000. They could probably manage the first with only $500,000. This latter sum they believe they could raise from a group of about fifteen friends and relatives including four physicians and two dentists, all of whom have previously invested in similar speculative ventures; three trial lawyers; a securities lawyer; Hooks' Aunt Minnie, a wealthy widow with no business experience; three business executives; and a stockbroker.

1. Flyer, Leader, and Hooks are anxious to avoid the expense and delay of registration. They have asked you to review for them the methods they might use to raise either $500,000 or $1,000,000 without registering. What should you tell them? (Consider §§ 3(a) (11), 4(2) and 4(6) and Rules 147 and 501–506.)

2. After discussing the various alternatives, your clients have decided to raise the full $1,000,000. They do not feel that among the three of them they know enough potential investors to raise that entire amount. They have discussed their plans with Sarah Sinker, a young stockbroker, and she has expressed an interest in assisting them. She has been involved in several small public offerings, but has never done a private placement before. At a meeting with the four of them you are asked to respond to the following questions:

a. Can Pisces pay Sinker a commission for her assistance in making the private placement? See Rule 501(h)(4).

b. Assuming that Sinker is retained, can she place an advertisement in the local newspaper describing briefly the nature of the offering and soliciting expressions of interest? Can she place a similar notice in the monthly newsletter her firm sends to its customers? Can she mention the offering in speeches she gives occasionally to private groups? Can she send a letter to investors on a list maintained by her firm of customers the firm knows to be interested in small, speculative offerings of this sort? Can she send a letter to other brokers in the community asking for similar lists they may maintain and circularize investors on those lists? What can be said in any such communications? See Rule 502(c).

c. Is there any limit to the number or qualifications of persons that may be approached about the stock? Are there any limits on the number or qualifications of purchasers? If so, what must Sinker do to ascertain whether particular prospects meet the qualifications? Can all of the prospects on the list prepared by Flyer, Leader and Hooks buy stock? See Rules 505(b)(2) and 506(b)(2).

d. What information must the company furnish prospective purchasers of stock? In what form should it be furnished? See Rule 502(b).

e. Are there any other precautions the company must take to comply with the exemption? See Rules 502(d) and 503.

The '33 Act provides for two types of exemptions: exempt *securities* and exempt *transactions*. The broadest of the exemptions is found in section 4(1), which exempts "[t]ransactions by any person other than the issuer, underwriter, or dealer." In this one simple clause the statute eliminates from its coverage the great bulk of ordinary trading by investors on the securities exchanges or the over-the-counter market after the initial issuance of a security.

The second class of exempt transactions, those "by an issuer not involving any public offering" (Section 4(2)), is also of substantial importance. Without this so-called "private offering exemption" the smallest closely held corporation would risk running afoul of the '33 Act when it first issues stock to its shareholders.* While the issuance of new shares of stock to the two or three shareholders of a closely held corporation, all of whom will participate actively in the business, would clearly fall within the exemption, describing the limits of a private offering when larger numbers of investors not all of whom are directly connected with the business are involved has proved a difficult task for the courts and the SEC. We shall examine below how they have dealt with that task.

In the Small Business Investment Incentive Act of 1980 Congress added a new exemption in Section 4(6), which exempts "transactions involving offers or sales * * * solely to one or more accredited investors" so long as the aggregate offering price does not exceed $5 million. The concept of an "accredited investor" was taken from the American Law Institute's Federal Securities Code, an effort to codify federal securities law in one statute and at the same time to clarify and simplify the law. The term is defined in Section 2(15) of the Act to include certain institutional investors such as banks, insurance companies, and investment companies, as well as other persons who, on the basis of such factors as wealth and financial sophistication, qualify under rules to be promulgated by the SEC.

---

* It is possible that one of the other exemptions, in particular the intrastate offering exemption of Section 3(11), discussed in greater detail below, might also apply.

The remaining classes of exempt transactions are relatively technical and need not concern us here.

Section 3 of the Act defines the types of securities that are exempt from the operation of Section 5. It begins with a lengthy list—including securities of banks, governments, and charitable organizations, as well as certain kinds of commercial paper, insurance contracts, and securities issued in recapitalization or reorganization transactions—that is of little general importance.

Section 3(a)(11) establishes the so-called "intrastate offering exemption," which, like the private offering exemption, may prove useful to the small company seeking to avoid the burdens of registering an offering of new securities. The exemption is available only for an issue *offered and sold* exclusively to "persons resident within" one state.*

The SEC interprets "residence" in the domiciliary sense (See SEC, Securities Act Release No. 4434 (Dec. 6, 1961)), and this creates some uncertainty in efforts to comply with the terms of the exemption. It is quite possible that a potential offeree reasonably believed by the issuer on the basis of objective appearance to have his principal residence in the state, may, in fact, be domiciled elsewhere. (This is often true, for example of persons in the military service.) The risk is more substantial than it might first appear, because the exemption is unavailable for not only that offer but also for the entire issue, thereby opening the seller to liability to every person who has purchased securities sold in the offering.

Until 1974 the lack of a clear definition of certain other key parts of the exemption also gave pause to careful lawyers considering the possibility of using it. The '33 Act requires, for example, that the issuer be "doing business within" the state in which the offer is made, but it gives no indication of how much business is required. There is also often considerable difficulty in determining what is "an issue." When the issuer has sold securities to nonresidents of the state previously, are those sales to be "integrated" into a subsequent offering made entirely within the state? In 1974 the SEC alleviated some of the problems faced by the lawyer trying to comply with the exemption by adopting Rule 147, which provides a set of more or less objective conditions within which an offer can be guaranteed exempt treatment.

In practice the utility of the exemption seems to depend largely on local conditions. It is obviously riskier to attempt such an offering in a metropolitan area that encompasses more than one state. Moreover in some states the failure to register an offering under the '33 Act increases the burden of complying with the local blue sky law (discussed more fully below), with the result that there is little or no

---

* The District of Columbia is not a "state" for the purposes of the exemption. 1 L. Loss, Securities Regulation 602 (2d ed. 1961).

net saving in time and expense. Finally, use of the intrastate offering exemption simply seems to have met with greater acceptance in some areas than in others, with some practitioners still deeming it too risky and others having found they could use it successfully.

The remaining statutory exemption of particular interest to counsel to a small corporation is Section 3(b), which empowers the SEC to exempt, according to such conditions as it sees fit to establish, other issues of up to $5 million.

The exemptions from the Securities Act's registration provisions that are of interest to smaller issuers have over the years been a source of some difficulty. The awkwardness of the statutory structure together with the lack of an adequate definition for a number of crucial terms (such as, for example, "public offering") have combined to provide considerable problems for issuers—and their counsel—wishing to avoid the expense and risk of registration. Beginning in 1974 the SEC and Congress took a number of steps intended to alleviate the burdens imposed by the securities laws on small issuers. Those efforts culminated in 1982 with the promulgation of a new Regulation D, which attempts to coordinate the various exemptions in a coherent scheme. The following excerpts from the release that proposed the new rules describes the background against which they were adopted.

SEC, SECURITIES ACT RELEASE NO. 6389 (Mar. 8, 1982).

I. BACKGROUND

Regulation D is the product of the Commission's evaluation of the impact of its rules and regulations on the ability of small businesses to raise capital. This study has revealed a particular concern that the registration requirements and the exemptive scheme of the Securities Act impose disproportionate restraints on small issuers. In response to this concern, the Commission has taken a number or actions, including a relaxation of certain aspects of Regulation A * [17 C.F.R. §§ 230.251–230.264], the adoption of Rule 242 **, and the introduction of Form S–18 [17 C.F.R. § 239.27], a simplified registration statement for certain first time issuers.

---

* Regulation A, although technically an exemption from the registration requirements, essentially amounts to an abbreviated form of registration in which the issuer prepares and distributes an "offering circular" that is, in effect, a short-form prospectus. The filing is made in the appropriate regional office of the SEC rather than in its Washington, D.C., headquarters. The offering is generally treated somewhat less formally by all concerned than a regular registration, in large part because the civil liability provisions of § 11 do not apply.—Eds.

** Rule 242, which was rescinded at the time of the adoption of Regulation D, provided an exemption for sales of up to $2 million worth of securities to up to 35 ordinary investors plus an unlimited number of "accredited persons." Rule 146 furnished a "safe harbor" definition of "private offering." Another exemption rescinded when Regulation D was adopted was Rule 240, which allowed sales of up to $100,000 worth of securities without registration for companies with 100 shareholders or less.—Eds.

Coincident with the Commission's small business program, Congress enacted the Small Business Investment Incentive Act of 1980 (the "Incentive Act") [94 Stat. 2275 (codified in scattered sections of 15 U.S.C.A.)]. The Incentive Act included three changes to the Securities Act: the addition of an exemption in Section 4(6) for offers and sales solely to accredited investors, the increase in the ceiling of Section 3(b) from $2,000,000 to $5,000,000, and the addition of Section 19 (c) which, among other things, authorized "the development of a uniform exemption from registration for small issuers which can be agreed upon among several States or between the States and the Federal Government."

II. DISCUSSION

A. Overview

Regulation D is a series of six rules, designated Rules 501–506, that establishes three exemptions from the registration requirements of the Securities Act and replaces exemptions that currently exist under Rules 146 *, 240 **, and 242.   *   *   *

Rules 501–503 set forth definitions, terms, and conditions that apply generally throughout the regulation. The exemptions of Regulation D are contained in Rules 504–506.   *   *   *

Rule 504 generally expands Rule 240 by increasing the amount of securities sold in a 12 month period from $100,000 to $500,000, eliminating the ceiling on the number of investors, and removing the prohibition on payment of commissions or similar remuneration. Rule 504 also removes restrictions on the manner of offering and on resale if an offering is conducted exclusively in states where it is registered and where a disclosure document is delivered under the applicable state law. Like Rule 240, Rule 504 does not prescribe specific disclosure requirements. Rule 504 is an effort by the Commission to set aside a clear and workable exemption for small offerings by small issuers to be regulated by state "Blue Sky" requirements and to be subject to federal antifraud provisions and civil liability provisions such as Section 12(2). Therefore, the exemption is not available to issuers that are subject to the reporting obligations of the Securities Exchange Act of 1934 (the "Exchange Act") [15 U.S.C.A. 78a *et seq.*] or are investment companies as defined under the Investment Company Act of 1940 (the "Investment Company Act") [15 U.S.C.A. 80a–1 *et seq.*].

---

* Rule 146 was a "safe harbor" codification of the "private offering exemption" provided by section 4(2) of the Act. It was rescinded when Regulation D was adopted and was replaced by Rule 506.

** Rule 240 was a "small offering" exemption that allowed an issuer to sell up to $100,000 worth of securities without registration. It, too, was rescinded with the adoption of Regulation D and was replaced by Rule 504.

Rule 505 replaces Rule 242. Its offering limit is $5,000,000 in a 12 month period, an increase from the $2,000,000 in six months ceiling in Rule 242. Like its predecessor, Rule 505 permits sales to 35 purchasers that are not accredited investors and to an unlimited number of accredited investors. However, the class of accredited investors has now been expanded. The exemption is available to all non–investment company issuers, and expansion of the restriction in Rule 242 that limited the exemption's availability to certain corporate entities. An issuer under Rule 505 may not use any general solicitation or general advertising. The informational requirements under Rule 505 are substantially similar to those in Rule 242.

Rule 506 takes the place of Rule 146. As under its predecessor, Rule 506 is available to all issuers for offerings sold to not more than 35 purchasers. Accredited investors, however, do not count towards that limit. Rule 506 requires an issuer to make a subjective determination that each purchaser meets certain sophistication standards, a provision that narrows a similar requirement as to all offerees under Rule 146. The new exemption retains the concept of the purchaser representative so that unsophisticated purchasers may participate in the offering if a purchaser representative is present. Like Rule 146, Rule 506 prohibits any general solicitation or general advertising.

B. Uniform Federal-State Limited Offering Exemptions

In conjunction with the proposal and adoption of Regulation D, the Commission * * * has coordinated with the North American Securities Administrators Association ("NASAA").[9] The objective of this process has been to develop a basic framework of limited offering exemptions that can apply uniformly at the federal and state levels. Regulation D is intended to be the principal element of this framework. Under Rule 504, offerings below $500,000 by a non-reporting company will not be required to be registered at the federal level. Moreover, if such offerings are registered in states requiring the delivery of a disclosure document the manner of offering limitations and the restrictions on resale will not apply. Because of the small amount of the offering and the likelihood that sales will occur in a limited geographic area, the Commission and NASAA believe that greater reliance on state securities laws is appropriate. Rules 505 and 506, and applicable definitions, terms and conditions in Rules 501–503, are intended to be uniform federal-state exemptions.

In October 1981, NASAA formally adopted a uniform limited offering exemption as an official policy guideline.[10] * * * The

9. NASAA is a voluntary organization composed of securities regulatory agencies of 49 states, the Commonwealth of Puerto Rico, Guam, as well as Mexico and 13 provinces of Canada.

10. An official policy guideline of NASAA represents endorsement of a principle which NASAA believes has general application. NASAA has no power to enact legislation, promulgate regula-

Commission understands that following its adoption of Regulation D, the NASAA Subcommittee will recommend adoption by NASAA of modifications to its uniform limited offering exemption to provide for a uniform exemptive system. This system will endorse Rule 505, with certain additional terms, and Rule 506.

C. STATE BLUE SKY LAWS

From 1870 to 1930, the public sale of corporate stocks and bonds increased dramatically, and so did the incidence of securities fraud. To counter the predation practiced by peddlers of securities on innocent investors, state legislatures began enacting securities laws. Better known as "blue sky" laws after an early judicial opinion comdemning "speculator schemes which have no more basis than so many feet of 'blue sky,' " these statutes regulate the sales of securities to purchasers within the jurisdiction.

The first such law, enacted in Kansas in 1911, provided for the registration of securities and securities salespeople. A security covered by the Act could not be sold until a state agency issued a permit. The Kansas statute governing the denial of permits provided:

> But, if said bank commissioner finds that such articles of incorporation or association, charter, constitution and by-laws, plan of business or proposed contract, contain any provision that is unfair, unjust, inequitable or oppressive to any class of contributors, or if he decides from his examination of its affairs that said investment company is not solvent and does not intend to do a fair and honest business, and in his judgment does not provide a fair return on the stocks, bonds, or other securities by it offered for sale, then he shall notify such investment company in writing of his findings, and it shall be unlawful for such company to do any further business in this state * * * . (Kan.L. 1911, c. 133, § 5).

State regulation of securities spread rapidly. By 1933 all states, except Nevada, had enacted blue sky laws.

Generally speaking these laws contain some form of one or more of three basic regulatory devices: (1) anti-fraud provisions which made it unlawful to make a false or misleading statement or to omit a material fact in connection with the sale of a security; (2) registration or licensing of certain persons engaged in the securities business prior to their trading in securities within a state; (3) registration or licensing of securities prior to any dealing in the securities, which frequently involves procedures and standards for an affirmative administrative approval of the merits of a particular issue. "Each of the three regulatory devices represents a somewhat different philosophical approach toward the same end of protecting the investing

tions, or otherwise bind the legislatures
or administrative agencies of its members.

public. Antifraud provisions are intended to enable the administrator to issue public warnings, to investigate suspected fraudulent activities, to take injunctive or other steps to stop them, and as a last resort to punish them. Registration of brokers, dealers, agents and investment advisers is intended to prevent fraudulent or unqualified persons from entering the securities business, to supervise their activities within the state once registration has been achieved, and to remove them from registration if they fall below any of the statutory standards. Registration of securities is intended to give the investor 'a run for his money' by excluding from the statute those securities which do not satisfy the statutory standards."* The Securities Act of 1933, Section 18, and the Securities Exchange Act of 1934, Section 28(a), expressly preserve the effect of the state securities laws.

Although there is not space here to discuss them further, the impact of blue sky laws on the selling of securities is often quite important. In a large public offering in which securities will be sold in many states, it is necessary for someone, usually counsel for the underwriters, to "blue sky" the issue, assuring that the requirements of the laws of every state in which it is to be offered have been complied with. As these laws vary considerably from one state to another, this is often a substantial task.

Blue sky laws also render the administration of the exemptions to the registration requirements of the 1933 Act quite complex. Even before the actions taken by Congress and the SEC in the last few years to expand the availability of exemptions under federal law, the exemptions under the various state laws that required registration were not always coordinated with the federal exemptions. Under the impetus of the Small Business Investment Incentive Act, the SEC has actively undertaken to encourage state legislatures and state securities administrators to develop exemptions that better harmonize with the federal system. Regulation D, the product of a cooperative effort between the Commission and the North American Securities Administrators Association, was the principal result.

D. CIVIL LIABILITIES UNDER THE SECURITIES ACT

The thing that the noninitiate observing a securities offering for the first time would find most striking is the care with which the participants approach the process of drafting the registration statement. (It might be noted that this care is reflected in the cost of the process. Although it varies widely from one offering to another, the average cost of the public offerings by relatively small firms during 1975 was $123,000.**) The seriousness with which the underwriters and representatives of the issuer and their lawyers, accountants, and

* L. Loss, Securities Regulation 34 (2d ed. 1961).

** SEC, Report of the Advisory Committee on Corporate Disclosure 27 (1977).

The major components are accounting and legal fees and printing costs. This figure does not include underwriters' commissions.

other experts treat a public offering is due in no small part to the Draconian liability provisions of the '33 Act.

The most significant of these provisions for a registered offering is found in Section 11, which was specifically intended to remove the common law obstacles to an action by a defrauded purchaser of securities such as the requirement that the plaintiff plead and prove privity, scienter, reliance and causation.* Under Section 11 the plaintiff need only show that he or she purchased a security covered by a registration statement (not necessarily from the issuer, an underwriter, or a participating dealer), that there was a material misstatement or omission in the registration statement, and that the plaintiff lost money on the purchase. The plaintiff may sue a variety of persons including:

1. the signers of the registration statement;

2. the directors and those who have been named with their consent as prospective directors;

3. the accountants, engineers, appraisers and other experts named as having prepared or certified some portion of the registration statement; and

4. the underwriters.

(Query: The issuer is not specifically named in Section 11 as one of the persons that might be liable under its provisions. Can you discover why the issuer may nevertheless be sued under Section 11? Are there any other potential defendants?)

Several of the other elements of a common law action for deceit may become issues in such a Section 11 action, but they take the form of defenses as to which the burden of proof is on the defendants. They can, for example, escape liability for all or part of the plaintiff's losses if they can show that the fall in the price of the security was due to causes other than the misleading portions of the registration statement. Section 11(e). With respect to those portions of the statement prepared or certified by experts (in the jargon of the profession the "expertised" portions), such as the financial statements, the other defendants are not liable if they can show that they had no reasonable ground to believe and did not believe that the portion in question was materially false. Section 11(b)(3)(C).

The most important defense, one that permeates the entire process of the preparation of a registration statement, is the so-called "due diligence defense" of Sections 11(b)(3) and 11(c). That defense is explored in the *BarChris* case, excerpts from which are set forth below. In practice it is interpreted as requiring all those who might be liable under Section 11 to review the registration statement and

* For a discussion of the elements of an action for fraud or deceit, *see* Chapter 19, Section B.

conduct a reasonable investigation in order to satisfy themselves of its accuracy.

The other principal liability provisions of the '33 Act are found in Section 12. Its first paragraph furnishes the principal "teeth" against violations of the registration requirements of Section 5. In effect it allows anyone who has purchased an illegally unregistered security from the issuer or an underwriter to rescind the transaction at any time within one year after the sale. This is true regardless of whether the buyer knew that the security was being sold in violation of Section 5. The operation of Section 12(1) is illustrated by Henderson v. Hayden, Stone, Inc., 461 F.2d 1069 (5th Cir. 1972) in which the court allowed the plaintiff, whom it said "can only be described as a sophisticated investor," to rescind a purchase of $180,000 worth of stock of a total offering of $300,000 for which the seller believed (wrongly as it turned out) that an exemption from the registration requirement was available.

Section 12(2), like Section 11, provides a basis of liability for false or misleading statements made in connection with the sale of a security through the use of the mails or the facilities of interstate commerce. It is broader than Section 11 in some respects, particularly in that it does not require that the security in question be registered or that the misstatement or omission have appeared in a registration statement. It applies to any communication, including oral communication. Like Section 12(1), the plaintiff may, in the first instance, sue only persons with whom he was in privity, although the liability of "controlling persons" under Section 15 and theories according to which liability may be imposed on those who have "aided and abetted" the principal violator may expand the available targets.

At the time the '33 Act was passed its liability provisions were considered by many participants in the securities industry to be so onerous that fear was expressed in many quarters that the financing of new ventures would cease altogether and "grass would grow in Wall Street." That has not, of course, proved to be the case. But securities professionals and their lawyers have continued to treat Section 11 with a great deal of respect. So great, indeed, that the first lawsuit brought under Section 11 to run its full course to a district court decision was not decided until 1968. The case, Escott v. BarChris Construction Corp., sent tremors throughout the financial community—not so much because of its strict application of the provisions of Section 11, which, after all was not more rigorous than the interpretation given to the section by most observers all along, but because the opinion was the first authoritative holding that Section 11 did indeed mean what it seemed to say. The case shocked issuers, directors, investment bankers, accountants, and their counsel into awareness that perhaps their practices had become a little sloppy during the "Go-Go Years" of the sixties and stimulated a searching reexamination of those practices by those involved.

ESCOTT v. BARCHRIS CONSTRUCTION CORP.

283 F.Supp. 643 (S.D.N.Y.1968).

McLEAN, District Judge.

This is an action by purchasers of 5 1/2 per cent convertible sub-ordinated fifteen year debentures of BarChris Construction Corporation (BarChris). Plaintiffs purport to sue on their own behalf and "on behalf of all other and present and former holders" of the debentures. When the action was begun on October 25, 1962, there were nine plaintiffs. Others were subsequently permitted to intervene. At the time of the trial, there were over sixty.

The action is brought under Section 11 of the Securities Act of 1933 (15 U.S.C.A. § 77k). Plaintiffs allege that the registration statement with respect to these debentures filed with the Securities and Exchange Commission, which became effective on May 16, 1961, contained material false statements and material omissions.

Defendants fall into three categories: (1) the persons who signed the registration statement; (2) the underwriters, consisting of eight investment banking firms, led by Drexel & Co. (Drexel); and (3) Bar-Chris's auditors, Peat, Marwick, Mitchell & Co. (Peat, Marwick).

The signers, in addition to BarChris itself, were the nine directors of BarChris, plus its controller, defendant Trilling, who was not a director. Of the nine directors, five were officers of BarChris, i.e., defendants Vitolo, president; Russo, executive vice president; Pugliese, vice president; Kircher, treasurer; and Birnbaum, secretary. Of the remaining four, defendant Grant was a member of the firm of Perkins, Daniels, McCormack & Collins, BarChris's attorneys. He became a director in October 1960. Defendant Coleman, a partner in Drexel, became a director on April 17, 1961, as did the other two, Auslander and Rose, who were not otherwise connected with Bar-Chris.

[The BarChris Construction Corp. was in the business of building bowling alleys. It had begun in 1946 as a partnership organized by Vitolo and Pugliese, which was incorporated in 1955. The advent of automatic pin setting machines in 1952 provided a powerful stimulus to the industry, from which BarChris benefitted handsomely. In 1960 it built some three percent of all of the bowling lanes constructed in the United States. Between 1956 and 1960 the company's sales leaped from $800,000 to over $9 million.]

*   *   *

In general, BarChris's method of operation was to enter into a contract with a customer, receive from him at that time a comparatively small down payment on the purchase price, and proceed to construct and equip the bowling alley. When the work was finished and the building delivered, the customer paid the balance of the contract price in notes, payable in installments over a period of years. Bar-

Chris discounted these notes with a factor and received part of their face amount in cash. The factor held back part as a reserve.

In 1960 BarChris began a practice which has been referred to throughout this case as the "alternative method of financing." In substance this was a sale and leaseback arrangement. * * * In instances in which this method applied, BarChris would build and install what it referred to as the "interior package." * * * When it was completed, it would sell the interior to a factor, James Talcott Inc. (Talcott), who would pay BarChris the full contract price therefor. The factor then proceeded to lease the interior either directly to BarChris's customer or back to a subsidiary of BarChris. In the latter case, the subsidiary in turn would lease it to the customer.

Under either financing method, BarChris was compelled to expend considerable sums in defraying the cost of construction before it received reimbursement. As a consequence, BarChris was in constant need of cash to finance its operations, a need which grew more pressing as operations expanded.

In December 1959, BarChris sold 560,000 shares of common stock to the public at $3.00 per share. * * *

By early 1961, BarChris needed additional working capital. The proceeds of the sale of the debentures involved in this action were to be devoted, in part at least, to fill that need.

The registration statement of the debentures, in preliminary form, was filed with the Securities and Exchange Commission on March 30, 1961. A first amendment was filed on May 11 and a second on May 16. The registration statement became effective on May 16. The closing of the financing took place on May 24. On that day BarChris received the net proceeds of the financing.

By that time BarChris was experiencing difficulties in collecting amounts due from some of its customers. Some of them were in arrears in payments due to factors on their discounted notes. As time went on those difficulties increased. Although BarChris continued to build alleys in 1961 and 1962, it became increasingly apparent that the industry was overbuilt. Operators of alleys, often inadequately financed, began to fail. Precisely when the tide turned is a matter of dispute, but at any rate, it was painfully apparent in 1962.

In May of that year BarChris made an abortive attempt to raise more money by the sale of common stock. It filed with the Securities and Exchange Commission a registration statement for the stock issue which it later withdrew. In October 1962 BarChris came to the end of the road. On October 29, 1962, it filed in this court a petition for an arrangement under Chapter XI of the Bankruptcy Act. BarChris defaulted in the payment of the interest due on November 1, 1962 on the debentures.

[The court here launches on a twenty-five page exposition of the facts. It finds that the prospectus contained a number of errors:

1. The earnings for 1960 were overstated as a result of inaccurate estimates of the percentage completion of some alleys under construction and treating as income certain amounts that should not have been so treated.

2. Because of the accounting treatment of several items of current assets, net current assets were overstated by a relatively small amount.

3. Under the "alternative method of financing" described by the court above, BarChris remained liable as guarantor of 100 percent of its subsidiary's obligations on leases of the bowling alleys that BarChris had constructed. The prospectus falsely stated that the contingent liabilities as of Dec. 31, 1960, to which the company was subject as a consequence amounted to only 25 percent of the unexpired lease payments.

4. For similar reasons, the contingent liabilities as of April 30, 1961 were also understated.

5. BarChris had acquired all of the stock of two customers with which it had contracts to build alleys. Payments on those contracts by the customers were improperly included in BarChris's income for the three months ended March 31, 1961 even though the payments were merely transfers from one segment of the company to another.

6. The prospectus gave a figure for a backlog of unfilled orders as of March 31, 1961 that was substantially overstated.

7. The statements in the prospectus regarding advances made by certain officers to the company were misleading and substantially understated the amount of those loans outstanding as of the date of the prospectus.

8. The "Use of Proceeds" section of the prospectus indicated that a substantial portion of the proceeds of the offering would be used for working capital. In fact, at the time of the offering the company's cash resources were already severely strained, and it used over $1 million of the proceeds to pay off outstanding obligations.

9. The prospectus stated that, "Since 1955, the Company has been required to repurchase less than $\frac{1}{2}$ of 1% of [the promissory notes discounted to factors and guaranteed by BarChris]." The truth was that by May, 1961 several of its customers were seriously delinquent in the payment of their notes, the situation was getting rapidly worse, and the factor had indicated that it might require BarChris to repurchase over $1,350,000 worth of notes.]

* * *

Summary

For convenience, the various falsities and omissions which I have discussed in the preceding pages are recapitulated here. They were as follows:

1. 1960 Earnings
   (a) Sales

As per prospectus	$9,165,320
Correct figure	8,511,420
Overstatement	$ 653,900

   (b) Net Operating Income

As per prospectus	$1,742,801
Correct figure	1,496,196
Overstatement	$ 246,605

   (c) Earnings per Share

As per prospectus	$ .75
Correct figure	.65
Overstatement	$ .10

2. 1960 Balance Sheet
   Current Assets

As per prospectus	$4,524,021
Correct figure	3,914,332
Overstatement	$ 609,689

3. Contingent Liabilities as of December 31, 1960 on Alternative Method of Financing

As per prospectus	$ 750,000
Correct figure	1,125,795
Understatement	$ 375,795
Capitol Lanes should have been shown as a direct liability	$ 325,000

4. Contingent Liabilities as of April 30, 1961

As per prospectus	$ 825,000
Correct figure	1,443,853
Understatement	$ 618,853
Capitol Lanes should have been shown as a direct liability	$ 314,166

5. Earnings Figures for Quarter ending March 31, 1961
   (a) Sales

As per prospectus	$2,138,455
Correct figure	1,618,645
Overstatement	$ 519,810

(b) <u>Gross Profit</u>

As per prospectus	$ 483,121
Correct figure	252,366
Overstatement	$ 230,755

6. <u>Backlog as of March 31, 1961</u>

As per prospectus	$6,905,000
Correct figure	2,415,000
Overstatement	$4,490,000

7. Failure to Disclose Officers' Loans Outstanding and Unpaid on May 16, 1961 $ 386,615

8. Failure to Disclose Use of Proceeds in Manner not Revealed in Prospectus

    Approximately $1,160,000

9. Failure to Disclose Customers' Delinquencies in May 1961 and BarChris's Potential Liability with Respect Thereto

      Over $1,350,000

10. Failure to Disclose the Fact that BarChris was Already Engaged, and was about to be More Heavily Engaged, in the Operation of Bowling Alleys

Materiality

It is a prerequisite to liability under Section 11 of the Act that the fact which is falsely stated in a registration statement, or the fact that is omitted when it should have been stated to avoid misleading, be "material." The regulations of the Securities and Exchange Commission pertaining to the registration of securities define the word as follows (17 C.F.R. § 230.405 (*l*)):

The term "material", when used to qualify a requirement for the furnishing of information as to any subject, limits the information required to those matters as to which an average prudent investor ought reasonably to be informed before purchasing the security registered.

What are "matters as to which an average prudent investor ought reasonably to be informed"? It seems obvious that they are matters which such an investor needs to know before he can make an intelligent, informed decision whether or not to buy the security.

Early in the history of the Act, a definition of materiality was given in Matter of Charles A. Howard, 1 S.E.C. 6, 8 (1934), which is still valid today. A material fact was there defined as:

> * * * a fact which if it had been correctly stated or disclosed would have deterred or tended to deter the average prudent investor from purchasing the securities in question.

The average prudent investor is not concerned with minor inaccuracies or with errors as to matters which are of no interest to him. The facts which tend to deter him from purchasing a security are facts which have an important bearing upon the nature or condition of the issuing corporation or its business.

Judged by this test, there is no doubt that many of the misstatements and omissions in this prospectus were material. * * *

* * *

The "Due Diligence" Defenses

[The court here quotes the provisions of Section 11 that set forth the defenses of due diligence and reliance on experts.]

Every defendant, except BarChris itself, to whom, as the issuer, these defenses are not available, and except Peat, Marwick, whose position rests on a different statutory provision, has pleaded these affirmative defenses. Each claims that (1) as to the part of the registration statement purporting to be made on the authority of an expert (which, for convenience, I shall refer to as the "expertised portion"), he had no reasonable ground to believe and did not believe that there were any untrue statements or material omissions, and (2) as to the other parts of the registration statement, he made a reasonable investigation, as a result of which he had reasonable ground to believe and did believe that the registration statement was true and that no material fact was omitted. * * *

Before considering the evidence, a preliminary matter should be disposed of. The defendants do not agree among themselves as to who the "experts" were or as to the parts of the registration statement which were expertised. Some defendants say that Peat, Marwick was the expert, others say that BarChris's attorneys, Perkins, Daniels, McCormack & Collins, and the underwriters' attorneys, Drinker, Biddle & Reath, were also the experts. On the first view, only those portions of the registration statement purporting to be made on Peat, Marwick's authority were expertised portions. On the other view, everything in the registration statement was within this category, because the two law firms were responsible for the entire document.

The first view is the correct one. To say that the entire registration statement is expertised because some lawyer prepared it would be an unreasonable construction of the statute. Neither the lawyer for the company nor the lawyer for the underwriters is an expert within the meaning of Section 11. The only expert, in the statutory sense, was Peat, Marwick, and the only parts of the registration statement which purported to be made upon the authority of an expert were the portions which purported to be made on Peat, Marwick's authority.

The parties also disagree as to what those portions were. Some defendants say that it was only the 1960 figures (and the figures for prior years, which are not in controversy here). Others say in substance that it was every figure in the prospectus. The plaintiffs take a somewhat intermediate view. They do not claim that Peat, Marwick expertised every figure, but they do maintain that Peat, Marwick is responsible for a portion of the text of the prospectus, i.e., that pertaining to "Methods of Operation," because a reference to it was made in footnote 9 to the balance sheet.

Here again, the more narrow view is the correct one. The registration statement contains a report of Peat, Marwick as independent public accountants dated February 23, 1961. This relates only to the consolidated balance sheet of BarChris and consolidated subsidiaries as of December 31, 1960, and the related statement of earnings and retained earnings for the five years then ended. This is all that Peat, Marwick purported to certify. It is perfectly clear that it did not purport to certify the 1961 figures, some of which are expressly stated in the prospectus to have been unaudited.

Moreover, plaintiffs' intermediate view is also incorrect. The cross reference in footnote 9 to the "Methods of Operation" passage in the prospectus was inserted merely for the convenience of the reader. It is not a fair construction to say that it thereby imported into the balance sheet everything in that portion of the text, much of which had nothing to do with the figures in the balance sheet.

I turn now to the question of whether defendants have proved their due diligence defenses. The position of each defendant will be separately considered.

   * * *

[Only representative portions of the court's discussion are included.]

Kircher

Kircher was treasurer of BarChris and its chief financial officer. He is a certified public accountant and an intelligent man. He was thoroughly familiar with BarChris's financial affairs. He knew the terms of BarChris's agreements with Talcott. He knew of the customers' delinquency problem. He participated actively with Russo in May 1961 in the successful effort to hold Talcott off until the financing proceeds came in. He knew how the financing proceeds were to be applied and he saw to it that they were so applied. He arranged the officers' loans and he knew all the facts concerning them.

Moreover, as a member of the executive committee, Kircher was kept informed as to those branches of the business of which he did not have direct charge. He knew about the operation of alleys, present and prospective. * * * In brief, Kircher knew all the relevant facts.

Kircher worked on the preparation of the registration statement. He conferred with Grant and on occasion with Ballard. He supplied information to them about the company's business. He read the prospectus and understood it. He knew what it said and what it did not say.

Kircher's contention is that he had never before dealt with a registration statement, that he did not know what it should contain, and that he relied wholly on Grant, Ballard and Peat, Marwick to guide him. He claims that it was their fault, not his, if there was anything wrong with it. He says that all the facts were recorded in BarChris's books where these "experts" could have seen them if they had looked. He says that he truthfully answered all their questions. In effect, he says that if they did not know enough to ask the right questions and to give him the proper instructions, that is not his responsibility.

There is an issue of credibility here. In fact, Kircher was not frank in dealing with Grant and Ballard. He withheld information from them. But even if he had told them all the facts, this would not have constituted the due diligence contemplated by the statute. Knowing the facts, Kircher had reason to believe that the expertised portion of the prospectus, i. e., the 1960 figures, was in part incorrect. He could not shut his eyes to the facts and rely on Peat, Marwick for that portion.

As to the rest of the prospectus, knowing the facts, he did not have a reasonable ground to believe it to be true. On the contrary, he must have known that in part it was untrue. Under these circumstances, he was not entitled to sit back and place the blame on the lawyers for not advising him about it.

Kircher has not proved his due diligence defenses.

* * *

Auslander

Auslander was an "outside" director, i.e., one who was not an officer of BarChris. He was chairman of the board of Valley Stream National Bank in Valley Stream, Long Island. In February 1961 Vitolo asked him to become a director of BarChris. Vitolo gave him an enthusiastic account of BarChris's progress and prospects. As an inducement, Vitolo said that when BarChris received the proceeds of a forthcoming issue of securities, it would deposit $1,000,000 in Auslander's bank.

In February and early March 1961, before accepting Vitolo's invitation, Auslander made some investigation of BarChris. He obtained Dun & Bradstreet reports which contained sales and earnings figures for periods earlier than December 31, 1960. He caused inquiry to be made of certain of BarChris's banks and was advised that they regarded BarChris favorably. He was informed that inquiry of Talcott had also produced a favorable response.

On March 3, 1961, Auslander indicated his willingness to accept a place on the board. Shortly thereafter, on March 14, Kircher sent him a copy of BarChris's annual report for 1960. Auslander observed that BarChris's auditors were Peat, Marwick. They were also the auditors for the Valley Stream National Bank. He thought well of them.

Auslander was elected a director on April 17, 1961. The registration statement in its original form had already been filed, of course, without his signature. On May 10, 1961, he signed a signature page for the first amendment to the registration statement which was filed on May 11, 1961. This was a separate sheet without any document attached. Auslander did not know that it was a signature page for a registration statement. He vaguely understood that it was something "for the SEC."

Auslander attended a meeting of BarChris's directors on May 15, 1961. At that meeting he, along with the other directors, signed the signature sheet for the second amendment which constituted the registration statement in its final form. Again, this was only a separate sheet without any document attached. Auslander never saw a copy of the registration statement in its final form.

At the May 15 directors' meeting, however, Auslander did realize that what he was signing was a signature sheet to a registration statement. This was the first time that he had appreciated that fact. A copy of the registration statement in its earlier form as amended on May 11, 1961 was passed around at the meeting. Auslander glanced at it briefly. He did not read it thoroughly.

At the May 15 meeting, Russo and Vitolo stated that everything was in order and that the prospectus was correct. Auslander believed this statement.

In considering Auslander's due diligence defenses, a distinction is to be drawn between the expertised and non-expertised portions of the prospectus. As to the former, Auslander knew that Peat, Marwick had audited the 1960 figures. He believed them to be correct because he had confidence in Peat, Marwick. He had no reasonable ground to believe otherwise.

As to the non-expertised portions, however, Auslander is in a different position. He seems to have been under the impression that Peat, Marwick was responsible for all the figures. This impression was not correct, as he would have realized if he had read the prospectus carefully. Auslander made no investigation of the accuracy of the prospectus. He relied on the assurance of Vitolo and Russo, and upon the information he had received in answer to his inquiries back in February and early March. These inquiries were general ones, in the nature of a credit check. The information which he received in answer to them was also general, without specific reference to the statements in the prospectus, which was not prepared until some time thereafter.

It is true that Auslander became a director on the eve of the financing. He had little opportunity to familiarize himself with the company's affairs. The question is whether, under such circumstances, Auslander did enough to establish his due diligence defense with respect to the non-expertised portions of the prospectus.

Although there is a dearth of authority under Section 11 on this point, an English case under the analogous Companies Act is of some value. In Adams v. Thrift, [1915] 1 Ch. 557, aff'd, [1915] 2 Ch. 21, it was held that a director who knew nothing about the prospectus and did not even read it, but who relied on the statement of the company's managing director that it was "all right," was liable for its untrue statements.

Section 11 imposes liability in the first instance upon a director, no matter how new he is. He is presumed to know his responsibility when he becomes a director. He can escape liability only by using that reasonable care to investigate the facts which a prudent man would employ in the management of his own property. In my opinion, a prudent man would not act in an important matter without any knowledge of the relevant facts, in sole reliance upon representations of persons who are comparative strangers and upon general information which does not purport to cover the particular case. To say that such minimal conduct measures up to the statutory standard would, to all intents and purposes, absolve new directors from responsibility merely because they are new. This is not a sensible construction of Section 11, when one bears in mind its fundamental purpose of requiring full and truthful disclosure for the protection of investors.

I find and conclude that Auslander has not established his due diligence defense with respect to the misstatements and omissions in those portions of the prospectus other than the audited 1960 figures.

* * *

Grant

Grant became a director of BarChris in October 1960. His law firm was counsel to BarChris in matters pertaining to the registration of securities. Grant drafted the registration statement for the stock issue in 1959 and for the warrants in January 1961. He also drafted the registration statement for the debentures. In the preliminary division of work between him and Ballard, the underwriters' counsel,

Grant took initial responsibility for preparing the registration statement, while Ballard devoted his efforts in the first instance to preparing the indenture.

Grant is sued as a director and as a signer of the registration statement. This is not an action against him for malpractice in his capacity as a lawyer. Nevertheless, in considering Grant's due diligence defenses, the unique position which he occupied cannot be disregarded. As the director most directly concerned with writing the registration statement and assuring its accuracy, more was required of him in the way of reasonable investigation than could fairly be expected of a director who had no connection with this work.

There is no valid basis for plaintiffs' accusation that Grant knew that the prospectus was false in some respects and incomplete and misleading in others. Having seen him testify at length, I am satisfied as to his integrity. I find that Grant honestly believed that the registration statement was true and that no material facts had been omitted from it.

In this belief he was mistaken, and the fact is that for all his work, he never discovered any of the errors or omissions which have been recounted at length in this opinion, with the single exception of Capitol Lanes. He knew that BarChris had not sold this alley and intended to operate it, but he appears to have been under the erroneous impression that Peat, Marwick had knowingly sanctioned its inclusion in sales because of the allegedly temporary nature of the operation.

Grant contends that a finding that he did not make a reasonable investigation would be equivalent to a holding that a lawyer for an issuing company, in order to show due diligence, must make an independent audit of the figures supplied to him by his client. I do not consider this to be a realistic statement of the issue. There were errors and omissions here which could have been detected without an audit. The question is whether, despite his failure to detect them, Grant made a reasonable effort to that end.

Much of this registration statement is a scissors and paste-pot job. Grant lifted large portions from the earlier prospectuses, modifying them in some instances to the extent that he considered necessary. But BarChris's affairs had changed for the worse by May 1961. Statements that were accurate in January were no longer accurate in May. Grant never discovered this. He accepted the assurances of Kircher and Russo that any change which might have occurred had been for the better, rather than the contrary.

It is claimed that a lawyer is entitled to rely on the statements of his client and that to require him to verify their accuracy would set an unreasonably high standard. This is too broad a generalization. It is all a matter of degree. To require an audit would obviously be unreasonable. On the other hand, to require a check of matters easily verifiable is not unreasonable. Even honest clients can make mistakes. The statute imposes liability for untrue statements regardless of whether they are intentionally untrue. The way to prevent mistakes is to test oral information by examining the original written record.

There were things which Grant could readily have checked which he did not check. For example, he was unaware of the provisions of the agreements between BarChris and Talcott. He never read them. Thus, he did not know, although he readily could have ascertained, that BarChris's contingent liability on Type B leaseback arrangements was 100 per cent, not 25 per cent. He did not appreciate that if BarChris defaulted in repurchasing delinquent customers' notes upon Talcott's demand, Talcott could accelerate all the customer paper in its hands, which amounted to over $3,000,000.

As to the backlog figure, Grant appreciated that scheduled unfilled orders on the company's books meant firm commitments, but he never asked to see the contracts which, according to the prospectus, added up to $6,905,000. Thus, he did not know that this figure was overstated by some $4,490,000.

Grant was unaware of the fact that BarChris was about to operate Bridge and Yonkers. He did not read the minutes of those subsidiaries which would have revealed that fact to him. On the subject of minutes, Grant knew that minutes of certain meetings of the BarChris executive committee held in 1961 had not been written up. Kircher, who had acted as secretary at those meetings, had complete notes of them. Kircher told Grant that there was no point in writing up the minutes because the matters discussed at those meetings were purely routine. Grant did not insist that the minutes be written up, nor did he look at Kircher's notes. If he had, he would have learned that on February 27, 1961 there was an extended discussion in the executive committee meeting about customers' delinquencies, that on March 8, 1961 the committee had discussed the pros and cons of alley operation by BarChris, that on March 18, 1961 the committee was informed that BarChris was constructing or about to begin constructing twelve alleys for which it had no contracts, and that on May 13, 1961 Dreyfuss, one of the worst delinquents, had filed a petition in Chapter X.

Grant knew that there had been loans from officers to BarChris in the past because that subject had been mentioned in the 1959 and January 1961 prospectuses. In March Grant prepared a questionnaire to be answered by officers and directors for the purpose of obtaining information to be used in the prospectus. The questionnaire did not inquire expressly about the existence of officers' loans. At approximately the same time, Grant prepared another questionnaire in order to obtain information on proxy statements for the annual stockholders' meeting. This questionnaire asked each officer to state whether he was indebted to BarChris, but it did not ask whether Bar-Chris was indebted to him.

* * *

The application of proceeds language in the prospectus was drafted by Kircher back in January. It may well have expressed his intent at that time, but his intent, and that of the other principal officers of BarChris, was very different in May. Grant did not appreciate that the earlier language was no longer appropriate. He never learned of the situation which the company faced in May. He knew that Bar-Chris was short of cash, but he had no idea how short. He did not know that BarChris was withholding delivery of checks already drawn and signed because there was not enough money in the bank to pay them. He did not know that the officers of the company intended to use immediately approximately one-third of the financing proceeds in a manner not disclosed in the prospectus, including approximately $1,000,000 in paying old debts.

* * *

As far as customers' delinquencies is concerned, although Grant discussed this with Kircher, he again accepted the assurances of Kircher and Russo that no serious problem existed. He did not examine the records as to delinquencies, although BarChris maintained such a record. Any inquiry on his part of Talcott or an examination of BarChris's correspondence with Talcott in April and May 1961 would have apprised him of the true facts. It would have led him to appreciate that the statement in this prospectus, carried over from earlier prospectuses, to the effect that since 1955 BarChris had been required to repurchase less than one-half of one per cent of discounted customers' notes could no longer properly be made without further explanation.

Grant was entitled to rely on Peat, Marwick for the 1960 figures. He had no reasonable ground to believe them to be inaccurate. But the matters which I have mentioned were not within the expertised portion of the prospectus. As to this, Grant was obliged to make a reasonable investigation. I am forced to find that he did not make one. After making all due allowances for the fact that BarChris's officers misled him, there are too many instances in which Grant failed to make an inquiry which he could easily have made which, if pursued, would have put him on his guard. In my opinion, this finding on the evidence in this case does not establish an unreasonably high standard in other cases for company counsel who are also directors. Each case must rest on its own facts. I conclude that Grant has not established his due diligence defenses except as to the audited 1960 figures.

* * *

NOTE—"MATERIALITY"

"Materiality" is a concept that is central to the securities laws. The term was originally drawn from the common law of fraud, which gives the plaintiff a cause of action only if the defendant has made a "material" misstatement. It appears throughout the securities statutes, both in the context of required disclosure and in the provision of rights of action to investors who have been misled by material misstatements or omissions. Nowhere in the statutes, however, is there a definition of the word "material." The Securities and Exchange Commission has sought to define it when used to qualify a requirement for disclosure under the '33 Act by saying that it "limits the information required to those matters as to which an average prudent investor ought reasonably to be informed before purchasing the security registered." Rule 405. The federal courts wrestled with the definition of materiality for years. One of the leading early attempts was given in List v. Fashion Park, Inc., 340 F.2d 457, 462 (2d Cir. 1965), cert. den. 382 U.S. 811, 86 S.Ct. 23, 15 L.Ed.2d 60, reh. denied 382 U.S. 933, 86 S.Ct. 305, 15 L.Ed.2d 344, in which the Second Circuit insisted on an *objective* test: "The basic test of 'materiality' * * * is whether 'a reasonable man would attach importance [to the fact misrepresented] in determining his choice of action in the transaction in question.'" (Citing Restatement, Torts § 546 (1938).)

In SEC v. Texas Gulf Sulphur Co., 401 F.2d 833 (2d Cir. 1968) cert. denied, 394 U.S. 976, 89 S.Ct. 1454, 22 L.Ed.2d 756, the same court created a problem that would plague judges and commentators for years. Quoting *List*, which had in turn quoted an earlier opinion, the court emphasized that a material fact is one " 'which in reasonable and objective contemplation *might* affect the value of the corporation's stocks or securities * * *.' List v. Fashion Park, Inc., supra at 462, quoting from Kohler v. Kohler Co., 319 F.2d 634, 642 (7th Cir. 1963). (Emphasis supplied.)" Thus was born a dispute over whether a fact was material only if a reasonable man "would" consider it important or whether it is enough that this hypothetical individual "might" consider it important. The Supreme Court exacerbated the problem in Mills v. Electric Auto-Lite Co., 396 U.S. 375, 384, 90 S. Ct. 616, 621, 24 L.Ed.2d 593, 602 (1970), in which it was claimed that shareholders had been misled in the exercise of their voting rights. The Court said that the alleged misstatement was material if "it might have been considered important by a reasonable shareholder," but went on to elaborate by indicating that this meant that such a misstatement must "have a significant *propensity* to affect the voting process * * *."

When the Court finally focussed on the "would-might" controversy, however, it decided not to choose at all but to lay down a somewhat different standard. In TSC Indus., Inc. v. Northway, 426 U.S. 438, 449, 96 S.Ct. 2126, 2132, 48 L.Ed.2d 757, 766 (1976), the Court, in what appears to be the last word on the matter, ruled that, "An omitted fact is material if there is a substantial likelihood that a reasonable shareholder would consider it important on deciding how to vote." Although *Northway* also involved shareholder voting rather than a decision to buy or sell a security, its standard presumably applies in the latter context as well.

Developing a (more or less) resolved verbal formulation of the standard of materiality, however, is only half the battle—if indeed it is that. For, as reading the opinion in *Escott* should bring home, it is still necessary to apply the standard to a particular set of facts. As with any other standard that calls on a court or jury to determine what some hypothetical and presumably objective reasonable person would or would not do, that is often a difficult task.

See also Chapter 13, Section B (Note: Materiality and Causation), *infra*.

E.   WHAT IS A "SECURITY"?

Until this point we have ignored a central question in the application of the securities laws: To what sort of financial instrument do the various requirements and prohibitions they embody apply? The definition of "security" in Section 2(1) of the '33 Act, as broad as it is, is only a starting point. The courts and the SEC have held the word to encompass not only the engraved piece of paper denominated "stock" or "bond" or "certificate" that the term would first bring to the mind of the ordinary person, but also to include such rather surprising "securities" as whiskey warehouse receipts (SEC Securities Act Release No. 33–5018 (Nov. 4, 1969)), "pyramid" sales schemes (SEC v. Glenn W. Turner Enterprises, Inc., 474 F.2d 476 (9th Cir. 1973)), condominium units (SEC Securities Act Release No. 5347 (Jan. 4, 1973)), chinchillas (Miller v. Central Chinchilla Group, Inc., 494 F.2d 414 (8th Cir. 1974) on remand 66 F.R.D. 411), beavers (Continental Marketing Corp. v. SEC, 387 F.2d 466 (10th Cir. 1967) cert. denied 391 U.S. 905, 88 S.Ct. 1655, 20 L.Ed.2d 419) and brood mares (Kentucky Blood Horses, [1973 Transfer Binder] Fed.Sec.L.Rep. (CCH) ¶ 79, 430). In fact the leading Supreme Court decision on the definition of "security" involved the sale of interests in an orange grove in Florida. In SEC v. W. J. Howey Co., 328 U.S. 293, 66 S.Ct. 1100, 90 L.Ed. 1244 (1946), reh. denied, 329 U.S. 819, 67 S.Ct. 27, 91 L.Ed. 697, the Court laid down the following general guidelines:

[A]n investment contract for purposes of the Securities Act means a contract, transaction, or scheme, whereby a person invests his money in a common enterprise and is led to expect profits solely from the efforts of the promoter or a third party, it being immaterial whether the shares in the enterprise are evidenced by formal certificates or by nominal interests in the physical assets employed in the enterprise.

*   *   *

The test is whether the scheme involves an investment of money in a common enterprise with profits to come solely from the efforts of others. If that test be satisfied, it is immaterial whether the enterprise is speculative or non-speculative or whether there is a sale of property with or without intrinsic value. * * * The statutory policy of affording broad protection to investors is not to be thwarted by unrealistic and irrelevant formulae.

The Court's repeated use of the phrase "solely from the efforts of" persons other than the investor has given the lower courts some difficulty in later cases. The current trend seems to be not to take the word "solely" too literally. In SEC v. Glenn W. Turner Enterprises, Inc., 474 F.2d 476 (9th Cir. 1973) the Ninth Circuit held that a "pyramid" scheme whereby investors purchased self-improvement plans and received the right to sell plans to others, involved the sale of a security for the purposes of the '33 Act. The court rejected the argument that there was no security because the investor was required to conduct some of the effort himself. "Rather," the court said, "we adopt a more realistic test, whether the efforts made by those other than the investor are the undeniably significant ones, those essential managerial efforts which affect the failure or success of the enterprise." 474 F.2d at 482. See also SEC v. Koscot Interplanetary, Inc., 497 F.2d 473 (5th Cir. 1974), another case involving a scheme developed by the flamboyant Mr. Turner which was also held to involve the sale of a security.

The limits as to how far the definition of "security" can be pushed were clarified substantially by two Supreme Court decisions. In United Housing Foundation, Inc. v. Forman, 421 U.S. 837, 95 S.Ct. 2051, 44 L.Ed.2d 621 (1975), reh. denied 423 U.S. 884, 96 S.Ct. 157, 46 L.Ed.2d 115, the Court held that shares of "stock" entitling a purchaser to lease an apartment in a state–subsidized and supervised non-profit housing cooperative were not securities. Although the shares were called stock, the name was not dispositive. The Court stated:

> In the present case respondents do not contend, nor could they, that they were misled by use of the word "stock" into believing that the federal securities laws governed their purchase. Common sense suggests that people who intend to acquire only a residential apartment in a state-subsidized cooperative, for their personal use, are not likely to believe that in reality they are purchasing investment securities simply because the transaction is evidenced by something called a share of stock. These shares have none of the characteristics "that in our commercial world fall within the ordinary concept of a security." Despite their name, they lack * * * the most common feature of stock: the right

to receive "dividends contingent upon an apportionment of profits." Nor do they possess the other characteristics traditionally associated with stock: they are not negotiable; they cannot be pledged or hypothecated; they confer no voting rights in proportion to the number of shares owned; and they cannot appreciate in value. In short, the inducement to purchase was solely to acquire subsidized low-cost living space; it was not to invest for profit.

Nor, the Court held, did the shares constitute an "investment contract." The Court concluded that the purchasers "were attracted solely by the prospect of acquiring a place to live, and not by financial returns on their investments."

In International Brotherhood of Teamsters v. Daniel, 439 U.S. 551, 99 S.Ct. 790, 58 L.Ed.2d 808 (1979) the Supreme Court held that an interest in a noncontributory, compulsory pension plan was not a security, reversing the contrary ruling of the Seventh Circuit. Using the *Howey* analysis as a starting point, the Court found that the pension plan in question lacked both an investment by the plaintiff and the expectation of profit from a common enterprise. The opinon said:

> In every decision of this Court recognizing the presence of a "security" under the Securities Acts, the person found to have been an investor chose to give up a specific consideration in return for a separable financial interest with the characteristics of a security. Even in those cases where the interest acquired had intermingled security and nonsecurity aspects, the interest obtained had "to a very substantial degree elements of investment contracts * * *." In every case the purchaser gave up some tangible and definable consideration in return for an interest that had substantially the characteristics of a security.

Rejecting the Court of Appeals' conclusion that there was an "expectation of profit" because pension benefits exceeded the contributions of the employer and depended in part on earnings from the funds assets, the Court said:

> It is true that the Fund, like other holders of large assets, depends to some extent on earnings from its assets. In the case of a pension fund, however, a far larger portion of its income comes from employer contributions, a source in no way dependent on the efforts of the Fund's managers. * * * Not only does the greater share of a pension plan's income ordinarily come from new contributions, but unlike most entrepreneurs who manage other people's money, a plan usually can count on increased employer contributions, over which the plan itself has no control, to cover shortfalls in earnings.
>
> The importance of asset earnings in relation to the other benefits received from employment is diminished further by the fact that where a plan has substantial preconditions to vesting, the principal barrier to an individual employee's realization of pension

benefits is not the financial health of the fund. Rather, it is his own ability to meet the fund's eligibility requirements.

F. PREPARATION OF THE REGISTRATION STATEMENT: AN OVERVIEW

SCHNEIDER AND MANKO, GOING PUBLIC—PRACTICE, PROCEDURE AND CONSEQUENCES

15 Vill.L.Rev. 283, 290–294, 296–300 (1970).

THE REGISTRATION STATEMENT

The registration statement is the disclosure document required to be filed with the SEC in connection with a registered offering. It consists physically of two principal parts. Part I of the registration statement is the prospectus, which is the only part that normally goes to the public offerees of the securities. It is the legal offering document. Part II of the registration statement contains supplemental information which is available for public inspection at the office of the SEC.

The registration "forms" contain a series of detailed "items" and instructions, in response to which disclosures must be made. But, they are not forms in the sense that they have blanks to be completed like a tax return. Traditionally, the prospectus describes the company's business and responds to all the disclosures required in narrative rather than item-and-answer form. It is prepared as a brochure describing the company and the securities to be offered. The usual prospectus is a fairly stylized document and there is a customary sequence for organizing the material.

In the typical first public offering, the items which are most difficult to respond to, and which require the most creative effort in preparation, deal with the description of the company's business, its properties, material transactions between the company and the insiders and how the proceeds will be used. Other matters required to be disclosed in the prospectus deal with the details of the underwriting, the plan for distributing the securities, capitalization, pending legal proceedings, description of securities being registered, identification of directors and officers and their remuneration, options to purchase securities and principal holders of securities. There are also detailed requirements concerning financial statements and financial information concerning the company's product lines.

* * *

The SEC, which reviews the registration statement, has no authority to pass on the merits of a particular offering. The SEC has no general power to prohibit an offering because it considers the investment opportunity to be a poor risk. The sole thrust of the Federal statute is disclosure of relevant information. No matter how speculative the investment, no matter how poor the risk, the offering will comply with Federal law *if* all the required facts are disclosed. By contrast, many state securities or "blue sky" laws, which are applicable in the jurisdictions where the distribution takes place, do regulate the merits of the securities.

* * *

The Commission has also evolved certain principles of emphasis in highlighting disclosures of adverse facts. * * * [It] cannot prohibit an offering from being made, but it can make the offering look highly unattractive. In particular, if there are sufficient adverse factors in an offering, these are required to be set forth in detail in the very beginning of the prospectus under a caption such as "Introductory Statement" or "Risk Factors of the Offering." * * *

To the same end, the SEC has required that boldface reference be made to certain adverse factors on the prospectus cover page. The cover page statements must cross reference disclosures within the prospectus on such matters as high risk factors, immediate equity dilution of the public's investment and various forms of underwriting compensation beyond the normal spread. To add to the brew, the Commission sometimes insists that certain factors be emphasized beyond what the attorneys working on the matter consider to be their true importance. A usual example is that prominent attention must be called to transactions between the company and its management. Often matters of relative insignificance, in terms of amounts involved, are made to appear very important by the amount of space given and placement in the prospectus.

The prospectus is a somewhat schizophrenic document, having two purposes which often present conflicting pulls. On the one hand, it is a selling document. It is used by the principal underwriters to form the underwriting syndicate and a dealer group, and by the underwriters and dealers to sell the securities to the public.

From this point of view, it is desirable to present the best possible image. On the other hand, the prospectus is a disclosure document, an insurance policy against liability. With the view toward protection against liability, there is a tendency to resolve all doubts against the company and to make things look as bleak as possible. In balancing the purposes, established underwriters and experienced counsel, guided at least in part by their knowledge of the SEC staff attitudes, traditionally lean to a very conservative presentation. They avoid glowing adjectives, subjective evaluations and predictions about the future. The prospectus is limited to provable statements of historic fact. The layman frequently complains that all the glamor and romance has been lost. "Why can't you tell them," he says, "that we have the most aggressive and imaginative management in the industry?" It takes considerable client education before an attorney can answer this question to his client's satisfaction.

The quarterback in preparing the registration statement is normally the attorney for the company. He is principally responsible for preparing the non-financial parts of the registration statement. Drafts are circulated to all concerned. There are normally several major revisions before sending the job to the printer, and at least a few more printed drafts before the final filing. Close cooperation is required among counsel for the company, the underwriters' counsel, the accountants and the printer. Unless each knows exactly what is expected of him by each of the others, additional delay, expense and irritation are inevitable.

Review by the SEC

After the registration statement is filed initially, the Commission reviews it to see that it appropriately responds to the applicable form and almost always finds some deficiencies which are communicated by its staff through the "deficiency letter" or "letter of comments." Amendments to the registration statement are then filed to meet the comments. When the deficiencies are cured, the SEC issues an order allowing the registration statement to become, to use the word of art, "effective." Only after the registration statement is effective may sales to the public take place.

If counsel, or the accountants, with respect to financial comments, feels that the staff's comments are inapposite or should not be met for some other reason, he will discuss them with the staff, usually by telephone but in person if the matter is sufficiently serious. The Commission's staff is generally reasonable in dealing with counsel's objections. However, as a practical matter, an offering cannot usually come to market unless an accommodation has been reached on all comments. Therefore, the staff usually has the last word on when the company has adequately met the comments, even if they are not legally binding in the formal sense.

* * *

Preliminary Preparation

For the average first offering, a very substantial amount of preliminary work is required which does not relate directly to preparing the registration statement as such. To have a vehicle for the offering, the business going public normally must be conducted by a single corporation or a parent corporation with subsidiaries. In most cases, the business is not already in such a neat package when the offering project commences. It is often conducted by a number of corporations under common ownership, by partnerships or by combinations of business entities. Considerable work must be done in order to reorganize the various entities by mergers, liquidations and capital contributions. Even where there is a single corporation, a recapitalization is almost always required so that the company will have an appropriate capital structure for the public offering. To mention a few other common projects in preparing to go public, it is often necessary to enter into, to revise or to terminate employment agreements, adopt stock option plans and grant options thereunder, transfer real estate, revise leases, rewrite the corporate charter and by-laws, prepare new stock certificates, engage a transfer agent and registrar, rearrange stockholdings of insiders, draw, revise or cancel agreements among shareholders and revamp financing arrangements.

TIMETABLE

Although laymen find it difficult to believe, the average first public offering normally requires six weeks to three months of intensive work before the registration statement can be filed. One reason so much time is required is the need to accomplish the preparatory steps just referred to at the same time the registration statement is being prepared. There are many important and often interrelated business decisions to be made and implemented, and rarely are all of these questions decided definitively at the outset. Some answers must await final figures, or negotiations with underwriters, and must be held open until the last minute. Inevitably, a businessman first exposed to these considerations will change his mind several times in the interim. Furthermore, drafting of the prospectus normally begins before the financial statements are available. Almost inevitably, some rewriting must be done in the non-financial parts after the financial statements are distributed in order to blend the financial and non-financial sections together. Laymen frequently have the frustrating feeling as the deadline approaches that everything is hopelessly confused. They are quite surprised to see that everything falls into place at the eleventh hour.

After the registration statement is filed with the Commission, the waiting period begins. It is during this interval that red herrings are distributed. The Commission reviews the registration statement and finally issues its letter of comments. There is a wide variation in the time required for the SEC to process a registration statement. * * * At times the delay in receiving a letter of comments from the Commission has exceeded 100 days. At other times, for relatively simple and well prepared registration statements, or for registration statements of companies which have filed previously, the letter of comments may be received in less than two weeks.

* * *

EXPENSES

The largest single expense in going public is usually the underwriters' compensation. The underwriting cash discount or cash commission on a new issue generally ranges from 7 percent to 10 percent of the public offering price. The maximum has been coming down in recent years as a result of pressure from the National Association of Securities Dealers, Inc. ("NASD"), a self-regulatory agency which has effective controls on the amount of compensation which under-writers may receive.

Normally, the three largest additional expenses are legal fees, accounting fees and printing costs.   *   *   *

For each registration statement, there is a filing fee at the rate of 1/50th of 1 percent of the maximum aggregate offering price of the securities, with a minimum fee of $100.   Among the other expenses to be borne are original issue and transfer taxes, if applicable, transfer agent and registrar fees, printing of stock certificates and "blue sky" expenses.   Sometimes the company must pay an expense allowance to the underwriters.   This is a negotiated figure which can be as high as $20,000 or possibly more.   The company frequently pays the underwriters' counsel a special fee for "blue sky" work, which can range up to several thousand dollars, depending on the number and identity of the jurisdictions involved.

*   *   *

Another cost of going public arises out of the heavy burden and time demand it may impose on the company's administrative and executive personnel.   Throughout the period of selecting the underwriters and preparing the registration statement, these activities can, and often do, absorb a significant amount of executive time.

*   *   *

G.   ATTORNEYS' RESPONSIBILITIES

PROBLEM

AEROBICS, INC.

For the past three months you have been working on the registration of a first issue of common stock by your client, Aerobics, Inc., a manufacturer of athletic shoes.   You recently completed working with the SEC staff on the last amendments to the preliminary prospectus, which you filed three weeks ago, all of the resulting changes have been set in type, and the staff has indicated its agreement to acceleration of the effectiveness of the registration.   A meeting has been scheduled for this afternoon between Aerobics' principal officers and representatives of the underwriters to negotiate the final price of the offering.   Aerobics' president, Clay Foote, a good friend and college classmate of yours told you he is worried about how the meeting will go because during the last week or so interest rates have experienced a small rise that ecnomists are predicting will soon accelerate, and the stock market has been behaving nervously. Foote is concerned that unless the offering, which he believes is critical to his company's future, is closed soon, it may have to be postponed indefinitely.

At lunch before the meeting, Foote breaks some troublesome news. Professor Arthur Pedicks, a specialist in athletic injuries who teaches at a local medical school, was retained by the company some months ago to assist in improving the company's products. In studying the running shoe that is Aerobics' principal revenue producer, he thinks he has found that a unique patented feature of the shoe, which has been advertised as its major virtue, under certain circumstances, substantially increases the risk of an unusual variety of knee injury in certain particularly susceptible runners. Dr. Pedicks has told Foote that the problem can readily be corrected for future production models of the shoe. The company has, however, sold nearly a million pairs of these shoes over the last several years, and Dr. Pedicks believes that the shoe may be a contributing cause of a sharp increase in this particular type of knee injury that had puzzled orthopedists for some time. Foote asks you whether there might be problems with liability should the connection between this injury and the Aerobics' shoe become known. Your immediate concern is somewhat different.

1.   Does the registration statement have to be amended to reflect any contingent liabilities arising from the problem with the shoe?

2.   Consider the alternative of having Foote tell the underwriters about the problem. If they were fully apprised of all the details and were willing to go ahead with the offering without amending the prospectus, would that resolve the situation?

3.   Foote does not want to tell the other directors yet as he is afraid that a leak might damage Aerobics' reputation unnecessarily if Dr. Pedicks' fears turn out to be unfounded. Should you encourage him to inform the board? Should you inform the board if he is unwilling to?

4.   Suppose that Foote does inform the underwriters, and they, after consulting with their attorney, decide to proceed with the offering without amending the prospectus. If you believe that the possible defect in the shoe is material to the accuracy of the prospectus, what are your obligations? May you inform the SEC of the facts? Should you? Must you? Is there anything else you ought to do?

SEC v. NATIONAL STUDENT MARKETING CORP.

457 F.Supp. 682 (D.D.C.1978).

BARRINGTON D. PARKER, District Judge.

[In August, 1969, National Student Marketing Corporation (NSMC) entered into a merger agreement with Interstate National Corporation (Interstate). Among the conditions of the merger recited in the agreement were that both corporations obtain opinion letters from their attorneys stating that all transactions in connection with the merger had been effected in compliance with the law and that each corporation would provide the other with a "comfort letter" from its independent public accountant. In accordance with standard practice the letter was to state: (1) that the accountants had no reason to believe that the unaudited interim financial statements presented at the closing had not been prepared in accordance with generally accepted accounting principles, (2) that the accountants had no reason to believe that any material adjustments to those statements were required fairly to present the results of the corporation's operations, and (3) that the company had experienced no material adverse changes in position between the last interim financial statement and the merger. Under the terms of the agreement, it could be terminated at any time prior to the effective date of the merger by the mutual consent of the boards of directors of the two corporations and any of the agreement's terms could be waived by either party. In the course of preparing their comfort letter, NSMC's accountants determined that certain substantial adjustments were required with respect to NSMC's interim financials that would cause the company to show a small loss for the nine-month period prior to the merger instead of a $700,000 profit. Although the accountants discussed these adjustments with NSMC officials, Interstate was not apprised of them until a draft of the comfort letter was delivered during the merger closing. At that time, Interstate representatives, including Meyer and Schauer, partners in Lord, Bissel & Brook (LBB), Interstate's outside counsel (Meyer was also an Interstate director) and the company's president (Brown), conferred privately and decided to proceed with the merger despite the fact that the approval of Interstate's shareholders had been solicited on the basis of information that painted a too-rosy picture of NSMC's financial health. No effort was made to disclose the content of the comfort letter to Interstate's former shareholders, to the SEC or to the public. Not long after the merger NSMC began experiencing substantial financial difficulties and ultimately went into receivership. The SEC commenced enforcement proceedings against a number of defendants involved with the NSMC—Interstate merger, including those discussed here. The charges against all of the other defendants were resolved by settlement.]

* * *

IV. AIDING AND ABETTING

The Court must now turn to the Commission's charges that the defendants aided and abetted * these two violations of the antifraud

---

* [Eds. note:] In Woodward v. Metro Bank of Dallas, 522 F.2d 84, 94–95 (5 Cir. 1975), the court explained the aider and abettor concept as follows: "The elements of an aiding and abetting claim have not yet crystallized into a set pattern; however, we find the Sixth Circuit's analysis in SEC v. Coffey (6 Cir. 1974) 493 F.2d 1304, cert. denied 420 U.S. 908, 95 S.Ct. 826, 42 L.Ed.2d 837 helpful: Without meaning to set forth an inflexible definition of aiding and abetting, we

provisions [§ 10(b) of the '34 Act * and § 17(a) of the '33 Act].   The violations themselves establish the first element of aiding and abetting liability, namely that another person has committed a securities law violation.   The remaining elements, though not set forth with any uniformity, are essentially that the alleged aider and abettor had a "general awareness that his role was part of an overall activity that is improper, and [that he] knowingly and substantially assisted the violation."

The Commission's allegations of aiding and abetting by the defendants, specified at page 700 *supra*, seem to fall into four basic categories: (1) the failure of the attorney defendants to take any action to interfere in the consummation of the merger; (2) the issuance by the attorneys of an opinion with respect to the merger; (3) the attorneys' subsequent failure to withdraw that opinion and inform the Interstate shareholders or the SEC of the inaccuracy of the nine-month financials;   *   *   *.   [The fourth allegation is omitted.]   The SEC's position is that the defendants acted or failed to act with an awareness of the fraudulent conduct by the principals, and thereby substantially assisted the two violations.   The Court concurs with regard to the attorneys' failure to interfere with the closing, but must conclude that the remaining actions or inaction alleged to constitute aiding and abetting did not substantially facilitate either the merger or the stock sales.

As noted, the first element of aiding and abetting liability has been established by the finding that Brown and Meyer committed primary violations of the securities laws.   Support for the second element, that the defendants were generally aware of the fraudulent activity, is provided by the previous discussion concerning scienter.   With the exception of LBB, which is charged with vicarious liability, each of the defendants was actually present at the closing of the merger when the comfort letter was delivered and the adjustments to the nine-month financials were revealed.   Each was present at the

find that a person may be held as an aider and abettor only if some other party has committed a securities law violation, if the accused party had general awareness that his role was part of an overall activity that is improper, and if the accused aider-abettor knowingly and substantially assisted the violation.   493 F. 2d at 1316.   The elements adopted by the Third Circuit in Landy v. Federal Deposit Ins. Corp. (3 Cir. 1973), 486 F.2d 139, cert. denied, 416 U.S. 960, 94 S.Ct. 1979, 40 L.Ed.2d 312, are similar to the *Coffey* test, but *Landy* refers to 'an independent wrong' instead of a securities law violation, and knowledge of the wrong's existence instead of awareness of a role in improper activity.   Finally, *Landy* omits the 'knowing' requirement for the substantial assistance aspect.   The first two *Landy* elements pose a danger of overinclusiveness and seem to lose sight of the necessary connection to the securities laws.   One could know of the existence of a 'wrong' without being aware of his role in the scheme, and it is the participation that is at issue.   The scienter requirement scales upward when activity is more remote; therefore, the assistance rendered should be both substantial and knowing.   A remote party must not only be aware of his role, but he should also know when and to what degree he is furthering the fraud."

* Section 10(b) and Rule 10b–5, adopted under its authority, are discussed at some length in Chapter 19, Section B, *infra*.—Eds.

Interstate caucus and the subsequent questioning of the NSMC representatives; each knew of the importance attributed to the adjustments by those present. They knew that the Interstate shareholders and the investing public were unaware of the adjustments and the inaccuracy of the financials. Despite the obvious materiality of the information, each knew that it had not been disclosed prior to the merger and stock sale transactions. Thus, this is not a situation where the aider and abettor merely failed to discover the fraud, or reasonably believed that the victims were already aware of the withheld information. The record amply demonstrates the "knowledge of the fraud, and not merely the undisclosed material facts," that is required to meet this element of secondary liability.

The final requirement for aiding and abetting liability is that the conduct provide knowing, substantial assistance to the violation. In addressing this issue, the Court will consider each of the SEC's allegations separately. The major problem arising with regard to the Commission's contention that the attorneys failed to interfere in the closing of the merger is whether inaction or silence constitutes substantial assistance. While there is no definitive answer to this question, courts have been willing to consider inaction as a form of substantial assistance when the accused aider and abettor had a duty to disclose. Although the duty to disclose in those cases is somewhat distinguishable, in that they contemplate disclosure to an opposing party and not to one's client, they are sufficiently analogous to provide support for a duty here.

Upon receipt of the unsigned comfort letter, it became clear that the merger had been approved by the Interstate shareholders on the basis of materially misleading information. In view of the obvious materiality of the information, especially to attorneys learned in securities law, the attorneys' responsibilities to their corporate client required them to take steps to ensure that the information would be disclosed to the shareholders. However, it is unnecessary to determine the precise extent of their obligations here, since it is undisputed that they took no steps whatsoever to delay the closing pending disclosure to and resolicitation of the Interstate shareholders. But, at the very least, they were required to speak out at the closing concerning the obvious materiality of the information and the concomitant requirement that the merger not be closed until the adjustments were disclosed and approval of the merger was again obtained from the Interstate shareholders. Their silence was not only a breach of this duty to speak, but in addition lent the appearance of legitimacy to the closing. The combination of these factors clearly provided substantial assistance to the closing of the merger.

Contrary to the attorney defendants' contention, imposition of such a duty will not require lawyers to go beyond their accepted role in securities transactions, nor will it compel them to "err on the side of conservatism,   *   *   *   thereby inhibiting clients' business judgments and candid attorney-client communications." Courts will not lightly overrule an attorney's determination of materiality and the need for disclosure. However, where, as here, the significance of the information clearly removes any doubt concerning the materiality of the information, attorneys cannot rest on asserted "business judgments" as justification for their failure to make a legal decision pursuant to their fiduciary responsibilities to client shareholders.

The Commission also asserts that the attorneys substantially assisted the merger violation through the issuance of an opinion that was false and misleading due to its omission of the receipt of the comfort letter and of the completion of the merger on the basis of the false and misleading nine-month financials. The defendants contend that a technical reading of the opinion demonstrates that it is not false and misleading, and that it provides accurate opinions as to Interstate's compliance with certain corporate formalities. Of concern to the Court, however, is not the truth or falsity of the opinion, but whether it substantially assisted the violation. Upon consideration of all the circumstances, the Court concludes that it did not.

Contrary to the implication made by the SEC, the opinion issued by the attorneys at the closing did not play a large part in the consummation of the merger. Instead, it was simply one of many conditions to the obligation of NSMC to complete the merger. It addressed a number of corporate formalities required of Interstate by the Merger Agreement, only a few of which could possibly involve compliance with the antifraud provisions of the securities laws. Moreover, the opinion was explicitly for the benefit of NSMC, which was already well aware of the adjustments contained in the comfort letter. Thus, this is not a case where an opinion of counsel addresses a specific issue and is undeniably relied on in completing the transaction. Under these circumstances, it is unreasonable to suggest that the opinion provided substantial assistance to the merger.

The SEC's contention with regard to counsel's alleged acquiescence in the merger transaction raises significant questions concerning the responsibility of counsel. The basis for the charge appears to be counsel's failure, after the merger, to withdraw their opinion, to demand resolicitation of the shareholders, to advise their clients concerning rights of rescission of the merger, and ultimately, to inform the Interstate shareholders or the SEC of the completion of the merger based on materially false and misleading financial statements. The defendants counter with the argument that their actions following the merger are not subject to the coverage of the securities laws.

The filing of the complaint in this proceeding generated significant interest and an almost overwhelming amount of comment within the legal profession on the scope of a securities lawyer's obligations to his client and to the investing public. The very initiation of this action, therefore, has provided a necessary and worthwhile impetus for the profession's recognition and assessment of its responsibilities in this area. The Court's examination, however, must be more limited. Although the complaint alleges varying instances of misconduct on the part of several attorneys and firms, the Court must narrow its focus to the present defendants and the charges against them.

Meyer, Schauer and Lord, Bissell & Brook are, in essence, here charged with failing to take any action to "undo" the merger. The Court has already concluded that counsel had a duty to the Interstate shareholders to delay the closing of the merger pending disclosure and resolicitation with corrected financials, and that the breach of that duty constituted a violation of the antifraud provisions through aiding and abetting the merger transaction. The Commission's charge, however, concerns the period following that transaction. Even if the attorneys' fiduciary responsiblities to the Interstate shareholders continued beyond the merger, the breach of such a duty would not have the requisite relationship to a securities transaction, since the merger had already been completed. It is equally obvious that such subsequent action or inaction by the attorneys could not substantially assist the merger.

* * *

Thus, the Court finds that the attorney defendants aided and abetted the violation of § 10(b), Rule 10b–5, and § 17(a) through their participation in the closing of the merger.

[The court goes on to discuss the appropriateness of the injunctive relief requested by the SEC. It states, "The crucial question * * * remains * * * whether there exists a reasonable likelihood of future illegal conduct by the defendant * * *." Finding that, "The Commission has not demonstrated that the defendants engaged in the type of repeated and persistent misconduct which usually justifies the issuance of injunctive relief," the court declined to issue the order requested and dismissed the complaint.]

AMERICAN BAR ASSOCIATION, CODE OF PROFESSIONAL RESPONSIBILITY

CANON 4

A Lawyer Should Preserve the Confidences and Secrets of a Client

ETHICAL CONSIDERATIONS

EC 4–1 Both the fiduciary relationship existing between lawyer and client and the proper functioning of the legal system require the preservation by the lawyer of confidences and secrets of one who has employed or sought to employ him. A client must feel free to discuss whatever he wishes with his lawyer and a lawyer must be equally free to obtain information beyond that volunteered by his client. A lawyer should be fully informed of all the facts of the matter he is handling in order for his client to obtain the full advantage of our legal system.   *   *   *

EC 4–2 The obligation to protect confidences and secrets obviously does not preclude a lawyer from revealing information when his client consents after full disclosure, when necessary to perform his professional employment, when permitted by a Disciplinary Rule, or when required by law.   *   *   *   If the obligation extends to two or more clients as to the same information, a lawyer should obtain the permission of all before revealing the information. A lawyer must always be sensitive to the rights and wishes of his client and act scrupulously in the making of decisions which may involve the disclosure of information obtained in his professional relationship.   *   *   *

DISCIPLINARY RULES

DR 4–101 Preservation of Confidences and Secrets of a Client.

(A) "Confidence" refers to information protected by the attorney-client privilege under applicable law, and "secret" refers to other information gained in the professional relationship that the client has requested be held inviolate or the disclosure of which would be embarrassing or would be likely to be detrimental to the client.

(B) Except when permitted under DR 4–101 (C), a lawyer shall not knowingly:

   (1) Reveal a confidence or secret of his client.

   (2) Use a confidence or secret of his client to the disadvantage of the client.

   (3) Use a confidence or secret of his client for the advantage of himself or of a third person, unless the client consents after full disclosure.

(C) A lawyer may reveal:

   (1) Confidences or secrets with the consent of the client or clients affected, but only after a full disclosure to them.

   (2) Confidences or secrets when permitted under Disciplinary Rules or required by law or court order.

   (3) The intention of his client to commit a crime and the information necessary to prevent the crime.

   (4) Confidences or secrets necessary to establish or collect his fee or to defend himself or his employees or associates against an accusation of wrongful conduct.

*   *   *

CANON 5

A Lawyer Should Exercise Independent Professional Judgment on Behalf of a Client

EC 5–18 A lawyer employed or retained by a corporation or similar entity owes his allegiance to the entity and not to a stockholder, director, officer, employee, representative, or other person connected with the entity. In advising the entity, a lawyer should keep paramount its interests and his professional judgment should not be influenced by the personal desires of any person or organization. Occasionally a lawyer for an entity is requested by a stockholder, director, officer, employee, representative, or other person connected with the entity to represent him in an individual capacity; in such case the lawyer may serve the individual only if the lawyer is convinced that differing interests are not present.

CANON 7

A Lawyer Should Represent a Client Zealously Within the Bounds of the Law

Duty of the Lawyer to a Client

EC 7–5 A lawyer as adviser furthers the interest of his client by giving his professional opinion as to what he believes would likely be the ultimate decision of the courts on the matter at hand and by informing his client of the practical effect of such decision. He may continue in the representation of his client even though his client has elected to pursue a course of conduct contrary to the advice of the lawyer so long as he does not thereby knowingly assist the client to engage in illegal conduct or to take a frivolous legal position. A lawyer should never encourage or aid his client to commit criminal acts or counsel his client on how to violate the law and avoid punishment therefor.

EC 7–8 A lawyer should exert his best efforts to insure that decisions of his client are made only after the client has been informed of relevant considerations. A lawyer ought to initiate this decision-making process if the client does not do so. Advice of a lawyer to his client need not be confined to purely legal considerations. A lawyer should advise his client of the possible effect of each legal alternative. A lawyer should bring to bear upon this decision-making process the fullness of his experience as well as his objective viewpoint. In assisting his client to reach a proper decision, it is often desirable for a lawyer to point out those factors which may lead to a decision that is morally just as well as legally permissible. He may emphasize the possibility of harsh consequences that might result from assertion of legally permissible positions. In the final analysis, however, the lawyer should always remember that the decision whether to forego legally available objectives or methods because of non-legal factors is ultimately for the client and not for himself. In the event that the client in a non-adjudicatory matter insists upon a course of conduct that is contrary to the judgment and advice of the lawyer but not prohibited by Disciplinary Rules, the lawyer may withdraw from the employment.

DISCIPLINARY RULES

DR 7–101 Representing a Client Zealously.

* * *

(B) In his representation of a client, a lawyer may:

* * *

(2) Refuse to aid or participate in conduct that he believes to be unlawful, even though there is some support for an argument that the conduct is legal.

DR 7–102 Representing a Client Within the Bounds of the Law.

(A) In his representation of a client, a lawyer shall not:

* * *

(3) Conceal or knowingly fail to disclose that which he is required by law to reveal.

* * *

(7) Counsel or assist his client in conduct that the lawyer knows to be illegal or fraudulent.

* * *

(B) A lawyer who receives information clearly establishing that:

(1) His client has, in the course of the representation, perpetrated a fraud upon a person or tribunal shall promptly call upon his client to rectify the same, and if his client refuses or is unable to do so, he shall reveal the fraud to the affected person or tribunal, except when the information is protected as a privileged communication.

* * *

AMERICAN BAR ASSOCIATION, PROPOSED FINAL DRAFT, MODEL RULES OF PROFESSIONAL CONDUCT (1981)

Rule 1.2 Scope of Representation

(a) A lawyer shall abide by a client's decisions concerning the objectives of representation, subject to paragraphs (c), (d) and (e), and shall consult with the client as to the means by which they are to be pursued. A lawyer shall abide by a client's decision whether to accept an offer of settlement of a matter. * * *

(b) A lawyer's representation of a client, including representation by appointment, does not constitute an endorsement of the client's political, economic, social or moral views or activities.

(c) A lawyer may limit the objectives of the representation if the client consents after disclosure. If a client insists upon pursuing an objective that the lawyer considers repugnant or imprudent, the lawyer may withdraw if doing so can be accomplished without material adverse effect on the interests of the client or as otherwise permitted by Rule 1.16(b).

(d) A lawyer shall not counsel or assist a client in conduct that the lawyer knows or reasonably should know is criminal or fraudulent, or in the preparation of a written instrument containing terms the lawyer knows or reasonably should know are legally prohibited, but a lawyer may counsel or assist a client in a good faith effort to determine the validity, scope, meaning or application of the law.

(e) When a lawyer knows or reasonably should know that a client expects assistance not permitted by the Rules of Professional Conduct or other law, the lawyer shall inform the client of the relevant limitations to which the lawyer is subject.

Rule 1.6   Confidentiality of Information

(a) A lawyer shall not reveal information relating to representation of a client except as stated in paragraph (b), unless the client consents after disclosure.

(b) A lawyer may reveal such information to the extent the lawyer believes necessary:

(1) To serve the client's interests, unless it is information the client has specifically requested not be disclosed;

(2) To prevent the client from committing a criminal or fraudulent act that the lawyer believes is likely to result in death or substantial bodily harm, or substantial injury to the financial interest or property of another;

(3) To rectify the consequences of a client's criminal or fraudulent act in the commission of which the lawyer's services had been used;

(4) To establish a claim or defense on behalf of the lawyer in a controversy between the lawyer and the client, or to establish a defense to a criminal charge or civil claim against the lawyer based upon conduct in which the client was involved; or

(5) To comply with the Rules of Professional Conduct or other law.

Comment:

A fundamental principle in the client-lawyer relationship is that the lawyer maintain confidentiality of information relating to the representation. The client is thereby encouraged to communicate fully and frankly with the lawyer even as to embarrassing or legally damaging subject matter.

The principle of confidentiality is given effect in two related bodies of law, the attorney-client privilege in the law of evidence and the rule of confidentiality established in professional ethics. The attorney-client privilege applies in judicial and other proceedings in which a lawyer may be called as a witness or otherwise required to produce evidence concerning a client. The rule of client-lawyer confidentiality applies in situations other than those where evidence is sought from the lawyer through compulsion of law. The confidentiality rule applies not merely to matters communicated in confidence by the client but also to all information relating to the representation, whatever its source. A lawyer may not disclose such information except as authorized or required by the Rules of Professional Conduct or other law.

Authorized Disclosure

A lawyer may disclose information about a client when necessary in the proper representation of the client. In litigation, for example, a lawyer may disclose information by admitting a fact that cannot properly be disputed, or in negotiation by making a disclosure that facilitates a satisfactory conclusion.

Lawyers in a firm may, in the course of the firm's practice, disclose to each other information relating to a client of the firm, unless the client has instructed that particular information be confined to specified lawyers.

Disclosure Adverse to Client

The confidentiality rule is subject to limited exceptions. In becoming privy to information about a client, a lawyer may foresee that the client intends serious and perhaps irreparable harm to another person. To the extent a lawyer is prohibited from making disclosure, the interests of the potential victim are sacrificed in favor of preserving the client's confidences even though the client's purpose is wrongful. To the extent a lawyer is required or permitted to disclose a client's purposes, the client may be inhibited from revealing facts which would enable the lawyer to counsel against a wrongful course of action. A rule governing disclosure of threatened harm thus involves balancing the interests of one group of potential victims against those of another. On the assumption that lawyers generally fulfill their duty to advise against the commission of deliberately wrongful acts, the public is better protected if full disclosure by the client is encouraged than if it is inhibited.

Generally speaking, information relating to the representation must be kept confidential, as stated in paragraph (a). However, where the client is or has been engaged in criminal or fraudulent conduct or the integrity of the lawyer's own conduct is involved, the principle of confidentiality may have to yield, depending on the lawyer's knowledge about and relationship to the conduct in question, and the seriousness of that conduct. Several situations must be distinguished.

First, the lawyer may not counsel or assist a client in conduct that is criminal or fraudulent. See Rule 1.2(d). As noted in the Comment to that Rule, there can be situations where the lawyer may have to reveal information relating to the representation in order to avoid assisting a client's criminal or fraudulent conduct.   *   *   *

Second, the lawyer may have been innocently involved in past conduct by the client that was criminal or fraudulent. In such a situation the lawyer has not violated Rule 1.2(d), because to "counsel or assist" criminal or fraudulent conduct requires knowing that the conduct is of that character. Even if the involvement was innocent, however, the fact remains that the lawyer's professional services were made the instrument of the client's crime or fraud. The lawyer, therefore, has a legitimate interest in being able to rectify the consequences of such conduct, and has the professional right although not a professional duty to rectify the situation. Exercising that right may require revealing information relating to the representation. Paragraph (b)(3) gives the lawyer professional discretion to reveal such information to the extent necessary to accomplish rectification.

Third, the lawyer may learn that a client intends prospective conduct that is criminal or fraudulent. Inaction by the lawyer is not a violation of Rule 1.2(d), except in the limited circumstances where failure to act constitutes assisting the client. See Comment to Rule 1.2(d). However, the lawyer's knowledge of the client's purpose may enable the lawyer to prevent commission of the prospective crime or fraud. If the prospective crime or fraud is likely to result in substantial injury, the lawyer may feel a moral obligation to take preventive action. When the threatened injury is grave, such as homicide or serious bodily injury, the lawyer may have an obligation under tort or criminal law to take reasonable preventive measures. Whether the lawyer's concern is based on moral or legal considerations, the interest in preventing the harm may be more compelling than the interest in preserving confidentiality of information relating to the client. As stated in paragraph (b)(2), the lawyer has professional discretion to reveal information in order to prevent substantial harm likely to result from a client's criminal or fraudulent act.

It is arguable that the lawyer should have a professional obligation to make a disclosure in order to prevent homicide or serious bodily injury which the lawyer knows is intended by a client. However, it is very difficult for a lawyer to "know" when such a heinous purpose will actually be carried out, for the client may have a change of mind. To require disclosure when the client intends such an act, at risk of disciplinary liability if the assessment of the client's purpose turns out to be wrong, would be to impose a penal risk that might interfere with the lawyer's resolution of an inherently difficult moral dilemma.

The lawyer's exercise of discretion requires consideration of such factors as the magnitude, proximity and likelihood of the contemplated wrong, the nature of the lawyer's relationship with the client and with those who might be injured by the client, the lawyer's own involvement in the transaction and factors that may extenuate the conduct in question. In any case, a disclosure adverse to the client's interest should be no greater than the lawyer believes necessary to the purpose. A lawyer's decision not to take preventive action permitted by paragraph (b)(2) does not violate this Rule.

Where the client is an organization, the lawyer may be in doubt whether contemplated conduct will actually be carried out and whether higher authority in the organization approves. Where necessary to guide his conduct in connection with this Rule, the lawyer should make inquiry within the organization as indicated in Rule 1.13(b).

The term "another" in paragraph (b)(2) includes a person, organization and government.

*   *   *

Rule 1.13 Organization as the Client

(a) A lawyer employed or retained to represent an organization represents the organization as distinct from its directors, officers, employees, members, shareholders or other constituents.

(b) If a lawyer for an organization knows that an officer, employee or other person associated with the organization is engaged in action, intends to act or refuses to act in a matter related to the representation that is a violation of a legal obligation to the organization, or a violation of law which reasonably might be imputed to the organization, and is likely to result in material injury to the organization, the lawyer shall proceed as is reasonably necessary in the best interest of the organization. In determining how to proceed, the lawyer shall give due consideration to the seriousness of the violation and its consequences, the scope and nature of the lawyer's representation, the responsibility in the organization and the apparent motivation of the person involved, the policies of the organization concerning such matters and any other relevant considerations. The measures taken shall be designed to minimize disruption of the organization and the risk of revealing information relating to the representation to persons outside the organization. Such measures may include:

(1) Asking reconsideration of the matter;

(2) Advising that a separate legal opinion on the matter be sought for presentation to appropriate authority in the organization; and

(3) Referring the matter to higher authority in the organization, including, if warranted by the seriousness of the matter, referral to the highest authority that can act in behalf of the organization as determined by applicable law.

(c) When a matter has been referred to the organization's highest authority in accordance with paragraph (b), and that authority insists upon action, or refuses to take action, that is clearly a violation of a legal obligation to the organization, or a violation of law which reasonably might be imputed to the organization, and is likely to result in substantial injury to the organization, the lawyer may take further remedial action that the lawyer reasonably believes to be in the best interest of the organization. Such action may include revealing information relating to the representation of the organization only if the lawyer reasonably believes that:

(1) The highest authority in the organization has acted to further the personal or financial interests of members of that authority which are in conflict with the interests of the organization; and

(2) Revealing the information is necessary in the best interest of the organization.

(d) In dealing with an organization's directors, officers, employees, members, shareholders or other constituents, a lawyer shall explain the identity of the client when necessary to avoid misunderstandings on their part.

(e) A lawyer representing an organization may also represent any of its directors, officers, employees, members, shareholders or other constituents, subject to the provisions regarding conflict of interest stated in Rule 1.7. If the organization's consent to the dual representation is required by Rule 1.7, the consent shall be given by an appropriate official of the organization other than the individual who is to be represented.

Comment:

The Entity as the Client

In transactions with their lawyers, clients who are individuals can speak and decide for themselves, finally and authoritatively. In transactions between an organization and its lawyer, however, the organization can speak and decide only through agents, such as its officers or employees. In effect, the client-lawyer relationship is maintained through an intermediary between the client and the lawyer. This fact requires the lawyer under certain conditions to be concerned whether the intermediary legitimately represents the client.

When officers or employees of the organization make decisions for it, the decisions ordinarily must be accepted by the lawyer even if their utility or prudence is doubtful. Decisions concerning policy and operations, including ones entailing serious risk, are not as such in the lawyer's province. However, different considerations arise when the lawyer knows that the organization may be materially harmed by action of an officer or employee that is in violation of law. In such a circumstance, the lawyer may seek to have the officer, employee or other agent reconsider the matter. If that fails, or if the matter is of sufficient seriousness and importance to the organization, the lawyer should take steps to have the matter reviewed by a higher authority in the organization. Clear justification should exist for seeking review over the head of the officer or employee normally responsible for it. The stated policy of the organization may define circumstances and prescribe channels for such review, and a lawyer should encourage the formulation of such a policy. Even in the absence of organization policy, however, the lawyer may have an obligation to refer a matter to higher authority, depending on the seriousness of the matter and whether the officer in question has apparent motives to act at variance with the organization's interest. Review by the chief executive officer or by the board of directors may be required when the matter is of importance commensurate with their authority. Somewhere along the line it may be useful or essential to obtain an independent legal opinion.

In an extreme case, the lawyer must refer the matter to the organization's highest authority. Ordinarily, that is the board of directors or similar governing body. However, applicable law may prescribe that under certain conditions highest authority reposes elsewhere; for example, in the independent directors of a corporation. The ultimately difficult question is whether the lawyer should be required to circumvent the organization's highest authority when it persists in a course of action that is clearly violative of law or a legal obligation to the organization and is likely to result in substantial injury to the organization.

In such a situation, if the lawyer can take remedial action without a disclosure of information that might adversely affect the organization, the lawyer as a matter of professional discretion should take such action as the lawyer reasonably believes to be in the best interest of the organization. For example, a lawyer for a close corporation may be obliged to disclose misconduct by the board to the shareholders. However, taking such action could entail disclosure of information relating to the representation with consequent risk of injury to the client. When such is the case, the organization is threatened by alternative injuries: the injury that may result from the governing board's action or refusal to act, and the injury that may result if the lawyer's remedial efforts entail disclosure of confidential information. The lawyer may pursue remedial efforts even at the risk of disclosure in the circumstances stated in subparagraphs (c) (1) and (c)(2).

H. DISCLOSURE POLICY

PROBLEM

A DINNER CONVERSATION

At a dinner party you fall into a conversation about the securities laws with an economics professor at a local university. He argues that the disclosure requirements of the '33 Act provide little or no social benefit, or at least that the substantial costs of registration under the Act are not nearly justified by any reductions in fraud or improvements in the efficiency of the capital markets. He is willing to admit that perhaps a federal statute simply prohibiting fraud in the sale of securities and establishing a civil action for damages (similar to Section 12(2) of the '33 Act) may serve some useful purpose, but he vigorously maintains that were it not for the entrenched interests of the securities bar and the accounting profession, whose members profit handsomely from the '33 Act, its registration requirements would long ago have been abolished.

Rising to the defense of your profession, you present a strong, lawyerlike argument to the contrary. What is it? Do you believe it? Consider the following:

R. POSNER, ECONOMIC ANALYSIS OF LAW 332 (2d ed. 1977).

The regulation of the securities markets has two main aspects, both intended to reduce the likelihood of a recurrence of a 1929-type crash. First, new issues of stock may be sold only by means of a prospectus, approved by the SEC in advance, that contains certain required information (including adverse information) deemed material to a purchaser. Second, trading in securities is subject to a variety of restrictions designed to dampen "speculative fever" and increase public confidence in the securities markets.

There is a serious question whether either branch of regulation is effective in achieving its formal objectives. Capital markets are competitive and competitive markets generate, without government prodding, information concerning the products sold. It is especially plausible to expect the capital markets to generate abundant and, on the whole, accurate information about new issues in view of the presence of (1) sophisticated middlemen—the underwriters who market new issues—between issuer and purchaser; (2) sophisticated purchasers such as trust companies, mutual funds, and pension funds; and (3) the many financial analysts employed by brokerage firms and by independent investment advisory services. Written in a forbidding legal and accounting jargon, prospectuses are of no direct value to the unsophisticated stock purchaser. Nor is it obvious that the disclosure requirements imposed by the SEC in fact increase the flow of information. By limiting selling efforts to the prospectus, and by taking a restrictive view of what may be properly included in a prospectus * * * the SEC limits the amount of information communicated by the issuer.

STIGLER, PUBLIC REGULATION OF THE SECURITIES MARKET, 19 Bus.Law. 721, 724–30 (1964).

2.   *A Test of Previous Regulation*

* * *

The paramount goal of the regulations in the security markets is to protect the innocent (but avaricious) investor. A partial test of the effects of the SEC on investors' fortunes will help to answer the question of whether testing a policy's effectiveness is an academic scruple or a genuine need. * * *

The basic test is simplicity itself: how did investors fare before and after the SEC was given control over the registration of new issues? We take all the new issues of industrial stocks with a value exceeding $2.5 million in 1923–1928, and exceeding $5 million in 1949–1955, and measure the values of these issues (compared to their offering price) in five subsequent years. It is obviously improper to credit or blame the SEC for the absolute differences between the periods in investors' fortunes, but if we measure stock prices relative to the market average, we shall have eliminated most of the effects of general market conditions. The price ratios * * * for each time span are divided by the ratio of the market average for the same period. Thus if from 1926 to 1928 a common stock rose from $20 to $30, the price ratio is 150 (per cent) or an increase of 50 per cent but relative to the market, which rose by 68.5 per cent over this two-year period, the new issue fell 12 per cent.

The prices of common * * * stocks were first analyzed to determine whether they varied with size of issue after one, three, or five years. In each case there was no systematic or statistically significant variation of price with size of issue. The elusiveness of quotations on small issues makes it difficult to answer this question for issues smaller than the minimum size of our samples ($2.5 million in the 1920's, $5 million in the 1950's). One small sample was made of 15 issues in 1923 of $500 thousand to $1 million for which quotations were available, and this was compared with the 22 larger issues of the same year. The differences were sufficient to leave open the question of the representativeness of our findings for smaller issues.

* * *

In both periods it was an unwise man who bought new issues of common stock: he lost about one-fifth of his investment in the first year relative to the market, and another fifth in the years that followed. The data reveal no risk aversion.

The average for the two periods reveal no difference in values after one year, and no significant difference after two years, but a significant difference in the third and fourth, but not fifth, years. The ambiguity in this pattern arises chiefly because the issues of 1928 did quite poorly, and the number of issues in this year was relatively large—one-third of all issues of the 1920's were made in 1928. It may well be that these enterprises did not have sufficient time to become well-launched before the beginning of the Great Depression. With an unweighted average of the various years, there would be no significant difference between the averages in the 1920's and the 1950's.

The "proper" period over which to hold a new stock in these comparisons is difficult to specify: presumably it is equal to the average period the purchasers held the new issues. With speculative new issues one would expect the one year period to be much the most relevant, for thereafter the information provided by this year of experience would become an important determinant of the investor's behavior.

These comparisons suggest that the investors in common stocks in the 1950's did little better than in the 1920's, indeed clearly no better if they held the securities only one or two years. This comparison is incomplete in that dividends are omitted from our reckoning, although this is probably a minor omission and may well work in favor of the 1920's.

The variance of the price ratios, however, was must larger in the 1920's than in the later period: in every year the difference between periods was significant at the 1 per cent level, and in four years at the 1 per cent level. This is a most puzzling finding: the simple-minded interpretation is that the SEC has succeeded in eliminating both unusually good and unusually bad new issues! This is difficult to believe as a matter of either intent or accident. A more plausible explanation lies in the fact that many more new companies used the market in the 1920's than in the 1950's—from one viewpoint a major effect of the SEC was to exclude new companies.

* * *

These studies suggest that the SEC registration requirements had no important effect on the quality of new securities sold to the public. A fuller statistical study—extending to lower sizes of issues and dividend records—should serve to confirm or qualify this conclusion but it is improbable that the qualification will be large, simply because the issues here included account for most of the dollar volume of industrial stocks issued in these periods. Our study is not exhaustive in another sense: we could investigate the changing industrial composition of new issues and other possible sources of differences in the market performance of new issues in the two periods.

But these admissions of the possibility of closer analysis can be made after any empirical study. They do not affect our two main conclusions: (1) it is possible to study the effects of public policies, and not merely to assume that they exist and are beneficial, and (2) grave doubts exist whether if account is taken of costs of regulation, the SEC has saved the purchasers of new issues one dollar.

FRIEND, DISCUSSION AND QUESTIONS FROM THE FLOOR IN ECONOMIC POLICY AND THE REGULATION OF CORPORATE SECURITIES, 115–117 (H. Manne ed. 1969).*

* * * Let me indicate the nature of Stigler's original test.

He took a period from 1923 through 1928 and compared the relative performance of new issues the first five years after issuance with a comparable period after the SEC was in business.

Now, we took Stigler's original test, corrected the data—he made a number of errors, roughly 25, virtually all of which favored his hypothesis—and we found out that with these corrections all five of his experiments were favorable to the post-SEC period; there were no exceptions.

Two of the experiments showed a statistically significant result favorable to the post-SEC period and the improvements ranged from 9 to 37 percent in all five of his experiments, which I would not consider inconsequential; totally apart from matters of statistics. Stigler then changed his original test and said 1923 to 1928 is not the period he should have taken; he really should have taken 1923 to 1927. It turns out that 1928 was the year when the new issues did the worst. So he took out the year in the pre-SEC period when the new issues did the worst.

He terminated his experiments at the year 1927, the year when new issues did best. This is inadmissible procedure. Remember that these new issue performance relatives were corrected for the developments in the market as a whole. Now, using these new tests we still played the game but pointed out that the game is rather biased against the SEC. In our rejoinder we showed that for the third, fourth, and fifth years after issuance the post-SEC results were still considerably better than the pre-SEC results, 6 to 17 percent better, even though not one of the single results was statistically significant. Results for the first two years were inconclusive.

* * * We noted that this post-SEC superiority was least marked in the first year or so after the issue date but that this finding can be explained by two facts: the extensive price-pegging and numerous manipulative pools in the 1920s which might be expected to be particularly active in the first year after the public sale of a new issue, and the extreme difficulty of security evaluation in the absence of full disclosure unless there is some record of operating experience.

* For a more detailed analysis see Friend and Herman, The SEC Through a Glass Darkly, 37 J.Bus. 382 (1964)—Eds.

In connection with the first of these two points, it might be noted that a large sample of new issues, which, according to the Pecora Hearings were subject to pool operations in the 1920s, had an above-average price performance in the first year after the issue date.

Now, a second point that Professor Benston mentions in connection with these Stigler tests is that the variance of these new issue price relatives for individual issues was smaller in the post-SEC period than in the pre-SEC period. Here he makes the same remark that Professor Stigler did commenting on this result and says that this simply shows that securities regulation had effectively precluded both the most successful and the least successful issues and—I think this is no longer Stigler but Professor Benston—who, what economist, wants to preclude the most successful issues?

Actually, I don't know any economist who would not argue that the only point of encouraging risky issues is to enhance average return for the whole set of issues. If you can simply maintain return and minimize risk, presumably this is what the shareholder wants. Of course, effectively what the SEC has been able to accomplish, if you take these figures at face value, is to do the almost impossible: first, increase the average returns on the new issues by making them closer to the returns on outstanding issues and, second, lower risks.

One thing that Professor Benston mentions not at all, and this is one of many, is that if you look at the post-SEC period and confine your attention, on the one hand, to issues which are subject to the full disclosure provisions of the SEC and on the other, to issues which are not subject to the full disclosure provisions, holding size approximately constant, you find out that those issues which are subject to the full disclosure issues of the SEC performed much closer to the market for outstanding issues than issues which were not subject to those disclosure provisions.

Actually, a scientist would find this much more relevant evidence than comparing post-SEC to the pre-SEC period for obvious reasons. There are many other things in addition to the advent of the SEC which affected the relative price performance of new and outstanding issues.

* * *

R. STEVENSON, CORPORATIONS AND INFORMATION: SECRECY, ACCESS AND DISCLOSURE 80–82 (1980).

It is quite clear that politically the '33 Act and the '34 Act were in large measure reactions to the troubled economic climate of the times. Everyone was looking for a scapegoat on which to blame the Depression. The savings of thousands of small investors who had flocked to the stock market in unprecedented numbers during and immediately after the boom years of the twenties had been wiped out. From 1932 to 1934 the Senate held a series of widely publicized hearings on the securities industry in which widespread financial fraud and abuse were uncovered. The debate that led to the passage of the securities laws contained little economic analysis, a lack due partly to the paucity of economic studies of the securities markets at the time and partly to the fact that the attention of most economists was directed at trying to understand the reasons underlying an economic crisis that had left the industrialized world reeling.

Influenced by free-market economic theory and the influential ideas of Louis Brandeis, the draftsmen of the '33 Act rejected direct regulatory intervention in the securities markets in favor of a scheme that emphasized disclosure as a cure for the imperfections and abuses found to be prevalent in the flotation of new issues of securities. Disclosure, it was thought, would principally serve to improve the functioning of the securities markets by providing to investors the information they needed to evaluate the merits of a potential investment. Moreover, although this goal was distinctly secondary, it was also recognized that disclosure would help to deter fraud and self-dealing, conduct which, as Justice Frankfurter put it, has a "shrinking quality."

Although the '34 Act represented a much more direct intervention in the substantive operations of the securities markets, it, too, relied heavily on disclosure as a device both for providing investors with reliable information about firms whose stocks and bonds were traded in the market and for discouraging stock manipulation and unethical management practices.

From the outset, then, the motives underlying the securities laws were mixed. They would, it was thought, improve the functioning of the market by making more readily available the facts about securities and their issuers that were essential to informed investment decisions; at the same time, the required disclosure of these facts would discourage illegal and unethical behavior by securities professionals and corporate managers and would thus protect the unwary investor from the sharp practices that had received so much publicity during the hearings that led to the passage of the statutes.

While on its face this ambivalence might seem perfectly innocuous—indeed, it must have seemed so to the proponents of the legislation—experience has shown that there is a tension between investor protection and facilitation of the efficient functioning of the securities markets. In the last few years this difficulty has been compounded by the evolution—in retrospect one might almost say the inevitable evolution—of an entirely new use of the securities laws. Originally, the improper conduct that disclosure was intended to discourage was conduct, to use the language of the famous Rule 10b–5, "in connection with the purchase or sale of any security"—in other words, "securities fraud"; but within the last decade or so the "connection" between required disclosure and securities trading (or the exercise of shareholder suffrage) has been stretched so thin that it can now be seen by only the most refined eye. Today the disclosure requirements of the securities laws are used, in a variety of ways, for the explicit purpose of influencing a wide range of corporate primary behavior that has only the most tenuous connection with the securities markets. The law, said Sir Henry Maine, evolves through the use of fiction; and although the fiction that this new use of disclosure is related to the original purposes of the securities laws has been steadfastly maintained, it is time that it be recognized for what it is—a new, and distinctive exercise of federal power. It is related to "the protection of investors" to be sure, but in a way that could hardly have been contemplated by the draftsmen of the '33 and '34 Acts.

In their current metamorphosis, then, the securities laws must be seen as serving a tripartite goal: (1) furnishing investors and stockholders with information that is useful in making decisions about investment and the exercise of shareholder suffrage; (2) protecting investors by discouraging fraudulent or deceptive practices in securities trading; and (3) protecting investors by modifying corporate primary conduct in ways that are only indirectly linked to securities transactions. This division of goals, which does not appear to be clearly understood even by the regulators at the Securities and Exchange Commission, has produced a great deal of unnecessary confusion in the interpretation and application of the law.

REPORT OF THE ADVISORY COMMITTEE ON CORPORATE DISCLOSURE TO THE SECURITIES AND EXCHANGE COMMISSION * 618–652 (1977).

THE NATURE OF MANDATED DISCLOSURE

(Prepared for the Advisory Committee by William H. Beaver)

I. *The Investment Setting*

The investment process involves the giving up of current consumption in exchange for securities, which are claims to future, uncertain cash flows. The investor must decide how to allocate wealth between current consumption and investment and how to allocate the funds set aside for investment among the various securities available. The investor naturally has a demand for information that will aid in assessing the future cash flows associated with the securities and the firms that offer those securities. However, the investor is not acting in isolation but within a larger investment environment. This environment consists of several attributes. (1) Investors, some perhaps with limited financial and accounting training, have the opportunity

---

* This report was the result of a major study of disclosure policy conducted by a panel composed of distinguished securities lawyers, law professors, accountants, securities analysts, economists, and others and chaired by former SEC Chairman A. A. Sommer, Jr. One of the Committee's specific mandates was to address the continuing utility of mandated disclosure in light of some of the modern learning summarized in this section. William Beaver is a professor of accounting.—Eds.

to avail themselves of the services of financial intermediaries, such as investment companies, to whom they can defer a portion of the investment process. (2) Investors, some perhaps with limited access to and ability to interpret financial information, have the opportunity to avail themselves of the services of information intermediaries, such as analysts, to whom they can defer a portion or all of the information gathering and processing function. (3) The information intermediaries compete with one another in the gathering and interpretation of investment information, including firm-specific information. Moreover, corporations, competing with one another for the investors' funds, have incentives to provide information to the investment community. (4) Investors and the intermediaries have a set of information available that is more comprehensive and, perhaps in some cases, more timely than the SEC filings. (5) Recent security price research, primarily on listed securities, indicates that, as a reasonable approximation, security prices fully reflect publicly available information (sometimes referred to as market efficiency).

By recent estimates, there are over 14,000 analysts. Corporate management has incentives to provide information to the analysts, and the analysts have incentives to seek out and disseminate such information. This private-sector information system appears to be large and active. * * * Moreover, private-sector information search may explain why security prices quickly reflect a broad set of information. For example, it has been argued that competition among analysts results in security prices that reflect a broad set of information. At the time of the enactment of the Securities Acts, statements of legislative intent indicate that at least some reliance was placed upon competition within the professional investment community to interpret the SEC filings and to effect efficiently determined security prices.

* * * There is an implicit reliance on the functioning of the professional investment community in order to justify the current system as an effective mechanism for disclosure. Moreover, this community often relies on investment information that is more comprehensive and in some cases more timely than that contained in the mandated filings. Under these conditions, the question arises concerning the role of the SEC and its mandated disclosure system in the entire framework. Why is it desirable to have a portion of that disclosure system contain a mandated set of disclosures?

II. *Role of Mandated Disclosure—Previous Rationale*

There have been two common forms of justification for the desirability of disclosure regulation.

The first approach consists of citing a litany of perceived abuses. Several questions can be raised in connection with such an approach. Were the actions in question in fact "abuses?" What one person might label "manipulation" another might label "arbitrage." In particular, what harm was inflicted as a result of such actions? Was inadequate disclosure a contributing factor to the abuses? In other words, will mandating disclosure of some form deter or reduce such activities? What was the frequency of abuses relative to some measure of total activity? This is potentially important because mandated disclosure tends to be imposed on broad classes of corporations, not merely those who committed the perceived abuse.

However, more fundamentally, the point is that perfection is unattainable. Any corporate disclosure system, even one with a mandated portion, will incur some frequency of abuse. It is not clear that there has been a decline in the frequency of abuse over the 44 years since the inception of the Acts, and in the presence of increased regulation of corporate disclosure. Moreover, it is as inappropriate to judge a disclosure system solely on the basis of its perceived abuses as it would be to judge the merits of a public agency, such as the SEC, solely on the basis of its perceived worst regulations. The central issue is whether there is some flaw in the private sector forces that would lead to the conclusion that governmental regulation is a more desirable solution.

A second approach is to define the objectives of the corporate disclosure system and by implication the role of mandated disclosure. For example, "informed, rational investment decisions" is one frequently cited objective. However, again the central issue is why is governmental regulation necessary or desirable to achieve this objective?

III. *Rationale for Disclosure Regulation*

This section will attempt to develop a framework for the consideration of issues regarding disclosure regulation. In order to do so, the nature of economic problems and the purpose of government with respect to those problems will be briefly discussed.

Economic issues fall into two major categories: issues of efficiency and issues of equity. The first category is concerned with the most efficient means of achieving some specified result, where movement to a more efficient solution could in principle result in everyone in the economy being in a more preferred position (or at least as preferred a position) with no one being in a less preferred position * * * . The second category deals with the choice among efficient solutions, where each solution will leave some individuals better off but others worse off. Issues as to how wealth should be distributed among individuals in the economy would be one example of an issue of equity. The government becomes involved in both types of issues. However, the rationale for governmental intervention can vary considerably depending upon the type of issue involved. Therefore it is imperative to state the extent to which the rationale for disclosure regulation rests on efficiency or equity considerations.

In general, the government has a variety of means available to deal with these issues, including the enforcement of private contracts, the definition and enforcement of property rights, taxation, regulation, and direct ownership. The Securities Acts provide two primary methods by which the flow of information to investors is effected. First are the general anti-fraud provisions; the second is the power to explicitly mandate corporate disclosure via the SEC filings and annual reports to shareholders.

With respect to the first method, the Securities Acts provide that it is unlawful to make a false or misleading statement or to omit a material fact in connection with the sale of a security. Laws against fraud are commonplace in the sale of a variety of commodities and they reflect concern over the pervasive problem that the quality of the product or service being sold is uncertain. Moreover, often one party to the transaction may naturally be in a position of superior information regarding the quality. Under anti-fraud provisions, certain parties to the transaction face the prospect of civil or criminal penalties when and if the quality of the commodity is eventually discovered and their behavior is deemed "fraudulent."

While the deterrence of fraud via legal liability is fairly commonplace, the presence of a regulatory mechanism that explicitly mandates the nature of what must be disclosed is a rather special feature of securities' regulations [sic]. For example, neither federal nor state laws require filing a prospectus when an individual sells a home, even though the seller is in a potentially superior position with respect to information regarding the quality of the home.

The subsection III–A deals with arguments that potentially provide a rationale for disclosure regulation, which by implication asserts that reliance solely on the anti-fraud provisions is inadequate. The arguments fall into three major categories. (1) Corporation disclosures induce externalities and therefore have aspects of a public good. (2) Left unregulated, market forces would lead to an asymmetrical or uneven possession of information among investors. (3) Corporate management has incentives to suppress unfavorable information.

III–A. *Corporate Disclosure Externalities*

An externality exists when the actions of one party have effects on other parties, who are not charged (or compensated) via the price mechanism. While in principle it would be possible to conceive of an elaborate price system that would charge or compensate the third parties for these effects, it may be undesirable to do so because it is too costly or simply infeasible.

However, without some form of collective action, the party undertaking the action has no incentive to internalize the effects on third parties, and it may lead to an inefficiency. For example, in the classic public good analysis with positive external effects on third parties, there will be an underproduction of the public good in the absence of a collective action that incorporates the third parties, who benefit from the public good but do not participate in the decision to produce or pay for it. For this reason, these third parties are often referred to as "free riders." In this situation, the private incentives are less than the social incentives to produce the public good.

In the disclosure context, two examples are frequently offered. Externalities could occur when information about the productive opportunities of one firm convey information about the productive opportunities of other firms. Shareholders in the disclosing firm pay the costs of disclosure but shareholders in the other firms do not, even though they are affected by the disclosure. For example, disclosure by a firm about its success (or lack thereof) with respect to some product development may provide information to other firms about their chances of success in similar product developments. In fact, it might even obviate their having to expend resources on product developments. Thus the familiar objection to disclosure on grounds of competitive disadvantage is one form of externality. In this setting there will be a lack of incentive to fully disclose because of the benefits of disclosure to other firms for which the disclosing firm is not being compensated.

The second example deals with positive external effects on prospective shareholders. Investors demand information in order to assess the risks and rewards (*i.e.*, the array of potential future cash flows) associated with alternative portfolios of securities. In making consumption and investment decisions, the investor finds information about a security useful whether or not that particular security ultimately is one of the securities in the portfolio chosen by the investor. The process of selecting the "best" portfolio inherently involves a consideration of investment alternatives (*i.e.*, alternative portfolios). Therefore information on securities in these alternative portfolios may be valuable at the decision making stage, even though after-the-fact some of those securities may not be included in the portfolio chosen. In this setting, current shareholders bear the costs of disclosure, yet prospective shareholders share in the benefits of disclosure (*i.e.*, they are free riders). If the prospective shareholders neither participate in the decision to disclose nor share in bearing the costs, there will tend to be less disclosure than there would be under a collective agreement which included them. They would be willing to pay for additional disclosure such that everyone (both current and prospective shareholders) would be in a more preferred position (*i.e.*, a more efficient solution would be attained).

III–B. *Additional Considerations*

There are a number of additional issues to be introduced in considering an externality or public good approach to disclosure regulation.

First, what is the materiality of the externality or public good aspects to corporate disclosure? Currently, little empirical evidence exists to assess the importance of potential externalities.

Second, issues of cost must be introduced. These include the direct costs of disclosure, the indirect costs of disclosure, and the costs of regulation. The direct costs of disclosure include the costs of the production, certification, dissemination, processing, and interpretation of disclosures. These costs are borne by the corporations and the analyst community and ultimately by investors. The indirect costs include the adverse effects of disclosure on competitive advantage (*e.g.*, creating a disincentive to innovate or invest in product development) and legal liability, which may induce an inefficient bearing of risk by management and auditors, among others. The costs of regulation include the costs involved in the development, compliance, enforcement, and litigation of disclosure regulations. These costs are borne by taxpayers and by shareholders (and perhaps indirectly by consumers and employees).

Third, there are issues related to the information demanded by the regulatory agency in order to develop and monitor the regulations. In the context of disclosure regulation, the SEC attempts to determine the amount and nature of corporate disclosure that would take place, absent the inefficiencies induced by the externalities. In the case where the prospective shareholders are free riders, this involves an attempt to determine their demand for information. In general, investor demand for information will be influenced by the wealth, risk preferences, and beliefs of investors, which is a nontrivial demand for information by the regulatory agency. Economic analyses which show the attainment of a more efficient solution via governmental regulation typically assume perfect knowledge on the part of the regulatory body, which is obviously an unrealistic assumption. Where it is too costly or simply infeasible to obtain the desired information, implementation error by the regulatory agency due to imperfect information may occur.

For example, individuals may not have incentives to honestly reveal their preference for corporate disclosure. They may understate or overstate the desirability of additional disclosure depending on the extent to which they perceive their indication of preference will be used as a basis to assess their share of the costs. A clear illustration is provided when there is no attempt to include the free riders in sharing in the costs of disclosures. In other words, suppose some groups are invited to participate in the process that determines the quantity and nature of corporate disclosure but are not invited to share in bearing the costs of those additional disclosures (*e.g.*, financial analysts). In this situation, the result may be excessive disclosure, rather than inadequate disclosure as suggested by the standard public good analysis. Issues of efficiency and equity are raised by such a process.

Fourth, there are issues that relate to the incentives of the regulatory agency itself. The economics of regulation offers two primary views of regulatory behavior. The first is the "public interest" view, which states that regulatory behavior is directed toward furthering the public interest. This view implicitly assumes the incentives of regulators are aligned so as to further the public interest and that the concept of public interest is well-defined. The second view is known as the "capture theory" and states that the prime beneficiaries of regulation are not the public (or investors, in the case of the Securities Acts) but rather those being regulated. This has led critics of the Securities Acts, such as Stigler, to argue that the primary beneficiaries of the Acts are various members in the professional investment industry rather than investors at large.

Fifth, there is the issue of alternatives to governmental regulation, such as private sector collective agreements. For example, many goods with externalities are dealt with in the private sector. Newspapers and television are two examples. The issue of whether to deal with the problem collectively in the private or public sector revolves around the issue of relative costs of the alternative approaches. It is generally felt that the government has a comparative advantage in dealing with certain types of collective agreements. In particular, where it would be extremely costly or infeasible to preclude free riders or where it would be extremely costly or infeasible to attempt to charge them, it is intuitively felt the comparative advantage favors governmental action.

III–C. *Uneven Possession of Information Among Investors*

A second major argument for disclosure regulation is that, left unregulated, market forces would lead to an uneven possession of information among investors. Selective disclosure is one example. In other words, the result would be a continuum of informed investors ranging from well informed to ill informed. It is further argued that such asymmetry of access to information is inherently unfair and violates the meaning of "fair" disclosure under the Securities Acts. Hence the basis of the argument is typically one of equity rather than efficiency. Simply stated, it is only fair that the less informed be protected from the more informed.

Recent economic analysis of the demand for privately held information suggests that considerable incentives exist to expend efforts searching for and obtaining nonpublicly available information for trading purposes.[12] Studies described elsewhere in the Report document the existence of a large informal information network, where information flows from management to the analysts. However, the unfairness of such a process is not self-evident.

Presumably, the analysts pass along the benefits of the information search to their clients, either directly or indirectly. In this sense, the clients of analysts become more informed investors. However,

---

12. The term, *information for trading purposes*, refers to the demand for information for speculative purposes. In other words, information is demanded for the purpose of earning abnormal returns due to superior information at the expense of uninformed investors. * * *

they pay for the analysts' services either directly or indirectly. As long as the services are available to anyone willing to pay for them, there is no obvious way in which harm is occurring. At the margin, investors will purchase analysts' services to that point where investors are indifferent between being more informed or less informed, given the costs of becoming more informed. In other words, the expected benefits of being more informed (e.g., in the form of expected superior returns due to better information) are equal to (or offset by) the costs incurred to obtain the additional information. A common argument is that some investors cannot afford to purchase the services of analysts. However, the existence of financial intermediaries makes the force of this argument unclear. Moreover, it ignores several alternatives open to relatively less informed investors. One such alternative is to partially insulate themselves from more informed traders via buy-and-hold strategies and index funds. Also the actions of the more informed may signal their information to the less informed and as a result prices may partially (in the limit, fully) reflect the information.

The purchase of analysts' information can be viewed as the decision to purchase a higher quality product (in this case, superior information). In general, quality differences exist with respect to any commodity, and usually it is not thought to be unfair when one consumer chooses to purchase a higher quality product while another chooses a lower quality item. The purchase of automobiles is one example, but illustrations could be provided for almost any commodity.

While selective disclosure is commonly cast as an equity issue, there are grounds for considering it on the basis of efficiency. * * * If there were no costs to forming private-sector collective agreements, investors would agree among themselves not to privately seek information. Everyone would gain in that society would no longer incur the costs of private search for information, whose sole purpose is to redistribute wealth among investors via trading on superior information. In other words, the trading gains in the form of superior returns due to privately held information net out to zero across all investors. It is a zero-sum gain in that every investor with superior returns is offset by other investors with inferior returns. However, to the extent that such search causes investors to incur real costs, it is not a zero-sum game but these costs constitute dead weight losses to investors as a whole. Investors would be better off to avoid such costs.

However reaching and enforcing such a collective agreement might be extremely costly or simply infeasible. In the absence of effective enforcement, the agreement would rapidly deteriorate, because there would always be a private incentive to cheat on the agreement. Therefore the SEC may have a comparative advantage in effectively eliminating private search for information. It could be accomplished by either or both of its two major means of regulation. (1) It could preempt private search by mandating the disclosure of the item in public filings or annual reports. (2) It could impose sufficient legal liability on transmittal of information from management to analysts such that information flows would be deterred (or in the limit eliminated).

This poses a dilemma. This argument suggests there will be a tendency for an excessive amount of information, as analysts and others privately search for information and disseminate it. However, this is the converse of the public good argument which implies an inadequate amount of disclosure. There are opposing forces operating. In one case the private incentives for disclosure fall short, while in the second case the private incentives are excessive. To the extent the former exists, it might be desirable to permit a certain amount of private search to compensate for the otherwise inadequate incentives to publicly disclose. However, permitting too much will lead to the inefficiencies described above.

III–D. *Management Incentives to Disclose*

A third major argument for disclosure regulation is that management has incentives to suppress unfavorable information. While there may be a general awareness of this potential among investors, investors would not know specifically the nature or materiality of the suppressed information. As a result, investors will be unable to distinguish quality differences among stocks to the same extent they would under fuller disclosure. Hence, security prices will not fully reflect quality differences among stocks and there will be uncertainty regarding the quality of each stock. There may be a tendency for lower quality stocks to be selling at a higher price than would prevail under fuller disclosure and conversely for the higher quality stocks.[19] This can lead to a phenomenon known as adverse selection, where the managements of poorer quality stocks have greater incentives to offer additional shares for sale than the managements of higher quality stocks.

Firms will tend to respond to this problem in a number of ways. (1) Higher quality firms will attempt to signal their higher quality by undertaking actions that would be irrational unless they were in fact of higher quality. The effectiveness of this signaling behavior will be influenced by the extent to which the lower quality firms can imitate the signaling behavior. Moreover, signaling may be a costly activity with no rewards beyond those of signaling. (2) Managements will offer to have their disclosure system monitored and certified by an independent party, leading to a demand for auditing services. (3) Managements may offer warrantees [*sic*] to shareholders whereby they will incur penalties if it is eventually discovered that unfavora-

---

19. A lower quality stock is one whose price is overstated relative to the price that would prevail if greater disclosures were available to investors, and conversely for a higher quality stock.

ble information was suppressed. In fact, managements' willingness to be auditied and to offer warrantees [*sic*] can be signals in themselves. Obviously both auditing services and warrantee [*sic*] contracts are not costless. One of the most important costs in the warrantee [*sic*] is that management may end up bearing more risk than that associated with failure to disclose.

After-the-fact it may be difficult to disentangle the deterioration in the stock price that was due to correcting inadequate disclosure as opposed to other unfavorable events. As a result, management may become an insurer for events in addition to those induced by management's disclosure policy. This may lead to an inefficient sharing of risks, relative to that that would attain if there were no uncertainty about the quality of the stocks. The costs may be prohibitive that such warrantees [*sic*] would not be offered.

The anti-fraud provisions can be viewed as requiring firms to provide disclosure warrantees [*sic*] to investors, where presumably the legal liability is sufficient to offset the incentives of management to suppress unfavorable information. The argument for governmental intervention as opposed to private sector contracting would be that the SEC has a comparative (cost) advantage in achieving the same result. However, while this argument forms a basis for anti-fraud statutes, it is not clear why a mandated disclosure system is desirable. In other words, why is reliance upon anti-fraud statutes deemed to be inadequate?

III–E. *Summary of Previous Discussion*

The purpose of the preceding discussion was to identify some of the issues involved in defining the role of mandated disclosures within the corporate disclosure system. Three rationale were provided for the potential desirability of the regulation of corporate disclosures. All three arguments rest on the premise that a public agency, such as the SEC, has a comparative advantage in forming collective agreements of a certain form (*i.e.*, where the potential beneficiaries or affected parties are numerous and difficult to identify and hence where it would be more costly or simply infeasible to attempt to deal with the same issue via private sector collective agreements).

IV. *Security Price Research and/or Implications*

Whether the potential desirability is likely to be realized depends upon a number of other considerations, including the ability of the regulatory agency to assess investor demand for information. Recent security price research in the areas of portfolio theory and efficient markets provides a framework within which to view the investor demand for information. These areas represent an important part of what is currently known about the investment decision and the environment within which that decision is made.

IV–A. *Portfolio Theory**

Portfolio theory characterizes the investment decision as a trade-off between expected return and risk (*i.e.*, as measured by the extent to which the actual return may differ from the expected return). Each portfolio of securities offers the investor a given combination of risk and expected return. Given the risk attitudes of the investor, the best portfolio is one that is the most preferred combination of risk and expected return. There are two immediate implications of portfolio theory for corporate disclosure. (1) Each individual security cannot be viewed in isolation but must be evaluated in the context of its membership in a portfolio consisting of other securities. The individual security is irrelevant, *except* insofar as it contributes to the overall risk and expected return of the portfolio. (2) The investor is concerned with *risk* as well as expected return (sometimes referred to as performance). Hence, corporate disclosure is concerned with the assessment of risk as well as the assessment of performance.

However, portfolio theory distinguishes between two types of risk. The first type is called unsystematic or diversifiable risk, because it can be virtually eliminated by diversification. The second type is called systematic or nondiversifiable risk, because it cannot be eliminated via diversification. The basis for this distinction rests on the view that two types of events affect the price of a security. There are economy-wide events, such as changes in anticipated inflation and interest rates, which affect the fortunes (and hence prices) of all securities with varying sensitivity. However, there are other events whose implications are largely firm-specific, such as changes in management, contract awards, and litigation. Unsystematic events by their very nature tend to be uncorrelated among firms at any point in time. To the extent that prices reflect only unsystematic or firm-specific events, returns among securities would be uncorrelated, and risk of the portfolio of such securities could be driven to zero via diversification across securities. However, to the extent that prices vary due to systematic events, security returns would be perfectly correlated, and diversification would not reduce the risk. Portfolio theory states that each security's return is subject to both types of risk. However, at the portfolio level only the systematic risk prevails, because the unsystematic risk has been diversified away. The investor is unnecessarily incurring unsystematic risk by failing to diversify. Therefore, there is a basic presumption in favor of diversification, unless the investor has some justification for choosing

---

* The economic literature classified under the general heading "portfolio theory" is voluminous. An accessible introduction is found in Chapter 6 of R. Posner and K. Scott, Economics of Corporate Law and Securities Regulation (1980).—Eds.

to remain undiversified. One reason for doing so would be superior information.

IV–B. *Investor Demand for Firm-Specific Information*

Portfolio theory stresses the importance of diversification in the reduction of much of the risk associated with holding a single security. It is unrealistic to believe that investors hold only one security (*e. g.,* the one being described in a registration statement). In fact, investors have the opportunity to purchase well diversified portfolios through financial intermediaries. * * * If the investor holds a well diversified portfolio, how, if at all, does this alter the way disclosure is viewed? It has been argued that diversification may substantially reduce the investor's demand for firm-specific information. The investor is concerned with firm-specific information only insofar as it is useful in assessing the portfolio attributes. While the investor may have considerable uncertainty about the risks and rewards associated with any one security, this uncertainty is considerably reduced at the portfolio level because of the effects of diversification. For example, while there may be considerable uncertainty as to the riskiness of any one security, typically the riskiness of the portfolio can be assessed with much greater confidence. In other words, an overestimate of the risk of one security will tend to be offset by an underestimation of the risk of another security. The effects of diversification are potentially powerful, and the benefits from incremental improvements in the precision of firm-specific information may be minimal.

In another context, suppose the investor is concerned that the security being purchased is mispriced, relative to the price at which it would sell if additional disclosures were available. From the point of view of the additional disclosure, some of the securities will be overpriced but some will be underpriced. A diversified portfolio will likely contain some of each and their effects will tend to be offsetting. Hence, the net effects of additional disclosure may differ considerably from the effects analyzed on a security-by-security basis.

This is not to suggest that portfolio theory implies that additional disclosure is valueless, but only that it can alter the way in which disclosure issues are viewed. There are a number of obvious additional considerations. (1) Many investors may choose to remain relatively undiversified, even though they have the opportunity to do so. These investors, for one reason or another, perceive that the disadvantages of diversification outweigh the advantages. The SEC faces a social choice question of to what extent to impose disclosure requirements on companies (and hence impose costs on all investors) in order to accommodate investors who have chosen not to diversify. (2) Not all investors may have access to a given item (*i.e.,* a problem of selective disclosure). (3) Management may use nondisclosure to obtain greater compensation than otherwise would be the case. (4)

There may be effects on resource allocation that are ignored when the investor setting is narrowly viewed.

IV–C. *Efficient Security Markets*

A securities market is said to be *efficient* with respect to some defined information if the security prices in that market "fully reflect" that information. The term, "fully reflect," is not a precise term. Operationally, if prices fully reflect a given set of information, then investors are playing a "fair game" with respect to that information. This means that all trading strategies based on that information will yield only the normal, expected return, commensurate with the risk involved.

A more precise definition is that the market is efficient with respect to a given piece of information if prices act *as if* everyone possessed that information and were able to interpret its implications for security prices. For example, several empirical studies have examined market efficiency with respect to changes in accounting methods. To say the market is efficient with respect to changes in accounting methods is to say that the stock prices behave as if all investors had knowledge of the change in method and knew how to interpret it.

The term, *market efficiency*, is unfortunate in some respects, because it may convey normative or value-laden connotations which have nothing to do with the concept itself. The concept of market efficiency refers to a relationship between stock prices and some defined information set. It is not to be confused with other uses of the term, *efficiency*, such as those which refer to how resources are allocated in the economy. It can also be misleading to use the term, *market efficiency*, without also specifying the information set. For example, to say simply that the market is efficient is an incomplete statement unless the intended implication is that the market is efficient with respect to any or all information. However, such an implication usually is not intended. Typically, when market efficiency is used in an unqualified manner, it is intended to imply that the market is efficient with respect to publicly available data, since most of the empirical research has been concerned with market efficiency of this form. Three major forms of market efficiency have been delineated: (1) weak form efficiency, which refers to market efficiency with respect to past security prices, (2) semi-strong form efficiency, which defines market efficiency with respect to publicly available information, and (3) strong form efficiency, which is concerned with market efficiency with respect to all information, including inside information.

There are several potential implications of market efficiency with respect to publicly available data. (1) Disclosure may still be a substantive issue. Merely because prices fully reflect publicly available information does not imply that prices necessarily reflect nonpublicly available information. (2) Once disclosure is provided, the method of formatting is unlikely to have an impact on stock prices. (3) Given the large, active private sector information system, many items may be reflected in prices even though they are not reported in annual reports, SEC filings, or any publicly available document. Moreover, any one type of data may have a number of substitutes which can provide similar information. Therefore, before proceeding to mandate any given item, it would be appropriate to consider if that item would be a material addition given the other data effectively being disseminated to the investment community and reflected in prices.

There is one nonimplication of the efficient market that deserves explicit recognition. Merely because prices reflect a broad information set does not preclude or presume the desirability of mandated disclosures. With respect to certain types of information, there still may be inadequate private incentives to gather and disseminate such data. Moreover, even if it is being disseminated via the private sector system, it may be deemed more efficient (*i.e.*, less costly) to have it disseminated via public disclosure by the corporation rather than via the private search activities for the reasons discussed earlier.

IV–D. *Empirical Evidence On The Effects Of Disclosure Regulation*

The empirical evidence falls into two major categories. The first deals with attempts to assess the immediate effects of the '33 and '34 Acts. The second type deals with attempts to assess the effects of some specific disclosure requirement imposed subsequent to the initial period.

Two prominent studies in the first category are Stigler's * * * analysis of the effects of the '33 Act on the return distributions of new issues, and Benston's * * * analysis of firms affected by the initial disclosure regulations of '34 Act. Both Stigler and Benston concluded that the securities legislation had little or no effect on the distribution of security price returns. The findings and the interpretations placed on the findings were highly controversial and have evoked a number of criticisms. The criticisms fall into three general categories. (1) The tests that were conducted are not appropriate tests of the effects. In other words, there was the lack of the development of a theory as to what security price return effects would be theoretically expected if the Securities Acts were or were not effective. Hence the tests are not capable of distinguishing whether the legislation was effective. (2) Even assuming that the tests were appropriate, a closer or more careful analysis of the findings would reveal that some effects were in fact observed in these studies. (3) Even assuming the tests were appropriate, the research design used was not powerful enough to detect the effects. * * *

V. *Concluding Remarks*

Empirical research of the sort described above may be useful in dealing with some aspects of mandated disclosure. If the particular item is being mandated because it is expected to add to the information used by the market, it seems reasonable to expect the disclosure of such data to impact on stock prices. If no stock price reaction is observed, then the question must be asked—what are the effects, if any, of requiring disclosure of that item? For example, one effect could be a lower cost to investors via mandating disclosure rather than relying on the private sector's informal information network.

In other words, it is virtually inconceivable that the SEC would not be able to find some disclosures that would have a price effect. * * * Merely because the private sector has chosen not to disseminate a given item cannot be taken as prima facie evidence that the incentives to disclose are inadequate. It may be that the "benefits" of disclosure of that item are perceived to be not commensurate with the costs, such that disclosure is not worthwhile. The crucial issue is how to distinguish nondisclosure on the basis of perceived insufficient benefits from nondisclosure due to some inadequacy in the market system.

Similarly, the observation that the current system incurs a certain level of abuse is a slim basis on which to justify the desirability of mandated disclosure. Other issues must be considered. (1) To what extent, if any, would abuse be reduced by mandating additional disclosure? (2) What are the additional costs associated with mandated disclosure? (3) Are there alternative methods of dealing with the problem that might be more effective and/or less costly? Reliance on anti-fraud statutes and private sector collective agreements are two possibilities. In any event, no system, even a mandated one, is likely to drive the level of abuse to zero nor is it likely such a result would be desirable, even it it were feasible, because of the costs of achieving that result. Implementation error caused by a lack of evidence on investors' demand for information and/or biases induced by reliance on vested interests must also be considered.

* * *

1 L. LOSS, SECURITIES REGULATION 124–26 (2d ed. 1961).

* * * The Securities Act became effective in May 1933. * * * Nine months later Professor William O. Douglas (who, like Brandeis, was to leave his mark on the Securities Act and the SEC) published a pungent critique of the act.

The battle on the act, he pointed out, was being waged by both sides on political lines, accompanied by a good deal of emotional thinking. Nevertheless, the act "is symbolic of a shift of political power." (It is important to remember when this was written.) Hence, Douglas said, "it is sheer nonsense to talk of repealing the

Securities Act or even of making substantial amendments." At the same time, he thought three propositions were "tolerably clear":

> First, that the Securities Act falls far short of accomplishing its purposes. Second, that in any programme for the protection of investors and in any genuine and permanent correction of the evils of high finance an Act like the Securities Act is of a decidedly secondary character. And, third, that a vigorous enforcement of the Act promises to spell its own defeat because it is so wholly antithetical to the programme of control envisaged in the New Deal and to the whole economy under which we are living.

As to the first two points, the "glaring light of publicity" on which the act is based is not enough, Douglas wrote, because

> those needing investment guidance will receive small comfort from the balance sheets, contracts, or compilation of other data revealed in the registration statement. They either lack the training or intelligence to assimilate them and find them useful, or are so concerned with a speculative profit as to consider them irrelevant.

This means that the results of the act for the investor are primarily twofold: the disclosure requirement will in itself prevent some fraudulent transactions that cannot stand the light of publicity, and the judgment of those who do understand will be reflected in the market price and will seep down to the investor through his advisers. In addition, the stringent civil liability provisions of the act are a great advance over the hypertechnical common law. But this chief virtue of the statute is also one of its greatest weaknesses. For history teaches that "terroristic methods are notoriously feeble instruments for continuous control." Witness the Eighteenth Amendment. The act is also "superficial." Registration will be hardest for well-established going concerns—"businesses with far flung units, with complicated details, with kaleidoscopic activities"—and easiest for "the oil well scheme, the gold mine venture, the holding company set-up, or the investment trust, in fact, any enterprise which is just beginning or whose activities, assets, and relations are simple." And at best the registration statement will be discounted shortly after its effectiveness "by a host of other bearish or bullish factors." There is * * * nothing to control the power of self-perpetuating management or to protect the rights of minorities, nothing on the soundness or unsoundness of capital structure or on "the problem of mobilizing the flow of capital to various productive channels."

To be sure, the act is but a first step. But this, said Douglas, is where the third point comes in. The whole business is essentially a "nineteenth-century piece of legislation" which unrealistically envisages a return to "Main Street business." This explains, among other things, "the great reliance placed on truth about securities, as if the truth could be told to people who could understand it—a supposition which might be justified if little units of business were seeking funds and people were buying shares with the modicum of intelligence with which they are supposed to buy wearing apparel or horses." We cannot "turn back the clock" to simpler days. We must perfect a plan for control of our present forms of organization so as to harness the "instruments of production not only for the ancient purpose of profit but also for the more slowly evolving purpose of service in the sense of the public good." Although the type of control embodied in the state blue sky laws should not be condemned, it would if transplanted to the federal scene engage a government agency in "activity a thousand fold more complex than the analogous activity of the Interstate Commerce Commission in the railroad field." "The control needed is one which would combine regulation by industry with supervision by government." For example, a company which had cleared its security through the Code Authority and the supervisory governmental agency (these were the days of the NRA) would gain the benefits of a moderated Securities Act. And ultimately there must be some form of control over access to the capital market.

Chapter 13

SHAREHOLDER ACTION AND PROXY REGULATION

A. THE POSITION OF THE SHAREHOLDER

1. THE ROLE OF THE SHAREHOLDERS IN LARGE CORPORATIONS

a. Separation of Ownership from Control

Stock ownership of large, publicly held corporations has become widely dispersed. In corporations with thousands or tens of thousands of shareholders, typically no single shareholder owns more than a fraction of a percent of a corporation's outstanding shares. As a result, ownership rarely possesses the attribute of management. Professors Adolf Berle and Gardiner Means in their classic work, The Modern Corporation and Private Property (1932), studied the characteristics of the two hundred largest corporations listed on the New York Stock Exchange and concluded that management and ownership had become separated; that existing management "controlled" most of these entities and was free to determine policies affecting prices, production, and employment with little, if any, effective constraint from the owners.

In developing their thesis of the separation of control from ownership in largely publicly held corporations, Berle and Means stated:

> [P]arallel with the growth in the size of the industrial unit has come a division in its ownership such that an important part of the wealth of individuals consists of interests in great enterprises of which no one individual owns a major part. [*Id.* at 66.]

> [A] large body of security holders has been created who exercise virtually no control over the wealth which they or their predecessors in interest have contributed to the enterprise. In case of management control, the ownership interest held by the controlling group amounts to but a very small fraction of the total ownership. [*Id.* at 5.]

> * * * [T]he position of ownership has changed from that of an active to that of a passive agent. In place of actual physical properties over which the owner could exercise direction and for which he was responsible, the owner now holds a piece of paper representing a set of rights and expectations with respect to an enterprise. But over the enterprise and over the physical property—the instruments of production—in which he has an interest, the owner has little control. At the same time he bears no responsibility with respect to the enterprise or its physical property. [*Id.* at 66.]

[I]n the corporate system, the "owner" of industrial wealth is left with a mere symbol of ownership while the power, the responsibility and the substance which have been an integral part of ownership in the past are being transferred to a separate group in whose hands lies control. * * * [*Id.* at 68.]

[In companies] in which ownership is so widely distributed that no individual or small group has even a minority interest large enough to dominate the affairs of the company. When the largest single interest amounts to but a fraction of one per cent—the case in several of the largest American corporations—no stockholder is in the position through his holdings alone to place important pressure upon the management or to use his holdings as a considerable nucleus for the accumulation of the majority to votes necessary to control. [*Id.* at 84.]

* * *

In such companies where does control lie? To answer this question, it is necessary to examine in greater detail the conditions surrounding the electing of the board of directors. In the election of the board the stockholder ordinarily has three alternatives. He can refrain from voting, he can attend the annual meeting and personally vote his stock, or he can sign a proxy transferring his voting power to certain individuals selected by the management of the corporation, the proxy committee. As his personal vote will count for little or nothing at the meeting unless he has a very large block of stock, the stockholder is practically reduced to the alternative of not voting at all or else of *handing over his vote to individuals over whom he has no control and in whose selection he did not participate.* In neither case will he be able to exercise any measure of control. Rather, control will tend to be in the hands of those who select the proxy committee by whom, in turn, the election of directors for the ensuing period may be made. Since the proxy committee is appointed by the existing management, the latter can virtually dictate their own successors. Where ownership is sufficiently sub-divided, the management can thus become a self-perpetuating body even though its share in the ownership is negligible. This form of control can properly be called "management control."* [*Id.* at 86–88.]

A recent significant study by Professor Edward S. Herman, Corporate Control, Corporate Power (1981), confirms the Berle and Means findings. Herman finds that "The power lacunae left by the diffusion of ownership is gradually occupied by those who exercise power on a daily basis and who are thereby well positioned to consoli-

---

* Later studies have confirmed the continuation of the same trends. In one study, management control of industrial companies increased from 40% to 76%. R. Larner, Management Control and the Large Corporation 12 (1970).

date it more firmly over time. Management's control is facilitated by its domination of the board selection processes and the resultant capacity of top officials to mold boards into friendly and compliant bodies." *Id.* at 52.

However, as Professor Herman adds, "Management's domination is not total, however—the owners do not disappear, nor do the lenders." *Id.* His further analysis demonstrated that the constraining force of other influences do not seriously constrain management, nor change its focus from that of profit maximization.

b. The Emergence of Institutional Investors as Shareholders

Another significant trend in the composition of share ownership has been the growing portion of stock held by institutional investors, particularly, bank trust departments of commercial banks and insurance companies. Financial institutions today hold substantial blocks of stock in many large corporations. A 1971 study by the Securities and Exchange Commission * of 213 financial institutions, including the 50 largest bank departments, 71 investment advisors managing the portfolios of the largest registered investment company complexes, the 26 largest life insurance companies, the 25 largest property and liability insurance company groups, and 41 self-administered portfolios belonging to the largest corporate employee benefit plans, educational endowments and foundations, reveal the following aggregate holdings by the selected financial institutions:

— 50 percent or more of the common stock of Xerox, Gulf Oil, Ford, Merck, Houston Lighting & Power, Middle South Utilities, Ampex, Trane, and National Airlines.

— 40 to 50 percent of the common stock of IBM, Eastman Kodak, Sears, Avon, Polaroid, Goodyear, International Paper, TRW, Celanese, National Steel, Upjohn, TWA, Tampa Electric, Lone Star Cement, Beckman Instruments, U.S. Freight, Northrop, and Hanes.

— 30 to 40 percent of the common stock of Standard Oil of New Jersey, Texaco, GE, 3–M, Mobil, Standard Oil of California, Proctor & Gamble, Standard Oil of Indiana, IT&T, American Home Products, International Nickel of Canada, J.C. Penney, Westinghouse, Owens-Corning, Chrysler, May Department Stores, Litton Industries, Schering, Kimberly-Clark, Hilton, Foremost-McKesson, Zayre, Metromedia, and General Portland Cement.

— 20 to 30 percent of the common stock of GM, DuPont, GT&E, RCA, Phillips Petroleum, Pacific Gas & Electric, Woolworth, Singer, Teledyne, Beatrice Foods, American Metal Climax, Standard Brands, Kaiser Aluminum, St. Regis Paper, Bendix, Continental Telephone, Long Island Lighting, Freeport

* SEC Institutional Investor Study Report, H.R.Doc. 92–64, Part 3, 92d Cong. 1st Sess., 1308–1309, 1364–1373 (Table IX–13) (1971).

Sulphur, Del Monte, Hart Schaffner & Marx, Emery Air Freight, Fluor, Arizona Public Service, Fuqua, Grand Union, Hammermill Paper, National Can, and Revere Copper & Brass.

———

An earlier Congressional staff study * of the 49 largest bank trust departments, found 176 companies in which one bank held 5 percent or more of the common stock of one or more of the 500 largest industrials, 20 companies in which one bank held 5 percent or more of the common stock of one or more of the 50 largest merchandisers, and 23 companies in which one bank held 5 percent or more of the common stock of one or more of the 50 largest transportation companies.

What accounts for the rise of financial institutions, especially bank trust departments, as shareholders? After World War II employee benefit plans grew rapidly, encouraged by favorable tax features and the drive by unions for increased employee protection. The development of employee benefit plans propelled bank trusts to a preeminent position among institutional investors, as banks manage about 80% of the assets of employee benefit plans.

Prior to World War II, bank trust funds were overwhelmingly invested in bonds. The then existing legal lists for investments by fiduciaries prohibited or severely limited equity holding. As a result of the inflationary pressures after World War II, which eroded the purchasing power of the trust principal and income, many states first increased the portion of trust principal which could be invested in common stock and then substituted a general "prudent investor" standard. Now, practically all the market value of pension trust portfolios is invested in common stocks.

The next excerpt summarizes a variety of public concerns with respect to share holdings by institutional shareholders.

SECURITIES AND EXCHANGE COMMISSION, INSTITUTIONAL INVESTOR STUDY REPORT, SUMMARY VOLUME, H.R. Doc. No. 92–64, Part 8, 92d Cong., 1st Sess. 127 (1971).

CONCLUSIONS

1. The prevailing legal framework does not distinguish materially between institutions and other holders of corporate shares in terms of shareholder prerogatives within the structure of corporate power, although there are significant practical and economic differences between them.

2. Institutions have the potential economic power to influence many companies, particularly large companies, because of their stock

* 1 Staff of Subcommittee on Domestic Finance, House Comm. on Banking and Currency, 90th Cong. 2d Sess, Commercial Banks and their Trust Activities: Emerging Influence on the American Economy 91 (Subcomm. Print 1968).

holdings.   Part two of the Study demonstrates that investment assets are concentrated in relatively few institutions.   These institutions in turn tend to concentrate their portfolios in relatively few stocks. Hence, it follows that institutional holdings may constitute a large percentage of the outstanding shares of certain companies.   Since institutions tend to invest primarily in the securities of larger companies, concentration is most pronounced in the shares of such companies.

3.   Some institutions, particularly banks, have personnel and business relationships with portfolio companies.   These relationships may tend to reinforce any power conferred as a result of stock holdings. They also create potential conflicts of interest and the possibility of misuse of inside information.   Although the Study can draw no general conclusions as to whether these adverse consequences actually occur or to what extent they may occur, it appears that there is a strong statistical correlation between bank stock holdings and personnel and business relationships.

4.   Institutions do not generally involve themselves directly in corporate decisionmaking, but instead have a policy of liquidating their holdings where corporate policies and proposals appear inappropriate.   They generally vote in favor of management proposals and only rarely report informal participation or consultation.   A number of institutions have a policy of always voting with management or of refraining from participation, particularly where general corporate matters (as opposed to acquisitions) are involved.   Participation is more likely to occur when the institution cannot readily liquidate its holdings in the company's shares and when the benefits of such participation are clear.

5.   Some institutions have been actively and significantly involved in facilitating contested transfers of corporate control.   In such cases, unlike ordinary corporate decisionmaking, the benefits to participating institutions may be more certain: in addition to trading and tendering profits, institutions may receive special inducements and benefits not made available to other shareholders of target companies.

For our purposes, the most significant development is the actual and potential impact of institutional investors on corporate decisionmaking.   One commentator summarized the debate with respect to the role of institutional investors as follows:

**MELVIN EISENBERG, THE STRUCTURE OF THE
CORPORATION: A LEGAL ANALYSIS
56–58 (1976).**

The appropriate relation between institutional shareholders and their portfolio corporations has prompted considerable debate.   Managers and their allies seek to constrain the discretion of such share-holders; shareholder democrats seek to expand it. One issue in the debate has been whether, considering their power and sophistication, institutional investors owe an obligation to their fellow shareholders to oversee corporate managers and to effect management changes when necessary. Generally speaking, the institutional investors have taken the position their primary obligation lies to their own benefi-ciaries, not to their fellow shareholders in portfolio companies; that they have neither the time nor the skills to exercise an oversight function; and that a company whose management should be changed is normally an unsound investment, so that an investor which does not like incumbent management should switch out of the investment as quickly as possible, rather than stay in and try to accomplish a change. Some of these arguments appear overstated. There are un-doubtedly many cases in which a corporation's assets outshine its management and an institution's position is too large to be liquidated except at a substantial loss, so that it would do better to try to change management than to sell the stock. It seems likely that there have been additional, unstated, reasons for the institutions' promanagement position, including obedience to the mores of the fi-nancial community, a desire to stay on good terms with management in order to promote a free flow of inside information, and in the case of certain institutions, particularly banks, a desire to obtain or retain business in their noninvestor capacities. Nevertheless, the position that the primary duty of a financial institution is to protect the inter-ests of its own beneficiaries, and that such institutions are in any event not equipped to oversee management, seems essentially sound.

2. THE SECURITIES MARKETS

In Chapter 12 you were introduced to the barest details of how securities are *issued* by a corporation. We turn now, with equal brevity, to the subject of how securities are *traded* by shareholders.

Investors usually acquire securities of a corporation from other investors rather than them from the company. Companies do not continuously sell new shares but do so only occasionally. Bringing buyers and sellers together is a vital economic function. Unless such a market exists companies will be unable to sell securities to the pub-lic except for low risk, high interest and early maturing loans. The market among shareholders is a *secondary* market. Actually, it is several markets.

The first type of market is the organized stock exchanges, such as the New York Stock Exchange, the American Stock Exchange, the Midwest Stock Exchange, the Pacific Coast Stock Exchange and about ten others. Securities are "listed" on the exchange, and trad-ing consists of a continuous auction. There is always a seller to match a buyer. All transactions are promptly reported on the "tape," which now is a computer screen. Trading occurs on the "floor" of the exchange and is accomplished by brokers (agents) who are members. They charge their customers a commission.

The other principal market is not a formal gathering place, but is called the over-the-counter market. It is the means by which securities that are not listed are traded, although sometimes listed securities are traded in this market. There is no continuous auction, but brokers negotiate on behalf of their customers for the best price. In fact the broker usually buys from one customer, and resells to another. Rather than receiving a commission, the broker (now acting as a dealer) makes a profit. Dealers communicate either by telephone or by computer connection.

There are also hybrid markets. Many transactions involve the sale of large blocks, usually between financial institutions, for which the customary mechanics are not suitable. In effect, special markets accommodate block trades.

Corporations need to devise a method to keep abreast of the trading in their securities. They must know where to send dividends and who has the rights of ownership at any given time. The beneficial owner of a security is the person entitled to the economic enjoyment of it, or who has the power to direct how the security will be voted or whether it will be sold. An individual owner usually possesses all of those attributes; in the case of an institution matters are more complicated. As we shall soon see, beneficial owners are not always the ones who appear as owners of record. It is sometimes more convenient to allow the broker who executed the transaction to keep possession of the certificate evidencing ownership. The company knows only of the record holder's existence and communicates with that person, who must, in turn, communicate with the beneficial owner.

3. HOW SHAREHOLDERS ACT

State corporation law provides a limited degree of shareholder participation in corporate affairs. We have observed how management and directors are chiefly responsible for running the business. [*See* Chapter 10.] But the shareholder role is nevertheless significant. Most corporation statutes provide that the corporation must hold an annual meeting of stockholders for the purpose of electing directors, who ordinarily are chosen for a term of one year. (*E.g.*, Delaware Gen.Corp.Law § 211). Certain transactions that affect the structure of a corporation must be approved by the stockholders, such as amendments to the articles of incorporation, mergers, and similar transactions. In addition, most corporation statutes permit the bylaws to be amended by the stockholders.

Some state corporation statutes specifically require an annual meeting to be held for the purpose of electing directors, and they provide remedies to shareholders to enforce this mandate. (*E.g.*, Del. Gen.Corp.L. § 211). State law also contains provisions with respect to notice, quorum, the vote required to take action at a meeting, and, of course, the voting rights of stock. Rules governing the conduct of a meeting are not found in statutes, but courts generally impose a standard of fair conduct. *See* Note, Corporate Meeting Procedure: A Rationale, 57 Va.L.Rev. 129 (1971). Thus, the chairman of the meeting could not arbitrarily rule out of order a motion to change the location of the next meeting, despite the absence of any provision in the statute specifically authorizing such a motion. Of course, there are practical inhibitions on the ability of an aggrieved shareholder to obtain redress in that situation.

In some instances, inspectors of election will be appointed prior to the meeting by the board of directors. Their function is to judge the validity of the votes that are cast. When there is a declared contest, the contestants may negotiate private arrangements setting forth rules for the conduct of the meeting and the counting of votes, and these agreements are legally enforceable. *See* Note: How the Proxy Process Works, *infra*.

In large companies many thousands of stockholders are scattered throughout the country, each holding a relatively small number of shares. It is simply impossible to convene the stockholders at one time or place to consider and act upon the matters that require their approval. A substitute process must be found to permit effective stockholder action. That substitute process is proxy voting.

The body of law which facilitates this process marks one of the great intersections of federal and state law. The authorization for stockholders to vote by proxy is found in the state corporation statutes, of which § 33 of the Model Business Corporation Act is typical. First, the statute permits shareholders to vote in person or by proxy. Second, it limits the validity of the proxy to a period of 11 months from the date of its execution. Under certain circumstances, the shareholder can make his appointment of a proxy irrevocable. Del. Gen.Corp.Law § 212.

"Proxy" is just another word for agent. Ordinarily, one thinks of a principal conferring power upon an agent to accomplish the principal's business. A third person's interest in that transaction extends only to the scope of the agent's authority. The shareholder appointment of a proxy, or agent, to act on his behalf at the shareholder meeting operates differently. Most striking, perhaps, is the fact that in large companies, the agent seeks out the principal to obtain the power necessary to conduct the meeting. Most often the management of the corporation is the agent. Management has a responsibility to conduct the company's business, and this requires the assembling of a quorum, but it is also true that management (the agent) derives a personal benefit—reelection to the board and retention of employment—from the shareholder vote. It is also plain that other principals are affected by the fact that fellow shareholders confer power on agents, thereby causing the election of directors who will govern the affairs of the corporation in which they own stock. Since these shareholders are scattered throughout the country, a federal interest arises in this transaction.

It is at this intersection that state law validates the process of proxy voting and federal law prescribes the conditions on which it may proceed. Congress delegated the specifics of federal regulation to the Securities and Exchange Commission, whose rules are summarized or quoted later in this section.

The main emphasis of federal securities law is disclosure. The legislative history of the SEC proxy regulations indicates that the Congressional concern was to provide "fair corporate suffrage." H. R.Rep. No. 1383, 73d Cong., 2d Sess. 2, 13–14 (1934). Since the meeting had become ceremonial, suffrage was actually exercised in the proxy process. The SEC's operating theory has been that fairness is achieved by adequately informing investors so they can make an informed choice. The SEC also has tried to neutralize, to a limited extent, the effect of management's control of the proxy soliciting process. The rules prescribe the form of the proxy document creating the formal agency power, define the scope of the agent's power, and require management to provide an opportunity to shareholders to vote on matters that other shareholders intend to bring before the meeting. Whether the regulation is sufficient to render corporate suffrage "fair" is something for students to evaluate after further study. Are the remedies for aggrieved stockholders sufficient? Can fairness be achieved while leaving the corporate treasury at the discretion of the management? On the other hand, can the problems and possible abuses be dealt with in a practical way?

The subtle extent of the federal involvement in corporate law, through its regulation of proxies is even more substantial than first appears. Federal law defines the information stockholders must have before they vote. Omission or inadequate disclosure of that material violates federal law. Subjective judgments of what is important are analyzed under federal law. For example, a merger requires shareholder approval and therefore the solicitation of proxies. State law provides remedies to shareholders if the terms of the merger are unfair to them. If shareholders contend that the terms were not fairly described to them, then they also have a federal claim. Federal courts must then decide whether the terms and conditions required disclosure—as a matter of federal law. Would certain aspects of the deal so significantly affect an investor's judgment that disclosure was required? This may entail a federal determination of whether the terms were substantively fair. Shareholders may prefer to argue over disclosure rather than substance, but the underlying issues are the same. However, framing the issue in terms of full disclosure federalizes the controversy. This development will become more apparent to you as we proceed through this section.

There is another path of some importance that crosses the federal-state intersection, and that is the role of self-regulatory organizations. While state law authorizes voting by proxies, and federal law conditions the solicitation of proxies upon compliance with federal law, nothing in either federal or state law requires management to solicit proxies. Yet the process of solicitation informs investors while it allows them a degree of participation. Both the New York Stock Exchange and the American Stock Exchange, in their general rules, policies, and procedures relating to listed companies, state that companies whose securities are listed on those exchanges are required to solicit proxies for all meetings of stockholders. The New York Stock Exchange adds, "The purpose and intent is to afford stockholders a convenient method of voting on matters that may be presented at stockholders meetings with adequate disclosure." This requirement is reflected in a contract between the Exchange and the company whose shares are listed, known as the "Listing Agreement." New York Stock Exchange Company Manual, p. A.134.

The issues that we will explore in this chapter are the following:

Who is subject to the proxy rules?

What conduct is subject to the proxy rules? That is, what is a "proxy" and a "solicitation?"

How does one comply with the rules?

What remedies are available when there has been a failure to comply?

Do the proxy rules allow an adequate opportunity to shareholders to participate in the governance of the corporation?

What balance is struck between federal and state law in the regulation of the shareholder participation process?

This section will not deal with one of the most important applications of the law concerning the solicitation of proxies, the contested election of directors, which will be taken up in Chapter 22. On some occasions management is confronted with an outsider who competes with the management for the votes of the shareholders. These elections are known as proxy contests. Special rules under the federal securities laws are applicable to those solicitations.

B. THE REGULATORY PATTERN

PROBLEM

NATIONAL METAL PRODUCTS: PART I

I

National Metal Products, Inc. ("National") is a Delaware corporation whose common stock is traded on the New York Stock Exchange. The company manufactures various types of specialized metal products. Its sales for the most recent year were $500 million. The annual meeting will be held on May 15, and proxy material will be distributed to the shareholders on or about April 1.

In February, the board of directors approved a merger with International Petroleum Corporation ("IPC") whereby National will issue additional shares of its common stock equal to 20% of the outstanding shares. The transaction requires shareholder approval by both companies under state law. Following board approval, National issued a press release announcing the proposed transaction and quoting the chief executive officer of the company expressing his great pleasure with the contemplated merger and forecasting a favorable impact on the future of National.

QUESTIONS

1. Rogers, the owner of 1,000 shares of common stock of National, is opposed to the merger. He questions whether National's press release violated the SEC proxy rules 14a–1 and 14a–3 governing the timing of solicitations. Put aside any questions you might have about possible violations of other provisions of the securities laws. How do you advise him?

II

The proxy material sought approval of the merger and the election of directors. The candidates for election were the incumbent directors of National and Sanford, the CEO of IPC. The shareholders voted overwhelming approval for both matters.

The proxy statement contained all the information required by SEC rules concerning the merger and the candidates for election to the board. Among the statements made about the merger was the following: "The board of directors recommends approval of the merger. The board's recommendation is based upon management's report and recommendations, and a review of the financial statements of IPC. It is the board's judgment, based on this information, that the merger is in the best interests of the company and its shareholders."

Several months later, the following facts became known:

A. The merger was negotiated between Meacham, the CEO of National, and Sanford, the CEO of IPC. It was taken up by National's board at a regular meeting where Meacham and other members of management made a brief presentation and answered questions. Financial statements of IPC had been given to each member of the board two days before the meeting. After about 30 minutes of discussion, the board voted unanimously in favor of the merger. This was the same procedure followed by National for three other acquisitions during the past two years.

B. The acquisition has proven costly to National, largely because of a price-fixing scheme that has recently come to light. Several years before the merger, management of IPC learned that its field managers had engaged in the scheme with several other independent oil producers. Senior management ordered the practice halted. Sanford informed Meacham of these past practices, which he said were hardly unknown in the industry, but Meacham made no mention of this to the board, nor was he asked any questions relating to this.

Several months after the merger, it was revealed that the price-fixing practices had continued even after the merger with National. As a result, substantial contracts between National (through IPC) and some refineries were cancelled, and there was a likelihood of large private suits under the anti-trust laws as well as criminal prosecutions. National has decided to dismiss some key managers who were engaged in this activity.

No mention of the past activity was made in the proxy statement.

C. National entered into a settlement of a claim by two local environmental protection agencies that the company violated their rules on emission controls. The violations were caused by furnaces in two older smelting plants of National, where management had decided to attempt compliance by patching up old emission control systems rather than replacing them with new and expensive electronic equipment. The Company was fined $500,000. At the time the proxy statement was issued, the board was aware of management's decision on the furnaces and the risks but decided, on advice of counsel, that no disclosure was necessary in the proxy statement.

2. Did the proxy statement violate Rule 14a–9 of the SEC proxy rules? Specifically, which statements, or omissions, if any, violated the rule, and why?

3. Assuming there were violations of the proxy rules, can Rogers bring suit, after he learns the facts, based on a violation of the proxy rules? Consider the following:

(a) Does Rogers have a claim based on federal law?

(b) In what capacity can Rogers sue?

(c) In what court can he sue?

(d) What causal connection can he show between the violations he can establish and the injury of which he complains?

(e) What degree of fault must he prove?

(f) What relief can he obtain?

(g) From whom can he obtain relief?

4. Suppose Rogers believes that the terms of the proposed merger are unfair to the shareholders of National, because they are too generous to the IPC holders. Can he obtain relief under the proxy rules, either before or after the vote by shareholders, based on a showing that the transaction is unfair, and that the unfairness is not plainly labeled?

5. Suppose Mr. Meacham owns or has voting control over a majority of the National stock. Does that change any of your answers to Questions 3 or 4? Consider whether any private right of action exists under those circumstances.

* * *

1. AN OVERVIEW OF THE PROXY RULES

See Chapter 12, Part A, for an overview of the Securities Exchange Act of 1934.

See the Statutory Supplement for § 14(a), (b) and (c) of the 1934 Act and Regulation 14A, containing the proxy rules. These rules apply to companies which have a class of securities listed on a stock exchange, pursuant to § 12(a) of the 1934 Act, or have a class of securities registered with the SEC under § 12(g) of the Act where the securities are owned by 500 or more holders of record and the issuer has $3,000,000 or more of assets.

A brief summary of the rules follows:[*]

SEC Regulation 14A currently consists of 12 "rules" and two "schedules" as follows:

Rule	
14a–1.	Definitions
14a–2.	Solicitations to which proxy rules apply
14a–3.	Information to be furnished security holders
14a–4.	Requirements as to proxy
14a–5.	Presentation of information in the proxy statement
14a–6.	Material required to be filed
14a–7.	Mailing communications for security holders
14a–8.	Proposals of security holders
14a–9.	False or misleading statements
14a–10.	Prohibition of certain solicitations
14a–11.	Special provisions applicable to election contests
14a–12.	Solicitation prior to furnishing proxy statement
Schedule 14A.	Information required in a proxy statement
Schedule 14B.	Information to be included in statements filed on behalf of a participant in an election contest

Rule 14a–1. Definitions

The term *solicitation* is defined to include: (1) any request for a proxy whether or not accompanied by or included in a form of proxy; (2) any request to execute or not to execute, or to revoke, a proxy; or (3) the furnishing of a form of proxy or other communication to se-

---

[*] Adapted from Hutson, The Annual Stockholders' Meetings, 12 C.P.S. (BNA) (1979).

curity holders under circumstances reasonably calculated to result in the procurement, withholding or revocation of a proxy.

Rule 14a–2. Solicitations to Which Proxy Rules Apply

The rules apply to all securities registered under the 1934 Act, including debt securities. In practice their principal application is to common stock because of its general voting power. The rules apply both to management and non-management solicitations, although there is an exemption for non-management solicitations of no more than 10 persons.

Rule 14a–3. Information to be Furnished Security Holders

The operative provision of this rule makes it unlawful to solicit a proxy unless each person is given, with or before the solicitation, a proxy statement containing the information specified in Schedule 14A. In addition, if the solicitation is made by management for an annual meeting, each proxy statement must be accompanied or preceded by an annual report containing information which is specified in part by the rule and in part is left to the discretion of management.

Rule 14a–4. Requirements as to Proxy

Security holders must be given an opportunity to vote either for or against each matter to be acted upon other than elections to office. If the proxy provides for both the election of directors and additional matters (other than approval of auditors) the proxy must provide a means by which the security holder may withhold a vote on directors as a group or individually. A proxy may confer discretionary authority with respect to matters as to which the security holder does not specify a choice if the form of proxy states in boldface type how it is intended to vote the shares in each such case. Shares may not be voted for any candidate not named in the proxy statement. The shares represented by the proxy must be voted at the meeting in accordance with instructions.

Rule 14a–5. Presentations of Information in the Proxy Statement

This rule deals with the manner in which the information specified in Schedule 14A is actually presented in the proxy statements. Matters addressed include the need for headings, the size of type used, the desirability of presenting information in tabular form, etc.

Rule 14a–6. Material Required to be Filed

This rule requires preliminary copies of the proxy statement and form of proxy to be filed with the Commission at least 10 days prior to their being sent or given to security holders. In practice, the staff of the Commission endeavors to review and comment on the proxy material within this 10-day period, and the party making the solicitation must provide in his schedule for whatever time is necessary for printing and enclosing the proxy material prior to its actual mailing. The preliminary proxy material must be accompanied by a filing fee, ordinarily $125 but more when there is a proxy contest, acquisition, or merger involved. The final proxy material must be mailed to the Commission for filing at or before the time it is released to security holders.

Rule 14a–7. Mailing Communications for Security Holders

A security holder who desires to solicit proxies may require management to mail proxy soliciting material. The cost must be paid by the security holder. As an alternative, the issuer may furnish the security holder with a list of names and addresses for such categories of security holders as may be specified by the person soliciting proxies.

Rule 14a–8. Proposals of Security Holders

This rule permits a security holder to submit to the company a proposed resolution that he will introduce at the shareholders meeting and have it included in the proxy material to be sent by the company to the shareholders. The proxy card must also permit an opportunity to vote in favor or against the proposal. The submission must be made in timely fashion, as defined in the rule. If management is opposed to the proposal, then the proponent is entitled to include a 200 word supporting statement that must also be printed in the proxy statement.

The key issue under the rule is whether the proposed resolution may be excluded from the proxy statement. Paragraph (c) of the rule sets forth 13 grounds for exclusion, the most important of which are as follows:

    1. The proposal, under the law of the state of incorporation is not a proper subject for action for security holders.

    3. The proposal, or supporting statement is contrary to one of the proxy rules, principally rule 14a–9, dealing with false or misleading statements.

    5. The proposal deals with a matter not significantly related to the company's business.

    7. The proposal deals with the conduct of ordinary business operations of the company.

The rule also describes the procedure for the company to object to the inclusion of the proposal, requiring an opinion of counsel that there are legal grounds to exclude the resolution. Notice must be given to the proponent.

Rule 14a–9. False or Misleading Statements

No solicitation subject to the rule can be made by means of a false or misleading statement with respect to any material fact. The rule illustrates several examples of such statements.

Rule 14a–10. Prohibitions of Certain Solicitations

This is the shortest of the 12 rules. It prohibits any undated or postdated proxy and any proxy which provides that it shall be deemed to be dated as of any date subsequent to the date it is signed by the shareholder.

Rule 14a–11. Special Provisions Application to Election Contests

This rule requires, in the case of solicitations opposing another solicitation concerning election of directors, the filing with the Commission and national securities exchanges of certain information concerning the participants in the solicitation. Required information includes the participants' occupations and employment history, interest in securities of the issuer, and understandings concerning future employment by or transactions with the issuer. The solicitation on behalf of competing nominees would be by separate proxy statement providing such information to the shareholders.

Rule 14a–12. Solicitation Prior to Furnishing Required Statement

This rule provides that certain solicitations made in opposition to a prior solicitation or an invitation for tenders may be made prior to furnishing the required proxy statement.

Schedule 14A. Information Required in Proxy Statement

This schedule identifies 22 items of information which must be included in the proxy statements under the conditions specified.

Item 1.   Revocability of proxy
Item 2.   Dissenters' rights of appraisal
Item 3.   Persons making the solicitations
Item 4.   Interest of certain persons in matters to be acted upon
Item 5.   Voting securities and ownership thereof by certain beneficial owners and management
Item 6.   Nominees and directors
Item 7.   Remuneration and other transactions with management and others
Item 8.   Relationship with independent public accountants
Item 9.   Bonus, profit sharing and other remuneration plans
Item 10.   Pension and retirement plans
Item 11.   Options, warrants or rights
Item 12.   Authorization or issuance of securities otherwise than for exchange
Item 13.   Modification or exchange of securities

NOTE—HOW THE PROXY PROCESS WORKS: LAW AND PRACTICE

A. *The Annual Meeting*

Annual stockholder meetings have become a rite of spring, since most corporations hold their annual meetings shortly after they have distributed their annual financial statements for the previous year. At that time the stockholders are barraged with documents from their companies—the notice of the annual meeting, a proxy statement, a proxy and an annual report. A sample form of proxy appears in the supplement as part of the proxy rules.

The mailing of these materials marks almost the culmination of the proxy process. How does it work?

The corporation, acting through its board of directors, must select the date of the annual meeting and then work backwards. Most often that date is fixed in the by-laws, and does not change from year to year. The corporation must decide which shareholders are entitled to vote, since the shareholder body changes from day to day. The board selects a "record date," meaning that those who are stockholders at the close of business on that date will be entitled to notice and to vote at the meeting. The corporation maintains a record of its stockholders, and when ownership of stock changes, the transfer agent, customarily a bank, records the change. Since the procedure usually requires several days to take effect, a number of persons who have sold their stock and no longer consider themselves as stockholders appear as stockholders of record on the record date and will be entitled to vote.

B. *Shareholder Voting*

The board of directors must select the nominees for election as directors on whose behalf proxies will be solicited. That is, the material sent to the stockholders solicits authorization for the proxy holder to vote in favor of specified persons who will be placed in nomination at the annual meeting. No one is actually nominated until the meeting has convened, but by that time the stockholder voters will have already instructed their proxy for whom to vote. SEC rules require those soliciting a proxy to disclose for whom they intend to vote, and not deviate from that choice (except in rare cases). Rule 14a–4 of the Proxy Rules. Other candidates may be nominated at the meeting but, in effect, the votes have been cast and the election decided before the candidates have been nominated. The reason for this ironic result is that the shareholders do not actually vote at the meeting—they authorize their agents to vote. The proxy on which they confer this authority is not a ballot on which they make choices (at least not as to the election of directors as no rival candidates are offered) but is a power of attorney.

The board of directors must also decide what other matters will be submitted for action at the meeting. Authority and instructions as to how to vote on those matters will have to be solicited, and disclosure must be made in the proxy material. The directors usually recommend how to vote, and the proxy gives authority to vote in accordance with the board's recommendations unless instructions are given to the contrary. Inertia works for the directors. Some of the matters on which directions are sought will be initiated by the board or by management, such as ratification of the board's choice of independent auditors who will examine and certify the financial statements, or proposed amendment to the articles of incorporation which have been approved by the board of directors. Other items might be matters that stockholders have told management they intend to present at the meeting.

C. *Filing Proxy Material*

After these decisions have been made, the proxy materials must be prepared for filing with the Securities and Exchange Commission. To some extent the preparation of the proxy materials constitutes a markup of the previous year's materials, but both the rules and the circumstances change from year to year and a substantial effort will be required to prepare the filings. Ordinarily these are reviewed by the board of directors but most of the work must be performed by management, which has the data, and by counsel who understands the legal requirements.

The materials are then filed with the Securities and Exchange Commission, pursuant to Rule 14a–6 of the proxy rules, and the filing is reviewed by the staff of the Division of Corporation Finance. These materials are marked as preliminary proxy materials, and they may not be sent to stockholders. Under Rule 14a–3, a proxy statement may not be sent to stockholders until it has been on file with the SEC for at least 10 days. In many cases, the staff review takes longer than 10 days and it is customary for the company to wait until it has received comments from the staff before sending anything to the stockholders. Otherwise, if the Commission staff has strong objections to material already sent to stockholders it may recommend a lawsuit to enjoin the meeting until corrective action is taken. This could prove terribly embarrassing and costly to the company and management considers it prudent to allow the Commission full opportunity to comment. As you can see, the relationship between the company and the SEC and its staff is partly adversary and partly cooperative, mainly the latter.

D. *Identifying the Shareholders: Street Names*

Who are the stockholders and how does one discover their identity in order to communicate with them? An examination of the corporation's stock records will not reveal all the information. Largely for reasons of convenience, a great many stockholders (approximately 30%) choose not to take possession of the stock certificate, but instead opt to leave their shares on deposit with their brokers. In addition, many shares are owned in trust or custodial accounts under the supervision of a bank. Furthermore, when shares are transferred from one brokerage firm to another, on behalf of a customer the change may be reflected only on the records of a central clearing house depository, which is used to minimize the danger of losing stock certificates by eliminating their physical movement. The result of all of these practices of convenience is to record the ownership of securities in what has become known as "street name," which has the further effect of leaving the corporation unaware of who are the beneficial owners of the stock. The corporation knows only the name of the record holder and it is able to communicate only with the record holder. Holders of large beneficial interests (5%), however, are required by §§ 13(d) and 13(g) of the 1934 Act to identify themselves in filings with the SEC.

In light of these practices it is necessary to devise a mechanism for corporations to communicate with beneficial owners so they may direct the voting of shares. The rules of the New York Stock Exchange require brokers to transmit the material which they receive from the company to the beneficial owners. Moreover, those rules prohibit the broker, even though it is the legal owner, from voting the shares without instructions from the beneficial owner unless the matter is completely routine and no controversy exists. Rules 451 and 452 of the New York Stock Exchange. Without instructions, therefore, the company may not receive enough proxies to achieve a quorum. This requires the company to send sufficient copies of the proxy material to the brokers in ample time for the material to be transmitted to the beneficial owners, and instructions returned. The Securities and Exchange Commission undertook a study of street name practices in 1976, on instructions from the Congress, and found that the practice of street name ownership served a number of useful purposes, despite the problems. Securities and Exchange Commission, Street Name Study (Fed.Sec.L.Rept. CCH, Sp.Report to No. 672) 61–63 (1976).

Strictly as a matter of convenience, when shares are held in "street name" the record holder will be a "nominee," usually a designated partnership whose sole function is to simplify stock transfers. The largest stockholder in the country is a nominee known as Cede &

Co., the nominee of the Central Depository Company. The latter acts as a clearing house between New York Stock Exchange brokerage firms. On the books of C.D. will appear the record of which firms own the shares held in the name of Cede & Co. In turn, the brokerage firms' books will indicate the interests of the beneficial owners.

E. *Control of the Machinery*

It should be obvious from the foregoing description that the solicitation of proxies, which is necessary if shareholders are to act as a body, requires an elaborate machinery. Detailed records of stockholders must be maintained, material must be prepared, reviewed, filed and mailed, and counsel must play a significant function. All of this is expensive. The expenses are borne by the company since they relate to a necessary function that management must discharge. If a shareholder seeks to oppose management's proposals, or if he wishes to offer a candidate in opposition to those nominated by the board of directors, he must duplicate the entire process and bear the expense on his own, subject to obtaining reimbursement of expenses in limited circumstances. Can the federal law attain its objective of "fair corporate suffrage" if state law gives management effective control over the solicitation process? On the other hand, is there a practical alternative? *See* Note: Should Shareholder Power be Enhanced?, *infra.*

F. *Counting the Proxies*

The final aspect of the proxy machinery involves the counting of the votes. The proxy holders present their proxies at the meeting and then, having established that they are the agent for the number of shares so evidenced, they cast their ballot. In an uncontested election, no one has any interest in challenging their count. However, if a contested election of directors is involved or if there has been opposition to a proposed transaction, or if approval of a transaction requires more than a majority vote, then the count of the proxies becomes crucial. There are several wrinkles that can make the count contentious. For one thing, proxies are revocable and they may be revoked either by notice to the company or by a later designation of someone else as a proxy to vote in a different way. In that case, the later dated proxy constitutes the valid designation of an agent, and it automatically cancels the earlier designation. But which one is the later proxy? How does one tell? Or, suppose one of the contestants argues that the proxy held by the other side is invalid because the proxy was not signed properly or because some other defect appears. Who settles this question? What law applies to determine the answer?

Ordinarily, the board of directors designates inspectors of election, and, in some cases, state law requires the appointment of inspectors of election. Generally, these people are not members of management, but are professionals hired to do the job. What law applies? Certainly not federal law, but there is no statutory body of state law which provides any answers. The practical answer is found in the practices of corporate lawyers who have developed such rules as those dealing with proper signatures, fiduciary voting, dating of proxies and the like. If there is an election campaign with two sides actively seeking proxies, it is customary for the lawyers for each side to draft a set of rules in advance of the meeting to serve as the ground rules applicable to that election. These unofficial documents have served as guides to courts in the rare instances where the issues are litigated. As you can see, the sources of law in this area are many and varied.

See Del.Gen.Corp.L. §§ 211 and 212; MBCA §§ 28 and 33; and Sample Proxy Forms.

NOTE—WHAT IS A SOLICITATION AND WHEN CAN YOU MAKE ONE?

The SEC, in its interpretations and enforcement of the proxy rules, has emphasized the requirement that the first communication in a proxy solicitation be a proxy statement. Even communications that are not identified as a "solicitation" of a "proxy" will be subjected to this requirement so long as they serve the same purpose and are likely to have the same effect.

A. *Communications Reasonably Calculated to Procure a Vote*

The broad swath of both operative terms—"proxy" and "solicitation"—were illustrated in Studebaker Corp. v. Gittlin, 360 F.2d 692 (2d Cir. 1966). A shareholder of Studebaker sought inspection of the company's shareholder list in order to prepare for a contest for control of the board of directors. As he was not a shareholder for six months, state law required that he own 5% of the stock in order to have a statutory right to obtain the list. He met the requirement by obtaining authorization from 42 other shareholders, and a state court ordered the company to allow inspection. The company went to federal court to obtain an injunction of the state court order, on grounds that the authorizations were obtained in violation of federal law.

The SEC argued, amicus curiae, that authorizations to inspect the shareholder list were subject to the proxy rules even if the request was not part of a planned subsequent solicitation of proxies. The Second Circuit observed:

> We need not go that far to uphold the order of the district court. In SEC v. Okin, 132 F.2d 784 (2d Cir. 1943), this court ruled that a letter which did not request the giving of any authorization was subject to the Proxy Rules if it was part of "a continuous plan" intended to end in solicitation and to prepare the way for success. This was the avowed purpose of Gittlin's demand for inspection of the stockholders list and, necessarily, for his soliciting authorizations sufficient to aggregate the 5% of the stock required by § 1315 of New York's Business Corporation Law. Presumably the stockholders who gave authorizations were told something

and, as Judge L. Hand said in Okin, "one need only spread the misinformation adequately before beginning to solicit, and the Commission would be powerless to protect shareholders." 132 F. 2d at 786. Moreover, the very fact that a copy of the stockholders list is a valuable instrument to a person seeking to gain control, * * * is a good reason for insuring that shareholders have full information before they aid its procurement. We see no reason why, in such a case, the words of the Act should be denied their literal meaning. [citations omitted.] 360 F.2d at 696.

The competing considerations that favor subjecting some communications to the formalities of the proxy rules and allowing others to go unregulated were presented in the controversy that surrounded the proposed merger of the Rock Island Railroad with the Union Pacific Railroad in 1963. On May 13, 1963, the management of both companies announced the agreement of a merger, but on June 24, 1963, the Chicago and Northwestern Railway announced a competing offer for the shares of the Rock Island. This gave shareholders of Rock Island a choice of offers between Union Pacific and the Northwestern. To accept the Northwestern offer they would have to vote down the Union Pacific merger at the shareholder meeting. On June 27, 1963 the boards of Rock Island and Union Pacific approved the merger, subject to shareholder approval. The Northwestern then applied to the ICC on July 3, 1963, for approval of *its* proposed offer to purchase.

On July 26, 1963, Union Pacific published an ad in newspapers around the country expressing its opposition to the Northwestern offer, largely on grounds that this would adversely affect railroad service. The ads appeared in newspapers in cities served by the Rock Island, but also in Washington and New York, which were not served by the Railroad.

A shareholder of Rock Island claimed that the ad was an unlawful proxy solicitation since it was a communication reasonably calculated to procure a vote which was not preceded by a proxy statement. The court disagreed, noting that the purpose of the ad was to inform the public rather than to solicit proxies, and a public interest independent of the shareholder decision existed. It was significant that the meeting had not been called at the time of the ad and was not called until October 1, 1963. The meeting was scheduled for November 15, almost four months after the ad. Brown v. Chicago R.I. & P.R.R. Co., 328 F.2d 122, 124–5. (7th Cir. 1964).

By contrast, once the contestants began their formal pursuit of proxies, a court was inclined to include within the net of solicitation all communications that had a bearing on the outcome. A brokerage firm prepared a report which concluded that the Northwestern offer was better for the stockholders of Rock Island than was the Union Pacific and distributed that report to its customers. Copies of the report were further distributed by Northwestern to other Rock Island shareholders, and in fact, Northwestern had assisted in the preparation of the report. The court held that the report was a communication reasonably calculated to result in the procurement of a proxy and therefore was a solicitation subject to the rules even though it was not prepared by a party to the formal solicitation. Union Pacific-Railroad Co. v. Chicago & N.W. Ry. Co., 226 F.Supp. 400 (N.D.Ill.1964).

In Smallwood v. Pearl Brewing Company, 489 F.2d 579 (5th Cir. 1974), a company solicited shareholder approval of a merger. However, approximately two months prior to mailing the proxy statement, the company advised its shareholders by mail of the proposed merger, indicating that the board favored its approval because they thought it was beneficial. The court held that the letter was not reasonably calculated to result in the procurement of a proxy. No proxies were actually mentioned and the correspondence "if not totally innocuous was not overwhelmingly prejudicial either." *Id.* at 601. The court also noted the value of prompt disclosure, which would be impeded by complete compliance with the proxy rules. *Id.* at 600–01.

This last point has great significance. A constant tension exists between the SEC disclosure policies and its formal filing requirements. Both the courts and the SEC recognize that the practical effect of labeling a communication to be a "solicitation" of a "proxy" is to stifle some communications completely. It is often impractical to furnish proxy solicitation material prior to the communication. Thus, in Calumet Industries, Inc. v. MacClure, 464 F.Supp. 19 (N.D.Ill.1978), there were organizational discussions among shareholders contemplating a proxy contest for control of a corporation. The court held that these were not "solicitations." It rejected the argument that the term should be broadly interpreted to cover any communication which may eventually influence the giving of proxies when they are actually sought.

In Cook United Inc. v. Stockholders Protective Committee, Fed. Sec.L.Reporter (CCH) ¶ 96,875 (S.D.N.Y.1979), the court denied relief to those objecting to the formation of a 13 member committee, in violation of the no-solicitation requirement, on ground that the violation was "technical" and was later cured.

In 1966 a group of AT&T shareholders formed a committee to oppose an investigation by the Federal Communications Commission of the company's rates and profits. The committee posted an advertisement asking shareholders to contribute 10 cents for each AT&T share owned so that the committee can "represent you (the shareholders) as an intervenor in the FCC proceedings." The SEC staff contended that the ad constituted the solicitation of a proxy that was not preceded by a proxy statement, and hence violated the SEC's rules. The committee organizers argued that no solicitation subject to SEC rules was made, and that it would exceed the Commission's powers to subject that ad to this restriction. Neither side pressed its position; the SEC took no action and the ad was not repeated. The controversy demonstrated the multiplicity of purposes served by communications to shareholders.

In another situation, management of a company was faced with a proposed resolution that a shareholder intended to offer at the meeting. In accordance with Rule 14a–8, the text of the shareholder proposal was included in the proxy statement mailed by the management. Management was asked by the Investor Responsibility Research Center to comment upon the proposal. The Center is a non-profit corporation that prepares and distributes reports analyzing stockholder proposals that are to be acted upon at meetings. Its subscribers are mainly large institutions, such as universities, foundations and bank trust departments. Management questioned whether the report was a proxy solicitation, which failed to comply with the rules, and whether management would be barred from responding, since its answer would be printed and circulated. The SEC's Division of Corporation Finance commented as follows:

> On the basis of the information presented to us in this matter, and in particular, the fact that the Center represents in its materials that it is a disinterested party with respect to the outcome of the stockholder proposal controversies upon which it reports; the fact that it has the stated intention and purpose of providing an objective discussion and analysis of relevant issues, with a balanced presentation of opposing viewpoints; and the fact that it makes no recommendations as to how its subscribers should vote on reported proposals; it is this Division's view that the Center's "Proxy Issues Service" reports do not constitute proxy soliciting materials that are within the purview of the Commission's proxy rules and regulations.

Interpretative letter to *Motorola Inc.*, June 9, 1975.

Does the participant in the corporate electoral process have a constitutionally protected right to speak? This question is most poignantly presented in the context of a proxy contest for control of a corporation, but it also arises on more neutral occasions when management or minority shareholders simply want to tell their story.

It was once commonly believed that "commercial speech," which mostly refers to advertising, was not protected by the First Amendment. *See* Valentine v. Chrestensen, 316 U.S. 52, 62 S.Ct. 920, 86 L. Ed. 1262 (1942). More recent Supreme Court decisions have eroded that belief. Virginia State Board of Pharmacy v. Virginia Consumer Council, 425 U.S. 748, 96 S.Ct. 1817, 48 L.Ed.2d 346 (1976), invalidated a state's restriction on advertising the price of prescription drugs. The following year the Court held that blanket suppression of advertising by lawyers was invalid under the First Amendment. Bates v. State Bar of Arizona, 433 U.S. 350, 97 S.Ct. 2691, 53 L.Ed.2d 810 (1977).

In both cases, however, the Court recognized that there are special characteristics to commercial speech, and some regulation to deal with deception was permissible. Prior restraint was also possible. Thus, a restriction on direct, in person, solicitation by a lawyer of a client in connection with a personal injury claim (*i.e.* "ambulance chasing") did not offend the First Amendment. Ohralik v. Ohio State Bar Association, 436 U.S. 447, 98 S.Ct. 1912, 56 L.Ed.2d 444 (1978). The Court sustained the right to impose "prophylactic measures whose objective is the prevention of harm before it occurs." 436 U.S. at 464.

The Court further explored the special characteristics of commercial speech in Central Hudson Gas & Electric Corp. v. Public Service Commission of New York, 447 U.S. 557, 100 S.Ct. 2343 (1980), involving a total ban on all advertising promoting the use of electricity. The Public Service Commission's concern was in promoting conservation and avoiding higher utility rates which might result if institutional advertising costs became part of the rate base. The Court acknowledged that its "decisions on commercial expression have rested on the premise that such speech, although meriting some protection, is of less constitutional moment than other forms of speech," 100 S. Ct. at 2349–50 n.5. Thus, the Court observed, "there can be no constitutional objection to the suppresion of commercial messages that do not accurately inform the public about lawful activity." *Id.* at 2350. *See also* Friedman v. Rogers, 440 U.S. 1, 99 S.Ct. 887, 59 L.Ed. 2d 100 (1979), sustaining a prohibition on the use of trade names by optometrists.

Justice Powell, in *Central Hudson*, suggested a four step analysis to determine the validity of restrictions on commercial speech. "At the outset, we must determine whether the expression is protected by the First Amendment. For commercial speech to come within that provision, it at least must concern lawful activity and not be misleading. Next, we ask whether the asserted governmental interest is substantial. If both inquiries yield positive answers, we must determine whether the regulation directly advances the government interest asserted, and whether it is not more extensive than is necessary to serve that interest." 100 S.Ct. at 2351. The Court then found the total ban was excessive, and struck down the restriction.

As applied to proxy regulation, the key question would seem to turn on the last step in Justice Powell's analysis. Can the SEC require prior scrutiny of soliciting material before participants in a proxy solicitation can communicate to investors? Is such regulation necessary in view of the fact that anti-fraud provisions exist in the proxy rules, furnishing an alternative to pre-clearance type of regulation? How sweeping is the regulation? Even conceding the SEC's right to closely examine proxy solicitations, are all communications that have some bearing on the matter to be voted upon subject to the restrictions? Are all participants subject to the same restrictions—

the company and the small stockholders alike? What about proxy solicitations that have political overtones, like Mr. Pillsbury's message to the Honeywell stockholders? Is prior SEC clearance necessary for those communications? By what standard will the courts judge the validity of SEC regulations? *See* Reich, Consumer Protection and the First Amendment: A Dilemma for the FTC, 61 Minn.L. Rev. 705 (1977); Jackson & Jeffries, Commercial Speech: Economic Due Process and the First Amendment, 65 Va.L.Rev. 1 (1979); Farber, Commercial Speech and First Amendment Theory, 74 Nw.U.L. Rev. 372 (1979).

2. CIVIL LIABILITIES UNDER THE PROXY RULES

a. Implied Private Rights of Action

NOTE—A STUDENT GUIDE TO J. I. CASE CO. v. BORAK

The case that follows this note, the *Borak* case, is one of the most significant decisions in the interpretation of the federal securities laws and one of the most important landmarks at the intersection of corporate and securities law. Understanding its full significance, however, requires some background in the business and procedural aspects of the case.

Plaintiff Carl Borak was a stockholder in a company that proposed to merge into the defendant company. A merger is a combination of two corporations in which the legal existence of one company terminates. The shareholders of that company may receive any of a variety of kinds of consideration—cash, debt securities or stock of the surviving corporation. Plaintiff objected to the merger because he contended that it involved improper self–dealing by the managers of his corporation and that the minority shareholders were treated unfairly. If true, Borak's allegations described a breach of fiduciary duty at common law.

His suit was brought in federal district court in Wisconsin, with jurisdiction based on diversity of citizenship. The injunction was denied and the merger was consummated. Thereafter, the complaint was amended to ask for broader relief.

A threshold issue was the capacity in which plaintiff was suing. Was the suit brought as a class action, which is an action brought directly on behalf of the stockholders, or was it brought as a derivative suit on behalf of the corporation? How does one discern the difference?

The chapter on derivative suits (Chapter 15) explores this issue. Suffice it to say at this point that a derivative suit asserts an injury to the corporation as opposed to injury to the shareholders. The corporation itself must be affected by the wrong that was committed. Most important, any relief runs to the corporation. It recovers damages if any are awarded. A proxy solicitation, which was involved in approving the merger, affects a corporate transaction, but the solicitation is used to enable a shareholder to exercise his individual right to vote. Thus, there are elements of both class and derivative actions involved.

Borak was decided before the 1966 revision of the Federal Rules of Civil Procedure. There was no Rule 23.1 at that time and Rule 23 as then in effect was a vastly different rule from the present version. At that time it was more difficult to distinguish class from derivative actions than under the new rules.

A key question involved the applicability of state substantive law. If the suit could be brought only as a derivative suit, would Borak have to comply with the special state law procedural limitations applicable to that type of suit even though he sued in federal court? One of the state law limitations on derivative suits is the requirement that a plaintiff must post security for expenses borne by defendant. This requirement is imposed in diversity cases if it is required by the law of the forum state, which, in turn, may refer to the law of the state of incorporation. The purpose of the requirement is to protect the corporation and the individual defendants from the expense of defending frivolous suits. Derivative suits were sometimes seen by courts and legislatures as having a potential for harassment, brought only for the purpose of forcing a settlement. These kinds of suits are colloquially known as "strike suits." Having a tiny economic stake in the corporation, the plaintiffs may lack the personal funds necessary to reimburse defendants for their expenses, if the court determines that is in order, and hence the law may require them to post a bond as security for their potential obligation. However, some critics note that the requirement can also discourage bona fide suits and is therefore discriminatory. The amount of security generally required covers not merely court costs, but, in the discretion of the court, may be used to repay defendants for attorneys fees and the other major expenses in defending a complex law suit. Posting a bond can be fairly expensive. The real risk, and deterrent, of course, is that the plaintiff may have to make good on the bond.

Such a requirement existed in Wisconsin and therefore was applicable to Mr. Borak's common law suit, if it was derivative. If the suit were seen as a direct action, even a class action, then no such security provisions were operative. The district court viewed the suit as derivative. Since Borak refused to post security, the court dismissed the complaint. Borak then amended his complaint (one of three amendments) and added another count, this time claiming a violation of the federal proxy rules. Now he claimed that the state law limits did not apply to his federal right and no security could be required of him.

The district court held, however, that the federal claim would only entitle Borak to prospective or declaratory relief. The pleas for other relief were dismissed because of the refusal to post security. The district court reasoned that insofar as Borak requested the kind of relief that could be obtained only from his common law claim, such relief converted his claim into a state claim. Borak appealed from all these rulings.

The Seventh Circuit reversed the district court. The common law claim was construed to be both derivative and direct and therefore not subject to the security for expenses requirements. More important, the court held that the relief available under the federal count, as to which no security could be demanded, could be either prospective or retrospective, whichever was necessary to make the federal substantive requirements effective. Consequently, plaintiff could obtain what he sought even if the state claim was dropped. The decision created a conflict with the Sixth Circuit which had earlier ruled that prospective relief alone could be granted for violation of the proxy rules. Dann v. Studebaker-Packard Corp., 288 F.2d 201 (6th Cir. 1960).

If the action is held to be a class or direct action, the issue of security for expenses vanishes, but the scope of relief issue does not entirely disappear. The district court's view as to the narrow scope of relief available under federal law remains important. As a class claimant Borak would be able to press both the common law and federal claim, and whatever relief could *not* be granted under federal law might still be granted under common law. Might, mind you; not necessarily would. Even though both the federal and state aspects of the case would be heard in the same court, that court would be sitting as a state court on the common law issues and as a federal court on the proxy issues. And there's the rub.

Under the narrow interpretation of federal remedies that was taken by the district court in this case, it is not clear that a court could dispense all the relief Borak requested, even though it had the powers of both federal and state courts. The reason for that is that Borak would be made to rely, very largely, on state remedies, and hope that state law would grant a full sweep of remedies in this context. Surely the result might vary from state to state. State corporation statutes differ from one another, and might not allow damages or post-merger equitable relief. State law might not tamper with a completed merger. There may be other differences between the relief that could be obtained from a federal court with full remedial powers and a state court. The statute of limitations might not be the same. The burden of proof might differ. The entitlement to attorney's fees might not be the same under state law as under federal law. Therefore, the result Borak sought was to have the suit construed to be a class action, so that he could press both federal and state claims, and, in addition, have the court rule that under both federal and state law, he would be entitled to both prospective relief or retrospective relief (damages). This would give him multiple bites at the apple. The more critical issue was one of relief. If federal law entitled him to broad remedies, he could probably win everything by maintaining the suit under federal law alone, whether it was a class action or a derivative suit.

What would Borak's position be if he was limited to prospective relief under federal law? Relief might take the form of a declaratory judgment that the proxy rules had been violated and an injunction against further violations. Armed with that judgment, Borak could then press his state remedies. He might do it in the same court, or go into state court and urge that common law remedies should follow from the violation of the federal law. That might or might not impress the state (or "state") court. State courts would not feel the need to protect the sanctity of the federal law and policy embodied in the proxy rules since it is not within their jurisdiction. Therefore, a state court could deny further relief. It might, of course, hold that a federal law violation tainted the transaction and set it aside, award damages, or award some other form of relief it thought appropriate to further the state law policy objectives that were involved in the case. That could make matters still more confusing, if that is possible.

J. I. CASE CO. v. BORAK

377 U.S. 426, 84 S.Ct. 1555, 12 L.Ed.2d 423 (1964).

Mr. Justice CLARK delivered the opinion of the Court.

This is a civil action brought by respondent, a stockholder of petitioner J. I. Case Company, charging deprivation of the pre-emptive rights of respondent and other shareholders by reason of a merger between Case and the American Tractor Corporation. It is alleged that the merger was effected through the circulation of a false and misleading proxy statement by those proposing the merger. The complaint was in two counts, the first based on diversity and claiming a breach of the directors' fiduciary duty to the stockholders. The second count alleged a violation of § 14(a) of the Securities Exchange Act of 1934 with reference to the proxy solicitation material. The trial court held that as to this count it had no power to redress the alleged violations of the Act but was limited solely to the granting of declaratory relief thereon under § 27 of the Act.[2] The court held

2. Section 27 of the Act, 48 Stat. 902–903, 15 U.S.C.A. § 78aa, provides in part: "The district courts of the United States, the Supreme Court of the District of Columbia, and the United States courts of any Territory or other place subject to the jurisdiction of the United States shall have exclusive jurisdiction of violations of this title or the rules and regulations thereunder, and of all suits in equity and actions at law brought to enforce any liability or duty created by this title or the rules and regulations thereunder. Any criminal proceeding may be brought in the district wherein any act or transaction constituting the violation occurred. Any suit or action to enforce any liability or duty created by this title or rules and regulations thereunder, or to enjoin any violation of such title or rules and regulations, may be brought in any such district or in the district wherein the defendant is found or is an inhabitant or transacts business, and process in such cases may be served in any other district of which the defendant is an inhabitant or wherever the defendant may be found."

Wis.Stat., 1961, § 180.405(4), which requires posting security for expenses in derivative actions, applicable to both counts, except that portion of Count 2 requesting declaratory relief. It ordered the respondent to furnish a bond in the amount of $75,000 thereunder and, upon his failure to do so, dismissed the complaint, save that part of Count 2 seeking a declaratory judgment. On interlocutory appeal the Court of Appeals reversed on both counts, holding that the District Court had the power to grant remedial relief and that the Wisconsin statute was not applicable. 317 F.2d 838. We granted certiorari. We consider only the question of whether § 27 of the Act authorizes a federal cause of action for rescission or damages to a corporate stockholder with respect to a consummated merger which was authorized pursuant to the use of a proxy statement alleged to contain false and misleading statements violative of § 14(a) of the Act.
* * *

I.

Respondent, the owner of 2,000 shares of common stock of Case acquired prior to the merger, brought this suit based on diversity jurisdiction seeking to enjoin a proposed merger between Case and the American Tractor Corporation (ATC) on various grounds, including breach of the fiduciary duties of the Case directors, self-dealing among the management of Case and ATC and misrepresentations contained in the material circulated to obtain proxies. The injunction was denied and the merger was thereafter consummated. Subsequently successive amended complaints were filed and the case was heard on the aforesaid two-count complaint. The claims pertinent to the asserted violation of the Securities Exchange Act were predicated on diversity jurisdiction as well as on § 27 of the Act. They alleged: that petitioners, or their predecessors, solicited or permitted their names to be used in the solicitation of proxies of Case stockholders for use at a special stockholders' meeting at which the proposed merger with ATC was to be voted upon; that the proxy solicitation material so circulated was false and misleading in violation of § 14(a) of the Act and Rule 14a–9 which the Commission had promulgated thereunder; that the merger was approved at the meeting by a small margin of votes and was thereafter consummated; that the merger would not have been approved but for the false and misleading statements in the proxy solicitation material; and that Case stockholders were damaged thereby. The respondent sought judgment holding the merger void and damages for himself and all other stockholders similarly situated, as well as such further relief "as equity shall require." The District Court ruled that the Wisconsin security for expenses statute did not apply to Count 2 since it arose under federal law. However, the court found that its jurisdiction was limited to declaratory relief in a private, as opposed to a government, suit alleging violation of § 14(a) of the Act. Since the additional equitable relief and damages prayed for by the respondent would, therefore, be available only under state law, it ruled those claims subject to the security for expenses statute. After setting the amount of security at $75,000 and upon the representation of counsel that the security would not be posted, the court dismissed the complaint, save that portion of Count 2 seeking a declaration that the proxy solicitation material was false and misleading and that the proxies and, hence, the merger were void.

II.

It appears clear that private parties have a right under § 27 to bring suit for violation of § 14(a) of the Act. Indeed, this section specifically grants the appropriate District Courts jurisdiction over "all suits in equity and actions at law brought to enforce any liability or duty created" under the Act. The petitioners make no concessions, however, emphasizing that Congress made no specific reference to a private right of action in § 14(a); that, in any event, the right would not extend to derivative suits and should be limited to prospective relief only. In addition, some of the petitioners argue that the merger can be dissolved only if it was fraudulent or nonbeneficial, issues upon which the proxy material would not bear. But the causal relationship of the proxy material and the merger are questions of fact to be resolved at trial, not here. We therefore do not discuss this point further.

III.

While the respondent contends that his Count 2 claim is not a derivative one, we need not embrace that view, for we believe that a right of action exists as to both derivative and direct causes.

The purpose of § 14(a) is to prevent management or others from obtaining authorization for corporate action by means of deceptive or inadequate disclosure in proxy solicitation. The section stemmed from the congressional belief that "[f]air corporate suffrage is an important right that should attach to every equity security bought on a public exchange." H.R.Rep. No. 1383, 73d Cong., 2d Sess., 13. It was intended to "control the conditions under which proxies may be solicited with a view to preventing the recurrence of abuses which * * * [had] frustrated the free exercise of the voting rights of stockholders." Id., at 14. "Too often proxies are solicited without explanation to the stockholder of the real nature of the questions for which authority to cast his vote is sought." S.Rep. No. 792, 73d Cong., 2d Sess., 12. These broad remedial purposes are evidenced in the language of the section which makes it "unlawful for any person * * * to solicit or to permit the use of his name to solicit any proxy or consent or authorization in respect of any security * * * registered on any national securities exchange in contravention of such rules and regulations as the Commission may prescribe as necessary or appropriate in the public interest *or for the protection of investors.*" (Italics supplied.) While this language makes no specific reference to a private right of action, among its chief purposes is "the protection of investors," which certainly implies the availability of judicial relief where necessary to achieve that result.

The injury which a stockholder suffers from corporate action pursuant to a deceptive proxy solicitation ordinarily flows from the damage done the corporation, rather than from the damage inflicted directly upon the stockholder. The damage suffered results not from the deceit practiced on him alone but rather from the deceit practiced on the stockholders as a group. To hold that derivative actions are not within the sweep of the section would therefore be tantamount to a denial of private relief. Private enforcement of the proxy rules provides a necessary supplement to Commission action. As in anti-trust treble damage litigation, the possibility of civil damages or injunctive relief serves as a most effective weapon in the enforcement of the proxy requirements. The Commission advises that it examines over 2,000 proxy statements annually and each of them must necessarily be expedited. Time does not permit an independent examination of the facts set out in the proxy material and this results in the Commission's acceptance of the representations contained therein at their face value, unless contrary to other material on file with it. Indeed, on the allegations of respondent's complaint, the proxy material failed to disclose alleged unlawful market manipulation of the stock of ATC, and this unlawful manipulation would not have been apparent to the Commission until after the merger.

We, therefore, believe that under the circumstances here it is the duty of the courts to be alert to provide such remedies as are necessary to make effective the congressional purpose. As was said in Sola Electric Co. v. Jefferson Electric Co., 317 U.S. 173, 176, 63 S.Ct. 172, 174, 87 L.Ed. 165 (1942):

> When a federal statute condemns an act as unlawful, the extent and nature of the legal consequences of the condemnation, though left by the statute to judicial determination, are nevertheless federal questions, the answers to which are to be derived from the statute and the federal policy which it has adopted.

It is for the federal courts "to adjust their remedies so as to grant the necessary relief" where federally secured rights are invaded. "And it is also well settled that where legal rights have been invaded, and a federal statute provides for a general right to sue for such invasion, federal courts may use any available remedy to make good the wrong done." Bell v. Hood, 327 U.S. 678, 684, 66 S.Ct. 773, 777, 90 L.Ed. 939 (1946). Section 27 grants the District Courts jurisdiction "of all suits in equity and actions at law brought to enforce any liability or duty created by this title   *   *   *." In passing on almost identical language found in the Securities Act of 1933, the Court found the words entirely sufficient to fashion a remedy to rescind a fraudulent sale, secure restitution and even to enforce the right to restitution against a third party holding assets of the vendor. Deckert v. Independence Shares Corp., 311 U.S. 282, 61 S.Ct. 229, 85 L.Ed. 189 (1940). This significant language was used:

> The power *to enforce* implies the power to make effective the right of recovery afforded by the Act. And the power to make the right of recovery effective implies the power to utilize any of the procedures or actions normally available to the litigant according to the exigencies of the particular case. At 288 of 311 U.S., at 233 of 61 S.Ct.

Nor do we find merit in the contention that such remedies are limited to prospective relief. This was the position taken in Dann v. Studebaker-Packard Corp., 6 Cir., 288 F.2d 201, where it was held that the "preponderance of questions of state law which would have to be interpreted and applied in order to grant the relief sought * * * is so great that the federal question involved * * * is really negligible in comparison." But we believe that the overriding federal law applicable here would, where the facts required, control the appropriateness of redress despite the provisions of state corporation law, for it "is not uncommon for federal courts to fashion federal law where federal rights are concerned." Textile Workers Union of America v. Lincoln Mills, 353 U.S. 448, 457, 77 S.Ct. 912, 918, 1 L.Ed. 2d 972 (1957). In addition, the fact that questions of state law must be decided does not change the character of the right; it remains federal. * * *

Moreover, if federal jurisdiction were limited to the granting of declaratory relief, victims of deceptive proxy statements would be obliged to go into state courts for remedial relief. And if the law of the State happened to attach no responsibility to the use of misleading proxy statements, the whole purpose of the section might be frustrated. Furthermore, the hurdles that the victim might face (such as separate suits, as contemplated by Dann v. Studebaker-Packard Corp., supra, security for expenses statutes, bringing in all parties necessary for complete relief, etc.) might well prove insuperable to effective relief.

IV.

Our finding that federal courts have the power to grant all necessary remedial relief is not to be construed as any indication of what we believe to be the necessary and appropriate relief in this case. We are concerned here only with a determination that federal jurisdiction for this purpose does exist. Whatever remedy is necessary must await the trial on the merits.

The other contentions of the petitioners are denied.

Affirmed.

NOTE—THE EXISTENCE OF IMPLIED PRIVATE
RIGHTS OF ACTION

You should note certain peculiarities of the *Borak* decision. The Court makes no reference to the legislative history of § 14 of the Securities Exchange Act of 1934, although the case holds that there is a private right of action under that section. No private right is provided in § 14; if it exists it must be implied. Since the action is one "arising under the laws of the United States," and therefore is predicated on legislative authority, this omission is surprising. In fact, an examination of the legislative history would have failed to turn up any indication of whether Congress contemplated that private suits could or could not be brought under that provision.

Nor does the Court discuss the fact that the same statute specifically provided in other sections for private remedies, none of which could have availed plaintiff. Congress authorized private suits by investors who were injured by manipulation (§ 9), for corporations whose insiders engaged in buying and selling the company's stock (§ 16) and, most pertinent, for investors who were injured as a result of any false or misleading information contained in a document filed with the Securities and Exchange Commission (§ 18). One might have expected some reference to the maxim of statutory interpretation known as "expressio unius est exclusio alterius"—literally, expression of one thing is the exclusion of another. The only other statutory provision that is analyzed in the opinion is § 27; which confers exclusive jurisdiction for violations of the statute in the federal courts, and provides for service of process and for venue. This provision was necessary in the statute, whether private rights of action were implied or not, since jurisdiction and venue had to be addressed with respect to the specific remedies contained in the statute. If *no* express remedies had been provided in the statute, then, of course, § 27 would have significant implications as to whether the courts should create remedies.

The Court does not discuss the carefully detailed pattern of express private remedies that is provided in the Securities Exchange Act of 1934 and its companion statute the Securities Act of 1933, or the effect that implied remedies would have on those provisions. Both of those statutes provide specific remedies for each of the substantive rights that are created in the statute. The remedies went beyond common law protections, but the tradeoff was tight procedural restrictions and a short statute of limitations. In other words, whenever Congress declared conduct was wrong, it specifically provided a remedy. Thus, the proxy statement which was the basis of the suit in *Borak* was a document filed with the Commission and a remedy in § 18 was provided for certain investors. In all likelihood, that remedy would have been of no use to the plaintiff in *Borak*, but that does not gainsay the fact that certain other investors would have been able to sue the Company in that case. Was the omission a pregnant one?

As written, the opinion seems to focus mainly on the result and the desirability of the easy enforcement of the proxy rules. This may indeed be the correct result, but it is difficult to avoid thinking of it more as a legislative decision than a judicial one. Or the Court may have strongly believed it was the right thing to do in light of the remedial purpose of the statutes. As Professor Louis Loss expressed it, "the Court reached the right result not for the wrong reason but for no reason at all." 5 L. Loss, Securities Regulation 2882 (1969).

Perhaps the same result could have been reached with more traditional judicial tools. In Kardon v. National Gypsum Co., 69 F.Supp. 512 (E.D.Pa.1946), a Federal District Court implied a private right of action under Rule 10b–5 of the same statute, which prohibits false or misleading statements, or deceptive or manipulative acts or practices in connection with the purchase or sale of securities. The court found that the violation of a statute was a tort, and in those circumstances courts have commonly granted relief under statutes in favor of members of the protected class. *See* § 286, Restatement of Torts. The tort theory expounded in *Kardon* finds support in Dean Ezra Ripley Thayer's seminal article, Public Wrong and Private Action, 27 Harv.L.Rev. 317 (1914). Some have traced its legacy to the Statute of Westminster in 1285. Subsequent to the *Borak* decision, the Supreme Court employed such an approach to imply a civil remedy under the Rivers & Harbors Act of 1899. Wyandotte Transportation Co. v. United States, 389 U.S. 191, 88 S.Ct. 379, 19 L.Ed.2d 407 (1967). This analysis would not only rest the existence of an implied right of action on something firmer than convenience of the parties and the desirability of the result, but would provide a handle for deciding the nature of the action, the burden of proof, damages, and a host of other issues. However, for *Borak* to have followed such a path would have required the Court to decide the capacity in which plaintiff was suing, a choice carefully avoided in the opinion.

Even this approach, though, may be questioned as applied to the proxy rules. The application of substantive statutory standards by the courts, to cases where those standards do not specifically apply is traditionally employed by courts that are already seized of jurisdiction on some basis other than the statute itself, such as in a common law court or in a federal court where there is diversity of citizenship. The effect of implying a private remedy in *Borak*, however, is not merely to furnish a standard for the court to apply, but is to confer jurisdiction that the court would otherwise lack.

Theory aside, in fact most litigation under the federal securities laws, certainly after *Borak*, has been brought under rules adopted by the Securities and Exchange Commission rather than under the express civil liability provisions found in the statutes. Most cases have been brought under Rule 10b–5, which was promulgated by the SEC to implement § 10(b) of the Securities Exchange Act of 1934 which authorizes the Commission to define manipulative and deceptive conduct in connection with the purchase or sale of securities. The broad reading given to the scope of that rule by the lower courts made it the favorite remedy of aggrieved plaintiffs. In the first ten years after *Borak*, the Supreme Court encouraged that development. In Mills v. Electric Auto-Lite Co., 396 U.S. 375, 90 S.Ct. 616, 24 L.Ed.2d 593 (1970), private stockholder actions to enforce the substantive provisions of the laws were hailed as "corporate therapeutics," 396 U.S. at 396. The Court in that case even awarded attorney's fees to be paid by the losing party just for establishing a violation of the law without regard to whether plaintiff could show harm. In Superintendent of Insurance v. Bankers Life & Casualty Co., 404 U.S. 6, 92 S.Ct. 165, 30 L.Ed.2d 128 (1971), the Court acknowledged the existence of implied private rights in cases under Rule 10b-5 without so much as any discussion in the main body of the opinion. Countless lower court rulings extended private rights without further analysis of whether such rights were contemplated under the statute.

Serious interpretive questions, however, remained unanswered after *Borak*. The elements of the federal claim that was created in *Borak* had to be explored. What statute of limitations would the court find for this claim for which Congress had not written any limitation? What was necessary to establish in order to show that the defendant's violations caused the injury? Was reliance on the defendant's misrepresentations or omissions necessary? What degree of fault had to be shown? What defenses were available to the defendants? Many of these questions were answered more or less, under the specific liability provisions in the federal securities laws, but of course they had to be judicially defined where the private cause of action was created by the courts rather than the legislature.

The popularity of the implied rights of action, which to some extent could be explained by plaintiff's desire to avoid the limitations found in the express remedies, put a severe strain on the federal courts, at least in some judicial districts. Complex cases could easily be initiated and withstand summary judgment motions. It is not surprising, therefore, that a judicial reaction set in against implied private rights of action, not only under the securities laws but as to a wide range of remedial federal legislation. Beginning in 1974, the Supreme Court seriously curtailed their availability.

In National Railroad Passenger Corp. v. National Association of Railroad Passengers, 414 U.S. 453, 94 S.Ct. 690, 38 L.Ed.2d 646 (1974), the Court denied the existence of an implied private right of action under the Rail Passenger Service Act of 1970 because the statutory scheme and the legislative history indicated that the express remedies in the statute were exclusive. The Attorney General was given enforcement authority in that statute and the Court found that private remedies would be inconsistent with the regulatory pattern.

The maxim of "expressio unius est exclusio alterius" was cited as authority for the rejection of implied private right.

The most frequently cited case involving implied private rights of action is Cort v. Ash, 422 U.S. 66, 95 S.Ct. 2080, 45 L.Ed.2d 12 (1975) where a unanimous Court denied a private right under the Federal Election Campaign Law. A stockholder of Bethlehem Steel Corporation asserted that the corporation had illegally expended funds in the 1972 Presidential election, and a derivative suit was brought to recover those amounts. In rejecting the claim that suit could be brought under the statute, the Court laid down four factors as relevant to determing whether an implied private right of action exists. These factors are:

1. Is the plaintiff one of the class for whose *especial* benefit the statute was enacted? (This was the question asked in Texas & Pacific R. Co. v. Rigsby, 241 U.S. 33, 36 S.Ct. 482, 60 L.Ed. 874 (1916), applying another maxim: Ubi jus, ibi remedium).

2. Is there any indication of legislative intent, explicit or implicit either to create or deny the private remedy?

3. Is it consistent with the underlying purposes of the legislative scheme to imply such a remedy?

4. Is the cause of action one traditionally relegated to state law, in an area basically the concern of the states, so that it would be inappropriate to infer a cause of action solely on federal law?

The decisions of the Supreme Court since *Cort* foretell a narrowing of the doctrine of implied private rights of action. In two securities law cases, Blue Chip Stamps v. Manor Drug Stores, 421 U.S. 723, 95 S.Ct. 1917, 44 L.Ed.2d 539 (1975) and Ernst & Ernst v. Hochfelder, 425 U.S. 185, 96 S.Ct. 1375, 47 L.Ed.2d 668 (1976), the Court expressed doubt as to the availability of the implied private right of action where an express remedy might be available. Thus, in *Ernst & Ernst*, the Court queried whether an implied right of action would be available to a plaintiff if § 18 could have provided a remedy. The question went unanswered because the claim fell for other reasons. Three courts of appeals have since affirmed the existence of an implied right notwithstanding the availability of an express remedy. Huddleston v. Herman & MacLean, 640 F.2d 534 (5th Cir. 1981); Ross v. A. H. Robins Co., 607 F.2d 545 (2d Cir. 1979), cert. denied 446 U.S. 946, 100 S.Ct. 2175, 64 L.Ed.2d 802 (1980); Wachovia Bank & Trust Co. v. National Student Marketing Corp., 650 F.2d 342 (D.C.Cir. 1980). However, the Supreme Court granted certiorari in *Huddleston* on the question of whether an implied remedy exists under Section 10(b) for purchasers who have express remedies under Section 11 of the 1933 Act by virtue of the fact that the securities they purchased were issued pursuant to a registration statement. 50 U.S.L.W. 3796–7 (1982). Reversal of the lower court on this ground would further curtail the scope of implied liabilities, and might even lead the Court to deny an implied remedy whenever any express remedy is available to the plaintiff.

Warning signals have been issued by the Court, in other contexts that it will consider carefully what effect the implication of remedies will have on the pattern of express remedies designed by Congress. Great American Federal Savings & Loan Association v. Novotny, 442 U.S. 366, 99 S.Ct. 2345, 60 L.Ed.2d 957 (1979). That case, denying a remedy under 42 U.S.C.A. § 1985 for a violation of Title VII of the Civil Rights Act because it would undercut the specific provisions in the latter Act, has a clear message for the development of implied remedies under the federal securities laws.

Further, the Court has narrowed or tightened the *Cort v. Ash* test. In Piper v. Chris Craft, 430 U.S. 1, 97 S.Ct. 926, 51 L.Ed.2d 124 (1977), standing was denied in a case brought under § 14(e) of the Securities Exchange Act of 1934, which deals with tender offers, a subject we will explore later. That statute prohibits certain conduct in connection with tender offers, but provides no express remedies. Two companies were competing with each other in a bid to acquire control of a third company and the one which was unsuccessful sued the successful suitor for violations of the tender offer provisions of the statute. The Supreme Court found that there was no standing to bring that suit, relying in part, on Cort v. Ash. The Supreme Court refined the *Cort* test, by asking whether an implied cause of action was *necessary* to effectuate the Congressional goals, posing a higher threshold than exists when the question is whether it was *consistent* with the legislative scheme. *See* Pitt, Standing to Sue Under the Williams Act After Chris Craft: A Leaky Ship on Troubled Waters, 34 Bus.Law. 117 (1978).

The Court has continued to refine the scope of implied private rights of action, granting some, but more often denying others. An implied right of action was sustained in two sex discrimination cases, Davis v. Passman, 441 U.S. 228, 99 S.Ct. 2264, 60 L.Ed.2d 846 (1979) based on the Fifth Amendment and in Cannon v. University of Chicago, 441 U.S. 667, 99 S.Ct. 1946, 60 L.Ed.2d 560 (1979), under Title IX of the Education Amendments of 1972. In the latter case, the Court followed the Cort v. Ash standards in determining that a private right existed but appeared to do so narrowly and reluctantly. A lengthy dissent by Mr. Justice Powell took issue with the Cort v. Ash tests as inappropriate because they amounted to judicial legislation.

Shortly thereafter, the Court decided Touche Ross & Co. v. Redington, 442 U.S. 560, 99 S.Ct. 2479, 61 L.Ed.2d 82 (1979) denying an implied private right of action under § 17 of the Securities Exchange Act of 1934, which requires stock brokers to file financial reports annually with the SEC. In that case the Court did not pursue the four part analysis of Cort v. Ash but said that its task "is limited solely to determining whether Congress intended to create the private rights of action asserted * * *." 442 U.S. at 568, 99 S.Ct. at 2485. It noted that § 17 "is flanked by provisions of the 1934 Act that explicitly grant private causes of action * * *. Obviously, then, when Congress wished to provide a private damage remedy, it knew how to do so and did so expressly." *Id.* at 571–2, 99 S.Ct. at 2487.

Addressing itself to the policy arguments found so persuasive in *Borak*, the Court said that "generalized references to the 'remedial purposes' of the 1934 Act will not justify reading a provision 'more broadly than its language and the statutory scheme reasonably permit.' * * * To the extent that our analysis in today's decision differs from that of the Court in *Borak* it suffices to say that in a series of cases since *Borak* we have adhered to a stricter standard for the implication of private causes of action, and we follow that stricter standard today * * *. The ultimate question is one of whether this Court thinks that it can improve upon the statutory scheme that Congress enacted into law." *Id.* at 578, 99 S.Ct. at 2490.

Further, in *Touche Ross*, the Court disposed of the § 27 argument that had been found so persuasive in *Borak*. Mr. Justice Rehnquist said in *Touche Ross*, that § 27 "creates no cause of action of its own force and effect; it imposes no liability. The source of plaintiff's rights must be found if at all, in the substantive provisions of the 1934 Act which they seek to enforce, not in the jurisdictional provision." *Id.* at 577, 99 S.Ct. at 2490.

In Transamerica Mortgage Advisors, Inc. v. Lewis, 444 U.S. 11, 100 S.Ct. 242, 62 L.Ed.2d 146 (1979) the Court recognized an implied right to equitable relief under a section of the Investment Advisors Act which declared contracts that violate that statute to be void.

The Court then rejected the plaintiff's principal contention that he was entitled to damages because the defendant violated a section of that statute which declares certain fraudulent practices to be illegal. The intention of Congress with respect to such a remedy was central to the inquiry. "Such an intent may appear implicitly in the language or the structure of the statute, or in the circumstances of its enactment." 444 U.S. at 19, 100 S.Ct. at 246. Since the Court found no language or pattern leading to the implication of a damages remedy, it denied it availability. It noted "the mere fact that the statute was designed to protect advisers' clients does not require the implication of a private cause of action for damages on their behalf."

The Court specifically addressed the continued viability of Cort v. Ash in State of California v. Sierra Club, 451 U.S. 287, 101 S.Ct. 1775, 68 L.Ed.2d 101 (1981), in a case involving an implied private right of action under the Rivers and Harbors Appropriations Act of 1899. The statute prohibited the creation of any obstruction not affirmatively authorized by Congress, to the navigable capacity of any of the waters of the United States, but did not create any private enforcement. The Sierra Club sought to enjoin the state from constructing a canal that would divert the flow of water. The Court unanimously held that no private remedy was available, even for an injunction. Nothing in the legislative history indicated that the statute was for the "especial benefit of a particular class." 451 U.S. at 294. Rather, the statute "was designed to benefit the public at large." *Id.* The Court then noted that it was not surprising that there was no indication of a legislative intent to create or deny a remedy. *Id.* at 295.

This decision assigned priorities to the *Cort* factors. Since the first two factors were not satisfied, "it is unnecessary to inquire further to determine whether the purpose of the statute would be advanced by the judicial implication of a private action or whether such a remedy is within the federal domain of interest. These factors are only of relevance if the first two factors give indication of congressional intent to create the remedy." *Id.* at 298.

Four justices would have gone further in minimizing the *Cort* factors, as "merely guides in ascertaining legislative intent."

There is support for the concurring justices' view in the Court's decision in Universities Research Association v. Coutu, 450 U.S. 754, 101 S.Ct. 1451, 67 L.Ed.2d 662 (1981) where a private remedy on behalf of construction workers claiming benefits under the Davis-Bacon Act was denied. The Court acknowledged that the plaintiffs were members of the class for whose especial benefit the law was enacted, but denied them a remedy because the language and approach of the statute provided no support for such an interpretation. In fact, the Court believed that a private remedy would upset the balance struck by Congress.

The Court's cautious approach toward implying private remedies was summed up in Northwest Airlines, Inc. v. Transport Workers Union, 451 U.S. 77, 101 S.Ct. 1571, 67 L.Ed.2d 750 (1981). "In almost any statutory scheme, there may be a need for judicial interpretation of ambiguous or incomplete provisions. But the authority to construe a statute is fundamentally different from the authority to fashion a new rule or to provide a new remedy which Congress decided not to adopt. [citation omitted.] The presumption that a remedy was deliberately omitted from a statute is strongest when Congress has enacted a comprehensive legislative scheme including an integrated system of procedures for enforcement."

The Court's recent rulings seem consistent with Mr. Justice Powell's dissent in *Cannon.* This leaves one to question the present viability of *Borak* (not to mention *Cort*) in light of Justice Powell's comment about *Borak* in which he said, "I find this decision both unprecedented and incomprehensible as a matter of public policy. The decision's rationale which lies ultimately in the judgment that 'private enforcement of the proxy rules provides a necessary supplement to Commission action,' * * * ignores the fact that Congress, in determining the degree of regulation to be imposed on companies covered by the Securities Exchange Act, already had decided that private enforcement was unnecessary. More significant for present purposes, however, is the fact that *Borak*, rather than signaling a start in the trend of this court, constitutes a singular and, I believe, aberrant interpretation of a federal regulatory statute." 441 U.S. at 735–36, 99 S.Ct. at 1977. However, Justice Powell added in a footnote, that he did not think that *Borak* should be overruled "at this late date." *Id.* at 735, n. 6, 99 S.Ct. at 1978.

If *Borak* and the availability of an implied private right of action under the proxy rules seems safe, and probably an implied private right of action under rule 10b–5 as well, it is more doubtful what will happen in other areas. Lower courts have continued to imply private rights even where the Supreme Court has not specifically sanctioned their availability. One court, in sustaining a private right for a suit against a stock exchange for failing to enforce its rules of supervision against an insolvent broker, interpreted the Supreme Court's decisions as militating against *extensions* of private rights, not overturning long recognized actions. Rich v. New York Stock Exchange, Inc., 509 F.Supp. 87 (S.D.N.Y.1981). Other courts have continued to expand private rights into new areas, relying on *Cort* and *Cannon*. Thus, the Third Circuit found a private right under the Trust Indenture Act of 1939, one of the statutes enforced by the SEC, in Zeffiro v. First Pennsylvania Banking & Trust Co., 623 F.2d 290 (3d Cir. 1980). More importantly, in Merrill Lynch, Pierce, Fenner & Smith, Inc. v. Curran, 50 U.S.L.W. 4457 (1982), the Court upheld a private right of action under the Commodity Exchange Act, a statute that is closely analogous to the securities laws. The majority found that Congress intended a private right of action (the paramount, if not the sole, test) on the grounds that the federal courts had uniformly held such a right to exist under the anti-fraud section at the time Congress substantially revised the Act in 1974. The decision was 5 to 4, with Justice Powell filing a vigorous dissent.

It should also be noted that the rules of the stock exchanges are another source of stockholder rights with respect to the solicitation of proxies. From time to time, investors have brought suit in federal court claiming that there was an implied private right of action for violation of the stock exchange rules to the same extent that the rules of the SEC provide an implied private right of action. The Supreme Court has not passed on this issue, and lower court decisions are widely split. *See* Jablon v. Dean Witter & Co., 614 F.2d 677 (9th Cir. 1980). A Supreme Court policy that looks begrudgingly on implied private rights of action will obviously have an effect on the extension of private rights of action for violation of stock exchange rules.

b. Elements of a Remedy

(i) *Materiality*

TSC INDUSTRIES, INC. V. NORTHWAY, INC.

426 U.S. 438, 96 S.Ct. 2126, 48 L.Ed.2d 757 (1976).

[National Industries acquired 34% of TSC Industries stock by purchase from the founding family, and then placed five of its nominees on TSC's board of directors. The two companies agreed to a sale of TSC's assets to National in exchange for stock and warrants of National. A joint proxy statement was issued by the two companies. A shareholder of TSC sued for violation of Section 14(a) of the Securities Exchange Act of 1934 and Rule 14a–9. The shareholder claimed, among other things, that the proxy statement failed to state that purchase of the 34% block of stock, which was disclosed, gave it control of TSC. The District Court found no material omissions from the proxy statement, but the Court of Appeals reversed.]

Mr. Justice MARSHALL delivered the opinion of the Court.

* * *

The question of materiality, it is universally agreed, is an objective one, involving the significance of an omitted or misrepresented fact to a reasonable investor. Variations in the formulation of a general test of materiality occur in the articulation of just how significant a fact must be or, put another way, how certain it must be that the fact would affect a reasonable investor's judgment.

The Court of Appeals in this case concluded that material facts include "all facts which a reasonable shareholder *might* consider important." 512 F.2d at 330 (emphasis added). This formulation of the test of materiality has been explicitly rejected by at least two courts as setting too low a threshold for the imposition of liability under Rule 14a–9. Gerstle v. Gamble-Skogmo, Inc., 478 F.2d 1281, 1301–1302 (C.A.2 1973); Smallwood v. Pearl Brewing Co., 489 F.2d 579, 603–604 (C.A.5 1974). In these cases, panels of the Second and Fifth Circuits opted for the conventional tort test of materiality— whether a reasonable man *would* attach importance to the fact misrepresented or omitted in determining his course of action. * * *

In arriving at its broad definition of a material fact as one that a reasonable shareholder *might* consider important, the Court of Appeals in this case relied heavily upon language of this Court in Mills v. Electric Auto-Lite Co., *supra*. That reliance was misplaced. The *Mills* Court did characterize a determination of materiality as at least "embod[ying] a conclusion that the defect was of such a character that it might have been considered important by a reasonable shareholder who was in the process of deciding how to vote." But if any language in *Mills* is to be read as suggesting a general notion of materiality, it can only be the opinion's subsequent reference to materiality as a "requirement that the defect have a significant *propensity* to affect the voting process." For it was that requirement that the Court said "adequately serves the purpose of ensuring that a cause of action cannot be established by proof of a defect so trivial, or so unrelated to the transaction for which approval is sought, that correction of the defect or imposition of liability would not further the interests protected by § 14(a)." Even this language must be read, however, with appreciation that the Court specifically declined to consider the materiality of the omissions in *Mills*. The references to materiality were simply preliminary to our consideration of the sole question in the case—whether proof of the materiality of an omission from a proxy statement must be supplemented by a showing that the defect actually caused the outcome of the vote. It is clear, then, that *Mills* did not intend to foreclose further inquiry into the meaning of materiality under Rule 14a–9.

C

In formulating a standard of materiality under Rule 14a–9, we are guided, of course, by the recognition in *Borak* and *Mills* of the Rule's broad remedial purpose. That purpose is not merely to ensure by judicial means that the transaction, when judged by its real terms, is fair and otherwise adequate, but to ensure disclosures by corporate management in order to enable the shareholders to make an informed choice. As an abstract proposition, the most desirable role for a court in a suit of this sort, coming after the consummation of the proposed transaction, would perhaps be to determine whether in fact the proposal would have been favored by the shareholders and consummated in the absence of any misstatement or omission. But as we recognized in *Mills*, such matters are not subject to determination with certainty. Doubts as to the critical nature of information misstated or omitted will be commonplace. And particularly in view of the prophylactic purpose of the Rule and the fact that the content of the proxy statement is within management's control, it is appropriate that these doubts be resolved in favor of those the statute is designed to protect.

We are aware, however, that the disclosure policy embodied in the proxy regulations is not without limit. Some information is of such dubious significance that insistence on its disclosure may accomplish more harm than good. The potential liability for Rule 14a–9 violation can be great indeed, and if the standard of materiality is unnecessarily low, not only may the corporation and its management be subjected to liability for insignificant omissions or misstatements, but also management's fear of exposing itself to substantial liability may cause it simply to bury the shareholders in an avalanche of trivial information—a result that is hardly conducive to informed decision-making. Precisely these dangers are presented, we think, by the definition of a material fact adopted by the Court of Appeals in this case—a fact which a reasonable shareholder *might* consider important. We agree with Judge Friendly, speaking for the Court of Appeals in *Gerstle*, that the "might" formulation is "too suggestive of mere possibility, however unlikely."

The general standard of materiality that we think best comports with the policies of Rule 14a–9 is as follows: An omitted fact is material if there is a substantial likelihood that a reasonable shareholder would consider it important in deciding how to vote. This standard is fully consistent with *Mills* general description of materiality as a requirement that "the defect have a significant *propensity* to affect the voting process." It does not require proof of a substantial likelihood that disclosure of the omitted fact would have caused the reasonable investor to change his vote. What the standard does contemplate is a showing of a substantial likelihood that, under all the circumstances, the omitted fact would have assumed actual significance in the deliberations of the reasonable shareholder. Put another way, there must be a substantial likelihood that the disclosure of the omitted fact would have been viewed by the reasonable investor as having significantly altered the "total mix" of information made available.

* * * In considering whether summary judgment on the issue is appropriate, we must bear in mind that the underlying objective facts, which will often be free from dispute, are merely the starting point for the ultimate determination of materiality. The determination requires delicate assessments of the inferences a "reasonable shareholder" would draw from a given set of facts and the significance of those inferences to him, and these assessments are peculiarly ones for the trier of fact. Only if the established omissions are "so obviously important to an investor, that reasonable minds cannot differ on the question of materiality" is the ultimate issue of materiality appropriately resolved "as a matter of law" by summary judgment.

III

The omissions found by the Court of Appeals to have been materially misleading as a matter of law involved two general issues—the degree of National's control over TSC at the time of the proxy solicitation, and the favorability of the terms of the proposed transaction to TSC shareholders.

A. *National's Control of TSC*

The Court of Appeals concluded that two omitted facts relating to National's potential influence, or control, over the management of TSC were material as a matter of law. First, the proxy statement failed to state that at the time the statement was issued, the chairman of the TSC board of directors was Stanley Yarmuth, National's president and chief executive officer, and the chairman of the TSC executive committee was Charles Simonelli, National's executive vice president. Second the statement did not disclose that in filing reports required by the SEC, both TSC and National had indicated that National "may be deemed to be a 'parent' of TSC as that term is defined in the Rules and Regulations under the Securities Act of 1933." The Court of Appeals noted that TSC shareholders were relying on the TSC board of directors to negotiate on their behalf for the best possible rate of exchange with National. It then concluded that the omitted facts were material because they were "persuasive indicators that the TSC board was in fact under the control of National, and that National thus 'sat on both sides of the table' in setting the terms of the exchange."

We do not agree that the omission of these facts, when viewed against the disclosures contained in the proxy statement, warrants the entry of summary judgment against TSC and National on this record. Our conclusion is the same whether the omissions are considered separately or together.

The proxy statement prominently displayed the facts that National owned 34% of the outstanding shares in TSC, and that no other person owned more than 10%. App. 262–263, 267. It also prominently revealed that 5 out of 10 TSC directors were National nominees, and it recited the positions of those National nominees with National—indicating, among other things, that Stanley Yarmuth was president and a director of National, and that Charles Simonelli was executive vice president and a director of National. These disclosures clearly revealed the nature of National's relationship with TSC and alerted the reasonable shareholder to the fact that National exercised a degree of influence over TSC. In view of these disclosures, we certainly cannot say that the additional facts that Yarmuth was chairman of the TSC board of directors and Simonelli chairman of its executive committee were, on this record, so obviously important that reasonable minds could not differ on their materiality.

* * *

[The court also found no material omissions with respect to the other allegations charged by the plaintiff.]

(ii) Causation

MILLS v. ELECTRIC AUTO–LITE CO.

396 U.S. 375, 90 S.Ct. 616, 24 L.Ed.2d 95 (1970).

Mr. Justice HARLAN delivered the opinion of the Court.

This case requires us to consider a basic aspect of the implied private right of action for violation of § 14(a) of the Securities Exchange Act of 1934, recognized by this Court in J. I. Case Co. v. Borak, 377 U.S. 426 (1964). As in *Borak* the asserted wrong is that a corporate merger was accomplished through the use of a proxy statement that was materially false or misleading. The question with which we deal is what causal relationship must be shown between such a statement and the merger to establish a cause of action based on the violation of the Act.

I

Petitioners were shareholders of the Electric Auto-Lite Company until 1963, when it was merged into Mergenthaler Linotype Company. They brought suit on the day before the shareholders' meeting at which the vote was to take place on the merger against Auto-Lite, Mergenthaler, and a third company, American Manufacturing Company, Inc. The complaint sought an injunction against the voting by Auto-Lite's management of all proxies obtained by means of an allegedly misleading proxy solicitation; however, it did not seek a temporary restraining order, and the voting went ahead as scheduled the following day. Several months later petitioners filed an amended complaint, seeking to have the merger set aside and to obtain such other relief as might be proper.

In Count II of the amended complaint, which is the only count before us, petitioners predicated jurisdiction on § 27 of the 1934 Act. They alleged that the proxy statement sent out by the Auto-Lite management to solicit shareholders' votes in favor of the merger was misleading, in violation of § 14(a) of the Act and SEC Rule 14a–9 thereunder. Petitioners recited that before the merger Mergenthaler owned over 50% of the outstanding shares of Auto-Lite common stock, and had been in control of Auto-Lite for two years. American Manufacturing in turn owned about one-third of the outstanding shares of Mergenthaler, and for two years had been in voting control of Mergenthaler and, through it, of Auto-Lite. Petitioners charged that in light of these circumstances the proxy statement was misleading in that it told Auto-Lite shareholders that their board of directors recommended approval of the merger without also informing them that all 11 of Auto-Lite's directors were nominees of Mergenthaler and were under the "control and domination of Mergenthaler." Petitioners asserted the right to complain of this alleged violation both derivatively on behalf of Auto-Lite and as representatives of the class of all its minority shareholders.

On petitioners' motion for summary judgment with respect to Count II, the District Court for the Northern District of Illinois ruled as a matter of law that the claimed defect in the proxy statement was, in light of the circumstances in which the statement was made, a material omission. The District Court concluded, from its reading of the *Borak* opinion, that it had to hold a hearing on the issue whether there was "a causal connection between the finding that there has been a violation of the disclosure requirements of § 14(a) and the alleged injury to the plaintiffs" before it could consider what remedies would be appropriate.

After holding such a hearing, the court found that under the terms of the merger agreement, an affirmative vote of two-thirds of the Auto-Lite shares was required for approval of the merger, and that the respondent companies owned and controlled about 54% of the outstanding shares. Therefore, to obtain authorization of the merger, respondents had to secure the approval of a substantial number of the minority shareholders. At the stockholders' meeting, approximately, 950,000 shares, out of 1,160,000 shares outstanding were voted in favor of the merger. This included 317,000 votes obtained by proxy from the minority shareholders, votes that were "necessary and indispensable to the approval of the merger." The District Court concluded that a causal relationship had thus been shown, and it granted an interlocutory judgment in favor of petitioners on the issue of liability, referring the case to a master for consideration of appropriate relief.

The District Court made the certification required by 28 U.S.C. § 1292(b), and respondents took an interlocutory appeal to the Court of Appeals for the Seventh Circuit. That court affirmed the District Court's conclusion that the proxy statement was materially deficient, but reversed on the question of causation. The court acknowledged that, if an injunction had been sought a sufficient time before the stockholders' meeting, "corrective measures would have been appropriate." 403 F.2d 429, 435 (1968). However, since this suit was brought too late for preventive action, the courts had to determine "whether the misleading statement and omission caused the submission of sufficient proxies," as a prerequisite to a determination of liability under the Act. If the respondents could show, "by a preponderance of probabilities, that the merger would have received a sufficient vote even if the proxy statement had not been misleading in the respect found," petitioners would be entitled to no relief of any kind. *Id.*, at 436.

The Court of Appeals acknowledged that this test corresponds to the common law fraud test of whether the injured party relied on the misrepresentation. However, rightly concluding that "[r]eliance by thousands of individuals, as here, can scarcely be inquired into" (*id.*, at 436 n.10), the court ruled that the issue was to be determined by proof of the fairness of the terms of the merger, If respondents could show that the merger had merit and was fair to the minority shareholders, the trial court would be justified in concluding that a sufficient number of shareholders would have approved the merger had there been no deficiency in the proxy statement. In that case respondents would be entitled to a judgment in their favor.

Claiming that the Court of Appeals has construed this Court's decision in *Borak* in a manner that frustrates the statute's policy of enforcement through private litigation, the petitioners then sought review in this Court. We granted certiorari, believing that resolution of this basic issue should be made at this stage of the litigation and not postponed until after a trial under the Court of Appeals' decision.

II

As we stressed in *Borak*, § 14(a) stemmed from a congressional belief that "[f]air corporate suffrage is an important right that should attach to every equity security bought on a public exchange." * * * The decision below, by permitting all liability to be foreclosed on the basis of a finding that the merger was fair, would allow the stockholders to be bypassed, at least where the only legal challenge to the merger is a suit for retrospective relief after the meeting has been held. A judicial appraisal of the merger's merits could be substituted for the actual and informed vote of the stockholders.

The result would be to insulate from private redress an entire category of proxy violations—those relating to matters other than the terms of the merger. Even outrageous misrepresentations in a proxy solicitation, if they did not relate to the terms of the transaction, would give rise to no cause of action under § 14(a). Particularly if carried over to enforcement actions by the Securities and Exchange Commission itself, such a result would subvert the congressional purpose of ensuring full and fair disclosure to shareholders.

Further, recognition of the fairness of the merger as a complete defense would confront small shareholders with an additional obstacle to making a successful challenge to a proposal recommended through a defective proxy statement. The risk that they would be unable to rebut the corporation's evidence of the fairness of the proposal, and thus to establish their cause of action, would be bound to discourage such shareholders from the private enforcement of the proxy rules that "provides a necessary supplement to Commission action." J. I. Case Co. v. Borak, 377 U.S., at 432, 84 S.Ct. at 1560.[5]

Such a frustration of the congressional policy is not required by anything in the wording of the statute or in our opinion in the *Borak* case. Section 14(a) declares it "unlawful" to solicit proxies in contravention of Commission rules, and SEC Rule 14a–9 prohibits solicitations "containing any statement which * * * is false or misleading with respect to any material fact, or which omits to state any

---

5. The Court of Appeals' ruling that "causation" may be negated by proof of the fairness of the merger also rests on a dubious behavioral assumption. There is no justification for presuming that the shareholders of every corporation are willing to accept any and every fair merger offer put before them; yet such a presumption is implicit in the opinion of the Court of Appeals. That court gave no indication of what evidence petitioners might adduce, once respondents had established that the merger proposal was equitable, in order to show that the shareholders would nevertheless have rejected it if the solicitation had not been misleading. Proof of actual reliance by thousands of individuals would, as the court acknowledged, not be feasible, see R. Jennings & H. Marsh, Securities Regulation, Cases and Materials 1001 (2d ed. 1968) * * *. In practice, therefore, the objective fairness of the proposal would seemingly be determinative of liability. But in view of the many other factors that might lead shareholders to prefer their current position to that of owners of a larger, combined enterprise, it is pure conjecture to assume that the fairness of the proposal will always be determinative of their vote.

---

material fact necessary in order to make the statements therein not false or misleading * * *." Use of a solicitation that is materially misleading is itself a violation of law, as the Court of Appeals recognized in stating that injunctive relief would be available to remedy such a defect if sought prior to the stockholders' meeting. In *Borak*, which came to this Court on a dismissal of the complaint, the Court limited its inquiry to whether a violation of § 14(a) gives rise to "a federal cause of action for rescission or damages," 377 U.S., at 428, 84 S.Ct. at 1558. Referring to the argument made by petitioners there "that the merger can be dissolved only if it was fraudulent or non-beneficial, issues upon which the proxy material would not bear," the Court stated: "But the causal relationship of the proxy material and the merger are questions of fact to be resolved at trial, not here. We therefore do not discuss this point further." *Id.*, at 431, 84 S.Ct. at 1559. In the present case there has been a hearing specifically directed to the causation problem. The question before the Court is whether the facts found on the basis of that hearing are sufficient in law to establish petitioners' cause of action, and we conclude that they are.

Where the misstatement or omission in a proxy statement has been shown to be "material," as it was found to be here, that determination itself indubitably embodies a conclusion that the defect was of such a character that it might have been considered important by a reasonable shareholder who was in the process of deciding how to vote.[6] This requirement that the defect have a significant *propensity* to affect the voting process is found in the express terms of Rule 14a–9, and it adequately serves the purpose of ensuring that a cause of action cannot be established by proof of a defect so trivial, or so unrelated to the transaction for which approval is sought, that correction of the defect or imposition of liability would not further the interests protected by § 14(a).

There is no need to supplement this requirement, as did the Court of Appeals, with a requirement of proof of whether the defect actually had a decisive effect on the voting. Where there has been a finding of materiality, a shareholder has made a sufficient showing of causal relationship between the violation and the injury for which he seeks redress, if, as here, he proves that the proxy solicitation itself,

---

6. In this case, where the misleading aspect of the solicitation involved failure to reveal a serious conflict of interest on the part of the directors, the Court of Appeals concluded that the crucial question in determining materiality was "whether the minority shareholders were sufficiently alerted to the board's relationship to their adversary to be on their guard." 403 F.2d, at 434. An adequate disclosure of this relationship would have warned the stockholders to give more careful scrutiny to the terms of the merger than they might to one recommended by an entirely disinterested board. Thus, the failure to make such a disclosure was found to be a material defect "as a matter of law," thwarting the informed decision at which the statute aims, regardless of whether the terms of the merger were such that a reasonable stockholder would have approved the transaction after more careful analysis. See also Swanson v. American Consumer Industries, Inc., 415 F.2d 1326 (C.A.7th Cir. 1969).

rather than the particular defect in the solicitation materials, was an essential link in the accomplishment of the transaction. This objective test will avoid the impracticalities of determining how many votes were affected, and, by resolving doubts in favor of those the statute is designed to protect, will effectuate the congressional policy of ensuring that the shareholders are able to make an informed choice when they are consulted on corporate transactions.[7]

III

Our conclusion that petitioners have established their case by showing that proxies necessary to approval of the merger were obtained by means of a materially misleading solicitation implies nothing about the form of relief to which they may be entitled. We held in *Borak* that upon finding a violation the courts were "to be alert to provide such remedies as are necessary to make effective the congressional purpose," noting specifically that such remedies are not to be limited to prospective relief.   *   *   *

*   *   *

IV

Although the question of relief must await further proceedings in the District Court, our conclusion that petitioners have established their cause of action indicates that the Court of Appeals should have affirmed the partial summary judgment on the issue of liability. The result would have been not only that respondents, rather than petitioners, would have borne the costs of the appeal, but also, we think, that petitioners would have been entitled to an interim award of litigation expenses and reasonable attorneys' fees. We agree with the position taken by petitioners, and by the United States as *amicus*, that petitioners, who have established a violation of the securities laws by their corporation and its officials, should be reimbursed by the corporation or its survivor for the costs of establishing the violation.

*   *   *

In many suits under § 14(a), particularly where the violation does not relate to the terms of the transaction for which proxies are solicited, it may be impossible to assign monetary value to the benefit. Nevertheless, the stress placed by Congress on the importance of fair and informed corporate suffrage leads to the conclusion that, in vindicating the statutory policy, petitioners have rendered a substantial

---

7. We need not decide in this case whether causation could be shown where the management controls a sufficient number of shares to approve the transaction without any votes from the minority. Even in that situation, if the management finds it necessary for legal or practical reasons to solicit proxies from minority shareholders, at least one court has held that the proxy solicitation might be sufficiently related to the merger to satisfy the causation requirement, *see* Laurenzano v. Einbender, 264 F.Supp. 356 (D.C.E.D.N.Y.1966).

service to the corporation and its shareholders. Whether petitioners are successful in showing a need for significant relief may be a factor in determining whether a further award should later be made. But regardless of the relief granted, private stockholders' actions of this sort "involve corporate therapeutics," and furnish a benefit to all shareholders by providing an important means of enforcement of the proxy statute. To award attorneys' fees in such a suit to a plaintiff who has succeeded in establishing a cause of action is not to saddle the unsuccessful party with the expenses but to impose them on the class that has benefited from them and that would have had to pay them had it brought the suit.

For the foregoing reasons we conclude that the judgment of the Court of Appeals should be vacated and the case remanded to that court for further proceedings consistent with this opinion.

It is so ordered.

NOTE—SUBSEQUENT DEVELOPMENTS IN MILLS

Once the Court found that a violation of the proxy rules had occurred, because of the material nature of the misstatement the infraction was held to have caused the injury, and thus the fairness of the transaction which was caused became relevant to the question of relief. The District Court found that the merger was unfair to the minority shareholders and awarded damages of $1,233,918, but the Court of Appeals reversed. 552 F.2d 1239 (7th Cir. 1977), cert. denied 434 U.S. 922, 98 S.Ct. 398, 54 L.Ed.2d 279 (1977). The court determined the transaction to be fair by looking at the market value of the stock owned by the minority stockholders relative to that held by the dominant stockholders to see if what the minority received amounted to the fair share of what they contributed, plus an amount equal to the enhanced, or "synergistic", value of the resulting enterprise.

The court also held that the attorneys would be entitled to fees from the corporation only for the period up to the Supreme Court decision. Lead counsel was awarded a fee of $250,000, not an overly generous amount considering the time devoted to the case. (Order dated May 14, 1978).

NOTE—MATERIALITY AND CAUSATION

1. *Materiality*

The proxy statement provides an unusually good opportunity to inform investors about the affairs of a company. Not only does this facilitate "fair corporate suffrage," it assists investors in making buy, sell or hold decisions. Thus, even in an election where there is no opposition to the management's recommendations, the proxy statement provides to the marketplace detailed information about the company's financial affairs, management compensation, the organization of the board of directors and other relevant data. Some of this information appears in the proxy statements and some appears in the annual report that the proxy rules require companies to deliver to their stockholders.

As the cases make clear, the Court has allowed stockholders to sue the company when the proxy statement fails to comply with the rules. *Borak* held that private recovery was predicated upon establishing a "causal relationship" between the proxy material and the transaction, a question of fact to be resolved at trial. *Mills* then held that "Where there has been a finding of materiality [of the omitted fact], a shareholder has made a sufficient showing of causal relationship between the violation and the injury for which he seeks redress * * *." *TSC* next provided an elaborate definition of "materiality." Clearly, not every false or misleading statement nor every omission will give rise to recovery by stockholders. One is then led to ask, to what objective of the proxy rules must the defect relate? Must the omission or false or misleading statement have played a significant role in bringing about the matter submitted to a vote? Do only those errors which bear upon the financial soundness of the investment have bearing on the investor's decision to grant a proxy? Do other factors, not easily quantifiable, have anything to do with an investor's decision? Do the proxy rules have any aim other than the protection of the investor's interest?

These questions are of large jurisdictional significance. To the extent that companies may be held liable for failing to disclose information that is material to the accomplishment of some goal other than investor protection, great sweep is given to the federal securities laws and to the SEC in its power to govern corporate conduct. Section 14(a) of the Securities Exchange Act of 1934 gives the Commission power to prescribe rules and regulations it deems "necessary or appropriate in the public interest or for the protection of investors." Presumably the words "in the public interest" have some meaning that, according to one writer, "would seem at least to permit the Commission to take into account the broader public interest when acting in areas near the margins of investor protection * * *." Stevenson, The SEC and Foreign Bribery, 32 Bus.Law. 53 (1976). However, the Supreme Court in NAACP v. Federal Power Commission, 425 U.S. 662, 96 S.Ct. 1806, 48 L.Ed. 284 (1976) held that similar language in another statute should be read to confine the agency's power close to its main purposes, which in the case of the SEC means the protection of investors.

To what extent can the SEC or a court find that a corporation's failure to disclose violations of the law become violations of the proxy rules? One answer might be that the violation is material if the penalty imposed on the corporation is of financial significance so as to be relevant to a conventional financial analysis. But suppose the violation results in relatively insignificant penalties or, even better from the company's standpoint, was incurred in the course of obtaining substantial benefits for the company. For example, a company might have violated some environmental law which enabled it to dispose of waste products at a great saving. Or it might have bribed a public official in return for which it received substantial economic benefits which it still retains. Are investors interested in requiring disclosure of that information especially where the disclosure might deter the company from securing the economic advantage?

The SEC found violations of its reporting requirement by United States Steel Corporation when it failed to disclose the company's frequent violations of environmental requirements, which resulted in fines to the company. In the Matter of United States Steel Corporation, Rel. No. 34–16223 (Sept. 27, 1979). Is this a compounding of the original violation, brought within the scope of securities laws because of a failure to disclose that violation? The *pattern* of behavior that created economic risks, not the isolated violation, probably caused the violations to come within the SEC's arena.

In the Report of the Securities and Exchange Commission on Questionable and Illegal Corporate Payments and Practices, submitted to the Senate Banking, Housing and Urban Affairs Committee in 1976, the Commission took the view that questionable or illegal payments were material facts that ought to be disclosed to investors regardless of the size of the payment or the impact on business because the disclosure requirements of the law are intended to facilitate the stockholders' evaluation of management's stewardship, and "investors should be vitally interested in the quality and integrity of management." Several courts have agreed with this in particular contexts. In SEC v. Kalvex, Inc., 425 F.Supp. 310 (S.D.N.Y.1975), the proxy statement's failure to disclose that a candidate for director had arranged for illegal kick-backs of a small amount was held to be a material omission because of the bearing that the information had on the candidate's integrity. Similarly, in Cooke v. Teleprompter Corp., 334 F.Supp. 467 (S.D.N.Y.1971), it was held to be a material omission to fail to disclose the conviction of a candidate for the board for bribing public officials. In that case, the company's operations depended upon receiving an FCC license, heightening the importance of information the FCC might deem important. In SEC v. Jos. Schlitz Brewing Co., 452 F.Supp. 824 (E.D.Wis.1978) the court found that the failure to disclose illegal or improper payments made to induce the sale of the company's products was material because of the bearing it had on the integrity of management. A failure of a proxy statement to disclose that several candidates for the board of directors had consented to a finding that they had violated certain provisions of the federal securities laws dealing with "insider trading" justified an injunction against the holding of an annual meeting until the proxy statement had been corrected to disclose that fact. Rafal v. Geneen, Fed.Sec.L.Rep. (CCH) ¶ 93,505 (E.D.Pa.1972).

The SEC has instituted a number of actions against corporations which made illegal and questionable payments, mainly abroad, and had failed to disclose that conduct in their proxy statements and in other reports filed with the Commission. Some strong opposition was voiced against this practice on grounds that the Commission was seeking to enforce other laws and other policies through its disclosure requirements but that these requirements should be confined to matters of relevance to investors. *See* Freeman, The Legality of the SEC's Management Fraud Program, 31 Bus.Law. 1295 (1976). To some extent this argument was mooted by the adoption in 1977 of the Foreign Corrupt Practices Act, which made it illegal to make such payments without regard to the financial materiality of the payments or of business impacted. However, that statute does not answer the question as to whether a violation of the federal securities laws occurs when there has been a failure to disclose the illegal activity.

A court refused to find a violation of the proxy rules when a corporation omitted a description of its policy to "thwart, resist and abuse" labor laws by opposing unionization. Amalgamated Clothing & Textile Workers Union v. J. P. Stevens & Co. Inc., 475 F.Supp. 328 (S.D.N.Y.1979). It found that omissions relating to a question of business judgment (as opposed to self dealing) are not actionable even if claims of illegality are involved. (Refer back to the Chesapeake Marine Problem, Part I, in Chapter 3.) Moreover, the court found that the proxy rules do not require directors to accuse themselves of violating the law. *See* SEC v. Chicago Helicopter, Civ. Action No. 79–C–0469 (N.D.Ill.1980).

A public interest group filed a petition with the SEC urging adoption of disclosure requirements of certain environmental and employment discrimination information, on grounds that this information was relevant to investors concerned with the social performance of the corporation. Among other things, the proponents urged that violations of the National Environmental Protection Act and employment discrimination law had bearing on the "integrity of management." After the SEC refused to adopt such a requirement, a federal district court required the Commission to consider the matter further and the SEC held hearings, after which it reaffirmed its position. Ultimately, the Commission was vindicated in the courts, mainly on grounds of deference to the expertise of the administrative agency, Natural Resources Defense Council v. SEC, 606 F.2d 1031 (D. C.Cir. 1979).

Can these different results be reconciled? If bribes are material without regard to their financial importance, why not environmental violations?

Disclosure serves more than one purpose. It can inform so that those who need to take action, such as stockholders voting at a meeting, have sufficient information on which to base a judgment, but it can also deter conduct. That is, disclosure has a therapeutic effect.

508   SHAREHOLDER ACTION   Ch. 13

The Advisory Committee on Corporate Disclosure to the SEC recommended that adoption of a position that "the Commission should not adopt disclosure requirements which have as their principal objective the regulation of corporate conduct." In commenting upon that report the Commission said "it does not believe, however, that the benefits to be derived from such a statement would, on balance outweigh the difficulties which it might create * * *. Decisions as to whether to require disclosure frequently do affect conduct and Congress was well aware of this consequence and thought it would often be beneficial." Preliminary Responses of the Commission to the Recommendations of the Advisory Committee on Corporate Disclosure, Securities Act Release No. 5906, Feb. 15, 1978, Fed.Sec.L.Rept. (CCH) par. 81,505.

The conduct itself may be the focus of shareholder attack, and the claim of inadequate disclosure merely the vehicle for attack. Thus, if a merger grossly unfair to one side was falsely presented, but rejected by the shareholders, no suit could follow. The shareholder could not show how any loss was caused by the violation. But suppose the converse appears: the facts establishing unfairness of the merger were fully, and painfully disclosed, but the shareholders approved. The loss is plain enough—the transaction was unfair—but has there been a violation of the proxy rules? Must the unfairness be disclosed? Must the merger be *characterized* as unfair, obviously a statement that would never appear in a proxy statement. In other words, do the rules require more than disclosure of facts from which the decision maker can draw his own conclusions?

In Golub v. PPD Corp., 576 F.2d 759 (8th Cir. 1978), plaintiffs alleged that a sale of assets from a corporation to a related person was unfair, and did not disclose management's improper motives. The court upheld dismissal of the complaint.

> As far as proxy statements are concerned * * * the federal purpose is served if the statement fully and fairly sets out such relevant and material facts as would enable a reasonably prudent stockholder to make an intelligent decision as to whether to grant the requested proxy or as to how he should vote on the questions mentioned in the proxy statement. * * *
>
> Actually, the plaintiffs are not complaining about any absence of facts in the proxy statement. Their complaint is that those who prepared the statement did not "disclose" what the plaintiffs say was the true motivation of * * * management in selling the assets of the company, and did not characterize the bonus aspects of the transaction as plaintiffs would have it characterized. Under the ['34] Act and regulations plaintiffs were not entitled to have such a "disclosure" or such a characterization.
>
> It is quite possible that plaintiffs may have a claim against the defendants or some of them under applicable state law. If so,

plaintiffs are free to pursue that claim in an appropriate forum.
* * *

576 F.2d at 764–65.

2. *Causation*

A finding that information about illegal activity constitutes material information, as some courts have held (see Ross v. Warner, Fed. Sec.L.Rep. (CCH) par. 97,735 (S.D.N.Y.1980) does not establish liability under the proxy rules. The plaintiff must still prove a causal connection between event and injury.

"Causation" is not one of the law's clearer concepts. It is often confused with "reliance," but a distinction between the two was drawn in *Mills*. There is a "but for" aspect to causation, but although that element is needed to establish causation in fact, it is not sufficient to establish liability. The added element that is needed is referred to as "legal" cause or "proximate" cause. That is, "but for" the misrepresentation" plaintiff might not have bought the property sold by defendant, but the loss might have resulted from a general economic decline. The Court in *Mills* did not find it necessary to explore all the ramifications of "cause." *See* Note, Causation and Liability in Private Actions for Proxy Violations, 81 Yale L.J. 107 (1970).

The concept of causation has been parsed into two tests: *transaction* causation and *loss* causation. In Schlick v. Penn-Dixie Cement Corp., 507 F.2d 374 (2d Cir. 1974), shareholders approved a merger between Penn Dixie and its 52% owned subsidiary, Continental. Minority shareholders of Continental complained about the terms of the deal and the inadequacy of disclosure to them. The court held that in order to establish a claim under the proxy rules (only one of the counts), both transaction and loss causation would have to be shown. Transaction causation means that the violations caused the company to engage in the transaction in question; loss causation means that the misrepresentations or omissions caused the economic harm.

Loss causation was relatively easy to demonstrate—showing that the minority shareholders received too little in the merger. But how does one demonstrate that the transaction was caused by defendants' conduct when defendants owned enough stock to cause the merger? This is the issue left open by footnote 7 in *Mills*. The court found that the proxy solicitation, and the approval of the minority shareholders, played a sufficiently operative role in the accomplishment of the transaction, on the terms proposed, so that there was a causal link between the misstatements and the deed. After all, management did not force the transaction on the minority which it possessed the power to do; it sought to win their approval. Apparently management determined that the "unnecessary" proxy solicitation was important. It is not clear that management would have chosen to go ahead with the deal without first seeking the approval of minority shareholders. To a large extent, the court was guided by policy considerations favoring accurate disclosure in proxy material, the informational value to the market and the constraint on management.

This expansive interpretation of transaction causation has been followed. In Cole v. Schenley Industries, Inc., 563 F.2d 35 (2d Cir. 1977), minority shareholders of Schenley complained about the disclosure provided them in a proxy statement seeking a merger, in effect, with its 84% parent, Glen Alden. The court explained why there was transaction causation, as follows:

> A Schenley minority shareholder had four options in May 1971: (1) accept Glen Alden's offer, (2) seek appraisal rights under Delaware law * (3) threaten to seek appraisal rights in an attempt to force Glen Alden to improve its offer, and (4) seek to enjoin the merger. The minority shareholders owned about 1.1 million shares of common stock and about 2.5 million shares of preferred stock of Schenley. If all, or a substantial portion, had exercised, or threatened to exercise, their appraisal rights, Schenley would have had to set aside a considerable sum of cash and the merger might not have been consummated. It was also possible that if additional information could be extracted the minority shareholders would have been able to enjoin the merger under Delaware law. * * * We need not decide whether such a suit would have been successful under Delaware law. In view of these three alternatives to accepting the Glen Alden offer, we hold that the proxy solicitation was an essential part of the merger.

563 F.2d at 39–40.

Where is the causal relationship between transactions allegedly improper, such as illegal payments by the corporation, and any false or misleading statements in the proxy material? The harm can be shown to be of two possible varieties: (1) the illegal payment, and (2) consequential side effects (the investigation, damage to reputation and the tax audit) from the violation. The shareholders did not vote to approve the transactions that caused these effects. Courts have found transaction causation lacking in these circumstances. Limmer v. General Telephone and Electronic Corp., Fed.Sec.L.Rep. (CCH) par. 96,111 (S.D.N.Y.1977); Herman v. Beretta, Fed.Sec.L.Rep. (CCH) par. 97,685 (S.D.N.Y.1980).

On the other hand, where shareholders challenged the election of directors because the proxy material failed to disclose their cover up of illegal payments, transaction causation was established. The issue of election of directors had been submitted to the stockholders. Of course, plaintiff still had to show that the omission had "a significant propensity to effect the voting process." This brings us back to ma-

---

* Appraisal rights are a statutory right, granted under state corporation law, enabling stockholders who oppose a merger (and sometimes similar transactions as well) to obtain the appraised value of their stock. A careful detailed procedure establishing the fair price is contained in the statute. See § 80, MBCA; Chapter 20, Introduction to Organic Change.

teriality. Weisberg v. Coastal States Gas Corp., 609 F.2d 650 (2d Cir. 1979).

The Ninth Circuit carried the analysis further in Gaines v. Haughton, 645 F.2d 761 (9th Cir. 1981). Agreeing that when the plaintiff attacks the election, not the improper payments, the analysis shifts from causation to materiality, the court drew a distinction between non-disclosure of self-dealing conduct, which is presumptively material, and "allegations of simple breach of fiduciary duty/waste of corporate assets—the non-disclosure of which is never material for § 14(a) purposes." *Id.* at 776–77.

The court elaborated on the point: "Many corporate actions taken by directors in the interest of the corporation might offend and engender controversy among some stockholders. Investors share the same diversity of social and political views that characterize the polity as a whole. The tenor of a company's labor relations policies, economic decisions to relocate or close established plants, commercial dealings with foreign countries which are disdained in certain circles, decisions to develop (or not to develop) particular natural resources or forms of energy technology, and the promulgation of corporate personnel policies that reject (or embrace) the principle of affirmative action, are just a few examples of business judgments, soundly entrusted to the broad discretion of the directors, which may nonetheless cause shareholder dissent and provoke claims of "wasteful," "unethical," or even "immoral" business dealings. Should corporate directors have a duty under § 14(a) to disclose all such corporate decisions in proxy solicitations for their re-election? We decline to extend the duty of disclosure under § 14(a) to these situations. While we neither condone nor condemn these and similar types of corporate conduct (including the now illegal practice of questionable foreign payments), we believe the aggrieved shareholders have sufficient recourse to state law claims against the responsible directors and, if all else fails, can sell or trade their stock in the offending corporation in favor of an enterprise more compatible with their own personal goals and values." *Id.* at 778–79.

3. *Scienter*

NOTE—THE DIRECTORS' RESPONSIBILITY FOR THE PROXY STATEMENT

Who has the responsibility for preparing and reviewing proxy material? No answer to that question is found in the statute or the Commission's rules. The question is likely to arise in a stockholder's claim for relief based on an assertion that the materials failed to comply with the proxy rules. The issue will also come up in enforcement proceedings by the SEC where an injunction may be sought against individuals as well as the company.

As you will see in the materials dealing with a director's duty, the burden on corporate directors has been increasing. The SEC has asserted that directors have a responsibility for the honesty and accuracy of materials sent to investors or filed with the Commission. (Rel. No. 33–6231, September 2, 1980). With respect to directors who are the principal executive officers of the company, this seems plain enough since the corporation is able to act only through the efforts of individuals. But what of those members of the board who are not part of management and who are "outside" directors? In Gould v. American Hawaiian Steamship Co., 535 F.2d 761 (3rd Cir. 1976), the court held that an outside director "was responsible with his fellow directors for the action of the board in which he participated as well as for his acts or failure to act * * *. The [lower] court held that in any event [the outside director] would have known that the proxy statement in its final form was false if he had read it, which it was his duty to do as a member of the board of directors which was issuing the document to solicit the shareholders' proxies. The [lower] court concluded that under these circumstances the [outside director] was liable for the materially false and misleading proxy statement * * *. As we have seen, the District Court held negligence to be the appropriate standard under § 14(a) and we agree." 535 F.2d at 776–77. Contra: Adams v. Standard Knitting Mills, 623 F.2d 472 (6th Cir. 1980) (accounting firm not liable for failure to detect error in proxy statement where there was no intent to deceive).

In Gould, the 3d Circuit rejected the more exacting standard of scienter as necessary to establish liability under the proxy rules. This standard has been applied with respect to other liability provisions of the securities laws. See Ernst & Ernst v. Hochfelder, 425 U. S. 185, 96 S.Ct. 1375, 47 L.Ed.2d 668 (1976). If liability is to be based on a standard that does not require some type of personal misconduct, either intentionally or recklessly, on the part of directors, then courts will have to develop objective standards for reasonable conduct. As in other areas of tortious behavior, standards are likely to evolve over time, and the law may come to demand a higher degree of diligence by directors as the price of avoiding a finding of negligence. The proxy materials will require closer scrutiny by all directors. Thus, the holding in Gould makes the regulation of proxies potentially one of the deeper penetrations of federal law into corporate affairs.

C. SHAREHOLDER PROPOSALS

PROBLEMS ON SHAREHOLDER PROPOSALS

A

Universal Motors Corporation maintains plants around the country, a number of which are old and inefficient. Recently rumors have circulated that the Company intends to close several factories in Ohio. One such plant is in Lima, Ohio, where UMC employs 5,000 workers, accounting for a substantial portion of the community payroll. The output at that plant contributes less than 1% to UMC's revenues and profits. The Company's policy, whenever it closes a plant, is to pay severance pay equal to three months wages or salary, and if possible, to offer continued employment at another facility.

A group of students at nearby State University have purchased ten shares of UMC stock, which is traded on the New York Stock Exchange, and have submitted a shareholder proposal for inclusion in the forthcoming proxy statement of UMC.

The text of this resolution is as follows:

RESOLVED, that the by-laws be amended to add the following provision: The corporation shall not substantially discontinue the use of any significant business or plant facility unless (1) the company gives one year notice in writing to the affected employees and community representatives of the extent of the proposed closing or reduction, (2) a hearing is conducted at which an opportunity is provided to employees and citizens of the affected communities to express their views on any aspect of the proposed closing or reduction and (3) the Board of Directors is furnished with a written report of a detailed study on the economic, environmental and social consequences of the proposed action upon the affected community. Such report shall become a record of the Corporation and copies shall be made available to shareholders upon payment of reasonable costs.

The following supporting statement was also submitted:

The power to discontinue a plant or other facility carries with it the power to visit major economic, environmental and social consequences upon a particular community—consequences that may be calamitous. The proposed new by-law simply requires the Board of Directors to be aware of these consequences before the Corporation acts on such matters, which are neither routine nor trivial, and enables the owners of the Corporation to acquire, in addition to already available financial information, some knowledge concerning the social impact of their company's activities. The Company's disregard for the welfare of its workers necessitates revised procedures in making these far-reaching decisions.

The by-law would impose requirements upon the Corporation that are similar to but far less extensive than those calling upon federal agencies to furnish environmental impact statements before undertaking certain projects, and for much the same reasons. Application of the by-law is limited to actions upon "significant" facilities so as to avoid harassment of the company. Implementation and interpretation will devolve upon the Board, which must decide the issue in good faith.

* * *

The proponents of the resolution have asked the University Board of Directors to support the resolution, and there has been editorial support in the student newspaper. In addition, the proponents have written letters to alumni and community leaders in Lima and vicinity to seek their support. The University owns a large bloc of UMC stock; it also receives large annual gifts from UMC. Local politicians have taken up the issue, and a bill has been introduced in the state legislature to require similar procedures.

QUESTIONS

1. On what grounds might UMC management object to the proposal?

2. If objection is made how should the matter be decided?

3. If you were a member of the University Board of Directors, how should you react to the proposal if it is included in the proxy statement?

B

Should the following resolution be included in the proxy statement of a company (assuming compliance with all procedural requirements) over the objection of management?

Resolved, that the by-laws of the Corporation be amended to provide as follows:

The Board of Directors shall recommend annually to the stockholders the selection of the Corporation General Counsel, which appointment shall become effective upon ratification by the stockholders.

C

Suppose the union which represented the employees at UMC wants to elect its president to the board of directors. The company's board has turned down the suggestion. The union is anxious to hold down its costs and asks whether it can make use of the company's proxy materials to solicit votes for their candidate. How do you advise the union?

1. EVOLUTION OF THE RULE

NOTE—AN INTRODUCTION TO THE SHAREHOLDER PROPOSAL RULE

The power that shareholders theoretically possess to rise up at the annual meeting and obtain action through the passage of a resolution is, by itself, illusory. A tiny fraction of the shareholders are present at the meeting. Practically all the shares are represented by proxy, and the rules of the Securities & Exchange Commission either bind the proxy holders to vote in a prescribed way, or give the proxy holder complete discretion. Management, therefore, can turn away any shareholder resolution it opposes.

What has happened, as we have already noted, is that the proxy soliciting process has become the surrogate for the meeting. The shareholder who wants his motion to succeed at the meeting must undertake to solicit proxies in advance. He must obtain the list of the shareholders, file proxy soliciting material, print the proxy statement, and mail it to all the shareholders. He may also want to use follow up material. If the shareholder wants to take control of the company, all of this effort can be cost justified. But suppose the shareholder wants only to have the shareholders approve an amendment to the by-laws changing the place of the next meeting. Or suppose he wants the company to cease doing business with a country that he believes oppresses human rights. Perhaps what the shareholder *really* wants is to rivet public attention on an issue, and spark some debate. The shareholder will derive no personal benefit from passage of the resolution. There is no way the expense of his own solicitation of proxies can be cost justified.

Nevertheless, our shareholder has a right (or *perhaps* he has a right) to make his motion from the floor of the meeting. That presupposes the matter is appropriate to raise in the corporate forum. Under those circumstances, perhaps he also has a right to have access to the surrogate corporate forum—the proxy statement—and have his intended resolution appear in the proxy statement sent to shareholders, thereby informing them that the matter will come before the meeting and giving them an opportunity to vote on the question by specific instructions to their proxy.

The SEC began to take the position that the shareholder had such a right in 1938, and in 1942 it formalized its views by adopting the first version of the shareholder proposal rule which is now Rule 14a–8. As originally adopted, the rule required management to include in its proxy statement a shareholder proposal that was going to be introduced at the meeting, so long as the proposal was a "proper subject for action by security holders." Matters that dealt with general political, social or economic matters were viewed by the SEC as not proper subjects for action by shareholders.

By what standard is the propriety of the subject matter of the proposal to be judged? SEC v. Transamerica Corp., 163 F.2d 511 (3d Cir. 1947) provided the key to the answer.

Lewis Gilbert, a shareholder of Transamerica, submitted several proposals that he asked to have included in the company's proxy statement. One of his proposals would have resulted in shareholder election of the independent public auditors of the company's financial statements; another would have amended the by-laws with respect to the procedure for by-law amendment. Another would have required the report of the annual meeting be sent to shareholders. The company excluded all the proposals, on grounds that the rule did not require their inclusion and the SEC sought an injunction against the solicitation of proxies with a proxy statement it believed to be deficient.

The court agreed with the SEC position that a "proper subject" is one in which the shareholders may properly be interested under the law of the state of incorporation. Applying that test, all of the above proposals were properly includible in Transamerica's proxy materials. The election of auditors was clearly within the stockholders' concern since it is for their benefit that the corporation is run, and the financial condition is at the heart of matters. The amendment to the by-laws was proper because Delaware law specifically allows shareholders to do that. The only basis for exclusion was the company's own by-law provision that required advance notice to be contained in the notice of the annual meeting, which was not done in this case. However, that self-imposed restriction did not diminish the power given by the state to the shareholders. The report of the meeting was proper because, the court said, "we can perceive no logical basis for concluding that it is not a proper subject for action by the security holders." *Id.* at 517.

Thus, the court and the SEC both viewed the shareholder proposal rule as a federal mechanism to enliven a state created right of the shareholder. While the SEC interprets its own rule hundreds of times each year, presumably it is applying state law. In fact, there are few state cases to provide guidance.

We have already examined Auer v. Dressel, 306 N.Y. 427, 118 N. E.2d 590 (1954) in Chapter 10, where the court permitted shareholders to compel the holding of a meeting to consider a recommendation. A narrower view of the shareholder's right was expressed in Carter v. Portland General Electric Co., 227 Or. 401, 362 P.2d 766 (1961) where the court affirmed management's refusal to include in the proxy statement a shareholder statement in opposition to management plans for the construction of a dam. A motion on the floor of the meeting was also ruled out of order, and the court refused to overturn any of these actions by management. In holding that the shareholder request was not a "proper subject" for stockholder consideration, the court observed:

> * * * "Granted, that the proposed dam project would commit a large part of the corporate defendant's assets and credit. By the same token, it also involved extensive engineering, economic, financial and even political considerations. It is impossible to believe that the obviously voluminous character of such data could have been abbreviated to the point that any communication with the stockholders or debate at the annual meeting could have resulted in any knowing or sensible vote by the stockholders."

362 P.2d at 769.

The SEC has amended the shareholder proposal rule over the years and has elaborated on the restrictions, or added new ones. The bases for exclusion fall into two categories. Some involve further interpretations of the phrase "proper subject for action by security holders." The others are directed at regulating the *process* so as to prevent abuse by the shareholders of the opportunity afforded under the rule.

In 1948, the SEC amended the rule to authorize the exclusion of proposals that were submitted "primarily for the purpose" of redressing personal claims or grievances. In 1952, management was permitted to exclude a proposal if it "clearly appears" that it was submitted "primarily for the purpose of promoting general economic, political, racial, religious, social or similar causes." Note that both of these amendments focused on the state of mind of the proponent, not on the objective subject matter of the proposal.

In 1954, several significant changes were made. Most important, management could exclude proposals "relating to the conduct of the ordinary business of the issuer." Management could also omit a proposal that had been submitted in either of the last two years if it failed to obtain a 3% vote, or a 6% vote the second time, or a 10% vote the third time. Finally, the shareholders were allowed the opportunity to put in a 100-word supporting statement if management opposed their proposal.

In 1972, the SEC responded to the increasing use of the shareholder proposal rule to raise issues of public policy importance. The Commission eliminated the subjective inquiry into the proponent's motivation and made includability turn on whether the proposal was "significantly related to the business of the issuer" and whether it was "within the control of the issuer." This amendment set the stage for a dramatic increase in shareholder proposals on social issues.

In 1976 the rule was again overhauled to approximate its present form. Later amendments have not affected the basic question of includability. The present version sets forth thirteen "substantive bases for omission of proposals." However, only seven of the thirteen subparagraphs in Rule 14a–8(c) are devoted to the issue of when a proposal, under the laws of the issuer's domicile, is a proper subject for action by security holders. The other six subparagraphs concern abuses of the process. *See* Schwartz and Weiss, An Assessment of the SEC Shareholder Proposal Rule, 65 Geo.L.J. 635 (1977).

It is the SEC's conclusion that the rule, following the 1976 amendments, "was operating well." Staff Report on Corporate Accountability to Senate Committee on Banking, Housing and Urban Affairs 133 (96th Cong., 2d Sess., Sept. 4, 1980). The Report noted that this was the general conclusion of witnesses who appeared in the Commission's Hearings on Corporate Governance. Furthermore, the feeling, in general, was that shareholder proposals were an effective tool of corporate accountability.

2. THE PARTICIPANTS

NOTE—THE STOCKHOLDER PROPONENTS

Approximately 500 stockholder proposals from about 100 different shareholders are submitted to more than 100 companies each year. Several of these shareholders have become well known in the corporate world as a result of their activities.

The stockholder movement began in the 1930's with an emphasis on shareholder democracy. The founding father was Lewis Gilbert, a New York investor who devotes full time to this activity and other shareholder-related matters. Gilbert and his associates, including his brother John, attend about 200 annual meetings a year. He relies not only on the proposals contained in the proxy material to express his concerns, but he is a vocal participant at annual meetings. The meetings are also much enlivened by the participation of Mr. Gilbert's long-time ally, Mrs. Wilma Soss, president of the Federation of Women Stockholders of America. The issues characteristically raised by Gilbert and Soss have included voting reforms, preemptive rights, management compensation and communication with stockholders. Mrs. Evelyn Davis is another activist who has campaigned against charitable contributions, corporate political activity and the influence of lawyers. All three have regarded themselves as watchdogs for the minority shareholders and their questions and occasional theatrical tactics have often been the highlight of the annual meeting.

Beginning in 1970, another type of shareholder proponent came forward. These were the shareholders, with few shares and little interest in conventional corporate matters, who raised issues of social concern, such as the impact on the environment, race and sex discrimination, and quite often, the conduct of business in places where human rights have not been respected. Often these critics, who management has described as "special interest" proponents, make management long for Gilbert, Soss, or Davis. The first such proponent was the Project on Corporate Responsibility, which created Campaign GM that is described in this chapter. Later the Project focused on issues relating to corporate governance. Various church groups soon followed with a very active program. The leading church group is the Interfaith Center on Corporate Responsibility, which has opposed corporate presence in South Africa. Individual church groups have also sponsored proposals to raise that issue, and the church groups have been active in other issues as well. One of their main concerns has been the sale and marketing of infant formula in less developed countries.

Numerous ad hoc groups have used the shareholder proposal process to advocate issues of concern to them, such as labor organizations opposing the union resistance efforts of J. P. Stevens & Co., Inc. or the American Jewish Congress opposing the Arab boycott.

Proposals of a more conservative hue have also been advanced, and with increasing frequency in recent years. Carl Olson, a California accountant, has put forth numerous proposals urging an end to trading with Communist countries, and the termination of gifts to universities that are insufficiently sympathetic to the corporation.

SCHWARTZ, THE PUBLIC–INTEREST PROXY CONTEST: REFLECTIONS ON CAMPAIGN GM

69 Mich.L.Rev. 419, 423–30 (1971).

What Was Campaign GM?

Campaign GM was an effort to obtain shareholder approval of several resolutions through the solicitation of proxies. These resolutions were formally offered by the Project on Corporate Responsibility (Project), a Washington-based nonprofit corporation that owned twelve shares of General Motors common stock. The Project was formed in late 1969 to promote corporate responsibility and to educate management and the public about the social role of corporations. Project leaders believed that a proxy contest with General Motors would afford them an opportunity to gain attention for their efforts and would provide a test of the ability of the corporate and economic system to reform itself. Campaign GM, directed by four young lawyers known as "coordinators," was a specially formed unit to carry out this program. Although nine resolutions were proposed to management, the campaign was mainly an effort to obtain support for two of them.

The first was a proposal to amend the bylaws of the company to increase the number of directors by three persons. The proposal did not define the types of persons who would be eligible for those seats. Thus, no effort was made to classify public-interest directors. Campaign GM revealed that, if this proposal passed, it intended to nominate for the three newly created directorships Miss Betty Furness, Dr. Rene Dubos, and the Reverend Channing Phillips. It also made clear that these persons would not be nominated unless the board was enlarged so that none of management's candidates were challenged.

The second was a proposal to create a Shareholders Committee for Corporate Responsibility (Committee). This Committee was to consist of fifteen to twenty-five representatives of a variety of interest areas, and it was to be selected by a three-member selection committee consisting of a representative of the board of directors of General Motors, a representative of the United Auto Workers, and a representative of Campaign GM. It was to act in the nature of a commission, serving for a period of one year and submitting a report directly to the shareholders—rather than to the board of directors—in time for the 1971 annual meeting. The Committee was supposed to gather facts and make recommendations on some basic questions concerning the corporation, such as its role in modern society and its prospects for and possible means of achieving a proper balance between the interests of shareholders, employees, consumers, and the general public. The Committee was also supposed to make recommendations on how the decision-making base of the company could be broadened, and specifically on how directors would be nominated and elected and board committee members selected. Finally, the Committee would evaluate the company's past and present efforts regarding air pollution, safety, mass transportation, and the manner in which General Motors had used its economic power to contribute to the social welfare of the Nation. In effect, the Committee was designed to conduct a social audit of the company's performance and make recommendations for the future.

The campaign was announced on February 7, 1970, by Ralph Nader at a press conference in Washington, D. C. Nader had no affiliation with Campaign GM or the Project, but he supported their goals. He disclosed that three shareholder resolutions (including the two described above) were being submitted to management for inclusion in the proxy statement to be sent to the shareholders of General Motors. After commenting that the legal structure of the corporation contributed to the growing gap between corporate performance and corporate responsibility, he called for "a new definition of the corporation's constituency." Commenting then upon the position of the shareholders, he stated that in theory they owned the corporation; in fact, they were treated as creditors. The result was that "[t]he procedures, the information, the organization, the manpower and the funds are management's to deploy. But the fiction of shareholder democracy continues to plague the reality. By highlighting the fiction a new reality can be borne that will tame the corporate tiger."
* * *

Voting at a shareholders meeting is by proxy, of course, but Campaign GM could not solicit proxies from all of the General Motors shareholders. The cost was simply prohibitive; postage costs alone for a single first-class mailing to each shareholder would have been close to 100,000 dollars. The strategy, however, as Nader announced it, was to reach all of the corporation's shareholders. This goal could be accomplished only if the resolutions proposed to be offered at the annual meeting were included in the proxy statement that management mailed to the shareholders. It was thus necessary that the legal machinery for regulating proxy solicitations and conducting shareholders meetings recognize the proposals both as valid subjects for corporate concern and, specifically, as matters of shareholder concern. In this manner, Campaign GM would achieve a legitimacy of presence to force debate and consideration of the issues. * * *

General Motors opposed the inclusion in the management proxy statement of any of the resolutions proposed by the Project, claiming that the proxy rules permitted their exclusion. This battle led to wide public interest in the campaign, for when the SEC declared that, in its opinion, the two resolutions dealing with the amendment of the bylaws and the creation of the shareholder committee on corporate responsibility were required to be included in the management proxy statement under Rule 14a–8, the news media widely reported the event. Thus, Campaign GM was creating a stir well before the scheduled annual meeting.

Because of the one-hundred-word limitation on the supporting statement, Campaign GM could not rely on management's proxy statement as its sole means of communication to shareholders. The coordinators regarded it as essential that they communicate with the public through the media, and with larger shareholders—particularly institutional shareholders, whom they regarded as the focal point in the campaign—through their own proxy statement. Consequently, they prepared a fifteen-page proxy statement, attached a form of proxy, and sent it to approximately 5,000 institutions and brokers. Meanwhile, national attention was much concerned with pollution, one of the major issues raised by Campaign GM. On April 22, 1970, a month before the General Motors annual meeting, there was the nationwide observance of Earth Day. At an early stage in the campaign, President Nixon submitted a legislative proposal dealing with environmental pollution. Scarcely a magazine or a newspaper in the country overlooked the problem of air pollution. Industry, including the automobile industry, announced new plans and programs to deal with air pollution. One result was that Campaign GM became identified in the press as a crusade against automobile air pollution. It was such a crusade, of course, but it was other things as well. The other issues in the campaign tended to become obscured by the attention to the air pollution issue.

Management responded to Campaign GM in a vigorous fashion. Its proxy statement accused the Project of seeking to harass the management and of trying "to promote the particular economic and social views espoused by the proponent of the resolution." Management took the unusual step of enclosing a twenty-one-page booklet entitled GM's Record of Progress with its proxy statement. This pamphlet defended management's record in all of the areas of social concern that were part of Campaign GM's program. It also contained an introduction by James Roche, the chairman of General Motors, stating, "The Project is using General Motors as a means through which it can challenge the entire system of corporate management in the United States." In addition, on April 10 General Motors published advertisements in about 150 newspapers throughout the country defending its record on air pollution. Management also telephoned larger shareholders and in other ways made clear that it earnestly desired the support of larger shareholders.   *   *   *

The meeting on May 22 lasted a record 6½ hours and was attended by an overflow audience of more than 3,000 shareholders—more than twice the number that had attended the previous meeting. The meeting was largely devoted to Campaign GM's issues, and there were many sharp exchanges between the Campaign's speakers and Mr. Roche, but unlike annual meetings at other companies there was no disruption. General Motors was obviously concerned about the challenge. The customary half-hour film did not discuss new products or profit activities, but rather was almost a point-by-point rebuttal to the charges of irresponsible behavior. The meeting received unusual attention from newspapers, magazines, and television. When it was over, each side complimented the other for the manner in which it behaved and this author, speaking on behalf of Campaign GM, informed management that "[w]e look forward to seeing you next year." * * *

The votes on the proposals were announced at the end of the meeting after most of the shareholders had long since departed. Management won overwhelmingly, of course. The proposal for the shareholder committee received 6,361,299 votes, representing 2.73 per cent of the votes cast, from 61,794 shareholders, representing 7.19 per cent of the shareholders voting. The proposal to amend the by-laws was supported by 5,691,130 shares, or 2.44 per cent of the votes cast, and 53,495, or 6.22 per cent of the shareholders voting.

NOTE—CAMPAIGN GM AFTERMATH

Within months after the annual meeting at which the shareholders overwhelmingly rejected the Campaign GM proposals, GM's board of directors created a Public Policy Committee and elected its first black member, Rev. Leon Sullivan. About a year later, it elected its first woman member.

A second round of Campaign GM was held in 1971, dealing with questions of board structure and disclosure, and the results were approximately the same. *See* Schwartz, Toward New Corporate Goals: Co-Existence with Society, 60 Geo.L.J. 57 (1971). However, as one commentator noted, "As a result of Campaign GM, American corporate electoral processes have become fundamentally changed." Blumberg, The Politicalization of the Corporation, 26 Bus.Law. 1551, 1561 (1971).

An important part of the change was the proliferation of the tactics inaugurated in Campaign GM. Several more rounds were conducted by the Project on Corporate Responsibility, but many other groups, or individuals, employed the shareholder proposal tactic to deal with a wide range of social concerns.

The use of shareholder proposals to advance social causes has been sharply criticized, of course. One of the harsher critics is Professor Henry G. Manne. In Shareholder Social Proposals Viewed by an Opponent, 24 Stan.L.Rev. 481, 492–3 (1972), Professor Manne drew the following conclusions:

> But the real importance of corporate activism does not lie in lengthy shareholder meetings or cosmetic business changes. The real significance of these moves can only be understood in terms of a broadly-waged propaganda war that has been going on in the United States against large-scale corporate capitalism since at least the early part of this century. The ultimate ramifications of this ideological struggle are presumably felt in the form of government supervision of the economy. The battles in this war may be fought on many grounds, including matters like shareholder social proposals, but the victories and defeats are measured by the amount of hostile or unflattering publicity one side scores against the other. Only in this sense do the issues of shareholder proposals or corporate social responsibility seem important. Taken alone they cannot be said to have created any fundamental change in the corporate system.

For a comprehensive chronicle of events see D. Vogel, Lobbying the Corporation: Citizen Challenges to Business Authority (1978).

NOTE—INSTITUTIONS AND SHAREHOLDER PROPOSALS

We have already noted that an increasing amount of stock is owned by institutional investors who traditionally eschewed any management role in their portfolio companies. However, there are pressures that are causing moderation of that policy.

Students are one pressure group that have caused universities to examine their voting policy or their stock ownership policy. Their activity began during the Vietnam War but has extended to embrace other issues as well (*e.g.*, American companies' investments in South Africa). *See* J. Simons, C. Powers, J. Gunnemann, The Ethical Investor (1972). Unionized employees are another pressure group that may cause trustees of pension plans to take positions on shareholder proposals. Charitable foundations may be disposed to become moderately involved by the very nature of their purpose. *See*, B. Longstreth and H. D. Rosenbloom, Corporate Social Responsibility and the Institutional Investor: A Report to the Ford Foundation (1973).

The extent of institutional activism and the manner in which they inform themselves and proceed are policy questions of considerable importance to individual companies and the economy in general. There are also significant legal questions: How does the prudent person rule apply to the voting of shares by fiduciaries? To what extent does that rule, or any other rule, require or permit a fiduciary to approve resolutions, or the proposed corporate action, that may reduce profits? Over what period of time is profit measured? If there is a clash between the interests of vested beneficiaries and those whose benefits lie on the future, who should the fiduciary favor? Should the fiduciary "pass through" the voting rights to the beneficiaries?

See Curzon & Pelesh, Revitalizing Corporate Democracy: Control of Investment Managers' Voting on Social Responsibility Proxy Issues, 93 Harv.L.Rev. 670 (1980).

3. RULES FOR INCLUSION

ADOPTION OF AMENDMENTS RELATING TO PROPOSALS BY SECURITY HOLDERS

Securities Exchange Act Release No. 12999 (November 22, 1976)

The Securities and Exchange Commission today announced that it has adopted certain amendments to Rule 14a–8 under Section 14(a) of the Securities Exchange Act of 1934 ("Exchange Act"). Rule 14a–8 is the provision in the Commission's proxy rules which sets forth the requirements applicable to proposals submitted by security holders for inclusion in the proxy soliciting materials of issuers.

* * *

SUBSTANTIVE BASES FOR OMISSION OF PROPOSALS—RULE 14a–8(c)

Paragraph (c) of the revised rule sets forth various substantive grounds for excluding a proposal from an issuer's proxy materials. As amended, paragraph (c) contains 13 separate grounds for omitting a proposal. Each of these grounds is discussed below in the order in which it appears in the revised paragraph.

(1) *State Law.* Subparagraph (c)(1) of the former rule allowed the management to omit a proposal "If the proposal as submitted is, under the laws of the issuer's domicile, not a proper subject for action by security holders." This provision has been based on the theory that no purpose is served by including in an issuer's proxy materials proposals which the issuer's security holders cannot properly act upon.

The Commission also has added a Note to subparagraph (c)(1) of the rule alerting proponents to the fact that the propriety of their proposals under the applicable state law may depend upon the form in which the proposal appears. Thus, the Note states that "A proposal that may be improper under the applicable state law when framed as a mandate or directive may be proper when framed as a recommendation or request."

The test of the above Note is in accord with the long standing interpretative view of the Commission and its staff under subparagraph (c)(1). In this regard, it is the Commission's understanding that the laws of most states do not, for the most part, explicitly indicate those matters which are proper for security holders to act upon but instead provide only that "the business and affairs of every corporation organized under this law shall be managed by its board of directors," or words to that effect. Under such a statute, the board may be considered to have exclusive discretion in corporate matters, absent a specific provision to the contrary in the statute itself, or the corporation's charter or by-laws. Accordingly, proposals by security holders that mandate or direct the board to take certain action may constitute an unlawful intrusion on the board's discretionary authority under the typical statute. On the other hand, however, proposals that merely recommend or request that the board take certain action would not appear to be contrary to the typical state statute, since such proposals are merely advisory in nature and would not be binding on the board even if adopted by the majority of the security holders. The Note will serve the purpose of alerting proponents to these distinctions and to the importance of framing their proposals in a form that is acceptable under the applicable state law.

* * *

(5) *Insignificant Matters.* Subparagraph (c)(2)(ii) of the former rule allowed an issuer to omit a proposal if it consisted of a "recommendation, request or mandate that action be taken with respect to any matter, including a general economic, political, racial, religious, social or similar cause, that is not significantly related to the business of the issuer * * *." The Commission has retained the substance of this provision in subparagraph (c)(5) of the revised rule.

A number of commentators expressed the view that the Commission should revise the subparagraph to allow the omission of a proposal whenever the matter involved therein does not bear a significant economic relation to the issuer's business. In this regard, the Commission does not believe that subparagraph (c)(5) should be hinged solely on the economic relativity of a proposal, since there are many instances in which the matter involved in a proposal is significant to an issuer's business, even though such significance is not apparent from an economic viewpoint. For example, proposals dealing with cumulative voting rights or the ratification of auditors in a sense may not be economically significant to an issuer's business but they nevertheless have a significance to security holders that would preclude their being omitted under this provision. And proposals relating to ethical issues such as political contributions also may be significant to the issuer's business, when viewed from a standpoint other than a purely economic one.

Notwithstanding the foregoing, the Commission recognizes that there are circumstances in which economic data may indicate a valid basis for omitting a proposal under this provision. The Commission wishes to emphasize, however, that the significance of a particular matter to an issuer's present or prospective business depends upon that issuer's individual circumstances, and that is applicable in all instances. Moreover, as previously indicated, the burden is on the issuer to demonstrate that this or any other provision of Rule 14a–8 may properly be relied upon to omit a proposal.

* * *

(7) *Routine Matters.* Subparagraph (c)(5) of the former rule permitted an issuer to omit a proposal from its proxy materials if the proposal consisted of a "recommendation or request that the management take action with respect to a matter relating to the conduct of the ordinary business operations of the issuer." The Commission proposed in Release No. 34–12598 to replace this provision with one that would have allowed the omission of a proposal if it dealt with a "routine, day-to-day matter relating to the conduct of the ordinary business operations of the issuer." The proposed new provision, which would have been more restrictive than the former one, was considered at the time to be appropriate for possible adoption because the former provision occasionally had been relied upon to exclude proposals of considerable importance to the issuer and its security holders. The Commission hoped that the new provision would produce results that were more in accord with the concept of shareholder democracy underlying Section 14(a) of the Exchange Act.

Commentators pointed out that many of the shareholder proposals under the new provision would necessarily deal with ordinary business matters of a complex nature that shareholders, as a group, would not be qualified to make an informed judgment on, due to their lack of business expertise and their lack of intimate knowledge of the issuer's business. In the view of these commentators, it would not be practicable in most instances for stockholders to decide management problems at corporate meetings. Further, they stated that the proposed new provision would be difficult to administer because of the subjective judgments that necessarily would be required in interpreting it.

After consideration of the above comments, the Commission has determined not to adopt proposed subparagraph (c)(7) in the form in which it was proposed for comment.

The Commission has decided to adopt a provision that essentially is the same as subparagraph (c)(5) of the former rule. That is, a proposal will be excludable if it "deals with a matter relating to the conduct of the ordinary business operations of the issuer." The Commission recognizes that this standard for omission has created some difficulties in the past, and that, on occasion, it has been relied upon to omit proposals of considerable importance to security holders. Nevertheless, the Commission believes that the provision is a workable one, as evidenced by the fact that it has been in operation for over 22 years and has not, until the past year or so, generated a significant amount of controversy.

The Commission is of the view that the provision adopted today can be effective in the future if it is interpreted somewhat more flexibly than in the past. Specifically, the term "ordinary business operations" has been deemed on occasion to include certain matters which have significant policy, economic or other implications inherent in them. For instance, a proposal that a utility company not construct a proposed nuclear power plant has in the past been considered excludable under former subparagraph (c)(5). In retrospect, however, it seems apparent that the economic and safety considerations attendant to nuclear power plants are of such magnitude that a determination whether to construct one is not an "ordinary" business matter. Accordingly, proposals of that nature, as well as others that have major implications, will in the future be considered beyond the realm of an issuer's ordinary business operations, and future interpretative letters of the Commission's staff will reflect that view.

NOTE—THE SHAREHOLDER ROLE AND *BELLOTTI*

In the Staff Report on Corporate Accountability, submitted to the Senate Committee on Banking, Housing and Urban Affairs (Sept. 4, 1980), the SEC considered the effect of First National Bank of Boston v. Bellotti, 435 U.S. 765, 98 S.Ct. 1407, 55 L.Ed.2d 707 (1978) on the role of shareholders. The Supreme Court assumed that shareholders would be able to exercise a degree of control over management use of the treasury for political purposes through the corporate democratic process. The SEC noted the significance of disclosure to that process and the fact that shareholder proposals were one means to obtain the information. The Report then questioned whether prevailing views of what is "significantly related," within the meaning of Rule 14a–8(c)(5) were adequate to meet the needs of the situation.

The staff's concern in the Report was whether shareholders would be able to use shareholder proposals to obtain information about corporate political activities, or perhaps to exercise some dominion over corporate political activities. However, the effects of *Bellotti* may go further. The First Amendment rights of corporations may enable them to express a corporate view on any subject it wishes. Who should direct corporate policy in this respect? If management does not wish the corporation to speak out, can the shareholder compel it to do so? In any event, are these legitimate issues for shareholders to raise through the proposal device?

NOTE—THE SEC INTERPRETATIONS

The flesh on the bones of Rule 14a–8 is provided by SEC interpretations of the rule. These interpretations are furnished in response to company inquiries to the Commission staff concerning omissions from the proxy material of a shareholder proposal. The company asks the staff to concur with its view, which is most often accompanied by an opinion of counsel, that omission of the proposal will not violate the proxy rules. The proponent of the proposal will often respond with an opposing opinion of counsel. Since the inquiry asks whether the staff will recommend any action by the Commission if the company does not include the proposal, the staff responses are known as "no action" letters.

Each year about 100 no-action letters interpreting Rule 14a–8 are issued, mostly from the staff and on rare occasions by the Commission. These letters are available at one of the SEC's offices in Washington and selected letters are printed in looseleaf services. They may also be retrieved through computer research services. The letters are the common law of Rule 14a–8.

Some letters are identified by the Commission staff as "significant" because they are of general interest. One of the most important of these is the letter to Motorola that follows. This letter was approved by the Commission unanimously, but Commissioner Roberta Karmel expressed serious concern that the SEC's action would politicize the process of shareholder proposals.

MOTOROLA, INC., SECURITIES AND EXCHANGE COMMISSION, DIVISION OF CORPORATE FINANCE, February 23, 1978. (Available February 23, 1978.)

[SEC Staff Reply]

This is in response to your letter of January 12, 1978 and a letter from John T. Hickey dated February 16, 1978 concerning a request made by Motorola, Inc., (The "Company") by the Eastern Province of Servites, Haverford College and the Interfaith Center on Corporate Responsibility to include a shareholder proposal in the Company's proxy soliciting material for the 1978 annual meeting of shareholders. Pursuant to Rule 14a–8(d) under the Securities Exchange Act of 1934, your letter indicated the management's intention to exclude this proposal from the Company's proxy material. Subsequently, we received a letter dated February 21, 1978 from Professor Paul Neuhauser, counsel for one of the proponents, suggesting that management's determination to omit the proposal was erroneous.

The proposal and related supporting statement, as submitted by the proponents, read as follows:

WHEREAS in South Africa the black majority is rigorously controlled and oppressed by a white minority which comprises 18% of the population;

WHEREAS South Africa's apartheid system legalizes racial discrimination in all aspects of life and deprives the black population of most basic human rights, e.g. Africans cannot vote, cannot collectively bargain, must live in racially segregated areas, are paid grossly discriminatory wages, are assigned 13% of the land which [sic] 87% of the land is reserved for the white population;

WHEREAS South Africa's system of white minority rule called apartheid is widely condemned by the U. S. government and numerous international bodies, and the United Nations requires a mandatory arms embargo since South Africa is a threat to world peace;

WHEREAS black opposition to apartheid and black demands for full political, legal, and social rights has risen dramatically within the last years;

WHEREAS widespread killing, arrests and repression has been the South African government's response to nationwide demonstrations for democratic rights;

WHEREAS as concerned investors we believe that U. S. business investments in South Africa, including our company's sales of equipment to South African police and armed forces provide significant economic support, international credibility and moral legitimacy to South Africa's apartheid government;

THEREFORE BE IT RESOLVED, the shareholders request the Board of Directors establish the following as corporate policy.

Motorola and any of its subsidiaries shall (1) cease further investment in the Republic of South Africa, (2) should terminate at once all sales to the South African government and (3) terminate its present operations there as expeditiously as possible unless and until the South African government commits itself to ending the legally enforced form of racism called apartheid and takes meaningful steps toward the achievement of full political, legal and social rights for the majority population (African, Asian and Coloured).

[Supporting Statement]

Motorola is one of the more significant U. S. investors in South Africa. As concerned investors in Motorola we believe that Motorola's investment in South Africa strengthens white minority rule and apartheid.

Motorola has sold equipment for use by South African police and military. In light of the U. S. supported arms embargo against South Africa we are fearful that Motorola's South African subsidiary may be undercutting the spirit, if not the letter, of this arms embargo.

In addition the South African government has invoked war powers legislation requiring foreign corporations to manufacture and provide strategic products when that government demands it. Thus, corporations such as Motorola can become virtual hostages of that government helping them to keep political power in the white minority's hands as their police and military are involved in vicious repression of any dissent. We do not believe Motorola should be involved in any way in supporting that government's police or military strength.

If Motorola is concerned about human rights it should, at the very least, immediately terminate all sales of equipment to the South African government that is being used to repress its black citizens.

[Staff's Views]

In your letter you have expressed the opinion that the foregoing proposal may be omitted from the Company's proxy material under paragraphs (c)(3) and (c)(5) of Rule 14a–8, and you cite certain reasons in support of that opinion. Professor Neuhauser, however, has indicated that for the reasons stated in his letter on the matter, he does not agree with your opinion.

With respect to your opinion that the proposal and related supporting statement, or portions thereof, may violate Rule 14a–9 and therefore be excludable pursuant to Rule 14a–8(c), the Division does not agree, with certain exceptions, that you have satisfied your burden of establishing the applicability of those rules to the subject proposal and related supporting statement.

* * *

This Division does not concur in your opinion that the proposal may be excluded under Rule 14a–8(c)(5). That provision allows the omission of a proposal that "deals with a matter that is not significantly related to the issuer's business." While you have provided information which could indicate that the amounts of the Company's business in South Africa is less than one percent of its total sales, earnings or assets, we would direct your attention to Securities Exchange Act Release 12999 (November 22, 1976) which states in part that "there are many instances in which the matter involved in a proposal is significant to an issuer's business, even though such significance is not apparent from an economic viewpoint." In that release the Commission went on to point out that "proposals * * * also may be significant to the issuer's business, when viewed from a standpoint other than a purely economic one." Moreover, the economic significance of such a proposal to a particular issuer's business may not always be apparent from an analysis of quantitative historical data, although such data is a factor to be considered. The Commission has also indicated that the burden is on the issuer to demonstrate that this or any other provision of Rule 14a–8 may properly be relied upon to omit a proposal. The Division is unable to conclude that you have met your burden of demonstrating that the subject matter of the instant proposal is not significantly related to the Company's business despite the Company's limited economic exposure in South Africa. Accordingly, we do not believe that the management may rely on Rule 14a–8(c)(5) as a basis for omitting this proposal.

MEDICAL COMMITTEE FOR HUMAN RIGHTS v. SECURITIES AND EXCHANGE COMMISSION

432 F.2d 659 (D.C.Cir. 1970).

TAMM, Circuit Judge.

The instant petition presents novel and significant questions concerning implementation of the concepts of corporate democracy embodied in section 14 of the Securities Exchange Act of 1934, and of the power of this court to review determinations of the Securities and Exchange Commission made pursuant to its proxy rules. For reasons to be stated more fully below, we hold that the Commission's action in the present case is reviewable, and that the cause must be remanded for further administrative proceedings.

I. PROCEDURAL HISTORY OF THE CASE

On March 11, 1968, Dr. Quentin D. Young, National Chairman of the Medical Committee for Human Rights, wrote to the Secretary of the Dow Chemical Company, stating that the Medical Committee had obtained by gift several shares of Dow stock and expressing concern regarding the company's manufacture of the chemical substance napalm. [It submitted the following proposal for inclusion in the proxy statement:]

* * *

RESOLVED, that the shareholders of the Dow Chemical Company request the Board of Directors, in accordance with the laws of the State of Delaware, and the Composite Certificate of Incorporation of the Dow Chemical Company, to adopt a resolution setting forth an amendment to the Composite Certificate of Incorporation of the Dow Chemical Company that napalm shall not be sold to any buyer unless that buyer gives reasonable assurance that the substance will not be used on or against human beings.

* * *

[T]he Commission's Chief Counsel of the Division of Corporation Finance [advised Dow and Medical Committee that it would take no action if the proposal were omitted from the proxy statement]. [The] Medical Committee again renewed its request for a Commission review of the Division's decision. On the same day, the Medical Committee filed with the Commission a memorandum of legal arguments in support of its resolution, urging numerous errors of law in the Division's decision. * * * [B]oth parties were informed that "[t]he Commission has approved the recommendation of the Division of Corporation Finance that no objection be raised if the Company omits the proposals from its proxy statements for the forthcoming meeting of shareholders." The petitioners thereupon instituted the present action, and on July 10, 1969, the Commission moved to dismiss the petition for lack of jurisdiction. On October 13 we denied the motion "without prejudice to renewal thereof in the briefs and at the argument on the merits."

*   *   * [T]he Commission has consistently and vigorously urged, to the exclusion of all other contentions, that this court is without jurisdiction to review its action.

[The Court rejected the SEC's argument that the petition was not timely filed. It held that the Commission's "decision" was a reviewable order because the administrative process had run its course with respect to the proxy proposal and that there was a substantial public interest in having important questions of corporate democracy raised before the Commission and the courts. It was held to be unimportant that the determination was made in the form of a "no-action" letter. Partial review of the merits was held to be appropriate.]

There is also, it seems to us, an independent public interest in having the controversy decided in its present posture rather than in the context of a private action against the company. The primary and explicit purpose of section 14(a) is "the protection of investors," and the primary method of implementing this goal is through Commission regulation of proxy statements, not through private actions by individual security holders. For the small investor, personal recourse to the Commission's proxy procedures without benefit of counsel may well be the only practicable method of contesting a management decision to exclude his proxy proposal.[12] In this situation, as our recent decisions make clear, it is particularly important that the Commission look carefully at the merits of the shareholder's proposal, and that it do so pursuant to an accurate perception of the Congressional intent underlying the proxy statute. Direct judicial review of Commission proxy decisions is unquestionably the most logical and efficient means of achieving this objective.

*   *   *

12. This contention was recently presented to the Commission in a proxy contest involving the General Motors Corporation. See Cong.Rec. E–2147 (daily ed., March 17, 1970):

It must be recognized that Management's proxy statement is the only effective vehicle through which all of the shareholders can have an opportunity to express themselves, and even to hear any arguments on the questions involved. *   *   * [T]he cost [of conducting a competing solicitation] is virtually prohibitive except to extremely well heeled shareholders. *   *   *

This is no ordinary dispute with Management; it is not an effort by insurgent shareholders to seize control of the corporation. If it were so, one could justify large expenditures because the individual rewards are great and because, if successful, the insurgents could obtain reimbursement of their expenses from the company. The issues here lack that personal pecuniary bias. Denial of access to the shareholders through management's proxy solicitation, practically speaking, is total denial.

III.   THE MERITS OF PETITIONER'S PROPOSAL

The Medical Committee's sole substantive contention in this petition is that its proposed resolution could not, consistently with the Congressional intent underlying section 14(a), be properly deemed a proposal which is either motivated by *general* political and moral concerns, or related to the conduct of Dow's ordinary business operations. These criteria are two of the established exceptions to the general rule that management must include all properly submitted shareholder proposals in its proxy materials. They are contained in Rule 14a–8(c), 17 C.F.R. § 240.14a–8(c) (1970), which provides in relevant part:

> * * * [M]anagement may omit a proposal * * * from its proxy statement and form of proxy under any of the following circumstances:

> * * *

> (2) [now ¶ ¶ (c)(5) and (6)] If it clearly appears that the proposal is submitted by the security holder * * * primarily for the purpose of promoting general economic, political, racial, religious, social or similar causes; or

> * * *

> (5) [now ¶ (c)(7)] If the proposal consists of a recommendation or request that the management take action with respect to a matter relating to the conduct of the ordinary business operations of the issuer.

Despite the fact that our October 13 order in this case deferred resolution of the jurisdictional issue pending full argument on the merits, the Commission has not deigned to address itself to any possible grounds for allowing management to exclude this proposal from its proxy statement. We confess to a similar puzzlement as to how the Commission reached the result which it did, and thus we are forced to remand the controversy for a more illuminating consideration and decision. In aid of this consideration on remand, we feel constrained to explain our difficulties with the position taken by the company and endorsed by the Commission.

It is obvious to the point of banality to restate the proposition that Congress intended by its enactment of section 14 of the Securities Exchange Act of 1934 to give true vitality to the concept of corporate democracy. The depth of this commitment is reflected in the strong language employed in the legislative history:

> Even those who in former days managed great corporations were by reason of their personal contacts with their shareholders constantly aware of their responsibilities. But as management became divorced from ownership and came under the control of

banking groups, men forgot that they were dealing with the savings of men and the making of profits became an impersonal thing. When men do not know the victims of their aggression they are not always conscious of their wrongs. * * *

* * *

Fair corporate suffrage is an important right that should attach to every equity security bought on a public exchange. Managements of properties owned by the investing public should not be permitted to perpetuate themselves by the misuse of corporate proxies.

H.R.Rep. No. 1383, 73d Cong., 2d Sess. 5, 13 (1934).

In striving to implement this open-ended mandate, the Commission has gradually evolved its present proxy rules. * * * It eventually became clear that the question of what constituted a "proper subject" for shareholder action was to be resolved by recourse to the law of the state in which the company had been incorporated; however, the paucity of applicable state law giving content to the concept of "proper subject" led the Commission to seek guidance from precedent existing in jurisdictions which had a highly developed commercial and corporate law and to develop its own "common law" relating to proper subjects for shareholder action.

Further areas of difficulty became apparent as experience was gained in administering the "proper subject" test, and these conflicts provided the Commission with opportunities to put a detailed gloss upon the general phraseology of its rules. Thus, in 1945 the Commission issued a release containing an opinion of the Director of the Division of Corporation Finance that was rendered in response to a management request to omit shareholder resolutions which bore little or no relationship to the company's affairs; for example, these shareholder resolutions included proposals "that the anti-trust laws and the enforcement thereof be revised," and "that all Federal legislation hereafter enacted providing for workers and farmers to be represented should be made to apply equally to investors." The Commission's release endorsed the Director's conclusion that "proposals which deal with general political, social or economic matters are not, within the meaning of the rule, 'proper subjects for action by security holders.'"

* * *

Several years after the Commission issued this release, it was confronted with the same kind of problem when the management of a national bus company sought to omit a shareholder proposal phrased as "A Recommendation that Management Consider the Advisability of Abolishing the Segregated Seating System in the South"—a proposal which, on its face, was ambiguous with respect to whether it was limited solely to company policy rather than attacking all segregated seating, and which quite likely would have brought the company into violation of state laws then assumed to be valid. The Commission staff approved management's decision to omit the proposal, and the shareholder then sought a temporary injunction against the company's solicitation in a federal district court. The injunction was denied because the plaintiff had failed to exhaust his administrative remedies or to show that he would be irreparably harmed by refusal to grant the requested relief. Peck v. Greyhound Corp., 97 F.Supp. 679 (S.D.N.Y.1951). The Commission amended its rules the following year to encompass the above-quoted exception for situations in which "it clearly appears that the proposal is submitted by the security holder * * * primarily for the purpose of promoting general economic, political, racial, religious, social or similar causes." So far as we have been able to determine, the Commission's interpretation or application of this rule has not been considered by the courts.

The origins and genesis of the exception for proposals "relating to the conduct of the ordinary business operations of the issuer" are somewhat more obscure. This provision was introduced into the proxy rules in 1954, as part of amendments which were made to clarify the general proposition that the primary source of authority for determining whether a proposal is a proper subject for shareholder action is state law. See 19 Fed.Reg. 246 (1954). * * *

These two exceptions are, on their face, consistent with the legislative purpose underlying section 14; for it seems fair to infer that Congress desired to make proxy solicitations a vehicle for *corporate* democracy rather than an all-purpose forum for malcontented shareholders to vent their spleen about irrelevant matters,[26] and also realized that management cannot exercise its specialized talents effectively if corporate investors assert the power to dictate the minutiae of daily business decisions. However, it is also apparent that the two exceptions which these rules carve out of the general requirement of inclusion can be construed so as to permit the exclusion of practically any shareholder proposal on the grounds that it is either "too general" or "too specific." Indeed, in the present case Dow Chemical Company attempted to impale the Medical Committee's proposal on both

---

26. *See, e.g.,* the following colloquy, which appears in House Hearings at 162–63:

Mr. Boren. So one man, if he owned one share in A.T. & T. * * * and another share in R.C.A. * * * if he decided deliberately * * * to become a professional stockholder in each one of the companies—he could have a hundred-word propaganda statement prepared and he could put it in every one of these proxy statements. Suppose he were a Communist.

Commissioner Purcell. That is possible. We have never seen such a case.

Mr. Boren. Suppose a man were a Communist and he wanted to send to

all of the stockholders of all of these firms, a philosophic statement of 100 words in length, or a propaganda statement. * * * He could by the mere device of buying one share of stock * * * have available to him the mailing list of all the stockholders in the Radio Corporation of America.

* * *

Commissioner Purcell. Of course, we have never seen such a case; and if such a case came before us, then we would have to deal with it and make such appropriate changes as might seem necessary. * * *

horns of this dilemma: in its memorandum of counsel, it argued that the Medical Committee's proposal was a matter of ordinary business operations properly within the sphere of management expertise and, at the same time, that the proposal clearly had been submitted primarily for the purpose of promoting general political or social causes. As noted above, the Division of Corporation Finance made no attempt to choose between these potentially conflicting arguments, but rather merely accepted Dow Chemical's decision to omit the proposal "[f]or reasons stated in [the company's] letter and the accompanying opinion of counsel, both dated January 17, 1969"; this determination was then adopted by the full Commission. Close examination of the company's arguments only increases doubt as to the reasoning processes which led the Commission to this result.

In contending that the Medical Committee's proposal was properly excludable under Rule 14a–8(c)(5), Dow's counsel asserted:

> It is my opinion that *the determination of the products which the company shall manufacture*, the customers to which it shall sell the products, and the conditions under which it shall make such sales are related to the conduct of the ordinary business operations of the Company and that any attempt to amend the Certificate of Incorporation to define the circumstances under which the management of the Company shall make such determinations is contrary to the concept of corporate management, which is inherent in the Delaware General Corporation Act under which the Company is organized.

In the first place, it seems extremely dubious that this superficial analysis complies with the Commission's longstanding requirements that management must sustain the burden of proof when asserting that a shareholder proposal may properly be omitted from the proxy statement, and that "[w]here management contends that a proposal may be omitted because it is not proper under State law, it will be incumbent upon management to refer to the applicable statute or case law." As noted above, the Commission has formally represented to Congress that Rule 14a–8(c)(5) is intended to make state law the governing authority in determining what matters are ordinary business operations immune from shareholder control; yet, the Delaware General Corporation law provides that a company's Certificate of Incorporation may be amended to "change, substitute, enlarge or diminish the nature of [the company's] business." If there are valid reasons why the Medical Committee's proposal does not fit within the language and spirit of this provision, they certainly do not appear in the record.

The possibility that the Medical Committee's proposal could properly be omitted under Rule 14a–8(c)(2) appears somewhat more substantial in the circumstances of the instant case. * * *

As our earlier discussion indicates, the clear import of the language, legislative history, and record of administration of section 14

(a) is that its overriding purpose is to assure to corporate shareholders the ability to exercise their right—some would say their duty—to control the important decisions which affect them in their capacity as stockholders and owners of the corporation. Thus, the Third Circuit has cogently summarized the philosophy of section 14(a) in the statement that "[a] corporation is run for the benefit of its stockholders and not for that of its managers." SEC v. Transamerica Corp., 163 F.2d 511, 517 (3d Cir. 1947), cert. denied, 332 U.S. 847, 68 S.Ct. 351, 92 L.Ed. 418 (1948). Here, in contrast to the situations detailed above which led to the promulgation of Rule 14a–8(c)(2), the proposal relates solely to a matter that is completely within the accepted sphere of corporate activity and control. No reason has been advanced in the present proceedings which leads to the conclusion that management may properly place obstacles in the path of shareholders who wish to present to their co-owners, in accord with applicable state law, the question of whether they wish to have their assets used in a manner which they believe to be more socially responsible but possibly less profitable than that which is dictated by present company policy. Thus, even accepting Dow's characterization of the purpose and intent of the Medical Committee's proposal, there is a strong argument that permitting the company to exclude it would contravene the purpose of section 14(a).

However, the record in this case contains indications that we are confronted with quite a different situation. The management of Dow Chemical Company is repeatedly quoted in sources which include the company's own publications as proclaiming that the decision to continue manufacturing and marketing napalm was made not *because* of business considerations, but *in spite of* them; that management in essence decided to pursue a course of activity which generated little profit for the shareholders and actively impaired the company's public relations and recruitment activities because management considered this action morally and politically desirable. The proper political and social role of modern corporations is, of course, a matter of philosophical argument extending far beyond the scope of our present concern; the substantive wisdom or propriety of particular corporate political decisions is also completely irrelevant to the resolution of the present controversy. What *is* of immediate concern, however, is the question of whether the corporate proxy rules can be employed as a shield to isolate such managerial decisions from shareholder control. After all, it must be remembered that "[t]he control of great corporations by a very few persons was the abuse at which Congress struck in enacting Section 14(a)." SEC v. Transamerica Corp., *supra*, 163 F. 2d at 518. We think that there is a clear and compelling distinction between management's legitimate need for freedom to apply its expertise in matters of day-to-day business judgment, and management's patently illegitimate claim of power to treat modern corporations with their vast resources as personal satrapies implementing personal political or moral predilections. It could scarcely be argued that management is more qualified or more entitled to make these kinds of decisions than the shareholders who are the true beneficial owners of the corporation; and it seems equally implausible that an application of the proxy rules which permitted such a result could be harmonized with the philosophy of corporate democracy which Congress embodied in section 14(a) of the Securities Exchange Act of 1934.

In light of these considerations, therefore, the cause must be remanded to the Commission so that it may reconsider petitioner's claim within the proper limits of its discretionary authority as set forth above, and so that "the basis for [its] decision [may] appear clearly on the record, not in conclusory terms but in sufficient detail to permit prompt and effective review."

NOTE

The decision in *Medical Committee* was vacated and remanded on grounds of mootness. 404 U.S. 403, 92 S.Ct. 977, 30 L.Ed.2d 560 (1972). In Kixmiller v. SEC, 492 F.2d 641 (D.C.Cir. 1974), the same court of appeals decided that if the Commission declines review of a staff opinion agreeing that a stockholder proposal could be omitted, there is no reviewable agency action. Evidently the court reacted to the observation of one of its members who said he believed that the Supreme Court had granted certiorari in *Medical Committee* in order to reverse only to have the decision saved "by the bell of mootness." Sec.Reg.L.Rep. (BNA), No. 184, p. A–8 (Jan. 10, 1973).

NOTE—SHAREHOLDER PROPOSALS AND TRANSACTION CAUSATION

Shareholder proposals are frequently submitted in precatory form, whereby the shareholders "request" action by the board. Adoption of the resolution would not, by itself, cause a corporate transaction to occur. Can a misleading comment by management opposing such a proposal ever give rise to a private claim under the proxy rules? Inasmuch as no actual corporate transaction was affected by the vote, can the aggrieved shareholder demonstrate "transaction causation" necessary to sustain a private right? In Sisters of the Precious Blood v. Bristol-Meyers, Inc., 431 F.Supp. 385 (S.D.N.Y.1977), appeal dismissed, (2d Cir. 1978), the district court dismissed a suit because of the lack of a causal link.

This decision would have no significance on an SEC action to enjoin the further solicitation of proxies until the proxy material complied with federal law, such as the Commission instituted in *SEC v. Transamerica*. But Commission cases are rare. In a boiler plate paragraph in no-action letters dealing with the includability of a shareholder proposal, the SEC reminds the parties that its own views are advisory only and that the parties have recourse to the federal courts to enforce their rights under the proxy rules. Thus, the Commission expects private litigation, or the possibility of it, to be the enforcement mechanism to carry out Rule 14a–8. Is this expectation realistic if precatory proposals, which account for a large percentage of all shareholder proposals, cannot be the subject of a suit because of a lack of transaction causation?

Consider what "transaction" is affected by misrepresentations in a proxy statement. When management submits a recommendation for a merger, as it did in *Borak* and *Mills*, the transaction which arguably injures the shareholder is the merger itself. That is the event that is "caused" by the proxy statement. In the case of a shareholder proposal, the event is the proposal—not the action it proposes. That is because the exercise of publicly airing the shareholder recommendation is the means by which action is accomplished, not the actual vote. The process is what counts, whereby the shareholders propose, management responds and the public listens. The vote is a foregone conclusion, and not the crucial part of the process. The medium is the message, if you will. However, the public airing is much affected by the facts surrounding the issue, and the facts are largely drawn from the proxy materials.

Thus, as the SEC observed in its *amicus* brief to the Second Circuit in *Sisters of the Precious Blood*, shareholders are injured by misleading statements relating to precatory proposals which deprive them of the opportunity to have their proposals considered fairly and, more practically, which possibly deprive them of their right to resubmit the proposal if it fails to achieve the 3% minimum vote. One could add that it might cost the proponents the symbolic significance of a 3% vote, an event of some importance and catalytic quality as shown by the fact that a big enough vote by shareholders has often persuaded management "voluntarily" to take the action that the shareholder proposed.

4. WHITHER (OR WITHER) THE SHAREHOLDERS?

NOTE—SHOULD SHAREHOLDER POWER BE ENHANCED?

The shareholders are the "owners" of the corporation, at least under the traditional view. To what extent can they exercise dominion over their property? To what extent should the law be interpreted, or amended, to enhance their power?

Suppose a shareholder wants to initiate certain action that the existing board of directors and management opposes. He wants the company to liquidate, because he believes that the value of the assets when sold will exceed the value of the stock of the going concern. Or, he may wish the company to accept an offer to merge with another company. What power does the shareholder have to achieve those goals?

A survey of state law by the staff of the SEC showed that shareholders are given few powers to initiate corporation action. Seventeen states, including New York, Ohio and Pennsylvania, permit shareholders to amend the certificate of incorporation without board approval, and two others, California and Connecticut, allow shareholders to initiate a charter amendment. No state permits shareholders to approve a merger without board action and five states allow shareholders to sell all of the assets. Fourteen states permit shareholders to dissolve the corporation without board approval. The principal shareholder power is to amend the by-laws, as thirty-two states give shareholders ultimate power in this respect. Wander, Shareholder Influence on Corporate Policy in Standards for Regulating Corporate Internal Affairs 91 (D. Fischel ed. 1981).

As to any other matter not dealt with in the statute, shareholders must argue for a common law power to take action, stemming largely from the inherent rights of owners. It is in this non-statutory area where many problems arise.

One power shareholders do have is to elect new directors who will agree with their program. Thus, in 1980 the Shareholders Protective Committee for SCM Corporation was formed to solicit proxies for the election of a slate of directors who advocated a program of at least partially liquidating the company. However, their proxy statement estimated that the cost of the solicitation was approximately $750,000, and that all of the expense would be borne by the individual members of the committee. Obviously this will present an insuperable obstacle to most shareholders, but the members of the SCM committee owned approximately three times as much stock as management. They lost the contest, it might be noted.

Can the shareholders utilize the existing proxy mechanism that management employs in connection with the annual meeting? In other words, can shareholders initiate action that is opposed by the board of directors, and take away from the board of directors or management the decision making power? If so, the cost is borne by the corporation, and it would be greatly reduced.

At this point the obstacle to enhanced stockholder power is more legal than practical. In Automatic Self-Cleaning Filter Syndicate Co., Ltd. v. Cunninghame, [1906] 2 Ch. 34 (C.A.), the Court denied a motion by a shareholder that would have compelled the sale of the company's assets. The shareholders had voted in favor of such a sale, but the directors were opposed. The court rejected the view that directors, as agents of the stockholders, were required to obey their principal and found that they had full power to run the corporation, subject to the statute and the charter, neither of which gave this power to the shareholders. That case would seem to express the American view of the law, as well. You will note that Rule 14a–8 limits the federal law right of shareholders to use the proxy machinery for matters that are proper under state law. *See* S.E.C. v. Transamerica Corporation *supra*.

Can the shareholder, barred from taking action that binds, recommend to the board of directors that the company be liquidated? If this can be done under state law, then the mechanism for achieving it is provided by federal law, so long as the company is subject to the '34 Act. A recommendation is not action, of course, and we have seen that state courts (Auer v. Dressel), and the Securities & Exchange Commission (in Rule 14a–8(c)(7)) are mindful of the distinction. The shareholder, about to crank up such an effort, might ponder what the effect of the recommendation would be if it were adopted. Could the board ignore it? Would that furnish any basis for acting against management or the board?

Using the company's proxy machinery, under the federal right created by Rule 14a–8, imposes significant limitations on the proponent of such a proposal. As a practical matter, the proponent must demonstrate the wisdom of the proposed course of action, that is, that the higher values exist in liquidation. Can that case be made out within the word limitation contained in Rule 14a–8? That seems hardly likely in view of the SEC's cautions against overstating the case and the need to elaborate upon and support any projections that are made. Without supporting data, there is a risk that the proposal will be considered misleading under Rule 14a–9, and therefore excludable under Rule 14a–8(c)(3).

Perhaps another approach to enhancing the shareholders' power is to allow them the opportunity to use the corporate proxy machinery for the solicitation of support for different candidates for election to the board of directors than those proposed by management. In other words, the proxy material sent by management to the shareholders could provide a choice to the shareholders. Arguably, such a right could be created under the federal proxy rules: the offering of a choice among candidates could be imposed as a condition to the interstate solicitation of proxies. More fundamentally, however, the question is one of organic corporation law. In that respect consider the following, an excerpt from Professor Melvin Eisenberg's The Structure of the Corporation (1975) pp. 113–21:

> Under the corporate statutes the power to elect the board is vested exclusively in the shareholders. The board does not have the power to elect its successor board (although it is often empowered to fill interim vacancies caused by death, resignation, or removal), and therefore cannot take actions for the purpose of perpetuating itself in office.   *   *   *
>
> As a corollary to this exclusive power to elect the board, shareholders have at least concurrent power to nominate candidates for directorship. It has already been shown that the proxy system is today's shareholders' meeting. Correspondingly, the designation of candidates in the proxy materials is today's nomination. The shareholder power to make nominations must therefore carry with it access to the basic corporate machinery used to make nomina-

tions, that is, the corporate proxy materials. Although it might be objected that nominations are not made in the proxy materials, but rather from the floor at the annual meeting, such an objection at best is based purely on form, and is not well-based even there. Normally, proxies are executed and mailed by shareholders before the date of the meeting, and proxies gathered in a solicitation subject to the Proxy Rules can be voted only in favor of persons named in the proxy. If nominations are not deemed to occur until the meeting, voting would precede nominations—a rather unusual format. Indeed, it appears that in actual corporate practice the bylaws usually do not fix the time for making nominations, and that in fact the predominant practice is to treat the proxy materials as the corporation's nominating machinery—so that, for example, persons in whose favor proxies are solicited are normally characterized in the proxy materials as "nominees" rather than merely as "candidates."

In light of the fact that the shareholders have exclusive power to elect the board, it might be questioned on what principle the board may use the corporate proxy machinery to designate candidates at all. Such use might be justified on two bases: as a derivative of the customary concurrent power to nominate, and through application of the principle that as far as reasonably practicable, personal campaign funds should not be permitted to determine corporate office. But neither basis would justify *exclusive* board access to the corporate proxy machinery for this purpose. Even assuming the board has a customary power to nominate candidates, it could not abrogate the shareholders' right to nominate, which inheres by law. And if personal campaign funds should not be permitted to determine corporate office, far less should the funds of the corporation itself, as would tend to be the case if the board's access were exclusive.

One argument, which stems from the conclusion's apparent unconventionality, is that even if shareholders might once have claimed the right to designate candidates in the corporate proxy materials, a contrary practice of denying that right has grown up which it is now too late to challenge.

* * *

A second possible argument against the right of shareholders to designate candidates in the corporate proxy materials is that such a result would be impracticable. Certainly, practicability should be considered in determining the rules governing access to the corporate proxy machinery. It does not seem impracticable, however, to permit the shareholders to designate candidates through that machinery. Such access need be triggered only when the corporate proxy machinery is set in motion for a similar purpose by management, and therefore would not entail the distribution of corporate proxy materials that would not otherwise be distributed; all that would be required is the addition of extra names to a proxy card and extra names and descriptions to a proxy statement being distributed anyway. Furthermore, since the corporate proxy machinery will predictably be set in motion at approximately the same date every year, a shareholder's exercise of this right could be conditioned on the submission of the names of his candidates a reasonable time in advance of this date. Thus where the right is exercised—and it will not always be exercised—it is doubtful that it would add materially to the basic solicitation cost. And corporations which deem an unrestricted shareholder right to designate candidates impracticable can adopt a bylaw limiting the right to shareholders owning in the aggregate some minimum percentage of the corporation's stock, say five percent.

* * *

A third possible argument is that as a matter of policy it is preferable to maximize managerial power and minimize the power of shareholders. Such an argument is normally made to rest on one of two different premises: (1) That management knows better than the shareholders themselves what is good for the shareholders, so that the shareholders' own best interests are promoted by limiting shareholders' rights; or (2) That the public interest is best advanced by scaling down the shareholders' interests in favor of corporate client-groups, such as labor or consumers, and that to accomplish this purpose it is necessary to weaken shareholder control over management, which is then in a position to recognize client-group claims. The first premise assumes that the average shareholder is economically naive. However, as pointed out earlier, while the average *shareholder* may be economically naive (although even this has not been proved), the great bulk of *shareholdings* are controlled by sophisticated and wealthy individual or institutional investors who are very well able to calculate their own interests. The second premise assumes that ultimate shareholder control reinforces a corporate orientation toward profit maximization, it does not prevent management from behaving decently. In the long run, the public interest might better be served by a corporate orientation toward maximizing profits within the limits of decent behavior than by dropping profit maximization as the principal corporate goal. But in any event, there is no sound basis for believing either that ultimate shareholder control significantly affects corporate orientation toward profits, or that present-day management could or would use a less circumscribed power self-lessly and wisely. Managers are no less self-interested than shareholders, and no more expert on the public interest, and whether shareholders are less apt to vote in the public interest than directors is presently indeterminable.

One perspective on the shareholder participation process, which is facilitated by a liberal interpretation of Rule 14a–8, is that it constitutes another device for rendering management accountable for the exercise of its power. All accountability devices have their limitations, whether we refer to regulation and law enforcement, annual elections or the marketplace. However, the existence of many systems may complement one another.

The shareholder proposal device is a means of raising issues about the management or the corporation in a public forum. Management cannot ignore a public accusation that it has neglected the public interest. Moreover, there follows a quick referendum. Surely all this is not without cost, but it is probably not great. Whether there is a sufficient benefit to justify even a modest cost, however, is the question.

The overwhelming majority of shareholders oppose the proposals submitted by their fellow shareholders. Does this prove that shareholder proposals are a waste of time and money? In particular, proposals that raise social issues, like cessation of business in South Africa, attract far less support than the elimination of charitable contributions. To conclude from that evidence that management enjoys respect and affection may not be an accurate way of reading the election returns, however. Inertia and the presumption of regularity create an enormous advantage in favor of management. If outsiders receive 3% or more of the vote, thereby winning the legal right to resubmit the proposal, management takes that as a signal that they should pay attention to the substance of the proposal. They understand that even that small a vote is a sign of rumblings in the ranks. With respect to those proposals that have political or social overtones, discontent among the general public may be even more important than unhappiness among the shareholders, because in a economic and political way, the general public is a constituency to which management must be accountable.

On the other hand, tinkering with the system which has relegated shareholders to an insignificant role may be hazardous. Shareholders have available to them the "Wall Street Rule." They can sell their shares if they are unhappy. They can avoid having their economic affairs governed by inefficient managers. Theoretically, if enough of them are unhappy, there will be more sellers than buyers, driving down the prices of the stock and sending the clearest of signals to management to change its ways. Can the law improve on the simplicity, directness and cost efficiency of this mechanism?

Yet, there remains doubt among many that the market works as efficiently in operations as it does in theory. It offers virtually no outlet for stockholders and others complaining of anti-social behavior. One more opportunity to those interested in the corporation to chip away at the absoluteness of management's power is believed by many to be healthy for the corporation and the economy in general.

Chapter 14

INTRODUCTION TO FIDUCIARY DUTIES

A. THE DUTY OF CARE

1. INTRODUCTION

Fiduciary duty is a central, indeed perhaps the most important, concept in the Anglo-American law of corporations. The word, "fiduciary", comes from the Latin *fides*, meaning faith or confidence, and was originally used in the common law to describe the nature of the duties imposed on a trustee. Perhaps because many of the earliest corporations cases involved charitable corporations, it seemed natural to analogize the duties of a director in managing corporate property to the duties of a trustee in managing trust property. Whatever the historical roots of the use of the fiduciary concept to delineate the duties of corporate directors, there is nothing inevitable about it. The whole concept of a trust, and the fiduciary principles that go with it, are absent from the civil law system, which has therefore had to find other sources on which to base its approach to the obligations of the officers, directors and controlling shareholders of a corporation.

The original analogy between a trustee and those who control a corporation was a close one. But as corporations began to play a role of increasing importance in an increasingly complex commercial world, the strictures imposed by the law on a true trustee, gradually eroded. Today little is left but the basic notion that officers, directors, controlling shareholders owe some sort of duty, one that will be enforced by the court, to the corporation, and through it to the shareholders. The precise definition of that duty is anything but clear. As Justice Frankfurter said in a frequently quoted passage from SEC v. Chenery Corp., 318 U.S. 80, 85, 63 S.Ct. 454, 458, 87 L.Ed. 626, 632 (1949):

> But to say that a man is a fiduciary only begins analysis; it gives direction to further inquiry. To whom is he a fiduciary? What obligations does he owe as a fiduciary? In what respect has he failed to discharge these obligations? And what are the consequences of his deviation from duty?

The fiduciary duty of officers and directors is traditionally subdivided into the duty of care and the duty of loyalty. In this chapter we will explore the duty of care and the duty of loyalty.

PROBLEM

NATIONAL METAL PRODUCTS—PART II

National Metal Products, Inc. (National) is described in Chapter 13, Section B (The Regulatory Pattern). Its board currently consists of eleven directors, five of whom are employed by the corporation and six of whom are "outside directors." The five inside directors are:

(1) Charles Meacham—son of the founder of the company, chairman of the board and chief executive officer, and owner of ten percent of National's outstanding stock;

(2) Glen Gray—secretary and general counsel;

(3) Ruth Brown—treasurer;

(4) James Green—vice president for operations;

(5) Ann White—vice president for finance;

The non-employee directors include:

(1) Sarah Meacham—widow of the founder and owner of five percent of National's stock. She has been on the board since it was founded. In recent years she has attended very few meetings because of her failing health, but has been retained on the board largely for sentimental reasons;

(2) Ernest Price—the partner in National's outside accounting firm who is principally responsible for the work for National;

(3) Beverly Samuels—a partner in the law firm that does most of National's legal work;

(4) Ralph Jordan—a partner in the investment banking firm that assisted in the acquisition of International Petroleum Corporation as well as doing other work for National;

(5) William Mays—former English professor now the president of Southeastern University, Charles Meacham's alma mater;

(6) "Red" Sanford—the controlling stockholder of the International Petroleum Corporation before it was merged into National and now owner of a substantial block of National shares.

Shortly after his father's death four years ago, Meacham worked out a merger with the International Petroleum Corporation (IPC), a closely-held, but very large oil producer that had been a substantial customer of National. In the merger IPC's shareholders were given National common stock amounting to 20 percent of the shares outstanding. National's board approved the transaction after a brief discussion based on financial statements prepared by IPC's accounting staff, a detailed study of IPC and the benefits of the acquisition prepared by Jordan, and a half-hour oral presentation by Meacham. During a brief discussion of the deal, Ernest Price raised a number of questions about the financial statements that Meacham was unable to answer. William Mays complained that he had not had sufficient time to study the transaction and wondered whether it would not be desirable to postpone a vote to the next board meeting. This, Meacham said would be impossible, because the merger agreement that he and "Red" Sanford had negotiated would expire before the transaction could be approved by the shareholders unless the steps necessary for a shareholder vote were commenced immediately. The final vote on the merger was 8 in favor and none against. Mays abstained, and Sarah Meacham was not present at the meeting. (Sanford had not yet become a member of the board.) The transaction was ultimately approved by the shareholders and was consumated three years ago.

The merger has proved to be very disadvantageous for National. During preliminary discussions with Charles Meacham, Sanford, who was chief executive officer of IPC, told Meacham of some "problems" that IPC had experienced with price fixing by its field managers. Sanford indicated that this sort of practice was widespread in the industry, but that he had taken steps to have it halted at IPC. After the merger, Meacham directed Gray to investigate the antitrust problems and to develop a program to prevent future difficulties in this area. Gray reported his findings to the board. His "program" consisted of a memorandum, signed by Meacham, to all field managers stating that the new top management would no longer condone price-fixing and that it should cease.

These measures apparently had little effect, and price-fixing continued after the merger. Eventually several private treble damage actions were filed against National, and the Justice Department instituted a criminal prosecution. Both the civil and the criminal suits alleged violations before and after the merger. The private actions were recently settled in an arrangement that will cost National $15 million over the next three years. The criminal action resulted in a $2 million dollar fine. Sanford, who was also prosecuted, entered a plea of nolo contendere and was fined $20,000.

In the wake of these problems, National dismissed several of the senior managers of the International Petroleum Division (which operates the assets of the former IPC). Because there was very little management depth, the Division has been floundering ever since and has sustained large operating losses for the last two years.

A committee of dissident stockholders has asked you for your advice on the feasibility of a derivative suit against the directors of National for breach of their duty of care.

They are upset about several things. First, they believe the board should have obtained more information and should have considered the merger more extensively before approving it. Second, the board should have discovered IPC's price-fixing problems before the merger. At the very least, having discovered them, the board should have acted more aggressively to prevent further price-fixing after the merger. Finally, the acquisition of a company with so little management depth in an industry about which National knew so little was so ill-advised as to be negligent.

QUESTIONS

1. Briefly describe on what claims, and on what theories, might a plaintiff sue.

2. Consider what defenses might be available to individual directors. For example:

a. Might Sarah Meacham argue successfully that she should not be held liable because she was not present at the meeting at which the merger was approved? Might she argue that she knew too little about business to have appreciated the deficiencies in IPC's management?

b. Might Mays argue that he is not liable for approving an ill-advised merger because he objected at the meeting and abstained from the final vote? What if he had voted against?

3. To what extent can directors rely on others? For example, can the remainder of the directors:

a. Rely on Meacham's recommendation of the transaction?

b. Rely on Jordan's study?

c. Rely on Gray's program to prevent further antitrust violations?

4. Are there directors whose conduct was more culpable? For example, in contrast to the other directors is there a greater likelihood that liability for negligence will be imposed on:

a. Charles Meacham, who negotiated the transaction?

b. Jordan, who prepared a detailed study of it?

c. Gray, who was charged with stopping the antitrust violations?

d. Sanford, who knew more about the problems than anyone else?

5. How does the business judgment rule enter into the defenses available to the directors?

6. Considering the likelihood of success of the proposed lawsuit, would you take the case on a contingent fee?

2. THE STANDARD OF CARE

a. The Basic Standard

FRANCIS v. UNITED JERSEY BANK

87 N.J. 15, 432 A.2d 814 (1981).

POLLOCK, J.

[Pritchard & Baird, Inc., was a reinsurance broker, a firm that arranged contracts between insurance companies by means of which companies that wrote large policies sold participations in those policies to other companies in order to share the risks. According to the custom in the industry, the selling company pays the applicable portion of the premium to the broker, which deducts its commission and forwards the balance to the reinsuring company. The broker thus handles large amounts of money as a fiduciary for its clients.

As of 1964, all the stock of Pritchard & Baird was owned by Charles Pritchard, Sr., one of the firm's founders, and his wife and two sons, Charles, Jr. and William. They were also the four directors. Charles, Sr., dominated the corporation until 1971, when he became ill and the two sons took over management of the business. Charles, Sr. died in 1973, leaving Mrs. Pritchard and the sons the only remaining directors.

Contrary to the industry practice, Pritchard & Baird did not segregate its operating funds from those of its clients, depositing all in the same account. From this account Charles, Sr. had drawn "loans," that correlated with corporate profits and were repaid at the end of each year. After his death, Charles, Jr. and William began to draw ever larger sums (still characterizing them as "loans") that greatly exceeded profits. They were able to do so by taking advantage of the "float" available to them during the period between the time they received a premium and the time they had to forward it (less commission) to the reinsurer.

By 1975 the corporation was bankrupt. This action was brought by the trustees in bankruptcy against Mrs. Pritchard and the bank as administrator of her husband's estate. She died during the pendency of the proceedings, and her executrix was substituted as defendant. As to Mrs. Pritchard, the principal claim was that she had been negligent in the conduct of her duties as a director of the corporation.]

The "loans" were reflected on financial statements that were prepared annually as of January 31, the end of the corporate fiscal year. Although an outside certified public accountant prepared the 1970 financial statement, the corporation prepared only internal financial statements from 1971–1975. In all instances, the statements were simple documents, consisting of three or four 8½ × 11 inch sheets.

The statements of financial condition from 1970 forward demonstrated:

	WORKING CAPITAL DEFICIT	SHAREHOLDERS' LOANS	NET BROKERAGE INCOME
1970	$ 389,022	$ 509,941	$ 807,229
1971	not available	not available	not available
1972	$ 1,684,289	$ 1,825,911	$ 1,546,263
1973	$ 3,506,460	$ 3,700,542	$ 1,736,349
1974	$ 6,939,007	$ 7,080,629	$ 876,182
1975	$10,176,419	$10,298,039	$ 551,598.

* * *

Mrs. Pritchard was not active in the business of Pritchard & Baird and knew virtually nothing of its corporate affairs. She briefly visited the corporate offices in Morristown on only one occasion, and she never read or obtained the annual financial statements. She was unfamiliar with the rudiments of reinsurance and made no effort to assure that the policies and practices of the corporation, particularly pertaining to the withdrawal of funds, complied with industry custom or relevant law. Although her husband had warned her that Charles, Jr. would "take the shirt off my back," Mrs. Pritchard did not pay any attention to her duties as a director or to the affairs of the corporation. 162 N.J.Super. at 370, 392 A.2d 1233.

After her husband died in December 1973, Mrs. Pritchard became incapacitated and was bedridden for a six-month period. She became listless at this time and started to drink rather heavily. Her physical condition deteriorated, and in 1978 she died. The trial court rejected testimony seeking to exonerate her because she "was old, was grief-stricken at the loss of her husband, sometimes consumed too much alcohol and was psychologically overborne by her sons." 162 N.J. Super. at 371, 392 A.2d 1233. That court found that she was competent to act and that the reason Mrs. Pritchard never knew what her sons "were doing was because she never made the slightest effort to discharge any of her responsibilities as a director of Pritchard & Baird." 162 N.J.Super. at 372, 392 A.2d 1233.

* * *

III

Individual liability of a corporate director for acts of the corporation is a prickly problem. Generally directors are accorded broad immunity and are not insurers of corporate activities. The problem is particularly nettlesome when a third party asserts that a director, because of nonfeasance, is liable for losses caused by acts of insiders, who in this case were officers, directors and shareholders. Determination of the liability of Mrs. Pritchard requires findings that she had a duty to the clients of Pritchard & Baird, that she breached that duty and that her breach was a proximate cause of their losses.

The New Jersey Business Corporation Act makes it incumbent upon directors to

> discharge their duties in good faith and with that degree of diligence, care and skill which ordinarily prudent men would exercise under similar circumstances in like positions. [N.J.S.A. 14A:6–14]

This provision was based primarily on section 43 of the Model Business Corporation Act and is derived also from section 717 of the New York Business Corporation Law. Before the enactment of N.J. S.A. 14A:6–14, there was no express statutory authority requiring directors to act as ordinarily prudent persons under similar circumstances in like positions. Nonetheless, the requirement had been expressed in New Jersey judicial decisions.

A leading New Jersey opinion is Campbell v. Watson, 62 N.J.Eq. 396, 50 A. 120 (Ch.1901), which, like many early decisions on director liability, involved directors of a bank that had become insolvent. A receiver of the bank charged the directors with negligence that allegedly led to insolvency. In the opinion, Vice Chancellor Pitney explained that bank depositors have a right to

> rely upon the character of the directors and officers [and upon the representation] that they will perform their sworn duty to manage the affairs of the bank according to law and devote to its affairs the same diligent attention which ordinary, prudent, diligent men pay to their own affairs; and * * * such diligence and attention as experience has shown it is proper and necessary that bank directors should give to that business in order to reasonably protect the bank and its creditors against loss. [*Id.* at 406, 50 A. 120]

* * *

Underlying the pronouncements in * * * Campbell v. Watson, *supra*, and N.J.S.A. 14A:6–14 is the principle that directors must discharge their duties in good faith and act as ordinarily prudent persons would under similar circumstances in like positions. Although specific duties in a given case can be determined only after consideration of all of the circumstances, the standard of ordinary care is the wellspring from which those more specific duties flow.

As a general rule, a director should acquire at least a rudimentary understanding of the business of the corporation. Accordingly, a director should become familiar with the fundamentals of the business in which the corporation is engaged. *Campbell, supra*, 62 N.J.Eq. at 416, 50 A. 120. Because directors are bound to exercise ordinary care, they cannot set up as a defense lack of the knowledge needed to exercise the requisite degree of care. If one "feels that he has not had sufficient business experience to qualify him to perform the duties of a director, he should either acquire the knowledge by inquiry, or refuse to act." *Ibid.*

Directors are under a continuing obligation to keep informed about the activities of the corporation. Otherwise, they may not be able to participate in the overall management of corporate affairs. * * * Directors may not shut their eyes to corporate misconduct and then claim that because they did not see the misconduct, they did not have a duty to look. The sentinel asleep at his post contributes nothing to the enterprise he is charged to protect.

Directorial management does not require a detailed inspection of day-to-day activities, but rather a general monitoring of corporate affairs and policies. Accordingly, a director is well advised to attend board meetings regularly. Indeed, a director who is absent from a board meeting is presumed to concur in action taken on a corporate matter, unless he files a "dissent with the secretary of the corporation within a reasonable time after learning of such action." N.J.S.A. 14A:6–13 (Supp.1981–1982). * * *

While directors are not required to audit corporate books, they should maintain familiarity with the financial status of the corporation by a regular review of financial statements. In some circumstances, directors may be charged with assuring that bookkeeping methods conform to industry custom and usage. The extent of review, as well as the nature and frequency of financial statements, depends not only on the customs of the industry, but also on the nature of the corporation and the business in which it is engaged. Financial statements of some small corporations may be prepared internally and only on an annual basis; in a large publicly held corporation, the statements may be produced monthly or at some other regular interval. Adequate financial review normally would be more informal in a private corporation than in a publicly held corporation.

Of some relevance in this case is the circumstance that the financial records disclose the "shareholders' loans". Generally directors are immune from liability if, in good faith,

> they rely upon the opinion of counsel for the corporation or upon written reports setting forth financial data concerning the corporation and prepared by an independent public accountant or certified public accountant or firm of such accountants or upon financial statements, books of account or reports of the corporation represented to them to be correct by the president, the officer of the corporation having charge of its books of account, or the person presiding at a meeting of the board. [N.J.S.A. 14A:6–14]

The review of financial statements, however, may give rise to a duty to inquire further into matters revealed by those statements. Upon discovery of an illegal course of action, a director has a duty to object and, if the corporation does not correct the conduct, to resign.

In certain circumstances, the fulfillment of the duty of a director may call for more than mere objection and resignation. Sometimes a director may be required to seek the advice of counsel. * * *

A director is not an ornament, but an essential component of corporate governance. Consequently, a director cannot protect himself behind a paper shield bearing the motto, "dummy director." * * * The New Jersey Business Corporation Act, in imposing a standard of ordinary care on all directors, confirms that dummy, figurehead and accommodation directors are anachronisms with no place in New Jersey law. * * *

The factors that impel expanded responsibility in the large, publicly held corporation may not be present in a small, close corporation. Nonetheless, a close corporation may, because of the nature of its business, be affected with a public interest. For example, the stock of a bank may be closely held, but because of the nature of banking the directors would be subject to greater liability than those of another close corporation. Even in a small corporation, a director is held to the standard of that degree of care that an ordinarily prudent director would use under the circumstances.

A director's duty of care does not exist in the abstract, but must be considered in relation to specific obligees. In general, the relationship of a corporate director to the corporation and its stockholders is that of a fiduciary. Shareholders have a right to expect that directors will exercise reasonable supervision and control over the policies and practices of a corporation. The institutional integrity of a corporation depends upon the proper discharge by directors of those duties.

While directors may owe a fiduciary duty to creditors also, that obligation generally has not been recognized in the absence of insolvency. With certain corporations, however, directors are seemed to owe a duty to creditors and other third parties even when the corporation is solvent. Although depositors of a bank are considered in some respects to be creditors, courts have recognized that directors may owe them a fiduciary duty. Directors of nonbanking corporations may owe a similar duty when the corporation holds funds of others in trust. * * *

* * *

As a reinsurance broker, Pritchard & Baird received annually as a fiduciary millions of dollars of clients' money which it was under a duty to segregate. To this extent, it resembled a bank rather than a small family business. Accordingly, Mrs. Pritchard's relationship to the clientele of Pritchard & Baird was akin to that of a director of a bank to its depositors. * * *

As a director of a substantial reinsurance brokerage corporation, she should have known that it received annually millions of dollars of loss and premium funds which it held in trust for ceding and reinsurance companies. Mrs. Pritchard should have obtained and read the annual statements of financial condition of Pritchard & Baird. Although she had a right to rely upon financial statements prepared in accordance with N.J.S.A. 14A:6–14, such reliance would not excuse her conduct. *   *   *

From those statements, she should have realized that, as of January 31, 1970, her sons were withdrawing substantial trust funds under the guise of "Shareholders' Loans." The financial statements for each fiscal year commencing with that of January 31, 1970, disclosed that the working capital deficits and the "loans" were escalating in tandem. Detecting a misappropriation of funds would not have required special expertise or extraordinary diligence; a cursory reading of the financial statements would have revealed the pillage. *   *   *

*   *   *

IV

Nonetheless, the negligence of Mrs. Pritchard does not result in liability unless it is a proximate cause of the loss. Analysis of proximate cause requires an initial determination of cause-in-fact. Causation-in-fact calls for a finding that the defendant's act or omission was a necessary antecedent of the loss, *i.e.*, that if the defendant had observed his or her duty of care, the loss would not have occurred. Further, the plaintiff has the burden of establishing the amount of the loss or damages caused by the negligence of the defendant. *   *   *

Cases involving nonfeasance present a much more difficult causation question than those in which the director has committed an affirmative act of negligence leading to the loss. Analysis in cases of negligent omissions calls for determination of the reasonable steps a director should have taken and whether that course of action would have averted the loss.

Usually a director can absolve himself from liability by informing the other directors of the impropriety and voting for a proper course of action. Conversely, a director who votes for or concurs in certain actions may be "liable to the corporation for the benefit of its creditors or shareholders, to the extent of any injuries suffered by such persons, respectively, as a result of any such action." N.J.S.A. 14A:6–12 (Supp.1981–1982). A director who is present at a board meeting is presumed to concur in corporate action taken at the meeting unless his dissent is entered in the minutes of the meeting or filed promptly after adjournment. N.J.S.A. 14:6–13. In many, if not most, instances an objecting director whose dissent is noted in accordance with N.J.S.A. 14:6–13 would be absolved after attempting to persuade fellow directors to follow a different course of action. *   *   *

*   *   *

In this case, the scope of Mrs. Pritchard's duties was determined by the precarious financial condition of Pritchard & Baird, its fiduciary relationship to its clients and the implied trust in which it held their funds. Thus viewed, the scope of her duties encompassed all reasonable action to stop the continuing conversion. Her duties extended beyond mere objection and resignation to reasonable attempts to prevent the misappropriation of the trust funds.

A leading case discussing causation where the director's liability is predicated upon a negligent failure to act is Barnes v. Andrews, 298 F. 614 (S.D.N.Y.1924). In that case the court exonerated a figurehead director who served for eight months on a board that held one meeting after his election, a meeting he was forced to miss because of the death of his mother. Writing for the court, Judge Learned Hand distinguished a director who fails to prevent general mismanagement from one such as Mrs. Pritchard who failed to stop an illegal "loan":

> When the corporate funds have been illegally lent, it is a fair inference that a protest would have stopped the loan, and that the director's neglect caused the loss. But when a business fails from general mismanagement, business incapacity, or bad judgment, how is it possible to say that a single director could have made the company successful, or how much in dollars he could have saved? [Id. at 616–617]

Pointing out the absence of proof of proximate cause between defendant's negligence and the company's insolvency, Judge Hand also wrote:

> The plaintiff must, however, go further than to show that [the director] should have been more active in his duties. This cause of action rests upon a tort, as much though it be a tort of omission as though it had rested upon a positive act. The plaintiff must accept the burden of showing that the performance of the defendant's duties would have avoided loss, and what loss it would have avoided. [Id. at 616]

* * *

Within Pritchard & Baird, several factors contributed to the loss of the funds: comingling of corporate and client monies, conversion of funds by Charles, Jr. and William and dereliction of her duties by Mrs. Pritchard. The wrongdoing of her sons, although the immediate cause of the loss, should not excuse Mrs. Pritchard from her negligence which also was a substantial factor contributing to the loss. Her sons knew that she, the only other director, was not reviewing their conduct; they spawned their fraud in the backwater of her neglect. Her neglect of duty contributed to the climate of corruption; her failure to act contributed to the continuation of that corruption. Consequently, her conduct was a substantial factor contributing to the loss.

Analysis of proximate cause is especially difficult in a corporate context where the allegation is that nonfeasance of a director is a proximate cause of damage to a third party. * * * Nonetheless, where it is reasonable to conclude that the failure to act would produce a particular result and that result has followed, causation may be inferred. We conclude that even if Mrs. Pritchard's mere objection had not stopped the depredations of her sons, her consultation with an attorney and the threat of suit would have deterred them. That conclusion flows as a matter of common sense and logic from the record. Whether in other situations a director has a duty to do more than protest and resign is best left to case-by-case determinations. In this case, we are satisfied that there was a duty to do more than object and resign. Consequently, we find that Mrs. Pritchard's negligence was a proximate cause of the misappropriations.

To conclude, by virtue of her office, Mrs. Pritchard had the power to prevent the losses sustained by the clients of Pritchard & Baird. With power comes responsibility. She had a duty to deter the depredation of the other insiders, her sons. She breached that duty and caused plaintiffs to sustain damages.

The judgment of the Appellate Division is affirmed.

NOTES AND QUESTIONS

1. In Selheimer v. Manganese Corp. of America, 423 Pa. 563, 224 A.2d 634 (1966), the Pennsylvania Supreme Court was called on to apply Section 408 of the Pennsylvania Business Corporation Law, which required that "Officers and directors shall * * * discharge the duties of their respective positions in good faith and with that diligence, care and skill which ordinarily prudent men would exercise under similar circumstances *in their personal business affairs.*" (Emphasis added.) By contrast, as the court pointed out, the statute applicable to bank directors replaced the italicized words with "in like position." Although admitting that the result was anomalous, the court held that Section 408 "imposes on a director of a *business* corporation a much *higher* degree of care than the law imposes on a director of a banking corporation * * *." Do you agree with this interpretation? In 1968 Pennsylvania amended Section 408 by deleting "in their personal business affairs."

2. In a much-cited article, Professor Bishop concludes:

The search for cases in which directors of industrial corporations have been held liable in derivative suits for negligence uncomplicated by self-dealing is a search for a very small number of needles in a very large haystack. Few are the cases in which the stockholders do not allege conflict of interest, still fewer those among them which achieve even such partial success as denial of the defendants' motion to dismiss the complaint. Still, it cannot be denied that there is a small number of relatively recent cases which do seem to lend a modicum of substance to the fears of directors of industrial or mercantile corporations that they may be struck for what they like to call "mere" or "honest" negligence. Bishop, Sitting Ducks and Decoy Ducks: New Trends in Indemnification of Corporate Directors and Officers, 77 Yale L.J. 1078, 1099 (1968).

Francis does not involve an industrial corporation. In fact the court makes much of the similarity between the corporation and a bank for some purposes. Suppose that Pritchard & Baird had, instead of brokering reinsurance transactions, manufactured widgets. And suppose further that there was a minority shareholder who was not a member of the Pritchard family. Would the court have held Mrs. Pritchard liable for the defalcations of her sons in a derivative suit by that shareholder?

b. A Unitary Standard?

Should the standard of care be a purely objective one, which makes reference only to a "reasonable director," or should it depend on the personal qualifications of a particular director? The common law has vacillated on this point. Courts typically have imposed one unitary standard of care. *See e.g.* Barnes v. Andrews, 298 F. 614 (2d Cir. 1924) (an inactive director must "inform himself of what was going on with some particularity"): Gamble v. Brown, 29 F.2d 366 (4th Cir. 1928) (aged and infirm director held liable); McDonnell v. American Leduc Petroleums, Limited, 491 F.2d 380 (2d Cir. 1974) (president and director who "had little business experience" and maintained "passive role" held liable to the extent that the corporation was damaged by conduct of others about which she knew or should have known by examining the corporation's books). Compare Anderson v. Akers, 7 F.Supp. 924 (W.D.Ky.1934) (director of "unsound mind" held not liable) aff'd in part and rev'd in part, 86 F.2d 518 (6th Cir. 1936), rev'd in part per curiam, 302 U.S. 643, 58 S.Ct. 53, 82 L.Ed. 500 (1937); Harman v. Willbern, 374 F.Supp. 1149 (D.Kan.1974) (director, who sold his shares and remained on the board "in name only" and who relied on the corporation's officers, while the corporation was looted, held not liable). Differing standards of care may be difficult to reconcile with the joint and several liability of directors for actionable negligence.

The trial court's opinion in Francis v. United Jersey Bank, 162 N.J. Super. 355, 392 A.2d 1233 contains the following passage:

> It has been urged in this case that Mrs. Pritchard should not be held responsible for what happened while she was a director of Pritchard & Baird because she was a simple housewife who served as a director as an accommodation to her husband and sons. Let me start by saying that I reject the sexism which is unintended but which is implicit in such an argument. There is no reason why the average housewife could not adequately discharge the functions of a director of a corporation such as Pritchard &

Baird, despite a lack of business career experience, if she gave some reasonable attention to what she was supposed to be doing. The problem is not that Mrs. Pritchard was a simple housewife. The problem is that she was a person who took a job which necessarily entailed certain responsibilities and she then failed to make any effort whatever to discharge those responsibilities. The ultimate insult to the fundamental dignity and equality of women would be to treat a grown woman as though she were a child not responsible for her acts and omissions.

It has been argued that allowance should be made for the fact that during the last years in question Mrs. Pritchard was old, was grief-stricken at the loss of her husband, sometimes consumed too much alcohol and was psychologically overborne by her sons. I was not impressed by the testimony supporting that argument. There is no proof whatever that Mrs. Pritchard ever ceased to be fully competent. There is no proof that she ever made any effort as a director to question or stop the unlawful activities of Charles, Jr. and William. The actions of the sons were so blatantly wrongful that it is hard to see how they could have resisted any moderately firm objection to what they were doing. The fact is that Mrs. Pritchard never knew what they were doing because she never made the slightest effort to discharge any of her responsibilities as a director of Pritchard & Baird.

c.   Reliance on Experts and Committees

Directors—in particular outside directors, who are necessarily more remote from the conduct of the everyday affairs of a corporation—must rely in making decisions on a variety of others to provide them with information and recommendations. Most notably they are largely at the mercy of the chief executive officer for their source of information, both routine and particular to especially important transactions on which they are asked to pass. It is quite obviously sound policy that they should in general be entitled to rely on that information as both accurate and complete. *See* Bates v. Dresser, 251 U.S. 524, 40 S.Ct. 247, 64 L.Ed. 388 (1920). But even here, there are probably limits. Reports to the board may contain on their face sufficient warning of their own inadequacy to put a reasonable director on notice that better information should be demanded. And reports prepared by or under the supervision of corporate employees who have a personal interest in the outcome of the decision on which they bear may require closer than usual scrutiny. *See* Gallin v. National City Bank, 155 Misc. 880, 281 N.Y.S. 795 (1935) (directors liable for excess payments made pursuant to bonus plan after relying on false figures prepared under supervision of beneficiaries of plan).

Directors must also frequently rely on opinions provided by attorneys, accountants, engineers, financial specialists, and other expert advisors. Here again the general rule is that such reliance is justified and protects directors who relied in good faith on such advice against liability if the advice turns out to be poor. In Gilbert v. Burnside, 216 N.Y.S.2d 430, 13 A.D.2d 982 (1961), aff'd 11 N.Y.2d 960, 229 N.Y.S.2d 10, 183 N.E.2d 325 (1962), for example, a shareholder brought a derivative suit seeking reimbursement by the directors of money expended by the corporation preparatory to an acquisition that was ultimately declared illegal in Farris v. Glen Alden Corp., 393 Pa. 427, 143 A.2d 25 (1958) (which we will take up in Chapter 20 of these materials). The trial court held for the plaintiff. In reversing that decision the Appellate Division said, "The judgment below determines, in effect, that these financiers (the Glen Alden directors) knew, or should have known, more Pennsylvania law than eminent Pennsylvania counsel." *See also* Spirt v. Bechtel, 232 F.2d 241 (2d Cir. 1956).

Consider the attempt at codification of the "somewhat diffuse common law standard" (American Bar Association, Corporate Director's Guidebook, 32 Bus.Law. 5, 16 (1976)) contained in Section 35 of the MBCA. Is the total insulation from liability in the circumstances described a satisfactory resolution of the problem? Does the language permit (or encourage) abdication of directorial responsibility? See also the last paragraph of MBCA § 42.

Increasingly greater emphasis has been placed in recent years on the role of committees in the operation of the board. The SEC, the New York Stock Exchange, and a large number of commentators have suggested that corporations at least have an audit committee, and perhaps certain others such as compensation and nominating committees. The New York Stock Exchange now requires that listed companies have independent audit committees. N.Y. Stock Exchange Rule 2495 H. To what extent can the directors delegate critical functions to such committees, and what amount of supervision or oversight of their work should be required? *See* Hahn & Manzoni, The Monitoring Committee and Outside Directors' Evolving Duty of Care, 9 Loyola University L.J. 585 (1979).

d. Current Trends

Although we have come a long way from the days when the Marquis of Bute could become a bank president at the tender age of six months, In re Cardiff Savings Bank, [1892] 2 Ch. 100, the standard of care suggested by the leading cases still appears to be a rather low one. The conventional view seems to be that conduct that approaches gross negligence, or at least falls below "mere" negligence, is required before liability will be imposed. The law to be found in the cases, however, may not present an altogether accurate picture of the way the law is today functioning in practice.

As one experienced corporate attorney put it, "I agree * * * that the number of adjudicated cases in which directors have been held liable for mere negligence is relatively small * * *. But I respectfully submit that the number of decided cases does not really tell the whole story. So far as I know, we have no reliable information concerning the number of shareholders' derivative suits against directors, based upon alleged negligence, which have been brought and subsequently settled out of court." Cary & Harris, Standards of Conduct Under Common Law, Present Day Statutes and the Model Act, 27 Bus.Law. (Special Ed. Feb.1972) 61 (remarks of Sam Harris). In short, regardless of how the standard of care has been applied in the principal reported cases, whether a particular pattern of directorial behavior was "negligent" is ultimately a question of fact. There are substantial indications that corporate directors and officers—and their attorneys—are more and more coming to *perceive* that the standard of care is, in practice, a great deal higher than it has conventionally been thought to be.

One contributing factor, at least where there is the possibility of an action in federal court, may be the Supreme Court's decision in Ross v. Bernhard, 396 U.S. 531, 90 S.Ct. 733, 24 L.Ed.2d 729 (1970), that the plaintiff in a stockholder's derivative suit is entitled to a jury trial as to questions of fact with respect to which the corporation would have been so entitled had it brought the suit.

The law of directors' and officers' duty of care was, until recently, largely developed by state courts. Often referring to the difficulties of attracting and retaining competent directors and officers, and perhaps caught up to some extent in Professor Cary's "race to the bottom", they have tended to be relatively solicitous toward corporate managers. In recent years, however, the federal courts have begun to develop, under the federal securities laws, rather different notions of the proper role of corporate fiduciaries. One of the earlier cases in which this tendency was manifested was Escott v. BarChris Construction Corp., 283 F.Supp. 643 (S.D.N.Y.1968), aff'd 416 F.2d 1189 (2d Cir. 1969), which we have already discussed. The general consensus about that case seems to be that "due diligence" under the Securities Act of 1933 was, as interpreted by the *BarChris* court, a good deal stricter than its common law cousin, the duty of care.

In Gould v. American-Hawaiian Steamship Co., 535 F.2d 761 (3d Cir. 1976), a case arising under the '34 Act, the Court of Appeals affirmed a decision holding an outside director liable for failing to prevent the issuance of a misleading proxy statement in connection with a merger. His failure to take action violated the duty of care he owed to the stockholders, the court held, a duty *implied* from the simple prohibition in the SEC's Rule 14a–9 against fraudulent proxy solicitations. Here again, it seems unlikely that a state court, at least not one applying the traditional common law standard, would have found the director to have acted in violation of his duties.

It remains to be seen to what extent the emerging standard of care applicable to directors under the federal securities laws will affect the future development of the state law duty.

3. PASSIVE NEGLIGENCE

There is an obvious conceptual distinction, occasionally recognized explicitly by the courts, between breach of the duty of care by misfeasance and by nonfeasance—between the active negligence and the passive negligence of simple inattention to the obligations that come with being a director. In the misfeasance cases it might be said that the general reluctance to hold directors liable for financial losses arising from their decisions is closely related to the policy underlying the business judgment rule. In the second variety of case, however, the problem is that no business judgment has been exercised. Here one has to look for other reasons to justify a similar tendency to treat directors rather gently.

GRAHAM v. ALLIS-CHALMERS MANUFACTURING CO.

41 Del.Ch. 78, 188 A.2d 125 (1963).

WOLCOTT, Justice.

This is a derivative action on behalf of Allis-Chalmers against its directors and four of its non-director employees. The complaint is based upon indictments of Allis-Chalmers and the four non-director employees named as defendants herein who, with the corporation, entered pleas of guilty to the indictments. The indictments, eight in number, charged violations of the Federal anti-trust laws. The suit seeks to recover damages which Allis-Chalmers is claimed to have suffered by reason of these violations.

The directors of Allis-Chalmers appeared in the cause voluntarily. The non-director defendants have neither appeared in the cause nor been served with process. Three of the non-director defendants are still employed by Allis-Chalmers. The fourth is under contract with it as a consultant.

The complaint alleges actual knowledge on the part of the director defendants of the anti-trust conduct upon which the indictments were based or, in the alternative, knowledge of facts which should have put them on notice of such conduct.

However, the hearing and depositions produced no evidence that any director had any actual knowledge of the anti-trust activity, or had actual knowledge of any facts which should have put them on notice that anti-trust activity was being carried on by some of their company's employees. The plaintiffs, appellants here, thereupon shifted the theory of the case to the proposition that the directors are liable as a matter of law by reason of their failure to take action designed to learn of and prevent anti-trust activity on the part of any employees of Allis-Chalmers.

By this appeal the plaintiffs seek to have us reverse the Vice Chancellor's ruling of non-liability of the defendant directors upon this theory, and also seek reversal of certain interlocutory rulings of the Vice Chancellor refusing to compel pre-trial production of documents, and refusing to compel the four non-director defendants to testify on oral depositions. We will in this opinion pass upon all the questions raised, but, as a preliminary, a summarized statement of the facts of the cause is required in order to fully understand the issues.

Allis-Chalmers is a manufacturer of a variety of electrical equipment. It employs in excess of 31,000 people, has a total of 24 plants, 145 sales offices, 5000 dealers and distributors, and its sales volume is in excess of $500,000,000 annually. The operations of the company are conducted by two groups, each of which is under the direction of a senior vice president. One of these groups is the Industries Group under the direction of Singleton, director defendant. This group is divided into five divisions. One of these, the Power Equipment Division, produced the products, the sale of which involved the anti-trust activities referred to in the indictments. The Power Equipment Division, presided over by McMullen, non-director defendant, contains ten departments, each of which is presided over by a manager or general manager.

The operating policy of Allis-Chalmers is to decentralize by the delegation of authority to the lowest possible management level capable of fulfilling the delegated responsibility. Thus, prices of products are ordinarily set by the particular department manager, except that if the product being priced is large and special, the department manager might confer with the general manager of the division. Products of a standard character involving repetitive manufacturing processes are sold out of a price list which is established by a price leader for the electrical equipment industry as a whole.

Annually, the Board of Directors reviews group and departmental profit goal budgets. On occasion, the Board considers general questions concerning price levels, but because of the complexity of the company's operations the Board does not participate in decisions fixing the prices of specific products.

The Board of Directors of fourteen members, four of whom are officers, meets once a month, October excepted, and considers a previously prepared agenda for the meeting. Supplied to the Directors at the meetings are financial and operating data relating to all phases of the company's activities. The Board meetings are customarily of several hours duration in which all the Directors participate actively. Apparently, the Board considers and decides matters concerning the general business policy of the company. By reason of the extent and complexity of the company's operations, it is not practicable for the Board to consider in detail specific problems of the various divisions.

The indictments to which Allis-Chalmers and the four non-director defendants pled guilty charge that the company and individual non-director defendants, commencing in 1956, conspired with other manufacturers and their employees to fix prices and to rig bids to private electric utilities and governmental agencies in violation of the anti-trust laws of the United States. None of the director defendants in this cause were named as defendants in the indictments. Indeed, the Federal Government acknowledged that it had uncovered no probative evidence which could lead to the conviction of the defendant directors.

The first actual knowledge the directors had of anti-trust violations by some of the company's employees was in the summer of 1959 from newspaper stories that TVA proposed an investigation of identical bids. Singleton, in charge of the Industries Group of the company, investigated but unearthed nothing. Thereafter, in November of 1959, some of the company's employees were subpoenaed before the Grand Jury. Further investigation by the company's Legal Division gave reason to suspect the illegal activity and all of the subpoenaed employees were instructed to tell the whole truth.

Thereafter, on February 8, 1960, at the direction of the Board, a policy statement relating to anti-trust problems was issued, and the Legal Division commenced a series of meetings with all employees of the company in possible areas of anti-trust activity. The purpose and effect of these steps was to eliminate any possibility of further and future violations of the anti-trust laws.

As we have pointed out, there is no evidence in the record that the defendant directors had actual knowledge of the illegal anti-trust actions of the company's employees. Plaintiffs, however, point to two FTC decrees of 1937 as warning to the directors that anti-trust activity by the company's employees had taken place in the past. It is argued that they were thus put on notice of their duty to ferret out such activity and to take active steps to insure that it would not be repeated.

The decrees in question were consent decrees entered in 1937 against Allis-Chalmers and nine others enjoining agreements to fix uniform prices on condensors and turbine generators. The decrees recited that they were consented to for the sole purpose of avoiding the trouble and expense of the proceeding.

None of the director defendants were directors or officers of Allis-Chalmers in 1937. The director defendants and now officers of the company either were employed in very subordinate capacities or had no connection with the company in 1937. At the time, copies of the decrees were circulated to the heads of concerned departments and were explained to the Managers Committee.

In 1943, Singleton, officer and director defendant, first learned of the decrees upon becoming Assistant Manager of the Steam Turbine Department, and consulted the company's General Counsel as to them. He investigated his department and learned the decrees were being complied with and, in any event, he concluded that the company had not in the first place been guilty of the practice enjoined.

Stevenson, officer and director defendant, first learned of the decrees in 1951 in a conversation with Singleton about their respective areas of the company's operations. He satisfied himself that the company was not then and in fact had not been guilty of quoting uniform prices and had consented to the decrees in order to avoid the expense and vexation of the proceeding.

Scholl, officer and director defendant, learned of the decrees in 1956 in a discussion with Singleton on matters affecting the Industries Group. He was informed that no similar problem was then in existence in the company.

Plaintiffs argue that because of the 1937 consent decrees, the directors were put on notice that they should take steps to ensure that no employee of Allis-Chalmers would violate the anti-trust laws. The difficulty the argument has is that only three of the present directors knew of the decrees, and all three of them satisfied themselves that Allis-Chalmers had not engaged in the practice enjoined and had consented to the decrees merely to avoid expense and the necessity of defending the company's position. Under the circumstances, we think knowledge by three of the directors that in 1937 the company had consented to the entry of decrees enjoining it from doing something they had satisfied themselves it had never done, did not put the Board on notice of the possibility of future illegal price fixing.

Plaintiffs have wholly failed to establish either actual notice or imputed notice to the Board of Directors of facts which should have put them on guard, and have caused them to take steps to prevent the future possibility of illegal price fixing and bid rigging. Plaintiffs say that as a minimum in this respect the Board should have taken the steps it took in 1960 when knowledge of the facts first actually came to their attention as a result of the Grand Jury investigation. Whatever duty, however, there was upon the Board to take such steps, the fact of the 1937 decrees has no bearing upon the question, for under the circumstances they were [put on] notice of nothing.

Plaintiffs are thus forced to rely solely upon the legal proposition advanced by them that directors of a corporation, as a matter of law, are liable for losses suffered by their corporations by reason of their gross inattention to the common law duty of actively supervising and managing the corporate affairs. Plaintiffs rely mainly upon Briggs v. Spaulding, 141 U.S. 132, 11 S.Ct. 924, 35 L.Ed. 662.

From the Briggs case and others * * * it appears that directors of a corporation in managing the corporate affairs are bound to use that amount of care which ordinarily careful and prudent men would use in similar circumstances. Their duties are those of control, and whether or not by neglect they have made themselves liable for failure to exercise proper control depends on the circumstances and facts of the particular case.

The precise charge made against these director defendants is that, even though they had no knowledge of any suspicion of wrongdoing on the part of the company's employees, they still should have put into effect a system of watchfulness which would have brought such misconduct to their attention in ample time to have brought it to an end. However, the Briggs case expressly rejects such an idea. On the contrary, it appears that directors are entitled to rely on the honesty and integrity of their subordinates until something occurs to put them on suspicion that something is wrong. If such occurs and goes unheeded, then liability of the directors might well follow, but absent cause for suspicion there is no duty upon the directors to install and operate a corporate system of espionage to ferret out wrongdoing which they have no reason to suspect exists.

The duties of the Allis-Chalmers Directors were fixed by the nature of the enterprise which employed in excess of 30,000 persons, and extended over a large geographical area. By force of necessity, the company's Directors could not know personally all the company's employees. The very magnitude of the enterprise required them to confine their control to the broad policy decisions. That they did this is clear from the record. At the meetings of the Board in which all Directors participated, these questions were considered and decided on the basis of summaries, reports and corporate records. These they were entitled to rely on, not only, we think, under general principles of the common law, but by reason of 8 Del.C. § 141(f) as well, which in terms fully protects a director who relies on such in the performance of his duties.

In the last analysis, the question of whether a corporate director has become liable for losses to the corporation through neglect of duty is determined by the circumstances. If he has recklessly reposed confidence in an obviously untrustworthy employee, has refused or neglected cavalierly to perform his duty as a director, or has ignored either willfully or through inattention obvious danger signs of employee wrongdoing, the law will cast the burden of liability upon him. This is not the case at bar, however, for as soon as it became evident that there were grounds for suspicion, the Board acted promptly to end it and prevent its recurrence.

Plaintiffs say these steps should have been taken long before, even in the absence of suspicion, but we think not, for we know of no rule of law which requires a corporate director to assume, with no justification whatsoever, that all corporate employees are incipient law violators who, but for a tight checkrein, will give free vent to their unlawful propensities.

We therefore affirm the Vice Chancellor's ruling that the individual director defendants are not liable as a matter of law merely because, unknown to them, some employees of Allis-Chalmers violated the anti-trust laws thus subjecting the corporation to loss.

* * *

The judgment of the court below is affirmed.

NOTES AND QUESTIONS

1. This case grew out of the heavy electrical equipment price fixing conspiracy, one of the first instances in which executives of major corporations received jail terms for violations of the antitrust laws. For discussions of those events see J. Brooks, Business Adventures, ch. 7 (1969); Smith, The Incredible Electrical Conspiracy, Fortune (April 1961) at 132, (May 1961) at 161. Notwithstanding the evidence given in the criminal cases and similar evidence in *Graham* that subordinate employees had concealed their illegal behavior from their supervisors, there was a good deal of skepticism in the press and in Congress that the higher-ups were, in fact, innocent of all knowledge of what was going on.

2. In fully understanding *Graham*, it may help to draw an organization chart of the company, locating the individual defendants within it. What is your evaluation of the plausibility of their claims of ignorance?

3. There was some indication that the decentralization of Allis-Chalmers discussed by the courts was accompanied by severe pressures on the heads of the various organizational units to show steadily increasing profits for the segment of the organization for which they were responsible. These pressures were apparently independent of the conditions in the particular markets in which the organizational unit operated; and it is obviously quite difficult to increase profits at a time of stagnant or declining demand. If this description of the mode of management in use at Allis-Chalmers is correct, was the court too quick to say that it is not necessary for a board of directors to establish "a corporate system of espionage"?

4. The Foreign Corrupt Practices Act of 1977 makes it a crime for U.S. businesses to make use of the mails or facilities of interstate commerce "corruptly" to offer or give anything of value to any "foreign official" to influence any act in his official capacity or inducing him to use his influence with a foreign government in order to assist the firm "in obtaining or retaining business." It also prohibits giving or paying anything to any other person "while knowing or having reason to know" that a part of the gift or payment will be used for such a purpose. Violations of these provisions are punishable by fines of up to $1 million for a corporation and up to $10,000 and five years imprisonment for any officer, director, stockholder or agent of the corporation found guilty of a willful violation. Compliance with the Act has been a matter of some concern to corporations doing business overseas. Consider the following views of a practicing attorney, presented during a panel discussion, as to what is necessary to prevent a violation. Every indication is that his views are widely-

shared and that, consequently, most affected corporations are doing something along the lines he suggests.

"I believe a corporate compliance program should be adopted by SEC reporting companies and by all companies operating in the foreign area. The key element of a good corporate compliance program is a corporate code of conduct. Such a code should cover matters both within and without the scope of the Foreign Corrupt Practices Act * * *. Indeed, it should extend beyond the subjects discussed here, to such areas as antitrust and trade regulation.

"A well-drafted code should provide a specific mechanism for employees to report violations to a senior officer of the company or perhaps directly to the internal audit group. Without such a mechanism, an employee is likely to be reluctant to report violations to persons above his supervisor. This reluctance could create obvious problems if the supervisor is involved in the violations or should have known about them in the proper exercise of his duties.

"A principal purpose of a code is to educate employees. If a company has a lengthy and complicated code of conduct, management should seriously consider coupling the dissemination of the code with a seminar program designed to assure that the code is truly understood by the company's managers and other affected employees. Such seminars are already a part of the compliance programs of many companies.

"It is extremely important that compliance with the code be monitored. In my opinion, an issuer with a code that is not enforced is probably in a worse position than an issuer with no code at all. One common feature of monitoring programs is the requirement that employees and agents certify annually that they have complied with the code and, in some cases, that they are not aware of violations by others in the company. Effective monitoring also requires spot checks by internal auditors.

"The type and scope of a preventive program for a company necessarily will depend on its particular business and operations. What is appropriate for one company may not be for another. But some form of corporate compliance program clearly setting forth the business rules which the board of directors expects management and other employees to observe is appropriate for all SEC reporting companies and non-reporting companies with foreign operations." Weiss, Foreign Corrupt Practices Act of 1977: The Anti-Bribery Provisions, in Practising Law Institute, Tenth Annual Institute on Securities Regulation, 71, 81–82 (A. Fleischer, M. Lipton, & R. Stevenson eds. 1979).

Would a court find the officers and directors of a company that failed to adopt something like the compliance mechanism sketched in the foregoing advice guilty of a breach of the duty of care if a foreign branch manager paid a bribe to a government official to get business, and the company was subsequently fined a substantial sum for violation of the Act?

5. What should be the relationship between the duty of care under state corporation law and the standard for criminal liability of corporate managers as a result of failures of supervision leading to unintentional violation by a corporation of a criminal statute? In United States v. Park, 421 U.S. 658, 95 S.Ct. 1903, 44 L.Ed.2d 489 (1975), the president of Acme Markets, Inc. was charged, along with his company, with five violations of the Federal Food, Drug, and Cosmetics Act in allowing food to be held in a company warehouse where it was exposed to contamination by rodents. The company pleaded guilty, but Park pleaded innocent and was tried before a jury, which convicted him. He was fined $50 on each of the five counts.

The Supreme Court described his testimony at the trial as follows:

"Respondent was the only defense witness. He testified that, although all of Acme's employees were in a sense under his general direction, the company has an 'organizational structure for responsibilities for certain functions' according to which different phases of its operation were 'assigned to individuals who, in turn, have staff and departments under them.' He identified those individuals responsible for sanitation and related that upon receipt of the January 1972 FDA letter, he had conferred with the vice president for legal affairs, who informed him that the Baltimore division vice president 'was investigating the situation immediately and would be taking corrective action and would be preparing a summary of the corrective action to reply to the letter.' Respondent stated that he did not 'believe there was anything [he] could have done more constructively than what [he] found was being done.' "

* * *

Park's conviction was ultimately affirmed by the Supreme Court in an opinion by Chief Justice Burger, who observed:

"[In] providing sanctions which reach and touch the individuals who execute the corporate mission—and this is by no means necessarily confined to a single corporate agent or employee—the Act imposes not only a positive duty to seek out and remedy violations when they occur but also, and primarily, a duty to implement measures that will insure that violations will not occur. The requirements of foresight and vigilance imposed on responsible corporate agents are beyond question demanding, and perhaps onerous, but they are no more stringent than the public has a right to expect of those who voluntarily assume positions of authority in business enterprises whose services and products affect the health and wellbeing of the public that supports them."

4. THE BUSINESS JUDGMENT RULE

GIMBEL v. THE SIGNAL COMPANIES, INC.

316 A.2d 599 (Del.Ch.1974).

[The facts of this case were set forth in Chapter 10, Part E. In brief, the case involves a shareholder objection to the sale by Signal of a wholly owned subsidiary representing about one-quarter of its assets for approximately $480 million in cash.]

I turn now to the second and more difficult question presented on this application for a preliminary injunction.

The plaintiff attacks the proposed transaction on the grounds that the 480 million dollar sale price is wholly inadequate compensation for the assets of Signal Oil.

In evaluating the merits of this allegation, precedent requires the Court to start from the normal presumption that Signal's Board of Directors acted in good faith in approving the sale of Signal Oil to Burmah. Chancellor Josiah Wolcott spoke thusly of this good faith presumption:

> * * * [T]he directors of the defendant [selling] corporation are clothed with that presumption which the law accords to them of being actuated in their conduct by a *bona fide* regard for the interests of the corporation whose affairs the stockholders have committed to their charge. This being so, the sale in question must be examined with the presumption in its favor that the directors who negotiated it honestly believed that they were securing terms and conditions which were expedient and for the corporation's best interests.

Robinson v. Pittsburgh Oil Ref. Corp., 14 Del.Ch. 193, 199, 126 A. 46, 48 (Ch.1924).

This presumption, an important aspect of what has generally come to be known as the "business judgment rule," has been consistently reaffirmed and broadened with respect to the sale of corporate assets over the past several decades. Application of the rule, of necessity, depends upon a showing that informed directors did, in fact, make a business judgment authorizing the transaction under review.

Although not dealing specifically with the sale of a substantial corporate asset, Chief Justice Daniel F. Wolcott recently recognized the strength of the presumption inherent in this rule:

> A board of directors enjoys a presumption of sound business judgment, and its decisions will not be disturbed if they can be attributed to any rational business purpose. A court under such circumstances will not substitute its own notions of what is or is not sound business judgment.

Sinclair Oil Corporation v. Levien, Del.Supr., 280 A.2d 717, 720 (1971). Quite recently, Vice Chancellor Brown also applied the business judgment rule when called upon to enjoin a large scale corporate merger. Muschel v. Western Union Corporation, Del.Ch., 310 A.2d 904, 908 (1973).

This does not mean, however, that the business judgment rule irrevocably shields the decisions of corporate directors from challenge. As Vice Chancellor Marvel explained in Marks v. Wolfson, the business judgment rule weighs in favor of the directors' decision to sell assets unless the complaining shareholders can prove fraud or a clearly inadequate sale price:

> In other words, it [is] incumbent on plaintiffs to prove that the defendants against whom relief is sought were either guilty of actual fraud or that the price fixed for the sale of Highway's assets was so clearly inadequate as constructively to carry the badge of fraud.

41 Del.Ch. 115, 123, 188 A.2d 680, 685 (Ch.1963).

In challenging the sale of Signal Oil to Burmah, the plaintiff here does not seriously charge that the proposed transaction constitutes fraudulent self-dealing on the part of Signal's Board of Directors. * * * At this stage, the Court can find no indication of self-dealing on the part of the Board of Directors such as would taint the proposed transaction or neutralize the effect of the business judgment rule. And, therefore, * * * that the usual presumption of director good faith ought not apply, must fail. * * *

Actual fraud, whether resulting from self-dealing or otherwise, is not necessary to challenge a sale of assets. And, although the language of "constructive fraud" or "badge of fraud" has frequently and almost traditionally been used, such language is not very helpful when fraud admittedly has not been established. There are limits on the business judgment rule which fall short of intentional or inferred fraudulent misconduct and which are based simply on gross inadequacy of price. This is clear even if language of fraud is used. The principles are familar and should start with the directors' discretion and the limits thereof when dealing with price under the business judgment rule:

> When the question is asked whether in a given case the price is adequate, it is readily seen that room is afforded for honest differences of opinion. While the parties to the controversy may be guilty of an intolerance of view towards each other, yet a court, when called upon to decide the question, must endeavor, as best it may, to arrive at the correct answer, making all due allowance for the range over which honestly inclined minds may wander. It is further true that inadequacy of price will not suffice to condemn the transaction as fraudulent, unless the inadequacy is so gross as to display itself as a badge of fraud. I take it that so long as the inadequacy of price may reasonably be referred to an honest exercise of sound judgment, it cannot be denominated as fraudulent.

When the price proposed to be accepted is so far below what is found to be a fair one that it can be explained only on the theory of fraud, or a reckless indifference to the rights of others interested, it would seem that it should not be allowed to stand.

Allied Chemical & Dye Corporation v. Steel & Tube Co., 14 Del.Ch. 1, 19, 120 A. 486, 494 (Ch.1923).

[F]airness or unfairness of the price * * * must be judged in the light of the conditions as they existed at the time of the execution of the contract.

Allied Chemical & Dye Corp. v. Steel & Tube Co., *supra*, 14 Del.Ch. 64, at 95, 122 A. 142, at 155.

It is not every disparity between price and value that will be allowed to upset a proposed sale. The disparity must be sufficiently great to indicate that it arises not so much from an honest mistake in judgment concerning the value of the assets, as from either improper motives underlying the judgment of those in whom the right to judge is vested or a reckless indifference to or a deliberate disregard of the interests of the whole body of stockholders including of course the minority.

Allaun v. Consolidated Oil Co., supra, 16 Del.Ch. at 325, 147 A. at 264 (Ch.1929).

One recognized test on the directors' business judgment is the free marketplace. In Marks v. Wolfson, Vice Chancellor Marvel employed "the classic test imposed in the early Delaware cases" in reaching his conclusion that the sale price established for corporate assets satisfied the law:

In actual point of fact the evidence sustains a finding, in my opinion, that the bargaining which resulted in the sale here in issue took place between a willing buyer who was not required to buy and a willing seller under no real compulsion to sell and that such bargaining was genuine and motivated by self-interest on the part of those on opposite sides of the bargaining table.

41 Del.Ch. at 124, 125, 188 A.2d at 686 (Ch.1963).

* * *

Keeping in mind this guidance and other similar precedent on valuation and director responsibility to obtain a fair price for corporate assets, the Court will now consider those allegations whereby the plaintiff seeks to hurdle the protections of the business judgment rule and successfully challenge the sale of Signal Oil. The question is: did the Signal directors act recklessly in accepting a wholly inadequate price for Signal Oil?

Factually, to support his claim of recklessness, the plaintiff basically relies on three related factors: the alleged gross inadequacy of price; the failure of the Board of Directors to act on such an important matter with informed reasonable deliberation; and specifically the failure of the Board of Directors to obtain an updated appraisal of Signal Oil's properties before agreeing to accept Burmah's offer. Except for the key question of value, there is not significant dispute over the factual chronology.

Prior to Burmah's first contact relating to this agreement, which was on October 17, 1973, Signal had been negotiating a proposed merger with United Aircraft. The deal fell through in September 1973. In connection with that transaction, a report was drafted by DeGolyer and MacNaughton, a prominent independent firm of petroleum geologists. The report valued Signal Oil's reserves as of June 30, 1973 at an approximate figure between 230 and 260 million dollars. There were other accounting reports prepared by Price Waterhouse and Company in connection with the proposed merger. In addition, Signal requested Kenneth E. Hill, an expert in the evaluation of oil properties, to undertake an evaluation of the petroleum properties of Signal Oil. Mr. Hill had done so and, as of September 13, 1973, his opinion of the fair market value of the oil properties was $350,000,000.

On October 17, 1973, in Houston, Texas, Max Roberts and Clifford Andrews, representatives of Burmah, approached Willis H. Thompson, President and Chief Executive Officer of Signal Oil, about the possibility of Burmah acquiring some or all of Signal Oil's properties. Thompson referred them to Forrest N. Shumway, the President and Chief Executive Officer of Signal and on October 24, 1973, there was a meeting in Los Angeles. At that time, N.J.D. Williams, Chief Executive Officer of Burmah Oil Co. Ltd., the British parent of Burmah, indicated that Burmah was interested in acquiring the assets of Signal Oil in a range of $400,000,000. Shumway said that any offer in excess of $400,000,000 would be submitted to the Board of Directors.

There followed an exchange of information including the DeGolyer and MacNaughton report and the accounting reports of Price Waterhouse. Negotiations continued through November, including extensive drafting sessions with Burmah's attorneys. The matter was not put before Signal's Board of Directors at the November 27, 1973 meeting although the Board was advised generally that management had other inquiries about subsidiaries since the United transaction fell through. A Burmah representative was invited to address a meeting of the Signal Oil Board, at which was discussed Burmah's history, business and operating policies. By early December, a third draft of the purchase agreement had been prepared, access to confidential data had been permitted and Burmah had sent Signal a draft of a press release to announce the transaction. All this occurred during a period when there was no notification to the Board of Directors in their capacity as Board members of the developments. An attorney for the minority, on the basis of rumors, wrote a letter dated December 3, 1973 indicating opposition to a sale of oil and gas properties, indicating further that shareholder approval was required, and requesting consultation.

Burmah's formal offer was communicated to Signal on December 18, 1973. The offer required acceptance on or before December 21, 1973. A special meeting of the Board of Directors of Signal was called for December 21. This meeting was called on notice of only a day and a half and the outside directors were not notified of the purpose of the meeting. At least three of the outside directors were confronted with the proposed sale for the first time at the special meeting itself. Plaintiff learned of the proposed sale when it was reported in the press on Saturday, December 22, 1973.

At the meeting, a handwritten outline of the transaction was submitted to the directors and an oral presentation was made in support of the transaction. There was no updated evaluation of the oil and gas reserves of Signal Oil presented. There was no effort made at that time to determine if other companies would offer a higher price. The meeting lasted a couple of hours and resulted in the approval of a transaction of over $480,000,000 and possibly one of the largest private cash sales ever to take place.

It is important to note what was discussed at the special Board of Director's meeting on December 21. * * * It is also important to note that the discussion took place with the background of aborted United negotiations and other inquiries. It appears that there was some review of the per share value of Signal stock and it was determined that, as of the market closing on December 20, the total market value of Signal stock was estimated at 440 million dollars. The terms of the contract were reviewed with an overall analysis of the tax consequences. There was discussion of the use of the proceeds to be gained from the sale of Signal Oil and, in particular, the advantage of pre-paying certain indebtedness, the advantage from increased interest income, and the needs of the other subsidiaries, which were giving a greater return. There was discussion of sales, income, cash flow, the balance sheet and the general financial status of the corporation. The current situation in the oil industry was discussed including the impact on price and profit and the potential for additional oil finds. Oil reserve values received substantial discussion. Price increases were contemplated. The risk of price controls and the limitations that could come from allocations and excess profit taxes were reviewed. Capital expenditure requirements of Signal Oil were reviewed and, particularly, the risk factor in the North Sea investment. The advantage of the Signal Oil investment was compared with the advantage of having the cash on hand. The advisability of waiting for a higher price was discussed. The Burmah offer was the best suggested price of any discussions with potential buyers and Burmah could pay it. In summary, while the meeting was short for a transaction of this size, there was an overall view of the situation, generally within the confines of the material the company already had available.

* * *

But having given full weight to the legitimate considerations of the Board, it is necessary, at the risk of repetition, to pinpoint elements which suggest imprudence. The circumstances are such as to raise the question as to whether the Signal Board, when the sale of Signal Oil stock was presented, were able to perform their fiduciary obligation as directors to make an informed judgment of approving the transaction. In particular, it is difficult to ignore the following facts.

The transaction had been in progress since October. I am satisfied that management decided early in the game, and probably in October, that the offer, when made, would be recommended to the Board. Certainly by early December the only reasonable assumption was that management would recommend the transaction to the Board.

To highlight the fact that management did not bring the proposed transaction to the attention of the Signal Board, it should be noted that in early December management did bring the transaction to the attention of the Signal Oil Board, evidently because personnel at Signal Oil were somewhat restless about the investigation being conducted by the Burmah people. But the point is management was ready to go out of its way of relieving anxiety in the subsidiary that was being transferred and yet made no advance effort to educate the directors whose responsibility it was to approve the transaction. The point is aggravated by the fact that there was a regular board meeting with one hundred per cent attendance on November 27, 1973.[9]

Even granting that management had prior legal difficulties with the minority group of which the plaintiff is a member, it is hard to overlook the fact the minority interest wrote to each board member, expressed opposition to the sale of the oil and gas interest, further stated its belief that any such transaction required shareholders' approval and further requested to be consulted. Except for obtaining an opinion of counsel to counter the legal position on the requirement of shareholder action, this request was totally ignored by management and by the Board. Such lack of consideration for a minority viewpoint of the substantial block of stock, and perhaps the largest single block of stock, gives rise to the allegation, which probably cannot be established as motivation, that management was trying to effectively freeze out a minority interest.

---

9. As early as October 24th, Burmah had indicated a price in the range of 400 million dollars, and was advised such an offer would be taken to the Board of Directors. Thompson deposition, docket number 24, p. 48. Shumway indicated the terms would be satisfactory in October.

There does not appear to be in the record any effort on the part of management to slow or seek a delay in the December 21st deadline which was imposed by the December 18th offer of Burmah. Rather the circumstances are consistent with Signal's management approval of the forced decision on a tight time schedule. It is clear that Burmah's strategy was to force a quick decision.

The decision to call a special meeting of the Board on approximately two days' notice highlights the failure of management to advise the Board in their capacity as Board members of this very important transaction. Only six directors * * * knew of the purpose of the meeting in advance. Not only was the call short but management failed to give any notice of the subject matter in advance. The question is not one of legality. The question is one of permitting the Board the opportunity to make a reasonable and reasoned decision.

There is no question that the energy crisis has created a drastic change in the value of oil and gas properties. Even granting that there may be wide divergence in expert viewpoint, the situation made desirable an updated evaluation since the Hill evaluation as of September 30 and the De Golyer and MacNaughton evaluation as of June 30. Indeed, the defendants' own expert in this proceeding, while he values Signal Oil at less than the sale price, also values Signal Oil at $60,000,000 more on December 21 than he did on September 30. Moreover, questions on fairness were naturally directed to Thompson, a director who will continue with Signal Oil after the sale to Burmah.

In addition, even though the directors knew of Signal's need for cash, there had been no precise analysis about the use of the money to be obtained from the sale. Indeed, the income projections which were presented at the director's meeting showed that income will decrease in the three years after the sale as compared with the projections prior to the sale. Even making allowance for the fact that Signal Oil has evidently failed to achieve projections, this presentation is somewhat out of the ordinary.

The factors, which suggest imprudence and perhaps some others such as the differences that Signal Oil personnel had with the De Golyer and MacNaughton report and certain potential liabilities of Signal which survive the sale, do not in my judgment raise at this stage a reasonable probability that the plaintiff will be able to pierce the "business judgment" standard. When considered in light of the whole case, they do not in themselves justify the conclusion that the "directors acted so far without information that they can be said to have passed an unintelligent and unadvised judgment." Mitchell v. Highland-Western Glass Co., *supra*, 19 Del.Ch. at 329–330, 167 A. at 833. But, and perhaps particularly on this preliminary application, the full circumstances surrounding the approval do relate to the overriding factual issue in the case. What was Signal Oil worth on December 21, 1973? Or to put the question in its legal context, did the

Signal directors act without the bounds of reason and recklessly in approving the price offer of Burmah?

Thus, the ultimate question is not one of method but one of value. The method does not appear so bad on its face as to alter the normal legal principles which control. But hasty method which produces a dollar result which appears perhaps to be shocking is significant. On the basis of affidavits relating to value,* the Court has the tentative belief that plaintiff would have a reasonable prospect of success on the merits since limited record indicates a gross disparity between the fair market value of Signal Oil on December 21, 1973 and what the Board of Directors were willing to sell the company for, namely, $480,000,000. To the extent the scale tips, on the present record, the nod is to the plaintiff.   *   *   *

*   *   *

In essence, notwithstanding the affidavits and the conflict in their content, there remains a serious question about the reasonable probability that the plaintiff will succeed in this action. Therefore, notwithstanding my tentative conclusion on reasonable probability, I am convinced that the discrepancy between the values is so great that an immediate fuller investigation into this matter of fair value should be had.   *   *   *

[The court granted a preliminary injunction restraining the sale until February 15, 1974 during which it directed a hearing on the question of the value of Signal Oil. "[M]indful of the possible injuries that may be done to the Corporation and to those shareholders which support the Board action," the court conditioned the injunction on the plaintiff's posting of a security bond in the amount of $25 million.]

NOTE—THE BUSINESS JUDGMENT RULE AND THE DUTY OF CARE

What, exactly, does Chancellor Quillen mean when he evaluates the decision of the Signal board in light of the "business judgment rule"? Is the result a reduced standard of care? Is the business judgment rule the reason for his statement, "The question is: did the Signal directors act *recklessly* in accepting a wholly inadequate price for Signal Oil?" (Emphasis supplied.) When, if ever, would a standard of ordinary care apply?

One well-known statement of the interaction between the business judgment rule and the duty of care is given in Casey v. Woodruff, 49 N.Y.S.2d 625, 643 (Sup.Ct.1944): "The question is frequently asked, how does the operation of the so-called 'business judgment rule' tie in with the concept of negligence? There is no conflict between the two. When the courts say that they will not interfere in matters of

---

* The plaintiff's expert has submitted an affidavit evaluating Signal Oil at $761 million. The defendant's expert said it was worth only $438 million.—Eds.

business judgment, it is presupposed that judgment—reasonable diligence—has in fact been exercised. A director cannot close his eyes to what is going on about him in the conduct of the business of the corporation and have it said that he is exercising business judgment. Courts have properly decided to give directors a wide latitude in the management of the affairs of a corporation provided always that judgment, and that means an honest, unbiased judgment, is reasonably exercised by them."

———

Puma v. Marriott, 283 A.2d 693 (Del.Ch.1971), involved the sale of shares of various real estate corporations to Marriott Corporation by members of the controlling family. The real estate corporations owned land that was leased to Marriott Corporation. The court applied the business judgment rule, rather than the stricter standards that govern self dealing transactions, and found in favor of the defendants. The transaction was considered only by the independent members of the board who obtained advice from outside counsel, tax advisors and accountants, and independent appraisals on each of the properties.

This careful process takes time. Was it available to the directors of Signal Oil? Must each decision be assessed in terms of its own time frame and consequences?

MILLER v. AMERICAN TELEPHONE & TELEGRAPH CO.

507 F.2d 759 (3rd Cir. 1974).

SEITZ, Chief Judge.

Plaintiffs, stockholders in American Telephone and Telegraph Company ("AT&T"), brought a stockholders' derivative action in the Eastern District of Pennsylvania against AT&T and all but one of its directors. The suit centered upon the failure of AT&T to collect an outstanding debt of some $1.5 million owed to the company by the Democratic National Committee ("DNC") for communications services provided by AT&T during the 1968 Democratic national convention. Federal diversity jurisdiction was invoked under 28 U.S.C.A. § 1332.

Plaintiffs' complaint alleged that "neither the officers or directors of AT&T have taken any action to recover the amount owed" from on or about August 20, 1968, when the debt was incurred, until May 31, 1972, the date plaintiffs' amended complaint was filed. The failure to collect was alleged to have involved a breach of the defendant directors' duty to exercise diligence in handling the affairs of the corporation, to have resulted in affording a preference to the DNC in collection procedures in violation of § 202(a) of the Communications Act of 1934, 47 U.S.C.A. § 202(a) (1970), and to have amounted to AT&T's

making a "contribution" to the DNC in violation of a federal prohibition on corporate campaign spending, 18 U.S.C.A. § 610 (1970).

* * *

On motion of the defendants, the district court dismissed the complaint for failure to state a claim upon which relief could be granted. 364 F.Supp. 648 (E.D.Pa.1973). The court stated that collection procedures were properly within the discretion of the directors whose determination would not be overturned by the court in the absence of an allegation that the conduct of the directors was "plainly illegal, unreasonable, or in breach of a fiduciary duty * * *." Id. at 651. Plaintiffs appeal from dismissal of their complaint.

* * *

I.

The pertinent law on the question of the defendant directors' fiduciary duties in this diversity action is that of New York, the state of AT&T's incorporation. The sound business judgment rule, the basis of the district court's dismissal of plaintiffs' complaint, expresses the unanimous decision of American courts to eschew intervention in corporate decision-making if the judgment of directors and officers is uninfluenced by personal considerations and is exercised in good faith. Pollitz v. Wabash Railroad Co., 207 N.Y. 113, 100 N.E. 721 (1912); Bayer v. Beran, 49 N.Y.S.2d 2, 4–7 (Sup.Ct.1944); 3 Fletcher, Private Corporations § 1039 (perm. ed. rev. vol. 1965). Underlying the rule is the assumption that reasonable diligence has been used in reaching the decision which the rule is invoked to justify. Casey v. Woodruff, 49 N.Y.S.2d 625, 643 (Sup.Ct.1944).

Had plaintiffs' complaint alleged only failure to pursue a corporate claim, application of the sound business judgment rule would support the district court's ruling that a shareholder could not attack the directors' decision. Where, however, the decision not to collect a debt owed the corporation is itself alleged to have been an illegal act, different rules apply. When New York law regarding such acts by directors is considered in conjunction with the underlying purposes of the particular statute involved here, we are convinced that the business judgment rule cannot insulate the defendant directors from liability if they did in fact breach 18 U.S.C.A. § 610, as plaintiffs have charged.

Roth v. Robertson, 64 Misc. 343, 118 N.Y.S. 351 (Sup.Ct.1909), illustrates the proposition that even though committed to benefit the corporation, illegal acts may amount to a breach of fiduciary duty in New York. In *Roth*, the managing director of an amusement park company had allegedly used corporate funds to purchase the silence of persons who threatened to complain about unlawful Sunday operation of the park. Recovery from the defendant director was sustained on the ground that the money was an illegal payment:

> For reasons of public policy, we are clearly of the opinion that payments of corporate funds for such purposes as those disclosed in this case must be condemned, and officers of a corporation making them held to a strict accountability, and be compelled to refund the amounts so wasted for the benefit of stockholders. * * * To hold any other rule would be establishing a dangerous precedent, tacitly countenancing the wasting of corporate funds for purposes of corrupting public morals. Id. at 346, 118 N. Y.S. at 353.

The plaintiffs' complaint in the instant case alleges a similar "waste" of $1.5 million through an illegal campaign contribution.

Abrams v. Allen, 297 N.Y. 52, 74 N.E.2d 305 (1947), reflects an affirmation by the New York Court of Appeals of the principle of *Roth* that directors must be restrained from engaging in activities which are against public policy. In *Abrams* the court held that a cause of action was stated by an allegation in a derivative complaint that the directors of Remington Rand, Inc., had relocated corporate plants and curtailed production solely for the purpose of intimidating and punishing employees for their involvement in a labor dispute. The Court of Appeals acknowledged that, "depending on the circumstances," proof of the allegations in the complaint might sustain recovery, *inter alia*, under the rule that directors are liable for corporate loss caused by the commission of an "unlawful or immoral act." Id. at 55, 74 N.E.2d at 306. In support of its holding, the court noted that the closing of factories for the purpose alleged was opposed to the public policy of the state and nation as embodied in the New York Labor Law and the National Labor Relations Act. Id. at 56, 74 N.E. 2d at 307.

The alleged violation of the federal prohibition against corporate political contributions not only involves the corporation in criminal activity but similarly contravenes a policy of Congress clearly enunciated in 18 U.S.C.A. § 610. That statute and its predecessor reflect congressional efforts: (1) to destroy the influence of corporations over elections through financial contributions and (2) to check the practice of using corporate funds to benefit political parties without the consent of the stockholders. United States v. CIO, 335 U.S. 106, 113, 68 S.Ct. 1349, 92 L.Ed. 1849 (1948).

The fact that shareholders are within the class for whose protection the statute was enacted gives force to the argument that the alleged breach of that statute should give rise to a cause of action in those shareholders to force the return to the corporation of illegally contributed funds. Since political contributions by corporations can be checked and shareholder control over the political use of general corporate funds effectuated only if directors are restrained from causing the corporation to violate the statute, such a violation seems a particularly appropriate basis for finding breach of the defendant directors' fiduciary duty to the corporation. Under such circumstances, the directors cannot be insulated from liability on the ground that the contribution was made in the exercise of sound business judgment.

Since plaintiffs have alleged actual damage to the corporation from the transaction in the form of the loss of a $1.5 million increment to AT&T's treasury, we conclude that the complaint does state a claim upon which relief can be granted sufficient to withstand a motion to dismiss.

II.

We have accepted plaintiffs' allegation of a violation of 18 U.S.C. A. § 610 as a shorthand designation of the elements necessary to establish a breach of that statute. This is consonant with the federal practice of notice pleading. That such a designation is sufficient for pleading purposes does not, however, relieve plaintiffs of their ultimate obligation to prove the elements of the statutory violation as part of their proof of breach of fiduciary duty. At the appropriate time, plaintiffs will be required to produce evidence sufficient to establish three distinct elements comprising a violation of 18 U.S.C.A. § 610: that AT&T (1) made a contribution of money or anything of value to the DNC (2) in connection with a federal election (3) for the purpose of influencing the outcome of that election. The first two of these elements are obvious from the face of the statute; the third was supplied by legislative history prior to being made explicit by 1972 amendments to definitions applicable to § 610.

* * *

The order of the district court will be reversed and the case remanded for further proceedings consistent with this opinion.

NOTE: THE AMERICAN LAW INSTITUTE PROJECT

Tentative Draft No. 1 of the American Law Institute's Principles of Corporate Governance and Structure: Restatement and Recommendations (April 1, 1982), offers the following statement of the duty of due care and the business judgment rule:*

§ 4.01. Duty of Care of Corporate Directors and Officers; The Business Judgment Rule

Corporate law should provide that:

(a) A corporate director or officer has a duty to his corporation to perform his functions in good faith, in a manner that he reasonably believes to be in the best interests of the corporation, and with the care that an ordinarily prudent person would reasonably

* Tent.Draft No. 1, at 140–41 (April 1, 1982).

be expected to exercise in a like position and under similar circumstances.

(b) The duty of care set forth in subsection (a) encompasses the obligation of a director or officer to make reasonable inquiry when acting upon corporate transactions or otherwise performing his functions and also encompasses the obligation of a corporate director to be reasonably concerned with the existence and effectiveness of monitoring programs, including law compliance programs.

(c) The duty of care set forth in subsections (a) and (b) encompasses the obligation of a director or officer to make reasonable efforts to cause his corporation to perform its duty under § 2.01 (a)* to obey the law.

(d) A corporate director or officer shall not be subject to liability under the duty of care standards set forth in subsections (a), (b), or (c) with respect to the consequences of a business judgment if he:

> (1) informed himself and made reasonable inquiry with respect to the business judgment;

> (2) acted in good faith and without a disabling conflict of interest; and

> (3) had a rational basis for the business judgment.

Except as expressly provided to the contrary in this Statement, an action or proceeding invoking the principles set forth in subsections (a), (b), or (c), to reverse, enjoin, or modify a business decision, should fail if the corporate decisionmaker [§ 1.06]** is protected against liability by this subsection.

The following excerpt from the Introduction Note on the Duty of Care and Business Judgment elaborates on the relationship between standard of due care and the business judgment rule.

> c. *The relationship between duty of care and the business judgment rule.* As § 4.01(d) indicates, the business judgment rule accords corporate directors and officers significant legal insulation from hindsight reviews of their unsuccessful decisions. Shareholders, with expectations of greater profit, accept the risk that a business decision—honestly and rationally taken—may not be vindicated by subsequent success. The business judgment rule also provides directors and officers with a rationale for justifying their business decisions in the face of a request to a court to en-

---

* Section 2.01(a) states that corporation law should provide that corporations should conduct their business "with a view to corporate profit and shareholder gain except that, even if such profit and gain are not enhanced, the corporation is obliged, to the same extent as a natural person, to act within the boundaries set by law."

** § 1.06. Corporate Decisionmaker

"Corporate decisionmaker" means that corporate official or body with the authority to make a particular decision for the corporation.

join what they intend to do. But the "safe harbor" provided by the business judgment rule presupposes a deliberative process and an informed decision. Although there is confusion in the cases and commentaries, the sound view is that "it is presupposed in this 'business judgment rule' that reasonable diligence and care have been exercised" by a corporate decisionmaker in preparing himself to make a business judgment. H. Ballantine, *Law of Corporations* § 63a at 161 (rev.ed.1946). This concept is encompassed in § 4.01(d)'s requirement that a director or officer inform himself and make reasonable inquiry with respect to a business judgment before he is afforded the legal insulation provided by the business judgment rule. It is only this socially desirable species of business decision that the law favors with the special protection afforded by § 4.01(d)'s standard which shields from liability business judgments that have "a rational basis." If a corporate director or officer cannot meet the criteria for a business judgment set forth in § 4.01(d), then his business decision will be reviewed under the more demanding reasonable care test set forth in § 4.01(a).

(Tent.Draft No. 1, at 133–4).

Comment (a) to § 4.01 provides:

In summary, the integration of the duty of care provisions in subsections (a)–(c) of § 4.01 and the business judgment rule in subsection (d) would basically work in the following ways: If a director or officer has complied with the standards of care set forth in § 4.01(a)–(c) as to any business decision or other function, he will be free of legal liability. If a director or officer has complied with the business judgment criteria set forth in § 4.01(d) as to a deliberative decision, he will again be free of legal liability. If, however, a shareholder can sustain the burden of proving that a business decision was made by a director or officer without informing himself and making reasonable inquiry with respect to the decision, then the safe harbor provided in § 4.01(d) will not be available, and the director or officer will be found to have violated the reasonable care standard set forth in § 4.01(a). If a shareholder can sustain the burden of proving the absence of good faith or a disabling conflict of interest, then the safe harbor provided by § 4.01(d) will also not be available, and the applicable substantive standard set forth in Parts V [Duty of Loyalty] or VI [Transactions in Control] will control. Finally, if a shareholder can sustain the burden of proving that a corporate director's or officer's judgment had no rational basis, then the protection provided by § 4.01(d) will again not be available, and the director or officer will be found to have violated the reasonable care standard set forth in § 4.01(a).

(Tent.Draft No. 1, at 147)

* * *

Comment (a) to § 4.01(d) states:

The business judgment rule has often been stated as a "presumption" (with various qualifications) that directors or officers have acted properly. Confusion has been created by the numerous varying formulations of the rule and the fact that courts have often stated the rule incompletely or with elliptical shorthand references. The relatively complex formulation of the business judgment rule set forth in § 4.01(d) is needed to cover the myriad of factual contexts in which business judgment issues arise.

In reality, although courts have not expressed it this way, the business judgment rule has offered a safe harbor for informed business decisions that are honestly and rationally undertaken. The traditional fear has been that such a business decision, if it turns out to be wrong and is judged in the harsh light of hindsight, might unfairly expose directors and officers to open-ended liability under the reasonable care, "ordinary negligence," culpability standard of duty of care provisions. Such an exposure might also have seriously counterproductive effects on corporate decisionmaking.

(Tent.Draft No. 1, at 193.)

B. THE DUTY OF LOYALTY—PART I

PROBLEM

MILTON CORPORATION

Milton Corporation, a Columbia corporation (the "Corporation"), constructs, owns and operates hotels and restaurants throughout the United States. It is a public company, listed on the New York Stock Exchange, but it is controlled by the Milton family, who founded it in 1935. For the first twenty years of the company's existence, its stock was owned entirely by members of the family.

Following the public offering of stock and at the present time, public investors own 60% of the Corporation's stock; the Milton family owns the remaining 40%. The board of directors of the Corporation consists of James Milton, the president and chief executive; Samuel Milton (James' brother); Janet Milton Hayes (their sister), the chief financial officer; John Quincy, the general counsel of the Corporation; and Michael Brown, Ruth Grey and Robert White, each of whom is a prominent business executive having no other connections with the Corporation.

The Milton family owns all the stock of Realty Investors Corporation ("RIC") which was formed in 1940. The three directors of RIC are: James Milton, Samuel Milton, and Janet Milton Hayes. RIC, from the beginning of its operations, has purchased the land on which the Corporation's hotels and restaurants are situated, and then leased it on a long term basis to the Corporation. RIC also buys and sells real estate to other real estate developers. Although some of the sites selected by the Corporation for construction are on property previously acquired by RIC in independent transactions, the Corporation initiates most transactions. RIC enters the picture to acquire the land and work out the rental terms with the Corporation. The rental arrangements between RIC and the Corporation have provided for approximately the same rents that generally prevailed in the local area, as a flat fee, and also provided for a flat percentage of the Corporation's revenues from operations. In some cases, this has resulted in RIC's deriving far greater profits from some units than did the Corporation. The board of directors of the Corporation has approved each such transaction at meetings at which all directors were present, but at which the Miltons did not vote. When the Corporation sold its shares to the public, in 1955, the transactions between RIC and the Corporation were fully disclosed in the prospectus.

The Corporation is considering leasing property from RIC on which it plans to build a new hotel. The terms of this proposed transaction are the same as the earlier deals, except that RIC will also receive a percentage of the profits from the concessionaires who will operate in the hotel. Accordingly, the Corporation will receive that much less from the operation of those concessions. RIC requires this added compensation because the RIC bought the parcel of land in question for speculation, and not in connection with a transaction initiated by the Corporation. RIC has received lucrative offers from unrelated parties to lease or sell the property. The arrangement RIC proposes to enter into with the Corporation will provide RIC with a smaller profit than it would have made from at least two of the other offers.

A special meeting of the board of directors of the Corporation will consider the proposed transaction. The board has asked you to analyze the situation and make your recommendations. Under MBCA § 41:

1. Who may be counted for a quorum of the board of directors at the meeting to consider the transaction?

2. How many votes will be required for the approval of the transaction? What procedures would you recommend be followed in order to minimize the risk of the transaction being set aside? Consider the *Shlensky* and *Remillard Brick* cases.

3. Suppose that the transaction is approved by a unanimous vote of Quincy, Brown, Gray, and White, meeting in the absence of the Milton family directors. May a shareholder of the Corporation succeed in enjoining the lease? What must the plaintiff show? Who will have the burden of proof? Suppose White votes against the transaction.

4. Suppose Robert White, a director, votes in favor of the transaction, what is his risk of liability?

5. Suppose the Corporation informs its shareholders of these facts and the shareholders, by an overwhelming vote, ratify the transaction. Can the members of the Milton family participate in the vote? What effect does ratification have on any claim for liability? Consider the *Fliegler* case and MBCA § 32.

6. What if the Corporation's articles of incorporation contain the following provision: "Section 9.02, *Transactions in Which Directors Have an Interest*. Any contract or other transaction between the Corporation and one or more of its directors or between the Corporation and any firm of which one or more of its directors are members or employees, or in which they are interested, or between the Corporation and any Corporation or association of which one or more of its directors are shareholders, members, directors, officers, or employees, or in which they are interested, shall be valid for all purposes, notwithstanding the presence of the director or directors at the meeting of the Board of Directors of the Corporation that acts upon, or in reference to, the contract or transaction, and notwithstanding his or their participation in the action, if the fact of such interest shall be disclosed or known to the Board of Directors and the Board of Directors shall, nevertheless, authorize or ratify the contract or transaction, the interested director or directors to be counted in determining whether a quorum is present and to be entitled to vote on such authorization or ratification. This section shall not be construed to invalidate any contract or other transaction that would otherwise be valid under the common and statutory law applicable to it."

7. To what extent can the directors rely on the business judgment rule in a suit challenging the transaction?

1. INTRODUCTION: EVOLUTION OF THE STANDARD

MARSH, ARE DIRECTORS TRUSTEES?, CONFLICT OF INTEREST AND CORPORATE MORALITY
22 Bus.Law 35, 36–44 (1966).

* * *

There have been several different rules adopted by courts and legislatures to deal with this problem of conflict of interest, which correspond roughly with successive periods in the legal history of this country. Therefore in the discussion immediately following, I propose to consider the principles which have been advanced at one time or another, in more or less chronological order, even though the earlier ones have been largely if not completely abandoned.

I. TYPES OF LEGAL REGULATIONS

a. *Prohibition*

In 1880 it could have been stated with confidence that in the United States the general rule was that any contract between a director and his corporation was voidable at the instance of the corporation or its shareholders, without regard to the fairness or unfairness of the transaction. This rule was stated in powerful terms by a number of highly regarded courts and judges in cases which arose generally out of the railroad frauds of the 1860's and 1870's.

*   *   *

Under this rule it mattered not the slightest that there was a majority of so-called disinterested directors who approved the contract. The courts stated that the corporation was entitled to the unprejudiced judgment and advice of all of its directors and therefore it did no good to say that the interested director did not participate in the making of the contract on behalf of the corporation. " *   *   *   the very words in which he asserts his right declare his wrong; he ought to have participated. *   *   * [6] Furthermore, the courts said that it was impossible to measure the influence which one director might have over his associates, even though ostensibly abstaining from participation in the discussion or vote. " *   *   *   a corporation, in order to defeat a contract entered into by directors, in which one or more of them had a private interest, is not bound to show that the influence of the director or directors having the private interest determined the action of the board. The law cannot accurately measure the influence of a trustee with his associates, nor will it enter into the inquiry. *   *   * " [7]

Perhaps the strongest reason for this inflexibility of the law was given by the Maryland Supreme Court which stated that, when a contract is made with even one of the directors, "the remaining directors are placed in the embarrassing and invidious position of having to pass upon, scrutinize and check the transactions and accounts of one of their own body, with whom they are associated on terms of equality in the general management of all the affairs of the corporation." [8] Or, as Justice Davies of the New York Supreme Court expressed the same thought: "The moment the directors permit one or more of their number to deal with the property of the stockholders, they surrender their own independence and self control." [9]

This rule applied not only to individual contracts with directors, but also to the situation of interlocking directorates where even a mi-

6. Stewart v. Lehigh Valley R. R. Co., 38 N.J.Law 505, at 523 (Ct. Err. & App. 1875).

7. Munson v. Syracuse, G. & C. Ry. Co., 103 N.Y. 58, at 74, 8 N.E. 355, at 358 (1886).

8. Cumberland Coal and Iron Co. v. Parish, 42 Md. 598, at 606 (1875).

9. Cumberland Coal and Iron Co. v. Sherman, 30 Barb. 553, at 573 (N.Y.Sup. Ct.1859).

nority of the boards were common to the two contracting corporations. Not only that, it was also applied to the situation where one
corporation owned a majority of the stock of another and appointed
its directors, even though they might not be the same men as sat on
the board of the parent corporation. It is interesting to note that the
courts during this era had no difficulty in identifying so-called dummy directors, even though their inability to do so was later given as
one of the reasons why this rule of law had to be abandoned.
* * *

This principle, absolutely inhibiting contracts between a corporation and its directors or any of them, appeared to be impregnable in
1880. It was stated in ringing terms by virtually every decided case,
with arguments which seemed irrefutable, and it was sanctioned by
age. * * *

* * *

Thirty years later this principle was dead.*

b. *Approval by a Disinterested Majority of the Board*

It could have been stated with reasonable confidence in 1910 that
the general rule was that a contract between a director and his corporation was valid if it was approved by a disinterested majority of his
fellow directors and was not found to be unfair or fraudulent by the
court if challenged; but that a contract in which a majority of the
board was interested was voidable at the instance of the corporation
or its shareholders without regard to any question of fairness.

One searches in vain in the decided cases for a reasoned defense
of this change in legal philosophy, or for the slightest attempt to refute the powerful arguments which had been made in support of the
previous rule. Did the courts discover in the last quarter of the Nineteenth Century that greed was no longer a factor in human conduct?
If so, they did not share the basis of this discovery with the public;
nor did they humbly admit their error when confronted with the next
wave of corporate frauds arising out of the era of the formation of
the "trusts" during the 1890's and early 1900's.

The only explanation which seems to have been given for this
change in position was the technical one that a trustee, while forbidden to deal with himself in connection with the trust property, could
deal directly with the cestui que trust if he made full disclosure and
took no unfair advantage; and that the case of a director who abstained from representing the corporation but dealt in his personal

---

* *But compare*, Johnson v. Duensing,
340 S.W.2d 758 (Mo.Ct.App.1960) ("However, notwithstanding the views expressed by the courts in some jurisdictions on the subject, the policy of the law
in this state has long continued to be
* * * [that] 'A director or other officer may not either directly or indirectly
profit by his position. * * *. It is immaterial that the corporation was not
damaged by the transaction in which the
profits were made or that he acted
throughout in the highest good faith and
without intent to injure the corporation.' ")—Eds.

capacity with a majority of disinterested directors was properly analogized to a trustee dealing with the cestui que trust.   *   *   *

But in no case is there any discussion or attempted refutation of the reasons previously given by the courts as to why it is impossible, in such a situation, for any director to be disinterested. Some courts seem simply to admit that the practice has grown too widespread for them to cope with.   *   *   *

And the New York Supreme Court stated in Genesee & W. V. Ry. Co. v. Retsof Min. Co.: [21]

> The rule contended for by the learned counsel for the defendant has been considerably relaxed of late years. Indeed, it would be difficult to conduct the affairs of the multifarious corporations of the country, many of which, although apparently sustaining the relations of rivals in business, are nevertheless practically controlled by the same directors, if the element of good faith, instead of individual interests, were not established as the basis of intercorporate action.

*   *   *

However, this apparent survival of the older rule was nothing but a meaningless facade. As early as 1903 the New Jersey courts decided that the strict rule did not apply to a case of "interlocking directorates." [25] Since the case of a contract between two corporations with common directors was thought to present an entirely different problem than a contract with a director individually, without any inquiry into the question whether the common director or directors owned more stock in one of the two corporations than the other, all that a director had to do in order to avoid the older rule was to incorporate the business in which he expected to have dealings with the corporation on whose board he sat. Since most such businesses would be incorporated anyway for other reasons, this meant that the older rule was virtually abrogated except with respect to approval of salaries.

*   *   *

Under the rule that a disinterested majority of the directors must approve a transaction with one of their number, the question arose whether this meant a disinterested quorum (i.e., normally a majority of the whole board) or merely a disinterested majority of a quorum, so that the interested director or directors could be counted to make up the quorum. Virtually all of the cases held that the interested director could not be counted for quorum purposes.   *   *   *

c. *Judicial Review of the Fairness of the Transaction*

By 1960 it could be said with some assurance that the general rule was that no transaction of a corporation with any or all of its direc-

---

21. 15 Misc. 187 at 195, 36 N.Y.Supp. 896 at 901 (Sup.Ct.1895).   *   *   *

25. Robotham v. Prudential Ins. Co. of America, 64 N.J.Eq. 673, 53 A. 842 (Ch.1903)   *   *   *.

tors was automatically voidable at the suit of a shareholder, whether there was a disinterested majority of the board or not; but that the courts would review such a contract and subject it to rigid and careful scrutiny, and would invalidate the contract if it was found to be unfair to the corporation.

It is difficult in most States to determine with exactness the point of time at which the rule changed again, or indeed to prove beyond a reasonable doubt that it has in fact changed in a particular State. There are a large number of cases which deal with situations where a majority of the board were interested and which discuss them solely in terms of a review of the fairness of the transaction, without bothering to cite or discuss any of the previous decisions, perhaps in the same State, enunciating the rule that there must be approval by a disinterested majority of the board. Some of these cases could be distinguished from the previous holdings on the basis that they deal with interlocking directorates rather than contracts with interested directors, if one wishes to take any stock in that distinction. There is another large group of cases which deal with situations where it does not appear that a majority of the board were interested in the transaction, but the opinions of the courts deal with the problem solely in terms of fairness, without mentioning any requirement of a disinterested majority. These cases are not necessarily inconsistent with such a requirement, but they in all probability indicate that these courts have gone over to the modern rule.

* * *

2. THE MODERN STANDARD

a. The Basic Rule

SHLENSKY v. SOUTH PARKWAY BUILDING CORP.

19 Ill.2d 268, 166 N.E.2d 793 (1960).

[The plaintiffs, minority shareholders of South Parkway Building Corporation (Building Corporation), sued to require defendant directors to personally account for damages suffered by the corporation in the various transactions. The trial court held that defendants breached their fiduciary duties in all of the challenged transactions and ordered an accounting for the benefit of the shareholders. The Appellate Court reversed on the ground that, under Illinois law, the plaintiffs had failed to sustain the burden of establishing that the transactions were fraudulent.

The main operating asset of the Building Corporation was a 3-story commercial building on a city lot in Chicago. Since the inception of Building Corporation, defendant Engelstein was a director and majority shareholder of the corporation. In each of the challenged transactions the second party was a corporation owned by Engelstein in which he acted as either an officer or director or both. In each case, the court found that the transactions were approved by an interested majority of the Building Corporation's board of directors.

In reversing the decision below and holding that the defendants failed to establish the fairness of the transaction in question and that their conduct constituted a breach of fiduciary duty for which the trial court properly ordered them to account, BRISTOW, J. stated:]

In [Dixmoor Golf Club, Inc. v. Evans, 325 Ill. 612, 156 N.E. 785 (1927)] this court stated at page 616 of 325 Ill., at page 787 of 156 N. E.: "The directors of a corporation are trustees of its business and property for the collective body of stockholders in respect to such business. They are subject to the general rule, in regard to trusts and trustees, that they cannot, in their dealings with the business or property of the trust, use their relation to it for their own personal gain. It is their duty to administer the corporate affairs for the common benefit of all the stockholders, and exercise their best care, skill, and judgment in the management of the corporate business *solely in the interest of the corporation.* * * * It is a breach of duty for the directors to place themselves in a position where their personal interests would prevent them from acting for the best interests of those they represent." (Italics ours.)

The court expounded that while a director is not disqualified from dealing with the corporation and buying its property, or selling property to it, the transaction will be subject to the closest scrutiny, and if not conducted with the utmost fairness, "to the end that the corporation shall have received full value," it will be set aside. The court then held that since the board of directors therein was dominated by one member, and had purchased land from him for the corporation at a price that was 2½ times more than required by his option, the transaction would be set aside, even though the corporation had use for the land, and had received some benefit from the transaction.

The same year, this court in White v. Stevens, 326 Ill. 528, 158 N. E. 101, 103, without referring to the Dixmoor case, reiterated that a director may deal with the corporation of which he is a member, provided he acts fairly and for the interest of the company. The court also recognized that corporations having directors in common may contract with each other "if the contracts are fair and reasonable," but emphasized that such transactions would be carefully scrutinized by equity. In the case before it, where the allegedly offending corporation had "procured the furniture for the hotel company at prices charged by manufacturers and wholesalers and furnished it to the hotel company at the same price," the court found that "the most careful scrutiny fails to disclose any unfairness to or overreaching of the hotel company in the entire transaction."

* * *

* * * [I]n Winger v. Chicago City Bank & Trust Co., 394 Ill. 94, 67 N.E.2d 265, * * * [a]fter reviewing the English and Ameri-

can authorities on the fiduciary status of corporate directors, the court in the Winger case reaffirmed the rule in the Dixmoor case, and noted further that the fact that directors do not deal directly with themselves, but deal with another corporation which they own or control, will not change the effect of the transaction. In fact, the court pointed out that it is practically the unanimous opinion of courts that, even if only one of the directors voting for the transaction profited thereby, and his vote was necessary, the transaction would be tainted with the same illegality and fraud as though they were all interested. Under those circumstances, the directors have the burden of overcoming the presumption against the validity of the transaction, by showing its fairness and propriety.

* * * [W]e find that the Winger case, construed in its entirety, holds that transactions between corporations with common directors may be avoided only *if unfair*, and that the directors who would sustain the challenged transaction have the burden of overcoming the presumption against the validity of the transaction by showing its fairness.

While the acts of the directors in the Winger case may have been a more flagrant breach of fiduciary duty, as defendants contend, than those involved in the instant case—depending upon one's view point— those circumstances do not change the rule of law applied by the court. Moreover, we agree with the court that no distinction should be made, as defendants suggest, between transactions of a director with his corporation and those in which he hides behind the corporate veil and deals through another corporation which he owns or controls.

* * *

In the leading case of Geddes v. Anaconda Copper Mining Co., 254 U.S. 590, 41 S.Ct. 209, 65 L.Ed. 425, followed by an imposing body of authority, the operative facts were somewhat analogous to those in the case at bar in that they involved transactions between corporations with common directors and allegedly inadequate consideration. The challenged transaction there, however, involved a sale of all the corporate property, whereas the transactions in the instant case involve agreements allegedly siphoning a substantial portion of the corporate assets. The United States Supreme Court, after noting that the record showed beyond controversy that Ryan was an officer and director and dominated the affairs of the buying and selling companies, as well as their boards of directors, set aside the transaction. In so doing, the court promulgated the oft quoted rule at page 599 of 254 U.S., at page 212 of 41 S.Ct.: "The relation of directors to corporations is of such a fiduciary nature that transactions between boards having common members are regarded as jealously by the law as are personal dealings between a director and his corporation, and where the fairness of such transactions is challenged the burden is upon those who would maintain them to show their entire fairness and where a sale is involved the full adequacy of the consideration. Espe-

INTRODUCTION TO FIDUCIARY DUTIES

cially is this true where a common director is dominating in influence
or in character. This court has been consistently emphatic in the application of this rule, which, it has declared, is founded in soundest
morality, and we now add in the soundest business policy."

In our judgment, the Geddes rule, which is essentially the same as
that applied in the Winger case, is not only legally cogent, but is consistent with the entire concept of the fiduciary relation in the fabric
of our commercial law. The contrary rule, urged by defendants,
whereby those attacking the transactions of fiduciaries would have
the burden of establishing its unfairness or fraudulency is not only
without substantial support in the case law, but would put a premium
on sharp practices by directors by putting the onus of proof on their
victims, and would also tend to further separate corporate management from ownership.

In contrast, the rule of the Geddes and Winger cases, insofar as it
provides that the directors shall have the burden of establishing the
fairness and propriety of the transactions, not only protects shareholders from exploitation, but permits flexibility in corporate dealings. While the concept of "fairness" is incapable of precise definition, courts have stressed such factors as whether the corporation
received in the transaction full value in all the commodities purchased; the corporation's need for the property; its ability to finance
the purchase; whether the transaction was at the market price, or
below, or constituted a better bargain than the corporation could have
otherwise obtained in dealings with others; whether there was a detriment to the corporation as a result of the transaction; whether
there was a possibility of corporate gain siphoned off by the directors
directly or through corporations they controlled; and whether there
was full disclosure—although neither disclosure nor shareholder assent can convert a dishonest transaction into a fair one.

Moreover, where the corporate directors fail to establish the fairness of the challenged transaction, it may either be set aside, or affirmed and damages recovered for the losses sustained by the corporation.

In the light of this analysis of the appropriate rules and guiding
considerations, we shall determine the propriety of the five challenged transactions of the board of the Building Corporation herein.

Inasmuch as the authorization of the payment of $100,000 to the
Store [one of the three tenants in the building owned by the Building
Corporation] for its fixtures was conditioned on the subsequent modi-
fication of its lease, we shall consider these transactions together. It
is undisputed that at the time of these transactions the board of the
Building Corporation consisted of seven members, and that director
Sturm resigned in protest of the payment of $100,000 to the Store.
The remaining six directors present and voting for that purchase in-
cluded Englestein, the owner and president of the Store; Mackie, a
Store director; and Bernstein, who was the lawyer for Englestein and

for the Store, as well as for Englestein's other business enterprises. We cannot, under the circumstances, perceive just how defendants can seriously characterize Bernstein as an independent and disinterested director representing only the Building Corporation.

It is therefore apparent that the fixture purchase authorized on March 18, 1948, could not conceivably be deemed to have been approved by an independent and disinterested majority of directors of the Building Corporation. Furthermore, as pointed out in the Geddes case, it is not the mere number of common directors which determines whether approval has been given by an independent and disinterested majority of directors, but rather whether a majority of the directors are dominated by an individual or a group.

Nor was the modification of the Store lease on May 4, 1948, effected by an independent and disinterested majority. At that time only five members of the board were present, Townsend being out of town and apparently informed by telephone, and the votes of approval included Englestein, Mackie and Bernstein, along with Teter, and Peyla, who thought that the Store rent was being increased. Therefore, in view of the lack of approval by a disinterested majority, it was incumbent upon defendants to sustain the burden of establishing the fairness of these transactions.

It is uncontroverted that the Building Corporation had no commercial use for the fixtures, which even included the asphalt tile and built-in partitions, all of which were continued to be used by the Store. Moreover, since the used fixtures had limited intrinsic value, as compared with their cost of $100,000, the only consideration which the corporation could realize from this substantial outlay would be through its rental charges. While the directors on May 4, 1948, increased the minimum rent payable by the Store by some $5,000, they eliminated practically all of the percentage rents, except the 1½ per cent on sales over $1,100,000, which was tantamount to a 40% reduction in future rents, and also waived some $24,316 of accrued rent owed by the Store.

In defense of this transaction, defendants and the Appellate Court stress that the economic health of the Store was of great value to the Building Corporation, since it meant the retention of a tenant and benefited all the other tenants, which were economically interdependent, and therefore justified pouring money into the Store. In our judgment, however, the economic interdependence of the tenancies (Neisner's, Walgreen's, and the Store) hardly justifies giving one of them—the Store owned by Englestein—all of the financial benefits, and requiring the other tenants to pay rents which were 10 to 20 times higher per square foot than the rent paid by Englestein's Store. In this connection, the evidence showed that the rent paid by the Store, even in 1948, was $20,737, or $.24 per square foot, as compared with rentals of $42,875 or $2.00 per square foot paid by Neisner's for similar space, and $30,708 or $5.44 per square foot paid by Walgreen's. It is also difficult for us to comprehend just why the Store was such a valuable tenant when other tenants paid much higher rentals, and when the record shows that the subsequent tenant of the premises willingly paid a rental over $2\frac{1}{2}$ times as much as that paid by the Store.

It is therefore patent from the evidence that defendants not merely failed to establish the fairness of this $100,000 used fixture purchase and rent reduction scheme, but that it was tantamount to a deliberate depletion of corporate assets, for the benefit of another corporation in which 3 of the 6 directors had adverse interests. Under those circumstances, the findings and orders of the master and chancellor that defendants' conduct constituted a breach of their fiduciary duty, for which they must account to the Building Corporation, were neither contrary to the manifest weight of the evidence, nor predicated on a conclusive presumption, as defendants argue. It was therefore error for the Appellate Court to have set aside those findings.

* * *

b. Shareholder Ratification

FLIEGLER v. LAWRENCE

361 A.2d 218 (Del.1976).

[Agau Mines, Inc. (Agau) was organized to explore and develop certain properties for mineable gold and silver ore. In November, 1969, defendant John Lawrence, President of Agau, acquired certain properties in his individual capacity. He offered the property to Agau, but its board of directors refused on the ground that the corporation's legal and financial position could not support the acquisition and development of the properties. At that point, Lawrence along with other Agau shareholders and officers, formed and transferred the property the United States Antimony Corp. (USAC) so that the capital needed for the development of the properties could be raised without risk to Agau through the sale of Agau stock. In January, 1970 Agau and USAC executed an agreement giving Agau an option to buy all of USAC's shares in exchange for 800,000 shares of Agau's restricted investment stock if the properties proved to be of commercial value.

After the decision to exercise the option, plaintiff brought a shareholder derivative action on behalf of Agau seeking to recover the 800,000 Agau shares and for an accounting. Defendants to the action were Agau's officers and directors and USAC.

The Delaware Supreme Court upheld the Vice-Chancellor's determination that the chance to acquire the properties was a corporate opportunity which was and should have been offered to Agau and that the individual defendants were entitled to acquire it for themselves after Agau properly rejected the properties. In holding that the defendants proved the intrinsic fairness of the exchange of Agau stock for the USAC shares, the court stated:]

Preliminarily, defendants argue that they have been relieved of the burden of proving fairness by reason of shareholder ratification of the Board's decision   *   *   *.   They rely on 8 Del.C. § 144(a)(2) and Gottlieb v. Heyden Chemical Corp., Del.Supr., 33 Del.Ch. 177, 91 A.2d 57 (1952).

In *Gottlieb*, this Court stated that shareholder ratification of an "interested transaction", although less than unanimous, shifts the burden of proof to an objecting shareholder to demonstrate that the terms are so unequal as to amount to a gift or waste of corporate assets. Also see Saxe v. Brady, 40 Del.Ch. 474, 184 A.2d 602 (1962). The Court explained:

> [T]he entire atmosphere is freshened and a new set of rules invoked where formal approval has been given by a majority of independent, fully informed [share]holders. 91 A.2d at 59.

The purported ratification by the Agau shareholders would not affect the burden of proof in this case because the majority of shares voted in favor of exercising the option were cast by defendants in their capacity as Agau shareholders. Only about one-third of the "disinterested" shareholders voted, and we cannot assume that such non-voting shareholders either approved or disapproved. Under these circumstances, we cannot say that "the entire atmosphere has been freshened" and that departure from the objective fairness test is permissible. Compare Schiff v. R. K. O. Pictures Corp., 37 Del.Ch. 21, 104 A.2d 267 (1954), with David J. Greene & Co. v. Dunhill International, Inc., *supra*, and Abelow v. Symonds, 40 Del.Ch. 462, 184 A. 2d 173 (1962). In short, defendants have not established factually a basis for applying *Gottlieb*.

Nor do we believe the Legislature intended a contrary policy and rule to prevail by enacting 8 Del.C. § 144, which provides, in part:

> (a) No contract or transaction between a corporation and 1 or more of its directors or officers, or between a corporation and any other corporation, partnership, association, or other organization in which 1 or more of its directors or officers, are directors or officers, or have a financial interest, shall be void or voidable solely for this reason, or solely because the director or officer is present at or participates in the meeting of the board or committee which authorizes the contract or transaction, or solely because his or their votes are counted for such purpose, if:

> (1) The material facts as to his relationship or interest and as to the contract or transaction are disclosed or are known to the board of directors or the committee, and the board [or] committee in good faith authorizes the contract or transaction by the affirmative votes of a majority of the disinterested directors, even though the disinterested directors be less than a quorum; or

(2) The material facts as his relationship or interest and as to the contract or transaction are disclosed or are known to the shareholders entitled to vote thereon, and the contract or transaction is specifically approved in good faith by vote of the shareholders; or

(3) The contract or transaction is fair as to the corporation as of the time it is authorized, approved or ratified, by the board of directors, a committee, or the shareholders.

Defendants argue that the transaction here in question is protected by § 144(a)(2) which, they contend, does not require that ratifying shareholders be "disinterested" or "independent"; nor, they argue, is there warrant for reading such a requirement into the statute. See Folk, The Delaware General Corporation Law—A Commentary and Analysis (1972), pp. 85–86. We do not read the statute as providing the broad immunity for which defendants contend. It merely removes an "interested director" cloud when its terms are met and provides against invalidation of an agreement "solely" because such a director or officer is involved. Nothing in the statute sanctions unfairness to Agau or removes the transaction from judicial scrutiny.

* * *

MARSH, ARE DIRECTORS TRUSTEES? CONFLICT OF INTEREST AND CORPORATE MORALITY
22 Bus.Law. 35, 48–49 (1966).

* * * All of the cases seem to hold that [shareholder ratification, after full disclosure] will suffice to validate the transaction with an interested director, at least in the absence of fraud or unfairness. Furthermore, the stock of the interested director or directors may be voted on the question of ratification, and *as shareholders* they may cast the deciding votes. Of course, under most of the cases even the shareholders may not effectively ratify a fraudulent transaction, although according to some courts they may decide that it is inadvisable to sue and thereby block any attempt by a minority shareholder to challenge a transaction alleged to be fraudulent.

The rule stated in the preceding paragraph has been justified on the basis that where there is shareholder ratification the case is precisely analogous to that of a trustee dealing with his cestui que trust after full disclosure, and is not at all a case of a trustee dealing with himself. However, the validity of this analogy may be seriously questioned. When a trustee deals with his cestui que trust who is an individual that is sui juris, after full disclosure, then the cestui que trust is able to negotiate for himself and there is no more danger of fraud or over-reaching than in any other business transaction. However, when the shareholders of a publicly-held company are asked to ratify a transaction with interested directors they cannot as a practical matter *negotiate* for the corporation. They are, they must be, limited to rejecting or accepting the deal formulated by the interested directors. Even if it be assumed that the deal is fair, that is not what the shareholders are entitled to. They are entitled to have someone negotiate the best deal obtainable for their corporation, fair or unfair. This the interested directors cannot do. As the New Hampshire court said, it is "impossible for common directors to procure the lowest rates for one party and the highest rates for the other. * * * They were not arbitrators, called in to adjust conflicting claims. * * * "

*　　*　　*

c.　The Role of the Statute

REMILLARD BRICK CO. v. REMILLARD-DANDINI CO.

109 Cal.App.2d 405, 241 P.2d 66, 73–77 (1952).

[Stanley and Sturgis controlled a majority of the shares of Remillard-Dandini Co. Remillard-Dandini Co. owned all the shares of San Jose Brick & Tile, Ltd. Stanley and Sturgis controlled the boards of directors of Remillard-Dandini Co. and San Jose Brick & Tile, Ltd. and were executive officers of both corporations and drew salaries from them. The court refers to Remillard-Dandini Co. and San Jose Brick & Tile, Ltd. as the "manufacturing companies." Stanley and Sturgis owned, controlled and operated Remillard-Dandini Sales Corp. which the court refers to as the "sales corporation."

Plaintiff, a minority shareholder of Remillard-Dandini Co., alleged that the majority directors of the manufacturing companies used their power to have the manufacturing companies enter into contracts with the sales corporation, so that the manufacturing companies were stripped of their sales function and that through the sales corporation Stanley and Sturgis realized profits which would have gone to the manufacturing companies. Stanley and Sturgis maintained that the minority shareholder and the minority directors of the manufacturing companies were informed of their interests in the contracts. In invalidating the contracts, PETERS, Presiding Justice, stated:]

It is argued that, since the fact of common directorship was fully known to the boards of the contracting corporations, and because the * * * majority stockholders consented to the transaction, the minority stockholder and directors of the manufacturing companies have no legal cause to complain. In other words, it is argued that if the majority directors and stockholders inform the minority that they are going to mulct the corporation, section 820 of the Corporations Code * constitutes an impervious armor against any attack on the

---

* Section 820 of the Corporations Code, enacted in 1947 and based on former section 311 of the Civil Code, provided:

Directors and officers shall exercise their powers in good faith, and with a view to the interests of the corporation. No contract or other transaction between a corporation and one or more of its directors, or between a corporation and any corporation, firm, or association in which one or more of its directors are directors or are financially interested, is either void or voidable because such director or directors are

transaction short of actual fraud. If this interpretation of the section were sound, it would be a shocking reflection on the law of California. It would completely disregard the first sentence of section 820 setting forth the elementary rule that "Directors and officers shall exercise their powers in good faith, and with a view to the interests of the corporation", and would mean that if conniving directors simply disclose their dereliction to the powerless minority, any transaction by which the majority desire to mulct the minority is immune from attack. That is not and cannot be the law.

Section 820 of the Corporations Code is based on former section 311 of the Civil Code, first added to our law in 1931. Stats. of 1931, Chap. 862, p. 1777. Before the adoption of that section it was the law that the mere existence of a common directorate, at least where the vote of the common director was essential to consummate the transaction, invalidated the contract. Caminetti v. Prudence etc. Ins. Ass'n, 62 Cal.App.2d 945, 950, 146 P.2d 15. That rule was changed in 1931 when section 311 was added to the Civil Code, and limited to a greater extent by the adoption of section 820 of the Corporations Code. If the conditions provided for in the section appear, the transaction cannot be set aside simply because there is a common directorate. Here, undoubtedly, there was a literal compliance with subdivision b of the section. The fact of the common directorship was disclosed to the stockholders, and the * * * majority stockholders, did approve the contracts.

But neither section 820 of the Corporations Code nor any other provision of the law automatically validates such transactions simply because there has been a disclosure and approval by the majority of the stockholders. That section does not operate to limit the fiduciary duties owed by a director to all the stockholders, nor does it operate to condone acts which, without the existence of a common directorate, would not be countenanced. That section does not permit an officer or director, by an abuse of his power, to obtain an unfair advantage or profit for himself at the expense of the corporation. The director cannot, by reason of his position, drive a harsh and unfair bargain

present at the meeting of the board of directors or a committee thereof which authorizes or approves the contract or transaction, or because his or their votes are counted for such purpose, if the circumstances specified in any of the following subdivisions exist:

(a) The fact of the common directorship or financial interest is disclosed or known to the board of directors or committee and noted in the minutes, and the board or committee authorizes, approves, or ratifies the contract or transaction in good faith by a vote sufficient for the purpose without counting the vote or votes of such director or directors.

(b) The fact of the common directorship or financial interest is disclosed or known to the shareholders, and they approve or ratify the contract or transaction in good faith by a majority vote or written consent of shareholders entitled to vote.

(c) The contract or transaction is just and reasonable as to the corporation at the time it is authorized or approved.

Common or interested directors may be counted in determining the presence of a quorum at a meeting of the board of directors or a committee thereof which authorizes, approves, or ratifies a contract or transaction.—Eds.

with the corporation he is supposed to represent. If he does so, he may be compelled to account for unfair profits made in disregard of his duty. Even though the requirements of section 820 are technically met, transactions that are unfair and unreasonable to the corporation may be avoided. California Corporation Laws by Ballantine and Sterling (1949 ed.), p. 102, § 84. It would be a shocking concept of corporate morality to hold that because the majority directors or stockholders disclose their purpose and interest, they may strip a corporation of its assets to their own financial advantage, and that the minority is without legal redress. Here the unchallenged findings demonstrate that Stanley and Sturgis used their majority power for their own personal advantage and to the detriment of the minority stockholder. They used it to strip the manufacturing companies of their sales functions—functions which it was their duty to carry out as officers and directors of those companies. There was not one thing done by them acting as the sales corporation that they could not and should not have done as officers and directors and in control of the stock of the manufacturing companies. It is no answer to say that the manufacturing companies made a profit on the deal, or that Stanley and Sturgis did a good job. The point is that those large profits that should have gone to the manufacturing companies were diverted to the sales corporation. The good job done by Stanley and Sturgis should and could have been done for the manufacturing companies. If Stanley and Sturgis, with control of the board of directors and the majority stock of the manufacturing companies, could thus lawfully, to their own advantage, strip the manufacturing companies of their sales functions, they could just as well strip them of their other functions. If the sales functions could be stripped from the companies in this fashion to the personal advantage of Stanley and Sturgis, there would be nothing to prevent them from next organizing a manufacturing company, and transferring to it the manufacturing functions of these companies, thus leaving the manufacturing companies but hollow shells. This should not, is not, and cannot be the law.

It is hornbook law that directors, while not strictly trustees, are fiduciaries, and bear a fiduciary relationship to the corporation, and to all the stockholders. They owe a duty to all stockholders, including the minority stockholders, and must administer their duties for the common benefit. The concept that a corporation is an entity cannot operate so as to lessen the duties owed to all of the stockholders. Directors owe a duty of highest good faith to the corporation and its stockholders. It is a cardinal principle of corporate law that a director cannot, at the expense of the corporation, make an unfair profit from his position. He is precluded from receiving any personal advantage without fullest disclosure to and consent of *all* those affected. The law zealously regards contracts between corporations with interlocking directorates, will carefully scrutinize all such transactions, and in case of unfair dealing to the detriment of minority stockholders, will grant appropriate relief. Where the transaction greatly benefits one corporation at the expense of another, and especially if it personally benefits the majority directors, it will and should be set aside. In other words, while the transaction is not voidable simply because an interested director participated, it will not be upheld if it is unfair to the minority stockholders. These principles are the law in practically all jurisdictions.

NOTE—CONFLICTS OF INTEREST AND STATUTORY PROVISIONS

Many states have enacted "interested director" statutes similar to MBCA § 41. As *Remillard Brick* says of the California provision, they are aimed generally at reversing the early common law rule according to which a contract or transaction between a corporation and one or more of its directors or between a corporation and another entity in which one or more directors had an interest was void or voidable. While these statutes clearly reverse the early common law rule, their effect on the more modern approach—which subjects such contracts or transactions to close judicial scrutiny—is less clear. Does compliance with the procedures outlined in the statute irrebuttably validate the transaction; does it shift the burden of proving unfairness to the challenging party; or is there some other effect?

Most of the interested director statutes, like MBCA § 41, set forth the methods for sustaining transactions in the alternative, *i.e.*, the transaction will not be void or voidable if it meets the requirements of disinterested director approval, *or* if it is approved by the shareholders *or* if the transaction is fair and reasonable. The use of the disjunctive might suggest that the transaction will be scrutinized for fairness only if disinterested director or shareholder approval has not been obtained. The inference seems to be countered by language in some statutes to the effect that a transaction that satisfies one or more of the tests will not be voidable *solely* because of the director's interest or the director's presence at a meeting at which the transaction is approved. *See, e.g.*, N.Y.Bus.Corp.Law § 713; Del.G.C.L. § 144. At least one court, in interpreting the New Jersey statute, indicated that "notwithstanding the use of 'or' to connect the subdivisions of the statute, the preferable construction is to require that a particular transaction pass muster under each subdivision." Scott v. Multi-Amp Corp., 386 F.Supp. 44, 67 (D.C.N.J.1977).

Unfortunately legislative history and official commentaries (where they are available) are seldom of any help. *See, e.g.*, MBCA § 41, Comment 2; *see also* the discussion of the legislative history of the New York provision in Note, The Status of the Fairness Test Under Section 713 of the New York Business Corporation Law, 76 Colum.L. Rev. 1156, 1166–74, 1179–82 (1976). Given the long-standing disfavor with which director conflict of interest transactions have been viewed, however, it might be thought that a legislative enactment purporting to shield them from scrutiny should do so explicitly.

An examination of the interested director statutes and the related case law suggests ways in which transactions may be structured so as to minimize the possibility that they will receive close judicial scrutiny, as well as ways in which such transactions may be attacked.

Disinterested Director Approval

Under both the California statute and the MBCA, where there are insufficient disinterested directors to act for the board, *e.g.*, where a majority of the directors present at the board or committee meeting are interested, the contract will be voidable unless it is fair and reasonable to the corporation. Under the New York statute, however, if there are insufficient disinterested directors to approve the transaction, the transaction may be authorized by unanimous vote of the disinterested directors, *see* N.Y.Bus.Corp.Law § 713(a)(1), while the Delaware statute requires only that the transaction be authorized "by the affirmative votes of a majority of the disinterested directors, even though the disinterested directors be less than a quorum." *See* Del. G.C.L. § 144. It could be argued that under either of the latter two provisions a "unanimous" or "majority" vote of one director would suffice to meet the requirements for disinterested director approval. Would you counsel reliance on such an interpretation?

The problem of interpretation stems at least in part from the varying stages of development of the case law at the time the statutes were enacted. Many jurisdictions had adopted a general rule that contracts between interested directors would not be automatically invalidated, but had not expressly overruled earlier cases applying an automatic voidability rule. Some jurisdictions retained vestiges of the automatic voidability rule to be applied in specific situations, *e.g.*, where the interested director represented both parties to the transaction in the bargaining process, where the interested director was counted for purposes of determining the presence of a quorum, or where the interested director's vote was necessary for approval of the transaction. Thus, if the statute was designed to reverse the case law, the question remains: what case law? Yet another source of confusion may be traced to the potentially broad applicability of the statutes to a multitude of situations in which director conflicts of interests might arise and in which separate lines of case law might have developed. A final source of difficulty is that the statutes may be applied to a spectrum of situations in which the degree of director interest may range from a single director merely sitting on the boards of more than one corporation to a situation where all directors stand to benefit financially from the challenged transaction.

While there is no one solution to the problems underlying the interested director statutes, it is possible to identify factors that the courts will consider relevant in determining what standard of review will be applied.

1. *Committee Approval.* The interested director statutes provide that disinterested director approval of conflict of interest transactions may be obtained at either a meeting of the board or at a committee meeting. Thus, it appears that even where there are insufficient disinterested directors to act for the board, a committee composed of a majority of disinterested directors could still approve a transaction. If there were no committee having a majority of disinterested directors in existence at the time the transaction was first proposed, could the board appoint such a committee solely for purposes of considering the transaction?

Where special committees composed of disinterested directors have recommended dismissal of shareholder derivative actions brought against directors, board action on such recommendations has, in several cases, been accorded deference under the business judgment doctrine, though it is not yet clear whether the board may dismiss actions alleging self-dealing. (These cases are discussed in greater detail in Chapter 15, Part E(3) *infra.* Should board action on a committee recommendation that an interested director transaction be approved be accorded similar deference? Even if such deference is accorded, a complaining shareholder should still be able to attack the independence of the approving committee or the effectiveness of disinterested director disclosure. Who should have the burden of proof on these issues?

2. *Director Abstention from the Negotiation and Approval Processes.* The "hard-core" conflict of interest cases arise where the interested director represents both the corporation and himself in the bargaining process. One court has suggested that "[i]ndispensable to liability for violation of his fiduciary obligation as to any personal transaction with the corporation is the demonstration that a director has acted in a dual capacity—for himself as well as the corporation." Borden v. Guthrie, 23 A.D. 313, 260 N.Y.S.2d 769, 774 (1965), aff'd 17 N.Y.2d 571, 268 N.Y.S.2d 330, 215 N.E.2d 511 (1966). *See also* Puma v. Marriott, 283 A.2d 693 (Del.Ch.1971). *Cf.* David J. Greene & Co. v. Dunhill International, Inc., 249 A.2d 427, 430–31 (Del.Ch.1969), in which the court indicated that

> [i]n the absence of divided interests, the judgment of the majority stockholders and/or the board of directors * * * is presumed made in good faith and inspired by a bona fides of purpose. But when the persons * * * who control the making of a transaction and the fixing of its terms, are on both sides, then the presumption and deference to sound business judgment are no longer present.

3. *Charter Provisions.* Might the possibility of a successful attack on an interested director transaction be minimized by including a provision in the corporate charter providing that such transactions

are valid for all purposes if ratified by the board of directors upon disclosure of the directors' interest? The few cases that have considered the impact of such a clause are in conflict. In Everett v. Phillips, 288 N.Y. 227, 43 N.E.2d 18, 22 (1942) (decided before adoption of the New York interested director statute) the court indicated that while transactions in which directors have acted in a dual capacity should be carefully scrutinized, it shifted the burden of proof on the question of fairness to the plaintiffs, holding that a charter provision "expressly authorizing the directors to act even in matters where they have dual interest, has the effect of exonerating the directors, at least in part, 'from adverse inferences which might otherwise be drawn against them.'" But in both Abeles v. Adams Engineering Co., 35 N.J. 411, 173 A.2d 246 (1961) and Pappas v. Moss, 393 F.2d 865 (3d Cir. 1968), the courts held that such charter provisions only authorized the directors to enter into conflict of interest transactions, and placed the burden of proving fairness on the interested directors.

Charter provisions have also been found to be effective in rebutting adverse inferences generally attaching to other aspects of conflict of interest transactions. Thus, in Sterling v. Mayflower Hotel Corp., 33 Del.Ch. 20, 89 A.2d 862 (1952), the court found that despite the common law rule that a transaction would be voidable if interested directors were counted in determining the presence of a quorum, where a charter provision authorized interested directors to be counted for such purposes, the board's approval of the transaction was not invalid, at least where the transaction would subsequently be submitted to the shareholders for approval, and where the transaction was fair to the corporation. *Cf.* Piccard v. Sperry Corp., 48 F. Supp. 465 (S.D.N.Y.1943), aff'd 152 F.2d 462 (C.C.A.2), cert. den. 328 U.S. 845, 66 S.Ct. 1024, 90 L.Ed. 1619 (1946), upholding board action under such a provision even in the absence of shareholder ratification.

4. *Timing of Approval.* Should different standards be applied to board action authorizing directors to enter into a transaction and board action "ratifying" a transaction already consummated? Professor Buxbaum suggests that it is only in the former situation that directors should be able to avail themselves of the benefits of disinterested director approval of conflict of interest transactions. Buxbaum, Conflict-of-Interest Statutes and the Need for a Demand on Directors in Derivative Actions, 68 Cal.L.Rev. 1122, 1125 (1980). Even if such a reading is not compelled by the statutory language, it does seem as Professor Buxbaum concludes, that

> [t]his distinction intuitively makes sense. One need not totally accept * * * comments about the difficult position of nominally independent directors who are expected cooly to judge their fellow directors' behavior to embrace the narrower proposition implicit in these statutes: that however difficult it may be to restrain fellow directors from a proposed course of conduct, it is excessively diffi-

cult to repudiate a transaction already effected by one's fellow directors, thereby subjecting them, among other things, to financial sanctions.

Id. at 1127 (footnote omitted).

5. *Domination of the Board.* Despite the development of more flexible rules governing interested director transactions, courts have continued to be sensitive to the possibility that an interested director might dominate the board. In Shlensky v. South Parkway Building Corp., 19 Ill.2d 268, 284, 166 N.E.2d 793, 802 (Ill.1960), the court stated, "[I]t is not the mere number of common directors which determines whether approval has been given by an independent and disinterested majority of directors, but rather whether a majority of the directors are dominated by an individual or group." The problem is especially acute where the director in question is also a major or controlling shareholder. Thus, in Borden v. Sinsky, 530 F.2d 478 (3d Cir. 1976), the president, director and controlling shareholder of a corporation contended that his personal acquisition of a corporate opportunity should have been tested against the business judgment rule rather than against an intrinsic fairness standard. The director argued that the transaction had been approved by a fully informed board, and that an intrinsic fairness test should only be applied upon a showing of an "interested" or "dominated" board, which in turn required that the board members be financially interested. In approving the application of the intrinsic fairness standard, the court stated that

> [o]ur examination of the relevant Delaware case law indicates that the issue of director "interest" or "domination" is largely a question of fact to be determined from all the relevant facts and circumstances of a particular case * * *. While a showing of financial interest is certainly relevant to, and often dispositive of, this question, it is only one factor to be considered by the trier of fact.

530 F.2d at 495.

See also Globe Woolen Co. v. Utica Gas & Electric Co., 224 N.Y. 483, 121 N.E. 378 (1918).

Shareholder Approval

At common law, an otherwise voidable transaction could be upheld if ratified by a majority of the shareholders, provided that the transaction was not unfair or fraudulent, and provided that the material facts as to the transaction and the director's interest were disclosed to the shareholders. Upon shareholder ratification, a presumption of fairness seems to have attached to the transactions. Thus, some courts indicated that shareholder ratification had the effect of shifting the burden of proof to the party challenging the transaction to show that the terms were so unequal as to amount to waste. *See* Gottlieb v. Heyden Chemical Corp., 33 Del.Ch. 177, 91 A.2d 57 (1952);

Eliasberg v. Standard Oil Co., 23 N.J.Super. 431, 92 A.2d 862 (Ch.Div. 1952), aff'd 12 N.J. 467, 97 A.2d 437 (1953). Nevertheless, as a general rule, where the interested directors own a majority of the shares, shareholder ratification does not shift the burden of proving unfairness to the challenging party. See Brundage v. New Jersey Zinc Co., 48 N.J. 450, 226 A.2d 585 (1967); Pappas v. Moss, 393 F.2d 865 (3d Cir. 1968); David J. Greene & Co. v. Dunhill International, Inc., 249 A.2d 427 (Del.Ch.1963).

It appears that the shareholder approval provision of the interested director statutes, at least as interpreted by Fliegler v. Lawrence and by Remillard Brick Co., codify the common law. Thus an interested director transaction is not voidable where the director's interest is disclosed to the shareholders and the shareholders approve the transaction, but technical compliance with the statutory procedures does not immunize a transaction from scrutiny for fairness where the interested directors are also majority shareholders who vote in favor of the transaction.

Would the rationale of *Fliegler* and *Remillard Brick* apply where the interested directors own a controlling but less than majority interest in the corporation; where they own less than a controlling interest, but their votes are necessary for majority approval of a transaction?

A long line of cases can be cited for the proposition that a shareholder may vote his stock as he pleases; that a shareholder has no fiduciary obligation to fellow shareholders. But there is a separate and growing body of cases holding that a majority or dominant shareholder does occupy a fiduciary position in relation to minority shareholders, and therefore a controlling shareholder may not exercise his control so as to defraud the majority. See Sneed, The Factors Affecting the Validity of Stockholder Votes in Adverse Interest, 13 Okla.L. Rev. 373 (1960); Sneed, Stockholder Votes Motivated by Adverse Interest: The Attack and the Defense, 58 Mich.L.Rev. 961 (1960); Sneed, The Stockholder May Vote as He Pleases: Theory and Fact, 22 U.Pitt.L.Rev. 23 (1960).

While the general rule appears to be that "[t]he personal interest and disqualification of the directors [acting as directors] does not restrict the voting of the same men as shareholders to ratify the contract, subject to limitations against fraud and oppression," H.W. Ballantine, Corporations 177 (Rev. ed. 1946); see also R.S. Stevens, Corporations 567 (2d ed. 1949), there is enough uncertainty in the area to suggest the prudence of structuring the transaction so as to permit a court to readily identify how may disinterested shareholders approved the transaction. In apparent recognition of the wisdom of taking such steps, there has been an increasing trend toward obtaining "majority of the minority" shareholder approval of transactions, especially in the context of parent-subsidiary mergers.

The California statute adopts a majority of the minority approach in situations in which the directors have a material financial interest. Professors Bulbulia and Pinto interpret the California statute as validating in effect, thus precluding judicial scrutiny for fairness. Bulbulia and Pinto, Statutory Responses to Interested Directors' Transactions: A Watering Down of Fiduciary Standards?, 53 Notre Dame Law. 201, 220 (1977).

Fairness

Where neither the requirements for disinterested director nor shareholder approval have been met, the interested director statutes provide that the transaction will not be voidable if it is fair to the corporation. In Point Trap Co. v. Manchester, 98 R.I. 49, 199 A.2d 592 (1964), the director, without informing either the remaining directors or the shareholders, sold corporate property to himself. He contended that under the Rhode Island statute, which provided that "[a] contract not otherwise void or voidable shall not be rendered void or voidable merely because not approved or ratified in accordance with the [disinterested director or shareholder approval] provisions," R.I. Gen.Laws § 7–4–7 (1956), the contract should be upheld because it was fair to the corporation. The court, basing its decision on the "not otherwise void or voidable" language, held the transaction to be voidable. *Id.* at 596. It indicated that an officer of a corporation occupies a fiduciary relationship, which

> "imposes the duty on the fiduciary to act with the utmost good faith. That good faith requirement forbids action on the part of a fiduciary without the knowledge and consent of his cestui que trust when he has an individual interest in the subject matter or when his interest is in conflict with that of the person for whom he acts." *Id.*

In State ex rel. Hayes Oyster Co. v. Keypoint Oyster Co., 64 Wash.2d 375, 391 P.2d 979 (1964), the president, a director and substantial shareholder, arranged for the sale of corporate properties to another corporation in which he was to have an interest. The transaction was submitted to the shareholders for their approval, but without disclosure of the director's interest. The director voted a majority of the stock, including his own, in favor of the sale. In invalidating the transaction, the court indicated that

> this court has abolished the mechanical rule whereby any transaction involving corporate property in which a director has an interest is voidable at the option of the corporation. Such a contract cannot be voided if the director or officer can show that the transaction was fair to the corporation. However, non-disclosure by an interested director or officer is, in itself, unfair.

391 P.2d 979.

It appears then, that there may be situations in which an otherwise fair transaction might still be avoided because of a lack of procedural fairness. *See* Bulbulia and Pinto, Statutory Responses to Interested Directors' Transactions: A Watering Down of Fiduciary Standards?, 53 Notre Dame Law. 201, 210 (1977). *See also* Chapter 21, Part A(2), Note—The Search for Fairness and Part A(3), Fairness: Process and Review, *infra*.

Fairness, Fraud and Waste—Burdens and Standards of Proof

Most commentators who have considered the interested director statutes agree that compliance with the procedures for board or shareholder approval of interested director transactions will not completely immunize those transactions from attack. *See*, Bulbulia and Pinto, Statutory Responses to Interested Directors' Transactions: A Watering Down of Fiduciary Standards?, 53 Notre Dame Law. 201 (1977); Note, The Status of the Fairness Test Under Section 713 of the New York Business Corporation Law, 76 Colum.L.Rev. 1156 (1976); E. L. Folk, The Delaware General Corporation Law, 74–75 (1972); C.L. Israels, Corporate Practice § 6.13 (3d ed., revised by A. M. Hoffman, 1974). But there is no consensus, among either the commentators or the courts, as to what is or should be the effect of compliance. And the effect might vary depending on which statute or section is considered, or depending upon the context in which the question arises, *e.g.*, whether a plaintiff is challenging a settlement, whether the issue is presented at a summary judgment stage or after trial on the merits. Much of the dispute appears to boil down to questions of burdens of proof (both burden of coming forward and of persuasion) and of standards of proof.

The language courts use to articulate standards of proof is hopelessly vague. They have indicated that, in seeking to uphold or to invalidate a transaction, a party will be required to prove the presence or absence of: fairness; good faith; a bona fide business purpose; justness and reasonableness; intrinsic fairness; constructive fraud; waste; or fraud. What is the quantum of proof required to satisfy each standard, and how does the quantum differ among standards? It may at times be difficult to avoid the conclusion that a court has made a decision on the merits of a case and has buttressed its decision by articulating a particular standard of proof which has or has not been met.

3. DUTIES OF MAJORITY OR CONTROLLING STOCKHOLD-ERS

ZAHN v. TRANSAMERICA CORP.

162 F.2d 36 (3d Cir. 1947).

BIGGS, Circuit Judge.

Zahn, a holder of Class A common stock of Axton-Fisher Tobacco Company, a corporation of Kentucky, sued Transamerica Corporation, a Delaware company, on his own behalf and on behalf of all stockholders similarly situated, in the District Court of the United States for the District of Delaware. His complaint as amended asserts that Transamerica caused Axton-Fisher to redeem its Class A stock at $80.80 per share on July 1, 1943, instead of permitting the Class A stockholders to participate in the assets on the liquidation of their company in June, 1944. He alleges in brief that if the Class A stockholders had been allowed to participate in the assets on liquidation of Axton-Fisher and had received their respective shares of the assets, he and the other Class A stockholders would have received $240 per share instead of $80.80. Zahn takes the position that he has two separate causes of action, one based on the Class A shares which were not turned back to the company for redemption; another based on the shares which were redeemed.[1] He prayed the court below to direct Transamerica to pay over to the shareholders who had not surrendered their stock the liquidation value and to pay over to those shareholders who had surrendered their stock the liquidation value less $80.80. Transamerica filed a motion to dismiss. The court below granted the motion holding that Zahn had failed to state a cause of action. See 63 F.Supp. 243. He appealed. *Reversed*

The facts follow as appear from the pleadings, which recite provisions of Axton-Fisher's charter. Prior to April 30, 1943, Axton-Fisher had authorized and outstanding three classes of stock, designated respectively as preferred stock, Class A stock and Class B stock. Each share of preferred stock had a par value of $100 and was entitled to cumulative dividends at the rate of $6 per annum and possessed a liquidation value of $105 plus accrued dividends. The Class A stock, specifically described in the charter as a "common" stock, was entitled to an annual cumulative dividend of $3.20 per share. The Class B stock was next entitled to receive an annual dividend of $1.60 per share. If further funds were made available by action of the board of directors by way of dividends, the Class A stock and the Class B stock were entitled to share equally therein. Upon liquidation of the company and the payment of the sums required by the preferred stock, the Class A stock was entitled to share with the Class B stock

---

1. The plaintiff was originally the holder of 235 shares of Class A stock purchased on four occasions between July 23 and August 10, 1943, inclusive. Between August 2 and August 20, 1943, the plaintiff surrendered for redemption 215 shares and retained 20 shares.

in the distribution of the remaining assets, but the Class A stock was entitled to receive twice as much per share as the Class B stock.[2]

Each share of Class A stock was convertible at the option of the shareholder into one share of Class B stock. All or any of the shares of Class A stock were callable by the corporation at any quarterly dividend date upon sixty days' notice to the shareholders, at $60 per share with accrued dividends.[3] The voting rights were vested in the Class B stock but if there were four successive defaults in the payment of quarterly dividends, the class or classes of stock as to which such defaults occurred gained voting rights equal share for share with the Class B stock. By reason of this provision the Class A stock had possessed equal voting rights with the Class B stock since on or about January 1, 1937.

On or about May 16, 1941, Transamerica purchased 80,160 shares of Axton-Fisher's Class B common stock. This was about 71.5% of the outstanding Class B stock and about 46.7% of the total voting stocks of Axton-Fisher. By August 15, 1942, Transamerica owned 5,332 shares of Class A stock and 82,610 shares of Class B stock. By March 31, 1943, the amount of Class A stock of Axton-Fisher owned by Transamerica had grown to 30,168 shares or about 66⅔% of the total amount of this stock outstanding, and the amount of Class B stock owned by Transamerica had increased to 90,768 shares or about 80% of the total outstanding. Additional shares of Class B stock were acquired by Transamerica after April 30, 1943, and Transamerica converted the Class A stock owned by it into Class B stock so that on or about the end of May, 1944 Transamerica owned virtually all of the outstanding Class B stock of Axton-Fisher. Since May 16, 1941, Transamerica had control of and had dominated the management, di-

---

2. The charter provides as follows:

In the event of the dissolution, liquidation, merger or consolidation of the corporation, or sale of substantially all its assets, whether voluntary or involuntary, there shall be paid to the holders of the preferred stock then outstanding $105 per share, together with all unpaid accrued dividends thereon, before any sum shall be paid to or any assets distributed among the holders of the Class A common stock and/or the holders of the Class B common stock. After such payment to the holders of the preferred stock, and all unpaid accrued dividends on the Class A common stock shall have been paid, then all remaining assets and funds of the corporation shall be divided among and paid to the holders of the Class A common stock and to the holders of the Class B common stock in the ratio of 2 to 1; that is to say, there shall be paid upon each share of Class A common stock twice the amount paid upon each share of Class B common stock, in any such event.

3. The charter provides as follows:

The whole or any part of the Class A common stock of the corporation, at the option of the Board of Directors, may be redeemed on any quarterly dividend payment date by paying therefor in cash Sixty dollars ($60.00) per share and all unpaid and accrued dividends thereon at the date fixed for such redemption, upon sending by mail to the registered holders of the Class A common stock at least sixty (60) days' notice of the exercise of such option. If at any time the Board of Directors shall determine to redeem less than the whole amount of Class A common stock then outstanding, the particular stock to be so redeemed shall be determined in such manner as the Board of Directors shall prescribe; provided, however, that no holder of Class A common stock shall be preferred over any other holder of such stock.

rectorate, financial policies, business and affairs of Axton-Fisher. Since the date last stated Transamerica had elected a majority of the board of directors of Axton-Fisher. These individuals are in large part officers or agents of Transamerica.

In the fall of 1942 and in the spring of 1943 Axton-Fisher possessed as its principal asset leaf tobacco which had cost it about $6,361,981. This asset was carried on Axton-Fisher's books in that amount. The value of leaf tobacco had risen sharply and, to quote the words of the complaint, "unbeknown to the public holders of * * * Class A common stock of Axton-Fisher, but known to Transamerica, the market value of * * * [the] tobacco had, in March and April of 1943, attained the huge sum of about $20,000,000."

The complaint then alleges the gist of the plaintiff's grievance, viz., that Transamerica, knowing of the great value of the tobacco which Axton-Fisher possessed, conceived a plan to appropriate the value of the tobacco to itself by redeeming the Class A stock at the price of $60 a share plus accrued dividends, the redemption being made to appear as if "incident to the continuance of the business of Axton-Fisher as a going concern," and thereafter, the redemption of the Class A stock being completed, to liquidate Axton-Fisher; that this would result, after the disbursal of the sum required to be paid to the preferred stock, in Transamerica gaining for itself most of the value of the warehouse tobacco. The complaint further alleges that in pursuit of this plan Transamerica, by a resolution of the Board of Directors of Axton-Fisher on April 30, 1943, called the Class A stock at $60 and, selling a large part of the tobacco to Phillip-Morris Company, Ltd., Inc., together with substantially all of the other assets of Axton-Fisher, thereafter liquidated Axton-Fisher, paid off the preferred stock and pocketed the balance of the proceeds of the sale. Warehouse receipts representing the remainder of the tobacco were distributed to the Class B stockholders.

* * *

The circumstances of the case at bar are *sui generis* and we can find no Kentucky decision squarely in point. In our opinion, however, the law of Kentucky imposes upon the directors of a corporation or upon those who are in charge of its affairs by virtue of majority stock ownership or otherwise the same fiduciary relationship in respect to the corporation and to its stockholders as is imposed generally by the laws of Kentucky's sister States or which was imposed by federal law prior to Erie R. Co. v. Tompkins, 304 U.S. 64, 58 S.Ct. 817, 82 L.Ed. 1188.

The tenor of the federal decisions in respect to the general fiduciary duty of those in control of a corporation is unmistakable. The Supreme Court in Southern Pacific Co. v. Bogert, 250 U.S. 483, 487, 488, 39 S.Ct. 533, 535, 63 L.Ed. 1099, said: "The rule of corporation law and of equity invoked is well settled and has been often applied. The majority has the right to control; but when it does so, it occupies a fiduciary relation toward the minority, as much so as the corporation itself or its officers and directors." In Pepper v. Litton, 308 U.S. 295, 306, 60 S.Ct. 238, 245, 84 L.Ed. 281, the Supreme Court stated: "A director is a fiduciary. * * * So is a dominant or controlling stockholder or group of stockholders. * * * Their powers are powers in trust. * * * Their dealings with the corporation are subjected to rigorous scrutiny and where any of their contracts or engagements with the corporation is challenged the burden is on the director or stockholder not only to prove the good faith of the transaction but also to show its inherent fairness from the viewpoint of the corporation and those interested therein."

* * *

There can be no doubt of the general law upon this question. It is succinctly stated in Thompson on Corporations, supra, Section 1337, as follows: "Very plainly a director is disqualified from voting on matters in which he has a personal interest or on matters concerning the personal interest of a director who controls his vote. The rule is that any resolution passed at a meeting of the directors at which a director having a personal interest in the matter voted, will be voidable at the instance of the corporation or the stockholders, without regard to its fairness, where the vote of such directors was necessary to the passage of such resolution." It is clear that under the law of Kentucky the fiduciary relationship of directors is such that a court of equity will not permit them to make a profit of their trust and that directors of a corporation are required to manage and conduct their trust so as to realize whatever profit may accrue in the course of the business for the benefit of their cestuis que trust.

It is appropriate to emphasize at this point that the right to call the Class A stock for redemption was confided by the charter of Axton-Fisher to the directors and not to the stockholders of that corporation. We must also re-emphasize * * * that there is a radical difference when a stockholder is voting strictly as a stockholder and when voting as a director; that when voting as a stockholder he may have the legal right to vote with a view of his own benefits and to represent himself only; but that when he votes as a director he represents all the stockholders in the capacity of a trustee for them and cannot use his office as a director for his personal benefit at the expense of the stockholders.

Two theories are presented on one of which the case at bar must be decided: One, vigorously asserted by Transamerica and based on its interpretation of the decision in the Taylor case, is that the board of directors of Axton-Fisher, whether or not dominated by Transamerica, the principal Class B stockholder, at any time and for any purpose, might call the Class A stock for redemption; the other, asserted with equal vigor by Zahn, is that the board of directors of Axton-Fisher as fiduciaries were not entitled to favor Transamerica, the

Class B stockholder, by employing the redemption provisions of the charter for its benefit.

* * *

The difficulty in accepting Transamerica's contentions in the case at bar is that the directors of Axton-Fisher, if the allegations of the complaint be accepted as true, were the instruments of Transamerica, were directors voting in favor of their special interest, that of Transamerica, could not and did not exercise an independent judgment in calling the Class A stock, but made the call for the purpose of profiting their true principal, Transamerica. In short a puppet-puppeteer relationship existed between the directors of Axton-Fisher and Transamerica.

The act of the board of directors in calling the Class A stock, an act which could have been legally consummated by a disinterested board of directors, was here effected at the direction of the principal Class B stockholder in order to profit it. Such a call is voidable in equity at the instance of a stockholder injured thereby. It must be pointed out that under the allegations of the complaint there was no reason for the redemption of the Class A stock to be followed by the liquidation of Axton-Fisher except to enable the Class B stock to profit at the expense of the Class A stock. As has been hereinbefore stated the function of the call was confided to the board of directors by the charter and was not vested by the charter in the stockholders of any class. It was the intention of the framers of Axton-Fisher's charter to require the board of directors to act disinterestedly if that body called the Class A stock, and to make the call with a due regard for its fiduciary obligations. If the allegations of the complaint be proved, it follows that the directors of Axton-Fisher, the instruments of Transamerica, have been derelict in that duty. Liability which flows from the dereliction must be imposed upon Transamerica which, under the allegations of the complaint, constituted the board of Axton-Fisher and controlled it.

* * *

As has been stated the plaintiff has endeavored to set up a "First Cause of Action" and a "Second Cause of Action" in his complaint. The first cause of action is based upon his ownership of shares of Class A stock not surrendered by him to Axton-Fisher for redemption and is asserted not only on his own behalf but also on behalf of other Class A stockholders retaining their stock. The second cause of action is asserted by him on his own behalf and on behalf of other Class A stockholders in respect to the value of the stock which was surrendered for redemption. The two alleged separate causes of action, however, are in reality one. In our opinion, if the allegations of the complaint be proved, Zahn may maintain his cause of action to recover from Transamerica the value of the stock retained by him as that shall be represented by its aliquot share of the proceeds of Axton-Fisher on dissolution. It is also our opinion that he may maintain a cause of action to recover the difference between the amount received by him for the shares already surrendered and the amount which he would have received on liquidation of Axton-Fisher if he had not surrendered his stock.   *   *   *

4. THE CORPORATE OPPORTUNITY DOCTRINE

The doctrine of corporate opportunity is a branch of the duty of loyalty owed by a corporate manager to his corporation. The doctrine forbids a manager from diverting to himself an opportunity that "belongs" to the corporation. Although that proposition sounds reasonable and relatively straightforward, it turns out in practice to be quite difficult to apply. The problem is to separate "opportunities" that should, in conscience be turned over to the corporation, from those that can properly be exploited by the individual. Courts often pose the question in terms of whether the corporation has some "expectancy" in the opportunity. As a leading case put it:

> This corporate right or expectancy, this mandate upon directors to act for the corporation, may arise from various circumstance, such as, for example, the fact that directors had undertaken to negotiate in the field on behalf of the corporation, or that the corporation was in need of the particular business opportunity to the knowledge of the directors, or that the business opportunity was seized and developed at the expense, and with the facilities of the corporation. It is noteworthy that in cases which have imposed this type of liability upon fiduciaries, the thing determined by the court to be the subject of the trust was a thing of special and unique value to the [beneficiary]; for example, real estate, a proprietary formula valuable to the corporation's business, patents indispensable or valuable to its business, a competing enterprise or one required for the growth and expansion of the corporation's business or the like. To put it quite simply, the question to be determined is, have the directors profited at the expense of their corporation; have they gained because of disloyalty to its interests and welfare?" Litwin v. Allen, 25 N.Y.S.2d 667, 686 (Sup.Ct.1940).

If a corporate opportunity has been usurped, the corporation can recover any damages it may have suffered or any profits realized by the corporate manager. A constructive trust may also be applied for the corporation's benefit on the subject matter of the corporate opportunity, particularly if the corporation's need for the property is substantial. Harmony Way Bridge Co. v. Leathers, 353 Ill. 378, 187 N.E. 432 (1933). If the corporate manager has been unjustly enriched, he or she will be liable even if the dealings of the corporate manager have not been harmful or caused a loss to the corporation.

PROBLEM

MILTON CORPORATION—PART II

A little over a year ago, the Milton Corporation began to discuss the possibility of buying or building a gambling casino. After a management presentation to the directors on the advantages and disadvantages of such a step, the board authorized the officers to begin an active search for specific prospects. Management's initial investigations turned up nothing that seemed appropriate.

Meanwhile, shortly after this process began, Ruth Grey, one of the directors, inherited from her great uncle a large parcel of land on the boardwalk in Atlantic City, New Jersey. She mentioned this fact to James Milton after a board meeting, and inquired if he thought that the property might be suitable for the corporation's casino project. Milton was favorably struck by the idea, and became enthusiastic about it when a preliminary study showed that the property would be ideal for a casino.

Grey had her personal attorney contact Milton, and the two entered into negotiations about the sale of the Atlantic City property. The board was informed about these negotiations. Eventually, Milton and Grey's lawyer arrived at a tentative agreement on a sale for $850,000, which Milton said was the highest the corporation would be willing to pay. The agreement was subject to approval by Grey and by the Milton Corporation's directors.

Before the matter could be brought before the board, however, Grey was approached by Resorts Unlimited, Inc., a large company that owns and operates numerous casinos and resorts throughout the world. Resorts offered Grey $1 million for the property. She immediately called Milton, who told her that he did not feel the property was worth that much and that he would not be willing to match the Resorts offer. Grey and Milton informed the board of these events at its next meeting. Grey later sold the property to Resorts for $1.1 million.

Besides being a director of the Milton Corporation, Robert White has extensive personal investments in a variety of fields, including substantial real estate holdings. He is also the president and chairman of the board of Petro Investments, Inc., a holding company whose assets are invested primarily in real estate. Shortly after the board meeting at which the directors of Milton were told of the possibility of buying Grey's property in Atlantic City, White met an old business acquaintance while on a trip to London. White's friend told him that a London casino had just come on the market at what the friend said was a very attractive price. White immediately called the real estate broker who was handling the casino, and within three weeks had signed a contract on behalf of Petro Investments to purchase it. Ten months later, Petro resold the casino at a $1.5 million profit.

You have been approached by Beatrice Rate, a shareholder in the Milton Corporation, who has recounted essentially these facts. She has asked you about the possibility of success of a derivative suit against Grey and White. How should you advise her? Would you take her case on a contingent-fee basis?

MILLER v. MILLER

302 Minn. 207, 222 N.W.2d 71 (1974).

ROGOSHESKE, Justice.

[Miller Waste Mills, Inc. (Miller Waste) was a closely-held family corporation. At the time of this action, plaintiff Oscar Miller was a minority shareholder of Miller Waste. The individual defendants were plaintiff's brothers, Benjamin and Rudolph who held a majority of the shares and who as officers and directors, actively controlled and managed the corporation. Other minority shares were held by the parties' mother, brother and sisters. Miller Waste was engaged in the business of high volume manufacture of "packing waste" and "wiping waste," products, respectively, used to lubricate railroad cars and to wipe engines and other heavy machinery. From 1943 until 1953 Rudolph and Benjamin financed six different corporations which were engaged in businesses related to Miller Waste. Plaintiff brought a shareholder's derivative action to recover assets and profits of the six corporations owned and controlled by his defendant brothers, alleging that they wrongfully diverted to the corporate defendants corporate opportunities properly belonging to Miller Waste. The trial court entered judgment dismissing plaintiff's complaint. On appeal the Supreme Court of Minnesota affirmed.

In dismissing plaintiff's complaint, the trial court found that none of the businesses of the defendant corporations was a corporate opportunity of Miller Waste, except business transfers to one corporation. However, the court determined in that instance no wrongful diversion was made since the transfers were made or the opportunities seized in good faith and duly ratified by the then officers and shareholders of Miller Waste.]

* * *

The principal issue raised by plaintiff, and the one on which our disposition of this appeal rests, concerns the proper standards to be applied in determining whether defendants Rudolph and Benjamin Miller appropriated to themselves business opportunities properly belonging to Miller Waste. Even though the various opportunities were developed by defendant corporations, all were owned and controlled by Rudolph and Benjamin. Thus, we approach the issue in the same way as if the opportunities were appropriated by the defendants personally.

Having conceded on oral argument, as plaintiff must, that the court's factual findings and the inference drawn therefrom which bear on this issue have ample evidentiary support, he vigorously argues that the trial court, constrained by our decision in Diedrick v. Helm, 217 Minn. 483, 14 N.W.2d 913 (1944), limited the holding of the landmark case of Guth v. Loft, Inc., 23 Del.Ch. 255, 5 A.2d 503 (1939), and thereby applied an unduly restrictive "line of business" test or standard in determining that defendants were not liable for any diversion of corporate opportunities, and that application of proper standards requires reversal.

At the outset we acknowledge the well-recognized, common-law principle that one entrusted with the active management of a corporation, such as an officer or director, occupies a fiduciary relationship to the corporation and may not exploit his position as an "insider" by appropriating to himself a business opportunity properly belonging to the corporation. If such a business opportunity is usurped for personal gain, it is equally well recognized that the opportunity and any property or profit acquired becomes subject to a constructive trust for the benefit of the corporation. Guth v. Loft, Inc. *supra*. This principle, usually referred to as the doctrine of corporate opportunity, is derived essentially from fundamental rules of agency concerning the duty of utmost good faith and loyalty owed by a fiduciary to his principal[6] and also from the law of constructive trusts embodying equitable principles of unjust enrichment.

Although the rule prohibiting usurpation of corporate opportunities is easy to state, difficulties arise in its application. The main problem confronting courts concerns the proper test or standards to apply in determining whether a business opportunity properly belongs to the corporation. Guth v. Loft, Inc., *supra*, cited by virtually all jurisdictions confronted with the problem, adopted the following standards (23 Del.Ch. 271, 5 A.2d 510):

> It is true that when a business opportunity comes to a corporate officer or director in his individual capacity rather than in his official capacity, and the opportunity is one which, because of the nature of the enterprise, is not essential to his corporation, and is one in which it has no interest or expectancy, the officer or director is entitled to treat the opportunity as his own, and the corporation has no interest in it, if, of course the officer or director has not wrongfully embarked the corporation's resources therein.
> * * *

> On the other hand, it is equally true that, if there is presented to a corporate officer or director a business opportunity which the corporation is financially able to undertake, is, from its nature, in

---

6. Cf. Minn.St. 301.31: "Officers and directors shall discharge the duties of their respective positions in good faith, and with that diligence and care which ordinarily prudent men would exercise under similar circumstances in like positions."

the line of the corporation's business and is of practical advantage to it, is one in which the corporation has an interest or a reasonable expectancy, and, by embracing the opportunity, the self-interest of the officer or director will be brought into conflict with that of his corporation, the law will not permit him to seize the opportunity for himself.

While this court has dealt with the problem and has acknowledged the general principles embodied in the doctrine of corporate opportunity, the necessity of adopting a specific formula for determining when a business opportunity properly belongs to the corporation has not previously been directly presented. In Diedrick, our leading case, we cited the principles and standards set forth in Guth and also in Solimine v. Hollander, 128 N.J.Eq. 228, 16 A.2d 203 (1940), but expressly deemed it unnecessary to formulate "an all-inclusive definition of what constitutes a 'corporate opportunity' " for the decision in that case. 217 Minn. 493, 14 N.W.2d 919, 153 A.L.R. 658. Even though the Diedrick case is cited as adopting what might be called the five-pronged Solimine test for determining the existence of corporate opportunities,[10] we interpret the court's opinion as relying mainly upon the "line of business" test enunciated in Guth.

Apart from our prior treatment of the problem, other jurisdictions have also experienced difficulties in applying proper standards. We have searched the case law and commentary in vain for an all-inclusive or "critical" test or standard by which a wrongful appropriation can be determined and are persuaded that the doctrine is not capable of precise definition. Rather, it appears that courts have opened or closed the business opportunity door to corporate managers upon the facts and circumstances of each case and by application of one or more of three variant but often overlapping tests or standards: (1) The "interest or expectancy" test, which precludes acquisition by corporate officers of the property of a business opportunity in which the corporation has a "beachhead" in the sense of a legal or equitable interest or expectancy growing out of a preexisting right or relationship;[11] (2) the "line of business" test, which characterizes an opportunity as corporate whenever a managing officer becomes involved in

---

10. According to Solimine v. Hollander, 128 N.J.Eq. 228, 246, 16 A.2d 203, 215 (1940), a business opportunity is not a corporate one "(a) wherever the fundamental fact of good faith is determined in favor of the director or officer charged with usurping the corporate opportunity, *or* (b) where the company is unable to avail itself of the opportunity, *or* (c) where availing itself of the opportunity is not *essential* to the company's business, *or* (d) where the accused fiduciary does not exploit the opportunity by the employment of his company's resources, *or* (e) where by embracing the opportunity personally the director or officer is not

brought into direct competition with his company and its business." Note that each of the above considerations is mutually exclusive and that the presence of any one consideration precludes the finding of a usurpation of a corporate opportunity.

11. For example, a corporation which possesses a lease on certain property or operates under a patent license is deemed to have an "interest" or "expectancy" in such property or license as to preclude the appropriation of such interests by the corporate fiduciaries.

an activity intimately or closely associated with the existing or prospective activities of the corporation; and (3) the "fairness" test, which determines the existence of a corporate opportunity by applying ethical standards of what is fair and equitable under the circumstances.

The Guth case, most often cited as establishing the "line of business" test—more flexible in scope than the restrictive "interest or expectancy" test of earlier decisions—also recognized the practical fairness approach which has been employed in more recent decisions (23 Del.Ch. 279, 5 A.2d 514):

> * * * [T]he appellants say that the expression, "in the line" of a business, is a phrase so elastic as to furnish no basis for a useful inference. The phrase is not within the field of precise definition, nor is it one that can be bounded by a set formula. *It has a flexible meaning, which is to be applied reasonably and sensibly to the facts and circumstances of the particular case. Where a corporation is engaged in a certain business, and an opportunity is presented to it embracing an activity as to which it has fundamental knowledge, practical experience and ability to pursue, which, logically and naturally, is adaptable to its business having regard for its financial position, and is one that is consonant with its reasonable needs and aspirations for expansion, it may be properly said that the opportunity is in the line of the corporation's business.* (Italics supplied.)

In Durfee v. Durfee & Canning, 323 Mass. 187, 199, 80 N.E.2d 522, 529 (1948), the court, which placed strong emphasis on factors of fairness, rejected the "interest or expectancy" test and declared:

> We do not concur in the argument of counsel for the defendant to the effect that the test is whether the corporation has an existing interest or an expectancy thereof in the property involved, being of the opinion that *the true basis of the governing doctrine rests fundamentally on the unfairness in the particular circumstances of a director, whose relation to the corporation is fiduciary, "taking advantage of an opportunity [for his personal profit] when the interest of the corporation justly calls for protection. This calls for the application of ethical standards of what is fair and equitable * * * [in] particular sets of facts."* Ballantine on Corporations (Rev. ed. 1946) 204–205. (Italics supplied.)

 In an effort hopefully to ameliorate the often-expressed criticism that the doctrine is vague and subjects today's corporate management to the danger of unpredictable liability, we believe a more helpful approach is to combine the "line of business" test with the "fairness" test and to adopt criteria involving a two-step process for determining the ultimate question of when liability for a wrongful appropriation of a corporate opportunity should be imposed. The threshold question to be answered is whether a business opportunity presented is also a "corporate" opportunity, i.e., whether the business opportunity is of sufficient importance and is so closely related to the existing or prospective activity of the corporation as to warrant judicial sanctions against its personal acquisition by a managing officer or director of the corporation. This question, necessarily one of fact, can best be resolved, we believe, by resort to a flexible application of the "line of business" test set forth in Guth v. Loft, Inc., *supra*. The inquiry of the factfinder should be directed to all facts and circumstances relevant to the question, the most significant being: Whether the business opportunity presented is one in which the complaining corporation has an interest or an expectancy growing out of an existing contractual right; the relationship of the opportunity to the corporation's business purposes and current activities—whether essential, necessary, or merely desirable to its reasonable needs and aspirations—; whether, within or without its corporate powers, the opportunity embraces areas adaptable to its business and into which the corporation might easily, naturally, or logically expand; the competitive nature of the opportunity—whether prospectively harmful or unfair—; whether the corporation, by reason of insolvency or lack of resources, has the financial ability to acquire the opportunity; and whether the opportunity includes activities as to which the corporation has fundamental knowledge, practical experience, facilities, equipment, personnel, and the ability to pursue. The fact that the opportunity is not within the scope of the corporation's powers, while a factor to be considered, should not be determinative, especially where the corporate fiduciary dominates the board of directors or is the majority shareholder.

[handwritten margin note: Step 1]

If the facts are undisputed that the business opportunity presented bears no logical or reasonable relation to the existing or prospective business activities of the corporation or that it lacks either the financial or fundamental practical or technical ability to pursue it, then such opportunity would have to be found to be noncorporate as a matter of law. If the facts are disputed or reasonable minds functioning judicially could disagree as to whether the opportunity is closely associated with the existing or prospective activities of the corporation or its financial or technical ability to pursue it, the question is one of fact with the burden of proof resting upon the party attacking the acquisition.

Absent any evidence of fraud or a breach of fiduciary duty, if it is determined that a business opportunity is not a corporate opportunity, the corporate officer should not be held liable for its acquisition. If, however, the opportunity is found to be a corporate one, liability should not be imposed upon the acquiring officer if the evidence establishes that his acquisition did not violate his fiduciary duties of loyalty, good faith, and fair dealing toward the corporation. Thus the second step in the two-step process leading to the determination of the ultimate question of liability involves close scrutiny of the equitable considerations existing prior to, at the time of, and following

[handwritten margin note: Step 2]

the officer's acquisition. Resolution will necessarily depend upon a consideration of all the facts and circumstances of each case considered in the light of those factors which control the decision that the opportunity was in fact a corporate opportunity. Significant factors which should be considered are the nature of the officer's relationship to the management and control of the corporation; whether the opportunity was presented to him in his official or individual capacity; his prior disclosure of the opportunity to the board of directors or shareholders and their response; whether or not he used or exploited corporate facilities, assets, or personnel in acquiring the opportunity; whether his acquisition harmed or benefited the corporation; and all other facts and circumstances bearing on the officer's good faith and whether he exercised the diligence, devotion, care, and fairness toward the corporation which ordinarily prudent men would exercise under similar circumstances in like positions. Minn.St. 301.31.

We are not to be understood, by adopting this two-step process, as suggesting that a finding of bad faith is essential to impose liability upon the acquiring officer. Nor, conversely, that good faith alone, apart from the officer's fiduciary duty requiring loyalty and fair dealing toward the corporation, will absolve him from liability. And it must be acknowledged, in adopting corporate opportunity doctrine expanded beyond the narrow preexisting property interest or expectancy standard, that there can be cases where the officer's personal seizure of an opportunity so clearly essential to the continuance of a corporation or so intimately related to its activities as to amount to a direct interference with its existing activities would negate any attempt by the officer to prove his good faith, loyalty, and fair dealing.

The burden of proof on the questions of good faith, fair dealing, and loyalty of the officer to the corporation should rest upon the officer who appropriated the business opportunity for his own advantage. Such a burden necessarily lies with the acquiring officer because a fiduciary with a conflict of interest should be required to justify his actions and because of the practical reality that the facts with regard to such questions are more apt to be within his knowledge.

* * *

[Applying the first tier of its analysis to the Miller case, the court held that whether the businesses of five of the corporate defendants were in the line of business of Miller Waste was a disputed question of fact and "clearly the trial court's finding that each was not [had] ample evidentiary support." Similarly, the findings that the individual defendants diverted from Miller Waste, corporate opportunities transferred to two of the defendant corporations were sustained by the evidence, and were in the court's view, "consistent with the proper application of the standards to be applied in determining the question of whether a business opportunity presented to a corporate fiduciary is a corporate opportunity." Finally, the trial court's conclusion that the defendants were not liable for usurping corporate opportunity was affirmed based on a consideration of the "equitable" factors enumerated in the second tier of the test, specifically the transfers "did not harm the corporation; that no corporate assets or facilities were used or exploited; that such diversions were made in good faith without concealment * * * and after full disclosure to and with the acquiescence, if not the approval, of all the then officers and shareholders of Miller Waste."].

Affirmed.

NOTE

Some facts considered by courts in determining whether a corporate manager may personally take an opportunity include whether:

1. corporate utilization is barred by State law or the corporation's articles of incorporation. Amending the articles may be a time-consuming procedure thereby causing both the corporation and the corporate executive to lose the opportunity;

2. the corporation is financially unable to take advantage of the opportunity because of financial difficulty or a lack of liquid assets. Actual financial insolvency leaves the corporate manager free to act. The court in Irving Trust Co. v. Deutsch, 73 F.2d 121, 124 (2d Cir. 1934), reversing in part 2 F.Supp. 971 (S.D.N.Y.1932), cert. denied 294 U.S. 708, 55 S.Ct. 405, 79 L.Ed. 1243 (1935), stated:

> Nevertheless, [these facts which raise some question whether the corporation actually lacked the funds or credit necessary for carrying out a contract] tend to show the wisdom of a rigid rule forbidding directors of a solvent corporation to take over for their own profit a corporate contract on the plea of the corporation's financial inability to perform. If the directors are uncertain whether the corporation can make the necessary outlays, they need not embark it upon the venture; if they do, they may not substitute themselves for the corporation any place along the line and divert possible benefits into their own pockets.

In more "liberal" jurisdictions, see e.g. Gauger v. Hintz, 262 Wis. 333, 55 N.W.2d 426 (1953), corporate managers may retain an opportunity because the corporation did not then "have the liquid funds available" to take advantage of it. Corporate managers must, however, use their best efforts to uncover the financing needed by their corporation to acquire an opportunity. A director or officer need not advance funds to enable a corporation to take advantage of a business opportunity. A. C. Petters Co. v. St. Cloud Enterprises, Inc., 301 Minn. 261, 222 N.W.2d 83 (1974).

3. the opportunity has been offered to and rejected by an independent board of directors after full disclosure. Gaynor v. Buckley, 203 F.Supp. 620 (D.Or.1962), aff'd on other grounds 318 F.2d 432 (9th Cir. 1963). Disclosure above may, however, be insufficient if the

transaction is unfair. Recall Fliegler v. Lawrence. See also the excerpt from Johnston v. Greene below.

What if the interested corporate manager dominated the board through stock ownership? Domination probably refers to the actual use of stock ownership to control or influence the board.* In Johnston v. Greene, 35 Del.Ch. 479, 121 A.2d 919 (1956), Odlum, the alleged wrongdoer, was a director of Airfleets and the president of Atlas Corp., a corporation of which he owned or controlled approximately 11% of its stock. Atlas, in turn, was the largest shareholder of Airfleets and owned about 18% of the latter's stock. The chancellor found that Odlum dominated the board of Airfleets on the basis of his stock ownership and as to the other directors, his "wishes were their commands." The Delaware Supreme Court accepted the chancellor's finding as to the existence of domination but declined to hold Odlum liable, holding that he had acted properly. 35 Del.Ch. at 489, 121 A.2d at 925.

Rejection by a controlled board, however, provides a defense if the directors exercise independent business judgment on a particular transaction.

4. the third party refuses to deal with the corporation but only if the corporate manager has not instigated that refusal. *See e.g.* Crittenden & Cowler Co. v. Cowles, 66 App.Div. 95, 72 N.Y.S. 701 (1901).

A difficult situation arises when a director or officer holds positions in two or more corporations or is a corporate manager in one corporation and a substantial shareholder in one corporation and dominates the second corporation by selecting directors and officers subservient to his or her will.

COMMENT, CORPORATE OPPORTUNITY

74 Harv.L.Rev. 765, 770–771 (1961).

* * *

In resolving the conflict of loyalties that may confront an executive participating in the affairs of several corporations, the initial step should be to determine which, if any, of the corporations has under the line-of-business test a prior claim to the opportunity as against the executive. If only one of the corporations has a prior claim, the executive would seem to violate his duty to that corporation as much by delivering the opportunity to a different corporation as by appropriating it for himself. However, if the opportunity is within the line of business of more than one of his corporations, two determinations must be made: first, whether the executive should ever be permitted to resolve the conflict by delivering the opportunity to one of the corporations, rather than disclosing it to the corporations and letting

* Walker, Legal Handles Used to Open
or Close the Corporate Opportunity Door,
56 Nw.U.L.Rev. 608, 622 (1961).

them compete for it; second, whether within the area of the line of business, there are degrees of obligation the existence of which will under certain circumstances compel the executive to recognize a paramount duty to one of the corporations. There does appear to be at least one functional criterion for distinguishing between corporate claimants, namely whether the opportunity is essential to the successful performance of the present operations of one of the corporations. To put this criterion in a slightly different form, the inquiry should be whether one corporation has a claim to the opportunity under the old definition of corporate opportunity while the others must rely on the modern definition to support their claims. Another possible criterion is whether the opportunity will relieve one corporation from serious financial difficulties while it would merely augment the profits of the other claimants. But this criterion is a questionable one, since profit and loss are on the same continuum, and to the corporation and its shareholders the loss of a possible profit may not appear intrinsically different from the loss which would result from the corporation's falling into insolvency.

Even if the suggested criterion for determining degrees of obligation is adopted, there will undoubtedly be cases where all the potentially interested corporations fall within or without it. Under those circumstances, it might seem fairest to require disclosure to all of them. Disclosure, however, may lead to competitive bidding which will drive up the cost of the opportunity. When the shareholders of the competing corporations are not substantially identical, each corporation would seemingly prefer the risk of a higher price to the risk of losing the opportunity. But where most of the stock of each corporation is held by the same group of shareholders, and the management groups are different enough to make competition likely, the interests of the vast majority of shareholders may be best served by permitting a common officer or director to allocate the opportunity at his discretion, as long as he acts in good faith.

Where the applicable law is uncertain, a corporation could perhaps assure its executives freedom to allocate opportunities among the corporations to which they are obligated by adoption of a charter provision. Such a provision might stipulate that "officers and directors of this corporation may hold positions as officers and directors of other corporations in related businesses and their efforts to advance such corporations will not constitute a breach of fiduciary loyalty to this corporation in the absence of a showing of bad faith." This type of provision should ordinarily be effective to relieve an executive of his obligation to make disclosure to all the corporations with which he is connected, although a court might not be inclined to construe it to allow him to ignore a paramount duty arising under the criterion mentioned above.

* * *

In Johnston v. Greene, 35 Del.Ch. 479, 121 A.2d 919 (1956), Odlum, a financier, who was an officer and director of numerous corporations, was offered, in his individual capacity, the chance to acquire the stock of Nutt-Shel, a corporation 100% owned by Hutson, and several patents pertaining to its business. The business of Nutt-Shel had no close relation to the business of Airfleets, Inc., of which Odlum was president. Odlum turned over to Airfleets the opportunity to buy the stock of Nutt-Shel, but purchased the patents for his friends and associates and, to a limited extent, for himself. Airfleets, a corporation with a large amount of cash, possessed the financial capability to buy the patents. The board of Airfleets, dominated by Odlum, voted to buy only the stock. A shareholders' derivative action was instituted against Odlum and the directors for an accounting of the profits realized on the sale of the patents. The Delaware Supreme Court stated:

The first important fact that appears is that Hutson's offer, which was to sell the patents and at least part of the stock, came to Odlum, not as a director of Airfleets, but in his individual capacity. The Chancellor so found. The second important fact is that the business of Nutt-Shel—the manufacture of self-locking nuts—had no direct or close relation to any business that Airfleets was engaged in or had ever been engaged in, and hence its acquisition was not essential to the conduct of Airfleets' business. Again, the Chancellor so found. The third fact is that Airfleets had no interest or expectancy in the Nutt-Shel business, in the sense that those words are used in the decisions dealing with the law of corporate opportunity. * * * For the corporation to have an actual or expectant interest in any specific property, there must be some tie between that property and the nature of the corporate business. Cf. Guth v. Loft, [23 Del.Ch. 255, 5 A.2d 503], in which the Court said: "The tie was close between the business of Loft and the Pepsi-Cola enterprise". 23 Del.Ch. 279, 5 A.2d 515. No such tie exists here. Airfleets had no interest, actual or in expectancy, in the Nutt-Shel business.

We accordingly find ourselves compelled to disagree with the Chancellor's decision. Recognizing that Airfleets had no expectancy in the Nutt-Shel business and that its acquisition was not essential to Airfleets, he nevertheless held that Airfleets' need for investments constituted an "interest" in the opportunity to acquire that business. Now, this is an application of the rule of corporate opportunity that requires careful examination. It is one thing to say that a corporation with funds to invest has a general interest in investing those funds; it is quite another to say that such a corporation has a specific interest attaching in equity to any and every business opportunity that may come to any of its directors in his individual capacity. This is what the Chancellor appears to have held. Such a sweeping extension of the rule of corporate opportunity finds no support in the decisions and is, we think, unsound.

It is, of course, entirely possible that a corporate opportunity might in some cases arise out of a corporate need to invest funds and the duty of the president or any other director to seek such an opportunity. But whether it does arise, in any particular case, depends on the facts—upon the existence of special circumstances that would make it unfair for him to take the opportunity for himself.

We cannot find any such circumstances in this case. At the time when the Nutt-Shel business was offered to Odlum, his position was this: He was the part-time president of Airfleets. He was also president of Atlas—an investment company. He was a director of other corporations and a trustee of foundations interested in making investments. If it was his fiduciary duty, upon being offered any investment opportunity, to submit it to a corporation of which he was a director, the question arises, Which corporation? Why Airfleets instead of Atlas? Why Airfleets instead of one of the foundations? So far as appears, there was no specific tie between the Nutt-Shel business and any of these corporations or foundations. Odlum testified that many of his companies had money to invest, and this appears entirely reasonable. How, then, can it be said that Odlum was under any obligation to offer the opportunity to one particular corporation? And if he was not under such an obligation, why could he not keep it for himself?

Plaintiff suggests that if Odlum elects to assume fiduciary relationships to competing corporations he must assume the obligations that are entailed by such relationships. So he must, but what are the obligations? The mere fact of having funds to invest does not ordinarily put the corporations "in competition" with each other, as that phrase is used in the law of corporate opportunity. There is nothing inherently wrong in a man of large business and financial interests serving as a director of two or more investment companies, and both Airfleets and Atlas (to mention only two companies) must reasonably have expected that Odlum would be free either to offer to any of his companies any business opportunity that came to him personally, or to retain it for himself—provided always that there was no tie between any of such companies and the new venture or any specific duty resting upon him with respect to it.

It is clear to us that the reason why the Nutt-Shel business was offered to Airfleets was because Odlum, having determined that he did not want it for himself, chose to place the investment in that one of his companies whose tax situation was best adapted to receive it. He chose to do so, although he could probably have sold the stock to an outside company at a profit to himself. If he had done so, who could have complained? If a stockholder of Airfleets could have done so, why not a stockholder of Atlas as well?

It is unnecessary to labor the point further. We are of opinion that the opportunity to purchase the Nutt-Shel business belonged to Odlum and not to any of his companies.

This conclusion requires the rejection of the plaintiffs' contention, and of the Chancellor's holding, that the opportunity to buy the Nutt-Shel business belonged to Airfleets. But it does not in itself dispose of the case.

The refusal of the directors of Airfleets to buy the patents was, under the Chancellor's finding, a transaction between the dominating director and his corporation. It is therefore subject to strict scrutiny, and the defendants have the burden of showing that it was fair.

* * *

Our conclusions upon a careful review of this record are: first, that the opportunity to acquire the Nutt-Shel business did not belong to Airfleets; second, that the transaction between Odlum and Airfleets involving the patents was fair and free of any overreaching or inequitable conduct.

* * *

5. EXECUTIVE COMPENSATION

a. Introduction

There are four basic forms of executive compensation: salaries; bonuses; stock options and other plans based on stock value; and deferred compensation (pension) plans. To this might be added the fringe benefits (or "perks") which, depending on which commentators you believe (and which companies you observe) are either outrageous wastes of corporate funds or are moderate and useful forms of inducing executives to work harder. From the point of view of the executive, there are a number of factors that enter into the structuring of the ideal compensation package, including income and estate tax considerations, the executive's age and retirement plans, outside income, and preference as to balance between risk and potential gain.

From the point of view of the corporation, the principal considerations are the obvious ones of minimizing the cash outlay involved and maximizing the incentive effect on the performance of the executive, maximizing the deductibility of the total compensation paid for the purposes of computing the corporation's income tax and limiting the dilution of capital resulting from the sale of stock at below-market prices.

Salary and Current Bonus. Executives receive a fixed base salary plus a bonus geared to a percentage of the corporation's profits. Salaries, if reasonable, are immediately deductible by the corporation for income tax purposes as ordinary and necessary business expenses.

Traditionally, directors served without compensation with their rewards coming from the increased value of their shares. Lacking a significant share ownership, corporations are increasingly providing directors with meaningful compensation. The median annual salary for outside directors of large, manufacturing corporations ranges from $5,000 to $15,000.

Stock Options. Stock options tie executive compensation to the performance of the corporation's stock. A stock option is an agreement by which a corporation grants an executive the right to buy a specified number of shares of the corporation's stock at a fixed price over a limited period of time. Stock options which were qualified under the Internal Revenue Code possessed a number of favorable income tax advantages. Currently, so-called incentive stock options offer income tax benefits.

Another compensation technique tied to the market performance of the corporation's stock may take the form of a phantom stock plan under which an executive is credited with units on the books of the corporation. The value of a unit equals the market value of a share of the corporation's stock when the unit is created increased by (1) the value of the stock until a specified date, such as the retirement or death of the executive and (2) the dividends paid on a share of stock during this time period. This arrangement provides the executive with an interest that appreciates with the rise in the value of the corporation's stock without any financial outlay. An executive need not bear the additional risk associated with the holding of shares purchased on the exercise of an option. Income taxation is deferred until the individual receives the funds from the corporation. The corporation, in turn, receives a deduction in the year the executive pays income taxes.

Deferred Compensation Plans. The most common form of deferred compensation plan is a retirement plan which provides cash payments after retirement and is designed to provide a source of income during retirement. Deferred compensation plans which are qualified under the Internal Revenue Code offer tax benefits for both corporations and executives. Corporations receive an immediate deduction for income tax purposes on cash contributions into the plan. Compensation deferred until retirement is taxable at a later date when presumably executives will be in a lower income tax bracket. The accumulation of income on the amounts paid into the plan is tax free.

Fringe Benefits ("Perks"). Corporations provide executives with an endless variety of fringe benefits, including group life insurance, health insurance, use of corporate autos and aircraft, and free lunches and vacations. Each form has its own income tax and financial considerations.

Executive Compensation: Corporate Law Consideration. Planning executive compensation raises four basic questions: shareholder approval; consideration; self-dealing; and waste. Corporate laws usually require shareholder approval with respect to rights or options entitling directors, officers or employees to acquire stock of the corporation. MBCA § 20. The executive must supply adequate consideration by means of an employment contract or the arrangement must be conditioned on continued service by the executive. *See e.g.* Beard v. Elster, 39 Del.Ch. 153, 160 A.2d 731 (1960). In Kerbs v. California Eastern Airways, Inc., 33 Del.Ch. 69, 90 A.2d 652, 656 (Del. 1952) the court stated:

> The validity of a stock option plan under which selected personnel of a corporation may acquire a stock interest in the corporation depends directly upon the existence of consideration to the corporation and the inclusion in the plan of conditions, or the existence of circumstances which may be expected to insure that the contemplated consideration will in fact pass to the corporation.
> * * *
>
> What is sufficient consideration to validate a plan depends upon the facts and circumstances of the particular case. Sufficient consideration to the corporation may be, *inter alia*, the retention of the services of an employee, or the gaining of the services of a new employee, provided there is a reasonable relationship between the value of the services to be rendered by the employee and the value of the options granted as an inducement or compensation.

Several avenues exist to surmount the self-dealing problem raised where directors are asked to approve compensation arrangements in which they are included as officers. A corporation could seek (1) shareholder approval or (2) the recommendations of the outside (disinterested) directors or a committee composed of outside directors, or (3) both (1) and (2). A disinterested quorum will not exist if the officer-directors act on each other's compensation arrangement, with each interested director withdrawing from the deliberations on his or her plan. Stoiber v. Miller Brewing Co., 257 Wis. 13, 42 N.W.2d 144 (1950). Where the compensation is authorized by the shareholders (a majority of whom are disinterested) or disinterested directors, the business judgment rule places the burden of proving waste on the party attacking the reasonableness of the compensation. What limits, however, do the concepts of waste and reasonableness impose on executive compensation?

b. Publicly Held Corporations

In Rogers v. Hill, 289 U.S. 582, 53 S.Ct. 731, 77 L.Ed. 1385 (1933), a shareholder brought a suit to recover for the company the allegedly excessive compensation paid its president, George W. Hill, and five Vice Presidents. In 1912 the shareholders of the American Tobacco Co. adopted a by-law providing for annual bonus payments to these corporate officers of amounts based on a percentage net profits in excess of a stated amount. The soaring fortunes of the American Tobacco Co. led to a swelling of the amount representing these bonuses. By 1930, Hill's percentage of net profits reached $842,507. In reversing the decision of the Second Circuit dismissing the complaint, the Supreme Court stated:

It follows from what has been shown that when adopted the by-law was valid. But plaintiff alleges that the measure of compensation fixed by it is not now equitable or fair. And he prays that the court fix and determine the fair and reasonable compensation of the individual defendants, respectively, for each of the years in question. The allegations of the complaint are not sufficient to permit consideration by the court of the validity or reasonableness of any of the payments of account of fixed salaries, or of special credits, or of the allotments of stock therein mentioned. Indeed, plaintiff alleges that other proceedings have been instituted for the restoration of special credits, and his suits to invalidate the stock allotments were recently considered here. Rogers v. Guaranty Trust Co., 288 U.S. 123, 53 S.Ct. 295, 77 L.Ed. 652. The only payments that plaintiff by this suit seeks to have restored to the company are the payments made to the individual defendants under the by-law.

We come to consider whether these amounts are subject to examination and revision in the District Court. As the amounts payable depend upon the gains of the business, the specified percentages are not per se unreasonable. The by-law was adopted in 1912 by an almost unanimous vote of the shares represented at the annual meeting and presumably the stockholders supporting the measure acted in good faith and according to their best judgment.   *   *   *   Plaintiff does not complain of any [payments] made prior to 1921. Regard is to be had to the enormous increase of the company's profits in recent years. The $2\frac{1}{2}$ per cent yielded President Hill $447,870.30 in 1929 and $842,507.72 in 1930. The $1\frac{1}{2}$ per cent yielded to each of the vice-presidents, Neiley and Riggio, $115,141.86 in 1929 and $409,495.25 in 1930 and for these years payments under the by-law were in addition to the cash credits and fixed salaries shown in the statement.

While the amounts produced by the application of the prescribed percentages give rise to no inference of actual or constructive fraud, the payments under the by-law have by reason of increase of profits become so large as to warrant investigation in equity in the interest of the company. Much weight is to be given to the action of the stockholders, and the by-law is supported by the presumption of regularity and continuity. But the rule prescribed by it cannot, against the protest of a shareholder, be used to justify payments of sums as salaries so large as in substance and effect to amount to spoliation or waste of corporate property.

The dissenting opinion of Judge Swan indicates the applicable rule: "If a bonus payment has no relation to the value of services for which it is given, it is in reality a gift in part and the majority stockholders have no power to give away corporate property against the protest of the minority." 60 F.2d 109, 113. The facts alleged by plaintiff are sufficient to require that the District Court, upon a consideration of all the relevant facts brought forward by the parties, determine whether and to what extent payments to the individual defendants under the by-law constitute misuse and waste of the money of the corporation. * * *

Other shareholders brought a separate action, Heller v. Boylan, 29 N.Y.S.2d 653 (Sup.Ct.1941), aff'd mem. 263 App.Div. 815, 32 N.Y.S.2d 131 (1st Dept.1941), challenging the bonus payments in later years. In rejecting the attack, the court stated:

> Yes, the Court possesses the *power* to prune these payments, but openness forces the confession that the pruning would be synthetic and artificial rather than analytic or scientific. Whether or not it would be fair and just, is highly dubious. Yet, merely because the problem is perplexing is no reason for eschewing it. It is not timidity, however, which perturbs me. It is finding a rational or just gauge for revising these figures were I inclined to do so. No blueprints are furnished. The elements to be weighed are incalculable; the imponderables, manifold. To act out of whimsy or caprice or arbitrariness would be more than inexact—it would be the precise antithesis of justice; it would be a farce.
>
> If comparisons are to be made, with whose compensation are they to be made—executives? Those connected with the motion picture industry? Radio artists? Justices of the Supreme Court of the United States? The President of the United States? Manifestly, the material at hand is not of adequate plasticity for fashioning into a pattern or standard. Many instances of positive underpayment will come to mind, just as instances of apparent rank overpayment abound. Haplessly, intrinsic worth is not always the criterion. A classic might perhaps produce trifling compensation for its author, whereas a popular novel might yield a titantic fortune. Merit is not always commensurately rewarded, whilst mediocrity sometimes unjustly brings incredibly lavish returns. Nothing is so divergent and contentious and inexplicable as values.
>
> Courts are ill-equipped to solve or even to grapple with these entangled economic problems. Indeed, their solution is not within the juridical province. Courts are concerned that corporations be honestly and fairly operated by its directors, with the observance of the formal requirements of the law; but what is reasonable compensation for its officers is primarily for the stockholders. This does not mean that fiduciaries are to commit waste, or misuse or abuse trust property, with impunity. A just cause will find the Courts at guard and implemented to grant redress. But the

stockholder must project a less amorphous plaint than is here presented.

On this branch of the case, I find for the defendants. Yet it does not follow that I affirmatively approve these huge payments. It means that I cannot by any reliable standard find them to be waste or spoliation; it means that I find no valid ground for disapproving what the great majority of stockholders have approved. In the circumstances, if a ceiling for these bonuses is to be erected, the stockholders who built and are responsible for the present structure must be the architects. Finally, it is not amiss to accent the antiseptic policy stressed by Judge Liebell in Winkelman et al. v. General Motors Corporation, D.C.S.D.N.Y. decided August 14, 1940, 39 F.Supp. 826, that: "The duty of the director executives participating in the bonus seems plain—they should be the first to consider unselfishly whether under all the circumstances their bonus allowances are fair and reasonable".

c. Closely-Held Corporations

RUETZ v. TOPPING

453 S.W.2d 624 (Mo.App.1970).

[In this case the court held that interested directors of a close corporation did not satisfy their burden of justifying the compensation they had received by showing its reasonableness. An expert witness (a certified public accountant) called by defendants, had testified, in answer to a hypothetical question, that in his opinion salaries of $26,000 per year paid by the company were reasonable. In discussing this issue the court observed:]

* * * It is said that, like the reasonableness of an attorney's fee, the reasonableness of the compensation paid to an employee is a question of fact. Ordinarily, like an attorney's fee, it is not subject to a precise determination by any known mathematical formula; there is no hard and fast rule to be used in deciding what is reasonable in all cases and each must be decided on its own facts and circumstances. Unlike the determination of a reasonable attorney's fee, where the elements which may properly be considered are specified in our Civil Rule 4.12, V.A.M.R., no authority has been found which undertakes to give an all-inclusive statement of the factors which may properly be used in arriving at a conclusion as to the reasonableness of an employee's compensation.

This is not to say that we are wholly without some guidelines, for the question of what is reasonable compensation, especially at the executive level, has received attention from both the text writers and the courts. Fletcher, in his Cyclopedia Corporations, Vol. 5, Section 2133, p. 577, quotes from a New York case that:

To come within the rule of reason the compensation must be in proportion to the executive's ability, services and time devoted to the company, difficulties involved, responsibilities assumed, success achieved, amounts under jurisdiction, corporate earnings, profits and prosperity, increase in volume or quality of business or both, and all other relevant facts and circumstances.

Section 162(a)(1) of the Internal Revenue Code, 1954, allows a corporation to deduct as an ordinary and necessary expense in carrying on a business "a reasonable allowance for salaries or other compensation for personal services actually rendered," and that provision has proven to be a more prolific source of litigation as to what was or was not reasonable compensation. In that area, also no set formula has been devised, and various factors to be considered are mentioned: the employee's qualifications; the nature, extent and scope of the employee's work; the size and complexities of the business; a comparison of salaries paid with the gross income and the net income; the prevailing general economic conditions; a comparison of salaries with distribution to stockholders; the prevailing rates of compensation for comparable positions in comparable concerns; the salary policy of the taxpayer as to all employees; and in the case of small corporations with a limited number of officers the amount of compensation paid to the particular employee in previous years.

Chapter 15

SHAREHOLDER LITIGATION

PROBLEM

MILTON CORPORATION—PART III

[handwritten: Milton Corp = Hilton]

Reread the facts of Part I of the Milton Corporation Problem set forth in Chapter 14, Part B.

Acting on advice of counsel, the corporation submitted the proposed lease transaction between it and RIC to the shareholders, who approved it overwhelmingly. The proxy statement estimated that the amounts that would be paid under the clause in the lease giving RIC a percentage of the profits of the concessionaires would equal approximately 50 percent of the base rent.

It is now three years later, and the hotel has been extremely successful. The percentages of the concessionaires' profits paid RIC under the lease have proved to be quite high, even exceeding the base rental payments in the last two years. This has resulted principally from the addition of several new concessions as the hotel has expanded.

A

Your firm represents Herman, who owns 100 shares of Milton stock he inherited from his father under the latter's will a year ago. Herman's father purchased the shares at the time the corporation first went public. He did not vote on the lease transaction.

Herman has come to you to ask about the possibility of bringing a suit to challenge the lease with RIC. He has reason to believe that Milton's management may have known that the revenues that would be paid under the lease were likely to exceed the estimates given in the proxy statement. In any case, he is convinced that the payments to RIC are so high as to be unfair to the Milton Corporation.

The Milton Corporation is incorporated in Columbia and has its principal offices in New York. RIC is incorporated in Delaware and also has its principal offices in New York. The directors of Milton all reside in New York or in Connecticut. Herman is a resident of New Jersey.

Wilma Gilbert, the partner for whom you work, has asked you to analyze several questions:

1. What are the most promising causes of action that might be available to Herman?

2. Should a suit be brought as a derivative suit or a direct suit (probably in the form of a class action)?

3. Are there any problems with respect to Herman's standing to bring a derivative suit?

4. Is there diversity jurisdiction for a derivative suit? In addition to his home in New Jersey, Herman maintains an apartment in New York. Were a federal court to decide that he "resides" in New York, would there still be diversity jurisdiction for a derivative suit? Suppose all the directors reside in Connecticut and Pennsylvania.

5. If the action is cast as a derivative suit, must Herman first make a demand on the directors? On the shareholders? If so what form should the demand take? Suppose that it were decided to bring the suit in Columbia naming only RIC as a defendant, and suppose further that the Columbia state courts have followed the Massachusetts rules with respect to demand. Would your answers be different?

B

Assume now that you are an associate at the firm that has done the Milton Corporation's corporate and securities work for some time. Will Carey, the partner for whom you work, advised Milton on the transaction in question. He discussed it with James Milton and with other top company officials and reviewed various corporate documents.

Herman has filed suit in the federal district court in Columbia, alleging both that the lease transaction violated state law and that its approval violated the federal proxy rules. Carey has asked you to research the following questions:

6. What would be the consequences of the board's appointing Brown, Grey, and White as a litigation committee to decide how to respond to the suit, having them retain Frank Berger, a retired justice of the Columbia Supreme Court, as special counsel? If the committee, after investigating the allegations of Herman's complaint concluded that it would not be in the best interest of the corporation for the suit to continue, and, on Berger's advice moved to dismiss it, what would be the likely result?

7. If the Milton Corporation requests the posting of security for expenses will Herman have to comply if the suit is brought in New York? In Columbia? In Delaware? Does it matter whether the cause of action is based on federal or state law? Would your answer be different if Milton were incorporated in Delaware?

8. Can your firm represent the Milton Corporation in the lawsuit? Can it represent James Milton?

9. Will Herman be able to depose Carey and question him about the transaction?

A. INTRODUCTION AND HISTORICAL DEVELOPMENT

1. INTRODUCTION

In 1963 Mrs. Dora Surowitz sued the management of Hilton Hotels Corporation, charging them with "frauds of the grossest kind against the corporation." She brought suit on behalf of herself and the other stockholders, alleging violations of the federal securities law and Delaware corporation law. The complaint accused the defendant officers and directors of defrauding the corporation out of several million dollars via two deceptive stock purchase schemes designed to enrich the individual defendants, while depriving the company of millions of dollars at a time that the company was in need of funds to operate the business. Surowitz v. Hilton Hotels Corp., 383 U.S. 363, 364, 86 S.Ct. 845, 846, 15 L.Ed.2d 807, 809 (1966).

The Supreme Court described Mrs. Surowitz as

* * * a Polish immigrant with a very limited English vocabulary and practically no formal education. For many years she has worked as a seamstress in New York where, by reason of frugality, she saved enough money to buy some thousands of dollars worth of stocks. She was, of course, not able to select stocks for herself with any degree of assurance of their value. Under these circumstances she had to receive advice and counsel and quite naturally she went to her son-in-law, Irving Brilliant.

Id. at 368, 86 S.Ct. at 848, 15 L.Ed.2d at 811.

Mrs. Surowitz had become disturbed by the decline in the value of her stock and the company's discontinuance of dividends, since she had purchased the stock for the specific purpose of gaining a source of income. After discussing the matter with Mr. Brilliant, who was an attorney, Mrs. Surowitz agreed that a suit be brought in her name to recover for the company the money that had been allegedly dissipated. Federal Rule of Civil Procedure 23.1 governs derivative suit procedure in the federal courts; among other things, it requires that the complaint be verified by the plaintiff-shareholder. The defendants asserted, on the basis of their deposition of Mrs. Surowitz, that she did not have a sufficient grasp of the complaint to have properly verified it.

The Supreme Court reversed the Seventh Circuit's dismissal of the suit. Conceding that procedural rules were necessary to discourage " 'strike suits' by people who might be interested in getting quick dollars by making charges without regard to their truth so as to coerce corporate managers to settle worthless claims in order to get rid of them," the Court also noted the salutary effect of derivative suits. *Id.* at 371, 86 S.Ct. at 850, 15 L.Ed.2d at 813. Mr. Justice Black commented:

> Derivative suits have played a rather important role in protecting shareholders of corporations from the designing schemes and wiles of insiders who are willing to betray their company's interests in order to enrich themselves. And it is not easy to conceive of anyone more in need of protection against such schemes than little investors like Mrs. Surowitz.

Id. The Court perceived the rules as "designed in large part to get away from some of the old procedural booby traps which common law pleaders could set to prevent unsophisticated litigants from having their day in court." *Id.* at 373, 86 S.Ct. at 851, 15 L.Ed.2d at 814.

The *Surowitz* case signified the recognition by the courts and by the corporate and legal community that, notwithstanding the recognized potential for abuse, the stockholders' derivative suit has won acceptance as an important tool in forging managerial accountability.

Nonetheless, certain problems inherent in the derivative suit have long troubled legislatures and the legal community. The derivative suit may, perhaps, be too readily brought on behalf of a very small stockholder, encouraged by a lawyer seeking quick rewards through coerced settlement. While this tactic can be used in other situations as well, the pejorative "strike suit" has been reserved for the derivative suit. The fact remains that the law has singled out derivative suits for the imposition of special procedural restrictions to discourage abuses of the process because of the large costs that may be imposed on corporations by persons purporting to act on its behalf. Among other things, this chapter looks at the reasons for the legal restrictions, examines how they operate, and evaluates them. The class action is the other tool of shareholder litigation, but it is a device that has broader applicability and will not be examined here. It should be noted, however, that the economics of litigation require shareholders to proceed not as individuals but as representatives; the economics likewise generally compel lawyers to look to entities or groups for their fees and expenses. This fact of life casts the plaintiff's lawyer in a central role which requires close examination.

What is a derivative suit? We have encountered derivative suits throughout the book, as most of the law that defines the duties of care and of loyalty has been shaped in derivative suits. Contrast a derivative suit with a direct action, either on an individual's own behalf or behalf of a class. In a direct action by shareholders, the plaintiff asserts his own rights or the rights of a whole class of persons similarly situated. Any recovery belongs to the shareholders and they pay their own fees. Most importantly, the shareholder in a direct action asserts that rights that are personal to him have been violated.

A derivative suit, on the other hand, is a suit on behalf of another "person," brought by one who has an interest in that person but who is not its normal decision maker. The plaintiff's rights are derivative in that he asserts an injury done to someone else and strives to recover for that person. The owner of shares (note, not bonds) is allowed to speak for the corporation on the theory that those ordinarily charged with that responsibility, the board of directors or the management, will not act because, in the usual case, they are the defendants. Any recovery from the suit belongs to the corporation. The lawyer acting for the plaintiff looks to the corporation for his fee. In a derivative suit the corporation is the real party in interest, while in the direct suit it is the defendant.

Derivative

The following example will illustrate the difference between the two types of suits. Suppose the directors in a corporation caused the company to sell some of its property to themselves at a price below fair market value. In this bargain purchase, the corporation may have been injured. The harm in that case can be redressed only in a derivative suit. By contrast, suppose the officers and directors in the corporation caused the company to sell stock to the public without disclosing all of the material facts, and when the truth is revealed the price of the stock drops. The harm in that case will be redressed in a direct action *against* the corporation rather than on behalf of the corporation.

Derivative v. Direct

Most of this book is concerned with the substantive merits of the cases presented; in this chapter, the focus is on procedural issues. We will deal with these questions from the point of view both of practicality and public policy. How much of a deviation from the normal principles of corporate governance should be allowed? How does one balance the costs of derivative suits with the burdens? These large questions are subsumed in smaller ones: What are the requirements for standing? What preliminary steps does the law require to be taken before the suit may be brought? What objections can be raised to the right of the particular plaintiff to act for the corporation? Can the directors prevent the suit from proceeding? How can settlement of a suit be achieved? When may defendants be indemnified by the corporation that is suing them? Who pays the counsel fees? What are the special responsibilities of lawyers in this type of litigation?

In a derivative suit, since any recovery will be on behalf of the corporation, any fees paid will be paid by it. But the corporation is a client that has not sought counsel in the usual way and the persons who ordinarily act as counsel for the corporation customarily oppose the plaintiffs. The question of "who is in charge?" can become confusing in a derivative suit.

The plaintiff who asserts the right of the corporation in a derivative suit rarely has much of a personal stake in the suit. The benefit to the plaintiff shareholder is only indirect and will come, if at all, from the enhancement of the value of his stock. Even in a class action where the recovery is direct, rarely will the amount recovered by the individuals come close to the expense of asserting those rights. Why, then, are such suits brought when the client has such a slight economic interest in the suit?

As a practical matter, the legal basis for stockholders derivative suits is often discovered by lawyers who then bring the suit in the name of a qualified shareholder. While the stakes for the individual shareholder may be small, for the lawyer they are very large. If the recovery on behalf of the corporation is substantial, then so is the legal fee. But the payment of any fee is contingent upon the success of the suit.

While much litigation in our courts is financed on a contigent basis (*e.g.*, negligence suits or plaintiff's antitrust actions), stockholder's derivative suits present unique concerns. First, in most litigation in which the lawyer's fee is contingent upon success, counsel must stay within the bounds set by his client. When the client tells counsel to litigate, he litigates; when the client prefers to settle, the lawyer settles. By contrast, the shareholder acting as plaintiff in a derivative suit gives no directions. Secondly, in most contigent litigation, the client knows he has been injured and seeks out a lawyer; in the derivative suit, the client may not realize he has been injured until counsel advises him. Finally, the client's stake in the outcome of most contingent litigation is at least as great as that of his counsel. In the derivative suit, the lawyer has far more at stake than the shareholder acting for the corporation. Settlements can benefit counsel without pain to the defendants and with little or no benefit to the individual. The potential for abuse by attorneys is rife.

Thus, in a derivative suit, judicial control, including approval of the terms of settlement and the fee of counsel, must substitute for client control. A form of legal control over attorney's prosecutions of derivative suits has developed that searches for a balance between total latitude for lawyers and excessive restrictions on the bringing of suits. As you read the following materials, consider how the courts and legislatures have grappled with this problem. Decide whether you think the derivative suit is appropriately viewed as the most effective weapon in the arsenal of corporate accountability—or whether the old appellation, "strike suit," is still appropriate.

2. ORIGINS OF THE DERIVATIVE SUIT

The modern derivative suit has its origins in mid 19th century English equity, but it was not long after the emergence of the British form of action that the American courts recognized, adopted and began to refine it.

Dean Bert S. Prunty, in his article The Shareholders' Derivative Suit: Notes on its Derivation, 32 N.Y.U.L.Rev. 980 (1957), asserts that early nineteenth century British courts saw an emergent "new pattern of human organization for the wealth production and distribution process," resulting from the expansion of the opportunity to invest in large scale enterprises. At the same time, shareholder participation in management declined. "The resulting concentration of power produced abuses * * * . The evolution of the derivative suit is the record of the efforts of judges and lawyers to enforce * * * [management] responsibility without destroying the right of a majority of the members of a corporate body to govern the affairs of that body and without assuming the burden of all intra-corporate conflict." *Id.* at 992–93. *See* Foss v. Harbottle, 2 Hare 461, 467 Eng. Rep. 189 (Ch. 1843) (Chancellor refused to intervene in business affairs of corporations which could be resolved effectively by members of the organization); *cf.* Preston v. The Grand Collier Dock Co., 11 Sim. 327, 59 Eng.Rep. 900 (Vice-Ch.1840) (majority of membership could not authorize directors' *ultra vires* acts); Atwool v. Merryweather, L.R. 5 Eq. 464 (1868) (majority of shareholders could not ratify promoters' fraudulant act); all discussed in Prunty, *supra*, at 982–85. The British cases focused on the mechanics of the courtroom; they did not analyze the new legal relationships developing among corporate participants.

The American courts focused from the start on the newborn relationship between corporate directors and shareholders. *Id.* at 994. Equity jurisdiction over corporations, based on a trust theory, was recognized as early as 1817 in the United States when, in dicta, Chancellor Kent noted that if complainant shareholders had brought suit against the directors "for a breach of trust * * * against individuals by name, calling them to account for the use, and benefit of the company at large," equity could have enjoined defendant bank's alleged misconduct. Attorney-General v. The Utica Insurance Co., 2 Johns.Ch. 317 (N.Y.1817) discussed in Prunty, *supra*, at 987. *See* Hornstein, The Shareholders' Derivative Suit in the United States, 1967 J.Bus.L. 282, 284 (1967). In Robinson v. Smith, 3 Paige Ch. 222 (N.Y.1832), the right of minority stockholders to establish directors' liability for losses was also grounded on a trust theory. Their right to institute suit on the corporation's behalf was upheld, although the suit was dismissed for failure to bring the corporation before the court as a party defendant. Prunty, *supra*, at 986; Hornstein, *supra*, at 284. And, in 1855, the Supreme Court recognized the right of a shareholder to set in motion the legal machinery to enjoin the State of Ohio from collecting a corporate tax. In Dodge v. Woolsey, 59 U. S. (18 How.) 331, 15 L.Ed. 401 (1855), the shareholder's "right to go beyond the corporate family and get relief against the outsider" was grounded on a breach of duty analysis. The shareholder could sue in the face of a managerial refusal to sue, which amounted to a breach of managerial trust. Prunty, *supra* at 991; Hornstein, *supra*, at 284–85.* Thus, the trust analogy led the shareholder to attempt the

---

* Actually Dodge v. Woolsey was a collusive suit, challenging the constitutionality of a state tax. The challenge took the form of a shareholder suing the corporation and the tax collector in a diversity suit because there was no general federal

enforcement of rights belonging to the corporation—attempts that were, by their nature, derivative.

B. POLICY OBJECTIVES

COFFEE AND SCHWARTZ, THE SURVIVAL OF THE DERIVATIVE SUIT: AN EVALUATION AND A PROPOSAL FOR LEGISLATIVE REFORM

81 Colum.L.Rev. 261, 302–9 (1981).

A. *The Choice of Rationales: Deterrence Versus Compensation*

At the outset, we must ask the most basic questions: What can the derivative action realistically accomplish? What is its purpose? To our minds, the organizing principle around which the derivative action should be reconstructed is a deterrent one: the derivative action should serve as the principal means by which to enforce the fiduciary duties of corporate officials [and entities] and to penalize the violation thereof. Of course, this may seem obvious. Yet, although a deterrent rationale for the derivative action has been occasionally recognized by courts * * * it has never been the dominant rationale, and indeed some decisions appear frankly skeptical of it. By and large, courts have instead assumed that a compensatory rationale underlies the derivative action. Such a rationale may have been appropriate when the derivative action first emerged, but the changed relationship between the shareholder and his corporation makes such a rationale seem increasingly anachronistic. In three critical respects, compensation is a goal that the derivative action realizes only imperfectly.

First, there is the problem of the constantly changing composition of the shareholders. A corporate recovery does not redress the injury to shareholders to the extent that the shareholders at the time of the injury subsequently disposed of their shares prior to the time of the recovery. To this extent, incoming shareholders receive a windfall gain. Somewhat inconsistently, the traditional theory of the derivative action both recognized and repressed this difficulty in identifying the "true" victim of the fiduciary abuse. On the one hand, it accepted the baldest of legal fictions, that it was the corporation itself that was the injured party; on the other hand, it disqualified noncontemporaneous shareholders from bringing a derivative action. Yet, to be consistent, this latter perception of the derivative action, as intended to benefit injured shareholders, would also dictate either that the corporate recovery be reduced by the percentage of noncontemporaneous holders or that some portion of the recovery be redirected to the individual shareholders who sold in the intervening period since the time of the wrong. This does not happen. Instead, the traditional theory glosses over this problem by pretending that the

question jurisdiction in federal courts at that time. The device was copied for more than 25 years, until federal question jurisdiction was established.

corporation has suffered the injury. But if this legal fiction were truly believed, it should also follow that noncontemporaneous shareholders be accepted as eligible plaintiffs. To some degree, the anthropomorphic fallacy inherent in viewing the corporation, rather than its shareholders, as the victim is probably a necessary fiction accepted by courts in order to avoid the potentially enormous problems involved in identifying the true victims. But to concede this is also to concede that courts are accepting an obvious fiction because they are less interested in compensation than in seeing that wrongdoers do not escape sanctions. In short, the fiction of compensation serves the reality of deterrence.

A second problem with a compensatory rationale is that the corporate injury resulting from a fiduciary breach is not necessarily the same as the injury suffered by shareholders. Even assuming an efficient securities market that automatically translates any injury suffered by the corporation into a decline in its share values, it is still plausible that the stockholders' aggregate loss will exceed that of the corporation—basically because the events will be seen by the marketplace as creating a risk of repetition. For example, a self-dealing transaction between a controlling shareholder and his corporation may result in a hypothetical loss of $1 million to the corporation. But to the extent that this signals to the marketplace that the shareholders in the corporation are vulnerable to such abuse, the market would rationally discount the aggregate value of the corporation's shares by more than $1 million in anticipation of future abuses. In short, for legal purposes, the corporation's loss is a historical concept, measured by accounting conventions and limited to injuries that have actually occurred; in contrast, the shareholder's loss may be greater, because in a securities market that discounts future possibilities, predictions of future loss are immediately converted into a present decline in share values.

* * *

A final, and partially countervailing, problem with a compensatory rationale is that the typical recovery in a derivative action, although large in absolute terms, is seldom more than de minimis on a per share basis. In some well-known cases, it has amounted only to a few pennies a share. If all the derivative suit accomplishes is the refund of a few cents per share to thousands of individual shareholders, it is difficult to conclude that such a result justifies the considerable drain on judicial time and court resources that the litigation of this complex form of action creates. Such a recovery will be neither much noticed by the individual shareholder nor responded to by the stock market. Of course, this objection applies as well to many class actions. In this light, the great achievement of both class and derivative actions is not that they yield meaningful compensation, but that by aggregating such individual losses, they produce a great enough sanction to create real deterrence.

These three objections—the likelihood of share transfers between the time of the wrong and that of the recovery, the lack of congruence between corporate gains and losses and those of shareholders, and the trivial size of the typical recovery on a pro-rated basis—do not imply that compensation is an illusory or insignificant goal. But they do cast considerable doubt on its ability to serve as the central rationale of the derivative action.

* * *

The differences between (deterrent) and (compensatory) rationales come into clearest focus when one poses the hardest practical questions about derivative litigation: Should a court dismiss an otherwise meritorious derivative action if it appears that costs of litigation will exceed the likely recovery? Should a defendant be permitted to raise the defense that the crime paid, that the benefits of illegal action undertaken by him on behalf of the corporation exceeded the costs and penalties imposed on the corporation as a result? Should a shareholder not injured by the misconduct be denied the ability to bring a meritorious derivative action that otherwise would not be pursued? In each of these cases, a deterrent perspective tends to answer in the negative, while a compensatory rationale tends to respond in the affirmative. At the same time, these questions also illustrate how unacceptable a legal system would be that took either position and applied it in a doctrinaire fashion to answer all questions that arose. Under a pure "bounty-hunter" rationale, nothing more would be required of a plaintiff than a willingness and competence to prosecute the action. If the supposed protector of the shareholders were to force the corporation to incur costs in connection with the litigation well in excess of even the maximum possible recovery, these costs would be simply rationalized as necessary to produce adequate deterrence. Conversely, under a pure compensatory rationale, the court would be placed in the morally compromising position of having to offset the fruits of misconduct against the penalties imposed therefor and possibly to acknowledge that, despite the best efforts of the state, crime did indeed pay. Both alternatives quickly produce absurd results.

C. WHAT IS A DERIVATIVE SUIT?

EISENBERG v. FLYING TIGER LINE, INC.

451 F.2d 267 (2d Cir. 1971).

IRVING R. KAUFMAN, Circuit Judge.

Max Eisenberg, a resident of New York, "as stockholder of The Flying Tiger Line, Inc. [Flying Tiger], on behalf of himself and all other stockholders of said corporation similarly situated" commenced this action in the Supreme Court of the State of New York to enjoin the effectuation of a plan of reorganization and merger. Flying Tiger, a Delaware corporation with its principal place of business in

California, removed the action to the District Court for the Eastern District of New York.

Flying Tiger pleaded several affirmative defenses and moved for an order to require Eisenberg to comply with New York Business Corporation Law § 627 (McKinney's Consol.Laws, c. 4 1963), which requires a plaintiff suing derivatively on behalf of a corporation to post security for the corporation's costs. Judge Travia granted the motion without opinion and afforded Eisenberg thirty days to post security in the sum of $35,000. Eisenberg did not comply, his action was dismissed and he appeals. We find Eisenberg's cause of action to be personal and not derivative within the meaning of § 627. We therefore reverse the dismissal.

In this action, Eisenberg is seeking to overturn a reorganization and merger which Flying Tiger effected in 1969. He charges that a series of corporate maneuvers were intended to dilute his voting rights. In order to achieve this end, he alleges, Flying Tiger in July 1969 organized a wholly owned Delaware subsidiary, the Flying Tiger Corporation ("FTC"). In August, FTC in turn organized a wholly owned subsidiary, FTL Air Freight Corporation ("FTL"). The three Delaware corporations then entered into a plan of reorganization, subject to stockholder approval, by which Flying Tiger merged into FTL and only FTL survived. A proxy statement dated August 11 was sent to stockholders, who approved the plan by the necessary two-thirds vote at the stockholders' meeting held on September 15.

Upon consummation of this merger Flying Tiger ceased as the operating company, FTL took over operations and Flying Tiger shares were converted into an identical number of FTC shares. Thereafter, FTL changed its name to "Flying Tiger Line, Inc.," for the obvious purpose of continuing without disruption the business previously conducted by Flying Tiger. The approximately 4,500,000 shares of the company traded on the New York and Pacific Coast stock exchanges are now those of the holding company, FTC, rather than those of the operating company, Flying Tiger. The effect of the merger is that business operations are now confined to a wholly owned subsidiary of a holding company whose stockholders are the former stockholders of Flying Tiger.

* * * We are called on to decide, assuming Eisenberg's complaint is sufficient on its face, only whether he should have been required to post security for costs as a condition to prosecuting his action.

* * *

Eisenberg argues * * * that New York courts would refuse to invoke § 627 in the instant case because the section applies exclusively to derivative actions specified in Business Corporation Law § 626. He urges that his class action is representative and not derivative.

We are told that if the gravamen of the complaint is injury to the corporation the suit is derivative, but "if the injury is one to the plaintiff as a stockholder and to him individually and not to the corporation," the suit is individual in nature and may take the form of a representative class action. 13 Fletcher, Private Corporation § 5911 (1970 Rev.Vol.). This generalization is of little use in our case which is one of those "borderline cases which are more or less troublesome to classify." *Id.* The essence of Eisenberg's claimed injury is that the reorganization has deprived him and fellow stockholders of their right to vote on the operating company affairs and that this right in no sense ever belonged to Flying Tiger itself. This right, he says, belonged to the stockholders *per se*. Flying Tiger notes, however, that the stockholders were harmed, if at all, only because their company was dissolved, and their vote can be restored only if that company is revived. It insists, therefore, that stockholders are affected only secondarily or derivatively because we must first breathe life back into their dissolved corporation before the stockholders can be helped.

Despite a leading New York case which would seem at first glance to support Flying Tiger's position, we find that its contention misses the mark by a wide margin in its failure to distinguish between derivative and non-derivative class actions. In Gordon v. Elliman, 306 N.Y. 456, 119 N.E.2d 331 (1954), by a vote of 4 to 3, the Court of Appeals took an expansive view of the coverage of § 627's predecessor, General Corporation Law § 61–b. The majority held that an action to compel the payment of a dividend was derivative in nature and security for costs could be required. The test formulated by the majority was "whether the object of the lawsuit is to recover upon a chose in action belonging directly to the stockholders, or whether it is to compel the performance of corporate acts which good faith requires the directors to take in order to perform a duty which they owe to the corporation, and through it, to its stockholders." 306 N.Y. at 459, 119 N.E.2d at 334. Pursuant to this test it is argued that, if Flying Tiger's directors had a duty not to merge the corporation, that duty was owed to the corporation and only derivatively to its stockholders. Both the 4–1 Appellate Division and the 4–3 Court of Appeals opinions evoked the quick and unanimous condemnation of commentators. Moreover, this test, "which appears to sweep away the distinction between a representative and a derivative action," in effect classifying all stockholder class actions as derivative, has been limited strictly to its facts by lower New York courts. * * *

Other New York cases which have distinguished between derivative and representative actions are of some interest. In Horowitz v. Balaban, 112 F.Supp. 99 (S.D.N.Y.1949), a stockholder sought to restrain the exercise of conversion rights that the corporation had granted to its president. The court found the action representative and refused to require security, setting forth the test as "[w]here the corporation has no right of action by reason of the transaction complained of, the suit is representative, not derivative." *Id.* at 101.

Similarly, actions to compel the dissolution of a corporation have been held representative, since the corporation could not possibly benefit therefrom. Fontheim v. Walker, 141 N.Y.S.2d 62 (Sup.Ct.1955); Davidson v. Rabinowitz, *supra*. Lennan v. Blakely, 80 N.Y.S.2d 288 (Sup.Ct.1948), teaches that an action by preferred stockholders against directors is not derivative. And Lehrman v. Godchaux Sugars, Inc., *supra*, discloses that an action by a stockholder complaining that a proposed recapitalization would unfairly benefit holders of another class of stock was representative. These cases and *Lazar, supra*, are totally consistent with the postulates of the leading treatises. *See, e.g.*, 13 W. Fletcher, Private Corporation § 5915 (Rev.Vol. 1970); 3B J. Moore, Federal Practice ¶ 23.1.16[1] (2d ed. 1969). Professor Moore instructs that "where a shareholder sues on behalf of himself and all others similarly situated to * * * enjoin a proposed merger or consolidation * * * he is not enforcing a derivative right; he is, by an appropriate type of class suit enforcing a right common to all the shareholders which runs against the corporation."

Eisenberg's position is even stronger than it would be in the ordinary merger case. In routine merger circumstances the stockholders retain a voice in the operation of the company, albeit a corporation other than their original choice. Here, however, the reorganization deprived him and other minority stockholders of any voice in the affairs of their previously existing operating company.

NOTE—FEATURES OF A DERIVATIVE SUIT

1. *Individual Recovery.* The nature of derivative suit—an assertion by a shareholder, in the name of a corporation, of a cause of action belonging to the corporation—normally results in the award of any monetary judgment to the corporation. Creditors and shareholders benefit indirectly by the strengthening of the corporation. If recovery were awarded to individual shareholders, it would constitute judicial interference in corporate management. A direct award of damages would, in effect, be a distribution of corporate assets to the shareholders either as a dividend or in partial liquidation of the corporation. Keenan v. Eshleman, 22 Del.Ch. 82, 194 A. 40 (1937), aff'd 23 Del.Ch. 234, 2 A.2d 904 (1938) (where the corporation is a going concern conducting a profitable business, individual recovery in a derivative action is inappropriate because it would interfere with the management responsibilities of the directors); Note, Distinguishing Between Direct and Derivative Shareholder Suits, 110 U.Pa.L.Rev. 1147, 1148 (1962).

There are, however, instances in which the courts have held that special circumstances require that the monetary judgment be awarded directly to the shareholders in a pro rata distribution. In Perlman v. Feldmann, 219 F.2d 173 (2d Cir. 1955), cert. denied 349 U.S. 952, 75 S.Ct. 880, 99 L.Ed. 1277, minority shareholders brought a derivative suit against Feldmann, the former controlling person of a steel manufacturer, and the persons to whom he sold his 37% interest. The court found a breach of fiduciary duty in the transaction and damages in the amount of the premium paid to Feldmann were awarded. The court granted pro rata recovery of the damages to the injured stockholders. If the corporation received the award, the syndicate that purchased the shares would have benefitted both from the return of the premium paid by it for the controlling shares as well as from having obtained control. Had *all* shareholders received their share of the award—not just the injured minority—the purchaser of the controlling block would have recovered a return of the premium it paid for control. Does the pro rata recovery granted here provide complete remedy for the breach of duty? *See* Note, Individual Pro Rata Recovery in Stockholders' Derivative Suits, 69 Harv.L.Rev. 1314 (1956).

Courts have awarded individual recovery in other circumstances where majority shareholders/directors voted themselves excessive salaries in a scheme to deprive derivative action plaintiffs of their share in a judgment if their litigation were successful, Eaton v. Robinson, 19 R.I. 146, 31 A. 1058 (1895); where successor controlling stockholders purchased their stock with full knowledge of excessive salaries paid by the corporation to their predecessor controlling stockholders, Matthews v. Headley Chocolate Co., 130 Md. 523, 100 A. 645 (1917); where the wrongdoers were themselves substantial shareholders of the corporation, Di Tomasso v. Loverro, 250 App.Div. 206, 293 N.Y.S. 912 (1937), aff'd 276 N.Y. 551, 12 N.E.2d 570; and where the corporation no longer was a going concern and the parties to the suit owned all the shares of the corporation, Sale v. Ambler, 335 Pa. 165, 6 A.2d 519 (1939).

Individual recovery in derivative suits presents a number of procedural difficulties. What would happen if not all the shareholders were parties to a suit? Must notice be given to all interested persons, including beneficial shareholders and creditors? Should the right to share in the recovery be limited to contemporaneous shareholders? If the corporation is publicly held, how can distribution be effected? *See* Grenier, Pro rata Recovery by Shareholders on Corporate Causes of Action as a Means of Achieving Corporate Justice, 19 Wash. & Lee L.Rev. 165 (1962).

2. *Jury Trial.* The derivative suit was originally a remedy available in equity, allowing shareholders to enforce a corporate cause of action against officers, directors or third parties. As with all suits in equity, parties had no right to a jury trial. At the time the Seventh Amendment was adopted, preserving the right to jury trial in suits at common law, a corporation's suit to enforce a legal right was an action carrying the right to a jury trial. Thus, partaking of the qualities of both an action at law and a suit in equity, the derivative suit's status under the Seventh Amendment was uncertain until Ross v. Bernhard, 396 U.S. 531, 90 S.Ct. 733, 24 L.Ed.2d 729 (1970), in which

the Supreme Court held that shareholder-plaintiffs were entitled to a jury trial as to those issues in derivative actions for which the corporation would have been so entitled had it sued in its own right. Shareholders brought suit against the directors of an investment company, Lehman Corporation, and its brokers, Lehman Brothers, alleging breach of fiduciary duty, ordinary breach of contract, gross negligence and violation of the Investment Company Act. The court noted that:

> Legal claims are not magically converted into equitable issues by their presentation to a court of equity in a derivative suit. The claim pressed by the stockholder against directors or third parties "is not his own but the corporation's." Koster v. Lumbermens Mut. Co., 330 U.S., at 522, 67 S.Ct., at 831. The corporation is a necessary party to the action; without it the case cannot proceed. Although named a defendant, it is the real party in interest, the stockholder being at best the nominal plaintiff. The proceeds of the action belong to the corporation and it is bound by the result of the suit. The heart of the action is the corporate claim. If it presents a legal issue, one entitling the corporation to a jury trial under the Seventh Amendment, the right to a jury is not forfeited merely because the stockholder's right to sue must first be adjudicated as an equitable issue triable to the court.

The Court also referred to the unitary civil action under the Federal Rules of Civil Procedure: "[I]t is no longer tenable for a district court, administering both law and equity in the same action, to deny legal remedies to a corporation, merely because the corporation's spokesman are its shareholders rather than its directors."

D. STANDING

BANGOR PUNTA OPERATIONS, INC. v. BANGOR & AROOSTOOK RAILROAD CO.

417 U.S. 703, 94 S.Ct. 2578, 41 L.Ed.2d 418 (1974).

Mr. Justice POWELL delivered the opinion of the Court.

This case involves an action by a Maine railroad corporation seeking damages from its former owners for violations of federal antitrust and securities laws, applicable state statutes, and common-law principles. The complaint alleged that the former owners had engaged in various acts of corporate waste and mismanagement during the period of their control. The shareholder presently in control of the railroad acquired more than 99% of the railroad's shares from the former owners long after the alleged wrongs occurred. We must decide whether equitable principles applicable under federal and state law preclude recovery by the railroad in these circumstances.

I

Respondent Bangor & Aroostook Railroad Co. (BAR), a Maine corporation, operates a railroad in the northern part of the State of Maine. Respondent Bangor Investment Co., also a Maine corporation, is a wholly owned subsidiary of BAR. Petitioner Bangor Punta Corp. (Bangor Punta), a Delaware corporation, is a diversified investment company with business operations in several areas. Petitioner Bangor Punta Operations, Inc. (BPO), a New York corporation, is a wholly owned subsidiary of Bangor Punta.

On October 13, 1964, Bangor Punta, through its subsidiary BPO, acquired 98.3% of the outstanding stock of BAR. This was accomplished by the subsidiary's purchase of all the assets of Bangor & Aroostook Corp. (B&A), a Maine corporation established in 1960 as the holding company of BAR. From 1964 to 1969, Bangor Punta controlled and directed BAR through its ownership of about 98.3% of the outstanding stock. On October 2, 1969, Bangor Punta, again through its subsidiary, sold all of its stock for $5,000,000 to Amoskeag Co., a Delaware investment corporation. Amoskeag assumed responsibility for the management of BAR and later acquired additional shares to give it ownership of more than 99% of all the outstanding stock.

In 1971, BAR and its subsidiary filed the present action against Bangor Punta and its subsidiary in the United States District Court for the District of Maine. The complaint specified 13 counts of alleged mismanagement, misappropriation, and waste of BAR's corporate assets occurring during the period from 1960 through 1967 when B&A and then Bangor Punta controlled BAR. Damages were sought in the amount of $7,000,000 for violations of both federal and state laws. *   *   *

*   *   *

The District Court granted petitioners' motion for summary judgment and dismissed the action. 353 F.Supp. 724 (1972). The court first observed that although the suit purported to be a primary action brought in the name of the corporation, the real party in interest and hence the actual beneficiary of any recovery, was Amoskeag, the present owner of more than 99% of the outstanding stock of BAR. The court then noted that Amoskeag had acquired all of its BAR stock long after the alleged wrongs occurred and that Amoskeag did not contend that it had not received full value for its purchase price, or that the purchase transaction was tainted by fraud or deceit. *   *   *

The United States Court of Appeals for the First Circuit reversed. 482 F.2d 865 (1973). *   *   *

We granted petitioners' application for certiorari. 414 U.S. 1127, 94 S.Ct. 863, 38 L.Ed.2d 752 (1974). We now reverse.

II

A

We first turn to the question whether respondent corporations may maintain the present action under § 10 of the Clayton Act, 15 U. S.C. § 20, and § 10(b) of the Securities Exchange Act of 1934, 15 U.S. C.A. § 78j(b), and Rule 10b–5, 17 CFR § 240.10b–5. The resolution of this issue depends upon the applicability of the settled principle of equity that a shareholder may not complain of acts of corporate mismanagement if he acquired his shares from those who participated or acquiesced in the allegedly wrongful transactions. This principle has been invoked with special force where a shareholder purchases all or substantially all the shares of a corporation from a vendor at a fair price, and then seeks to have the corporation recover against that vendor for prior corporate mismanagement. The equitable considerations precluding recovery in such cases were explicated long ago by Dean (then Commissioner) Roscoe Pound in Home Fire Insurance Co. v. Barber [67 Neb. 644, 93 N.W. 1024 (1903).] Dean Pound, writing for the Supreme Court of Nebraska, observed that the shareholders of the plaintiff corporation in that case had sustained no injury since they had acquired their shares from the alleged wrongdoers after the disputed transactions occurred and had received full value for their purchase price. Thus, any recovery on their part would constitute a windfall, for it would enable them to obtain funds to which they had no just title or claim. Moreover, it would in effect allow the shareholders to recoup a large part of the price they agreed to pay for their shares, notwithstanding the fact that they received all they had bargained for. Finally, it would permit the shareholders to reap a profit from wrongs done to others, thus encouraging further such speculation. Dean Pound stated that these consequences rendered any recovery highly inequitable and mandated dismissal of the suit.

The considerations supporting the *Home Fire* principle are especially pertinent in the present case. As the District Court pointed out, Amoskeag, the present owner of more than 99% of the BAR shares, would be the principal beneficiary of any recovery obtained by BAR. Amoskeag, however, acquired 98.3% of the outstanding shares of BAR from petitioner Bangor Punta in 1969, well after the alleged wrongs were said to have occurred. Amoskeag does not contend that the purchase transaction was tainted by fraud or deceit, or that it received less than full value for its money. Indeed, it does not assert that it has sustained any injury at all. Nor does it appear that the alleged acts of prior mismanagement have had any continuing effect on the corporations involved or the value of their shares. Nevertheless, by causing the present action to be brought in the name of respondent corporations, Amoskeag seeks to recover indirectly an amount equal to the $5,000,000 it paid for its stock, plus an additional $2,000,000. All this would be in the form of damages for wrongs petitioner Bangor Punta is said to have inflicted, not upon Amoskeag, but upon respondent corporations during the period in which Bangor Punta owned 98.3% of the BAR shares. In other words, Amoskeag seeks to recover for wrongs Bangor Punta did to *itself* as owner of the railroad. At the same time it reaps this windfall, Amoskeag desires to retain all its BAR stock. Under *Home Fire*, it is evident that Amoskeag would have no standing in equity to maintain the present action.

We are met with the argument, however, that since the present action is brought in the name of respondent corporations, we may not look behind the corporate entity to the true substance of the claims and the actual beneficiaries. The established law is to the contrary. Although a corporation and its shareholders are deemed separate entities for most purposes, the corporate form may be disregarded in the interests of justice where it is used to defeat an overriding public policy. In such cases, courts of equity, piercing all fictions and disguises, will deal with the substance of the action and not blindly adhere to the corporate form. Thus, where equity would preclude the shareholders from maintaining an action in their own right, the corporation would also be precluded. It follows that Amoskeag, the principal beneficiary of any recovery and itself estopped from complaining of petitioners' alleged wrongs, cannot avoid the command of equity through the guise of proceeding in the name of respondent corporations which it owns and controls.

*   *   *

III

In reaching the contrary conclusion, the Court of Appeals stated that it could not accept the proposition that Amoskeag would be the "sole beneficiary" of any recovery by BAR. 482 F.2d, at 868. The court noted that in view of the railroad's status as a "quasi-public" corporation and the essential nature of the services it provides, the public had an identifiable interest in BAR's financial health. Thus, any recovery by BAR would accrue to the benefit of the public through the improvement in BAR's economic position and the quality of its services. The court thought that this factor rendered any windfall to Amoskeag irrelevant.

At the outset, we note that the Court of Appeals' assumption that any recovery would necessarily benefit the public is unwarranted. As that court explicitly recognized, any recovery by BAR could be diverted to its shareholders, namely Amoskeag, rather than reinvested in the railroad for the benefit of the public. Nor do we believe this possibility can be avoided by respondents' suggestion that the District Court impose limitations on the use BAR might make of the recovery. There is no support for such a result under either federal or state law. BAR would be entitled to distribute the recovery in any lawful manner it may choose, even if such distribution resulted only in private enrichment. In sum, there is no assurance that the public would receive any benefit at all from these funds.

The Court of Appeals' position also appears to overlook the fact that Amoskeag, the actual beneficiary of any recovery through its ownership of more than 99% of the BAR shares, would be unjustly enriched since it has sustained no injury. It acquired substantially all the BAR shares from Bangor Punta subsequent to the alleged wrongs and does not deny that it received full value for its purchase price. No fraud or deceit of any kind is alleged to have been involved in the transaction. The equitable principles of *Home Fire* preclude Amoskeag from reaping a windfall by enhancing the value of its bargain to the extent of the entire purchase price plus an additional $2,000,000. Amoskeag would in effect have acquired a railroad worth $12,000,000 for only $5,000,000. Neither the federal antitrust or securities laws nor the applicable state laws contemplate recovery by Amoskeag in these circumstances.

The Court of Appeals further stated that it was important to insure that petitioners would not be immune from liability for their wrongful conduct and noted that BAR's recovery would provide a needed deterrent to mismanagement of railroads. Our difficulty with this argument is that it proves too much. If deterrence were the only objective, then in logic any plaintiff willing to file a complaint would suffice. No injury or violation of a legal duty to the particular plaintiff would have to be alleged. The only prerequisite would be that the plaintiff agree to accept the recovery, lest the supposed wrongdoer be allowed to escape a reckoning. Suffice it to say that we have been referred to no authority which would support so novel a result, and we decline to adopt it.

We therefore conclude that respondent corporations may not maintain the present action. The judgment of the Court of Appeals is reversed.

So ordered.

Mr. Justice MARSHALL, with whom Mr. Justice DOUGLAS, Mr. Justice BRENNAN, and Mr. Justice WHITE join, dissenting.

* * *

I cannot agree. Having read the precedents relied upon by the majority, I respectfully submit that they not only do not support, but indeed directly contradict the result reached today. While purporting to rely on settled principles of equity, the Court sadly mistakes the facts of this case and the established powers of an equity court. In my view, no windfall recovery to Amoskeag is inevitable, or even likely, on the facts of this case. But even if recovery by respondents would in fact be a windfall to Amoskeag, the Court disregards the interests of the railroad's creditors, as well as the substantial public interest in the continued financial viability of the Nation's railroads which have been so heavily plagued by corporate mismanagement, and ignores the powers of the court to impose equitable conditions on a corporation's recovery so as to insure that these interests are protected. The Court's decision is also inconsistent with prior decisions of this Court limiting the application of equitable defenses when they impede the vindication, through private damage actions, of the important policies of the federal antitrust laws.

* * *

* * * Although first Bangor Punta and then Amoskeag owned the great majority of the shares of respondent railroad, the record shows that there are many minority shareholders who owned BAR stock during the period from 1960 through 1967 when the transactions underlying the railroad's complaint took place, and who still owned that stock in 1971 when the complaint was filed. Any one of these minority shareholders would have had the right, during the 1960–1967 period, as well as thereafter, to bring a derivative action on behalf of the corporation against the majority shareholder for misappropriation of corporate assets. * * *

* * *

But let us assume that the majority is correct in finding some windfall recovery to Amoskeag inevitable in this case. This is still but one of several factors which a court of equity should consider in determining whether the public interest would best be served by piercing the corporate veil in order to bar this action. The public interest against windfall recoveries is no doubt a significant factor which a court of equity should consider. But in this case it is clearly outweighed by other considerations, equally deserving the recognition of a court of equity, supporting the maintenance of the railroad's action against those who have defrauded it of its assets.

Surely the corporation, as an entity independent of its shareholders, has an interest of its own in assuring that it can meet its responsibility to its creditors. And I do not see how it can do so unless it remains free to bring suit against those who have defrauded it of its assets. The Court's result, I fear, only gives added incentive to abuses of the corporate form which equity has long sought to discourage—allowing a majority shareholder to take advantage of the protections of the corporate form while bleeding the corporation to the detriment of its creditors, and then permitting the majority shareholder to sell the corporation and remain free from any liability for its wrongdoing.

More importantly, equity should take into account the public interest at stake in this litigation. * * *

The significance of the public interest in the financial well-being of railroads should be self-evident in these times, with many of our Nation's railroads in dire financial straits and with some of the most important lines thrown into reorganization proceedings. Indeed, the prospect of large-scale railroad insolvency in the Northeast United States was deemed by Congress to present a national emergency, prompting enactment of the Regional Rail Reorganization Act of 1973, in which the Federal Government, for the first time, committed tax dollars to a long-term commitment to preserve adequate railroad service for the Nation.   *   *   *

The Court gives short shrift, however, to the public interest. While recognizing that respondents' complaint is based primarily on federal antitrust and securities statutes designed to benefit the public, and while conceding that the statutorily designated plaintiffs are respondent corporations, the Court nevertheless holds that these plaintiffs cannot maintain this action because any recovery by Amoskeag would violate established principles of equity. I cannot agree, for the public interest and the legislative purpose should always be heavily weighed by a court of equity. As this Court has frequently recognized, equity should pierce the corporate veil only when necessary to serve some paramount public interest, or "where it otherwise would present an obstacle to the due protection or enforcement of public or private rights." New Colonial Ice Co. v. Helvering, 292 U. S., at 442, 54 S.Ct. at 791. Here, however, it is the failure to recognize the railroad's own right to maintain this suit which undercuts the public interest.

———

NOTE—THE STANDING REQUIREMENT

1. *Federal Law.* Rule 23.1 of the Federal Rules of Civil Procedure contains the standing requirements for derivative suits in federal courts, whether they are brought to enforce a federally created right or a state law right in a diversity case. Some states have no statutory provision governing standing; elsewhere the requirements vary. See § 49 MBCA; § 626 of the New York Bus.Corp.L. The rule may be found in the corporate statute or in the procedure statute, which does seem more logical. The Federal Rules govern the federal forum, however, and are not subject to Erie Railroad Co. v. Tompkins, 304 U.S. 64, 58 S.Ct. 817, 82 L.Ed. 1188 (1938). Hanna v. Plumer, 380 U.S. 460, 85 S.Ct. 1136, 14 L.Ed.2d 8 (1965). (But see Walker v. Armco Steel Corp., 446 U.S. 740, 100 S.Ct. 1978, 64 L.Ed.2d 659 (1980), where court held that state statute as to time an action commenced was an integral part of statute of limitations and did not conflict with FRCP, which provided a different time for commencement of action).

2. *Ownership by Operation of Law.* Federal law and a significant number of state statutes (New York and California among them, as well as the Model Act) permit suit by persons whose ownership was acquired by operation of law from a contemporaneous owner.

What is the "operation"? Are shares acquired by intestate succession in a different category from shares acquired under a will?

3. *Continuing Wrong.* What constitutes ownership "at the time of the transaction of which [the shareholder] complains" is not always clear. For example, a plaintiff alleged that the wrong was committed when defendants caused the corporation to purchase certain bonds, at a time when plaintiff was not a shareholder, but that the wrong continued when the defendants caused the corporation to retain the bonds. The court found that the actionable wrong was only the purchase, not its retention, or else the limitation on standing would have no meaning at all. Nickson v. Filtrol Corp., 262 A.2d 267 (Del.Ch.1970).

On the other hand, the "continuing wrong" theory prevented dismissal of a derivative suit which challenged a contract that had been entered upon prior to the complaining shareholder's purchase, but under which payments were still being made. The attack was not against the initial transaction, but against the current payments. Palmer v. Morris, 316 F.2d 649 (5th Cir. 1963). Does this distinction make any sense? Bear in mind that the main purpose of the contemporaneous ownership requirement is to prevent persons from "buying lawsuits."

In Forbes v. Wells Beach Casino, Inc., 307 A.2d 210 (Me.1973), plaintiff was denied a contractual right to purchase property from a corporation, which right he claimed was improperly diverted to the defendant at a price below plaintiff's bid. Defendant continued to hold the property. Plaintiff then bought stock in the corporation and initiated a derivative suit against the defendant for the loss to the corporation. Following a detailed analysis of the standing requirement and the continuing wrong exception, the court found that a plaintiff who purchased shares after a wrongful taking of property, but remained a shareholder while a wrongful holding continued was not barred from bringing the suit. Moreover, the court saw nothing wrong in the plaintiff's purchase of shares to gain a base from which he could redress a grievance, as he claimed that fraud and mismanagement had deprived him of his property.

4. *Double Derivative Suits.* Suppose the plaintiff is not a shareholder, and never was a shareholder of the company that was involved in the transaction of which he complains, but instead owns stock in a corporation which owns stock of that corporation. The action would then be a double derivative suit, or possibly a triple derivative suit. Thus, in Kaufman v. Wolfson, 132 F.Supp. 733 (S.D.N.Y. 1955), the complaining shareholder complained of an act that injured D Corporation, whose controlling interest was owned by M Corporation. Plaintiff owned shares of S Corporation, which owned a substantial amount of M Corporation shares.

There could be no doubt that the plaintiff's interest in S Corporation was economically affected by what happened to D Corporation.

The justification for allowing a remote derivative suit is that the corporation that is said to have suffered wrong, and its shareholder corporation which had the right to bring the derivative suit, were in the control of those charged with inflicting the injury. United States Lines, Inc. v. United States Lines Co., 96 F.2d 148 (C.C.A.1938).

5. *Equitable Shareholder.* Must a shareholder be a shareholder of record in order to institute and maintain a stockholder's derivative action? *See* Marco v. Dulles, 177 F.Supp. 533 (S.D.N.Y.1959), (holding that a non-record or equitable owner may maintain a derivative action under New York law and citing both federal and state opinions supporting the holding). A great deal of stock is owned in "street name," *i.e.,* a stockbroker's name, but the beneficial owner is allowed to maintain an action. The rights of other beneficial owners are not so clear. Can the beneficiary of a trust sue? What about the life tenant as compared to the remainderman? Contingent remainder interests? Should the trust instrument control?

In Jones v. Taylor, 348 A.2d 188 (Del.Ch.1975), the court allowed a daughter who held an expectant legacy in stock enforceable in equity after her mother's death to maintain suit in her own name. Would a person who simply had a future interest in stock at the time of the occurrence complained of have sufficient equitable interest in the stock to qualify as a derivative suit plaintiff?

6. *Convertible-Debenture Holders.* In Harff v. Kerkorian, 324 A.2d 215 (Del.Ch.1974), the Court of Chancery of Delaware held that holders of convertible subordinated debentures had no standing to sue because only one who was a shareholder at the time of the transaction at issue could maintain a derivative action. For purposes of a derivative action, the court noted, an equitable owner of stock is considered a stockholder; a holder of convertible debentures, however, is not an equitable owner of the shares into which the debentures are convertible. Rather, he is a holder of a debt instrument and cannot bring suit on behalf of the corporation. Is this argument sound? Does it ignore the probable intent of a holder of convertible debentures (that is, to convert the low-interest bonds into stock at a favorable time)? Does it ignore the economic nature of convertible debentures and the economic impact on those securities resulting from an impairment to the equity in the corporation? *See* Note, Derivative Actions—Harff v. Kerkorian—Standing of Convertible Holders in Delaware, 1 J.Corp.L. 413 (1976).

7. *Merged Corporations.* Can stockholders of a merged corporation derivatively sue on behalf of the corporation into which the original corporation has been merged? The District Court for the Southern District of New York, applying Delaware law, found the merged corporation and its shareholders lost their capacity to sue in Basch v. Talley Industries, Inc., 53 F.R.D. 9 (S.D.N.Y.1971). By virtue of the merger, the original corporation's rights, privileges and identity were merged into the surviving corporation, and likewise, the

stockholders of the merged corporation lost the right to sue derivatively on its behalf. However, where a corporation sold all its assets to another corporation, and then dissolved, shareholders were found to have standing to sue the erstwhile directors of their now dissolved corporation. Independent Investor Protective League v. Time, Inc., 50 N.Y.2d 259, 428 N.Y.S.2d 671, 406 N.E.2d 486 (1980). The New York statute recognized a continuing interest of shareholders in a dissolving corporation to at least secure full benefits of the dissolution. In a merger, however, the rights of the merged corporation terminate instantly. Is this hanging too large a distinction on a small technicality that has no economic significance?

8. *Shareholder of Successor Corporations.* In Marco v. Dulles, *supra,* suit was brought by shareholders of a corporation, which was a successor to the corporation which originally had the cause of action. The court allowed the shareholders to maintain suit because the cause of action was one in which the shareholders had precisely the same interest.

9. *Other Statutory Limits.* There are important statutory limitations on the contemporaneous ownership requirement. Section 800 (b)(1) of the California Corporations Code provides an exception if (1) there is a strong prima facie case in favor of the claim; (2) no other similar action has been or is likely to be instituted; (3) the plaintiff acquired the shares before there was public disclosure or disclosure to the plaintiff of the act which he complains; (4) the suit is necessary to prevent a windfall to the defendants; and (5) the requested relief will not result in unjust enrichment.

Section 516 of the Business Corporation Law of Pennsylvania allows suit, in the discretion of the court, if the shareholder or beneficial owner can maintain on a preliminary showing to the court, by petition, and upon affidavits and depositions that there is a strong prima facie case and that without the suit a serious injustice will result.

Neither of these statutes provide any history to indicate how they might operate.

E.   PROCEDURAL REQUIREMENTS

1. INTRODUCTION—DEMAND ON DIRECTORS

Directors, not shareholders manage the corporation. Certainly individual, self-appointed shareholders, do not manage the corporation. Decisions to litigate are managerial judgments. In recognition of the fact that derivative suits depart from the norm, the courts and legislatures have fashioned the requirement that shareholders must exhaust intra-corporate remedies before bringing suit. The intra-corporate remedy most commonly required is a *demand on directors* (see Rule 23.1 of FRCP); in some states the plaintiff must also make *demand on shareholders*. The demand informs the board that if the corporation does not enforce its rights, the shareholder will institute a derivative action against the alleged wrongdoers. The statutes do not set forth any specific procedure, and any timely effort (written or oral) that effectively communicates the shareholder's request and submits the facts on which an action would be maintained will satisfy the requirement. *See* Comment, The Demand and Standing Requirements in Stockholder Derivative Actions, 44 U.Chi.L.Rev. 168, 172 (1976); Note, Demand on Directors and Shareholders as a Prerequisite to a Derivative Suit, 73 Harv.L.Rev. 746, 752 (1960).

But what if a shareholder does not make a demand on directors? Consider why the shareholder might want to omit this step. What if he thinks that demand would be useless because the board would reject it?

IN RE KAUFFMAN MUTUAL FUND ACTIONS

479 F.2d 257 (1st Cir. 1973).

ALDRICH, Senior Circuit Judge.

This appeal challenges two rulings of the district court that plaintiff's derivative suit on behalf of certain mutual funds of which he is a shareholder is not maintainable because of failure to allege sufficient reason to excuse a prior demand on the directors, and, as to two funds, on the shareholder. F.R.Civ.P.Rule 23.1. We reach only the first issue.

Plaintiff is a shareholder in four mutual funds, the Dreyfus Fund, Inc., Manhattan Fund, Inc., Fidelity Trend Fund, Inc., and the Putnam Growth Fund, the latter two being, respectively, a Massachusetts corporation and a Massachusetts business trust. In December, 1968 he filed this suit in the District of New Jersey in several capacities—not only as a shareholder of the above funds, but also, *inter alia*, as a representative of shareholders of other funds—alleging antitrust and Investment Company Act causes of action against many large mutual funds, their external investment advisers, directors affiliated with both funds and advisers, and the Investment Company Institute, the trade association for the mutual fund industry. The thrust of the antitrust claim, the only one relevant to this proceeding, is that defendant fund directors, who were also affiliated with investment advisers, conspired with funds, advisers, and others to set excessive noncompetitive management fee schedules based solely on the average net assets of the funds. In April, 1969 defense counsel submitted a list of fifteen preliminary motions, divided into three groups, the second group including a Rule 23.1 attack on plaintiff's failure to make a demand on directors and shareholders. * * *

* * * Defendants then brought forward, (1) a Rule 23.1 motion to dismiss for failure of plaintiff to make a demand on directors of the Kauffman funds, (2) a Rule 23.1 motion to dismiss, on behalf of the two Massachusetts Kauffman funds, for failure of plaintiff to

make a demand on stockholders; (3) a Rule 23.1 motion to dismiss because of plaintiff's inability to give fair representation, and (4) a motion by non-Kauffman funds to dismiss for failure to state or waiver of any claim upon which relief could be granted. The court, 56 F. R.D. 128, though denying the latter two motions, granted the first two and dismissed the complaint on July 7, 1972. This appeal followed; there being no cross-appeal.

* * *

For lawyers and judges accustomed to the liberalized "notice" pleading of the Federal Rules, F.R.Civ.P. 8, a brief review of the background of Rule 23.1 is in order. Rule 23.1 is not an ordinary, but an exceptional rule of pleading, serving a special purpose, and requiring a different judicial approach. Socially desirable as minority stockholders' actions may be thought to be, it is normally the directors, not the stockholders, who conduct the affairs of the company. Hence, to be allowed, sua sponte, to place himself in charge without first affording the directors the opportunity to occupy their normal status, a stockholder must show that his case is exceptional. His initial burden is to demonstrate why the directors are incapable of doing their duty, or as the Court has put it, to show that "the antagonism between the directory and the corporate interest * * * be unmistakable." Delaware & Hudson Co. v. Albany & Susquehanna R. R., 1909, 213 U.S. 435, 447, 29 S.Ct. 540, 543, 53 L.Ed. 862. This has long meant, as the Court stated in Hawes v. Oakland, 1881, 104 U.S. 450, 26 L.Ed. 827, cited in *Delaware*, that the "cause of failure [to induce corporate action] * * * should be stated with particularity." 104 U.S. at 461, 26 L.Ed. 827.

* * *

1. *An allegation of domination and control, unsupported by underlying facts, does not satisfy the requirement of particularity.*

The complaint asserts that the directors affiliated with the management advisers "dominate and control" the directorates of the funds. It is conceded, however, that in each instance the self-interested, affiliated director-defendants constitute less than a majority of the membership of the board. Were there a majority, this is a particularity from which a conclusion of control might follow. Plaintiff must allege specific facts demonstrating the unmistakable link between the unaffiliated majority and the affiliated and allegedly wrongdoing minority.

In this circumstance plaintiff's brief seeks to infer collective hostility to his claims by dwelling on the fact that his suit has met extended resistance. Whatever might be the effect if the resistance were on substantive grounds, to attempt to capitalize on the circumstance that the corporations are seeking to dismiss because of plaintiff's failure to make demand is classic bootstrap. Domination is not established by insistence on the right to have plaintiff plead a valid basis for suit.

2. *The fact that the named defendants participated is not enough to excuse demand upon the directorate.*

Apart from "control," only the affiliated directors—a minority of each board—are alleged to have "acquiesced, encouraged, cooperated and assisted in the effectuation and maintenance" of the conspiracy. The unaffiliated directors are not named as defendants, or even as the ones who approved the acts complained of. * * * The complaint alleges that the "funds" participated in the conspiracy, but does not specify in what manner. What is basically important, the complaint does not allege that those who were unaffiliated directors at the time of suit participated; viz., that the unaffiliated directors who would have voted on plaintiff's demand in 1968, had he made one, were the same ones (and hence, assertedly, impervious to a demand) that composed the boards when the contracts in question were approved.

There is no burden on the court to make such assumptions. Were we, in disregard of the rule, to add to the complaint, we could only wonder whether we were not making interpolations that plaintiff could not in good faith sustain. Plaintiff's explanation made in argument why he sued only the affiliated directors, whatever its value, cannot meet his burden of showing that as to the majority of the board at the time of suit demand would have been futile. Even were we mistaken with respect to our next point, on which, essentially, he grounds his claim of particularity, there are thus no sufficient allegations of futility relating to a majority of the board.

3. *Approval by the directors of action alleged to be injurious to the corporation is not sufficient to excuse demand, except in circumstances not here alleged.*

There is a further reason that, in the light of the extensive argumentation that has been made to us, we feel we should deal with. Even if we could assume that there had never been a change in the complement of the boards of directors, and that those who were the directors at the time of the suit had approved of the transactions presently attacked, it would not follow that mere prior participation would excuse making the demand. Where mere approval of the corporate action, absent self-interest or other indication of bias, is the sole basis for establishing the directors' "wrongdoing" and hence for excusing demand on them, plaintiff's suit should ordinarily be dismissed. In fact, only a single court, has held otherwise.

In this respect, the nature of the alleged misconduct must be considered. Logic suggests a sharp distinction between a transaction completely undirected to a corporate purpose and one which, while perhaps vulnerable to criticism, is of a character that could be thought to serve the interests of the company. If the transaction attacked was one solely for the benefit of minority, interested directors—taking out a sham loan, trading in worthless real estate—the approval of the other, nominally disinterested, directors is prima facie inexplicable. If a director goes along with a colleague in an act on its face advantageous only to that colleague and not to the corporation, this in itself is a circumstance, or particularity, supporting the claim that he is under that colleague's control. It may be assumed that he would remain so when the directorate votes on plaintiff's demand. It does not follow, however, that a director who merely made an erroneous business judgment in connection with what was plainly a corporate act will "refuse to do [his] duty in behalf of the corporation if [he] were asked to do so." Bartlett v. New York, N. H. & H. R. R., 221 Mass. at 536, 109 N.E. at 455. Indeed, to excuse demand in these circumstances—majority of the board approval of an allegedly injurious corporate act—would lead to serious dilution of Rule 23.1.

A minority stockholder, unless his claim is worthless on its face, necessarily alleges some illegal transaction or conduct harmful to the corporation. If demand is to be excused merely because the directors participated, the same could be said with respect to those who had failed to oppose, or, indeed, who, as new directors, had merely neglected to take action against their predecessors. If by plaintiff's merely alleging error, the directors are to be presumed incapable of exercising sound business judgment, Rule 23.1 would become virtually meaningless—a stockholder would be entitled to try the case on the merits, (viz., to establish that the fees were excessive, or improperly arrived at, or in violation of the antitrust laws) to show that he had a right to bring it.

We recognize the social desirability of bona fide, well founded minority suits. We also recognize the tremendous waste involved in suits that are not well founded. We do not accept the dictum in de-Haas v. Empire Petroleum Co., 10 Cir., 1970, 435 F.2d 1223, at 1228, that "[c]ourts have generally been lenient in excusing demand" if it is to be applied to allegations as substantively deficient as the present. Such easy remarks overlook the requirement that the directors' "antagonism * * * be unmistakable." Delaware & Hudson Co. v. Albany R. R. If, as plaintiff suggests, this frustrates his ability to prosecute a worthwhile suit, the answer is that he was not entitled to bring it.

* * *

Affirmed.

COFFIN, Chief Judge (concurring).

I concur in the judgment of affirmance. While agreeing that unsupported allegations of domination of a majority by a minority are insufficient, I would, but for one defect, find such support in the allegations that the named defendants, which include the mutual funds (and necessarily their boards of directors), "acquiesced, encouraged, cooperated and assisted in the effectuation and maintenance" of the conspiracy to establish exorbitant basic fee agreements benefiting fund advisers (and thus affiliated directors) to the detriment of the funds and in violation of the antitrust laws. But I view as fatal the absence of an allegation or indication in the affidavits, to use the court's phrasing, "that the unaffiliated directors who would have voted on plaintiff's demand in 1968, had he made one, were the same ones (and hence, assertedly, impervious to a demand) that composed the boards when the contracts in question were approved." We cannot assume that new unaffiliated directors would be unwilling to reconsider the wisdom or legality of their predecessors' actions and, if appropriate, bring suit.

I would, however, not go so far as the court does in delineating "the sharp distinction", for purposes of excusing demand under Rule 23.1, between actions which "could be thought to serve the interests of the company" and those of a fraudulent or self-dealing nature. The distinction has not been so articulated in almost a century of derivative suit jurisprudence, although concededly most of the prominent cases have involved just such factual situations. Yet the language of a number of cases traces a wider compass. Moreover, these are times when corporations are exceeding in size and impact even the giantism of the past, when new layers and dimensions of corporate obligation are being recognized, and when the importance of directorate oversight of the management technocracy is greater than ever. A higher degree of professionalism, sensitivity, and scrutiny may fairly be expected on the part of directors today than in a simpler era. I am therefore reluctant, by resort to formula, to set boundaries to the action or inaction of directors, beyond which demand on them shall always be required.

* * *

I also note that the management fee contracts are not attacked as simply ultra vires or as the product of mere negligence or even of "unsound" or "erroneous business judgment". They are alleged to be illegal under federal antitrust laws. If I were to calibrate a scale to measure the impact of varying improprieties, I would rate such an allegation fairly high. I find it hard to imagine that a director, however, unaffiliated, who had participated, or under these circumstances knowingly acquiesced, in a major transaction, albeit for a corporate purpose, would authorize a suit, effectively against himself, claiming that the transaction violated the federal antitrust laws. Even independent watchdogs cannot be thought ready to sign a confession of that magnitude.

NOTE—OTHER APPROACHES TO THE REQUIREMENT OF DEMAND ON DIRECTORS

In Barr v. Wackman, 36 N.Y.2d 371, 368 N.Y.S.2d 497, 329 N.E.2d 180 (1975), the New York court was called upon to interpret the demand requirement of Section 626(c) of the Bus.Corp.Law (requiring demand on directors unless it is futile) in an action in which a majority of the directors had no interest in the transaction in question but were nevertheless charged with a breach of their duty of due care by permitting the transaction. The Court of Appeals affirmed the holding of the trial court that under the circumstances no demand was necessary. Judge Fuchsberg explained the decision as follows:

The basic question is whether from the particular circumstances of the liability charged it may be inferred that the making of such a demand would indeed be futile. Thus, it is well established that a demand will be excused where the alleged wrongdoers control or comprise a majority of the directors. * * * And, while justification for failure to give directors notice prior to the institution of a derivative action is not automatically to be found in bare allegations which merely set forth prima facie personal liability of directors without spelling out some detail, such justification may be found when the claim of liability is based on formal action of the board in which the individual directors were participants.

It is not sufficient, however, merely to name a majority of the directors as parties defendant with conclusory allegations of wrongdoing or control by wrongdoers. This pleading tactic would only beg the question of actual futility and ignore the particularity requirement of the statute. The complaint here does much more than simply name the individual board members as defendants. It sets out, with particularity, a series of transactions allegedly for the benefit of Gulf & Western and the affiliated directors. Though there are no allegations that the unaffiliated directors personally benefited from the transactions, they are claimed to have disregarded Talcott's interests for the sole purpose of accommodating Gulf & Western, which, in turn, would allegedly reciprocate by promoting the self-interest of the affiliated directors. Acting officially, the board, qua board, is claimed to have participated or acquiesced in assertedly wrongful transactions. * * *

If true, the allegations of the complaint * * * state a cause of action against the defendants, including the unaffiliated directors, for breach of their duties of due care and diligence to the corporation. Plaintiff may prove that the exercise of reasonable diligence and independent judgment under all the circumstances by the unaffiliated directors, at least to meaningfully check the decisions of the active corporate managers, would have put them on notice of the claimed self-dealing of the affiliated directors and avoided the alleged damage to Talcott. If the unaffiliated directors abdicated their responsibility, they may be liable for their omissions. Taking their potential liability from the face of the complaint, plaintiff's failure to make a demand on the board was warranted.

We reject appellants' proposition that allegations of directorial fraud or self-interest is, in every case, a prerequisite to excusing a derivative shareholder from making a demand upon the board. (Compare, *e.g.*, Matter of Kauffman Mut. Fund Actions * * *) Directors undertake affirmative duties of due care and diligence to a corporation and its shareholders in addition to their obligation merely to avoid self-dealing. That unaffiliated directors may not have personally profited from challenged actions does not necessarily end the question of their potential liability to the corporation and the consequent unlikelihood that they would prosecute the action. * * *

As a consequence, a derivative shareholder's complaint may, in a particular case, withstand a motion to dismiss for failure to make a demand upon the board, even though a majority of the board are not individually charged with fraud or self-dealing. Particular allegations of formal board participation in and approval of active wrongdoing may, as here, suffice to defeat a motion to dismiss. We believe the better approach in these cases is to rest the determination of the necessity for a demand in the sound discretion of the court to which the issue is first presented, to be determined from the sufficiency of the complaint, liberally construed.

368 N.Y.S.2d at 505–08.

If mere approval of an allegedly injurious transaction by otherwise disinterested directors is insufficient to excuse demand, under what circumstances will it be enough? In Lewis v. Curtis, 671 F.2d 779 (3d Cir. 1982), Judge Seitz attempted to provide guidance in a situation where, if demand were required, the suit would be barred.

"The board will lack such disinterestedness if plaintiff's allegations, taken as true, would show that under state law, a court could not defer to the board's decision not to pursue the lawsuit."

* * *

"We do not think to excuse demand, plaintiff must allege that the transaction could not under any circumstances ultimately be considered the product of business judgment. Rather, the court in determining whether demand is necessary should consider whether a demand on directors is likely to prod them to correct a wrong. With this as the focus, the interestedness of the directors in the transaction is more relevant to our inquiry than the character of the alleged wrong * * *. Thus, to determine whether a decision not to sue the interested directors would be immunized from scrutiny, it is necessary to determine whether the directors who would make that decision were involved in the allegedly wrongful transaction."

Are there situations, apart from those where directors were "involved in the allegedly wrongful decision" where demand is not "likely to prod them to correct a wrong"?

NOTES

1. *Defendant-Directors.* The fact that the directors are defendants is not sufficient in and of itself to excuse demand. Thus, the requirement of Rule 23.1 that the complaint allege with particularity that demand was made and the reasons that demand failed will not be automatically excused by naming directors as defendants. If plaintiffs allege futility of demand based on directors' status as defendants, they must specify details going beyond that status which support their assertion of futility. Lewis v. Valley, 476 F.Supp. 62 (S.D. N.Y.1979). The plaintiffs will not be able to bootstrap themselves out of the demand requirement by manufacturing the pleadings.

2. *Evenly Divided Board.* The First Circuit, acknowledging its strict standard, says no demand is needed where the board is evenly divided between independent and nonindependent directors. Untermeyer v. Fidelity Daily Income Trust, 580 F.2d 22 (1st Cir. 1978).

3. *Change of Directors.* When the membership of the board of directors changes during the course of the lawsuit, must demand be made on the new board? The Second Circuit, in Brody v. Chemical Bank, 517 F.2d 932 (2d Cir. 1975), required plaintiffs to make demand on a new board where they had not made demand initially because they were suing the original board and had alleged the futility of making demand. The court cited In re Kauffman Mutual Fund Action, *supra* in support of its assertion that demand must be made to give the new board the chance to take over the litigation and thus fulfill its duty to manage the corporation's affairs. What if demand is made on the original board, that board refuses, the shareholder continues in his prosecution of the suit, and then the board membership changes. Would a second demand be required?

4. *Consequences of a Board's Refusal to Sue.* If a shareholder-plaintiff makes a demand on the board, and the board refuses to bring the suit, what consequences result? Does the shareholder still have a right to further pursue the suit? Does the board refusal act as a bar to the derivative suit? Do certain variations in the facts (*e.g.*, whether or not directors are named as directors) produce different consequences? Note that if the demand is "accepted," the derivative suit is automatically barred, since the directors will bring suit in the name of the corporation.

These significant questions are unsettled. Generally, the courts will not interfere in a decision by a board of directors that establishes or carries out corporate management policy. This doctrine of noninterference stems from the business judgment rule, which carries with it a presumption of reasonableness. This presumption spills over to the area of responses to demands to institute litigation. In cases where the alleged wrongdoer in a derivative suit is a third party (and no board involvement in the misdeed is alleged), rejection of demand has generally precluded further pursuit of the derivative claim. This result is strengthened by the fact that directors usually have some financial interest in the corporation and so they would rarely have reason to allow such malfeasance. Ash v. IBM, 353 F.2d 491 (3d Cir. 1965).

This doctrine of noninterference could extend beyond reasonable bounds if courts were to extend it to suits claiming wrongdoing by board members, officers or other agents of the corporation. There is little case law on the question. In principle it appears that these board refusals could be laid on a spectrum, with suits against third party defendants on one end and those against an entire board on the other. What result would you foresee if one director of a large board were sued? A minority of directors? The majority of directors? The corporation's chief executive officer? Other senior management? A controlling shareholder? Should other factors affect the result—*e.g.*, public policy considerations, probability of the suit's success, size and importance of the cause of action? *See* Note, Demand on Directors and Shareholders as a Prerequisite to a Derivative Suit, 73 Harv.L.Rev. 746 (1960). In fact, courts have tended to regard the demand requirement as a housekeeping requirement, having little substantive significance. That attitude may be changing as courts cooperate with management's efforts to impose some constraint on a shareholder's power to launch complex and costly litigation.

We will encounter a variation of this problem in the context of corporate motions to dismiss based on action by the board or a committee of the board that holds the suit not to be in the best interest of the corporation. *See* Zapata Corporation v. Maldonado and Note: Decisions to Terminate Derivative Suits.

2. DEMAND ON SHAREHOLDERS

MAYER v. ADAMS

37 Del.Ch. 298, 141 A.2d 458 (1958).

SOUTHERLAND, Chief Justice.

The case concerns Rule 23(b) of the Rules of the Court of Chancery, Del.C.Ann. relating to stockholders' derivative suits. The second sentence of paragraph (b) provides:

> The complaint shall also set forth with particularity the efforts of the plaintiff to secure from the managing directors or trustees and, if necessary, from the shareholders such action as he desires,

and the reasons for his failure to obtain such action or the reasons for not making such effort.

The question is:

Under what circumstance is a preliminary demand on shareholders necessary?

Plaintiff is a stockholder of the defendant Phillips Petroleum Company. She brought an action to redress alleged frauds and wrongs committed by the defendant directors upon the corporation. They concern dealings between Phillips and defendant Ada Oil Company, in which one of the defendant directors is alleged to have a majority stock interest.

The amended complaint set forth reasons why demand on the directors for action would be futile and the sufficiency of these reasons was not challenged. It also set forth reasons seeking to excuse failure to demand stockholder action. The principal reasons were (1) that fraud was charged, which no majority of stockholders could ratify; and (2) that to require a minority stockholder to circularize more than 100,000 stockholders—in effect, to engage a proxy fight with the management—would be an intolerably oppressive and unreasonably rule, and in any event would be a futile proceeding. All defendants moved to dismiss on the ground that the reasons set forth were insufficient in law to excuse such failure.

The Vice Chancellor was of opinion that, notwithstanding these allegations, demand on stockholders would not necessarily have been futile. He accordingly dismissed the complaint. Plaintiff appeals.

In the view we take of the case, the issue between the litigants narrows itself to this:

If the ground of the derivative suit is fraud, is demand for stockholder action necessary under the rule?

When it is said that a demand on stockholders is necessary in a case involving fraud, the inquiry naturally arises: demand to do what?

Let us suppose that the objecting stockholder submits to a stockholders' meeting a proposal that a suit be brought to redress alleged wrongs. He may do so either by attending the meeting, or, if the regulations of the Securities and Exchange Commission are applicable, by requiring the management to mail copies of the proposal to the other stockholders. * * * Let us further suppose—a result quite unlikely—that the stockholders approve the resolution. What is accomplished by such approval? The stockholder is about to file his suit. What additional force is given to the suit by the approval?

Let us suppose again that the proposal is disapproved by the majority stockholders—as common knowledge tells us it will ordinarily be. What of it? They cannot ratify the alleged fraud. Keenan v. Eshleman, 23 Del.Ch. 234, 2 A.2d 904, 120 A.L.R. 227; Loft, Inc. v.

Guth, 23 Del.Ch. 138, 2 A.2d 225. The stockholder files his suit, which proceeds notwithstanding the disapproval.

If the foregoing is a correct analysis of the matter, it follows that the whole process of stockholder demand in a case of alleged fraud is futile and avails nothing. * * *

The defendants vigorously assail this view of the matter. They say that the rule requires demand for action to be made upon the stockholders in all cases in which the board of directors is disqualified (as here) to pass upon the matter of bringing suit, because in such a case the power to determine the question of policy passes to the body of the stockholders. The stockholders may determine, when the matter is presented to them, upon any one of a number of courses. Thus, defendants say, they may authorize plaintiff's suit; they may determine to file the suit collectively—"take it over", so to speak; they may take other remedial action; they may remove the directors; and, finally, they may decide that the suit has no merit, or, as a matter of corporate policy, that it should not in any event be brought.

These answers do not impress us. As we have said, why is it "necessary" to have stockholders' approval of plaintiff's suit? Defendants say: to comply with the rule. This is arguing in a circle. The question is, does the rule make it necessary?

Again, what is gained (except, perhaps, "moral" support) by having the suit brought by a group of stockholders, however large, rather than by a single individual? A more serious objection to this suggestion is that under Delaware law the directors manage the corporation—not the stockholders. It is certainly gravely to be doubted whether the majority stockholders, as such, may take over the duties of the directors in respect of litigation.

The suggestion that the directors could be removed is a suggestion that the objecting stockholder could engage in a proxy fight with the management. Of all defendants' suggestions, this seems to us to be the most unrealistic. How often is a minority stockholder equipped to take on such a formidable task? And why should a proxy fight be made a condition precedent to a minority stockholder's suit to redress an alleged fraud?

Finally it is suggested that the stockholders may (1) determine that the suit has no merit, or (2) that it is not good policy to press it.

As to the first suggestion, we think it clear that in the ordinary case the stockholders in meeting could not satisfactorily determine the probable merits of a minority stockholder's suit without a reasonably complete presentation and consideration of evidentiary facts. Perhaps some very simple cases might be handled in another manner, but they must be few. A stockholders' meeting is not an appropriate forum for such a proceeding.

The second suggestion, that the stockholders may, as a matter of policy, determine that the claim shall not be enforced and bind the minority not to sue, is really the crux of this case. If the majority stockholders have this power, there would be much to be said for defendants' argument that in case of a disqualified or non-functioning board, the stockholders should decide the matter.

But a decision not to press a claim for alleged fraud committed by the directors means, in effect, that the wrong cannot be remedied. It is conceded that the wrong cannot be ratified by the majority stockholders, but it is said that refusal to sue is a different thing from ratification. Strictly speaking, this is true, but the practical result is the same. To construe Rule 23(b) as making necessary a submission of the matter to stockholders, because the stockholders have the power to prevent the enforcement of the claim, is to import into our law a procedure that would inevitably have the effect of seriously impairing the minority stockholder's now existing right to seek redress for frauds committed by directors of the corporation. This right he has always had under the Delaware law and practice. The policy of the General Corporation law for many years has been to grant to the directors, and to the majority stockholders in certain matters, very broad powers to determine corporate management and policy. But, correlatively, the policy of our courts has always been to hold the directors and the majority stockholders to strict accountability for any breach of good faith in the exercise of these powers, and to permit any minority stockholder to seek redress in equity on behalf of the corporation for wrongs committed by the directors or by the majority stockholders. We cannot believe that Rule 23(b) was intended to import into our law and procedure a radical change of this judicial policy.

* * *

We hold that if a minority stockholder's complaint is based upon an alleged wrong committed by the directors against the corporation, of such a nature as to be beyond ratification by a majority of the stockholders, it is not necessary to allege or prove an effort to obtain action by the stockholders to redress the wrong.

The question may be asked: In what circumstances is such demand necessary? Obviously the rule contemplates that in some cases a demand is necessary; otherwise, it would have not been adopted.

We are not called upon in this case to attempt to enumerate the various circumstances in which demand on stockholders is excused; and likewise we do not undertake to enumerate all the cases in which demand is necessary. It seems clear that one instance of necessary demand is a case involving only an irregularity or lack of authority in directorate action.

The phrase "if necessary" is thus, we think, susceptible of a reasonable construction that comports with Delaware law and practice.

We are accordingly compelled to disagree with the holding of the Vice Chancellor that the bill should be dismissed as to all the defendants for failure to comply with Rule 23(b).

NOTE—DEMAND ON SHAREHOLDERS

S. Solomont & Sons Trust, Inc. v. New England Theatres Operating Corp., 326 Mass. 99, 93 N.E.2d 241 (1950), exemplifies the so-called "Massachusetts" or "strict" rule according to which a demand on shareholders must always be made as a precondition to the bringing of a derivative suit. Ohio follows the same rule. Claman v. Robertson, 164 Ohio St. 61, 128 N.E.2d 429 (1955).

In commenting on *Solomont* in a suit where jurisdiction was based on diversity, Judge Charles Wyzanski had the following to say:

The eminence of the Massachusetts Supreme Judicial Court, an eminence not surpassed by any American tribunal, is in large measure due to its steadiness, learning and understanding of the durable values long prized in this community. Subtle variations and blurred lines are not characteristic of that court. Principles are announced and adhered to in broad magisterial terms. The emphasis is on precedent and adherence to the older ways, not on creating new causes of action or encouraging the use of novel judicial remedies that have sprung up in less conservative communities. Here abides the ancient faith in the right of men to choose their own associates, make their own arrangements, govern themselves and thus grow in responsibility without much in the way of either hindrance or help from the state. This basic philosophy permeates the Massachusetts rules governing derivative suits and makes the state court reluctant to intervene in internal controversies unless parties are obviously prevented from getting fair treatment at the hands of those with whom they chose to be associated and by whose judgment they once desired to be bound.

In the state court there is also an evident if not declared skepticism about the effectiveness of minority stockholders' suits in promoting the welfare, enhancing the reputation or enriching the coffers of those corporations which are supposed to have been wronged. Where there have been abuses, the cooperative action of the majority of the corporate members, the criminal law, and the administrative and judicial remedies available to executive officers of the state have evidently been regarded as adequate. Unsupported minority stockholder suits have been considered appropriate only where no fair forum except the court was available.

Another philosophy prevails in many places. There it is recognized that while minority corporate members are often actuated by selfish interests, they are sometimes useful gadflies which become the most effective instruments for ferreting out wrongdoing, for pursuing it publicly and for giving point to the only sanctions actual and potential wrongdoers fear. To prevent these minority members from suing until they have acquired the support of a majority of their fellows is in most cases to throttle them. They must move against inevitable inertia which always favors the *status quo*, the respectable and the powerful, particularly if, regardless of wrongdoing, a particular company has prospered. They rarely have large funds at their command to circularize and arouse their fellows. And, above all, they are not in a position to state the details of wrongdoing which would persuade unprejudiced men until after they have brought suit and had the advantage of testimonial compulsion. Moreover, courts in some states have been affected in their equity and common law rules by the noticeable shift in statutory rules in the direction of a larger role in corporate affairs for the minority stockholder and in the direction of greater legal protection of his interests from the overreaching, collusion or indifference of his fellows.

But this other philosophy—this reliance on the minority member as the instrument for maintaining corporate order and this use of judicial power to investigate and decide upon his claims—is not the usual Massachusetts view. * * *

Pomerantz v. Clark, 101 F.Supp. 341, 346 (D.C.Mass.1951).

Federal Rule 23.1 requires the complaint to allege what efforts have been made to seek action by the stockholders "if necessary." A similar provision in Colorado law was interpreted to mean that even if the shareholders could not ratify the acts, that did not excuse plaintiff from making a demand. "The purpose of making demand on the shareholders is to inform them of the alleged nonratifiable wrongs; to seek their participation in available courses of action, such as, the removal of the directors and the election of new directors who will seek the redress required in the circumstances; or to secure shareholder approval of an action for damages to the corporation caused by the alleged wrongdoing directors." Bell v. Arnold, 175 Colo. 277, 487 P.2d 545 (1971). *See* Annot: Circumstances Excusing Demand Upon Other Shareholders Which is Otherwise Prerequisite to Bringing of Stockholder's Derivative Suit on Behalf of Corporation, 48 A.L. R.3d 595 (1973).

See Note on Choice of Law, *infra* this Chapter for consideration of the issue as which law governs the requirement of demand on stockholders.

3. THE BOARD'S DISCRETION

Suppose the board makes an explicit decision not to sue. This decision may be made in the form of a rejection of a demand to bring suit, by a board vote at a later time, or in a case where no demand was made. Is the shareholder's right to bring a derivative suit barred because of this act? It may be argued that even where demand is not required, the board still possesses the power to cause the corporation to elect not to sue. A refusal to bring suit following a demand is generally not regarded as a positive business judgment; a studied decision not to sue may be viewed more as an act of business management. Some courts, as you will see in the cases that follow, refer to this act as coming within the business judgment *rule*, a concept which provides a shield against liability. However, the decision not to sue, used as a sword against a derivative suit, may be justified because it comes within the board's power to manage. It might better be classified as coming within the business judgment *doctrine*, not the rule. *See* Hinsey, Maldonado (NY) v. Maldonado (DE): Which Prevails? Legal Times (Wash.) Aug. 4, 1980, at 18.

This issue of the board's power to deprive a shareholder of the right to sue was infrequently articulated until 1976. At about that time many corporations revealed that they had made illegal political contributions or other illegal or questionable payments, mostly overseas, to obtain favorable treatment. These revelations were often followed by derivative suits against members of management and the board charging them with failure to prevent these occurrences. In addition, many of the suits alleged violations of the proxy rules since the activities had not been contemporaneously disclosed. A common response by boards was to appoint a committee of outside directors to study the charges and make binding recommendations. Most committees recommended that no action be taken against the defendants and that the cases should be dismissed.

All of these cases involved charges that management and the directors were negligent or otherwise failed in their duty of due care; none charged any self-dealing or self-enrichment by the defendants. The device of using internal procedures to dispose of the charge was seen by management as a great boon; and to the derivative suit bar, as nothing less than a threat to the very existence of the derivative suit as an institution. The issue of whether the board can resort to this device to assert control over the suit is a question of state law. For public companies no law is more important, therefore, than Delaware law.

ZAPATA CORP. v. MALDONADO

430 A.2d 779 (Del.1981).

[In 1970, Zapata Corporation granted options to certain of its officers and directors to purchase stock at $12.15 per share. The options could be exercised in installments, with the final installment exercisable not before July 14, 1974. At around that time, when the stock had reached a price of between $18–19, the Company planned to make a tender offer for its own shares at $25.00 per share. The company planned to announce the tender offer just prior to July 14, 1974. The effect of the announcement would be to increase the market value of the shares to approximately $25.00 per share. As a result, there would be an additional federal income tax liability on persons who exercised the option, since the tax liability was measured as the difference between the option price ($12.15) and the market price at the time of exercise (about $25).

It was alleged that in order to reduce their individual income tax liability, the board of directors voted to accelerate the exercise date to a time prior to the announcement of the tender offer. The optionees could then exercise when a lower market price prevailed. However, this had the further effect of reducing the corporation's corresponding tax deduction for officers' compensation (*i.e.*, the corporation would only get to deduct $18.00 per share although the price would appreciate on announcement of the offer to $25.00). In effect, the option holders and the corporation were caught in a zero sum game: one could not win without the other losing. A majority of the directors had a direct interest in the outcome of the game since they were option holders.

In 1975, derivative suits were filed in both state and federal courts, alleging breach of fiduciary duty by directors who voted to accelerate the option exercise date and federal proxy rule violations in connection with the re-election of the directors who had so benefitted at the expense of the Corporation. Both of these suits were styled Maldonado v. Flynn.

Four years after the filing of these suits, the Zapata Board appointed two new directors and constituted them as the "Independent Investigation Committee of Zapata Corporation." The committee retained as counsel the law firm of one of the directors. Within three months of their appointment, the Committee filed a "Report and Determination" to the effect that all of the law suits should be dismissed. At their direction, the Corporation's counsel then moved for dismissal of the action.

The Federal District Court in New York concluded that the board of a Delaware corporation had authority to terminate derivative litigation.

The court observed, with respect to the exercise of business judgment in this case:

> [T]he Committee labored under no compulsion to conclude that the actions were lacking in merit. Such a finding is not a prerequisite to the exercise of business judgment though of course it is a factor that may well be considered. To the contrary, the essence of the business judgment rule in this context is that directors may freely find that certain *meritorious* actions are not in the corporation's best interests to pursue. Indeed, here liability is not a foregone conclusion as the issue of materiality remains for trial determination.

> The final substantive judgment whether a particular lawsuit should be maintained requires a balance of many factors—ethical, commercial, promotional, public relations, employee relations, fiscal as well as legal. The factors to be taken into account and

their evaluation are for the Committee expressly appointed to consider them and are beyond the judicial reach. In the last analysis the decision required to be made and that in fact was made is not a legal but a business judgment. * * *

Judge Weinfeld declined to find a conflict with the policy of the federal proxy rules. Maldonado v. Flynn, S.D.N.Y., 485 F.Supp. 274 (1980).

The Delaware Chancery Court held otherwise and ruled that the case could not be dismissed. Maldonado v. Flynn, Del.Ch., 413 A.2d 1251 (1980). ("*Maldonado.*")

However, after its ruling that the board of directors could not exercise its judgment to dismiss the law suit, the Court of Chancery ruled that the shareholder claim arose out of the same transaction as his claim in the district court in New York and thus, was barred by the doctrine of res judicata. However, Vice Chancellor Hartnett stayed the dismissal because the federal claim in New York was then on appeal. If the district court was reversed by the Second Circuit, its determination could have no res judicata effect because there would have been no adverse final judgment. Maldonado v. Flynn, Del.Ch., 417 A.2d 378 (1980).]

QUILLEN, Justice.

* * * Zapata's observation that it sits "in a procedural gridlock" appears quite accurate, and we agree that this Court can and should attempt to resolve the particular question of Delaware law. *. * * We limit our review in this interlocutory appeal to whether the Committee has the power to cause the present action to be dismissed.

We begin with an examination of the carefully considered opinion of the Vice Chancellor which states, in part, that the "business judgment" rule does not confer power "to a corporate board of directors to terminate a derivative suit", 413 A.2d at 1257. His conclusion is particularly pertinent because several federal courts, applying Delaware law, have held that the business judgment rule enables boards (or their committees) to terminate derivative suits, decisions now in conflict with the holding below.

As the term is most commonly used, and given the disposition below, we can understand the Vice Chancellor's comment that "the business judgment rule is irrelevant to the question of whether the Committee has the authority to compel the dismissal of this suit". 413 A.2d at 1257. Corporations, existing because of legislative grace, possess authority as granted by the legislature. Directors of Delaware corporations derive their managerial decision making power, which encompasses decisions whether to initiate, or refrain from entering, litigation, from 8 Del.C. § 141(a). This statute is the fount of directorial powers. The "business judgment" rule is a judicial creation that presumes propriety, under certain circumstances, in a board's decision. Viewed defensively, it does not create authority. In this sense the "business judgment" rule is not relevant in corporate decision making until after a decision is made. It is generally used as a defense to an attack on the decision's soundness. The board's managerial decision making power, however, comes from § 141(a). The judicial creation and legislative grant are related because the "business judgment" rule evolved to give recognition and deference to directors' business expertise when exercising their managerial power under § 141(a).

In the case before us, although the corporation's decision to move to dismiss or for summary judgment was, literally, a decision resulting from an exercise of the directors' (as delegated to the Committee) business judgment, the question of "business judgment", in a defensive sense, would not become relevant until and unless the decision to seek termination of the derivative lawsuit was attacked as improper. *Maldonado*, 413 A.2d at 1257. Accord, Abella v. Universal Leaf Tobacco Co., Inc., E.D.Va., 495 F.Supp. 713 (1980) (applying Virginia law); Maher v. Zapata Corp., S.D.Tex., 490 F.Supp. 348 (1980) (applying Delaware law). This question was not reached by the Vice Chancellor because he determined that the stockholder had an individual right to maintain this derivative action. *Maldonado*, 413 A.2d at 1262.

Thus, the focus in this case is on the power to speak for the corporation as to whether the lawsuit should be continued or terminated. As we see it, this issue in the current appellate posture of this case has three aspects: the conclusions of the Court below concerning the continuing right of a stockholder to maintain a derivative action; the corporate power under Delaware law of an authorized board committee to cause dismissal of litigation instituted for the benefit of the corporation; and the role of the Court of Chancery in resolving conflicts between the stockholder and the committee.

Accordingly, we turn first to the Court of Chancery's conclusions concerning the right of a plaintiff stockholder in a derivative action. We find that its determination that a stockholder, once demand is made and refused, possesses an independent, individual right to continue a derivative suit for breaches of fiduciary duty over objection by the corporation, *Maldonado*, 413 A.2d at 1262–63, as an absolute rule, is erroneous. The Court of Chancery relied principally upon Sohland v. Baker, Del.Supr., 141 A. 277 (1927), for this statement of the Delaware rule. *Maldonado*, 413 A.2d at 1260–61. *Sohland* is sound law. But *Sohland* cannot be fairly read as supporting the broad proposition which evolved in the opinion below.

* * *

Moreover, McKee v. Rogers, Del.Ch., 156 A. 191 (1931), stated "as a general rule" that "a stockholder cannot be permitted * * * to invade the discretionary field committed to the judgment of the directors and sue in the corporation's behalf when the managing body refuses. This rule is a well settled one." 156 A. at 193.

The *McKee* rule, of course, should not be read so broadly that the board's refusal will be determinative in every instance. Board members, owing a well-established fiduciary duty to the corporation, will not be allowed to cause a derivative suit to be dismissed when it would be a breach of their fiduciary duty. Generally disputes pertaining to control of the suit arise in two contexts.

Consistent with the purpose of requiring a demand, a board decision to cause a derivative suit to be dismissed as detrimental to the company, after demand has been made and refused, will be respected unless it was wrongful.[10] A claim of a wrongful decision not to sue is thus the first exception and the first context of dispute. Absent a wrongful refusal, the stockholder in such a situation simply lacks legal managerial power.

But it cannot be implied that, absent a wrongful board refusal, a stockholder can never have an individual right to initiate an action. For, as is stated in *McKee*, a "well settled" exception exists to the general rule.

[A] stockholder may sue in equity in his derivative right to assert a cause of action in behalf of the corporation, *without prior demand* upon the directors to sue, when it is apparent that a demand would be futile, that the officers are under an influence that sterilizes discretion and could not be proper persons to conduct the litigation.

156 A. at 193 (emphasis added). This exception, the second context for dispute, is consistent with the Court of Chancery's statement below, that "[t]he stockholder's individual right to bring the action does not ripen, however, * * * unless he can show a demand to be futile." *Maldonado*, 413 A.2d at 1262.

These comments in *McKee* and in the opinion below make obvious sense. A demand, when required and refused (if not wrongful), terminates a stockholder's legal ability to initiate a derivative action.[12] But where demand is properly excused, the stockholder does possess the ability to initiate the action on his corporation's behalf.

10. In other words, when stockholders, after making demand and having their suit rejected, attack the board's decision as improper, the board's decision falls under the "business judgment" rule and will be respected if the requirements of the rule are met. *See* Dent, *supra* note 5, 75 Nw.U.L.Rev. at 100–01 & nn. 24–25. That situation should be distinguished from the instant case, where demand was not made, and the *power* of the board to seek a dismissal, due to disqualification, presents a threshold issue. For examples of what has been held to be a wrongful decision not to sue, *see* Stockholder Derivative Actions, *supra* note 5, 44 U.Chi.L.Rev. at 193–98. We recognize that the two contexts can overlap in practice.

12. Even in this situation, it may take litigation to determine the stockholder's lack of power, *i.e.*, standing.

These conclusions, however, do not determine the question before us. Rather, they merely bring us to the question to be decided. It is here that we part company with the Court below. * * * We see no inherent reason why the "two phases" of a derivative suit, the stockholder's suit to compel the corporation to sue and the corporation's suit (see 413 A.2d at 1261–62), should automatically result in the placement in the hands of the litigating stockholder sole control of the corporate right throughout the litigation. To the contrary, it seems to us that such an inflexible rule would recognize the interest of one person or group to the exclusion of all others within the corporate entity. Thus, we reject the view of the Vice Chancellor as to the first aspect of the issue on appeal.

The question to be decided becomes: When, if at all, should an authorized board committee be permitted to cause litigation, properly initiated by a derivative stockholder in his own right, to be dismissed? As noted above, a board has the power to choose not to pursue litigation when demand is made upon it, so long as the decision is not wrongful. If the board determines that a suit would be detrimental to the company, the board's determination prevails. Even when demand is excusable, circumstances may arise when continuation of the litigation would not be in the corporation's best interests. Our inquiry is whether, under such circumstances, there is a permissible procedure under § 141(a) by which a corporation can rid itself of detrimental litigation. If there is not, a single stockholder in an extreme case might control the destiny of the entire corporation. This concern was bluntly expressed by the Ninth Circuit in Lewis v. Anderson, 9th Cir., 615 F.2d 778, 783 (1979), cert. denied, 449 U.S. 869, 101 S.Ct. 206, 66 L.Ed.2d 89 (1980): "To allow one shareholder to incapacitate an entire board of directors merely by leveling charges against them gives too much leverage to dissident shareholders." But, when examining the means, including the committee mechanism examined in this case, potentials for abuse must be recognized. This takes us to the second and third aspects of the issue on appeal.

Before we pass to equitable considerations as to the mechanism at issue here, it must be clear that an independent committee possesses the corporate power to seek the termination of a derivative suit. Section 141(c) allows a board to delegate all of its authority to a committee. Accordingly, a committee with properly delegated authority would have the power to move for dismissal or summary judgment if the entire board did.

Even though demand was not made in this case and the initial decision of whether to litigate was not placed before the board, Zapata's board, it seems to us, retained all of its corporate power concerning litigation decisions. If Maldonado had made demand on the board in this case, it could have refused to bring suit. Maldonado could then have asserted that the decision not to sue was wrongful and, if correct, would have been allowed to maintain the suit. The board, however, never would have lost its statutory managerial authority. The demand requirement itself evidences that the managerial power is retained by the board. When a derivative plaintiff is allowed to bring suit after a wrongful refusal, the board's authority to choose whether to pursue the litigation is not challenged although its conclusion—reached through the exercise of that authority—is not respected since it is wrongful. Similarly, Rule 23.1, by excusing demand in certain instances, does not strip the board of its corporate power. It merely saves the plaintiff the expense and delay of making a futile demand resulting in a probable tainted exercise of that authority in a refusal by the board or in giving control of litigation to the opposing side. But the board entity remains empowered under § 141(a) to make decisions regarding corporate litigation. The problem is one of member disqualification, not the absence of power in the board.

The corporate power inquiry then focuses on whether the board, tainted by the self-interest of a majority of its members, can legally delegate its authority to a committee of two disinterested directors. We find our statute clearly requires an affirmative answer to this question. As has been noted, under an express provision of the statute, § 141(c), a committee can exercise all of the authority of the board to the extent provided in the resolution of the board. Moreover, at least by analogy to our statutory section on interested directors, 8 Del.C. § 141, it seems clear that the Delaware statute is designed to permit disinterested directors to act for the board.

We do not think that the interest taint of the board majority is per se a legal bar to the delegation of the board's power to an independent committee composed of disinterested board members. The committee can properly act for the corporation to move to dismiss derivative litigation that is believed to be detrimental to the corporation's best interest.

Our focus now switches to the Court of Chancery which is faced with a stockholder assertion that a derivative suit, properly instituted, should continue for the benefit of the corporation and a corporate assertion, properly made by a board committee acting with board authority, that the same derivative suit should be dismissed as inimical to the best interests of the corporation.

At the risk of stating the obvious, the problem is relatively simple. If, on the one hand, corporations can consistently wrest bona fide derivative actions away from well-meaning derivative plaintiffs through the use of the committee mechanism, the derivative suit will lose much, if not all, of its generally-recognized effectiveness as an intracorporate means of policing boards of directors. If, on the other hand, corporations are unable to rid themselves of meritless or harmful litigation and strike suits, the derivative action, created to benefit the corporation, will produce the opposite, unintended result. It thus appears desirable to us to find a balancing point where bona fide stockholder power to bring corporate causes of action cannot be unfairly trampled on by the board of directors, but the corporation can rid itself of detrimental litigation.

As we noted, the question has been treated by other courts as one of the "business judgment" of the board committee. If a "committee, composed of independent and disinterested directors, conducted a proper review of the matters before it, considered a variety of factors and reached, in good faith, a business judgment that [the] action was not in the best interest of [the corporation]", the action must be dismissed. *See, e.g.,* Maldonado v. Flynn, *supra,* 485 F.Supp. at 282, 286. The issues become solely independence, good faith, and reasonable investigation. The ultimate conclusion of the committee, under that view, is not subject to judicial review.

We are not satisfied, however, that acceptance of the "business judgment" rationale at this stage of derivative litigation is a proper balancing point. While we admit an analogy with a normal case respecting board judgment, it seems to us that there is sufficient risk in the realities of a situation like the one presented in this case to justify caution beyond adherence to the theory of business judgment.

The context here is a suit against directors where demand on the board is excused. We think some tribute must be paid to the fact that the lawsuit was properly initiated. It is not a board refusal case. Moreover, this complaint was filed in June of 1975 and, while the parties undoubtedly would take differing views on the degree of litigation activity, we have to be concerned about the creation of an "Independent Investigation Committee" four years later, after the election of two new outside directors. Situations could develop where such motions could be filed after years of vigorous litigation for reasons unconnected with the merits of the lawsuit.

Moreover, notwithstanding our conviction that Delaware law entrusts the corporate power to a properly authorized committee, we must be mindful that directors are passing judgment on fellow directors in the same corporation and fellow directors, in this instance, who designated them to serve both as directors and committee members. The question naturally arises whether a "there but for the grace of God go I" empathy might not play a role. And the further question arises whether inquiry as to independence, good faith and reasonable investigation is sufficient safeguard against abuse, perhaps subconscious abuse.

* * *

It seems to us that there are two other procedural analogies that are helpful in addition to reference to Rules 12 and 56. There is some analogy to a settlement in that there is a request to terminate litigation without a judicial determination of the merits. *See* Perrine v. Pennroad Corp., Del.Supr., 47 A.2d 479, 487 (1946). "In determining whether or not to approve a proposed settlement of a derivative stockholders' action [when directors are on both sides of the transaction], the Court of Chancery is called upon to exercise its own business judgment." Neponsit Investment Co. v. Abramson, Del.Supr., 405 A.2d 97, 100 (1979) and cases therein cited. In this case, the litigating stockholder plaintiff facing dismissal of a lawsuit properly commenced ought, in our judgment, to have sufficient status for strict Court review.

Finally, if the committee is in effect given status to speak for the corporation as the plaintiff in interest, then it seems to us there is an analogy to Court of Chancery Rule 41(a)(2) where the plaintiff seeks a dismissal after an answer. Certainly, the position of record of the litigating stockholder is adverse to the position advocated by the corporation in the motion to dismiss. Accordingly, there is perhaps some wisdom to be gained by the direction in Rule 41(a)(2) that "an action shall not be dismissed at the plaintiff's instance save upon order of the Court and upon such terms and conditions as the Court deems proper."

Whether the Court of Chancery will be persuaded by the exercise of a committee power resulting in a summary motion for dismissal of a derivative action, where a demand has not been initially made, should rest, in our judgment, in the independent discretion of the Court of Chancery. We thus steer a middle course between those cases which yield to the independent business judgment of a board committee and this case as determined below which would yield to unbridled plaintiff stockholder control. In pursuit of the course, we recognize that "[t]he final substantive judgment whether a particular lawsuit should be maintained requires a balance of many factors— ethical, commercial, promotional, public relations, employee relations, fiscal as well as legal." Maldonado v. Flynn, *supra*, 485 F.Supp. at 285. But we are content that such factors are not "beyond the judicial reach" of the Court of Chancery which regularly and competently deals with fiduciary relationships, disposition of trust property, approval of settlements and scores of similar problems. We recognize the danger of judicial overreaching but the alternatives seem to us to be outweighed by the fresh view of a judicial outsider. Moreover, if we failed to balance all the interests involved, we would in the name of practicality and judicial economy foreclose a judicial decision on the merits. At this point, we are not convinced that is necessary or desirable.

After an objective and thorough investigation of a derivative suit, an independent committee may cause its corporation to file a pretrial motion to dismiss in the Court of Chancery. The basis of the motion is the best interests of the corporation, as determined by the committee. The motion should include a thorough written record of the investigation and its findings and recommendations. Under appropriate Court supervision, akin to proceedings on summary judgment, each side should have an opportunity to make a record on the motion. As to the limited issues presented by the motion noted below, the moving party should be prepared to meet the normal burden under Rule 56 that there is no genuine issue as to any material fact and that the moving party is entitled to dismiss as a matter of law. The Court should apply a two-step test to the motion.

First, the Court should inquire into the independence and good faith of the committee and the bases supporting its conclusions. Limited discovery may be ordered to facilitate such inquiries. The corporation should have the burden of proving independence, good faith and a reasonable investigation, rather than presuming independence, good faith and reasonableness. If the Court determines either that the committee is not independent or has not shown reasonable bases for its conclusions, or, if the Court is not satisfied for other reasons relating to the process, including but not limited to the good faith of the committee, the Court shall deny the corporation's motion. If, however, the Court is satisfied under Rule 56 standards that the committee was independent and showed reasonable bases for good faith findings and recommendations, the Court may proceed, in its discretion, to the next step.

The second step provides, we believe, the essential key in striking the balance between legitimate corporate claims as expressed in a derivative stockholder suit and a corporation's best interests as expressed by an independent investigating committee. The Court should determine, applying its own independent business judgment, whether the motion should be granted.[18] This means, of course, that instances could arise where a committee can establish its independence and sound bases for its good faith decisions and still have the corporation's motion denied. The second step is intended to thwart instances where corporate actions meet the criteria of step one, but the result does not appear to satisfy its spirit, or where corporate actions would simply prematurely terminate a stockholder grievance deserving of further consideration in the corporation's interest. The Court of Chancery of course must carefully consider and weigh how compelling the corporate interest in dismissal is when faced with a non-frivolous lawsuit. The Court of Chancery should, when appropriate, give special consideration to matters of law and public policy in addition to the corporation's best interests.

If the Court's independent business judgment is satisfied, the Court may proceed to grant the motion, subject, of course, to any equitable terms or conditions the Court finds necessary or desirable.

The interlocutory order of the Court of Chancery is reversed and the cause is remanded for further proceedings consistent with this opinion.

18. This step shares some of the same spirit and philosophy of the statement by the Vice Chancellor: "Under our system of law, courts and not litigants should decide the merits of litigation." 413 A.2d at 1263.

NOTE—POSTLOGUE

Since the federal district in New York did not guess the correct outcome of the Delaware Supreme Court's disposition of the termination issue, the Second Circuit was compelled to remand the case. Maldonado v. Flynn, 671 F.2d 729 (2d Cir. 1982). However, the scope of the remand was narrow.

The court held Delaware law to be consistent with the policies underlying sections 10(b) and 14(a) of the Securities Exchange Act. Since the court agreed with Judge Weinfeld's earlier findings that the board members who recommended termination of the suit acted independently and in good faith, it only remained to have the district judge exercise his own independent business judgment to determine whether the suit should be dismissed.

Is this a correct interpretation of *Zapata*? Must the trial court, on instructions from the appellate court, apply its own business judgment to the issue, or is this left to the discretion of the lower court?

More important, is the Second Circuit's affirmance that the directors' initial decision should be accorded the benefits of the business judgment rule, once independence is established, consistent with *Zapata*? Does this depart from the spirit of the Delaware decision that expressed an unwillingness to apply the business judgment rule to a case where demand on directors was excused?

NOTE—DECISIONS TO TERMINATE DERIVATIVE SUITS

The cases that have considered the board's power to terminate derivative suits may be broadly categorized as those that involve allegations of a breach of the duty of due care and those that allege a breach of the duty of loyalty. The attempt to use a committee for purposes of terminating a derivative suit was first presented in the due care cases. When it was later used in self-dealing cases, courts did not always note the distinction between the two situations. Is the distinction a relevant one? Is it important in the *Zapata* decision?

Gall v. Exxon, 418 F.Supp. 508 (S.D.N.Y.1976), was the first case in which a decision by a board committee that a derivative suit was not in the best interest of the corporation was used as a basis for seeking dismissal of the suit. In July, 1975 an Exxon Corporation shareholder made a demand on the Board of Directors in anticipation of bringing a derivative suit. He referred in his demand to claims made by other shareholders in their recently-brought derivative suits. These claims related to transactions involving Esso Italiana, a wholly owned subsidiary of Exxon, which purportedly made periodic and sizeable contributions to support Italian political parties. The shareholder alleged that corporate assets had been wasted and misused as bribes; that Exxon's Board of Directors had permitted or acquiesced in a cover-up of the payments; and that the directors had failed to control adequately the chief executive of Esso Italiana, who made the payments.

Responding to the demand, the Exxon Board established a "Special Committee on Litigation," comprised of three board members: two of them newly-elected outside directors, and the third a senior vice-president of Exxon. The Committee retained as counsel the retired chief justice of the New Jersey Supreme Court. The resolution creating the committee provided that it would conduct an investigation into the claims and circumstances which were the focus of the demand and would determine whether Exxon Corporation should undertake the litigation. The Committee's findings revealed that Exxon had authorized the expenditure of approximately twenty-seven million dollars in questionable payments to Italian political parties between 1963 and 1972. An estimated twenty-nine million dollars in unauthorized payments also had been made during that period. Noting, however, that no Exxon officials had engaged in bribery, the Special Committee exercised its business judgment and decided not to bring suit.

When a suit was later filed and the plaintiff challenged the effectiveness of the Special Committee's determination, the court held that, if the decision was in fact a bona fide judgment of independent directors, the suit would be dismissed. Plaintiff was allowed an opportunity to challenge the independence of the committee and the bona fides of its determination.

The court reasoned that the Special Committee's determination should be accorded the same deference under the business judgment rule as if it was made by the whole board. Plaintiffs argued that, because the board, which included seven defendants in the suit, could have rejected the committee's determination, the committee was not truly independent. The court rejected this argument, claiming that the Special Committee exercised the full powers of the Board in investigating and deciding the matter. According to the court, the "focus of the business judgment rule inquiry is on those who actually wield the decision-making authority, not on those who might have possessed such authority at different times and under different circumstances."

Burks v. Lasker, 441 U.S. 471, 99 S.Ct. 1831, 60 L.Ed.2d 404 (1979), was a derivative suit by shareholders of a mutual fund, against several directors of the fund and its investment adviser. Plaintiffs alleged violations of the Investment Company Act of 1940 (one of the federal securities laws) as well as common law breach of duty of due care, centering around the fund's substantial purchases of the commercial paper of Penn Central just prior to Penn Central's insolvency. The complaint did not allege any self-dealing on the part of the defendants, but rather charged that defendants had failed to exercise due care in relying almost exclusively upon the advice of a third party brokerage firm. Five members of the 11 person board, who were not affiliated with the fund's investment adviser and not defendants in the suit, convened as a quorum pursuant to the company's by-laws, retained a retired chief judge of the New York Court of Appeals as independent counsel, and on the basis of their investigation, decided that the litigation was adverse to the company's best interest and moved to dismiss. After permitting discovery on the question of the directors' independence, the district court granted the motion. The Court of Appeals for the Second Circuit reversed.

The Supreme Court reversed. First, it held that state law governed the question of whether disinterested directors possessed the power to terminate a derivative suit if they concluded that the litigation was adverse to the corporation's best interest. Second, the Court acknowledged that, even if state law permitted such a decision there could be circumstances in which such a state policy was inconsistent with a federal policy underlying the cause of action. But, it declined to find any conflict between the federal statutes involved in the case and the board action.

Burks and *Gall* encouraged the use of independent committees as a device to obtain dismissal of derivative suits. Even more fundamentally, they buttressed the assertion by boards that they possess power to terminate derivative suits in the exercise of their business judgment. The New York Court of Appeals carried that doctrine perhaps as far as it could stretch in Auerbach v. Bennett, 47 N.Y.2d 619, 419 N.Y.S.2d 920, 393 N.E.2d 994 (1979). A derivative suit was brought against directors and the independent auditor of General Telephone & Electronics Corporation. The suit was based on a report by the Company's audit committee, following an investigation, that the company had made illegal payments and bribes, and that some of the individual defendants had been personally involved. The board appointed a Special Litigation Committee consisting of three directors who had joined the board after the transactions in question. One member of the committee joined the board after the suit was brought. A former chief judge of the New York Court of Appeals (not the same one as in *Burks*) was chosen as independent counsel. The Committee concluded that none of the defendants had violated the New York law governing due care, that none had profited personally and that it was not in the best interests of the corporation for the derivative action to proceed. Counsel was directed to move to dismiss and the trial court granted the motion. The intermediate court reversed, but the Court of Appeals overruled it and sustained the motion to dismiss.

The court held that the business judgment rule bars judicial inquiry into good faith actions of the directors which are an exercise of honest judgment. Derivative actions belong to the corporation and the decision whether to pursue a claim requires the weighing and balancing of many factors. Thus, the court refused to look at the merits of the decision of the committee. It did, however, probe into the independence of the committee and the procedures it followed, and was satisfied as to both.

Five days after *Zapata*, the Ninth Circuit (without citing the Delaware Supreme Court) interpreted California law to permit a committee of independent directors to dismiss a derivative suit involving questionable payments by Lockheed officials, in the exercise of the committee's business judgment. Gaines v. Haughton, 645 F.2d 761 (9th Cir. 1981). The only requirement was that the committee be independent, its procedures adequate and its actions taken in good faith. The court saw this as a clear trend of the law.

All of these cases relied on *Burks* as well on a trilogy of early Supreme Court decisions: Hawes v. City of Oakland, 104 U.S. 450, 26 L.Ed. 827 (1882); Corbus v. Alaska Treadwell Gold Mining Co., 187 U. S. 455, 23 S.Ct. 157, 47 L.Ed. 256 (1903); and United Copper Securities Co. v. Amalgamated Copper Co., 244 U.S. 261, 37 S.Ct. 509, 61 L. Ed. 1119 (1917). All three of these earlier cases were suits against third parties who were separate and unaffiliated entities. Writing for the Court in *United Copper*, Justice Brandeis noted:

> In the instant case there is no allegation that the United Copper Company is in control of the alleged wrongdoers or that its directors stand in any relation to them or that they have been guilty of any misconduct whatsoever. Nor is there even an allegation that their action in refusing to bring suit is unwise.

The most frequently cited authority for the director's power to refuse to sue is Justice Brandeis' concurring opinion in Ashwander v. Tennessee Valley Authority, 297 U.S. 288, 56 S.Ct. 466, 80 L.Ed. 688 (1936). The Court sustained the constitutionality of the Tennessee Valley Authority in a challenge by a stockholder of an involved corporation. Chief Justice Hughes' opinion of the Court upheld the stockholder's standing to sue the directors who had caused the corporation to comply with the allegedly invalid law. Justice Brandeis, for himself and three others, disputed the stockholder's standing. He wrote:

> Within recognized limits, stockholders may invoke the judicial remedy to enjoin acts of the management which threaten their property interest. But they cannot secure the aid of a court to correct what appear to them to be mistakes of judgment on the part of the officers. Courts may not interfere with the management of the corporation, unless there is bad faith, disregard of the relative rights of its members, or other action seriously threatening their property rights. This rule applies whether the mistake is due to error of fact or of law, or merely to bad business judgment. It applies, among other things, where the mistake alleged is the refusal to assert a seemingly clear cause of action, or the compromise of it. [Citing *United Copper*.] If a stockholder could compel the officers to enforce every legal right, courts, instead of chosen officers, would be the arbiters of the corporation's fate. 288 U.S. at 343.

Burks, Gall, and *Auerbach* are one step removed from these earlier decisions in that, instead of being third parties, the defendants were officers and directors charged with breach of the duty of care. Another line of cases that has developed since *Burks* is still one more step removed from the historical precedent. In these cases the defendants are officers and directors charged with self-dealing, or breach of the duty of loyalty. What is particularly significant about this development is that most derivative suits are of this nature. Only the rare case challenges the directors' diligence; the case that challenges their integrity is the one that appeals to the derivative suit bar. Hence, the use of the committee device, or the application of the business judgment rule in this context, strikes the derivative suit bar where it lives.

The *Zapata* cases involved such a situation, of course. The federal judge who dismissed the district court action, however, gave no indication that he recognized any distinction from *Burks*. Without any qualifications, Judge Weinfeld found that Abbey v. Control Data Corp., 603 F.2d 724 (8th Cir. 1979), which interpreted Delaware law to allow dismissal of a case involving illegal foreign payments, was authority for finding that Delaware would apply the business judgment rule in a case that concerned self-dealing. Does *Zapata* put that notion to rest under Delaware law?

Lewis v. Anderson, 615 F.2d 778 (9th Cir. 1980), was a derivative suit that also challenged the grant of new stock options to the defendant directors of Walt Disney Productions, allegedly in breach of fiduciary duty and the proxy rules. A special litigation committee was appointed, consisting of two outside directors who joined the board after the challenged transactions and one director who was a defendant but who did not derive personal benefit from the transaction. The committee retained independent counsel, conducted an investigation and decided it would not be in the best interests of the corporation to pursue the litigation. It instructed counsel to move to dismiss; the trial court ruled that the committee possessed the power to do so, but reserved for later decision whether it had made a good faith determination. The Court of Appeals affirmed. Applying California law, it found that the business judgment rule applies to all discretionary decisions of the board, including the decision not to pursue a cause of action. The only requirement is that the board, or the committee acting for it, be independent, and that factual issue must be resolved on remand. The court saw no frustration of federal policy in allowing independent directors the power to decide not to pursue a possible claim under the proxy rules. That decision was reaffirmed by the Ninth Circuit in *Gaines*.

Galef v. Alexander, 615 F.2d 51 (2d Cir. 1980), denied power to the full board to exercise its business judgment to dismiss, also in a case involving stock options. Plaintiff complained about the board's decision to replace outstanding options with new ones with a lower exercise price, for the benefit of management and certain directors. Six directors had benefited from this act; the other nine directors, after hearing reports from outside counsel, decided that the best interests of the company required dismissal of the law suit.

The court found that there was doubt as to whether the board was independent in view of the fact that even the non-recipients of the options were named as defendants. Even assuming their independence, however, Judge Kearse found that the federal proxy rule claim could not be dismissed by the board's exercise of its discretion because this would frustrate the federal policy underlying the integrity of proxy statement disclosure, particularly as the defect related to a self-dealing transaction.

It must be clear that corporate boards will resort to the exercise of their business judgment whenever possible because it provides a means of neatly disposing of litigation that promises to be lengthy, costly, and risky. To stand any chance of success, they will need to employ independent directors and outside counsel and undertake careful investigation. Obviously, there are certain benefits to the corporation and its shareholders from the regularization of such procedures. Indeed, the most profound impact of *Burks* and its progeny may be felt in the governance structure of the corporation.

How courts will deal with these efforts is still unclear—to us if not to some judges. *Zapata*, critically important because it is Delaware law, leaves unanswered many questions as to its scope and the procedure it demands. Whether courts will draw distinctions based on the nature of the claim is unclear. What is proper procedure, and who is "independent" must be defined. Whether boards can simply add new directors who are independent as to these suits is not certain, although *Zapata* casts doubt on that. Whether courts will review the substance of directors' judgments—the issue separating *Zapata* and *Auerbach*—is perhaps the largest uncertainty.

Burks posed one further question in cases involving a federal claim—whether the policies underlying the federal claim would be undercut by allowing the directors' decision to terminate the derivative suit to stand. Most frequently the federal claim will arise under rule 10b–5 or 14a–9 of the Securities Exchange Act of 1934. In Abramowitz v. Posner, 672 F.2d 1025 (2d Cir. 1982), the court found "no threat to the purity of the securities market in applying the business judgment rule to allow disinterested, independent directors to terminate derivative litigation." In that case the court said that the policies of both Section 10(b) and Section 14(a) were served by allowing the informed judgment of independent directors to control corporate litigation. Accord, Lewis v. Anderson, *supra*; Abbey v. Control Data Corp., *supra*.

4. SECURITY FOR EXPENSES

KAUFMAN v. WOLFSON

136 F.Supp. 939 (S.D.N.Y.1955).

DIMOCK, District Judge.

This is a motion by plaintiff to vacate a stay of a stockholder's derivative action brought in this court under the diversity jurisdiction. The action was stayed until plaintiff should furnish security in the amount of $50,000 pursuant to section 61–b of the New York General Corporation Law [now § 627 of the Bus.Corp.Law.] That section requires in substance that a plaintiff in a stockholder's derivative action shall give security for defendant's expenses unless he owns at least 5% of the outstanding stock or stock having a market value in excess of $50,000. Plaintiff bases his plea for the vacating of the stay on an allegation that he has been joined by other named stockholders with the result that they together hold 3,058 shares of stock of defendant New York Shipbuilding Company, which have a value in excess of $50,000. He asks that they be allowed to intervene as parties plaintiff and that, upon their intervention and joinder, all plaintiffs be permitted to serve an amended supplemental complaint a copy of which is attached to the moving affidavit.

Defendants oppose the motion on the ground, among others, that plaintiff does not allege that the proposed new plaintiffs meet the requirement of Rule 23(b) F.R.C.P., 28 U.S.C.A., that the "plaintiff was a shareholder at the time of the transaction of which he complains". If defendants are correct in their position that Rule 23(b) requires that all of the stockholders whose stock is necessary to make up the requisite $50,000 market value must have owned their shares at the time of the transaction complained of, the motion must be denied.

At a time when the New York law permitted suit by stockholders who had acquired their shares after the transaction complained of, it was held in this court that Rule 23(b) applied even though the case was governed by New York law. Accordingly the requirement of ownership contemporaneous with the transaction complained of was enforced. Piccard v. Sperry Corp., D.C.S.D.N.Y., 36 F.Supp. 1006, affirmed without opinion, 2 Cir., 120 F.2d 328; Winkelman v. General Motors Corp., D.C.S.D.N.Y., 44 F.Supp. 960, and Lissauer v. Bertles, D.C.S.D.N.Y., 37 F.Supp. 881.

Those cases have been supported by a later dictum by Mr. Justice Jackson in Cohen v. Beneficial Industrial Loan Corp., 337 U.S. 541, 69 S.Ct. 1221, 93 L.Ed. 1528. In that case it was held that provisions of New Jersey law similar to section 61–b of the New York General Corporation Law requiring the giving of security in stockholders' derivative actions were applicable in an action brought in the United States District Court for the District of New Jersey under the diversity jurisdiction. The ground for the decision was that such provisions were not merely procedural. Against this position it had been urged, 337 U.S. at page 556, 69 S.Ct. at page 1230, "that Federal Rule of Civil Procedure No. 23 deals with plaintiff's right to maintain such an action in federal court and that therefore the subject is recognized as procedural and the federal rule alone prevails." Mr. Justice Jackson answered as follows, 337 U.S. at page 556, 69 S.Ct. at page 1230:

> Rule 23 requires the stockholder's complaint to be verified by oath and to show that the plaintiff was a stockholder at the time of the transaction of which he complains or that his share thereafter devolved upon him by operation of law. In other words, the federal court will not permit itself to be used to litigate a purchased grievance or become a party to speculation in wrongs done to corporations.   *   *   *   These provisions neither create nor exempt from liabilities   *   *   *   . None conflict with the statute in question and all may be observed by a federal court, even if not applicable in state court.

It is true that Mr. Justice Jackson had before him the New Jersey statute which contained a "time of ownership" provision substantially similar to that in Rule 23(b) F.R.C.P. but he was clearly of opinion that its provisions should be applied in federal court "even if not applicable in state court".

The "time of ownership" provision of Rule 23(b) must be applied in federal court, therefore, even if no such provision is part of the state law which is being enforced.

Since the decision of Piccard v. Sperry Corp., Winkelman v. General Motors Corp., and Lissauer v. Bertles, the above cited federal cases dealing with New York law, the New York statutes have been amended by the addition of the provisions of section 61–b of the General Corporation Law above referred to. They have been interpreted by a New York court in Noel Associates v. Merrill, 184 Misc. 646, 655, 53 N.Y.S.2d 143, to permit, in effect, a suit, without security, by one plaintiff who held his stock contemporaneously with the transaction complained of plus a group of other plaintiffs who acquired their stock thereafter, where the aggregate market value of the shares exceeded $50,000.

Fuller v. American Machine & Foundry Co., D.C.S.D.N.Y., 95 F. Supp. 764, holds that the rule of the Noel case must be applied in federal court. I regret that, for the reasons hereinafter stated, I cannot agree.

In the Cohen case Mr. Justice Jackson said in effect that, despite substantive state law that the claim could be maintained by plaintiffs who purchased their stock subsequent to the alleged injury, Rule 23 (b) F.R.C.P. had the effect of prohibiting the maintenance of the claim in the federal court except by plaintiffs whose ownership of their stock was contemporaneous with the alleged injury.

In the instant case plaintiffs rely on the substantive state law that the claim can be maintained by plaintiffs who own in the aggregate $50,000 worth of stock and all but one of whom purchased their stock subsequent to the alleged injury. If, as was said in the Cohen opinion, Rule 23(b) prevents suit in the federal court by a group of subsequent purchasers all by themselves even though the state law would have permitted it, I can perceive no reason why Rule 23(b) should not prevent suit in the federal court by a group of subsequent purchasers and one contemporaneous owner even though the state law would have permitted it.

If the question of adding plaintiffs to make up a requisite aggregate value of stock held by plaintiffs had never come up, no one would have had the temerity to argue that Rule 23(b) F.R.C.P. permitted the joinder of plaintiffs who did not own stock at the time of the alleged injury. The mere fact that the New York courts construe the New York statutes as permitting such joinder for the purpose of making up the requisite $50,000 worth, has no tendency to alter the construction of Rule 23(b).

Plaintiff's motion is denied without prejudice to renewal upon a showing of compliance with the "time of ownership" provision of Rule 23(b) F.R.C.P. and the provisions of section 61–b of the New York General Corporation Law as to the alternatives to furnishing security. Such action must be taken within 20 days of the date of the publication of a note of this opinion in the New York Law Journal. For that period the stay restraining plaintiff from initiating any proceedings in this action, heretofore granted, is continued on the existing terms.

NOTE—SECURITY FOR EXPENSES LEGISLATION

The policy considerations underlying security for expenses legislation were stated in the opinion of Mr. Justice Jackson in Cohen v. Beneficial Industrial Loan Corp., 337 U.S. 541, 69 S.Ct. 1221, 93 L.Ed. 1528 (1949), in which the Supreme Court upheld such statutes against a constitutional attack and furthermore found that the *Erie* doctrine required their application in diversity suits. (*See*, Note Choice of Law, infra this Chapter.) Mr. Justice Jackson wrote:

> The background of stockholder litigation with which this statute deals requires no more than general notice. As business enterprises increasingly sought the advantages of incorporation, management became vested with almost uncontrolled discretion in handling other people's money. The vast aggregate of funds committed to corporate control came to be drawn to a considerable extent from numerous and scattered holders of small interests. The director was not subject to an effective accountability. That created strong temptation for managers to profit personally at the expense of their trust. The business code became all too tolerant of such practices. Corporate laws were lax and were not self-en-

forcing, and stockholders, in face of gravest abuses, were singularly impotent in obtaining redress of abuses of trust.

Equity came to the relief of the stockholder, who had no standing to bring civil action at law against faithless directors and managers. Equity, however, allowed him to step into the corporation's shoes and seek in its right the restitution he could not demand in his own. It required him first to demand that the corporation vindicate its own rights, but when, as was usual, those who perpetrated the wrongs also were able to obstruct any remedy, equity would hear and adjudge the corporation's cause through its stockholder with the corporation as a defendant, albeit a rather nominal one. This remedy, born of stockholder helplessness, was long the chief regulator of corporate management and has afforded no small incentive to avoid at least grosser forms of betrayal of stockholders' interests. It is argued, and not without reason, that without it there would be little practical check on such abuses.

Unfortunately, the remedy itself provided opportunity for abuse, which was not neglected. Suits sometimes were brought not to redress real wrongs, but to realize upon their nuisance value. They were bought off by secret settlements in which any wrongs to the general body of share owners were compounded by the suing stockholder, who was mollified by payments from corporate assets. These litigations were aptly characterized in professional slang as "strike suits." And it was said that these suits were more commonly brought by small and irresponsible than by large stockholders, because the former put less to risk and a small interest was more often within the capacity and readiness of management to compromise than a large one.

337 U.S. at 547–48.

New York adopted the first security for expenses statute (now found in N.Y.Bus.Corp.Law § 627) in 1944 in reaction to complaints against abuses of the derivative suit. The New York statute threw a substantial obstacle in the path of the derivative suit plaintiff by requiring the posting of a bond in a substantial amount sufficient to cover the expenses, including attorneys' fees, of the corporation and other defendants (to the extent that the corporation might have to indemnify them). In addition, the rule created a new source of liability by reversing the standard American rule that a successful defendant is not entitled to reimbursement of his costs and attorneys' fees from the plaintiff. This statute was intended to have a chilling effect on potential derivative suit plaintiffs.

The New York statute followed on the heels of a study of derivative suit litigation sponsored by the New York State Chamber of Commerce, which produced a lengthy report, the "Wood Report," highly critical of the abuses that it claimed had been committed. Wood, Survey and Report Regarding Stockholders' Derivative Suits

(1944).* The Wood Report listed the following as among the "common and principal abuses most frequently criticized:"

(a) Most derivative actions are brought by stockholders having no real financial interest in the corporation and accordingly so little stake in any possible recovery by it that it is not credible to suppose that they would have undertaken investigation or prosecution of the sort in their own interest, it being obvious that the only one likely to profit substantially in the event of success is the attorney.

(b) Under the present New York Rule, suit may be and often is brought by a stockholder purchasing his stock immediately prior to suit for the purpose of giving him or his attorneys status to bring suit.

(c) The bulk of this litigation is in the hands of a limited group of attorneys, so limited that it cannot be believed that the nominal plaintiffs have ascertained that they have a cause of action, and brought it to the particular lawyers.

(d) The present practice permits such cases to be handled as if they were the private concern of the individual plaintiffs and defendants and their attorneys.

(e) In practically every case involving a large corporation, the original action as soon as known by a reported decision on motion in the New York Law Journal or otherwise discovered by attorneys specializing in this field (such as by examination of filed cases in the New York County Clerk's Office), is followed by other actions on substantially identical complaints or motions are made to intervene on behalf of other stockholders. In neither of these instances is it reasonable to suppose that the nominal stockholder plaintiff initiated the action or intervention.

New York's lead has been followed by some, but by no means a majority of other states.** California takes a somewhat different approach. California General Corporation Law (1976), Section 800 permits a motion at any time within 30 days after service of summons upon the corporation or upon any defendant who is or was at the relevant time an officer or director of the corporation to require the plaintiff to furnish security.

The motion may be based upon one or both of the following grounds: (1) That there is no reasonable possibility that the prosecution of the cause of action alleged in the complaint against the moving party will benefit the corporation or its shareholders. (2) That the moving party, if other than the corporation, did not participate in the transaction complained of in any capacity.

---

* For discussion and criticism of the Wood Report see Hornstein, New Aspects of Stockholders' Derivative Suits, 47 Colum.L.Rev. 1 (1947); Hornstein, The Death Knell of Stockholders' Derivative Suits in New York, 32 Calif.L.Rev. 123 (1944).

** The Corporate Laws Committee of the ABA proposed elimination of security for expenses in April 1981.

The Court must hold a hearing upon the motion to consider evidence and may in its discretion fix security at no more than $50,000, which may be thereafter changed.*

Discussing the security for expenses statutes, one commentator suggested, "Had the legislators really been concerned with the so-called 'abuse' of stockholders' suits, the extortionate secret settlement, the remedy was painfully obvious: to bar secret settlements." Hornstein, New Aspects of Shareholders' Derivative Suits, 47 Colum. L.Rev. 1, 3 (1947). Do you agree?

The impact of the legislation has been less than expected. One reason is that a plaintiff confronted with a motion for security may request a shareholder list for the purpose of circularizing the stockholder body to enlist co-plaintiffs who will own in the aggregate enough stock to avoid the statute's application. *See*, Baker v. McFadden Publications, 300 N.Y. 325, 90 N.E.2d 876 (1960). Corporate management, when they are defendants, are likely to blanch at the idea of the circulation of a letter to shareholders describing, in forceful terms, their alleged misdeeds. Abe Pomerantz, the dean of the shareholder plaintiff's bar, is quoted as saying that with that prospect in mind, "In most cases, the sophisticated defendant will not make the motion." Note, Security for Expense in Shareholders' Derivative Suits, 4 Colum.J.L. & Soc.Prob. 50, 65 (1968).

Delaware, otherwise enjoying a reputation as generally favorable to management, has no security for expenses legislation. It has been suggested, perhaps too cynically, that the reason for this otherwise paradoxical omission is that Delaware is better able to attract shareholder litigation before its bench and bar.

The application of security for expenses legislation raises a surprising number of complexities on which there is no general agreement. For example, can a shareholder who, at the time the complaint was filed, did not own a sufficient number of shares to be exempt from the operation of the statute resist a motion for security by purchasing more stock? *Compare*, Weinstein v. Behn, 68 N.Y.S.2d 199 (1947), aff'd mem. 272 App.Div. 1045, 75 N.Y.S.2d 284 (1st Dept. 1947), with Richman v. Felmus, 8 App.Div.2d 985, 190 N.Y.S.2d 920 (2d Dept. 1959) and Purdy v. Humphrey, 187 Misc. 40, 60 N.Y.S.2d 535 (1946). *See* Haberman v. Tobin, 480 F.Supp. 425 (S.D.N.Y.1979). Kaufman v. Wolfson, *supra*, raises the issue of joinder with non-contemporaneous owners as a device to get around the state statute on security for expenses.

In a suit in federal court based on diversity jurisdiction, should the court apply the security for expenses statute of the state of incorporation even where there is no similar requirement in the forum state? Suppose the situation is the reverse? In Berkwitz v. Humphrey, 130

---

* Note that the California statute, unlike most, permits motions for security by certain defendants, other than the corporation.

F.Supp. 142 (N.D.Ohio 1955), the court held that, under *Erie*, the state of incorporation's security for expenses statute would not be applied by the forum state and therefore would not be applied by the federal court in that state. In other words, the statute was "substantive" for *Erie* purposes (*i.e*, federal court would follow state court), but not substantive for purposes of the internal affairs rule (*i.e.*, it did not follow the corporation.)

It is, finally, important to note that state security for expenses statutes are inapplicable in federal courts where the action is founded on a federal question. Fielding v. Allen, 181 F.2d 163 (2d Cir. 1948), *cert. denied* 340 U.S. 817, 71 S.Ct. 46, 95 L.Ed. 600 (1950). Where the plaintiff also asserts a claim arising under state law, relying either on pendent jurisdiction or diversity of citizenship to establish jurisdiction, the usual practice is to require the posting of security for only that portion of the costs expected to arise out of the defense of the state law portion of the complaint. *See, e.g.*, Epstein v. Solitron Devices, Inc., 388 F.2d 310 (2d Cir. 1968); Fielding v. Allen, *supra*.

F. JURISDICTION AND VENUE

1. PERSONAL JURISDICTION

Most shareholder litigation involves some or all of the officers and directors of a corporation as defendants. Obtaining personal jurisdiction over all of the individual defendants in the same action may pose severe practical problems. In many large corporations (and in some not so large) at least some of the directors, and occasionally some of the officers, reside and work in jurisdictions other than the one in which the corporation has its home office and may not be easily amenable to service of process. While the plaintiff could, presumably, attempt to serve the directors when they come into the state—to attend a board meeting, for example—such a procedure presents certain obvious difficulties. The shareholder is likely, therefore, to cast about for some more convenient means of obtaining personal jurisdiction over the defendants.

The Securities Exchange Act of 1934 supplies a partial answer for suits brought under its provisions in § 27, which provides that suits based on the Act "may be brought in any district where an act or transaction constituting the violation alleged occurred or in the district wherein the defendant is found or is an inhabitant or transacts business, and process in such cases may be served in any other district of which the defendant is an inhabitant or wherever the defendant may be found." This unusual provision for literally worldwide service of process is a distinct advantage for plaintiffs suing under the 1934 Act and explains in part the popularity of Rule 10b–5 with plaintiffs' lawyers.

Several states have enacted some form of "long-arm" statute designed to permit personal jurisdiction over nonresident directors of corporations organized under the laws of those states. One form of such a statute provides that nonresident directors are deemed to have appointed the Secretary of State as their agent for service of process in actions relating to the corporation. *E.g.*, Ind.Code §§ 34–2–2–1, 34–2–2–2 (1969); S.C.Bus.Corp.Act § 13.7 (1962).

The law of Delaware on this question is of more than ordinary interest. Until 1977 the Delaware statute provided for the sequestration of the shares owned by directors of a Delaware corporation, an action that was accomplished by placing a "stop transfer order" on the corporation's stock ledger. The "situs" of the stock was deemed to be in Delaware, regardless of the location of the actual certificates. In Shaffer v. Heitner, 433 U.S. 186, 97 S.Ct. 2569, 53 L.Ed.2d 683 (1977), however, the Supreme Court, held that this procedure was unconstitutional, ruling that the "minimum contacts" doctrine of International Shoe Co. v. Washington, 326 U.S. 310, 66 S.Ct. 154, 90 L.Ed. 95 (1945), should be extended to *quasi in rem* as well as to *in personam* jurisdiction. Mere ownership of stock in a Delaware corporation would not suffice for jurisdiction.

The Supreme Court rendered its decision in *Shaffer* on June 24, 1977. On July 7, 1977, the Delaware General Assembly unanimously enacted a new statute (Del.Code tit. 10, § 3114) "to fill the void." * The statute deems non-resident *directors* (not officers) of Delaware corporations to have consented to service of process in Delaware and to have appointed the registered agent of the corporation (or in default of a registered agent, the Secretary of State) as agent for service of process. Its constitutionality was sustained in Armstrong v. Pomerance, 423 A.2d 174 (Del.1980).

2. JURISDICTION OVER THE CORPORATION

The corporation is almost always an indispensable party to a derivative suit both because recovery normally runs in its favor and so that it will be bound by *res judicata*. *See*, Dean v. Kellogg, 294 Mich. 200, 292 N.W. 704 (1940). The usual practice is to name the corporation as a defendant. But for some purposes the corporation is more like a plaintiff. How should the corporation be treated for purposes of diversity of citizenship and venue?

In Smith v. Sperling, 354 U.S. 91, 77 S.Ct. 1112, 1 L.Ed.2d 1205 (1957), the Supreme Court held that the corporation should be aligned as a defendant if it is "antagonistic" to the plaintiff, which is usually the case as evidenced by its refusal to bring the action on its own. The determination is made on the basis of the pleadings. As a practical matter, therefore, in any true derivative suit, the corporation will almost always be aligned as a defendant in determining whether the requisite diversity exists for federal jurisdiction.

* Jacobs & Stargatt, The New Delaware Director-Consent-to-Service Statute. 33 Bus.Law 701 (1978).

The federal provisions dealing with venue and service of process are set forth in §§ 1332, 1391, 1401 and 1695 of 28 U.S.C.A. See the statutory supplement.

G. CHOICE OF LAW

What law governs the procedural and substantive issues presented in stockholder derivative suits? If a corporation formed under the laws of state X is sued in state court in X the problem ordinarily does not arise. (A cautionary note: Sometimes a court will apply the law of the principal place of business. See California Gen.Corp.Law § 2115.) But if a corporation is sued in federal court, or in a state court of another jurisdiction, some difficult questions arise. Problems of federalism doubtless complicate the issue. A federal court not only has to consider which state law might apply, but whether *any* state law applies.

Here are a few governing principles (if not rules):

(1) Corporation law matters are customarily governed by the "internal affairs rule." The effect of the rule is to make the corporate law of the state of incorporation follow a corporation wherever the suit is brought.

In Hausman v. Buckley, 299 F.2d 696 (2d Cir. 1962), cert. denied 369 U.S. 885, 82 S.Ct. 1157, 8 L.Ed.2d 286 plaintiff brought a derivative suit on behalf of a Venezuelan corporation in federal court in New York. The case was governed by the state law of the forum, including the forum state's conflict of laws rules. New York law applies the internal affairs rule. The issue of whether a suit of this type could be maintained was held to be a substantive issue, and under New York conflict of law rules, the law of Venezuela applied. Thus, even though the forum state allowed derivative suits, the place of incorporation did not, and the suit was dismissed.

Messinger v. United Canso Oil and Gas Ltd., 486 F.Supp. 788 (D. Conn.1980), held a requirement for demand on stockholders, in a diversity case in Connecticut, to be governed by Canadian law, as that was where the corporation was formed, and that was the law a Connecticut court would follow.

Whether a suit is to be characterized as direct or derivative is determined not by the forum state but by the place of incorporation. Gadd v. Pearson, 351 F.Supp. 895 (M.D.Fla.1972).

The strength of the internal affairs rule is seen in Shaffer v. Heitner, 433 U.S. 186, 97 S.Ct. 2569, 53 L.Ed.2d 683 (1977). After finding that Delaware's interest in a corporation formed under Delaware law was insufficient to support quasi-in-rem jurisdiction, the Supreme Court noted, "In general, the law of the state of incorporation is held to govern the liability of officers or directors to the corporation and its stockholders * * *. The rationale for the general rule appears to be based more on the need for a uniform and certain standard to govern the internal affairs of a corporation than on the perceived interest of the state of incorporation."

(2) Erie Railroad Co. v. Tompkins, 304 U.S. 64, 58 S.Ct. 817, 82 L. Ed. 1188 (1938), compels a federal court to follow the substantive law of the forum state in a diversity case, including the forum state's conflicts rules. Less clear is the effect on the "procedural" issues in a derivative suit.

In Cohen v. Beneficial Industrial Loan Corp., 337 U.S. 541, 69 S. Ct. 1221, 93 L.Ed. 1528 (1949), a suit involving a Delaware corporation was brought in federal district court in New Jersey. Delaware has no provision for posting security for expenses; New Jersey had a rule similar to New York's requiring such security upon demand. The Court held the New Jersey rule applicable. "A plaintiff cannot avail himself of the New Jersey forum and at the same time escape the terms on which it is made available."

Mr. Justice Jackson later expanded: "Even if we were to agree that the New Jersey statute is procedural, it would not determine that it is not applicable. Rules which lawyers call procedural do not always exhaust their effect by regulating procedure. But this statute is not merely a regulation of procedure. With it or without it the main action takes the same course. However, it creates a new liability where none existed before, for it makes a stockholder who institutes a derivative action liable for the expense to which he puts the corporation and other defendants, if he does not make good his claims. Such liability is not usual and it goes beyond payment of what we know as "costs". If all the Act did was to create this liability, it would clearly be substantive. But this new liability would be without meaning and value in many cases if it resulted in nothing but a judgment for expenses at or after the end of the case. Therefore, a procedure is prescribed by which the liability is insured by entitling the corporate defendant to a bond of indemnity before the outlay is incurred. We do not think a statute which so conditions the stockholder's action can be disregarded by the federal court as a mere procedural device." 337 U.S. at 555-6.

(3) The Federal Rules of Civil Procedure, which apply to all federal court actions, would appear not to be controlled by *Erie*, so that to the extent matters are governed by Rule 23.1, that is the applicable law. Hanna v. Plumer, 380 U.S. 460, 85 S.Ct. 1136, 14 L.Ed.2d 8 (1965). Some qualification of that statement is necessary, however. Mr. Justice Harlan, who was victorious counsel in *Cohen*, wrote a concurring opinion in *Hanna* in which he expressed the view that the Court was departing from the principles of *Cohen*. He said state rules which reflect policy considerations should be allowed to operate. Thus, in Walker v. Armco Steel Corp., 446 U.S. 740, 100 S.Ct. 1978, 64 L.Ed.2d 659 (1980), the Supreme Court found that an action had not been timely commenced for purposes of the Oklahoma statute of limitations even though it was timely commenced under the standards of

Rule 3 of the Federal Rules. Federal rules which purport to affect substantive rights may exceed the power of the rule makers, and therefore, may require a narrow interpretation. Rule 23.1 certainly presents some situations where this issue is raised.

(4) If federal substantive policies are involved in a case, they must be allowed to operate. *Erie* will not impose state law restrictions on federal rights. In Levitt v. Johnson, 334 F.2d 815 (1st Cir. 1964), plaintiff brought suit under the federal Investment Company Act of 1940 in federal district court of Massachusetts. He made no demand on stockholders. Massachusetts, which was both the forum state and the state of incorporation required such a demand, and the federal rules require demand to be made "if necessary." The federal statute was silent on the subject. The district court found that under the internal affairs rule, the shareholder's rights are determined by the state of incorporation, and demand was required. The Court of Appeals reversed. A federal right was asserted and its availability could not be made to turn on compliance with state law. The court also rejected the idea that, in the face of Congressional silence, it should adopt a federal judicial policy of requiring demand that was similar to that followed by the forum state. Noting that the subject corporation had 48,000 stockholders, the court said that such a policy would frustrate the purposes of the federal act. The result is interesting in light of the enthusiasm with which the First Circuit had applied the Massachusetts rule in diversity cases.

The following questions test the principles:

(1) Suppose a Delaware corporation is sued in federal district court in New York. The defendants demand that plaintiff post security for expenses under § 627 of the New York Business Corporation Law. Neither Delaware law nor the Federal Rules of Civil Procedure refer to security for expenses. What law applies?

(2) A New York corporation is sued in a Delaware court. May security be demanded? That is, does this particular New York law follow the corporation?

(3) Suppose suit is brought in federal district court in New York, involving a New York corporation, and plaintiff alleges a common law breach of fiduciary duty and violation of federal securities laws. May security be demanded?

(4) Suppose suit is brought in federal district court by a shareholder of a California corporation who acquired his shares after the transaction of which he complains. California permits a non-contemporaneous shareholder to bring suit upon a proper showing. Rule 23.1 of the Federal Rules of Civil Procedure requires contemporaneous ownership of a plaintiff. May the suit be maintained?

(5) Suppose the shareholder in the previous paragraph brings suit in state court in New York, where contemporaneous ownership is required. Will the New York court apply its law or California law?

(6) Suppose the shareholder above brings suit in California court and the defendants remove the case to federal court. Must the suit be dismissed? Can removal be prevented? Is it dismissed with prejudice? What difference does it make?

(7) Suppose the corporation is a New York corporation, but its principal place of business and the plaintiff's residence is California. Suit is brought in California. May it be maintained by the plaintiff?

(8) Suppose the stockholder complains of a continuing wrong that commenced prior to his acquisition of shares but which still continues. The case law of the state of incorporation has held that standing would not be proper under the circumstances alleged. Is the federal court where the case is brought bound by this interpretation?

(9) Suppose a derivative suit is brought on behalf of a Maryland corporation in federal district court. No allegation as to demand on directors is made in the complaint. Maryland does not require a demand on directors or shareholders, but Rule 23.1 of the FRCP does. Is a demand necessary?

(10) Suppose the suit in the preceding paragraph is brought in New York, which requires of a demand on directors in § 626(c). Is demand required? That is, does the court follow the forum state rule or the rule of the state of incorporation?

(11) Suppose the New York corporation is sued in Maryland. Is demand required?

(12) Suppose a New York corporation is sued in federal district court in Massachusetts, where defendants reside. New York's statute makes no reference to demand on stockholders, and case law indicates none is required. Rule 23.1 of the FRCP requires that the making of a demand must be alleged "if necessary." Massachusetts law requires such a demand be made. Is demand required?

(13) Suppose a Massachusetts corporation is sued in Delaware, where the defendants reside, and which has a rule similar to FRCP 23.1. Is demand on the stockholders necessary?

H. ROLE OF COUNSEL

Can the lawyer who has represented the corporation now represent the individual directors—who very often will be the management of the corporation—in a derivative suit? While counsel represented the corporation, nonetheless he rendered advice to the individuals relating to the transaction that is in question. It is natural for those defendants now to turn to that lawyer and ask that he represent them when their conduct is challenged. But is such representation in conflict with the lawyer's responsibility to the corporation—which has been his client? Will representation of the individual defendants necessarily cause the counsel to reveal confidences of the corporation in breach of his professional responsibility?

The law is evolving in this respect, as the following two excerpts reveal.

DEVELOPMENTS IN THE LAW—CONFLICTS OF INTEREST IN THE LEGAL PROFESSION

94 Harv.L.Rev. 1244, 1339–1342 (1981).

Shareholder Derivative Suits

A derivative suit is nominally brought "to enforce a right of the corporation against a third party, and recovery in the suit must generally go to the corporation. But it may nevertheless be in the entity's interest to oppose a derivative suit. The entity's decision to oppose the suit or merely remain a passive bystander is of more than academic interest, because various potentially decisive procedural defenses can be raised only by the entity. The corporate attorney directed by management to resist such a suit, when the real defendant to the suit is a corporate insider, must be concerned that opposing the suit may be in the insider's—but not in the shareholders'—best interest.

The possibility for conflict of interest here is universally recognized. Although early cases found joint representation permissible where no conflict of interest was obvious, the emerging rule is against dual representation in all derivative actions. Outside counsel must thus be retained to represent one of the defendants. The cases and ethics opinions differ on whether there must be separate representation from the outset or merely from the time the corporation seeks to take an active role. Furthermore, this restriction on dual representation should not be waivable by consent in the usual way; the corporation should be presumptively incapable of giving valid consent.

It has been suggested that the outside lawyer should represent the individual defendants, perhaps as an indirect means of ensuring that their legal fees are not borne by the corporation. The better rule is to require that outside counsel represent the corporation, while the corporate attorney represents the insider defendant; the question of expenses would be decided separately. This rule recognizes that while the in-house attorney is nominally the representative of the corporation, his personal loyalties will inevitably be to the individual executives who hired him.

A corollary of the principle that the entity interests do not necessarily coincide with the position taken by the plaintiff in a derivative suit is that a former corporate attorney may not represent a shareholder in a derivative suit against the same corporation. If one looks only to the form of the suit, there would appear to be no conflict here—after all, the derivative suit purportedly seeks to advance the interests of the attorney's former client—but in reality these suits are often opposed to the entity's true interests.

CANNON v. UNITED STATES ACOUSTICS CORP.

398 F.Supp. 209 (N.D.Ill.1975), aff'd in relevant part per curiam
532 F.2d 1118 (7th Cir. 1976).

[This case was a stockholder's derivative suit in which the plaintiff alleged that the individual defendants committed numerous violations of the federal securities laws: granting themselves illegal stock options; causing the corporation to issue them additional shares based upon false claims that the stock was paid for rent, services and other expenses; usurpation of corporate opportunities; and the payment of illegal compensation.

Plaintiff sought to disqualify the law firm that represented both the corporation and the individual defendants. The defendants asserted that the conflict was theoretical only, and that if any real conflict did arise, they would withdraw.

The court disqualified counsel from representing the corporation. It found the thrust of the rules to be that "The interest of the corporate client is paramount and should not be influenced by any interest of the individual corporate officials." It summarized the law as follows:]

MARSHALL, District Judge.

* * * These are serious charges. If they are proved, the corporations stand to gain substantially. The CPR unquestionably prohibits one lawyer from representing multiple clients when their interests are in conflict. The code goes so far as to say that if the clients' interests are potentially differing, the preferable course is for the lawyer to refuse the employment initially. In addition, at least one influential bar association has issued an opinion stating that dual representation is subject to conflicts of interest even when the corporation takes a passive role in the litigation. The case law on the question is not consistent; older cases hold dual representation is not improper, while more recent decisions hold that it is, both in derivative shareholder suits and in suits under 29 U.S.C.A. § 501 (1970).

As previously discussed the court is bound to apply the CPR to lawyers practicing before it. The code is clear that multiple representation is improper when the client's interests are adverse. Nevertheless, defendants' counsel argue there is no present conflict and should one arise they will withdraw their representation of the individual defendants and represent only the corporations. There are a number of problems with this solution. First, the complaint on its face establishes a conflict that cannot be ignored despite counsel's good faith representations. Second, counsel overlooks the hardship on the court and the parties if in the middle of this litigation new counsel must be obtained because a conflict arises. Lastly, although counsel offers to withdraw its representation of the individual defendants and remain counsel for the corporations if a conflict should arise, the appropriate course, as suggested by [Lewis v. Shaffer Stores Co., 218 F.Supp. 238 (S.D.N.Y.1963)] and [Murphy v. Washington American League Base Ball Club, Inc., 324 F.2d 394 (D.C. Cir. 1963)], is for the corporation to retain independent counsel. Under this procedure, once counsel has examined the evidence, a decision can be made regarding the role the corporation will play in the litigation. This decision will be made without the possibility of any influence emanating from the representation of the individual defendants, and will also eliminate the potential problem of confidences and secrets reposed by the individual defendants being used adverse to their interests by former counsel should new counsel have had to have been selected under the approach suggested by defense counsel. This solution, concededly, is not without its disabilities. The corporations' rights to counsel of their choice are infringed and in a closely held corporation, as here, the financial burden is increased. Nevertheless, on balance, the corporations must obtain independent counsel.

* * *

NOTE—ATTORNEY–CLIENT PRIVILEGE

Perhaps the most difficult operational questions for counsel concern the scope of the attorney-client privilege and the work product rule. Counsel has consulted with individual members of management in his role as counsel to the corporation. Were those conversations privileged? Do they remain privileged when a shareholder seeks to discover them? Was counsel engaged in a meeting with the "client" when he spoke to the managers?

The present version of the Code of Professional Responsibility states:

EC 5–18 A lawyer employed or retained by a corporation or similar entity owes his allegiance to the entity and not to a stockholder, director, officer, employee, representative, or other person connected with the entity. In advising the entity, a lawyer should keep paramount its interests and his professional judgment should not be influenced by the personal desires of any person or organization. Occasionally a lawyer for an entity is requested by a stockholder, director, officer, employee, representative, or other person connected with the entity to represent him in an individual capacity; in such case the lawyer may serve the individual only if the lawyer is convinced that differing interests are not present.

In Garner v. Wolfinbarger, 430 F.2d 1093 (5th Cir. 1970), counsel asserted that the attorney-client privilege prevented him from testifying as to the advice he gave the "corporation" in a transaction involving the sale of securities. The sale was attacked in a shareholder suit

alleging violation of the federal securities laws.   Judge Godbold's
opinion of the court stated:

> The corporation says that its right to assert the privilege is abso-
> lute and of special importance where disclosure is sought in a suit
> brought by the shareholders, those who might second-guess or
> even harass in matters purely of judgment.   But in assessing
> management assertions of injury to the corporation it must be
> borne in mind that management does not manage for itself and
> that the beneficiaries of its action are the stockholders.   Conceptu-
> alistic phrases describing the corporation as an entity separate
> from its stockholders are not useful tools of analysis.   They serve
> only to obscure the fact that management has duties which run to
> the benefit ultimately of the stockholders.   For example, it is diffi-
> cult to rationally defend the assertion of the privilege if all, or
> substantially all, stockholders desire to inquire into the attorney's
> communications with corporate representatives who have only
> nominal ownership interests, or even none at all.   There may be
> reasonable differences over the manner of characterizing in legal
> terminology the duties of management, and over the extent to
> which corporate management is less of a fiduciary than the com-
> mon law trustee.   There may be many situations in which the cor-
> porate entity or its management, or both, have interests adverse
> to those of some or all stockholders.   But when all is said and
> done management is not managing for itself.

*   *   *

In summary, we say this.   The attorney-client privilege still has
viability for the corporate client.   The corporation is not barred
from asserting it merely because those demanding information enjoy the status of stockholders.   But where the corporation is in
suit against its stockholders on charges of acting inimically to
stockholder interests, protection of those interests as well as those
of the corporation and of the public require that the availability of
the privilege be subject to the right of the stockholders to show
cause why it should not be invoked in the particular instance.

[The case was remanded to the lower court to determine the issue
of "good cause."]

_____

In re LTV Securities Litigation, 89 F.R.D. 595 (N.D.Tex.1981),
found "good cause" to deny shareholder discovery where the communication took place "post-event."   Once accused of wrong-doing, management's need to consult counsel in confidence is "self evident."

The extent of the privilege was interpreted in Upjohn Co. v. United States, 449 U.S. 383, 101 S.Ct. 677, 66 L.Ed.2d 584 (1981).   Counsel
undertook an investigation of reports that the company had made
questionable payments to foreign officials to secure business.   Coun-

sel sent questionnaires to foreign managers and conducted interviews. The government subpoenaed the resulting documents, and
counsel resisted the subpoena on the basis of the attorney-client privilege. The Sixth Circuit rejected the claim on grounds that it was limited to discussions with members of the "control group" of the corporation.

Justice REHNQUIST delivered the opinion of the Court: *gives wider range to the privilege*

In the case of the individual client the provider of information
and the person who acts on the lawyer's advice are one and the
same. In the corporate context, however, it will frequently be employees beyond the control group as defined by the court below—
"officers and agents   *   *   *   responsible for directing [the company's] actions in response to legal advice"—who will possess the
information needed by the corporation's lawyers. Middle-level—
and indeed lower-level—employees can, by actions within the
scope of their employment, embroil the corporation in serious legal difficulties, and it is only natural that these employees would
have the relevant information needed by corporate counsel if he is
adequately to advise the client with respect to such actual or potential difficulties.

*   *   *

The control group test adopted by the court below thus frustrates the very purpose of the privilege by discouraging the communication of relevant information by employees of the client to
attorneys seeking to render legal advice to the client corporation.
The attorney's advice will also frequently be more significant to
noncontrol group members than to those who officially sanction
the advice, and the control group test makes it more difficult to
convey full and frank legal advice to the employees who will put
into effect the client corporation's policy.

The narrow scope given the attorney-client privilege by the
court below not only makes it difficult for corporate attorneys to
formulate sound advice when their client is faced with a specific
legal problem but also threatens to limit the valuable efforts of
corporate counsel to ensure their client's compliance with the law.
In light of the vast and complicated array of regulatory legislation
confronting the modern corporation, corporations, unlike most individuals, "constantly go to lawyers to find out how to obey the
law," Burnham, The Attorney-Client Privilege in the Corporate
Arena, 24 Bus.Law. 901, 913 (1969), particularly since compliance
with the law in this area is hardly an instinctive matter   *   *   *   .
The test adopted by the court below is difficult to apply in practice, though no abstractly formulated and unvarying "test" will
necessarily enable courts to decide questions such as this with
mathematical precision. But if the purpose of the attorney-client
privilege is to be served, the attorney and client must be able to
predict with some degree of certainty whether particular discus-

sions will be protected. An uncertain privilege, or one which purports to be certain but results in widely varying applications by the courts, is little better than no privilege at all. The very terms of the test adopted by the court below suggest the unpredictability of its application. The test restricts the availability of the privilege to those officers who play a "substantial role" in deciding and directing a corporation's legal response.

I. SETTLEMENT AND COUNSEL FEES

Class actions and derivative suits that are brought in federal court, and in some state courts as well, may not be dismissed or settled without notice to shareholders and approval by the court. Why?

HAUDEK, THE SETTLEMENT AND DISMISSAL OF STOCKHOLDERS ACTIONS, Part I

22 Sw.L.J. 767, 768–70 (1968).

The Federal Rule: Its History and Purpose

History. The evils which Federal Rule 23(c) was designed to cure have often been recited. From the early days of the class suit, it had been widely accepted doctrine that a representative or derivative plaintiff owed no duties to his class or corporation. He was the *dominus litis*; since he bore all the expenses of the action, he could dismiss or compromise it at pleasure and on any terms he saw fit. That right continued until intervention by another class member or entry of a decree in favor of the class. Thus, the class plaintiff could drop his suit in return for the payment to him of a "private settlement" in an amount vastly exceeding his individual interest. Other class members had no right to share in the proceeds of the private settlement and had no standing to object to the dismissal of the suit. Once the action was abandoned, they could not intervene and revive it. There apparently was only one restriction to the class plaintiff's freedom from control: A compromise by the plaintiff of the corporation or class rights could be enjoined or rescinded for fraud or bad faith. To forestall that possibility, the *voluntary* submission of corporate settlements for judicial approval came into increasing use in the 1930's.

The prevailing state of the law plainly invited abuse. Most stockholders' suits involve corporate or class claims of considerable magnitude. The temptation for the defendants to buy off the plaintiff by a relatively modest private settlement was therefore great. Many stockholders' actions of doubtful merit were brought simply to secure private settlements for the plaintiff and his lawyer. Private settlements also were employed to stifle meritorious suits brought initially in good faith. In derivative suits, the corporation, frequently controlled by the alleged wrongdoers or their allies, could not be expected to resist by direct action. Even without a private settlement, complaining stockholders often dropped their suits simply to avoid further expense and trouble. By the time the class suit was dismissed, the statute of limitations or laches often barred other stockholders from bringing actions of their own; advantages already gained in the litigation were lost. The termination of the action without notice to the class also served to conceal whatever wrongs had been done, so that uninformed class members were unable to safeguard their rights. The stockholder's suit was in danger of becoming a tool for defeating the class rights it was intended to protect.

Such, in broad outline, was the law before Rule 23(c) forbade the dismissal or compromise of a class action without the approval of the court. Under the Rule as originally phrased, notice to the class members of a proposed dismissal or compromise was mandatory only in derivative and other "true" class actions; in other types of class suits notice was to be given only if the court required it. In either case the manner of notice was left to the court's direction. The 1966 amendment of the Federal Rules has segregated representative and derivative actions for separate treatment in Rules 23 and 23.1, respectively; but the substance of old Rule 23(c) has been preserved, except that class notice of a proposed dismissal or compromise is now mandatory in all types of class suits.

———

In Wolf v. Barkes, 348 F.2d 994 (2d Cir. 1965), plaintiff in a stockholder's derivative suit sought to enjoin a settlement by the corporation with defendant-officers. Judge Friendly concluded that the notice and approval provisions of the Federal Rule did not apply to this settlement. No derivative suit was being settled; the corporation retained the power to settle its own litigation.

The plaintiff's concern was that the corporate settlement would provide a presumptively valid defense to the derivative suit, on the basis of which the defendants could move to dismiss it even though the settlement between the corporation and the defendants was without judicial approval. But Judge Friendly noted that the plaintiff could still attack the settlement on grounds of waste, or fraud in a self-dealing transaction. Query: Would the court have the same scope of review in *that* suit as it would have in a settlement approval proceeding?

In Clark v. Lomas & Nettleton Financial Corp., 625 F.2d 49 (5th Cir. 1980), cert. denied 450 U.S. 1029, 101 S.Ct.1738, 68 L.Ed.2d 224 (1981), the court vacated the settlement between the corporation and individual defendants, made on the eve of a scheduled trial of a derivative suit because the corporation's board was not independent. The court did not even consider the fairness of the settlement terms.

The shareholder who attacks the out-of-court settlement by the corporation (and who may have to shoulder the burden of proof), is the same shareholder who would have to defend any settlement he made with defendants on the same issue. Is his burden in defending a settlement greater or lighter than his burden in attacking the out-of-court settlement? Which proceeding is better calculated to protect the rights of the stockholders?

A key factor to bear in mind is that the judicially approved settlement constitutes *res judicata* of the claims asserted in the suit. *See* Note, Res Judicata in the Derivative Action: Adequacy of Representation and the Inadequate Plaintiff, 71 Mich.L.Rev. 1042 (1973).

SHLENSKY v. DORSEY

574 F.2d 131 (3d Cir. 1978).

OPINION OF THE COURT

MARIS, Circuit Judge.

* * *

The eight actions comprising the consolidated derivative suit now before us were instituted between March and November of 1975 in five separate district courts, including the District Court for the Western District of Pennsylvania to which the suits were eventually transferred and there consolidated. Named as defendants are Gulf, eighteen of its present and former officers and directors, an officer of a former Gulf subsidiary, and Price Waterhouse, Gulf's former independent certified public accountant and auditor. The shareholders seek recovery on behalf of Gulf of allegedly illegally expended corporate funds in excess of $18,800,000, incidental monetary damages and costs incurred by Gulf, equitable relief and the plaintiffs' litigation expenses.

The derivative suits arose out of public revelations in 1973 and 1975 by Gulf officials and the Securities and Exchange Commission of alleged illegal corporate action. Investigation by the Watergate Special Prosecution Force into the activities of the Finance Committee to Re-Elect the President (in 1972) precipitated Gulf's disclosure in 1973 that its vice president in charge of government relations, Claude C. Wild, Jr., had, in 1971 and 1972, donated out of corporate funds $100,000, $15,000 and $10,000 to the 1972 presidential election campaigns of President Nixon, Representative Mills and Senator Jackson, respectively. The contributions amounting to $125,000 were subsequently returned to Gulf. In November 1973 Gulf and Wild pleaded guilty to criminal charges of violations of the Federal Election Campaign Act, 18 U.S.C. § 610. Gulf was fined $5,000 and Wild, $1,000.

* * *

Opting to settle the case rather than proceed to trial, the parties, with the exception of Price Waterhouse, entered into a "Stipulation of Compromise and Settlement" and on September 29, 1976, petitioned the district court for its approval.

* * *

Gulf agreed to reimburse and indemnify the settling defendants * * * as to their reasonable expenses, including counsel fees, incurred in connection with the consolidated action or any other action, judgment or penalty arising out of the matters * * *. Gulf also agreed to the adoption of and further implementation of already initiated internal auditing and reporting procedures designed to avoid a recurrence of unlawful political contributions.

The North River Insurance Company, the insurance carrier under Gulf's directors' and officers' liability and corporate reimbursement policy, agreed to pay $2,000,000 to Gulf conditioned on the execution of releases by Gulf and the defendants named as insured in the policy.

Certain of the individual defendants agreed not to contest the rescission by Gulf's board of directors on July 13, 1976, of stock option rights and attendant stock appreciation rights previously granted them under the 1974 stock option plan and the board's denial of incentive compensation awards for 1975 amounting to $370,000. Gulf agreed to refuse delivery to other defendants of Gulf stock valued at $250,000 previously awarded them. Other Gulf employees, not defendants, consented to the denial of incentive compensation due them aggregating $23,882.28. A retired employee * * * was denied all future payments to him under a 1964 agreement with Gulf. Gulf admitted reimbursement by recipients of illegal or unauthorized contributions from Gulf funds amounting to $57,261.55.

Lastly, based upon the complexity of the litigation, the competence of the attorneys and accountants involved and the benefits to Gulf and its shareholders from the compromise and settlement of the case, Gulf agreed not to oppose an application, with supporting data, to the district court by the plaintiffs' attorneys and accountants for payment by Gulf of their reasonable fees and reimbursement of their expenses in an amount not to exceed $600,000 for fees and $25,000 for expenses.

A summary of the settlement terms was sent to the more than 300,000 Gulf shareholders of record with directions to file in advance of a settlement hearing to be held November 18, 1976, their written objections, if any, to the settlement and notice of their intention to appear if they desired to do so. * * *

* * * [T]he district court conducted a hearing on the plaintiffs' application for accountants' and attorneys' fees and expenses. The district court found the objective value of the time spent by the persons involved in representing the plaintiffs to be in the aggregate $407,429.50. That amount was increased by the court by $167,570.50 in consideration of such factors as the contingent nature of success in the litigation, the benefits achieved by the settlement terms and the quality of the services performed. The court accordingly found

$575,000 to be representative of fair and reasonable fees. The court also approved reimbursement of the attorneys' and accountants' expenses in the amount of $32,777.95 and directed by order entered November 19, 1976, payment by Gulf of a total of $607,777.95 for fees and reimbursement of expenses of the plaintiffs' accountants and attorneys.

* * *

Turning to the district court's determination that the settlement was fair and reasonable, we bear in mind that the scope of our review is very limited. For the district court has wide discretion in making that decision * * *.

The principal factor to be considered in determining the fairness of a settlement concluding a shareholders' derivative action is the extent of the benefit to be derived from the proposed settlement by the corporation, the real party in interest. The adequacy of the recovery provided the corporation by the settlement must be considered in the light of the best possible recovery, of the risks of establishing liability and proving damages in the event the case is not settled, and of the cost of prolonging the litigation.

Given the amount of unlawfully disbursed corporate funds alleged to total $18,800,000 and taking into consideration the risks of establishing liability and damages, set forth at length in the district court's findings of fact and conclusions of law, we cannot say that it was an abuse of the district court's discretion to conclude that $3,500,000 represented a fair and reasonable settlement amount even without taking into consideration the additional nonmonetary benefits to Gulf referred to but not valued by the district court. * * *

One of the factors to be considered in determining the fairness of a settlement disposing of a class action is the reaction of the members of the class. * * * Here the overwhelming majority of Gulf shareholders have not objected to the settlement and Gulf, for the benefit of which the suit was filed, has agreed to its terms.

Bearing in mind all of the factors—the $2,000,000 contribution to Gulf by its insurer under a directors' and officers' liability insurance policy in exchange for its release from further liability under the policy, the agreements of the individual defendants to give up their claims against Gulf for compensation and stock option rights valued by the district court at approximately $1,500,000, the additional cost of protracted litigation, the risk of successful prosecution of the claims given up, the fact that so very few shareholders objected to the settlement, the corporation's approval of the settlement, and the fact that the settlement provides a substantial net benefit to Gulf after payment of plaintiffs' counsel fees and expenses—we cannot say that the district court abused its discretion in approving the settlement as a fair compromise and settlement of the action before it.

* * *

IV. AWARD OF ATTORNEYS' AND ACCOUNTANTS' FEES AND EXPENSES

Under the "American" rule ordinarily applied in our courts, a prevailing litigant is not entitled to recover attorneys' fees from a losing party absent statutory authority. However, the courts, exercising their equitable powers, have permitted a plaintiff whose efforts have created a fund benefiting others as well as himself to recoup some of the costs of the litigation, including attorneys' fees, out of the common fund or directly from the other parties enjoying the benefits who are required to pay their proportionate share of the costs. *Alyeska Pipeline Co. v. Wilderness Society*, 421 U.S. 240, 257, 95 S.Ct. 1612, 44 L.Ed.2d 141 (1975); *Trustees v. Greenough*, 105 U.S. 527, 26 L.Ed. 1157 (1882). The plaintiffs in a shareholders' derivative action may, thus, recover their expenses, including attorneys' fees, from the corporation on whose behalf their action is taken if the corporation derives a benefit, which may be monetary or nonmonetary, from their successful prosecution or settlement of the case. *Mills v. Electric Auto-Lite Co.*, 396 U.S. 375, 391–395, 90 S.Ct. 616, 24 L.Ed.2d 593 (1970); *Levine v. Bradlee*, 378 F.2d 620, 622 (3d Cir. 1967).

In the present case, as we have seen, the district court awarded to the attorneys and accountants of the plaintiffs the total sum of $607,777.95 for fees and reimbursement of expenses to be paid by Gulf. Pat S. Holloway, at our No. 77–1158, and the Project, at our No. 77–1157, appeal from the order making this award. Their contentions are essentially that the settlement did not result in a net benefit to Gulf and that, therefore, the plaintiffs are not entitled to any award of attorneys' fees and expenses. In the alternative, they contend that the district court failed to adhere to the standards set forth in *Lindy Bros. Builders, Inc. v. American Radiator & Standard Sanitary Corp.*, 487 F.2d 161 (3d Cir. 1973) (*Lindy I*), and *Lindy Bros. Builders, Inc. v. American Radiator & Standard Sanitary Corp.*, 540 F.2d 102 (3d Cir. 1976) (*Lindy II*), and erred in awarding fees in excess of the objective value of the attorneys' services.

* * *

In this circuit, as we have already pointed out, the district court, in the exercise of its discretion to award reasonable attorneys' fees in an appropriate case, is required to follow the guidelines for determining the reasonable value of the attorneys' services set forth in the *Lindy* cases. Moreover, we have held that failure of the district court to follow these guidelines constitutes an abuse of discretion. Under these guidelines the court is required first to arrive at the objective value of the individual attorneys' services by multiplying their hours of work by their normal billing rates per hour. The resulting basic or "lodestar" figure may be increased or decreased depending upon the applicability of other factors, primarily, the contingent nature of success in the litigation and the quality of the attorneys' efforts. The district court must make a separate inquiry and findings of fact with respect to each of those factors. *Lindy II*, 540 F.2d 102, 116. *Lindy II* requires that if the district court decided that consideration of the contingency of success justifies a change in the basic fee, it must indicate the elements of contingency involved, examples of which it mentions, 540 F.2d at 117. Also, it must state the specific amount of the increase or decrease to be made in the fees by reason of the contingency feature and the reasons supporting such increase or decrease. *Lindy II*, 540 F.2d 102, 117. The same procedure must be followed in evaluating the quality of the attorneys' work with a view to an increase or decrease in the lodestar figure to reflect the effect of that factor. *Lindy II*, 540 F.2d 102, 117–118.

The district court's calculation of the objective value of the plaintiffs' attorneys' services benefiting Gulf is not in dispute. The court accepted, with some modification, the statement of the hours spent on the case by the various attorneys, accountants and paraprofessionals and the normal hourly billing rates of those individuals contained in the plaintiffs' verified petition for fees. The court found that the aggregate objective value of the services of all the individuals entitled to compensation amounted to $407,429.50.

The district court then applied percentage increases, ranging from 7% to 82%, to the lodestar figures for the various lawyers and accountants involved. The aggregate increase over the total produced by the lodestar figures brought the fee award to $575,000, with an award of $32,777.95 for reimbursement of expenses producing a total of $607,777.95 which the court awarded to the attorneys and accountants of the plaintiffs for their fees and expenses.

* * *

NOTE—ATTORNEYS' FEES

The older approach to counsel fees is known as the "salvage value" approach, according to which courts calculated the fee as a percentage of the total recovery. Typically, the awards ranged between 20%–35% when the award was below $1 million; 15%–20% when it was more. The approach followed in *Dorsey* is favored by the Federal Judicial Manual for Complex Litigation, but disliked by many derivative suit lawyers.

Chapter 16

INDEMNIFICATION AND INSURANCE

PROBLEM

NATIONAL METAL PRODUCTS—PART III

Your law firm is outside counsel to National Metal Products, Inc., the corporation described in the problems in Chapters 13 and 14. The Department of Justice recently instituted criminal proceedings against the corporation and "Red" Sanford, a vice-president and member of the board of directors, for violating the antitrust laws by fixing prices. Sanford is represented by another law firm. In order to prepare himself for discussions with the Antitrust Division, Bayless Lee, the partner handling the case for the corporation, has asked you whether the corporation (a) can, or (b) must, indemnify Sanford for (1) fines, and (2) attorneys' fees and costs of litigation paid by him in connection with the proceedings. Lee has asked you to consider four possibilities. First, Sanford contests the charges against him and is found innocent. Second, he contests the charges and is found guilty and fined. Third, at the corporation's request, in order to avoid the costs and possible embarrassment of protracted litigation, Sanford pleads nolo contendere and is fined. Fourth, Sanford decides on his own to plead nolo contendere and is fined. You should answer these questions under the following assumptions: First, that National is incorporated under the MBCA; second, that it is incorporated in New York; third, that it is incorporated under the MBCA and the articles of incorporation include a provision identical to Section 5 of the Ford Motor Company Composite Certificate of Incorporation; infra; and fourth, that its by-laws include a provision identical to Section 30 of the General Motors Corporation by-laws.

PROBLEM

NATIONAL METAL PRODUCTS—PART IV

Several shareholders of National Metal Products have recently filed a derivative suit naming as defendants all of the directors of the company. The suit alleges that the defendants are liable to the corporation for causing or failing to prevent violations of the antitrust laws that led to the company's being required to pay $15 million in civil damages and $2 million in fines.

The complaint alleges that "Red" Sanford knowingly violated the antitrust laws; that Charles Meacham, the president of National, and Glen Gray, the secretary and general counsel, recklessly failed to prevent the violations; and that all the other directors were negligent in failing to prevent them. Settlement negotiations are now underway, and it appears that one of the questions that is relevant to the corporation's willingness to settle is the extent to which it will be required or permitted to indemnify the various defendants. There appear to be four possible scenarios to be considered. First, the defendants litigate the case and some or all win a judgment on the merits. Second, some or all of the defendants succeed in having the case against them dismissed on procedural grounds. Third, some or all of the defendants are adjudged liable after trial. Fourth, the case is settled, the defendants paying damages to the corporation. How should you reply to Lee's query whether the corporation (a) can, or (b) must indemnify the directors for (1) damages, and (2) attorneys' fees and costs for each of these scenarios? You should again answer these questions under the varying assumptions as to the applicable law described in Part III, above.

PROBLEM

MILTON CORPORATION—PART V

Your firm represents the Milton Corporation in a derivative suit brought by Beatrice Rate against Robert White arising out of the facts described in Part II of the Milton Corporation problem, supra, Chapter 14. You have been asked to prepare a memorandum discussing whether the corporation (a) can, or (b) must indemnify White for attorneys' fees and costs sustained by him in defending the action. Again, you are to answer the question assuming first, that White wins the case on the merits; second, that he succeeds in having it dismissed on procedural grounds; third, that he settles the case; and fourth, that he is found liable after trial. Again, also, you should make the varying assumptions about the applicable law you were asked to make in the preceding problems.

A. INTRODUCTION

The officers and directors of corporations, particularly large, publicly-held corporations, are exposed to a wide variety of potential liabilities. In light of the growing litigiousness of our society, the risks of loss entailed, already substantial, appear to many to be increasing steadily. Corporate executives may find themselves defendants or potential defendants in derivative suits or direct actions by shareholders, in civil actions brought by others who deal with the corporation, or in civil or criminal actions instituted by the government. They are occasionally required to pay substantial sums in the way of damages, penalties, or fines, and, more frequently, must incur large expenses for legal counsel in the defense of actions or threatened actions against them.

It has frequently been observed that the fear of being subject to such costs acts as a real deterrent to corporations' ability to attract and retain competent executives. At least in part to overcome this deterrent, most large and many small corporations seek to offer some measure of protection against both the amounts that their officers and directors might be required to pay in damages, penalties, and fines and the legal fees and other costs they incur in defending themselves. This protection takes two forms: indemnification by corporations against losses sustained by an executive in legal proceedings arising out of the executive's corporate role, and insurance against such losses.

With respect to both indemnification and insurance, there are a number of corporate law questions, including:

(1) Against *what sort of losses* (*i.e.*, damages, penalties, fines, amounts paid in settlement, attorneys' fees, other litigation costs, etc.) *must* a corporation indemnify its executives?

(2) Against what sort of losses *may* it indemnify?

(3) Against what sort of losses may it insure its executives? *

(4) Under *what conditions* must or may a corporation indemnify its executives? For example may it reimburse an executive for damages paid as a result of an adverse civil judgment? For penalties imposed in a civil proceeding? For criminal fines? What if the damages, penalties, or fines are paid as a result of the settlement of an action and are not assessed after a trial on the merits?

B.　INDEMNIFICATION

The right of a corporate officer or director to be indemnified, and the power of the corporation voluntarily to indemnify him or her against damages, fines, or penalties growing out of the performance of corporate duties are governed by both common law and corporate statutes and are often dealt with in provisions of the charter or by-laws as well.

1.　COMMON LAW

IN RE E. C. WARNER CO.

232 Minn. 207, 45 N.W.2d 388 (1950).

MATSON, Justice.

[A. E. Wilson, the president and treasurer and a director of the E. C. Warner Company, was sued in three similar derivative suits by shareholders of the corporation. All were dismissed on the pleadings, resulting in judgments on the merits in Wilson's favor. The corporation subsequently petitioned for voluntary dissolution, and in the ensuing proceedings, the law firms that had represented Wilson in the derivative suits filed claims for their legal fees. The receiver

---

* As posed, this is strictly a legal question. There are also the associated practical questions of the extent of coverage that insurance companies are willing to offer and how much coverage a corporation is willing to pay for.

in dissolution requested the district court to determine whether the claims were valid. When the district court ruled, over the objection of the stockholder-plaintiffs in the derivative suits, that the attorneys should be paid, the stockholders appealed.]

1. * * * It is uniformly held that if in his derivative action a plaintiff stockholder is successful upon the merits so as to confer a tangible corporate benefit he is entitled to be reimbursed by the corporation for his reasonable expenses, inclusive of attorney's fees. But what is the position of a defendant director if he is successful in securing a vindication upon the merits in such action? May he look to the corporation for reimbursement for his attorney's fees and expenses? If he may, is his right of recovery dependent upon being able to show that his successful defense has conferred a specific corporate benefit? Clearly, neither party to a derivative action is entitled to payment or reimbursement of any expenses incurred, or to be incurred, prior to, and in the absence of, a successful result upon the merits. The ultimate result of the litigation is controlling. In the interim, as a matter of fair play, the corporation with all its assets stands impounded as a neutral.

" * * * There is a vast difference between letting a director fight the battle at his own expense—with reimbursement if he is vindicated—and using the power of the corporation to aid in the fight before it is shown whether or not he is a faithful servant who deserves indemnity. * * * The rule under discussion is designed to produce fair play—to prevent the plaintiff from being overwhelmed by the company's financial power before the real defendants have shown their guilt or innocence." 40 Col.L.Rev. 431, 438–439.

2. The question as to the right of a judicially vindicated director to reimbursement is an open one in this jurisdiction.

Relatively few courts have dealt with the problem, and their decisions are by no means uniform in conclusion or as to the theory upon which they have proceeded. In Figge v. Bergenthal, 130 Wis. 594, 625, 109 N.W. 581, 592, 110 N.W. 798, the court allowed a recovery for no other reason than that "if no case is made against defendants it is not improper or unjust that the corporation should pay for the defense of the action." In Griesse v. Lang, 37 Ohio App. 553, 175 N. E. 222, a right of recovery was denied principally on the basis that the vindicated directors had not thereby conferred a benefit on the corporation. In Solimine v. Hollander, 129 N.J.Eq. 264, 19 A.2d 344, the court, although it found a corporate benefit, held such benefit not to be essential to a right of recovery and allowed recovery on the basis of sound policy. In New York Dock Co. Inc. v. McCollom, 173 Misc. 106, 16 N.Y.S.2d 844, a right of recovery was denied, in that no substantial benefit accrued to the corporation.[5] * * *

5. It is interesting to note that in 1941 as a result of the case of New York Dock Co., Inc. v. McCollom, 173 Misc. 106, 16 N.Y.S.2d 844, the New York legislature passed a statute validating (a) charter provisions or bylaws authorizing reim-

3. * * * If we are not to do violence to the practical necessities of responsible corporate management, we cannot fit the *sui generis* position of officers and directors into old fiduciary forms. The law as to trustee and *cestui*—as well as the law governing principal and agent and guardian and ward—had taken fairly definite form before the modern type of corporation had become a factor in the business world and before its influence and its obligations as a social factor had been recognized. If in keeping with the "benefit theory," applied by some jurisdictions to the trustee of an express trust, we hold that liability to charges of misconduct is one of the inherent hazards impliedly assumed in accepting a corporate directorship, and that therefore a director is not entitled, after a *successful defense upon the merits*, to reimbursement for his reasonable expenses *unless he can show a specific benefit to the corporation*, we shall have then, in contravention of sound public policy, placed a premium upon faithless and irresponsible corporate leadership and action. In the first place, directors and officers have not only a right but a fiduciary duty to stand their ground against any unjust attack which, if permitted to go unchallenged, will ultimately remove the guidance of the corporate activity from the hands of those to whom the stockholders had previously committed it. In the light of this obligation of faithful stewardship, the policy of the law should be to encourage directors to resist unjust charges in the confidence that ultimately, if their innocence be judicially established, they will be reimbursed for their necessary expenses of defense. Solimine v. Hollander, 129 N.J.Eq. 264, 19 A.2d 344, 348. Unless this is the rule, we have the further result that it is not likely that men of substance will be willing to assume the responsibility of corporate directors.

" * * * Such a rule enables the director of limited means to enlist the professional service and aid of competent counsel who will be willing to undertake the defense upon the assurance that, if successful, payment would be forthcoming from the corporate treasury. The withholding of such assurance might well have the effect of denying the financially disabled director the opportunity of adequate representation in the suit against him. *But what is more important than this is the fact that the right to reimbursement is a circumstance that would actuate and induce responsible business men to accept the posts of directors*, the emoluments of which would otherwise never be commensurate with the risk of loss involved in paying out of their own pocket the costs involved in defending their conduct. *The right of reimbursement carries with it the added virtue that it is likely to discourage in large measure stockholders' litigation of the strike variety with which the courts are not unfamiliar.*

bursement of directors for expenses except when adjudged liable for negligence or misconduct, and (b) authorizing payment by the corporation of expenses of officers or directors in successfully prosecuting or defending an action. 22 Mc-

Kinney's Consol.Laws New York Ann., c. 23, General Corporation Law, § 27–a, as amended by L.1941, c. 350, L.1944, c. 711, and renumbered § 63 by L.1945, c. 869; 30 Cornell L.Q. 249, note.

Solimine v. Hollander, 129 N.J.Eq. 272, 19 A.2d 348. (Italics supplied.) This right of reimbursement has its foundation in the maintenance of a sound public policy favorable to the development of sound corporate management as a prerequisite for responsible corporate action.

It follows that irrespective of any showing of direct or tangible benefit to the corporation, a corporate director, *after he has been vindicated on the merits* in a shareholder's derivative suit charging him with dereliction of duty, is entitled to be repaid his reasonable expenses out of corporate funds. Undoubtedly, a vindication of the integrity of the corporate management is in a certain general sense beneficial to the corporation from the standpoint of preserving the confidence of its creditors and of its prospective investors, as well as in the maintenance of the morale of its employes and stockholders, but such a general benefit is not the foundation of the right of recovery. A general benefit of this nature is but an incident of sound corporate management.

*   *   *

The order appealed from is affirmed.

Affirmed.

2. STATE STATUTES

As the *Warner* opinion suggests, the common law as to the *right* of a corporate officer or director to indemnification was at best confused. And there was little precedent as to the limitations on the power of a corporation to indemnify. Dissatisfaction with the judicial handling of the problem of indemnification eventually sparked legislative action. New York enacted the first indemnification statute in 1941. Today all jurisdictions in the United States have adopted some statutory provision dealing with the matter, and most have enacted comprehensive indemnification statutes.

Indemnification provisions are of two types, permissive and mandatory. The comprehensive statutes include both. A permissive, or enabling provision gives a corporation the power to indemnify its corporate managers under certain circumstances. Mandatory statutes accord a director or officer, who meets the statutory standards, a right to indemnification.

Some indemnification statutes are exclusive, that is, they permit indemnification only as prescribed by statute. *E.g.*, N.Y. BCL § 721. According to the legislative history of N.Y. BCL § 721, the "purpose of this section is to make clear that the provisions which follow relative to the indemnification of directors and officers are exclusive and establish a policy from which no material deviation [by way of increased indemnification] is permissible." * The more common non-ex-

---

* Joint Legislative Committee to Study Revision of Corporate Laws, Supplement to Fifth Interim Report to 1961 Session of New York State Legislature, Doc. No. 12 (1961) at 53.

clusive statutes permit a corporation to indemnify corporate managers in circumstances not expressly described in the statute. *See, e.g.,* MBCA § 5.

3.　CHARTER AND BY-LAW PROVISIONS

Whether because of uncertainty as to the scope of indemnification allowed or required under the applicable statutory and case law or because of a desire to amplify or clarify the various rights and obligations of the corporate and its executives, many corporations include in their articles of incorporation or by-laws some provision relating to indemnification. Such provisions are clearly authorized in principle by the non-exclusive statutes, although the validity of particular terms that go beyond what is expressly permitted under the statute is less certain. Consider the following excerpts from the articles of incorporation of the Ford Motor Company and the by-laws of General Motors, both Delaware corporations. What do they add to the Delaware statutory provisions, which are essentially identical to MBCA 5? If you conclude that they add nothing, what is the reason for the provisions? Would you advise a corporate client to include in its articles or by-laws some similar provision?

FORD MOTOR COMPANY
COMPOSITE CERTIFICATE OF INCORPORATION

SECTION 5

INDEMNIFICATION

5.1 *Directors, Officers and Employees of the Corporation.* Every person now or hereafter serving as a director, officer or employee of the corporation shall be indemnified and held harmless by the corporation from and against any and all loss, cost, liability and expense that may be imposed upon or incurred by him in connection with or resulting from any claim, action, suit, or proceeding, civil or criminal, in which he becomes involved, as a party or otherwise, by reason of his being or having been a director, officer or employee of the corporation, whether or not he continues to be such at the time such loss, cost, liability or expense shall have been imposed or incurred. As used herein, the term "loss, cost, liability and expense" shall include, but shall not be limited to, counsel fees and disbursements and amounts of judgments, fines or penalties against, and amounts paid in settlement by, any such director, officer or employee; provided, however, that no such director, officer or employee shall be entitled to claim such indemnity: (1) with respect to any matter as to which there shall have been a final adjudication that he has committed or allowed some act or omission, (a) otherwise than in good faith in what he considered to be the best interests of the corporation, and (b) without reasonable cause to believe that such act or omission was proper and legal; or (2) in the event of a settlement of such claim, action, suit, or proceeding unless (a) the court having jurisdiction thereof shall have approved of such settlement with knowledge of the indemnity provided herein, or (b) a written opinion of independent legal counsel, selected by or in a manner determined by the Board of Directors, shall have been rendered substantially concurrently with such settlement, to the effect that it was not probable that the matter as to which indemnification is being made would have resulted in a final adjudication as specified in clause (1) above, and that the said loss, cost, liability or expense may properly be borne by the corporation. A conviction or judgment (whether based on a plea of guilty or *nolo contendere* or its equivalent or after trial) in a criminal action, suit or proceeding shall not be deemed an adjudication that such director, officer or employee has committed or allowed some act or omission as hereinabove provided if independent legal counsel, selected as hereinabove set forth, shall substantially concurrently with such conviction or judgment give to the corporation a written opinion that such director, officer or employee was acting in good faith in what he considered to be the best interests of the corporation or was not without reasonable cause to believe that such act or omission was proper and legal.

5.2 *Directors, Officers and Employees of Subsidiaries.* Every person (including a director, officer or employee of the corporation) who at the request of the corporation acts as a director, officer or employee of any other corporation in which the corporation owns shares of stock or of which it is a creditor shall be indemnified to the same extent and subject to the same conditions that the directors, officers and employees of the corporation are indemnified under the preceding paragraph, except that the amounts of such loss, cost, liability or expense paid to any such director, officer or employee shall be reduced by and to the extent of any amounts which may be collected by him from such other corporation.

5.3 *Miscellaneous.* The provisions of this Section 5 of Article NINTH shall cover claims, actions, suits and proceedings, civil or criminal, whether now pending or hereafter commenced and shall be retroactive to cover acts or omissions or alleged acts or omissions which heretofore have taken place. In the event of death of any person having a right of indemnification under the provisions of this Section 5 of Article NINTH, such right shall inure to the benefit of his heirs, executors, administrators and personal representatives. If any part of this Section 5 of Article NINTH should be found to be invalid or ineffective in any proceeding, the validity and effect of the remaining provisions shall not be affected.

5.4 *Indemnification Not Exclusive.* The foregoing right of indemnification shall not be deemed exclusive of any other right to which those indemnified may be entitled, and the corporation may provide additional indemnity and rights to its directors, officers or employees.

GENERAL MOTORS CORPORATION
BY–LAWS

30. *Indemnification of Directors and Officers.* The corporation may indemnify every person, his heirs, executors and administrators, against any and all judgments, fines, amounts paid in settlement and reasonable expenses, including attorneys' fees, incurred by him in connection with any claim, action, suit or proceeding (whether actual or threatened, brought by or in the right of the corporation or otherwise, civil, criminal, administrative or investigative, including appeals), to which he may be or is made a party by reason of his being or having been a director or officer of the corporation, or at its request of any other corporation.

There shall be no indemnification (i) as to amounts paid in settlement or other disposition of any threatened or pending action by or in the right of the corporation or such other corporation, or (ii) as to matters in respect of which it shall be determined by judgment or otherwise that such director or officer was derelict in the performance of his duties to the corporation or such other corporation, and, in the case of any criminal action or proceeding, that he had reasonable cause to believe that his conduct was unlawful.

Any such person shall be entitled to indemnification as of right (i) if he has been wholly successful, on the merits or otherwise, with respect to any claim, action, suit or proceeding or, (ii) except as hereinabove provided in respect of matters as to which a court or independent legal counsel shall have determined that he acted in good faith for a purpose which he reasonably believed to be in the best interests of the corporation or such other corporation and, in addition, in the case of any criminal action or proceeding, had no reasonable cause to believe that his conduct was unlawful. Such court or independent counsel shall have the power to determine that such director or officer is entitled to indemnification as to some matters even though he is not so entitled as to others. The termination of any claim, action, suit or proceeding by judgment, settlement, conviction or upon a plea of nolo contendere or its equivalent, shall not in itself create a presumption that any such director or officer did not act in good faith for a purpose which he reasonably believed to be in the best interests of the corporation and, in the case of any criminal action or proceeding, that he had reasonable cause to believe that his conduct was unlawful.

Amounts paid in indemnification shall include, but shall not be limited to, counsel and other fees and disbursements and judgments, fines or penalties against, and amounts paid in settlement by, such director or officer. The corporation may advance expenses to, or where appropriate may itself at its expense undertake the defense of, any such director or officer provided that he shall have undertaken to repay or to reimburse such expenses if it should be ultimately determined that he is not entitled to indemnification under this article.

Payments of indemnification made pursuant to this article shall be reported to the stockholders in the next proxy statement or otherwise, except that no such payments need be reported if such director or officer has been wholly successful on the merits or otherwise.

The provisions of this article shall be applicable to claims, actions, suits or proceedings made or commenced after the adoption hereof, whether arising from acts or omissions to act occurring before or after the adoption hereof.

The rights of indemnification provided in this Article 30 shall not be exclusive of any rights to which any such director or officer may otherwise be entitled by contract or as a matter of law.

4. INDEMNIFICATION UNDER THE FEDERAL SECURITIES LAWS

The consistent administrative policy of the SEC has been that indemnification of officers, directors, and controlling shareholders for violations of the 1933 Act is against the policy of the Act in that indemnification would reduce or eliminate its deterrent effect against negligence and other misconduct in the sale of securities. 3 L. Loss, Securities Regulation 1831 (1961).

The SEC enforces this administrative policy through the exercise of its power to grant acceleration of the effective date of registration statements. The SEC's rules state that it may not grant acceleration unless the registration statement (1) describes any relevant indemnification provisions, (2) indicates that the SEC's view is that such provisions are contrary to public policy insofar as they purport to cover liabilities arising under the securities laws, and (3) undertakes in case a claim for indemnification is made to "submit to a court of appropriate jurisdiction the question whether such indemnification * * * is against public policy as expressed in the Act and will be governed by the final adjudication of such issue." SEC Rule 460, Note.

The judicial precedent on indemnification for securities law liabilities is scanty, but the courts that have addressed the problem have tended to agree with the position taken by the SEC. One of the leading cases is Globus v. Law Research Service, Inc., 418 F.2d 1276, 1287–1289 (2d Cir. 1969), which involved a claim by an underwriter under an indemnification provision in the underwriting agreement. The trial court found that the underwriter had had actual knowledge of the omission of material facts from an offering circular. In barring recovery under the indemnification clause, the court said:

> * * * It is well established that one cannot insure himself against his own reckless, willful or criminal misconduct. * * *

Civil liability under section 11 and similar provisions was designed not so much to compensate the defrauded purchaser as to promote enforcement of the Act and to deter negligence by providing a penalty for those who fail in their duties. And Congress intended to impose a "high standard of trusteeship" on underwriters. * * * Thus, what Professor Loss terms the "in terrorem effect" of civil liability, 3 Loss, [Securities Regulation] at 1831, might well be thwarted if underwriters were free to pass their liability on to the issuer. Underwriters who knew they could be indemnified simply by showing that the issuer was "more liable" than they (a process not too difficult when the issuer is inevitably closer to the facts) would have a tendency to be lax in their independent investigations. * * * Cases upholding indemnity for negligence in other fields are not necessarily apposite. The goal in such cases is to compensate the injured party. But the Securities Act is more concerned with prevention than cure.

Finally, it has been suggested that indemnification of the underwriter by the issuer is particularly suspect. Although in form the underwriter is reimbursed by the issuer, the recovery ultimately comes out of the pockets of the issuer's stockholders. Many of these stockholders may be the very purchasers to whom the underwriter should have been initially liable. The 1933 Act prohibits agreements with purchasers which purport to exempt individuals from liability arising under the Act. [§ 14]. The situation before us is at least reminiscent of the evil this section was designed to avoid.

In *Globus* the violation of the securities laws was a knowing one. The case for indemnification becomes somewhat stronger when the violation is merely negligent. In Odette v. Shearson, Hammill & Co., Inc., 394 F.Supp. 946, 954–957 (S.D.N.Y.1975), however, the court ruled that an underwriter that was the primary defendant in an action alleging omission of material facts in connection with a sale of securities could not recover indemnification from another party alleged to have participated in concealing the omitted facts. The court considered itself bound by *Globus* not to permit indemnification if the primary liability was based on an intentional or reckless violation. But even if the underwriter's conduct was merely negligent, the opinion went on, to allow indemnification would defeat the policy of the securities laws.

The court reached a similar result in Gould v. American-Hawaiian Steamship Co., 387 F.Supp. 163 (D.C.Del.1974), vac'd on other grounds 535 F.2d 761 (3d Cir. 1976), which imposed liability under Rule 14a–9 on directors of a corporation that issued a misleading proxy statement. The court denied a group of directors who had not been involved in the actual preparation of the proxy statement, and were thus found to have been negligent in allowing it to be published, indemnification against those directors who had helped draft the statement and were thus more culpable. The opinion stated:

> In short, most of the cases on indemnity under the Securities Act can be read to support the proposition that an unsuccessful defendant may obtain indemnity from one significantly more responsible for the injury to the plaintiff. This indemnification doctrine, however, was developed in § 10(b) and § 17(a) cases, where the gravamen of the wrongdoing is fraudulent and intentional conduct, and is not necessarily applicable to indemnity under § 14(a). It may be that one joint tortfeasor whose conduct has been of limited culpability should be entitled to shift his loss to another joint tortfeasor whose conduct has been deliberately fraudulent in cases arising under sections of the Securities Acts prohibiting fraud. Shifting liability to the more culpable tortfeasor in such cases may adequately serve the deterrent purposes of those sections. But § 14(a) reaches negligent as well as deliberately deceptive conduct, and the considerations governing indemnity thereunder are, accordingly, somewhat different. * * * Thus, the question of who pays the damages to the plaintiffs is of as great concern as the issue of whether the plaintiffs are compensated at all. To allow indemnity to those who have breached responsibilities squarely placed upon them by the statute would vitiate the remedial purposes of § 14(a). Only a realistic possibility of liability for damages will encourage due diligence by those who solicit proxies and will protect the interests of informed corporate suffrage. Consequently, even if one concurrent tortfeasor bears greater responsibility for preparation or approval of false or misleading proxy materials, a person who breaches § 14(a) duties should not thereby be entitled to indemnity.

C. INSURANCE

Directors' and officers' liability insurance (known in the trade as "D & O insurance") is a relatively recent development. It was not until the mid-1960's, when an increasing number of lawsuits began to generate fears of liability, that these policies began to find favor among large numbers of corporations.

D & O premiums are high, and in the long run at least, they are probably substantially more costly to the large corporation than simply indemnifying executives for their losses to the extent permitted by law. *See* A. Conard, Corporations in Perspective 410–11 (1976). Nevertheless, beyond the usual risk-spreading advantages of insurance, D & O policies offer executives the additional comfort of coverage of losses that an indemnification statute would not require, or even permit, the corporation to pay. One of the most common policies, for example, insures against liabilities, actual or asserted, for "wrongful acts" (a broadly defined term), and includes "damages judgments, settlements and costs, charges and expenses incurred in the defense of actions, suits or proceedings." (The policy does exclude, however, "fines and penalties imposed by law or other matters which are uninsurable under the law pursuant to which this policy shall be construed.") *See* Hinsey, The New Lloyd's Policy Form for Directors and Officers Liability Insurance—An Analysis, 33 Bus.Law. 1961, 1965–66 (1978); Johnston, Corporate Indemnification and Liability Insurance for Directors and Officers, 33 Bus.Law. 1993, 2016 (1978). This means, therefore, that a corporation may insure its officers and directors against, among other non-indemnifiable losses, (1) judgments or settlements in derivative suits based on negligence and (2) judgments or settlements in suits based on negligent violation of the federal securities laws. It is less clear, but it may also be possible to insure against at least some liabilities arising out of conduct that would fail to meet the statutory standard for indemnification. *See* Johnston, *supra*, at 2034.

Most state statutes contain express authorization for corporations to purchase "D & O" insurance. *E.g.,* MBCA § 5(g). New York's statute, although slightly more restrictive than the broader language of the nearly identical MBCA and Delaware provisions, states that it "is the public policy of this state to spread the risk of corporate management, notwithstanding any other general or special law of this state or of any other jurisdiction including the federal government." N.Y. BCL § 727(e).

A "D & O" policy consists of two separate, but integral parts. *See* Johnston, *supra*, at 2013. The first part is designed to reimburse the corporation for its lawful expenses in connection with indemnifying its directors and officers, not the corporation's liability to a plaintiff in an action. This part of a "D & O" policy reduces the amounts which corporate directors or officers would otherwise be required to pay in those instances where the corporation is unable, or less likely, unwilling to indemnify. It thus encourages and facilitates corporate indemnification of directors and officers. The second part insures individuals, acting in their capacity as officers or directors of the insured corporation, against losses, including judgments and settlements. Their coverage under "D & O" policies is limited in a number of ways. A deductible amount for each director and officer and for the corporation serves as a deterrent to carelessness or misconduct. Directors and officers also usually bear a certain percentage, typically 5%, of the loss above the deductible amount. The coinsurance provision provides an additional deterrent to negligence or misconduct and an incentive to defend questionable or unfounded claims. The payment of fines and penalties imposed in a criminal suit or action are excluded from the definition of "loss" as are other fines, penalties, and punitive damages imposed by a final adjudication which are uninsurable under the law pursuant to which the policy is construed. Specific exclusions include: claims based on environmental damage; violations of the Employee Retirement Income Security Act of 1974; libel and slander; claims based on gaining personal profit or advantage to which a director or officer is not legally entitled; and claims brought about or attributable to their dishonesty. Thus, the personal profit exclusion would exclude self-dealing or a breach of duty of loyalty, and claims under Section 16(b) of the 1934 Act which result in a return of profits to the corporation, or under Rule 10b–5. The advantage exclusion would bar, for example, claims arising out of a director or officer misspending corporate funds to preserve himself or herself in office.

The premiums for a "D & O" policy are "costly" and are set on a case-by-case basis taking into account the size of the corporation, its type of business, financial condition and merger and acquisition history, the number of directors and officers, the corporation's past litigation history, and special circumstances, such as governmental investigations, adverse publicity potential and political activity. Small corporations have experienced difficulty in obtaining "D & O" policies because fewer checks and balances are built into their corporate structures. The premiums for a "D & O" policy are generally split between the corporation and the individual on a ninety-ten basis, with the corporation bearing the larger share.

D. POLICY CONSIDERATIONS

PROBLEM

LEGISLATIVE POLICYMAKING

You have recently joined the staff of the Corporate Accountability Research project, a public interest organization devoted principally to the reform of corporation law. As your first project you have been asked to draft testimony in support of a federal incorporation statute that would apply to large, publicly-held companies. One of the principal justifications for such a statute is the perception that state corporation law is inadequate in a number of respects to protect the interests of shareholders and the public. As background for your work on the section of the bill dealing with indemnification, you have been given the following excerpts with the suggestion that you might base much of your draft on them. In light of what you have already learned, how much of what they say remains true today? How should the differences between them be resolved? Is state law in this area in need of reform? What changes do you believe should be made?

R. NADER, M. GREEN, J. SELIGMAN, TAMING THE GIANT CORPORATION, 108 (1976).

There is, to be sure, a persuasive case for indemnifying corporate directors against the costs of nonmeritorious legal claims. If innocent directors had to settle such suits because they lacked the resources to hire competent attorneys, responsible men and women would be discouraged from becoming directors. But current indemnity statutes are not limited to the purpose of protecting innocent officers from the costs of nonmeritorious suits. They also protect guilty officers from accountability for their wrongs and reduce incentives for lawful conduct.

Delaware's statute * exemplifies this overbreadth. It allows a corporation

> to purchase and maintain insurance on behalf of any person who is or was a director, officer, employee or agent of the corporation * * * against any liability asserted against him and incurred by him in any such capacity, or arising out of his status as such, whether or not the corporation would have the power to indemnify him against any such liability under the provisions of this section.

As written, this provision permits the corporation to insulate its officers from *all* potential liabilities. Officers may be insured against any negligence, self-dealing, looting the corporation or embezzlement, all conflicts of interest, and deliberate statutory violations. They may be reimbursed for violations of federal safety, civil rights, environmental, tax, or antitrust laws. They may even be insured against the same judgments in derivative actions that an earlier provision of the same statute provided a corporation could not indemnify directly.

Delaware defends such insurance as a form of compensation, arguing that the corporation could make a larger compensation arrangement with the executive and let him pay for the insurance himself. But the question is not how much officers' compensation should be, but rather whether wrongful acts *should* be indemnified at all. Why should an executive of a drug company be indemnified for the costs of a criminal fine if he is convicted of allowing a harmful drug to injure several thousand people when the same act as a private individual would send him to jail? An untenable double standard has been created. The more powerful an executive becomes, the less likely he is to pay for an abuse of power.

QUESTION

Is the excerpt correct in saying that an executive could be indemnified for a criminal fine?

CONARD, A BEHAVIORAL ANALYSIS OF DIRECTORS' LIABILITY FOR NEGLIGENCE

1972 Duke L.J. 895, 899–903, 907–909, 912–916.

* * *

1. *Indemnification.* Directors are likely to share the propensity of other human beings to regard their mistakes as the products of the unforeseeability of human events, rather than as failures to exercise

---

* Section 145 of the Delaware General Corporation Law is essentially identical to MBCA § 5.—Eds.

the skill and care of normally prudent managers. Consequently, directors are likely to regard it as only fair that their corporations reimburse them for the expenses they incur in defending against claims of negligence and for any amounts for which they may be required to reimburse the corporation. Corporation laws have been generously amended to permit such indemnification, and directors can reasonably be expected to make the fullest permissible use of them.

There are, however, some obstacles to the indemnification procedure. First, the directors who are to be reimbursed cannot vote on their own claims; nevertheless, if there are disinterested directors, they may be expected to hold a favorable view of their fellow-directors, since otherwise they would not be serving on the same board. The sympathetic attitude of disinterested directors will naturally be reinforced by the fact that they owe their positions to the votes of the proxy committee, which usually includes the principal executives who must have concurred in whatever decisions the board has made. If the matter requires shareholder approval, the stockholders may be expected to vote as recommended by the directors since, if the shareholders did not have confidence in the management, most would have sold their shares and invested in another company.

The second obstacle to the indemnification procedure will be the terms of the indemnification statutes which preclude indemnification when directors have been found to be at fault. However, no such finding can be made if the case is settled before judgment. Relevant data suggest that more than 90 percent of such cases will be terminated prior to judgment. A survey in the 1930's and early 1940's showed that 95 percent of shareholders' derivative suits were terminated otherwise than by a judgment for the plaintiff. Most of these suits were probably against directors, although the report on the survey does not so specify. More recent data on automobile injury litigation show that over 85 percent of the cases terminated otherwise than by a judgment for the claimant. Thus, indemnification is likely to be permissible in 90 percent or more of the suits against directors. Consequently, it may be hypothesized that directors will escape payment from their own pockets in a very high percentage of the cases where claims are made and prosecuted.

2. *Liability Insurance.* To the extent that risks of directors' negligence liability persist in spite of indemnification practice, liability risks may be further reduced by officers' and directors' liability insurance. Before the 1960's, this form of insurance seems to have been used infrequently, probably because the threat of liability was not credible to most directors. Among the developments which stimulated the great leap forward of liability insurance, the most dramatic was the decision of Escott v. BarChris Construction Corp., which demonstrated how ordinary businessmen could become personally liable for the aggregate amount of a stock or bond flotation.

No data seem to be available on the number of corporations carrying this type of insurance, but casual conversations with corporation counsel indicate that such insurance is nearly universal among publicly-held companies. A typical answer to an inquiry is "of course we take officers' and directors' liability insurance. Anybody would be crazy to be a director for a company that does not." Although Professor Bishop has attacked this attitude as unsound, his observations serve to confirm that this point of view is prevalent.[27]

* * *

3. *Refusal to Serve.* If the available indemnification procedures and insurance coverage do not provide a sense of security, people may refuse to serve as directors. A frequent observation of corporate counsel is that respected directors are harder to obtain these days. In practice, this seems to mean that many directorial candidates initially decline to serve and can be persuaded to do so only by assurances that the company carries liability insurance to protect them and by the existence of a substantial level of directors' fees. When these considerations fail to persuade a potential director, the explanations for the failure are often that insurance does not cover all risks, it never pays for the time lost if a liability suit is brought, and it is inherently incapable of neutralizing the injury to prestige and peace of mind occasioned by a liability suit.

Ironically, indemnification and insurance may even aggravate the danger of lost time, reputation, and composure caused by liability suits. As juries and judges become aware that the amounts which they assess against directors are not taken from the defendants' personal wealth, there is a likelihood that larger sums will be awarded, further stimulating the litigiousness of plaintiffs' attorneys.

Unfortunately, it is not certain that the nominees who refuse to serve are the least competent ones, as hypothesized in the "idealistic model" presented above. The greater the wealth and reputation of a candidate, the less willing he may be to assume a position of risk. The quality of "prudence," so valued in a money manager, is highly incompatible with incurring risks of million-dollar liabilities. An enterprise with stains on its corporate history and badly in need of better advisers may thus be peculiarly handicapped in procuring competent directors.

Some critics of directors' liability insurance seem to assume that the right kind of director would be one who would have no fear of liability, because he would plan to exercise due care. By similar reasoning, the right kind of automobile driver would be one who fails to

27. Vincent Stahl, speaking in March, 1969, stated that he was surprised to find that 50 percent of a sample of large corporations were carrying such insurance. ALI-ABA Course of Study on Insuring Corporate Personnel and Professional Advisers under Expanding Concepts of Professional Responsibility 8 (1970). * * *

carry automobile liability insurance, because he intends to have no accidents.

* * *

TRANSACTION COSTS

Coercive measures generally involve high transaction costs since people do not willingly give up their money or their freedom. Directors' liability cases are no exception. Some data on the amounts of attorneys' fees in this area are available because the fees of successful plaintiffs' attorneys are usually assessed against the corporation by court order. Professor Hornstein determined from a survey of court records that the average allowance for all expenses was about 20 percent of the benefit conferred on the corporation. The percentage allowed was lower for the larger recoveries and higher for the smaller ones. Some very large awards have been made, such as the $1,876,000 recovery in Zenn v. Anzalone, a case which involved Alleghany Corporation's control of Investors' Diversified Services, Inc.
* * *

In addition to plaintiffs' collection costs, corresponding expenses are incurred by the defense, whether borne by the individual defendants, by the corporations of which they are directors, or by liability insurers. Data on these costs are not a matter of record, and can only be estimated. They include the costs of defense not only in the cases where plaintiffs prevail but also in the numerous cases where the plaintiffs fail and their lawyers obtain nothing. In the aggregate, defense expenses seem likely to be as great as claimants' expenses, although to be on the safe side one might estimate them to be 10 percent of the benefits conferred by payments and settlements. Defensive and offensive expenses combined must, therefore, be equal to at least 30 percent of the benefits received by corporations and investors on account of directors' negligence liability.

When directors' liability is covered by insurance, the transactional costs increase by the costs of insurance acquisition and administration. These costs vary with different kinds of insurance and are conveniently viewed as the "retained premium"—that is, the fraction of the premium which the company does not pay out in benefits or settlements. In automobile liability insurance, the retained fraction is approximately 40 percent. In fidelity insurance, which resembles directors' liability insurance in that it is concerned with employees' misfeasance, the retention rises to approximately 50 percent. In suretyship, it reaches approximately 65 percent.

No published figures are available on loss ratios in officers' and directors' liability insurance. Even if available, such figures would not be decisive because experience with this line of underwriting is limited. One can assume, however, that the premium retention will be high because this form of liability insurance coverage is quite uncompetitive.   Very few companies are offering directors' liability insurance, and so there is very little competitive pressure on premiums.

Under present circumstances, it seems likely that the retention rate will be at least 50 percent; of the remaining 50 percent paid out in settlements, claimants' lawyers will probably retain one fifth, so that the net benefits may be approximately 40 percent of the premium costs.

The premiums are usually paid in the ratio of 90 percent from the corporation and 10 percent from the directors.   However, the necessity of paying premiums necessarily increases the costs of being a director, and it seems likely that directors' fees are increased, even if not explicitly, to the extent necessary to pay the premiums.   Consequently, all the premiums are paid at the ultimate expense of the persons interested in the corporation.   In a healthy corporation, this means principally at the expense of the shareholders; to the extent that the executives share profits, such payment would also be at their expense.   In corporations which are experiencing financial difficulties, the expense may be ultimately borne by creditors, suppliers and employees, all of whom suffer in various ways from the ill fortunes of the enterprise.

*   *   *

AN ALTERNATIVE STRUCTURE OF DIRECTORS' LIABILITY

Although directors' liability seems to operate in a clumsy and expensive way, it does not necessarily deserve to be abolished.   Even a very small percentage of improvement in the wisdom of directors' decisions would be well worth buying.   Indeed, in a trillion-dollar corporate-oriented economy, it is clear that even a minimal improvement in the wisdom of directorial decision making would be well worth achieving.

However, the low net output of the system suggests that it may be desirable to devise a more efficient mechanism for achieving the same goals.   There is an immense waste in litigating over million-dollar liabilities, with lawyers' fees in proportion, when only a tiny fraction of the redistribution operates to punish directors or to benefit injured investors.

To eliminate the waste, and vitalize the deterrent, it would be sufficient to abolish indemnification and insurance.   However, this approach would deter responsible persons from serving as directors.   The objective, therefore, must be to find a means of dispensing with indemnification and insurance, while simultaneously restraining the destructive effects of the deterrent.

An imaginable solution would be a return to the legal principles of a less complicated era, when Judges Holmes and Hand applied the "business judgment rule."   Although their decisions were probably wiser than analyses which attempt to assess the entire corporate loss against each single director, their results will not provide satisfaction today. Few modern judges share the faith of Holmes and Hand that businessmen will do well enough if left to themselves   *   *   *.

The solution, if there is one, must be to reduce the extent of director liability to the amount which a prudent man is willing to risk. The difficulty arises from the fact that courts have mechanically applied to directors' liability the classic measure of damages evolved in tort law—that is, the full measure of loss resulting from the tortfeasor's wrongful conduct.

The necessity of reducing the extent of director liability is evidenced by the current form of liability insurance, with its upper and lower limits and coinsurance in the middle. Professor Loss also acknowledges the necessity of setting a limit on individual liability—$25,000—in the current revision of the federal securities acts. Whether the liability limit (and the insurance deductible) is set at $5,000 or at $25,000, the limit will be derisively small in some cases, and draconically large in others. In order to be effective but not catastrophic, the measure of liability must stand in a proper relation to what a director gains from his position. If his annual fees of $10,000 drop to $5,000 after taxes, his maximum liability could be limited to this amount. Perhaps it should be twice this amount, or perhaps one-half, but it should vary depending upon the director's compensation. For the director who is motivated by financial considerations, this limit should be sufficient; for others, it is irrelevant.

The risk of losing one's annual compensation would also bear very differently on outside than on inside directors. Since outside directors are presumed to have some other primary source of income, the loss of their directors' fees would mean only that such directors had rendered a gratuitous service. For inside directors, who are not presumed to have substantial outside income, the loss would be much more serious; but since insiders are directly dependent upon the well-being of the corporation, they also have much greater incentives to bear the risk.

To carry out this plan, Congress could pass a law limiting the negligence liability of a director in a registered corporation to his net after-tax income from the corporation for the year in which one or more violations of duty occurred. This might result in a liability of $5,000 for an outside director and $100,000 for an officer-director. At the same time, the statute would forbid indemnification of such liabilities, as well as prohibit insurance coverage against them. The law should cover not only the federal securities laws but also state securities laws and common-law principles of negligence and fiduciary duty. This coverage is appropriate because interstate corporations need to be liberated from the dual entanglements of catastrophic directors' liabilities and the expensive but useless encumbrances of indemnification and insurance. Like other federal liabilities, this form of directors' liability should be assertable by a shareholder without the impediment of state law requirements of contemporaneous shareholding and security for expenses. Payment of indemnification and insurance premiums would stop, but this would have no noticeable effect on corporate profits.

The effect of such a law would be to reduce immensely the amount of litigation over negligence. Since prospects of million-dollar verdicts would no longer exist, there would be no point in either side's incurring a quarter of a million dollars in legal expenses. As a result, questions of director negligence would be settled much more expeditiously and cheaply.

The total effect of the change on liability suits cannot be estimated without considering at the same time what would be done with regard to directors' liability for illicit profits obtained through self-dealing, short term trading, or trading on inside information. This engaging study would require another article as long as the present one. Consequently, the complete design of a legislative reform and a model of its aftermath must be left for another occasion.

An Alternative Insurance Structure: No Fault?

Since directors' liability insurance tends to spread the costs of directors' mistakes throughout the community of corporate investors, one is tempted to consider a system of "no-fault" insurance whereby corporations would simply insure themselves and their investors against loss. However, "loss" is too undefineable to lend itself to insurance coverage. To give the coverage any effective definition, it would have to be restricted to losses caused by blamable [sic] mistakes, which takes us right back to directors' liability insurance.

Perhaps a no-fault coverage could be designed for securities flotations which are accompanied by material misrepresentations, as in the *BarChris* case. It is hardly conceivable that buyers could be protected against all losses for all time on condition of finding a flaw in the registration statement. It is conceivable, however, that buyers could be insured against a market loss of more than 50 percent within twelve months if a misrepresentation were discovered within that time. This result would have the merit of mitigating the most unexpected losses of many investors. The cost would be borne by the entire community of security buyers, augmented by the expenses of insurance underwriting and administration. The function of this type of insurance would be similar to that of Federal Deposit Insurance on bank accounts. To deter misrepresentation, we would rely on administrative remedies—for example, stop orders—and on criminal penalties.

If security buyers were like bank depositors—embracing the rank and file of humanity and relying on their securities as their principal shelter against a rainy day—such insurance could be recommended. If, however, security buyers are generally among the financially stronger individuals and institutions, with their own programs of di-

versification, they would probably be better off bearing their own
risks. The latter hypothesis seems more likely to be true, and no-
fault insurance for directors' errors appears to be a needless encum-
brance on the money markets.

* * *

Chapter 17

THE LARGE CORPORATION IN SOCIETY

PROBLEMS

In each of the following problems, assume first that you are outside counsel to the corporation and have been called upon to give your advice on the matters in question. Second, assume that you have also been a member of the board of directors of the corporation for several years and that your law firm does some work for it but is not principal outside counsel. In this second role, consider whether your function as a director who is also an attorney is different from that of any other outside director. For each problem you should answer these questions:

1. As a matter of corporation law, does the board have any discretion, or is its decision compelled by its fiduciary duties to the shareholders? To the extent that the profitability of the corporation is relevant to these decisions, is it helpful to think in terms of "long term" profitability?

2. What interests, if any, besides those of shareholders, is it appropriate for the board to consider? May it (or should it, or must it) take into account the interests of employees? Of the community in which it does business? The "national" interest?

3. To the extent that the board may or must consider interests other than those of the shareholders, how should it determine what those interests are? Should it look to federal legislation, for example, to ascertain national public policy? To Consumers' Union to determine the interests of consumers? To the individual consciences of the board members for what is "right" for society?

4. What persons or groups that might be affected by the board's decision would have standing to sue to challenge that decision? Shareholders? Employees? Members of the affected community? Consumers? Others?

5. Should shareholder approval be required for any of the actions taken? If specific authorization is not required, should there be a provision in the charter authorizing any departure from profit maximization?

6. Is there a requirement that the decision or facts of relevance to the decision be disclosed? Under what mandate?

7. Besides bringing a suit, what other actions might affected parties take to challenge the corporation's conduct? Are such possibilities relevant to the board's decision? Legally? Practically?

8.   If your conclusion is that the law of corporations does not deal with the social consequences of the corporate decision in question, what, if anything should be done to remedy the situation?   Should the law be called upon to guide corporate decisions like these, or can the free market and individual conscience provide sufficient direction?

I

U.S. DRUGS, INC.

U.S. Drugs, Inc., produces a broad line of pharmaceutical products.   It has recently developed a new drug that is extremely effective in treating certain liver disorders.   Unfortunately, the drug appears to lead to heart failure in a small, but significant proportion of those who use it.   As a consequence, the U.S. Food and Drug Administration has refused to permit it to be sold in this country.   The company has invested a substantial amount of money in the development and testing of the drug, and would like to recoup that investment if possible.   Its international division has proposed to manufacture and sell the new drug in certain Latin American countries whose drug laws are substantially less restrictive than those of the United States. The question has been brought to the board of directors.   Would you vote in favor of selling the drug abroad (assuming that the sales violated no U.S. or foreign law)?   Would your answer depend on whether the potential side effects of the drug were conspicuously indicated on the label, on package inserts, and in all selling literature given to physicians?

II

STANDARD OIL COMPANY OF NEW ENGLAND (SONE)

Standard Oil Company of New England (SONE) is a major international oil company.   Its stock is listed on the New York Stock Exchange.   SONE also has significant investments in leases of western United States coal lands and in oil shale.

The time is the present; the oil companies are under political attack on a number of fronts in the United States, with the main efforts of the attackers being the introduction of measures that will limit oil company profits.   SONE and other members of the industry are countering these attacks with a major advertising and public relations campaign to develop more energy so as to make the United States more self-sufficient in energy supply.

SONE has an opportunity to purchase and operate extensive coal mining operations in South Africa.   Management estimates that the rate of return on the proposed investment will be considerably higher than it would be for any other use of the funds available to SONE. This is true in large part because of the low wages paid to black miners and the low level of government safety standards at South Afri-

can mines. Moreover, the return on investment would remain very
attractive even if SONE ran a model mine and paid miners minimum
wages approximately double those now paid in South Africa.

III

INTERNATIONAL ELECTRONICS, INC.

International Electronics, Inc., has a large assembly plant located
in a small town in New England. With over 1,000 workers, it is the
town's major employer. For the last several years, the plant has
been only marginally profitable, and projections for the future show
that situation continuing. The corporation's planning department has
recommended to the board that the New England plant be closed and
that a new plant be built in Malaysia that would employ nearly 3,000
people to do the same work. Because the going wage rate in Malaysia is only one-tenth that in New England, the new operation could be
expected to return close to twenty percent on the invested capital,
considerably in excess of the company's average return on investment.

Can the Board take into consideration the devastating effect on
the New England town of closing the plant there? Should it? What
weight should be given the fact that the Malaysian plant would employ a large number of people who now live in extreme poverty? Are
there other "non-economic" considerations that should be taken into
account by the board?

IV

ENGULF & DeVOWER, INC.

The chief executive of Engulf and DeVower, Inc., a large multina-
tional conglomerate based in the United States, is quite concerned
about the lack of employment opportunities for ghetto youth, a problem of which he has become particularly aware as a member of the
President's Task Force on Unemployment. He has proposed that one
of the company's subsidiaries, which has a plant located in St. Louis,
Missouri, establish a program of hiring and training unemployed
ghetto teenagers. The total cost of the program, including training
and efficiency losses, is expected to be approximately $250,000 a
year, or about two percent of the plant's total payroll. The plant
presently has no trouble in hiring skilled, experienced workers. The
company's public relations department believes it could get a great
deal of mileage out of the program by making it the focus of a series
of "corporate image" advertisements. These ads would be expected
to cost about $500,000 over a two-year period.

A. INTRODUCTION

In the early 1930's two of the leading corporate scholars in America, Adolf Berle and E. Merrick Dodd, debated the role of corporate management and of the corporation. Berle's view was that corporate powers were held in trust "at all times exercisable only for the ratable benefit of all the shareholders * * *." Berle, Corporate Powers as Powers in Trust, 44 Harv.L.Rev. 1049 (1931). Dodd's thesis was that the business corporation was properly seen "as an economic institution which has a social service as well as a profit making function." Dodd, For Whom Are Corporate Managers Trustees?, 45 Harv.L.Rev. 1145, 1148 (1932). *See* Weiner, The Berle-Dodd Dialogue on the Concept of the Corporation, 64 Colum.L.Rev. 1458 (1964).

Twenty years later, following the New Jersey decision in A. P. Smith Manufacturing Co. v. Barlow, 13 N.J. 145, 98 A.2d 581 (1953), appeal dism'd 346 U.S. 861, 74 S.Ct. 107, 98 L.Ed. 373 (1953), upholding the validity of a corporate charitable contribution*, Berle concluded, "the argument has been settled (at least for the time being) squarely in favor of Professor Dodd's contention." A. Berle, The 20th Century Capitalist Revolution 169 (1954). As Berle later commented, "[m]odern directors are not limited to running business enterprise for maximum profit, but are in fact and recognized in law as administrators of a community system." The Corporation in Modern Society xii (E. Mason, ed. 1960).

Although corporations may be permitted to make limited donations to charity, managers are not given license to ignore stockholder interests. They are after all, not the owners of the corporation, and, like other employees, they must account to someone for their stewardship. Nevertheless, their discretion is considerable. The debate over the corporation's place in society suggests several key questions: Who comprises the constituency of those who manage the corporation? By what standard are the managers held accountable for the discharge of their functions? By what means is the standard enforced?

The point of view with which Professor Dodd became associated has been referred to as the school of managerialism, recognizing as it did that business managers were professionals and that their duties demanded almost statesmanlike responsibilities. The Berle view became more associated with the notion of corporate democracy, although the political analogy it suggests was never meant to apply literally. However, other corporate commentators have drawn the political analogy closely. To some, this has meant greater participation by shareholders, who are seen as the only constituency to whom loyalty is owed. Others, such as Professor Robert Dahl, a political

* You may want to review at this point the excerpts from Theodora Holding Corp. v. Henderson and Union Pacific Railroad Co. v. Trustees, Inc., set forth in Section D.3 of Chapter 4, *supra.*

scientist, have described the corporation as a political entity, imposing its will on affected citizens who have no voice in its policies, unless they are stockholders. The remedy, then, is to provide representation to the affected constituencies of the corporation, perhaps by allowing them to vote or by providing representation on the board of directors for special constituencies.* A Ralph Nader task force looked at the corporation in much the same manner, and urged the "constitutionalizing" of the corporation.** In the same vein, Professor Abram Chayes urged that the "rule of law" be applied to corporations, which would allow the governed to participate in the selection of the governors.*** Of course, to all of these additional constituencies who would partake in corporate affairs, the notion of "long term profitability," not to mention profit maximization, is less important than it is to stockholders.

While all business affects the public in one way or another, providing employment for its workers, products and services for its consumers, and utilizing limited resources of the nation, the focus of the debate is on large corporate enterprises. The reasons are essentially twofold. In the first instance, large businesses have larger impact on the public, a self-evident fact. In the second place, large businesses have public stockholders who have relinquished their control over the use of their property to professional managers. Rarely do we see among this group of companies individually or family owned major businesses; few shades of Henry Ford remain. What we have is the separation of ownership from control, a phenomenon closely analyzed by Professors Berle and Gardiner Means in their classic study, The Modern Corporation and Private Property (1932).

One implication of the Berle and Means observation is that the value of the shareholder's property is very much determined by the market where stock is traded. In 1932 there was much reason to doubt the integrity and effectiveness of the market. Many of the proposals they suggested were embodied in the federal securities laws, the first of which was adopted in 1933.

Our purpose in this section is to focus on some of the legal implications surrounding the issue of corporate accountability.**** Obvi-

---

* R. Dahl, After the Revolution? 115 et seq. (1970).

** R. Nader, M. Green & J. Seligman, Constitutionalizing the Corporation: The Case for the Federal Chartering of Giant Corporations (1976).

*** A. Chayes, The Modern Corporation and the Rule of Law, in The Corporation in Modern Society 25 (E. Mason, ed. 1966).

**** We have used the term "corporate accountability" in preference to the more common "corporate responsibility." The latter term has come to signify so many

aspects of the problems of the large corporation in society that it tends to confuse rather than clarify discussion, meaning one thing to some observers and quite another thing to others. In particular, "corporate responsibility" is often used to denote corporate voluntarism—such as, for example, making charitable donations or efforts to employ and train the "hardcore" unemployed—as well as simply conducting normal corporate affairs in an ethical manner. "Corporate accountability," as it is used here excludes corporate voluntarism. It denotes a relationship between the corporation

ously, the issue affects more than lawyers and it is mainly a question of business policy. What do we want our corporations to be and what functions do we want them to perform? How broad should the horizons of corporate managers stretch?

There is a serious and perplexing question as to the meaning of corporate accountability. All persons, including corporations, are required to obey the law. Does accountability to the public mean anything more than that? Is the responsibility of corporate management to exploit all profit opportunity permitted by law? What implications has the answer to that question for the role of corporations in the legislative and regulatory processes? Should they oppose changes in statutes or regulations that would impose additional costs on their operations, even if the change would affect all within the industry? Or do managers have the right—or even the obligation on occasion— to support such changes? At the same time, do business managers have a privilege—or a responsibility—to support changes in the law that would impose costly restrictions on their profit opportunities so as to compel both their own company and all its competitors to conduct business in a manner that does less harm to the public?

"Corporate responsibility," the term often used to refer to this set of problems is an unfortunate one. It is so ill-defined that it has come to mean entirely different things to different people. Not infrequently the difference between advocates and critics of greater corporate responsibility turn out, on examination, to involve little more than different understandings of what it means. It would probably be best if we were to banish the term altogether from our lexicon, (indeed it is for that reason that we have chosen to replace it for the most part with the term "corporate accountability"), but that appears at this late date to be a practical impossibility. It would help, at least to attempt some refinement in the use of the term, "corporate responsibility."

One possible way of reducing the broad coverage of "social responsibility" is to limit it to questions involving the social consequences of the way in which corporations carry on their normal business affairs. Such a limitation would exclude from the meaning of the term questions involving violations of the law (which are, for the most part, trivial, the answer almost always being, "the corporation, like everyone else, should obey the law"). It would also exclude activities undertaken (or avoided) by a corporation because of their social consequences but having no direct relation to the firm's normal operations. Such problems as whether corporations should give to charities, and how much, would thus fall outside of this more precise meaning of "corporate responsibility."

and its environment that tends to conform corporate behavior to serve, or at least not to injure, the interests of the society at large. For an enlightening discussion of this problem (which uses the term "corporate voluntarism" in a slightly different and more precise sense) *see* Engel, An Approach to Corporate Social Responsibility, 32 Stan.L.Rev. 1 (1979).

Even thus narrowed the term still encompasses a broad spectrum of questions. Consider the following illustrations, for example: Should a corporation undertake a costly pollution control program that exceeds the requirements of the law? Should a corporation undertake affirmative antidiscrimination programs, even where not compelled to do so, because its managers believe it is the right thing to do? Should a corporation keep a factory in a community, where the factory is a marginal operation, because to do so preserves the economic structure of that community, even though it has an opportunity to move its facility elsewhere and derive a larger profit? Should an oil company take advantage of the present petroleum market to make higher than usual profits or should it reduce its prices to the consumer? Should an agricultural company provide better facilities to migrant workers than it is required by law or by contract?

The question is not only one of determining what is the right thing to do in any given situation—never an easy issue to resolve—but it is also a question of process. Since we do not always know what is the right thing to do in any given situation, perhaps the best that can be expected of any corporation is that its procedures for decision-making provide us with confidence in the process. In fact, much of the focus on the corporate responsibility debate in recent years has been on the question of corporate governance. This is an area to which we will return in the next chapter. For the time being, we can say certain things about the corporate decision-making process.

The board of directors of most public companies consists mainly of so-called outside directors, that is, persons who are not full-time employees of the company. In addition, the board includes the chief executive officer of the company and several other high-ranking officials. The outside directors are usually drawn from the ranks of business and tend to be predominantly white males who are busily engaged in their own major pursuits. They devote a relatively small amount of time to the affairs of companies on whose boards they sit as outside directors and rely principally on information that is furnished to them by the management. Customarily, they have no independent staff of their own. In form, they are elected by the stockholders of the company, but in fact, their nomination is virtually tantamount to election because in the overwhelming number of cases they are unopposed for election. Directors are nominated for the board by the board itself, and are initially selected by the management, except in some cases where a nominating committee of the board of directors is composed entirely of outside directors. For the most part, it is safe to say that the directors are self-selected, self-perpetuating, loyal to management, and able to devote only part-time to their positions. It might also be added that they are generally paid fairly nominal sums for their efforts, usually only a small fraction of their total incomes.

Company counsel usually plays a considerable role in the decision-making process. The lawyer will advise management, and sometimes directly the board of directors, about the legal implications of a contemplated action. Lawyers often become confidants of those they advise and therefore have a larger influence than their formal relationship would indicate. They tend to advise not only on the strict requirements of law, but often as to areas of judgment extending beyond their legal expertise. Because public companies live in a goldfish bowl, and must comply with extensive disclosure requirements imposed by the federal securities laws and, in some cases, the stock exchange where their shares are traded, the lawyer is looked to as the person who advises on disclosure requirements. Disclosure is largely intended to serve an information role for investors so they can decide whether to buy, sell, or hold securities of any particular company, but it is well known that disclosure has effects on behavior as well. That is, there are some things people are willing to do when they do not have to make full disclosure that they would not do if they had to disclose.

DODGE v. FORD MOTOR CO.

204 Mich. 459, 170 N.W. 668 (1919).

[The facts of this famous case were set forth in Chapter 8. Although the principal issue in the case was whether the corporation could be compelled to pay a dividend, the case is best remembered for its discussion of the role of a corporation in society, a discussion that was elicited by Henry Ford's insistence in describing the motives behind his plans for the business in social rather than narrowly economic terms. The "plan" to which the following excerpt refers is the retention of much of the profits earned by the corporation to finance a rapid expansion rather than distributing them to the shareholders.]

It is the contention of plaintiffs that the apparent effect of the plan is intended to be the continued and continuing effect of it, and that it is deliberately proposed, not of record and not by official corporate declaration, but nevertheless proposed, to continue the corporation henceforth as a semi-eleemosynary institution and not as a business institution. In support of this contention, they point to the attitude and to the expressions of Mr. Henry Ford.

Mr. Henry Ford is the dominant force in the business of the Ford Motor Company. No plan of operations could be adopted unless he consented, and no board of directors can be elected whom he does not favor. One of the directors of the company has no stock. One share was assigned to him to qualify him for the position, but it is not claimed that he owns it. A business, one of the largest in the world, and one of the most profitable, has been built up. It employs many men, at good pay.

"My ambition," said Mr. Ford, "is to employ still more men, to spread the benefits of this industrial system to the greatest possible number, to help them build up their lives and their homes. To do this we are putting the greatest share of our profits back in the business."

"With regard to dividends, the company paid sixty per cent. on its capitalization of two million dollars, or $1,200,000, leaving $58,000,000 to reinvest for the growth of the company. This is Mr. Ford's policy at present, and it is understood that the other stockholders cheerfully accede to this plan."

He had made up his mind in the summer of 1916 that no dividends other than the regular dividends should be paid, "for the present."

"Q. For how long? Had you fixed in your mind any time in the future, when you were going to pay— A. No.

"Q. That was indefinite in the future? A. That was indefinite; yes, sir."

The record, and especially the testimony of Mr. Ford, convinces that he has to some extent the attitude towards shareholders of one who has dispensed and distributed to them large gains and that they should be content to take what he chooses to give. His testimony creates the impression, also, that he thinks the Ford Motor Company has made too much money, has had too large profits, and that, although large profits might be still earned, a sharing of them with the public, by reducing the price of the output of the company, ought to be undertaken. We have no doubt that certain sentiments, philanthropic and altruistic, creditable to Mr. Ford, had large influence in determining the policy to be pursued by the Ford Motor Company— the policy which has been herein referred to.

It is said by his counsel that—

Although a manufacturing corporation cannot engage in humanitarian works as its principal business, the fact that it is organized for profit does not prevent the existence of implied powers to carry on with humanitarian motives such charitable works as are incidental to the main business of the corporation.

And again:

As the expenditures complained of are being made in an expansion of the business which the company is organized to carry on, and for purposes within the powers of the corporation as hereinbefore shown, the question is as to whether such expenditures are rendered illegal because influenced to some extent by humanitarian motives and purposes on the part of the members of the board of directors.

* * * [The cases referred to by counsel], after all, like all others in which the subject is treated, turn finally upon the point, the question, whether it appears that the directors were not acting for

the best interests of the corporation. We do not draw in question, nor do counsel for the plaintiffs do so, the validity of the general proposition stated by counsel nor the soundness of the opinions delivered in the cases cited. The case presented here is not like any of them. The difference between an incidental humanitarian expenditure of corporate funds for the benefit of the employés, like the building of a hospital for their use and the employment of agencies for the betterment of their condition, and a general purpose and plan to benefit mankind at the expense of others, is obvious. There should be no confusion (of which there is evidence) of the duties which Mr. Ford conceives that he and the stockholders owe to the general public and the duties which in law he and his codirectors owe to protesting, minority stockholders. A business corporation is organized and carried on primarily for the profit of the stockholders. The powers of the directors are to be employed for that end. The discretion of directors is to be exercised in the choice of means to attain that end, and does not extend to a change in the end itself, to the reduction of profits, or to the nondistribution of profits among stockholders in order to devote them to other purposes.

* * *

NOTE—DODGE v. FORD

To a large extent Henry Ford argued his case in the press. Ford said that he wanted only a small profit from his venture.

> I hold this [view] because it enables a large number of people to buy and enjoy the use of a car and because it gives a larger number of men employment at good wages. Those are the two aims I have in life. But I would not be counted a success * * * if I could not accomplish that and at the same time make a fair amount of profit for myself and the men associated with me in the business.

> And let me say right here [Ford continued], that I do not believe that we should make such an awful profit on our cars. A reasonable profit is right, but not too much. So it has been my policy to force the price of the car down as fast as production would permit, and give the benefits to users and laborers, with resulting surprisingly enormous benefits to ourselves. A. Nevins & F. Hill, Ford: Expansion and Challenge 1915–1933, 97 (1957).

Mr. Ford was challenged on cross-examination by counsel for the Dodge brothers, Ellicott G. Stevenson, producing the following colloquy:

STEVENSON: Now, I will ask you again, do you still think that those profits were "awful profits?"

FORD: Well, I guess I do, yes.

STEVENSON: And for that reason you were not satisfied to continue to make such awful profits?

FORD: We don't seem to be able to keep the profits down.

STEVENSON: * * * Are you trying to keep them down? What is the Ford Motor Company organized for except profits, will you tell me, Mr. Ford?

FORD: Organized to do as much good as we can, everywhere, for everybody concerned.

What, demanded Stevenson, was the purpose of the company? "To do as much as possible for everybody concerned," replied Ford. "* * * To make money and use it, give employment, and send out the car where the people can use it." He added, "And incidentally to make money."

STEVENSON: Incidentally make money?

FORD: Yes, sir.

STEVENSON: But your controlling feature * * * is to employ a great army of men at high wages, to reduce the selling price of your car, so that a lot of people can buy it at a cheap price, and give everybody a car that wants one.

FORD: If you give all that, the money will fall into your hands; you can't get out of it.*

On close reading, Ford does not seem to be saying that he intended to carry on the corporation's business for anything other than the "profit of the stockholders," although the Supreme Court of Michigan felt otherwise. Indeed, Ford sees no clash in objectives; service to the public rewards stockholders. His manner of saying it, however, obviously bothered the court, but then Ford was never known for being flannel-mouthed. His most damaging statement was his admission that the special dividends were to be postponed "indefinitely." That view seemed too cavalier to the judges. Ford was playing to another public, and that focus caused him to characterize passive stockholders as "parasites."

Ford triumphed on most of the issues in the case. He was permitted to go ahead with the expansion and was required to pay out only half of the available surplus, not the 75% the Dodges demanded. But he might have won more. His biographers say:

Suppose he had said, for example: Our entire policy is for the ultimate good of the stockholders. Expansion is purely a business necessity. In the long run it will be immensely profitable to the company [as, indeed, history proved it to be]. The facts that it provides new jobs and makes possible a lower-priced car for the

---

* A. Nevins & F. Hill, Ford: Expansion and Challenge 1915–1933, 99–100 (1957).

nation is incidental. As to dividends, we have already resumed payment of special ones, and as the company's position permits, these will be larger. Such a statement would have left [the other shareholders], considering his attitude on other points, small ground for interference. But Ford wanted credit for serving the public, wanted to be a hero to the millions. He also had a firm instinct against paying further large sums to the stockholders. He won the plaudits he craved, but was penalized for refusing to pay the parasites. A. Nevins & F. Hill, Ford: Expansion and Challenge 1915–1933, 105 (1957).

SHLENSKY v. WRIGLEY

95 Ill.App.2d 173, 237 N.E.2d 776 (1968).

SULLIVAN, Justice.

This is an appeal from a dismissal of plaintiff's amended complaint on motion of the defendants. The action was a stockholders' derivative suit against the directors for negligence and mismanagement. The corporation was also made a defendant. Plaintiff sought damages and an order that defendants cause the installation of lights in Wrigley Field and the scheduling of night baseball games.

Plaintiff is a minority stockholder of defendant corporation, Chicago National League Ball Club (Inc.), a Delaware corporation with its principal place of business in Chicago, Illinois. Defendant corporation owns and operates the major league professional baseball team known as the Chicago Cubs. The corporation also engages in the operation of Wrigley Field, the Cubs' home park, the concessionaire sales during Cubs' home games, television and radio broadcasts of Cubs' home games, the leasing of the field for football games and other events and receives its share, as visiting team, of admission moneys from games played in other National League stadia. The individual defendants are directors of the Cubs and have served for varying periods of years. Defendant Philip K. Wrigley is also president of the corporation and owner of approximately 80% of the stock therein.

Plaintiff alleges that since night baseball was first played in 1935 nineteen of the twenty major league teams have scheduled night games. In 1966, out of a total of 1620 games in the major leagues, 932 were played at night. Plaintiff alleges that every member of the major leagues, other than the Cubs, scheduled substantially all of its home games in 1966 at night, exclusive of opening days, Saturdays, Sundays, holidays and days prohibited by league rules. Allegedly this has been done for the specific purpose of maximizing attendance and thereby maximizing revenue and income.

The Cubs, in the years 1961–65, sustained operating losses from its direct baseball operations. Plaintiff attributes those losses to inadequate attendance at Cubs' home games. He concludes that if the directors continue to refuse to install lights at Wrigley Field and schedule night baseball games, the Cubs will continue to sustain comparable losses and its financial condition will continue to deteriorate.

Plaintiff alleges that, except for the year 1963, attendance at Cubs' home games has been substantially below that at their road games, many of which were played at night.

Plaintiff compares attendance at Cubs' games with that of the Chicago White Sox, an American League club, whose weekday games were generally played at night. The weekend attendance figures for the two teams was similar; however, the White Sox week-night games drew many more patrons than did the Cubs' weekday games.

Plaintiff alleges that the funds for the installation of lights can be readily obtained through financing and the cost of installation would be far more than offset and recaptured by increased revenues and incomes resulting from the increased attendance.

Plaintiff further alleges that defendant Wrigley has refused to install lights, not because of interest in the welfare of the corporation but because of his personal opinions "that baseball is a 'daytime sport' and that the installation of lights and night baseball games will have a deteriorating effect upon the surrounding neighborhood." It is alleged that he has admitted that he is not interested in whether the Cubs would benefit financially from such action because of his concern for the neighborhood, and that he would be willing for the team to play night games if a new stadium were built in Chicago.

Plaintiff alleges that the other defendant directors, with full knowledge of the foregoing matters, have acquiesced in the policy laid down by Wrigley and have permitted him to dominate the board of directors in matters involving the installation of lights and scheduling of night games, even though they knew he was not motivated by a good faith concern as to the best interests of defendant corporation, but solely by his personal views set forth above. It is charged that the directors are acting for a reason or reasons contrary and wholly unrelated to the business interests of the corporation; that such arbitrary and capricious acts constitute mismanagement and waste of corporate assets, and that the directors have been negligent in failing to exercise reasonable care and prudence in the management of the corporate affairs.

The question on appeal is whether plaintiff's amended complaint states a cause of action. It is plaintiff's position that fraud, illegality and conflict of interest are not the only bases for a stockholder's derivative action against the directors. Contrariwise, defendants argue that the courts will not step in and interfere with honest business judgment of the directors unless there is a showing of fraud, illegality or conflict of interest.

The cases in this area are numerous and each differs from the others on a factual basis. However, the courts have pronounced certain ground rules which appear in all cases and which are then applied to the given factual situation. The court in Wheeler v. Pullman Iron and Steel Company, 143 Ill. 197, 207, 32 N.E. 420, 423, said:

> It is, however, fundamental in the law of corporations, that the majority of its stockholders shall control the policy of the corporation, and regulate and govern the lawful exercise of its franchise and business. * * * Every one purchasing or subscribing for stock in a corporation impliedly agrees that he will be bound by the acts and proceedings done or sanctioned by a majority of the shareholders, or by the agents of the corporation duly chosen by such majority, within the scope of the powers conferred by the charter, and courts of equity will not undertake to control the policy or business methods of a corporation, although it may be seen that a wiser policy might be adopted and the business more successful if other methods were pursued. The majority of shares of its stock, or the agents by the holders thereof lawfully chosen, must be permitted to control the business of the corporation in their discretion, when not in violation of its charter or some public law, or corruptly and fraudulently subversive of the rights and interests of the corporation or of a shareholder.

The standards set in Delaware are also clearly stated in the cases. In Davis v. Louisville Gas & Electric Co., 16 Del.Ch. 157, 142 A. 654, a minority shareholder sought to have the directors enjoined from amending the certificate of incorporation. The court said on page 659:

> We have then a conflict in view between the responsible managers of a corporation and an overwhelming majority of its stockholders on the one hand and a dissenting minority on the other—a conflict touching matters of business policy, such as has occasioned innumerable applications to courts to intervene and determine which of the two conflicting views should prevail. The response which courts make to such applications is that it is not their function to resolve for corporations questions of policy and business management. The directors are chosen to pass upon such questions and their judgment *unless shown to be tainted with fraud* is accepted as final. The judgment of the directors of corporations enjoys the benefit of a presumption that it was formed in good faith and was designed to promote the best interests of the corporation they serve. (Emphasis supplied)

* * *

Plaintiff argues that the allegations of his amended complaint are sufficient to set forth a cause of action under the principles set out in Dodge v. Ford Motor Co., 204 Mich. 459, 170 N.W. 668. In that case plaintiff, owner of about 10% of the outstanding stock, brought suit against the directors seeking payment of additional dividends and the enjoining of further business expansion. In ruling on the request for dividends the court indicated that the motives of Ford in keeping so much money in the corporation for expansion and security were to benefit the public generally and spread the profits out by means of more jobs, etc. The court felt that these were not only far from related to the good of the stockholders, but amounted to a change in the ends of the corporation and that this was not a purpose contemplated or allowed by the corporate charter. The court relied on language found in Hunter v. Roberts, Throp & Co., 83 Mich. 63, 47 N.W. 131, 134, wherein it was said:

> Courts of equity will not interfere in the management of the directors unless it is clearly made to appear that they are guilty of fraud or misappropriation of the corporate funds, or refuse to declare a dividend when the corporation has a surplus of net profits which it can, without detriment to its business, divide among its stockholders, and when a refusal to do so would amount to such an abuse of discretion as would constitute a fraud or breach of that good faith which they are bound to exercise toward the stockholders.

From the authority relied upon in that case it is clear that the court felt that there must be fraud or a breach of that good faith which directors are bound to exercise toward the stockholders in order to justify the courts entering into the internal affairs of corporations. This is made clear when the court refused to interfere with the directors decision to expand the business. The following appears on page 684 of 170 N.W.:

> We are not, however, persuaded that we should interfere with the proposed expansion of the business of the Ford Motor Company. In view of the fact that the selling price of products may be increased at any time, the ultimate results of the larger business cannot be certainly estimated. *The judges are not business experts.* It is recognized that plans must often be made for a long future, for expected competition, for a continuing as well as an immediately profitable venture. * * * We are not satisfied that the alleged motives of the directors, in so far as they are reflected in the conduct of business, menace the interests of the shareholders. (Emphasis supplied)

Plaintiff in the instant case argues that the directors are acting for reasons unrelated to the financial interest and welfare of the Cubs. However, we are not satisfied that the motives assigned to Philip K. Wrigley, and through him to the other directors, are contrary to the best interests of the corporation and the stockholders. For example, it appears to us that the effect on the surrounding neighborhood might well be considered by a director who was considering the patrons who would or would not attend the games if the park were in a poor neighborhood. Furthermore, the long run interest of the corporation in its property value at Wrigley Field might demand all efforts to keep the neighborhood from deteriorating. By these thoughts we do not mean to say that we have decided that the decision of the directors was a correct one. That is beyond our jurisdiction and ability. We are merely saying that the decision is one properly before directors and the motives alleged in the amended complaint showed no fraud, illegality or conflict of interest in their making of that decision.

While all the courts do not insist that one or more of the three elements must be present for a stockholder's derivative action to lie, nevertheless we feel that unless the conduct of the defendants at least borders on one of the elements, the courts should not interfere. The trial court in the instant case acted properly in dismissing plaintiff's amended complaint.

* * *

There is no allegation that the night games played by the other nineteen teams enhanced their financial position or that the profits, if any, of those teams were directly related to the number of night games scheduled. There is an allegation that the installation of lights and scheduling of night games in Wrigley Field would have resulted in large amounts of additional revenues and incomes from increased attendance and related sources of income. Further, the cost of installation of lights, funds for which are allegedly readily available by financing, would be more than offset and recaptured by increased revenues. However, no allegation is made that there will be a net benefit to the corporation from such action, considering all increased costs.

Plaintiff claims that the losses of defendant corporation are due to poor attendance at home games. However, it appears from the amended complaint, taken as a whole, that factors other than attendance affect the net earnings or losses. For example, in 1962, attendance at home and road games decreased appreciably as compared with 1961, and yet the loss from direct baseball operation and of the whole corporation was considerably less.

The record shows that plaintiff did not feel he could allege that the increased revenues would be sufficient to cure the corporate deficit. The only cost plaintiff was at all concerned with was that of installation of lights. No mention was made of operation and maintenance of the lights or other possible increases in operating costs of night games and we cannot speculate as to what other factors might influence the increase or decrease of profits if the Cubs were to play night home games.

* * *

Finally, we do not agree with plaintiff's contention that failure to follow the example of the other major league clubs in scheduling night games constituted negligence. Plaintiff made no allegation that these teams' night schedules were profitable or that the purpose for which night baseball had been undertaken was fulfilled. Furthermore, it cannot be said that directors, even those of corporations that are losing money, must follow the lead of the other corporations in the field. Directors are elected for their business capabilities and judgment and the courts cannot require them to forego their judgment because of the decisions of directors of other companies. Courts may not decide these questions in the absence of a clear showing of dereliction of duty on the part of the specific directors and mere failure to "follow the crowd" is not such a dereliction.

For the foregoing reasons the order of dismissal entered by the trial court is affirmed.

Affirmed.

————

In Sylvia Martin Foundation v. Swearingen, 260 F.Supp. 231 (S.D. N.Y.1966), a stockholder brought a derivative suit against officers and directors of Standard Oil Company of Indiana seeking to hold defendants liable for having financed expansion by borrowing in Europe at higher interest rates than would have been available in the United States, solely for the purpose of alleviating the United States balance of payments—as had been urged by President Johnson of all American companies. The complaint was dismissed on jurisdictional grounds.

However, Judge Ryan added the following thought: "Because of our dismissal of the complaint as against Standard for failure to obtain personal jurisdiction over it, we do not reach its motion to dismiss for failure to state a claim and for summary judgment on the merits. But had our decision on service been otherwise, the ultimate result would not have differed since, as a matter of law, the complaint does not plead a claim over which the Court would presume to act involving as it does an attack on a matter of business judgment and policy of defendant's directors in the management of corporate affairs for which, absent an allegation of fraud, personal profit or gain, the undisputed facts show complete justification."

B. BUSINESS SELF–PERCEPTION

A STATEMENT ON NATIONAL POLICY BY THE RESEARCH AND POLICY COMMITTEE OF THE COMMITTEE FOR ECONOMIC DEVELOPMENT*: SOCIAL RESPONSIBILITIES OF BUSINESS CORPORATIONS 19–23, 26, 28–33 (1971).

CORPORATE GROWTH AND RESPONSIBILITIES

*   *   *

As corporations have grown, they also have developed sizable constituencies of people whose interests and welfare are inexorably linked with the company and whose support is vital to its success.
*   *   *

*   *   *

Community Neighbors *   *   *.

In fact, the constituencies of large corporations have become so sizable and diversified—encompassing millions of employees, stockholders, customers, and community neighbors in all sections of the country and in all classes of society—that they actually constitute a microcosm of the entire society.

*   *   *

In relations with their constituencies and with the larger society, American corporations operate today in an intricate matrix of obligations and responsibilities that far exceed in scope and complexity those of most other institutions and are analogous in many respects to government itself. *The great growth of corporations in size, market power, and impact on society has naturally brought with it a commensurate growth in responsibilities; in a democratic society, power sooner or later begets equivalent accountability.*

The growth of corporate responsibilities has been reflected in part by the growth of formal and informal constraints on the exercise of corporate power. A considerable body of law and government regulation has been developed to ensure that *all* corporations conduct business ethically, compete vigorously, treat employees fairly, advertise honestly, and so on. Corporations are also expected to behave in accordance with social customs, high moral standards, and humane values. Not all corporations have lived up to these standards, and increasingly the public reacts very strongly against those in positions of great power who are arrogant or insensitive to either their legal or social responsibilities.

---

* The Committee for Economic Development is a prestigious organization, composed largely of the chief executives of major U.S. corporations, devoted to the study of issues of public policy.

THE NEW MANAGERIAL OUTLOOK

* * *

As a permanent institution, the large corporation is developing long-term goals such as survival, growth, and increasing respect and acceptance by the public. Current profitability, once regarded as the dominant if not exclusive objective, is now often seen more as a vital means and powerful motivating force for achieving broader ends, rather than as an end in itself. Thus, modern managers are prepared to trade off short-run profits to achieve qualitative improvements in the institution which can be expected to contribute to the long-run profitable growth of the corporation.

The modern professional manager also regards himself, not as an owner disposing of personal property as he sees fit, but as a trustee balancing the interests of many diverse participants and constituents in the enterprise, whose interests sometimes conflict with those of others. The chief executive of a large corporation has the problem of reconciling the demands of employees for more wages and improved benefit plans, customers for lower prices and greater values, vendors for higher prices, government for more taxes, stockholders for higher dividends and greater capital appreciation—all within a framework that will be constructive and acceptable to society.

* * *

THE DOCTRINE OF ENLIGHTENED SELF–INTEREST

In classical economic thought, the fundamental drive of business to maximize profits was automatically regulated by the competitive marketplace. As Adam Smith put it, each individual left to pursue his own selfish interest (*laissez-faire*) would be guided "as by an unseen hand" to promote the public good.

The competitive marketplace remains the principal method of harmonizing business and public interests, because it has proved over a very long time to be an efficient way of allocating economic resources to society's needs. Yet governmental intervention has been required to promote and regulate the conditions of competition. Government also has intervened to guide economic activity toward major public objectives, as determined by the political process, when these cannot be achieved through the normal working of the marketplace.

* * *

Indeed, the corporate interest broadly defined by management can support involvement in helping to solve virtually any social problem, because people who have a good environment, education, and opportunity make better employees, customers, and neighbors for business than those who are poor, ignorant, and oppressed. It is obviously in the interest of business to enlarge its markets and to improve its work force by helping disadvantaged people to develop and employ their economic potential. Likewise, it is in the interest of business to help reduce the mounting costs of welfare, crime, disease, and waste of human potential—a good part of which business pays for.

The doctrine of enlightened self-interest is also based on the proposition that if business does not accept a fair measure of responsibility for social improvement, the interests of the corporation may actually be jeopardized. Insensitivity to changing demands of society sooner or later results in public pressures for governmental intervention and regulation to require business to do what it was reluctant or unable to do voluntarily. Today, the public strongly wants the environment cleaned up and Congress is responding by enacting stringent antipollution measures which will require substantial technological and economic changes in many industries.

* * *

REDEFINING STOCKHOLDER INTEREST

* * *

Inasmuch as the business community as a whole clearly has a vital stake in a good, well-functioning society, it can be argued that the stockholder's interest in the long run is best served by corporate policies which contribute to the development of the kind of society in which business can grow and prosper. Indeed, this long-range stockholder interest would justify governmental regulation to bring about improved environmental operating conditions—in, for example, pollution abatement—if corporations singly or as a group cannot achieve such results on their own.

SOCIAL IMPROVEMENT AND PROFITABILITY

The positive perspective of enlightened self-interest provides the framework for reconciling social improvement with profitability. Changing public expectations and the urgent quest for a good society are beginning to generate new demands for the kind of goods and services that in many respects business is demonstrably well qualified to provide. Some of these markets will come into existence fairly naturally, some will have to be created by business initiative, and others will have to be fashioned primarily by government. Altogether, they will provide substantial opportunities for business to profit by serving society's new requirements.

* * *

LIMITATIONS ON CORPORATE SOCIAL ACTIVITIES

* * *

Cost-benefit considerations are a very important factor. No company of any size can willingly incur costs which would jeopardize its competitive position and threaten its survival. While companies may well be able to absorb modest costs or undertake some social activities on a break-even basis, any substantial expenditure must be justified in terms of the benefits, tangible and intangible, that are expected to be produced. Since major corporations have especially long planning horizons, they may be able to incur costs and forego profits in the short run for social improvements that are expected to enhance profits or improve the corporate environment in the long run. But the corporation that sacrifices too much in the way of earnings in the short run will soon find itself with no long run to worry about.

Thus, management must concern itself with realizing a level of profitability which its stockholders and the financial market consider to be reasonable under the circumstances. This means that substantial investments in social improvement will have to contribute to earnings, and the extent of such earnings will be a major factor in determining the mix of a company's commercial and social activities.

* * *

STEVENSON, CORPORATIONS AND SOCIAL RESPONSIBILITY: IN SEARCH OF THE CORPORATE SOUL
42 Geo.Wash.L.Rev. 709, 718–20 (1974).

* * * [T]he new rhetoric of corporate social responsibility frequently exceeds the reality. The corporate "urban affairs" programs that flowered after the civil disorders of the mid-sixties provide an instructive example of this phenomenon. Many large corporations, urged on by government and private groups, promised to hire and train large numbers of socially disadvantaged, mostly black, city-dwellers. Many of the promises were, in fact, kept. But the recession at the end of the decade caused many layoffs. And by and large, the first to be laid off were the "hard-core unemployed" who had been hired in fulfillment of the large corporations' "social obligations." The situation appears to be no better today than when the program started.

Moreover, there is a good deal of evidence that much of the corporate activity was selfishly motivated. In a recently published study describing the results of a survey of nearly half of the Fortune 500 firms, 80 percent of the corporations surveyed indicated that a principal reason for their initiation of "urban affairs" programs was the hope of improving their public image. Many companies spent more on publicizing their programs than they spent on the programs themselves. * * *

A closer examination of the "social" activities of corporations leaves one with the firm impression that not only are they not overwhelming in magnitude, but they are generally not very successful either. Solutions to social problems tend to be political and economic in nature, not technological. Corporations are good at using and manipulating technology, but are not always so adept at politics. The efforts in the late sixties of many aerospace firms to apply their technological abilities to the newly recognized problems of the cities turned out for the most part to be miserable failures. The Office of Education has now all but abandoned its experiments with contracting the running of schools out to private businesses—corporations turned out not to be any better at educating children than school boards.

But even were corporations possessed of unique abilities to deal effectively with nonbusiness problems, is it really so clear that ties which, at least nominally, bind the corporation to the exigencies of the profit motive should be cut? How comforting is the notion of corporate giants, freed of whatever constraints are now imposed on them by the market mechanism, galloping about the countryside on white horses rescuing women and children and bringing succor to the needy and the aged?   *   *   *

C.   WHAT IS CORPORATE RESPONSIBILITY?: ANOTHER VIEW

MILTON FRIEDMAN, CAPITALISM & FREEDOM 133–34 (1962).

The view has been gaining widespread acceptance that corporate officials   *   *   *   have a "social responsibility" that goes beyond serving the interest of their stockholders   *   *   *. This view shows a fundamental misconception of the character and nature of a free economy. In such an economy, there is one and only one social responsibility of business—to use its resources and engage in activities designed to increase its profits so long as it stays within the rules of the game, which is to say, engages in open and free competition, without deception or fraud.   *   *   *   It is the responsibility of the rest of us to establish a framework of law such that an individual in pursuing his own interest is, to quote Adam Smith again, "led by an invisible hand to promote an end which was no part of his intention. Nor is it always the worse for the society that it was no part of it. By pursuing his own interest, he frequently promotes that of the society more effectually than when he really intends to promote it. I have never known much good done by those who affected to trade for the public good."

Few trends could so thoroughly undermine the very foundations of our free society as the acceptance by corporate officials of a social responsibility other than to make as much money for their stockholders as possible. This is a fundamentally subversive doctrine. If businessmen do have a social responsibility other than making maximum profits for stockholders, how are they to know what it is? Can self-selected private individuals decide what the social interest is? Can they decide how great a burden they are justified in placing on themselves or their stockholders to serve that social interest? Is it tolerable that these public functions of taxation, expenditure, and control be exercised by the people who happen at the moment to be in charge of particular enterprises, chosen for those posts by strictly private groups? If businessmen are civil servants rather than the employees of their stockholders then in a democracy they will, sooner or later, be chosen by the public techniques of election and appointment.

D. THE ROLE OF COUNSEL

NORMAL REDLICH, LAWYERS, THE TEMPLE, AND THE MARKET PLACE
30 Bus.Lawyer 65 (March 1975).

* * *

* * * We may sometimes resent the fact that the public is pointing to the lawyers and holding us responsible for many of the moral shortcomings of the country, but there is no way that the legal profession can avoid bearing this burden. We play too crucial a role in government and corporate life to avoid this responsibility. I have been the chief legal officer of a very large corporation—one with an eleven billion dollar a year budget—the municipal corporation which we call New York City. I believe firmly that if the legal arm of a corporate enterprise loses its moral strength, that decline will be reflected throughout that enterprise.

It is both our burden and our glory that we are expected to live by a high professional standard and earn a living at the same time. We do not have the luxury of the clergy who can live in the temple and condemn the market place. Nor do we have the more flexible standard of those who live solely in the market place. We have to carry the standards of the temple into the market place and practice our trade there. That is why a country which questions its moral behavior inevitably questions its lawyers.

Lawyers in this country do not act, as do barristers, as a professional class removed from the day-to-day affairs of their clients. We are, as the title of this Institute indicates, advisors to management. As such we are involved in what management does, as advisors and as defenders. We are accountable to a Code of Professional Responsibility and to a body of law which has interpreted that Code. We are both enforcers of law and defenders of those who violate it.

* * *

Let me state the problem. Lawyers, including house counsel, are both a part of, and also professionally removed from, corporate and governmental entities which have engaged, and will continue to engage, in actions which may be illegal and immoral. These entities require our advice and are entitled to our services. Moreover, society has a profound interest in having a corps of professionals giving competent legal advice to these corporate and governmental entities.

The question we face is this. How does that corps of profession-als—we lawyers—so carry out our mission that we can hold our heads high and say to the public, "We have done all that we can to prevent the wrongdoings of our clients consistent with our responsi-bility to advise them as to the law"? That is the question I wish to explore briefly with you. For upon its answer depends our ability satisfactorily to resolve some of the more serious problems facing our profession today.

Lawyers have a natural way of quickly moving to the outer limits of any question. This is understandable because these uncertain ar-eas are troublesome to us. *   *   *

*   *   *

First, let us talk about our clear professional responsibility to say, "No." We all operate under a canon which commands us to " *   *   * exercise independent professional judgment on behalf of a client." I know how difficult it sometimes is, when an important and powerful client is embarking on some course of action which every-one is convinced is in the best interests of the company only to have the lawyer insist on some step—such as a disclosure—which he feels is legally required. This happens in the governmental context as well.

A lawyer can be under enormous pressure to "go along" with a transaction when he knows that the facts are simply not as they are portrayed to a government agency or to another private party. We have all heard the seductive serpent-like song. It has many refrains: "Who will ever know?" "You're not the judge, you're only the law-yer." "I didn't hire you to tell me what I can't do." "Whose lawyer are you, anyway?" You've heard these and many more. Often noth-ing at all needs to be said. Everyone is going along on the basis of certain assumptions, and it is so difficult to speak up and announce, as in the famous fable, "Look, the Emperor has no clothes."

But if there is anything which is clear, it is our professional duty to refuse to approve of, or participate in, transactions which we be-lieve to be unlawful, even if it means that we have to delay or thwart a major program of a client, or cause a considerable loss of money, or embarrass management—or even cause us to lose a major client. *   *   *

*   *   *

Moreover, lawyers in this situation are constantly underestimating their own power. They speak not from weakness but from strength. Very often the client wants the lawyer's stamp of approval and will not proceed without it. Despite all of the pressuring, and occasional bullying, the lawyer does hold the passkey and only he can turn it. In the final analysis, we cannot expect the public to respect lawyers as independent professionals if they run for cover when a powerful

client wants them to go along with a shady transaction on grounds
that "everyone is doing it" or that "no one will find out."

* * *

Another * * * role is the advisor's responsibility to speak out
in the public interest regardless of the views of his clients. The Code
of Professional Responsibility specifically authorizes such expression
of views provided it does not adversely affect a client's interest on a
particular matter the lawyer may be handling. * * *

* * *

POTTER STEWART, PROFESSIONAL ETHICS
FOR THE BUSINESS LAWYER: THE
MORALS OF THE MARKET PLACE
31 Bus.Lawyer 463 (November 1975).

* * * I must remind you that it has been more than 20 years
since I last practiced as a business lawyer. My comments today on
Professional Ethics for the Business Lawyer are necessarily based,
therefore, on imperfect recollections of the practical aspects of the
problems involved, distorted by more recent observations from the
judicial sidelines.

But not all of my memories of the practical ethical problems facing practicing business lawyers have dimmed. I still vividly remember, for example, many conversations with the wise old senior partner
of my Cincinnati law firm, a man old enough to be my grandfather.
He was an unwavering believer in total independence for the business
lawyer. Although our firm represented a number of corporate clients, he steadfastly refused for many years to serve on the Board of
Directors of any of them. To have done so, he firmly believed, would
have compromised his independence and his professional integrity.
Indeed, he felt so strongly about not only the reality but also the
appearance of professional objectivity and independence that he
would not leave his office to see a business client. Since the client
was seeking his professional legal advice, the client came to our office to see him. And this was true even though the client was the
President of the largest company in town, which also happened to be
one of the largest corporations in the United States.

These ideas seemed somewhat old-fashioned and eccentric even a
generation ago, and today probably no business lawyer in a large
metropolitan area could realistically practice his profession in that
way. But these ideas reflected, nonetheless, I think, a remarkably
clear perception of the need for the brightest possible line of demarcation between the function of a lawyer in giving professional counsel
to his client, and the function of corporate management in carrying
on the corporation's business in the profit-making interests of its
stockholders. And I remind you that the propriety of a lawyer serv-

ing as a member of the Board of Directors of his corporate client remains, even today, a vexing problem of professional responsibility.

What I want to discuss this afternoon, however, stems from an event of more recent vintage, an event in which I was directly involved only a few weeks ago. I refer to the Supreme Court's unanimous decision, announced last June 16 in the case of Goldfarb v. Virginia State Bar, 421 U.S. 773 (1975). [The case held that minimum fee schedules for lawyers violated § 1 of the Sherman Act.]

* * *

* * * [T]he *Goldfarb* opinion amounts to a new look at the legal profession—a look less exalted, perhaps, than what we are used to, but one that is consonant, I think, with what lawyers actually do. The *Goldfarb* case says that lawyers are primarily economic actors, men and women who perform a service for profit. When lawyers, like plumbers, get together and impose restrictions on the prices they will charge, the kind of work they will do, the markets they will serve, the merchandising practices they will follow, or any number of similar subjects, the antitrust laws may well be implicated. For lawyers are subject to the same temptations and pressures that, in all other areas of economic life, can lead to concerted activity destructive of a free and competitive market. And the members of the public, the consumers of lawyers' services, are best served if there is true competition among lawyers for their patronage.

In this view of the legal profession, what is left for a code of professional responsibility for the business lawyer? Are professional ethics now to be no more elevated than the standards of a Better Business Bureau? Are we now to exalt the morals of the market place into a model of professional respectability? These are fundamental and difficult questions, but I submit that affirmative answers to them, rhetoric aside, may not be so calamitous as might be supposed.

* * *

But beyond * * * a few * * * precepts of decency and common sense, a good case can be made, I think, for the proposition that the ethics of the business lawyer are indeed, and perhaps should be, no more than the morals of the market place. The first rule for a business lawyer is to provide his total ability and effort to his client. But is this an ethical standard, or no more than a response to the economic forces of the market place? After all the first rule in *any* occupation is to be competent. The business lawyer is in the business of providing legal advice for a businessman. If he performs that job with diligence, conscientiousness, and knowledgeable ability, his client will reap the benefits and will reward him accordingly. If not, unless he is particularly lucky or married to the boss' daughter, the lawyer will find his client less than eager to retain indefinitely a professional adviser who habitually directs him down the wrong path.

In short, it can fairly be argued that many aspects of what we call "ethics" are not really ethics at all, but are merely corollaries of the axiom of the better mousetrap, an axiom that is itself derived from enlightened self-interest.

* * *

There are, as I have said, some ethical constraints upon the business lawyer that are *not* directly derived from the principle of competitive success. It may be that, in order to drum those standards into the heads of the obtuse, there is a need for the kind of rhetoric that describes the business lawyer as a "priest of the Law," who brings to the market place the "standards of the temple," to use the phrases of Dean Redlich at the National Institute last fall. But aside from the inescapable responsibility that his profession places upon every lawyer to act as a wholly honorable and trustworthy person and a good and law abiding citizen, is there any way in which a business lawyer can better serve the public interest than by giving the best possible legal advice to his clients? Is it the duty of a lawyer, by contrast, to try to impose upon his clients his own notions of social, or political or economic morality? Is it indeed even "ethical" for him to try to impose his own system of moral priorities and social values on his clients' business decisions, in the guise of neutral legal advice?

* * *

THOMAS SHAFFER, LEGAL INTERVIEWING AND COUNSELING, 39–45 (1976).

DILEMMAS IN THE IDEAL OF CLIENT SELF–DETERMINATION

Client self-determination is a more complex subject than the professional literature represents it to be. The ideal and the legal profession's guidelines for professional conduct are stated in the Code of Professional Responsibility, Ethical Consideration 7–8:

> A lawyer should exert his best efforts to insure that decisions of his client are made only after the client has been informed of relevant considerations. A lawyer ought to initiate this decision-making process if the client does not do so. Advice of a lawyer to his client need not be confined to purely legal considerations. A lawyer should advise his client of the possible effect of each legal alternative. A lawyer should bring to bear upon this decision-making process the fullness of his experience as well as his objective viewpoint. In assisting his client to reach a proper decision, it is often desirable for a lawyer to point out those factors which may lead to a decision that is morally just as well as legally permissible. He may emphasize the possibility of harsh consequences that might result from assertion of legally permissible positions. *In the final analysis, however, the lawyer should always remember that the decision whether to forego legally*

available objectives or methods because of non-legal factors is ultimately for the client and not for himself. In the event that the client in a non-adjudicatory matter insists upon a course of conduct that is contrary to the judgment and advice of the lawyer but not prohibited by the Disciplinary Rules, the lawyer may withdraw from the employment. (Emphasis added.)

The *Code* states the principle in the clearest possible manner. It also recognizes a duty in lawyers to supply information available from their experience, from their learning, and from their "objective" observation; this includes moral considerations and consideration of what John Dewey called "the logic of consequences." The *Code* says that lawyers have a duty to initiate this broad decision-making process—that is, to insist upon it, regardless, apparently, of how docile or uncommunicative the client is. Finally, the *Code* notices (albeit timidly) that lawyers also have consciences. It affirms a freedom to withdraw from employment if the client seems to the lawyer to be wrong.

Lawyer theories about client self-determination, from a somewhat different perspective, occupy a spectrum which is broader than the cool, rational dialogue contemplated by the *Code*. At one extreme, for example, there is often a species of interpersonal demand on the lawyer which is usually—and, no doubt, properly—excluded from client choice. In Frank Cihlar's example, "such limitations may take the shape of a decision to avoid becoming * * * friend or lover." At the other extreme, most lawyers (including your author) insist, more vehemently than the *Code*, that a lawyer need not lend his talents to client objectives he regards as immoral. This latter limitation has taken on atypical insistence after "Watergate" and an increase in public doubt about the moral decency of lawyers. Many today resist the principle often attributed to John W. Davis: "The lawyer's duty [is] to represent his client's interests to the limit of the law, [and] not to moralize on the social and economic implications of the client's lawful action." However convenient that dictum may be to the lawyer's economy of emotion, many of us doubt its depth, both in cases involving legal conduct which seems immoral and in cases involving moral conduct which seems illegal. Examples cover (1) cases where the lawyer's moral influence is invoked even beyond the informational level contemplated by the *Code*; (2) cases where the client proposes conduct which seems moral to the client but not to the lawyer * * *.

1. *Lawyer's Moral Influence Invoked.* This example is from Brown and Shaffer: "We had a corporate client with large industrial plants in the Deep South. Our client was a fourth-tier contractor with the federal government, which meant then that it had some, but very slight, duties to racially integrate its work force. Our client had discussed this with my senior in the firm, who asked me to research

the client's duties under a presidential executive order on equal employment opportunity.

"I drafted a memorandum outlining the client's minimal duties. My senior, with memo in hand, telephoned the secretary of the corporation; he explained my memo ('the law'). The secretary—who was himself a lawyer—said he understood this advice but still wondered what the corporation should do. My senior in the firm then said we had reviewed the situation, and that our advice was to integrate fully in all plants. This advice had all the jurisprudential clarity and economy of Brown v. Board of Education. This law-office decision went beyond the letter of the law, as most law-office decisions, from income taxes to the corrupt practices act, do. Lawyer-client decision-making is not, after all, a form of technical journalism. I have often wondered why my senior gave the advice he did:

"He may have been putting his own social opinions into the decision-making process.

"He may have believed that the law was in a process which would soon reach this client with full-integration requirements; that is, he may have been simply predictive.

"He may, in addition, have assessed the economic and human costs of compliance (which were great in this case) and have decided that early compliance was cheapest.

"He may, finally, have assessed the moral implications of full integration, minimal integration, and no integration, in terms of his own and the client's ethical posture. This last is my preferred speculation; it involves consideration of a wide array of factors—the consciences of the executives we were advising (the decision-makers); corporate image; the welfare of the workers (white and black); the social posture in the South and the nation at that time; and, most important, his own perception of the moral openness of the people he was advising. Any of these factors implies a recognition of the fact that the corporation was inevitably a moral leader in the community."

The client in this example took the lawyer's advice; all plants were fully integrated, about a decade before "the law" began to require integration of them. The lawyer's behavior here seems, by the way, to have gone beyond advice on what the law required, but to have been fully within two phrases in E.C. 7–8: " * * * a decision that is morally just as well as legally permissible" and " * * * the possibility of harsh consequences that might result from assertion of legally permissible positions." Its defect is its failure to respect what the *Code* calls a "decision-making process." There was a good decision here, but the process was poor. The moral decision, for all that appeared, came solely from the lawyer. The client may have done the right thing, but its officers were deprived of the important human satisfaction which comes from considering alternatives and making a righteous and praiseworthy choice. The lawyer also took upon himself moral, as well as legal, responsibility for the client's behavior. That could have turned out to be professionally and emotionally uneconomic; is seems to me to have demonstrated too little regard for the conscience of the client. Regard for the conscience of the client would not have posed problems for the conscience of the lawyer since there was, at the point where "advice" was given, no indication that the client would make a choice which would have posed a moral dilemma for the lawyer. * * *

2. Client Conduct Which Seems Immoral to the Lawyer. Cihlar gives this example, which I edit slightly: "Mr. D., a lawyer, received a call from one of his clients who indicated that he had decided to commit suicide. Mr. D.'s response to this information was not one of hysteria or of immediate activity designed to get his caller into the protective embrace of some life-sustaining authority. He simply indicated that he hoped his caller would not *choose* to take his life since Mr. D. regarded him as a friend whom he liked very much and would regret not having around. * * * Mr. D. did not urge his caller not to take his life nor did he endeavor to reach him in person. Instead, he merely expressed his concern over the potential loss but stressed the fact that he thought the decision was ultimately his caller's. * * * With this, Mr. D. concluded the conversation and returned to sleep. * * *" Mr. D. said later that he felt his client "had sufficient command of his faculties so as to permit him to make up his own mind in the matter." He said he would regard killing himself as immoral, but that he felt it appropriate only to intervene in his client's decision on the matter, and inappropriate to interfere with it. The example is probably more dramatic than the present point requires, but it suggests a host of less dramatic cases where clients make choices which seem wrong but which a person-oriented lawyer feels bound to respect. * * *

In fact, though, moral impulses are subtle, often difficult to understand, and even more difficult to articulate. This is another instance * * * where effective legal counseling requires a resolute effort to achieve self-awareness.

E.   STATUTORY REFORM

PROBLEM

You have been retained as a consultant to a state law revision commission. Would you recommend the enactment of the following standard of corporate accountability:

All corporate powers shall be exercised by or under the authority of, and the business and affairs of a corporation shall be managed under the direction of a board of directors as the good of the enterprise, its employees, and the public interest demand.

Consider the following excerpt:

GREAT BRITAIN, DEPARTMENT OF TRADE AND INDUSTRY, COMPANY LAW REFORM, CMND. 5391, 19–20 (1973).

[This document was a "white paper" giving the British Government's considered views, preparatory to legislative or administrative action.]

The Public Responsibility of the Company

* * *

56.   Statute law has over the years defined and limited the areas and directions in which profit may be pursued.   The directors of a company owe a fiduciary duty to do their best for those whose financial resources they are using; but in an increasingly complex industrial society this is no longer taken to mean that the aim must be the simple one of immediate profitability.   A board of directors has to reconcile several different interests, of which profit is the main but cannot be the only one.   Any company must behave as a responsible part of the society in which it exists, but, as for an individual, responsibilities are of two kinds—one specific and one general.   The law sets limits to the pursuit of profit—be they limits on acts affecting the public generally, such as fraudulent dealing, exploiting monopolies or polluting the atmosphere, or domestic matters such as the amount of redundancy payment and the keeping of books of account. These are in the main specifically identifiable duties or proscriptions; and it is for society, through the general body of the law, to alter those limits for all companies if it is thought right that they should be altered.   The other kind of responsibility, a more general and moral kind, is much more difficult to specify and define in terms that can assist any board to decide in any particular situation just where that responsibility leads them, or that can be translated into law.

57.   For these wider responsibilities, a Code of Conduct might be appropriate, but to be effective, a Code needs some external sanction. The Watkinson Committee suggest, for instance, that companies should consider adding to their memoranda a clause allowing directors to take wider considerations into account when exercising their judgment as directors, and that a Code would set such judgments in a general frame of reference.   That would no doubt protect the directors against any claim by shareholders seeking compensation for loss caused by directors' actions not taken directly and clearly in the shareholders' interest.   What also needs to be considered is whether it would give the positive guidance which a company might feel it needed, or might feel that its competitors needed, if it were to deviate safely from the straightforward most profitable course.   For a Code to be effective in that area of responsibility which this Paper has described as "social" or "moral"—and given that by its nature much of the material cannot be put in specific and precise form—some independent source of judgment may be necessary.   The Take-Over Panel

suggests a precedent, but the Panel has of course the sanctions of the Stock Exchange behind it, and it is not at present easy to see what counterpart might exist in relation to the general run of industrial decisions. It is evident that boards of directors can and do have regard to such matters as the interests of customers, or employees and of the general public, since these matters bear upon the reputation and well-being of the company as well as upon short-term profit. The more public disclosure there is of companies' conduct the more will that be true. It is, however, important to set criteria for judging whether in any particular case they have done so to an acceptable degree.

58. A useful step forward would be to impose a duty on directors to report to the shareholders on specific parts of the company's response to the social environment. As indicated above the Government intends to use for this purpose the powers which they seek to require additional disclosure in directors' reports. Administrative and drafting problems for directors may be involved, but these are matters of legitimate public concern. There is no lack of informed and interested people (including the employees of a company) to mark what is said. And the cumulative effect would have real and increasing value both in making companies more aware of their duty to and dependence on the community of which they are a part, and in helping the community to appreciate the real extent to which companies individually and collectively are contributing to social progress.

The Company and Its Employees

59. The duty that a company owes to its employees has already been emphasized. The role of the employees in the conduct of the company's affairs is a matter to which the Government attaches the greatest importance and which they have under urgent examination. The Government believes that is in the interests of all concerned, including those who provide the capital, that the employees should have an appropriate opportunity of influencing decisions which can closely affect their own interest. These matters extend beyond the field of company law and have a significant part to play in the improvement of industrial relations. The debate on this subject is proceeding alongside the debate on company law as a whole. The Government therefore intends to publish later this year a separate Green Paper on employee participation, discussing proposals for ensuring the closer involvement of employees in company affairs; decisions about any new legislation which may be needed will be taken only when there has been full opportunity for public debate on the proposals and after consultation with both sides of industry.

Chapter 18

THE GOVERNANCE OF THE CORPORATION

PROBLEM

A POSITION PAPER

You have recently become a member of the staff of the general counsel of a large manufacturing corporation. Your boss has been asked to present a paper at a conference on "The Governance of the Large Corporation in the Year 2000." The paper is to give an overview of the principal issues of corporate governance that corporations and policy makers can be expected to grapple with during the rest of the century and to outline the major changes, if any, that should be made in the governance structure as it now exists. Knowing of your interest in the topic, your boss has asked you to prepare a memorandum to serve as a starting point for discussion in a series of seminars she plans to hold on the subject within the corporation. You have been requested to address four questions:

1. Considering the large corporation as an institution that responds to economic, social, and political forces, what are the principal mechanisms through which those forces are translated into responses?

2. Are there any weaknesses in the way those mechanisms presently operate, either from the point of view of shareholders or of the society at large?

3. What changes should be made in the present governance structure to deal with any weaknesses that do exist?

4. How should those changes be accomplished? By changes in state corporation law? By changes in federal law? By corporations themselves?

A. INTRODUCTION: THE MEANING OF CORPORATE GOVERNANCE

The last several years have seen an increasing amount of attention devoted to the problems of "corporate governance": Articles on the topic by both scholars and practitioners have appeared in law reviews and other legal periodicals with growing frequency; a chairman of the Securities and Exchange Commission made it one of the dominant themes of his administration (see Grienenberger and McGrath, Reduction in Credibility Stems from Commission Stand on Accountability, N.Y.L.J., Dec. 17, 1979 at 29 (tracing the evolution of the views on corporate governance of former SEC Chairman Harold M. Williams)); the SEC staff undertook a major study of corporate gov-

765

ernance culminating in a 782 page report (Staff Report on Corporate Accountability, Comm. Print, Senate Comm. on Banking, Housing, and Urban Affairs (1980)); and the American Law Institute launched a project to produce a "restatement" of the law on this topic.

Unfortunately, as with the term "corporate social responsibility" there is no clear agreement on just what "corporate governance" means. A starting point for a definition of the expression—as it is used in this book at any rate—is that it describes a portion of the set of all of those forces, and the mechanisms through which they operate that, taken together, dictate the behavior of large * corporations. The principal part of the larger set excluded by the definition consists of regulatory laws that, by threat of criminal or civil sanctions, seek to achieve certain substantive results *directly*, by requiring the corporation to act or prohibiting it from acting in particular ways. They are, thus, "substantive" in their content. Governance mechanisms, by contrast, act *indirectly*, attempting to attain the desired behavior by altering the forces operating on the corporation or the mechanisms through which they are felt. They can therefore be thought of as "formal" or "procedural" in nature.

A good example of the distinction is found in the two techniques used by Congress in the Foreign Corrupt Practices Act to restrain U. S. corporations from paying bribes to officials of foreign governments. The "regulatory" (in the sense used above) portion of the statute simply prohibits such conduct and imposes criminal penalties for violations of the prohibition. Securities Exchange Act of 1934, § 30A. Not content with this direct approach, however, Congress also required that corporations subject to the statute keep records that, "in reasonable detail, accurately and fairly reflect" their transactions, and that they maintain internal accounting controls "sufficient to provide reasonable assurances that" their transactions are in accordance with management directions. *Id.* § 13(b)(2). The problem Congress sought to correct in passing these provisions was obviously not just sloppy record keeping. Many of the much-publicized improper corporate payments that prompted the passage of the statute had been made by subordinate officials without the knowledge or authorization of top management. The record keeping and auditing provisions of the statute were intended to support the direct prohibition of bribery by insuring that management would learn of improper behavior by corporate employees and could not turn a blind eye to their violations of the substantive parts of the statute. These "procedural" provisions are thus excellent examples of a "governance mechanism" as that term is used in this chapter.

* We are concerned here only about *large* corporations, both because their behavior is of considerably greater importance to the society than that of their smaller cousins and because many of the mechanisms of interest operate differently, or not at all, in the small firm.

Why should the law of corporations (broadly defined) include governance mechanisms? There are those who seem to believe it should not. Many commentators of the "Chicago School" persuasion, for example, would argue that even the conventional impositions of the usual corporate statute, such as the provisions governing shareholder voting, are warranted only as a means of reducing "transaction costs" to facilitate what are essentially creations of private contract. Otherwise, the terms of these private arrangements are no business of the state. *See, e.g.,* Winter, State Law, Shareholder Protection, and the Theory of the Corporation, 6 J. Legal Stud. 251 (1977). And insofar as the conduct of corporations occasionally has socially undesirable consequences, the way for society to deal with them is to enact and enforce appropriate regulations. A former SEC chairman argues, for example,

> I would suggest that using the corporation laws to correct either the deficiencies of present legislation or deficiencies in enforcement is to seek remedy in the wrong place. The right way to correct those deficiencies, quite simply, is by tightening up the laws, if they are too loose, by substituting new laws if the old ones are conceptually inadequate, and by stepping up enforcement with a larger commitment of money and people, if the fault lies there." Sommer, Should Corporation Laws Function to Restrain Antisocial and Illegal Conduct? in Commentaries on Corporate Structure and Governance 257 (D. Schwartz, ed., 1979).

Although they do not always recognize it expressly, those who advocate changes in corporate governance implicitly reject these views. They believe that the combination of regulation and the governance mechanisms that have naturally and voluntarily been adopted by corporations in the pursuit of their own interests (or perhaps more precisely, the interests of those who control them) are inadequate to protect some or all of the other interests affected by corporate behavior, including those of shareholders, employees, and the society at large.

There are two principal explanations that might be offered for why this should be true. First, there may be a gap between the substantive norms imposed by regulation directed at corporate conduct and the somewhat higher standards of behavior we desire from large corporations. A society in which every individual acted always and exclusively in his or her own *economic* self-interest, constrained only by the limits imposed by law, would hardly be a desirable one in which to live. It may be further argued—although the proposition would not be without controversy—that a society in which business corporations behaved in the same fashion could also be improved. Even Milton Friedman seems implicitly to have recognized this when he wrote that the responsibility of the management of a corporation is "generally * * * to make as much money as possible while conforming to the basic rules of the society, both those embodied in law *and those embodied in ethical customs.*" Friedman, The Social

Responsibility of Business Is to Increase Its Profits, New York Times Magazine, Sept. 13, 1970 at 33 (emphasis added). Governance mechanisms may be aimed at encouraging corporations to behave more in accordance with "ethical customs", presumably even though the consequences might sometimes be lower profits than would be produced by bare compliance with the law.

The second basic reason for the possible failure of regulation and voluntary governance measures to provide entirely satisfactory means of directing corporate behavior into the most socially-desirable channels is found in the weaknesses of regulation. The enforcement of the law is not costless. The more we seek, as Mr. Sommer suggests, to fill in the chinks in the existing pattern of regulation and to pour resources into enforcing existing laws, the greater the cost becomes. It may well be that in some circumstances the desired standard of conduct may be achieved at less cost by changes in governance patterns than by increasing enforcement efforts. This would seem to be the judgment reached by Congress in passing the Foreign Corrupt Practices Act.

The discussion of corporate governance has often been diffuse; and there is, at least as yet, no generally accepted framework for analysis of the issues. The sections that follow examine what seem to be emerging as some of the more important questions about several of the major governance mechanisms. In particular, we will consider the roles played by some of the principal actors within the corporate institution, and certain of the more important "procedural" techniques that have been suggested as tools for improving governance.

B. THE CORPORATE ACTORS

1. THE SHAREHOLDERS

Reconsider Chapter 13, Section A, Subsection 1 and Section C, Subsection 4.

2. THE MANAGERS

Reconsider Chapter 17, Section A.

MANNING, A TAXONOMY OF CORPORATE LAW REFORM, IN COMMENTARIES ON CORPORATE STRUCTURE AND GOVERNANCE 124, 128–29 (D. Schwartz, ed., 1979).

* * * [Another] group that seeks change in the nation's present corporate system takes as its watchword "management accountability." This group * * * argues that in any soundly run institution everyone should be accountable to someone else; and that the leader of any institution who is accountable to no one, whose word is law, and who is not in jeopardy of removal from power will in time become arbitrary, arrogant, self-aggrandizing, prodigal, and despotic

and will, further, lose contact with reality, isolate himself from unpleasant information, and make increasingly erratic judgements, to the misery of those around him and ultimately to the disaster of the organization that he heads. The fear of [these] critics is that the top officers of large-scale American corporations have achieved, or at least approximated, such a status of nonaccountability and that the situation is both dangerous and morally unacceptable.

In the view of the author, these propositions of human psychology are valid. Indeed those who agree with this author that the centralized strong-management system of the modern large-scale enterprise is essential to its economic effectiveness must recognize that on the other side of the same coin it is written that: (1) the society should set external legal ground rules for the behavior of enterprises; (2) the society should do what it can to distribute the human costs of economic dislocation; and (3) external and internal forces of accountability must be effectively brought to bear upon corporate managers. The question is whether the existing set of accountability constraints upon corporate management is, in fact, adequate. That is a key and central subject for public debate.

* * *

Reflection on the content of the concept of accountability reveals that it contains several quite different components, each of them important and each perhaps calling for special processes of monitoring, reporting, review, or check and balance. Consider the following corporate situations, which raise four different aspects of the problem of accountability:

(1) A company's officers improperly line their own pockets with assets of the company or its shareholders by self-dealing contracts at unfair prices, by paying themselves undeserved compensation, by trading in the company's stock on inside information, or the like;

(2) In a misguided but unselfish effort to advance the interests of the company, its officers lead the company to violate the law, to infringe standards of decent business practice, or to behave in a socially irresponsible manner;

(3) Through laziness or incompetence, the company's officers operate the enterprise inefficiently and let it go to pot financially;

(4) The board of directors of the company fails to exercise due care to keep itself informed about the company's affairs; or fails to exercise due care to prevent management's cheating, illegal conduct, poor profit performance, or reprehensible social behavior; or fails to exercise due care to see to it that appropriate timely disclosure about the company's affairs is made to the public, the market, and the appropriate authorities.

To enact laws against these different categories of blameworthy corporate and managerial behavior is helpful, but not in itself enough. Prosecution can catch only a few evildoers, and it also has the disadvantage of coming after the fact. The criminal sanction is also clearly inappropriate to deal with simple managerial inefficiency. What is needed is a set of built-in institutional arrangements that on a daily, ongoing basis prevent, or at least contain within tolerable limits, undesirable conduct or ineffective performance by corporate managers, directors, and their companies. To achieve that result while retaining the important advantages of our strong-management corporate system requires several conditions, some of which are external to the corporate enterprise, and some of which are internal to it.

Requisite conditions external to the corporation are: an effective SEC, honest and exacting public accountants, a competent and skeptical corps of financial analysts and commentators, and a body of rigorous legal doctrine invocable in shareholders' suits by an able corporate plaintiffs' bar. What are the facts? The SEC has been consistently vigorous and activist. The profession of independent accounting (with a little prodding help from others) has of late been experiencing, and is still experiencing, a major evolution toward more scrupulous procedures and greater independence from corporate management. The financial press and analysts have become increasingly sophisticated and gimlet-eyed in recent years. The plaintiffs' bar is alive and well, and shareholder litigation flourishes, despite some recently demonstrated indispositions by the Supreme Court to continue to expand the reach of class actions and Rule 10b–5. So far, so good.

The other two requisites of management accountability are internal to the corporate structure. They are a board of directors that is not controlled by management and a flow of reliable information. Those two elements are essential. *If the strong-executive model of corporate governance is to be maintained, it must be accompanied by a flow of solid and honest data sufficient to permit management's stewardship to be evaluated in all respects, and that flow must go (in the first instance) to a board of directors made up of members who are able and willing to evaluate management's performance objectively from the perspective of the interests of the enterprise as a whole.* Contained in that single sentence, it seems to me, is the crux of current policy questions about corporate reform.

Read Chapter 22, Section C.

3. THE BOARD OF DIRECTORS

Much of the discussion of the need for or means of accomplishing improvements in corporate governance has focused on the role played—or that might be played—by the board of directors. Most of those who agree with the proposition that some changes are necessary would begin by increasing the importance of the board in the governance structure. There is, however, less agreement as to precisely what this might mean.

a. Reconceptualizing the Role of the Board

There appear to be at least three different views of the proper role of the board, which is seen as functioning either (1) as a monitor of management, (2) as an active participant in management, or (3) as an adversary to management.* In the first role the board could monitor the performance of top executives against established financial, social and legal goals. Corporate officers and the board presumably would be involved in goal setting. As part of its monitoring role, a board would identify and discharge mediocre top executives who failed to meet specified standards. Such a board could also assess the corporation's structure, the decision-making techniques used by an organization, and the process by which management functions.

A more active board might participate more directly in corporate governance. This type of board could carefully review and approve (or disapprove) major corporate policies and long-range objectives by analyzing and discussing management proposals. The board could ask discerning and critical questions of management with respect to a variety of items, such as, the corporation's goals, its constituencies, and the desired rate of corporate growth and profitability.

In contrast to a board working with management, a board could serve as an adversary to management. The board, as a watchdog, could investigate management and report to the corporation's shareholders and its other constituencies whether top management has complied with the legal and social demands on corporate conduct.** But the adversary role runs against the widely perceived need to preserve a working, cooperative relationship between management and the board. A combative, investigatory board might bring a corporation to a standstill by stimulating divisiveness within the corporation, intimidating management, and inhibiting management's ability to initiate and implement programs. A far-reaching role for the board in corporate governance rests on directors having a sufficient flow of information and time to fulfill their expanded responsibilities. Will the new role(s) assumed by the board further aggravate information blockages? Directors, with limited time to devote to the corporation, probably cannot initiate or significantly shape corporate policies. A

* Statement of The Business Roundtable, The Role and Composition of the Board of Directors of the Large Publicly Owned Corporation, 33 Bus.Law. 2083, 2096–2103 (1978) sets forth the following four key board functions: providing for management and board succession, considering decisions and actions with a potential for major economic impact, considering social impacts, and establishing policies and procedures to assure law compliance. *See also* P. Drucker, Management: Tasks, Responsibilities, Practices 631 (1974); M. Eisenberg, The Structure of the Corporation: A Legal Analysis 164–65 (1976); N. Leech & R. Mundheim, The Outside Public Director (1976); ABA Corporate Director's Guidebook, 33 Bus.Law. 1595 (1978).

** R. Nader, M. Green, & J. Seligman, Taming of the Giant Corporation 120 (1976).

board which constantly raises questions and inputs into major decisions would be slow-moving and perhaps indecisive.

Even the modest and perhaps more realistic monitoring role poses troublesome questions. Will directors, in reviewing management and its decisions, seek to substitute their judgment for managements'? How involved would a board be in the corporate governance process—not in the day-to-day decisions, but in the setting of long-run or intermediary objectives, policies, and strategies? The line between an adversary posture and an examination of the corporation's "best interests" is admittedly imprecise. Monitoring may, in the eyes of some directors, imply an adversary posture vis-a-vis management thereby posing the problem of a slowdown in corporate decision-making as the board assays management's performance. The effective implementation of a monitoring function rests on the establishment of acceptable, specific, and measurable standards of management performance. Even if performance criteria can be set, the fast-moving pace of business may render such guidelines out-of-date, necessitating periodic revisions. Standards would be difficult to administer and measurements might require information not supplied by management. In addition, the directors would have to decide whom to hold responsible if the standards were not satisfied. Is the chief executive officer (or someone else), individually, or is top management as a group, collectively responsible? Or will the board conclude that the failure to achieve the targeted goals resulted from factors beyond the control of the top executives?

To create an "independent" board of directors with the resources and the will for critical judgments, a board prepared at least to monitor effectively the performance of management, three significant changes in corporate boards have occurred: increased percentage of outside directors; greater use of board committees, particularly audit and nominating committees; and better information flows for directors. Shifts in the composition and organization of the board may point to a greater degree of "independence" on the part of corporate boards.

b. Outside Directors

Corporate boards are increasingly composed of outsiders. Studies show that an increasing percentage of corporations prefer that a majority of board members be from the outside *, and that the number of directors with strong ties to management has decreased **. How-

* Korn/Ferry International, Board of Directors: Seventh Annual Study 3 (February, 1980). The actual results were: 73 percent of the companies surveyed preferred that the majority of board members should be from outside the company, as compared to 65 percent in the 1978 study. Also, 31 percent preferred that three-quarters or more should be from outside the company, as compared to 25 percent in the 1979 study.

** L. Smith, The Boardroom is Becoming a Different Scene, Fortune, May 8, 1978, at 150, 154; Small, The Evolving Role of the Director in Corporate Governance, 30 Hastings L.J. 1353 (1979).

ever, there are different views on how many outside directors should be on a board and on what constitutes an "independent" director. A definition of "insider" limited to any person presently employed by the corporation, would make "outsider" include former or retired executives of the corporation in question and individuals having a business or professional relationship with the corporation, such as partners in the corporation's outside law firms, executives of the commercial banks or investment firms which serve the corporation, or corporate suppliers and customers. Such nominal "outsiders" are economically dependent on the corporation and may be no less independent than employees of the corporation. The SEC has recently required detailed information with respect to board composition which presents a profile of the current makeup of boards of directors. An average of 35 percent of the boards of all companies were directors employed by the company or an affiliate, and an additional 29.4 percent were in a position that required disclosure under Item 6(b) of Regulation 14A*. So even though an average of 65 percent of the members of boards consisted of non-management directors, nearly half of those directors were still in a relationship with the company that could impair their ability to exercise truly independent judgment. Large corporations tended to have fewer employees and persons with Item 6(b) relationships on the board, but the overall average of totally independent directors is still lower than many commentators consider desirable.

Even if the outside directors are technically independent of the corporation, in terms of non-affiliation, a "mind set" in the form of a corporate orientation may exist on the part of many of the new directors. Outsiders who themselves are current or former chief executive officers or professionals (with some exceptions) who deal principally with corporate clients, tend, in most instances, to identify with and support management interests and viewpoints; outsiders remain almost instinctively pro-management. Outside directors, even if nominally independent of past or present ties with the corporation, generally comprise part of the "corporate club." Senior corporate officers or professionals who comprise the corporate retinue are sympathetic to pressures and uncertainties that confront chief executive officers; they empathize with the difficulties facing a chief executive officer.

Several additional practical impediments to "independence" may surface. Corporate-oriented types generally will be governed by the protocol of the club which restrains a director from trespassing on the chief executive officer's turf. Many independent directors presently serve as chief executive officers in their own right, and must face their own boards. These individuals simply do not want to cre-

* Securities and Exchange Commission, Division of Corporate Finance, Staff Report on Corporate Accountability, F6 (1980). The SEC proxy rules now require corporations to disclose significant relationships of corporate directors with the company, including employment, material business dealings, professional and investment banking relationships. Item 6 (b) to Schedule 14A.

ate activist precedents for their boards. The composition of a re-structured board in terms of the background of the new directors may, therefore, render the outsiders less effective in performing the monitoring or checking functions.

In redirecting the search for "independent directors" it may be advisable to select directors from among individuals who are not part of the corporate club. Non-establishment directors would offer many benefits. Specifically, they likely would broaden the perspective of management by providing corporate executives, who all too often are isolated, with a better understanding of the feelings and attitudes of the corporation's various constituencies—its public. These individuals would provide a window onto the world in which the corporation functions as well as serving as window for more groups into the corporation and bringing a different perspective to bear on board decisions.

But mandating the selection of non-establishment individuals raises serious difficulties. Well-meaning individuals may lack the requisite expertise and experience to make corporate decisions. They may be unaware of a corporation's problems and the dynamics of board meetings. These individuals may offer little constructive input or may be co-opted into the existing corporate apparatus, its goals and functions. From a business viewpoint, non-establishment directors may be perceived of as an obstructive, disruptive force among board members and between the board and management. Will the interests of these individuals conflict with those of the corporation? Suspicions exist that non-club members would use information acquired through service on a board in a manner hostile to the best interest of the corporation, for example, by chanelling information for litigation purposes to public agencies, public interest groups, or corporate shareholders. Even if guidelines could be established for secrecy and the release of information by directors, an adverse relationship among board members would likely reduce board effectiveness. Management would filter less information to a board or take board action through an executive committee which would not include the non-members of the "corporate club." Management could also informally converse with selected directors on matters requiring board evaluation or advice. The amount of business that would come before a board, even on a formal level, would be reduced and board discussions would become less candid. Meetings would be empty rituals. The board's monitoring function would likely be short-circuited and management might be freer from evaluation by the board even with respect to the traditional corporate goals of long-term profit maximization in the interest of the shareholders.

c. **Constituency Directors**

MANNING, A TAXONOMY OF CORPORATE LAW REFORM, IN COMMENTARIES ON CORPORATE STRUCTURE AND GOVERNANCE 120–22 (D. Schwartz, ed., 1979).

A small group of critics of the American corporation * * * takes as an immutable axiom that for all institutions and for all time, the only institutional decisions that are legitimate are those that are arrived at on the basis of a consensus of all persons who have an interest in, or are affected by, the outcome. Thus, in their view, a board of directors of a corporation should not be allowed to decide to close a plant, since many other people will be affected by that decision. The solution * * * under the bland name "co-determination" is that boards of directors should be required by law to include representatives of labor unions. It is pointed out that a variant of this feature has been introduced in Germany * * *.

One immediate question raised by this proposal relates to its internal philosophic consistency. If one were truly serious about including on a board of directors representatives of the various parties who have an economic interest in the enterprise, then it would include not only representatives of shareholders and employees but also representatives of lenders, suppliers, customers, contractors, lessors (and lessees), municipalities, states, school districts, charities, the U.S. Treasury, etc., all of which have a stake in the enterprise's income stream. Would all these groups be enthusiastic to see their interests guarded by labor union representatives?

* * *

But the split-board concept is faulty at a more fundamental level. Must special-interest participationism be accepted as a universal axiom to be applied unthinkingly to every form of organized human behavior? Aside from the question of its wide application to other institutions (armies, churches, schools, ship crews, courts, etc.), the core of the question as addressed to commercial enterprises is whether one recognizes and accepts that the commercial corporation—whether small or large—should be first and foremost an organization designed to operate efficiently to produce goods and services for the society, rather than a political organization designed to maximize political expression. To the degree that the managerial and decision-making structure of the incorporated enterprise is altered to resemble a New England town meeting, a Quaker consensus session, an Italian Parliament, or a two-party power negotiation, the capacity of the enterprise to carry out its basic economic function cannot fail to be impeded.

* * *

Seen from [the perspective of economic efficiency], the role of common shareholders as the ultimate constituency of the corporation makes a great deal of sense. Unlike any of the other constituents who tap the income stream of the enterprise—workers, creditors, tax collectors, suppliers, etc.—the common shareholder is playing for the entrepreneurial margin and only the entrepreneurial margin. Nothing so clears the mind and sharpens his taste for efficiency as the recognition that everyone else gets paid ahead of him and that he gets nothing unless there is something left over. No other constituency of the enterprise has the same incentive to achieve a high level of efficiency for the enterprise as a whole, since the economic interest of each other constituency is narrower or has a limiting cap on it or runs directly counter to the interest of the aggregate enterprise's cost control. Shareholders—particularly the professional sharp-eyed investors with a nervous focus on the bottom line—perform a vital function for the enterprise and for the efficiency of the economy as a whole.

It is the responsibility of the board of directors and management of an enterprise, and it is to the special economic interest of the common shareholders, to attend to the operating efficiency of the enterprise as a whole. No other group has that perspective of the aggregate. To lodge within the board of directors a cell whose commitment is to a single constituency of the enterprise—whether to employees, lenders, consumers, or any other group—rather than to the interest of the aggregate enterprise is a certain way to dilute and in time to destroy the feature of the corporate form that, more than any other, has accounted for its extraordinary economic success.

A movement for employee representation in corporate governance has developed in Western Europe. In West Germany, for example, the corporate legal system is based on a two-tier board structure consisting of an executive board composed of the firm's top executives, which manages the corporation, and a supervisory board, from which members of the executive board are excluded, which selects corporate managers.* In industrial companies with 2000 or more employees, the employees elect one-half of the members of the supervisory board. The shareholders elect the other half. In case of a deadlock, the chairman of the board, elected by the shareholder members of the board, casts an additional vote. The executive board and the supervisory board meet separately. The executive board resolves business matters outside the presence of less informed outsiders. The supervisory board can discuss the performance of the corporate managers

* For a recent survey *see*, Gruson and Meillicke, The New Co-Determination Law in Germany, 32 Bus.Law. 571 (1971). *See also*, Schoenbaum and Lieser, Reform of the Structure of the American Corporation: The "Two-Tier" Board Model, 62 Ky.L.J. 91, 110–112, 115–116, 121–129, (1973); Vagts, Reforming the "Modern" Corporation: Perspectives from the German, 80 Harv.L.Rev. 23, 68–78 (1966).

without the embarrassment of the presence of corporate management.

SOLOMON, TOWARD A FEDERAL POLICY ON WORK: RESTRUCTURING THE GOVERNANCE OF CORPORATIONS

43 Geo.Wash.L.Rev. 1263, 1320–21 (1975).

The conduct of German enterprise has not been greatly affected by the codetermination system. Rarely do differences exist between the management board and the supervisory board or between members of the supervisory board. A custom has arisen whereby the management board informally solicits the opinion of the supervisory board prior to formal decision-making. Informal discussions also take place on the supervisory board level. Through these informal solicitations of views, the supervisory board may influence decision-making by the managerial board. Management retains the initiative, possesses the greater technical expertise, and controls the flow of information to the supervisory board. These factors impede the independence of the supervisory board in overseeing and evaluating management. The labor representatives have repeatedly placed plant interests ahead of those of consumers, workers, and shareholders. Few efforts have been undertaken with respect to job redesign. Price increases, especially if coupled with wage or fringe benefit gains, have not been opposed by the labor members of the supervisory board. In sum, the so-called worker representatives, who usually speak for national labor unions instead of the employees of the firm, have served as means to facilitate managerial decision-making. The rank-and-file employees have remained indifferent to the participatory structure.

Even if it has not greatly changed worker participation in management, however, the codetermination system has great potential for reducing labor-management tensions and increasing cooperation of employees and management. Management can also evidence a greater concern for employee interest. At the very least, worker morale and job satisfaction have improved slightly. These advantages accrue from a better communications and information interchange, not from the government-mandated, formal worker involvement in a two-tier structure.

If constituency representation allows new voices to call attention to social factors in corporate decision-making, what groups, in addition to employees, should be represented? Other possible groups include suppliers, customers, both immediate and ultimate, and cohabitants, that is, the people affected by a corporation's actions. If the constituencies can be designated, how many representatives on the board would each constituency have and how will the constituencies select their representatives? What weight would be given to the interests of the various constituencies when they conflict with each other or with the interests of the shareholders? How will the interests of the various constituency groups be adjusted within the corporation? Will directors responsible to different interests create a divisive, adversary atmosphere? Will the board become a political organ working out conflicts through shifting alliance among directors representing different interests? The tug-of-war among competing groups may damage the board's collegiality and result in a board's inability to reach timely decisions. Consider the following assessment of "public interest" directors.

CONARD, REFLECTIONS ON PUBLIC INTEREST DIRECTORS

75 Mich.L.Rev. 941, 959–960 (1977).

Putting together the pieces of the puzzle, we can draw some plausible conclusions about various kinds of public interest directors.

Environmental interest directors are the least likely to be useful, even to environmentalists. Since defenders of the environment have few interests in common with representatives of investors, employees, customers, or consumers, they have little chance of making effective alliances with other constituencies. Having no constituency within the ambit of corporate operations, they have nothing to trade off. Although they might serve as gadflies, their energies would be more productively spent in the political arena, where their influence over voters gives them a position of greater strength. Their presence on corporate boards may even be detrimental to the environmental cause, for such presence might nourish the supposition that environmental interests are fairly weighed inside the corporation, which can never be true because of the weight of the interests arrayed against them.

Consumer interest directors have a slightly better chance of operating effectively, because the other corporate constituencies—investors, employees, and customers—have a lively interest in consumer favor. But there are two obstacles for which no solutions have been suggested. One is the difficulty of finding the consumers and persuading them to concern themselves with their representation. The other is that if the consumers speak their minds, their minds may be devoid of any real concern for the prosperity and continuity of the enterprise. The mind of the consumer is usually on the marketplace where he pays the price for the product. Consumer interests are likely to be better served by improving their access to information, suppressing restraints on competition, and invoking criminal laws against purveyors of dangerous or fraudulent products.

On the other hand, customer-interest directors and employee-interest directors seem to be structurally practicable. In the giant enterprises that are envisioned in all discussions of public interest directors, it will usually be possible to identify and mobilize the constituencies involved. Both customers and employees have an interest in the long-term welfare of the enterprise even greater than that of many shareholders, who can switch their loyalties as fast as they can dial Merrill Lynch. Employees and customers are much less likely than investors to display the apathy toward corporate affairs that has turned shareholders' meetings into empty charades.

The danger in a system of governance shared by the representatives of employees, customers and investors is not so much that it would not work as that it would work too well. The normal impulse of investors to hold down wage costs and maximize sales might give way to conspiracies to provide higher wages, more restricted outlets, and higher profits, all at the expense of consumers. But this outcome seems no more likely to take place when employees and customers are represented in governance than when they are not. If employees and customers were represented, the former would have a chance to influence marketing in a direction that would maximize employment, and the latter would have an opportunity to influence wage policy in the direction of minimizing prices. The tendency of these constituencies to balance one another would depend in large part on the competitiveness of the industry. Representation of employees and customers might make rigorous competition even more essential to public welfare than it is today.

d. "Public" Directors

Rather than directors who represent various constituencies, should "public directors" * be appointed who will represent, at least in theory, the community at large? Who will select such directors? A government agency, a legislative body, a vote by means of the electoral process, or a corporate board? Selection by a federal agency would increase governmental intrusion in the private sector and would centralize political power. Concern exists about the politicalization of the process, that is, the appointments would likely be used

* C. Stone, Where the Law Ends: The Social Control of Corporate Behavior 158–173 (1975) advocates that at least 10% of a company's general public directors would represent the public interest and would be charged with specific duties, among other functions, of reminding the board of its legal and ethical concerns, reviewing the effectiveness of the corporation's internal information systems, and serving as a receptive audience for employees who seek to bring information to the board's attention. Stone also advocates special public directors to be appointed by a federal court or administrative agency, in cases of a demonstrated delinquency situation which arises when a corporation has repeatedly violated the law, or in cases where chronic, in-

dustry-wide problems exist. A special public director, who would have special qualifications for his or her task, for example, an environmental engineer in cases of environmental problems, would be charged with a narrowly focused mandate. A special public director would oversee the correction of the behavior and seek to prevent its recurrence. *Id.* at 179–181.

R. Nader, M. Green, and J. Seligman, Taming the Giant Corporation 125 (1976) would require that each director have responsibility for a particular area of social concern with an identifiable constituency, such as environmental or consumer protection.

for political patronage and the type of person selected may lack experience. An inexperienced public director would encounter difficulty in exercising or imposing any degree of critical judgment. The prospect of appointments for a short term, coupled with part-time service and the likelihood of a high turnover of public directors minimizes the opportunity to acquire, through service on a board, the requisite experience and expertise. Absent an explicit delineation of functions and powers, public directors probably will not automatically take upon themselves a special responsibility to the public. Public directors may also face the hostility of their fellow directors thereby lessening their effectiveness. Government-appointed public directors serving on the board of the Union Pacific Railroad in the nineteenth century claimed that "they were treated as spies and antagonists and kept in the dark about many things." *   In sum, one commentator has concluded:

> [W]e have some limited American experience in the case of the Union Pacific Railroad, the Illinois Central Railroad and the Prudential Insurance Company. I might add that none of these institutions have shown any change whatsoever, as a result of the unusual feature of its board. Blumberg, The Role of the Corporation In Society Today, 31 Bus.Law. 1403, 1406 (1976).

The difficulties of using non-corporate club members as corporate directors led proponents of board restructuring, such as Prof. Christopher Stone, to recommend that "public directors," even if selected by a governmental commission, should be approved by a majority of the board of the involved corporation and be removable by the corporation without cause by a unanimous vote of the board, or for cause by a two-thirds vote of the board. The need for public directors to develop a working relationship with other members of the board forms the basis for the requirement of a board veto. As Stone states, "[I]f the public director and his staff are to succeed, the arrangement will have to be one that suggests to the other directors (and, through them, to the corporate organization) that their particular public director is there because they have approved his being there." C. Stone, Where the Law Ends: The Social Control of Corporate Behavior 159 (1976). In short, legitimacy and support from the board constitute a requisite for the effective functioning of directors. Participation by the corporation in the selection process, is, however, not without pitfalls. As Abraham Pomerantz, counsel for plaintiffs in corporate matters, acidly noted, "[I]f you [corporate management] are choosing * * * independent directors you are not going to choose anybody who is going to be too hard on you." Abraham Pomerantz, University of Pennsylvania Law School, Conference on Mutual Funds, 115 U.Pa.L.R. 662, 739 (1967) (statement with reference to non-affiliated mutual fund directors).

* Schwartz, Governmentally Appointed Directors in a Private Corporation—The Communications Satellite Act of 1962, 79 Harv.L.Rev. 350, 359 (1965).

If we settle for the board which strives to monitor management, delineation and analysis of qualifications for outside "independent" directors may be critical. A balance must be struck between: (1) the need to develop a working relationship among board members, on one hand, and the management and the board, on the other hand, and (2) a willingness on the part of directors to offer constructive criticism of the corporation and its management. Beyond the formal requisites of independence, a director should possess three paramount attributes. First, a director must be familiar with the management of complex organizations, at policy-making or management levels or both, including an understanding of business and finance, and be sensitive to the concerns of social policy. Corporations may also have a need for directors with expertise in specific areas. Second, individuals with integrity are needed who will be "polite skeptics." Lewis, Choosing and Using Outside Directors, Har.Bus.Rev., July-Aug. 1974, at 70, 72. A director must be able to raise tough, unwelcome questions without losing the respect of other board members and management. Third, a director must be willing to spend the time needed to do the job properly.

Even if revised criteria are delineated for "independent" directors, do enough qualified and willing candidates exist? Three groups are readily apparent: professionals, executives, and academics. Executives and professionals with the necessary degree of flexibility could make significant contributions based on their years of experience, but are unlikely to be independent of the corporate ethos. Academics are generally inexperienced in corporate affairs and as outsiders to the corporation might be thought untrustworthy or lacking in judgment. Active professionals, corporate executives or academics are probably too busy. A preponderance of retired or semi-retired executives or professionals on a board may upset the need for a balanced age distribution needed to insure continuity and vitality. Although generalizations are impossible, retired or semi-retired individuals may be just as much, if not more so, imbued with the corporate outlook as their active counterparts.

Two techniques exist to fill the void: professional directors (*see, e. g.,* W. Douglas, Democracy and Finance 52–55 (1940)) or full-time inside directors. Well-paid professional directors, who would be experienced in business, could serve on the boards of a limited number of non-competing corporations and be reasonably protected from dismissal during their terms. These seasoned business or professional individuals, who would have no current business interests, could achieve a high degree of knowledge of a company and become proficient in their responsibilities, including the exercise of analytical skills, the identification of problem areas, the raising of questions, and the taking on assignments to study problem areas. To prevent a dependency on or co-optation by management, or too great an identification with a corporation, it might be desirable to bar professional directors from serving consecutive terms in the same corporation.

Several problems exist. Professional directors might take their commissions too zealously and meddle in day-to-day operations of a corporation or incessantly call upon management to account for itself. Will talented individuals with relevant experience be drawn to service as a professional director and will the compensation be high enough even if the calling is attractive? Will professional directors bring a broad public perspective to the boardroom, particularly if they are dependent for a significant part of their income on fees earned from service on a few corporate boards?

e. Restructuring the Board

The foregoing materials examined proposals for changes in the board that stem largely from a "political" perspective. Another approach treats the board and its relationship to management as part of a bureaucratic structure and seeks to modify that structure to the end that the board might better perform the functions assigned to it. The change in board structure that has been most widely accepted, both in theory and in practice, is the division of the board into specialized committees charged with principal responsibility for certain key areas of corporate management. Such a system:*

— "compensates for the fact that outside directors can function only part-time,

— permits a better focus on particular problems and a more intensive exploration of those problems, and

— permits development and utilization of specialized knowledge and experience."

As a result of pressure by the SEC**, and stock exchange requirements***, the use of standing board committees, particularly the audit committee, has increased dramatically among large corporations. The current SEC proxy monitoring data show that 84.5 percent of the companies analyzed have audit committees†. As recently as 1973,

---

* Statement of the Business Roundtable, The Role and Composition of the Board of Directors of Large Publicly Held Corporations, 33 Bus.Law. 2083, 2109 (1978).

** SEC Rules require corporations to disclose in their proxy statements:

  1. whether the corporation has an audit, nominating or compensation committee,

  2. describe the functions performed by each such committee,

  3. the names of the committee members,

  4. and the number of committee meetings held by each such committee during the last fiscal year.

Item 6(d)(1) of Schedule 14A. CCH Fed. Sec.L.R. ¶ 24,037.

*** The New York Stock Exchange requires as a condition of continued listing that every domestic listed company establish and maintain an audit committee composed of one or more directors who are independent of management. Officers, employees and affiliates would not be qualified for audit committee membership, but a former officer may qualify if the board determines that he or she will exercise independent judgment and will materially assist in the function of the committee. New York Stock Exchange Company Manual, A–29.

† Securities and Exchange Commission, Division of Corporate Finance Staff Report on Corporate Accountability, F62 (1980). The breakdown is as follows: 99.4 percent of NYSE-listed companies;

fewer than 50 percent of the companies studied did. Today, even among the smallest companies studied ($0–$50 million in assets), 59.6 percent have an audit committee.

The audit committee, which monitors and investigates a corporation's financial transactions, is designed to prevent financial improprieties. The audit committee is a direct line between the corporation's independent accounting firm and the board of directors. It can perform a wide range of tasks under the rubric of its general responsibility for coordinating and evaluating internal and external audits. Audit committees recommend an auditing firm to the full board; confer with the auditors before, during, and after audit about its scope, procedures, problems, and results; and discuss with the corporation's internal auditors the nature and effectiveness of their work. Audit committees have also frequently investigated suspect payments and other financial irregularities.

The audit committees assist outside directors, management and the auditors. Through its independent access to financial information and its contact with the independent auditors, the audit committee can better inform the board of the company's financial activities and improve the board's supervision of management. The committee offers management an opportunity to review the company's financial reporting and controls. The audit committee gives the internal auditors direct access to the board. It shields the external auditors from undue management influence by providing a forum in which they can confer directly with board members about their accounting practices, the quality of internal accountability, or suspicious financial transactions.

The effectiveness of the contribution of the audit committee to corporate governance remains unclear.* Audit committees have on several notable occasions exposed an executive's malefactions. For example, the audit committee created by the SEC's consent decree with Firestone Tire & Rubber Co. reported that a former vice-chairman and chief financial officer of the corporation controlled but could not account for an approximately one million dollar company fund for illegal domestic political contributions. At Gulf Oil a special "ad hoc" audit committee of two outside directors and a nondirector attorney chronicled fourteen years of clandestine and illegal expenditures in the United States and abroad. Partly as a result of this report, the board of directors ousted the chairman and three senior executives.

Yet, audit committees have not always functioned as effectively. Audit committees at Gulf Oil and Lockheed failed to discover illegal uses of corporate funds. At Lockheed, members of the audit committee inquired about commissions paid to foreign agents but evidently

79.5 percent of AMEX-listed companies; and 75.3 percent of NASDAQ-companies.

* See Greene and Falk, The Audit Committee—A Measured Contribution to Corporate Governance: A Realistic Appraisal of Its Objectives and Functions, 34 Bus.Law. 1229, 1238–1246 (1979).

were satisfied with management's assurance that the payments were legal. The failures at Gulf and Lockheed may be attributable to the fact that the outside directors were personal friends of top management. Nevertheless, management can probably hide fraud from an audit committee if it wants to. Not only has the sophistication of misfeasance reached new heights, but it is difficult for audit committee members to remain alert to the rare but flagrant situations in which they are needed. At best, an active, independent audit committee composed of seasoned, knowledgeable business executives may lessen opportunities for improprieties. The mere presence of an audit committee may deter questionable activities by management. But the efficacy of the deterrence may be difficult, if not impossible, to measure.

The role of audit committees, and other committees as well, is still somewhat undefined. This, as much as anything else, may account for failures to discover improprieties. The proposed (but unenacted) "Protection of Shareholders' Rights Act of 1980" (S. 2567, 96th Cong., 2d Sess. (1980)) set forth a detailed list of audit committee responsibilities that would be required of all larger companies. The current SEC proxy monitoring data indicate that these functions are being carried out, at least in part, by many audit committees; however, there are other companies where the committee review is less complete.

The bill provided:

(b) It shall be the function of the audit committee, in addition to any other functions agreed to by the board of directors, to

   (1) review the arrangements and scope of the independent audit examination;

   (2) review, upon completion of the audit, the following items with the principal firm of independent auditors engaged by the affected corporation:

      (A) any report of opinion proposed to be rendered in connection with the audit;

      (B) the extent to which the resources of the affected corporation were and should be utilized to minimize the time spent by the independent auditors;

      (C) any significant transactions detected during the audit which were unrecorded, unauthorized, or not adequately supported;

      (D) any material change in the affected corporation's accounting principles;

      (E) all significant adjustments proposed by the auditor;

      (F) the scope of the auditor's examination; and

(G) any recommendations which the independent auditors may have with respect to improving internal accounting controls and choice of accounting principles;

(3) investigate and make recommendations concerning the cooperation which the independent auditors received from officers and employees of the affected corporation during the conduct of the audit;

(4) subject to the approval of a majority of the outstanding shares of the affected corporation, hire and dismiss the independent auditors and determine the compensation which they shall be paid;

(5) inquire of appropriate company personnel and the independent auditors as to any instances of deviations from the affected corporation's established codes of conduct and periodically review such policies;

(6) meet with the affected corporation's chief financial officer and other appropriate personnel at least twice a year to review and discuss with them the general policies and procedures utilized or proposed to be utilized by the affected corporation with respect to internal accounting controls, including the internal audit function;

(7) direct and supervise an investigation into any matters brought to its attention within the scope of its duties;

(8) review executive perquisites;

(9) report on the committee's activities in the annual report to shareholders; and

(10) review, either as a committee of the whole or by a designated member, all releases and other information to be disseminated by the affected corporation to the press media, the public, or its shareholders which concern disclosures of financial condition and results of operation, or forecasts of such information, of the affected corporation and its subsidiaries.

Where the audit committee functions in a reasonably thorough manner, the non-committee members of the board of directors can be expected to rely on the recommendations and information provided by that committee. This in itself would suggest that there should be emphasis on establishing proper audit committee procedures. *See,* for example, MBCA § 35. *See also* Report of the Committee on Corporate Laws: Changes in the Model Business Corporation Act, 30 Bus.Law. 501, 507 (1975).

Another interesting proposal regarding the restructuring of the board—one that has not, however, met with wide acceptance—is described in the following excerpt.

COFFEE, BEYOND THE SHUT–EYED SENTRY: TOWARD A THEORETICAL VIEW OF CORPORATE MISCONDUCT AND AN EFFECTIVE LEGAL RESPONSE

63 Va.L.Rev. 1099, 1148–50 (1977).

* * * [A]s long as the board's manpower is limited, as in the present structure, it cannot both engage in strategic planning and simultaneously monitor internal and external problems with any real effectiveness. This, however, is the same problem of limited management capacity that confronted the corporation earlier in this century, and that was resolved successfully by decentralization. The unitary corporate structure gave way to the multidivisional form * * *. [Recall Graham v. Allis Chalmers, Chapter 14.] In effect, to solve a problem of information overload analogous to that now faced by the board, the chief executive officer surrendered his day to day control over operational matters and allocated this authority to several mini-chief executives, positioned at the apexes of their respective autonomous divisions.

If we wish to institutionalize a stronger corporate superego, a similar strategy of decentralization seems in order: the board's monitoring function might be decentralized by creating "mini-boards" that would correspond with these same divisional chief executives. Just as the corporation's "ego" was divisionalized several decades ago, so might be its "superego" today. This suggested satellite board structure would involve the introduction of a miniature board of directors at the apex of each division, chiefly to serve as antennae for the central board. In theory, such a change would produce the same reduction in organizational distance between operational levels and the board superego as would "flattening" the entire structure. Moreover, it could do so without creating an information overload on the central board. Such mini-boards might be staffed by independent "outsiders" and chaired by members of the central board, thus creating a direct link between them and the central board. In contrast to a system under which committees of the central board review activities in specialized areas, the mini-board approach would neither rely on "inside" corporate officials, who are subject to conflicting pressures, nor further overwhelm the already heavily burdened "outside" director. Rather, the board would be in effect replicating itself. In so doing, the board would be reducing its own "span of control," thereby gaining a heightened monitoring capacity. It also would be gaining a second information net, paralleling the formal channels of communication already in existence, which would provide the board with a potential means of checking the degree of distortion in the information reaching it through the normal channels. Additionally, such mini-boards might serve as an apprenticeship or proving ground for future outside directors. Finally, the additional expense created by such a system would not be too costly for a large public corporation.

———

One recent experiment in the restructuring of corporate boards grew out of the revelations in the mid-1970's of the payment of bribes by a large number of U.S. corporations. The settlements of several of the numerous lawsuits—some brought by shareholders and some by the Securities and Exchange Commission—growing out of those revelations involved agreements by the corporate defendants to undertake certain management reforms. One of the most dramatic of those settlements involved the Northrop Corporation. The following excerpt describes the results.

SOLOMON, RESTRUCTURING THE CORPORATE BOARD OF DIRECTORS: FOND HOPE—FAINT PROMISE

76 Mich.L.Rev. 581, 594–97 (1978).

* * * The settlement required the company to elect four new outside directors as well as to amend the certificate of incorporation by adopting a provision which increased the size of the board and assured that outsiders would comprise a majority of it. Candidates for the new directorships were to be selected by the existing board subject only to the court's determination that the candidates met the settlement's vague command that they have "experience, independence, integrity and ability to make significant contributions as directors of Northrop and to fulfill the special responsibilities of New Directors."

The settlement also reconstituted the Board's executive, audit, and nominating committees. The executive committee was directed to report on Northrop's relationships with its emissaries and consultants at home and abroad and to recommend reforms in the company's organization which would prevent future wrongdoing. To insure that the committee would distance itself from management during the inquiry, the settlement provided that for a specified time five of the six committee members would be outside directors and that three of these, including the chairman, would be new outside directors. The settlement further provided that the audit and nominating committees would permanently consist entirely of outside directors.

* * *

The private [settlement] at Northrop * * * gave the plaintiffs a voice in the selection of new directors. The Northrop plaintiffs suggested ten candidates who, the plaintiffs believed, would be aggressively independent and acceptable to Northrop. The undertaking required the company to interview and consider these candidates as it did other candidates. The selection of candidates was entrusted to Northrop's nominating committee, subject to the court's supervision.

This committee, which was composed of the six outside directors then on Northrop's board, considered candidates of its own choice as well as plaintiffs' and announced its intention to nominate the candidates most likely to perform significant directorial services and best able to fulfill the special responsibilities of the new directors.

The selection was a process of "horse trading" in which each side possessed a veto power. According to one of the plaintiffs' lawyers, Northrop understood (without ever having been explicitly told) that if the corporation rejected plaintiffs' nominees out of hand, the plaintiffs would vigorously attack the nominees in open court. Although each side placed two candidates on the final slate of four, it is questionable whether this process produced different directors than the corporation would have chosen on its own. Both of the plaintiffs' nominees were members of the corporate club. One, William Balhaus, was in fact a former executive and director of Northrop, although since he had been a rival of Jones [the president of Northrop] he might have been expected to keep a close eye on Northrop's management. Nevertheless, Northrop regarded Balhaus, the president of Beckman Industries, Inc., who had a board of directors of his own to deal with, to be "safe." One of Northrop's lawyers was able to say that "the plaintiff nominated [selected] many of the same people as the corporation would have."

* * *

4. COUNSEL

American Bar Association, Model Rules of Professional Conduct (Proposed Final Draft, May 30, 1981).

Reread *Rule 1.13 Organization as the Client* (See Chapter 12, Section G).

————

PALMIERI, LAWYERS ARE THE KEY TO CORPORATE GOVERNANCE, IN COMMENTARIES ON CORPORATE STRUCTURE AND GOVERNANCE 365, 367–68 (D. Schwartz, ed., 1979).

* * * [Lawyers] are the key to corporate governance. * * *

* * *

Based on my own experience with corporate disasters, in almost every case you come out of the records asking yourself, "Where were the lawyers on this problem?" They were in the boardroom. They were there month after month as the disaster developed. I cite you the classic example of the Penn Central, where a fair share of the nation's business elite, whose net worth collectively outstripped that of the company, sat around the table for two years while that company lurched steadily toward the biggest bankruptcy in history. The reason for such disasters is that lawyers are not doing their job.

Part of the reason for this failure is that lawyers may not be able to do it in the management relationship that they have, either as outside counsel or as corporate general counsel employed by the company.

How do you solve that problem? Well, the answer seems to me to be that the prime function of an independent director is to assure that corporate counsel relates to the independent directors and to the board as a client. Now that may seem shocking. The code of professional responsibility, after all, prescribes that the client is the company. In fact, lawyers, and corporate lawyers in particular, tend to function as the chief executives' lawyers; and that is true for obvious reasons. They develop close personal relationships and take their directions from the CEO. Furthermore, it is absolutely essential that the chief executive be able to enjoy a relationship of confidence with the company's general counsel. At the same time I believe that it is absolutely essential that counsel be able to relate to the board, particularly the independent directors, as the client. How can this be done?

CUTLER, REMARKS, IN COMMENTARIES ON CORPORATE STRUCTURE AND GOVERNANCE
374 (D. Schwartz, ed., 1979).

*   *   *   There are three solutions to [the] problem   *   *   *.

Another, that has actually been employed, is to permit various committees of the board, like the audit committee, to have their own outside counsel. Ford Motor Company's audit committee has its own outside counsel. The General Motors' compensation committee has its own outside counsel. And in both of those cases it works.

But the third way, and one which could be done and I think some companies are beginning to do, is to have a committee of the board, either the audit committee or some other committee, conduct a legal audit. And periodically, just as the audit committee does, such a committee meet with inside counsel and outside counsel out of the presence of the rest of the management.

C.   SOME PROCEDURAL MECHANISMS

1.   IMPROVING INFORMATION FLOW

It is clear, as several of the preceding excerpts have highlighted, that for any mechanism of governance to function effectively, there must be an adequate flow of information to the principal decision makers. In recent years there has been increasing attention to efforts to improve information flow, both within and without the corporation. In particular, there have been a number of efforts, many of which have produced practical results, to provide a greater flow of information to directors so that the board may perform a more active role in the corporate governance structure. Some of the corporate failures in the past are attributable, at least in part, to the fact that the directors were unaware of serious problems until it was too late to do anything. The ignorance of the board of directors of the Penn Central is perhaps an extreme example, but it suggests management's unwillingness to keep the directors informed about even massive problems, as well as the board's lack of interest in the affairs of the corporation. According to an SEC staff study,

> Pennsylvania Railroad and New York Central directors were accustomed to a generally inactive role in company affairs. They never changed their view of their role. Both before and after the merger [on February 1, 1968] they relied on oral descriptions of company affairs. They failed to perceive the complexities of the merger or the fact that appropriate groundwork and planning had not been done. After the merger they claim to have been unaware of the magnitude of the fundamental operational problems or the critical financial situation until near the end. [The Penn Central Co. went into bankruptcy on June 21, 1970.] They did not receive or request written budgets or cash flow information which were essential to understanding the condition of the company or the performance of management. Only late in 1969 did they begin requesting such information and even then it was not made available in a form that was meaningful or useful. SEC Staff Study of the Financial Collapse of the Penn Central Co.—Summary [1972–73 Transfer Binder] Fed.Sec.L.Rept. (CCH) ¶ 78,931 at 82, 2 (August 3, 1972).

Indeed, a study of 474 industrial corporations showed that in 1970 only 17.2 percent sent directors manufacturing data prior to a meeting, only 21.3 percent sent marketing data, only 5.7 percent sent the agenda, and 11 percent failed to send any information at all. Securities and Exchange Commission, Division of Corporate Finance, Staff Report on Corporate Accountability, F135 (1980), citing Heidrick and Struggles, Inc., Profile of the Board of Directors 5 (1971). However, by 1976 the amount of information made available to the directors had increased substantially. In the same group of industrial corporations, 23.3 percent sent manufacturing data, 28.7 percent sent marketing data, 75.7 percent an agenda, and only 2.9 percent sent nothing. *Id.*, citing Heidrick and Struggles, Inc., The Changing Board: Profile of the Board of Directors 11 (1977). Audit committees now also provide information to directors serving on them through meetings with a corporation's auditors and internal auditing staff. This information eventually filters up to the entire board.

The increased flow of information poses a number of questions. Does the information furnished provide relevant facts and figures and present the major policy viewpoints and options, yet treat the line between skimpiness and overpowering detail? Should the outside directors act on the information provided by top management, which presumably screens out and arranges the data to present an optimistic picture of the corporation and its management thereby retaining, in large measure, management's ultimate power over the decision-making process? Or should the directors have unrestricted or at least a greater degree of access to information throughout the corporation? Chief executive officers are reluctant to accord directors direct contact, for example with subordinate officers, for fear of undercutting management's chain of command. Is the extent of danger overrated, particularly if top executives explain the process which, in turn, is channeled through an institutional mechanism, such as regular visits or informal contacts by directors with lower echelon executives, and is designed to focus on specific inquiries, such as corporate issues within the expertise of the subordinate executives?

COFFEE, BEYOND THE SHUT–EYED SENTRY: TOWARD A THEORETICAL VIEW OF CORPORATE MISCONDUCT AND AN EFFECTIVE LEGAL RESPONSE

63 Va.L.Rev. 1099, 1131–39 (1977).

Adverse information, particularly information relating to contingent liabilities, appears not to be reaching the board until a crisis has become unavoidable. * * *

A variety of reasons appear to share responsibility for these information blockages: (a) a shared feeling on the part of subordinate officials that they owe their loyalty chiefly to senior management and not to the board; (b) a belief that the board is interested only in "hard" quantitative information, such as capital costs, financial ratios, and expected rates of return; (c) a sense that "everybody knows anyway," coupled with the perception that the board would rather not be put on formal notice as to the ugly "facts of life" of doing business abroad; and (d) a "lack of congruence" between the interests of the corporation and the career aspirations of individual corporate officials. More simply, this last point means that what is good for General Motors is not necessarily good for its Assistant Vice President. If he fails to use sensitive payments, or if he discloses to his superiors any questionable practices he does use, he may appear less successful than his compatriots who hide such information from their superiors. To be sure, the tendency to report information selectively, emphasizing the positive while filtering out the negative, is characteristic of all bureaucratic organizations (whether the information relates to * * * environmental hazards of a major governmental project, or the illegal means by which a profitable contract has been secured). But distinguishing the corporate context is the comparative absence of any institutionalized mechanisms by which to penetrate and break down these information blockages. While armies have inspectors general, and governmental projects face the necessity of environmental impact studies, no currently enforced legal norm requires the corporation to internalize a means of forcing potentially adverse information to the attention of the board.

How serious is the need for a legal strategy tailored to these problems? To answer this question, we need to take a broader look.

E. *An Overview of Internal Corporate Decisionmaking*

[Coffee here refers to the electrical equipment conspiracy that gave rise to *Allis-Chalmers.*]

In the aftermath of that scandal, both congressional committees and commentators identified several common root causes within the structure of the participating corporations that had permitted the conspiracy to continue undetected for a substantial period. First, senior management had been unable to communicate to the operating levels of the corporation its concern about exposure to antitrust liabilities. Second, this failure of internal communications was compounded by a fixed belief on the part of subordinates aware of the formal corporate policy that senior management did not really mean what it said. Third, senior management was so isolated from those at operational levels as to be effectively unable to monitor or control closely conduct at operational levels.

The problem of management isolation from operations was in turn found to be the product of a series of factors, such as a decentralized corporate structure, a hierarchical command system that required orders and responses to travel along narrow linear channels of communication, and a technical orientation of those at operational levels that made them inattentive to both the signs and risks of illegality. One study of that conspiracy found that even when subordinates had sought to protest orders they considered questionable, they found themselves checked by the linear structure of authority, which effectively denied them any means by which to appeal. For example, one almost Kafkaesque ploy utilized to prevent an appeal by a subordinate was to have a person substantially above the level of his immediate superior ask him to engage in the questionable practice. The immediate superior would then be told not to supervise the activities of the subordinate in the given area. Thus, both the subordinate and the supervisor would be left in the dark regarding the level of authority from which the order had come, to whom an appeal might lie, and whether they would violate company policy by even discussing the matter between themselves. By in effect removing the subject employee from his normal organizational terrain, this stratagem effectively structured an information blockage into the corporate communication system. *   *   *

*   *   *   [T]he problem is hardly unique to the area of corporate misconduct. Recent SEC studies of such corporate collapses as Penn Central and Stirling Homex have found the boards to have been unaware of the impending disasters. While the SEC has cited these instances as evidence of inadequate diligence by the outside directors, others have identified a different pattern: the systematic censorship by those controlling the flow of information to the board of warning signals that might have alerted outside directors. Surveying a host of examples, Peter Drucker, the acknowledged dean of American theorists on management, has observed that the board "was always the last group to hear of trouble in the great business catastrophes of the century."

But why? An example * * * is the * * * insolvency of W.T. Grant Co., the giant retailer. A major cause of the collapse was Grant's lack of even rudimentary internal controls over inventory or credit. Those at lower echelons within the corporation exploited this lack of central control by deliberately contriving an upward flow of misinformation. As the final collapse approached, for example, the company's buying department appears actually to have increased its purchases of large capital goods items, where profit was least likely, in order to prevent cutbacks in its own staff. Similarly, individual store managers unrealistically extended credit to meet their own sales quotas. In some cases, vendors were even deliberately overpaid, subject to an oral agreement to treat the overpayment as a loan, so that store managers could manipulate their fourth quarter profits to show a rising trend at year's end by recalling these loans. Given the weakness of the internal controls, it should not be surprising that there also was evidence of suspicious payments resembling kickbacks. This pattern of conflict between the interests of the subunit and those of the firm equally characterizes corporations not on the brink of insolvency. Recently, the Washington Post uncovered a similar example, involving two wholly owned subsidiaries of U.S. Steel. Both of the subsidiaries have been actively lobbying with regard to proposed legislation, *but on opposite sides.*

Economists and other theorists have termed this type of organizational schizophrenia "subgoal pursuit." The theory is that given an opportunity to exercise discretion, managers at lower levels within a firm will tend to act not to maximize the firm's welfare, but rather the interests and autonomy of their own unit or division. Such behavior is virtually inevitable, organization theorists have found, because the subunit chief executive who fails to act as the zealous advocate of the interests of his own unit, even when those interests conflict with the firm's overall welfare, "is not apt to be viable for long." The captive of his constituency, he must act as the partisan representative of its interests or risk abandonment by his own subordinates. Thus, even at his still mild level of abstraction, the problem of information blockages ceases to be only a technical failure of communications or the consequence of careless inattention, but becomes instead part of a predictable and deliberate strategy rationally employed by lower echelons to protect their own interests from both senior management and the board alike.

* * *

Studying governmental bureaucracies in the 1960's, Gordon Tullock observed the phenomenon of "authority leakage." He described this as a progressive loss of control over subordinate units within the same bureaucracy as the organization expanded and the distance between such units and those at the agency's top became greater. Subsequently, another student of bureaucracies, Anthony Downs, formalized Tullock's perception into a general law, the "Law of Diminishing Control," which states: "The larger any organization becomes, the weaker is the control over its actions exercised by those at the top."

* * *

On the reverse side of the coin to the problem of "authority leakage" are the problems associated with the upward transmission of adverse information within the corporate hierarchy. To the extent that corporate communications are basically serial in nature, so that information is retransmitted from each hierarchical level to the next, the Theory of Cognitive Dissonance suggests one problem. That theory simply states the much-observed phenomenon that recipients of information unconsciously focus on and relay only the information that reinforces their preexisting attitudes, while filtering out conflicting information. To the extent that adverse information conflicts with the recipient's basic attitudes by showing failure, it is particularly subject to this unconscious filtering.

Even absent the distorting impact of preexisting attitudes on information flow, experimental evidence suggests that serial relay of information results in significant information loss. Information theorists have formulated the rule that each additional relay in a communications system halves the message while doubling the "noise." Significantly, some corporations have today between twelve and fifteen hierarchical levels between the first-line supervisor and the company president, suggesting that much "noise" and only a very diluted message will reach the top through regular lines of communication.

* * *

2. THE CRIMINAL LAW

Perhaps the oldest, and certainly the most straightforward, reaction to society to aberrant behavior is to make it a crime. The use of the criminal law to regulate corporate conduct, however, has certain difficulties. Corporations cannot be imprisoned and statutory fines may be inadequate to deter undesirable conduct when practiced by corporations. This had led to a search for other means to address the problem. In United States v. Atlantic Richfield Co., 465 F.2d 58 (7th Cir. 1972), a corporation was found guilty of discharging refuse into the Chicago Sanitary and Ship Canal, in violation of an 1899 law. Rather than impose the maximum statutory fine of $2,500, the court placed the corporation on probation for a period of 6 months and required the corporation to set up a program for handling oil spillage. The corporation objected to the idea of probation and to the terms of the probation. The court of appeals found that the trial judge had the right to suspend the fine and to place the corporation on probation, although it held that the terms of probation were not addressed to the purpose of rehabilitation, and were unreasonable. The court did not address the question of whether probation could be imposed on a defendant that preferred to pay the penalty provided by the law.

Another problem with applying criminal statutes to corporations is that the corporation acts only through live individuals. Therefore, to make deterrence believable, some feel that penalties must be assessed against individuals rather than on the fictional entity. The bureaucratic nature of corporate action, however, often obscures actual responsibility. The existence of the corporate machinery makes it difficult to impose sanctions on senior managers whose "crime" may be their ignorance of corporate wrongdoing, and, hence, their failure to prevent it. In United States v. Park, 421 U.S. 658, 95 S.Ct. 1903, 44 L.Ed.2d 489 (1975), the Supreme Court sustained the conviction of the president of a retail food chain because of impurities in the food resulting from rodent infestation in one of its warehouses. It is clear that the president of the company had no personal knowledge of warehouse conditions and that functional responsibility for such matters had been delegated to others. But the Court said his guilt could be based on his relationship to the situation. He had a positive duty to seek out and remedy violations—a requirement the Court acknowledged was demanding and "perhaps onerous". 421 U.S. at 672. The very harshness of the result makes it unusual to find remote actors in the corporation held criminally responsible for what amounts to their negligence. *See generally*, Corporate Crime: Regulating Corporate Behavior Through Criminal Sanctions, 92 Harv.L.Rev. 1227 (1979).

COFFEE, CORPORATE CRIME AND PUNISHMENT: A NON–CHICAGO VIEW OF THE ECONOMICS OF CRIMINAL SANCTIONS

17 Am.Crim.L.Rev. 419, 456–61 (1980).

A distinctive feature of organizational crime is that it is committed by agents for the primary benefit of a principal. Axiomatically, although the corporation must act through its agents, the profit accrues primarily to the firm and its owners. Thus, the cost of deterring the agent may be less than that of deterring the firm. Not only will the organization incur greater gain from crime than will its agents, but, if there exists no monetary equivalent to a harsh prison sentence, then the organization also faces a lesser deterrent threat.

In terms of a cost-effective strategy, therefore, it seems strange that the Free Market economists agree that the organization should be the cost bearer. It may be revealing that they give substantially different reasons why this should be so. Elzinga and Breit use as their starting point the persistent unwillingness of the federal courts to impose imprisonment on antitrust violators, even in blatant cases of price fixing. They noted that, as of 1976, no such organizational offender appeared to have ever served as much as a year in prison. This pattern has continued even though the Antitrust Division now regularly submits a sentencing memorandum recommending imprisonment. * * *

Professor Posner * * * argues that because the firm is the decision-maker, it is the firm's utility function, not the individual's, that should be altered. From this perspective, the individual is little more than an anonymous cog within the firm, and if he misbehaves in a manner adverse to the firm, the firm will discipline or fire him.

There are several counter-arguments to this analysis. First, as already noted, it may be less expensive to punish the individual rather than the organization, because the individual's expected benefit is lower. Second, because the corporation is better positioned than the individual to pass along the cost in the form of higher prices, it will be less deterred. Attempts by the state to impose higher penalties against the corporation may also require higher transaction costs, because the corporate defendant may be expected to expend more resources resisting conviction. In contrast, the transaction costs associated with mounting a legal defense are far more significant to the individual defendant, who accordingly has a greater incentive to plea-bargain. Thus, it may be more cost efficient to focus on the individual decision-maker.

Third, there is little evidence that fines in fact trigger any internal disciplinary mechanism within the firm, even if they should do so in theory. In the electrical equipment price fixing conspiracy of the late 1950's, the convicted defendants were eventually obliged to settle civil actions by paying approximately $600 million to the private plaintiffs. Despite criminal trials, congressional investigations, derivative suits, and research by a legion of journalists, no credible evidence was uncovered linking senior executives of any of the major corporations to the conspiracy. On the contrary, the participants were basically middle level managers who hid their involvement from their superiors. According to Professor Posner's theory, the organization is expected in such a situation to discipline the individuals who have exposed it to such an extraordinary loss by firing them. Rarely would there have been greater justification for such an action.

But what in fact happened? Westinghouse "imposed absolutely no disciplinary treatment upon the individuals responsible." General Electric demoted some and asked for the resignation of others, but retained still others who had been convicted. The other corporate conspirators appear to have taken no punitive action against any employees. Even those fired by General Electric were able to find similar positions in other firms. Thus, even in the case when the organization has disciplined the employee, there is reason to doubt that he has suffered a sufficiently significant penalty to deter others from engaging in future frolics and detours. In overview, the loyalty shown by the corporations involved in the electrical equipment conspiracy to their convicted employees was remarkable: most were retained even in the face of derivative suits against their corporation's directors for negligent supervision, and shareholder proxy proposals seeking their dismissal were soundly defeated. Those convicted generally were seen as unfortunate scapegoats who merited special treatment by their companies—in effect, corporate prisoners of war.

This same pattern is reflected in the experience of corporations convicted of offenses growing out of the Watergate investigation. A follow-up survey in 1975 by the New York Times found that "most of the 21 business executives who admitted their guilt" to the Special Prosecutor were "still presiding over these companies."

The economist can attempt to account for this pattern by arguing that the illegal behavior was in the best interests of the corporation (or at least appeared to be at the time) and thus did not warrant disciplinary action. In some cases this may be true, but it fails to give a persuasive explanation for the foregoing cases. Antitrust violations, because of the potential treble damages liability, cannot safely be assumed to maximize the utility of the corporation as a whole, although they may well advance the interests of a particular division or group of employees by freeing them from the anxieties of interfirm competition. Similarly, the political contributions prosecuted in the wake of Watergate may have been motivated as much by the interests or political sympathies of the chief executive as by any specific corporate benefit sought.

If the corporation was not benefitted by the criminal acts of its officials, however, what explains the general absence in these cases of disciplinary action against the convicted employees? A multitude of explanations, of course, are possible. * * * Whatever the reasons, the ultimate conclusion is that evidence of internal disciplinary measures is conspicuous by its absence. Thus, exclusive reliance on penalties aimed at the firm seems dangerously unrealistic.

This last observation, that stockholders may be powerless to remove management even if there is conclusive evidence of wrongdoing, leads to a more generalized problem which criminal justice policy must confront. A significant number of economists no longer accept two of the fundamental assumptions of the neoclassical school: (1) that the individual decision-maker will predictably act in the interest of the firm; and (2) that the firm will seek to maximize profits (and thus will respond quickly to increased penalties that make illegal activity too costly to be profitable). Rather, these economists stress the relative autonomy and opportunities for discretionary decision-making possessed by the individual manager within the firm.

* * *

Concededly, neoclassical economists have never accepted the managerialists' argument that the lack of congruence between the motives of the manager and his organization may cause the manager to act in a manner that is in fact adverse to the corporation's interests. Their answer has been that the disciplining force of the market will prevent the manager from engaging for long in discretionary behavior contrary to the corporation's interests. If persistent, such frolics and detours away from the central goal of profit maximization will attract a hostile take-over by another firm, which realizes that it can obtain a "bigger bang for the buck" from the assets of the mismanaged firm.

Although this theory sounds logical, the disciplinary powers of the market have eroded. A combination of developments—state anti-takeover laws, high transaction costs, increasingly restrictive judicial interpretations of the federal securities laws applicable to tender offers—has diluted the incentive for the tenderor and raised the odds against a hostile tender. * * * Even if the disciplinary powers of the capital markets were considerably greater, they would be unlikely to have a significant impact upon managerial behavior in this context. By becoming involved in a protracted criminal episode, the would-be target corporation in effect renders itself the monarch butterfly of the corporate world, which none can swallow without experiencing acute indigestion. * * *

The key implication to be drawn from the managerialists' position is that a penalty structure that is high enough to deter the corporation may still not deter its managers (who may be intent on maximizing a quite different utility function). * * * [For example] the corporate official may be more intent than is the corporation on maximizing profits within a shorter time period. Such a motivation would be rational if the manager's compensation, fringe benefits, and opportunities for promotion were tied to short-run performance or if he foresaw a hostile take-over which could be averted by an increase in short-run profitability. To a considerable degree, this seems inevitable because, to paraphrase Lord Keynes, in the long run the manager, unlike the corporation, is dead.

R. POSNER, ANTITRUST LAW: AN ECONOMIC PERSPECTIVE 225–26 (1976).

[T]he actual remedial scheme found in the antitrust statutes leaves much to be desired. There is, to begin with, the unnecessary and therefore inappropriate reliance on the criminal sanction, including imprisonment (now for as long as three years). Imprisonment should be regarded as a sanction of last resort, in general and with particular reference to antitrust. First, it is difficult to translate a monetary sum (the costs of a particular price-fixing conspiracy, say) into a nonpecuniary cost—so many days in prison. The effort to do so is almost certain to lead to excessive leniency. Second, imprisonment is a much costlier sanction for society to administer than the collection of a fine. Imprisonment consumes real resources, not the least of which is the legitimate production of the imprisoned individual, which is lost during his term of imprisonment. Fines involve no such waste. Apart from (ordinarily slight) collection costs, the entire loss to the defendant who is fined is offset by an equal benefit to the taxpayers (or whoever else receives the fine). A fine is a transfer payment that only negligibly reduces the aggregate wealth of the society. Not so with imprisonment: the cost to the defendant of being imprisoned is a deadweight loss to society.

Where violators are judgment-proof, society is compelled to resort to imprisonment or some other method of nonpecuniary sanction despite the advantages of the fine. But inability to pay judgments is not a problem in the antitrust field. True, individuals are frequently joined as defendants in antitrust suits—the individuals who participated actively in whatever violation the corporate defendant is accused of having committed—and, although they are a good deal more affluent than the common criminal, they might sometimes be unable to pay judgments measured by the social costs of their violations. But I consider this a detail, for it is in general unimportant whether the individual corporate employees are joined as defendants in antitrust cases. A corporation has effective methods of preventing its employees from commiting acts that impose huge liabilities on it. A sales manager whose unauthorized participation in a price-fixing scheme resulted in the imposition of a $1-million fine on his employer would thereafter, I predict, have great difficulty finding responsible employment, and this prospect would appear to be sufficient to exert a substantial deterrent effect, one at least comparable to the generally light individual fines and very short prison sentences of existing law.

3. EXTERNAL POLITICAL FORCES

STEVENSON, THE CORPORATION AS A POLITICAL INSTITUTION

8 Hofstra L.Rev. 39, 40–1, 45, 50–1 (1979).

* * * In the last decade or so the lamp of reason has finally awakened the business community and its observers to the reality that the corporation, that preeminently *economic* institution, has become—nay, has always been—a *political* institution as well. It has become inescapably clear that while the forces of economics do indeed play a crucial role in shaping corporate behavior, large corporations respond—sometimes with an alacrity that is startling in such bureaucratic behemoths—to the vagarious currents of political forces as well.

The "political" forces of which I speak are perhaps best defined in the negative: Those extrinsic influences on corporate behavior, arising out of popular feelings, that are not expressed *directly* through the market mechanism. These forces often have economic aspects. A corporation may, for example, seek to build a favorable public image, or to avoid an unfavorable one, because of that image's potential impact on the corporation's sales, its ability to recruit executive talent, or the morale of its employees. A corporation may choose or refrain from a particular course of action out of fear of inviting governmental regulation. But the calculus that leads a company to improve its pollution control program, to stop manufacturing napalm, or to withdraw from South Africa is not related to the laws of supply and demand in the conventional manner in which most corporate economic decisions are made.

*   *   *

The Mechanisms of Politicization

Traditional modes of political analysis do not translate well into a corporate context for the self-evident reason that the electoral mechanism, to which all democratic political analysis must ultimately refer, occupies a place in corporate politics that is, if not negligible, very nearly so.

*   *   * We must, therefore, look elsewhere for the mechanisms by which political forces operate on the corporation. I would suggest three such mechanisms as among the most important: The impact of public opinion on the managerial psyche; the effects, real or imagined, actual or potential, of public opinion on the economic welfare of the corporation; and the fear of regulation.

Public Opinion and the Managerial Psyche

The corporation, that "mere legal entity," has, as Blackstone put it, no soul. It is not subject to social pressures, cannot be shamed or embarrassed, and cannot be conditioned to behave in a given way. That is not, however, true of its managers. Corporate executives live in the communities in which their firms operate. They enjoy whatever measure of prestige—or obloquy—comes from their corporate affiliation. And of course they must, in the end, live with their own consciences.

*   *   *

The Economic Effects of Public Opinion

It is not just management psyches that suffer from a negative corporate image. Corporations are also affected in more conventional ways by hostile public opinion generated by adverse publicity. Corporate managers justify the large sums they spend on public relations with the rationale that a favorable public image promotes sales.

Particularly in oligopolistic markets where competing goods are very similar in quality, a firm's share of the market depends in large part on its brand image. This image in turn depends on a complex blend of factors, only one of which is the overall standing of the corporation in the public favor; but a manager who ignores public opinion does so at his or her peril.

Even firms that do not sell directly to the public are usually concerned about their images. United States Steel, for example, is anxious to let us know "We're involved." Dupont tells us about "Better things for better living through chemistry," and Union Carbide claims "Something we make will touch your life." Some of this concern can be traced to management's desire for association with a prestigious company; however, there can be no doubt that a prime motivation for improving the corporate image is the belief in its relation to profitability.

* * *

Fear of Regulation

Corporate executives have learned that if their manner of conducting business creates problems of sufficient concern to a sufficient number of people, the government will eventually react by changing the rules. Gone are the days of "the public be damned."

* * *

Business executives do not like regulation except when it serves to reduce the pressures of competition. Their reasons are complex. In part they object to the economic costs imposed by regulation. But the negative reaction of corporate executives is, perhaps, more often a product of the limitations on their flexibility, the challenge to their self-image as lords of their own dominion, the insult to their ideological view of the world, and other "psychic" costs of regulation. Whatever the reasons, and however valid, it is clear that executives are averse to regulation. Their aversion is an important factor in determining the corporate response to those political forces that carry a credible threat of regulation.

Chapter 19

REGULATION OF SECURITIES TRADING

A. INTRODUCTION TO SECURITIES TRADING

In this chapter we will consider some of the legal problems associated with sales of securities after their initial issue by a corporation. Federal law, in particular that growing from the Securities Exchange Act of 1934, is the source of the most important body of rules governing these trading transactions. State law is not without its importance, however, and a knowledge of the common law background is important to an understanding of the federal law. Our consideration of the legal issues, therefore, will begin with a look at state law. But since an elementary familiarity with the functioning of the stock market is essential to a comprehension of its legal regulation, there follows a very brief description of how the stock market functions.

The organized securities markets can be divided into two types: the stock exchanges and the over-the-counter (OTC) market. A stock exchange is a physically central marketplace, the "floor" of the exchange, where a limited number of broker-dealers who are members of the exchange buy and sell for the accounts of their customers and for their own accounts securities that are listed on the exchange ("listed securities"). The principal exchanges are the New York Stock Exchange and the American Stock Exchange; there are also several regional exchanges that mostly handle the shares of smaller companies.

An investor who wishes to buy or sell shares on an exchange places an order with a broker which, if a member of an exchange on which the issue is traded, will handle the transaction itself; otherwise the broker will forward the order to a firm that is an exchange member. The commission broker that handles the execution of the order sends it to a floor trader who is physically present on the floor of the exchange. The floor trader goes to the place on the floor at which the security is traded (the "post") where the order is executed. At the post are always a number of other floor traders (the "crowd") and a "specialist" who "makes a market" in the security. The specialist trades both for his own account (in which case he is acting as a "dealer") and for the accounts of others who have given him orders to execute (in which case he is acting as a "broker"). The specialist's role is an important one; his market-making furnishes liquidity in the trading of the security, permitting easier matching of buy and sell orders and causing the price of the stock to move more smoothly.

There are two principal types of customers' orders: "limit orders" and "market orders." The former direct the broker to buy or sell at a particular price. The latter call for a trade at the prevailing price. When a market order is brought to the post it is executed immediately at the prevailing market price. It may be matched with a countervailing order held by another broker in the crowd, or, if there is no such order, it will be accepted by the specialist either for his own account or carrying out a limit order. The specialist maintains a limit order book to keep track of limit orders left with him by brokers who cannot always be continuously present at one post.

The OTC market consists of a network of telephone lines and a computerized quotation system through which broker-dealers trade in securities that are, for the most part, not listed on an exchange. One or more broker-dealers may make a market in a given OTC security by giving continuous quotations of prices at which they will buy and sell. Thus the price of an OTC security is usually given in the form "20 bid, $20\frac{1}{2}$ asked." That is, the market-maker is offering to buy a reasonable number of shares for $20 per share and to sell a reasonable number at $20.50 per share. (The difference between the bid and asked prices may vary, but it is usually under $1.) These quotations are communicated to other broker-dealers either through the National Association of Securities Dealers Automated Quotation System (NASDAQ), a computerized network that furnishes continuous quotations, or through printed "sheets" that are revised daily. There may be no market-maker for lightly traded securities; but for more heavily-traded issues there may be several.

Like the specialist in the exchanges, a market-maker provides liquidity for a security. The degree of liquidity depends on the number of shares, on balance, bought or sold, the size of the market maker's spread (that is, the difference between the bid and asked prices), and the effect of the market maker's transactions on succeeding quotations and the transactions.

Transactions in the OTC market are usually negotiated and consummated by telephone, not on the floor of an exchange. A broker-dealer may act as a broker on an agency basis and negotiate with the market maker offering the best price quotation in a relevant stock. A broker-dealer may also act as a dealer (principal) and match public orders from its own inventory. In confirming a transaction, a broker-dealer will state whether it acted as a broker or a dealer. The name of the person or entity from whom the market maker or the dealer acquired the shares is not indicated. Transactions on stock exchanges or on the OTC market, therefore, are faceless exchanges.

The system described here is presently in flux. The Congress has directed the SEC to establish a so-called "national market system" that would link all of the exchanges and much of the OTC market in one computerized system that would allow a given order to be executed wherever the best price was then available. The final shape of such a system is not yet clear, but it would substantially reduce, if not eliminate, the roles presently played by floor traders and specialists, much of whose functions would be taken over by computers. The need for such a revision of the existing system, which by and large works pretty well, is a matter of some controversy. Uncertainty about the potential for problems with the new system combined with opposition by some of those who have vested interests in the way the business is now conducted have slowed the pace of change, and the implementation of the new system has been slower than was originally expected.

B. LIABILITY FOR MISLEADING STATEMENTS OR OMISSIONS

PROBLEM

ALTERNATIVE ENERGY CORPORATION—PART I

You represent the Alternative Energy Corporation (AEC), a substantial company whose common stock is actively traded on the New York Stock Exchange. Among other activities, the corporation is engaged in research and development on solar cells used to convert the sun's energy into electricity. In recent weeks engineers working on one of the more promising devices have made several important breakthroughs that have led many of them to believe that they are on the verge of being able to produce commercially a cell that is three or four times more efficient than anything now available. If their predictions are correct, the company's marketing department estimates that revenues from the new technology should increase the company's profits between one quarter and one third over the next two years. Burns, AEC's president, himself an engineer, is of the opinion, however, that the technology will require considerable further work and investment before it is commercially practicable, and that it may never be successful. It is generally known in the financial community that AEC is doing work on solar cells, but the company has made no public statements about the state of its research.

A

Burns has called you to say that he is scheduled to discuss AEC's prospects with a group of securities analysts and financial reporters on Friday. He would like to know whether he has any obligation to say anything about the recent developments in the company's work on the solar cell, and, if so, how much he should say. What should you advise him?

B

At the meeting on Friday, Burns was not feeling well. Toward the end of the meeting, in response to a question about the solar cells, he said, "As you may know, we have been working on solar cells for over five years. In the course of our work, we have developed one particular type of cell that, to the best of my knowledge, is known to no one else in the industry. I believe that, if it can be made to work, this technology could revolutionize the energy business. Recently our engineers have informed me that they have made enormous progress toward the commercialization of the device and, although I am not at all sure about this personally, many of them believe that success is imminent."

The next day the financial pages of a leading newspaper carried a short article describing Burns' talk of the preceding day and headlined, "AEC SAYS NEW SOLAR CELL 'IMMINENT'". On Monday, AEC's stock, which had been trading at about $40 a share, went up to $50.

Burns has called you to ask what, if anything, he should do. He is particularly concerned about the possibility of liability for losses sustained by investors who bought AEC stock in reliance on the newspaper article or the favorable recommendation he understands several analysts who were at the meeting are giving. He wants to know:

(a) if his statement violated the law, and, if so, what the consequences might be;

(b) if he has a legal obligation to correct the misleading impression now circulating; and

(c) whether there is any possibility of liability if he issues a corrective press release and it turns out that his engineers are right after all.

1. INTRODUCTION: THE COMMON LAW BACKGROUND

The law governing the trading of securities is today largely federal law, more specifically, law developed under § 10(b) of the Securities Exchange Act and Rule 10b–5. That state law has largely been supplanted in this area is due in part to the procedural advantages of suing under the 1934 Act. Perhaps the most important of these are the provisions of § 27 that allow worldwide service of process on the defendant and an extremely liberal choice of venue. Suing under federal law in federal court also has other procedural advantages, particularly with respect to derivative suits, where state law often poses significant obstacles to a plaintiff. In addition federal discovery rules are often more liberal than their state counterparts.

The development of the law under Rule 10b–5 is also, however, a result of the unsatisfactory nature of the substantive rights afforded by the common law, which depend in large measure on the tort action of fraud or deceit.

The contours of the common law tort of deceit are fuzzy at best, varying considerably from one state to another, and containing a host of qualifications and conditions that depend on the particular fact pattern. It is nevertheless useful to review the basic outlines of the traditional common law tort, both in order to understand why it proved an inadequate tool for dealing with securities fraud and because the federal courts have constructed their analysis of Rule 10b–5 using the elements of an action for deceit, omitting or modifying them as it has seemed desirable.

The traditional action for deceit required the plaintiff to prove five elements: (1) The plaintiff justifiably relied (2) to his detriment (3) on a misrepresentation of a material fact (4) made by the defendant with the knowledge of its falsity or with reckless disregard for the truth and (5) with the intention that the plaintiff rely. In abbreviated form these elements may be listed as (1) reliance, (2) causation, (3) materiality, and (4) scienter (a combination of the last two).

In the context of transactions in securities, particularly when they took place through the impersonal medium of a securities exchange and not in a face-to-face transaction, the proof of these elements often presented the plaintiff with insuperable barriers to recovery. It was often difficult, for example, to show that the defendant had intended for the plaintiff to rely on the misstatement. Cases in which the defendant had misled the plaintiff by *omitting* to tell him a crucial fact also provided difficulties because in commercial transactions the accepted principle is that mere silence does not give rise to an action for deceit. (Although courts often found reasons not to apply this doctrine too strictly when it led to "unappetizing" results.*) As we shall see, this rule presented particular problems for recovery in cases in which an "insider" in possession of some special bit of knowledge engaged in a securities transaction with someone unaware of that information.

In the early days of the development of the law under Rule 10b–5 the federal courts, while paying deference to the general analytical structure of the traditional common law action, felt relatively free to disregard the traditional elements of the tort. In more recent times, however, the Supreme Court has increasingly insisted that Congress meant "fraud" when it said "fraud" and that therefore the federal law should not depart too far from its common law antecedents.

2. RULE 10b–5

a. Introduction

The SEC's Rule 10b–5 (which you should read at this point) is an acorn from which has grown a very large judicial oak. It is responsible for a large portion of that body of law that is often referred to "federal corporation law"—almost always in quotation marks because of the implications of such a phrase in a post-*Erie* legal system.

The authority for the adoption of the rule is § 10(b) of the Securities Exchange Act, itself no more than a brief and cryptic statement of a broad anti-fraud principle. The legislative history of that section

---

* Prosser, Torts 696 (4th ed. 1971).

is described in SEC v. Texas Gulf Sulphur Co., 401 F.2d 833, 859 (2d Cir. 1968):

> Section 10(b) of the Act * * * was taken by the Conference Committee from Section 10(b) of the proposed Senate bill, S. 3420, and taken from it verbatim insofar as here pertinent. The only alteration made by the Conference Committee was to substitute the present closing language of Section 10(b), " * * * in contravention of such rules and regulations as the Commission may prescribe as necessary or appropriate in the public interest or for the protection of investors" for the closing language of the original Section 10(b) of S. 3420, " * * * which the Commission may declare to be detrimental to the interests of investors." 78 Cong.Rec. 10261 (1934).

> The Report of the Senate Committee which presented S. 3420 to the Senate summarized Section 10(b) as follows:

> Subsection (b) authorizes the Commission by rules and regulations to prohibit or regulate the use of *any other manipulative or deceptive practices which it finds detrimental to the interests of the investor.* (Emphasis supplied.)

> S.Rep. No. 792, 73rd Cong., 2d Sess. 18 (1934).

> Indeed, from its very inception, Section 10(b), and the proposed sections in H.R. 1383 and S. 3420 from which it was derived, have always been acknowledged as catchalls. *See* Bromberg, Securities Law: SEC Rule 10b–5, p. 19 (1967). In the House Committee hearings on the proposed House bill, Thomas G. Corcoran, Counsel with the Reconstruction Finance Corporation and a spokesman for the Roosevelt Administration, described the broad prohibitions contained in § 9(c), the section which corresponded to Section 10(b) of S. 3420 and eventually to Section 10(b) of the Act, as follows: "Subsection (c) says, 'Thou shalt not devise any other cunning devices' * * * Of course subsection (c) is a catchall clause to prevent manipulative devices. I do not think there is any objection to that kind of a clause. The Commission should have the authority to deal with new manipulative devices." Stock Exchange Regulation, Hearings before the House Committee on Interstate and Foreign Commerce, 73rd Cong., 2d Sess. 115 (1934). Although several other witnesses objected to the breadth of the proposed prohibition that Corcoran was supporting, the section as enacted did not in any way limit the broad scope of the "in connection with" phrase. *See* 3 Loss, Securities Regulation, 1424 n. 7 (2d ed. 1961).

Milton Freeman, who claims authorship of the rule itself, described the circumstances of its origin in Conference on Codification of the Federal Securities Laws, 22 Bus.Lawyer 793, 922 (1967):

> It was one day in the year 1943, I believe. I was sitting in my office in the SEC building in Philadelphia* and I received a call from Jim Treanor who was then the Director of the Trading and Exchange Division. He said, "I have just been on the telephone with Paul Rowen," who was then the SEC Regional Administrator in Boston, "and he has told me about the president of some company in Boston who is going around buying up the stock of his company from his own shareholders at $4.00 a share, and he has been telling them that the company is doing very badly, whereas, in fact, the earnings are going to be quadrupled and will be $2.00 a share for this coming year. Is there anything we can do about it?" So he came upstairs and I called in my secretary and I looked at Section 10(b) and I looked at Section 17, and I put them together, and the only discussion we had there was where "in connection with the purchase or sale" should be, and we decided it should be at the end.

> We called the Commission and we got on the calendar, and I don't remember whether we got there that morning or after lunch. We passed a piece of paper around to all the commissioners. All the commissioners read the rule and they tossed it on the table, indicating approval. Nobody said anything except Sumner Pike who said, "Well," he said, "we are against fraud, aren't we?" That is how it happened.

The SEC probably had no idea in 1942 (the correct date of adoption of Rule 10b–5) what the courts, at the urging of its successors and private litigants would make of this short, innocent prohibition against fraud and deceit. One of its most important early applications, and the first time it was held to support an implied private action, was in Kardon v. National Gypsum Co., 69 F.Supp. 512 (E.D.Pa. 1946). The principal parties in the suit were two family groups, each of which owned 50 percent of the stock of a corporation. The defendants learned that National Gypsum was interested in purchasing the corporation and bought the shares of the plaintiffs without telling them of that fact. The defendants then conveyed the corporation's assets to National Gypsum, reaping a substantial profit. The court held, that, although neither § 10(b) nor Rule 10b–5 explicitly provided a private remedy for a violation of their prohibitions, it was appropriate for the court to create one, citing the principle of tort law that the violation of a statute resulting in an injury to another is a tort.

The lower courts generally followed *Kardon* in implying the existence of a private right of action for damages under Rule 10b–5, and the Supreme Court finally confirmed it in Superintendent of Insur-

---

* Then the seat of the SEC—Eds.

ance v. Bankers Life & Casualty Co., 404 U.S. 6, 92 S.Ct. 165, 30 L. Ed.2d 128 (1971). The scope of such an action will be taken up in Chapter 22.

b. Rule 10b–5 and Corporate Publicity

SEC v. TEXAS GULF SULPHUR CO.

401 F.2d 833 (2d Cir. 1968), cert. denied 394 U.S. 976, 89 S.Ct. 1454,
22 L.Ed.2d 756 (1969).

WATERMAN, Circuit Judge:

[From 1957 to 1963 Texas Gulf Sulphur (TGS) conducted various geophysical explorations in eastern Canada which gave preliminary indications that there might be a body of mineral ore located in the northeast portion of an area designated as Kidd 55, near Timmins, Ontario. On November 12, 1963, TGS geologists completed a test hole, K–55–1, in the most promising part of the area. The drill core proved to contain an unusually high level of copper, zinc, and silver. The geologists in the field concealed the test hole and intentionally drilled a barren core away from the site. Those who knew of the first core were instructed to keep the knowledge confidential in order that TGS could acquire mineral rights to the surrounding land.

TGS completed its acquisition program and resumed drilling in March of 1964. By the evening of April 10, several more holes had been completed, all of which tended to confirm the existence of a substantial body of ore.

Meanwhile, rumors that TGS had made a major ore strike finally surfaced in the newspapers. On the morning of Saturday, April 12, Stephens, the president of TGS, read two separate reports of the drilling which seemed to infer a rich strike from the fact that the drill cores had been flown to the United States for chemical assay. Stephens immediately telephoned this information to Fogarty, the Executive Vice President, who later conferred with Mollison, the Vice President most directly in contact with the operations in Timmins. The next day, Sunday, April 12, Fogarty drafted a press release, approved by Stephens and a company attorney, designed to quell the rumors. The release was issued that afternoon, and appeared in the next morning's papers. The release read, in pertinent part:

"NEW YORK, April 12—The following statement was made today by Dr. Charles F. Fogarty, executive vice president of Texas Gulf Sulphur Company, in regard to the company's drilling operations near Timmins, Ontario, Canada. Dr. Fogarty said:

" 'During the past few days, the exploration activities of Texas Gulf Sulphur in the area of Timmins, Ontario, have been widely reported in the press, coupled with rumors of a substantial copper discovery there. These reports exaggerate the scale of operations, and mention plans and statistics of size and grade of ore that are without factual basis and have evidently originated by speculation of people not connected with TGS.

" 'The facts are as follows. TGS has been exploring in the Timmins area for six years as part of its overall search in Canada and elsewhere for various minerals—lead, copper, zinc, etc. During the course of this work, in Timmins as well as in Eastern Canada, TGS has conducted exploration entirely on its own, without the participation by others. Numerous prospects have been investigated by geophysical means and a large number of selected ones have been core-drilled. These cores are sent to the United States for assay and detailed examination as a matter of routine and on advice of expert Canadian legal counsel. No inferences as to grade can be drawn from this procedure.

" 'Most of the areas drilled in Eastern Canada have revealed either barren pyrite or graphite without value; a few have resulted in discoveries of small or marginal sulphide ore bodies.

" 'Recent drilling on one property near Timmins has led to preliminary indications that more drilling would be required for proper evaluation of this prospect. The drilling done to date has not been conclusive, but the statements made by many outside quarters are unreliable and include information and figures that are not available to TGS.

" 'The work done to date has not been sufficient to reach definite conclusions and any statement as to size and grade of ore would be premature and possibly misleading. When we have progressed to the point where reasonable and logical conclusions can be made, TGS will issue a definite statement to its stockholders and to the public in order to clarify the Timmins project.' "

The effect of this release was equivocal. One newspaper headlined its story on the release, "Copper Rumor Deflated." But some witnesses testified that they had interpreted the release as encouraging. On April 16, after more drilling, TGS finally made a public announcement confirming an ore find of major proportions.

The SEC brought suit against the corporation and various individual defendants. The complaint alleged that the individuals had violated Rule 10b–5 by purchasing TGS stock while they knew of the ore strike but before it had been announced to the public. (We will take up this "insider trading" branch of the case later.) As to the corporate defendant, the SEC alleged that it had violated the Rule by issuing a materially misleading press release on April 12.]

* * * The SEC argued below and maintains on this appeal that this release painted a misleading and deceptive picture of the drilling progress at the time of its issuance, and hence violated Rule 10b–5(2). TGS relies on the holding of the court below that "The issuance of the release produced no unusual market action" and "In the absence of a showing that the purpose of the April 12 press release was to

affect the market price of TGS stock to the advantage of TGS or its insiders, the issuance of the press release did not constitute a violation of Section 10(b) or Rule 10b–5 since it was not issued 'in connection with the purchase or sale of any security' " and, alternatively, "even if it had been established that the April 12 release was issued in connection with the purchase or sale of any security, the Commission has failed to demonstrate that it was false, misleading or deceptive." 258 F.Supp. at 294.

Before further discussing this matter it seems desirable to state exactly what the SEC claimed in its complaint and what it seeks. The specific SEC allegation in its complaint is that this April 12 press release " * * * was materially false and misleading and was known by certain of defendant Texas Gulf's officers and employees, including defendants Fogarty, Mollison, Holyk, Darke and Clayton, to be materially false and misleading."

The specific relief the SEC seeks is, pursuant to Section 21(e) of Securities Exchange Act of 1934, 15 U.S.C.A. § 78u(e), a permanent injunction restraining the issuance of any further materially false and misleading publicly distributed informative items.

B. *The "In Connection With * * *" Requirement.*

In adjudicating upon the relationship of this phrase to the case before us it would appear that the court below used a standard that does not reflect the congressional purpose that prompted the passage of the Securities Exchange Act of 1934.

The dominant congressional purposes underlying the Securities Exchange Act of 1934 were to promote free and open public securities markets and to protect the investing public from suffering inequities in trading, including, specifically, inequities that follow from trading that has been stimulated by the publication of false or misleading corporate information releases. * * *

Therefore it seems clear from the legislative purpose Congress expressed in the Act, and the legislative history of Section 10(b) that Congress when it used the phrase "in connection with the purchase or sale of any security" intended only that the device employed, whatever it might be, be of a sort that would cause reasonable investors to rely thereon, and, in connection therewith, so relying, cause them to purchase or sell a corporation's securities. There is no indication that Congress intended that the corporations or persons responsible for the issuance of a misleading statement would not violate the section unless they engaged in related securities transactions or otherwise acted with wrongful motives; indeed, the obvious purposes of the Act to protect the investing public and to secure fair dealing in the securities markets would be seriously undermined by applying such a gloss onto the legislative language. Absent a securities transaction by an insider it is almost impossible to prove that a wrongful purpose motivated the issuance of the misleading statement. The mere fact that an insider did not engage in securities transactions does not negate the possibility of wrongful purpose; perhaps the market did not react to the misleading statement as much as was anticipated or perhaps the wrongful purpose was something other than the desire to buy at a low price or sell at a high price. Of even greater relevance to the Congressional purpose of investor protection is the fact that the investing public may be injured as much by one's misleading statement containing inaccuracies caused by negligence as by a misleading statement published intentionally to further a wrongful purpose. We do not believe that Congress intended that the proscriptions of the Act would not be violated unless the makers of a misleading statement also participated in pertinent securities transactions in connection therewith, or unless it could be shown that the issuance of the statement was motivated by a plan to benefit the corporation or themselves at the expense of a duped investing public.

*   *   *

*   *   *   Accordingly, we hold that Rule 10b–5 is violated whenever assertions are made, as here, in a manner reasonably calculated to influence the investing public, e.g., by means of the financial media, if such assertions are false or misleading or are so incomplete as to mislead irrespective of whether the issuance of the release was motivated by corporate officials for ulterior purposes. It seems clear, however, that if corporate management demonstrates that it was diligent in ascertaining that the information it published was the whole truth and that such diligently obtained information was disseminated in good faith, Rule 10b–5 would not have been violated.

C. *Did the Issuance of the April 12 Release Violate Rule 10b–5?*

Turning first to the question of whether the release was misleading, i.e., whether it conveyed to the public a false impression of the drilling situation at the time of its issuance, we note initially that the trial court did not actually decide this question. Its conclusion that "the Commission has failed to demonstrate that it was false, misleading or deceptive," 258 F.Supp. at 294, seems to have derived from its views that "The defendants are to be judged *on the facts known to them* when the April 12 release was issued," 258 F.Supp. at 295 (emphasis supplied), that the draftsmen "exercised reasonable business judgment under the circumstances," 258 F.Supp. at 296, and that the release was not "misleading or deceptive *on the basis of the facts then known,*" 258 F.Supp. at 296 (emphasis supplied) rather than from an appropriate primary inquiry into the meaning of the statement to the reasonable investor and its relationship to truth. While we certainly agree with the trial court that "in retrospect, the press release may appear gloomy or incomplete," 258 F.Supp. at 296, we cannot, from the present record, by applying the standard Congress intended, definitively conclude that it was deceptive or misleading to the reasonable investor, or that he would have been misled by it. Certain newspaper accounts of the release viewed the release as confirming the existence of preliminary favorable developments, and this optimistic view was held by some brokers, so it could be that the reasonable investor would have read between the lines of what appears to us to be an inconclusive and negative statement and would have envisoned the actual situation at the Kidd segment on April 12. On the other hand, in view of the decline of the market price of TGS stock from a high of 32 on the morning of April 13 when the release was disseminated to $29^3/_8$ by the close of trading on April 15, and the reaction to the release by other brokers, it is far from certain that the release was generally interpreted as a highly encouraging report or even encouraging at all. Accordingly, we remand this issue to the district court that took testimony and heard and saw the witnesses for a determination of the character of the release in the light of the facts existing at the time of the release, by applying the standard of whether the reasonable investor, in the exercise of due care, would have been misled by it.

In the event that it is found that the statement was misleading to the reasonable investor it will then become necessary to determine whether its issuance resulted from a lack of due diligence. The only remedy the Commission seeks against the corporation is an injunction, and therefore we do not find it necessary to decide whether just a lack of due diligence on the part of TGS, absent a showing of bad faith, would subject the corporation to any liability for damages. We have recently stated in a case involving a private suit under Rule 10b–5 in which damages and an injunction were sought, " 'It is not necessary in a suit for equitable or prophylactic relief to establish all the elements required in a suit for monetary damages.' " Mutual Shares Corp. v. Genesco, Inc., 384 F.2d 540, 547, quoting from SEC v. Capital Gains Research Bureau, Inc., 375 U.S. 180, 193, 84 S.Ct. 275, 11 L.Ed.2d 237 (1963).

We hold only that, in an action for injunctive relief, the district court has the discretionary power under Rule 10b–5 and Section 10(b) to issue an injunction, if the misleading statement resulted from a lack of due diligence on the part of TGS. The trial court did not find it necessary to decide whether TGS exercised such diligence and has not yet attempted to resolve this issue. While the trial court concluded that TGS had exercised "reasonable *business* judgment under the circumstances," 258 F.Supp. at 296 (emphasis supplied) it applied an incorrect *legal* standard in appraising whether TGS should have issued its April 12 release on the basis of the facts known to its draftsmen at the time of its preparation, 258 F.Supp. at 295, and in assuming that disclosure of the full underlying facts of the Timmins situation was not a viable alternative to the vague generalities which were asserted. 258 F.Supp. at 296.

It is not altogether certain from the present record that the draftsmen could, as the SEC suggests, have readily obtained current reports of the drilling progress over the weekend of April 10–12, but they certainly should have obtained them if at all possible for them to do so. However, even if it were not possible to evaluate and transmit current data in time to prepare the release on April 12, it would seem that TGS could have delayed the preparation a bit until an accurate report of a rapidly changing situation was posssible. See 258 F.Supp. at 296. At the very least, if TGS felt compelled to respond to the spreading rumors of a spectacular discovery, it would have been more accurate to have stated that the situation was in flux and that the release was prepared as of April 10 information rather than purporting to report the progress "to date." Moreover, it would have obviously been better to have specifically described the known drilling progress as of April 10 by stating the basic facts. Such an explicit disclosure would have permitted the investing public to evaluate the "prospect" of a mine at Timmins without having to read between the lines to understand that preliminary indications were favorable— in itself an understatement.

The choice of an ambiguous general statement rather than a summary of the specific facts cannot reasonably be justified by any claimed urgency. The avoidance of liability for misrepresentation in the event that the Timmins project failed, a highly unlikely event as of April 12 or April 13, did not forbid the accurate and truthful divulgence of detailed results which need not, of course, have been accompanied by conclusory assertions of success. Nor is it any justification that such an explicit disclosure of the truth might have "encouraged the rumor mill which they were seeking to allay." 258 F.Supp. at 296.

We conclude, then, that, having established that the release was issued in a manner reasonably calculated to affect the market price of TGS stock and to influence the investing public, we must remand to the district court to decide whether the release was misleading to the reasonable investor and if found to be misleading, whether the court in its discretion should issue the injunction the SEC seeks.

* * *

* * * [W]e reverse the judgment dismissing the complaint against Texas Gulf Sulphur Company, remand the cause as to it for a further determination below, in the light of the approach explicated by us in the foregoing opinion, as to whether, in the exercise of its discretion, the injunction against it which the Commission seeks should be ordered.

On remand, the court found that "some reasonable investors, exercising due care, were misled by the press release" and that it was not the product of due diligence on the part of those responsible for it. SEC v. Texas Gulf Sulphur Co., 312 F.Supp. 77 (S.D.N.Y.1970), aff'd 446 F.2d 1301 (2d Cir. 1971).

3. IS THERE AN AFFIRMATIVE DUTY TO DISCLOSE?

SEC. EXCH. ACT RELEASE NO. 8995 (1970).

The Securities and Exchange Commission today reiterated the need for publicly held companies to make prompt and accurate disclosure of information, both favorable and unfavorable, to security holders and the investing public. Companies subject to the reporting requirements of the Securities Exchange Act of 1934 are, at the present time, generally required to file annual reports within 120 days after the end of their fiscal years, semi-annual reports within 45 days after the end of the 6-month period and current reports within 10 days after the end of the month in which a reportable event has occurred * * *.

Notwithstanding the fact a company complies with such reporting requirements, it still has an obligation to make full and prompt announcements of material facts regarding the company's financial condition. The responsibility for making such announcement rests, and properly so, with the management of the company. They are intimately aware of the factors affecting the operations of the business. Management of noninvestment companies are cognizant of factors affecting profits and losses, such as curtailment of operations, decline of orders, or costs overruns on major contracts. They are also cognizant of liquidity problems such as a decreased inflow of collections from sales to customers, the availability or lack of availability of credit from suppliers, banks, and other financial institutions, and the inability to meet maturing obligations when they fall due * * *.

The policy of prompt corporate disclosure of material business events is embodied in the rules and directives of the major exchanges. It should be noted that unless adequate and accurate information is available, a company may not be able to purchase its own securities or make acquisitions using its securities, and its insiders may not be able to trade its securities without running a serious risk of violating Section 10(b) of the Securities Exchange Act of 1934 and Rule 10b-5 thereunder.

Corporate managements are urged to review their policies with respect to corporate disclosure and endeavor to set up procedures which will insure that prompt disclosure be made of material corporate developments, both favorable and unfavorable, so that investor confidence can be maintained in an orderly and effective securities market.

NEW YORK STOCK EXCHANGE COMPANY MANUAL A–18 (1977).

SECTION A 2

Part 1

TIMELY DISCLOSURE

Timely and Adequate Disclosure of Corporate News

A corporation whose securities are listed on the New York Stock Exchange Inc. is expected to release quickly to the public any news or information which might reasonably be expected to materially affect the market for those securities. * * *

A corporation should also act promptly to dispel unfounded rumors which result in unusual market activity or price variations.

* * *

Exchange Market Surveillance

For its part, the Exchange maintains a continuous market surveillance program through its Division of Regulation and Surveillance. An "on-line" computer system has been developed which monitors the price movement of every listed stock—on a trade-to-trade basis—throughout the trading session. The program is designed to closely review the markets in those securities in which unusual price and volume changes occur or where there is a large unexplained influx of buy or sell orders. If the price movement of a stock exceeds a predetermined guideline, it is immediately "flagged" and a review of the situation is immediately undertaken to seek out the causes of the exceptional activity. Under such circumstances, the Company may be called by its Liaison Representative in the Division of Stock List to inquire about any company developments which have not been publicly announced but which could be responsible for unusual market activity. Where the market appears to be reflecting undisclosed information, the Corporation will normally be requested to make such information public immediately. * * *

* * *

Internal Handling of Confidential Corporate Matters

Unusual market activity or a substantial price change has on occasion occurred in a company's securities shortly before the announcement of an important corporate action or development. Such incidents are extremely embarrassing and damaging to both the Company and the Exchange since the public may quickly conclude that someone acted on the basis of "inside" information.

Negotiations leading to acquisitions and mergers, stock splits, the making of arrangements preparatory to an exchange or tender offer, changes in dividend rates or earnings, calls for redemption, new contracts, products, or discoveries, are the type of developments where the risk of untimely and inadvertent disclosure of corporate plans is most likely to occur. Frequently, these matters require discussion and study by corporate officials before final decisions can be made. Accordingly, extreme care must be used in order to keep the information on a confidential basis.

WHERE IT IS POSSIBLE TO CONFINE FORMAL OR INFORMAL DISCUSSIONS TO A SMALL GROUP OF THE TOP MANAGEMENT OF THE COMPANY OR COMPANIES INVOLVED, AND THEIR INDIVIDUAL CONFIDENTIAL ADVISORS WHERE ADEQUATE SECURITY CAN BE MAINTAINED, PREMATURE PUBLIC ANNOUNCEMENT MAY PROPERLY BE AVOIDED. In this regard, the market action of a company's securities should be closely watched at a time when consideration is being given to important corporate matters. If unusual market activity should arise, the Company should be prepared to make an immediate public announcement of the matter.

At some point it usually becomes necessary to involve other persons to conduct preliminary studies or assist in other preparations for contemplated transactions, e.g., business appraisals, tentative financing arrangements, attitude of large outside holders, availability of major blocks of stock, engineering studies, market analysis and surveys, etc. Experience has shown that maintaining security at this point is virtually impossible. Accordingly, fairness requires that the Company make an immediate public announcement as soon as confidential disclosures relating to such important matters are made to "outsiders."

The extent of the disclosures will depend upon the stage of discussion, studies, or negotiations. So far as possible, public statements should be definite as to price, ratio, timing and/or any other pertinent information necessary to permit a reasonable evaluation of the matter. As a minimum, they should include those disclosures made to "outsiders." Where an initial announcement cannot be specific or complete, it will need to be supplemented from time to time as more definitive or different terms are discussed or determined.

Corporate employees, as well as directors and officers, should be regularly reminded as a matter of policy that they must not disclose confidential information they may receive in the course of their duties and must not attempt to take advantage of such information themselves.

In view of the importance of this matter and the potential difficulties involved, the Exchange suggests that a periodic review be made by each company of the manner in which confidential information is being handled within its own organization. A reminder notice of the Company's policy to those in sensitive areas might also be helpful from time to time.

The effective implementation of the foregoing is essential to the maintenance of a fair and orderly securities market for the benefit of a company and its shareholders. It should minimize the occasions where the Exchange finds it necessary to temporarily halt trading in a security due to information leaks or rumors in connection with significant corporate transactions.

* * *

Part II

PROCEDURE FOR PUBLIC RELEASE OF INFORMATION

Immediate Release Policy

The normal method of publication of important corporate data is by means of a press release. This may be either by telephone or in written form. Any release of information that could reasonably be expected to have an impact on the market for a company's securities should be given to the wire services and the press FOR IMMEDIATE RELEASE. Clearly, a corporation cannot properly assume responsibility for the security of such important information in the hands of persons or organizations beyond its control.

The spirit of the IMMEDIATE RELEASE policy is not considered to be violated on weekends where a "Hold for Sunday or Monday A. M.'s" is used to obtain a broad public release of the news. This procedure facilitates the combination of a press release with a mailing to shareholders.

Annual and quarterly earnings, dividend announcements, acquisitions, mergers, tender offers, stock splits, and major management changes, and any substantive items of unusual or non-recurrent nature are examples of news items that should be handled on an immediate release basis. News of major new products, contract awards, expansion plans, and discoveries very often fall into the same category. Unfavorable news should be reported as promptly and candidly as the favorable. Reluctance or unwillingness to release a negative story or an attempt to disguise unfavorable news endangers a management's reputation for integrity. Changes in accounting methods to mask such occurrences can have a similar long-term impact.

It should be a corporation's primary concern to assure that news will be handled in proper perspective. This necessitates appropriate restraint, good judgment, and careful adherence to the facts. Any projections of financial data, for instance, should be soundly based, appropriately qualified, conservative and factual. Excessive or misleading conservatism should be avoided. Likewise, the repetitive release of essentially the same information is not appropriate.

* * *

Premature announcements of new products whose commercial application cannot yet be realistically evaluated should be avoided. So should overly optimistic forecasts, exaggerated claims and unwarranted promises. And should subsequent developments indicate that performance will not match earlier projections, this too should be reported and explained.

Judgment must be exercised as to the timing of a public release on those corporate developments where the immediate release policy is not involved or where disclosure would endanger the company's goals or provide information helpful to a competitor. In these cases, it is helpful to weigh the fairness to both present and potential stockholders who at any given moment may be considering buying or selling the company's stock.

STATE TEACHERS RETIREMENT BOARD v. FLUOR CORP.

654 F.2d 843 (2d Cir. 1981).

[The plaintiff, a public pension fund, sued Fluor Corporation, a large engineering and construction firm, for alleged violations of Rule 10b–5 and of the New York Stock Exchange Listing Agreement and Company Manual. On February 28, 1975 it signed a $1 billion contract to build a large coal gasification plant in South Africa known as SASOL II. The agreement provided for an "embargo" on all publicity about the contract until March 10, 1975, apparently to allow the South African party to complete delicate negotiations with the French government for financing.

During the week of March 3, the volume of trading in Fluor stock grew and the price moved up slightly. Rumors began to circulate that Fluor had received a large contract, and several securities professionals called the company to inquire about them. On March 6 a representative of the New York Stock Exchange contacted Fluor and suggested that it might be advisable to suspend trading. Fluor agreed, and trading was suspended on March 7.

Meanwhile, between March 3 and March 6, State Teachers sold, according to a decision made in January, some $6.4 million worth of Fluor stock.

The Court of Appeals held, among other things, that Fluor had not breached a duty to disclose its contract or to halt trading in its stock pending an announcement and that there is no implied private right of action under the portions of the New York Stock Exchange Company Manual set forth above. The section of the opinion dealing with the former issue follows.]

1. *Duty to Disclose or Halt Trading*

State Teachers asserts that Fluor had a duty to disclose the signing of the SASOL II contract during the week of March 3 when rumors became rampant and the price and volume of its stock shot upward. We disagree. Under all the circumstances, and particularly in light of its agreement with SASOL to make no announcement until

March 10, Fluor was under no obligation to disclose the contract. A company has no duty to correct or verify rumors in the marketplace unless those rumors can be attributed to the company. Elkind v. Liggett & Myers, Inc., 635 F.2d 156 (2d Cir. 1980). There is no evidence that the rumors affecting the volume and price of Fluor stock can be attributed to Fluor. Fluor responded to inquiries from analysts between March 4 and March 6 without comment on the veracity of the rumors and without making any material misrepresentation.

Moreover, even if the facts here give rise to a duty to disclose, there is no showing of any intent to defraud investors or any conduct which was reckless in any degree. Fluor's actions between March 3 and March 6 were made in a good faith effort to comply with the publicity embargo. The record completely lacks any evidence of *scienter*—a prerequisite to liability under section 10(b). Ernst & Ernst v. Hochfelder, *supra*. Indeed, at oral argument, counsel for State Teachers conceded that Fluor may not have had a duty to disclose the SASOL II contract under the circumstances.

State Teachers argues that, in any event, Fluor was under a duty to do what it could to halt trading in its stock once it learned that rumors regarding the SASOL II contract were affecting the price of the stock. This issue was not specifically addressed by the district court. State Teachers now argues that once an issuer decides as a matter of business judgment to withhold material information, it then assumes a duty to protect that news from selective disclosure which may disrupt the public market in its stock. In such a circumstance, the issuer must notify the Exchange and request a trading suspension until the news may be made public. State Teachers argues that this duty arises where, as here, the issuer becomes aware that the precise details of the material information are circulating in the market. It submits that this duty (i) is assumed by any issuer who has its stock traded on a public stock exchange and (ii) is consonant with the purpose of the Securities Exchange Act of 1934 to insure the integrity of the marketplace.

* * * State Teachers further argues that an issuer who fails to fulfill this duty to request a halt in trading, knowing that a selling stockholder may suffer a loss, is reckless; therefore, the *scienter* requirement for liability to attach in a section 10(b) private action is satisfied.

Under the circumstances presented in this case, we find that Fluor had no duty under section 10(b) to notify the Exchange and request that trading in its shares be suspended. Fluor first heard of rumors in the marketplace regarding the SASOL II contract on March 4. At that point, the volume of trading in Fluor stock had increased over previous weeks but there was no significant change in price. It was not until March 6 that the volume of trading in the stock and its price increased dramatically. The record indicates that no one at Fluor knew the reason for these market developments. That day, Fluor told the New York Stock Exchange that the signing of the SASOL II contract might be an explanation for the activity, and it agreed to the suggestion of the Exchange that trading be suspended. There was no trading on March 7. These facts obviate any suggestion that Fluor acted recklessly, much less with the fraudulent intent necessary for liability under section 10(b). *See, e.g.,* Chiarella v. United States, 445 U.S. 222, 100 S.Ct. 1108, 63 L.Ed.2d 348 (1980); Ernst & Ernst v. Hochfelder, *supra.* Fluor acted scrupulously when it revealed to the Exchange that the signing of the SASOL II contract might be an explanation for what the Exchange perceived as unusual market activity in Fluor stock. Fluor's good faith is further evidenced by its endorsement of the Exchange's decision to halt trading. For us to say that Fluor should have notified the Exchange at some earlier time would be to create a standard of liability under section 10 (b) which gives undue weight to hindsight.

In addition to the absence of an intent to defraud investors, the difficulty of establishing causation also supports our conclusion that a section 10(b) claim does not exist here for Fluor's failure to request a halt in trading. *See* Affiliated Ute Citizens v. United States, 406 U. S. 128, 154, 92 S.Ct. 1456, 1472, 31 L.Ed.2d 741 (1972). Although the Exchange likely would have honored a request by Fluor to halt trading, the decision rests entirely in the hands of the Exchange. It would be impossible for State Teachers to show on the record before us that had Fluor acted sooner to request a halt in trading the Exchange would have suspended trading before March 7.

* * *

NOTE: BUSINESS JUDGMENT AND THE DUTY TO DISCLOSE

In Financial Industrial Fund, Inc. v. McDonnell Douglas Corp., 474 F.2d 514 (10th Cir. 1973), a mutual fund bought shares of Douglas Aircraft (which later merged to become McDonnell Douglas) a week prior to the issuance of a press release by the company revealing a substantial drop in profits below previously published forecasts. The decline was due to shortages of materials and skilled workers and incorrect costing estimates. Plaintiff argued that all this was known to management well before the publication of its report and should have been disclosed.

The company successfully defended on grounds that the timing of the disclosure of negative performance was, under the facts, within management's discretion. The court held that material information must be "available and ripe for publication" before the duty to disclose arises. In this case, while management had an inkling of the situation prior to disclosure, it did not have reliable specific figures. The court further held that the defendant exercised "good faith and due diligence" in ascertaining and verifying the information. The court analogized the duty to the business judgment rule in determining the proper time to disclose.

C. PRIVATE ACTIONS

PROBLEM

ALTERNATIVE ENERGY CORPORATION—PART II

AEC did issue a press release to quell the speculation generated by stories about Burns' mention of the company's progress on a new solar cell. In reaction to that press release, AEC's stock dropped back to $40. It traded about that price for two months after which it began to creep back up, partly in response to more rumors about the new technology. Last week it was trading at $45.

Meanwhile, the engineers working on the new device made progress that exceeded even their most optimistic expectations. On Friday they informed Burns that all the technical problems had been resolved, that the new solar cell worked, and that they expected that the company would be able to commence full-scale production within six months. Burns immediately sent a memorandum to AEC's public relations director which read, "From what R&D tells me, I guess I was wrong about the new solar cell. This is a big one. Get a release out on it right away. You know how to handle it." Burns then left on a one week sailing vacation.

Unbeknownst to Burns, the public relations director had become seriously ill and had gone to the hospital Friday morning. The memorandum was delivered to the assistant director, an eager, but inexperienced young woman. Although Burns had discussed the possible need for a press release about the new solar cell with the director in some detail, the assistant knew very little about the matter. Moreover, she had been at AEC for only two weeks, and did not know who to discuss the matter with in the research and development department, and she could not reach her boss, who was in a coma at the hospital. She had heard, however, about the earlier difficulties with publicity about the solar technology, and was determined not to repeat them. Accordingly, over the weekend she issued a press release announcing that rumors about AEC's progress on a new solar cell were unfounded and that, although the company was continuing its research, it had experienced a setback in the work on one device that had appeared promising. That story was carried in Monday's newspapers. AEC's stock fell to $42 per and remained there until the next Monday, when Burns, returning from his vacation, issued a release giving the correct facts. The stock rose to $55 on that news.

Your firm represents University Professors' Retirement Fund (UPRF), a pension plan whose assets are invested principally in corporate securities. It held an option to purchase 50,000 shares of AEC stock at $45 per share. The option expired the Friday after the erroneous press release. UPRF has asked the firm to study the possibility of suing AEC for violating Rule 10b–5. You have been asked to prepare a memorandum on the legal questions that such a suit would raise. Among other things, you should consider whether UPRF has standing and whether it can show the necessary materiality, scienter, reliance, and causation.

1. INTRODUCTION

In the wake of the SEC's enforcement proceedings in the *Texas Gulf Sulphur* case there followed a large number of private suits seeking damages from the corporation and its officials for alleged violation of Rule 10b–5, principally the misleading press release of April 12. Cannon v. Texas Gulf Sulphur Co., 55 F.R.D. 308 (S.D.N.Y. 1972) reports the settlement of "63 private actions pending in this court; 13 such actions pending in the Supreme Court of New York, New York County; 2 derivative actions pending in this court; and 3 derivative actions pending in the Supreme Court of New York, New York County."

Another significant private action was Mitchell v. Texas Gulf Sulphur Co., 446 F.2d 90 (10th Cir. 1971), cert. denied 404 U.S. 1004, 92 S.Ct. 564, 30 L.Ed.2d 558, reh. denied 404 U.S. 1064, 92 S.Ct. 734, 30 L.Ed.2d 754 (1972), which was an action against TGS and Fogarty, by three TGS shareholders who had sold their shares allegedly in reliance on the April 12 release. The court began its analysis by saying, "in civil action instituted on the basis of 10b–5 violations, the keynote of which is fraud, the full panoply of common law fraud elements—misrepresentation or nondisclosure, materiality, scienter, intent to defraud, reliance and causation—have crept in and played varying roles of significance." The court then went on to consider the "varying roles" of these elements as they applied to the facts of the case. It is particularly interesting to note the court's acceptance of the trial judge's finding, that "[T]he record here discloses that the press release issued by defendants was misleading, intentionally deceptive, inaccurate and knowingly deficient in material facts."

The elements of common law fraud-materiality, scienter, reliance, and causation are not set forth explicitly in Rule 10b–5, but have been imported into its jurisprudence by the courts in the course of fashioning private remedies for violations of the rule. Even at common law, the precise nature of these elements is a matter of some confusion; and, as the court said in Mitchell v. Texas Gulf Sulphur, 446 F.2d 90 (10th Cir. 1971), cert. denied 404 U.S. 1004, 92 S.Ct. 564, 30 L.Ed.2d 558, as applied to private actions under Rule 10b–5, "a number of these elements have diminished in importance."

The *Huddleston* case sets forth the state of the law on each of these elements at length. Blue Chip Stamps v. Manor Drug Stores considers the issue of the plaintiff's standing to sue, on which the *Huddleston* court did not comment. Meanwhile, however, there are two elements of a 10b–5 action not present in an action for common law fraud that require our attention.

Use of the Jurisdictional Means. Rule 10b–5 applies only to prohibited acts committed "by the use of any means or instrumentality of interstate commerce, or of the mails, or any facility of any national securities exchange." The courts have been extremely liberal in interpreting this requirement. They have generally held that there is no necessity that the misrepresentation or omission have itself been made through means of interstate commerce, but only that there be *some* use of such means "in connection with" the transaction. *E.g.,* Ellis v. Carter, 291 F.2d 270 (9th Cir. 1961) (securities delivered interstate by airplanes); Rude v. Cambell Square, Inc., 411 F.Supp. 1040 (D.C.S.D.1976) (payment for securities delivered by mail). Moreover, it does not appear necessary that there actually be an interstate communication; it is enough that there be a communication that employs some "means or instrumentality of interstate commerce." Thus, for example, it has been held that an intrastate telephone call using lines that are part of an interstate system of communication satisfies the rule's jurisdictional requirement. Dupuy v. Dupuy, 511 F.2d 641 (5th Cir. 1975).

The "In Connection With" Requirement. The Second Circuit's broad approach to the requirement that the violation of the substantive prohibitions of Rule 10b–5 be "in connection with" a securities transaction has gained general acceptance in the courts that have considered the issue subsequently. Defendants in insider trading cases have argued, for example, that the plaintiff must show some "connection" between the defendant's failure to disclose a material fact before trading and the plaintiff's decision to trade—in the sense that the defendant's conduct caused the plaintiff's purchase or sale. The courts have rejected that argument. *See, e.g.,* Shapiro v. Merrill Lynch, Pierce, Fenner & Smith, 495 F.2d 228, 239 (2d Cir. 1974).

Perhaps the best indication of the remoteness of the "connection" that the courts have been willing to accept as establishing federal jurisdiction is found in Superintendent of Insurance v. Bankers Life & Casualty Co., 300 F.Supp. 1083 (S.D.N.Y.1969), aff'd 430 F.2d 355 (2d Cir. 1970), rev'd 404 U.S. 6, 92 S.Ct. 165, 30 L.Ed. 128 (1971). The "fraud" in that case was a complex scheme by which the defendants purchased all of the stock of a life insurance company using its own assets. The securities transaction to which it was claimed the fraud was "connected" was a sale by the insurance company of United States Treasury bonds effected by the defendants as part of their scheme. The district court held 10b–5 to be inapplicable, saying:

> The purity of the security transaction and the purity of the trading process are the sole objectives of federal concern. Therefore, the consummation of a security transaction as a mere incident of a fraudulent scheme and the mere fact of injury caused by the fraud, in the absence of any possibility that the fraud might materially effect the purity of the security transaction and the purity

of the trading process would not make the fraud federally cognizable. 300 F.Supp. 1083, 1101 (S.D.N.Y.1969).

In reversing the Second Circuit's affirmance of this view, Mr. Justice Douglas wrote, "[Section 10(b)] is not 'limited to preserving the integrity of the securities markets' (430 F.2d, at 361), though that purpose is included * * *. The crux of the present case is that [the defrauded corporation] suffered an injury as a result of deceptive practices touching its sale of securities as an investor."

Query: Is this interpretation broad enough to encompass misleading statements about the value of a parcel of real property made by a defendant who sold it to the plaintiff in exchange for securities? *See* Errion v. Connell, 236 F.2d 447 (9th Cir. 1956), which gives an affirmative answer. *But see* Note, 9 Stan.L.Rev. 589, 596 (1957).

HUDDLESTON v. HERMAN & MacLEAN

640 F.2d 534 (5th Cir. 1981), cert. granted 50 U.S.L.W. 3796–7 (1982).

ALVIN B. RUBIN, Circuit Judge.

* * *

I.

FACTS

Texas International Speedway, Inc. [TIS] filed a registration statement and prospectus with the Securities and Exchange Commission [SEC] and the Texas State Securities Board offering a total of $4,398,900 in securities, the proceeds of which were to be used to construct an automobile racetrack called the Texas International Speedway. The entire issue was sold on the offering date, October 30, 1969. The corporation was nonetheless short-lived, for on November 30, 1970, TIS filed a petition for bankruptcy under Chapter X of the Bankruptcy Act.

In 1972, the plaintiffs on behalf of themselves and other purchasers of TIS securities filed this class action alleging claims under Section 10(b) of the Securities Exchange Act of 1934 [the 1934 Act] and Rule 10b–5 promulgated pursuant to that statute. * * * The complaint sought damages from LoPatin, the former President, Treasurer and Director of TIS; Share, the former Executive Vice-President and Director of TIS; Herman and MacLean [H&M], the accountants who had participated in preparation of the prospectus, and others.

* * *

The issues that now concern us focus on statements made in the TIS prospectus. It contained an audited balance sheet dated May 31, 1969, and an unaudited balance sheet dated August 31, 1969. It related that the speedway was under construction and the proceeds of the securities issue would be used to pay the costs of that construction. It also contained a pro forma balance sheet dated May 31, 1969, showing that, upon completion of the public offering of the securities and the application of the proceeds to the construction costs of the speedway, TIS would on the speedway's opening date have $93,870 in cash on hand after allocation of $295,771 for general administrative expenses.

The trial judge submitted the case to the jury on special issues concerning whether the prospectus was materially misleading and, if so, whether this was done with scienter of various defendants. Despite the defendants' requests, he refused to submit special issues relating to reliance and causation.

The jury found that the prospectus was materially misleading as to the cost of constructing the speedway and that the defendants had "failed to disclose" the true facts with reckless disregard for the truth. The trial judge then himself determined the amount of damages and entered judgment for the plaintiffs and against LoPatin, Share and H&M.

* * *

III.

ELEMENTS OF THE CAUSE OF ACTION UNDER SECTION 10(b) AND RULE 10b–5

The elements necessary to prove a Section 10(b) claim have been so often applied by the lower federal courts that they can be stated in black letter fashion. To make out a claim under Section 10(b), which is based on the common law action of deceit, the plaintiff must establish (1) a misstatement or an omission (2) of material fact (3) made with scienter (4) on which the plaintiff relied (5) that proximately caused his injury. We discuss each of these prerequisites in turn.

A. *Materiality*

Considering the definition of a material fact under Section 14(a) of the 1934 Act and the SEC rules governing proxy statements, the Supreme Court, in TSC Industries, Inc. v. Northway, Inc., 426 U.S. 438, 96 S.Ct. 2126, 48 L.Ed.2d 757 (1976), adopted a "general standard of materiality * * * as follows: An omitted fact is material if there is a substantial likelihood that a reasonable shareholder *would* [not *might*] consider it important in deciding how to vote." TSC Industries, Inc. v. Northway, Inc., 426 U.S. at 449, 96 S.Ct. at 2132, 48 L. Ed.2d at 766 (emphasis added). "[T]here must be a substantial likelihood that the disclosure of the omitted fact would have been viewed by the reasonable investor as having significantly altered the 'total mix' of information made available." *Id.* at 449, 96 S.Ct. at 2132, 48 L.Ed.2d at 766. "In this circuit, the test of materiality [under Rule 10b–5] is 'whether a reasonable man would attach importance to the fact misrepresented in determining his course of action.' Smallwood

v. Pearl Brewing Co., 489 F.2d 579, 603–04 (5th Cir.), cert. denied, 419
U.S. 873, 95 S.Ct. 134, 42 L.Ed.2d 113 (1974)." Falls v. Fickling, 621
F.2d 1362, 1365 n.9 (5th Cir. 1980).

The TIS prospectus warned the potential investor that "THESE
SECURITIES INVOLVE A HIGH DEGREE OF RISK" and that the
construction costs might be underestimated. Nonetheless, there was
evidence from which the jury might have inferred that, on the effective date of the registration statement, LoPatin, Share and H&M already knew that the cost of construction was understated and that
consequently the Company's working capital position would not be as
favorable as the prospectus reflected. To warn that the untoward
may occur when the event is contingent is prudent; to caution that it
is only possible for the unfavorable events to happen when they have
already occurred is deceit.

Considering the evidence presented, the jury could justifiably conclude that the prospectus misstated the costs of completion of the
speedway, the amount of working capital that would be available to
the Company and the urgency of TIS's need to generate funds from
the operation of the speedway.

Each of these facts, and, certainly their combined significance
could all be considered important in the total mix of information considered by the securities purchaser. * * * We conclude, therefore, that there was sufficient evidence to warrant the finding of materiality of the misstatements.

B. Scienter

In Ernst & Ernst v. Hochfelder, 425 U.S. 185, 96 S.Ct. 1375, 47 L.
Ed.2d 668 (1976), the Supreme Court held that the Rule 10b–5 implied
cause of action requires a showing of scienter. See also Aaron v.
SEC, 446 U.S. 680, 100 S.Ct. 1945, 64 L.Ed.2d 611 (1980). The Court
defined the term as "a mental state embracing intent to deceive manipulate, or defraud." Ernst & Ernst v. Hochfelder, 425 U.S. at 193
n.12, 96 S.Ct. at 1381 n.12, 47 L.Ed.2d at 677 n.12. In Aaron the
Court expressly did not "address the question, reserved in Hochfelder, * * * whether, under some circumstances, scienter may
also include reckless behavior." 446 U.S. at 686 n.5, 100 S.Ct. at 1950
n.5, 64 L.Ed.2d at 620 n.5.

This circuit's position on whether reckless behavior is sufficient to
establish scienter is presently uncertain because the panel decision in
Broad v. Rockwell International Corp., 614 F.2d 418 (5th Cir. 1980),
was vacated by the granting of a rehearing en banc in that case, 618
F.2d 396 (5th Cir. 1980). See Dwoskin v. Rollins, Inc., 634 F.2d 285,
289 (5th Cir. 1981). The panel in Broad, concurring in the position
accepted by a number of other circuits, had expressly held that recklessness was sufficient to establish scienter. In cases decided both
before and after the Broad decision, we have referred to establishing
scienter by proof of reckless conduct. We here conclude that reck-

lessness can, under certain circumstances, be sufficient to establish scienter for purposes of the cause of action under Rule 10b–5. *See* G. A. Thompson & Co., Inc. v. Partridge, 636 F.2d 945 (5th Cir. 1981), in which another panel of this court recently reached this same conclusion and adopted the recklessness standard.

Reckless conduct sufficient to serve as scienter must involve more than simple, or even inexcusable negligence. It requires "an extreme departure from the standards of ordinary care, * * * which presents a danger of misleading buyers or sellers that is either known to the defendant or is so obvious that the actor must have been aware of it." SEC v. Southwest Coal & Energy Co., 624 F.2d 1312, 1321 n.17 (5th Cir. 1980) [quoting Franke v. Midwestern Oklahoma Development Authority, 428 F.Supp. 719, 725 (W.D.Okl.1976)] (SEC enforcement case).

* * *

Whether a defendant's actions in a Rule 10b–5 case violate the standard of care imposed by the Rule, thus establishing scienter, is a question of fact to be determined as of the time of the actions about which the plaintiff is complaining. The evidence was sufficient to warrant, although it did not compel, the inference that each of the defendants acted with the requisite state of mind.

Herman contends that the evidence failed to establish scienter on his part because he was not privy to all the information available to LoPatin and Share and because he relied on the construction cost figures they submitted to him and was not aware of the inaccuracy of those estimated costs. There was expert testimony that H&M was, to some degree, negligent in its accounting procedures. Although such negligence could not, under the standard articulated in *Hochfelder*, establish the requisite scienter, the jury might reasonably have concluded from Herman's testimony and from any inference to be drawn from his involvement in the preparation of the Use of Proceeds section of the prospectus, as well as from the refusal of H&M in October, 1969, to provide a comfort letter to the underwriters referring to the construction costs in the prospectus, that H&M acted with the requisite scienter. "Proof of a defendant's knowledge or intent [in a Rule 10b–5 action] will often be inferential * * *." Rolf v. Blyth, Eastman Dillon & Co., Inc., 570 F.2d 38, 47 (2d Cir.), cert. denied, 439 U.S. 1039, 99 S.Ct. 642, 58 L.Ed.2d 698 (1978). We conclude that the circumstantial evidence was sufficient to preclude a directed verdict in favor of H&M.

C. *Reliance and Causation*

Reliance and causation are related concepts. In the common law deceit action from which the Rule 10b–5 claim is derived, it was necessary for the plaintiff to show reliance on the defendant's fraudulent representations as a prerequisite to recovery. Establishing reliance, however, merely proves that the plaintiff was induced to act by the defendant's conduct. It is a nonsequitur to conclude that the representation that induced action necessarily caused the consequences of that action. As we have seen, the general statement of the elements of recovery under Rule 10b–5 requires proof both that the plaintiff relied on the misstatement and that the misstatement was the cause of his loss.

In Affiliated Ute Citizens of Utah v. United States, 406 U.S. 128, 92 S.Ct. 1456, 31 L.Ed.2d 741 (1972), the Supreme Court held that in some circumstances affirmative proof of reliance is not necessary. It distinguished the three subparagraphs of Rule 10b–5, pointing out that the first and third subparagraphs are not restricted to the misstatement or omission of a material fact but forbid a "course of business" or a "device, scheme, or artifice" that operates as a fraud. If a person who has an "affirmative duty under the Rule to disclose" a material fact to the holder of a security devises a plan to induce the holder to sell the securities without disclosing to him material facts that reasonably could be expected to influence his decision to sell, positive proof of reliance, it held, is not a prerequisite to recovery. Under the circumstances of that case, "involving primarily a failure to disclose * * * [a]ll that is necessary is that the facts withheld be material in the sense that a reasonable investor might have considered them important in the making of this decision. * * * This obligation to disclose and this withholding of a material fact establish the requisite element of causation in fact." 406 U.S. at 153–54, 92 S. Ct. at 1472, 31 L.Ed.2d at 761.

While *Affiliated Ute* relieves the investor in certain circumstances of the necessity of proving affirmatively that he relied on a prospectus or other representation, it does not eliminate the reliance element from the Rule 10b–5 case altogether. *See* Simon v. Merrill Lynch, Pierce, Fenner and Smith, Inc., 482 F.2d 880 (5th Cir. 1973). In Rifkin v. Crow, 574 F.2d 256, 262 (5th Cir. 1978), we restated our understanding of the *Affiliated Ute* rationale as it relates to proof of reliance in a Rule 10b–5 action:

> [W]here a 10b–5 action alleges defendant made positive misrepresentations of material information, proof of reliance by the plaintiff upon the misrepresentation is required. Upon an absence of proof on the issue, plaintiff loses. On the other hand, where a plaintiff alleges deception by defendant's nondisclosure of material information, the *Ute* presumption obviates the need for plaintiff to prove actual reliance on the omitted information. Upon a failure of proof on the issue, defendant loses. But this presumption of reliance in nondisclosure cases is not conclusive. If defendant can prove that plaintiff did not rely, that is, that plaintiff's decision would not have been affected even if defendant had disclosed the omitted facts, then plaintiff's recovery is barred.

Thus, reliance is an issue in *all* Rule 10b–5 cases. The difference between misrepresentation and non-disclosure cases relates only to whether proof of reliance is prerequisite to recovery or whether proof of non-reliance is an affirmative defense.

It is, therefore, necessary to characterize the facts in a Rule 10b–5 case as involving either primarily a failure to disclose, implicating the first or third subparagraph of the Rule and invoking the *Affiliated Ute* presumption of reliance, or, on the other hand, primarily a misstatement or failure to state a fact necessary to make those statements made not misleading, classified under the second subparagraph of the Rule and as to which no presumption of reliance is applicable. This case, involving alleged misstatements and omissions in a prospectus published pursuant to a public offering, cannot properly be characterized as an omissions case of the type for which the *Affiliated Ute* presumption was fashioned. The defendants did not "stand mute" in the face of a duty to disclose as did the defendants in *Affiliated Ute*. 406 U.S. at 153, 92 S.Ct. at 1472, 31 L.Ed.2d at 761. They undertook instead to disclose relevant information in an offering statement now alleged to contain certain misstatements of fact and to fail to contain other facts necessary to make the statements made, in light of the circumstances, not misleading. This is not a case in which difficulties of proof of reliance require the application of the *Affiliated Ute* presumption. Because the plaintiffs were not entitled to a presumption of reliance, a jury finding that the plaintiffs relied upon the misstatements and omissions in the prospectus was essential to the plaintiffs' recovery.

This circuit, according to *Simon v. Merrill Lynch, Pierce, Fenner and Smith, Inc.*, 482 F.2d 880 (5th Cir. 1973), requires "reasonable reliance" by the Rule 10b–5 plaintiff; "subjective reliance" alone does not suffice. 482 F.2d at 885. "[S]ome element of general reliance by plaintiff, even in nondisclosure cases, is essential to a Rule 10b–5 action." 482 F.2d at 884.

Subjective reliance is determined by the mental state of the individual. Another measure of reliance used by some courts, "justifiable reliance," requires an objective or "reasonable man" test. Although our prior decisions have not been completely clear on this point, we think "reasonable reliance," the test referred to by the *Simon* court, contemplates a subjective reliance standard, tempered by the requirement of due diligence on the part of the plaintiff, rather than the objective reliance test applicable under the justifiable reliance concept.

The district court, induced by counsel, confused materiality with reliance. The concepts are distinct and must be separately proved or disproved. Materiality does not necessarily imply that, were the truth known, the decision would be different. Thus, recovery is not permitted solely because the investor has relied on an immaterial misstatement or omission. On the other hand, even if a misstatement or omission might have been material to a reasonable investor, the plaintiff might not have relied on it, because, for example, he would have considered other factors more important or would have taken the same action even had he known the full truth. Consequently, in a class action, while the materiality element can be established for the class as a whole, reliance, like damages, is a matter of individual proof.

The district court compounded its failure to submit the reliance issue to the jury by failing also to submit the question of causation. Causation is related to but distinct from reliance. Reliance is a *causa sine qua non*, a type of "but for" requirement: had the investor known the truth he would not have acted. Causation requires one further step in the analysis: even if the investor would not otherwise have acted, was the misrepresented fact a *proximate* cause of the loss? The plaintiff must prove not only that, had he known the truth, he would not have acted, but in addition that the untruth was in some reasonably direct, or proximate, way responsible for his loss. The causation requirement is satisfied in a Rule 10b–5 case only if the misrepresentation touches upon the reasons for the investment's decline in value. If the investment decision is induced by misstatements or omissions that are material and that were relied on by the claimant, but are not the proximate reason for his pecuniary loss, recovery under the Rule is not permitted. Absent the requirement of causation, Rule 10b–5 would become an insurance plan for the cost of every security purchased in reliance upon a material misstatement or omission.

LoPatin and Share claim that the failure of TIS and the consequent economic loss of the plaintiff's investment are attributable to the materialization of risks described in the prospectus such as bad weather conditions and lack of spectator attendance at the racetrack. To prevail in their Rule 10b–5 action, the plaintiffs must establish that their economic loss was proximately caused by the fraudulent misstatements and omissions in the prospectus. This issue, the resolution of which is crucial to the plaintiffs' recovery, was not submitted to the trier of fact. Hence the elements of the Rule 10b–5 claim were not established and the judgment against the defendants must be reversed.

* * *

The trial court's failure to submit the reliance and causation issues to the jury requires us to grant a new trial.

For these reasons the judgment is reversed and the case is remanded for further proceedings consistent with this opinion.

2. STANDING

BLUE CHIP STAMPS v. MANOR DRUG STORES

421 U.S. 723, 95 S.Ct. 1917, 44 L.Ed.2d 539 (1975).

Mr. Justice REHNQUIST delivered the opinion of the Court.

This case requires us to consider whether the offerees of a stock offering, made pursuant to an antitrust consent decree and registered under the Securities Act of 1933, 48 Stat. 74, as amended, 15 U.S.C.A. § 77a et seq. (1933 Act), may maintain a private cause of action for money damages where they allege that the offeror has violated the provisions of Rule 10b–5 of the Securities and Exchange Commission, but where they have neither purchased nor sold any of the offered shares. See Birnbaum v. Newport Steel Corp., 193 F.2d 461 (CA2), cert. denied, 343 U.S. 956, 72 S.Ct. 1051, 96 L.Ed. 1356 (1952).

I

In 1963 the United States filed a civil antitrust action against Blue Chip Stamp Co. (Old Blue Chip), a company in the business of providing trading stamps to retailers, and nine retailers who owned 90% of its shares. In 1967 the action was terminated by the entry of a consent decree. United States v. Blue Chip Stamp Co., 272 F.Supp. 432 (C.D.Cal.), aff'd sub nom. Thrifty Shoppers Scrip Co. v. United States, 389 U.S. 580, 88 S.Ct. 693, 19 L.Ed.2d 781 (1968). The decree contemplated a plan of reorganization whereby Old Blue Chip was to be merged into a newly formed corporation, Blue Chip Stamps (New Blue Chip). The holdings of the majority shareholders of Old Blue Chip were to be reduced, and New Blue Chip, one of the petitioners here, was required under the plan to offer a substantial number of its shares of common stock to retailers who had used the stamp service in the past but who were not shareholders in the old company. Under the terms of the plan, the offering to nonshareholder users was to be proportional to past stamp usage and the shares were to be offered in units consisting of common stock and debentures.

The reorganization plan was carried out, the offering was registered with the SEC as required by the 1933 Act, and a prospectus was distributed to all offerees as required by § 5 of that Act, 15 U.S.C.A. § 77e. Somewhat, more than 50% of the offered units were actually purchased. In 1970, two years after the offering, respondent, a former user of the stamp service and therefore an offeree of the 1968 offering, filed this suit in the United States District Court for the Central District of California. Defendants below and petitioners here are Old and New Blue Chip, eight of the nine majority shareholders of Old Blue Chip, and the directors of New Blue Chip (collectively called Blue Chip).

Respondent's complaint alleged, *inter alia*, that the prospectus prepared and distributed by Blue Chip in connection with the offering was materially misleading in its overly pessimistic appraisal of Blue Chip's status and future prospects. It alleged that Blue Chip intentionally made the prospectus overly pessimistic in order to discourage respondent and other members of the allegedly large class whom it represents from accepting what was intended to be a bargain offer, so that the rejected shares might later be offered to the public at a higher price. The complaint alleged that class members because of and in reliance on the false and misleading prospectus failed to purchase the offered units. Respondent therefore sought on behalf of the alleged class some $21,400,000 in damages representing the lost opportunity to purchase the units; the right to purchase the previously rejected units at the 1968 price; and in addition, it sought some $25,000,000 in exemplary damages.

The only portion of the litigation thus initiated which is before us is whether respondent may base its action on Rule 10b–5 of the Securities and Exchange Commission without having either bought or sold the securities described in the allegedly misleading prospectus.
* * *

II

*   *   *

Within a few years after the seminal *Kardon* decision the Court of Appeals for the Second Circuit concluded that the plaintiff class for purposes of a private damage action under § 10(b) and Rule 10b–5 was limited to actual purchasers and sellers of securities. Birnbaum v. Newport Steel Corp., *supra.*

The Court of Appeals in this case did not repudiate *Birnbaum;* indeed, another panel of that court (in an opinion by Judge Ely) had but a short time earlier affirmed the rule of that case. Mount Clemens Industries, Inc. v. Bell, 464 F.2d 339 (1972). But in this case a majority of the Court of Appeals found that the facts warranted an exception to the *Birnbaum* rule. For the reasons hereinafter stated, we are of the opinion that *Birnbaum* was rightly decided, and that it bars respondent from maintaining this suit under Rule 10b–5.

III

The panel which decided *Birnbaum* consisted of Chief Judge Swan and Judges Learned Hand and Augustus Hand: the opinion was written by the last named. Since both § 10(b) and Rule 10b–5 proscribed only fraud "in connection with the purchase or sale" of securities, and since the history of § 10(b) revealed no congressional intention to extend a private civil remedy for money damages to other than defrauded purchasers or sellers of securities, in contrast to the express civil remedy provided by § 16(b) of the 1934 Act, the court concluded that the plaintiff class in a Rule 10b–5 action was limited to actual purchasers and sellers.   193 F.2d at 463–464.

* * *

The longstanding acceptance by the courts, coupled with Congress' failure to reject *Birnbaum's* reasonable interpretation of the wording of § 10(b), wording which is directed toward injury suffered "in connection with the purchase or sale" of securities, argues significantly in favor of acceptance of the *Birnbaum* rule by this Court.

Available evidence from the texts of the 1933 and 1934 Acts as to the congressional scheme in this regard, though not conclusive, supports the result reached by the *Birnbaum* court.   The wording of § 10(b) directed at fraud "in connection with the purchase or sale" of securities stands in contrast with the parallel antifraud provision of the 1933 Act, § 17(a), as amended, 68 Stat. 686, 15 U.S.C.A. § 77q, reaching fraud "in the offer or sale" of securities.   Cf. § 5 of the 1933 Act, 15 U.S.C.A. § 77e.   When Congress wished to provide a remedy to those who neither purchase nor sell securities, it had little trouble in doing so expressly.   Cf. § 16(b) of the 1934 Act, 15 U.S.C.A. § 78p(b).

* * *

Having said all this, we would by no means be understood as suggesting that we are able to divine from the language of § 10(b) the express "intent of Congress" as to the contours of a private cause of action under Rule 10b–5.   When we deal with private actions under Rule 10b–5, we deal with a judicial oak which has grown from little more than a legislative acorn.   Such growth may be quite consistent with the congressional enactment and with the role of the federal judiciary in interpreting it, see J. I. Case Co. v. Borak, *supra*, but it would be disingenuous to suggest that either Congress in 1934 or the Securities and Exchange Commission in 1942 foreordained the present state of the law with respect to Rule 10b–5.   It is therefore proper that we consider, in addition to the factors already discussed, what may be described as policy considerations when we come to flesh out the portions of the law with respect to which neither the congressional enactment nor the administrative regulations offer conclusive guidance.

Three principal classes of potential plaintiffs are presently barred by the *Birnbaum* rule.   First are potential purchasers of shares, either in a new offering or on the Nation's post-distribution trading markets, who allege that they decided not to purchase because of an unduly gloomy representation or the omission of favorable material which made the issuer appear to be a less favorable investment vehicle than it actually was.   Second are actual shareholders in the issuer who allege that they decided not to sell their shares because of an unduly rosy representation or a failure to disclose unfavorable material.   Third are shareholders, creditors, and perhaps others related to an issuer who suffered loss in the value of their investment due to corporate or insider activities in connection with the purchase or sale of securities which violate Rule 10b–5. It has been held that shareholder members of the second and third of these classes may frequently be able to circumvent the *Birnbaum* limitation through bringing a derivative action on behalf of the corporate issuer if the latter is itself a purchaser or seller of securities. See, *e.g.*, Schoenbaum v. Firstbrook, 405 F.2d 215, 219 (CA2 1968), cert. denied sub nom. Manley v. Schoenbaum, 395 U.S. 906, 89 S.Ct. 1747, 23 L.Ed. 2d 219 (1969). But the first of these classes, of which respondent is a member, cannot claim the benefit of such a rule.

A great majority of the many commentators on the issue before us have taken the view that the *Birnbaum* limitation on the plaintiff class in a Rule 10b–5 action for damages is an arbitrary restriction which unreasonably prevents some deserving plaintiffs from recovering damages which have in fact been caused by violations of Rule 10b–5. The Securities and Exchange Commission has filed an *amicus* brief in this case espousing that same view. We have no doubt that this is indeed a disadvantage of the *Birnbaum* rule, and if it had no countervailing advantages it would be undesirable as a matter of policy, however much it might be supported by precedent and legislative history. But we are of the opinion that there are countervailing advantages to the *Birnbaum* rule, purely as a matter of policy, although those advantages are more difficult to articulate than is the disadvantage.

There has been widespread recognition that litigation under Rule 10b–5 presents a danger of vexatiousness different in degree and in kind from that which accompanies litigation in general.   *   *   *

*   *   *

We believe that the concern expressed for the danger of vexatious litigation which could result from a widely expanded class of plaintiffs under Rule 10b–5 is founded in something more substantial than the common complaint of the many defendants who would prefer avoiding lawsuits entirely to either settling them or trying them. These concerns have two largely separate grounds.

The first of these concerns is that in the field of federal securities laws governing disclosure of information even a complaint which by objective standards may have very little chance of success at trial has a settlement value to the plaintiff out of any proportion to its prospect of success at trial so long as he may prevent the suit from being resolved against him by dismissal or summary judgment. The very pendency of the lawsuit may frustrate or delay normal business activity of the defendant which is totally unrelated to the lawsuit.

*   *   *

The potential for possible abuse of the liberal discovery provisions of the Federal Rules of Civil Procedure may likewise exist in this type of case to a greater extent than they do in other litigation. The prospect of extensive deposition of the defendant's officers and associates and the concomitant opportunity for extensive discovery of business documents, is a common occurrence in this and similar types of litigation. To the extent that this process eventually produces relevant evidence which is useful in determining the merits of the claims asserted by the parties, it bears the imprimatur of those Rules and of the many cases liberally interpreting them. But to the extent that it permits a plaintiff with a largely groundless claim to simply take up the time of a number of other people, with the right to do so representing an *in terrorem* increment of the settlement value, rather than a reasonably founded hope that the process will reveal relevant evidence, it is a social cost rather than a benefit. Yet to broadly expand the class of plaintiffs who may sue under Rule 10b–5 would appear to encourage the least appealing aspect of the use of the discovery rules.

Without the *Birnbaum* rule, an action under Rule 10b–5 will turn largely on which oral version of a series of occurrences the jury may decide to credit, and therefore no matter how improbable the allegations of the plaintiff, the case will be virtually impossible to dispose of prior to trial other than by settlement. In the words of Judge Hufstedler's dissenting opinion in the Court of Appeals:

> The great ease with which plaintiffs can allege the requirements for the majority's standing rule and the greater difficulty that plaintiffs are going to have proving the allegations suggests that the majority's rule will allow a relatively high proportion of "bad" cases into court. The risk of strike suits is particularly high in such cases; although they are difficult to prove at trial, they are even more difficult to dispose of before trial. 492 F.2d, at 147 n. 9.

The *Birnbaum* rule, on the other hand, permits exclusion prior to trial of those plaintiffs who were not themselves purchasers or sellers of the stock in question. The fact of purchase of stock and the fact of sale of stock are generally matters which are verifiable by documentation, and do not depend upon oral recollection, so that failure to qualify under the *Birnbaum* rule is a matter that can normally be established by the defendant either on a motion to dismiss or on a motion for summary judgment.

Obviously there is no general legal principle that courts in fashioning substantive law should do so in a manner which makes it easier, rather than more difficult, for a defendant to obtain a summary judgment. But in this type of litigation, where the mere existence of an unresolved lawsuit has settlement value to the plaintiff not only because of the possibility that he may prevail on the merits, an entirely legitimate component of settlement value, but because of the threat of extensive discovery and disruption of normal business activities which may accompany a lawsuit which is groundless in any event, but cannot be proved so before trial, such a factor is not to be totally dismissed. The *Birnbaum* rule undoubtedly excludes plaintiffs who have in fact been damaged by violations of Rule 10b–5, and to that extent it is undesirable. But it also separates in a readily demonstrable manner the group of plaintiffs who actually purchased or actually sold, and whose version of the facts is therefore more likely to be believed by the trier of fact, from the vastly larger world of potential plaintiffs who might successfully allege a claim but could seldom succeed in proving it. And this fact is one of its advantages.

The second ground for fear of vexatious litigation is based on the concern that, given the generalized contours of liability, the abolition of the *Birnbaum* rule would throw open to the trier of fact many rather hazy issues of historical fact the proof of which depended almost entirely on oral testimony. We in no way disparage the worth and frequent high value of oral testimony when we say that dangers of its abuse appear to exist in this type of action to a peculiarly high degree. * * *

* * *

In today's universe of transactions governed by the 1934 Act, privity of dealing or even personal contact between potential defendant and potential plaintiff is the exception and not the rule. The stock of issuers is listed on financial exchanges utilized by tens of millions of investors, and corporate representations reach a potential audience, encompassing not only the diligent few who peruse filed corporate reports or the sizable number of subscribers to financial journals, but the readership of the Nation's daily newspapers. Obviously neither the fact that issuers or other potential defendants under Rule 10b–5 reach a large number of potential investors, or the fact that they are required by law to make their disclosures conform to certain standards, should in any way absolve them from liability for misconduct which is proscribed by Rule 10b–5.

But in the absence of the *Birnbaum* rule, it would be sufficient for a plaintiff to prove that he had failed to purchase or sell stock by reason of a defendant's violation of Rule 10b–5. The manner in which the defendant's violation caused the plaintiff to fail to act could be as a result of the reading of a prospectus, as respondent claims here, but it could just as easily come as a result of a claimed reading of information contained in the financial pages of a local newspaper. Plaintiff's proof would not be that he purchased or sold stock, a fact which would be capable of documentary verification in most situations, but instead that he decided *not* to purchase or sell stock. Plaintiff's entire testimony could be dependent upon uncorroborated oral evidence of many of the crucial elements of his claim, and still be sufficient to go to the jury. The jury would not even have the benefit of weighing the plaintiff's version against the defendant's version, since the elements to which the plaintiff would testify would be in many cases totally unknown and unknowable to the defendant. The very real risk in permitting those in respondent's position to sue under Rule 10b–5 is that the door will be open to recovery of substantial damages on the part of one who offers only his own testimony to prove that he ever consulted a prospectus of the issuer, that he paid any attention to it, or that the representations contained in it damaged him. The virtue of the *Birnbaum* rule, simply stated, in this situation, is that it limits the class of plaintiffs to those who have at least dealt in the security to which the prospectus, representation, or omission relates. And their dealing in the security, whether by way of purchase or sale, will generally be an objectively demonstrable fact in an area of the law otherwise very much dependent upon oral testimony. In the absence of the *Birnbaum* doctrine, bystanders to the securities marketing process could await developments on the sidelines without risk, claiming that inaccuracies in disclosure caused nonselling in a falling market and that unduly pessimistic predictions by the issuer followed by a rising market caused them to allow retrospectively golden opportunities to pass.

*   *   *

We are dealing with a private cause of action which has been judicially found to exist, and which will have to be judicially delimited one way or another unless and until Congress addresses the question. Given the peculiar blend of legislative, administrative, and judicial history which now surrounds Rule 10b–5, we believe that practical factors to which we have adverted, and to which other courts have referred, are entitled to a good deal of weight.

Thus we conclude that what may be called considerations of policy, which we are free to weigh in deciding this case, are by no means entirely on one side of the scale. Taken together with the precedential support for the *Birnbaum* rule over a period of more than 20 years, and the consistency of that rule with what we can glean from the intent of Congress, they lead us to conclude that it is a sound rule and should be followed.

IV

The majority of the Court of Appeals in this case expressed no disagreement with the general proposition that one asserting a claim for damages based on the violation of Rule 10b–5 must be either a purchaser or seller of securities. However, it noted that prior cases have held that persons owning contractual rights to buy or sell securities are not excluded by the *Birnbaum* rule. Relying on these cases, it concluded that respondent's status as an offeree pursuant to the terms of the consent decree served the same function, for purposes of delimiting the class of plaintiffs, as is normally performed by the requirement of a contractual relationship.

*   *   *

* * * As a purely practical matter, it is doubtless true that respondent and the members of its class, as offerees and recipients of the prospectus of New Blue Chip, are a smaller class of potential plaintiffs than would be all those who might conceivably assert that they obtained information violative of Rule 10b–5 and attributable to the issuer in the financial pages of their local newspaper. And since respondent likewise had a prior connection with some of petitioners as a result of using the trading stamps marketed by Old Blue Chip, and was intended to benefit from the provisions of the consent decree, there is doubtless more likelihood that its managers read and were damaged by the allegedly misleading statements in the prospectus than there would be in a case filed by a complete stranger to the corporation.

But respondent and the members of its class are neither "purchasers" nor "sellers," as those terms are defined in the 1934 Act, and therefore to the extent that their claim of standing to sue were recognized, it would mean that the lesser practical difficulties of corroborating at least some elements of their proof would be regarded as sufficient to avoid the *Birnbaum* rule. While we have noted that these practical difficulties, particularly in the case of a complete stranger to the corporation, support the retention of that rule, they are by no means the only factor which does so. The general adoption of the rule by other federal courts in the 25 years since it was announced, and the consistency of the rule with the statutes involved and their legislative history, are likewise bases for retaining the rule. Were we to agree with the Court of Appeals in this case, we would leave the *Birnbaum* rule open to endless case-by-case erosion depending on whether a particular group of plaintiffs was thought by the court in which the issue was being litigated to be sufficiently more discrete than the world of potential purchasers at large to justify an exception. We do not believe that such a shifting and highly fact-oriented disposition of the issue of who may bring a damages claim for violation of Rule 10b–5 is a satisfactory basis for a rule of liability imposed on the conduct of business transactions. Nor is it as consistent as a straightforward application of the *Birnbaum* rule with the other factors which support the retention of that rule. We therefore hold that respondent was not entitled to sue for violation of Rule 10b–5, and the judgment of the Court of Appeals is reversed.

Reversed.

3. SCIENTER

ERNST & ERNST v. HOCHFELDER

425 U.S. 185, 96 S.Ct. 1375, 47 L.Ed.2d 668 (1976).

Mr. Justice POWELL delivered the opinion of the Court.

* * *

I

Petitioner, Ernst & Ernst, is an accounting firm. From 1946 through 1967 it was retained by First Securities Company of Chicago (First Securities), a small brokerage firm and member of the Midwest Stock Exchange and of the National Association of Securities Dealers, to perform periodic audits of the firm's books and records. In connection with these audits Ernst & Ernst prepared for filing with the Securities and Exchange Commission (Commission) the annual reports required of First Securities under § 17(a) of the 1934 Act, 15 U.S.C.A. § 78q(a). It also prepared for First Securities responses to the financial questionnaires of the Midwest Stock Exchange (Exchange).

Repondents were customers of First Securities who invested in a fraudulent securities scheme perpetrated by Leston B. Nay, president of the firm and owner of 92% of its stock. Nay induced the respondents to invest funds in "escrow" accounts that he represented would yield a high rate of return. * * * In fact, there were no escrow accounts as Nay converted respondents' funds to his own use immediately upon receipt. * * *

This fraud came to light in 1968 when Nay committed suicide, leaving a note that described First Securities as bankrupt and the escrow accounts as "spurious." Respondents subsequently filed this action for damages against Ernst & Ernst in the United States District Court for the Northern District of Illinois under § 10(b) of the 1934 Act. The complaint charged that Nay's escrow scheme violated § 10(b) and Commission Rule 10b–5, and that Ernst & Ernst had "aided and abetted" Nay's violations by its "failure" to conduct proper audits of First Securities. As revealed through discovery, respondents' cause of action rested on a theory of negligent nonfeasance. The premise was that Ernst & Ernst had failed to utilize "appropriate auditing procedures" in its audits of First Securities, thereby failing to discover internal practices of the firm said to prevent an effective audit. The practice principally relied on was Nay's rule that only he could open mail addressed to him at First Securities or addressed to First Securities to his attention, even if it arrived in his absence. Respondents contended that if Ernst & Ernst had conducted a proper audit, it would have discovered this "mail rule." The existence of the rule then would have been disclosed in reports to the Exchange and to the Commission by Ernst & Ernst as an irregular procedure that prevented an effective audit. This would have led to an investigation of Nay that would have revealed the fraudulent scheme. Respondents specifically disclaimed the existence of fraud or intentional misconduct on the part of Ernst & Ernst.

After extensive discovery the District Court granted Ernst & Ernst's motion for summary judgment and dismissed the action. * * *

The Court of Appeals for the Seventh Circuit reversed and remanded, holding that one who breaches a duty of inquiry and disclosure owed another is liable in damages for aiding and abetting a third party's violation of Rule 10b–5 if the fraud would have been discovered or prevented but for the breach. 503 F.2d 1100 (1974).

We granted certiorari to resolve the question whether a private cause of action for damages will lie under § 10(b) and Rule 10b–5 in the absence of any allegation of "scienter"—intent to deceive, manipulate, or defraud.[12] 421 U.S. 909, 95 S.Ct. 1557, 43 L.Ed.2d 773 (1975). We conclude that it will not and therefore we reverse.

II

Although § 10(b) does not by its terms create an express civil remedy for its violation, and there is no indication that Congress, or the Commission when adopting Rule 10b–5, contemplated such a remedy, the existence of a private cause of action for violations of the statute and the Rule is now well established. * * * Courts and commentators long have differed with regard to whether scienter is a necessary element of such a cause of action, or whether negligent conduct alone is sufficient. In addressing this question, we turn first to the language of § 10(b), for "[t]he starting point in every case involving construction of a statute is the language itself." *Blue Chip Stamps, supra,* at 756, 95 S.Ct. at 1935, 44 L.Ed.2d at 561 (Powell, J., concurring).

---

12. Although the verbal formulations of the standard to be applied have varied, several Courts of Appeals have held in substance that negligence alone is sufficient for civil liability under § 10(b) and Rule 10b–5. *See, e.g.,* White v. Abrams, 495 F.2d 724, 730 (CA9 1974) ("flexible duty" standard); Myzel v. Fields, 386 F.2d 718, 735 (CA8 1967), cert. denied, 390 U.S. 951, 88 S.Ct. 1043, 19 L.Ed.2d 1143 (1968) (negligence sufficient); Kohler v. Kohler Co., 319 F.2d 634, 637 (CA7 1963) (knowledge not required). Other Courts of Appeals have held that some type of scienter—*i.e.,* intent to defraud, reckless disregard for the truth, or knowing use of some practice to defraud—is necessary in such an action. *See, e.g.,* Clegg v. Conk, 507 F.2d 1351, 1361–1362 (CA10 1974), cert. denied, 422 U.S. 1007, 95 S.Ct. 2628, 45 L.Ed.2d 669 (1975) (an element of "scienter or conscious fault"); Lanza v. Drexel & Co., 479 F.2d 1277, 1306 (CA2 1973) ("willful or reckless disregard" of the truth). But few of the decisions announcing that some form of negligence suffices for civil liability under § 10(b) and Rule 10b–5 actually have involved only negligent conduct.

Smallwood v. Pearl Brewing Co., 489 F.2d 579, 606 (CA5), cert. denied, 419 U.S. 873, 95 S.Ct. 134, 42 L.Ed.2d 113 (1974); Kohn v. American Metal Climax, Inc., 458 F.2d 255, 286 (CA3 1973) (Adams, J., concurring and dissenting); Bucklo, Scienter and Rule 10b–5, 67 Nw.U.L.Rev. 562, 568–570 (1972).

In this opinion the term "scienter" refers to a mental state embracing intent to deceive, manipulate, or defraud. In certain areas of the law recklessness is considered to be a form of intentional conduct for purposes of imposing liability for some act. We need not address here the question whether, in some circumstances, reckless behavior is sufficient for civil liability under § 10(b) and Rule 10b–5.

Since this case concerns an action for damages we also need not consider the question whether scienter is a necessary element in an action for injunctive relief under § 10(b) and Rule 10b–5. Cf. SEC v. Capital Gains Research Bureau, 375 U.S. 180, 84 S.Ct. 275, 11 L.Ed.2d 237 (1963).

A

Section 10(b) makes unlawful the use or employment of "any manipulative or deceptive device or contrivance" in contravention of Commission rules. The words "manipulative or deceptive" used in conjunction with "device or contrivance" strongly suggest that § 10 (b) was intended to proscribe knowing or intentional misconduct.

In its *amicus curiae* brief, however, the Commission contends that nothing in the language "manipulative or deceptive device or contrivance" limits its operation to knowing or intentional practices. In support of its view, the Commission cites the overall congressional purpose in the 1933 and 1934 Acts to protect investors against false and deceptive practices that might injure them. *See* Affiliated Ute Citizens v. United States, *supra*, at 151, 92 S.Ct. at 1470, 31 L.Ed.2d at 760; Superintendent of Insurance v. Bankers Life & Cas. Co., *supra*, 404 U.S., at 11–12, 92 S.Ct. at 168, 30 L.Ed.2d at 134; J.I. Case Co. v. Borak, 377 U.S. 426, 432–433, 84 S.Ct. 1555, 1559–1560, 12 L. Ed.2d 423, 427–428 (1964). *See also* SEC v. Capital Gains Res. Bur., 375 U.S. 180, 195, 84 S.Ct. 275, 284, 11 L.Ed.2d 237, 248 (1963). The Commission then reasons that since the "effect" upon investors of given conduct is the same regardless of whether the conduct is negligent or intentional, Congress must have intended to bar all such practices and not just those done knowingly or intentionally. The logic of this effect-oriented approach would impose liability for wholly faultless conduct where such conduct results in harm to investors, a result the Commission would be unlikely to support. But apart from where its logic might lead, the Commission would add a gloss to the operative language of the statute quite different from its commonly accepted meaning. The argument simply ignores the use of the words "manipulative," "device," and "contrivance"—terms that make unmistakable a congressional intent to proscribe a type of conduct quite different from negligence. Use of the word "manipulative" is especially significant. It is and was virtually a term of art when used in connection with securities markets. It connotes intentional or willful conduct designed to deceive or defraud investors by controlling or artifically affecting the price of securities.

In addition to relying upon the Commission's argument with respect to the operative language of the statute, respondents contend that since we are dealing with "remedial legislation," Tcherepnin v. Knight, 389 U.S. 332, 336, 88 S.Ct. 548, 553, 19 L.Ed.2d 564, 569 (1967), it must be construed " 'not technically and restrictively, but flexibly to effectuate its remedial purposes.' " Affiliated Ute Citizens v. United States, 406 U.S., at 151, 92 S.Ct., at 1470, 31 L.Ed.2d, at 760 quoting SEC v. Capital Gains Research Bureau, *supra*, 375 U. S., at 195, 84 S.Ct., at 285, 11 L.Ed.2d, at 248. They argue that the "remedial purposes" of the Acts demand a construction of § 10(b) that embraces negligence as a standard of liability. But in seeking to accomplish its broad remedial goals, Congress did not adopt uniformly a negligence standard even as to express civil remedies.   *   *   *

It is thus evident that Congress fashioned standards of fault in the express civil remedies in the 1933 and 1934 Acts on a particularized basis. Ascertainment of congressional intent with respect to the standard of liability created by a particular section of the Acts must therefore rest primarily on the language of that section. Where, as here, we deal with a judicially implied liability, the statutory language certainly is no less important.

*   *   *

[The Court next reviews the legislative history of § 10(b), concluding that it lends no support for an argument that Congress intended § 10(b) to embrace negligent conduct.]

*   *   *

C

The 1933 and 1934 Acts constitute interrelated components of the federal regulatory scheme governing transactions in securities. *See Blue Chip Stamps*, 421 U.S., at 727–730, 95 S.Ct. 1917, 1921–1922, 46 L.Ed.2d 539, 544–546. As the Court indicated in SEC v. National Securities, Inc., 393 U.S. 453, 466, 89 S.Ct. 564, 571, 21 L.Ed.2d 668 (1969), "the interdependence of the various sections of the securities laws is certainly a relevant factor in any interpretation of the language Congress has chosen   *   *   *."   *   *   *

The Commission argues that Congress has been explicit in requiring willful conduct when that was the standard of fault intended, citing § 9 of the 1934 Act, 48 Stat. 889, 15 U.S.C.A. § 78i, which generally proscribes manipulation of securities prices.   *   *   *

The structure of the Acts does not support the Commission's argument. In each instance that Congress created express civil liability in favor of purchasers or sellers of securities it clearly specified whether recovery was to be premised on knowing or intentional conduct, negligence, or entirely innocent mistake. See 1933 Act §§ 11, 12, 15, 48 Stat. 82, 84, as amended, 15 U.S.C.A. §§ 77k, 77*l*, 77*o*; 1934 Act §§ 9, 18, 20, 48 Stat. 889, 897, 899, as amended, 15 U.S.C.A. §§ 78i, 78r, 78t.   *   *   *

We also consider it significant that each of the express civil remedies in the 1933 Act allowing recovery for negligent conduct, see §§ 11, 12(2), 15, 15 U.S.C.A. §§ 77k, 77*l*(2), 77*o*, is subject to significant procedural restrictions not applicable under § 10(b).   *   *   * We think these procedural limitations indicate that the judicially created private damages remedy under § 10(b)—which has no comparable restrictions [29]—cannot be extended, consistently with the intent of Con-

---

29. Since no statute of limitations is provided for civil actions under § 10(b), the law of limitations of the forum State is followed as in other cases of judicially

gress, to actions premised on negligent wrongdoing. Such extension would allow causes of action covered by §§ 11, 12(2), and 15 to be brought instead under § 10(b) and thereby nullify the effectiveness of the carefully drawn procedural restrictions on these express actions. * * *

D

We have addressed, to this point, primarily the language and history of § 10(b). The Commission contends, however, that subsections (b) and (c) of Rule 10b–5 are cast in language which—if standing alone—could encompass both intentional and negligent behavior. * * *

Viewed in isolation the language of subsection (b), and arguably that of subsection (c), could be read as proscribing, respectively, any type of material misstatement or omission, and any course of conduct, that has the effect of defrauding investors, whether the wrongdoing was intentional or not.

We note first that such a reading cannot be harmonized with the administrative history of the Rule, a history making clear that when the Commission adopted the Rule it was intended to apply only to activities that involved scienter. More importantly, Rule 10b–5 was adopted pursuant to authority granted the Commission under § 10(b). The rulemaking power granted to an administrative agency charged with the administration of a federal statute is not the power to make law. Rather, it is " 'the power to adopt regulations to carry into effect the will of Congress as expressed by the statute.' " *Dixon v. United States*, 381 U.S. 68, 74, 85 S.Ct. 1301, 1305, 14 L.Ed.2d 223, 228 (1965), quoting Manhattan General Equipment Co. v. Commissioner, 297 U.S. 129, 134, 56 S.Ct. 397, 399, 80 L.Ed. 528, 531 (1936). * * * When a statute speaks so specifically in terms of manipulation and deception, and of implementing devices and contrivances—the commonly understood terminology of intentional wrongdoing—and when its history reflects no more expansive intent, we are quite unwilling to extend the scope of the statute to negligent conduct.[33]

* * *

implied remedies. *See* Holmberg v. Armbrecht, 327 U.S. 392, 395, 66 S.Ct. 582, 584, 90 L.Ed. 743, 746 (1946), and cases cited therein. Although it is not always certain which state statute of limitations should be followed, such statutes of limitations usually are longer than the period provided under § 13.

33. As we find the language and history of § 10(b) dispositive of the appropriate standard of liability, there is no occasion to examine the additional considerations of "policy," set forth by the parties, that may have influenced the lawmakers in their formulation of the

statute. We do note that the standard urged by respondents would significantly broaden the class of plaintiffs who may seek to impose liability upon accountants and other experts who perform services or express opinions with respect to matters under the Acts. Last Term, in *Blue Chip Stamps*, 421 U.S., at 747–748, 95 S.Ct., at 1931, 46 L.Ed.2d, at 556, the Court pertinently observed:

While much of the development of the law of deceit has been the elimination of artificial barriers to recovery on just claims, we are not the first court to express concern that the inexorable

The judgment of the Court of Appeals is
Reversed.

NOTE—SCIENTER IN INJUNCTIVE ACTIONS

In footnote 12 of *Hochfelder* the Court specifically reserved decision on the necessity of a showing of scienter in an action for an injunction. The question was of particular interest to the SEC, for which injunctive proceedings are an important enforcement tool. The Supreme Court finally answered the question definitively in Aaron v. SEC, 446 U.S. 680, 100 S.Ct. 1945, 64 L.Ed.2d 611 (1980). Taking the same literal approach to a linguistic analysis of the statute as it had in *Hochfelder*, the Court held that there was no action under § 10(b) (or, therefore, under Rule 10b–5) without scienter. By contrast, however, using the same sort of analysis, the Court held that the SEC could sue for an injunction under §§ 17(a)(2) and 17(a)(3) of the 1933 Act with only a showing of negligence. Because it uses the word "defraud," however, § 17(a)(1) requires a showing of scienter. Since § 17(a) applies only to *sales* of securities, however, neither the SEC nor a defrauded seller may get an injunction against negligently misleading statements made by a *purchaser*.

D. INSIDER TRADING

PROBLEM

ALTERNATIVE ENERGY CORPORATION—PART III

Sunny Powers is the assistant treasurer of AEC, where she has worked since graduating from business school five years ago. Her responsibilities at the company are strictly financial, and she has little or no contact with the technical side of the business.

For several months she has been going out occasionally with Jack Apollo, a young engineer who also works for AEC. The other night

broadening of the class of plaintiff who may sue in this area of the law will ultimately result in more harm than good. In Ultramares Corp. v. Touche, 255 N.Y. 170, 174 N.E. 441 (1931), Chief Judge Cardozo observed with respect to 'a liability in an indeterminate amount for an indeterminate time to an indeterminate class:

> The hazards of a business conducted on these terms are so extreme as to enkindle doubt whether a flaw may not exist in the implication of a duty that exposes to these consequences. *Id.*, at 179–180, 174 N.E., at 444.

This case, on its facts, illustrates the extreme reach of the standard urged by respondents. As investors in transactions initiated by Nay, not First Securities, they were not foreseeable users of the financial statements prepared by Ernst & Ernst. Respondents conceded that they did not rely on either these financial statements or Ernst & Ernst's certificates of opinion. The class of persons eligible to benefit from such a standard, though small in this case, could be numbered in the thousands in other cases. Acceptance of respondents' view would extend to new frontiers the "hazards" of rendering expert advice under the Acts, raising serious policy questions not yet addressed by Congress.

at dinner Apollo excitedly told her that he and his colleagues were nearing completion of their work on a new solar cell and were on the verge of informing AEC's top management that the device was ready for production. He told her that, although some people who were working on the cell felt that it was likely to be expensive to produce and would therefore be only marginally profitable, he was of the opinion that it had the potential to increase AEC's earnings substantially over the next few years. The two joked that the stock market apparently agreed with him rather than his colleagues because AEC's stock had risen ten points a few months before on the basis of an erroneous report about progress on the device.

A

Powers now owns 500 shares of AEC common stock. Four months ago, she sold 500 shares at $40 in order to make a downpayment on a house. She recently inherited $50,000 and is considering using it to purchase more AEC stock. After her conversation with Apollo, she has even thought of buying calls on the stock, or at least purchasing it on margin. She is concerned, however, about legal restrictions against insider trading. She has called you to ask your advice.

If she were to buy now, would she violate (a) state law? (b) Section 16(b) of the 1934 Act? (c) Rule 10b–5? What would be the legal consequences of her violating any of these restrictions? Could she buy AEC debentures? Does it matter if they are convertible?

B

Assume that you have advised Powers that in your opinion her knowledge about the state of the new solar cell is material non-public information and that she should therefore not buy before AEC makes a public announcement. On Friday morning she learns from AEC's president that there will be a press release about the device at the beginning of the following week. She calls you to tell you that she will be leaving the following day for a two-week raft trip down the Colorado river. She asks if she can tell her stock broker to watch for a favorable news item about AEC and to buy 2000 shares of AEC stock on margin as soon as the news comes across the Dow Jones broad tape. Alternatively, she asks whether she can place an order to buy AEC if its price rises from $45, where it is now trading, to $48.

C

That night Powers paid a visit to her favorite bar where she fell into a conversation about AEC with the bartender, Phil Draft, who goes to business school during the day. She told Draft everything she knew about the new solar device. Later that evening Draft recounted his conversation with Powers, whom he identified as a "junior executive at AEC", to Shorty Swing, a stock broker. The next day Swing (1) bought 1000 shares of AEC common for his own account and 5000 shares each for three discretionary accounts, and (2) got a haircut, during which he told his barber what he had learned about AEC. The barber repeated this information to his next customer, Ted Trader, who purchased 1000 shares of AEC immediately upon returning to his office. Did any of these individuals violate Rule 10b–5?

1. COMMON LAW

a. Duty to Shareholders and Investors

GOODWIN v. AGASSIZ

283 Mass. 358, 186 N.E. 659 (1933).

RUGG, Chief Justice.

[A stockholder of the Cliff Mining Company, the stock of which was listed on the Boston Stock Exchange, sought relief for losses suffered in the sale through the exchange of 700 shares of the company's stock to the defendants, who were officers and directors of the corporation. The court accepted the trial judge's findings that Cliff had started exploration for copper on its land in 1925, acting on certain geological surveys. The exploration was not successful, however, and the company removed its equipment in May, 1926.

Meanwhile, in March, 1926, an experienced geologist wrote a report theorizing as to the existence of copper deposits in the region of the company's holdings. The defendants, believing there was merit to the theory, secured options to land adjacent to the copper belt. Also, anticipating an increase in the value of the stock if the theory proved correct, the defendants purchased shares of the company's stock through an agent.

When the plaintiff learned of the termination of the original exploratory operations from a newspaper article—for which defendants were in no way responsible—he immediately sold his stock.]

The contention of the plaintiff is that the purchase of his stock in the company by the defendants without disclosing to him as a stockholder their knowledge of the geologist's theory, their belief that the theory was true, had value, the keeping secret the existence of the theory, discontinuance by the defendants of exploratory operations begun in 1925 on property of the Cliff Mining Company and their plan ultimately to test the value of the theory, constitute actionable wrong for which he as stockholder can recover.

The trial judge ruled that conditions may exist which would make it the duty of an officer of a corporation purchasing its stock from a stockholder to inform him as to knowledge possessed by the buyer and not by the seller, but found, on all the circumstances developed by the trial and set out at some length by him in his decision, that there was no fiduciary relation requiring such disclosure by the defendants to the plaintiff before buying his stock in the manner in which they did.

The question presented is whether the decree dismissing the bill rightly was entered on the facts found.

The directors of a commercial corporation stand in a relation of trust to the corporation and are bound to exercise the strictest good faith in respect to its property and business. The contention that directors also occupy the position of trustee toward individual stockholders in the corporation is plainly contrary to repeated decisions of this court and cannot be supported. In Smith v. Hurd, 12 Metc. 371, 384, 46 Am.Dec. 690, it was said by Chief Justice Shaw: "There is no legal privity, relation, or immediate connexion, between the holders of shares in a bank, in their individual capacity, on the one side, and the directors of the bank on the other. The directors are not the bailees, the factors, agents or trustees of such individual stockholders."
* * *

The principle thus established is supported by an imposing weight of authority in other jurisdictions. A rule holding that directors are trustees for individual stockholders with respect to their stock prevails in comparatively few states; but in view of our own adjudications it is not necessary to review decisions to that effect.

While the general principle is as stated, circumstances may exist requiring that transactions between a director and a stockholder as to stock in the corporation be set aside. The knowledge naturally in the possession of a director as to the condition of a corporation places upon him a peculiar obligation to observe every requirement of fair dealing when directly buying or selling its stock. Mere silence does not usually amount to a breach of duty, but parties may stand in such relation to each other than an equitable responsibility arises to communicate facts. Wellington v. Rugg, 243 Mass. 30, 35, 136 N.E. 831. Purchases and sales of stock dealt in on the stock exchange are commonly impersonal affairs. An honest director would be in a difficult situation if he could neither buy nor sell on the stock exchange shares of stock in his corporation without first seeking out the other actual ultimate party to the transaction and disclosing to him everything which a court or jury might later find that he then knew affecting the real or speculative value of such shares. Business of that nature is a matter to be governed by practical rules. Fiduciary obligations of directors ought not to be made so onerous that men of experience and ability will be deterred from accepting such office. Law in its sanctions is not coextensive with morality. It cannot undertake to put all parties to every contract on an equality as to knowledge, experience, skill and shrewdness. It cannot undertake to relieve against hard bargains made between competent parties without fraud. On the other hand, directors cannot rightly be allowed to indulge with impunity in practices which do violence to prevailing standards of upright businessmen. Therefore, where a director personally seeks a stockholder for the purpose of buying his shares without making disclosure of material facts within his peculiar knowledge and not within reach of the stockholder, the transaction will be closely scrutinized and relief may be granted in appropriate instances. Strong v. Repide, 213 U.S. 419, 29 S.Ct. 521, 53 L.Ed. 853 * * *.

The precise question to be decided in the case at bar is whether on the facts found the defendants as directors had a right to buy stock of the plaintiff, a stockholder. Every element of actual fraud or misdoing by the defendants is negatived by the findings. Fraud cannot be presumed; it must be proved. Brown v. Little, Brown & Co., Inc., 269 Mass. 102, 117, 168 N.E. 521. The facts found afford no ground for inferring fraud or conspiracy. The only knowledge possessed by the defendants not open to the plaintiff was the existence of a theory formulated in a thesis by a geologist as to the possible existence of copper deposits where certain geological conditions existed common to the property of the Cliff Mining Company and that of other mining companies in its neighborhood. This thesis did not express an opinion that copper deposits would be found at any particular spot or on property of any specified owner. Whether that theory was sound or fallacious, no one knew, and so far as appears has never been demonstrated. The defendants made no representations to anybody about the theory. No facts found placed upon them any obligation to disclose the theory. A few days after the thesis expounding the theory was brought to the attention of the defendants, the annual report by the directors of the Cliff Mining Company for the calendar year 1925, signed by Agassiz for the directors, was issued. It did not cover the time when the theory was formulated. The report described the status of the operations under the exploration which had been begun in 1925. At the annual meeting of the stockholders of the company held early in April, 1926, no reference was made to the theory. It was then at most a hope, possibly an expectation. It had not passed the nebulous stage. No disclosure was made of it. The Cliff Mining Company was not harmed by the nondisclosure. There would have been no advantage to it, so far as appears, from a disclosure. * * * In the circumstances there was no duty on the part of the defendants to set forth to the stockholders at the annual meeting their faith, aspirations and plans for the future. Events as they developed might render advisable radical changes in such views. Disclosure of the theory, if it ultimately was proved to be erroneous or without foundation in fact, might involve the defendants in litigation with those who might act on the hypothesis that it was correct. The stock of the Cliff Mining Company was bought and sold on the stock exchange. The identity of buyers and seller of the stock in question in fact was not known to the parties and perhaps could not readily have been ascertained. The defendants caused the shares to be bought through brokers on the stock exchange. They said nothing to anybody as to the reasons actuating them. The plaintiff was no novice. He was a member of the Boston stock exchange and had kept a record of sales of Cliff Mining Company stock. He acted upon his own judgment in selling his stock. He made no inquiries of the defendants or of other officers of the company. The result is that the plaintiff cannot prevail.

Decree dismissing bill affirmed with costs.

———

NOTE

The conventional analysis holds that there are at common law three basic rules with respect to an insider's duty in trading in the corporation's stock. What is generally described as "the majority rule" takes the position that directors and officers owe a fiduciary duty only to the corporation; and accordingly they are under no affirmative obligation to disclose material non-public information when dealing with others who are unaware of it.

A second rule, developed in reaction to the sometimes harsh consequences of this approach, is the "special facts doctrine" enunciated in Strong v. Repide, 213 U.S. 419, 29 S.Ct. 521, 53 L.Ed. 853 (1909). This rule accepts that there may normally be no fiduciary duty owing by the insider to individual shareholders. But when, because of the particular circumstances surrounding a given transaction, nondisclosure amounts to unconscionable behavior on the insider's part, the plaintiff will be allowed a remedy.

In *Strong* the defendant was a director, the majority stockholder, and general manager of the corporation. He was authorized by the board of directors to conduct negotiations leading to the sale to the United States government of otherwise worthless land that was one of the corporation's principal assets. At the time of the transaction in question, he, alone, knew that the successful completion of the negotiations was near at hand. Without revealing his identity, he purchased through an agent, the shares of another stockholder for one-tenth what the shares were to become worth when the property was sold three months later. The Supreme Court granted rescission of the sale of stock, saying, "That the defendant was a director of the corporation is but one of the facts upon which the liability is asserted, the existence of all the others in addition making such a combination as rendered it the plain duty of the defendant to speak." 213 U.S. at 431. Other courts have invoked the "special facts doctrine" often enough to erode significantly the strict majority rule.

According to the third "rule," one that has steadily attracted more adherents among state courts, officers and directors owe a fiduciary duty to individual shareholders as well as to the corporation, regardless of whether there are special circumstances and thus have a duty to disclose material nonpublic information in any face-to-face stock transaction with a shareholder. This duty "exists because the stockholders have placed the directors in a strategic position where they

can secure firsthand knowledge of important developments. * * *
[T]he detailed information a director has of corporate affairs is in a
very real sense property of the corporation, and * * * no director
should be permitted to use such information for his own benefit at
the expense of his stockholders." Taylor v. Wright, 69 Cal.App.2d
371, 159 P.2d 980, 984–85 (1945).

This "strict" or "Kansas" rule had its origin in Hotchkiss v. Fischer, 136 Kan. 530, 16 P.2d 531 (1932). The plaintiff, an impoverished
widow from Burr Oak, Kansas, came to Topeka shortly before a
board meeting to inquire of the defendant, who was president and a
director of the corporation, whether she could expect a dividend. If
not, she felt she would have to sell her stock. The president replied
that he could not say whether a dividend would be declared until the
board met. He showed her the corporation's financial statements, explained them, but maintained a rather pessimistic stance. The widow
sold her stock to him for $1.25 per share. Three days later, the cor-
poration declared a dividend of $1 per share. The court held that in
such a transaction, the officer or director "acts in a relation of
scrupulous trust and confidence," and his behavior is therefore subject to the closest scrutiny.

Whether arising out of the "Kansas rule" or the "special facts
doctrine," the fiduciary duty of the insider, narrowly conceived,
would apply only in dealings with a shareholder. It could therefore
be thought to impose an obligation to disclose in the normal case only
when the plaintiff is selling stock to the insider since a buyer of stock
would not usually become a stockholder until after the transaction.
Judge Learned Hand called this a "sorry distinction," Gratz v.
Claughton, 187 F.2d 46, 49 (2d Cir. 1951), cert. denied 341 U.S. 920, 71
S.Ct. 741, 95 L.Ed. 1353. It is one that has not been applied at least
under federal law. See, e.g., Elkind v. Liggett & Myers, Inc., 635 F.
2d 156 (2d Cir. 1980).

b. Duty to the Corporation

DIAMOND v. OREAMUNO

24 N.Y.2d 494, 301 N.Y.S.2d 78, 248 N.E.2d 910 (1969).

FULD, Chief Judge.

Upon this appeal from an order denying a motion to dismiss the
complaint as insufficient on its face, the question presented—one of
first impression in this court—is whether officers and directors may
be held accountable to their corporation for gains realized by them
from transactions in the company's stock as a result of their use of
material inside information.

The complaint was filed by a shareholder of Management Assistance, Inc. (MAI) asserting a derivative action against a number of its
officers and directors to compel an accounting for profits allegedly
acquired as a result of a breach of fiduciary duty. It charges that

two of the defendants—Oreamuno, chairman of the board of directors, and Gonzalez, its president—had used inside information, acquired by them solely by virtue of their positions, in order to reap large personal profits from the sale of MAI shares and that these profits rightfully belong to the corporation. Other officers and directors were joined as defendants on the ground that they acquiesced in or ratified the assertedly wrongful transactions.

MAI is in the business of financing computer installations through sale and lease back arrangements with various commercial and industrial users. Under its lease provisions, MAI was required to maintain and repair the computers but, at the time of this suit, it lacked the capacity to perform this function itself and was forced to engage the manufacturer of the computers, International Business Machines (IBM), to service the machines. As a result of a sharp increase by IBM of its charges for such service, MAI's expenses for August of 1966 rose considerably and its net earnings declined from $262,253 in July to $66,233 in August, a decrease of about 75%. This information, although earlier known to the defendants, was not made public until October of 1966. Prior to the release of the information, however, Oreamuno and Gonzalez sold off a total of 56,500 shares of their MAI stock at the then current market price of $28 a share.

After the information concerning the drop in earnings was made available to the public, the value of a share of MAI stock immediately fell from the $28 realized by the defendants to $11. Thus, the plaintiff alleges, by taking advantage of their privileged position and their access to confidential information, Oreamuno and Gonzalez were able to realize $800,000 more for their securities than they would have had this inside information not been available to them. * * * A motion by the defendants to dismiss the complaint * * * for failure to state a cause of action was granted by the court at Special Term. * * *

It is well established, as a general proposition, that a person who acquires special knowledge or information by virtue of a confidential or fiduciary relationship with another is not free to exploit that knowledge or information for his own personal benefit but must account to his principal for any profits derived therefrom. This, in turn, is merely a corollary of the broader principle, inherent in the nature of the fiduciary relationship, that prohibits a trustee or agent from extracting secret profits from his position of trust.

In support of their claim that the complaint fails to state a cause of action, the defendants take the position that, although it is admittedly wrong for an officer or director to use his position to obtain trading profits for himself in the stock of his corporation, the action ascribed to them did not injure or damage MAI in any way. Accordingly, the defendants continue, the corporation should not be permitted to recover the proceeds. They acknowledge that, by virtue of the exclusive access which officers and directors have to inside information, they possess an unfair advantage over other shareholders and, particularly, the persons who had purchased the stock from them but, they contend, the corporation itself was unaffected and, for that reason, a derivative action is an inappropriate remedy.

It is true that the complaint before us does not contain any allegation of damages to the corporation but this has never been considered to be an essential requirement for a cause of action founded on a breach of fiduciary duty. This is because the function of such an action, unlike an ordinary tort or contract case, is not merely to compensate the plaintiff for wrongs committed by the defendant but, as this court declared many years ago (Dutton v. Willner, 52 N.Y. 312, 319) "to *prevent* them, by removing from agents and trustees all inducement to attempt dealing for their own benefit in matters which they have undertaken for others, or to which their agency or trust relates." (Emphasis supplied.)

Just as a trustee has no right to retain for himself the profits yielded by property placed in his possession but must account to his beneficiaries, a corporate fiduciary, who is entrusted with potentially valuable information, may not appropriate that asset for his own use even though, in so doing, he causes no injury to the corporation. The primary concern, in a case such as this, is not to determine whether the corporation has been damaged but to decide, as between the corporation and the defendants, who has a higher claim to the proceeds derived from the exploitation of the information. In our opinion, there can be no justification for permitting officers and directors, such as the defendants, to retain for themselves profits which, it is alleged, they derived solely from exploiting information gained by virtue of their inside position as corporate officials.

In addition, it is pertinent to observe that, despite the lack of any specific allegation of damage, it may well be inferred that the defendants' actions might have caused some harm to the enterprise. Although the corporation may have little concern with the day-to-day transactions in its shares, it has a great interest in maintaining a reputation of integrity, an image of probity, for its management and in insuring the continued public acceptance and marketability of its stock. When officers and directors abuse their position in order to gain personal profits, the effect may be to cast a cloud on the corporation's name, injure stockholder relations and undermine public regard for the corporation's securities. As Presiding Justice Botein aptly put it, in the course of his opinion for the Appellate Division, "[t]he prestige and good will of a corporation, so vital to its prosperity, may be undermined by the revelation that its chief officers had been making personal profits out of corporate events which they had not disclosed to the community of stockholders." (29 A.D.2d at p. 287, 287 N.Y.S.2d at p. 303.)

The defendants maintain that extending the prohibition against personal exploitation of a fiduciary relationship to officers and directors of a corporation will discourage such officials from maintaining a stake in the success of the corporate venture through share ownership, which, they urge, is an important incentive to proper performance of their duties. There is, however, a considerable difference between corporate officers who assume the same risks and obtain the same benefits as other shareholders and those who use their privileged position to gain special advantages not available to others. The sale of shares by the defendants for the reasons charged was not merely a wise investment decision which any prudent investor might have made. Rather, they were assertedly able in this case to profit solely because they had information which was not available to any one else—including the other shareholders whose interests they, as corporate fiduciaries, were bound to protect.

Although no appellate court in this State has had occasion to pass upon the precise question before us, the concept underlying the present cause of action is hardly a new one. (See, e.g., Securities Exchange Act of 1934 [48 U.S.Stat. 881], § 16[b]; U.S.Code, tit. 15, § 78p, subd. [b]; Brophy v. Cities Serv. Co., 31 Del.Ch. 241; Restatement, 2d, Agency, § 388, comment c.) Under Federal law (Securities Exchange Act of 1934, § 16[b]), for example, it is conclusively presumed that, when a director, officer or 10% shareholder buys and sells securities of his corporation within a six-month period, he is trading on inside information. The remedy which the Federal statute provides in that situation is precisely the same as that sought in the present case under State law, namely, an action brought by the corporation or on its behalf to recover all profits derived from the transactions.

In providing this remedy, Congress accomplished a dual purpose. It not only provided for an efficient and effective method of accomplishing its primary goal—the protection of the investing public from unfair treatment at the hands of corporate insiders—but extended to the corporation the right to secure for itself benefits derived by those insiders from their exploitation of their privileged position. * * *

Although the provisions of section 16(b) may not apply to all cases of trading on inside information, it demonstrates that a derivative action can be an effective method for dealing with such abuses which may be used to accomplish a similar purpose in cases not specifically covered by the statute. In Brophy v. Cities Serv. Co. (31 Del.Ch. 241, 70 A.2d 5, *supra*), for example, the Chancery Court of Delaware allowed a similar remedy in a situation not covered by the Federal legislation. One of the defendants in that case was an employee who had acquired inside information that the corporate plaintiff was about to enter the market and purchase its own shares. On the basis of this confidential information, the employee, who was not an officer and, hence, not liable under Federal law, bought a large block of shares and, after the corporation's purchases had caused the price to rise, resold them at a profit. The court sustained the complaint in a derivative action brought for an accounting, stating that "[p]ublic policy will not permit an employee occupying a position of trust and confidence toward his employer to abuse that relation to his own profit, regardless of whether his employer suffers a loss" (31 Del.Ch., at p. 246, 70 A.2d, at p. 8). And a similar view has been expressed in the Restatement, 2d, Agency (§ 388, comment c):

> c. *Use of confidential information.* An agent who acquires confidential information in the course of his employment or in violation of his duties has a duty * * * to account for any profits made by the use of such information, although this does not harm the principal. * * * So, if [a corporate officer] has 'inside' information that the corporation is about to purchase or sell securities, or to declare or to pass a dividend, profits made by him in stock transactions undertaken because of his knowledge are held in constructive trust for the principal.

In the present case, the defendants may be able to avoid liability to the corporation under section 16(b) of the Federal law since they had held the MAI shares for more than six months prior to the sales. Nevertheless, the alleged use of the inside information to dispose of their stock at a price considerably higher than its known value constituted the same sort of "abuse of a fiduciary relationship" as is condemned by the Federal law. Sitting as we are in this case as a court of equity, we should not hesitate to permit an action to prevent any unjust enrichment realized by the defendants from their allegedly wrongful act.

The defendants recognize that the conduct charged against them directly contravened the policy embodied in the Securities Exchange Act but, they maintain, the Federal legislation constitutes a comprehensive and carefully wrought plan for dealing with the abuse of inside information and that allowing a derivative action to be maintained under State law would interfere with the Federal scheme. Moreover, they urge, the existence of dual Federal and State remedies for the same act would create the possibility of double liability.

An examination of the Federal regulatory scheme refutes the contention that it was designed to establish any particular remedy as exclusive. In addition to the specific provisions of section 16(b), the Securities and Exchange Act contains a general anti-fraud provision in section 10(b) (U.S.Code, tit. 15, § 78j, subd. [b]) which, as implemented by rule 10b–5 (Code of Fed.Reg., tit. 17, § 240.10b–5) under that section, renders it unlawful to engage in a variety of acts considered to be fraudulent. In interpreting this rule, the Securities and Exchange Commission and the Federal courts have extended the common-law definition of fraud to include not only affirmative misrepresentations, relied upon by the purchaser or seller, but also a failure to disclose material information which might have affected the transaction.

Accepting the truth of the complainant's allegations, there is no question but that the defendants were guilty of withholding material information from the purchasers of the shares and, indeed, the defendants acknowledge that the facts asserted constitute a violation of rule 10b–5. The remedies which the Federal law provides for such violation, however, are rather limited. An action could be brought, in an exceptional case, by the SEC for injunctive relief. This, in fact, is what happened in the *Texas Gulf Sulphur* case (401 F.2d 833). The purpose of such an action, however, would appear to be more to establish a principle than to provide a regular method of enforcement. A class action under the Federal rule might be a more effective remedy but the mechanics of such an action have, as far as we have been able to ascertain, not yet been worked out by the Federal courts and several questions relating thereto have never been resolved. These include the definition of the class entitled to bring such an action, the measure of damages, the administration of the fund which would be recovered and its distribution to the members of the class. Of course, any individual purchaser, who could prove an injury as a result of a rule 10b–5 violation can bring his own action for rescission but we have not been referred to a single case in which such an action has been successfully prosecuted where the public sale of securities is involved. The reason for this is that sales of securities, whether through a stock exchange or over-the-counter, are characteristically anonymous transactions, usually handled through brokers, and the matching of the ultimate buyer with the ultimate seller presents virtually insurmountable obstacles. Thus, unless a section 16(b) violation is also present, the Federal law does not yet provide a really effective remedy.

In view of the practical difficulties inherent in an action under the Federal law, the desirability of creating an effective common-law remedy is manifest. "Dishonest directors should not find absolution from retributive justice", Ballantine observed in his work on Corporations ([rev.ed., 1946], p. 216), "by concealing their identity from their victims under the mask of the stock exchange." There is ample room in a situation such as is here presented for a "private Attorney General" to come forward and enforce proper behavior on the part of corporate officials through the medium of the derivative action brought in the name of the corporation. Only by sanctioning such a cause of action will there be any effective method to prevent the type type of abuse of corporate office complained of in this case.

There is nothing in the Federal law which indicates that it was intended to limit the power of the States to fashion additional remedies to effectuate similar purposes. Although the impact of Federal securities regulation has on occasion been said to have created a "Federal corporation law," in fact, its effect on the duties and obligations of directors and officers and their relation to the corporation and its shareholders is only occasional and peripheral. The primary source of the law in this area ever remains that of the State which created the corporation. Indeed, Congress expressly provided against any implication that it intended to pre-empt the field by declaring, in section 28(a) of the Securities Exchange Act of 1934 (48 U. S.Stat. 903), that "[t]he rights and remedies provided by this title shall be in addition to any and all other rights and remedies that may exist at law or in equity".

Nor should we be deterred, in formulating a State remedy, by the defendants' claim of possible double liability. Certainly, as already indicated, if the sales in question were publicly made, the likelihood that a suit will be brought by purchasers of the shares is quite remote. But, even if it were not, the mere possibility of such a suit is not a defense nor does it render the complaint insufficient. It is not unusual for an action to be brought to recover a fund which may be subject to a superior claim by a third party. If that be the situation, a defendant should not be permitted to retain the fund for his own use on the chance that such a party may eventually appear. A defendant's course, if he wishes to protect himself against double liability, is to interplead any and all possible claimants and bind them to the judgment.

In any event, though, no suggestion has been made either in brief or on oral argument that any purchaser has come forward with a claim against the defendants or even that anyone is in a position to advance such a claim. As we have stated, the defendants' assertion that such a party may come forward at some future date is not a basis for permitting them to retain for their own benefit the fruits of their allegedly wrongful acts. For all that appears, the present derivative action is the only effective remedy now available against the abuse by these defendants of their privileged position.

* * *

The order appealed from should be affirmed, with costs, and the question certified answered in the affirmative.

2. POLICY ASPECTS

PROBLEM

LEGISLATIVE POLICYMAKING

You have recently joined the staff of a United States Senator who is a member of the Committee on Banking, Housing, and Urban Affairs, which has jurisdiction over the securities laws. (a) The Senator is concerned over criticisms of the substance and the effectiveness of the restrictions on insider trading and has asked you to prepare a memorandum discussing the issues and making recommendations as to whether Congress should repeal, strengthen, or modify the law as it has developed under Rule 10b–5. (b) The Senator has also asked for an analysis of whether § 16(b) should be strengthened, left alone, or repealed. (c) You have also been asked to consider the alternative of requiring corporations regulated by the '34 Act to disclose their policies with respect to trading by their employees and directors on the basis of material inside information. Such a statement of policy would indicate whether the corporation would take no action against employees who engaged in insider trading, would dismiss them, would proceed against them to recover any profits so earned, or would take some other action.

What are your recommendations?

FREEMAN v. DECIO

584 F.2d 186 (7th Cir. 1978).

* * *

I.

Diamond v. Oreamuno and Indiana Law

Both parties agree that there is no Indiana precedent directly dealing with the question of whether a corporation may recover the profits of corporate officials who trade in the corporation's securities on the basis of inside information. However, the plaintiff suggests that were the question to be presented to the Indiana courts, they would adopt the holding of the New York Court of Appeals in Diamond v. Oreamuno, 24 N.Y.2d 494, 301 N.Y.S.2d 78, 248 N.E.2d 910 (1969). There, building on the Delaware case of Brophy v. Cities Service Co., 31 Del.Ch. 241, 70 A.2d 5 (1949), the court held that the officers and directors of a corporation breached their fiduciary duties owed to the corporation by trading in its stock on the basis of material non-public information acquired by virtue of their official positions and that they should account to the corporation for their profits from those transactions. Since *Diamond* was decided, few courts have had an opportunity to consider the problem there presented. In fact, only one case has been brought to our attention which raised the question of whether *Diamond* would be followed in another jurisdiction. In Schein v. Chasen, 478 F.2d 817 (2d Cir. 1973), vacated and remanded sub nom., Lehman Bros. v. Schein, 416 U.S. 386, 94 S.Ct. 1741, 40 L.Ed.2d 215 (1974), on certification to the Fla.Sup.Ct., 313 So.2d 739 (Fla.1975), the Second Circuit, sitting in diversity, considered whether the Florida courts would permit a *Diamond*-type action to be brought on behalf of a corporation. The majority not only tacitly concluded that Florida would adopt *Diamond*, but that the *Diamond* cause of action should be extended so as to permit recovery of the profits of non-insiders who traded in the corporation's stock on the basis of inside information received as tips from insiders. Judge Kaufman, dissenting, agreed with the policies underlying a *Diamond*-type cause of action, but disagreed with the extension of liability to outsiders. He also failed to understand why the panel was not willing to utilize Florida's certified question statute so as to bring the question of law before the Florida Supreme Court. Granting *certiorari*, the United States Supreme Court agreed with the dissent on this last point and on remand the case was certified to the Florida Supreme Court. That court not only stated that it would not "give the unprecedented expansive reading to *Diamond* sought by appellants" but that, furthermore, it did not "choose to adopt the innovative ruling of the New York Court of Appeals in *Diamond* [itself]." 313 So.2d 739, 746 (Fla. 1975). Thus, the question here is whether the Indiana courts are more likely to follow the New York Court of Appeals or to join the Florida Supreme Court in refusing to undertake such a change from existing law.

It appears that from a policy point of view it is widely accepted that insider trading should be deterred because it is unfair to other investors who do not enjoy the benefits of access to inside information. The goal is not one of equality of possession of information—since some traders will always be better "informed" than others by dint of greater expenditures of time and resources, greater experience, or greater analytical abilities—but rather equality of access to information.[9] Thus, in *Cady, Roberts & Co.*, 40 S.E.C. 907, 912 (1961), the SEC gave the following explanation of its view of the obligation of corporate insiders to disclose material inside information when trading in the corporation's stock:

> Analytically, the obligation rests on two principal elements: first, the existence of a relationship giving access, directly or indirectly, to information intended to be available only for a corporate purpose and not for the personal benefit of anyone, and second, the inherent unfairness involved where a party takes advantage of such information knowing it is unavailable to those with whom he is dealing.

Yet, a growing body of commentary suggests that pursuit of this goal of "market egalitarianism" may be costly. In addition to the costs associated with enforcement of the laws prohibiting insider trading, there may be a loss in the efficiency of the securities markets in their capital allocation function. The basic insight of economic analysis here is that securities prices act as signals helping to route capital to its most productive uses and that insider trading helps assure that those prices will reflect the best information available (i.e., inside information) as to where the best opportunities lie.[13] However, even when confronted with the possibility of a trade-off between fair-

9. As was stated by Professor Hetherington, "[u]nder any 'game' theory of the market a player is likely to consider unfair any advantage gained by his competitors that he not only does not have, but that he cannot obtain." J. Hetherington, Insider Trading and the Logic of the Law, 1967 Wis.L.Rev. 720, 721 (1967).

13. * * *

However, it has been suggested that insider trading may harm the securities markets in indirect ways. For one thing, outsiders might be less willing to invest in securities markets marked by the prevalence of a practice which they consider unfair. In addition an equal, if not greater degree of allocative efficiency can normally be achieved if the inside information is made public.

ness and economic efficiency, most authorities appear to find that the balance tips in favor of discouraging insider trading.

Over 40 years ago Congress was stirred by examples of flagrant abuse of inside information unearthed during the hearings preceding the 1933 and 1934 Securities Acts to include in the latter a section aimed at insider trading. Section 16(b) provides for the automatic recovery by corporations of profits made by insiders in short-swing transactions within a six-month period. This automatic accountability makes the rule one of relatively easy application and avoids very difficult problems concerning the measurement of damages, yet upon occasion leads to harsh results. The section has been characterized as a "crude rule of thumb." It is too narrow in that only short-swing trading and short selling are covered, leaving untouched other ways of profiting from inside information in the securities market. It is too broad in that short-swing trades not actually made on the basis of inside information are also caught in the Section's web of liability.

The SEC has also used its full panoply of powers to police insider trading through enforcement actions and civil actions. The agency has relied, *inter alia*, on Section 17(a) of the 1933 Act, Section 15(c)(1) of the 1934 Act, and Rule 10b–5. The relief obtained has included not only injunctions and suspension orders, but also disgorgement of profits earned in insider trading.

Lastly, the "victims" [20] of insider trading may recover damages from the insiders in many instances. Absent fraud, the traditional common law approach has been to permit officers and directors of corporations to trade in their corporation's securities free from liability to other traders for failing to disclose inside information. However, there has been a movement towards the imposition of a common law duty to disclose in a number of jurisdictions, at least where the insider is dealing with an existing stockholder. A few jurisdictions now require disclosure where certain "special facts" exist, and some even impose a strict fiduciary duty on the insider *vis-à-vis* the selling shareholder. But the most important remedies available to those injured by insider trading are found in the federal securities laws and

---

20. There is a good deal of ambiguity as to who should be considered a direct victim of insider trading. Those investors who actually bought from or sold securities to the insiders in face-to-face transactions may well feel cheated when they find out that the insiders were trading on the basis of material information unknown to the public. But what about traders involved in impersonal market transactions who were probably not even aware that insiders were trading in the market. These investors would have traded even if the insiders had stayed out of the market. However, if one instead asks the question of who might have act-

ed differently if the insiders had made public their inside information at the time that they dealt with the market, these investors might be considered to have been injured by the inside trading, even if they were unaware of the insiders' activity. This latter class is capable of a variety of definitions, such as "all persons who traded at the same time as did the insiders" or, at the limit, "all persons who traded from the time that the insiders entered the market until the time that the inside information became public or was otherwise fully reflected in the stock price."

in particular Rule 10b–5. Judicial development of a private right of action under that rule has led to significant relaxation of many of the elements of common law fraud, including privity, reliance, and the distinction between misrepresentation and non-disclosure. The rule has proven a favorite vehicle for damage suits against insiders for failing to disclose material information while trading in their corporation's stock. Section 17(a) of the 1933 Act may also provide a means of recovering damages from insiders in some cases. Lastly, persons injured by insider trading may be able to take advantage of the liability sections of state securities laws. A number of states, including Indiana, have enacted laws containing antifraud provisions modeled on Rule 10b–5. See Burns Ind.Stat.Ann. § 23–2–1–12.

Yet, the New York Court of Appeals in *Diamond* found the existing remedies for controlling insider trading to be inadequate. Although the court felt that the device of a class action under the federal securities laws held out hope of a more effective remedy in the future, it concluded that "the desirability of creating an effective common-law remedy is manifest." 301 N.Y.S.2d at 85, 248 N.E.2d at 915. It went on to do so by engineering an innovative extension of the law governing the relation between a corporation and its officers and directors. The court held that corporate officials who deal in their corporation's securities on the basis of non-public information gained by virtue of their inside position commit a breach of their fiduciary duties to the corporation. This holding represents a departure from the traditional common law approach, which was that a corporate insider did not ordinarily violate his fiduciary duty to the corporation by dealing in the corporation's stock, unless the corporation was thereby harmed.

The *Diamond* court relied heavily on the Delaware case of Brophy v. Cities Service Co., 31 Del.Ch. 241, 70 A.2d 5 (1949), the most significant departure from the traditional common law approach prior to *Diamond* itself. There, the confidential secretary to a director of a corporation purchased a number of shares of the company's stock after finding out that the corporation was about to enter the market to make purchases of its stock itself, and then sold at a profit after the corporation began its purchases. The Delaware Court of Chancery upheld the complaint in a derivative action on behalf of the corporation to recover those profits. The court stated that the employee occupied a position of trust and confidence toward his employer and that public policy would not permit him to abuse that relation for his own profit, regardless of whether or not the employer suffered a loss. 70 A.2d at 8. The *Diamond* court also relied on Section 388 of the Restatement (Second) of Agency. * * *

Accordingly, the *Diamond* court at least impliedly assimilated inside information to a corporate asset with respect to which corporate officers and directors owe the corporation a duty of loyalty.

There are a number of difficulties with the *Diamond* court's ruling. Perhaps the thorniest problem was posed by the defendants' objection that whatever the ethical status of insider trading, there is no injury to the corporation which can serve as a basis for recognizing a right of recovery in favor of the latter. The Court of Appeals' response to this argument was two-fold, suggesting first that no harm to the corporation need be shown and second that it might well be inferred that the insiders' activities did in fact cause some harm to the corporation. * * * Some might see the *Diamond* court's decision as resting on a broad, strict-trust notion of the fiduciary duty owed to the corporation: no director is to receive any profit, beyond what he receives from the corporation, solely because of his position. Although, once accepted, this basis for the *Diamond* rule would obviate the need for finding a potential for injury to the corporation, it is not at all clear that current corporation law contemplates such an extensive notion of fiduciary duty. It is customary to view the *Diamond* result as resting on a characterization of inside information as a corporate asset. The lack of necessity for looking for an injury to the corporation is then justified by the traditional "no inquiry" rule with respect to profits made by trustees from assets belonging to the trust *res*. However, to start from the premise that all inside information should be considered a corporate asset may presuppose an answer to the inquiry at hand. It might be better to ask whether there is any potential loss to the corporation from the use of such information in insider trading before deciding to characterize the inside information as an asset with respect to which the insider owes the corporation a duty of loyalty (as opposed to a duty of care). This approach would be in keeping with the modern view of another area of application of the duty of loyalty—the corporate opportunity doctrine. Thus, while courts will require a director or officer to automatically account to the corporation for diversion of a corporate opportunity to personal use, they will first inquire to see whether there was a possibility of a loss to the corporation—i.e., whether the corporation was in a position to potentially avail itself of the opportunity—before deciding that a corporate opportunity in fact existed. Similarly, when scrutinizing transactions between a director or officer and the corporation under the light of the duty of loyalty, most courts now inquire as to whether there was any injury to the corporation, i.e., whether the transaction was fair and in good faith, before permitting the latter to avoid the transaction. An analogous question might be posed with respect to the *Diamond* court's unjust enrichment analysis: is it proper to conclude that an insider has been unjustly enriched *vis-à-vis* the corporation (as compared to other traders in the market) when there is no way that the corporation could have used the information to its own profit, just because the insider's trading was made possible by virtue of his corporate position?

Not all information generated in the course of carrying on a business fits snugly into the corporate asset mold. Information in the form of trade secrets, customer lists, etc., can easily be categorized as a valuable or potentially valuable corporate "possession," in that it can be directly used by the corporation to its own economic advantage. However, most information involved in insider trading is not of this ilk, e.g., knowledge of an impending merger, a decline in earnings, etc. If the corporation were to attempt to exploit such non-public information by dealing in its own securities, it would open itself up to potential liability under federal and state securities laws, just as do the insiders when they engage in insider trading. This is not to say that the corporation does not have any interests with regard to such information. It may have an interest in either preventing the information from becoming public or in regulating the timing of disclosure. However, insider trading does not entail the disclosure of inside information, but rather its use in a manner in which the corporation itself is prohibited from exploiting it.

Yet, the *Diamond* court concluded that it might well be inferred that insider trading causes some harm to the corporation * * *. It must be conceded that the unfairness that is the basis of the widespread disapproval of insider trading is borne primarily by participants in the securities markets, rather than by the corporation itself. By comparison, the harm to corporate goodwill posited by the *Diamond* court pales in significance. At this point, the existence of such an indirect injury must be considered speculative, as there is no actual evidence of such a reaction. Furthermore, it is less than clear to us that the nature of this harm would form an adequate basis for an action for an accounting based on a breach of the insiders' duty of loyalty, as opposed to an action for damages based on a breach of the duty of care. The injury hypothesized by the *Diamond* court seems little different from the harm to the corporation that might be inferred whenever a responsible corporate official commits an illegal or unethical act using a corporate asset. Absent is the element of loss of opportunity or potential susceptibility to outside influence that generally is present when a corporate fiduciary is required to account to the corporation.

The *Brophy* case is capable of being distinguished on this basis. Although the court there did not openly rely on the existence of a potential harm to the corporation, such a harm was possible. Since the corporation was about to begin buying its own shares in the market, by purchasing stock for his own account the insider placed himself in direct competition with the corporation. To the degree that his purchases might have caused the stock price to rise, the corporation was directly injured in that it had to pay more for its purchases. The other cases cited by the *Diamond* court also tended to involve an agent's competition with his principal, harm to it, disregard for its instructions, or the like. * * *

A second problem presented by the recognition of a cause of action in favor of the corporation is that of potential double liability.

864   REGULATION OF SECURITIES TRADING   Ch. 19

The *Diamond* court thought that this problem would seldom arise, since it thought it unlikely that a damage suit would be brought by investors where the insiders traded on impersonal exchanges. * * *. The Second Circuit also gave consideration to the possibility of double liability in Schein v. Chasen, 478 F.2d at 824–25, but concluded that double liability could be avoided by methods such as that employed in SEC v. Texas Gulf Sulphur Co., 312 F.Supp. 77, 93 (S.D. N.Y.1970), where the defendants' disgorged profits were placed in a fund subject first to the claims of injured investors, with the residue payable to the corporation. The efficacy of the *Diamond* court's suggestion of resort to an interpleader action is open to question. The creation of a fund subject to the superior claims of injured investors also poses some difficulties. Although some observers have suggested that double liability be imposed so as to more effectively deter insider trading and that it is analytically justifiable since the two causes of action involved are based on separate legal wrongs, the *Diamond* and *Schein* courts' concern for avoiding double liability may implicitly reflect the view that a right of recovery in favor of the corporation was being created because of the perceived likelihood that the investors who are the true victims of insider trading would not be able to bring suit. When the latter in fact bring an action seeking damages from the insiders, thereby creating the possibility of double liability, the need for a surrogate plaintiff disappears and the corporation's claim is implicitly relegated to the back seat.

Since the *Diamond* court's action was motivated in large part by its perception of the inadequacy of existing remedies for insider trading, it is noteworthy that over the decade since *Diamond* was decided, the 10b–5 class action has made substantial advances toward becoming the kind of effective remedy for insider trading that the court of appeals hoped that it might become. Most importantly, recovery of damages from insiders has been allowed by, or on the behalf of, market investors even when the insiders dealt only through impersonal stock exchanges, although this is not yet a well-settled area of the law. In spite of other recent developments indicating that such class actions will not become as easy to maintain as some plaintiffs had perhaps hoped, it is clear the the remedies for insider trading under the federal securities laws now constitute a more effective deterrent than they did when *Diamond* was decided.

* * * [H]aving carefully examined the decision of the New York Court of Appeals in *Diamond*, we are of the opinion that although the court sought to ground its ruling in accepted principles of corporate common law, that decision can best be understood as an example of judicial securities regulation. Although the question is a close one, we believe that were the issue to be presented to the Indiana courts at the present time, they would most likely join the Florida

Supreme Court in refusing to adopt the New York court's innovative ruling.

* * *

The judgment of the district court is affirmed.

MANNE, WHAT KIND OF CONTROLS ON INSIDER TRADING DO WE NEED IN THE ATTACK ON CORPORATE AMERICA? 121–124 (M. Johnson ed. 1978).

THE PRACTICAL CASE AGAINST THE RULES

* * *

First, if the SEC allows shareholders to believe that it does effectively prevent insider trading, it is practicing a shameful deception. Or, alternately, the market is composed of a greater number of idiots than we have any reason to believe.

Second, individual confidence is *not* shaken by the belief or knowledge that insider trading occurs. During the frenzied period of popular participation in the stock market in the 1920s, news about pools using undisclosed information was published regularly in the financial press, with no apparent loss of investor confidence. Third, it is well known that the one and only thing that does cause investors to lose confidence is losses. After any period of significant downturn in market prices, the number of investors regularly declines, and there seems to be no other factor significantly influencing this variable.

THE ECONOMIC ARGUMENT AGAINST THE RULES

A proper economic excursion into the rather complex subject of insider trading necessitates a brief detour to explain two developments in modern finance economics. One of these is called the "efficient market hypothesis" and the other the "random walk theory" of stock prices. * * *

An "efficient" stock market is one that rapidly and correctly evaluates new information and integrates that information into the market price of shares. Study after study demonstrates the almost unbelievable efficiency with which our major stock markets perform this function. Indeed, no matter at what point econometricians test to see whether a given new development has yet impacted a share price, the impact always seems to have already occurred. This finding has even led some slightly incredulous researchers to conclude that the stock market instantaneously reflects any available information relevant to stock price.

Since stock prices do rapidly and correctly reflect new developments in a corporation's affairs, the movements of stock prices (apart from general industry or market movements and certain other oscillations or "noise" not relevant here) should follow a course dictated by these exogenous events.   *   *   *   They would include, for instance, with infinitely varying degrees of severity and with no predictable pattern, reactions from competitive products, changes in demand, changes in political rulings, international events, changes in the weather, managerial changes, and production difficulties.

These two theories, the efficient market hypothesis and the random walk theory, suggest two problems in connection with the subject of insider trading. The first problem is how the market can possibly be as efficient as has been suggested, and the second is how, if stock prices follow a random movement, shareholders can be injured by insider trading.

The answer to the first question, why the market is so efficient, probably relates in some fashion to insider trading, though the exact nature and characteristics of this relationship have not been clearly isolated or described. It does seem apparent, however, that information in most instances develops an increasing probability of its assumed impact as the time of the event draws closer. That is, the probability that the value of unanticipated earnings actually will be realized only becomes 100 percent on the day that the board of directors announces the fact. But, many weeks earlier those earnings may have appeared to some people to have a 20 percent probability of occurring. Such people include accountants or financial analysts who have information that could not, in and of itself, be said to be significant or material inside information. This information might include, for example, knowledge of an increase in sales, a disabling power struggle within a competitor company, or an important but early technological breakthrough. If this increasing-probability-of-truth hypothesis is correct, the closer one reaches to the actual development, the greater will be the extent to which the assumed value of the information has already been incorporated into the share's price. This reasoning helps to explain why we often see that an important news announcement meets with little or no change in the day's stock price quotations.

Whatever the mechanism by which information is being impacted efficiently into share prices, so long as the information generates a random movement of those prices, there is really no way in which insider trading can injure shareholders, even though shareholders are not privy to the information. This is not to say, of course, that shareholders could not be richer if they had the information. But, that is merely a truism. What it does suggest is this line of reasoning. First, people trade anonymously in an organized stock market. Second, by definition, prior (random) price movements tell "outsiders" nothing about subsequent price movements. Therefore, that a subsequent movement may have been predicted by an "insider" cannot affect the average rate of return investors realize from trading in corporate securities. Whether an insider was on the other side of the trade or not is utterly irrelevant to the noninsider's calculations about whether the stock market is a fair game.

But, one still may complain that there seems to be an immoral windfall profit gained by the insider in these situations. Thus, some believe that insider trading allows corporate officials to secure greater gains than they bargained for, or are entitled to. This argument would have merit if—and only if—the availability of possible trading gains resulting from access to information could not be known or recognized by others. That possibility, to say the least, is very unlikely. Once it is recognized that a special possibility for gain inheres in a given position, competition necessarily will drive down the total remuneration for that position to the competitive level indicated by the discounted value of all future income, including both salary and trading profits.

This observation about competition and bargaining for remuneration is relevant to the charge that allowing insider trading encourages manipulation and lessened attention to business affairs. If profitable opportunities for such activities were common, there should be considerably fewer corporate financial scandals today than there were, for example, in the 1920s. Yet, the evidence points the other way. A rational market theory of corporations reinforces the view that an unregulated corporate system's incentive structure generates efficient (and therefore honest) managerial action. This is not to say, of course, that dishonesty, fraud, and embezzlement do not occur. But, it does mean that the amount of such criminal activity is not a function of the insider trading rule.

There is tremendous uncertainty and variability, of course, in opportunities for profits from insider trading. And, while this uncertainty and variability mean that the competition for access to information is not as efficient as we might like, they also indicate that the entire topic may hardly be worth the posturing and moralizing it has engendered. Even if one agrees that there is a fundamental issue of business morality involved with insider trading, the seriousness of the problem, the possibility of correcting it, and the costs of enforcing rules against the practice still must be taken into account before a rational policy can be adopted. We seem to have evolved, instead, regulatory positions far worse than the evils sought to be cured.

SCHOTLAND, UNSAFE AT ANY PRICE: A REPLY TO MANNE, INSIDER TRADING AND THE STOCK MARKET

53 Va.L.R. 1425, 1440–43, 1447–51 (1967).

* * *

* * * [L]et us put aside all these reservations and examine the defense of unfettered insider trading on its own terms. The prime objection to such a practice is the impact it would have on the public's

confidence in the stock markets. An underlying premise of all our governmental involvement in this area has been that the stock markets are an essential part of our commercial and financial structure, and that their health will be sustained only if the public feels they are not a jungle, but rather are a safe place for investment. The main effort of the New York Stock Exchange * * * was to draw more of the public into the markets—to persuade the public to "own your share of America." Broker-dealers throughout the nation have bent their efforts and funds in the same direction. * * *

It must be acknowledged that what may be good for stockbrokers is not necessarily good for the stock market; that the stock market is only one of our capital markets; that the stock market is vigorous even though less than one-eighth of our population participates in it; and that probably many do participate despite their belief that the market is something of a jungle, where insiders—both of corporations and of the market—enjoy unfair advantages. But as long as the brokerage community and the Government continue to promote the idea that the stock market offers the advantages of reasonable safety for investment, reasonable likelihood of appreciation and the highest liquidity available for invested funds, so long will it be inconsistent and self-defeating to abandon restrictions on insider trading. This is made strikingly clear by the repeated acknowledgment in Manne's book that the less frequently outside shareholders trade, the less they will lose as a result of the exploitation of valuable information by insiders. Telling that to stockholders and potential stockholders will tend to discourage their participation in the stock market, which in turn will tend to reduce the health of that market and have a negative impact on corporations already held publicly, on smaller corporations which may need more capital to grow and on the economy as a whole. If free insider trading has that impact, the answer to "But who gets hurt?" is clear.

Apparently we have no studies on why some people participate in the stock market and others do not. Therefore one can only speculate on how important it is that the market not only be fair but also appear to be fair, and one can only conjecture about whether freeing insider trading would be injurious to the market, and if so, how injurious. But it is most interesting to note that in 1941, when a proposal to amend the Exchange Act was under consideration, a committee of the American Bar Association said that "[a] persistent cause of lack of public confidence in the exchanges has been the popular impression that they can be traded in profitably only by persons specially informed"; significantly, the committee concluded that section 16(b) should be retained.

Our conjecture can be guided also by the experience in other nations, where capital markets are less vigorous than our own, and where efforts are being made to encourage public participation. William Cary, who recently reminded an audience that "integrity in the capital markets is essential for mass capitalism," recounted his discussion with an ambassador from a South American country who wanted his country to have more public participation in stock ownership: "My first concern," said the ambassador, "is whether the public investor there can trust anyone." * * *

A second flaw in the hands-off thesis is its dependence on the notion that insider trading will improve price performance in the stock market by causing prices to reflect underlying values more accurately and by causing gradual instead of sudden price movements. There are at least three published reports of empirical research by economists on the market impact of insider trading, all strongly suggesting the absence of any substantial impact.

* * *

The third flaw in the defense of unfettered insider trading is the notion that it does no harm, or no significant harm, to long-term investors. This notion rests on the assumption that a long-term investor makes transactions on a "time" basis—he makes investment decisions on the basis that they are timely in his circumstances or in his evaluation of the overall market, and he is not influenced by the price of the security in question. The assumption seems counter-factual. Most investors own more than one security, and if they need cash, they will consider price in deciding which to sell; even long-term investors reach points when they decide to "take a profit" or "cut the loss"; and a prospective buyer for long-term investment will often wait until he considers the price "right." * * *

* * *

It is of the utmost importance to note, however, that any insider trading on undisclosed material information should be held unlawful, even though a particular course of such trading might have caused neither price movement nor delayed disclosure and so could not have caused any investor to act or refrain from acting. Several reasons compel this conclusion.

(1) Allowing any trading on undisclosed material information makes improper delay of disclosure more likely. We must not forget that if disclosure is improperly delayed, we cannot find out until all or at least some of the harm is done, and often we will not find out at all. To ensure timely disclosure—an end to which the SEC and the self-regulatory bodies are equally dedicated—it is obvious that we must avoid encouraging motivations for improper delay, however subconscious they may be. If we abandon restraints on insider trading, we tempt insiders to delay disclosure so that they can buy more shares or arrange financing for more buying; we also invite the timing of disclosure to get maximum market response. * * *

(2) Allowing insider trading on undisclosed material information makes unlawful manipulation more likely. This is because it allows (and in the Manne thesis encourages) an insider to have an unusually

large personal stake in the impact of public disclosure upon the price of his corporation's stock. And here again, we cannot detect the evil until it is under way, and often we will fail to detect it at all. * * *

* * *

(3) The harm from allowing insider trading on undisclosed material information is seen most clearly when we consider the effect on the long-term investor. Of all participants in the stock markets, he is most likely to have a sense of "unfairness" and thus to feel less willing to continue to participate in that stock or that market. Once again, assume there are no restraints on insider trading and, to take the hardest case, assume also that the insider trading in question did not affect the stock price or cause delayed disclosure. When the long-term holder sells shares, he understands as well as anyone else that soon after his sale a significantly favorable corporate event may be announced. If that does happen, he may be unhappy about having sold, but he knows that this is the way the game goes, and it is a fair game. But his feelings are likely to be different if he suspects that insiders may have been buying when he was selling. The long-term stockholder, above all others, is likely to expect fair dealing and perhaps even something of a fiduciary relationship between himself and the personnel of "his" corporation. Certainly he is subjected to enough propaganda to the effect that the personnel are working in his behalf and that he should have faith in the company and its management. He is likely to believe that the insiders are appropriately compensated in salary, stock options, etc., and that although it is fine for them to have stock investments in the corporation, (a) they are not entitled to trading profits won from the use of confidential knowledge accruing to their positions, (b) their trading in the shares, as differentiated from investing in them, raises the danger that they may be distracted from single-minded devotion to their work for the corporation, and (c) there is no reason they should benefit more than the stockholder from trading on good news about their corporation. And when there is bad news, and the long-term holder has not sold though the insiders have, the sense of unfairness sharpens.

* * *

In Enforcement of Insider Trading Restrictions, 66 Va.L.Rev. 1 (1980), Professor Michael Dooley argues that efforts to control insider trading under existing law are costly, sporadic, ineffective, and not justified by the results. He reports that, "The incidents of insider trading is clearly high; the available evidence suggests that it is the most common violation of the federal securities laws." In the face of that fact, however, he finds a relatively small number of SEC enforcement actions; * and even fewer private damage actions, which

* The SEC has undertaken to crack down on insider trading. According to a 1980 Wall Street Journal article, it was "filing civil suits at a rate of more than

are largely "parasitic", in the sense that they are instituted after, and as a result of, an action brought by the SEC. This is because, he says, enforcement actions are complex and expensive to bring, violations are difficult to detect, and the limitations on private damage actions (such as those imposed in Elkind v. Liggett & Myers, *infra*) make their pursuit unrewarding. In sum, Professor Dooley writes:

> The existing enforcement system consists of a combination of inputs that guarantees minimal success in apprehending and punishing offenders. The number of potential violations is high, as are the incentives to commit them. The potential offender must choose either to forego a certain profit or to take it and run a slight risk of modest penalty. In most SEC cases the effective sanction will be less than the offender's expected utility in violating the law. This is true not only when the SEC seeks disgorgement of profits (the probability of apprehension and punishment invariably is less than utility), but also when the offender theoretically faces penalties having a high monetary equivalent value such as imprisonment or license revocation. Existing budget constraints and past practice virtually assure offenders that the Commission will settle for less than the maximum sanction. The tendency of securities industry professionals to share inside information with one another despite the fact that this increases the probability that they will be detected and subjected to possibly severe sanctions graphically illustrates the confidence offenders have in leniency. Although private actions may threaten higher monetary sanctions, they have not increased the probability of apprehension and punishment. Even when the SEC has apprehended the offender and thus exposed him to private claims, many offenders will not be sued because they cannot pay the nominal sanction. (Dooley, Enforcement of Insider Trading Restrictions, 66 Va.L.Rev. 1, 24–5 (1980)).

On the other side of ledger, Dooley finds the case for enforcing the present proscriptions against insider trading a weak one. Because the law is based on section 10(b) and Rule 10b–5, "The existing system cannot be justified by showing that insider trading is 'wrong' in the sense of being undesirable, unethical, or even unfair. Insider trading must be shown to harm investors, directly or indirectly, in a particular way to fall within the proscriptive scope of section 10(b)." Dooley divides the case in favor of the current rules into two sets of arguments (most of which are discussed in the excerpts above)— those based on "direct harm" to investors and those based on "indirect harm." He concludes as to the former that "In the end, there is no satisfactory compensatory rationale for regulating insider trading. There is no evidence that insider trading causes direct harm to inves-

one a month." Wall Street Journal, Nov. 12, 1980, at 38, col. 4. The same article reports that the cases brought "represent a miniscule portion of all infractions."

tors or, even assuming that it does, that the extent of injury warrants the cost of regulation."

The latter category of arguments are based largely on the assertion that "insider trading is bad because it has bad effects on the market", an assertion that derives from the language of *Texas Gulf Sulphur*. But to the extent that that case and its progeny sought to ban insider trading simply because it was considered "unfair", that justification did not survive subsequent Supreme Court decisions[*] holding that "fraud" or "deceit" in the common law are essential elements of a violation of 10b–5; "unfairness" alone is not enough.

The more substantive arguments that purport to find some relation between insider trading and erosion of "market integrity" and "investor confidence" are without factual support according to Dooley. If there were any basis to these fears, he argues, the shares of any company susceptible to insider trading would trade at a discount from what they would otherwise be worth; investors, being averse to behavior they considered reprehensible, would pay less for the shares of a company managed by those who engaged in it. But this in turn would provide an incentive for "honest" managers to furnish guarantees to the market that their companies would not tolerate such behavior, the simplest example of which would be the adoption of a corporate rule prohibiting insiders from trading in the corporation's stock. The result, if the fears about the effects of insider trading on investor confidence were true, would logically be an increase in the price of the shares of companies that engaged in this sort of "bonding". Since corporations do not undertake to signal investors that their executives do not engage in insider trading, investors must not perceive that it does them any harm.

3. FEDERAL REGULATION—SECTION 16(b)

One of the principal evils of the securities markets addressed by Congress in the passage of the 1934 Act was the use by corporate insiders of nonpublic information to reap large profits in trading in the shares of their companies. The practice was so widespread that, although publicly condemned, it had come to be accepted by many in the financial world as one of the forms of compensation to which corporate officials were entitled. This view was abetted by the common law, which, as we have seen, did little to prevent insider trading. Moreover, even had the common law prohibited it, the prohibition would have been difficult to enforce in the anonymity of the stock exchanges.

Determined to make a strong statement against insider trading, Congress seized on a prophylactic device that, instead of establishing a rule against trading on the basis of material nonpublic information,

---

[*] *E.g.*, Santa Fe Industries, Inc. v. Green, 430 U.S. 462, 97 S.Ct. 1292, 51 L. Ed.2d 480 (1977); Ernst & Ernst v. Hoch- felder, 425 U.S. 185, 96 S.Ct. 1375, 47 L. Ed.2d 668 (1976).

and then casting about for an effective enforcement mechanism, simply attacked a narrow type of stock trading often associated with the misuse of inside information. In many, if not most of the more flagrant cases of insider trading, it was thought, the insider bought and sold (or, more rarely sold and bought) stock of his company within a relatively short period of time. Since the capital gains period of the tax laws was then six months, there was good reason to suspect that in most cases someone with access to inside information who bought and sold within six months (and therefore forewent the favorable tax treatment available for profits made on trades separated by a longer period) was doing so to take advantage of some special knowledge. It was only a step from this perception to the simple and readily enforceable, if crude, principle of § 16(b), which provides that any profits realized by an insider (as defined) on a purchase followed by a sale, or a sale followed by a purchase, within a six-month period, "shall inure to and be recoverable by the issuer." Although the section explicitly states that its purpose is "preventing the unfair use of information which may have been obtained by [the insider] by reason of his relationship to the issuer," there is no need to show any such "unfair use." All that is necessary is offsetting trades within six months by someone with the necessary relationship to the corporation.

As there would be reason to suspect that corporations would not always sue their officers or directors to recover the forbidden short-swing profits, the section carefully specifies that an action may be instituted by "the owner of any security of the issuer," in the form of a derivative suit. But why should a shareholder bother to bring such a suit when the proceeds will go to the corporation whose gain will normally be of only the remotest benefit to the shareholder? For better or for worse, and it might as well be put bluntly, it is not the shareholder who is the moving force in § 16(b) actions, but the shareholder's lawyer, to whom the courts—recognizing that this champertous behavior is essential to the operation of the statutory scheme—are quite generous in their awards of attorneys' fees. There are, in fact, a number of lawyers who make a good livelihood from bringing suits under § 16(b). And their troubled lives are made easier by their not even having to search out a plaintiff who was, to comply with Rule 23.1, a stockholder "at the time of the wrong complained of;" Congress carefully designed the statute to provide that the plaintiff only own securities of the corporation at the time of suit. Thus the 16(b) attorney need only find someone, often even himself, willing to buy a share or two and lend his name as plaintiff.

To make sure that potential plaintiffs (or their lawyers) were able to learn about potential violations of § 16(b), Congress provided in § 16(a) that the insiders covered by the statute must file with the SEC reports of any changes in their holdings within ten days after the end of the month in which the transaction takes place. The Commission publishes a monthly compilation of these reports, and summaries appear regularly in a number of financial publications.

For a statute that was intended to avoid the pitfalls of scienter, materiality, privity, and so forth that a more subtle approach to the problem of insider trading would have entailed by a clear, easily-applied rule, § 16(b) has presented the courts with a remarkable number of interpretational problems. To begin with, it has not proved as easy as it might first sound to define the class of insiders to whom the section applies. They include "the beneficial owner" of more than 10 per cent of any equity security and any director or officer. Rule 3b–2 defines "officer" as "a president, vice president, treasurer, secretary, comptroller, and any other person who performs for an issuer * * * functions corresponding to those performed by the foregoing officers." In Colby v. Klune, 178 F.2d 872 (2d Cir. 1949), however, the term was broadened to include "a corporate employee performing important executive duties of such character that he would be likely, in discharging these duties, to obtain confidentially information about the company's affairs that would aid him if he engaged in personal market transactions." See also Merrill Lynch, Pierce, Fenner & Smith, Inc. v. Livingston, 566 F.2d 1119, 1122–1123 (9th Cir. 1978).

The term, "beneficial owner" has been "read more expansively than it [is] in the law of trusts. For purposes of the family unit, shares to which legal title is held by one spouse may be said to be 'beneficially owned' by the other, the insider, if the ordinary rewards or ownership are used for their joint benefit." Whiting v. Dow Chemical Co., 523 F.2d 680, 688 (2d Cir. 1975). See also SEC, Securities Exchange Act Rel. No. 7793 (1966).

A beneficial owner may be liable only if he owned more than 10 per cent of the stock at the time of both purchase and sale transactions. Thus where a 10 per cent shareholder sells enough shares to reduce his holdings to a fraction less than 10 per cent and then in a separate transaction, sells the remaining shares, all within six months, the profit realized from the first sale is recoverable by the corporation but the profit from the second is not. Reliance Electric Co. v. Emerson Electric Co., 404 U.S. 418, 92 S.Ct. 596, 30 L.Ed.2d 575 (1972). Applying the same principle, one who purchases enough shares to become a 10 per cent shareholder and then sells some shares within six months, is not liable for any profit realized.* Foremost-McKesson v. Provident Securities, 423 U.S. 232, 96 S.Ct. 508, 46 L.Ed.2d 464 (1976).

By contrast, an officer or director is subject to the strictures of § 16(b) even though he may not have been in office at the time of both

---

* By contrast a 10 per cent shareholder who purchases more stock and then, within 6 months, sells enough stock to reduce his holding below 10 per cent is liable under § 16(b) because he was a 10 per cent shareholder at the time of *both* transactions.

purchase and sale. *See, e.g.* Feder v. Martin Marietta Corp., 406 F.2d 260 (2d Cir. 1969); Adler v. Klawans, 267 F.2d 840 (2d Cir. 1959). The reason for treating officers and directors differently from owners of more than 10 per cent of the stock is that "officers and directors have more ready access to the intimate business secrets of corporations and factors which can effect the market value of stock * * *. * * * Moreover, a director or officer can usually stimulate more directly actions which affect stock values * * *." Adler v. Klawans, *supra* at 845.

A partnership or corporation may be deemed to be a director if one of its members or officers serves as a director of the corporation whose shares it trades and is found to have been "deputized" to represent the partnership or corporation. Deputization is a question of fact and must be proved by the plaintiff. Where a partner had not been deputized to represent the partnership on a corporate board, liability under Section 16(b) will attach only to his or her share of the partnership's profits from the partnership's trading activities. Blau v. Lehman, 368 U.S. 403, 82 S.Ct. 451, 7 L.Ed.2d 403 (1962); Feder v. Martin Marietta Corp., 406 F.2d 260 (2d Cir. 1969).

In order to increase the deterrent effect of the statute, the courts compute the "profits" from a series of several purchases and sales within six months so as to produce the maximum damages. In the leading case of Smolowe v. Delendo Corp., 136 F.2d 231 (2d Cir. 1943), the defendants argued that their profits should be computed as for income tax purposes, *i.e.*, stock certificate numbers should be used to determine the actual profits earned from the purchase and sale of particular shares; if the certificate numbers are not known, profits should be calculated on a first-in-first-out basis. The *Smolowe* Court rejected this approach holding that, to give the statute its full effect the court should match the shares with the lowest purchase price against those with the highest sale price, ignoring any losses this would produce. This has achieved some bizarre results. In one case the defendant was required to pay $300,000 to the corporation for "profits" earned over several six month periods of trading although he had actually incurred a net loss of $400,000 on the transactions. Gratz v. Claughton, 187 F.2d 46 (2d Cir. 1951), cert. denied 341 U.S. 920, 71 S.Ct. 741, 95 L.Ed. 1353.

The problems that have generated the greatest amount of litigation under § 16(b) are probably those related to the definitions of "purchase" and "sale." In a merger transaction, for example, the shareholders of the acquired corporation normally exchange their shares for shares of the surviving corporation. It is not clear under § 16(b), however, whether this exchange involves a "sale" of the stock of the old corporation and a "purchase" of shares of the new. The courts have generally taken the approach that it depends on whether the transaction presents a possibility for the abuse of inside information. *See e.g.* Kern County Land Co. v. Occidental Petroleum Corp.,

411 U.S. 582, 93 S.Ct. 1736, 36 L.Ed.2d 503 (1973). Thus when officers or directors of the acquired corporation become officers or directors of the acquiring corporation after the merger, the exchange is a "purchase" because of their access to inside information. Gold v. Sloan, 486 F.2d 340 (4th Cir. 1973). *See also* Newmark v. RKO General, Inc., 425 F.2d 348 (2d Cir. 1970). On the other hand, when a tender offeror that lost out to a competing offer is forced to exchange shares acquired in the contest in a merger forced by the successful bidder, the transaction is not a "sale." Kern County Land Co. v. Occidental Petroleum Corp., supra.

Other transactions that have been held not to be purchases or sales include: gifts, Shaw v. Dreyfus, 172 F.2d 140 (2d Cir. 1949); certain stock reclassifications, Roberts v. Eaton, 212 F.2d 82 (2d Cir. 1954); and some conversions of securities, Petteys v. Butler, 367 F.2d 528 (8th Cir. 1966), cert. denied 385 U.S. 1006, 87 S.Ct. 712, 17 L.Ed.2d 545 (1967), and Blau v. Lamb, 363 F.2d 507 (2d Cir. 1966), cert. denied 385 U.S. 1002, 87 S.Ct. 707, 17 L.Ed.2d 542 (1967).

4. FEDERAL REGULATION—RULE 10b–5

SECURITIES AND EXCHANGE COMMISSION v. TEXAS GULF SULPHUR CO.

401 F.2d 833 (2d Cir. 1968), cert. denied 394 U.S. 976, 89 S.Ct. 1454, 22 L.Ed.2d 756 (1969).

[The drilling of hole K–55–1 in Timmins, Ontario, and the subsequent developments are summarized in Part B 2, above. In addition to charging the corporation with issuing a misleading press release, the SEC also charged various individuals with trading on the basis of material non-public information. The following portions of the court's opinion discusses those charges.]

[F]rom November 12, 1963 when K–55–1 was completed, to March 31, 1964 when drilling was resumed, certain of the individual defendants   *   *   *   and persons   *   *   *   said to have received "tips" from them, purchased TGS stock or calls thereon. Prior to these transactions these persons had owned 1135 shares of TGS stock and possessed no calls; thereafter they owned a total of 8235 shares and possessed 12,300 calls.

On February 20, 1964, also during this period, TGS issued stock options to 26 of its officers and employees whose salaries exceeded a specified amount, five of whom were the individual defendants Stephens, Fogarty, Mollison, Holyk, and Kline. Of these, only Kline was unaware of the detailed results of K–55–1, but he, too, knew that a hole containing favorable bodies of copper and zinc ore had been drilled in Timmins. At this time, neither the TGS Stock Option Committee nor its Board of Directors had been informed of the results of K–55–1, presumably because of the pending land acquisition program which required confidentiality. All of the foregoing defendants accepted the options granted them.

* * *

While drilling activity ensued to completion, TGS officials were taking steps toward ultimate disclosure of the discovery. On April 13, a previously-invited reporter for The Northern Miner, a Canadian mining industry journal, visited the drillsite, interviewed Mollison, Holyk and Darke, and prepared an article which confirmed a 10 million ton ore strike. This report, after having been submitted to Mollison and returned to the reporter unamended on April 15, was published in the April 16 issue. A statement relative to the extent of the discovery, in substantial part drafted by Mollison, was given to the Ontario Minister of Mines for release to the Canadian media. Mollison and Holyk expected it to be released over the airways at 11 P.M. on April 15th, but, for undisclosed reasons, it was not released until 9:40 A.M. on the 16th. An official detailed statement, announcing a strike of at least 25 million tons of ore, based on the drilling data set forth above, was read to representatives of American financial media from 10:00 A.M. to 10:10 or 10:15 A.M. on April 16, and appeared over Merrill Lynch's private wire at 10:29 A.M. and, somewhat later than expected, over the Dow Jones ticker tape at 10:54 A.M.

Between the time the first press release was issued on April 12 and the dissemination of the TGS official announcement on the morning of April 16, the only defendants before us on appeal who engaged in market activity were Clayton and Crawford and TGS director Coates. Clayton ordered 200 shares of TGS stock through his Canadian broker on April 15 and the order was executed that day over the Midwest Stock Exchange. Crawford ordered 300 shares at midnight on the 15th and another 300 shares at 8:30 A.M. the next day, and these orders were executed over the Midwest Exchange in Chicago at its opening on April 16. Coates left the TGS press conference and called his broker son-in-law Haemisegger shortly before 10:20 A.M. on the 16th and ordered 2,000 shares of TGS for family trust accounts of which Coates was a trustee but not a beneficiary; Haemisegger executed this order over the New York and Midwest Exchanges, and he and his customers purchased 1500 additional shares.

During the period of drilling in Timmins, the market price of TGS stock fluctuated but steadily gained overall. On Friday, November 8, when the drilling began the stock closed at $17^3/_8$; on Friday, November 15, after K–55–1 had been completed, it closed at 18. After a slight decline to $16^3/_8$ by Friday, November 22, the price rose to $20^7/_8$ by December 13, when the chemical assay results of K–55–1 were received, and closed at a high of $24^1/_8$ on February 21, the day after the stock options had been issued. It had reached a price of 26 by March 31, after the land acquisition program had been completed and drilling had been resumed, and continued to ascend to $30^1/_8$ by the close of trading on April 10, at which time the drilling progress up to then was evaluated for the April 12th press release. On April 13, the day on which the April 12 release was disseminated, TGS opened at $30\frac{1}{8}$, rose immediately to a high of 32 and gradually tapered off to close at $30\frac{7}{8}$. It closed at $30\frac{1}{4}$ the next day, and at $29\frac{3}{8}$ on April 15. On April 16, the day of the official announcement of the Timmins discovery, the price climbed to a high of 37 and closed at $36\frac{3}{8}$. By May 15, TGS stock was selling at $58\frac{1}{4}$.

I. THE INDIVIDUAL DEFENDANTS

A. *Introductory*

* * *

Rule 10b–5 was promulgated pursuant to the grant of authority given the SEC by Congress in Section 10(b) of the Securities Exchange Act of 1934 (15 U.S.C.A. § 78j(b)). By that Act Congress proposed to prevent inequitable and unfair practices and to insure fairness in securities transactions generally, whether conducted face-to-face, over the counter, or on exchanges, see 3 Loss, Securities Regulation 1455–56 (2d ed. 1961). The Act and the Rule apply to the transactions here, all of which were consummated on exchanges. Whether predicated on traditional fiduciary concepts, see, e.g., Hotchkiss v. Fischer, 136 Kan. 530, 16 P.2d 531 (Kan.1932), or on the "special facts" doctrine, see, e.g., Strong v. Repide, 213 U.S. 419, 29 S.Ct. 521, 53 L. Ed. 853 (1909), the Rule is based in policy on the justifiable expectation of the securities marketplace that all investors trading on impersonal exchanges have relatively equal access to material information, see Cary, Insider Trading in Stocks, 21 Bus.Law. 1009, 1010 (1966), Fleischer, Securities Trading and Corporation Information Practices: The Implications of the Texas Gulf Sulphur Proceeding, 51 Va.L.Rev. 1271, 1278–80 (1965). The essence of the Rule is that anyone who, trading for his own account in the securities of a corporation has "access, directly or indirectly, to information intended to be available only for a corporate purpose and not for the personal benefit of anyone" may not take "advantage of such information knowing it is unavailable to those with whom he is dealing," i.e., the investing public. Matter of Cady, Roberts & Co., 40 SEC 907, 912 (1961). Insiders, as directors or management officers are, of course, by this Rule, precluded from so unfairly dealing, but the Rule is also applicable to one possessing the information who may not be strictly termed an "insider" within the meaning of Sec. 16(b) of the Act. Cady, Roberts, supra. Thus, anyone in possession of material inside information must either disclose it to the investing public, or, if he is disabled from disclosing it in order to protect a corporate confidence, or he chooses not to do so, must abstain from trading in or recommending the securities concerned while such inside information remains undisclosed. So, it is here no justification for insider activity that disclosure was forbidden by the legitimate corporate objective of acquiring options to purchase the land surrounding the exploration site; if the information was, as the SEC contends, material, its possessors should have kept out of the market until disclosure was accomplished. Cady, Roberts, supra at 911.

B. *Material Inside Information*

An insider is not, of course, always foreclosed from investing in his own company merely because he may be more familiar with company operations than are outside investors. An insider's duty to disclose information or his duty to abstain from dealing in his company's securities arises only in "those situations which are essentially extraordinary in nature and which are reasonably certain to have a substantial effect on the market price of the security if [the extraordinary situation is] disclosed." Fleischer, Securities Trading and Corporate Information Practices: The Implications of the Texas Gulf Sulphur Proceeding, 51 Va.L.Rev. 1271, 1289.

Nor is an insider obligated to confer upon outside investors the benefit of his superior financial or other expert analysis by disclosing his educated guesses or predictions. The only regulatory objective is that access to material information be enjoyed equally, but this objective requires nothing more than the disclosure of basic facts so that outsiders may draw upon their own evaluative expertise in reaching their own investment decisions with knowledge equal to that of the insiders.

This is not to suggest, however, as did the trial court, that "the test of materiality must necessarily be a conservative one, particularly since many actions under Section 10(b) are brought on the basis of hindsight," 258 F.Supp. 262 at 280, in the sense that the materiality of facts is to be assessed solely by measuring the effect the knowledge of the facts would have upon prudent or conservative investors. As we stated in List v. Fashion Park, Inc., 340 F.2d 457, 462, "The basic test of materiality * * * is whether a *reasonable* man would attach importance * * * in determining his choice of action in the transaction in question. Restatement, Torts § 538(2)(a); accord Prosser, Torts 554–55; I Harper & James, Torts 565–66." (Emphasis supplied.) This, of course, encompasses any fact " * * * which in reasonable and objective contemplation *might* affect the value of the corporation's stock or securities * * *." List v. Fashion Park, Inc., supra at 462, quoting from Kohler v. Kohler Co., 319 F.2d 634, 642 (7 Cir. 1963). (Emphasis supplied.) Such a fact is a material fact and must be effectively disclosed to the investing public prior to the commencement of insider trading in the corporation's securities. The speculators and chartists of Wall and Bay Streets are also "reasonable" investors entitled to the same legal protection afforded conservative traders. Thus, material facts include not only information disclosing the earnings and distributions of a company but also those facts which affect the probable future of the company and those which may affect the desire of investors to buy, sell, or hold the company's securities.

In each case, then, whether facts are material within Rule 10b–5 when the facts relate to a particular event and are undisclosed by those persons who are knowledgeable thereof will depend at any given time upon a balancing of both the indicated probability that the event will occur and the anticipated magnitude of the event in light of the totality of the company activity. Here, notwithstanding the trial court's conclusion that the results of the first drill core, K–55–1, were "too 'remote' * * *   to have had any significant impact on the market, i.e., to be deemed material," 258 F.Supp. at 283, knowledge of the possibility, which surely was more than marginal, of the existence of a mine of the vast magnitude indicated by the remarkably rich drill core located rather close to the surface (suggesting mineability by the less expensive open-pit method) within the confines of a large anomaly (suggesting an extensive region of mineralization) might well have affected the price of TGS stock and would certainly have been an important fact to a reasonable, if speculative, investor in deciding whether he should buy, sell, or hold. After all, this first drill core was "unusually good and * * *   excited the interest and speculation of those who knew about it." 258 F.Supp. at 282.

Our disagreement with the district judge on the issue does not, then, go to his findings of basic fact, as to which the "clearly erroneous" rule would apply, but to his understanding of the legal standard applicable to them. Our survey of the facts found below conclusively establishes that knowledge of the results of the discovery hole, K–55–1, would have been important to a reasonable investor and might have affected the price of the stock.[12] On April 16, The Northern Miner, a trade publication in wide circulation among mining stock specialists, called K–55–1, the discovery hole, "one of the most impressive drill holes completed in modern times." Roche, a Canadian broker whose firm specialized in mining securities, characterized the importance to investors of the results of K–55–1. He stated that the completion of "the first drill hole" with "a 600 foot drill core is very very significant * * *   anything over 200 feet is considered very significant and 600 feet is just beyond your wildest imagination." He added, however, that it "is a natural thing to buy more stock once they give you the first drill hole." Additional testimony revealed that the prices of stocks of other companies, albeit less diversified, smaller firms, had increased substantially solely on the basis of the discovery

---

12. We do not suggest that material facts must be disclosed immediately; the timing of disclosure is a matter for the business judgment of the corporate officers entrusted with the management of the corporation within the affirmative disclosure requirements promulgated by the exchanges and by the SEC. Here, a valuable corporate purpose was served by delaying the publication of the K–55–1 discovery. We do intend to convey, however, that where a corporate purpose is thus served by withholding the news of a material fact, those persons who are thus quite properly true to their corporate trust must not during the period of nondisclosure deal personally in the corporation's securities or give to outsiders confidential information not generally available to all the corporations' stockholders and to the public at large.

of good anomalies or even because of the proximity of their lands to the situs of a potentially major strike.

Finally, a major factor in determining whether the K–55–1 discovery was a material fact is the importance attached to the drilling results by those who knew about it. In view of other unrelated recent developments favorably affecting TGS, participation by an informed person in a regular stock-purchase program, or even sporadic trading by an informed person, might lend only nominal support to the inference of the materiality of the K–55–1 discovery; nevertheless, the timing by those who knew of it, of their stock purchases and their purchases of *short-term* calls—purchases in some cases by individuals who had never before purchased calls or even TGS stock—virtually compels the inference that the insiders were influenced by the drilling results. This insider trading activity, which surely constitutes highly pertinent evidence and the only truly objective evidence of the materiality of the K–55–1 discovery, was apparently disregarded by the court below in favor of the testimony of defendants' expert witnesses, all of whom "agreed that one drill core does not establish an ore body, much less a mine," 258 F.Supp. at 282–283. Significantly, however, the court below, while relying upon what these defense experts said the defendant insiders *ought* to have thought about the worth to TGS of the K–55–1 discovery, and finding that from November 12, 1963 to April 6, 1964 Fogarty, Murray, Holyk and Darke spent more than $100,000 in purchasing TGS stock and calls on that stock, made no finding that the insiders were motivated by any factor other than the extraordinary K–55–1 discovery when they bought their stock and their calls. No reason appears why outside investors, perhaps better acquainted with speculative modes of investment and with, in many cases, perhaps more capital at their disposal for intelligent speculation, would have been less influenced, and would not have been similarly motivated to invest if they had known what the insider investors knew about the K–55–1 discovery.

Our decision to expand the limited protection afforded outside investors by the trial court's narrow definition of materiality is not at all shaken by fears that the elimination of insider trading benefits will deplete the ranks of capable corporate managers by taking away an incentive to accept such employment. Such benefits, in essence, are forms of secret corporate compensation, see Cary, Corporate Standards and Legal Rules, 50 Calif.L.Rev. 408, 409–10 (1962), derived at the expense of the uninformed investing public and not at the expense of the corporation which receives the sole benefit from insider incentives. Moveover, adequate incentives for corporate officers may be provided by properly administered stock options and employee purchase plans of which there are many in existence. In any event, the normal motivation induced by stock ownership, i.e., the identification of an individual with corporate progress, is ill-promoted by condoning the sort of speculative insider activity which occurred here; for example, some of the corporation's stock was sold at market in order to purchase short-term calls upon that stock, calls which would never be exercised to increase a stockholder equity in TGS unless the market price of that stock rose sharply.

The core of Rule 10b–5 is the implementation of the Congressional purpose that all investors should have equal access to the rewards of participation in securities transactions. It was the intent of Congress that all members of the investing public should be subject to identical market risks,—which market risks include, of course, the risk that one's evaluative capacity or one's capital available to put at risk may exceed another's capacity or capital. The insiders here were not trading on an equal footing with the outside investors. They alone were in a position to evaluate the probability and magnitude of what seemed from the outset to be a major ore strike; they alone could invest safely, secure in the expectation that the price of TGS stock would rise substantially in the event such a major strike should materialize, but would decline little, if at all, in the event of failure, for the public, ignorant at the outset of the favorable probabilities would likewise be unaware of the unproductive exploration, and the additional exploration costs would not significantly affect TGS market prices. Such inequities based upon unequal access to knowledge should not be shrugged off as inevitable in our way of life, or, in view of the congressional concern in the area, remain uncorrected.

We hold, therefore, that all transactions in TGS stock or calls by individuals apprised of the drilling results of K–55–1 were made in violation of Rule 10b–5. Inasmuch as the visual evaluation of that drill core (a generally reliable estimate though less accurate than a chemical assay) constituted material information, those advised of the results of the visual evaluation as well as those informed of the chemical assay traded in violation of law. The geologist Darke possessed undisclosed material information and traded in TGS securities. Therefore we reverse the dismissal of the action as to him and his personal transactions. The trial court also found, 258 F.Supp. at 284, that Darke, after the drilling of K–55–1 had been completed and with detailed knowledge of the results thereof, told certain outside individuals that TGS "was a good buy." These individuals thereafter acquired TGS stock and calls. The trial court also found that later, as of March 30, 1964, Darke not only used his material knowledge for his own purchases but that the substantial amounts of TGS stock and calls purchased by these outside individuals on that day, was "strong circumstantial evidence that Darke must have passed the word to one or more of his 'tippees' that drilling on the Kidd 55 segment was about to be resumed." 258 F.Supp. at 284. Obviously if such a resumption were to have any meaning to such "tippees," they must have previously been told of K–55–1.

Unfortunately, however, there was no definitive resolution below of Darke's liability in these premises for the trial court held as to him, as it held as to all the other individual defendants, that this "undisclosed information" never became material until April 9. As it is our holding that the information acquired after the drilling of K–55–1 was material, we, on the basis of the findings of direct and circumstantial evidence on the issue that the trial court has already expressed, hold that Darke violated Rule 10b–5(3) and Section 10(b) by "tipping" and we remand, pursuant to the agreement of the parties, for a determination of the appropriate remedy. As Darke's "tippees" are not defendants in this action, we need not decide whether, if they acted with actual or constructive knowledge that the material information was undisclosed, their conduct is as equally violative of the Rule as the conduct of their insider source, though we note that it certainly could be equally reprehensible.

With reference to Huntington, the trial court found that he "had no detailed knowledge as to the work" on the Kidd–55 segment, 258 F.Supp. 281. Nevertheless, the evidence shows that he knew about and participated in TGS's land acquisition program which followed the receipt of the K–55–1 drilling results, and that on February 26, 1964 he purchased 50 shares of TGS stock. Later, on March 16, he helped prepare a letter for Dr. Holyk's signature in which TGS made a substantial offer for lands near K–55–1, and on the same day he, who had never before purchased calls on any stock, purchased a call on 100 shares of TGS stock. We are satisfied that these purchases in February and March, coupled with his readily inferable and probably reliable, understanding of the highly favorable nature of preliminary operations on the Kidd segment, demonstrate that Huntington possessed material inside information such as to make his purchase violative of the Rule and the Act.

C. *When May Insiders Act?*

Appellant Crawford, who ordered the purchase of TGS stock shortly before the TGS April 16 official announcement, and defendant Coates, who placed orders with and communicated the news to his broker immediately after the official announcement was read at the TGS-called press conference, concede that they were in possession of material information. They contend, however, that their purchases were not proscribed purchases for the news had already been effectively disclosed. We disagree.

Crawford telephoned his orders to his Chicago broker about midnight on April 15 and again at 8:30 in the morning of the 16th, with instructions to buy at the opening of the Midwest Stock Exchange that morning. The trial court's finding that "he sought to, and did, 'beat the news,'" 258 F.Supp. at 287, is well documented by the record. The rumors of a major ore strike which had been circulated in Canada and, to a lesser extent, in New York, had been disclaimed by the TGS press release of April 12, which significantly promised the public an official detailed announcement when possibilities had ripened into actualities. The abbreviated announcement to the Canadian press at 9:40 A.M. on the 16th by the Ontario Minister of Mines and the report carried by The Northern Miner, parts of which had sporadically reached New York on the morning of the 16th through reports from Canadian affiliates to a few New York investment firms, are assuredly not the equivalent of the official 10–15 minute announcement which was not released to the American financial press until after 10:00 A.M. Crawford's orders had been placed before that. Before insiders may act upon material information, such information must have been effectively disclosed in a manner sufficient to insure its availability to the investing public. Particularly here, where a formal announcement to the entire financial news media had been promised in a prior official release known to the media, all insider activity must await dissemination of the promised official announcement.

Coates was absolved by the court below because his telephone order was placed shortly before 10:20 A.M. on April 16, which was after the announcement had been made even though the news could not be considered already a matter of public information. 258 F.Supp. at 288. This result seems to have been predicated upon a misinterpretation of dicta in *Cady, Roberts*, where the SEC instructed insiders to "keep out of the market until the established procedures for public release of the information are *carried out* instead of hastening to execute transactions in advance of, and in frustration of, the objectives of the release," 40 S.E.C. at 915 (emphasis supplied). The reading of a news release, which prompted Coates into action, is merely the first step in the process of dissemination required for compliance with the regulatory objective of providing all investors with an equal opportunity to make informed investment judgments. Assuming that the contents of the official release could instantaneously be acted upon,[18] at the minimum Coates should have waited until the news could reasonably have been expected to appear over the media of widest circulation, the Dow Jones broad tape, rather than hastening to insure an advantage to himself and his broker son-in-law.

* * *

CONCLUSION

In summary, therefore, we affirm the finding of the court below that appellants Richard H. Clayton and David M. Crawford have violated 15 U.S.C.A. § 78j(b) and Rule 10b–5; we reverse the judgment

18. Although the only insider who acted after the news appeared over the Dow Jones broad tape is not an appellant and therefore we need not discuss the necessity of considering the advisability of a "reasonable waiting period" during which outsiders may absorb and evaluate disclosures, we note in passing that, where the news is of a sort which is not readily translatable into investment action, insiders may not take advantage of their advance opportunity to evaluate the information by acting immediately upon dissemination. In any event, the permissible timing of insider transactions after disclosures of various sorts is one of the many areas of expertise for appropriate exercise of the SEC's rule-making power, which we hope will be utilized in the future to provide some predictability of certainty for the business community.

order entered below dismissing the complaint against appellees Charles F. Fogarty, Richard H. Clayton, Richard D. Mollison, Walter Holyk, Kenneth H. Darke, Earl L. Huntington, and Francis G. Coates, as we find that they have violated 15 U.S.C.A. § 78j(b) and Rule 10b–5. As to these eight individuals we remand so that in accordance with the agreement between the parties the Commission may notice a hearing before the court below to determine the remedies to be applied against them. We reverse the judgment order dismissing the complaint against Claude O. Stephens, Charles F. Fogarty, and Harold B. Kline as recipients of stock options, direct the district court to consider in its discretion whether to issue injunction orders against Stephens and Fogarty, and direct that an order issue rescinding the option granted Kline and that such further remedy be applied against him as may be proper by way of an order of restitution   *   *   *.

NOTE—TEXAS GULF SULPHUR AND BEYOND

On remand, the district court ordered those TGS insiders who had, prior to April 16, purchased TGS stock or recommended its purchase to others to disgorge the profits that they and their tippees had realized, paying them over to the corporation. The profits were held to be "the difference between the mean average price of TGS common stock on the New York Stock Exchange on April 17, 1964, which has been stipulated by the parties to be 40⅜, and the purchase price of their shares." The Second Circuit affirmed. SEC v. Texas Gulf Sulphur Co., 312 F.Supp. 77 (S.D.N.Y.1970), aff'd 446 F.2d 1301 (2d Cir. 1971). The decree made no provision for attempting to contact the defrauded sellers from whom the defendants or their tippees had bought. The damages paid by the defendants were, however, to be held in an escrow account, subject to court order, for five years after which any amount that had not been paid out to private claimants would become the property of the corporation. The settlement of some of the private actions arising from the insider trading aspects of the case is set forth in Cannon v. Texas Gulf Sulphur Co., 55 F.R.D. 308 (S.D.N.Y.1972).

Texas Gulf Sulphur is a landmark in the development of Rule 10b–5 and securities law in general. The opinions, including three concurring opinions and a lengthy dissent by Judge Moore, are still cited with some regularity. The case has two principal branches, the duty of corporate insiders (and their tippees) to "disclose or abstain" discussed above, and the obligation of the corporation and its responsible officials to assure that disclosures of material corporate events are both timely and accurate, which is considered in a subsequent portion of this chapter.

Subsequent cases have explored the limits of the prohibition on insider trading left unsettled by *Texas Gulf Sulphur*. Some of the most difficult problems arise in the context of private suits for damages. To begin with, there is the basic question, what is the purpose of the prohibition against insider trading? Is it (1) to protect investors from being "defrauded?" Is it (2) to protect the "integrity" of the securities markets in order to assure all investors that they are not playing in a game in which there are other players who have a substantial advantage over them in the form of inside information? Or is it (3) a "federalization" of a purported common law fiduciary standard that prohibits officers and directors from taking unfair advantage of shareholders in their corporation (a standard that, as we have seen, is anything but universally accepted in the state courts)?

A clear understanding of the purpose of the prohibition against insider trading is critical to answering two of the most difficult practical questions in administering it. The first is, to whom does the prohibition extend? If the purpose is (1) or (2), then it would seem that anyone who possesses knowledge of a material fact not available to the general public (or at least to anyone clever enough or diligent enough to find it out) should be prohibited from trading without disclosure of the fact. If the purpose is (3), on the other hand, only true insiders—or those who can be said to have some fiduciary duty toward investors in the marketplace—would be subject to the "disclose or abstain" rule.

The second, and perhaps even more difficult problem is what measure of damages should be employed? A narrow view of the purpose of the prohibition would suggest that only those actually in privity with the wrongdoers should be entitled to recover damages. They would be limited in their recovery to the difference between what they paid—if they bought from a defendant—and the "real" value of the security had disclosure been made and the market been given time to reflect the new facts. Conversely, if the plaintiffs *sold* to an insider, the measure of damages would be the difference between the price paid and the value of the security taking into account the effect on the market of the information withheld.

There are two difficulties with this relatively straightforward application of common law principles. First, it is often difficult or impossible to reconstruct a particular exchange transaction to determine the identity of the buyer and the seller. Even if it were possible, most investors would lack both the knowledge and the incentive to attempt to determine if they were, in fact, the lucky one to have bought from or sold to the guilty insider. Thus the private damage remedy would be of little effect in deterring insider trading. Second, since the matching of any given pair of buy and sell orders is a matter of pure fortuity, there is little logic in allowing one particular investor, who just happened to be in privity with someone trading on inside information, to recover while others who may have traded within minutes or even seconds go without a remedy. This reasoning has led the courts generally to reject a requirement of privity in such actions (*but see* Fridrich v. Bradford, *infra*), but then to find themselves in the even more difficult dilemma of deciding how to define the class of investors to whom a remedy is to be afforded. Is it all investors who traded during the same hour as the insider? During the same day? Or is it perhaps, as one of the leading cases held, all those who bought between the time the defendants first traded and the time the information was made public?

This last approach was taken by the courts in one of the best-known insider trading cases, Shapiro v. Merrill Lynch, Pierce, Fenner & Smith, Inc., 495 F.2d 228 (2d Cir. 1974), in which the brokerage firm learned, in its capacity as managing underwriter of a new issue of debentures of the Douglas Aircraft Co., that Douglas's earnings would be substantially lower than had been earlier projected. Merrill Lynch divulged this information to several of its institutional clients, who sold or took short positions in some 165,000 shares of Douglas common stock during a four-day period before the bad news was made public. In affirming a denial of the defendants' motion for judgment on the pleadings, the court of appeals said, "We hold that defendants owed a duty—for the breach of which they may be held liable in this private action for damages—not only to the purchasers of the actual shares sold by the defendants (in the unlikely event they can be identified) but to all persons who during the same period purchased Douglas stock in the open market without knowledge of the material inside information which was in the possession of the defendants." On remand the district court defined the class of plaintiffs to include all those who had purchased Douglas stock on the four days beginning on the day of the first allegedly illegal sale through the day on which the reduced earnings were announced. The court observed that liability "begins at the time 10b–5 is violated * * * and continues until the non-public material information * * * is effectively publicly disseminated." CCH Fed.Sec.L.Rep. ¶ 95,377 (S.D.N.Y.1975).

The difficulty with such an approach is that it can lead to damages that are out of all reasonable proportion to the wrong. In another leading case, Fridrich v. Bradford, 542 F.2d 307 (6th Cir. 1976), the defendant, son of a principal stockholder of Old Line Life Insurance Company, acting on a tip from his father about an impending merger, purchased 1225 shares of Old Line common stock on April 27, 1972. He sold the shares on July 27, making a profit of $13,000. The Sixth Circuit reversed a judgment for the plaintiffs, holding that as they were not in privity with the defendant, they were entitled to no relief. A contrary rule, the court said would lead "inexorably to an unjust and unworkable result * * * creating a windfall for those fortuitous enough to be aware of their nebulous legal rights, and imposing what essentially must be considered punitive damages almost unlimited in their potential scope." On the facts of the case, the court noted, had all of those who sold their stock on the same three days in June when the plaintiffs had sold joined the lawsuit, "Bradford Jr.'s potential liability in damages would have totalled approximately $800,000. If a class action had been brought which included all investors who sold Old Line stock between April 21 and June 29, 1972 [the date the merger was publicly announced], the damages could have totalled approximately $3,700,000. If the class had been further expanded to those selling up to November 20, 1972 [the date the merger was approved by the SEC] (and the holding appealed from admits of no limitation short thereof), the damages would have run in excess of $7,000,000."

In the following case, the Second Circuit was again called on to wrestle with some of these issues. Consider whether you think the solution it reaches is a sound one.

ELKIND v. LIGGETT & MYERS, INC.

635 F.2d 156 (2d Cir. 1980).

MANSFIELD, Circuit Judge.

This case presents a number of issues arising out of what has become a form of corporate brinkmanship-non-public disclosure of business-related information to financial analysts. The action is a class suit by Arnold B. Elkind on behalf of certain purchasers (more fully described below) of the stock of Liggett & Myers, Inc. (Liggett) against it. They seek damages for alleged failure of its officers to disclose certain material information with respect to its earnings and operations and for their alleged wrongful tipping of inside information to certain persons who then sold Liggett shares on the open market.

After a non jury trial Judge Constance Baker Motley held in posttrial findings and conclusions that Liggett did not violate Section 10 (b) of the Securities Exchange Act of 1934, 15 U.S.C.A. § 78j(b), or Rule 10b–5 promulgated thereunder, 17 C.F.R. § 240.10b–5, by failing prior to July 18, 1972, to release figures showing a substantial downturn in earnings or to correct erroneous projections of financial analysts which it had allegedly fostered. The court found, however, that on July 10, 1972, and July 17, 1972, officers of Liggett disclosed material inside information to individual financial analysts, leading to sale of Liggett stock by investors to whom this information was conveyed. Damages were computed on the basis of the difference between the price which members of the plaintiff class (uninformed buyers of Liggett stock between the time of the first tip and subsequent public disclosure) paid and what the stock sold for after the later disclosure. See 472 F.Supp. 123 (S.D.N.Y.1978). We affirm the dismissal of the counts alleging failure to disclose or correct. We reverse the finding of liability based on the alleged July 10, 1972, tip for want of materiality and scienter. We remand the determination of liability based on the July 17, 1972, tip for determination of damages. In all other respects the judgment is affirmed.

The plaintiffs consist of two classes: (1) with respect to Count I, which alleges misleading statements, nondisclosure of material information and failure to correct analysts' projections, all purchasers of Liggett stock between June 19, 1972, and July 18, 1972; (2) with respect to Count II, which alleges unlawful trading on the basis of tipped inside information, all purchasers of Liggett stock between June 28, 1972, and July 18, 1972. See 66 F.R.D. 36 (S.D.N.Y.1975); 77 F.R.D. 708 (S.D.N.Y.1977).

Liggett is a diversified company, with traditional business in the tobacco industry supplemented by acquisitions in such industries as liquor (Paddington Corp., importer of J&B Scotch), pet food (Allen Products Co. and Perk Foods Co., manufacturer of Alpo dog food), cereal, watchbands, cleansers and rugs. Its common stock is listed on the New York Stock Exchange.

In 1969 Liggett officers concluded that the company's stock was underpriced, due in part to lack of appreciation in the financial community for the breadth of its market activity. To cure this perceived deficiency, Liggett initiated an "analyst program," hiring a public relations firm and encouraging closer contact between analysts and company management. This included meetings with analysts at which Liggett officials discussed operations. Liggett also reviewed and commented on reports which the analysts were preparing, to correct errors and other misunderstandings.

Liggett had a record year in 1971, with earnings of $4.22 per share (up from $3.56 in 1970). The first quarter of 1972 was equally auspicious. On March 22, Liggett issued a press release reporting that sales of the non-tobacco lines had continued to increase in the first two months, but noting that current stockpiling of J&B Scotch by customers (in anticipation of a price increase) could affect sales. On May 3, 1972, the company released its first quarter figures, showing earnings of $1.00 per share (compared to $.81 in the first quarter of 1971).

This quarterly operations report led to considerable optimism in the financial community over Liggett's prospects. Management did nothing to deflate the enthusiasm. A number of reports containing predictions that 1972 earnings would increase about 10% over 1971 earnings were reviewed by officials of Liggett during the first five months of 1972. While company personnel corrected factual errors in these reports, they did not comment (or made noncommittal or evasive comments) on the earnings projections, according to the findings below, which are supported by the record. At group meetings with analysts in February and March, management indicated that it was making "good progress" with certain products and that it was "well-positioned" to take advantage of industry trends. At the end of March, Liggett successfully made a public offering of $50 million of debentures. At an April 25 stockholders' meeting, Liggett's Executive Vice President expressed general optimism that the company was continuing to make good progress. On May 3, the first quarter earnings were released. At a May 16 meeting with analysts in New York, officials reiterated their vague but quieting pronouncements. Similar comments, to the effect that 1972 was expected to be a "good year," were voiced at a June 5 presentation in London.

Despite the company's outward appearance of strength, Liggett's management was less sanguine intramurally. Internal budget projections called for only a two percent increase in earnings in 1972. In April and May, a full compilation of updated figures was ordered, and new projections were presented to the Board of Directors on May 15. April was marked by a sharp decline, with earnings of only $.03 per share (compared to $.30 the previous April). The 1972 earnings projection was revised downward from $4.30 to $3.95 per share. May earnings, which the Board received on June 19, rebounded somewhat to $.23 per share (compared to $.27 in May 1971 and original budget projections of $.34). At meetings with analysts during this period, Liggett officials took a more negative tone, emphasizing, for example, various cost pressures. There was no public disclosure of the adverse financial developments at this time. Beginning in late June, 1972, the price of Liggett's common stock steadily declined.

On July 17, preliminary earnings data for June and six-month totals became available to the Board of Directors. June earnings were $.20 per share (compared to $.44 in June 1971). The first half earnings for 1972 were approximately $1.46 per share, down from $1.82 the previous year. The Board decided to issue a press release the following day. That release, issued at about 2:15 P.M. on July 18, disclosed the preliminary earnings figures and attributed the decline to shortcomings in all of Liggett's product lines.

The district court found two "tips" of material inside information in the days before the July 18 press release. On July 10, analyst Peter Barry of Kuhn Loeb & Co. spoke by telephone with Daniel Provost, Liggett's Director of Corporate Communications. According to Barry's deposition testimony, apparently adopted by the court below, Provost confirmed Barry's suggestions that J&B sales were slowing due to earlier stockpiling and that a new competing dog food was affecting Alpo sales adversely. Barry asked if a projection of a 10% earnings decline would be realistic, and received what he characterized as a noncommittal response. Barry testified that Provost told him that a preliminary earnings statement would be coming out in a week or so. Since Barry knew of no prior instances in which Liggett had issued such a preliminary statement, he deduced that the figures would be lower than expected. Barry sent a wire * * * to Kuhn Loeb's offices. The information was conveyed to three clients. Two of them, holders of a total of over 600,000 shares did not sell. A third client sold the 100 shares he owned. No other Kuhn Loeb customers sold between the time of the July 10 "tip" and the release of preliminary earnings figures on July 18; Kuhn Loeb customers bought some 5,000 shares during this period.

The second "tip" occurred on July 17, one day before the preliminary earnings figures for the first half were released. Analyst Robert Cummins of Loeb Rhoades & Co. questioned Ralph Moore, Liggett's chief financial officer, about the recent decline in price of Liggett's common stock, as well as performance of the various subsidiaries. According to Cummins' deposition, he asked Moore whether there was a good possibility that earnings would be down, and received an affirmative ("grudging") response. Moore added that this information was confidential. Cummins sent a wire to his firm, and spoke with a stockholder who promptly sold 1,800 shares of Liggett stock on behalf of his customers.

The district court held that each of these disclosures was a tip of material information in violation of Rule 10b–5, rendering Liggett liable to all persons who bought the company's stock during the period from July 11 to July 18, 1972, inclusive, without knowledge of the tipped information. * * *

In computing damages for the July 10 and 17 tips, the court attempted to award the difference between the amount plaintiff class members paid for their stock and the value they received. The latter was interpreted to be the price at which the stock would have sold had there been public disclosure of the tipped information. The court ruled that plaintiff's expert testimony on this point was speculative and unsupported by the record. Instead, following Mitchell v. Texas Gulf Sulphur Co., 446 F.2d 90 (10th Cir.), cert. denied, 404 U.S. 1004, 92 S.Ct. 564, 30 L.Ed.2d 558 (1971), it looked to the actual market price at the end of "a reasonable period" (eight trading days) following the July 18 release of earnings figures as an approximation of what the price would have been had the tipped information been disclosed publicly. Thus damages amounted to the difference between the plaintiff class members' purchase prices (generally in the vicinity of $60 per share) and $43, the price of the stock eight trading days after disclosure. Based on the total volume of trading transactions from July 11 to July 18, the court awarded damages amounting to $740,000 on condition that any unclaimed portion would revert to Liggett. To this the court added prejudgment interest of approximately $300,000.

Liggett now appeals from the finding of liability on the tipping count, the computation of damages and the award of prejudgment interest. * * *

DISCUSSION

The issues before us on this appeal are * * * (3) whether the private disclosures of July 10 and 17 amounted to tips forbidden by the rule; and (4) if so, whether damages were properly assessed.

3. *Tipping Liability*

The knowing use by corporate insiders of non-public information for their own benefit or that of "tippees" by trading in corporate securities amounts to a violation of Rule 10b–5, SEC v. Texas Gulf Sulphur Co., 401 F.2d 833 (2d Cir. 1968) (en banc), cert. denied, 394 U. S. 976, 89 S.Ct. 1454, 22 L.Ed.2d 756 (1969); In re Cady, Roberts & Co., 40 S.E.C. 907 (1961), which may give rise to a suit for damages by uninformed outsiders who trade during a period of tippee trading. Shapiro v. Merrill Lynch, Pierce, Fenner & Smith, 495 F.2d 228 (2d Cir. 1974). See Chiarella v. United States, 445 U.S. 222, 100 S.Ct. 1108, 63 L.Ed.2d 348 (1980).[14]

The duty imposed on a company and its officers is an alternative one: they must disclose material inside information either to no outsiders or to all outsiders equally. As with any claim under Rule 10b–5, scienter must be proven. Ernst & Ernst v. Hochfelder, 425 U. S. 185, 96 S.Ct. 1375, 47 L.Ed.2d 668 (1976). However, if there is no trading by tippees (or those to whom the tippees convey their information), there can be no damages for tipping under § 10(b). See Shapiro v. Merrill Lynch, Pierce, Fenner & Smith, 353 F.Supp. 264, 278 (S.D.N.Y.1972), affd., 495 F.2d 228 (2d Cir. 1974). Trades by tippees are attributed to the tipper. Cf. Mosser v. Darrow, 341 U.S. 267, 71 S.Ct. 680, 95 L.Ed. 927 (1951); SEC v. Texas Gulf Sulphur Co., 446 F. 2d 1301, 1308 (2d Cir.), cert. denied, 404 U.S. 1005, 92 S.Ct. 561, 30 L. Ed.2d 558 (1971). Tippee trading, therefore, is the primary and essential element of the offense. The investor otherwise has no right to confidential undisclosed data from the company's files even though it might, if disclosed, influence his investment decision.[15]

The corporate officer dealing with financial analysts inevitably finds himself in a precarious position, which we have analogized to "a fencing match conducted on a tightrope." SEC v. Bausch & Lomb, Inc., 565 F.2d 8, 9 (2d Cir. 1977). A skilled analyst with knowledge of the company and the industry may piece seemingly inconsequential data together with public information into a mosaic which reveals material non-public information. Whenever managers and analysts meet elsewhere than in public, there is a risk that the analysts will emerge with knowledge of material information which is not publicly available.

---

14. The Supreme Court ruled in *Chiarella* that there can be no violation of § 10(b) unless the party so charged has violated a duty arising out of a relationship of trust. A corporate insider who tips confidential information clearly violates a fiduciary obligation, see *Chiarella, supra,* 445 U.S. at 229 & n. 12, 100 S.Ct. at 1115 & n. 12. This obligation is breached by insider selling, *e.g., Shapiro, supra; cf.* Gratz v. Claughton,

187 F.2d 46, 49 (2d Cir.) (L. Hand, J.), cert. denied, 341 U.S. 920, 71 S.Ct. 741, 95 L.Ed. 1353 (1951), as well as buying, *e.g.,* SEC v. Texas Gulf Sulphur Co., *supra.*

15. Whether the SEC may seek injunctive relief against tipping which has not been shown to have resulted in tippee trading is an issue not before us, and we do not wish our formulation of the duty involved to be taken to imply a view.

Despite the risks attendant upon these contacts, the SEC and the stock exchanges as well as some commentators have taken the view that meetings and discussions with analysts serve an important function in collecting, evaluating and disseminating corporate information for public use. The reconciliation of this outlook with the SEC's mandate that material facts may be disclosed to investors, provided they are made available to all (through filings with the SEC) and not merely to analysts, has led to a case-by-case approach.

The prerequisites of tipping liability, in addition to the revelation of non-public information about a company to someone who then takes advantage of this superior knowledge by trading in the company's stock, are that the tipped information must be *material*, and that the tipper-defendant must have acted with *scienter*.

(a) *Materiality*. We discussed the meaning of "materiality" in the *Bausch & Lomb* case, *supra*, reiterating the language of *Texas Gulf Sulphur* that the disclosed information must be "reasonably certain to have a substantial effect on the market price of the security." 565 F.2d at 15. We further applied the Supreme Court's definition of materiality from TSC Industries, Inc. v. Northway, Inc., 426 U.S. 438, 449, 96 S.Ct. 2126, 2132, 48 L.Ed.2d 757 (1976):

> What the standard [of materiality] does contemplate is a showing of a substantial likelihood that, under all the circumstances, the omitted fact would have assumed actual significance in the deliberations of the reasonable shareholder. Put another way, there must be a substantial likelihood that the disclosure of the omitted fact would have been viewed by the reasonable investor as having significantly altered the "total mix" of information made available.

Thus a relevant question in determining materiality in a case of alleged tipping to analysts is whether the tipped information, if divulged to the public, would have been likely to affect the decision of potential buyers and sellers.

Viewed under this standard, we cannot agree that the July 10 "tip" was material. The disclosure in that conversation consisted of confirmation that J&B sales were slowing due to earlier stockpiling and that Alpo sales were being adversely affected by Campbell's competing product and by the information that a preliminary earnings statement would be coming out in a week. The "news" about J&B and Alpo was already common knowledge among the analysts—indeed, Liggett had publicly stated that a decline in J&B sales was expected. The confirmation of these facts, which were fairly obvious to all who followed the stock and were not accompanied by any quantification of the downturns, cannot be deemed "reasonably certain to have a substantial effect on the market price of the security." Similarly, we cannot agree that in this context the bare announcement that preliminary earnings would be released in a week was material. No information concerning the amount of those earnings was disclosed, and the mere fact that there would be a release added little to the already available wisdom of the market place (reflected by stock prices which had been falling for two weeks) that Liggett might be in a downturn. It would serve little purpose to require a corporation to call a press conference in order to announce that it would be making an announcement in another week.

Further indication of the lack of materiality may be found in the reaction of those who were exposed to the inside information. The institutional investors, holders of 600,000 shares of Liggett, did not sell any of them. Indeed, the wire sent out by analyst Barry, was equivocal in its drawing of adverse inferences. * * *

The July 17 tip, however, was sufficiently directed to the matter of earnings to sustain the district court's finding of materiality. According to the deposition of Robert Cummins, the tippee, he inquired whether there was a "possibility" that earnings for the second quarter would be down, and received an affirmative response. He then inquired whether this was a "good possibility," and was again told yes. He was asked to keep the information confidential. Cummins then sent off a wire, stating that second quarter earnings, and probably first half earnings as well, would be lower than the previous year's totals.

While there is considerable room for doubt concerning the materiality of this disclosure, particularly in view of the lack of specificity and the fact that Cummins' wire was substantially the same as the wire sent by Barry after receiving information which we have concluded was not material, there are sufficient indicia of materiality to support the district court's conclusion. The request by Moore (Liggett's chief financial officer) that Cummins not repeat what he had been told added to the impression that the earnings were worse than those following the stock expected them to be. Moreover, 1,800 shares were sold by a stockbroker on behalf of his customers, after speaking with Cummins by telephone. The stockbroker was left with the impression that "the second quarter was going to be very poor," which he considered significant enough to prompt the sale. We therefore conclude that the July 17 tip was one of material inside information.

(b) *Scienter.* The Supreme Court, in Ernst & Ernst v. Hochfelder, *supra,* ruled that scienter is an essential element of a § 10(b) violation, leaving to the lower courts the meaning of scienter in various contexts. In this case we must apply the scienter requirement to the alleged tipping of material inside information. * * *

The Supreme Court defined scienter as "knowing or intentional misconduct," 425 U.S. at 197, 96 S.Ct. at 1382, leaving open the possibility that recklessness might suffice, *id.* at 193 n. 12, 96 S.Ct. at 1380 n. 12. We need go no further than the term "knowing" to resolve this case. One who deliberately tips information which he knows to be material and non-public to an outsider who may reasonably be expected to use it to his advantage has the requisite scienter. This action amounts to knowing misconduct. One who intentionally places such ammunition in the hands of individuals able to use it to their advantage on the market has the requisite state of mind for liability under § 10(b) and Rule 10b–5.

Applying this standard to the present case, we conclude that the July 10 tip was not accompanied by scienter. * * *

There was ample evidence of scienter in connection with the July 17 tip. One could reasonably infer that an official commenting on earnings shortly before their public release will know that the tip could reasonably be expected to be used by the tippee for trading advantages. It is therefore material. Indeed, Moore's request that the disclosure be kept confidential strongly supports this inference. The district court's finding that the information was disclosed in order to keep the analysts (whose job it was to advise clients in their trading of stock) a step ahead of public knowledge supports this conclusion.

We therefore conclude that the tip of July 10 was not material and was not accompanied by the requisite scienter to furnish the basis for liability under Rule 10b–5. The tip of July 17, however, was material and made with scienter. We turn, then, to the computation of damages.

4. *Damages*

This case presents a question of measurement of damages which we have previously deferred, believing that damages are best addressed in a concrete setting. See Shapiro v. Merrill Lynch, Pierce, Fenner & Smith, Inc., *supra*, 495 F.2d at 241–42; Heit v. Weitzen, 402 F.2d 909, 917 & n. 8 (2d Cir. 1968), cert. denied, 395 U.S. 903, 89 S.Ct. 1740, 23 L.Ed.2d 217 (1969). We ruled in *Shapiro* that defendants selling on inside information would be liable to those who bought on the open market and sustained "substantial losses" during the period of insider trading.[23]

The district court looked to the measure of damages used in cases where a buyer was induced to purchase a company's stock by materially misleading statements or omissions. In such cases of fraud by a fiduciary intended to induce others to buy or sell stock the accepted measure of damages is the "out-of-pocket" measure. This consists of the difference between the price paid and the "value" of the stock when brought (or when the buyer committed himself to buy, if earlier).[25] Except in rare face-to-face transactions, however, uninformed

---

23. The Sixth Circuit has since reached the opposite conclusion. Fridrich v. Bradford, 542 F.2d 307, 318 (6th Cir. 1976), cert. denied, 429 U.S. 1053, 97 S.Ct. 767, 50 L.Ed.2d 769 (1977).

25. Some cases have suggested the availability as an alternative measure of damages of a modified rescissionary measure, consisting of the difference between the price the defrauded party paid and the price at the time he learned or should have learned the true state of affairs. The theory of this measure is to restore the plaintiff to the position where

traders on an open, impersonal market are not induced by representations on the part of the tipper or tippee to buy or sell. Usually they are wholly unacquainted with and uninfluenced by the tippee's misconduct. They trade independently and voluntarily but without the benefit of information known to the trading tippee.

In determining what is the appropriate measure of damages to be awarded to the outside uninformed investor as the result of tippee-trading through use of information that is not equally available to all investors it must be remembered that investors who trade in a stock on the open market have no absolute right to know inside information. They are, however, entitled to an honest market in which those with whom they trade have no confidential corporate information. *See* SEC v. Texas Gulf Sulphur Co., *supra*, 401 F.2d at 848, 851–02.

> The primary object of the exchange is to afford facilities for trading in securities under the safest and fairest conditions attainable. In order that parties may trade on even terms they should have, as far as practicable, the same opportunities for knowledge in regard to the subject matter of the trade. H.R.Rep. No. 1383, 73d Cong., 2d Sess. 12 (1934).

It is the combination of the tip and the tippee's trading that poses the evil against which the open market investor must be protected. The reason for the "disclose or abstain" rule is the unfairness in permitting an insider to trade for his own account on the basis of material inside information not available to others. The tipping of material information is a violation of the fiduciary's duty but no injury occurs until the information is used by the tippee. The entry into the market of a tippee with superior knowledge poses the threat that if he trades on the basis of the inside information he may profit at the expense of investors who are disadvantaged by lack of the inside information. For this both the tipper and the tippee are liable. *See* SEC v. Texas Gulf Sulphur Co., 312 F.Supp. 77, 95 (S.D.N.Y.1970), affd., 446 F.2d 1301, 1308 (2d Cir. 1971). If the insider chooses not to trade, on the other hand, no injury may be claimed by the outside investor, since the public has no right to the undisclosed information.

Recognizing the foregoing, we in *Shapiro* suggested that the district court must be accorded flexibility in assessing damages, after considering

> the extent of the selling defendants' trading in Douglas stock, whether such trading effectively impaired the integrity of the

he would have been had he not been fraudulently induced to trade. *See, e.g.,* Mitchell v. Texas Gulf Sulphur Co., 446 F.2d 90, 104–06 (10th Cir.), cert. denied, 404 U.S. 1004, 92 S.Ct. 564, 30 L.Ed.2d 558 (1971). The soundness of this measure has been vigorously disputed in the case of open market trading. Green v. Occidental Petroleum Corp., 541 F.2d 1335, 1341–44 (9th Cir. 1976) (Sneed, J., concurring). While the district court cited to *Mitchell*, its opinion makes clear that it was applying the out-of-pocket measure of damages. Since the district court did not apply this modified rescissionary measure, we need not pass on it here.

market, * * * what profits or other benefits were realized by defendants [and] what expenses were incurred and what losses were sustained by plaintiffs. * * * Moreover, we do not foreclose the possibility that an analysis by the district court of the nature and character of the Rule 10b–5 violations committed may require limiting the extent of liability imposed on either class of defendants. 495 F.2d at 242.

We thus gave heed to the guidance provided by the Supreme Court in Affiliated Ute Citizens v. United States, 406 U.S. 128, 151, 92 S.Ct. 1456, 1471, 31 L.Ed.2d 741 (1972), to the effect that "Congress intended securities legislation enacted for the purpose of avoiding frauds to be construed 'not technically and restrictively, but flexibly to effectuate its remedial purposes.' *Id.* [SEC v. Capital Gains Research Bureau, 375 U.S. 180], at 195 [84 S.Ct. 275 at 284, 11 L.Ed.2d 237 (1963)]. This was recently said once again in Superintendent of Insurance v. Bankers Life & Casualty Co., 404 U.S. 6, 12 [92 S.Ct. 165, 168, 30 L.Ed.2d 128] (1971)." *See also* Mills v. Electric Auto-Lite Co., 396 U.S. 375, 386, 391, 90 S.Ct. 616, 622, 625, 24 L.Ed.2d 593 (1970) (1934 Act does not "circumscribe the courts' power to grant appropriate remedies").

Within the flexible framework thus authorized for determining what amounts should be recoverable by the uninformed trader from the tipper and tippee trader, several measures are possible. First, there is the traditional out-of-pocket measure used by the district court in this case. For several reasons this measure appears to be inappropriate. In the first place, as we have noted, it is directed toward compensating a person for losses directly traceable to the defendant's fraud upon him. No such fraud or inducement may be attributed to a tipper or tippee trading on an impersonal market. Aside from this the measure poses serious proof problems that may often be insurmountable in a tippee-trading case. The "value" of the stock traded during the period of nondisclosure of the tipped information (i. e., the price at which the market would have valued the stock if there had been a disclosure) is hypothetical. Expert testimony regarding that "value" may, as the district court found in the present case, be entirely speculative. This has led some courts to conclude that the drop in price of the stock after actual disclosure and after allowing a period of time to elapse for the market to absorb the news may sometimes approximate the drop which would have occurred earlier had the tip been disclosed. * * *

Whatever may be the reasonableness of the * * * "value" method of calculating damages in other contexts, it has serious vulnerabilities here. It rests on the fundamental assumptions (1) that the tipped information is substantially the same as that later disclosed publicly, and (2) that one can determine how the market would have reacted to the public release of the tipped information at an earlier time by its reaction to that information at a later, proximate time.

This theory depends on the parity of the "tip" and the "disclosure." When they differ, the basis of the damage calculation evaporates. One could not reasonably estimate how the public would have reacted to the news that the Titanic was near an iceberg from how it reacted to news that the ship had struck an iceberg and sunk. In the present case, the July 10 tip that preliminary earnings would be released in a week is not comparable to the later release of the estimated earnings figures on July 18. Nor was the July 17 tipped information that there was a good possibility that earnings would be down comparable to the next day's release of the estimated earnings figures.

An equally compelling reason for rejecting the theory is its potential for imposition of Draconian, exorbitant damages, out of all proportion to the wrong committed, lining the pockets of all interim investors and their counsel at the expense of innocent corporate stockholders. Logic would compel application of the theory to a case where a tippee sells only 10 shares of a heavily traded stock (e.g., IBM), which then drops substantially when the tipped information is publicly disclosed. To hold the tipper and tippee liable for the losses suffered by every open market buyer of the stock as a result of the later decline in value of the stock after the news became public would be grossly unfair. While the securities laws do occasionally allow for potentially ruinous recovery, we will not readily adopt a measure mandating "large judgments, payable in the last instance by innocent investors [here, Liggett shareholders], for the benefit of speculators and their lawyers," SEC v. Texas Gulf Sulphur Co., *supra*, 401 F.2d at 867 (Friendly, J., concurring), unless the statute so requires.

An alternative measure would be to permit recovery of damages caused by erosion of the market price of the security that is traceable to the tippee's wrongful trading, i.e., to compensate the uninformed investor for the loss in market value that he suffered as a direct result of the tippee's conduct. Under this measure an innocent trader who bought Liggett shares at or after a tippee sold on the basis of inside information would recover any decline in value of his shares caused by the tippee's trading. Assuming the impact of the tippee's trading on the market is measurable, this approach has the advantage of limiting the plaintiffs to the amount of damage actually caused in fact by the defendant's wrongdoing and avoiding windfall recoveries by investors at the expense of stockholders other than the tippee trader, which could happen in the present action against Liggett. The rationale is that if the market price is not affected by the tippee's trading, the uninformed investor is in the same position as he would have been had the insider abstained from trading. In such event the equilibrium of the market has not been disturbed and the outside investor has not been harmed by the informational imbalance. Only where the market has been contaminated by the wrongful conduct would damages be recoverable.

This causation-in-fact approach has some disadvantages. It allows no recovery for the tippee's violation of his duty to disclose the inside information before trading. Had he fulfilled this duty, others, including holders of the stock, could then have traded on an equal informational basis. Another disadvantage of such a measure lies in the difficult if not impossible burden it would impose on the uninformed trader of proving the time when and extent to which the integrity of the market was affected by the tippee's conduct.[28] In some cases, such as *Mitchell, supra* and *Shapiro, supra*, the existence of very substantial trading by the tippee, coupled with a sharp change in market price over a short period, would provide the basis for measuring a market price movement attributable to the wrongful trading. On the other hand, in a case where there was only a modest amount of tippee trading in a heavy-volume market in the stock, accompanied by other unrelated factors affecting the market price, it would be impossible as a practical matter to isolate such rise or decline in market price, if any, as was caused by the tippee's wrongful conduct. Moreover, even assuming market erosion caused by this trading to be provable and that the uninformed investor could show that it continued after his purchase, there remains the question of whether the plaintiff would not be precluded from recovery on the ground that any post-purchase decline in market price attributable to the tippee's trading would not be injury to him as a purchaser, i.e., "in connection with the purchase and sale of securities," but injury to him as a stockholder due to a breach of fiduciary duty by the company's officers, which is not actionable under § 10(b) of the 1934 Act or Rule 10b–5 promulgated thereunder. For these reasons, we reject this strict direct market-repercussion theory of damages.

A third alternative is (1) to allow any uninformed investor, where a reasonable investor would either have delayed his purchase or not purchased at all if he had had the benefit of the tipped information, to recover any post-purchase decline in market value of his shares up to a reasonable time after he learns of the tipped information or after there is a public disclosure of it but (2) limit his recovery to the amount gained by the tippee as a result of his selling at the earlier date rather than delaying his sale until the parties could trade on an equal informational basis. Under this measure if the tippee sold 5,000 shares at $50 per share on the basis of inside information and the stock thereafter declined to $40 per share within a reasonable time after public disclosure, an uninformed purchaser, buying shares during the interim (e.g., at $45 per share) would recover the difference between his purchase price and the amount at which he could have sold the shares on an equal informational basis (i.e., the market

---

28. Although the approach that damages cannot be recovered unless causally connected with the trading on inside information has been recognized, it has also been observed that such connection is difficult to establish. Fridrich v. Bradford, 542 F.2d 307, 320 n. 27 (1976), cert. denied, 429 U.S. 1053, 97 S.Ct. 767, 50 L. Ed.2d 769 (1977).

price within a reasonable time after public disclosure of the tip), subject to a limit of $50,000, which is the amount gained by the tippee as a result of his trading on the inside information rather than on an equal basis. Should the intervening buyers, because of the volume and price of their purchases, claim more than the tippee's gain, their recovery (limited to that gain) would be shared *pro rata.*

This third alternative, which may be described as the disgorgement measure, has in substance been recommended by the American Law Institute in its 1978 Proposed Draft of a Federal Securities Code, §§ 1603, 1703(b), 1708(b), 1711(j). It offers several advantages. To the extent that it makes the tipper and tippees liable up to the amount gained by their misconduct, it should deter tipping of inside information and tippee-trading. On the other hand, by limiting the total recovery to the tippee's gain, the measure bars windfall recoveries of exorbitant amounts bearing no relation to the seriousness of the misconduct. It also avoids the extraordinary difficulties faced in trying to prove traditional out-of-pocket damages based on the true "value" of the shares purchased or damages claimed by reason of market erosion attributable to tippee trading. A plaintiff would simply be required to prove (1) the time, amount, and price per share of his purchase, (2) that a reasonable investor would not have paid as high a price or made the purchase at all if he had had the information in the tippee's possession, and (3) the price to which the security had declined by the time he learned the tipped information or at a reasonable time after it became public, whichever event first occurred. He would then have a claim and, up to the limits of the tippee's gain, could recover the decline in market value of his shares before the information became public or known to him. In most cases the damages recoverable under the disgorgement measure would be roughly commensurate to the actual harm caused by the tippee's wrongful conduct. In a case where the tippee sold only a few shares, for instance, the likelihood of his conduct causing any substantial injury to intervening investors buying without benefit of his confidential information would be small. If, on the other hand, the tippee sold large amounts of stock, realizing substantial profits, the likelihood of injury to intervening uninformed purchasers would be greater and the amount of potential recovery thereby proportionately enlarged.

We recognize that there cannot be any perfect measure of damages caused by tippee trading. The disgorgement measure, like others we have described, does have some disadvantages. It modifies the principle that ordinarily gain to the wrongdoer should not be a prerequisite to liability for violation of Rule 10b–5. It partially duplicates disgorgement remedies available in proceedings by the SEC or others. Under some market conditions such as where the market price is depressed by wholly unrelated causes, the tippee might be vulnerable to heavy damages, permitting some plaintiffs to recover undeserved windfalls. In some instances the total claims could exceed the wrongdoer's gain, limiting each claimant to a pro rata share of the gain. In other situations, after deducting the cost of recovery, including attorneys' fees, the remainder might be inadequate to make a class action worthwhile. However, as between the various alternatives we are persuaded, after weighing the pros and cons, that the disgorgement measure, despite some disadvantages, offers the most equitable resolution of the difficult problems created by conflicting interests.

* * *

The finding of liability based on the July 10, 1972, tip is reversed. The award of damages is also reversed and the case is remanded for a determination of damages recoverable for tippee-trading based on the July 17, 1972, tip, to be measured in accordance with the foregoing. Each party will bear his own costs.

5. MARKET INFORMATION

PROBLEM

ALTERNATIVE ENERGY CORPORATION—PART IV

A

You are having lunch with an old friend from law school who has become a patent attorney. Over the lobster bisque, he tells you that he would like your advice on a legal question that he is sure you know more about than he. His firm represents Alternative Energy Corporation, a New York Stock Exchange Corporation. A few days ago the company asked him to do a patent search on a new device for converting solar energy to electricity. The chief engineer of the company is very excited about the new technique. He told your friend that it is more efficient than any previously known and that the device can be manufactured relatively inexpensively. Your friend knows the patents in the field fairly well and even without doing a search is almost sure AEC's device is patentable. His question is whether he would violate any legal duty if he bought stock in AEC.

B

This time the friend with whom you are dining is an official in the Department of Energy who is responsible for managing energy research grants. She tells you over her vichyssoise that she is responsible for the research grant under which AEC has been doing much of its work on the new solar cell. In that capacity she has just learned of the success of AEC's efforts (which has not yet been publicly announced). She asks you whether she would be violating the law if she were to purchase AEC stock and to advise her parents to do likewise. (You may assume that government regulations relating to conflicts of interest would pose no obstacle.)

C

In a busy social week, you are now having lunch with a journalist friend who works for a major metropolitan daily. Over her gazpacho, she tells you that she learned from the paper's financial columnist this morning that his column for tomorrow will tout the stock of Alternative Energy Corporation. The columnist has learned from interviews with company officials that the firm has made a major breakthrough in solar energy technology. The article will be the first public announcement of this development. Your friend asks whether she would violate the securities laws if she were to purchase some AEC stock this afternoon. She also wonders whether you would not like to buy some.

CHIARELLA v. UNITED STATES

445 U.S. 222, 100 S.Ct. 1108, 63 L.Ed.2d 348 (1980).

Mr. Justice POWELL delivered the opinion of the Court.

The question in this case is whether a person who learns from the confidential documents of one corporation that it is planning an attempt to secure control of a second corporation violates § 10(b) of the Securities Exchange Act of 1934 if he fails to disclose the impending takeover before trading in the target company's securities.

I

Petitioner is a printer by trade. In 1975 and 1976, he worked as a "markup man" in the New York composing room of Pandick Press, a financial printer. Among documents that petitioner handled were five announcements of corporate takeover bids. When these documents were delivered to the printer, the identities of the acquiring and target corporations were concealed by blank spaces or false names. The true names were sent to the printer on the night of the final printing.

The petitioner, however, was able to deduce the names of the target companies before the final printing from other information contained in the documents. Without disclosing his knowledge, petitioner purchased stock in the target companies and sold the shares immediately after the takeover attempts were made public. By this method, petitioner realized a gain of slightly more than $30,000 in the course of 14 months. Subsequently, the Securities and Exchange Commission (Commission or SEC) began an investigation of his trading activities. In May 1977, petitioner entered into a consent decree with the Commission in which he agreed to return his profits to the sellers of the shares. On the same day, he was discharged by Pandick Press.

In January 1978, petitioner was indicted on 17 counts of violating § 10(b) of the Securities Exchange Act of 1934 (1934 Act) and SEC

Rule 10b–5. After petitioner unsuccessfully moved to dismiss the indictment, he was brought to trial and convicted on all counts.

The Court of Appeals for the Second Circuit affirmed petitioner's conviction.   588 F.2d 1358 (1978).   We granted certiorari, 441 U.S. 942, 99 S.Ct. 2158, 60 L.Ed.2d 1043 (1979), and we now reverse.

II

* * *

This case concerns the legal effect of the petitioner's silence.   The District Court's charge permitted the jury to convict the petitioner if it found that he willfully failed to inform sellers of target company securities that he knew of a forthcoming takeover bid that would make their shares more valuable.   In order to decide whether silence in such circumstances violates § 10(b), it is necessary to review the language and legislative history of that statute as well as its interpretation by the Commission and the federal courts.

Although the starting point of our inquiry is the language of the statute, Ernst & Ernst v. Hochfelder, 425 U.S. 185, 197, 96 S.Ct. 1375, 1382, 47 L.Ed.2d 668 (1976), § 10(b) does not state whether silence may constitute a manipulative or deceptive device.   Section 10(b) was designed as a catchall clause to prevent fraudulent practices.   *Id.*, at 202, 206.   But neither the legislative history nor the statute itself affords specific guidance for the resolution of this case.   When Rule 10b–5 was promulgated in 1942, the SEC did not discuss the possibility that failure to provide information might run afoul of § 10(b).

The SEC took an important step in the development of § 10(b) when it held that a broker-dealer and his firm violated that section by selling securities on the basis of undisclosed information obtained from a director of the issuer corporation who was also a registered representative of the brokerage firm.   In *Cady, Roberts & Co.*, 40 S. E.C. 907 (1961), the Commission decided that a corporate insider must abstain from trading in the shares of his corporation unless he has first disclosed all material inside information known to him.   The obligation to disclose or abstain derives from

> [a]n affirmative duty to disclose material information[,] [which] has been traditionally imposed on corporate "insiders," particular officers, directors, or controlling stockholders.   We, and the courts have consistently held that insiders must disclose material facts which are known to them by virtue of their position but which are not known to persons with whom they deal and which, if known, would affect their investment judgment.   *Id.*, at 911.

The Commission emphasized that the duty arose from (i) The existence of a relationship affording access to inside information intended to be available only for a corporate purpose, and (ii) the unfairness of allowing a corporate insider to take advantage of that information by trading without disclosure.   *Id.*, at 912, and n. 15.

That the relationship between a corporate insider and the stockholders of his corporation gives rise to a disclosure obligation is not a novel twist of the law. At common law, misrepresentation made for the purpose of inducing reliance upon the false statement is fraudulent. But one who fails to disclose material information prior to the consummation of a transaction commits fraud only when he is under a duty to do so. And the duty to disclose arises when one party has information "that the other [party] is entitled to know because of a fiduciary or similar relation of trust and confidence between them." [9] In its *Cady, Roberts* decision, the Commission recognized a relationship of trust and confidence between the shareholders of a corporation and those insiders who have obtained confidential information by reason of their position with that corporation. This relationship gives rise to a duty to disclose because of the "necessity of preventing a corporate insider from [taking] * * * unfair advantage of the uninformed minority stockholders." Speed v. Transamerica Corp., 99 F. Supp. 808, 829 (D.Del.1951).

The Federal courts have found violations of § 10(b) where corporate insiders used undisclosed information for their own benefit. *E. g.*, SEC v. Texas Gulf Sulphur Co., 401 F.2d 833 (CA2 1968), cert. denied, 404 U.S. 1005, 92 S.Ct. 561, 30 L.Ed.2d 558 (1972). The cases also have emphasized, in accordance with the common-law rule, that "[t]he party charged with failing to disclose market information must be under a duty to disclose it." Frigitemp Corp. v. Financial Dynamics Fund, Inc., 524 F.2d 275, 282 (CA2 1975). Accordingly, a purchaser of stock who has no duty to a prospective seller because he is neither an insider nor a fiduciary has been held to have no obligation to reveal material facts.

This Court followed the same approach in Affiliated Ute Citizens v. United States, 406 U.S. 128, 92 S.Ct. 1456, 31 L.Ed.2d 741 (1972). A group of American Indians formed a corporation to manage joint assets derived from tribal holdings. The corporation issued stock to its Indian shareholders and designated a local bank as its transfer agent. Because of the speculative nature of the corporate assets and the difficulty of ascertaining the true value of a share, the corporation requested the bank to stress to its stockholders the importance of retaining the stock. *Id.*, at 146, 92 S.Ct., at 1468. Two of the bank's assistant managers aided the shareholders in disposing of stock which the managers knew was traded in two separate markets—a primary market of Indians selling to non-Indians through the bank and a resale market consisting entirely of non-Indians. Indian sellers charged that the assistant managers had violated § 10(b) and Rule 10b-5 by failing to inform them of the higher prices prevailing

---

9. Restatement of the Law 2d, Torts § 551(2)(a) (1976). *See* James & Gray, Misrepresentation—Part II, 37 Md.L.Rev. 488, 523–527 (1978). As regards securities transactions, the American Law Institute recognizes that "silence when there is a duty to speak may be a fraudulent act." ALI, Federal Securities Code § 262(b) (Proposed Official Draft 1978).

in the resale market. The Court recognized that no duty of disclosure would exist if the bank merely had acted as a transfer agent. But the bank also had assumed a duty to act on behalf of the shareholders, and the Indian sellers had relied upon its personnel when they sold their stock. *Id.*, at 152, 92 S.Ct., at 1471. Because these officers of the bank were charged with a responsibility to the shareholders, they could not act as market makers inducing the Indians to sell their stock without disclosing the existence of the more favorable non-Indian market. *Id.*, at 152–153, 92 S.Ct., at 1471–1472.

Thus, administrative and judicial interpretations have established that silence in connection with the purchase or sale of securities may operate as a fraud actionable under § 10(b) despite the absence of statutory language or legislative history specifically addressing the legality of nondisclosure. But such liability is premised upon a duty to disclose arising from a relationship of trust and confidence between parties to a transaction. Application of a duty to disclose prior to trading guarantees that corporate insiders, who have an obligation to place the shareholder's welfare before their own, will not benefit personally through fraudulent use of material nonpublic information.[12]

III

In this case, the petitioner was convicted of violating § 10(b) although he was not a corporate insider and he received no confidential information from the target company. Moreover, the "market information" upon which he relied did not concern the earning power or operations of the target company, but only the plans of the acquiring company. Petitioner's use of that information was not a fraud under § 10(b) unless he was subject to an affirmative duty to disclose it before trading. In this case, the jury instructions failed to specify any such duty. In effect, the trial court instructed the jury that petitioner owed a duty to everyone; to all sellers, indeed, to the market as a whole. The jury simply was told to decide whether petitioner used material, nonpublic information at a time when "he knew other people trading in the securities market did not have access to the same information." Record, at 677.

The Court of Appeals affirmed the conviction by holding that "*[a]nyone*—corporate insider or not—who regularly receives material nonpublic information may not use that information to trade in securities without incurring an affirmative duty to disclose." 588 F.2d

12. "Tippees" of corporate insiders have been held liable under § 10(b) because they have a duty not to profit from the use of inside information that they know is confidential and know or should know came from a corporate insider, Shapiro v. Merrill Lynch, Pierce, Fenner & Smith, 495 F.2d 228, 237–238 (CA2 1974). The tippee's obligation has been viewed as arising from his role as a participant after the fact in the insider's breach of a fiduciary duty. Subcommittees of American Bar Association Section of Corporation, Banking, and Business Law, Comment Letter on Material, Non-Public Information (Oct. 15, 1973) reprinted in BNA, Securities Regulation & Law Report No. 233, at D–1, D–2 (Jan. 2, 1974).

1358, 1365 (CA2 1978) (emphasis in original). Although the court said that its test would include only persons who regularly receive material nonpublic information, *id.*, at 1366, its rationale for that limitation is unrelated to the existence of a duty to disclose.[14] The Court of Appeals, like the trial court, failed to identify a relationship between petitioner and the sellers that could give rise to a duty. Its decision thus rested solely upon its belief that the federal securities laws have "created a system providing equal access to information necessary for reasoned and intelligent investment decisions." 588 F.2d, at 1362. The use by anyone of material information not generally available is fraudulent, this theory suggests, because such information gives certain buyers or sellers an unfair advantage over less informed buyers and sellers.

This reasoning suffers from two defects. First not every instance of financial unfairness constitutes fraudulent activity under § 10(b). See Santa Fe Industries Inc. v. Green, 430 U.S. 462, 474–477, 97 S.Ct. 1292, 1301–1303, 51 L.Ed.2d 480 (1977). Second, the element required to make silence fraudulent—a duty to disclose—is absent in this case. No duty could arise from petitioner's relationship with the sellers of the target company's securities, for petitioner had no prior dealings with them. He was not their agent, he was not a fiduciary, he was not a person in whom the sellers had placed their trust and confidence. He was, in fact, a complete stranger who dealt with the sellers only through impersonal market transactions.

We cannot affirm petitioner's conviction without recognizing a general duty between all participants in market transactions to forgo actions based on material, nonpublic information. Formulation of such a broad duty, which departs radically from the established doctrine that duty arises from a specific relationship between two parties, see n. 9, *supra*, should not be undertaken absent some explicit evidence of congressional intent.

14. The Court of Appeals said that its "regular access to market information" test would create a workable rule embracing "those who occupy * * * strategic places in the market mechanism." United States v. Chiarella, 588 F.2d 1358, 1365 (CA2 1978). These considerations are insufficient to support a duty to disclose. A duty arises from the relationship between parties, see n. 9, *supra*, and accompanying text, and not merely from one's ability to acquire information because of his position in the market.

The Court of Appeals also suggested that the acquiring corporation itself would not be a "market insider" because a tender offeror creates, rather than receives, information and takes a substantial economic risk that its offer will be unsuccessful. *Id.*, at 1366–1367. Again, the Court of Appeals departed from the analysis appropriate to recognition of a duty. The Court of Appeals for the Second Circuit previously held, in a manner consistent with our analysis here, that a tender offeror does not violate § 10(b) when it makes preannouncement purchases precisely because there is no relationship between the offeror and the seller. "We know of no rule of law * * * that a purchaser of stock, who was not an 'insider' and had no fiduciary relation to a prospective seller, had any obligation to reveal circumstances that might raise a seller's demands and thus abort the sale." General Time Corp. v. Talley Industries, 403 F.2d 159, 164 (CA2 1968), cert. denied, 393 U.S. 1026, 89 S. Ct. 631, 21 L.Ed.2d 570 (1969).

As we have seen, no such evidence emerges from the language or legislative history of § 10(b). Moreover, neither the Congress nor the Commission ever has adopted a parity-of-information rule. Instead the problems caused by misuse of market information have been addressed by detailed and sophisticated regulation that recognizes when use of market information may not harm operation of the securities markets. For example, the Williams Act limits but does not completely prohibit a tender offeror's purchases of target corporation stock before public announcement of the offer. Congress' careful action in this and other areas contrasts, and is in some tension, with the broad rule of liability we are asked to adopt in this case.

Indeed, the theory upon which the petitioner was convicted is at odds with the Commission's view of § 10(b) as applied to activity that has the same effect on sellers as the petitioner's purchases. "Warehousing" takes place when a corporation gives advance notice of its intention to launch a tender offer to institutional investors who then are able to purchase stock in the target company before the tender offer is made public and the price of shares rises. In this case, as in warehousing, a buyer of securities purchases stock in a target corporation on the basis of market information which is unknown to the seller. In both of these situations, the seller's behavior presumably would be altered if he had the nonpublic information. Significantly, however, the Commission has acted to bar warehousing under its authority to regulate tender offers after recognizing that action under § 10(b) would rest on a "somewhat different theory" than that previously used to regulate insider trading as fraudulent activity.

We see no basis for applying such a new and different theory of liability in this case. As we have emphasized before, the 1934 Act cannot be read " 'more broadly than its language and the statutory scheme reasonably permit.' " Touche Ross & Co. v. Redington, 442 U.S. 560, 578, 99 S.Ct. 2479, 2490, 61 L.Ed.2d 82 (June 18, 1979), quoting SEC v. Sloan, 436 U.S. 103, 116, 98 S.Ct. 1702, 1711, 56 L.Ed.2d 148 (1978). Section 10(b) is aptly described as a catch-all provision, but what it catches must be fraud. When an allegation of fraud is based upon nondisclosure, there can be no fraud absent a duty to speak. We hold that a duty to disclose under § 10(b) does not arise from the mere possession of nonpublic market information. The contrary result is without support in the legislative history of § 10(b) and would be inconsistent with the careful plan that Congress has enacted for regulation of the securities markets. Cf. Santa Fe Industries Inc. v. Green, 430 U.S., at 479, 97 S.Ct., at 1304.

* * *

The judgment of the Court of Appeals is reversed.

NOTE—MARKET INFORMATION

There seems to be no longer any serious question that corporate insiders, themselves, are forbidden from trading on the basis of material information that is not public, whether that information relates to the corporation itself or to the market for its securities. The same prohibition almost certainly extends to the immediate "tippees" of the insiders who, by trading on such information, participate in the wrong committed in the giving of the tip. *See* Shapiro v. Merrill Lynch, Pierce, Fenner & Smith, Inc., 495 F.2d 228 (2d Cir. 1974). In either case it can be said that the insider—and derivatively his tippees—have breached a fiduciary duty owing to the corporation's security holders (or purchasers who are to become security holders, *see* Gratz v. Claughton, 187 F.2d 46, 49 (2d Cir. 1951), cert. denied 341 U. S. 920, 71 S.Ct. 741, 95 L.Ed. 1353. When the source of the information is not a corporate insider, however, the problem becomes more difficult. Counterbalanced against the trend toward insisting on something approaching equal opportunity for all traders in the securities markets in order to promote a fair market that enjoys investor confidence, there is the need not to discourage legitimate efforts to uncover facts relevant to the value of a security; it is trading based on those efforts that tends to push the price in an appropriate direction and therefore to make the securities markets more "efficient". See Fleischer, Mundheim & Murphy, An Initial Inquiry Into the Responsibility to Disclose Market Information, 121 U.Pa.L.Rev. 798 (1973).

The term "market information" has been used to describe two different sorts of information related to the price of a corporation's securities. In the more linguistically precise usage, it refers to information bearing on the future course of the market for the securities as opposed to information about the fortunes of the corporation itself. *See* Koeltl and Longstreth, Market Information Revisited, 11 Rev. Sec.Reg. 843 (Oct. 11, 1978). That is the sort of information at issue in *Chiarella*. The term has also been used to refer to information bearing on a potential movement in price that is not obtained from a corporate source. *See* Oppenheimer & Co., Exchange Act Release No. 12319 (April 12, 1976) [1975–76 Transfer Binder] Fed.Sec.L.Rep. (CCH) ¶ 80,511 at 86,415, n. 2.

With respect to market information in the first sense, the need not to deprive investors of the fruits of legitimate research appears less strong. Allowing a privileged group who have access to the knowledge that, for example, a tender offer is about to be announced, to profit by betting on a "sure thing" strikes many as unfair and out of harmony with a desire to promote investor confidence. The SEC has reacted to that perception by promulgating Rule 14e–3 which, among other things, reverses the result in *Chiarella*. The rule was issued under the Commission's authority to regulate tender offers. It prohibits trading in securities to be acquired in a tender offer by any person (other than the prospective tender offeror) "who is in possession of material information relating to such tender offer which information he knows or has reason to know is nonpublic and which he knows or has reason to know has been acquired directly or indirectly from (1) the offering person, (2) the issuer of the securities sought or to be sought by such tender offer, or (3) any officer, director, partner or employee or any other person acting on behalf of the offering person or such issuer * * *." The rule also prohibits insiders of the offeror and the target, as well as their "tippees", from tipping others about a tender offer.

It should go without saying that lawyers who in the course of their practice learn about impending tender offers are no less subject to the constraints against trading on that information than others. For example, the SEC obtained a consent order against David Hall, a New York attorney, a large portion of whose practice consisted of representing public corporations as "special shareholder relations counsel", enjoining him from violating Rule 10b–5 and requiring him to disgorge some $33,000 in profits he allegedly made from trading on information about tender offers involving his clients. He subsequently pled guilty to criminal charges growing out of the same incidents.

NOTE—DUTY TO EMPLOYERS

The decision in *Chiarella* puts in question whether inside knowledge of significant market developments can ever be the basis of liability under § 10(b) and Rule 10b–5. Commonly that information is possessed not by corporate insiders owing a duty to shareholders, but rather by outsiders who contemplate a transaction that might affect the market for that stock. The most dramatic example occurs with respect to tender offers, as was the case in *Chiarella*.

However, the prosecution argued that Mr. Chiarella breached a duty he owed to the market place, which was too broad and loose to satisfy the Court. The argument was not made that by appropriating the information he received in the course of his employment, Mr. Chiarella violated a duty he owed to his employer.

United States v. Newman, 664 F.2d 12 (2d Cir. 1981), concerned several persons associated with investment banking firms who conspired to use their non-public knowledge of contemplated tender offers to reap large gains. The trial court dismissed a criminal prosecution against a stockbroker charged with trading on information about takeovers passed to him by Courtois and Antonio, employees of major investment banking firms on the ground that the defendants lacked sufficient notice that this conduct might violate the federal securities laws. The Second Circuit reversed the district court's dismissal of the indictment. The court held that the charge of the indictment that Newman had "aided, participated in and facilitated Courtois and Antonio in violating the fiduciary duties of honesty, loyalty and silence owed directly to Morgan Stanley, Kuhn Loeb, and clients of those investment banks" was adequate to allege a criminal violation of section 10(b) and Rule 10b–5. However, it should be noted that the offending conduct directly impacted not on those to whom they owed a duty, but rather on strangers to whom they did not.

E.   THE RESPONSIBILITIES OF COUNSEL

PROBLEM

ALTERNATIVE ENERGY CORPORATION—PART V

You represent the Alternative Energy Corporation, a New York Stock Exchange company. Burns, the company's president, recently received an attractive offer from another large corporation in the energy business. AEC's board considers Burns an extremely valuable asset to the company, and, in order to retain his services, offered him a substantial increase in compensation. Included in the revised compensation package were options to purchase 200,000 shares of AEC stock at $40 per share, the current market price. An outside consultant for the firm has valued the options at $300,000.

Because of a provision in the company's by-laws, it is necessary for the shareholders to approve the options, and a resolution to do so appears in the proxy statement you have drafted in preparation for the upcoming annual meeting. The proxy statement discloses the reasons for the additional compensation, describes the terms of the options, and states that an independent consultant has valued them at $300,000. You filed the proxy statement with the SEC two weeks ago, and it has been mailed out to the shareholders.

Yesterday you learned from Burns that AEC's research and development department has just made a dramatic breakthrough in the design of a new solar cell. It appears that the new device will enable AEC to increase its profits substantially over the next several years. Burns indicated that he planned to save the announcement of the good news for the annual shareholders' meeting, which will be held in about a month. You told him that this development had made the portion of the proxy statement dealing with his stock options no longer accurate since they would become substantially more valuable with the announcement of the new solar cell.

Burns responded, "I don't see any reason to make any change to the proxy statement now. I'm sure the shareholders will be even more willing to give me a raise now then they would have before. Anyway, that proxy statement was entirely accurate when it was sent out. No one ever meant to mislead anyone else. I don't see how we've done anything wrong that needs correcting."

You suggested that he at least take the matter to the board of directors. He replied that he saw no need to and that he was afraid that if he told them, the news would be more likely to leak out before the annual meeting.

Although you insisted that he and AEC would violate the law by proceeding with the proxy solicitation without a correction, he would not budge.

Assume that in your opinion, the outstanding proxy statement is materially misleading and that to continue without correcting it would violate the proxy rules. What do you do? May you, should you, or must you:

1. Tell the board?

2. Tell the shareholders?

3. Tell the SEC?

4. Withdraw your representation?

5. Do something else?

IN THE MATTER OF CARTER AND JOHNSON

Securities and Exchange Commission, 1981. Securities
Exchange Act Release No. 17597.

William R. Carter and Charles J. Johnson, Jr., respondents, appeal from the initial decision of the Administrative Law Judge in this proceeding brought under Rule 2(e) of the Commission's Rules of Practice.[1] In an opinion dated March 7, 1979, the Administrative Law Judge found that, in connection with their representation of National Telephone Company, Inc. during the period from May 1974 to May 1975, Carter and Johnson willfully violated and willfully aided and abetted violations of Sections 10(b) and 13(a) of the Securities Exchange Act of 1934 (the "Exchange Act") and Rules 10b–5, 12b–20 and 13a–11 thereunder and that they engaged in unethical and improper professional conduct. In light of these findings, the Administrative Law Judge concluded that Carter and Johnson should be suspended from appearing or practicing before the Commission for periods of one year and nine months, respectively.

For the reasons stated more fully below, we reverse the decision of the Administrative Law Judge with respect to both respondents. We have concluded that the record does not adequately support the Administrative Law Judge's findings of violative conduct by respondents. Moreover, we conclude that certain concepts of proper ethical

1. Rule 2(e), 17 CFR 201.2(e), provides in paragraph (1):

The Commission may deny, temporarily or permanently, the privilege of appearing or practicing before it in any way to any person who is found by the Commission after notice of and opportunity for hearing in the matter (i) not to possess the requisite qualifications to represent others, or (ii) to be lacking in character or integrity or to have engaged in unethical or improper professional conduct, or (iii) to have willfully violated, or willfully aided and abetted the violation of any provision of the federal securities laws (15 U.S.C. 77a to 80b–20), or the rules and regulations thereunder.

and professional conduct were not sufficiently developed, at the time of the conduct here at issue, to permit a finding that either respondent breached applicable ethical or professional standards. In addition, we are today giving notice of an interpretation by the Commission of the term "unethical or improper professional conduct," as that term is used in Rule 2(e)(1)(ii). This interpretation will be applicable prospectively in cases of this kind.

* * *

III.

RESPONDENTS' CONDUCT

A. *National Telephone Company.* The conduct at issue in these proceedings occurred in connection with respondents' legal representation of National Telephone Company, Inc. ("National") during the period from mid-1974 through mid-1975. National, a Connecticut corporation with its principal offices located in East Hartford, Connecticut, was founded in 1971 to lease sophisticated telephone equipment systems to commercial customers pursuant to long-term (5- to 10-year) leases.[23] National enjoyed an impressive growth rate in its first three years, increasing its total assets from $320,123 to $19,028,613 and its net income from $2,390 to $633,485 during this period. At the same time, the company's backlog grew from $66,000 to $2,610,000 and the value of equipment leases written by it increased from $255,422 to $13,292,549.

The architect of National's meteoric rise was Sheldon L. Hart, one of its founders and, at all times relevant to these proceedings, its controlling stockholder. From its incorporation until his resignation on May 24, 1975, Hart was National's chief executive officer, chairman of the board of directors, president and treasurer. National's chief in-house counsel was Mark I. Lurie who, assisted by Brian Kay, was one of respondents' principal contracts with the company.

In large measure, National was a prisoner of its own success. As is commonly the case with equipment leasing companies, the greater part of National's costs in connection with a new lease, including equipment marketing and installation expenses, was incurred well before rental payments commenced. Since rental payments were National's only significant source of revenues, the company's cash flow

---

23. Since 1973, National's common stock has been registered with the Commission under Section 12(g) of the Exchange Act, rendering National subject to, among other things, the periodic reporting obligations imposed by Section 13 (a) of the Act, and the rules and regulations thereunder. During this period, National's common stock was quoted in the National Association of Securities Dealers Automated Quotation System, and the record indicates that an active trading market existed during the relevant period. In addition, from August 7, 1974 until March 31, 1975, National had on file with the Commission an effective registration statement on Form S–8 with respect to 200,000 shares of its common stock to be offered to its employees pursuant to National's Qualified Savings Investment Plan.

situation worsened with each new lease, and continued growth and operations could only be sustained through external financing. Between 1971 and 1973, National managed to obtain needed capital from an initial public offering of stock under Regulation A, short-term loans from local banks, and an offering of convertible debentures in September of 1973.

National's last successful effort to secure significant outside financing resulted in the execution, in May and June of 1974, of a $15 million credit agreement (the "Credit Agreement") with a group of five banks. Although the Credit Agreement was not closed (in amended form) until December 1974, the banks were willing to advance substantial sums to National under a variety of demand arrangements prior to the closing. In fact, by the time of the closing on December 20, 1974, these advances totaled some $16.8 million. The Credit Agreement was amended to cover this amount, plus $2.2 million for general corporate purposes and an additional $2 million available only upon the implementation of a special business plan limiting National's business growth if other sources of money could not be located. Unfortunately, funds available under the Credit Agreement, as amended, were not sufficient to finance National's expansion and operations much beyond the closing, and the pressure on National's cash flow continued.

National finally ran out of time in July of 1975, after being unable to secure sufficient external financing after the closing of the Credit Agreement. On July 2, 1975, National was forced to file a petition for an arrangement under Chapter XI of the Bankruptcy Act, 11 U.S. C.A. 701, *et seq.*; in March of 1976 this proceeding was converted into a reorganization under Chapter X of the Bankruptcy Act, 11 U.S.C.A. 501, *et seq.*

On November 26, 1975, the Commission authorized a formal investigation into the facts and circumstances surrounding National's collapse in order to determine whether any violations of the federal securities laws had occurred. This investigation covered the involvement of respondents, as well as of their law firm.

An injunctive proceeding was initiated by the Commission on January 16, 1978, in the United States District Court for the District of Columbia, against Hart, Lurie, the company's management directors, the company's independent auditors and others, alleging violations of the antifraud and reporting provisions of the Exchange Act, and the rules thereunder. That action has now been settled by all named defendants, without admitting or denying the allegations in the complaint, through issuance of permanent injunctions against future violations of the federal securities laws and the ordering of certain ancillary equitable relief.   *   *   *

B. *Respondents and Their Law Firm.* Carter, an attorney admitted to practice in the State of New York, was born in 1917. He received his law degree from Harvard Law School and has been working for the law firm known as Brown, Wood, Ivey, Mitchell & Petty ("Brown, Wood") since 1945, having become a partner of the firm in 1954. Carter's principal areas of practice have been securities, general corporate and antitrust law.

Johnson, also admitted to practice as an attorney in the State of New York, as well as in the State of Connecticut, was born in 1932. He received his legal education at Harvard Law School and joined Brown, Wood's predecessor firm in 1956, becoming a partner in 1967. Johnson's principal areas of practice have been corporate and securities law.

Kenneth M. Socha worked with Carter and Johnson on a variety of legal matters affecting National, including all of the matters which are the basis of these proceedings. Socha joined Brown, Wood as an associate in 1970 and continued in that capacity during all periods relevant to these proceedings.

*   *   *

During 1974 and 1975, Brown, Wood, principally through Carter, Johnson and Socha, provided a wide range of legal services to National, including the preparation of a Form S–8 registration statement, proxy materials and an annual report for the company's 1974 annual stockholders meeting, other Commission filings, press releases and communications to National's stockholders. Johnson was charged with the overall coordination of Brown, Wood's legal efforts on National's behalf and was generally kept aware of progress on all significant projects. In March of 1974, after another Brown, Wood partner left the firm, Johnson asked Carter to assist Socha in working on the Credit Agreement. Thereafter Carter assumed primary responsibility for that project.

In July of 1974, Johnson was elected secretary of National, agreeing to serve in such capacity at Hart's urging. Although his principal duty as secretary was to attend meetings of the board of directors and prepare appropriate minutes, Johnson testified that he attended a total of only four meetings during this period: those of his election on July 1, 1974 and his resignation on May 24, 1975, and two additional meetings which were held on August 19, 1974 and October 15, 1974. The National board of directors held at least three additional meetings during Johnson's tenure as secretary at which he was not present.

In addition to matters as to which they were directly consulted, Brown, Wood, and thus both respondents, appear to have been informed about all matters as to which National made public disclosure.
*   *   *

C. *Chronology of National's Final Year: May 1974 to May 1975.* In order fully to appreciate respondents' role in the events at issue here, it is necessary to set forth the following rather lengthy description of the 12 months immediately preceding public disclosure of the circumstances that led to National's bankruptcy. * * *

1. *May to August 1974: National Executes a $15 Million Credit Agreement; the Annual Report Projections; the Continuing Need for Additional Financing.* National's story lies in its unrelenting need to secure ever greater amounts of outside financing. As explained above, given the nature of its leasing business, the more installations the company contracted for, the greater became the gap between internally generated cash flow and the soaring needs of front-end equipment installation costs. * * *

In May and June of 1974, negotiations with a consortium of five banks, in which Carter, Johnson and Socha were all participants, culminated in the execution of the Credit Agreement, which was dated as of April 30, 1974. The Credit Agreement provided for an interim revolving loan of up to $15 million, evidenced by rolling 90-day notes, until November 29, 1974, at which time National had the option to convert the principal amount then outstanding into six-year term notes. As discussed below, the Credit Agreement (as amended) was not formally closed until December 20, 1974, in part because National was unable to satisfy the closing conditions relating to its liquidity and debt-to-net-worth ratios. Ultimately the banks agreed to waive these conditions.

Since the Credit Agreement contemplated that the loans thereunder [32] would be secured by substantially all of National's assets, it was necessary for National to transfer these assets to Systems, a transfer which in turn required the approval of National's stockholders. In order to secure this approval, National called its annual stockholders meeting for June 27, 1974, and Brown, Wood was asked to prepare the proxy materials for this meeting. Carter and Johnson also participated in the preparation of National's 1974 Annual Report. These proxy materials, along with National's 1974 Annual Report, were sent to National's stockholders on June 17 and filed with the Commission on June 19.

* * *

National's 1974 Annual Report contained projections of future lease installations which showed, by each quarter, a doubling of annual installations from approximately $13.3 million in fiscal 1974 to approximately $27 million in fiscal 1975. In response to a specific request from Hart, Carter advised National orally and in writing that * * * it was permissible to include projections in the Annual Report, but that the assumptions underlying the projections should also

32. Since National was prohibited by Connecticut law from obtaining secured loans from banks whose principal offices were located outside the state, it created a New York subsidiary, National Telecommunications Systems, Inc. ("Systems"), to enter into the Credit Agreement with the banks. National agreed to transfer its leases and title to the underlying equipment to Systems to be pledged as security for the Credit Agreement loans, for which National was to act as guarantor.

be disclosed. Hart ignored this advice and the Annual Report was distributed without assumptions. This incident is the first example in the record of Hart's uncooperative reaction to respondents' advice concerning the disclosure demands of the federal securities laws.

National's management, as well as Carter and Johnson, were well aware that the company would need substantial outside financing in addition to that provided by the Credit Agreement to realize the Annual Report projections. As early as the July 1 meeting of National's board of directors, the company had already borrowed $10 million of the $15 million which would be available under the Credit Agreement. At that meeting, which was attended by Johnson in his new capacity as corporate secretary, Hart announced that National needed at least $17 million in new financing to achieve the new lease installation projections in the Annual Report. After Hart reported to the meeting on the various alternatives being explored for additional funds, the directors focused on the importance of this issue to the continuing growth and viability of the company. The minutes of that meeting reflect the board's conclusion that "it [was] essential   *   *   *   to continue to explore all appropriate means for obtaining financing for the Corporation's operations."

*   *   *

As the summer of 1974 wore on, both the severity of and concern for National's financial predicament intensified, fueled in large measure by the deteriorating credit markets. At an August 19 meeting of National's board of directors—the second board meeting attended by Johnson—Hart once again reported on his continuing attempts to raise more capital.

At that August 19 board meeting, several directors expressed serious concern over National's growth rate in light of its need for additional money, high financing costs and lack of available cash. Dr. Eli Shapiro, one of National's nonmanagement directors, presented a memorandum which was discussed at some length. It suggested that National had over-estimated its borrowing ability and overstated its growth projections, concluding that the company had to seek additional equity financing immediately if it were to ensure its ability to survive financial adversity. The board determined that the company's rate of growth was a matter of major importance; that the growth rate should be carefully monitored by management and the board; and that management should be prepared to proceed at a slower rate if advisable.

*   *   *

2. *September to December 1974: National's Growing Cash Crises; Preparations for the Closing under the Credit Agreement.* By early fall of 1974, National's cash needs outstripped its existing financing sources and a severe cash crises ensued. A meeting between National and its bankers was held on September 11, 1974; neither

respondent was present. By that date, National had already received from the bank group more than $13.2 million of the $15 million contemplated by the Credit Agreement, which had yet to be closed. Moreover, in the preceding months, National had borrowed an additional $1.5 million from two of the lending banks, an amount that was not originally contemplated by the pending agreement, thus bringing the total funds already advanced by the banks to something approximating the $15 million provided for under the original agreement.

At the September 11 meeting with the banks, Hart indicated that the projected equity offering had been ruled out by National's investment bankers, due to deteriorating market conditions. He further reported that National's cash flow problems had caused the company voluntarily to institute a "wind-down" program, effective September 1: As he described it, this program, projected to last five months, was a severe retrenchment, designed to protect the banks' existing investment. Under it, National would limit its operations to the conversion of present inventory—approximately $5 million—into installed systems under new leases, phase out further marketing and installation efforts and reduce the company to a "pure maintenance organization." Hart requested an increase in the total amount of the banks' planned loan from $15 to $21 million in order to finance this wind-down program. The banks, however, hesitated, agreeing only that no decision would be made on lending National additional funds until the pending $15 million Credit Agreement was closed.

Hart, in fact, had lied to the banks. No wind-down program had been instituted or, as it turned out, would be until almost eight months later, in May of 1975. There is, however, no evidence in the record that respondents were, or ever became, aware of Hart's September 11, 1974 deception.

* * *

At the October 15, 1974 meeting of National's board of directors, attended by Johnson, there was a further discussion of National's "tight cash position," its inability to secure additional credit despite vigorous efforts, and its continued need for external financing. By that time, National had already increased its borrowing from the bank group from $13.2 million (the September 11 figure) to $14.3 million of the initially planned $15 million loan, with the additional $1.5 million in separate loans from two of the banks still outstanding. Hart stated to the board that he had discussed with the banks a "contingency plan" for the orderly "wind-down" of National's sales activities, but apparently did not disclose to the board or to Johnson who was present that he had falsely represented to the banks that such a program was already being implemented.

The board of directors became increasingly concerned about the company's financial situation, recognizing that a curtailment of National's operations and a termination of its sales would soon become necessary unless significant additional financing were obtained, and that one of the major impediments to obtaining such financing was the failure to close the Credit Agreement. The board therefore instructed Hart to take immediate steps to close the Credit Agreement.

Two days later, on October 17, National issued a press release reporting its results for the second fiscal quarter ended September 30, 1974. The release, which respondents did not prepare or review, but which they did receive after the fact, disclosed a substantial increase in lease installations, net income and earnings per share over the corresponding fiscal quarter in 1973, but once again made no mention of the financial crisis when facing the company. Thus the gap between National's public posture and the private realities continued to widen.

The banks' position and the concerned reaction of National's board of directors made closing the Credit Agreement the first order of the day for National. As a result, on October 18, respondents both attended a meeting with various representatives of National and the lending banks to discuss what remained to be done to close the Credit Agreement. The extent of the company's unsecured borrowings, its unsuccessful efforts to obtain other financing and its past due operating expenses were also discussed, along with the steps the company had purportedly taken to curtail operations. Significantly, a winddown plan—this time characterized as a "contingency" plan—was also discussed, with Hart again asking the banks to increase the Credit Agreement coverage by $6 million to fund such a plan, in order to protect their existing $15 million investment.

In light of his presence at the July 1, August 19 and October 15 board meetings, as well as the October 18 bank meeting, Johnson was well aware of National's cash crisis, its continuing failure to obtain needed financing and its purported "wind-down" program. This, in addition to the well-known depressed state of the credit markets and the fact that National had projected, confirmed and continued to report, without obviously relevant qualifications, rapidly growing sales and earnings, undoubtedly prompted Johnson to instruct Socha to draft a disclosure letter to National's stockholders approximately two days after the October 18 bank meeting.

The proposed stockholders letter, which was reviewed by both Carter and Johnson and sent to the company in early November, was a candid summary of National's financial predicament, noting that National would "in the near future" have to obtain significant financing in addition to the Credit Agreement. It concluded:

> The Company's efforts to obtain additional financing have been adversely affected by tight credit conditions, increased interest costs, a generally unfavorable equity market and certain factors that are peculiar to its business such as the negative cash flow described above. In view of these factors the Company has determined that it would be prudent to curtail its sales operations and, therefore, to emphasize the liquidity rather than growth until such time as additional debt or equity financing can be obtained.

Johnson subsequently told Lurie that this was the type of communication "that a company * * * interested in keeping its stockholders advised on a regular basis should be making." [40] Despite this advice, National's management declined to issue the letter. Neither
respondent elected to pursue the matter.

* * *

[O]n November 26, a draft of an amendment to the Credit Agreement (the "Amendment"), prepared by the banks' counsel, White &
Case, but worked on and reviewed by Carter, treated the wind-down
plan as an attached exhibit. The November 26 draft of the Amendment also reflected a new total commitment of $21 million—indicating
that Hart's $6 million request had been agreed to—but provided that
National had to implement the plan to wind-down its operations, and
thus terminate sales, if it desired to borrow more than $17 million.

It is important to note, at this point, that both Carter and Johnson
must have been aware that, if National were to implement the wind-
down plan, the company would have no reasonable opportunity to
meet the projections of $27 million in lease installations which were
set forth in the 1974 Annual Report and indirectly reconfirmed in the
company's September 12 letter to its stockholders. The wind-down
plan, which Socha summarized in a December 2 memorandum to
Johnson, provided that National would not be permitted to enter into
any further leases. Obviously, under these circumstances, the company's sales and earnings growth would be halted—short of projected
levels.

In early December, Socha received from National a draft of the
company's quarterly report to its stockholders for the second fiscal
quarter ended September 30, 1974. The report contained a series of
graphs, illustrating the successful results of National's operations,
but once again made no mention of the dire financial straights in
which the company found itself in December. Such an omission was
especially significant in light of the disclosure recommendations
which Brown, Wood had by then made to National. When Socha inquired whether the use of the graphs had been cleared by Johnson,
Lurie informed him that they had. This was not true, as Johnson
noted on the copy of the draft report circulated to him by Socha. The
quarterly report was mailed as proposed, and neither respondent ever
spoke with the company's management about the disclosure problems
it presented or about Lurie's misrepresentation to Socha.

It thus appears that, by early December, Carter and Johnson were
both fully aware that (1) National was experiencing a cash crises severe enough to threaten the continued viability of the company if further financing could not be found, (2) when closed, the Credit Agreement, as modified by the Amendment, would not provide the

40. Johnson testified that, in his opinion, distribution of the letter was not *required* by the federal securities laws.

necessary additional financing, (3) National's earlier projections could no longer be achieved if the Credit Agreement's wind-down plan were to be implemented, and (4) National's management was unreceptive when confronted with respondents' advice to disclose the company's financial problems.

* * *

3. *December 1974 to January 1975: The Lease Maintenance Plan; the Closing; Related Public Disclosure.* In the final days leading to the closing, National's "wind-down" plan was renegotiated somewhat and finally emerged with a new name, the lease maintenance plan ("LMP"). All the witnesses speaking to the question agreed that the term "lease maintenance plan" had no generally accepted meaning in the industry and that they had never used or heard this term before. * * *

* * *

At a meeting held on December 11, with Carter and representatives of National and the banks present, final details of the Amendment were negotiated. A draft of the Amendment dated December 13, 1974, which was prepared by White & Case, contemplated an arrangement under which the banks would permit Systems to borrow up to $19 million at any time on or before April 30, 1975. These borrowings were to be secured by the telephone leases and equipment transferred to Systems by National and guaranteed by National. If either (1) National and/or Systems attempted to borrow in excess of $19 million from the existing bank group or (2) National failed to meet a specified liquidity test, National and Systems were required to implement the LMP. Their failure to do so in accordance with the provisions of the LMP was an event of default under the Credit Agreement, as modified by the Amendment (the "Amended Credit Agreement"), and resulted in all outstanding indebtedness under that Agreement becoming due and payable upon demand.

The December 13 draft of the Amendment for the first time contained a reference to a "lease maintenance plan" and indicated that the LMP was to be attached as an exhibit to the Amendment. The effect of the implementation of the LMP on National's operations and growth would obviously be both dramatic and devastating. Indeed, as one expert called by respondents testified, the LMP was "a sort of a holding pattern short of bankruptcy or levy by the creditors." The LMP required National to terminate all sales activities, dismiss all sales personnel, and limit its operations to those necessary to service existing leases. In effect, the company would be transformed into a mere service agency, maintaining existing leases, but writing no new ones. Moreover, the final $2 million of the funds to be provided by the banks was only available until June 30, 1975 and could only be used to implement the LMP, principally by financing the installation of equipment already in inventory to complete existing orders.

* * *

On December 19, the day immediately preceding the closing under the Amended Credit Agreement, at a day-long pre-closing meeting, Hart told Carter that he did not want the terms of the LMP made public or filed with the Commission. Although Carter testified that he could not recall the reason for this request, he speculated that Hart sought not to publicize the LMP because he was concerned that the disclosure of the LMP's effects on the company's business would have a negative impact on the morale of National's sales personnel. After reading the LMP, Carter advised Hart that the LMP would have to be filed with the Commission if it were an exhibit to the Amendment, as originally had been contemplated. However, Carter added that the LMP need not be filed with the Commission or publicized if it were not an exhibit but rather merely referred to in the Amendment. Hart agreed, and the Amendment was modified to delete the LMP as an exhibit.

Also at the December 19 pre-closing conference, Carter reviewed and extensively revised a press release prepared by National announcing the closing of the Amended Credit Agreement. The revised press release was reviewed by all parties at the meeting, including the company's management. No one raised any objections to the revisions proposed by Carter.

On December 20, the Amended Credit Agreement was closed and National immediately borrowed $18 million from the banks. Of this amount, over $16.8 million was used to repay existing demand indebtedness based on advances the banks had made to National since the original Credit Agreement had been signed six months earlier. All or virtually all of the remainder was used to pay various operating expenses which National had already incurred. Even after these expenses were discharged, National was left with substantial short-term debt totalling almost $2 million. The record is ambiguous as to the degree to which Carter was aware of this situation.

Whatever the state of Carter's knowledge concerning National's past-due obligations, the record makes it clear that Carter understood that the December 20 financing in no way extricated National from its financial dilemma. At the time of his testimony in the Commission's investigation, Carter stated that he understood that, if National did not obtain significant additional financing, it would soon be "right back in the soup."

Immediately after the closing, National issued the press release that Carter had redrafted the day before. The release stated, in its entirety:

PRESS RELEASE—FOR IMMEDIATE RELEASE

EAST HARTFORD, CONN., DECEMBER 20, 1974

National Telephone Company today announced the execution of a $6,000,000 extension of a $15,000,000 Credit Agreement with a group of banks headed by Bankers Trust Company of New York. Included in the $21 million is a contingency fund of $2 million which is available until June 30, 1975 and which may be utilized by the Company only for the purpose of funding a lease maintenance program in the event additional financing is not otherwise available.

Of the $21 million, the Company has borrowed $18 million pursuant to a seven-year term loan, of which approximately $16,500,000 was used to repay outstanding short-term loans. The balance will be used for general operating expenses. Participating in the loans are Bankers Trust Company of New York, Mellon Bank N.A. of Pittsburgh, Central National Bank of Cleveland, The Connecticut Bank and Trust Company and The Hartford National Bank and Trust Company of Hartford, Connecticut.

The press release did not discuss either of the following matters each of which was then within the knowledge of Carter and Johnson.

(1) The precise nature and effects on National's business of the LMP and the likelihood that National would be required to implement the LMP within a short period of time; and

(2) The substantial limitations placed on National's operations by the Amended Credit Agreement.

It is also apparent from the record that the press release's statement indicating that the balance of the financing remaining after the repayment of outstanding bank debt "will be used for general operating expenses" was misleading, in light of the substantial overdue obligations of National then existing.

The second major item of public disclosure concerning the closing was a stockholders' letter mailed, without respondents' knowledge, by National on or about December 23. This letter, which was issued in the face of Socha's advice to National that no further public statements should be issued concerning the Amended Credit Agreement unless such statements were cleared by Brown, Wood, contained numerous misstatements and omissions, including the following:

(1) The letter indicated that the company "was stronger now than ever before in its history" and that it had "a greater availability of capital, expanding productivity and growing earnings" and was "looking forward to an outstanding year in calendar 1975."

(2) The letter indicated that the entire additional $6 million loan to National could be used for future operating expenses.

(3) The letter made no reference to National's repayment of existing bank loans and other pre-existing debts with the proceeds of the financing, its continuing cash needs and shortages, or the LMP.

Respondents first learned of the letter on December 27, when Brian Kay, who was aware that National had ignored Socha's advice that all public disclosure should be reviewed by them, voluntarily telephoned Socha and dictated the letter to him. Socha thought that the letter's description of the Amended Credit Agreement was "seriously inadequate" and immediately gave a copy of it to Johnson. Carter, too, was consulted. While respondents felt that the letter did not make "adequate disclosure" with respect to the Amended Credit Agreement, they concluded that, when read together with the earlier December 20 press release which Carter had revised, it was not materially false or misleading, and that no corrective action by National was therefore required. Johnson later did, however, orally express his dissatisfaction with the letter to Lurie.

With the close of 1974, the record reveals that respondents were in the uncomfortable position of attempting to provide disclosure advice to an aggressive client whose unreceptive management actively frustrated the giving of advice and ignored what advice managed to get through. It is in the context of this attitude that respondents and National moved into the new year, with the final efforts to save the company and the resulting sharp needs to attend to the company's public disclosure obligations.

4. *January to March 1975: National's December 1974 Form 8–K; the Triggering of the LMP; Disclosure Pressures from the Banks.* On January 9, 1975, National filed a current report on Form 8–K for the month of December 1974, reporting on the closing under the Amended Credit Agreement. This document was drafted by Carter, who accepted full responsibility for it.

The Amended Credit Agreement, which was attached to the Form 8–K as an exhibit, made frequent reference to the LMP. And the 8–K itself stated that $2 million of National's recent $21 million loan arrangement was "a contingency fund available until June 30, 1975 only for the purpose of financing a lease maintenance program in the event additional financing is not otherwise available." As previously requested by Hart, however, the LMP itself was not included as an exhibit to the Agreement or the filing; nor was the term "lease maintenance plan" specifically defined or the effects which it would have on the company discussed.

Between the January 9, 1975 filing of National's form 8–K and mid-March, National's financial condition deteriorated even further, to a degree requiring the implementation of the LMP. In addition, the gap between National's public disclosure posture and its private financial condition continued to widen and National's board of directors was becoming increasingly uncomfortable with the situation.

There is no indication in the record that either respondent directly or indirectly became aware of the growing seriousness of the situation until a March 17 telephone call from the banks' counsel, * * *

* * *

On March 17, * * * over six weeks after the LMP had in fact been triggered—Brown, Wood was informed for the first time, by the *banks'* lawyers, White & Case, that events requiring implementation of the LMP had occurred. The White & Case lawyers had received a telephone call from a vice president of one of the banks informing them of this fact and reporting that no public disclosure had been made by National. The bank vice president also sought White & Case's advice on how to respond to trade creditors of National who were making inquiries to the banks about the company.

During their March 17 conversation, the White & Case lawyers advised Carter that National and its counsel, Brown, Wood, had the responsibility to determine what disclosure, if any, would be appropriate under the circumstances, and they sought assurances that, if proper disclosure were deemed necessary, it would be forthcoming. Carter, who admittedly considered the triggering of the LMP clearly material, assured White & Case that, if what they said were true, Brown, Wood would contact National and "get a statement out." The White & Case lawyers then called the bank's vice president and relayed the content of their conversation with Carter.

On the following day, March 18, Carter telephoned Lurie and informed him of the call from the White & Case lawyers. Lurie neither confirmed nor denied that the LMP had been triggered. Rather, he dissembled, stating that the situation was "tight," but adding that, "if they were careful, they would all be right." Carter advised Lurie that, if the LMP had indeed been triggered, the fact should be disclosed publicly, although he did not press Lurie for a definite answer on whether the LMP had in fact been triggered, or on whether National's management was in fact implementing the LMP as required by the Amended Credit Agreement.

Carter informed Johnson both of the telephone call from the banks' lawyers and the subsequent conversations with Lurie. While Johnson's first reaction was to find out what the facts were, neither he nor anyone else at Brown, Wood sought to verify the facts by contacting anyone at National. Nor did they seek to contact anyone outside of National, such as the consulting firm, which they knew had been charged by the parties with responsibility for monitoring National's compliance with the terms of the Amended Credit Agreement.

5. *April to May 1975: Respondents' Disclosure Advice; National's Board Acts; Hart's Resignation; Public Disclosure.* In early April, Carter and Johnson once again discussed the need to disclose National's obligation to implement the LMP. As a result of a conversation with Hart, Johnson had become "morally certain" that

National was required to implement the LMP, and that the failure to do so would result in National's being in default under the Amended Credit Agreement, although he did not believe, nor did Carter, that Hart intended to implement the LMP even though it was required.

* * *

On April 23, 1975 both respondents met with Hart and advised him in no uncertain terms that immediate disclosure was required. In response to Hart's protestations that National would soon obtain additional financing, respondents advised him that these hopes, as well as any negotiations for a waiver of the LMP by the banks, did not serve to excuse National's legal obligation to make prompt disclosure.

Shortly before the April 23 meeting, the vice president of one of the lending banks had written to Hart requesting, among other things, a "written response from your counsel regarding [National's] obligation to make public disclosure regarding significant transactions which may have transpired during the last several months, particularly with regard to the implementing of the lease maintenance plan." Presumably as a result of this request, Hart telephoned Johnson on April 28—only five days after having received the unambiguous and forceful advice that disclosure was required—to request that Johnson issue a legal opinion for the banks to the effect that disclosure of the triggering of the LMP was *not* necessary. Johnson testified that he replied as follows:

> I'm incredulous. I just can't believe this. You sat in my office last week and I told you as clearly and positively and precisely as I could that my advice was that you should disclose that you had gone into the lease maintenance mode.

Ultimately, Hart responded to the bank's request for an opinion of counsel with a letter from National stating that no disclosure had been made because, "in the opinion of the company," none was required.

In late April, after the telephone encounter with Hart described above, Johnson instructed Socha to draft a disclosure document for National to issue, either in its next report to the Commission or in a special letter to the stockholders. In doing so, Johnson specified that the draft should be one that would be "acceptable to a person as emotionally involved as Hart." Both respondents reviewed and approved the draft prepared by Socha and it was forwarded to Hart on or about May 1, with the suggestion that Hart call Carter or Johnson about it.

The proposed document indicated that, under the Amended Credit Agreement, National was required to cease writing new leases when its borrowings exceeded $19 million; that the company was seeking a waiver of this requirement by the banks, as well as new financing; that the company was hopeful that both of these efforts would succeed; and that the company had curtailed its sales operations because it had not obtained essential additional financing. National did not issue this disclosure document in any form and the record does not indicate any response to Brown, Wood's disclosure advice. Neither respondent questioned anyone at the company about management's failure to make the suggested disclosure.

On May 9, Kay called Socha to seek his approval of a draft of the company's proposed current report on Form 8–K for the month of April. Socha reiterated Brown, Wood's earlier advice that disclosure should be made concerning National's present status under the Amended Credit Agreement and of the event of default that resulted from the company's failure to implement the LMP. Although Kay agreed to include the suggested disclosure, the report actually filed with the Commission did not contain any such disclosure, because Lurie would not permit it.

* * *

During this period, outside the knowledge of the respondents, the relationship between National's outside directors and its management was deteriorating rapidly. * * *

* * *

The internal and external tensions which had been developing around National came to a head on Saturday afternoon, May 24, at the special meeting of the board of directors in Hartford, Connecticut. Johnson was there, acting as secretary, having been asked to attend by Hart. * * * It was at this meeting that the outside directors learned for the first time that, for over a month, Brown, Wood had been recommending disclosure and Johnson read a draft of the letter which Brown, Wood had sent to Hart on May 1, disclosing that the LMP had been triggered and its effect on the company. One of the nonmanagement directors testified that he had no prior indication that Brown, Wood had been recommending this disclosure to Hart and that when he heard the letter read by Johnson he "was shocked to the core."

At the May 24 meeting, Hart resigned each of his corporate offices, although he remained a director of the company, Johnson prepared a press release which was unanimously approved by the Board and it was decided that Brown, Wood would continue as company counsel. Johnson, however, resigned as secretary of the company.

The press release prepared by Johnson during the May 24 meeting announced that National would immediately curtail the writing of new leases, and described the management changes and the company's need for outside financing. It also expressed the company's hope that its growth structure could be resumed in the future. The release made no mention of the fact that the company had defaulted under the Amended Credit Agreement. The release was made public on May 27, 1975.

6. *May to July 1975: The Events Following Public Disclosure.* Following the disclosure contained in the May 27 press release and the company's subsequent current report on Form 8–K for the month of May 1975, the market price for National's common stock declined from the $13 bid, $14 asked range to the $3 bid, $4 asked range and the market for the company's common stock became virtually nonexistent. On July 2, National initiated proceedings for an arrangement under the bankruptcy laws. Among the creditors in the resulting proceeding was Brown, Wood, which submitted a claim for legal fees in excess of $200,000.

IV.

AIDING AND ABETTING

Rule 2(e)(1)(iii) provides that the Commission may deny, temporarily or permanently, the privilege of appearing or practicing before it to any person who is found by the Commission, after notice of and opportunity for hearing, to have *willfully violated*, or *willfully aided and abetted the violation* of, any provision of the federal securities laws or the rules and regulations thereunder.

* * *

B. *Securities Law Violations by National.* We have no doubt that National's failure to disclose the nature of the LMP in the December 20 press release and the December Form 8–K constituted a violation of Sections 10(b) and 13(a) of the Exchange Act and Rules 10b–5, 12b–20 and 13a–11 thereunder. * * *

* * *

C. *Aiding and Abetting.* Our primary concern, however, is with the respondents' relationship to these violations of the securities laws. Although "[t]he elements of an aiding and abetting claim have not yet crystallized into a set pattern," [56] we have examined the decisions of the various circuits and conclude that certain legal principles are common to all the decisions.

In the context of the federal securities laws, these principles hold generally that one may be found to have aided and abetted a violation when the following three elements are present:

    1. there exists an independent securities law violation committed by some other party;

    2. the aider and abettor knowingly and substantially assisted the conduct that constitutes the violation; and

    3. the aider and abettor was aware or knew that his role was part of an activity that was improper or illegal.

56. Woodward v. Metro Bank of Dallas, 522 F.2d 84, 94 (C.A.5 1975).

928   REGULATION OF SECURITIES TRADING   Ch. 19

As noted above, we have no difficulty in finding that National committed numerous substantial securities law violations. The second element—substantial assistance—is generally satisfied in the context of a securities lawyer performing professional duties, for he is inevitably deeply involved in his client's disclosure activities and often participates in the drafting of the documents, as was the case with Carter. And he does so knowing that he is participating in the preparation of disclosure documents—that is his job.

In this connection, we do not distinguish between the professional advice of a lawyer given orally or in writing and similar advice which is embodied in drafting documents to be filed with the Commission. Liability in these circumstances should not turn on such artificial distinctions, particularly in light of the almost limitless range of forms which legal advice may take. Moreover, the opposite approach, which would permit a lawyer to avoid or reduce his liability simply by avoiding participation in the drafting process, may well have the undesirable effect of reducing the quality of the disclosure by the many to protect against the defalcations of the few.

For these reasons, the crucial inquiry in a Rule 2(e) proceeding against a lawyer inevitably tends to focus on the awareness or the intent element of the offense of aiding and abetting. It is that element which has been the source of the most disagreement among commentators and the courts. We do not seek to resolve that disagreement today. We do hold, however, that a finding of *willful aiding and abetting* within the meaning of Rule 2(e)(1)(iii) requires a showing that respondents were aware or knew that their role was part of an activity that was improper or illegal.

It is axiomatic that a lawyer will not be liable as an aider and abettor merely because his advice, followed by the client, is ultimately determined to be wrong. What is missing in that instance is a wrongful intent on the part of the lawyer. It is that element of intent which provides the basis for distinguishing between those professionals who may be appropriately considered as subjects of professional discipline and those who, acting in good faith, have merely made errors of judgment or have been careless.

Significant public benefits flow from the effective performance of the securities lawyer's role. The exercise of independent, careful and informed legal judgment on difficult issues is critical to the flow of material information to the securities markets. Moreover, we are aware of the difficulties and limitations attendant upon that role. In the course of rendering securities law advice, the lawyer is called upon to make difficult judgments, often under great pressure and in areas where the legal signposts are far apart and only faintly discernible.

If a securities lawyer is to bring his best independent judgment to bear on a disclosure problem, he must have the freedom to make innocent—or even, in certain cases, careless—mistakes without fear of legal liability or loss of the ability to practice before the Commission. Concern about his own liability may alter the balance of his judgment in one direction as surely as an unseemly obeisance to the wishes of his client can do so in the other. While one imbalance results in disclosure rather than concealment, neither is, in the end, truly in the public interest. Lawyers who are seen by their clients as being motivated by fears for their personal liability will not be consulted on difficult issues.

Although it is a close judgment, after careful review, we conclude that the available evidence is insufficient to establish that either respondent acted with sufficient knowledge and awareness or recklessness to satisfy the test for willful aiding and abetting liability.
* * *

D. *The December Press Release and Form 8–K.* In drafting the December press release and Form 8–K, Carter advised National that the provisions of the LMP were not required to be disclosed. There is ample evidence in the record indicating both respondents' knowledge about National's financial condition and the importance of the LMP. Johnson attended the Board meetings held on July 1, August 19, and October 15, 1974 at which the directors emphasized the importance of new financing and reviewed Socha's draft shareholders' letter in October that explained the significance of a proposed informal "wind-down" phase in National's corporate life. Johnson informed Carter of these matters in connection with their joint responsibilities for the representation of National. Carter focused on the details of the LMP when he advised Hart that the document embodying the plan did not have to be filed with the Commission if it were not an exhibit to the Amended Credit Agreement. Respondents were clearly aware of the company's lack of success in raising new capital, and the increasingly critical impact of its negative cash flow.

On the other hand, the record also contains no direct evidence of Carter's knowledge that the details of the LMP were material and we decline to infer such knowledge because of facts in the record on which Carter's erroneous judgment as to its immateriality is claimed to have been based. Carter had been told by Hart and others about numerous potential sources for additional financing. * * * Moreover, the banks were willing to close the Amended Credit Agreement and convert their $16.8 million in demand debt to six-year notes, which suggests they did not believe that National was in serious and immediate financial difficulty.

It is also significant that the December 20 press release, while originally drafted by National's management, was entirely rewritten by Carter in longhand at the December 19 pre-closing meeting. Having thus revised the document, Carter showed it to all present at the pre-closing and no one suggested any change. In fact, the only comment recalled by Carter was to the effect of, "Boy, that's full disclosure."

In view of the foregoing, we are unable to conclude that it has been demonstrated by sufficient evidence that Carter willfully aided and abetted violations of the securities laws in connection with the December 20 press release and the December Form 8–K.

E. *Subsequent Conduct.* The Administrative Law Judge found that, in addition to the violations resulting from the December 20, 1974 press release and the Form 8–K filed on January 8, 1975, National violated the federal securities laws through its continued failure to make adequate disclosures in public statements and Commission filings regarding its deteriorating cash position, its inability to meet earlier growth projections, the triggering of the LMP, and the impact the LMP would have on National. The Administrative Law Judge also found that respondents willfully aided and abetted these violations by failing to ensure that the required disclosures were made or to communicate to National's board of directors concerning management's refusal to make such disclosures. Our review of the record does not reveal a sufficient basis for sustaining respondents' liability as aiders and abettors of these violations.

* * *

On the basis of the record before us, we think that it is a close question, but in the final analysis we are unable to infer that respondents intended to aid the violations by not acting. The level of intent required by this test is higher than that required by some courts to show the appropriate mental state for the third element of aiding and abetting. There, some courts require only that an aider and abettor be "aware" that his role was part of an illegal or improper activity. Here, the test requires a showing that he "intended" to foster the illegal activity. This is a fine distinction, but we think it is an important one.

Our review of the record, which includes respondents' periodic exhortations to Hart to improve the quality of National's disclosure, leads us to believe that respondents did not intend to assist the violations by their inaction or silence. Rather, they seemed to be at a loss for how to deal with a difficult client.

Association of a law firm with a client lends an air of legitimacy and authority to the actions of a client. There are occasions when, but for the law firm's association, a violation could not have occurred. Under those circumstances, if the firm were cognizant of how it was being used and acquiesced, or if it gained some benefit from the violation beyond that normally obtained in a legal relationship, inaction would probably give rise to an inference of intent. This, however, is not such a case, and we find that respondents did not intend to assist the violation by their inaction.

V.

ETHICAL AND PROFESSIONAL RESPONSIBILITIES

A. *The Findings of the Administrative Law Judge.* The Administrative Law Judge found that both respondents "failed to carry out their professional responsibilities with respect to appropriate disclosure to all concerned, including stockholders, directors and the investing public * * * and thus knowingly engaged in unethical and improper professional conduct, as charged in the Order." In particular, he held that respondents' failure to advise National's board of directors of Hart's refusal to disclose adequately the company's perilous financial condition was itself a violation of ethical and professional standards referred to in Rule 2(e)(1)(ii).

Respondents argue that the Commission has never promulgated standards of professional conduct for lawyers and that the Commission's application in hindsight of new standards would be fundamentally unfair. Moreover, even if it is permissible for the Commission to apply—without specific adoption or notice—generally recognized professional standards, they argue that no such standards applicable to respondents' conduct existed in 1974–75, nor do they exist today.

We agree that, in general, elemental notions of fairness dictate that the Commission should not establish new rules of conduct and impose them retroactively upon professionals who acted at the time without reason to believe that their conduct was unethical or improper. At the same time, however, we perceive no unfairness whatsoever in holding those professionals who practice before us to generally recognized norms of professional conduct, whether or not such norms had previously been explicitly adopted or endorsed by the Commission. To do so upsets no justifiable expectations, since the professional is already subject to those norms.

The ethical and professional responsibilities of lawyers who become aware that their client is engaging in violations of the securities laws have not been so firmly and unambiguously established that we believe all practicing lawyers can be held to an awareness of generally recognized norms. We also recognize that the Commission has never articulated or endorsed any such standards. That being the case, we reverse the Administrative Law Judge's findings under subparagraph (ii) of Rule 2(e)(1) with respect to both respondents. Nevertheless, we believe that respondents' conduct raises serious questions about the obligations of securities lawyers, and the Commission is hereby giving notice of its interpretation of "unethical or improper professional conduct" as that term is used in Rule 2(e)(1)(ii). * * *

B. *Interpretive Background.* Our concern focuses on the professional obligations of the lawyer who gives essentially correct disclosure advice to a client that does not follow that advice and as a result violates the federal securities laws. The subject of our inquiry is not a new one by any means and has received extensive scholarly treatment as well as consideration by a number of local bar ethics committees and disciplinary bodies. Similar issues are also presently under consideration by the ABA's Commission on Evaluation of Professional Standards in connection with the review and proposed revision of the ABA's Code of Professional Responsibility.

While precise standards have not yet emerged, it is fair to say that there exists considerable acceptance of the proposition that a lawyer must, in order to discharge his professional responsibilities, make all efforts within reason to persuade his client to avoid or terminate proposed illegal action. Such efforts could include, where appropriate, notification to the board of directors of a corporate client. * * *

We are mindful that, when a lawyer represents a corporate client, the client—and the entity to which he owes his allegiance—is the corporation itself and not management or any other individual connected with the corporation.[73] Moreover, the lawyer should try to "insure that decisions of his client are made only after the client has been informed of relevant considerations."[74] These unexceptionable principles take on a special coloration when a lawyer becomes aware that one or more specific members of a corporate client's management is deciding not to follow his disclosure advice, especially if he knows that those in control, such as the board of directors, may not have participated in or been aware of that decision. Moreover, it is well established that no lawyer, even in the most zealous pursuit of his client's interests, is privileged to assist his client in conduct the lawyer knows to be illegal.[75] The application of these recognized principles to the special role of the securities lawyer giving disclosure advice, however, is not a simple task.

The securities lawyer who is an active participant in a company's ongoing disclosure program will ordinarily draft and revise disclosure documents, comment on them and file them with the Commission. He is often involved on an intimate, day-to-day basis in the judgments that determine what will be disclosed and what will be withheld from the public markets. When a lawyer serving in such a capacity concludes that his client's disclosures are not adequate to comply with the law, and so advises his client, he is "aware," in a literal sense, of a continuing violation of the securities laws. On the other hand, the lawyer is only an adviser, and the final judgment—and, indeed, responsibility—as to what course of conduct is to be taken must lie with the client. Moreover, disclosure issues often present difficult choices between multiple shades of gray, and while a lawyer's judgment may be to draw the disclosure obligation more broadly than his client, both parties recognize the degree of uncertainty involved.

73. *See* ABA Code of Professional Responsibility, Ethical Consideration ("ABA E.C.") 5–18.

74. ABA E.C. 7–8.

75. ABA D.R. 7–102(A)(7).

The problems of professional conduct that arise in this relationship are well-illustrated by the facts of this case. In rejecting Brown, Wood's advice to include the assumptions underlying its projections in its 1974 Annual Report, in declining to issue two draft stockholders letters offered by respondents and in ignoring the numerous more informal urgings by both respondents and Socha to make disclosure, Hart and Lurie indicated that they were inclined to resist any public pronouncements that were at odds with the rapid growth which had been projected and reported for the company.

If the record ended there, we would be hesitant to suggest that any unprofessional conduct might be involved. Hart and Lurie were, in effect, pressing the company's lawyers hard for the minimum disclosure required by law. That fact alone is not an appropriate basis for a finding that a lawyer must resign or take some extraordinary action. Such a finding would inevitably drive a wedge between reporting companies and their outside lawyers; the more sophisticated members of management would soon realize that there is nothing to gain in consulting outside lawyers.

However, much more was involved in this case. In sending out a patently misleading letter to stockholders on December 23 in contravention of Socha's plain and express advice to clear all such disclosure with Brown, Wood, in deceiving respondents about Johnson's approval of the company's quarterly report to its stockholders in early December and in dissembling in response to respondents' questions about the implementation of the LMP, the company's management erected a wall between National and its outside lawyers—a wall apparently designed to keep out good legal advice in conflict with management's improper disclosure plans.

Any ambiguity in the situation plainly evaporated in late April and early May of 1975 when Hart first asked Johnson for a legal opinion flatly contrary to the express disclosure advice Johnson had given Hart only five days earlier, and when Lurie soon thereafter prohibited Kay from delivering a copy of the company's April 1975 Form 8–K to Brown, Wood.

These actions reveal a conscious desire on the part of National's management no longer to look to Brown, Wood for independent disclosure advice, but rather to embrace the firm within Hart's fraud and use it as a shield to avoid the pressures exerted by the banks toward disclosure. Such a role is a perversion of the normal lawyer-client relationship, and no lawyer may claim that, in these circumstances, he need do no more than stubbornly continue to suggest disclosure when he knows his suggestions are falling on deaf ears.

C. *"Unethical or Improper Professional Conduct."* The Commission is of the view that a lawyer engages in "unethical or improper professional conduct" under the following circumstances: When a lawyer with significant responsibilities in the effectuation of a company's compliance with the disclosure requirements of the federal securities laws becomes aware that his client is engaged in a substantial and continuing failure to satisfy those disclosure requirements, his continued participation violates professional standards unless he takes prompt steps to end the client's noncompliance. The Commission has determined that this interpretation will be applicable only to conduct occurring after the date of this opinion.

We do not imply that a lawyer is obliged, at the risk of being held to have violated Rule 2(e), to seek to correct every isolated disclosure action or inaction which he believes to be at variance with applicable disclosure standards, although there may be isolated disclosure failures that are so serious that their correction becomes a matter of primary professional concern. It is also clear, however, that a lawyer is not privileged to unthinkingly permit himself to be co-opted into an ongoing fraud and cast as a dupe or a shield for a wrongdoing client.

Initially, counselling accurate disclosure is sufficient, even if his advice is not accepted. But there comes a point at which a reasonable lawyer must conclude that his advice is not being followed, or even sought in good faith, and that his client is involved in a continuing course of violating the securities laws. At this critical juncture, the lawyer must take further, more affirmative steps in order to avoid the inference that he has been co-opted, willingly or unwillingly, into the scheme of nondisclosure.

The lawyer is in the best position to choose his next step. Resignation is one option, although we recognize that other considerations, including the protection of the client against forseeable prejudice, must be taken into account in the case of withdrawal. A direct approach to the board of directors or one or more individual directors or officers may be appropriate; or he may choose to try to enlist the aid of other members of the firm's management. What is required, in short, is some prompt action that leads to the conclusion that the lawyer is engaged in efforts to correct the underlying problem, rather than having capitulated to the desires of a strong-willed, but misguided client.

Some have argued that resignation is the only permissible course when a client chooses not to comply with disclosure advice. We do not agree. Premature resignation serves neither the end of an effective lawyer-client relationship nor, in most cases, the effective administration of the securities laws. The lawyer's continued interaction with his client will ordinarily hold the greatest promise of corrective action. So long as a lawyer is acting in good faith and exerting reasonable efforts to prevent violations of the law by his client, his professional obligations have been met. In general, the best result is that which promotes the continued, strong-minded and independent participation by the lawyer.

We recognize, however, that the "best result" is not always obtainable, and that there may occur situations where the lawyer must conclude that the misconduct is so extreme or irretrievable, or the involvement of his client's management and board of directors in the misconduct is so thoroughgoing and pervasive that any action short of resignation would be futile. We would anticipate that cases where a lawyer has no choice but to resign would be rare and of an egregious nature.[78]

D. *Conclusion.* As noted above, because the Commission has never adopted or endorsed standards of professional conduct which would have applied to respondents' activities during the period here in question, and since generally accepted norms of professional conduct which existed outside the scope of Rule 2(e) did not, during the relevant time period, unambiguously cover the situation in which respondents found themselves in 1974–75, no finding of unethical or unprofessional conduct would be appropriate. That being the case, we reverse the findings of the Administrative Law Judge under Rule 2(e)(1)(ii). In future proceedings of this nature, however, the Commission will apply the interpretation of subparagraph (ii) of Rule 2(e)(1) set forth in this opinion.

An appropriate order will issue.

By the Commission (Chairman WILLIAMS and Commissioners LOOMIS and FRIEDMAN); Commissioner EVANS concurring in part and dissenting in part; and Commissioner THOMAS not participating.

Commissioner EVANS, concurring in part and dissenting in part:

* * *

* * * I find the conclusion inescapable that Carter knew that the unique requirements of the LMP were highly material and that the mere reference to this term in the press release and the Form 8–K was inadequate disclosure. I might have been less inclined to make this finding had National's financial position been more secure, the probable triggering of the LMP more remote, or the Company's public posture not so misleading. However, Carter was fully aware that, while a triggering of the LMP in the very near future was not inevitable, it was a reasonable probability and very much within the concern of all parties. It was apparent to Carter that the reasonable probability of the LMP being triggered, combined with the magnitude of its effect on National, compelled disclosure of the true meaning of the LMP. In other words, I conclude that Carter knew that the significance of the LMP, which was not apparent to the public, was information that a reasonable investor would view as having significantly altered the total mix of information available to the public. At the very least, Carter acted recklessly in failing to disclose the import

---

78. This case does not involve, nor do we here deal with, the additional question of when a lawyer, aware of his client's intention to commit fraud or an illegal act, has a professional duty to disclose that fact either publicly or to an affected third party. Our interpretation today does not require such action at any point, although other existing standards of professional conduct might be so interpreted. *See, e.g.,* ABA D.R. 7–102(B).

of the LMP. Thus, I find that Carter acted with scienter and should be liable as an aider and abettor to National's securities laws violations with regard to the Form 8–K and December 20 press release.

F.   A CONCLUDING NOTE—10b–5 AS OPERA

Professor David Ratner has suggested that recent Supreme Court cases interpreting Rule 10b–5 might best be understood as scenes from an opera:

The heroine of the opera is Dieci Becinque (10b–5), a beautiful 30-year-old rule, much beloved by securities lawyers everywhere. In the first act, we find her in a marble temple surrounded by nine high priests who sing her praises. First Willio, the eldest priest, sings his famous patter song, "Il Sovrintendente d'Assicurazione" ("The Superintendent of Insurance"), in which he eulogizes 10b–5 as the solution to all the wrongs of mankind. The act closes with Blackmunio's aria, "I Uti Affiliati", in which he lauds her as the savior of the oppressed Indian tribes of the American West.

After a three-year intermission, the curtain rises on the second act. We find our heroine in the same marble temple, but the mood has changed dramatically. Two new priests, Paolo and Rehnquistio, are sworn to destroy her. In the opening aria, "La Scheggia Azzurra" ("The Blue Chip"), Rehnquistio tells her that only one who has paid the price may enjoy her affections. This is followed by the rousing "Ride of the Hochfelder," in which Paolo tells her that she was born in manipulation and deception and may only deal with wicked people. Next, in the haunting aria "O Santa Fe" (Oh, Holy Faith"), Bianco declares that she must have nothing to do with corporate managers, no matter how wicked they are. Finally, in "La Chiarella" ("The Little Printer"), sung again by Paola, she is told that nobody must have anything to do with her unless he has first breached a specific duty to his fellow man.

We do not know how the second act will end but, despite Blackmunio's cry of protest, "Dissento," at the end of each aria, it appears that the heroine will finally be banished from the temple. However, there may yet be a third act in which she is restored to her former position of glory. Time will tell.

Chapter 20

INTRODUCTION TO ORGANIC CHANGE

PROBLEM

PRODUCTION, INC.—PART I

Production, Inc., a relatively small conglomerate, is an American Stock Exchange listed company organized under the laws of Columbia. Its articles of incorporation authorize 10 million shares of common stock, 5,000,000 of which are issued and outstanding. The stock is currently trading at $10 per share.

Production's most recent consolidated balance sheet can be summarized as follows:

ASSETS		LIABILITIES AND SHARE-HOLDERS' EQUITY	
Current Assets	$ 15,000,000	Current liabilities	$ 17,000,000
Fixed assets	110,000,000	Long term debt	52,000,000
		Total liabilities	69,000,000
Total assets	$125,000,000	Shareholders' Equity	
		Stated capital	$ 50,000,000
		Earned surplus	6,000,000
		Total shareholders' equity	$ 56,000,000
		Total liabilities and shareholders' equity	$125,000,000

Production's earnings for the last five years have been (in chronological order):

$20,000,000
18,000,000
6,000,000
7,000,000
7,000,000

Production recently approached Electronica, Inc., also a Columbia corporation, about a merger. Electronica has 2 million authorized shares of which 1 million are issued and outstanding. Its stock is presently trading in the over-the-counter market for 74 bid, 76 asked.

Electronica's most recent balance sheet can be summarized as follows:

ASSETS		LIABILITIES AND SHARE-HOLDERS' EQUITY	
Current assets	$ 10,000,000	Current liabilities	$ 3,000,000
Fixed assets	50,000,000	Long term debt	17,000,000
		Total liabilities	20,000,000
Total assets	$ 60,000,000	Shareholders' Equity	
		Stated capital	$ 25,000,000
		Earned surplus	15,000,000
		Total shareholders' equity	$ 40,000,000
		Total liabilities and shareholders' equity	$ 60,000,000

Electronica's profits for the last five years have been (in chronological order):

$ 2,000,000
2,000,000
2,500,000
4,000,000
5,000,000

About 35 percent of Electronica's stock is held by Homer Faraday, the founder and president of the company, or other members of his family. Another 5 percent is held by two senior executives, and the balance is in the hands of about a thousand public shareholders.

Faraday is 48 years old. He is not only a successful engineer, but he has proved to have a real flair for management, as is shown by the rapid growth of his company over the last several years. He has also assembled a very capable management team. One of the principal reasons that the board of Production is interested in Electronica is that Production's president and board chairman, Walters, is 67 years old and has been in poor health for the last several years. Production's directors are anxious to bring in some new managerial talent, and believe that Faraday and his team would provide it.

During preliminary negotiations Faraday and Walters have tentatively agreed on an exchange ratio of 8 shares of Production common for each share of common stock of Electronica. Faraday has insisted on a 5-year employment contract as president of Electronica beginning at $150,000 per year and increasing by 20 percent each year. Walters would resign as president but remain chairman of the board, with the understanding that he would relinquish the role of chief executive officer to Faraday after one year.

As counsel to Production, you have been asked to advise on alternative ways of structuring the combination between the two firms. Production's management is concerned about the possibility that its shareholders may not be happy with the transaction and that a substantial number may seek appraisal; and they would therefore like your advice for each possible alternative as to 1) the mechanics, including shareholder vote, required to accomplish the combination (Consider MBCA §§ 71, 72, 72A, 73, 79, and 59); 2) the extent to which shareholders would be entitled to appraisal rights (Consider MBCA § 80); 3) the possibility that a shareholder might be able to sue to block the transaction. The alternatives under consideration are:

A. Electronica merges into Production; or, alternatively, Production and Electronica are consolidated into the P.E. Corporation.

B. Production issues its common stock to Electronica shareholders in exchange for their Electronica shares.

C. Production issues its common stock to Electronica in exchange for all of Electronica's assets. Production assumes all of Electronica's liabilities. Electronica dissolves and distributes the Production stock received in the sale of assets transaction to its shareholders.

D. Electronica acquires Production in a stock for assets transaction. Assume Electronica's management is concerned about the possibility that its shareholders may be unhappy with the transaction, and a substantial number may seek appraisal causing a heavy cash drain. Assume the shareholders of Production present no problem with respect to appraisal rights. Consider especially the *Farris* and *Hariton* cases.

E. Production establishes a subsidiary and transfers to it enough Production common to engage in one of the transactions described in A, B, or C.

A. OVERVIEW

There are a variety of fundamental changes in the structure of a corporation that fall within the classification, "organic." They may be undertaken for a wide variety of reasons, and their impact on the practical affairs of the corporation may range from revolutionary to insignificant. They are organic in the sense that most, but not all, affect in some way the articles of incorporation, the "organic" document of the corporation. Among the common transactions that are usually considered within this category are:

(1) changes in the rights, preferences, or privileges of shares, usually, but not necessarily, undertaken by amendment of the articles of incorporation; * these alterations may be independent of changes in the entity or may be part of a change in the entity; and

---

* We have already examined such a case in the Chesapeake Marine Services problem.

(2) changes which affect the form, scope, or continuity of the enterprise, typically, mergers, consolidations, sales of all or substantially all of the corporation's assets and finally, dissolution,* (organically speaking, "decomposition"?).

The procedures required for the accomplishment of any of these changes are generally dictated by statute; and while the statutory mechanics may vary, both from one state to another and as among the various types of organic change, the standard pattern involves the adoption of the board of directors of a resolution recommending the transaction followed by a ratification by the shareholders. There are usually a number of procedural formalities, also dictated by statute governing such things as the contents of the resolution and the notice required to be given to the stockholders.

Until the 1960's most states required approval of such changes by an extraordinary majority—usually either two-thirds or three-quarters—of the stock. In 1969 Delaware amended its statute to reduce the necessary vote to a majority of the outstanding shares entitled to vote.** The Model Business Corporation Act was changed in 1969 to adopt the same rule. Many, but by no means all, of the states have since followed this "liberalization."

Since, in corporations having more than one class of stock, organic changes may affect different classes of stock differently, it is usual to require separate approval by each class of stock in such instances.

Besides the requirement of shareholder approval, corporation statutes typically provide that stockholders may, in effect, "opt out" of a transaction that significantly affects their relationship to the corporation by dissenting from the transaction and requiring the corporation to pay them in cash the value of their shares as determined by appraisal.

Neither of these two means of protecting the interest of the shareholders has proved always to satisfy all of the shareholders affected by major changes. With some frequency dissident shareholders have turned to the courts to seek alternative relief by way of injunctions or damages. One of the most active controversies in corporation law revolves around whether the appraisal remedy provided by statute should be treated as exclusive or whether the courts may conduct an examination of an organic change and fashion judicial remedies for transactions they find to be unfair or improperly motivated. As we shall see, at least if the Delaware courts are to be taken as leading the way, the current trend seems to be distinctly in the latter direction.

* For a more extensive consideration of dissolution, see Chapter 11, part F, *supra*.

** General Corporation Law of Delaware, §§ 242, 251, 271, 275. This "absolute majority" vote is still higher than the "simple majority" of the shares represented and voting at a shareholders meeting, which is all that is necessary to pass an ordinary resolution.

B. THE MECHANICS OF CORPORATE COMBINATIONS

1. CORPORATE LAW CONSIDERATIONS

The basic end of all corporate combinations is to put the assets of two (or occasionally more) corporations under the control of one management. The combined enterprise may be one legal entity, in which case the former legal separation of the constituent parts usually continues to be reflected in the organization of the entity into separate operating divisions; or the combined enterprise may continue to have two (or more) distinct legal entities related to each other as parent and subsidiary corporations. The ultimate decision as to which of these two end products is desired is principally a business decision depending on the preferences and operating style of management and on such legally related considerations as the extent to which it is desirable to separate the liabilities and legal obligations of the component parts of the new enterprise by retaining distinct corporations. On the whole, the form selected is just that—a form—and has little effect on the manner in which the enterprise is operated.

It should be no surprise that there is more than one way to accomplish the combination of two corporations. To illustrate, let us consider the most common situation in which one corporation (often called the acquiring corporation) desires to obtain control of the assets of a second, usually, but not always, smaller corporation (often called the target). There are three basic techniques of accomplishing this change in control that fall within the class of transactions under consideration here.

2. MERGER AND CONSOLIDATION

The first of these techniques has two variants, the statutory merger * and the consolidation. Both are statutory procedures that result in the combination of two (or more) corporations into one. The only difference is that in a merger one corporation merges into another with the former ceasing to exist as a separate legal entity and the latter (the surviving corporation) continuing in existence as owner of all the assets and subject to all the liabilities of both. In a consolidation both corporations cease to exist and a new legal entity is created.

---

* The term "*statutory* merger" is used here to distinguish this transaction from term "merger" which is often employed loosely to encompass all three techniques.

The two types of transaction may be illustrated in graphic terms:

Statutory merger:

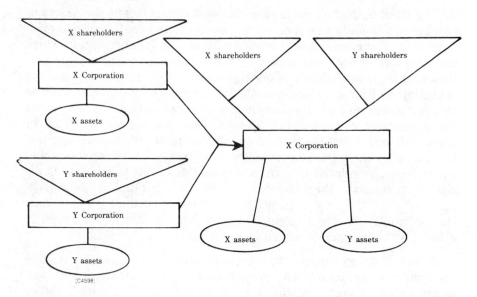

Consolidation:

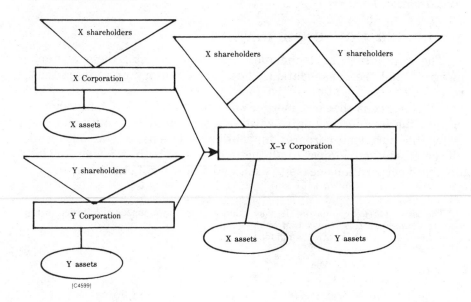

You should note that in both forms the former shareholders of the two corporations become shareholders of the surviving or newly created corporation, which automatically succeeds to all the assets and all the liabilities of both. In the merger, the shareholders of the surviving corporation retain their shares and those of the disappearing corporation exchange theirs for new shares in the surviving corporation. In a consolidation, both sets of shareholders must exchange their stock for shares in the new entity. In both cases assets are transferred and obligations are assumed by operation of law, there is no need to execute formal conveyances or assignments. See MBCA § 79(d). With two exceptions, approval of the shareholders of both corporations is required and both sets of shareholders are entitled to appraisal rights. MBCA §§ 71, 72, 73, 80 and 81.

The first exception from the usual requirement a shareholder vote relates to the so-called short-form merger, which is designed to accommodate the practicalities of the merger of an almost-wholly-owned subsidiary into its parent. Under the Model Act this procedure is available where the parent holds at least 90 percent of the subsidiary's stock. MBCA § 75. Under these circumstances, the vote of the shareholders of the subsidiary would be a useless formality since the parent has more than enough shares to approve the transaction. Moreover, whether the subsidiary continues as a separate entity or is combined with the parent is of little interest to the shareholders of the parent, and a requirement that they give their assent would likewise be an empty formality. In theory, at least, the interests of the minority shareholders of the subsidiary are adequately protected by their right to dissent from the transaction and seek appraisal of their shares. That theory, as we shall see, has not always been adequate to console the minority shareholders, who have with some regularity challenged these transactions on non-statutory grounds.

The second exception, embodied in MBCA § 73(d), is for mergers between corporations of relatively disparate size. If the number of outstanding shares of the larger corporation will increase by no more than 20 percent, and if there is no significant change in its articles of incorporation in the wake of the merger, there seems little need for the submission of the merger to its shareholders for their approval. Section 73(d) accommodates that principle. It also coordinates, for listed corporations at least, the merger provisions with those applicable to the other two basic forms of combination. As we shall shortly see, it is often possible to accomplish a stock-swap or a sale of assets without the approval of the shareholders of the acquiring corporation, at least if that corporation is not listed on the New York or American Stock Exchanges. The rules of these exchanges, however, may, as a practical matter, require such a vote—even though it would not be required by state law—where in the course of the transaction the acquiring corporation will issue additional shares in a number greater than 20 percent of the shares outstanding before the transaction.

Unless such a vote is taken, the new shares may not be listed on the exchange. *See e.g.* N.Y.S.E. Company Manual, A–283–284.

3. EXCHANGE OF SHARES

The second basic form of combination, by which a nearly identical result can be achieved, is an exchange of shares or "stock swap." If this technique is used, the acquiring corporation issues new shares to shareholders of the target in exchange for their stock in the target. The target then becomes a subsidiary of the parent. Graphically, the transaction looks like this:

Stock swap:

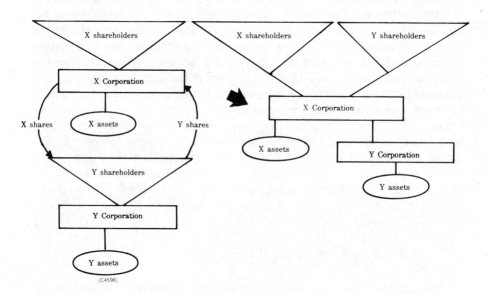

If the X Corporation does not desire to operate the Y Corporation as a subsidiary, but wishes to end with precisely the same structure as if Y had been merged into X, the exchange of shares may be followed by 1) a dissolution of Y in which it distributes all of its assets to X and X assumes all of its liabilities, or 2) a merger of Y into X, usually according to the "short form" merger discussed above.

One difficulty with this form of transaction is that not all of the Y shareholders may be willing to go along. When this is so X will hold only a majority, although perhaps an overwhelming majority of the Y shares, with some remaining in the hands of the original Y shareholders. The presence of this minority interest in Y may create headaches for the management of X, which will want to manage the two corporations as one economic entity, without having to be bothered about whether intercorporate transactions, such as the payment (or nonpayment) by Y of dividends, are fair to Y's minority shareholders. This uncomfortable situation often leads to efforts by the X corporation to "freeze out" the Y minority in a transaction in which they are forced to accept cash or debt instruments in exchange for their stock. This, as might be imagined, is not always to the liking of the Y minority, and frequently leads to litigation of a sort we shall examine in a later chapter.

Another solution to this difficulty is provided by MBCA § 72A. This section, which was added to the Model Act in 1976, in effect compels all of the shareholders of the acquired corporation (unless they choose to exercise their appraisal rights) to accept a share exchange approved by a majority of the acquired corporation's outstanding shares. The draftsmen of this provision, recognizing that the differences between a merger or consolidation and a stock swap were almost entirely formal, sought to make the two more equivalent in practice by depriving would-be "hold-outs" among the acquired corporation's shareholders of an option that they would have if the transaction were cast in the form of a merger. Giving the planners of corporate combination this option also eliminates the practical and legal difficulties that often lead to freeze-outs.

Although a vote of the shareholders of the target corporation is necessary under this alternative form of share exchange, in the traditional form, shareholders of the acquired corporation "voted" simply by deciding whether to exchange their shares or to hold on to them. Under most statutes no vote by the shareholders of the acquiring corporation is necessary, so long as it has sufficient authorized but unissued shares to complete the transaction. Their approval would of course be necessary if it were necessary to amend the articles of incorporation in order to create more shares.

Even if the acquiring corporation does have a sufficient number of authorized but unissued shares, however, if it is listed on either the New York Stock Exchange or the American Stock Exchange, shareholder approval may still be required where the new shares to be issued represent a 20 percent or greater increase in the issuer's outstanding shares. *See e.g.*, N.Y.S.E. Company Manual, A–283–284.

4. EXCHANGE OF STOCK FOR ASSETS

In the third type of acquisition, the acquiring corporation buys the assets of the target corporation for stock (or some combination of stock, cash, and occasionally, other securities) of the acquiring corporation. The result is that the acquiring corporation has obtained control over the target's assets (which is the only real end of any of these transactions) and the target has become a shell or holding company whose assets consist of the stock or other securities and any cash transferred in the exchange. The target may then dissolve, distributing these assets to its shareholders. Graphically the series of transactions looks like this:

Exchange of stock for assets:

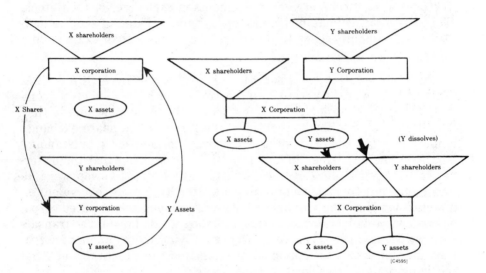

In this sort of transaction the assets of the acquired corporation must be transferred by deed or by other form of conveyance, a process that can generate a good deal of paperwork. The acquiring corporation usually, though not always, assumes the liabilities of the acquired corporation. The liabilities may also be provided for by having the target retain sufficient liquid assets to pay them off. Under certain circumstances, the acquiring corporation may be held responsible for obligations of the target under common law principles of transferee liability after a fraudulent conveyance even though there was no explicit assumption of liabilities under the terms of the transfer. In any case, most such transactions are subject to state bulk sales laws designed to give protection to creditors when an obligor sells all or substantially all of its assets.

Most state statutes require the approval of the shareholders of the target corporation for any sale of "all or substantially all" of its assets "if not in the usual and regular course of its business." See MBCA § 79. In most states this right to vote is accompanied by appraisal rights for those shareholders who do not approve of the transaction. See MBCA §§ 80 and 81.

If the acquiring corporation has enough authorized but unissued shares (and therefore does not have to amend its articles of incorporation to create more), state law does not normally require that its shareholders approve the transaction. This general observation is again subject to the qualification that, if the number of new shares to be issued is more than 20 percent of those outstanding, stock exchange rules may nevertheless force such approval.

5. TRIANGULAR COMBINATIONS

In some cases the acquiring corporation may not be content with the corporate structure that would result from a straightforward transaction of one of these types. In particular, the corporation may want to use the statutory merger technique because of the relative ease with which assets may be transferred and liabilities assumed, but may be concerned about subjecting its own assets to some unknown or contingent liability that has not yet materialized. Some years ago corporation lawyers developed the so-called "triangular merger" to deal with this problem.

In a triangular merger the acquiring corporation creates a subsidiary, taking all of the subsidiary's stock in exchange for the amount of the acquiring corporation's stock that is to be transferred to the shareholders of the target corporation in the merger. The target is then merged into the new subsidiary, with the target's shareholders receiving, instead of shares in the subsidiary, as in an ordinary merger, shares of its parent, the acquiring corporation. The result is then that the subsidiary becomes the owner of the target's business. Graphically, the transaction looks like this:

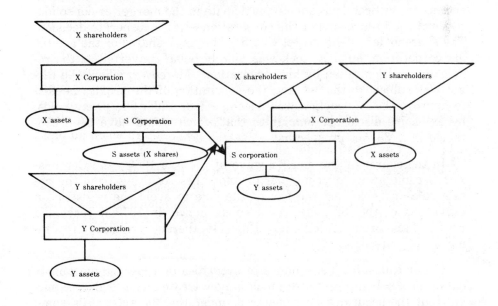

Note that the end result is exactly what would have been achieved had the transaction been structured as an exchange of shares (except that in this case there is no possibility of a remaining minority interest in the S Corporation). Not only, then, is it possible to make an exchange of shares produce the same result as a merger or consolidation, but the reverse is also true.

It will readily be seen that the device of a "merger subsidiary" can easily be adapted to use in either of the other two basic forms of combination (although there is little need for it in an exchange of shares). Subsection (B) of § 75 of the MBCA provides explicit authorization for exchanging for the shares of the acquired corporation "shares * * * of the surviving corporation or of any other corporation * * *."

6. SECURITIES LAW CONSIDERATIONS

Prior to 1972, under the SEC's Rule 133, statutory mergers or consolidations and exchanges of assets for stock were, in general, treated as not involving the "sale" of a security for the purposes of the '33 Act, and it was therefore not necessary to register the securities of the acquiring corporation that were issued in the transaction, even when the target was a publicly held corporation with a large number of shareholders. The principal justification for this "no-sale" rule was that, in both merger/consolidation and sale of assets transactions the critical decision—to participate in the merger or consolidation or to sell the assets of the corporation—was a corporate decision. The shareholder of the target was not "buying" shares of the acquiring corporation, but his stock was merely being converted as the result of an action taken by his corporation. Moreover, where the target was subject to the '34 Act, the solicitation of the proxies needed to approve the transaction was accompanied, under the proxy rules, by extensive disclosure similar to that which would have been contained in a '33 Act prospectus.

In the course of the merger wave of the late 1960's the Commission became aware of a number of anomalies resulting from the no-sale rule and observed the use of the rule to avoid the registration provisions of the '33 Act. As a consequence, in 1972 it rescinded Rule 133 and promulgated a new Rule 145, thereby essentially reversing its prior position.

Under Rule 145, the issuance of securities in a merger or consolidation or a sale of assets for stock is now treated as a "sale" requiring that the securities be registered under the '33 Act unless some exemption for the transaction is available. (The issuance of shares in a stock-for-stock exchange was always treated as a "sale" and continues to be.) The "sale" or "offer" is deemed to take place when the plan of the transaction is submitted to the shareholders of the target corporation for their approval. Where this involves a solicitation of proxies subject to Section 14 the communication sent to the shareholders is, therefore, both a '33 Act prospectus and a '34 Act proxy solicitation and is, in theory, subject to both sets of rules. In order to minimize the disclosure burdens involved, the Commission has established a Form S–14, designed particularly for merger or stock-for-asset exchanges, the disclosure requirements of which are somewhat less demanding than the ordinary '33 Act prospectus.

7. FEDERAL INCOME TAX CONSIDERATIONS

The federal income tax treatment of corporate reorganizations, which include the various transactions we have been discussing as well as recapitalizations and liquidations, is one of the most complex areas in the entire field of tax. Since, as is usually the case, however, tax considerations often play a substantial role in planning corporate combinations, it may be useful to sketch here the major outlines of ways the Internal Revenue Code deals with them.

The basic philosophy of the reorganization sections of the Code is that, to the extent possible, the tax laws should not influence the form in which businesses choose to carry on their operations. The effort of the drafters, therefore, was to permit reorganization transactions to be carried on without tax consequences, even though most of them involve some "sale or exchange" of assets that would ordinarily require the taxpayers—both the corporations involved and their shareholders—to recognize some gain or loss. Those reorganizations that qualify, therefore, are treated as "nonrecognition" transactions in which, in general, no gains or losses are realized for tax purposes. It is also necessary, however, for these gains (or losses) not to escape taxation altogether, otherwise it would be possible to avoid taxation by simply engaging periodically in some form of reorganization that qualified for nonrecognition treatment. As a corollary to nonrecognition, therefore, the Code provides, in effect, for deferral of the taxation of these gains through its treatment of the basis of the assets transferred in the reorganization. As a general rule the Code provides that the basis of such an asset is "carried over" in the transaction. The surviving corporation in a merger or consolidation holds the assets it receives in the transaction at the same basis those assets had in the hands of the transferor corporation (or corporations). Thus, although any appreciation in the value of those assets goes untaxed at the time of the transaction, it will eventually be taxed upon any subsequent transfer of the assets by the surviving corporation in a taxable transaction.

To illustrate, assume that the balance sheet of the acquired corporation looks like this:

ASSETS		LIABILITIES AND SHARE–HOLDERS' EQUITY	
Current Assets	$1000	Current Liabilities	$ 500
Fixed Assets	3000	Long-term Debt	2000
		Shareholders' Equity	1500
Total assets	$4000	Total	$4000

Now suppose that the acquiring corporation is willing to pay $5000 to acquire the assets of the acquired corporation ($1000 in excess of their book value). This $5000 is made up of $2500 worth of stock issued by the acquiring corporation and the assumption of all of the $2500 of liabilities owed by the acquired corporation. If the acquisition qualifies as a tax-free transaction, the assets transferred are held, for tax purposes, by the acquiring corporation at the same basis as they had in the hands of the acquired corporation: $1000 for current assets and $3000 for fixed assets. Moreover, even though the $1000 paid for the assets in excess of their basis would normally be taxable as a gain on the disposition of property, no tax is paid because the gain is not recognized. Should the acquiring corporation subsequently sell the assets for $5000, it would have to pay a tax on the $1000 "profit" from the sale, a profit that it has earned only in the eyes of the I.R.S.

By the same token, the shareholders of the corporations that are parties to a reorganization are in general deemed to hold any securities they receive as a result of the transaction at a basis equal in the securities they surrendered. Thus, although they, too, recognize no gain or loss in the transaction even though their original securities may have increased or decreased in value, the carryover of their basis to the new securities means that they will eventually be taxed (or be allowed to take whatever loss deductions they would be entitled to) on the change in value when they eventually dispose of the new securities.

To continue the illustration, assume that the acquired corporation has two equal shareholders, Able and Baker. Able originally paid $1000 for his stock; Baker paid $1500 for hers. In the acquisition transaction, each receives stock of the acquiring transaction worth $1250. Neither, however, recognizes any gain or loss on the exchange. And they hold the new stock at a basis equal to the stock they gave up. Thus if they each sell later for $1600, Able realizes a taxable gain of $600, and Baker a gain of $100.

Just as the Code provides for the carryover of the basis of assets transferred from one corporation to another, the transferee corporation also succeeds to certain other tax attributes of the transferor corporation in a merger, consolidation, or sale of assets. Since the acquired corporation remains in existence, continuing to hold its assets, in a stock-swap transaction, there is no need for special treatment of its tax attributes. The relevant provisions of the Code here are those providing for the filing of one consolidated return by a parent and its subsidiaries. The effect of these provisions on a stock-swap is quite similar to the effect of the carryover provisions on the transactions to which they apply.

It should be emphasized that this brief description greatly oversimplifies an extremely complex topic, and that, notwithstanding the Internal Revenue Code's underlying philosophy of "tax neutrality" toward reorganizations, it is impossible to plan such transactions without careful attention to their tax aspects.

C. REMEDIES FOR THE PROTECTION OF SHAREHOLDER

1. AT COMMON LAW

It was not always true that a merger or sale of assets could be accomplished by a majority (whether simple, absolute, or extraordinary) vote of the shareholders. In an earlier day the common law held that each shareholder has a vested right to continue as a participant in precisely that entity in which he or she has originally invested and that, as a consequence, any fundamental change in that corporation— amendment of the articles, merger, sale of assets, or dissolution— required the unanimous consent of all of the shareholders for its accomplishment.

In time, however, the concept of a corporation on which the premise of vested rights was founded, eroded. As corporations grew in size, the number of shareholders increased. Corporations were no longer composed of a small group of actively participating shareholders. A split developed between the shareholder whose relationship to the corporation was that of a passive investor and the larger, more active shareholders (as well as managers) who had a more personal stake in the enterprise. As the pace and complexity of economic growth accelerated and share ownership became increasingly dispersed, the dynamism of the corporation was more and more often threatened by the obstinacy of one or a few small shareholders who insisted on blocking changes that appeared desirable for the corporation.

The struggle to prevent the strangulation of corporate growth by this common law rule was cast first in constitutional form. A corporate charter, argued the proponents of the "vested rights" doctrine, was a contract between the state, the shareholders, and the corporation. This view was perhaps more plausible at a time when corporate charters were granted one by one by the legislature. Any modification of such a charter by act of the legislature was an unconstitutional impairment of the obligations of that contract. The issue was joined in Trustees of Dartmouth College v. Woodward, 17 U.S. (4 Wheat.) 518, 4 L.Ed. 629 (1819), in which the Supreme Court accepted that view, striking down a legislative amendment to the charter of Dartmouth College. The practical effect of the case on the operation of corporations proved, however, to be short-lived. Justice Story's concurring opinion suggested that by the simple device of reserving in the grant of the charter the right to amend it, the legislature could avoid any problems of impairment of contract should some alteration subsequently seem desirable. Thereafter it became standard practice to insert such a "reservation of powers" clause in virtually all corporate charters.

As the grant of special charters gave way to general incorporation statutes, states continued to make provision in the statutes for amendments, but now they began to provide for amendment by act of the corporation, as well as by act of the legislature. The vested rights doctrine was still to be dealt with, however. It was still open to the shareholders to argue that the "contract" to which they had become party by purchasing stock in a corporation could not be amended by some shareholders over the objection of others. The United States Supreme Court addressed the issue in Coombes v. Getz, 285 U.S. 434, 441–442, 52 S.Ct. 435, 436, 76 L.Ed. 866, 871 (1932):

> The authority of a state under the so-called reserve power is wide; but it is not unlimited. The corporate charter may be repealed or amended, and within limits not now necessary to define, the interrelation of the state, corporation, and stockholders may be changed; but neither vested property rights nor the obligation of contracts of third persons may be destroyed or impaired.

Eventually it became increasingly clear that the "vested rights" doctrine was unworkable and unnecessary. There was no clear answer to the question, "What rights are vested?" And the courts, with assistance from the legislatures and scholarly works began to view the problem from an altered perspective. The court in Dentel v. Fidelity Savings and Loan Association, 273 Or. 31, 539 P.2d 649, 651 (1975) commented:

> Some years ago when a court held that a right granted by the articles or bylaws could not be taken away by an amendment, the court stated that the right could not be taken because it was a "vested right," a "property right," or a "contract right." * * *

> The "vested rights" terminology has been attacked as being confusing and meaningless. * * * A corporation scholar has stated: " 'Vestedness' is the legal conclusion rather than the reason." Latty, Fairness—The Focal Point in Preferred Stock Arrearage Elimination, 29 Va.L.Rev. 1, 4 (1942). Section 58 of the Model Business Corporation Act has in essence, swept away the "vested rights" doctrine.[1] * * *

---

1. The comment to the Model Business Corporation Act states: "The broad power to amend conferred by the Model Act is intended to lay at rest the 'vested rights' doctrine * * *.

However, even with the decline of the "vested rights" approach, the courts have not held that a member of a corporation can be deprived, by amendment, of all rights created in the articles or bylaws. No definitive terminology has been developed. The courts and the writers have turned to the more indefinite tests of "fairness," "good faith," "reasonableness," and lack of "constructive fraud."

2. THE APPRAISAL REMEDY

a. Introduction

As the gradual transformation of the law from a doctrine of vested rights that permitted any shareholder to veto a transaction to a more flexible approach that permitted the holders of a majority of the shares to vary the terms of the contract unfolded, it became increasingly necessary to find some means to protect minority shareholders from the abuse the potential for which was clearly recognized from the beginning. One of the principal devices that emerged to serve this purpose was the appraisal remedy. Originally developed by the courts of equity, appraisal was ultimately assimilated into the statutory schemes of virtually all states. In Chicago Corp. v. Munds, 20 Del.Ch. 142, 149, 172 A. 452, 455 (1934), a Delaware court described this development as follows:

> At common law it was in the power of any single stockholder to prevent a merger. When the idea became generally accepted that, in the interest of adjusting corporate mechanisms to the requirements of business and commercial growth, mergers should be permitted in spite of the opposition of minorities, statutes were enacted in state after state which took from the individual stockholder the right theretofore existing to defeat the welding of his corporation with another. In compensation for the lost right a provision was written into the modern statutes giving the dissenting stockholder the option completely to retire from the enterprise and receive the value of his stock in money.

The appraisal remedy permits shareholders in a corporation that is undergoing some fundamental change to dissent from the transaction and insist on being paid in cash the value of their shares as determined by appraisal. The availability of the remedy varies from state to state. It is most often applicable in mergers, consolidations, or sales of all or substantially all of a corporation's assets. *See, e.g.,* MBCA § 80. It may also be available in certain recapitalizations. It is often unavailable to the shareholders of the parent corporation in a short-form merger. *E.g.,* MBCA § 80(c). Delaware excludes mergers for stock or sales of assets for stock where the stock in question

---

"One of the major purposes of the Model Act was to sweep aside the complexities of judicial decisions on vested rights which were increasingly handicap- ping the conduct of business through the corporate form. * * *." 2 Model Business Corporation Act Annotated (2d ed.), 225, § 58.

is listed on a national securities exchange on the theory that in those cases the ability to sell on the open market provides an adequate means of escape for the dissenting shareholder. Although the Model Act took more or less the same position, the Committee on Corporate Laws recently eliminated the exception for listed stock because, among other things, of a belief that the market does not always reflect the "true" or "fair" value of a stock. See Conard, Changes in the Model Business Corporation Act Affecting Dissenters' Rights, 32 Bus.Law. 1855 (1977). See also Buxbaum, The Dissenter's Appraisal Remedy, 23 U.C.L.A.L.Rev. 1229, 1247–48 (1976).

The procedural requirements to be followed before a shareholder may use the appraisal remedy also vary from jurisdiction to jurisdiction and are typically fairly complex. The statutes ordinarily require dissenters to give advance written notice of their intent to dissent, to refrain from voting in favor of the corporate action, to demand payment, and to tender their certificates. Shareholders generally lose their appraisal rights if the time periods and procedures are not strictly followed.

Contested appraisal proceedings can be lengthy. Pending the outcome of the proceedings, dissenters have no status as shareholders and do not receive any dividends although they may be entitled to interest on the value of their shares. *E.g.*, MBCA § 81(a)(4).

b. Valuation

As we have seen, there is no simple way to value property or corporate shares. The price a dissenting shareholder receives in an appraisal proceeding therefore, becomes the critical, yet perplexing, question. Statutes typically provide that the price paid shall equal the "fair value" of the shares. Under accumulated case law, appraisers determine "fair value" of the shares by using the market value corrected to eliminate the effect of the proposed change (assuming a trading market exists to provide a reliable estimate), capitalizing the past earnings using an appropriate multiplier to reflect the relative risks of the two enterprises, and valuing the corporation's assets (using "book value," "going-concern" value, or liquidating value as the measure). The corporation's pattern of dividend distributions may also be taken into account. A weight is assigned to each factor depending on the reliability of the data and its importance in each case. Application of Delaware Racing Association, 42 Del.Ch. 406, 213 A.2d 203 (1965). Asset value and earnings value usually receive the greatest weight; dividend value is used infrequently. In Francis I. duPont & Co. v. Universal City Studios, Inc., 312 A.2d 344 (Del.Ch. 1973), aff'd 334 A.2d 216 (Del.1975), the court weighed the asset values and earnings value, but disregarded market value as too speculative. In Swanton v. State Guaranty Corp., 42 Del.Ch. 477, 215 A.2d 242 (1965), the weights were as follows: asset value 60%; earnings value 30%;

market value 10%. *See* Note, Valuation of Dissenters, Stock under Appraisal Statutes, 79 Harv.L.Rev. 1453 (1966).

It must be noted that the appraiser's focus is usually retrospective. The court in Francis I. duPont & Co. v. Universal City Studios, *supra*, stated, "The determination must be based upon historical earnings rather than on the basis of prospective earnings." * (312 A.2d at 348) Del.Gen.Corp. Law § 262(f) specifically provides that the award shall be the "fair value [of the shares] exclusive of any element of value arising from the accomplishment or expectation of the merger." MBCA § 81(a)(3) defines the term "fair value". The comment to Section 81 indicates:

> The exception [for equitable considerations] is inserted to deal with "squeeze-out" situations in which the dissenter is excluded against his will from continued participation in the altered enterprise, by some method such as a "cash merger." In the more usual situation where the dissenter refuses to maintain a continuing interest in the altered enterprise, the general rule should prevail. The general rule does not of course, exclude consideration of appreciation or depreciation which might result from other corporate actions; these effects may be reflected either in market value or in the capitalization rate.**

c. Exclusivity of the Appraisal Remedy

Some statutes specify that the right to dissent and seek appraisal is the exclusive remedy available to shareholders who are dissatisfied with a fundamental change in the corporation.*** *E.g.*, Pa.Bus.Corp. L. § 1515(B)(K); Conn.Gen.Stat. § 33–373. *See* In re Jones & Laughlin Steel Corp., 263 Pa.Super. 378, 398 A.2d 186 (1979), aff'd 488 Pa. 524, 412 A.2d 1099 (1980) and Yanow v. Teal Industries, Inc., 178 Conn. 263, 422 A.2d 311 (1979). In the absence of an explicit statutory provision, the cases are in a state of some confusion as to whether, and under what circumstances, a shareholder may have another form of relief. *See generally*, Vorenberg, Exclusiveness of the Dissenting Stockholder's Appraisal Right, 77 Harv.L.Rev. 1189 (1964). It is clear that a shareholder can attack a merger as not authorized by the applicable statute, *e.g.*, Eisenberg v. Central Zone Property Corp., 306 N.Y. 58, 115 N.E.2d 652 (1953), as having been implemented without

---

* The multiple applied to the past earnings is usually considerably less than used in a commercial transaction.

** Conrad, Amendments of Model Business Corporation Act Affecting Dissenters' Rights (Sections 73, 74, 80 and 81), 33 Bus.Law. 2587, 2600–2601 (1978).

*** The California statute, § 1312 makes appraisal the exclusive remedy unless (1) two of the parties to a reorganization are affiliated with each other (as, for example, when a subsidiary is merged in-

to a parent corporation) thereby raising the possibility of self-dealing; (2) it is alleged that the shareholder vote approving the transaction was insufficient; or (3) it is alleged the reorganization violates a charter provision. The Model Act makes what it calls "cashout rights" (intentionally avoiding the term, "appraisal rights") exclusive "except when the corporate action is illegal or fraudulent with regard to the complaining shareholder or to the corporation." MBCA § 80(d).

the necessary procedural steps, *e.g.*, In re MacDonald, 205 App.Div. 579, 199 N.Y.S. 873 (2d Dept. 1923), or as resulting from fraud in the procurement of shareholder approval. On the other hand, older cases generally held that a shareholder whose sole complaint was that the terms of a merger or other fundamental change were "unfair" had no remedy other than appraisal. *E.g.*, Stauffer v. Standard Brands, Inc., 41 Del.Ch. 7, 187 A.2d 78 (1962); Blumenthal v. Roosevelt Hotel, Inc., 202 Misc. 988, 115 N.Y.S.2d 52 (1952).* But this rule seems not to apply in transactions in which there is an element of self-dealing that may raise questions of breach of fiduciary duty or in which "fraud" in its broadest sense can be alleged. In the much-discussed case, Singer v. Magnavox Co., set forth in Chapter 21, the Delaware Supreme Court held that in a merger designed to eliminate minority shareholders from future participation in the continuing entity, the fact that the dominant shareholder was on both sides of the transaction and was treated differently from the minority raised sufficient possibility of a breach of fiduciary duty that the minority were not limited to appraisal rights but could call on the court to scrutinize the fairness of the transaction.

Even in an arm's-length transaction it may be possible for a plaintiff to raise a successful challenge by proving that the treatment he received is so unfair as to constitute "constructive fraud." In Baron v. Pressed Metals of America, Inc., 35 Del.Ch. 581, 123 A.2d 848, 855 (1956) the court stated that, "When disparity is alleged between the value of the assets sold and the consideration received, plaintiff has the burden of showing such a gross disparity as will raise an inference of improper motives or reckless indifference to or intentional disregard of stockholders' interests." See also Gimbel v. Signal Companies set forth in Chapter 10, supra.

3. JUDICIAL RE-CASTING OF TRANSACTIONS: THE DE FACTO MERGER DOCTRINE

FARRIS v. GLEN ALDEN CORP.

393 Pa. 427, 143 A.2d 25 (1958).

COHEN, Justice.

We are required to determine on this appeal whether, as a result of a "Reorganization Agreement" executed by the officers of Glen Alden Corporation and List Industries Corporation, and approved by the shareholders of the former company, the rights and remedies of a dissenting shareholder accrue to the plaintiff.

Glen Alden is a Pennsylvania corporation engaged principally in the mining of anthracite coal and lately in the manufacture of air conditioning units and fire-fighting equipment. In recent years the company's operating revenue has declined substantially, and in fact, its

---

* *Blumenthal* has apparently been overruled by N.Y. BCL § 623 (k).

coal operations have resulted in tax loss carryovers of approximately $14,000,000. In October 1957, List, a Delaware holding company owning interests in motion picture theaters, textile companies and real estate, and to a lesser extent, in oil and gas operations, warehouses and aluminum piston manufacturing, purchased through a wholly owned subsidiary 38.5% of Glen Alden's outstanding stock.[1] This acquisition enabled List to place three of its directors on the Glen Alden board.

On March 20, 1958, the two corporations entered into a "reorganization agreement," subject to stockholder approval, which contemplated the following actions:

1.   Glen Alden is to acquire all of the assets of List, excepting a small amount of cash reserved for the payment of List's expenses in connection with the transaction. These assets include over $8,000,000 in cash held chiefly in the treasuries of List's wholly owned subsidiaries.

2.   In consideration of the transfer, Glen Alden is to issue 3,621,703 shares of stock to List. List in turn is to distribute the stock to its shareholders at a ratio of five shares of Glen Alden stock for each six shares of List stock. In order to accomplish the necessary distribution, Glen Alden is to increase the authorized number of its shares of capital stock from 2,500,000 shares to 7,500,000 shares without according pre-emptive rights to the present shareholders upon the issuance of any such shares.

3.   Further, Glen Alden is to assume all of List's liabilities including a $5,000,000 note incurred by List in order to purchase Glen Alden stock in 1957, outstanding stock options, incentive stock options plans, and pension obligations.

4.   Glen Alden is to change its corporate name from Glen Alden Corporation to List Alden Corporation.

5.   The present directors of both corporations are to become directors of List Alden.

6.   List is to be dissolved and List Alden is to then carry on the operations of both former corporations.

Two days after the agreement was executed notice of the annual meeting of Glen Alden to be held on April 11, 1958, was mailed to the shareholders together with a proxy statement analyzing the reorganization agreement and recommending its approval as well as approval of certain amendments to Glen Alden's articles of incorporation and bylaws necessary to implement the agreement. At this meeting the holders of a majority of the outstanding shares, (not including those owned by List), voted in favor of a resolution approving the reorganization agreement.

---

1. Of   the   purchase   price   of $8,719,109, $5,000,000 was borrowed.

On the day of the shareholders' meeting, plaintiff, a shareholder of Glen Alden, filed a complaint in equity against the corporation and its officers seeking to enjoin them temporarily until final hearing, and perpetually thereafter, from executing and carrying out the agreement.

The gravamen of the complaint was that the notice of the annual shareholders' meeting did not conform to the requirements of the Business Corporation Law, 15 P.S. § 2852–1 et seq., in three respects: (1) It did not give notice to the shareholders that the true intent and purpose of the meeting was to effect a merger or consolidation of Glen Alden and List; (2) It failed to give notice to the shareholders of their right to dissent to the plan of merger or consolidation and claim fair value for their shares, and (3) It did not contain copies of the text of certain sections of the Business Corporation Law as required.[3]

By reason of these omissions, plaintiff contended that the approval of the reorganization agreement by the shareholders at the annual meeting was invalid and unless the carrying out of the plan were enjoined, he would suffer irreparable loss by being deprived of substantial property rights.[4]

The defendants answered admitting the material allegations of fact in the complaint but denying that they gave rise to a cause of action because the transaction complained of was a purchase of corporate assets as to which shareholders had no rights of dissent or appraisal. For these reasons the defendants then moved for judgment on the pleadings.[5]

The court below concluded that the reorganization agreement entered into between the two corporations was a plan for a *de facto* merger, and that therefore the failure of the notice of the annual meeting to conform to the pertinent requirements of the merger provisions of the Business Corporation Law rendered the notice defective and all proceedings in furtherance of the agreement void. Wherefore, the court entered a final decree denying defendants' motion for judgment on the pleadings, entering judgment upon plaintiff's com-

---

3. The proxy statement included the following declaration: "Appraisal Rights.

"In the opinion of counsel, the shareholders of neither Glen Alden nor List Industries will have any rights of appraisal or similar rights of dissenters with respect to any matter to be acted upon at their respective meetings."

4. The complaint also set forth that the exchange of shares of Glen Alden's stock for those of List would constitute a violation of the pre-emptive rights of Glen Alden shareholders as established by the law of Pennsylvania at the time of Glen Alden's incorporation in 1917. The defendants answered that under both statute and prior common law no pre-emptive rights existed with respect to stock issued in exchange for property.

5. Counsel for the defendants concedes that if the corporation is required to pay the dissenting shareholders the appraised fair value of their shares, the resultant drain of cash would prevent Glen Alden from carrying out the agreement. On the other hand, plaintiff contends that if the shareholders had been told of their rights as dissenters, rather than specifically advised that they had no such rights, the resolution approving the reorganization agreement would have been defeated.

plaint and granting the injunctive relief therein sought. This appeal followed.

When use of the corporate form of business organization first became widespread, it was relatively easy for courts to define a "merger" or a "sale of assets" and to label a particular transaction as one or the other. But prompted by the desire to avoid the impact of adverse, and to obtain the benefits of favorable, government regulations, particularly federal tax laws, new accounting and legal techniques were developed by lawyers and accountants which interwove the elements characteristic of each, thereby creating hybrid forms of corporate amalgamation. Thus, it is no longer helpful to consider an individual transaction in the abstract and solely by reference to the various elements therein determine whether it is a "merger" or a "sale". Instead, to determine properly the nature of a corporate transaction, we must refer not only to all the provisions of the agreement, but also to the consequences of the transaction and to the purposes of the provisions of the corporation law said to be applicable. We shall apply this principle to the instant case.

Section 908, subd. A of the Pennsylvania Business Corporation Law provides: "If any shareholder of a domestic corporation which becomes a party to a plan of merger or consolidation shall object to such plan of merger or consolidation * * * such shareholder shall be entitled to * * * [the fair value of his shares upon surrender of the share certificate or certificates representing his shares]." Act of May 5, 1933, P.L. 364, as amended, 15 P.S. § 2852–908, subd. A.[6]

This provision had its origin in the early decision of this Court in Lauman v. Lebanon Valley R. R. Co., 1858, 30 Pa. 42. There a shareholder who objected to the consolidation of his company with another was held to have a right in the absence of statute to treat the consolidation as a dissolution of his company and to receive the value of his shares upon their surrender.

The rationale of the Lauman case, and of the present section of the Business Corporation Law based thereon, is that when a corporation combines with another so as to lose its essential nature and alter the original fundamental relationships of the shareholders among themselves and to the corporation, a shareholder who does not wish to continue his membership therein may treat his membership in the original corporation as terminated and have the value of his shares paid to him.

Does the combination outlined in the present "reorganization" agreement so fundamentally change the corporate character of Glen

---

6. Furthermore, section 902, subd. B provides that notice of the proposed merger and of the right to dissent thereto must be given the shareholders. "There shall be included in, or enclosed with * * * notice [of meeting of shareholders to vote on plan of merger] a copy or a summary of the plan of merger or plan of consolidation, as the case may be, and * * * a copy of subsection A of section 908 and of subsections B, C and D of section 515 of this act." Act of May 5, 1933, P.L. 364, § 902, subd. B, as amended, 15 P.S. § 2852–902, subd. B.

Alden and the interest of the plaintiff as a shareholder therein, that to refuse him the rights and remedies of a dissenting shareholder would in reality force him to give up his stock in one corporation and against his will accept shares in another? If so, the combination is a merger within the meaning of section 908, subd. A of the corporation law.

If the reorganization agreement were consummated plaintiff would find that the "List Alden" resulting from the amalgamation would be quite a different corporation than the "Glen Alden" in which he is now a shareholder. Instead of continuing primarily as a coal mining company, Glen Alden would be transformed, after amendment of its articles of incorporation, into a diversified holding company whose interests would range from motion picture theaters to textile companies[.] Plaintiff would find himself a member of a company with assets of $169,000,000 and a long-term debt of $38,000,000 in lieu of a company one-half that size and with but one-seventh the long-term debt.

While the administration of the operations and properties of Glen Alden as well as List would be in the hands of management common to both companies, since all executives of List would be retained in List Alden, the control of Glen Alden would pass to the directors of List; for List would hold eleven of the seventeen directorships on the new board of directors.

As an aftermath of the transaction plaintiff's proportionate interest in Glen Alden would have been reduced to only two-fifths of what it presently is because of the issuance of an additional 3,621,703 shares to List which would not be subject to pre-emptive rights. In fact, ownership of Glen Alden would pass to the stockholders of List who would hold 76.5% of the outstanding shares as compared with but 23.5% retained by the present Glen Alden shareholders.

Perhaps the most important consequence to the plaintiff, if he were denied the right to have his shares redeemed at their fair value, would be the serious financial loss suffered upon consummation of the agreement. While the present book value of his stock is $38 a share after combination it would be worth only $21 a share. In contrast, the shareholders of List who presently hold stock with a total book value of $33,000,000 or $7.50 a share, would receive stock with a book value of $76,000,000 or $21 a share.

Under these circumstances it may well be said that if the proposed combination is allowed to take place without right of dissent, plaintiff would have his stock in Glen Alden taken away from him and the stock of a new company thrust upon him in its place. He would be projected against his will into a new enterprise under terms not of his own choosing. It was to protect dissident shareholders against just such a result that this Court one hundred years ago in the Lauman case, and the legislature thereafter in section 908, subd. A, granted the right of dissent. And it is to accord that protection to the plaintiff that we conclude that the combination proposed in the case at hand is a merger within the intendment of section 908, subd. A.

Nevertheless, defendants contend that the 1957 amendments to sections 311 and 908 of the corporation law preclude us from reaching this result and require the entry of judgment in their favor. Subsection F of section 311 dealing with the voluntary transfer of corporate assets provides: "The shareholders of a business corporation which acquires by sale, lease or exchange all or substantially all of the property of another corporation by the issuance of stock, securities or otherwise shall not be entitled to the rights and remedies of dissenting shareholders * * * ."

And the amendment to section 908 reads as follows: "The right of dissenting shareholders * * * shall not apply to the purchase by a corporation of assets whether or not the consideration therefor be money or property, real or personal, including shares or bonds or other evidences of indebtedness of such corporation. The shareholders of such corporation shall have no right to dissent from any such purchase."

Defendants view these amendments as abridging the right of shareholders to dissent to a transaction between two corporations which involves a transfer of assets for a consideration even though the transfer has all the legal incidents of a merger. They claim that only if the merger is accomplished in accordance with the prescribed statutory procedure does the right of dissent accrue. In support of this position they cite to us the comment on the amendments by the Committee on Corporation Law of the Pennsylvania Bar Association, the committee which originally drafted these provisions. The comment states that the provisions were intended to overrule cases which granted shareholders the right to dissent to a sale of assets when accompanied by the legal incidents of a merger. See 61 Ann.Rep.Pa. Bar Ass'n 277, 284 (1957). Whatever may have been the intent of the *committee*, there is no evidence to indicate that the *legislature* intended the 1957 amendments to have the effect contended for. But furthermore, the language of these two provisions does not support the opinion of the committee and is inapt to achieve any such purpose. The amendments of 1957 do not provide that a transaction between two corporations which has the effect of a merger but which includes a transfer of assets for consideration is to be exempt from the protective provisions of sections 908, subd. A and 515. They provide only that the shareholders of a corporation which acquires the property or purchases the assets of another corporation, *without more*, are not entitled to the right to dissent from the transaction. So, as in the present case, when as part of a transaction between two corporations, one corporation dissolves, its liabilities are assumed by the survivor, its executives and directors take over the management and control of the survivor, and, as consideration for the transfer, its stockholders acquire a majority of the shares of stock of the survivor, then the transaction is no longer simply a purchase of assets or acquisition of property to which sections 311, subd. F and 908, subd. C apply, but a merger governed by section 908, subd. A of the corporation law. To divest shareholders of their right of dissent under such circumstances would require express language which is absent from the 1957 amendments.

Even were we to assume that the combination provided for in the reorganization agreement is a "sale of assets" to which section 908, subd. A does not apply, it would avail the defendants nothing; we will not blind our eyes to the realities of the transaction. Despite the designation of the parties and the form employed, Glen Alden does not in fact acquire List, rather, List acquires Glen Alden, cf. Metropolitan Edison Co. v. Commissioner, 3 Cir., 1938, 98 F.2d 807, affirmed sub nom., Helvering v. Metropolitan Edison Co., 1939, 306 U.S. 522, 59 S.Ct. 634, 83 L.Ed. 957, and under section 311, subd. D [8] the right of dissent would remain with the shareholders of Glen Alden.

We hold that the combination contemplated by the reorganization agreement, although consummated by contract rather than in accordance with the statutory procedure, is a merger within the protective purview of sections 908, subd. A and 515 of the corporation law. The shareholders of Glen Alden should have been notified accordingly and advised of their statutory rights of dissent and appraisal. The failure of the corporate officers to take these steps renders the stockholder approval of the agreement at the 1958 shareholders' meeting invalid. The lower court did not err in enjoining the officers and directors of Glen Alden from carrying out this agreement.

Decree affirmed at appellants' cost.

The real fight in *Farris* was over whether the plaintiff should have been given appraisal rights in the transaction. Although the court says little about it, the answer to that question seems logically to depend on an assessment of the appraisal remedy. In that regard, consider the following excerpt from a classic article on the subject:

MANNING, THE SHAREHOLDER'S APPRAISAL REMEDY:
AN ESSAY FOR FRANK COKER
72 Yale L.J. 223, 246–247 (1962).

[O]ne's history is a part of his present. Monuments often outlive the philosophies they were built to glorify. The pyramids are one example. The appraisal statutes are another. To the nine-

8. "If any shareholder of a business corporation which sells, leases or exchanges all or substantially all of its property and assets otherwise than (1) in the usual and regular course of its business, (2) for the purpose of relocating its business, or (3) in connection with its dissolution and liquidation, shall object to such sale, lease or exchange and comply with the provisions of section 515 of this act, such shareholder shall be entitled to the rights and remedies of dissenting shareholders as therein provided."

teenth century mind contemplating such matters, a corporate merger was a major and significant event. In the first place it involved a species of corporate assassination. A "corporation" died. A three-dimensional thing, created by the sovereign legislature, had passed away. These things were not matters to be taken casually. But something else happened, too. The shareholders of corporation A somehow became shareholders of corporation B and no longer shareholders of corporation A. The mere statement of such a preposterous proposition did violence to fundamental principles. How could a man who owned a horse suddenly find that he owned a cow? Furthermore—or perhaps this is but another statement of the same point—even if this transmutation could somehow be brought off, surely it could not constitutionally be done without the owner's consent. You might try to persuade him to sell his horse or to exchange it for a cow, but surely you could not whisk it away from him. Freedom of contract, rights of property, Constitution, law, and morals would forbid it, even if the *leger demain* for the conversion had been mastered. Given a nineteenth century view of freedom of contract this line of reasoning required only one premise: a "corporation" is just like a horse. The law of the last century had no doubt that it was. * * *

HARITON v. ARCO ELECTRONICS, INC.

40 Del. Ch. 326, 182 A.2d 22 (1962), aff'd
41 Del. Ch. 74, 188 A.2d 123 (1963).

SHORT, Vice Chancellor.

Plaintiff is a stockholder of defendant Arco Electronics, Inc., a Delaware corporation. The complaint challenges the validity of the purchase by Loral Electronics Corporation, a New York corporation, of all the assets of Arco. Two causes of action are asserted, namely (1) that the transaction is unfair to Arco stockholders, and (2) that the transaction constituted a de facto merger and is unlawful since the merger provisions of the Delaware law were not complied with.

* * *

Plaintiff now concedes that he is unable to sustain the charge of unfairness. The only issue before the court, therefore, is whether the transaction was by its nature a de facto merger with a consequent right of appraisal in plaintiff.

Prior to the transaction of which plaintiff complains Arco was principally engaged in the business of the wholesale distribution of components or parts for electronics and electrical equipment. It had outstanding 486,500 shares of Class A common stock and 362,500 shares of Class B common stock. The rights of the holders of the Class A and Class B common stock differed only as to preferences in dividends. Arco's balance sheet as of September 30, 1961 shows total assets of $3,013,642. Its net income for the preceding year was $273,466.

Loral was engaged, primarily, in the research, development and production of electronic equipment. Its balance sheet shows total assets of $16,453,479. Its net income for the year ending March 31, 1961 was $1,301,618.

In the summer of 1961 Arco commenced negotiations with Loral with a view to the purchase by Loral of all of the assets of Arco in exchange for shares of Loral common stock.   *   *   *   [A]n agreement for the purchase was entered into between Loral and Arco on October 27, 1961. This agreement provides, among other things, as follows:

1.   Arco will convey and transfer to Loral all of its assets and property of every kind, tangible and intangible; and will grant to Loral the use of its name and slogans.

2.   Loral will assume and pay all of Arco's debts and liabilities.

3.   Loral will issue to Arco 283,000 shares of its common stock.

4.   Upon the closing of the transaction Arco will dissolve and distribute to its shareholders, pro rata, the shares of the common stock of Loral.

5.   Arco will call a meeting of its stockholders to be held December 21, 1961 to authorize and approve the conveyance and delivery of all the assets of Arco to Loral.

6.   After the closing date Arco will not engage in any business or activity except as may be required to complete the liquidation and dissolution of Arco.

Pursuant to its undertaking in the agreement for purchase and sale Arco caused a special meeting of its stockholders to be called for December 27, 1961. The notice of such meeting set forth three specific purposes therefor: (1) to vote upon a proposal to ratify the agreement of purchase and sale, a copy of which was attached to the notice; (2) to vote upon a proposal to change the name of the corporation; and (3) if Proposals (1) and (2) should be adopted, to vote upon a proposal to liquidate and dissolve the corporation and to distribute the Loral shares to Arco shareholders. Proxies for this special meeting were not solicited. At the meeting 652,050 shares were voted in favor of the sale and none against. The proposals to change the name of the corporation and to dissolve it and distribute the Loral stock were also approved. The transaction was thereafter consummated.

Plaintiff contends that the transaction, though in form a sale of assets of Arco, is in substance and effect a merger, and that it is unlawful because the merger statute has not been complied with, thereby depriving plaintiff of his right of appraisal.

Defendant contends that since all the formalities of a sale of assets pursuant to 8 Del.C. § 271 have been complied with the transaction is in fact a sale of assets and not a merger. In this connection it is to be noted that plaintiffs nowhere allege or claim that defendant has not complied to the letter with the provisions of said section.

The question here presented is one which has not been heretofore passed upon by any court in this state. In Heilbrunn v. Sun Chemical Corporation, Del., 150 A.2d 755, the Supreme Court was called upon to determine whether or not a stockholder of the *purchasing* corporation could, in circumstances like those here presented, obtain relief on the theory of a de facto merger. The court held that relief was not available to such a stockholder.* It expressly observed that the question here presented was not before the court for determination. It pointed out also that while Delaware does not grant appraisal rights to a stockholder dissenting from a sale, citing Argenbright v. Phoenix Finance Co., 21 Del.Ch. 288, 187 A. 124, and Finch v. Warrior Cement Corp., 16 Del.Ch. 44, 141 A. 54, those cases are distinguishable from the facts here presented, "because dissolution of the seller and distribution of the stock of the purchaser were not required as a part of the sale in either case." In speaking of the form of the transaction the Supreme Court observes:

> The argument that the result of this transaction is substantially the same as the result that would have followed a merger may be readily accepted. As plaintiffs correctly say, the Ansbacher enterprise [seller] is continued in altered form as a part of Sun [purchaser]. This is ordinarily a typical characteristic of a merger. Sterling v. Mayflower Hotel Corp., 33 Del. 293, 303, 93 A.2d 107, 38 A.L.R.2d 425. Moreover the plan of reorganization *requires* the dissolution of Ansbacher and the distribution to its stockholders of the Sun stock received by it for the assets. As a part of the plan, the Ansbacher stockholders are compelled to receive Sun stock. From the viewpoint of Ansbacher, the result is the same as if Ansbacher had formally merged into Sun.

> This result is made possible, of course, by the overlapping scope of the merger statute and the statute authorizing the sale of

---

* In Heilbrunn v. Sun Chemical Corp., 38 Del.Ch. 321, 150 A.2d 755 (1959), two corporations agreed to a plan under which the larger one would purchase with stock all the assets of the much smaller enterprise and assume all of its liabilities; the selling corporation would then dissolve and distribute its assets (the acquiring corporation's stock) to its shareholders who would become shareholders of the acquiring corporation. A shareholder of the acquiring corporation attacked the plan as a de facto merger. The court held the plan valid. The de facto merger doctrine was inapplicable. The court stated: "[W]e fail to see how any injury has been inflicted upon the [stockholders of the purchasing corporation]. Their corporation has simply acquired property and paid for it in shares of stock. The business of [the purchasing corporation] will go on as before, with additional assets. The [stockholder of the purchasing corporation] is not forced to accept stock in another corporation. Nor has the reorganization changed the essential nature of the enterprise of the purchasing corporation, as in Farris * * *." (150 A.2d at 758)— Eds.

all the corporate assets. This possibility of overlapping was noticed in our opinion in the Mayflower case.

There is nothing new about such a result. For many years drafters of plans of corporate reorganization have increasingly resorted to the use of the sale-of-assets method in preference to the method by merger. Historically at least, there were reasons for this quite apart from the avoidance of the appraisal right given to stockholders dissenting from a merger.

Though it is said in the Heilbrunn case that the doctrine of de facto merger has been recognized in Delaware, it is to be noted that in each of the cases cited as recognizing the doctrine, namely, Drug, Inc. v. Hunt, 35 Del. 339, 168 A. 87 and Finch v. Warrior Cement Corp., supra, there was a failure to comply with the statute governing sale of assets. In both cases the sales agreement required delivery of the shares of the purchasing corporation to be made directly to the shareholders of the selling corporation. It was, of course, held in each case that no consideration passed to the selling corporation and that therefore the transaction did not constitute a sale of the assets of the selling corporation to the purchasing corporation. No such failure to comply with the provisions of the sale of assets statute is present in this case. On the contrary, as heretofore observed there was a literal compliance with the terms of the statute by this defendant.

The doctrine of de facto merger in comparable circumstances has been recognized and applied by the Pennsylvania courts, both state and federal, Lauman v. Lebanon Valley Railroad Co., 30 Pa. 42; Marks v. Autocar Co., D.C., 153 F.Supp. 768; Farris v. Glen Alden Corporation, 393 Pa. 427, 143 A.2d 25. * * * The Farris case demonstrates the length to which the Pennsylvania courts have gone in applying this principle. It was there applied in favor of a stockholder of the purchasing corporation, an application which our Supreme Court expressly rejected in Heilbrunn.

The right of appraisal accorded to a dissenting stockholder by the merger statutes is in compensation for the right which he had at common law to prevent a merger. Chicago Corporation v. Munds, 20 Del. Ch. 142, 172 A. 452. At common law a single dissenting stockholder could also prevent a sale of all of the assets of a corporation. The Legislatures of many states have seen fit to grant the appraisal right to a dissenting stockholder not only under the merger statutes but as well under the sale of assets statutes. Our Legislature has seen fit to expressly grant the appraisal right only under the merger statutes. This difference in treatment of the rights of dissenting stockholders may well have been deliberate, in order "to allow even greater freedom of action to corporate majorities in arranging combinations than is possible under the merger statutes." 72 Harv.L.Rev. 1132, "The Right of Shareholders Dissenting From Corporate Combinations To Demand Cash Payment For Their Shares."

While plaintiff's contention that the doctrine of de facto merger should be applied in the present circumstances is not without appeal, the subject is one which, in my opinion, is within the legislative domain. * * * The argument underlying the applicability of the doctrine of de facto merger, namely, that the stockholder is forced against his will to accept a new investment in an enterprise foreign to that of which he was a part has little pertinency. The right of the corporation to sell all of its assets for stock in another corporation was expressly accorded to Arco by § 271 of Title 8, Del.C. The stockholder was, in contemplation of law, aware of this right when he acquired his stock. He was also aware of the fact that the situation might develop whereby he would be ultimately forced to accept a new investment, as would have been the case here had the resolution authorizing dissolution followed consummation of the sale. * * *

There is authority in decisions of courts of this state for the proposition that the various sections of the Delaware Corporation Law conferring authority for corporate action are independent of each other and that a given result may be accomplished by proceeding under one section which is not possible, or is even forbidden under another. * * *

In a footnote to Judge Leahy's opinion [in Langfelder v. Universal Laboratories, 68 F.Supp. 209, 211 n. 5 (D.C.Del.1946), aff'd 163 F.2d 804 (3d Cir. 1947)] the following comment appears:

The text is but a particularization of the general theory of the Delaware Corporation Law that action taken pursuant to the authority of the various sections of that law constitute acts of independent legal significance and their validity is not dependent on other sections of the Act. Havender v. Federal United Corporation proves the correctness of this interpretation. Under Keller v. Wilson & Co. accrued dividends are regarded as matured rights and must be paid. But, this does not prevent a merger, good under the provisions of Sec. 59, from having the incidental effect of wiping out such dividend rights, i.e., Sec. 59 is complete in itself and is not dependent upon any other section, absent fraud. The same thing is true with most other sections of the Corporation Law.

The situation posed by the present case is even stronger than that presented in the Havender and [Hottenstein v.] York Ice cases. In those cases the court permitted the circumvention of matured rights by proceeding under the merger statute. Here, the stockholder has no rights unless another and independent statute is invoked to create a right. A holding in the stockholder's favor would be directly contrary to the theory of the cited cases.

I conclude that the transaction complained of was not a de facto merger, either in the sense that there was a failure to comply with one or more of the requirements of § 271 of the Delaware Corporation Law, or that the result accomplished was in effect a merger entitling plaintiff to a right of appraisal.

Defendant's motion for summary judgment is granted. Order on notice.

FOLK, DE FACTO MERGERS IN DELAWARE: HARITON v. ARCO ELECTRONICS, INC.

49 Va.L.Rev. 1261, 1280–81 (1963).

The basic premise implicitly adopted in *Hariton* may perhaps be stated more affirmatively. One does not invest in a unique corporate entity or even a particular business operation, but rather in a continuous course of business which changes over a long period of time. Certainly the best investments are growth investments— investments in enterprises which change with time, technology, business opportunities, and altered demand; and the worst investments are those which diminish in value because the type of business has lost importance and the corporation has been unable to adapt to the changed conditions. Although a shareholder's enthusiasm dwindles when an enterprise changes internally for the worst, no one suggests that he should have an option to compel the return of his investment. Viewed this way, the fact that the change—for better or for worse—comes through marriage, whether by merger or assets sale, seems purely incidental. The fact that the corporate entity in which one invested disappears as a result of a merger or of a sale of assets coupled with dissolution is also beside the point. One's investment may gain immortality when it takes a new form, i.e., a share in a successor enterprise.

M. EISENBERG, THE STRUCTURE OF THE CORPORATION 77–84 (1976).

The Place of Appraisal Rights in Closely Held Corporations

To understand the real utility—and perhaps the real origin—of the appraisal right, we must return once more to the partnership form. It will be recalled that absent contrary agreement, decisions on matters outside the scope of the partnership business can be made only by unanimous consent, new partners cannot be admitted without unanimous consent, and partnerships are normally short-lived and easy to dissolve. These various partnership incidents, although apparently disparate, are actually complementary. The veto power of each partner in matters outside the scope of the partnership business seriously restricts his copartners' freedom of action to make changes in the business that seem to them desirable and even necessary to meet changing conditions. This restriction might be intolerable except for the fact that each partner has agreed to the identity of his fellow veto-bearers, and that the timespan of such a veto is ordinarily short, since the remaining partners can either dissolve the partnership or await the end of its term and then reconstitute the enterprise along the desired lines.

But neither of the conditions making a veto tolerable in the partnership is normally present in the corporation: absent contrary agreement, the identity of fellow shareholders is not within a shareholder's control, and the duration of the enterprise is normally perpetual. Given those elements it is predictable that corporate law would permit a majority, or at least a high majority, to make structural changes even over the objection of minority shareholders. But just as a veto power might be intolerable in a corporation, so might be an unrestricted power in the majority to make structural changes, unless some method was provided whereby minority shareholders would not be locked into the restructured enterprise over their objections. The minority, in other words, should have the right to say to the majority, "We recognize your right to restructure the enterprise, provided you are willing to buy us out at a fair price if we object, so that we are not forced to participate in an enterprise other than the one contemplated at the outset of our mutual association." Seen from this perspective, the appraisal right is a mechanism admirably suited to reconcile, in the corporate context, the need to give the majority the right to make drastic changes in the enterprise to meet new conditions as they arise, with the need to protect the minority against being involuntarily dragged along into a drastically restructured enterprise in which it has no confidence.

This rationale does not explain all the legislative variations in appraisal rights, but it explains a good many. * * * It explains why a sale of substantially all assets usually triggers appraisal rights: the transaction invariably involves a complete restructuring of the nature of the seller's business (unless it is in the ordinary course of business, in which case it would not ordinarily trigger appraisal rights). Finally, it explains why dissolution does not trigger appraisal rights: in a dissolution everybody is getting out, and the minority shareholder does not need the protection of a mechanism which is designed to protect him against being locked into a restructured enterprise.

* * *

The Place of Appraisal Rights in Publicly Held Corporations

A shareholder in a closely held corporation ordinarily cannot withdrawn from the enterprise in response to a structural change unless he has an appraisal right: there will normally be no market for his shares. In contrast, a shareholder in a publicly held corporation normally can withdraw by selling his shares on the market. The need of such shareholders for an appraisal right is therefore certainly less compelling. Furthermore, the expectations of many shareholders in publicly held corporations undoubtedly revolve around the market rather than the enterprise. Is the appraisal right therefore unnecessary in the case of publicly held corporations?

* * * While it is true that many shareholders in publicly-held corporations are market-oriented, it has already been seen that many others are likely to own an amount of stock sufficient to orient their expectations around the long-term prospects of the enterprise rather than around a market which tends to fluctuate severely over any given short-run period. It may be questioned whether such shareholders should be remitted to the market to find relief from structural changes to which they object, unless the market to which they are remitted is not only continuous and deep, but is likely to reflect fairly the value of the enterprise. It seems clear, however, that the stock markets as presently constituted do not serve that function. As the Delaware Chancery court itself has pointed out:

> When it is said that the appraisal which the market puts upon the value of the stock of an active corporation as evidenced by its daily quotations, is an accurate, fair reflection of its intrinsic value, no more than a moment's reflection is needed to refute it. There are too many accidental circumstances entering into the making of market prices to admit them as sure and exclusive reflectors of fair value. The experience of recent years is enough to convince the most casual observer that the market in its appraisal of values must have been woefully wrong in its estimates at one time or another within the interval of a space of time so brief that fundamental conditions could not possibly have become so altered as to affect true worth. Markets are known to gyrate in a single day. The numerous causes that contribute to their nervous leaps from dejected melancholy to exhilarated enthusiasm and then back again from joy to grief, need not be reviewed. * * * Even when conditions are normal and no economic forces are at work unduly to exalt or depress the financial hopes of man, market quotations are not safe to accept as unerring expressions of value.[31]

That was written in 1934, but things have not changed much, in this regard, since then. To give a random illustration, Table 7–1 shows the highs and lows for the first ten common stocks, alphabetically, on the New York Stock Exchange, in 1974. Another example, also random—the first ten common stocks for the first eight months of 1968—is given in Table 7–2.

When fluctuations like these occur within a twelve-month or even eight-month period, it seems arbitrary, to say the least, to remit an enterprise-oriented shareholder to the market for relief.

Furthermore, even assuming that a market fairly reflects the value of stock in its normal operation, remitting a dissenting shareholder to the market will fail to adequately protect him where (1) his

31. Chicago Corp. v. Munds, 20 Del. Ch. 143, 150–151, 172 A. 452, 455 (Ch. 1934).

Table 7–1 *

Corporation	High	Low
Abbt Lb	61–1/4	30–1/2
ACF In	61–1/4	28–3/4
Acme Clev	14–5/8	7
Adm Dg	5–5/8	1–3/8
Adm E	13–1/4	7–3/8
Ad Mill	5–1/4	1–3/4
Addres	11–3/4	3
Adv Inv.	11–7/8	6–1/2
Aetna Lf.	31	15–1/8
Aquirre Co.	9–1/8	4–3/8

* N.Y. Times, Jan. 5, 1974, § 3, at 50, col. 3.

Table 7–2 *

Corporation	High	Low
Abacus	17–3/4	15–1/2
Abbott Lab	66–7/8	41–7/8
Abex Co.	42–1/8	28
ACF Ind.	68–3/8	39–1/2
Acme Mkt.	44	36
Adam Ex.	18–7/8	16
Ad Millis	30–5/8	18–3/4
Address	91–1/2	52
Admiral	25–1/8	16–1/2
Aeroquip	77	47–1/4

* N.Y. Times, Sept. 4, 1968, at 60, col. 2.

block is so large that the mere act of selling the block will depress the market—and it has already been seen that large blocks are common even in stocks listed on the New York Stock Exchange; (2) the very effect of the structural change is to depress the market price of the stock because the change is an ill-considered one; or (3) so many shareholders want to opt out that the market is flooded with sell orders.

A final problem with eliminating appraisal rights in publicly held corporations is that in such corporations the appraisal right not only serves the function of permitting shareholders to withdraw under certain circumstances at a fair price, but also serves as a check on management. Granted that a certain proportion of shareholders in publicly held corporations will vote in favor of any management proposal, no matter how ill-conceived, and granted that management is not necessarily either highly skilled or disinterested in the making of structural changes, it may be appropriate to structure the decisionmaking process in publicly held corporations so that something more than a majority—or even a two-thirds majority—is needed to carry a structural decision. As Professor Folk has pointed out:

> [I]t is important to maintain some internal or external control to offset the power of the directors, unless one assumes that directors, especially when backed by a shareholder majority, should have unrestrained discretion. Appraisal rights * * * have, in the past, served as a countervailing power to force the insiders to tailor their plans to minimize the number of dissenters by getting the best deal possible. A high vote requirement (including a class vote) plays the same sort of role. When either weapon is removed, the insiders lack the real self-interest to fashion a plan acceptable to a sufficient number of shareholders.[34]

It has already been seen that the appraisal right presents many difficulties from the shareholder's perspective: it is always technical; it may be expensive; it is uncertain in result; in the case of a publicly held corporation, is unlikely to produce a better result than could have been obtained on the market; and the ultimate award is taxable. It is, in short, a remedy of desperation. Generally speaking, no shareholder in a publicly held corporation will invoke the appraisal right unless he feels that the structural change from which he dissents is shockingly improvident and that the fair value of his shares before the change will far exceed the value of his shares thereafter. But may not the existence of just such a right—a switch which will be pulled only in case of emergency—be desirable in connection with transactions of the utmost gravity, in which self-interest and lack of financial skills may seriously obscure management's vision? While it would not be irrational to eliminate appraisal rights as to shares which are traded under conditions which are likely to insure the existence of a continuous and relatively deep market, it therefore seems more advisable to retain the appraisal right even in such cases, partly to protect the fair expectations of those shareholders whose legitimate expectations center on the enterprise rather than on the market, and partly to serve as a check on self-interested and unwise structural changes.

4. REMEDIES FOR THE PROTECTION OF CREDITORS

In a stock for assets transition, the acquiring corporation, on the theory that it is purchasing assets, only assumes those liabilities of the acquired corporation it selects. In Knapp v. North American Rockwell Corp., 506 F.2d 361, 363–364 (3d Cir. 1974), cert. denied 421 U.S. 965, 95 S.Ct. 1955, 44 L.Ed.2d 452 (1975), the court stated:

> The general rule is that "a mere sale of corporate property by one company to another does not make the purchaser liable for the

---

34. Folk, De Facto Mergers in Delaware: Hariton v. Arco Electronics, Inc., 49 Va.L.Rev. 1261, 1293 (1963).

liabilities of the seller not assumed by it." * * * There are, however, certain exceptions to this rule. Liability for obligations of a selling corporation may be imposed on the purchasing corporation when (1) the purchaser expressly or impliedly agrees to assume such obligations; (2) the transaction amounts to a consolidation or merger of the selling corporation with or into the purchasing corporation; (3) the purchasing corporation is merely a continuation of the selling corporation; or (4) the transaction is entered into fraudulently to escape liability for such obligations.

Under the second and third exceptions, many courts have imposed liability on the acquiring corporation a stock for assets transaction under the de facto merger doctrine.

For a further development of this trend, see Ramirez v. Amsted Industries, Inc., 171 N.J.Super. 261, 408 A.2d 818 (1979). In that case the power press that injured the plaintiff in 1975 had been manufactured in 1948 or 1949 by one corporation, which sold all of its assets to a second corporation in 1956, surviving only as a shell. The second corporation in turn sold its assets to the defendant in 1962, the contract of sale evidencing an intention for the purchaser to avoid assuming any product liabilities of the seller. Finding a "recent trend towards imposing liability where the successor continues the predecessor's product line and manufacturing operations * * *", the court explicitly rejected the traditional corporate law analysis in favor of the "social desirability of spreading the risk of defective products at the expense of the marketing enterprise which is supposedly better equipped to absorb the sting of unexpected injuries and damages." 408 A.2d at 823.

Consider the effect of statutes such as MBCA § 105. Which way should such a statute cut if the transferor corporation dissolves shortly after the sale of all of its assets? If it quickly distributes the consideration (stock) received in the sale to its shareholders as a dividend but remains in existence as a shell? Is it possible for the acquiring corporation to minimize its exposure to claims such as those in *Ramirez* by adjusting the structure of the transaction?

For a contrasting view see Leannais v. Cincinnati, Inc., 565 F.2d 437 (7th Cir. 1977).

D. OTHER FORMS OF ORGANIC CHANGE: RECAPITALIZATION

PROBLEM

PRODUCTION, INC.—PART II

Assume Production, Inc. also has outstanding 180,000 shares of cumulative preferred stock with a par value of $100. The $10 pre-

INTRODUCTION TO ORGANIC CHANGE   Ch. 20

ferred dividend has been skipped for the past two years. The arrearages equal $3,600,000. The preferred stock is presently traded at about $50 per share.

Production's most recent consolidated balance sheet can be summarized as follows:

ASSETS		LIABILITIES AND SHAREHOLDERS' EQUITY	
Current assets	$ 15,000,000	Current liabilities	$ 7,000,000
Fixed assets	110,000,000	Long term debt	44,000,000
		Total liabilities	51,000,000
Total assets	$125,000,000	Shareholders' equity	
		Stated capital	
		Common stock	$50,000,000
		Preferred stock	18,000,000
		Earned surplus	6,000,000
		Total shareholders' equity	74,000,000
		Total liabilities and shareholders' equity	$125,000,000

During the preliminary negotiations Faraday and Walters have tentatively agreed on an exchange ratio of eight shares of Production common or 1.5 shares of preferred stock for each share of common stock of Electronica.

The parties would like, if possible, to simplify the capital structure of whatever corporation or corporations survive the transaction by doing away with the Production preferred. At the least they would like to rid themselves of the obligation represented by the $3.6 million in accrued dividends.

Could the transaction be accomplished in such a way as to eliminate (1) the preferred stock of Production and (2) the accrued dividends on that stock?

1. INTRODUCTION

A corporation with substantial arrearages in dividends on preferred stock may be unable to pay these dividends now and in the future. The corporation seeks by a recapitalization, that is, a material adjustment in the rights of the preferred stock, to eliminate the accrued preferred dividends. As a business matter, this may be very desirable for the corporation as a whole, particularly if it needs to raise new capital. The arrearages block the payment of dividends to the common shareholders in the face of prior claim of the preferred shareholders. Whether the recapitalization is in the interest of the preferred shareholders depends on what they receive in exchange for giving up the dividends, and sometimes their preferred shares. Two techniques were and are used: (1) direct amendment to the articles of incorporation; (2) merger as an indirect means.

2. DIRECT TECHNIQUE: AMENDMENT OF ARTICLES

Modern statutes explicitly state a corporation may amend its articles to eliminate preferred dividend arrearages. *See e.g.* MBCA § 58 (k). Amendments to the articles that would cancel accrued dividends must be approved by the preferred shareholders, even if they cannot otherwise vote. MBCA § 60. An amendment gives rise to appraisal rights if it adversely affects a shareholder's interest, *e.g.*, by altering or abolishing a preference right. MBCA § 80(a)(4).

What if the corporation was organized before the enactment of the statute authorizing the amendment? Can the statute be applied retroactively? In McNulty v. W. & J. Sloane, 184 Misc. 835, 54 N.Y. S.2d 253 (1945), the court was asked to rule that the elimination of accrued preferred dividends under a New York statute that specifically authorized such recapitalizations by amendment to the corporation's articles of incorporation amounted to an unconstitutional taking of property without due process of law. In upholding the statute, the court stated the problem as follows:

> The importance of this problem from a legal, a financial and an economic standpoint is reflected in the many scholarly articles in law reviews in recent years concerning it. The courts have realized that the problem was a knotty one and that it involved important questions of public policy. On the one hand, there was the interest of the state, in the welfare of corporations organized under its sanction, in permitting them a certain flexibility in their capital structure to meet business and financial needs; on the other hand there was the concern to protect the rights of small investors, chargeable with an unrealistic, constructive knowledge of the "reserved power" of the Legislature.

> There was the possibility of improper domination by large stockholders to be weighed against the power of a small stockholder to force the majority to buy his stock at exorbitant prices and to threaten to use his voting rights in such a way as to injure the business of the corporation and thus impair the rights of others. There was the necessity for allowing financial rejuvenation and at the same time there was the realization that there might result the possible enrichment of a junior class of stockholders at the expense of a senior class. In short, the problem was one of balancing intertwining and conflicting interests and of determining what was conducive to the good of society. Such a problem, involving as it does, questions of sound public policy, is primarily for the Legislature and not for the courts.

> With the wisdom of legislation permitting the abolition of accrued cumulative but undeclared dividends the court can have no concern. That is the province of the law-maker and we cannot say that there is not reasonable basis for the law that was passed.

Differences of opinion there may reasonably exist as to whether the legislation, in the form in which it was enacted, is adequate for the purpose sought to be accomplished or whether there are sufficient safeguards surrounding a measure so fraught with danger and so susceptible to abuse. Some may say that supervision should have been given to an administrative agency; others that prior judicial approval should have been required; but these likewise are matters of legislative rather than judicial concern. The Legislature sought to guard against possible evil consequences by requiring a sufficient notice to stockholders, and a vote by the holders of record of two-thirds of the outstanding shares of each class of stock and by giving dissenting stockholders the right to an appraisal of their holdings and payment for them in case. There also exists the inherent power of a court of equity, a power limited generally to the test of good faith rather than a test objective in character, a power the exercise of which may be circumscribed, because too often what is an accomplished fact is presented to the court; but it is a significant, restraining influence nevertheless.*

The next question is, may a shareholder challenge a recapitalization for unfairness. In Barrett v. Denver Tramway Corp., 53 F.Supp. 198 (D.Del.1943), aff'd 146 F.2d 701 (3d Cir. 1944), the corporation proposed to eliminate its accumulated preferred dividends by creating the new preferred, with no arrearages but with preferences superior to the old preferred, which would be offered in exchange for the old preferred stock. In concluding that the recapitalization was objectively unfair, but could not be enjoined the court stated:

> * * * [U]nder Delaware law, where required statutory majorities have the right to take action looking to reclassification or re-

---

* In contrast, the court in Keller v. Wilson & Co., 21 Del.Ch. 391, 190 A. 115, 124–125 (1936), found an arrearage to be like a tangible property right, stating:

It may be conceded, as a general proposition, that the State, as a matter of public policy, is concerned in the welfare of its corporate creatures to the end that they may have reasonable powers wherewith to advance their interests by permitting adequate financing. It may also be conceded that there has been an increasing departure from the conception which formerly prevailed when the right of individual veto in matters of corporate government operated as a dangerous obstruction to proper functioning. But in determining whether the rights of the complainants herein are such as ought to be regarded as property rights, all aspects of the question must be considered to ascertain what is conducive to the best interests of society. The State is concerned also with the welfare of those who invest their money, the very essence of generation, in corporate enterprises. Some measure of protection should be accorded them. While many interrelations of the State, the corporation, and the shareholders may be changed, there is a limit beyond which the State may not go. Property rights may not be destroyed; and when the nature and character of the right of a holder of cumulative preferred stock to unpaid dividends, which have accrued thereon through passage of time, is examined in a case where that right was accorded protection when the corporation was formed and the stock was issued, a just public policy, which seeks the equal and impartial protection of the interests of all, demands that the right be regarded as a vested right of property secured against destruction by the Federal and State Constitutions.

arrangement of stockholders' rights, a presumption arises of bona fides of purpose with a resultant burden on dissidents to prove that the action taken is so palpably unfair as to amount to constructive fraud. The most recent announcement from the Delaware courts declares that "When fraud of this nature is charged, the unfairness must be of such character and must be so clearly demonstrated as to impel the conclusion that it emanates from acts of bad faith, or a reckless indifference to the rights of others interested, rather than from an honest error of judgment." [Porges v. Vadsco Sales Corp., 27 Del.Ch. 127, 32 A.2d 148, 151 (Ch. 1943)] * * * The proof in the case at bar clearly indicates that no such fraud has been practiced by management and the majority stockholders * * *. * * *

If a federal court is free to indulge an independent view of what constitutes unfairness * * * then I conclude the present plan is unfair to the preferred stockholders. * * * [W]here a plan of reclassification fails to call on the junior stock to contribute pari passu with the preferred stock, especially where the junior shares have no present equity but merely a hope for asset appreciation and increased earnings, I fail to see, in the fact of objection, why a state or federal jural dichotomy should sit idly by and sentence preferred shares to make the exclusive contribution when all rights should be whittled proportionately. Regardless of fraud and bad-faith questions, I believe it inequitable to allow the lower class to benefit to the detriment of the higher, in view of the traditional contract between preferred and common stockholders.

* * *

An independent examination of the plan shows the way will be clear for the payment of dividends on all classes of stock provided the present rate of earnings continues. This substantially benefits the common stock. Under defendant's capital structure, common has no value where the cumulative dividend arrearage charge is in the amount of $7,295,788.50. This item must be paid before common can receive anything. * * * [Under the plan,] [e]xisting preferred [would] lose the right to be paid any of its accumulated dividends out of current earnings until after the dividend requirements of the new preferred are met in full. The loss of such right is substantial in the face of the fact that present rate of earnings is large enough to permit a payment on account of accumulated dividends. Preferred is accorded no compensation for the surrender of this right. If defendant fails to operate at a profit in the future, which seems probable, preferred will have suffered a detriment for it would not only have failed to receive the dividends which the abnormal earnings might have justified, but it is also possible that part of the earnings may have been dissipated in the form of dividends to the common stock.

* * *

* * * [W]hile one may detect a faint intimation from the Porges case that a plan which exclusively promotes the interest of one class of stock to the detriment of another would be held unfair by the Delaware courts, after applying the Erie R. Co. v. Tompkins litmus paper, I cannot truly say that such intimation gleaned from the particular facts of Porges is sufficient to sustain a conclusion that the Delaware courts have abandoned and no longer insist, in order to find unfairness, upon the presence of "constructive fraud," "bad faith," or "gross unfairness." * * *

New Jersey courts, on the other hand, have freely granted relief on grounds of unfairness. *See e.g.* Kamena v. Janssen Dairy Corp., 133 N.J.Eq. 214, 31 A.2d 200 (Ch. 1943), aff'd without opinion 134 N.J. Eq. 359, 35 A.2d 894 (1944).

3. INDIRECT TECHNIQUES: MERGER

Alternatively, a merger may be used to revamp the capital structure of the surviving corporation, *e.g.*, cancel its accrued preferred dividends. Typically, a preferred shareholder must approve a merger which cancels accrued dividends, if they are not otherwise entitled to vote. MBCA § 73, but compare Del. GCL § 251.

BOVE v. COMMUNITY HOTEL CORP. OF NEWPORT, RHODE ISLAND

105 R.I. 136, 249 A.2d 89 (1969).

JOSLIN, Justice.

This civil action was brought * * * to enjoin a proposed merger of The Community Hotel Corporation of Newport, Rhode Island, [Community Hotel] a defendant herein, into Newport Hotel Corp., [Newport]. Both corporations were organized under the general corporation law of this state * * *. The case is here on the plaintiffs' appeal from a judgment denying injunctive relief and dismissing the action.

Community Hotel was incorporated on October 21, 1924, for the stated purpose of erecting, maintaining, operating, managing and leasing hotels; and it commenced operations in 1927 with the opening of the Viking Hotel in Newport. Its authorized capital stock consists of 6,000 shares of $100 par value six per cent prior preference cumulative preferred stock, and 6,000 shares of no par common stock of which 2,106 shares are issued and outstanding. The plaintiffs as well as the individual defendants are holders and owners of preferred stock, plaintiffs having acquired their holdings of approximately 900 shares not later than 1930. At the time this suit was commenced, dividends on the 4,335 then-issued and outstanding preferred shares had accrued, but had not been declared, for approximately 24 years, and totalled about $645,000 or $148.75 per share.

Newport was organized at the instance and request of the board of directors of Community Hotel solely for the purpose of effectuating the merger which is the subject matter of this action. Its authorized capital stock consists of 80,000 shares of common stock, par value $1.00, of which only one share has been issued, and that to Community Hotel for a consideration of $10.

The essentials of the merger plan call for Community Hotel to merge into Newport, which will then become the surviving corporation. Although previously without assets, Newport will, if the contemplated merger is effectuated, acquire the sole ownership of all the property and assets now owned by Community Hotel. The plan also calls for the outstanding shares of Community Hotel's capital stock to be converted into shares of the capital stock of Newport upon the following basis: Each outstanding share of the constituent corporation's preferred stock, together with all accrued dividends thereon, will be changed and converted into five shares of the $1.00 par value common stock of the surviving corporation; and each share of the constituent corporation's no par common stock will be changed and converted into one share of the common stock, $1.00 par value, of the surviving corporation.

Consistent with the requirements of G.L. 1956, § 7–5–3,[1] the merger will become effective only if the plan receives the affirmative votes of the stockholders of each of the corporations representing at least two-thirds of the shares of each class of its capital stock. For the purpose of obtaining the required approval, notice was given to both common and preferred stockholders of Community Hotel that a special meeting would be held for the purpose of considering and voting upon the proposed merger. Before the scheduled meeting date arrived, this action was commenced and the meeting was postponed to a future time and place. So far as the record before us indicates, it has not yet been held.

The plaintiffs argue that the primary, and indeed, the only purpose of the proposed merger is to eliminate the priorities of the preferred stock with less than the unanimous consent of its holders. Assuming that premise, a preliminary matter for our consideration

---

1. Section 7–5–3 in pertinent part provides:

Said agreement shall be submitted to the stockholders of each constituent corporation at a meeting thereof called separately for the purpose of taking the same into consideration. * * * At said meeting said agreement shall be considered and the stockholders of said corporation shall vote by ballot, in person or by proxy, for the adoption or rejection of the said agreement, each share entitling the holder thereof to one (1) vote, and if the votes of the stockholders of each such corporation representing at least two-thirds of the shares of each class of its capital stock shall be for the adoption of said agreement * * * the agreement so adopted and certified * * * shall thence be taken and deemed to be the agreement and act of consolidation or merger of said corporations * * *.

concerns the merger of a parent corporation into a wholly-owned subsidiary created for the sole purpose of achieving a recapitalization
which will eliminate the parent's preferred stock and the dividends
accumulated thereon, and whether such a merger qualifies within the
contemplation of the statute permitting any two or more corporations
to merge into a single corporation.

It is true, of course, that to accomplish the proposed recapitalization by amending Community Hotel's articles of association under relevant provisions of the general corporation law [2] would require the
unanimous vote of the preferred shareholders, whereas under the
merger statute, only a two-third vote of those stockholders will be
needed. Concededly, unanimity of the preferred stockholders is un-
obtainable in this case, and plaintiffs argue, therefore, that to permit
the less restrictive provisions of the merger statute to be used to accomplish indirectly what otherwise would be incapable of being accomplished directly by the more stringent amendment procedures of
the general corporation law is tantamount to sanctioning a circumvention or perversion of that law.

The question, however, is not whether recapitalization by the
merger route is a subterfuge, but whether a merger which is designed for the sole purpose of cancelling the rights of preferred
stockholders with the consent of less than all has been authorized by
the legislature. The controlling statute is § 7–5–2. Its language is
clear, all-embracing and unqualified. It authorizes any two or more
business corporations *which were or might have been organized* under the general corporation law to merge into a single corporation;
and it provides that the merger agreement shall prescribe " *   *   *
the terms and conditions of consolidation or merger, the mode of carrying the same into effect   *   *   * *as well as the manner of converting the shares of each of the constituent corporations into
shares or other securities of the corporation resulting from or surviving such consolidation or merger,* with such other details and
provisions as are deemed necessary." [3] (italics ours) Nothing in that
language even suggests that the legislature intended to make *underlying purpose* a standard for determining permissibility. Indeed, the
contrary is apparent since the very breadth of the language selected

---

2. Section 7–2–18, as amended, provides that a corporation may " *   *   *
from time to time when and as desired
amend its articles of association
*   *   *" and § 7–2–19, as amended,
provides that "Unless otherwise provided
in the articles of association, every such
amendment shall require the affirmative
vote of the following proportion of the
stockholders, passed at a meeting duly
called for the purpose:

"(a) *   *   *

"(b) Where the amendment diminish-
es the stipulated rate of dividends on

any class of stock or the stipulated
amount to be paid thereon in case of
call or liquidation, the unanimous vote
of the stockholders of such class and
the vote of a majority in interest of all
other stockholders entitled to vote."

3. The quoted provision is substantially identical to the Delaware merger statute (Del.Rev.Code (1935) C. 65, § 2091)
construed in Federal United Corp. v.
Havender, 24 Del.Ch. 318, 11 A.2d 331.

presupposes a complete lack of concern with whether the merger is designed to further the mutual interests of two existing and nonaffiliated corporations or whether alternatively it is purposed solely upon effecting a substantial change in an existing corporation's capital structure.

Moreover, that a possible effect of corporate action under the merger statute is not possible, or is even forbidden, under another section of the general corporation law is of no import, it being settled that the several sections of that law may have independent legal significance, and that the validity of corporate action taken pursuant to one section is not necessarily dependent upon its being valid under another. Hariton v. Arco Electronics, Inc., 40 Del.Ch. 326, 182 A.2d 22, aff'd, 41 Del.Ch. 74, 188 A.2d 123; Langfelder v. Universal Laboratories Inc., D.C., 68 F.Supp. 209, aff'd, 3 Cir., 163 F.2d 804.

We hold, therefore, that nothing within the purview of our statute forbids a merger between a parent and a subsidiary corporation even under circumstances where the merger device has been resorted to solely for the purpose of obviating the necessity for the unanimous vote which would otherwise be required in order to cancel the priorities of preferred shareholders. Federal United Corp. v. Havender, supra; Hottenstein v. York Ice Machinery Corp., 3 Cir., 136 F.2d 944.

A more basic problem narrowed so as to bring it within the factual context of this case, is whether the right of a holder of cumulative preferred stock to dividend arrearages and other preferences may be cancelled by a statutory merger. That precise problem has not heretofore been before this court, but elsewhere there is a considerable body of law on the subject. There is no need to discuss all of the authorities. For illustrative purposes it is sufficient that we refer principally to cases involving Delaware corporations. That state is important as a state of incorporation, and the decisions of its courts on the precise problem are not only referred to and relied on by the parties, but are generally considered to be the leading ones in the field.

The earliest case in point of time is Keller v. Wilson & Co., 21 Del. Ch. 391, 190 A. 115 (1936). Wilson & Company was formed and its stock was issued in 1925 and the law then in effect protected against charter amendments which might destroy a preferred shareholder's right to accumulated dividends. In 1927 that law was amended so as to permit such destruction, and thereafter the stockholders of Wilson & Company, by the required majorities, voted to cancel the dividends which had by then accrued on its preferred stock. In invalidating that action the rationale of the Delaware court was that the right of a holder of a corporation's cumulative preferred stock to eventual payment of dividend arrearages was a fixed contractual right, that it was a property right in the nature of a debt, that it was vested, and that it could not be destroyed by corporate action taken under legislative authority subsequently conferred, without the consent of all of the shareholders.

Consolidated Film Industries, Inc. v. Johnson, 22 Del.Ch. 407, 197 A. 489 (1937), decided a year later, was an almost precisely similar case. The only difference was that Consolidated Film Industries, Inc. was not created until after the adoption of the 1927 amendment, whereas in the earlier case the statutory amendment upon which Wilson & Company purported to act postdated both its creation and the issuance of its stock. Notwithstanding the *Keller* rationale that an investor should be entitled to rely upon the law in existence at the time the preferred stock was issued, the court in this case was " * * * unable to discover a difference in principle between the two cases." In refusing to allow the proposed reclassification, it reasoned that a shareholder's fixed contractual right to unpaid dividends is of such dignity that it cannot be diminished or eliminated retrospectively even if the authorizing legislation precedes the issuance of its stock.

Two years elapsed before Federal United Corp. v. Havender, supra, was decided. The issue was substantially the same as that in the two cases which preceded. The dissenting stockholders had argued, as might have been expected, that the proposed corporate action, even though styled a "merger," was in effect a *Keller* type recapitalization and was entitled to no different treatment. Notwithstanding that argument, the court did not refer to the preferred stockholder's right as "vested" or as "a property right in the nature of a debt." Neither did it reject the use of *Keller*-type nomenclature as creating "confusion" or as "substitutes for reason and analysis" which are the characterizations used respectively in Davison v. Parke, Austin & Lipscomb, Inc., 285 N.Y. 500, 509, 35 N.E.2d 618, 622; Meck, Accrued Dividends on Cumulative Preferred Stocks; The Legal Doctrine, 55 Harv.L.Rev. 7, 76. Instead, it talked about the extent of the corporate power under the merger statute; and it held that the statute in existence when Federal United Corp. was organized had in effect been written into its charter, and that its preferred shareholders had thereby been advised and informed that their rights to accrued dividends might be extinguished by corporate action taken pursuant thereto.

Faced with a question of corporate action adjusting preferred stock dividends, and required to apply Delaware law under Erie R.R. v. Tompkins, 304 U.S. 64, 58 Sup.Ct. 817, 82 L.Ed. 1188, it is understandable that a federal court in Hottenstein v. York Ice Machinery Corp., 3 Cir., 136 F.2d 944, 950, found *Keller, Johnson* and *Havender* irreconcilable and said,

If it is fair to say that the decision of the Supreme Court of Delaware in the Keller case astonished the corporate world, it is just to state that the decision of the Supreme Court in Havender astounded it, for shorn of rationalization the decision constitutes a repudiation of principles enunicated in the Keller case and in Consolidated Film Industries v. Johnson, supra, at 950.

With Keller's back thus broken, *Hottenstein* went on to say that under Delaware law a parent corporation may merge with a wholly-owned inactive subsidiary pursuant to a plan cancelling preferred stock and the rights of holders thereof to unpaid accumulated dividends and substituting in lieu thereof stock of the surviving corporation.

Only four years intervened between *Keller* and *Havender*, but that was long enough for Delaware to have discarded "vested rights" as the test for determining the power of a corporation to eliminate a shareholder's right to preferred stock dividend accumulation, and to have adopted in its stead a standard calling for judicial inquiry into whether the proposed interference with a preferred stockholder's contract has been authorized by the legislature. The *Havender* approach is the one to which we subscribe as being the sounder, and it has support in the authorities.

[The court here considers and rejects the argument that, because the corporation was created and the stock issued before the adoption of the merger statute, the elimination of preferred dividends is prohibited by the "Dartmouth College Case," Trustees of Dartmouth College v. Woodward, 17 U.S. 518 (1819).]

*   *   *

In addition to arguing that the proposed plan suffers from a constitutional infirmity, plaintiffs also contend that it is unfair and inequitable to them, and that its consummation should, therefore, be enjoined. By that assertion they raise the problem of whether equity should heed the request of a dissenting stockholder and intervene to prevent a merger notwithstanding that it has received the vote of the designated proportions of the various classes of stock of the constituent corporations.

In looking to the authorities for assistance on this question, we avoided those involving recapitalization by charter amendment where a dissident's only remedy against allegedly unfair treatment was in equity. In those situations the authorities generally permit equitable intervention to protect against unfair or inequitable treatment. Kamena v. Janssen Dairy Corp., 133 N.J.Eq. 214, 31 A.2d 200, aff'd, 134 N.J.Eq. 359, 35 A.2d 894. They are founded on the concept that otherwise there might be confiscation without recompense. The same rationale, however, is not available in the case of a merger, because there the dissenting stockholders usually can find a measure of protection in the statutory procedures giving them the option to compel the corporation to purchase their shares at an appraised value. This is a significant difference and is ample reason for considering the two situations as raising separate and distinct issues.

This case involves a merger, not a recapitalization by charter amendment, and in this state the legislature, looking to the possibility that there might be those who would not be agreeable to the proposed merger, provided a means whereby a dissatisfied stockholder might demand and the corporation be compelled to pay the fair value of his securities. G.L.1956, §§ 7–5–8 through 7–5–16 inclusive. Our inquiry then is to the effect of that remedy upon plaintiff's right to challenge the proposed merger on the ground that it is unfair and inequitable because it dictates what shall be their proportionate interests in the corporate assets. Once again there is no agreement among the authorities. Vorenberg, "Exclusiveness of the Dissenting Stockholder's Appraisal Right," 77 Harv.L.Rev. 1189. Some authorities appear to say that the statutory remedy of appraisal is exclusive. Beloff v. Consolidated Edison Co., 300 N.Y. 11, 87 N.E.2d 561. Others say that it may be disregarded and that equity may intervene if the minority is treated oppressively or unfairly, Barnett v. Philadelphia Market Co., 218 Pa. 649, 67 A. 912; May v. Midwest Refining Co., 1 Cir., 121 F.2d 431, cert. denied 314 U.S. 668, 62 Sup.Ct. 129, 86 L.Ed. 534, or if the merger is tainted with fraud or illegality, Adams v. United States Distributing Corp., 184 Va. 134, 147, 34 S.E.2d 244, 250, 162 A.L.R. 1227; Porges v. Vadsco Sales Corp., 27 Del.Ch. 127, 32 A.2d 148. To these differing views must also be added the divergence of opinion on whether those in control or those dissenting must bear the burden of establishing that the plan meets whatever the required standard may be. Vorenberg, supra; 77 Harv.L.Rev. 1189, 1210–1215.

In this case we do not choose as between the varying views, nor is there any need for us to do so. Even were we to accept that view which is most favorable to plaintiffs we still would not be able to find that they have been either unfairly or inequitably treated. The record insofar as it relates to the unfairness issue is at best sparse. In substance it consists of the corporation's balance sheet as of September 1967, together with supporting schedules. That statement uses book, rather than the appraised, values, and neither it nor any other evidentiary matter in any way indicates, except as the same may be reflected in the surplus account, the corporation's earning history or its prospects for profitable operations in the future.

Going to the figures we find a capital and surplus account of $669,948 of which $453,000 is allocable to the 4,530 issued and outstanding shares of $100 par value preferred stock and the balance of $216,948 to surplus. Obviously, a realization of the book value of the assets in the event of liquidation, forced or otherwise, would not only leave nothing for the common stockholders, but would not even suffice to pay the preferred shareholders the par value of their stock plus the accrued dividends of $645,000.

If we were to follow a rule of absolute priority, any proposal which would give anything to common stockholders without first providing for full payment of stated value plus dividend accruals would be unfair to the preferred shareholders. It could be argued that the proposal in this case violates that rule because an exchange of one share of Community Hotel's preferred stock for five shares of Newport's common stock would give the preferred shareholders securities worth less than the amount of their liquidation preference rights while at the same time the one to one exchange ratio on the common would enrich Community Hotel's common stockholders by allowing them to participate in its surplus.

An inherent fallacy in applying the rule of absolute priority to the circumstances of this case, however, is its assumption that assets would be liquidated and that nothing more than their book value will be realized. But Community Hotel is not in liquidation. Instead it is a going concern which, because of its present capitalization, cannot obtain the modern debt-financing needed to meet threatened competition. Moreover, management, in the call of the meeting at which it was intended to consider and vote on the plan, said that the proposed recapitalization plan was conceived only " * * * after careful consideration by your Board of Directors and a review of the relative values of the preferred and common stocks by the independent public accountants of the Corporation. The exchange ratio of five new common shares for each share of the existing preferred stock was determined on the basis of the book and market values of the preferred and the inherent value of the unpaid preferred dividends." Those assertions are contained in a document admitted as an exhibit and they have testimonial value.

When the varying considerations—both balance sheet figures and management's assertions—are taken into account, we are unable to conclude, at least at this stage of the proceedings, that the proposed plan is unfair and inequitable, particularly because plaintiffs as dissidents may avail themselves of the opportunity to receive the fair market value of their securities under the appraisal methods prescribed in § 7–5–8 through § 7–5–16 inclusive.

* * *

For the reasons stated, the judgment appealed from is affirmed.

Chapter 21

DUTIES OF MAJORITY STOCKHOLDERS

A. THE RESPONSIBILITIES OF CONTROLLING STOCKHOLDERS

No analysis of corporate power or of fiduciary responsibilities is complete without examining the position of controlling stockholders. Directors and officers ostensibly exercise the corporation's power, but they hold their power at the sufferance of the stockholders. If a single stockholder is able to exercise the power of the stockholder body, that person effectively controls the corporation.

The key to this power position is that corporations act by majority vote. A majority of the voting stock elects the board, which chooses management. A stockholder, whether an individual or another corporation, that can assemble a majority of votes wields *control* over property that is owned by others. This would seem to suggest that the controlling stockholder is one who owns more than 50% of the stock. In large corporations such persons, or even affiliated groups of persons, rarely exist. Ownership of large blocks, but less than 50% of the stock usually can result in the exercise of the same power as a majority. This is because not all the stockholders participate in the voting process, ownership is widely diffused and, once in control, the controlling persons usually command the loyalty of other stockholders. In fact, in most large corporations control usually stems not from ownership, but rather from incumbency and control of the proxy machinery. In this chapter, however, we address the responsibilities of those persons whose source of power is their ownership of stock and who can surmount the power of incumbency if necessary.

In our earlier discussion of fiduciary obligations, we focused on directors and officers. But the controlling person may be subject to the same obligations if he chooses to wield the same power, even without the formal trappings of office. For example, a parent corporation obviously controls its majority-owned subsidiary. The Supreme Court has said of dominant and controlling stockholders, "Their powers are powers in trust. * * * Their dealings with the corporation are subjected to rigorous scrutiny and where any of their contracts or engagements with the corporation is challenged the burden is on the director or stockholder not only to prove the good faith of the transaction but also to show its inherent fairness from the view point of the corporation and those interested therein." Pepper v. Litton, 308 U.S. 295, 306, 60 S.Ct. 238, 245, 84 L.Ed. 281 (1939).

986

In this chapter we will discuss first the fiduciary duties of controlling stockholders and when the duties arise. In the next chapter we will analyze how control is changed, and how it is preserved.

PROBLEM
PARENT–SUBSIDIARY RELATIONS

Phillips Corporation (P) is a diversified corporation, operating in a wide variety of industries either directly or through subsidiaries. It manufacturers ball bearings and machine tools, produces writing instruments and power tools, and operates hotels and a travel agency.

Slick Corporation, (S) a subsidiary of Phillips Corporation is a producer and distributor of motion pictures. Eighty percent of Slick Corporation's stock is owned by Phillips Corporation and the other 20% is owned by 2,500 public investors, whose shares are traded in the over the counter market. P acquired its holdings over a number of years, through some large transactions and in regular purchases. P shares are traded on the New York Stock Exchange. Both corporations are registered with the SEC pursuant to § 12 of the Securities Exchange Act of 1934.

A

P now has an opportunity to acquire all the shares of Triad Corporation, (T) a privately owned business. T produces oil drilling equipment, and that business is presently enjoying a tremendous boom. T's shareholders are willing to sell for $40 million, for cash or notes. The management of P is anxious to make the deal because they estimate that the return on their investment would yield annual profits of 15% the first year, and probably more in subsequent years. The return from P's other businesses varies from 5% to 18%.

To obtain the necessary funds to make the acquisition, P could borrow the money under a line of credit arrangement (at 14% interest rates), sell corporate debt instruments (at approximately 13% interest, plus related costs), sell additional shares of stock, which would probably require the sale of 15% interest in the company (remember the leverage effect?) or liquidate certain operations of the company for cash.

Management decides that it would be best to liquidate S, since the return on that investment is 5%. This would provide P with most of the funds it needs in order to make the T acquisition, it would improve the overall profitability of P, and doubtless have a favorable effect on P stock. S's assets consist mainly of cash and real estate; the library of old films and the movie studio equipment cannot realize much cash in the marketplace. This structure to the transaction has tax advantages for P.

The board of directors of S, a majority of whom are affiliated with P, votes to liquidate the corporation and hold a stockholder meeting to consider the question, in accordance with § 84 of the MBCA. The proxy statement of S sets forth accurate information about the composition of the board of directors, the financial condition of S and the fact that P intends to invest the proceeds of the liquidation into purchasing T. The book value of the S assets are $40 million (or $40 per share) and the liquidation sales would yield about $35 million, or $35 per share. The current market price of the stock that is traded is $30 per share.

The proxy statement also discloses that the stockholders will receive their pro-rata share of the proceeds from the sale of the assets. Since the plan adopted by the board requires the liquidating sales to be made within one year and the proceeds distributed within that time, in order to obtain tax advantages, the proxy statement also discloses that the shareholders who dissent from the transaction are not entitled to receive the appraised value of their shares under § 80 of the MBCA.

Smith, the owner of 200 shares of S, is unhappy about the proposed liquidation. He thought that the prospects for improved earnings in the movie industry were favorable, particularly if the company was prepared to make the necessary investment to produce blockbuster films, such as *Star Wars, Jaws, Superman* and a few others that it had declined to risk in the past. And, of course, the major investment that is now contemplated is of no benefit to the minority stockholders of S.

Smith has sought counsel as to what remedies, under either federal or state law, he might have to prevent this transaction or to recover damages. The shareholder meeting is scheduled for next week.

You are an associate in the law firm that Smith has consulted. The partner in charge of this case has dispatched a memorandum to you, asking you to think about this case over the weekend, do some background reading, and talk to her about the case on Monday. Her memo makes the following points:

"Let's try to look at our client's objections to the transaction from the standpoint of the other side. This should better enable us to prepare our case.

"1. The liquidation will produce $35 per share at the time that the market price of Slick stock is $30 per share. Do the shareholders have anything to complain about?

"2. Are the majority shareholders forbidden from liquidating a corporation, in accordance with the statute, just because it is operating profitably? Do they need any reason at all? If they do, doesn't the fundamental good sense of liquidating property that produces a 5% return on investment and reinvesting the proceeds at three times the profit provide legal protection?

"3. The shareholders may vote on this transaction. Isn't that all the protection contemplated by the law? The parent is not deprived of *its* right to vote, is it? And can't it vote the same way all the other stockholders vote, *i.e.*, 'what is best for me'?

"4. The elimination of the minority interest makes perfectly good sense to the parent. Is there anything wrong with their acting accordingly? Is the parent stuck with the minority shareholders forever?

"5. Smith thinks that management could have done a better job in the past, and that there are numerous things they could do to improve profitability, if Slick were not liquidated. Is any of this relevant? Are the sins of omission punishable in the courts?

"6. Wouldn't Smith have to shoulder a heavy burden of proof?

"7. If we went into federal court and claimed federal securities law violations, wouldn't we be thrown out on the basis of the fact that Phillips and Slick made full disclosure of the terms of the transaction? Even if we could prove a defect in their disclosure documents, could we show any connection between that violation and the transaction?"

B

Assume that several months before the Triad opportunity arose, Slick's board of directors had voted in favor of a policy of aggressive expansion. The board decided that the cash resources of the company greatly exceeded its cash needs, and the management should go in search of fresh opportunities.

Soon thereafter, the CEO of Triad approached the chief financial officer of Slick (who is also an officer of Phillips and a director of both companies) about the possibility of selling Triad. The man from Triad told the Phillips-Slick officer that he thought one or the other of his companies might be interested, and it was a matter of indifference to Triad which one it was.

The officer presented the facts to both the Phillips and Slick boards. The two boards agreed as follows: Phillips would purchase the Triad stock, and cause Slick to merge into Phillips. The shareholders of Slick would receive shares of Phillips in the merger. The value of the Phillips shares received would be an amount equal to the present fair market value of the Slick shares surrendered in the merger.

If you were asked by a minority shareholder of Slick to analyze this transaction (on which he now has an opportunity to vote) how would you comment? Is there any legally required basis for the exchange of Slick shares other than the one proposed in the transaction? What would you have to show in order to state a federal claim?

B. THE COMMON LAW

1. WHAT CONSTITUTES SELF DEALING

SINCLAIR OIL CORP. v. LEVIEN

280 A.2d 717 (Del.1971).

WOLCOTT, Chief Justice.

This is an appeal by the defendant, Sinclair Oil Corporation (here-after Sinclair), from an order of the Court of Chancery, 261 A.2d 911 in a derivative action requiring Sinclair to account for damages sustained by its subsidiary, Sinclair Venezuelan Oil Company (hereafter Sinven), organized by Sinclair for the purpose of operating in Venezuela, as a result of dividends paid by Sinven, the denial to Sinven of industrial development, and a breach of contract between Sinclair's wholly-owned subsidiary, Sinclair International Oil Company, and Sinven.

Sinclair, operating primarily as a holding company, is in the business of exploring for oil and of producing and marketing crude oil and oil products. At all times relevant to this litigation, it owned about 97% of Sinven's stock. The plaintiff owns about 3000 of 120,000 publicly held shares of Sinven. Sinven, incorporated in 1922, has been engaged in petroleum operations primarily in Venezuela and since 1959 has operated exclusively in Venezuela.

Sinclair nominates all members of Sinven's board of directors. The Chancellor found as a fact that the directors were not independent of Sinclair. Almost without exception, they were officers, directors, or employees of corporations in the Sinclair complex. By reason of Sinclair's domination, it is clear that Sinclair owed Sinven a fiduciary duty. Sinclair concedes this.

The Chancellor held that because of Sinclair's fiduciary duty and its control over Sinven, its relationship with Sinven must meet the test of intrinsic fairness. The standard of intrinsic fairness involves both a high degree of fairness and a shift in the burden of proof. Under this standard the burden is on Sinclair to prove, subject to careful judicial scrutiny, that its transactions with Sinven were objectively fair.

Sinclair argues that the transactions between it and Sinven should be tested, not by the test of intrinsic fairness with the accompanying shift of the burden of proof, but by the business judgment rule under which a court will not interfere with the judgment of a board of directors unless there is a showing of gross and palpable overreaching. Meyerson v. El Paso Natural Gas Co., 246 A.2d 789 (Del.Ch.1967). A board of directors enjoys a presumption of sound business judgment, and its decisions will not be disturbed if they can be attributed to any rational business purpose. A court under such circumstances will not substitute its own notions of what is or is not sound business judgment.

We think, however, that Sinclair's argument in this respect is misconceived. When the situation involves a parent and a subsidiary, with the parent controlling the transaction and fixing the terms, the test of intrinsic fairness, with its resulting shifting of the burden of proof, is applied. Sterling v. Mayflower Hotel Corp., supra; David J. Greene & Co. v. Dunhill International, Inc., 249 A.2d 427 (Del.Ch. 1968); Bastian v. Bourns, Inc., 256 A.2d 680 (Del.Ch.1969) aff'd. Per Curiam (unreported) (Del.Supr.1970). The basic situation for the application of the rule is the one in which the parent has received a benefit to the exclusion and at the expense of the subsidiary.

Recently, this court dealt with the question of fairness in parent-subsidiary dealings in Getty Oil Co. v. Skelly Oil Co., 267 A.2d 883 (Del.Supr.1970). In that case, both parent and subsidiary were in the business of refining and marketing crude oil and crude oil products. The Oil Import Board ruled that the subsidiary, because it was controlled by the parent, was no longer entitled to a separate allocation of imported crude oil. The subsidiary then contended that it had a right to share the quota of crude oil allotted to the parent. We ruled that the business judgment standard should be applied to determine this contention. Although the subsidiary suffered a loss through the administration of the oil import quotas, the parent gained nothing. The parent's quota was derived solely from its own past use. The past use of the subsidiary did not cause an increase in the parent's quota. Nor did the parent usurp a quota of the subsidiary. Since the parent received nothing from the subsidiary to the exclusion of the minority stockholders of the subsidiary, there was no self-dealing. Therefore, the business judgment standard was properly applied.

A parent does indeed owe a fiduciary duty to its subsidiary when there are parent-subsidiary dealings. However, this alone will not evoke the intrinsic fairness standard. This standard will be applied only when the fiduciary duty is accompanied by self-dealing—the situation when a parent is on both sides of a transaction with its subsidiary. Self-dealing occurs when the parent, by virtue of its domination of the subsidiary, causes the subsidiary to act in such a way that the parent receives something from the subsidiary to the exclusion of, and detriment to, the minority stockholders of the subsidiary.

We turn now to the facts. The plaintiff argues that, from 1960 through 1966, Sinclair caused Sinven to pay out such excessive dividends that the industrial development of Sinven was effectively prevented, and it became in reality a corporation in dissolution.

From 1960 through 1966, Sinven paid out $108,000,000 in dividends ($38,000,000 in excess of Sinven's earnings during the same period). The Chancellor held that Sinclair caused these dividends to be paid during a period when it had a need for large amounts of cash. Although the dividends paid exceeded earnings, the plaintiff concedes that the payments were made in compliance with 8 Del.C. § 170, authorizing payment of dividends out of surplus or net profits.

However, the plaintiff attacks these dividends on the ground that they resulted from an improper motive—Sinclair's need for cash. The Chancellor, applying the intrinsic fairness standard, held that Sinclair did not sustain its burden of proving that these dividends were intrinsically fair to the minority stockholders of Sinven.

Since it is admitted that the dividends were paid in strict compliance with 8 Del.C. § 170, the alleged excessiveness of the payments alone would not state a cause of action. Nevertheless, compliance with the applicable statute may not, under all circumstances, justify all dividend payments. If a plaintiff can meet his burden of proving that a dividend cannot be grounded on any reasonable business objective, then the courts can and will interfere with the board's decision to pay the dividend.

Sinclair contends that it is improper to apply the intrinsic fairness standard to dividend payments even when the board which voted for the dividends is completely dominated. In support of this contention, Sinclair relies heavily on American District Telegraph Co. [ADT] v. Grinnell Corp., (N.Y.Sup.Ct.1969) aff'd. 33 A.D.2d 769, 306 N.Y.S.2d 209 (1969). Plaintiffs were minority stockholders of ADT, a subsidiary of Grinnell. The plaintiffs alleged that Grinnell, realizing that it would soon have to sell its ADT stock because of a pending anti-trust action, caused ADT to pay excessive dividends. Because the dividend payments conformed with applicable statutory law, and the plaintiffs could not prove an abuse of discretion, the court ruled that the complaint did not state a cause of action. Other decisions seem to support Sinclair's contention.

We do not accept the argument that the intrinsic fairness test can never be applied to a dividend declaration by a dominated board, although a dividend declaration by a dominated board will not inevitably demand the application of the intrinsic fairness standard. If such a dividend is in essence self-dealing by the parent, then the intrinsic fairness standard is the proper standard. For example, suppose a parent dominates a subsidiary and its board of directors. The subsidiary has outstanding two classes of stock, X and Y. Class X is owned by the parent and Class Y is owned by minority stockholders of the subsidiary. If the subsidiary, at the direction of the parent, declares a dividend on its Class X stock only, this might well be self-dealing by the parent. It would be receiving something from the subsidiary to the exclusion of and detrimental to its minority stockholders. This self-dealing, coupled with the parent's fiduciary duty, would make intrinsic fairness the proper standard by which to evaluate the dividend payments.

Consequently it must be determined whether the dividend payments by Sinven were, in essence, self-dealing by Sinclair. The dividends resulted in great sums of money being transferred from Sinven to Sinclair. However, a proportionate share of this money was received by the minority shareholders of Sinven. Sinclair received nothing from Sinven to the exclusion of its minority stockholders. As such, these dividends were not self-dealing. We hold therefore that the Chancellor erred in applying the intrinsic fairness test as to these dividend payments. The business judgment standard should have been applied.

We conclude that the facts demonstrate that the dividend payments complied with the business judgment standard and with 8 Del. C. § 170. The motives for causing the declaration of dividends are immaterial unless the plaintiff can show that the dividend payments resulted from improper motives and amounted to waste. The plaintiff contends only that the dividend payments drained Sinven of cash to such an extent that it was prevented from expanding.

The plaintiff proved no business opportunities which came to Sinven independently and which Sinclair either took to itself or denied to Sinven. As a matter of fact, with two minor exceptions which resulted in losses, all of Sinven's operations have been conducted in Venezuela, and Sinclair had a policy of exploiting its oil properties located in different countries by subsidiaries located in the particular countries.

From 1960 to 1966 Sinclair purchased or developed oil fields in Alaska, Canada, Paraguay, and other places around the world. The plaintiff contends that these were all opportunities which could have been taken by Sinven. The Chancellor concluded that Sinclair had not proved that its denial of expansion opportunities to Sinven was intrinsically fair. He based this conclusion on the following findings of fact. Sinclair made no real effort to expand Sinven. The excessive dividends paid by Sinven resulted in so great a cash drain as to effectively deny to Sinven any ability to expand. During this same period Sinclair actively pursued a company-wide policy of developing through its subsidiaries new sources of revenue, but Sinven was not permitted to participate and was confined in its activities to Venezuela.

However, the plaintiff could point to no opportunities which came to Sinven. Therefore, Sinclair usurped no business opportunity belonging to Sinven. Since Sinclair received nothing from Sinven to the exclusion of and detriment to Sinven's minority stockholders, there was no self-dealing. Therefore, business judgment is the proper standard by which to evaluate Sinclair's expansion policies.

Since there is no proof of self-dealing on the part of Sinclair, it follows that the expansion policy of Sinclair and the methods used to achieve the desired result must, as far as Sinclair's treatment of Sinven is concerned, be tested by the standards of the business judgment rule. Accordingly, Sinclair's decision, absent fraud or gross overreaching, to achieve expansion through the medium of its subsidiaries, other than Sinven, must be upheld.

Even if Sinclair was wrong in developing these opportunities as it did, the question arises, with which subsidiaries should these opportunities have been shared? No evidence indicates a unique need or ability of Sinven to develop these opportunities. The decision of which subsidiaries would be used to implement Sinclair's expansion policy was one of business judgment with which a court will not interfere absent a showing of gross and palpable overreaching. Meyerson v. El Paso Natural Gas Co., 246 A.2d 789 (Del.Ch.1967). No such showing has been made here.

* * *

NOTE

The *Meyerson* case referred to in *Sinclair*, concerned the fairness of a parent corporation's filing a consolidated tax return with its subsidiary and using the losses of the subsidiary to offset the parent's gains, and reduce the parent's tax. The court rejected a minority shareholder's contention that this practice was unfair. Does the ruling of the court to leave that decision to the judgment of the board reflect a view that there is no self-dealing involved, or is the court saying that there are no established legal standards to invoke? *Meyerson* relies heavily on a New York case, which discussed the difficulty of making a fair allocation between parent and subsidiary corporations.

CASE v. NEW YORK CENTRAL RAILROAD CO.

15 N.Y.2d 150, 256 N.Y.S.2d 607, 204 N.E.2d 643 (1965).

[New York Central, which for years had owned a majority of the stock of Mahoning Coal Railroad Company, acquired 80% of Mahoning's stock and the two companies then entered into a tax allocation plan. Central had losses, but Mahoning had profits. Because of Central's 80% ownership, the companies could file a consolidated tax return. Central's losses offset Mahoning profits, and the latter was relieved of having to pay $3,825,717 in taxes. Under the allocation agreement Mahoning paid $3,556,992 to Central and retained $268,725.

Plaintiff was a minority shareholder of Mahoning who objected to the allocation. The Supreme Court ruled that the agreement was not unfair, but the Appellate Division reversed.

The Court of Appeals in turn reversed the Appellate Division.]

BERGAN, Judge.

* * *

Exercising, as it did by its majority stock ownership, effective control over Mahoning's affairs, Central was required to follow a course of fair dealing toward minority holders in the way it managed the corporation's business. It could not use its power to gain undue advantage to itself at the expense of the minority. This is the standard of responsibility of corporate officers who, in a relationship of this kind, are able to exert this kind of a corporate power as it has been laid down in many cases.

* * *

The arrangement made by Central had greater advantage to itself than to Mahoning. But there was no loss or disadvantage to Mahoning. The basic complaint of Mahoning's minority is that they should have gotten a larger share of the benefits of Central's tax losses than the agreement gave them. Plaintiffs do not spell out what would be the right amount.

The Judge at Special and Trial Term regarded the agreement as fair; the Appellate Division, as we have noted, was divided in opinion. It is true enough that in the years under scrutiny Central gained very large proportionate advantages in relation to Mahoning's advantage. But the agreement must be looked at with the knowledge which those who entered into it had when it was executed; and even the Appellate Division majority felt itself unable to say what would be a fair proportion of the distribution of Central's tax loss looking forward from the date of judgment.

Had the agreement not been signed at all, Mahoning would have paid the Government in taxes $268,725.28 more than it paid Central on being relieved of all tax liability. It gained this much; Central gained much more; but the pattern of managerial disloyalty to a corporation by which the stronger side takes what the weaker side loses is entirely absent from this record.

Moreover, Central could not have taken advantage of the consolidated return provisions of the Federal statute unless it were suffering substantial losses and the stockholders of Mahoning had a vital interest in Central's continued ability to pay the rent and operate the lines owned and leased by Mahoning. If that ability failed the entire profit basis of Mahoning's business might have fallen in jeopardy.

Thus, without loss to itself, and, indeed, at the equivalent of a fairly substantial rebate of its tax obligation, Mahoning was able to help a lessee suffering losses whose solvency was vital to Mahoning's interests. The argument of plaintiffs that Central got too large a share is not on this record a demonstration of such unfairness as to warrant judicial intervention.

Besides this, the loss shown by Central was under some rather flexible circumstances an asset to Central. It could have been carried forward for seven years [Internal Revenue Code 172(b)(1)(C)] and there is nothing about the financial history of Central to suggest that it was clear in 1957 when the agreement was made by Mahoning that Central itself could have not believed it would have carried forward and utilized the loss in future years.

TRANS WORLD AIRLINES, INC. v. SUMMA CORP.

374 A.2d 5 (Del.Ch.1977).

[Howard Hughes owned all the stock of Hughes Tool Company ("Toolco") which owned 78% of the stock of TWA. While competitive airlines were acquiring jet aircraft from Boeing and Douglas in the late 1950's, TWA was not allowed to negotiate for the purchase of planes by itself but instead was forced to rely on Toolco which was unable to arrange financing for a long while. TWA sought an accounting and damages for the delay it suffered from Toolco's refusal to allow TWA to bargain for itself, which it charged was motivated by Toolco's desire to secure a tax advantage from the transaction. Toolco said that this was not a self-dealing transaction because the parent derived no benefit to the detriment of the minority.]

MARVEL, Chancellor.

* * *

First of all, I am satisifed that the mere fact that Toolco engaged in the acquisition, financing, leasing, and ultimately in the sale of jet aircraft is not, in itself, of significance in this case because a parent company may concern itself with the purchase and sale of equipment to be used by a subsidiary, the basic question being rather whether or not TWA suffered injury by reason of being barred from dealing in such area on its own.

I conclude that the basic prerequisites to the application of the intrinsic fairness rule (Sinclair Oil Corp. v. Levien, *supra*) are found in the instant case. First of all, it is conceded that Toolco and Hughes exercised control over the affairs of TWA during the period in question, particularly in the area of the financing and acquisition of jet aircraft, the policy for which over a substantial period was dictated by the defendants, jet aircraft having been leased by Toolco to TWA on a day to day basis prior to agreement on a satisfactory financing arrangement. Furthermore, while Toolco ultimately turned over to TWA the jet aircraft in question once a financing plan was agreed upon, there is no doubt but that the defendants bargained on both sides of such transactions, causing TWA to act in such a way as to cause defendants to derive advantages at the expense of TWA to the exclusion of and to the detriment of the latter's minority shareholders. Accordingly, by refusing to allow TWA to select and finance the purchase of its own jet aircraft, the defendants were in a position to mete out to TWA such jet aircraft as they chose. In other words, by preventing TWA from making its own arrangements for the acquisition of jet planes, the defendants retained the capability of arranging the terms of such acquisitions so as to benefit themselves. In addition, in the event of the development of problems in connection with such acquisitions, as ultimately came to pass, in the task of obtaining long term financing for TWA, the defendants remained free to dispose of such aircraft to other air carriers.

Thus, it is clear on the present record that the minority shareholders of TWA received nothing in exchange for the strictures imposed by defendants on plaintiff's operations and that such stockholders may have suffered injury as a result of the loss of TWA's freedom to compete. As charged in the complaint, TWA might well have been able to earn substantially more income for its minority as well as majority stockholders through increased business activity during the period of its being dominated had it not been subject to the strictures imposed by the defendants.

* * *

[The Court ordered defendants to account to TWA for the damages sustained by the latter for those transactions not approved by the Civil Aeronautics Board.]

2. WHAT CONSTITUTES FAIR DEALING

SINGER v. MAGNAVOX CO.

380 A.2d 969 (Del.1977).

DUFFY, Justice (for the majority).

I

The litigation centers on a merger in July 1975 of The Magnavox Company (Magnavox) with T.M.C. Development Corporation (T.M.C.). Plaintiffs owned common stock of Magnavox at the time of the merger and they bring this class action for all persons who held such shares on the day before the merger. Defendants are: Magnavox, North American Philips Corporation (North American), North American Philips Development Corporation (Development), and individual members of Magnavox management who held their positions in July 1975. All corporations involved are chartered in Delaware. T.M.C. is a wholly-owned subsidiary of Development, which in turn is owned entirely by North American. Apparently, Development's only function was to assist North American in the acquisition of Magnavox.

II

The salient facts appear in the complaint and in a stipulation of the parties. These develop the following scenario:

On August 21, 1974, North American incorporated Development for the purpose of making a tender offer for the Magnavox common shares. Prior to that time, North American and Magnavox were independent, unaffiliated corporations. On August 28, Development offered to buy all Magnavox shares at a price of $8 per share.

* * *

In September 1974, the respective managements of Magnavox, North American and Development compromised their differences over the terms of the tender offer. They agreed to terms which included an increase in the offer price to $9 per share and, at the request of North American and Development, two-year employment contracts for sixteen officers of Magnavox (including some of the individual defendants) at existing salary levels. As part of the agreement, Magnavox withdrew its opposition to the tender offer. As modified, the offer was thus not opposed by Magnavox and, in response thereto, Development acquired approximately 84.1% of Magnavox's outstanding common stock.

With Development firmly in control of Magnavox, the managements of those two companies, and of North American, then set about acquiring all equity interest in Magnavox through a merger. In May 1975, Development caused the creation of T.M.C. for that purpose.

The directors of Magnavox unanimously agreed to the merger with T.M.C. and scheduled a special stockholders meeting for July 24, 1975, to vote on the plan. At the time of this action, four of the nine Magnavox directors were also directors of North American, and three others each had an employment contract, referred to above, with Magnavox and an option to purchase five thousand of North American's common shares, effective on the date of merger. In June 1975, the shareholders of Magnavox were given notice of the meeting with a proxy statement advising on the book value ($10.16) and merger price ($9.00) of the shares, and they were told that approval of the merger was assured since Development's holding alone was large enough to provide the requisite statutory majority. The proxy statement also advised the shareholders of their respective options to accept the merger price or to seek an appraisal under 8 Del.C. § 262.*

The meeting was held in Delaware as scheduled, the proxies were voted here, stockholder approval was given, and the merger was accomplished.

*   *   *

Thereafter, plaintiffs filed a complaint in the Court of Chancery alleging that: (1) the merger was fraudulent in that it did not serve any business purpose other than the forced removal of public minority shareholders from an equity position in Magnavox at a grossly inadequate price to enable North American, through Development, to obtain sole ownership of Magnavox; (2) in approving the merger, at a cash price per share to the minority which they knew to be grossly inadequate, defendants breached their fiduciary duties to the minority shareholders; and (3) the merger was accomplished in a manner violative of the antifraud provision of the Delaware Securities Act. 6

---

* Section 262 provides that shareholders who dissent to a merger, in accordance with certain procedures, are entitled to be paid the appraised value of their shares, exclusive of any element of value arising from the accomplishment of the merger. The Court of Chancery is directed to appraise the stock. Certain exceptions are provided not relevant to this case.—(Eds.)

Del.C. § 7303. Plaintiffs seek an order nullifying the merger and compensatory damages.

Defendants moved to dismiss the complaint on the ground that it fails to state a claim upon which relief may be granted, arguing that: (1) their actions are expressly authorized by 8 Del.C. § 251, and they fully complied therewith; (2) the exclusive remedy for dissatisfaction with the merger is an appraisal under 8 Del.C. § 262; and (3) plaintiffs are not entitled to relief under the Securities Act because they did not rely on any purported material misrepresentations, and because they lack standing to sue under the Act and status to maintain a class action.

The Court of Chancery granted the motion to dismiss, ruling that: (1) the merger was not fraudulent merely because it was accomplished without any business purpose other than to eliminate the Magnavox minority shareholders; (2) in any event, plaintiffs' remedy for dissatisfaction with the merger is to seek an appraisal; and (3) plaintiffs are not entitled to relief under the Securities Act because the proxy materials did not have a significant impact on accomplishment of the merger.

III

We turn, first, to what we regard as the principal consideration in this appeal; namely, the obligation owed by majority shareholders in control of the corporate process to minority shareholders, in the context of a merger under 8 Del.C. § 251, of two related Delaware corporations. It is, in other words, another round in the development of the law governing a parent corporation and minority shareholders in its subsidiary.

A.

To state the obvious, under § 251 two (or more) Delaware corporations "may merge into a single corporation." Generally speaking, whether such a transaction is good or bad, enlightened or ill-advised, selfish or generous—these considerations are beside the point. Section 251 authorizes a merger and any judicial consideration of that kind of togetherness must begin from that premise.

Section 251 also specifies in detail the procedures to be followed in accomplishing a merger. Briefly, these include approvals by the directors of each corporation and by "majority [vote] of the outstanding stock of" each corporation, followed by the execution and filing of formal documents. The consideration given to the shareholders of a constituent corporation in exchange for their stock may take the form of "cash, property, rights or securities of any other corporation." § 251(b)(4). A shareholder who objects to the merger and is dissatisfied with the value of the consideration given for his shares may seek an appraisal under 8 Del.C. § 262.

B.

In this appeal it is uncontroverted that defendants complied with the stated requirements of § 251. Thus there is both statutory authorization for the Magnavox merger and compliance with the procedural requirements. But, contrary to defendants' contention, it does not necessarily follow that the merger is legally unassailable. We say this because, (a) plaintiffs invoke the fiduciary duty rule which allegedly binds defendants; and (b) Delaware case law clearly teaches that even complete compliance with the mandate of a statute does not, in every case, make the action valid in law.

* * *

C.

From this premise we must now analyze the encounter between the exercise of a statutory right and the performance of the alleged fiduciary duty. As we have noted, § 251, by its terms, makes permissible that which the North American side of this dispute caused to be done: the merger of T.M.C. into Magnavox. We must ascertain, however, what restraint, if any, the duty to minority stockholders placed on the exercise of that right.

Plaintiffs contend that the Magnavox merger was fraudulent because it was made without any ascertainable corporate business purpose and was designed solely to freeze out of the minority stockholders. After a review of the cases, the Trial Court concluded that to the extent the complaint charges that the merger was fraudulent because it did not serve a business purpose of Magnavox, it fails to state a claim upon which relief may be granted. Our analysis leads to a different result, not on the basis of fraud but on application of the law governing corporate fiduciaries.

* * *

Any inquiry into the business purpose of a merger immediately leads to such questions as: "Whose purpose?" or "Whose business?" Is it that of the corporations whose shares are (or were) held by the minority? If so, it may well be that the business purpose of that company (*qua* company) is advanced by the merger, but that could be an academic result if the complainants (as here) are no longer shareholders because they have been cashed-out. On the other hand, if the corporation in which the complainants held shares "vanishes" in the merger, inquiry as to purpose may be unrealistic if not academic. And if the business purpose of the parent (or dominant) corporation should be examined (as defendants argue), minority shareholders of the subsidiary (or controlled corporation) may have undue difficulty in raising and maintaining the issue.

The point of this discussion is not that an exploration of the business purpose for a merger is without merit. It may well be necessary to examine that purpose in many mergers under judicial review. But as a threshold consideration in this opinion, it is not helpful in sorting out rights of the parties. It seems to us, rather, that the approach to the purpose issue should be made by first examining the competing claims between the majority and minority stockholders of Magnavox. That is what is really up for decision here, and so we look to the standards governing that relationship.

D.

It is a settled rule of law in Delaware that Development, as the majority stockholder of Magnavox, owed to the minority stockholders of that corporation, a fiduciary obligation in dealing with the latter's property. Sterling v. Mayflower Hotel Corp., Del.Supr., 33 Del.Ch. 293, 93 A.2d 107, 109–10(1952). In that leading "interested merger" case, this Court recognized as established law in this State that the dominant corporation, as a majority stockholder standing on both sides of a merger transaction, has "the burden of establishing its entire fairness" to the minority stockholders, sufficiently to "pass the test of careful scrutiny by the courts." See 93 A.2d at 109, 110. The fiduciary obligation is the cornerstone of plaintiffs' rights in this controversy and the corollary, of course, is that it is likewise the measure of the duty owed by defendants.

The classic definition of the duty was stated by Chief Justice Layton in Guth [v. Loft, Inc., Del.Supr., 23 Del.Ch. 255, 5 A.2d 503 (1939)] where he wrote:

> * * * While technically not trustees, * * * [corporate directors] stand in a fiduciary relation to the corporation and its stockholders. A public policy, existing through the years, and derived from a profound knowledge of human characteristics and motives, has established a rule that demands of a corporate officer or director, peremptorily and inexorably, the most scrupulous observance of his duty, not only affirmatively to protect the interests of the corporation committed to his charge, but also to refrain from doing anything that would work injury to the corporation, or to deprive it of profit or advantage which his skill and ability might properly bring to it, or to enable it to make in the reasonable and lawful exercise of its powers. The rule that requires an undivided and unselfish loyalty to the corporation demands that there shall be no conflict between duty and self-interest. The occasions for the determination of honesty, good faith and loyal conduct are many and varied, and no hard and fast rule can be formulated. The standard of loyalty is measured by no fixed scale.

5 A.2d at 510. While that comment was about directors, the spirit of the definition is equally applicable to a majority stockholder in any context in which the law imposes a fiduciary duty on that stockholder for the benefit of minority stockholders. We so hold.

* * *

Defendants concede that they owe plaintiffs a fiduciary duty but contend that, in the context of the present transaction, they have met that obligation by offering fair value for the Magnavox shares. And, say defendants, plaintiffs' exclusive remedy for dissatisfaction with the merger is to seek an appraisal under § 262. We disagree. In our view, defendants cannot meet their fiduciary obligations to plaintiffs simply by relegating them to a statutory appraisal proceeding.

At the core of defendants' contention is the premise that a shareholder's right is exclusively in the *value* of his investment, not its *form*. And, they argue, that right is protected by a § 262 appraisal which, by definition, results in fair value for the shares. This argument assumes that the right to take is coextensive with the power to take and that a dissenting stockholder has no legally protected right in his shares, his certificate or his company beyond a right to be paid fair value when the majority is ready to do this. Simply stated, such an argument does not square with the duty stated so eloquently and so forcefully by Chief Justice Layton in *Guth.*

We agree that, because the power to merge is conferred by statute, every stockholder in a Delaware corporation accepts his shares with notice thereof. See Federal United Corporation v. Havender, Del.Supr., 24 Del.Ch. 318, 11 A.2d 331, 338 (1940). Beyond question, the common law right of a single stockholder to simply veto a merger is gone. *Id.* at 331. But it by no means follows that those in control of a corporation may invoke the statutory power conferred by § 251, a power which this Court in *Havender, supra,* said was "somewhat analogous to the right of eminent domain," 11 A.2d at 338, when their purpose is simply to get rid of a minority. On the contrary, as we shall ultimately conclude here, just as a minority shareholder may not thwart a merger without cause, neither may a majority cause a merger to be made for the sole purpose of eliminating a minority on a cash-out basis.

E.

Plaintiffs allege that defendants violated their respective fiduciary duties by participating in the tender offer and other acts which led to the merger and which were designed to enable Development and North American to, among other things:

> [C]onsummate a merger which did not serve any valid corporate purpose or compelling business need of Magnavox and whose sole purpose was to enable Development and North American to obtain sole ownership of the business and assets of Magnavox at a price determined by defendants which was grossly inadequate and unfair and which was designed to give Development and North American a disproportionate amount of the gain said defendants anticipated would be recognized from consummation of the merger.

Defendants contend, and the Court of Chancery agreed, that the "business purpose" rule does not have a place in Delaware's merger law.

We hold the law to be that a Delaware Court will not be indifferent to the purpose of a merger when a freeze-out of minority stockholders on a cash-out basis is alleged to be its sole purpose. In such a situation, if it is alleged that the purpose is improper because of the fiduciary obligation owed to the minority, the Court is duty-bound to closely examine that allegation even when all of the relevant statutory formalities have been satisfied.

Consistent with this conclusion is Bennett v. Breuil Petroleum Corp., *supra*, wherein plaintiff alleged that the dominant shareholder caused the issuance of new shares to impair his interest and to force him out of the corporation upon management's terms. At the outset the Court said:

> As a starting point it must be conceded that action by majority stockholders having as its primary purpose the "freezing out" of a minority interest is actionable without regard to the fairness of the price.

And in Condec Corporation v. Lunkenheimer Company, *supra*, the Court applied a similar approach in an action for cancellation of stock alleged to be issued for the purpose of retaining corporate control, stating that "shares may not be issued for an improper purpose such as a take-over of voting control from others." 230 A.2d at 775.

Similarly, in Schnell v. Chris-Craft Industries, Inc., *supra*, this Court examined the purpose for advancement of the date of an annual meeting when it was allegedly done to perpetuate management in office. In ordering that the advanced date be nullified, Chief Justice (then Justice) Herrmann answered management's claim that strict statutory compliance insulated its action from attack by saying "that inequitable action does not become permissible simply because it is legally possible." 285 A.2d at 439.

Read as a whole, those opinions illustrate two principles of law which we approve: First, it is within the responsibility of an equity court to scrutinize a corporate act when it is alleged that its purpose violates the fiduciary duty owed to minority stockholders; and second, those who control the corporate machinery owe a fiduciary duty to the minority in the exercise thereof over corporate powers and property, and the use of such power to perpetuate control is a violation of that duty.

By analogy, if not *a fortiori*, use of corporate power solely to *eliminate* the minority is a violation of that duty. Accordingly, while we agree with the conclusion of the Court of Chancery that this merger was not fraudulent merely because it was accomplished without any purpose other than elimination of the minority stockholders, we conclude that, for that reason, it was violative of the fiduciary duty owed by the majority to the minority stockholders.

We hold, therefore, that a § 251 merger, made for the sole purpose of freezing out minority stockholders, is an abuse of the corporate process; and the complaint, which so alleges in this suit, states a cause of action for violation of a fiduciary duty for which the Court may grant such relief as it deems appropriate under the circumstances.

This is not to say, however, that merely because the Court finds that a cash-out merger was not made for the sole purpose of freezing out minority stockholders, all relief must be denied to the minority stockholders in a § 251 merger. On the contrary, the fiduciary obligation of the majority to the minority stockholders remains and proof of a purpose, other than such freeze-out, without more, will not necessarily discharge it. In such case the Court will scrutinize the circumstances for compliance with the *Sterling* rule of "entire fairness" and, if it finds a violation thereof, will grant such relief as equity may require. Any statement in *Stauffer* inconsistent herewith is held inapplicable to a § 251 merger.

* * *

Accordingly, as to this facet of the appeal, we reverse.

NOTE—THE SINGER TRILOGY

Several weeks after the decision in *Singer,* the Delaware Supreme Court decided Tanzer v. International General Industries, Inc., 379 A. 2d 1121 (Del. 1977)—a case that has been labeled the second of the Singer Trilogy. The case involved the merger of IGI with its 81% owned subsidiary, Kliklok Corporation which resulted in the elimination of the minority interest for cash. The plaintiffs contended that the transaction was lacking in business purpose.

The court stated, "While the focus here and in *Singer* has been on the rights of minority stockholders, we are well aware that a majority stockholder has rights too. And among these is exercising a fundamental right of a stockholder in a Delaware corporation; namely, the right to vote its shares." 379 A.2d at 1123.

The standard imposed by the court in assessing whether the transaction was proper was stated as follows:

As a stockholder, IGI need not sacrifice its own interest in dealing with a subsidiary; but that interest must not be suspect as a subterfuge, the real purpose of which is to rid itself of unwanted minority shareholders in the subsidiary. That would be a violation of *Singer* and any subterfuge or effort to escape its mandate must be scrutinized with care and dealt with by the Trial Court. And, of course, in any event, a *bona fide* purpose notwithstanding, IGI must be prepared to show that it has met its duty

imposed by Singer and Sterling v. Mayflower Hotel Corp.
* * * of "entire fairness" to the minority.

Id. at 1124.

Since the lower court found that IGI was not freezing out the minority "just for the purpose of freezing out the minority" but had undertaken the merger to facilitate long term debt financing, there existed a bona fide purpose for the merger.

On remand, to consider the fairness of the transaction the Chancellor entered summary judgment for IGI. Tanzer v. International General Industries, Inc., 402 A.2d 382 (Del. 1979). The court considered the following eight indicia of fairness (See *id.* at 390–95):

1. IGI had a bona fide purpose for merger.

2. The alternatives to a cash-out merger were not compelling. A stock-for-stock exchange would have been viewed as unfair by many stockholders. The court did note, however, that perhaps the fairest mode would have been to provide an option in either cash or stock.

3. There was an independent recommendation as to the fairness of the price from a reputable investment banker.

4. There was adequate notice to the minority stockholders in the proxy statement.

5. This was not a transaction in which the majority stockholder had obtained funds through a public offering at a high price followed by a repurchase at a significantly lower price.

6. While the subsidiary will be obligated, as the surviving corporation, to repay the loan used to repurchase the shares, this was found by the Chancellor not to inject a "detriment to its corporate purpose, nor indicate unfairness to the minority shareholders."

7. The minority stockholders will be entitled to their appraisal rights under the Delaware statute.

8. While IGI did not share any of the "synergistic benefits" accomplished in the merger this was not required to be weighed in the merger transaction itself. There will be an opportunity to examine the value of those benefits in the appraisal proceeding. Moreover, the minority shareholders received a premium over the present value of their shares.

The third case in the *Singer* Trilogy is Roland International Corp. v. Najjar, 407 A.2d 1032 (Del. 1979). This case involved a so-called short form merger—a transaction involving a parent and a 90% or more owned subsidiary. Such a merger does not require a shareholder vote, but only notice after the fact to minority shareholders that the boards of directors have agreed upon a merger. Del. Gen. Corp. Law § 253.

Relying on prior Delaware holdings, defendants argued that appraisal was the plaintiff's sole remedy and that § 253 "conclusively presumes" a proper purpose for a short term merger. Judge Duffy (who authored *Singer*) responded:

> That argument misses the point of *Singer*. The law of fiduciary duty, on which *Singer* is based, arises not from the operation of § 251 but independent of it. Indeed, *Singer* presupposes full compliance with the terms of § 251, and its impact begins at that point. As we have attempted to make plain, the duty arises from long-standing principles of equity and is superimposed on many sections of Corporation Law, including, we think, § 251.

407 A.2d at 1036.

The Court then affirmed the Vice Chancellor's denial of the defendants' motion to dismiss because the complaint alleged that the purpose of the merger was simply to squeeze out the minority interests, described by the court as the "classic going private transaction," and that required defendants to establish a proper purpose for the merger as a threshold requirement.

The significance of the *Singer* trilogy is clear, and its influence spreads beyond Delaware. But as the judge who coined the phrase "Singer Trilogy" added, Sterling v. Mayflower Hotel Corp., 33 Del. Ch. 293, 93 A.2d 107 (Del. 1952) "is the bedrock on which *Singer, Tanzer* and *Roland International* are built." Weinberger v. UOP, Inc., 426 A.2d 1333, 1344 (Del.Ch.1981). Vice Chancellor Brown summarized *Sterling* as follows:

> *Sterling* stands for the proposition that where a majority shareholder stands on both sides of a merger transaction which will result in the forced removal of the minority shareholders of the subsidiary in exchange for something of value for minority shares, and where the transaction is attacked in a suit in this Court by or on behalf of the minority shareholders on the grounds that the value being offered is inadequate and that the majority shareholder has breached its fiduciary duty in some way because of the manner in which the exchange or conversion value was agreed upon or determined, then this Court has a duty to examine all pertinent elements of the entire transaction so as to make sure that the minority is being treated fairly.

Id. at 1345.

A STUDENT'S GUIDE TO AHMANSON

Judge Traynor's opinion in Jones v. Ahmanson is widely heralded as a landmark in the law of corporations and corporate fiduciaries. It is often cited as evidence that state courts, interpreting common law duties, can provide adequate protection for the interests of shareholders without the intervention of federal law. No small part of the decision's significance is the eloquence of the opinion, and the great reputation of its author.

Some understanding of the workings of the marketplace are necessary to understand the transaction that occurred and the court's reaction to it. Plaintiff was a minority shareholder of United Savings & Loan Association of California ("Association") which became a public company in 1956 when it issued 6,568 shares. Association was controlled by Howard Ahmanson, a successful banker and philanthropist. (Visit the Ahmanson Art Museum when you are next in Los Angeles.) By 1959, the book value of the Association stock was $1,131, which was the result of its great success. However, the minority shareholders enjoyed little of the fruits of success because the market for their stock was very thin. At that price level, there were few buyers for the stock, and also few shares available for sale. Moreover, the company furnished no information to its shareholders, brokers or the public. The 1964 amendments to the Securities Exchange Act, requiring information from some companies whose stock is traded over the counter, was several years away. This situation occurred at a time when stocks of savings and loan associations, particularly the California ones, were the darlings of the stock market and they sold at premium prices well above their book value. But not so the Association.

Ahmanson then formed a holding company called United Financial Corporation ("United") which proceeded to acquire 87% of the stock of the Association through an exchange with invited shareholders. United became a public company, with many shares outstanding selling at prices that would attract buyers. Thus Ahmanson and friends had a public market for their interest in Association; the plaintiff was still standing at the gate waiting for the race to begin. She contended that Ahmanson could have accomplished the same result simply by splitting the Association stock on the basis of 250 for one which would have caused 1,642,000 shares of highly marketable stock to be outstanding. This would have created a market for all, not just some, of the shareholders. The defendants said that device would not have succeeded because it was preferable to sell stock of a holding company that owned more than one savings and loan company. The fact is, the holding company succeeded spectacularly. At a time that the Association book value—and the market value of its stock— was $1,411, an equivalent block of United had a market value of $3,711. The premium over book value was achieved, but only for those to whom Ahmanson made the offer to exchange shares of United for Association.

In the lower courts, the defendants argued that they had "an absolute right to use and dispose of their stock as they saw fit so long as they violated no right of the corporation or the other stockholders." As they saw it, no violation occurred because defendants had no obligation to permit the minority shareholders to participate on the same basis with them in the disposition of their stock. What was done, in other words, did not deprive the minority shareholders of any property right.

The lower courts agreed. As the intermediate appellate court observed, "To act in good faith one does not have to be a 'good neighbor' nor does the law demand of a fiduciary that he should in all matters do unto his beneficiary as he would be done by." Jones v. H. F. Ahmanson & Co., 76 Cal.Rptr. 293, 297 (Cal.App.1969), vacated 1 Cal. 3d 93, 81 Cal.Rptr. 592, 460 P.2d 464.

Judge Traynor, writing for the Supreme Court, used his rhetoric to accomplish a vastly different purpose. He criticized the existing state of the law as inadequate for the present day complex corporation, and he extended the duties of fiduciaries.

Note that the case is a class action, involving an assertion by the plaintiff that the defendants violated some duty owed to her—not to the corporation—and that she, and other members of her class, were entitled to personal recovery. That result demanded an expansion of fiduciary duties.

One commentator calculated that six different intracorporate relationships can be posited:

A. *With Respect to Management Activities*

    1. Between directors and the corporation.

    2. Between the controlling shareholders and the corporation.

    3. Between directors and the minority shareholders.

    4. Between the controlling shareholder and the minority shareholders.

B. *With Respect to Shareholder Activities*

    5. Between the controlling shareholder and the corporation.

    6. Between the controlling shareholder and the minority shareholders.

See Note, Jones v. Ahmanson: The Fiduciary Obligations of Majority Shareholders, 70 Colum.L.Rev. 1079 (1970).

Ahmanson involved only number 6. As to the other five, traditional theory recognized a fiduciary obligation. But the plaintiff could not fit within any of those categories because she stipulated that the corporation had suffered no harm. That might have been a tactical error since the notion of appropriation of corporate opportunity arguably applied to these facts. As it turned out, her stipulation presented Judge Traynor with the opportunity to mete out justice to remedy what he regarded as highly improper and unethical conduct.

Of course, *Ahmanson* raises many questions as to scope and meaning. The defendants controlled the Association both before and after the transaction. They realized value not in disposing of their controlling position, but nonetheless because of it. Judge Traynor finds a duty where control was a material factor. Give some thought to the many situations in which that might be true. Will defendants be wedded to their minority participants in all those cases? Is it appropriate to utilize remedies in this case that are generally used when a corporation merges or liquidates? Is the opinion an overreaction?

JONES v. H. F. AHMANSON & CO.

1 Cal.3d 93, 81 Cal.Rptr. 592, 460 P.2d 464 (1969).

[Plaintiff, the owner of 25 shares of United Savings and Loan Association ("Association") brought a class action for herself and all other similarly situated stockholders. The defendants were the principal stockholders and executives of the Association who controlled a holding company known as United Financial Corporation ("United") which owned 87% of the Association stock.

As noted, there was little activity in the marketplace for its shares, although savings and loan stocks were popular.

The defendants determined to increase investor interest in the stock of the Association, but not through means that would render the Association shares more marketable. Instead, defendants formed United and transferred their shares of the Association to that corporation on the basis of 250 shares for one (a "derived block"). Following the exchange, United owned 85% of the Association's stock. United soon thereafter publicly offered units consisting of shares of its stock and a debenture. In order to pay the interest and principal on the debenture, United was dependent on dividends from the Association. Most of the proceeds from the public offering of United stock was distributed to the original shareholders of United, who had been the former majority stockholders of the Association. A second public offering of additional shares of United was made several months later at which time a large number of shares were sold by the defendants. Obviously, the best way for the public to invest in the Association was to purchase shares of United.

Shortly after the first public offering by United, the defendants caused that company to offer to purchase up to 350 shares of the Association's stock at $1,000 per share when the book value of those shares was $1,411 and earnings were $301 per share. At the time, a derived block of United sold at an aggregate price of $3,700, exclusive of the amount of $927 that had been paid out from the proceeds of the public offering as a return of capital. An additional 130 shares of Association stock were acquired by United Financial as a result of this offer.

In 1959 and in 1960 the Association paid extra dividends of $75 and $57 per share, but in December 1960, after the offer from United to acquire shares had been made, the defendants caused the Association to notify each of the minority stockholders that the only dividends that would thereafter be paid would be $4 per share.

Defendants then proposed to exchange United shares with each of the minority shareholders of the Association on the basis of 51 United shares, of a total value of $2,400, for each Association share. The

book value of each Association share was then $1,700 per share and
the earnings were $615 per share compared to book value of $210 and
earnings of $134 for a block of 51 United shares. The defendants
subsequently withdrew the offer.]

TRAYNOR, J.

I

Plaintiff's Capacity to Sue

We are faced at the outset with defendants' contention that if a
cause of action is stated, it is derivative in nature since any injury
suffered is common to all minority stockholders of the Association.
Therefore, defendants urge, plaintiff may not sue in an individual capacity or on behalf of a class made up of stockholders excluded from
the United Financial exchange, and in any case may not maintain a
derivative action without complying with Financial Code, section
7616. * * *

* * *

It is clear from the stipulated facts and plaintiff's allegations that
she does not seek to recover on behalf of the corporation for injury
done to the corporation by defendants. Although she does allege
that the value of her stock has been diminished by defendants' actions, she does not contend that the diminished value reflects an injury to the corporation and resultant depreciation in the value of the
stock. Thus the gravamen of her cause of action is injury to herself
and the other minority stockholders.

II

Majority Shareholders' Fiduciary Responsibility

Defendants take the position that as shareholders they owe no fiduciary obligation to other shareholders, absent reliance on inside information, use of corporate assets, or fraud. This view has long been
repudiated in California. The Courts of Appeal have often recognized that majority shareholders, either singly or acting in concert to
accomplish a joint purpose, have a fiduciary responsibility to the minority and to the corporation to use their ability to control the corporation in a fair, just, and equitable manner. Majority shareholders
may not use their power to control corporate activities to benefit
themselves alone or in a manner detrimental to the minority. Any
use to which they put the corporation or their power to control the
corporation must benefit all shareholders proportionately and must
not conflict with the proper conduct of the corporation's business.

* * *

Defendants assert, however, that in the use of their own shares
they owed no fiduciary duty to the minority stockholders of the Asso-

ciation. They maintain that they made full disclosure of the circumstances surrounding the formation of United Financial, that the creation of United Financial and its share offers in no way affected the control of the Association, that plaintiff's proportionate interest in the Association was not affected, that the Association was not harmed, and that the market for Association stock was not affected. Therefore, they conclude, they have breached no fiduciary duty to plaintiff and the other minority stockholders.

Defendants would have us retreat from a position demanding equitable treatment of all shareholders by those exercising control over a corporation to a philosophy much criticized by commentators and modified by courts in other jurisdictions as well as our own. In essence defendants suggest that we reaffirm the so-called "majority" rule reflected in our early decisions. This rule, exemplified by the decision in Ryder v. Bamberger, 172 Cal. 791, 158 P. 753 but since severely limited, recognized the "perfect right [of majority shareholders] to dispose of their stock * * * without the slightest regard to the wishes and desires or knowledge of the minority stockholders; * * *" (p. 806, 158 P. p. 759) and held that such fiduciary duty as did exist in officers and directors was to the corporation only. The duty of shareholders as such was not recognized unless they, like officers and directors, by virtue of their position were possessed of information relative to the value of the corporation's shares that was not available to outside shareholders. In such case the existence of special facts permitted a finding that a fiduciary relationship to the corporation and other shareholders existed. (Hobart v. Hobart Estate Co., 26 Cal.2d 412, 159 P.2d 958.)

* * * The rule applies alike to officers, directors, and controlling shareholders in the exercise of powers that are theirs by virtue of their position and to transactions wherein controlling shareholders seek to gain an advantage in the sale or transfer or use of their controlling block of shares. Thus we held in In re Security Finance, 49 Cal.2d 370, 317 P.2d 1, that majority shareholders do not have an absolute right to dissolve a corporation, although ostensibly permitted to do so by Corporations Code, section 4600, because their statutory power is subject to equitable limitations in favor of the minority. We recognized that the majority had the right to dissolve the corporation to protect their investment *if* no alternative means were available *and* no advantage was secured over other shareholders, and noted that "there is nothing sacred in the life of a corporation that transcends the interests of its shareholders, but because dissolution falls with such finality on those interests, above all corporate powers it is subject to equitable limitations." (49 Cal.2d 370, 377, 317 P.2d 1, 5.)

* * *

The increasingly complex transactions of the business and financial communities demonstrate the inadequacy of the traditional theories of fiduciary obligation as tests of majority shareholder responsibility to the minority. These theories have failed to afford adequate protection to minority shareholders and particularly to those in closely held corporations whose disadvantageous and often precarious position renders them particularly vulnerable to the vagaries of the majority. Although courts have recognized the potential for abuse or unfair advantage when a controlling shareholder sells his shares at a premium over investment value (Perlman v. Feldmann, 219 F.2d 173, 50 A.L.R.2d 1134) or in a controlling shareholder's use of control to avoid equitable distribution of corporate assets (Zahn v. Transamerica Corporation (3rd Cir. 1946) 162 F.2d 36, 172 A.L.R. 495 [use of control to cause subsidiary to redeem stock prior to liquidation and distribution of assets]), no comprehensive rule has emerged in other jurisdictions. Nor have most commentators approached the problem from a perspective other than that of the advantage gained in the sale of control. Some have suggested that the price paid for control shares over their investment value be treated as an asset belonging to the corporation itself (Berle and Means, The Modern Corporation and Private Property (1932) p. 243), or as an asset that should be shared proportionately with all shareholders through a general offer (Jennings, Trading in Corporate Control (1956) 44 Cal.L.Rev. 1, 39), and another contends that the sale of control at a premium is always evil (Bayne, The Sale-of-Control Premium: the Intrinsic Illegitimacy (1969) 47 Tex.L.Rev. 215).

* * * The case before us, in which no sale or transfer of actual control is directly involved, demonstrates that the injury anticipated by these authors can be inflicted with impunity under the traditional rules and supports our conclusion that the comprehensive rule of good faith and inherent fairness to the minority in any transaction where control of the corporation is material properly governs controlling shareholders in this state.

We turn now to defendants' conduct to ascertain whether this test is met.

III

Formation of United Financial and Marketing its Shares

Defendants created United Financial during a period of unusual investor interest in the stock of savings and loan associations. They then owned a majority of the outstanding stock of the Association. This stock was not readily marketable owing to a high book value, lack of investor information and facilities, and the closely held nature of the Association. The management of the Association had made no effort to create a market for the stock or to split the shares and reduce their market price to a more attractive level. Two courses were available to defendants in their effort to exploit the bull market in savings and loan stock. Both were made possible by defendants' status as controlling stockholders. The first was either to cause the Association to effect a stock split (Corp.Code, § 1507) and create a market for the Association stock or to create a holding company for Association shares and permit all stockholders to exchange their shares before offering holding company shares to the public. All stockholders would have benefited alike had this been done, but in realizing their gain on the sale of their stock the majority stockholders would of necessity have had to relinquish some of their control shares. Because a public market would have been created, however, the minority stockholders would have been able to extricate themselves without sacrificing their investment had they elected not to remain with the new management.

The second course was that taken by defendants. A new corporation was formed whose major asset was to be the control block of Association stock owned by defendants, but from which minority shareholders were to be excluded. The unmarketable Association stock held by the majority was transferred to the newly formed corporation at an exchange rate equivalent to a 250 for 1 stock split. The new corporation thereupon set out to create a market for its own shares. Association stock constituted 85 percent of the holding company's assets and produced an equivalent proportion of its income. The same individuals controlled both corporations. It appears therefrom that the market created by defendants for United Financial shares was a market that would have been available for Association stock had defendants taken the first course of action.

After United Financial shares became available to the public it became a virtual certainty that no equivalent market could or would be created for Association stock. United Financial had become the controlling stockholder and neither it nor the other defendants would benefit from public trading in Association stock in competition with United Financial shares. Investors afforded an opportunity to acquire United Financial shares would not be likely to choose the less marketable and expensive Association stock in preference. Thus defendants chose a course of action in which they used their control of the Association to obtain an advantage not made available to all stockholders. They did so without regard to the resulting detriment to the minority stockholders and in the absence of any compelling business purpose. Such conduct is not consistent with their duty of good faith and inherent fairness to the minority stockholders. Had defendants afforded the minority an opportunity to exchange their stock on the same basis or offered to purchase them at a price arrived at by independent appraisal, their burden of establishing good faith and inherent fairness would have been much less. At the trial they may present evidence tending to show such good faith or compelling business purpose that would render their action fair under the circumstances. On appeal from the judgment of dismissal after the defendants' demurrer was sustained we decide only that the complaint states a cause of action entitling plaintiff to relief.

Defendants gained an additional advantage for themselves through their use of control of the Association when they pledged that control over the Association's assets and earnings to secure the holding company's debt, a debt that had been incurred for their own benefit.[14] In so doing the defendants breached their fiduciary obligation to the minority once again and caused United Financial and its controlling shareholders to become inextricably wedded to a conflict of interest between the minority stockholders of each corporation. Alternatives were available to them that would have benefited all stockholders proportionately. The course they chose affected the minority stockholders with no less finality than does dissolution (In re Security Finance, *supra*, 49 Cal.2d 370, 317 P.2d 1) and demands no less concern for minority interests.

In so holding we do not suggest that the duties of corporate fiduciaries include in all cases an obligation to make a market for and to facilitate public trading in the stock of the corporation. But when, as here, no market exists, the controlling shareholders may not use their power to control the corporation for the purpose of promoting a marketing scheme that benefits themselves alone to the detriment of the minority. Nor do we suggest that a control block of shares may not be sold or transferred to a holding company. We decide only that the circumstances of any transfer of controlling shares will be subject to judicial scrutiny when it appears that the controlling shareholders may have breached their fiduciary obligation to the corporation or the remaining shareholders.

IV

Damages

From the perspective of the minority stockholders of the Association, the transfer of control under these circumstances to another corporation and the resulting impact on their position as minority stockholders accomplished a fundamental corporate change as to them. Control of a closely held savings and loan association, the major portion of whose earnings had been retained over a long period while its stockholders remained stable, became an asset of a publicly held holding company. The position of the minority shareholder was drastically changed thereby. His practical ability to influence corporate decisionmaking was diminished substantially when control was transferred to a publicly held corporation that was in turn controlled by the owners of more than 750,000 shares. The future business

14. Should it become necessary to encumber or liquidate Association assets to service this debt or to depart from a dividend policy consistent with the business needs of the Association, damage to the Association itself may occur. We need not resolve here, but note with some concern, the problem facing United Financial, which owes the same fiduciary duty to its own shareholders as to those of the Association. Any decision regarding use of Association assets and earnings to service the holding company debt must be made in the context of these potentially conflicting interests.

goals of the Association could reasonably be expected to reflect the needs and interest of the holding company rather than the aims of the Association stockholders thereafter. In short, the enterprise into which the minority stockholders were now locked was not that in which they had invested.

* * *

Appraisal rights protect the dissenting minority shareholder against being forced to either remain an investor in an enterprise fundamentally different than that in which he invested or sacrifice his investment by sale of his shares at less than a fair value. (O'Neal and Derwin, Expulsion or Oppression of Business Associates (1961), *supra*, 62.) Plaintiff here was entitled to no less. But she was entitled to more. In the circumstances of this case she should have been accorded the same opportunity to exchange her Association stock for that of United Financial accorded the majority.

Although a controlling shareholder who sells or exchanges his shares is not under an obligation to obtain for the minority the consideration that he receives in all cases, when he does sell or exchange his shares the transaction is subject to close scrutiny. When the majority receives a premium over market value for its shares, the consideration for which that premium is paid will be examined. If it reflects payment for that which is properly a corporate asset all shareholders may demand to share proportionately. (Perlman v. Feldmann, *supra*, 219 F.2d 173.) Here the exchange was an integral part of a scheme that the defendants could reasonably foresee would have as an incidental effect the destruction of the potential public market for Association stock. The remaining stockholders would thus be deprived of the opportunity to realize a profit from those intangible characteristics that attach to publicly marketed stock and enhance its value above book value. Receipt of an appraised value reflecting book value and earnings alone could not compensate the minority shareholders for the loss of this potential. Since the damage is real, although the amount is speculative, equity demands that the minority stockholders be placed in a position at least as favorable as that the majority created for themselves.

If, after trial of the cause, plaintiff has established facts in conformity with the allegations of the complaint and stipulation, then upon tender of her Association stock to defendants she will be entitled to receive at her election either the appraised value of her shares on the date of the exchange, May 14, 1959, with interest at 7 percent a year from the date of this action or a sum equivalent to the fair market value of a "derived block" of United Financial stock on the date of this action with interest thereon from that date, and the sum of $927.50 (the return of capital paid to the original United Financial shareholders) with interest thereon from the date United Financial first made such payments to its original shareholders, for each share tendered. The appraised or fair market value shall be reduced, however, by the amount by which dividends paid on Association shares during the period from May 14, 1959 to the present exceeds the dividends paid on a corresponding block of United Financial shares during the same period.

* * *

NOTE—THE SEARCH FOR FAIRNESS

If fairness is the test in parent-subsidiary transactions, what constitutes fair treatment of the minority by the majority? In one context, a merger of the subsidiary into the parent, the courts have usually found that fairness requires that the minority shareholders receive an amount of consideration equal to the value of the stock which they surrender. *See,* for example, Tanzer v. International General Industries in Note: The Singer Trilogy. That has been criticized as inadequate. It has been urged that if the merger creates values over and above those that previously existed, through some efficiency of operation (the whole being greater than the sum of the parts), then the synergistic gains should be shared proportionately. Sharing should be accomplished by allocating market value of securities based on *relative* pre-merger values. (Brudney & Chirelstein, Fair Shares in Corporate Mergers and Takeovers, 88 Harv.L.Rev. 297 (1974).)

Sounds good, answers another commentator, but it does not withstand actual application. The benefit cannot be readily measured, and one must look closely at the source from which it emanates in order to see what allocation should be made. Thus, the "fair shares" approach rejects the virtue of a simple and predictable test for one that improperly holds out a promise of illusory precision. (Lorne, A Reappraisal of Fair Shares in Controlled Mergers, 126 U.Pa.L.Rev. 955 (1978).)

Moreover, Mr. Lorne notes another particularly significant factor inherent in so-called cash out mergers—the element of risk. It is fundamental to the operation of the stock market that rewards are yielded in some proportion to the risks taken. When minority shareholders are removed from the risk of stock ownership by a cash out merger, Lorne doubts the validity of their entitlement to a participation in potential future rewards.

However, the Delaware Supreme Court has rejected the appraisal value as a basis for damages when a breach of fiduciary duty has occurred. In that situation, rescission or its monetary substitute is needed. That remedy would "equal the increment in value that [the defendant] enjoyed as a result of acquiring [the subsidiary's] stock in issue." Lynch v. Vickers Energy Corp., 429 A.2d 497 (Del.1981). Is that award the equivalent of "fair shares?"

Weinberger v. UOP, Inc., 426 A.2d 1333 (Del.Ch.1981) involved the merger of Signal Companies Inc. ("Signal") with its 50.5% owned subsidiary, UOP, Inc. The majority interest was acquired in a tender offer at $21 per share. Three years later Signal decided that its best interests would be served by acquiring 100% of the stock. Signal then entered into an agreement with UOP's board, six of whose 13 members (including the president) were affiliated with Signal, to acquire the minority interest through a merger in which the minority shareholders would receive $21 in cash.

Among other things plaintiff objected to the fairness of the price. Plaintiff introduced expert testimony to show that the fair value was $26, a figure arrived at mainly on an analysis of discounted cash flow. (Recall The Parable in Chapter 5). The court was troubled by "the fortuitous selection of a discount factor which is not necessarily related to any objective standard."

426 A.2d at 1358. The expert also based his analysis on an assumption of enhanced value to the buyer from acquiring full ownership.

The Court observed:

* * * [I] have difficulty with the entire concept employed by plaintiff's expert. * * * Thus, as I perceive it, plaintiff seems to be arguing that in order for the transaction to be fair to UOP's minority shareholders, they must be paid the value of the stock to Signal. And this would appear to be in contrast to the value of a share of UOP in the hands of all shareholders as of the time of the merger.

"This position of the plaintiff, if I have perceived it correctly, stems from the admonishment in *Singer, Tanzer* and *Roland International*, that a majority shareholder cannot be absolved from the scrutiny of the courts simply because minority shareholders who are unhappy with the cash out price have the right to seek judicial determination of the value of their shares under the appraisal statute * * *. As a consequence, plaintiff seems to be contending that the factors which go into a determination of the value of stock under a[n] * * * appraisal proceeding are not those which apply in a proceeding such as this wherein a minority shareholder is attacking the fairness, and thus the validity of the merger itself, on the grounds that the price paid for the minority interests is grossly inadequate. Thus, plaintiff seems to be suggesting that in evaluating the fairness of the merger terms to the minority in such a proceeding as this, one must look to what it is reasonably worth to the former majority shareholder to be rid of all other shareholders so as to become the sole owner of the enterprise, and then, using that as a basis or starting point, determine what is a fair amount for it to have paid the minority for the right to become sole shareholder. The resulting figure the plaintiff, through the approach employed by his expert, would transform into the fair value of the minority shares in the context of a cash out merger.

"I do not find this approach to correspond with either logic or the existing law. In the first place, it assumes that a stock has more than one value in the hands of a minority shareholder. That is to say, if he has no complaints as to how the merger came about and no complaints as to the good faith effort of those in fiduciary position to discharge their duties, but if he nonetheless has an honest difference of opinion as to the price and for that reason desires an appraisal, then the Court hears evidence and values his shares under one standard. But if the same shareholder feels that those in a fiduciary position to his interests have acted in disregard of their duty, or if he feels that a concentration of all the corporate stock in the hands of the former majority shareholder will unjustly enrich the former majority shareholder when compared against that which he is paying for it, then the Court is to hear evidence and value his shares under a different standard. I cannot believe that the policy of our law contemplates the application of such a dual standard.

"Aside from this, the case law does not support the distinction that plaintiff is attempting to make. Again, as directed by *Singer*, *Tanzer* and *Roland International*, I return to Sterling v. Mayflower Hotel Corp., for the final analysis. There it was stated by the Supreme Court that upon the conversion of the Mayflower stock into Hilton stock a minority shareholder of Mayflower was entitled to receive 'the substantial equivalent in value of the shares he held before the merger.' 93 A.2d at 110. That was the test. A Mayflower shareholder was not entitled to 'something that he did not have before the merger and could not obtain'—in that case the liquidating value of his stock. 93 A.2d at 111.

* * *

"Thus, to the extent that plaintiff is suggesting that in the context of a cash out merger the fairness of the price paid to the minority is to be determined by reference to that which the former majority shareholder will have immediately after the merger as a result of being the 100 per cent owner of the corporation, I reject the argument as being unsound and not in accord with the existing law.

"At the same time, it is presumably proper to view the benefits that may flow to the majority shareholder as a result of becoming the 100 per cent owner as one of the elements to be considered in determining the fairness of the transaction. * * *

" * * * [I]t can be argued that the Supreme Court [in *Sterling*] tacitly recognized that as a part of 'entire fairness' it was proper to allow the minority some element of value over and above the otherwise provable value of the minority shares for the benefit that would come to the majority shareholder as a result of becoming the 100 per cent of the subsidiary through the merger process. This is not to say that it is an absolute requirement, however, and it does not mean that the value of the minority shares to the majority shareholder is the standard to be applied."

426 A.2d at 1359–61.

3. FAIRNESS: PROCESS AND REVIEW

"Fairness" is a fact-specific judgment. In a transaction where a controlling person is on both sides, with power to impose the result, courts closely scrutinize the economic terms and the business reason. But there are constraints on the court's ability to second-guess business people. Moreover, the most the court can do is to determine whether the economic terms come within the range of fairness; the court cannot renegotiate a deal to assure that it is fairer than fair.

In addition to examining substance, courts view the process by which the deal was struck. Process is something that courts understand better than business. Consideration of the process focuses on the board of directors, and the relevant questions include the following:

1. Who are the directors? Do they appear to be independent?

2. What did the board do in considering the transaction? How much time did they spend on it? What documentation did they examine?

3. Were experts used? Were their efforts apparently professional?

4. What disclosure was made to the shareholders? Were communications marked by total candor?

These considerations are similar to those applied to all self-dealing transactions. *See* Chapter 14. However, in transactions between a corporation and a controlling person, there is simply no way that business can be conducted on an arm's length basis. We hasten to add that this does not mean that they cannot deal fairly with one another. But directors, however well-intentioned and honest and strong they may be can never be truly independent of the controlling person who possesses unchecked power to hire and fire them.

In other instances of self dealing, the fact of shareholder approval has significance. In Michelson v. Duncan, 407 A.2d 211 (Del.1979), the court held that a well-pleaded complaint alleging waste of corporate assets could not be dismissed on summary judgment, but that the burden of proof was shifted to the plaintiff after the shareholders ratified the transaction.

However, suppose ratification was a foregone conclusion because the controlling person had the votes to assure it. Will a court attach the same legal significance to ratification as if the shareholder body was independent? If not, what then is meant by the oft repeated contention that shareholders have a right to vote their stock as they please, including their own self-interest?

Weinberger v. UOP, Inc., 426 A.2d 1333 (Del.Ch.1981), as previously noted, involved the merger of Signal with its 50.5% owned subsidiary. The court observed, "Of significance, Signal's proposal required that the merger would have to be approved by a majority of

UOP's outstanding minority shares voting at the shareholders meeting at which the merger would be considered and, in addition, that the minority shares voting in favor of the merger, when coupled with Signal's 50.5 per cent interest, would have to comprise at least two-thirds of the UOP shares. Otherwise the proposed merger would be deemed disapproved." Id, at 1339.

The defendants argued that this structure to the transaction placed the burden on the plaintiff to establish unfairness—a difficult task. The court had granted an earlier motion to dismiss the complaint on grounds that it failed to state a cause of action. Weinberger v. UOP, Inc., 409 A.2d 1262 (Del.Ch.1979), noting that the fact that the minority shareholders were given power to reject the transaction meant that the unfairness of which the plaintiff complained was not imposed by the controlling shareholder. However, after an amended complaint, and a trial on the merits, Vice Chancellor Brown now observed:

"The ultimate burden is on the majority shareholder to show by a preponderence of the evidence that the transaction is fair. However, it is not the obligation of the majority shareholder to come forward with evidence in the first instance. Rather, it is the burden of the plaintiff attacking the fairness of the merger to demonstrate some need to invoke this obligation on the part of the majority shareholder. The plaintiff must charge that for some reason the terms of the merger are unfair to the minority, and must come forward initially with some proof and argument in support thereof *   *   * . It is the responsibility of the plaintiff to demonstrate some basis for the charge that the terms are unfair to the minority. Once done, the majority shareholder has the burden of coming forward with evidence to refute such charges and to demonstrate on all the evidence that the minority shareholders have been treated fairly.

*   *   *

"The fact that Signal and UOP structured the merger so that it had to be approved by a majority of the minority shareholders voting on the issue does not remove them from the burden [of establishing fairness]. The dismissal of the original complaint for failure to state a claim because of the manner in which the vote was structured simply ruled out that one element or factor, namely the use of its controlling voting position by Signal, from being potentially determinative of the matter. It was simply a finding that Signal did not use its *voting power* to bring about the merger for an improper purpose, as proscribed by *Singer*. It was not a finding that Signal in no way whatever used its majority position so as to cause UOP's minority to be merged out, nor did it represent any finding as to Signal's purpose.

"Since the merger terms were proposed by Signal and agreed to by UOP's board which at least it superficially controlled, Signal (as it has always conceded) still stood on both sides of the transaction and therefore, under *Sterling*, still owed a fiduciary duty to UOP's minority in dealing with UOP's property. The evaluation of the purpose element as required by *Tanzer*, as well as a consideration of the other challenged factors which went into the decision to fix the merger price at $21 per share, was not obviated by Signal's decision to leave the vote in the hands of the minority."

C.   FEDERAL LAW AND MAJORITY STOCKHOLDERS

1.   FIDUCIARY STANDARDS UNDER RULE 10b–5

The fiduciary obligations of managers and controlling persons are customarily governed by state law. Federal securities law governs a limited aspect of fiduciary conduct, that is, the duty to make full disclosure to shareholders and potential investors. At first glance, therefore, the substantive conduct of corporate fiduciaries does not come within the scope of the federal securities law.

However, the language of Rule 10b–5 invites another interpretation. The rule does prohibit, in paragraphs (a) and (c), fraudulent conduct "in connection with the purchase or sale" of any security. Fraudulent conduct, it might be argued, can take the form of unfair transactions that a dominant person is able to impose on the corporation or on its stockholders. This has been referred to as "equitable fraud." For example, the corporation might be compelled by its controlling person to sell its shares for less than fair market value, or the corporation might be forced to purchase shares from the controlling persons at more than fair market value. While suit could be brought under state law for breach of fiduciary duty, a plaintiff, suing on behalf of the corporation in a derivative suit, might prefer to sue under Rule 10b–5.

A Federal law might offer a plaintiff the advantages of worldwide service of process, more favorable discovery rules, or a result on the merits that could not be won in state courts. Thus, despite the early reaction of the courts that Rule 10b–5 was limited to "garden variety fraud" in the marketplace and not breaches of fiduciary duty, Birnbaum v. Newport Steel Corp., 193 F.2d 461 (2d Cir. 1952), cert. denied 343 U.S. 956, 72 S.Ct. 1051, 96 L.Ed. 1356, the drive to bring mismanagement cases into federal court picked up pace.

Plaintiffs' major obstacle, in this context, involved the issue of deception. While it was not difficult to find that a fiduciary, who misled the board of directors into issuing stock to him for spurious consideration, was liable to the corporation under Rule 10b–5 for fraudulent conduct. Hooper v. Mountain State Securities Corp., 282 F.2d 195 (5th Cir. 1960), cert. denied 365 U.S. 814, 81 S.Ct. 695, 5 L. Ed. 2d 693, a different case was presented when all the directors knew the pertinent facts. Thus, in O'Neill v. Maytag, 339 F.2d 764 (2d Cir. 1964), the plaintiff accused the board of directors of repurchasing the company's shares at a premium price in order to maintain their own control. The court agreed with defendants that no violation of Rule 10b–5 had occurred because all members of the board of directors were fully informed as to all of the relevant facts about the transaction. Thus, the federal purpose of providing full disclosure to the decision makers had been served—however differently the transaction might be viewed under state law. By contrast, the same court, in Ruckle v. Roto American Corp., 339 F.2d 24 (2d Cir. 1964), decided several weeks earlier, had found that a violation of Rule 10b–5 occurred when *one* of the directors had been misled about a similar transaction, even though a majority of the decisionmaking body was fully informed.

In this view, where the stockholders of the corporation perform no role in the decision—because state law so determines—then no deception of the corporation had occurred. Some courts [the Third Circuit in Pappas v. Moss, 393 F.2d 865 (3rd Cir. 1968), and the Seventh Circuit in Dasho v. Susquehanna Corp., 380 F.2d 262 (7th Cir. 1967)] took the position that it was possible for all of the directors to deceive both the corporation and the stockholders in a fraudulent self-dealing transaction. In effect, what these courts held was that the knowledge of the deceiving directors was not attributed to the corporation and therefore there was deception of the corporation.

The Second Circuit took another look at this issue in Schoenbaum v. Firstbrook, 405 F.2d 215 (2d Cir. 1968). A majority-owned subsidiary issued some of its shares to the parent corporation, allegedly for inadequate consideration. A minority of the directors of the subsidiary were affiliated with the parent corporation but they abstained from voting on the transaction. A panel of the Second Circuit affirmed the dismissal of the action under Rule 10b–5 on grounds that there had been no deception. The court asked whether it was appropriate to impute to the corporation the knowledge of its agents and found that under the circumstances it was required to do so. The court, *en banc*, reversed the summary dismissal of the complaint. The key language in Judge Hays' opinion is as follows:

> In the present case it is alleged that [parent] exercised controlling influence over the issuance to it of treasury stock of [subsidiary] for a wholly inadequate consideration. If it is established that the transaction took place as alleged, it constituted a violation of Rule 10b–5, Subdivision (3) because [parent] engaged in an "act, practice or course of business which operates or would operate as a fraud or deceit upon any person, in connection with the purchase or sale of any security." Moreover, [parent] and the directors of

[subsidiary] were guilty of deceiving the stockholders of [subsidiary] (other than parent).   405 F.2d at 219–20.

Those who favored an expansion of Rule 10b–5 so as to cover breaches of fiduciary duty, whether or not accompanied by deception, pointed out that the court found that there had been a violation and then added, *"moreover"* that there had been deception.   Thus, it would seem that the violation was not made to turn on whether there was deception.   Such an interpretation of *Schoenbaum* could lead to the creation of a federal body of fiduciary law and greatly reduce the significance of state corporation law.   The only qualification was that the transaction had to involve a securities transaction, which usually was not difficult to find.

Subsequent cases in the Second Circuit and elsewhere pondered the meaning of *Schoenbaum*, with some courts pointing out that the case was at heart a deception case, while other courts emphasized the nature of the transaction in which a dominant stockholder imposed an unfair transaction on the corporation by means of its undue influence.   Thus, in Popkin v. Bishop, 464 F.2d 714 (2d Cir. 1972), plaintiff acknowledged that the proxy statement made full disclosure of the facts bearing upon the fairness of a merger but contended that the allegedly unfair exchange ratio imposed on the minority shareholders constituted a violation of the anti-fraud rules.   The court held that federal law was satisfied by full disclosure to the stockholders.   *See* Note, The Controlling Influence Standard in Rule 10b–5 Corporate Mismanagement Cases, 86 Harv.L.Rev. 107 (1973).   The Supreme Court recognized an implied private right of action under Rule 10b–5 in Superintendent of Insurance v. Bankers Life & Casualty Co., 404 U.S. 6, 92 S.Ct. 165, 30 L.Ed.2d 128 (1971), a complex case where the wrongdoer sold securities owned by the company of which he was the sole stockholder and embezzled the proceeds.   For the most part, the transaction in question was not one of "garden variety fraud" in the marketplace, but a classic example of mismanagement.   However, the Court found the elements of deception in the case, and the debate remained open.

The high-water mark for 10b–5 as a rule proscribing improper conduct was Green v. Santa Fe Industries, Inc., 533 F.2d 1283 (2d Cir. 1976), where the court found that a violation had occurred in a "going private" transaction.   The majority stockholder eliminated the minority interest for cash, allegedly for no proper corporate purpose and for inadequate consideration.   The transaction was accomplished in a "short form merger" which did not require a vote of the stockholders under Delaware law.   Thus, there was no deception of stockholders since there was no communication to them.   Furthermore, Delaware law at that time rejected any remedy for minority stockholders except appraisal, (a view Delaware courts have since rejected in Roland International Corp. v. Najjar, 407 A.2d 1032 (Del.1979)) so that the lack of proper purpose was irrelevant under state law.   The defendants prevailed in the district court on grounds that there had been no deception. The Second Circuit reversed. Judge Medina, who interestingly enough had dissented in *Schoenbaum*, now wrote, "Lest there be any lingering doubt on this point, we now hold that [in cases involving breach of fiduciary duty], including that one now before us, no allegation or proof of misrepresentation or non-disclosure is necessary." 533 F.2d, at 1287. This time the issue was unmistakenly presented to the Supreme Court.

Although the Supreme Court in *Santa Fe, infra*, provided a firm answer to the "deception" issue, important definitional and application questions remained, which are presented in the two succeeding court of appeals decisions.

SANTA FE INDUSTRIES, INC. v. GREEN

430 U.S. 462, 97 S.Ct. 1292, 51 L.Ed.2d 480 (1977).

Mr. Justice WHITE delivered the opinion of the Court.

The issue in this case involves the reach and coverage of § 10(b) of the Securities Exchange Act of 1934 and Rule 10b–5 thereunder in the context of a Delaware short-form merger transaction used by the majority stockholder of a corporation to eliminate the minority interest.

I

In 1936, petitioner Santa Fe Industries, Inc. (Santa Fe), acquired control of 60% of the stock of Kirby Lumber Corp. (Kirby), a Delaware corporation. Through a series of purchases over the succeeding years, Santa Fe increased its control of Kirby's stock to 95%; the purchase prices during the period 1968–1973 ranged from $65 to $92.50 per share. In 1974, wishing to acquire 100% ownership of Kirby, Santa Fe availed itself of § 253 of the Delaware Corporation Law, known as the "short-form merger" statute. Section 253 permits a parent corporation owning at least 90% of the stock of a subsidiary to merge with that subsidiary, upon approval by the parent's board of directors, and to make payment in cash for the shares of the minority stockholders. The statute does not require the consent of, or advance notice to, the minority stockholders. However, notice of the merger must be given within 10 days after its effective date, and any stockholder who is dissatisfied with the terms of the merger may petition the Delaware Court of Chancery for a decree ordering the surviving corporation to pay him the fair value of his shares, as determined by a court-appointed appraiser subject to review by the court.

Santa Fe obtained independent appraisals of the physical assets of Kirby—land, timber, buildings, and machinery—and of Kirby's oil, gas, and mineral interests. These appraisals, together with other financial information, were submitted to Morgan Stanley & Co. (Morgan Stanley), an investment banking firm retained to appraise the fair market value of Kirby stock. Kirby's physical assets were appraised at $320 million (amounting to $640 for each of the 500,000 shares); Kirby's stock was valued by Morgan Stanley at $125 per share. Under the terms of the merger, minority stockholders were offered $150 per share.

The provisions of the short-form merger statute were fully complied with. The minority stockholders of Kirby were notified the day after the merger became effective and were advised of their right to obtain an appraisal in Delaware court if dissatisfied with the offer of $150 per share. They also received an information statement containing, in addition to the relevant financial data about Kirby, the appraisals of the value of Kirby's assets and the Morgan Stanley appraisal concluding that the fair market value of the stock was $125 per share.

Respondents, minority stockholders of Kirby, objected to the terms of the merger, but did not pursue their appraisal remedy in the Delaware Court of Chancery. Instead, they brought this action in federal court on behalf of the corporation and other minority stockholders, seeking to set aside the merger or to recover what they claimed to be the fair value of their shares. The amended complaint asserted that, based on the fair market value of Kirby's physical assets as revealed by the appraisal included in the information statement sent to minority shareholders, Kirby's stock was worth at least $772 per share. The complaint alleged further that the merger took place without prior notice to minority stockholders; that the purpose of the merger was to appropriate the difference between the "conceded pro rata value of the physical assets," and the offer of $150 per share—to "freez[e] out the minority stockholders at a wholly inadequate price," and that Santa Fe, knowing the appraised value of the physical assets, obtained a "fraudulent appraisal" of the stock from Morgan Stanley and offered $25 above that appraisal "in order to lull the minority stockholders into erroneously believing that [Santa Fe was] generous." This course of conduct was alleged to be "a violation of Rule 10b–5 because defendants employed a 'device, scheme, or artifice to defraud' and engaged in an 'act, practice or course of business which operates or would operate as a fraud or deceit upon any person, in connection with the purchase or sale of any security.'" Morgan Stanley assertedly participated in the fraud as an accessory by submitting its appraisal of $125 per share although knowing the appraised value of the physical assets.

The District Court dismissed the complaint for failure to state a claim upon which relief could be granted. 391 F.Supp. 849 (SDNY 1975). * * *

* * *

A divided Court of Appeals for the Second Circuit reversed. 533 F.2d 1283 (1976). It first agreed that there was a double aspect to the case: first, the claim that gross undervaluation of the minority stock itself violated Rule 10b–5; and second, that "without any misrepresentation or failure to disclose relevant facts, the merger itself constitutes a violation of Rule 10b–5" because it was accomplished without any corporate purpose and without prior notice to the minority stockholders. Id., at 1285. As to the first aspect of the case, the Court of Appeals did not disturb the District Court's conclusion that the complaint did not allege a material misrepresentation or nondisclosure with respect to the value of the stock; and the court declined to rule that a claim of gross undervaluation itself would suffice to make out a Rule 10b–5 case. With respect to the second aspect of the case, however, the court fundamentally disagreed with the District Court as to the reach and coverage of Rule 10b–5. The Court of Appeals' view was that, although the Rule plainly reached material misrepresentations and nondisclosures in connection with the purchase or sale of securities, neither misrepresentation nor nondisclosure was a necessary element of a Rule 10b–5 action; the Rule reached "breaches of fiduciary duty by a majority against minority shareholders without any charge of misrepresentation or lack of disclosure."

* * *

II

* * * The Court of Appeals' approach to the interpretation of Rule 10b–5 is inconsistent with that taken by the Court last Term in Ernst & Ernst v. Hochfelder, 425 U.S. 185, 96 S.Ct. 1375, 47 L.Ed.2d 668 (1976).

Ernst & Ernst makes clear that in deciding whether a complaint states a cause of action for "fraud" under Rule 10b–5, "we turn first to the language of § 10(b), for '[t]he starting point in every case involving construction of a statute is the language itself.'" In holding that a cause of action under Rule 10b–5 does not lie for mere negligence, the Court began with the principle that "[a]scertainment of congressional intent with respect to the standard of liability created by a particular section of the [1933 and 1934] Acts must * * * rest primarily on the language of that section," 425 U.S., at 200, 96 S. Ct., at 1384, and then focused on the statutory language of § 10(b)— "[t]he words 'manipulative or deceptive' used in conjunction with 'device or contrivance.'" The same language and the same principle apply to this case.

To the extent that the Court of Appeals would rely on the use of the term "fraud" in Rule 10b–5 to bring within the ambit of the Rule all breaches of fiduciary duty in connection with a securities transaction, its interpretation would, like the interpretation rejected by the Court in *Ernst & Ernst*, "add a gloss to the operative language of the statute quite different from its commonly accepted meaning."

But, as the Court there held, the language of the statute must control the interpretation of the Rule:

> Rule 10b–5 was adopted pursuant to authority granted the [Securities and Exchange] Commission under § 10(b). The rulemaking power granted to an administrative agency charged with the administration of a federal statute is not the power to make law. Rather, it is "the power to adopt regulations to carry into effect the will of Congress as expressed by the statute." * * * [The scope of the Rule] cannot exceed the power granted the Commission by Congress under § 10(b).

The language of § 10(b) gives no indication that Congress meant to prohibit any conduct not involving manipulation or deception. Nor have we been cited to any evidence in the legislative history that would support a departure from the language of the statute. "When a statute speaks so specifically in terms of manipulation and deception, * * * and when its history reflects no more expansive intent, we are quite unwilling to extend the scope of the statute * * *." Thus the claim of fraud and fiduciary breach in this complaint states a cause of action under any part of Rule 10b–5 only if the conduct alleged can be fairly viewed as "manipulative or deceptive" within the meaning of the statute.

III

It is our judgment that the transaction, if carried out as alleged in the complaint, was neither deceptive nor manipulative and therefore did not violate either § 10(b) of the Act or Rule 10b–5.

As we have indicated, the case comes to us on the premise that the complaint failed to allege a material misrepresentation or material failure to disclose. The finding of the District Court, undisturbed by the Court of Appeals, was that there was no "omission" or "misstatement" in the information statement accompanying the notice of merger. On the basis of the information provided, minority shareholders could either accept the price offered or reject it and seek an appraisal in the Delaware Court of Chancery. Their choice was fairly presented, and they were furnished with all relevant information on which to base their decision.[14]

---

14. In addition to their principal argument that the complaint alleges a fraud under clauses (a) and (c) of Rule 10b–5, respondents also argue that the complaint alleges nondisclosure and misrepresentation in violation of clause (b) of the Rule. Their major contention in this respect is that the majority stockholder's failure to give the minority advance notice of the merger was a material nondisclosure, even though the Delaware short-form merger statute does not require such notice. Brief for Respondents 27. But respondents do not indicate how they might have acted differently had they had prior notice of the merger. Indeed, they accept the conclusion of both courts below that under Delaware law they could not have enjoined the merger because an appraisal proceeding is their sole remedy in the Delaware courts for any alleged unfairness in the terms of the merger. Thus, the failure to give advance notice was not a material nondisclosure within the meaning of the statute or the Rule. Cf. TSC Industries, Inc. v. Northway, Inc., 426 U.S. 438, 96 S.Ct. 2126, 48 L.Ed.2d 757 (1976).

We therefore find inapposite the cases relied upon by respondents and the court below, in which the breaches of fiduciary duty held violative of Rule 10b–5 included some element of deception. Those cases forcefully reflect the principle that "[§] 10(b) must be read flexibly, not technically and restrictively" and that the statute provides a cause of action for any plaintiff who "suffer[s] an injury as a result of deceptive practices touching its sale [or purchase] of securities * * *." Superintendent of Insurance v. Bankers Life & Cas. Co., 404 U.S. 6, 12–13, 92 S.Ct. 165, 169, 30 L.Ed.2d 128 (1971). But the cases do not support the proposition, adopted by the Court of Appeals below and urged by respondents here, that a breach of fiduciary duty by majority stockholders, without any deception, misrepresentation, or nondisclosure, violates the statute and the Rule.

It is also readily apparent that the conduct alleged in the complaint was not "manipulative" within the meaning of the statute. "Manipulation" is "virtually a term of art when used in connection with securities markets." Ernst & Ernst, 425 U.S., at 199, 96 S.Ct., at 1384. * * * No doubt Congress meant to prohibit the full range of ingenious devices that might be used to manipulate securities prices. But we do not think it would have chosen this "term of art" if it had meant to bring within the scope of § 10(b) instances of corporate mismanagement such as this, in which the essence of the complaint is that shareholders were treated unfairly by a fiduciary.

IV

The language of the statute is, we think, "sufficiently clear in its context" to be dispositive here, but even if it were not, there are additional considerations that weigh heavily against permitting a cause of action under Rule 10b–5 for the breach of corporate fiduciary duty alleged in this complaint. Congress did not expressly provide a private cause of action for violations of § 10(b). Although we have recognized an implied cause of action under that section in some circumstances, Superintendent of Insurance v. Bankers Life & Cas. Co., *supra*, 404 U.S., at 13 n. 9, 92 S.Ct., at 169, we have also recognized that a private cause of action under the antifraud provisions of the Securities Exchange Act should not be implied where it is "unnecessary to ensure the fulfillment of Congress' purposes" in adopting the Act. Piper v. Chris-Craft Industries, 430 U.S., at 41, 97 S.Ct., at 949. Cf. J. I. Case Co. v. Borak, 377 U.S. 426, 431–433, 84 S.Ct. 1555, 12 L. Ed.2d 423 (1964). As we noted earlier, the Court repeatedly has described the "fundamental purpose" of the Act as implementing a "philosophy of full disclosure"; once full and fair disclosure has occurred, the fairness of the terms of the transaction is at most a tangential concern of the statute. As in Cort v. Ash, 422 U.S. 66, 78, 80, 95 S.Ct. 2080, 2087, 2090, 45 L.Ed.2d 26 (1975), we are reluctant to recognize a cause of action here to serve what is "at best a subsidiary purpose" of the federal legislation.

A second factor in determining whether Congress intended to create a federal cause of action in these circumstances is "whether 'the cause of action [is] one traditionally relegated to state law * * *.'" Piper v. Chris-Craft Industries, Inc., 430 U.S., at 40, 97 S.Ct., at 949, quoting Cort v. Ash, *supra*, at 78, 95 S.Ct., at 2087. The Delaware Legislature has supplied minority shareholders with a cause of action in the Delaware Court of Chancery to recover the fair value of shares allegedly undervalued in a short-form merger. Of course, the existence of a particular state-law remedy is not dispositive of the question whether Congress meant to provide a similar federal remedy, but as in *Cort* and *Piper*, we conclude that "it is entirely appropriate in this instance to relegate respondent and others in his situation to whatever remedy is created by state law." 422 U.S., at 84, 95 S.Ct., at 2091; 430 U.S., at 41, 97 S.Ct., at 949.

The reasoning behind a holding that the complaint in this case alleged fraud under Rule 10b–5 could not be easily contained. It is difficult to imagine how a court could distinguish, for purposes of Rule 10b–5 fraud, between a majority stockholder's use of a short-form merger to eliminate the minority at an unfair price and the use of some other device, such as a long-form merger, tender offer, or liquidation, to achieve the same result; or indeed how a court could distinguish the alleged abuses in these going private transactions from other types of fiduciary self-dealing involving transactions in securities. The result would be to bring within the Rule a wide variety of corporate conduct traditionally left to state regulation. In addition to posing a "danger of vexatious litigation which could result from a widely expanded class of plaintiffs under Rule 10b–5," Blue Chip Stamps v. Manor Drug Stores, 421 U.S., at 740, 95 S.Ct., at 1927, this extension of the federal securities laws would overlap and quite possibly interfere with state corporate law. Federal courts applying a "federal fiduciary principle" under Rule 10b–5 could be expected to depart from state fiduciary standards at least to the extent necessary to ensure uniformity within the federal system. Absent a clear indication of congressional intent, we are reluctant to federalize the substantial portion of the law of corporations that deals with transactions in securities, particularly where established state policies of corporate regulation would be overridden. As the Court stated in Cort v. Ash, *supra*: "Corporations are creatures of state law, and investors commit their funds to corporate directors on the understanding that, except where federal law *expressly* requires certain responsibilities of directors with respect to stockholders, state law will govern the internal affairs of the corporation." 422 U.S., at 84, 95 S. Ct., at 2091 (emphasis added).

We thus adhere to the position that "Congress by § 10(b) did not seek to regulate transactions which constitute no more than internal corporate mismanagement." Superintendent of Insurance v. Bankers Life & Cas. Co., 404 U.S., at 12, 92 S.Ct., at 169. There may well be a need for uniform federal fiduciary standards to govern mergers such as that challenged in this complaint. But those standards should not be supplied by judicial extension of § 10(b) and Rule 10b–5 to "cover the corporate universe." [17]

The judgment of the Court of Appeals is reversed, and the case is remanded for further proceedings consistent with this opinion.

So ordered.

Mr. Justice BRENNAN dissents and would affirm for substantially the reasons stated in the majority and concurring opinions in the Court of Appeals, 533 F.2d 1283 (CA2 1976).

* * *

2. POST SANTA FE DEVELOPMENT

GOLDBERG v. MERIDOR

567 F.2d 209 (2d Cir. 1977), cert. denied 434 U.S. 1069,
98 S.Ct. 1249, 55 L.Ed.2d 771 (1978).

[Goldberg, a stockholder of Universal Gas & Oil Company, Inc. (UGO), brought a derivative suit against UGO's controlling parent, Maritimecor, S.A.; Maritime Fruit Carriers Company Ltd., an Israeli corporation; several individuals who were directors of one or more of the corporations; an investment firm; and an accounting firm. Both UGO and Maritimecor are Panama corporations. The complaint alleged a series of actions, the critical one of which was the sale to UGO of essentially all of Maritimecor's assets in exchange for up to 4,200,000 shares of UGO stock and the assumption by UGO of Maritimecor's debts. The plaintiff alleged that this transaction violated both New York law and Rule 10b–5, although he dropped the state claim after the defendants moved for the posting of security for expenses pursuant to § 627 of the New York Business Corporation Law.

The essence of the amended complaint was that the assets transferred by Maritimecor, less the debts assumed by UGO, were worth less than the value of the UGO stock. When the defendants moved to dismiss, claiming that the amended complaint failed to state a claim under Rule 10b–5 since "deception and non-disclosure is (sic) a requirement for a 10b–5 case", plaintiff's counsel submitted an affidavit which asserted that "insofar as plaintiff Goldberg, a minority shareholder, is concerned, there has been no disclosure to him of the fraudulent nature of the transfer of Maritimecor assets and liabilities

17. Cary, Federalism and Corporate Law: Reflections Upon Delaware, 83 Yale L.J. 663, 700 (1974) (footnote omitted). Professor Cary argues vigorously for comprehensive federal fiduciary standards, but urges a "frontal" attack by a new federal statute rather than an extension of Rule 10b–5. He writes: "It seems anomalous to jig-saw every kind of corporate dispute into the federal courts through the securities acts as they are presently written." *Ibid. See also* Note, Going Private, 84 Yale L.J. 903 (1975) (proposing the application of traditional doctrines of substantive corporate law to problems of fairness raised by "going private" transactions such as short-form mergers).

for stock of UGO." Annexed to the affidavit were two press releases describing the agreement. It was asserted that these two press releases failed to disclose certain conflicts of interest; that current liabilities of Maritimecor exceeded the shareholder's net equity; and that Maritimecor had, in fact, overstated its assets since they showed a higher value than appropriate for UGO shares. Counsel asked leave to amend again if the court should find the pleading defective.

The District Court denied leave to amend and dismissed the case, finding that no deception was alleged. The Court of Appeals held that the amendment should be permitted and that the complaint should be treated as if it had alleged that the press releases were materially misleading and that one of UGO's directors claimed to have been deceived or not to have been fully informed as to the effects of the transaction. The court then went on to discuss the merits:]

FRIENDLY, Circuit Judge.

* * *

II.

If the complaint were thus amended, we would deem it clear that, so far as this court's decisions are concerned, the case would be governed by *Schoenbaum* rather than by *Popkin*. The August 1 press release held out an inviting picture that

> As a result of the transaction, UGO will replace Maritimecor as the principal operating subsidiary of MFC and, as such, will engage in a diversified line of shipping and shipping related activities including the sale of ships and ship-building contracts, the operation of reefers and tankers, and upon their delivery, product carriers and oil drilling rigs, and underwriting marine insurance.

when allegedly the truth was that UGO had entered into a transaction that would ensure its doom. *Popkin* was specifically rested on its special facts. The plaintiff was taken to have conceded that the complaint did not allege misrepresentation or non-disclosure and that he relied solely on the unfairness of the merger terms. * * * The observation in *Popkin*, 464 F.2d at 719, that "our emphasis on improper self-dealing did not eliminate nondisclosure as a key issue in the Rule 10b–5 cases" followed a statement that when, as here, state law does not demand prior shareholder approval of a transaction, "it makes sense to concentrate on the impropriety of the conduct itself rather than on the 'failure to disclose' it because full and fair disclosure in a real sense will rarely occur. It will be equally rare in the legal sense once the view is taken—as we did in *Schoenbaum*—that under federal securities law disclosure to interested insiders does not prevent a valid claim that fraud was committed upon 'outsiders' (such as minority shareholders) whatever the requirements of state corporate law may be." *Id.* The ruling of *Popkin* was that in the *opposite* situation, where "merger transactions * * *, under state law, must be subjected to shareholder approval * * * if federal law ensures that shareholder approval is fairly sought and freely given, the principal federal interest is at an end," 464 F.2d at 720, see also *id.* n.17. Clearly that is not this case.

III.

The ruling that this case is attracted by *Schoenbaum* rather than by *Popkin* by no means ends our inquiry. Rather it brings us to the serious question whether *Schoenbaum* can be here applied consistently with the Supreme Court's decision in Santa Fe Industries, Inc. v. Green, *supra*. We think it can be and should.

* * *

The problem with the application of § 10(b) and Rule 10b–5 to derivative actions has lain in the degree to which the knowledge of officers and directors must be attributed to the corporation, thereby negating the element of deception. * * *

* * *

Schoenbaum, then, can rest solidly on the now widely recognized ground that there is deception of the corporation (in effect, of its minority shareholders) when the corporation is influenced by its controlling shareholder to engage in a transaction adverse to the corporation's interests (in effect, the minority shareholders' interests) and there is nondisclosure or misleading disclosures as to the material facts of the transaction. Assuming that, in light of the decision in *Green*, the existence of "controlling influence" and "wholly inadequate consideration"—an aspect of the *Schoenbaum* decision that perhaps attracted more attention, see 405 F.2d at 219–20—can no longer alone form the basis for Rule 10b–5 liability, we do not read *Green* as ruling that no action lies under Rule 10b–5 when a controlling corporation causes a partly owned subsidiary to sell its securities to the parent in a fraudulent transaction and fails to make a disclosure or, as can be alleged here, makes a misleading disclosure. The Supreme Court noted in *Green* that the court of appeals "did not disturb the District Court's conclusion that the complaint did not allege a material misrepresentation or nondisclosure with respect to the value of the stock" of Kirby; the Court's quarrel was with this court's holding that "neither misrepresentation nor nondisclosure was a necessary element of a Rule 10b–5 action", 430 U.S. at 470, 97 S.Ct. at 1299, and that a breach of fiduciary duty would alone suffice. It was because "the complaint failed to allege a material misrepresentation or material failure to disclose" that the Court found "inapposite the cases [including *Schoenbaum*] relied upon by respondents and the court below, in which the breaches of fiduciary duty held violative of Rule 10b–5 included some element of deception", 430 U.S. at 475, 97 S.Ct. at 1301, see fn. 15. * * *

Here the complaint alleged "deceit * * * upon UGO's minority shareholders" and, if amendment had been allowed as it should have been, would have alleged misrepresentation as to the UGO-Maritimecor transaction at least in the sense of failure to state material facts "necessary in order to make the statements made, in the light of the circumstances under which they were made, not misleading," Rule 10b–5(b).[8] The nub of the matter is that the conduct attacked in *Green* did not violate the " 'fundamental purpose' of the Act as implementing a 'philosophy of full disclosure' ", 430 U.S. at 478, 97 S.Ct. at 1303; the conduct here attacked does.

Defendants contend that even if all this is true, the failure to make a public disclosure or even the making of a misleading disclosure would have no effect, since no action by stockholders to approve the UGO-Maritimecor transaction was required. Along the same lines our brother Meskill invoking the opinion in *Green*, 430 U.S. at 474 n.14, 97 S.Ct. at 1301 n.14, contends that the defendants' acts were not material since plaintiff has failed adequately to allege what would have been done had he known the truth.

In TSC Industries, Inc. v. Northway, Inc., 426 U.S. 438, 449, 96 S. Ct. 2126, 2133, 48 L.Ed.2d 757 (1976), a case arising under Rule 14a–9, the Court laid down the standard of materiality as "a showing of a substantial likelihood that, under all the circumstances, the omitted fact would have assumed actual significance in the deliberations of the reasonable shareholder" or, putting the matter in another way, "a substantial likelihood that the disclosure of the omitted fact would have been viewed by the reasonable investor as having significantly altered the 'total mix' of information made available." When, as in a derivative action, the deception is alleged to have been practiced on the corporation, even though all the directors were parties to it, the test must be whether the facts that were not disclosed or were misleadingly disclosed to the shareholders "would have assumed actual significance in the deliberations" of reasonable and disinterested directors or created "a substantial likelihood" that such directors would have considered the "total mix" of information available to have been "significantly altered." That was the basis for liability in *Schoenbaum*; it was likely that a reasonable director of Banff, knowing the facts as to the oil discovery that had been withheld from minority shareholders, would not have voted to issue the shares to Aquitaine at a price below their true value. Here there is surely a significant likelihood that if a reasonable director of UGO had known the facts alleged by plaintiff rather than the barebones of the press releases, he would not have voted for the transaction with Maritimecor.

---

8. We do not mean to suggest that § 10(b) or Rule 10b–5 requires insiders to characterize conflict of interest transactions with pejorative nouns or adjectives. However, if Maritimecor was in the parlous financial condition alleged in the opposing affidavit of plaintiff's counsel, a disclosure of the acquisition of Maritimecor that omitted these *facts* would be seriously misleading.

Beyond this Goldberg and other minority shareholders would not have been without remedy if the alleged facts had been disclosed. The doubts entertained by our brother as to the existence of injunctive remedies in New York, * * * are unfounded. Blumenthal v. Roosevelt Hotel, Inc., 202 Misc. 988, 115 N.Y.S.2d 52 (Sup.Ct.N.Y. Co.1952), and Williams v. Bartell, 34 Misc.2d 552, 226 N.Y.S.2d 187 (Sup.Ct.N.Y.Co.), modified, 16 A.D.2d 21, 225 N.Y.S.2d 351 (1st Dept. 1962), were suits by stockholders acting in their own behalf to enjoin the sale of all corporate assets or a merger transaction as to which New York afforded dissenters the remedy of an appraisal. Where an appraisal remedy is not available, the courts of New York have displayed no hesitancy in granting injunctive relief. * * *

* * *

The availability of injunctive relief if the defendants had not lulled the minority stockholders of UGO into security by a deceptive disclosure, as they allegedly did, is in sharp contrast to *Green*, where the disclosure following the merger transaction was full and fair, and, as to the pre-merger period, respondents accepted "the conclusion of both courts below that under Delaware law they could not have enjoined the merger because an appraisal proceeding is their sole remedy in the Delaware courts for any alleged unfairness in the terms of the merger," fn. 14.

Defendants also rely on statements in Part IV of the *Green* opinion which lend them some support if taken in isolation and out of context. Thus the Court, quoting from Piper v. Chris-Craft Industries, Inc., 430 U.S. 1, 40, 97 S.Ct. 926, 51 L.Ed.2d 124 (1977), said that one factor in determining whether a case was covered by § 10(b) and Rule 10b–5, was "whether 'the cause of action [is] one traditionally relegated to state law * * * .' " But the Court quickly added, after referring to the Delaware appraisal statue, that "Of course, the existence of a particular state law remedy is not dispositive of the question whether Congress meant to provide a similar federal remedy," and it would be hard to think of a cause of action more "traditionally relegated to state law" than the one asserted in the *Superintendent of Insurance* case, which, as has been said, made "just plain stealing" a fraud under Rule 10b–5, on the basis that Begole failed to tell the directors "in advance that he was going to steal". Defendants rely also on the Court's fears of the difficulty of future line-drawing among various kinds of breach of fiduciary duty involving securities transactions. But this was said in support of drawing the line so as to require plaintiffs to make claims of nondisclosure or misleading disclosure, not as directing the lower courts to dismiss cases where it was claimed that fiduciaries had failed to disclose their self-dealing or had made a misleading disclosure, even though no disclosure was required by state law. Similarly we fail to see how defendants gain from the Court's quotation of its statement in the *Superintendent of Insurance* case, 404 U.S. at 12, 92 S.Ct. at 169, that

"Congress by § 10(b) did not seek to regulate transactions which constitute no more than internal corporate mismanagement"—a statement that originally seemed intended only to remove *negligent* corporate misconduct from the reach of the statute. We readily agree that if all that was here alleged was that UGO had been injured by "internal corporate mismanagement", no federal claim would have been stated. But a parent's looting of a subsidiary with securities outstanding in the hands of the public in a securities transaction is a different matter; in such cases disclosure or at least the absence of misleading disclosure is required. * * *

The order dismissing the complaint is reversed and the case is remanded to the district court for further proceedings, including amendment of the complaint, consistent with this opinion.

* * *

HEALEY v. CATALYST RECOVERY OF PENNSYLVANIA, INC.

616 F.2d 641 (3rd Cir. 1980).

[Plaintiff was president and a 20% shareholder of Catalyst Regeneration Services, Inc. ("CRS") which became the object of a takeover bid by SCR, Inc. SCR purchased all the shares except those owned by plaintiff. SCR then proposed a merger and conducted negotiations with plaintiff. In the course of discussions, certain information was withheld from the plaintiff. The merger was accomplished, as was inevitable in view of SCR's holdings. Plaintiff sued under Rule 10b–5, and the court found that Goldberg v. Meridor provided an exception to *Santa Fe*.]

SEITZ, Chief Judge.

It is important to note at the outset the difference between *Goldberg* and *Santa Fe*. The mere existence of a state injunctive remedy would be insufficient, by itself, to distinguish *Santa Fe*. The crucial difference is whether there was misrepresentation or omission in the flow of information between the majority and minority shareholders. In *Santa Fe*, the Supreme Court expressly noted that there had been no misinformation connected with the merger. By contrast, in *Goldberg*, the plaintiffs claimed that a parent corporation had either not disclosed or misleadingly disclosed information concerning its sale of the overvalued assets of its controlled subsidiary, some of the shares of which were held by the public.

We believe that this distinction concerning the flow of information between the majority and minority shareholders is persuasive. There is a strong federal interest, evidenced by the entire field of federal securities regulation, in ensuring a proper flow of information between the parties to a securities transaction. The Supreme Court has sanctioned a private cause of action under rule 10b–5 on behalf of sellers to enforce that federal interest. *See Santa Fe, supra,* 430 U.

S. at 477, 97 S.Ct. 1292, citing Superintendent of Insurance v. Bankers Life & Casualty Co., 404 U.S. 6, 13 n.9, 92 S.Ct. 165, 30 L.Ed.2d 128 (1971). All that *Goldberg* holds is that if some misrepresentation or omission by the defendant prevents the plaintiff from stopping the merger through a state injunction, then there is a cause of action under rule 10b–5. Because this result flows from misinformation that harms the plaintiff, it is precisely the type of situation to which rule 10b–5 is addressed.

*   *   *

Accordingly, we hold that where a misrepresentation or omission of material information deprives a proper plaintiff minority shareholder of an opportunity under state law to enjoin a merger, there is a cause of action under rule 10b–5.

The defendants argue that a plaintiff must make some type of showing on the question of whether he would have actually been granted the injunction had he been given the information in question. The United States Court of Appeals for the Ninth Circuit in Kidwell ex rel. Penfold v. Meikle, 597 F.2d 1273 (9th Cir. 1979), adopted this rule on the theory that to hold otherwise would be inconsistent with *Santa Fe's* concern over federal judicial encroachment on areas of law traditionally left to the states.

We feel it is better to view this question as an aspect of the materiality requirement. As already noted, once a sufficient disruption in the flow of information is alleged, as in *Goldberg* and here, the concerns expressed in Part IV of *Santa Fe* are not present. Therefore, *Santa Fe* is not particularly helpful in deciding whether there must be proof that the plaintiff had some chance of success in his injunctive suit. The theory of *Goldberg* is that the plaintiff wanted the information to make a decision whether to apply for a state injunction. Accordingly, we think a doctrine that is geared to the plaintiff's decisionmaking process is more suitable for analyzing the question the defendants have raised here.

Under rule 10b–5, misinformation by misrepresentation or omission is not by itself sufficient; the information in question must be material. The Supreme Court has defined materiality as: "a substantial likelihood that, under all the circumstances, the omitted fact would have assumed actual significance in the deliberations of the reasonable shareholder." TSC Industries, Inc. v. Northway, Inc., 426 U.S. 438, 449, 96 S.Ct. 2126, 2132, 48 L.Ed.2d 757 (1976). Because this test is geared to the plaintiff's decisionmaking process, we think it is the relevant framework for analyzing the present question.

Applying this standard to the present case, the question is what information would be deemed to be material by the reasonable investor who contemplates seeking an injunction against a merger. Seen as a question of materiality, the issue of the plaintiff's ability to secure an injunction is easily resolved. Unless there is a reasonable probability that a shareholder could have used the information to obtain an injunction, then the information would not be important to the decisionmaking process of a reasonable investor. We therefore hold that in a case such as this the plaintiff must demonstrate that at the time of the misrepresentation or omission, there was a reasonable probability of ultimate success in securing an injunction had there been no misrepresentation or omission. Although *Meikle* speaks in terms of actual success, we frame the test in terms of a reasonable probability for two reasons. First, we believe absolute certainty to be both an impossible goal as well as an impracticable standard for a jury to implement. Second, in most cases the state remedy will be a preliminary injunction, which looks to the likelihood of ultimate success.

It is important to stress here the relationship of the information to the injunction. As already noted, the mere existence of an injunctive remedy is not enough; the information must be of a type that if the plaintiff had the information not supplied, he could use it to seek an injunction. For example, in a case of omitted information, the question is whether, if the plaintiff had received the information, it would have been significant to the determination of the reasonable probability of ultimate success.

Applying these principles to the facts here, we find that a remand is necessary. One can enjoin a merger for any of several reasons: fraud, illegality, ultra vires act, or unfairness.

In any event, we cannot decide the question here because the district court did not address this issue and it has not been fully briefed in this court. Therefore, we remand to the district court to consider in the first instance whether there was sufficient evidence to create a jury issue on the question of the plaintiff's reasonable probability of ultimate success under Texas law. This requires a two-step inquiry. First, the court should determine what information the jury could reasonably believe was withheld. Second, it should determine whether any of that information could have been used to obtain a Texas injunction. If there was as a matter of law no reasonable probability of ultimate success, the information is not material.

Because there may be a new trial, we feel it is necessary to give some guidance as to the submission of the question to the jury.
* * *

* * *

ALDISERT, Circuit Judge, dissenting.

* * *

I disagree with the majority on several critical points. First, I believe they improperly apply the standards for materiality in securities actions, and thus deem Healey's allegations of materiality sufficient; in my view, the nondisclosures were actually not material as a matter of law. Second, the majority disregard the alternative rationale presented in *Santa Fe*. My reading of part IV of that decision indicates that Healey's action should be dismissed because it does not promote the policies of the federal securities laws and because it interferes with and usurps functions traditionally relegated to state corporate law. Finally, the majority err by implicitly assuming that only the federal courts can effectively protect minority shareholders from breaches of fiduciary duty owed them under state law by majority shareholders.

* * *

Healey's private action does not further the policies embodied in the securities laws. As the Court noted in *Santa Fe*, "the 'fundamental purpose' of the Act [is to implement] a 'philosophy of full disclosure'; once full and fair disclosure has occurred, the fairness of the terms of the transaction is at most a tangential concern of the statute." 430 U.S. at 477–78, 97 S.Ct. at 1303 (citation omitted). Although Healey does allege nondisclosure, the entire thrust of his state claim for injunctive relief would have been that the terms of the merger were unfair to him. By requiring him to demonstrate a reasonable probability of success in the state action, the majority require him to demonstrate unfairness to prevail on his federal claim. The majority thus deem concern for fairness, under the guise of nondisclosure, sufficient under the federal statutory schema to serve as a passport into a federal courtroom. Apart from its unjustified assumption that the concern for fairness cannot be vindicated in the state court system, see part IV *infra*, the failure of this approach is dramatically demonstrated by the effect of the federal action. Healey's action serves only to protect his state breach of fiduciary duty action, which deals with a concern—fairness—that is " 'at best a subsidiary purpose' of the federal legislation." 430 U.S. at 478, 97 S.Ct. at 1303 (citation omitted). Thus, Healey has succeeded in slipping through the back door what federal courts are loathe to let him do directly: He challenges the fairness of a state corporate transaction, using the majority's test of "a reasonable probability of ultimate success" in the state action, by asserting his claim under the federal securities laws.

B

Healey's action also enters an area traditionally relegated to state law, making his implied federal remedy inappropriate under the fourth test of Cort v. Ash. A clearer instance of a plaintiff asking federal courts to usurp state functions is difficult to imagine. The allegation is that the defendants violated federal law by withholding information critical to Healey's state claim. Not only does Healey's claim present an unpersuasive case for a federal remedy, it creates a startling irony. Under the majority's formulation, only if a plaintiff has a state claim for an injunction can he recover under federal Rule

10b–5 for breach of fiduciary duty. If state injunctive relief is unavailable, as in *Santa Fe*, the plaintiff also has no federal remedy. Thus, rather than aiding plaintiffs under federal law who have no state remedy, the majority's formulation provides federal relief to plaintiffs who have state remedies, but denies federal relief to plaintiffs who have no state remedy!

* * *

IV

Most bothersome, however, is the implicit assumption by the majority that only federal courts can grant proper relief to an injured party whenever transactions in securities are involved. Traditional state remedies guarantee the plaintiff an appraisal procedure through which he can obtain the fair value of his stock. An action under Rule 10b–5 guarantees him no more. Because it assures the plaintiff of no greater recovery than he could obtain in his state action, I cannot see how it promotes greater disclosure than the state action. Absent explicit legislative sanction, therefore, federal encroachment into this area is justified only if the federal courts do a superior job of administering the remedy.

* * *

NOTE—THE NEW APPLICATION OF RULE 10b–5

A. *Reversing the Trend*

1. *Santa Fe* furnishes a narrow reading of the scope of Rule 10b–5, particularly in Part IV of the opinion. Thus, the Court refers to the danger of encouraging "vexatious litigation," citing Blue Chip Stamps v. Manor Drug Stores, 421 U.S. 723, 95 S.Ct. 1917, 44 L.Ed.2d 539 (1975). *Blue Chip*, decided in 1975, marked the beginning of an apparently heightened interest by the Supreme Court in federal securities cases, as well as a departure from previous interpretations. Litigation once viewed as "therapeutic" [(Mills v. Electric Auto-Lite Co., 396 U.S. 375, 90 S.Ct. 616, 24 L.Ed.2d 593 (1970)] was now seen as "vexatious."

Between 1936 and 1975, the SEC reigned supreme among federal agencies before the Supreme Court. Not only did the SEC lose no case of substantive content in the Court, but the Court generally reviewed only those cases the Commission wanted reviewed and decided virtually every private case in accordance with the SEC's amicus briefs.

Since 1975 those statistics have been almost completely turned around. The Court has decided more than a score of cases since 1975, and the SEC, or the side it favored, has lost practically all of them. The Court has come to speak of the agency's experience as its "alleged expertise." The Court narrowly interprets definitions, curtails implied private rights, imposes high standards of proof on plaintiffs, including the SEC, and gives a narrow reading of fraud. This is not to say the new decisions are incorrect, but surely they are different.

In *Blue Chip* the Court referred to the highly esteemed panel of the Second Circuit that decided Birnbaum v. Newport Steel Corp., 193 F.2d 461 (2d Cir. 1952), cert. denied 343 U.S. 956, 72 S.Ct. 1051, 96 L. Ed. 1356, which the Court upheld. (It did not pause for compliments when it reversed another distinguished panel of the Second Circuit in *Santa Fe*.) The Supreme Court can only review a small fraction of the federal securities cases decided in the lower courts, of course, and prior to 1975 the number of securities cases heard by the Supreme Court was quite small. The Second Circuit decisions were particularly significant at that time for several reasons. Obviously, New York, as the hub of the financial markets, was the center of litigation activity affecting finance and commerce. The docket of the district court in Manhattan bulged with securities cases in the 1960's. The Second Circuit enjoyed a reputation as an uncommonly high quality court, with some of the most distinguished judges of their time then sitting: Learned Hand, Augustus Hand, Jerome Frank, Charles Clark, Thomas Swan and Henry Friendly. By and large the Second Circuit was in tune with the Supreme Court, at least on securities cases. Thus, because of the combination of experience, ability, and the responsibility of usually being final, the Second Circuit opinions merit close reading. Since 1975, however, the Supreme Court has asserted its role more forcefully, thereby diminishing the preeminence of any lower court.

B. *Deception of the Corporation*

While *Santa Fe* put to rest the "lingering doubt" on the question of deception, albeit very differently from the Second Circuit's disposition of this issue, there remains considerable room for controversy. True, deception is a necessary element of the claim for relief. But how is deception accomplished? If all of the directors are fully informed about the allegedly improper transactions, does that mean that no deception of the corporation has occurred? In a derivative suit, it is the knowledge or deception of the corporation that matters. Of course, a corporation only has "constructive knowledge" of anything; perhaps it is possible to "constructively deceive" a corporation by failing to inform the minority shareholders even though the board is informed. While this principle was recognized before *Santa Fe*, the question is whether it survives *Santa Fe*.

In Maldonado v. Flynn, 597 F.2d 789 (2d Cir. 1979), plaintiffs alleged unfairness to the corporation in the administration of the stock option plan. The defendants countered with the argument that no deception had taken place, as all directors knew the facts and no shareholder approval was needed. The Court agreed with the defendants. Judge Mansfield wrote:

> Where approval by the shareholders is not necessary, however, full disclosure to a disinterested board of directors is equivalent to full disclosure to the shareholders * * * . Even if some directors have an interest in the transaction, absent domination or control of a corporation or of its board by the officer-beneficiaries, approval of the transaction by a disinterested majority of the board possessing authority to act and fully informed of all relevant facts will suffice to bar a Rule 10b–5 claim that the corporation or its stockholders were deceived. [Citing Goldberg v. Meridor, Schoenbaum v. Firstbrook and Ruckle v. Roto American Corp.].

> The knowledge of the disinterested majority must in such event be attributed to the corporation and its stockholders, precluding deception. For this purpose "disinterest" is defined as lack of any financial stake by a director in the transaction under consideration. Delaware law, although not controlling, is to the same effect. 597 F.2d at 793.

It is particularly interesting to note the characteristics of the "disinterested" directors in that case. The board consisted of eight members of whom five were present at the meeting. One director, admittedly interested, abstained from voting. The transaction was approved by the four directors who were considered disinterested. One was a partner in a law firm that received substantial fees from the corporation. However, the court found that absent a claim that the director voted in favor of the transaction in exchange for a promise of continued legal fees or some other quid pro quo, he would not be considered interested. The court observed, "Unless and until board membership on the part of a corporation's outside counsel, or of anyone with a commercial relationship with the corporation, is outlawed, we cannot assume that a counsel-director acts for reasons that are against the corporation's interest, as distinguished from the private interests of its officers. Moreover, the shareholders were aware of [the director's] relationship as legal counsel to the Corporation when they elected him as a director, and presumably were willing to trust his judgment notwithstanding this fact." Id. at 794.

Another of the so-called disinterested directors had engaged in the same kind of conduct that the plaintiff alleged to be improper in this case. Thus, he had used inside information for personal profit, and plaintiffs said he therefore could not be disinterested, since he had reason to profit himself by seeking to gain the favor of senior management who would benefit from his vote. The plaintiff argued that he could not make a disinterested judgment adverse to management without prejudice to himself. The court said it did not have to decide the question because there was sufficient approval by disinterested directors even without his vote.

Is this a satisfactory approach to disinterestedness? According to the authors of one criticism, "The crucial criterion should not be whether a director is financially interested, but whether he can exercise *independent judgment* on behalf of the corporation and its shareholders. Any conflict or disability that impairs a director's judgment poses the same threat to the best interests of the corporation and shareholders, regardless of whether it is financially based. Thus, a showing that a director has a conflict of interest—whether financially related, status oriented, or otherwise—or that he is acting under some other disability, should prevent him from representing the corporation for purposes of Rule 10b–5 disclosure." Ferrara and Steinberg, A Reappraisal of Santa Fe: Rule 10b–5 and the New Federalism, 129 U.Pa.L.Rev. 263, 290 (1980).

On the other hand, if even a single disinterested director is on the board, has not full disclosure been made? Such a director possesses the same power as the shareholders to seek judicial remedies in state court to protect the corporate interest.

C. *Causation and Materiality*

Deception alone is not sufficient to establish a claim under Rule 10b–5. There must be a causal connection between the deception and the harm to the plaintiff. *See Santa Fe*, footnote 14. In *Santa Fe* the parties conceded that disclosure to stockholders would have served no function, not only because the shareholders had no vote but because it was conceded that they had no remedy except for appraisal. That result has since been change in Delaware by *Singer* and *Roland*. If the stockholders play no formal role in the transaction, does that mean that it is of no consequence when they are misinformed or uninformed about the transaction because "deception" of the shareholders played no role in effectuating the transaction? Is non-disclosure to the stockholders, in situations where they have no vote, ever relevant to the accomplishment of the transaction?

The decisions in *Goldberg* and *Healey*, which contain subtle distinctions, show that deception may occur despite full disclosure to decision-makers. Other courts have split on the issue that subtly divides the Second and Third Circuits. The Fifth Circuit, in Alabama Farm Bureau Mutual Casualty Co., Inc. v. American Fidelity Life Insurance Co., 606 F.2d 602 (5th Cir. 1979), cert. denied 446 U.S. 933, 100 S.Ct. 2149, 64 L.Ed.2d 785 (1980), held that "all that is required to establish 10b–5 liability is a showing that state law remedies are available, and that the facts shown make out a prima facie case for relief; it is not necessary to go further and prove that the state action would have been successful." 606 F.2d at 614.

However, both the Seventh and Ninth Circuits have demanded a higher threshold than *Healey*, although a claim under Rule 10b–5 was allowed. Both of these courts insisted that the plaintiff show not only the availability of a claim under state law, but that the plaintiff demonstrate that the state court would have granted the requested relief. Wright v. Heizer Corp., 560 F.2d 236 (7th Cir. 1977), cert. denied 434 U.S. 1066, 98 S.Ct. 1243, 55 L.Ed.2d 767 (1978); Kidwell ex rel. Penfold v. Meikle, 597 F.2d 1273 (9th Cir. 1979).

The latter approach has been criticized as unsound. One commentator observed that the federal court would be required to make a determination of fairness as part of deciding whether federal liability is established—precisely what *Santa Fe* sought to avoid. *See* Note, Suits for Breach of Fiduciary Duty Under Rule 10b–5 after Santa Fe Industries Inc. v. Green, 91 Harv.L.Rev. 1874 (1978). Another comment notes that "making a federal claim completely dependent on state law would emasculate the federal interest in uniformity * * *." Ferrara and Steinberg, A Reappraisal of Santa Fe: Rule 10b–5 and the New Federalism, 129 U.Pa.L.Rev. 263, 293 (1980).

On the other hand, others view the *Goldberg* line of authority as an end run around *Santa Fe*, bringing back into federal court issues that the Supreme Court found to be properly left to state law.

Several other courts have looked at the "deception" issue somewhat differently. Focusing on materiality as an element of proof, some courts have ruled that no deception has been practiced if the alleged misstatements went not to the facts but to the inferences. In Goldberger v. Baker, 442 F.Supp. 659 (S.D.N.Y.1977), the court found that there was no deception when the defendants failed to state that the terms of the transaction were "unfair" to the minority stockholders. It was sufficient if the facts were disclosed from which the stockholders could draw their own conclusion.

In Rodman v. The Grant Foundation, 608 F.2d 64 (2d Cir. 1979), the corporation repurchased its own shares, allegedly for the improper purpose of strengthening management's control position. That "purpose" was not disclosed to the stockholders. The court held that it was plain on its facts that the transaction was going to have an impact on control, and consequently there was no requirement to disclose the subjective purpose of the defendants.

In Biesenbach v. Guenther, 588 F.2d 400 (3d Cir. 1978), the court found no violation from the defendants' failure to state that the defendants breached their fiduciary duty. The court observed that "this approach would clearly circumvent the Supreme Court's holding in *Santa Fe*." 588 F.2d at 402.

We have already seen that proxy regulation can affect substantive corporate conduct, and suits under Rule 14a–9 may provide another battleground for claims of breach of fiduciary. How are those claims affected by *Santa Fe*?

Chapter 22

TRANSACTIONS IN CORPORATE CONTROL

A. SALES OF CONTROL

1. INTRODUCTION: THE CONSEQUENCES OF A SALE OF CONTROL

An analysis of the legal issues involved in the "sale of control" begins with an understanding of the nature of the transaction and its value to the parties. "Control" means the power to use the assets of a corporation as the controlling person chooses. The controlling person, unlike non-controlling stockholders, has direct power over his investment, and this reduces the risk of his investment. In actual fact, the power can be used in a manner that benefits the enterprise and all the stockholders alike, or it may be abused to serve only the benefit of the controlling person.

The controlling person is able to profit from a corporation in several ways, some of which are unique to his controlling position. As an investor in the corporation the controlling stockholder is in the same boat as all other investors, and will profit (or lose) proportionately the same as all others do from the affairs of the company. But the controlling person can profit in other ways as well. He can decide to hire himself and to pay himself a salary. The controlling person can cause the corporation to buy and sell property from himself. He can cause other transactions, in which he or favored friends can profit. Most important, he can impose his will on the corporation to make the business decisions he believes are best. The controlling stockholder, in effect, has the keys to the corporate treasury, and this is immense power which can be used properly or improperly. Of course, power and right are not always the same, and the law can impose barriers to improper use and impose costs on those who abuse their power, but these are not guarantees against abuse. Some exercises of power will always occur in the seams of the zone between proper and improper conduct.

The non-controlling stockholder, whose investment is vital for the success of the business, must rely upon the good business judgment of the controlling person. The non-controlling shareholder gains a measure of protection if it is possible to change control readily. If control is lodged securely with a majority stockholder, the non-controlling stockholders cannot cause a change. In that event, those without control must have a means to dispose of their interest in the corporation. In other words, where minority shareholders have no voice in the corporation, their protection lies in their having a means of exiting from the corporation. But even where the non-controlling

1044

stockholders can easily sell their interest they would favor legal rules that minimize impediments to the voluntary change of control in order to permit the possibility that inefficient management can be displaced by more efficient managers.

Not only is it in the interest of a particular corporation to have means to change control swiftly and with little cost, it benefits the economy as a whole to relocate management in more efficient hands. A business that is inefficiently managed may not be able to survive against its competitors in the marketplace. This may lead to another firm acquiring the inefficient company or it may mean the liquidation of the business and the sale of its assets to others who will then use them in some other way. Competition fosters efficiency. This is the theory; in practice the marketplace may not be so ruthlessly effective and some firms are able to continue to operate at less than optimal performance.

Outsiders may perceive a unique investment opportunity in the chance to acquire control of a corporation and operate it more efficiently than the present controlling person, and thereby derive a higher return on their investment than is offered elsewhere. In other words, a poorly managed company may represent a bargain for one who can change management. The outsider may purchase a sufficient number of shares to become the controlling person, and this transaction may or may not involve the cooperation of the incumbent controlling person. If the incumbent controlling person owns more than 50% of the stock, change can only be achieved with his cooperation. The incumbent controlling person will realize that if he sells the stock that keeps him in control, he will be disposing of a property interest (his shares) that have not only entitled him to enjoy the same benefits as all others stockholders, but also gave him the power to deal with the corporate property for his own benefit. Thus, he will want something for his stock and something for the power that goes with it. Unless he gets something for both, *i.e.*, a premium over what the noncontrolling person can obtain, he has a disincentive to sell, because his power to gain for himself the fruits of control can compensate him (but not the other shareholders) despite his inefficient management. Low dividends can be more than offset by a high salary. To the extent that the law imposes a barrier to payment of a premium to the seller, it may impede the negotiated sale of control. And in the case of a company where the controlling person cannot be dislodged without his consent, prohibition on receiving a control premium may impose a complete barrier to a change in control.

The buyer then faces the need to make the investment worth the price. If a premium has been paid to the seller, say the publicly traded stock owned by the minority interests sells for $10 and the buyer paid the controlling person $12, the buyer is out $2 a share immediately following the purchase. How does he recoup the premium? One way is to improve the market price of the stock by superior management. As economists Jensen and Meckling put it, the new controlling person hopes to eliminate the "agency costs"—the costs associated with suboptimal performance. (Jensen and Meckling, Theory of the Firm: Managerial Behavior, Agency Costs and Ownership Structure, 3 J.Fin.Econ. 305 (1976).) This result benefits everyone. Another way is to unlock the treasury and carry off the assets, that is, to loot the corporation. A premium that bears little relationship to potential investment values may signify that the buyer intends the latter. But obviously the payment of a premium does not always put the buyer at odds with the other stockholders.

We must examine the form in which negotiated control transfer situations occur to see what legal rules govern them.

The value of control is determined by the value of the assets of the corporation over which control is exercised. It is those assets, or the profit opportunities from their use, which the buyer of control is seeking. Those assets can be purchased directly from the corporation, and the entire proceeds of the sale will go to the corporation. If the transaction takes that form, then the controlling person would benefit only in the same proportions as the non-controlling persons of the corporation. However, the controlling person would have lost something that the other shareholders never possessed, which was dominion over the assets.

Suppose a corporation has assets for which the buyer of control would be willing to pay one million dollars. The controlling person owns, say, 60% of the stock. A sale of all the assets followed by a tax free liquidation would produce a benefit of $600,000 to the controlling person. Suppose he suggests to the buyer that the latter purchase all of the controlling person's stock for $700,000, which would then enable the buyer to exercise the same dominion over the assets as the seller formerly exercised. Indeed, he can cause the corporation to now sell all of the assets to himself for $750,000, liquidate the business, and receive back $450,000 so that the total purchase price of those assets would have been the same as he originally offered. However, in this sale, the controlling person received $100,000 more than he would have under the terms of the first offer, the non-controlling stockholders $100,000 less.

Suppose the controlling person of the corporation with one million dollars of assets owns stock representing a fraction of 1%. Buying that person's stock would accomplish nothing for the buyer. But if the controlling person is the chief executive officer of the company, he exercises practical, or working control, if there are no other large stockholders. Suppose the controlling person suggests to the buyer that instead of buying the assets from the corporation, which would provide virtually nothing for the controlling person while depriving him of his dominion and his employment, the buyer purchase the seller's directorship and officership in the company (along with the shares) for $100,000 and then proceed to exercise control over the assets. Again, the buyer might be able to cause the corporation to sell him the assets for $900,000, which would result in the same costs for those assets that he originally contemplated.

Both of those transactions appear highly suspicious and we could readily develop theories to impose liability on the parties. In the first place, we might say that the transaction constitutes a corporate transaction when we compress both of its components. Commonwealth Title Insurance & Trust Co. v. Seltzer, 227 Pa. 410, 76 A. 77 (1910); Dunnett v. Arn, 71 F.2d 912 (C.C.A.10 1934); Low v. Wheeler, 207 Cal.App.2d 44, 24 Cal.Rptr. 538 (1962). One would expect that the recovery under this theory belongs to the corporation and that it would be obtained in a stockholder's derivative suit.

The second situation would be attacked as the sale of an office, and only the corporation can do this, not the holder of the office. McClure v. Law, 161 N.Y. 78, 55 N.E. 388 (1874); Porter v. Healy, 244 Pa. 427, 91 A. 428 (1914); Rosenfeld v. Black, 445 F.2d 1337 (2d Cir. 1971).

The great difficulty with the application of these theories is that every sale of stock by a controlling person, at least if it is accompanied by the departure of the controlling person from the company, necessarily carries with it a change in management and dominion over the assets. If the amount of stock that is sold is more than 50%, then the investment properties and the control properties of that stock are inseparable. It is impossible to sell one without selling the other. It almost defies nature under those circumstances to define a legal theory which permits the sale of stock but does not permit a sale of control. But, as Professor Thomas Reed Powell once observed, "If A is inextricably related to B, and if you can think of A without thinking of B, then you have what can only be described as a legal mind."

Transactions involving the sale of corporate stock carrying with it a sale of control of the corporation have troubled legal commentators for years. The concern is easy enough to understand. The selection by the controlling person of a successor in control is one of the most important decisions that the controlling person makes. It may profoundly affect the welfare of the corporation. Assuming that the new controlling person has only honest intentions with respect to the management of the business, that does not necessarily equip him as a proper successor. The opportunity to sell stock owned by a controlling person for a premium price can cloud the seller's thinking and lead him to confer control upon an ill suited manager. Once entrenched in control, it may be impossible, or at least difficult, to dislodge the new controlling person. Therefore, it is vital that the choice of a successor controlling person should be made free of any temptation for personal benefit that comes at the expense of the corporation or the other stockholders.

One noted commentator, Professor David C. Bayne, S.J., has written numerous articles in which he has described the extra price paid to the controlling person, the premium, as a bribe made to induce the sale. Clearly, the receipt of such a bribe would be contrary to the fiduciary obligation of the controlling person.

Bayne's theories originate from the earlier writings of Professor Adolf A. Berle who described the control element of a controlling person's stock as an asset belonging to the corporation. Berle observed that the value of control stemmed from the fact that corporations may act on less than unanimous consent of the stockholders. Therefore, it was the corporate mechanism that imparted value to some stock, when combined in sufficient numbers, that was not possessed by other stock. Since it was the corporate machinery that gave value to the stock, that added value belonged to the corporation. Presumably, Berle's theory would allow the seller of a controlling block to receive the payment of a premium from the seller representing what has been called the blockage, or block assembly cost. There is an efficiency in purchasing a large block from one owner in order to eliminate the cost of putting together an equivalent block from many sources of smaller stockholders. It would seem that the premium there does not derive from the corporate machinery but from market factors, and properly belongs to the individual. Block assembly cost is also not a very large amount.

Under the analysis of either Berle or Bayne, the controlling person could maintain for himself only the investment value of the stock, that is, the same value that the stock had when owned by non-controlling persons. Thus, despite the fact that there were buyers in the market who recognize that 50% of the stock, when owned by a single person, was worth more per share than a minor percentage of the stock, and despite the fact that these persons could not be shown to have any improper designs on the corporation, the Berle and Bayne approaches would deprive the controlling person of a value acknowledged by the marketplace. It remains for further analysis and examination to see the extent to which courts have accepted these theories.

A partial list of writings in this field are: A. Berle and G. Means, The Modern Corporation and Private Property, 207–52 (rev. ed. 1968); Andrews, The Stockholder's Right to Equal Opportunity in the Sale of Shares, 78 Harv.L.Rev. 505 (1965); Jaravas, Equal Opportunity in the Sale of Controlling Shares: A Reply to Professor Andrews, 32 U. Chi.L.Rev. 430 (1965); Bayne, Corporate Control as a Strict Trustee, 53 Geo.L.J. 543 (1965); Bayne, The Sale-of-Control Premium: The Definition, 53 Minn.L.Rev. 485 (1969); Berle, The Price of Power: Sale of Corporate Control, 50 Cornell L.Q. 628 (1965); Brudney, Fiduciary Ideology in Transactions Affecting Corporate Control, 65 Mich. L.Rev. 259 (1966); Hazen, Transfers of Corporate Control and Duties of Controlling Shareholders, 25 U.Pa.L.Rev. 1023 (1977); Hill, The Sale of Controlling Shares, 70 Harv.L.Rev. 986 (1957); Jennings,

Trading in Corporate Control, 44 Calif.L.Rev. 1 (1956); Leech, Trans-
actions in Corporate Control, 104 U.Pa.L.Rev. 725 (1956); O'Neal,
Sale of a Controlling Interest: Bases of Possible Seller Liability, 38
U.Pitt.L.Rev. 9 (1976); Schwartz, The Sale of Control and the 1934
Act: New Directions for Federal Corporate Law, 15 N.Y.L.F. 674
(1969).

2. MANAGEMENT ACCOUNTABILITY

Accountability is a much pursued goal in corporate law. Although political devices play some role, perhaps no structure works
as efficiently as the marketplace. The fact that corporations act by
majority vote and that most trading stock has voting power makes it
possible for outsiders to gain control through purchase of a majority
of the stock. Professor Manne has identified the market for voting
power as the market for control. Some facets of it are explained below.

Excerpt from MANNE, MERGERS AND THE
MARKET FOR CORPORATE CONTROL
73 J. Pol. Econ. 110–114 (1965).

A fundamental premise underlying the market for corporate control is the existence of a high positive correlation between corporate
managerial efficiency and the market price of shares of that company. As an existing company is poorly managed—in the sense of not
making as great a return for the shareholders as could be accomplished under other feasible managements—the market price of the
shares declines relative to the shares of other companies in the same
industry or relative to the market as a whole. This phenomenon has
a dual importance for the market for corporate control.

In the first place, a lower share price facilitates any effort to take
over high-paying managerial positions. The compensation from these
positions may take the usual forms of salary, bonuses, pensions, expense accounts, and stock options. Perhaps more important, it may
take the form of information useful in trading in the company's
shares; or, if that is illegal, information may be exchanged and the
trading done in other companies' shares. But it is extremely doubtful that the full compensation recoverable by executives for managing their corporations explains more than a small fraction of outsider
attempts to take over control. Take-overs of corporations are too expensive generally to make the "purchase" of management compensation an attractive proposition.

It is far more likely that a second kind of reward provides the
primary motivation for most take-over attempts. The market price of
shares does more than measure the price at which the normal compensation of executives can be "sold" to new individuals. Share
price, or that part reflecting managerial efficiency, also measures the
potential capital gain inherent in the corporate stock. The lower the

stock price, relative to what it could be with more efficient management, the more attractive the take-over becomes to those who believe that they can manage the company more efficiently. And the potential return from the successful take-over and revitalization of a poorly run company can be enormous.

Additional leverage in this operation can be obtained by borrowing the funds with which the shares are purchased, although American commercial banks are generally forbidden to lend money for this purpose. A comparable advantage can be had from using other shares rather than cash as the exchange medium. Given the fact of special tax treatment for capital gains, we can see how this mechanism for taking over control of badly run corporations is one of the most important "get-rich-quick" opportunities in our economy today.

But the greatest benefits of the take-over scheme probably inure to those least conscious of it. Apart from the stock market, we have no objective standard of managerial efficiency. Courts, as indicated by the so-called business-judgment rule, are loath to second-guess business decisions or remove directors from office. Only the take-over scheme provides some assurance of competitive efficiency among corporate managers and thereby affords strong protection to the interests of vast numbers of small, non-controlling shareholders. Compared to this mechanism, the efforts of the SEC and the courts to protect shareholders through the development of a fiduciary duty concept and the shareholder's derivative suit seem small indeed. It is true that sales by dissatisfied shareholders are necessary to trigger the mechanism and that these shareholders may suffer considerable losses. On the other hand, even greater capital losses are prevented by the existence of a competitive market for corporate control.

There are several mechanisms for taking over the control of corporations. The three basic techniques are the proxy fight, direct purchase of shares, and the merger. The costs, practical difficulties, and legal consequences of these approaches vary widely. The selection of one or another or some combination of these techniques frequently represents a difficult strategy decision.

PROBLEM

GOTHAM TRIBUNE

Gotham Tribune, Inc., publisher of the Gotham Tribune, is a publicly owned Delaware corporation whose stock is traded on the New York Stock Exchange. In recent months the price of the stock has been fairly stable at about $15 per share. Burt and Ernie, sons of the founder of the paper, each own 7½% of the stock, and hold executive positions with the company. There are 10,000,000 shares of common stock (the only authorized class) outstanding.

A wholly owned subsidiary of the company owns substantial timber property in Canada, and is a large producer of newsprint. It supplies all of the Tribune's needs, and sells to other users as well. The Tribune pays the same price as anyone else. There is a growing shortage of newsprint in the industry, and prices are on the rise. Over the years, the newspaper has contributed a relatively declining amount to corporate profits; the newsprint and timber business, increasingly more. The company earned $15 million, or $1.50 per share last year, of which one-third was attributed to the newsprint subsidiary. If not for the subsidiary, the company would have earned $1 per share, but it is likely that the stock would then sell for $6 or $7 per share instead of its present price. Therefore, the 50 cents per share of newsprint earnings sells for 16 or 18 times earnings. However, the newspaper is the pride of the management, as it is generally acclaimed to be one of the country's best.

World Publishers, Inc. publishes over 50 newspapers that it has acquired. While *most* of its newspapers are among the most profitable in the country (a couple of them presently are short of cash), they are very different from the Tribune. Some of the differences, in fact, contribute to the reason why World's papers are more profitable. In general, they have the largest circulation in the areas they service, and they are directed at the mass market. They rely heavily on wire services and do not maintain separate and expensive newsgathering bureaus.

World recently offered to buy the Tribune's subsidiary for $50 million in cash and long term debentures. Since newsprint is in short supply, World wanted to be assured of an adequate long term source. World agreed to continue to supply the needs of the Tribune, on favorable terms. That offer was carefully weighed by the Tribune's nine person board, which is composed of Burt, Ernie, the company's attorney, the president of the newsprint subsidiary, the executive vice president of Tribune, Inc. and four business people in the community who have no other connection with Gotham Tribune, Inc. The board, at a meeting at which all were present and concurred, decided to reject the offer because it did not believe the price was sufficient, since it was only ten times last year's earnings attributable to that segment of the business.

World Publishers, Inc. then offered to buy Burt's and Ernie's shares for $21 per share. Since each owns 750,000 shares, that offer amounted to $15,750,000 each. Burt was anxious to get out of the business and enter politics, and he favored acceptance of the offer. However, Ernie initially was opposed to the offer, and since it was for the total of their shares, each possessed a veto power.

However, Ernie became apprehensive that Burt might separately accept another offer, thus leaving Ernie in an isolated position. Rumors circulated that World would make a tender offer to the public shareholders at $18 per share for between 750,000 and one million shares if it could get either Burt or Ernie to sell. The success of that offer would have put Ernie in a minority stock position with little influence. Under these circumstances, Ernie agreed with Burt to accept the $21 offer, and they agreed to sell their shares. No tender offer is contemplated for the public shares. World has agreed to continue Ernie as a director and as publisher of the Tribune, at a salary higher than his present salary, under a long term contract. He will resign as chief executive officer of the company.

Burt and Ernie have agreed to arrange for the resignation of the directors seriatim* and to submit World's slate of candidates to the Board. Burt and Ernie have examined the list of names, and they are not familiar with them. They are familiar with top management of World, and the manager who is second in command in the company is well known to the public after an expose in the Tribune of his links to organized crime figures. He was never indicted for any crime, though.

Ernie has asked for an opinion of counsel with respect to the contract prior to the closing which is scheduled for next week.

The partner in charge of this matter has asked you to work with him on it. After reciting the facts set forth above, his memorandum to you reads as follows:

"This is the kind of situation for which shareholder's suits are made, and I have advised our clients of the high probability of litigation. That does not mean that they will lose, of course, but let us start to prepare for the inevitable legal challenge.

"Do our clients have any responsibility for what happens to the company or the shareholders under the stewardship of World? What should they do to protect themselves at this time?

"If they are selling control, the old Berle argument about control belonging to the corporation comes up. If they are not selling control, then why are they getting a premium for their shares? Is this just like the sale of assets that got our old client, C. Russell Feldmann, into trouble years ago?

"Is a sale of control involved in this case? They each own 7½%, which I think is below any threshold point I have ever seen.

"The newsprint component of the Tribune's business requires careful analysis. We know that's why World is interested in this deal. Does that mean that our clients, in selling their stock, have merely turned a corporate opportunity into a personally profitable stock sale? The board turned it down, true, but is that rejection vulnerable for any reason? Look at it closely, particularly the economics of the deal.

---

* Seriatim replacement of directors works as follows: If the board consists of A, B and C, who agree to elect X, Y and Z in their place, first A resigns and B and C elect X. Then B resigns and C and X elect Y. C resigns and X and Y elect Z.

"Is there any problem with the resignations? The clients advise me that this is a necessary element of the deal (in case you were thinking of recommending restructuring the transaction), and this is understandable. Would you want to spend all that money and still be on the outside looking in? Be careful, however, that you link your conclusion on the control issue with your analysis of the resignation issue.

"Where will the burden of proof lie in any suit? If the burden is on your clients, what must they show?

"Ever since our experience in the *Feldmann* case I have cautioned our clients to be wary of selling their stock without making sure all the other shareholders have the same opportunity. I believe this to be proper business behavior, and I am usually able to convince our clients to see things that way. It is not in the cards here. When clients have pressed the issue I have had to allow that the comparable offer was not legally mandated (in my opinion) but that it afforded legal protection. Have another look at this in the light of the facts as we know them.

"Is there any potential liability of the other directors, who are neither selling anything nor personally benefiting? I don't mean to suggest that the answer lies in their lack of profit, but it would sure surprise them if they were considered to be acting wrongfully. But better surprises now than later.

"And of course we have to check into the Rule 10b–5 aspects of this deal. Would anybody have standing to complain? Assuming that they would, and further assuming no advance public announcement of any kind is made, what would anybody be able to complain about? I think we are on firm ground here because it is my understanding that *Blue Chip* and *Santa Fe* constitute a double whammy on any stockholder suit. Am I missing something?"

Prepare for the meeting with the partner.

3. THE DUTY OF CARE IN THE SALE OF CONTROL

SWINNEY v. KEEBLER CO.

480 F.2d 573 (4th Cir. 1973).

WINTER, Circuit Judge.

[Plaintiffs were holders of defaulted debentures of Meadors, Inc. (Meadors), who brought a class action against the corporate issuer and the prior owners of the stock, to obtain payment of the debtures or recover damages equal to the amounts unpaid. The district court found for the plaintiffs.]

Since Keebler is the only defendant who has appealed, we will confine our consideration to the case against it. The district court found that, in connection with the successive sales of Meadors' stock from Keebler to Atlantic to Flora Mir Distributing, Meadors had been looted by Atlantic and its corporate assets dissipated, with the result, among others, that the interest and principal of the debentures were in default. Although the district court made no finding that Keebler had looted Meadors and, indeed, made no finding of any intentional wrongdoing on the part of Keebler, it nevertheless held Keebler liable for violation of its obligation to Meadors and Meadors' debenture holders "[i]n light of all the circumstances known to Keebler * * * to conduct such investigation of the purchaser [Atlantic] as would convince a reasonable man that the sale was legitimate, or to refrain from making the sale." Swinney v. Keebler Company, 329 F.Supp. 216, 224 (D.S.C.1971).

We disagree that the circumstances were such as to give rise to an obligation on the part of Keebler to conduct an investigation of Atlantic beyond that which was actually conducted or to refrain from making the sale. Accordingly, we reverse and direct the entry of judgment for Keebler.

I.

* * *

Briefly stated, Keebler bought the stock of Meadors, a candy manufacturer, on August 7, 1963. At the time of the purchase, Meadors was in serious financial trouble and its debentures had a book value of less than one-half of their principal amount. Keebler operated Meadors, manufacturing and distributing candy and causing it to engage in other profitable operations so as to utilize a substantial tax loss carryback. By February, 1968, Meadors had total assets of $581,491, including cash of $321,337, and a net worth of $230,000.

Prior to February, 1968, Keebler decided to withdraw from the manufacturer of candy, but not its sale and distribution, and it concluded to sell Meadors. It employed a broker to find a buyer and subsequently began negotiations with Flora Mir Candy.

Negotiations with Flora Mir Candy proceeded to the point where the buyer was preparing to purchase Meadors for $176,000, although not all aspects of the transaction had been agreed upon, when on February 9, 1968, a Keebler officer, Mr. Chester Burchsted, received a telephone call from a broker, Mr. Olen, who indicated that Atlantic might be interested in purchasing Meadors.

* * *

Burchsted and Olen met in the Newark airport on the morning of February 14, 1968, and as a result of the meeting an afternoon session was arranged in New York at the offices of Keebler's lawyers between Atlantic's counsel, Ivan Ezrine, Esquire, and several representatives of Keebler, including Edward Vincek, Esquire, Keebler's general counsel. In the meantime, Keebler's negotiations with Flora Mir Candy were suspended.

During the afternoon meeting, Keebler's various representatives questioned Ezrine concerning Atlantic, its financing structure and its corporate and financial history. Ezrine told Keebler that Atlantic was a prospering small holding company which was becoming a conglomerate and wanted to diversify by expanding into the candy business. Ezrine gave Keebler recent unaudited financial statements, prepared by certified public accountants, which showed that Atlantic had a net worth of $997,000 as of December 31, 1967, and net income of $158,588 for that calendar year.

At the February 14 meeting, Keebler and Atlantic negotiated an agreement for the sale of Meadors' stock, and the agreement was executed that day or the next. The contract documents were patterned largely on those which had been prepared while the negotiations with Flora Mir Candy were continuing. Among other things, the following agreements were reached: (1) the sales price was set at $235,000, (2) Atlantic represented its financial statement of December 31, 1967 as true, correct, and prepared in accordance with generally accepted accounting principles, (3) Atlantic promised, as a condition of the sale, that its financial strength on the closing date would be substantially the same or better than shown in its December 31, 1967 statements, (4) Atlantic agreed to guarantee Meadors' accounts payable and accruals, (5) Atlantic agreed to guarantee payment of the interest and principal of the Meadors' seven percent subordinated debentures, and (6) Atlantic agreed to indemnify Keebler from any liability arising out of the sale.

Keebler, for its part, warranted as true and correct its representations including the Meadors' balance sheet, the list of outstanding contracts and the list of Meadors' tangible properties. Keebler promised to use its best efforts to retain Meadors' personnel except officers and directors who were Keebler's nominees, and it agreed to purchase $562,000 worth of candy from Meadors within the ensuing nine-month period.

The closing was held in Greenville, South Carolina, on February 19. Prior thereto, Atlantic sent its certified public accountant to the Meadors' plant twice to inspect it. The accountant found a minor discrepancy in the properties of Meadors and the parties agreed to a $5,000 reduction in the ultimate purchase price paid by Atlantic on that account. Once at the negotiating session and once prior to the closing, Ezrine inquired of Vincek as to the possibility of making some arrangement to avoid Atlantic's bringing the funds for consummation of the transaction from New York. Both times Vincek rejected the suggestion and advised Ezrine that it was Atlantic's responsibility to finance the purchase.

At the closing, various documents were executed and delivered, including a licensing agreement which permitted Meadors to use Keebler's "Kitchen Rich" trademark under which Meadors' candy had been sold, and a detailed bill of sale conveying to Meadors all machinery and equipment theretofore on lease from Keebler. Although there was no evidence to show that Keebler was aware of what had transpired, Atlantic made a one-day borrowing of $235,000 from the People's National Bank, a bank in Greenville where Meadors had its account. Atlantic deposited the loan proceeds in an account in its name, then bought a $230,000 banker's check drawn on a New York bank in favor of Keebler for the adjusted purchase price. After the closing, Atlantic transferred $310,000 from the Meadors' account to its own account and repaid the loan. The transfer of funds was shown on Meadors' books as a loan to Atlantic—an account receivable—and on Atlantic's books as a loan from Meadors—an account payable.

Keebler had nothing further to do with Meadors after the closing except for the purchase of candy pursuant to the candy contract.

Atlantic retained ownership of Meadors for approximately four months and repaid approximately $33,200 of its loan. During this period, Meadors paid its trade accounts and made a profit of approximately $19,000. Atlantic's efforts to build up an independent sales force and find markets for its candy other than Keebler were largely unsuccessful, and Atlantic then sold the stock to Flora Mir Distributing, a subsidiary of Flora Mir Candy, on June 25, 1968, for a purchase price of $352,000. At that closing, Atlantic's accounts payable to Meadors was repaid; but Flora Mir Distributing, perpetuating the pattern established by Atlantic, thereafter withdrew funds from Meadors, reflected on Meadors' books as a loan to Flora Mir Distributing. Flora Mir Distributing acquired other candy companies, and Flora Mir Distributing treated itself and its subsidiaries as a single company, transferring monies and properties from one to the other. Initially, the group experienced success with their combined operations, but ultimately the combination became short of working capital and went into bankruptcy.

II.

The parties do not seriously dispute the applicable law. The district court correctly, we think, drew upon the leading case of Insuranshares Corporation v. Northern Fiscal Corporation, 35 F.Supp. 22 (E. D.Pa.1940), which held the sellers of a controlling interest in a corporation liable to the corporation when the buyers proceeded to loot it after their acquisition of control. Liability was predicated upon breach of a duty not to transfer control since the circumstances surrounding the transfer were "such as to awaken suspicion and put a prudent man on his guard—unless a reasonably adequate investigation discloses such facts as would convince a reasonable person that no fraud is intended or likely to result." 35 F.Supp. at 25.

In *Insuranshares*, the suspicious circumstances included (1) the defendants' probable knowledge that the purchase was to be financed by a pledge of the corporation's assets, (2) the corporation's president's clear predisposition to allow a sale to be financed by pledging those assets as security, (3) defendants' awareness of the purchasers' plan to have a large part of the corporation's assets converted into cash prior to the sale, (4) the inflated price or premium paid for control, especially given the nature of the business which was an investment trust with no physical assets but only the ready equivalent of cash in the form of marketable securities, (5) warnings from the sellers' attorneys as to their potential liabilities for dealing with little-known purchasers, and (6) the fact that the corporation had been looted five years before by a different group who had gained control by using the same method of financing.

The standard of conduct to which *Insuranshares* holds controlling transferors had been widely accepted. Generally, the owner of corporate stock may dispose of his shares as he sees fit. A dominant or majority stockholder does not become a fiduciary for other stockholders *merely* by owning stock. In selling their stock, the stockholders necessarily act for themselves, and not as trustees for the other stockholders. But majority stockholders who assume the management of the corporation, as Keebler did here, can be said to stand in fiduciary relation to the minority under certain circumstances. Thus, while the majority is not an absolute insurer against any wrongs which may be done to the corporation after the transfer of control or against any decisions by the new owners that may not be in the best interest of the minority, if the sellers of control are in a position to foresee the likelihood of fraud on the corporation, including its creditors, or on the remaining stockholders, at the hands of the transferee, their fiduciary duty imposes a positive duty to investigate the motives and reputation of the would-be purchaser; and unless such a reasonable investigation shows that to a reasonable man no fraud is intended or likely to result, the sellers must refrain from the transfer of control.

III.

In light of the facts and applicable law, plaintiffs' right to recover turns on whether Keebler had sufficient knowledge to foresee the likelihood of fraud so as to give rise to a duty to conduct a further investigation and to satisfy itself, by the test of a reasonable man, that no fraud was intended or likely to result before it consummated the sale of control. The district court identified essentially seven circumstances which "might have indicated [to Keebler] that Atlantic Services had no intention of operating Meadors * * *." 329 F. Supp. at 220. These factors were: (1) no one from Atlantic had any experience in the candy business, (2) at the time the contract was executed no one from Atlantic had inspected the "Meadors operation," (3) by the time of the closing, only Atlantic's accountant had examined Meadors to "any appreciable extent and he was interested principally in the books and inventory," (4) Meadors had no market of its own and the "profit as shown could not have been accepted at face value by an outsider," (5) prior to the closing Atlantic had no negotiations with Meadors' key employees concerning the continuation of the business, (6) the sale was consummated with dispatch, and (7) Atlantic had inquired as to the availability of Meadors' funds for payment of the purchase price. Although the district court concluded that the first five factors were "not necessarily inconsistent with a legitimate sale of a business the size of Meadors," it held that when coupled with facts six and seven, they "were more than sufficient to arouse the suspicion of Keebler."

We think that the findings of fact relied on by the district court to conclude that Keebler was liable to Meadors' debenture holders were insufficient to support that result. We will comment on them seriatim.

From Keebler's point of view, the fact that no one from Atlantic had any experience in the candy business should not have been suspicious. Atlantic was represented to Keebler as a holding and investment company which did business through subsidiaries. A conglomerate, which Atlantic professed to be aspiring, regularly acquires diverse businesses; and in any event, it is not unusual for any corporation to venture into a new business field. Meadors was an integrated functioning enterprise with management and equipment in place, and Keebler agreed, except with respect to Meadors' officers and directors, which were Keebler personnel, to use its best efforts to maintain intact other personnel of Meadors then on Meadors' payroll. As a result of Keebler's agreement to purchase candy for a nine-month period, Keebler could assume that Meadors would have, at least for the short run, a ready market for candy and an opportunity to recruit and train a sales force.

No suspicion should have been aroused from the fact that no one from Atlantic inspected the Meadors' operation prior to execution of the contract, and that at the time of closing, only Atlantic's accountant had examined Meadors to any appreciable extent. Atlantic's broker, Olen, who first telephoned Keebler's Burchsted, had some familiarity with Meadors, albeit apparently obtained from the broker retained by Keebler. Keebler made extensive warranties concerning the plant and its financial operations and were these warranties untrue, Atlantic might have rescinded the sale or sued for damages. A sufficient inspection prior to closing was made so that the parties agreed to a $5,000 reduction in the purchase price. From Keebler's point of view, Atlantic's reliance on its broker, on Keebler's warranties, and on Atlantic's accountant's inspections was hardly a circumstance indicative of an intention not to operate, much less of an intention to loot.

We see nothing suspicious in the fact that Meadors had no market of its own, and we do not agree that the profit as shown on Meadors' financial statements could not have been accepted at face value by an outsider. While Meadors' past profit history may have been somewhat questionable, its operation by Keebler was profitable, and Keebler warranted Meadors' balance sheet at the time of closing. There is no question but that Keebler's agreement to purchase candy provided Meadors with a substantial initial market, and Keebler could have reasonably assumed that during the period and with the financial support of its purchase of candy, Meadors could build up its own market. Keebler cannot be held liable as a result of its failure to sell Meadors to a company with a candy market already well developed. Only a small portion of the business community could live under such a restrictive rule with regard to the purchase and sale of business enterprises.

Nor do we find significant the fact that prior to closing, Atlantic conducted no negotiations with key employees then operating Meadors relative to their continuation of the business. Keebler contracted to use its best efforts to retain them as employees, and Atlantic did retain them after it took over. The wisdom of Atlantic's failure to negotiate with them prior to closing is not in issue—only its impact on Keebler as a "suspicious circumstance" is significant. Since Keebler owned Meadors, had full power to sell the company, and agreed to do its part in keeping the enterprise intact, we do not think that Keebler was confronted with a suspicious circumstance.

The dispatch with which the sale was consummated was not suspicious. In the first place, no reason to delay closing has been suggested. In any event, any haste was principally that of Keebler's making and not that of Atlantic. Keebler had been prepared to sell Meadors to Flora Mir Candy; active negotiations were being carried on and legal papers to consummate the transaction were in the course of preparation when Atlantic appeared on the scene. When agreement with Atlantic was reached, Keebler was pressing to consummate a more profitable transaction in lieu of a less profitable one before the latter was irrevocably lost.

The inquiries made by Atlantic with regard to the availability of Meadors' funds for payment of the purchase price were not such as to provide a basis on which Keebler could suspect how payment would be made, especially since Keebler made its position clear that Atlantic must consummate the purchase with its own funds. It is true that the record shows that Atlantic did not do so, but the record does not disclose an evidentiary basis to find, nor did the district court find, that Keebler knew or had reason to know of Atlantic's one-day loan and its immediate repayment with Meadors' funds. Whatever inkling Keebler may have had that Atlantic was interested in using Meadors' cash did not rise to a level sufficient to necessitate further investigation, especially in light of Atlantic's seemingly strong financial position and its apparent ability to finance the transaction with its own monies.

Overall, we conclude that the seven factors considered singly or in concert, were not sufficient to suggest to Keebler that Atlantic did not intend to operate Meadors, but rather intended to loot it. As our discussion of the findings relied on to support the contrary conclusion discloses, there were many positive indications that Atlantic intended to operate Meadors and to operate it profitably. In addition, Atlantic's guarantee of the payment of principal of and interest on Meadors' debentures was significant, especially in the light of Atlantic's apparent financial ability to fulfill that commitment. It follows, we think, that Keebler's obligation to conduct a further investigation sufficient to satisfy a reasonable man that no fraud was intended or likely to result, or to refrain from the transfer of control, did not arise. The obligation could not have been breached, so that there was therefore no basis to impose liability on Keebler.

Reversed.

In Clagett v. Hutchison, 583 F.2d 1259 (4th Cir. 1978), the majority stockholder sold shares of a racetrack corporation for $43.75 per share, at a time when the prevailing market price for the stock was between $7.50 and $10 per share. Among other things, minority stockholders sued the majority stockholder for breach of fiduciary duty in failing to investigate the buyers. Plaintiffs contended that the circumstances of the transaction were suspicious, and warranted investigation. The court disagreed. With respect to the price, Judge Hall observed:

> *First.* While the price paid for Hutchison's shares was indeed a premium price, it was nevertheless a premium paid for the element of control of the corporation. McDaniel v. Painter, 418 F.2d at 548. The premium payment is further justifiable since Laurel was a commercial business subject to further development as an ongoing business. Thus, the premium price paid to Hutchison cannot be said to be so unreasonable as to place him on notice of the likelihood of fraud on the corporation or the remaining stockholders. * * * Finally, as a matter of logic, it seems far-fetched to pay a 400% premium for stock simply in order to acquire control of a corporation in order to loot it. Certainly a cheaper corporate enterprise could be acquired for such malevolent purposes.

583 F.2d at 1262.

4. THE DUTY OF LOYALTY: CONTROL AS A CORPORATE ASSET

PERLMAN v. FELDMANN

219 F.2d 173 (2d Cir. 1955), cert. denied 349 U.S. 952, 75 S.Ct. 880, 99 L.Ed. 1277.

CLARK, Chief Judge.

This is a derivative action brought by minority stockholders of Newport Steel Corporation to compel accounting for, and restitution of, allegedly illegal gains which accrued to defendants as a result of the sale in August, 1950, of their controlling interest in the corporation. The principal defendant, C. Russell Feldmann, who represented and acted for the others, members of his family [owning a total of 37%], was at that time not only the dominant stockholder, but also the chairman of the board of directors and the president of the corporation. Newport, an Indiana corporation, operated mills for the production of steel sheets for sale to manufacturers of steel products, first at Newport, Kentucky, and later also at other places in Kentucky and Ohio. The buyers, a syndicate organized as Wilport Company, a Delaware corporation, consisted of end-users of steel who were interested in securing a source of supply in a market becoming ever tighter in the Korean War. Plaintiffs contend that the consideration paid for the stock included compensation for the sale of a corporate asset, a power held in trust for the corporation by Feldmann as its fiduciary. This power was the ability to control the allocation of the corporate product in a time of short supply, through control of the board of directors; and it was effectively transferred in this sale by having Feldmann procure the resignation of his own board and the election of Wilport's nominees immediately upon consummation of the sale.

* * *

The essential facts found by the trial judge are not in dispute. Newport was a relative newcomer in the steel industry with predominantly old installations which were in the process of being supplemented by more modern facilities. Except in times of extreme shortage Newport was not in a position to compete profitably with other steel mills for customers not in its immediate geographical area. Wilport, the purchasing syndicate, consisted of geographically remote end-users of steel who were interested in buying more steel from Newport than they had been able to obtain during recent periods of tight supply. The price of $20 per share was found by Judge Hincks to be a fair one for a control block of stock, although the over-the-counter market price had not exceeded $12 and the book value per share was $17.03. But this finding was limited by Judge Hincks' statement that "[w]hat value the block would have had if shorn of its appurtenant power to control distribution of the corporate product, the evidence does not show." It was also conditioned by his earlier ruling that the burden was on plaintiffs to prove a lesser value for the stock.

Both as director and as dominant stockholder, Feldmann stood in a fiduciary relationship to the corporation and to the minority stockholders as beneficiaries thereof. Although there is no Indiana case directly in point, the most closely analogous one emphasizes the close scrutiny to which Indiana subjects the conduct of fiduciaries when personal benefit may stand in the way of fulfillment of trust obligations. * * *

In Indiana, then, as elsewhere, the responsibility of the fiduciary is not limited to a proper regard for the tangible balance sheet assets of the corporation, but includes the dedication of his uncorrupted business judgment for the sole benefit of the corporation, in any dealings which may adversely affect it. * * *

It is true, as defendants have been at pains to point out, that this is not the ordinary case of breach of fiduciary duty. We have here no fraud, no misuse of confidential information, no outright looting of a helpless corporation. But on the other hand, we do not find compliance with that high standard which we have just stated and which we and other courts have come to expect and demand of corporate fiduciaries. In the often-quoted words of Judge Cardozo: "Many forms of conduct permissible in a workaday world for those acting at arm's length, are forbidden to those bound by fiduciary ties. A trustee is held to something stricter than the morals of the market place. Not honesty alone, but the punctilio of an honor the most sensitive, is then the standard of behavior. As to this there has developed a tradition that is unbending and inveterate. Uncompromising rigidity has been the attitude of courts of equity when petitioned to undermine the rule of undivided loyalty by the 'disintegrating erosion' of particular exceptions." Meinhard v. Salmon, supra, 249 N.Y. 458, 464, 164 N.E. 545, 546, 62 A.L.R. 1. The actions of defendants in siphoning off for personal gain corporate advantages to be derived from a favorable market situation do not betoken the necessary undivided loyalty owed by the fiduciary to his principal.

The corporate opportunities of whose misappropriation the minority stockholders complain need not have been an absolute certainty in order to support this action against Feldmann. If there was possibility of corporate gain, they are entitled to recover. * * *

This rationale is equally appropriate to a consideration of the benefits which Newport might have derived from the steel shortage. In the past Newport had used and profited by its market leverage by operation of what the industry had come to call the "Feldmann Plan." This consisted of securing interest-free advances from prospective purchasers of steel in return for firm commitments to them from future production. The funds thus acquired were used to finance improvements in existing plants and to acquire new installations. In the summer of 1950 Newport had been negotiating for cold-rolling facilities which it needed for a more fully integrated operation and a more marketable product, and Feldmann plan funds might well have been used toward this end.

Further, as plaintiffs alternatively suggest, Newport might have used the period of short supply to build up patronage in the geographical area in which it could compete profitably even when steel was more abundant. Either of these opportunities was Newport's, to be used to its advantage only. Only if defendants had been able to negate completely any possibility of gain by Newport could they have prevailed. It is true that a trial court finding states: "Whether or not, in August, 1950, Newport's position was such that it could have entered into 'Feldmann Plan' type transactions to procure funds and financing for the further expansion and integration of its steel facilities and whether such expansion would have been desirable for Newport, the evidence does not show." This, however, cannot avail the defendants, who—contrary to the ruling below—had the burden of proof on this issue, since fiduciaries always have the burden of proof in establishing the fairness of their dealings with trust property.

Defendants seek to categorize the corporate opportunities which might have accrued to Newport as too unethical to warrant further consideration. It is true that reputable steel producers were not participating in the gray market brought about by the Korean War and were refraining from advancing their prices, although to do so would not have been illegal. But Feldmann plan transactions were not considered within this self-imposed interdiction; the trial court found that around the time of the Feldmann sale Jones & Laughlin Steel Corporation, Republic Steel Company, and Pittsburgh Steel Corporation were all participating in such arrangements. In any event, it ill becomes the defendants to disparage as unethical the market advantages from which they themselves reaped rich benefits.

We do not mean to suggest that a majority stockholder cannot dispose of his controlling block of stock to outsiders without having to account to his corporation for profits or even never do this with impunity when the buyer is an interested customer, actual or potential for the corporation's product. But when the sale necessarily results in a sacrifice of this element of corporate good will and consequent unusual profit to the fiduciary who has caused the sacrifice, he should account for his gains. So in a time of market shortage, where a call on a corporation's product commands an unusually large premium, in one form or another, we think it sound law that a fiduciary may not appropriate to himself the value of this premium. Such personal gain at the expense of his coventurers seems particular reprehensible when made by the trusted president and director of his company. In this case the violation of duty seems to be all the clearer because of this triple role in which Feldmann appears, though we are unwilling to say, and are not to be understood as saying, that we should accept a lesser obligation for any one of his roles alone.

Hence to the extent that the price received by Feldmann and his codefendants included such a bonus, he is accountable to the minority stockholders who sue here. And plaintiffs, as they contend, are entitled to a recovery in their own right, instead of in right of the corporation (as in the usual derivative actions), since neither Wilport nor their successors in interest should share in any judgment which may be rendered. Defendants cannot well object to this form of recovery, since the only alternative, recovery for the corporation as a whole, would subject them to a greater total liability.

The case will therefore be remanded to the district court for a determination of the question expressly left open below, namely, the value of defendants' stock without the appurtenant control over the corporation's output of steel. We reiterate that on this issue, as on all others, relating to a breach of fiduciary duty, the burden of proof must rest on the defendants. Judgment should go to these plaintiffs and those whom they represent for any premium value so shown to the extent of their respective stock interests.

The judgment is therefore reversed and the action remanded for further proceedings pursuant to this opinion.

SWAN, Circuit Judge (dissenting).

With the general principles enunciated in the majority opinion as to the duties of fiduciaries I am, of course, in thorough accord. But, as Mr. Justice Frankfurter stated in Securities and Exchange Comm. v. Chenery Corp., 318 U.S. 80, 85, 63 S.Ct. 454, 458, 87 L.Ed. 626, "to say that a man is a fiduciary only begins analysis; it gives direction to further inquiry. To whom is he a fiduciary? What obligations does he owe as a fiduciary? In what respect has he failed to discharge these obligations?" My brothers' opinion does not specify precisely what fiduciary duty Feldmann is held to have violated or whether it was a duty imposed upon him as the dominant stockholder or as a director of Newport. Without such specification I think that both the legal profession and the business world will find the decision confusing and will be unable to foretell the extent of its impact upon customary practices in the sale of stock.

The power to control the management of a corporation, that is, to elect directors to manage its affairs, is an inseparable incident to the ownership of a majority of its stock, or sometimes, as in the present instance, to the ownership of enough shares, less than a majority, to control an election. Concededly a majority or dominant shareholder is ordinarily privileged to sell his stock at the best price obtainable from the purchaser. In so doing he acts on his own behalf, not as an agent of the corporation. If he knows or has reason to believe that the purchaser intends to exercise to the detriment of the corporation the power of management acquired by the purchase, such knowledge or reasonable suspicion will terminate the dominant shareholder's privilege to sell and will create a duty not to transfer the power of management to such purchaser. The duty seems to me to resemble the obligation which everyone is under not to assist another to commit a tort rather than the obligation of a fiduciary. But whatever the nature of the duty, a violation of it will subject the violator to liability for damages sustained by the corporation. Judge Hincks found that Feldmann had no reason to think that Wilport would use the power of management it would acquire by the purchase to injure Newport, and that there was no proof that it ever was so used. Feldmann did know, it is true, that the reason Wilport wanted the stock was to put in a board of directors who would be likely to permit Wilport's members to purchase more of Newport's steel than they might otherwise be able to get. But there is nothing illegal in a dominant shareholder purchasing from his own corporation at the same prices it offers to other customers. That is what the members of Wilport did, and there is no proof that Newport suffered any detriment therefrom.

My brothers say that "the consideration paid for the stock included compensation for the sale of a corporate asset", which they describe as "the ability to control the allocation of the corporate product in a time of short supply, through control of the board of directors; and it was effectively transferred in this sale by having Feldmann procure the resignation of his own board and the election of Wilport's nominees immediately upon consummation of the sale." The implications of this are not clear to me. If it means that when market conditions are such as to induce users of a corporation's product to wish to buy a controlling block of stock in order to be able to purchase part of the corporation's output at the same mill list prices as are offered to other customers, the dominant stockholder is under a fiduciary duty not to sell his stock, I cannot agree. For reasons already stated, in my opinion Feldmann was not proved to be under any fiduciary duty as a stockholder not to sell the stock he controlled.

* * *

NOTE

On remand, the District Court in *Perlman* computed the investment value of the common stock on the basis of a capitalization of the earnings, and awarded as damages the amount by which the purchase price exceeded that figure. 154 F.Supp. 436 (D.C.Conn. 1957). As the Court of Appeals ruled, this amount was paid to the minority shareholders, not to the corporation. That is highly unusual in a derivative suit. How is the corporation benefited by this action? Who should pay the plaintiff's counsel fees? Under the majority's analysis would Feldmann have been liable even if he did not receive a premium? Would not the "harm" to the corporation have been the same?

In Honigman v. Green Giant Co., 309 F.2d 667 (8th Cir. 1962), a plan of recapitalization was effected to change nonvoting stock into voting shares. The old voting shares were reduced to 9.3% of the voting power (from 100%) and their share of the net worth increased from .01% to 9.3%. Minority stockholders argued that the voting stockholders were paid a premium for their control, and that this was held to be improper in Perlman v. Feldmann. The court responded, "when fairly read, Perlman does not go to the extent of supporting the rule * * * that control should be considered a corporate asset * * * we are satisfied that plaintiff has wholly failed to demonstrate that the court's failure to apply the Berle rule * * * misapplied or misinterpreted the applicable Minnesota law." 309 F.2d at 670.

5. SALE OF A CORPORATE OFFICE

ESSEX UNIVERSAL CORP. v. YATES

305 F.2d 572 (2d Cir. 1962).

[Plaintiff contracted to purchase defendant's 28.3% interest in Republic Pictures for $8 per share, approximately $2 above the price at which the stock sold on the New York Stock Exchange. The contract required the seller to deliver resignations of a majority of Republic's directors and to cause the election of persons designated by the buyer. The seller refused to go ahead with this condition and claimed as a defense in a suit for breach of contract that to do so would be illegal.

The court unanimously reversed a judgment for plaintiff, but its decision is reflected in three separate opinions.]

LUMBARD, Chief Judge.

* * *

It is established beyond question under New York law that it is illegal to sell corporate office or management control by itself (that is, accompanied by no stock or insufficient stock to carry voting control). The rationale of the rule is undisputable: persons enjoying management control hold it on behalf of the corporation's stockholders, and therefore may not regard it as their own personal property to dispose of as they wish. Any other rule would violate the most fundamental principal of corporate democracy, that management must represent and be chosen by, or at least with the consent of, those who own the corporation.

Essex was, however, contracting with Yates for the purchase of a very substantial percentage of Republic stock. If, by virtue of the voting power carried by this stock, it could have elected a majority of the board of directors, then the contract was not a simple agreement for the sale of office to one having no ownership interest in the corporation, and the question of its legality would require further analysis. Such stock voting control would incontestably belong to the owner of a majority of the voting stock, and it is commonly known that equivalent power usually accrues to the owner of 28.3% of the stock.

For the purpose of this analysis, I shall assume that Essex was contracting to acquire a majority of the Republic stock, deferring consideration of the situation where, as here, only 28.3% is to be acquired.

Republic's board of directors at the time of the aborted closing
had fourteen members divided into three classes, each class being "as
nearly as may be" of the same size. Directors were elected for terms
of three years, one class being elected at each annual shareholder
meeting on the first Tuesday in April. Thus, absent the immediate
replacement of directors provided for in this contract, Essex as the
hypothetical new majority shareholder of the corporation could not
have obtained managing control in the form of a majority of the
board in the normal course of events until April 1959, some eighteen
months after the sale of the stock. The first question before us then
is whether an agreement to accelerate the transfer of management
control, in a manner legal in form under the corporation's charter and
by-laws, violates the public policy of New York.

There is no question of the right of a controlling shareholder under New York law normally to derive a premium from the sale of a
controlling block of stock. In other words, there was no impropriety
per se in the fact that Yates was to receive more per share than the
generally prevailing market price for Republic stock.

The next question is whether it is legal to give and receive payment for the immediate transfer of management control to one who
has achieved majority share control but would not otherwise be able
to convert that share control into operating control for some time. I
think that it is.

* * *

A fair generalization from these cases may be that a holder of
corporate control will not, as a fiduciary, be permitted to profit from
facilitating actions on the part of the purchasers of control which are
detrimental to the interests of the corporation or the remaining shareholders. There is, however, no suggestion that the transfer of control over Republic to Essex carried any such threat to the interests of
the corporation or its other shareholders.

Given this principle that it is permissible for a seller thus to
choose to facilitate immediate transfer of management control, I can
see no objection to a contractual provision requiring him to do so as a
condition of the sale. Indeed, a New York court has upheld an analogous contractual term requiring the board of directors to elect the
nominees of the purchasers of a majority stock interest to officerships. San Remo Copper Mining Co. v. Moneuse, 149 App.Div. 26,
133 N.Y.S. 509 (1st Dept. 1912). The court said that since the purchaser was about to acquire "absolute control" of the corporation, "it
certainly did not destroy the validity of the contract that by one of its
terms defendant was to be invested with this power of control at

once, upon acquiring the stock, instead of waiting for the next annual meeting."

* * *

The easy and immediate transfer of corporate control to new interests is ordinarily beneficial to the economy and it seems inevitable that such transactions would be discouraged if the purchaser of a majority stock interest were required to wait some period before his purchase of control could become effective. Conversely it would greatly hamper the efforts of any existing majority group to dispose of its interest if it could not assure the purchaser of immediate control over corporation operations. I can see no reason why a purchaser of majority control should not ordinarily be permitted to make his control effective from the moment of the transfer of stock.

* * *

Because 28.3 per cent of the voting stock of a publicly owned corporation is usually tantamount to majority control, I would place the burden of proof on this issue on Yates as the party attacking the legality of the transaction. Thus, unless on remand Yates chooses to raise the question whether the block of stock in question carried the equivalent of majority control, it is my view that the trial court should regard the contract as legal and proceed to consider the other issues raised by the pleadings. If Yates chooses to raise the issue, it will, on my view, be necessary for him to prove the existence of circumstances which would have prevented Essex from electing a majority of the Republic board of directors in due course. It will not be enough for Yates to raise merely hypothetical possibilities of opposition by the other Republic shareholders to Essex' assumption of management control. Rather, it will be necessary for him to show that, assuming neutrality on the part of the retiring management, there was at the time some concretely foreseeable reason why Essex' wishes would not have prevailed in shareholder voting held in due course. In other words, I would require him to show that there was at the time of the contract some other organized block of stock of sufficient size to outvote the block Essex was buying, or else some circumstance making it likely that enough of the holders of the remaining Republic stock would band together to keep Essex from control.

Reversed and remanded for further proceedings not inconsistent with the judgment of this court.

CLARK, Circuit Judge (concurring in the result).

Since Barnes v. Brown, 80 N.Y. 527, teaches us that not all contracts like the one before us are necessarily illegal, summary judgment seems definitely improper and the action should be remanded for trial. But particularly in view of our lack of knowledge of corporate realities and the current standards of business morality, I should prefer to avoid too precise instructions to the district court in the hope that if the action again comes before us the record will be generally more instructive on this important issue than it now is. I share all the doubts and questions stated by my brothers in their opinions and perhaps have some additional ones of my own. My concern is lest we may be announcing abstract moral principles which have little validity in daily business practice other than to excuse a defaulting vendor from performance of his contract of sale. Thus for fear of a possible occasional contract inimical to general stockholder interest we may be condemning out of hand what are more often normal and even desirable business relationships. As at present advised I would think that the best we can do is to consider each case on its own facts and with the normal presumption that he who asserts illegality must prove it.

* * *

FRIENDLY, Circuit Judge (concurring).

Chief Judge Lumbard's thoughtful opinion illustrates a difficulty, inherent in our dual judicial system, which has led at least one state to authorize its courts to answer questions about its law that a Federal court may ask. Here we are forced to decide a question of New York law, of enormous importance to all New York corporations and their stockholders, on which there is hardly enough New York authority for a really informed prediction what the New York Court of Appeals would decide on the facts here presented.

I have no doubt that many contracts, drawn by competent and responsible counsel, for the purchase of blocks of stock from interests thought to "control" a corporation although owning less than a majority, have contained provisions like paragraph 6 of the contract* *sub judice*. However, developments over the past decades seem to me to show that such a clause violates basic principles of corporate democracy. To be sure, stockholders who have allowed a set of directors to be placed in office, whether by their vote or their failure to vote, must recognize that death, incapacity or other hazard may prevent a director from serving a full term, and that they will have no voice as to his immediate successor. But the stockholders are entitled to expect that, in that event, the remaining directors will fill the vacancy in the exercise of their fiduciary responsibility. A mass seriatim resignation directed by a selling stockholder, and the filling of vacancies by his henchmen at the dictation of a purchaser and without any consideration of the character of the latter's nominees, are beyond what the stockholders contemplated or should have been expected to contemplate. This seems to me a wrong to the corporation and the other stockholders which the law ought not countenance, whether the selling stockholder has received a premium or not.

* Paragraph 6 provided for the resignation of the old board and the election of new directors designated by the buyer.

Right in this Court we have seen many cases where sudden shifts of corporate control have caused serious injury. To hold the seller for delinquencies of the new directors only if he knew the purchaser was an intending looter is not a sufficient sanction. The difficulties of proof are formidable even if receipt of too high a premium creates a presumption of such knowledge, and, all too often, the doors are locked only after the horses have been stolen. Stronger medicines are needed—refusal to enforce a contract with such a clause, even though this confers an unwarranted benefit on a defaulter, and continuing responsibility of the former directors for negligence of the new ones until an election has been held. Such prophylactics are not contraindicated, as Judge Lumbard suggests, by the conceded desirability of preventing the dead hand of a former "controlling" group from continuing to dominate the board after a sale, or of protecting a would-be purchaser from finding himself without a majority of the board after he has spent his money. A special meeting of stockholders to replace a board may always be called, and there could be no objection to making the closing of a purchase contingent on the results of such an election. I perceive some of the difficulties of mechanics such a procedure presents, but I have enough confidence in the ingenuity of the corporate bar to believe these would be surmounted.

Hence, I am inclined to think that if I were sitting on the New York Court of Appeals, I would hold a provision like Paragraph 6 violative of public policy save when it was entirely plain that a new election would be a mere formality—i.e., when the seller owned more than 50% of the stock. I put it thus tentatively because, before making such a decision, I would want the help of briefs, including those of *amici curiae*, dealing with the serious problems of corporate policy and practice more fully than did those here, which were primarily devoted to argument as to what the New York law has been rather than what it ought to be. Moreover, in view of the perhaps unexpected character of such a holding, I doubt that I would give it retrospective effect.

As a judge of this Court, my task is the more modest one of predicting how the judges of the New York Court of Appeals would rule, and I must make this prediction on the basis of legal materials rather than of personal acquaintance or hunch. Also, for obvious reasons, the prospective technique is unavailable when a Federal court is deciding an issue of state law. Although Barnes v. Brown, 80 N.Y. 527 (1880), dealt with the sale of a majority interest, I am unable to find any real indication that the doctrine there announced has been thus limited. True, there are New York cases saying that the sale of corporate offices is forbidden; but the New York decisions do not tell us what this means and I can find nothing, save perhaps one unexplained sentence in the opinion of a trial court in Ballantine v. Ferretti, 28 N.Y.S.2d 668, 682 (Sup.Ct.N.Y.Co.1941), to indicate that New York would not apply Barnes v. Brown to a case where a stockholder with much less than a majority conditioned a sale on his causing the resignation of a majority of the directors and the election of the purchaser's nominees.

Chief Judge Lumbard's proposal goes part of the way toward meeting the policy problem I have suggested. Doubtless proceeding from what, as it seems to me, is the only justification in principle for permitting even a majority stockholder to condition a sale on delivery of control of the board—namely that in such a case a vote of the stockholders would be a useless formality, he sets the allowable bounds at the line where there is "a practical certainty" that the buyer would be able to elect his nominees and, in this case, puts the burden of disproving that on the person claiming illegality.

Attractive as the proposal is in some respects, I find difficulties with it. One is that I discern no sufficient intimation of the distinction in the New York cases, or even in the writers, who either would go further in voiding such a clause. * * * When an issue does arise, the "practical certainty" test is difficult to apply. * * * Judge Lumbard correctly recognizes that, from a policy standpoint, the pertinent question must be the buyer's prospects of election, not the seller's—yet this inevitably requires the court to canvass the likely reaction of stockholders to a group of whom they know nothing and seems rather hard to reconcile with a position that it is "right" to insert such a condition if a seller has a larger proportion of the stock and "wrong" if he has a smaller. At the very least the problems and uncertainties arising from the proposed line of demarcation are great enough, and its advantages small enough, that in my view a Federal court would do better simply to overrule the defense here, thereby accomplishing what is obviously the "just" result in this particular case, and leave the development of doctrine in this area to the State, which has primary concern for it.

I would reverse the grant of summary judgment and remand for consideration of defenses other than a claim that the inclusion of paragraph 6 *ex mero motu* renders the contract void.

NOTE—SELLING THE OFFICE

Stockholders of Republic Corporation challenged the validity of the election of a majority of the board, chosen by directors as part of a transaction where 9.7% of the stock was sold by former management to a new controlling person. The stock was sold at a price slightly above market. The transaction occurred approximately nine months before the next regularly scheduled election, and an interim report was furnished to stockholders. At the next meeting the stockholders reelected all the directors. The petition to set aside the election was filed after the stockholders meeting had elected the directors; not after the initial election by directors.

The court found that the election was proper. "When a situation involving less than 50% of the ownership of stock exists, the question of what percentage of stock is sufficient to constitute working control is likely to be a matter of fact, at least in most circumstances." The interim notice and subsequent election establish that there was no deception of stockholders. The court does not say how it would have reacted to a petition challenging the election by the the board had it been promptly filed. Carter v. Muscat, 21 A.D.2d 543, 251 N. Y.S.2d 378 (1st Dept. 1964).

A different situation was presented in Brecher v. Gregg, 89 Misc. 2d 457, 392 N.Y.S.2d 776 (1975). Gregg, the president of Lin Broadcasting Corporation (LIN) sold his 4% stock interest to the Saturday Evening Post and promised to resign and cause the election of the Post's president and two others to the board, and the selection of the Post's president to succeed him in office. The price paid to Gregg was $3,500,000, approximately $1,260,000 above the market value of the stock. The agreement was carried out, but several weeks later the LIN board terminated the new president's tenure, and all the Post directors resigned and the Post sued for a refund of the premium paid for the stock. That suit was dismissed on grounds of the illegality of the payment.

A shareholder of LIN then sued Gregg and the other directors for the premium paid by the Post. The court held that Gregg was liable to the corporation for the premium, but that the other directors were not. Among other things, the court found as follows:

> The Court concludes as a matter of law that the agreement insofar as it provided for a premium in exchange for a promise of control, with only 4% of the outstanding shares actually being transferred, was contrary to public policy and illegal.
>
>   *   *   *
>
> The remedy is an equitable one and only available to the extent of actual profits realized by the defendant.   *   *   *
>
> In summary, an officer's transfer of fewer than a majority of his corporation's shares, at a price in excess of that prevailing in the market, accompanied by his promise to effect the transfer of offices and control in the corporation to the vendee, is a transaction which breaches the fiduciary duty owed the corporation and upon application to a court of equity; the officer will be made to forfeit that portion of his profit ascribable to the unlawful promise as he has been unjustly enriched; and an accounting made on behalf of the corporation, since it is, of the two, the party more entitled to the proceeds.
>
> Since there has been no showing that the actions of any directors other than Gregg either led to any pecuniary loss to the corporation or to the realization of any personal profit or gain to themselves, it follows that they cannot be held liable jointly, or severally, with Gregg for the payment of the premium over to the corporation.

392 N.Y.S.2d at 779–82.

NOTE—WHAT CONSTITUTES "CONTROL"?

While holders of relatively small blocks of stock may possess functional control, it is paradoxically a fact that holders of large stock holdings sometimes do not possess control. What is the responsibility of a large shareholder, even a director, who is not the controlling person?

TREADWAY COMPANIES, INC. v. CARE CORP.

638 F.2d 357 (2d Cir. 1980).

[Cowin owned 14% of the stock of Treadway Companies, Inc. (Treadway) which became the target of a take-over attempt by Care Corporation. He was the largest shareholder, and also a director. Cowin had contacts with Care concerning the sale of his stock, but while negotiations were proceeding he accepted renomination for election to the board. At about this time he rejected an invitation to sell his stock back to the company because, as he stated, he did not think the company could afford to make this purchase, and he doubted the propriety of a director making such a sale to the company. He subsequently sold his shares to Care for consideration having a present value of $8, equal to a 35% premium over the market price. In one part of a complex litigation, Treadway sought a judgment against Cowin for his profits on the stock sale. The court ruled in favor of Cowin.]

KEARSE, Circuit Judge.

* * *

We also conclude that Cowin breached no duty in selling his own shares to Care at a premium. Apparently Treadway's argument is that Cowin had a duty to afford the other shareholders an opportunity to participate in the sale, either because he was a director or because he was Treadway's "largest shareholder." We find both theories unpersuasive.

Treadway has pointed us to no case, and we know of none, in which a director was required, solely by reason of his status as director to account to the shareholders for profits earned on the sale of his shares.

> Ordinarily a director possesses the same right as any other stockholder to deal freely with his shares of stock and to dispose of them at such a price as he may be able to obtain, provided the director acts in good faith, since the corporation as such has no interest in its outstanding stock or in dealing in its shares among its stockholders.

3 Fletcher, [Cyclopedia of the Law of Private Corporations at § 900]. There is no indication that Cowin acted other than in good faith to-

ward Treadway and its shareholders. The district court found that Cowin did not misuse confidential information and that he did not usurp any corporate opportunity. Cowin's sale permitted Care to increase its stake in Treadway, but the district court found that neither Treadway nor its shareholders were thereby harmed in any way. Thus, we see nothing that would take this case outside the general principle that a director is free to sell his stock at whatever price he may obtain.

Nor do we find that Cowin's status as Treadway's "largest shareholder" carried with it a duty to share his premium with the other shareholders. It is true that in certain circumstances, a *controlling* shareholder may be required to account to the minority shareholders for the "control premium" he obtains upon selling his controlling shares. But Cowin was not a controlling shareholder. At the time of his sale, Cowin owned only 14% of Treadway's outstanding stock; the district court specifically found that Cowin did not have control of the corporation. Since Cowin therefore did not transfer control, he was under no duty to account for the premium he obtained.

* * *

6. EQUAL OPPORTUNITY

Professor William D. Andrews has interpreted the result of Perlman v. Feldmann as predicated on the fact that Feldmann did not share the favorable opportunity with his fellow shareholders. To deal with sales of control Professor Andrews has proposed the following rule:

> Whenever a controlling stockholder sells his shares, every other holder of shares (of the same class) is entitled to have an equal opportunity to sell his shares, or a pro rata part of them, on substantially the same terms. Or in terms of the correlative duty: Before a controlling stockholder may sell his shares to an outsider, he must assure his fellow stockholders an equal opportunity to sell their shares, or as high a proportion of theirs as he ultimately sells of his own.

Andrews, The Stockholders' Right to Equal Opportunity in the Sale of Shares, 78 Harv.L.Rev. 505, 515–16 (1965).

Professor Andrews believes that the "equal opportunity rule" contains self-enforcing mechanisms to prevent potential abuses, such as the subsequent looting of the corporation, whenever controlling shares are sold. After analysis of whether this rule might prevent sales that produce more efficient management, Professor Andrews concludes it would not and observes that "the problems with which the rule would deal are sufficiently serious to warrant the costs of enforcement."

One critic of Professor Andrews' approach writes that the rule would impose higher capital requirements on purchasers and would discourage transactions that benefit corporations and minority stock-holders. The argument is that the principle of equality cannot be shown to improve the functioning of the securities market. Javaras, Equal Opportunity in the Sale of Controlling Shares: A Reply to Professor Andrews, 32 U.Chi.L.Rev. 420 (1965).

Professor Berle criticized Andrews' rule because it rejects the notion that control is a corporate asset and the corollary that the premium belongs to the corporation. Berle believed that the Andrews' approach provides an adequate remedy, at least in some cases, although it should be recognized that it does not describe a right. Berle, The Price of Power: Sale of Corporate Control, 50 Corn.L.Q. 628 (1965).

The New York Court of Appeals recently observed: "This rule would profoundly affect the manner in which controlling stock interests are now transferred. It would require, essentially, that a controlling interest be transferred only by means of an offer to all stockholders, i.e., a tender offer. This would be contrary to existing law and if so radical a change is to be effected it would best be done by the Legislature." Zetlin v. Hanson Holdings, 48 N.Y.2d 684, 685, 421 N.Y.S.2d 877, 878, 397 N.E.2d 387 (1979).

However, in Donahue v. Rodd Electrotype Co. of New England, Inc., 367 Mass. 578, 328 N.E.2d 505 (1975), a *close corporation* redeemed the shares of the controlling person. In such a transaction, the court said that the directors or controlling stockholders must have acted with the "utmost good faith and loyalty" to the other stockholders. 328 N.E.2d at 515 citing Cardullo v. Landau, 329 Mass. 5, 8, 105 N.E.2d 843, 845 (1952).

The court then added:

"To meet this test, if the stockholder whose shares were purchased was a member of the controlling group, the controlling stockholder must cause the corporation to offer each stockholder an equal opportunity to sell a ratable number of his shares to the corporation at an identical price. Purchase by the corporation confers substantial benefits on the members of the controlling group whose shares were purchased. These benefits are not available to the minority stockholders if the corporation does not also offer them an opportunity to sell their shares. The controlling group may not, consistent with its strict duty to the minority, utilize its control of the corporation to obtain special advantages and disproportionate benefit from its share ownership. * * *

"The benefits conferred by the purchase are twofold: (1) provisions of a market for shares, (2) access to corporate assets for personal use. By definition, there is no ready market for shares of a close corporation. The purchase creates a market for shares which previously had been unmarketable. It transforms a previously illiquid investment into a liquid one. If the close corporation purchases shares only from a member of the controlling group, the controlling stockholder can convert his shares into cash at a time when none of the other stockholders can. Consistent with its strict fiduciary duty, the controlling group may not utilize its control of the corporation to establish an exclusive market in previously unmarketable shares from which the minority stockholders are excluded. * * *

"The purchase also distributes corporate assets to the stockholder whose shares were purchased. Unless an equal opportunity is given to all stockholders, the purchase of shares from a member of the controlling group operates as a *preferential* distribution of assets. In exchange for his shares, he receives a percentage of the contributed capital and accumulated profits of the enterprise. The funds he so receives are available for his personal use. The other stockholders benefit from no such access to corporate property and cannot withdraw their shares of the corporate profits and capital in this manner unless the controlling group acquiesces. Although the purchase price for the controlling stockholder's shares may seem fair to the corporation and other stockholders under the tests established in the prior case law, the controlling stockholder whose stock has been purchased has still received a relative advantage over his fellow stockholders, inconsistent with his strict fiduciary duty—an opportunity to turn corporate funds to personal use.

"The rule of equal opportunity in stock purchases by close corporations provides equal access to these benefits for all stockholders. We hold that, in any case in which the controlling stockholders have exercised their power over the corporation to deny the minority shall be entitled to appropriate relief."

328 N.E.2d at 518–19.

In Jones v. H. F. Ahmanson & Co., 1 Cal.3d 93, 81 Cal.Rptr. 592, 460 P.2d 464 (1969), the court applied the equal opportunity rule as a remedy once it found that there was a breach of fiduciary duty in the sale by the controlling person, an approach consistent with the one suggested by Professor Berle in his criticism of the Andrews' article.

Consider the following questions:

1. How would the equal opportunity rule prevent the feared worst consequences of a sale of control?

2. Is a suit alleging a failure to follow the equal opportunity rule a derivative or a direct action? If the corporate interest is allegedly protected by following the rule, as Professor Andrews claims, then isn't the failure to observe it damaging to the corporation, and may not (must not?) the suit be brought derivatively?

3. Consider the mechanics of the equal opportunity rule. Would it discourage changes in control? Would it affect the price?

4. Would you counsel a client to follow the rule? Why should he expend money (there are some costs) to restructure the transaction in that manner? What legal protection would he gain?

5. How far does the *Donahue* case go? Does it apply only to transactions where the corporation is a party? Does it apply only to close corporations or do some public companies fall within the scope of its reasoning?

7. DISCLOSURE AND FEDERAL LAW

In Christophides v. Porco, 289 F.Supp. 403 (S.D.N.Y.1968), plaintiffs brought suit under Rule 10b–5 to challenge a sale of a controlling person's shares at a premium. The court dismissed the complaint explaining:

> [A] purchaser is free to offer a premium for a block of control stock. This is so even though control stock is purchased pursuant to a plan to acquire the remainder of the shares at a low price, if, by private purchase or the normal economies of the market place, this can be achieved. It is only where fraud, deceit or manipulation enter that a violation of state law or of Rule 10b–5 occurs.

289 F.Supp. at 405.

There may be some basis for a federal claim arising out of a sale of control. A failure to disclose must be the touchstone. In Ferraioli v. Cantor, 281 F.Supp. 354 (S.D.N.Y.1967), a plaintiff who sold his shares at the market sued a controlling person who sold at a higher price, under Rule 10b–5, on a theory approximating a denial of equal opportunity. A motion to dismiss was denied. But lest this be viewed as acceptance of the equal opportunity rule, a more likely rationale is that the court viewed the controlling person as having a duty to speak when he invites a selected group of stockholders to join in a favorable opportunity and leaves the other stockholders to the market. Such an affirmative duty to speak, if held to exist under Rule 10b–5, would go beyond the holdings of state courts. *See* Tryon v. Smith, 191 Or. 172, 229 P.2d 251 (1951). The Second Circuit repudiated an interpretation of Ferraioli v. Cantor that would create a federal "equal opportunity" rule. Haberman v. Murchison, 468 F.2d 1305, 1312 (2d Cir. 1972).

However, some state courts have found inadequate disclosure to be a breach of fiduciary duty by a controlling person. In Brown v. Halbert, 271 Cal.App.2d 252, 76 Cal.Rptr. 781 (1969), the controlling person sold his shares at a favorable price. After obtaining an agreement for the price he desired for his own stock and while still an officer-director, he failed to make any effort to obtain for the minority substantially the same price he received and, in fact, worked actively for the buyers in assisting them to acquire all the stock at a low figure by recommending to the minority holders that they sell at below book value.

Apart from the substantive issue of whether federal law imposes a disclosure requirement or whether a sale of control constitutes some other kind of securities law violation, there is the practical issue of who can sue. Rule 10b–5 requires plaintiff to be a purchaser or seller. Blue Chip Stamps v. Manor Drug Stores, 421 U.S. 723, 95 S. Ct. 1917, 44 L.Ed.2d 539 (1975). If an action is brought under Rule 10b–5, alleging inadequate disclosure in a controlling person's sale of his stock, can the corporation sue in a derivative suit? Can the stockholders sue in a class action asserting a failure to provide an equal opportunity? Can they claim that the controlling person's sale prevented an offer to them? Where is there a causal connection between injury to the class and defendant's deception?

Suppose a suit charges that corporate funds were used, or would be used, by the purchaser, after he gained control, to fund the loans he had made to buy the stock? What missing element is furnished by that allegation? Does *Santa Fe* loom as an obstacle to such a suit?

Consider whether suit could be brought under the proxy rules. The "standing" issue changes, but what about the requirement that some "deception" cause some injury?

B. CONTESTS FOR CONTROL

PROBLEM

GENERAL INDUSTRIES CORPORATION—PART I

General Industries Corporation (GIC), a Delaware corporation whose stock is listed on the New York Stock Exchange, enjoyed stock market favor for several years as it experienced impressive growth in earnings. Its stock market price rose to a high of $90 per share. However, for the last three years, earnings have leveled off or declined. The stock is now selling for $35 and trading activity has subsided considerably.

The board of directors is composed of 15 members, of whom seven are management personnel. Members of the board own a total of 5% of the 5,000,000 shares outstanding. The remaining shares are owned by 30,000 holders of record. Approximately 35% of the stock is owned in "street name."

Danton, a wealthy oil magnate who owns 40,000 shares of GIC, is concerned about the declining fortunes of GIC. He recently met with Lee and Saunders, bank trust department executives whose trust funds each own 50,000 shares of GIC, to discuss various possibilities for bringing about a change in GIC management, which they feel is essential. Among the approaches they considered were: a meeting between Danton and company officials to persuade them to institute management changes; a request that Danton be elected to the board and the executive committee; the election of Danton as a minority director chosen through cumulative voting; and a full scale battle for control. Lee and Saunders suggested that Danton retain Joseph

Tetley, a well known lawyer who specializes in corporate control fights.

Danton made an appointment to see Tetley. In the meantime, to get an idea of his strength among stockholders, Danton arranged to meet with about fifteen large individual stockholders and representatives of stockholding institutions to discuss the situation. All agreed that something ought to be done, but there was no consensus as to what was the best course. They all agreed to meet again after Danton had talked with Tetley.

Following the meeting of investors, one of the individuals met with a reporter for the Wall Street Journal and furnished him with some information about GIC. The reporter used it as background for a story analyzing "what is wrong at GIC." Some of the description was inaccurate and it prompted a correction from the company. However, the price of GIC declined several points following publication, and Danton decided to test the market. He found stock easily available, and purchased 3,000 shares at declining prices down to $31 per share.

Danton then met with Tetley. He told Tetley that he was sure that a tender offer at $42 per share would succeed in acquiring a majority of the GIC stock and he was confident that the directors of Apex Petroleum Corp., of which he is CEO, would agree to make such an offer. He also expressed his view that GIC stockholders would vote in favor of him in preference to management, if given the opportunity.

Danton now wants advice on the best course of action to follow. He wants to know what legal considerations enter the decision, and what legal impediments could prevent his success. He also believes that GIC, the beneficiary of the change in control, ought to pay all his expenses.

Tetley has asked you, a young lawyer in his firm, to work with him on this. Danton is coming in to the office tomorrow and he wants to go over all the issues. Prepare for the meeting.

The lawyer's problem in our situation is to weigh alternative courses that lead to the same objective. Keep the objective in mind, *i.e.*, to gain control of GIC. There are strengths and weaknesses to each course, but they should never be considered in isolation from one another. We suggest that you first set out the relevant factors in the choice, and then study separately the proxy contest and the tender offer, and apply the questions to each.

First, analyze the client's needs if he is to succeed. He needs: (1) money, (2) a means to contact the stockholders and (3) a winning approach that will persuade others to go along with what he wants. The last item subdivides: in the case of asking people for their vote, he needs persuasive arguments; in the case of asking people to sell their stock, he needs to come up with the right price, and perhaps the

1080 TRANSACTIONS IN CONTROL Ch. 22

best competitive price. He must also head off competitive bids and other strategies to counteract resistance to his offer. In both cases he needs to come up with the right staff support. Consider those needs; they are relevant to cost.

Second, assess the likelihood of success with respect to each approach. Does entrenched management already have so many votes that it will be impossible to unseat them? What advantages are there to incumbency?

Now take up the specific issues. This will require close reading of the Federal securities law provisions relating to proxy contests and tender offers, summarized in section 2.

1. Can Danton get a list of stockholders? Do the same rules apply for proxy contests and tender offers? Under which course of action is Danton hurt *less* if there are delays in obtaining the list? When should he try to get the list (*See* paragraph 3, below.)

2. How much money is Danton likely to need for each course? Can funds be borrowed? Can Danton get at the corporate treasury? Can he keep management from using it?

3. Is there any tactical advantage to surprise? Consider the time frame and tactics in which the two different courses operate. Are there some things that one would want to do before the other side knows that there is a contest? Will Danton be able to buy shares, put together allies and raise money before the management must be told of his plan? Is any disclosure to management required now? What SEC filings are required, and when?

4. What strategies can management use against Danton? Consider the counter-tactics to management moves. What SEC filings or other disclosures will be required of management?

5. What are the liability risks to Danton? Can he be sued in federal court? What kind of relief is likely to be awarded? What activity by Danton poses the most serious liability threat? What are the realistic dangers, including the danger of delay? Very important—has anything been done which already creates a liability danger under either course?

6. Which type of bid creates a greater economic risk to Danton? What happens if he loses a tender offer? A proxy contest?

1. BUSINESS CONSIDERATIONS

Most changes in control are negotiated. One corporation "buys" another corporation. The management of the two corporations bargain over the terms, conditions, future management, and the precise legal forms which are decided in an arm's length session. If no deal is struck, that is usually the end of the matter.

In negotiated transactions the shareholder interests are represented by the management of the two companies. Although corporate law may require shareholder approval, and federal securities law may require full disclosure to shareholders, in a truly arm's length transaction, the business judgment rule largely insulates management from liability for mistakes. If the board exercises due care and no self dealing is involved, management has little to fear from a stockholder suit.

But if the management of a corporation is unable to agree to acceptable terms, or unwilling to negotiate in the first place, the would-be acquiror may seek to gain control through a hostile take-over by going over the heads of the management to the stockholders. As a matter of public policy, the ability to do so is critical to maintaining the accountability of the management and preventing managers from becoming too safely entrenched.

The bidder selects the mode of challenge. It has two choices: a proxy contest or a tender offer. If the target company is subject to the reporting requirements of § 12 of the Securities Exchange Act of 1934, the challenger must comply with federal securities law, principally §§ 13 and 14 of the '34 Act.

Many factors will bear on the challenger's decision, which requires a highly particularized analysis of the situation. The target must be closely scrutinized. How big is it? How many shares and shareholders does it have? Are there large blocks of stock? It is difficult to wage a successful proxy contest for a large public company, with widely scattered holdings. Institutions, as voters, tend to favor management. Are the stockholders unhappy with the management and inclined to vote for a change, or must they be induced to change control by the prospect of a large gain from the sale of their shares? Does the bidder have, or have available to it, sufficient funds to purchase the shares? Some tender offers require hundreds of millions of dollars, or more. If not, how much will it cost to wage an election contest? Are there legal impediments within the structure of the target to discourage one form or the other of challenge? Is suprise a necessary element of success? Surprise is almost impossible for a proxy contest; more possible in the case of a tender offer. What are the relevant tax and accounting considerations, and can the form of the challenge affect those considerations?

Fashion doubtless plays a role. Tender offers were virtually unheard of in the United States until the mid 1960's. They have now become the dominant form of hostile takeover.

We will examine these factors as we analyze the problem, looking first at the choices faced by the bidder and then by the target.

2. FEDERAL SECURITIES LAW PROVISIONS RELATING TO PROXY CONTESTS AND TENDER OFFERS

The Securities Exchange Act of 1934 has always authorized the regulation of proxy contests, and since 1954, the Securities and Exchange Commission has had special rules dealing with solicitations of proxies in that context. The statutory provisions dealing with tender offers [sections 13(d), (e), (f) and 14(d), (e), (f)], known as the Williams Act, were enacted in 1968. The pertinent statutes and rules are summarized below, but this is not a complete summary.

a. Identification of 5% Stockholders

Section 13(d)(1)—as implemented by Rule 13d–1—imposes a reporting requirement on any person who, after acquiring beneficial ownership of an equity security, owns 5% of that class. The equity securities covered under this provision are those registered under section 12, securities of an insurance company not exempt from registration under section 12(g)(2)(G), and securities issued by a closed-end investment company registered under the Investment Company Act of 1940. The 5% purchaser must submit the following information on Schedule 13D to the issuer of the security, to each exchange where the security is traded, and to the Commission within 10 days after the acquisition:

> (1) background information identifying the beneficial owner, and all other persons on whose behalf the person has made purchases;

> (2) the source and amount of funds expended;

> (3) if the purpose of the acquisition is to acquire control, any plans the person may have to liquidate, merge or effect any other major change in the issuer, *e.g.*, changes in the corporate charter, by-laws or board of directors;

> (4) the aggregate number and percentage of the class of securities owned by the person;

> (5) information as to any arrangements for the transfer of any securities of the issuer that were acquired.

Section 13(d)(2)—imposes a continuing duty on the person to amend Schedule 13D whenever material changes occur in the facts reported.

Section 13(d)(3)—provides that if two or more persons act as "a partnership, limited partnership, syndicate, or other group for the purpose of acquiring, holding or disposing of securities of an issuer, such syndicate or group shall be deemed a 'person' " for purposes of determining whether it is the owner of 5% of the stock. This provision is interpreted in Rule 13d–5(b)(1) as meaning, "When two or more persons agree to act together for the purpose of acquiring, holding, voting or disposing of equity securities of an issuer, the group formed thereby shall be deemed to have acquired beneficial ownership, for purpose of section 13(d) *   *   * of the Act, as of the date of such agreement of all equity securities of that issuer beneficially owned by any such persons." Thus, the date an agreement is made, which is an uncertain event, triggers the requirement for filing a Schedule 13D provided that the members of the "group" owned an aggregate of 5% of the stock on that date.

The rules additionally contain definitions of beneficial ownership and, the designation of separate forms for certain types of owners, and provisions for amendments.

b. Purchases by an Issuer of its Own Shares

Section 13(e)(1)—makes it unlawful for a company registered under Section 12 (or a closed-end investment company registered under the Investment Company Act of 1940) to purchase its own securities in contravention of rules that the Commission may adopt in order to prevent fraud, deception or manipulation.

Rule 13e–1 prohibits repurchases by an issuer of its own shares after a tender offer has been made for those shares unless the issuer files a statement with the Commission and notifies its stockholders of the purpose of the repurchase and the source of the funds.

Rule 13e–3 deals with certain practices of so-called "going private" transactions, whereby a public corporation terminates the stock interests of all or most of the public shareholders.

Rule 13e–4 deals with tender offers by an issuer for its own shares.

Rule 13e–2 is still only a proposed rule.

c. Proxy Contests

Rule 14a–7 applies to more than proxy contests, but it has particular application in that context. An issuer must make available to a security holder who seeks to solicit the security holders of the issuer an estimate of the number of record holders, and beneficial owners whose shares are owned in street name, and the cost of mailing proxy materials to the holders. If the security holder defrays the reasonable costs of mailing to the holders, the issuer must promptly mail the shareholders' proxy materials to the shareholders. In lieu of that mailing, the issuer may choose to furnish the security holder with a shareholder list, setting forth names and addresses but not necessarily the number of shares.

Rule 14a–11 is a special rule dealing with election contests, which are defined as solicitations in opposition to another candidate.

"Participants" including the issuer, directors, nominees, committees or groups soliciting proxies or financing the solicitation, must file a Schedule 14B five business days before making a solicitation to which the rule applies. The form must set forth biographical information about the participant, any interest in the securities of the subject company or in any transaction with the company, and a description of how the person became a participant.

The scope of the proxy rules is extended to cover parts of annual reports and reprints and reproductions of other articles bearing on the contest. Bear in mind that all other provisions of the proxy rules are also applicable to proxy contests, in particular, Rule 14a–9, which prohibits false or misleading statements in proxy solicitations.

d. Tender Offers

Section 14(d)(1)—prohibits the making of a tender offer (which is not defined in the statute), for a class of securities registered under section 12, of an insurance company not exempt from registration under section 12(g)(2)(G), or of a closed-end investment company registered under the Investment Company Act of 1940, if the bidder would then own 5% of that class, unless, "at the time copies of the offer or request of invitation [for tenders] are first published or sent or given to security holders [the bidder] has filed with the Commission a statement containing such of the information specified in section 13(d) of this title, and such additional information as the Commission may by rules and regulations prescribe as necessary or appropriate in the public interest or for the protection of investors *   *   * . Copies of all statements, in the form in which material is furnished to security holders and the Commission, shall be sent to the issuer not later than the date such material is first published or sent or given to any security holders."

Schedule 14D–1 is the required form and calls for information similar to that set forth in Schedule 13D, including the description of the bidder's purposes and plans for the target. In addition, when the bidder is a corporation and its "financial condition is material to a decision by a security holder of the [target] company whether to sell, tender or hold securities being sought in the tender offer," certain financial information about the bidder is required.

Rule 14d–2(a) states that a tender offer commences at 12:01 a.m. on the earlier date of either the first publication of a long-form or summary publication, or when the offer is given to security holders by any other means.

Rule 14d–2(b) states that if an issuer makes a bare bones public announcement of an intention to make a tender offer (and adds a few specified details) it has not commenced a tender offer, but it must do so within five business days by filing a Schedule 14D–1 and disseminate certain information to security holders. If it fails to do so, it must discontinue the offer.

Filing with a state agency triggers the requirement that a tender offer commence in five days, which may conflict with the law of most states that an offer cannot commence until 20 days after filing. The Commission believes that Rule 14d–2(b) preempts state takeover laws.

Rule 14d–5 requires the target company to either (1) mail the bidder's tender material to all persons on the shareholder list or (2) furnish the bidder with a list of names and addresses (but not including number of shares) of all shareholders. The choice belongs to the target company. It is the tender offer counterpart to Rule 14a–7.

The Williams Act also added certain substantive provisions relating to the making of tender offers, some of which have been modified by rules adopted by the Commission in 1979.

Section 14(d)(5) permits the security holders to withdraw any shares they may have tendered until after seven days have elapsed since the publication of the tender offer, or after 60 days from the commencement of the tender offer.

Section 14(d)(6) provides that if the tender offer is for less than all the securities of the class, and where a greater number have been deposited pursuant to the offer, then the bidder is required to take up tendered shares on a pro-rata basis from all shareholders who tendered their shares.

Section 14(d)(7) provides that if the bidder varies the terms of the offer before it expires, by increasing the consideration offered, then the increased consideration shall be paid to those who previously tendered their shares.

Rule 14d–9 requires certain persons to file a Schedule 14D–9 with the Commission on the date of a solicitation or recommendation with respect to a tender offer. These persons include the subject company, its management, affiliates, the bidder and persons acting on the bidder's behalf. Under the rule the subject company may issue a "stop-look-and-listen" communication to security holders without filing a Schedule 14D–9, provided that the company also informs holders of a date by which it will advise them of its position on the tender offer.

Section 14(e) makes it unlawful "for any person to make any untrue statement of a material fact or omit to state any material fact necessary in order to make the statements made, in the light of the circumstances under which they are made, not misleading, or to engage in any fraudulent, deceptive, or manipulative acts or practices, in connection with any tender offer or request or invitation for tenders, or any solicitation of security holders in opposition to or in favor of any such offer, request or invitation.

Rule 14e–1 requires that a tender offer must be held open for a minimum period of 20 business days. In the event that the bidder increases the consideration or the soliciting dealer's fee, the offer must remain open for 10 business days after the increase.

Rule 14e–2 requires a subject company's position with respect to a tender offer be disclosed to security holders in a statement no later than ten business days from the dissemination of a tender offer. The statement must include the reasons for the company's position. If the company takes no position on the offer, it must explain why.

Rule 14e–3 addresses the problem of persons who have advance knowledge of a pending tender offer, where the bidder has taken substantial steps to commence an offer. With some exceptions to exclude the bidder itself, it is a fraudulent, deceptive or manipulative act or practice for a person with such knowledge gained from the bidder, the issuer or an officer, director or employee of such person, to buy or sell shares of the target unless the information has been publicly disclosed a reasonable time before the purchase. The structure of the rule contains a number of detailed operational provisions.

Other Rules Affecting Tender Offers

Rule 10b–4 prohibits what is known as "short tendering," meaning that no one can tender shares (which can be achieved by borrowing certificates) that he does not own. The purpose of Rule 10b–4 is to prevent circumvention of the pro-rata provision of section 14(d)(6).

Rule 10b–13 prohibits purchases, directly or indirectly, by a bidder of shares of the target except pursuant to a tender offer once a tender offer has been made. Certain exceptions are provided in the rule. In Rel. No. 34–16385, the Commission published for comment Proposed Rule 14e–5 to replace current Rule 10b–13. The proposed rule would extend the prohibitive period to 10 business days after the termination of the tender offer so that a bidder would not be able to take advantage of unsettled market conditions following termination of the offer.

e. Change of Control

Section 14(f) requires a filing with the Commission and notice to all voting security holders of pertinent information that would be contained in a proxy statement whenever person comprising a majority of the directors are chosen other than at a stockholders' meeting, pursuant to an agreement of or understanding with a person acquiring shares in a tender offer or a transaction required to be reported under section 13(d).

3. PROXY CONTESTS

a. Introduction

A proxy contest provides the stockholders a choice in the selection of management. Stockholders receive proxy statements and forms of proxies from two different slates of candidates; one favored by incumbent management and the other favored by challengers. In addition, both sides may contact shareholders personally, and run newspaper advertisements that make strenuous appeals for votes.

Despite what appears to be a full opportunity for this contentious process to provide adequate information to voters, this form of corporate warfare is subject to close regulation by the SEC. In addition, the parties have access to the courts for private lawsuits (recall J. I. Case Co. v. Borak). Consequently, proxy contests cannot be fought without the assistance of counsel. Indeed, the lawyers are customarily the generals in this fight.

Tactics. The goal of a proxy contest is to win the voting support of the stockholders, not to acquire their shares. This requires the framing of the issues, the selection of candidates, and the construction of a platform. By habit, shareholders tend to vote in favor of management. Disaffected shareholders have often sold their stock before the mounting of a contest; those that remain have, in effect, accepted the incumbent management.

Waging an effective campaign to overcome this tendency requires time. But the amount of time available is limited, fixed by the annual meeting date established in the by-laws.

Although proxy contests are fought openly, the challengers probably welcome some period when management knows little about them and their plans. They would like to contact potential supporters, particularly those who can finance the campaign, before management can create certain defenses. The proxy rules, however, require early identification of the challenge, mainly through two devices. First, Rule 14a–11 requires a filing on Schedule 14B by participants in a proxy contest before any solicitations are made. The term "solicitation" is broadly defined in Rule 14a–2, although it permits a limited exemption for non-management solicitations. Second, section 13(d) requires a filing of a Schedule 13D whenever any person becomes the owner of 5% of the stock of a registered company, following an acquisition. "Person" includes a "group" and the SEC rules state that a "group" is defined to have "acquired" the shares of its members once the "group" is formed. Thus, despite the first rule's approval of limited contact not requiring any disclosure, the second rule might require that same conduct to trigger a filing obligation.

What is a Group? The leading case interpreting the statute is GAF Corp. v. Milstein, 453 F.2d 709 (2d Cir. 1971). At that time Section 13(d) required the filing of a schedule whenever a person owned 10% or more of the stock. Four Milstein family members owned in excess of 10%, and the question was whether their coming together as a group for the purpose of acquiring control of GAF constituted an "acquisition" of stock so that the group would have to file the required schedule. The Milsteins argued that purchases by the individuals were necessary before the group could be considered to have acquired anything. The court rejected that argument, relying heavily on the passage in the Senate Report that read as follows:

> The group would be deemed to have become the beneficial owners, directly, or indirectly, or more than 10 percent of a class of securities at the time they agreed to act in concert. Consequently, the group would be required to file the information called

for in section 13(d)(1) within 10 days after they agreed to act together, whether or not any member of the group had acquired any securities at that time.

453 F.2d at 716, citing S.Rep. No. 550, 90th Cong., 1st Sess. 8 (1967).

The court noted that the purpose of the Act is to alert the marketplace about rapid accumulations that might represent a shift in control, and the alleged conspiracy among the Milsteins was an example of what was intended to be disclosed. Subsequent holdings have applied the filing requirement to management groups organized to prevent a shift in control.

Management's Advantages. Management begins a proxy contest with certain distinct advantages. We have already mentioned the usual shareholder propensities to vote for management out of habit. In addition, management knows who the stockholders are and how many shares they own because it has the list. Secondly, management has a ready source of funds—the corporate treasury. Whether there are limits to their use of the treasury or whether challengers will be permitted to gain equal access at some point is explored in the material that follows, but even if the challengers can do so, this will not diminish management's *initial* edge.

Shareholder List. The challengers have a right to obtain a copy of the stockholders list, as a matter of state law, providing they have a "proper purpose." See Chapter 10, Section F. Some states require stockholders to have owned their shares for six months before they can obtain the list (Model Business Corporation Act, § 52); some permit any stockholder with a proper purpose to see the list (Del.Gen. Corp. Law § 220). A contestant in a proxy contest *has* a proper purpose to examine the list, but nonetheless management may force the challenger to sue, thereby delaying its delivery. At that stage of the proxy contest, the delay can be very damaging. There is no federal right to see the list. Read Rule 14a–7 closely to see what right it *does* provide.

Waging the Fight. After the existence of proxy contest has been publicly acknowledged, customarily with a news story announcing the formation of a challenger group (usually designated "The Shareholder Protective Committee of X Corp."), both sides will rush to communicate first with the stockholders. Each will send proxy cards in their own special color, to avoid confusion, and will hope to line up support. Both sides also hope to be the *last* to furnish stockholders with a proxy. Why? Under state law, a later conferral of agency power cancels any prior inconsistent grant of power. Therefore, if a stockholder has given both sides a proxy, the later one cancels the earlier one. When the proxies are counted, and both sides claim the vote of a particular stockholder, they will each try to prove that theirs was granted later, by looking at the date on the proxy card or on the envelope in which it was mailed. They will also seek to cancel the other sides' votes for various imperfections, such as defects in the signature, or the failure to indicate that the proxy was signed in a fiduciary capacity. There is virtually no law to govern this subject, and certainly no federal law. The legal issue is the validity of an election of directors, and that is a matter of state law. Mainly, however, it is a matter of corporate practice, and both sides usually agree in advance on a set of ground rules to govern the election.

But the main effort to impede the efforts of the other side is by showing that their solicitations violated the federal securities laws. Rule 14a–9 prohibits false and misleading statements in connection with the solicitation of a proxy. The notion of "false or misleading" is stretched by litigants, by SEC views, and sometimes by courts. *But see* TSC Industries, Inc. v. Northway. Each side reads the soliciting material of the other side closely, and tries to convince the staff of the SEC that it should seek to enjoin their opponent's solicitations. And, of course, the contestants may go to court on their own to seek an injunction against further violations and to cancel the fruits of the previously improper solicitations. The threat of such a remedy is a check against excessive statements in the soliciting material.

Significantly, it has been held that the fact that each side is able to counter the other side's arguments does not relieve a participant from the anti-fraud rules. Solicitations are not left to the policing effect of the election market place; each side must still abide by the rules. In SEC v. May, 229 F.2d 123, 124 (2d Cir. 1956), Judge Clark commented, "Appellants' fundamental complaint appears to be that stockholders disputes should be viewed in the eyes of the law just as are political contests, with each side free to hurl charges with comparative unrestraint, the assumption being that the opposing side is then at liberty to refute and thus effectively deflate the 'campaign oratory' of its adversary. Such, however, was not the policy of Congress as enacted in the Securities Exchange Act. There, Congress has clearly entrusted to the Commission the duty of protecting the investing public against misleading statements made in the course of a struggle for corporate control." (Recall, however, that in *TSC* the Court considered "the total mix of information" in determining whether the misstatement or omission was material.)

Many of the shares will be held in street name, and this will require the involvement of brokers in the voting of those shares. When a contest is involved, stock exchange rules prevent the brokers from voting the shares without specific authority from the beneficial owner. The contestants will make sure that they send enough copies of soliciting materials to the brokers so they can contact their customers.

Resoliciting efforts are a very significant part of the effort to counter the opponent. Since stockholders are offered not just one opportunity to vote, but many—each time they receive a proxy card from either side—there is a chance for confusion to reign and for accidents of timing to be determinative of the outcome. The last contestant to put a proxy in the hands of a stockholder may come away with some support inadvertently provided.

A major target of both sides will be the large institutional owners of stock. In some cases, as much as 40 or 50% of the stock may be owned by institutions. Clearly, these investors will be courted frequently by both sides, much as presidential candidates spend most of their campaign time in New York, California, Pennsylvania and Illinois.

Some Policy Considerations. Proxy contests occur with considerably less frequency than tender offers although they are, relatively speaking, much easier to mount. For the 12 months ended September 30, 1977, for example, there were 134 tender offers and only 37 proxy contests. *See* SEC, 43d Annual Report, 107–108 (1977).

Why should this be? For one reason, proxy contests have proved generally less successful as a means for outsiders to take control of a corporation than tender offers. It is apparently easier to convince investors to sell out (at a price above the market) than to convince them to vote for a change in management. Second, in the end, proxy contests often prove more costly for the challenger. If the contest fails, the expenses incurred represent a net loss. An unsuccessful tender offeror, on the other hand, may lay out a considerable amount of money in the purchase of stock, but is usually able to make a large enough profit on disposing of the stock to cover the expenses of the effort with some left over.

The regulatory approach to protecting the corporate electorate precedes some recent developments concerning the status of commercial speech under the First Amendment. These implications have rarely been a consideration in the application of the proxy rules, but this liberty is not likely to continue. Probably the most vulnerable SEC rules are the provisions in Rules 14a–6 and 14a–11 that require prepublication filing for proxy statements and other solicitations. While on balance this requirement might be sustained as not an excessive restraint on free speech, it is probably more difficult to defend the proposition in the context of a contest where opposing solicitations are made, and opponent's excesses are not unnoticed. Thus, the rules may restrain expression deemed highly valuable by the contestants. *See* Givens, Free Speech and Proxy Contests, N.Y.L.J., Feb. 16, 1978, p. 1.

b. Costs

ROSENFELD v. FAIRCHILD ENGINE AND AIRPLANE CORP.
309 N.Y. 168, 128 N.E.2d 291 (1955).

FROESSEL, Judge.

In a stockholder's derivative action brought by plaintiff, an attorney, who owns 25 out of the company's over 2,300,000 shares, he seeks to compel the return of $261,522, paid out of the corporate treasury to reimburse both sides in a proxy contest for their expenses. The Appellate Division, 284 App.Div. 201, 132 N.Y.S.2d 273, has unanimously affirmed a judgment of an Official Referee, Sup., 116 N.Y.S. 2d 840, dismissing plaintiff's complaint on the merits, and we agree. Exhaustive opinions were written by both courts below, and it will serve no useful purpose to review the facts again.

Of the amount in controversy $106,000 was spent out of corporate funds by the old board of directors while still in office in defense of their position in said contest; $28,000 were paid to the old board by the new board after the change of management following the proxy contest, to compensate the former directors for such of the remaining expenses of their unsuccessful defense as the new board found was fair and reasonable; payment of $127,000, representing reimbursement of expenses to members of the prevailing group, was expressly ratified by a 16 to 1 majority vote of the stockholders.

The essential facts are not in dispute, and, since the determinations below are amply supported by the evidence, we are bound by the findings affirmed by the Appellate Division. The Appellate Division found that the difference between plaintiff's group and the old board "went deep into the policies of the company", and that among these Ward's contract was one of the "main points of contention". The Official Referee found that the controversy "was based on an understandable difference in policy between the two groups, at the very bottom of which was the Ward employment contract".

By way of contrast with the findings here, in Lawyers' Advertising Co. v. Consolidated Ry., Lighting & Refrigerating Co., 187 N.Y. 395, at page 399, 80 N.E. 199, at page 200, which was an action to recover for the cost of publishing newspaper notices not authorized by the board of directors, it was expressly found that the proxy contest there involved was "by one faction in its contest with another for the control of the corporation * * * a contest for the perpetuation of their offices and control." We there said by way of *dicta* that under *such* circumstances the publication of certain notices on behalf of the management faction was not a corporate expenditure which the directors had the power to authorize.

Other jurisdictions and our own lower courts have held that management may look to the corporate treasury for the reasonable expenses of soliciting proxies to defend its position in a bona fide policy contest.

It should be noted that plaintiff does not argue that the aforementioned sums were fraudulently extracted from the corporation; indeed, his counsel conceded that "the charges were fair and reasonable", but denied "they were legal charges which may be reimbursed for". This is therefore not a case where a stockholder challenges specific items, which, on examination, the trial court may find unwarranted, excessive or otherwise improper. Had plaintiff made such objections here, the trial court would have been required to examine the items challenged.

If directors of a corporation may not in good faith incur reasonable and proper expenses in soliciting proxies in these days of giant corporations with vast numbers of stockholders, the corporate business might be seriously interfered with because of stockholder indifference and the difficulty of procuring a quorum, where there is no contest. In the event of a proxy contest, if the directors may not freely answer the challenges of outside groups and in good faith defend their actions with respect to corporate policy for the information of the stockholders, they and the corporation may be at the mercy of persons seeking to wrest control for their own purposes, so long as such persons have ample funds to conduct a proxy contest. The test is clear. When the directors act in good faith in a contest over policy, they have the right to incur reasonable and proper expenses for solicitation of proxies and in defense of their corporate policies, and are not obliged to sit idly by. The courts are entirely competent to pass upon their *bona fides* in any given case, as well as the nature of their expenditures when duly challenged.

It is also our view that the members of the so-called new group could be reimbursed by the corporation for their expenditures in this contest by affirmative vote of the stockholders. With regard to these ultimately successful contestants, as the Appellate Division below has noted, there was, of course, "no duty * * * to set forth the facts, with corresponding obligation of the corporation to pay for such expense". However, where a majority of the stockholders chose—in this case by a vote of 16 to 1—to reimburse the successful contestants for achieving the very end sought and voted for by them as owners of the corporation, we see no reason to deny the effect of their ratification nor to hold the corporate body powerless to determine how its own moneys shall be spent.

The rule then which we adopt is simply this: In a contest over policy, as compared to a purely personal power contest, corporate directors have the right to make reasonable and proper expenditures, subject to the scrutiny of the courts when duly challenged, from the corporate treasury for the purpose of persuading the stockholders of the correctness of their position and soliciting their support for policies which the directors believe, in all good faith, are in the best interests of the corporation. The stockholders, moreover, have the right to reimburse successful contestants for the reasonable and bona fide expenses incurred by them in any such policy contest, subject to like court scrutiny. That is not to say, however, that corporate directors can, under any circumstances, disport themselves in a proxy contest with the corporation's moneys to an unlimited extent. Where it is established that such moneys have been spent for personal power, individual gain or private advantage, and not in the belief that such expenditures are in the best interests of the stockholders and the corporation, or where the fairness and reasonableness of the amounts allegedly expended are duly and successfully challenged, the courts will not hesitate to disallow them.

The judgment of the Appellate Division should be affirmed, without costs.

DESMOND, Judge (concurring).

* * *

Plaintiff asserts that it was illegal for the directors (unless by unanimous consent of stockholders) to expend corporate moneys in the proxy contest beyond the amounts necessary to give to stockholders bare notice of the meeting and of the matters to be voted on thereat. Defendants say that the proxy contest revolved around disputes over corporate policies and that it was, accordingly, proper not only to assess against the corporation the expense of serving formal notices and of routine proxy solicitation, but to go further and spend corporate moneys, on behalf of each group, thoroughly to inform the stockholders. The reason why that important question is, perhaps, not directly before us in this lawsuit is because, as the Appellate Division properly held, plaintiff failed "to urge liability as to specific expenditures." The cost of giving routinely necessary notice is, of course, chargeable to the corporation. It is just as clear, we think, that payment by a corporation of the expense of "proceedings by one faction in its contest with another for the control of the corporation" is *ultra vires*, and unlawful. Approval by directors or by a majority stock vote could not validate such gratuitous expenditures. Some of the payments attacked in this suit were, on their face, for lawful purposes and apparently reasonable in amount but, as to others, the record simply does not contain evidentiary bases for a determination as to either lawfulness or reasonableness. Surely, the burden was on plaintiff to go forward to some extent with such particularization and proof. It failed to do so, and so failed to make out a prima facie case.

We are, therefore, reaching the same result as did the Appellate Division but on one only of the grounds listed by that court, that is, failure of proof. * * *

VAN VOORHIS, Judge (dissenting).

* * *

The Appellate Division acknowledged in the instant case that "It is obvious that the management group here incurred a substantial amount of needless expense which was charged to the corporation," but this conclusion should have led to a direction that those defendants who were incumbent directors should be required to come forward with an explanation of their expenditures under the familiar rule that where it has been established that directors have expended corporate money for their own purposes, the burden of going forward with evidence of the propriety and reasonableness of specific items rests upon the directors.   *   *   *

*   *   *

The main question of "policy" in the instant corporate election, as is stated in the opinions below and frankly admitted, concerns the long-term contract with pension rights of a former officer and director, Mr. J. Carlton Ward, Jr. The insurgents' chief claim of benefit to the corporation from their victory consists in the termination of that agreement, resulting in an alleged actuarial saving of $350,000 to $825,000 to the corporation, and the reduction of other salaries and rent by more than $300,000 per year. The insurgents had contended in the proxy contest that these payments should be substantially reduced so that members of the incumbent group would not continue to profit personally at the expense of the corporation. If these charges were true, which appear to have been believed by a majority of the shareholders, then the disbursements by the management group in the proxy contest fall under the condemnation of the English and the Delaware rule.

These circumstances are mentioned primarily to illustrate how impossible it is to distinguish between "policy" and "personnel", as Judge Rifkind expressed it, but they also indicate that personal factors are deeply rooted in this contest. That is certanly true insofar as the former management group is concerned.   *   *   *

Some expenditures may concededly be made by a corporation represented by its management so as to inform the stockholders, but there is a clear distinction between such expenditures by management and by mere groups of stockholders. The latter are under no legal obligation to assume duties of managing the corporation. They may endeavor to supersede the management for any reason, regardless of whether it be advantageous or detrimental to the corporation but, if they succeed, that is not a determination that the company was previously mismanaged or that it may not be mismanaged in the future. A change in control is in no sense analogous to an adjudication that the former directors have been guilty of misconduct. The analogy of allowing expenses of suit to minority stockholders who have been successful in a derivative action based on misconduct of officers or directors, is entirely without foundation.

Insofar as a management group is concerned, it may charge the corporation with any expenses within reasonable limits incurred in giving widespread notice to stockholders of questions affecting the welfare of the corporation. Expenditures in excess of these limits are *ultra vires*. The corporation lacks power to defray them. The corporation lacks power to defray the expenses of the insurgents in their entirety. The insurgents were not charged with responsibility for operating the company. No appellate court case is cited from any jurisdiction holding otherwise. No contention is made that such disbursements could be made, in any event, without stockholder ratification; they could not be ratified except by unanimous vote if they were *ultra vires*. The insurgents, in this instance, repeatedly announced to the stockholders in their campaign literature that their proxy contest was being waged at their own personal expense. If reimbursement of such items were permitted upon majority stockholder ratification, no court or other tribunal could pass upon which types of expenditure were "needless", to employ the characterization of the Appellate Division in this case. Whether the insurgents should be paid would be made to depend upon whether they win the stockholders election and obtain control of the corporation. It would be entirely irrelevant whether the corporation is "benefitted" by their efforts or by the outcome of such an election. The courts could not indulge in a speculative inquiry into that issue. That would truly be a matter of business judgment. In some instances corporations are better governed by the existing management and in others by some other group which supersedes the existing management. Courts of law have no jurisdiction to decide such questions, and successful insurgent stockholders may confidently be relied upon to reimburse themselves whatever may be the real merits of the controversy. The losers in a proxy fight may understand the interests of the corporation more accurately than their successful adversaries, and agitation of this character may ultimately result in corporate advantage even if there be no change in management. Nevertheless, under the judgment which is appealed from, success in a proxy contest is the indispensable condition upon which reimbursement of the insurgents depends. Adventurers are not infrequent who are ready to take advantage of economic recessions, reduction of dividends or failure to increase them, or other sources of stockholder discontent to wage contests in order to obtain control of well-managed corporations, so as to divert their funds through legal channels into other corporations in which they may be interested, or to discharge former officers and employees to make room for favored newcomers according to the fashion of political patronage, or for other objectives that are unrelated to the sound prosperity of the enterprise. The way is open and will be kept open for stockholders and groups of stockholders to contest corporate elections, but if the promoters of such movements choose to employ the costly modern media of mass persuasion, they should look for reimbursement to themselves and to the stockholders who are aligned with them. If the law be that they can be recompensed by the corporation in case of success, and only in that event, it will operate as a powerful incentive to persons accustomed to taking calculated risks to increase this form of high-powered salesmanship to such a degree that, action provoking reaction, stockholders' meetings will be very costly. To the financial advantages promised by control of a prosperous corporation, would be added the knowledge that the winner takes all insofar as the campaign expenses are concerned. To the victor, indeed, would belong the spoils.

The questions involved in this case assume mounting importance as the capital stock of corporations becomes more widely distributed. To an enlarged extent the campaign methods consequently come more to resemble those of political campaigns, but, as in the latter, campaign expenses should be borne by those who are waging the campaign and their followers, instead of being met out of the corporate or the public treasury. Especially is this true when campaign promises have been made that the expenses would not be charged to the corporation.

* * *

NOTE ON EXPENSES

What is the substantive rule adopted in *Rosenfeld*? Is it that a corporation may properly pay management's expenses in a proxy contest waged to protect corporate policies but not to protect corporate personnel? Or is it that a corporation may properly pay only the expenses incurred to inform shareholders about the issues but may not reimburse management for "campaign" expenses? The prevailing opinion supports the former rule. But a majority of the judges seem to favor the latter.

What few cases there are support the result in *Rosenfeld*. See Steinberg v. Adams, 90 F.Supp. 604 (S.D.N.Y.1950), and Levin v. Metro-Goldwyn-Mayer, Inc., 264 F.Supp. 797 (S.D.N.Y.1967) (both interpreting Delaware law). In January 1981, shareholders of Alexander's Inc. voted to pay $150,000 of expenses of dissidents who *threatened* to wage a proxy contest but did not. Management, instead, elected the dissidents to the board. Wall Street Journal, January 8, 1981, p. 12.

If the amounts involved in *Rosenfeld* hardly seem worth the trouble of extended litigation, one must remember that they were incurred at a time when the highest paid athlete received $100,000 a year, and associates at Wall Street law firms were paid $3,600 a year. Where have you gone, Joe DiMaggio?

Lawyers' fees are probably the single largest item in a control contest, and these can run very high. In the American Express Company bid for McGraw-Hill, management was reported to have spent approximately $3,500,000 in legal fees; the challengers over $2,000,000.

All the other expenses have risen, as well. These include the costs of accountants, financial analysts, public relations experts and stockholder soliciting firms, whose professional skills are always found to be necessary for success. Printing costs are probably the other major expense in a proxy contest; less so in a tender offer. These alone, could exceed the total expenses in *Rosenfeld*. There are incidental expenses of a lesser nature, but still often reaching into tens of thousands of dollars. Mailing, telephone, travel, photocopying, extra clerical help and other minor items are cumulatively significant. The stakes are high in a control contest, as in a war, and the costs are rarely questioned.

Perhaps a more important issue than the objection Judge Van Voorhis raises about the validity of compensating successful challenges is whether unsuccessful challengers have a right to be reimbursed. Can the board decide to make such payment? Can a proxy contest be settled by the contestants on this basis? Would shareholder approval be needed? Does that help if the payment is ultra vires? Or waste?

c. Litigation

Contestants are quick to seek help from the courts in a proxy contest. Some battles are fought in state court, e.g., to obtain the shareholder list or to challenge the validity of the meeting procedure, but most litigation is conducted in federal courts, which have exclusive jurisdiction over the federal proxy rules. While they have an obvious role to play in enforcing the '34 Act, courts are naturally reluctant to interfere in the election process. Judges realize the tactical significance of delay caused by litigation, and the public relations significance of a court ruling. Therefore, relief is granted only in the rare case. This does not deter clients from imploring their lawyers to sue or lawyers from recommending litigation to their clients. The stakes are high, the parties are eager and emotionally charged, the contest offers many opportunities for alleging wrong doing, and knockout punches are occasionally scored. Even unsuccessful litigation can be tactically useful.

The usual pre-election remedy sought is an injunction; in the first instance a preliminary injunction or a temporary restraining order. The tightness of the election schedule mandates the need to obtain temporary or preliminary relief rather than await the results of a trial on the merits. The most important, and the most common, allegation is that the proxy soliciting materials of the opponent are false and misleading in violation of Rule 14a–9. The plaintiff in a proxy contest suit will often assert violations of the various filing rules, relating to Schedules 14B, or 13D or Rule 14a–3. The court must then decide on the basis of allegations, affidavits and documents whether to enjoin the meeting, cancel proxies, order a resolicitation or some other appropriate relief.

Because of the serious nature of the litigation and its consequences, the courts have imposed a high threshold for relief. As one experienced trial judge summarized the standards (at least in the Second Circuit), "Plaintiff must show (a) either (1) likelihood of success on the merits, or (2) sufficiently serious questions going to the merits to make them a fair ground for litigation and a balance of hardships tipping decidedly toward the plaintiff; and (b) in either case, irreparable injury." Plant Industries, Inc. v. Bregman, 490 F.Supp. 265, 267 (S.D.N.Y.1980) (Weinfeld, J.).

Courts will indulge the parties, at least to a point. In Kennecott Copper Corp. v. Curtiss-Wright Corp., 584 F.2d 1195 (2d Cir. 1978), the court reversed a district court finding that the challenger's proxy materials were misleading. "Rare indeed is the proxy statement whose language could not be improved upon by a judicial craftsman sitting in the serenity of his chambers * * * . This is particularly so where the statement is prepared in the 'hurly-burly of a contested election. Not every corporate counsel is a Benjamin Cardozo * * * and nit picking should not become the name of the game." 584 F.2d at 1200.

Nevertheless, even with a close reading of the materiality standard of TSC Industries Inc. v. Northway, instances will arise where the court will determine that continuation of the contest without judicial intervention is unfair. The most dangerous misleading statements concern the economic performance of the subject company, or the track record of the challengers. Management may fail to reveal an unfavorable sharp drop in the earnings, (e.g. Kass v. Arden-Mayfair, Inc., 431 F.Supp. 1037 (D.C.Cal.1977), where unreported losses had increased by 100% over the comparable period of the year before) or the challengers neglect to disclose their own prior failures (e.g. Bertoglio v. Texas International Co., 488 F.Supp. 630 (D.C.Del.1980), where the challenger had been involved in securities fraud matters).

While it is true that a person soliciting proxies is required to make full disclosure, and not omit negative facts with the expectation that the other side can counter, nonetheless courts are mindful of the dynamics of a contest where each side is responding to the other. In Kennecott Copper Corp. v. Curtiss-Wright Corp., supra, the court observed that the omission from the challenger's proxy statement that it had not made a thorough investigation of its recommended future action, if it won, had been "thoroughly aired in this contested proceeding." 584 F.2d at 1200.

What the Kennecott court was most sensitive to was the effect of the judicial intrusion. The lower court had granted an injunction against Curtiss-Wright from voting its proxies because of the misleading statements it had allegedly made. That injunction was stayed on the eve of the meeting, but Curtiss-Wright's slate of candidates was narrowly defeated. "There is a strong likelihood, however, that the election results were influenced by the criticism of Curtiss-Wright contained in the district court's election-eve decision * * *. Equity demands therefore, that the proceedings of the 1978 annual meeting be voided in whole or in part so as to permit a new election of directors." Id.

Post election relief may be even more of a rarity than injunctive relief. At that juncture all that a court can do is void the election and nullify what the stockholders have done. It is not hard to find violations on both sides, and the tendency, is to leave the parties where the court found them. Chris-Craft Industries, Inc. v. Independent Stockholders Committee, 354 F.Supp. 895 (D.Del.1973). In Bertoglio v. Texas International Co., *supra*, the court voided the election of directors chosen for a three year term because it found that the shareholders would have to wait too long before the electoral process could undo the damage caused by an election conducted with false statements.

4. TENDER OFFERS

a. Introduction: Why, How and What

The tender offer—an offer to stockholders of a publicly owned corporation to exchange their shares for cash or securities at a price above the quoted market price—has become the most popular form of takeover device. The cash tender, in particular, has become common. In recent years it has replaced the proxy contest as the favored method for a contested takeover.

Tender offers come in various forms. A tender offer may be used in combination with a sale of control in a negotiated transaction. Thus, a purchase of a large, or controlling block of stock may be followed by a tender offer to the public shareholders on the same terms and conditions. Those few remaining shareholders who do not accept are usually "cashed out" in a merger that follows, *i.e.*, forced to accept cash as the consideration in a merger that is binding on all shareholders. Freund and Easton, The Three-Piece Suitor: An Alternative Approach to Negotiated Corporate Acquisitions, 34 Bus.Law. 1969 (1979). A tender offer may be made to the shareholders with the approval of the target company management, when there can be no prior purchase of a large block because none exists. Some tender offers present an option to the stockholders: cash or shares or debt securities of the bidder. Tax factors will greatly influence the choice of medium of consideration. Additionally, companies sometimes tender for their own shares.

Our focus is on the contested cash tender offer. Why have these become so popular? How do they operate, and how are they regulated? We will first try to explain the mechanical and business aspects of a tender offer, addressing two basic questions: (1) What is a tender offer in the eyes of the law? and (2) What kind of companies become targets of tender offers?

b. The Workings of the Cash Tender Offer

A corporation, through its management or board, decides it wants to expand. To oversimplify the choices, it can either build or buy. The psychology of instant gratification, and perhaps sound business as well, favors the choice of buying new capacity. Negotiation is the most favored form of purchase, but if it fails, a management that is intent on making the acquisition still has another card to play. That card is the hostile takeover—a tactic once spurned by "gentlemen executives" in the United States, although long practiced in the United Kingdom. The hostile takeover is no longer a "dirty trick" in American business, but an everyday occurrence.

As we have already observed, the cash tender offer is the most important of the hostile takeover devices. The cash tender offer is attractive to the bidder if it has a surfeit of cash or a line of credit and if it believes an investment can produce a rate of return in excess of the cost of borrowed money or of the interest received from idle cash. A cash tender offer is a relatively fast process, and permits the bidder to unilaterally determine the conditions on which it will make the investment.

A hostile takeover is a traumatic event in the life of a target corporation and its personnel. The managers of the target will no longer be in charge of their own business lives if the takeover succeeds, but rather they will be working for other managers. Indeed, some of them may not be working for the target company at all. The directors are likely to be replaced. The professional advisors, whether they are investment bankers or lawyers, are likely to lose a client, and, especially in the case of a lawyer, the loss may have serious consequences. The employees of the company face uncertainty and perhaps dismissal. The shareholders, oddly enough, are probably the least affected. It is true that their investment in the company that they may have owned for many years is liquidated, but that investment was at all times only a cash equivalent, and by tendering they have received the cash. They can spend it, save it, or re-invest, perhaps in the company that now owns the company in which they once owned stock. Their lives go on pretty much as before. Yet, whether the hostile takeover is to succeed and all these other drastic consequences occur is, in most cases, entirely up to them.

Selecting the Target. The first decision in the tender offer is made quietly by the bidder. It must select the target for its affection. One approach is to look for bargains. Typically, that would be a company with potential for growth in its earnings which the market place has not perceived or whose growth has been impeded by ineffective management. This search requires the bidder to analyze a large universe of companies, although it may narrow the field to specified industries. That is, the bidder may decide that it is not capable of absorbing business in some areas and therefore must concentrate its efforts on potential targets in fields that it knows and is able to manage. The size of the company is also important because every bidder has its own financial limitations, although it is not unusual for a small bidder to swallow a larger target. If the target has a large pool of liquid assets, sometimes the bidder will plan on liquidating those assets after the acquisition, in effect purchasing the target company with its own money.

In this search for bargains, the bidder will typically look for a company whose stock sells at a relatively low price/earnings ratio, a company that has significantly depressed or declining earnings as compared with competitors, liquidation value of its assets in excess of the market value of its stock, assets undervalued by the market place, little or no debt, and usually an asset size not exceeding one hundred million dollars.

In addition to looking closely at the financial and business information about the potential target, the bidder will have a close look at the demographics of the shareholder body. How many stockholders are there? Are there large blocks of stock concentrated in a few hands? How much stock does management own? Are there special characteristics to the composition of the shareholder body that make it less likely that a tender offer might succeed?

The bidder will also look for any legal impediments that might make the target either unattractive or too expensive. For example, the target may own a television station and a change in control will require approval by the Federal Communications Commission, a lengthy and uncertain process. If the target is a manufacturer of military defense materials its acquisition by a foreign dominated company may be unlawful. The target company may have certain provisions in its certificate of incorporation that discourage a change in control at least on a quick basis, which in fact are designed to repel potential suitors. Although the bidder may feel that these provisions may not ultimately provide a defense, it may also believe that its time and resources are better spent pursuing other, more readily available, targets. In fact, that analysis by the bidder may be precisely what the target had in mind when it inserted certain provisions in its governing instruments to make tender offers more difficult.

See E. Aranow & H. Einhorn, Tender Offers for Corporate Control (1972); A. Fleischer, Jr., Tender Offers: Defenses, Responses, and Planning (1978); Steinberg 5 C.P.S. (BNA), The Contested Cash Tender Offer: Practical, Economic and Legal Consideration of the Offer (1978).

Since the late 1970's the search for takeover targets has been enlarged to cover large and successful companies where a change in management does not necessarily mean improved management. Presumably, the bidder still believes it is acquiring a bargain in the sense that it is getting at least fair value for the cash it is paying, but that may only reflect the fact that the stock market has not caught up with the reality of the target company's worth. In a significant number of situations, very large companies have become the target of a cash tender offer, usually made by other equally large or even larger companies, and it is no longer unusual to see the total cash offered in a tender offer exceeding one billion dollars. Such targets are frequently companies with large amounts of natural resources. We will explore the public policy issues involved in tender offers in a later

note, but we should pause to observe that there are clearly significant differences between tender offers that displace inefficient management from those that change ownership of successful companies.

The Team. The bidder will have to assemble a team of professionals to guide it through the contest. Hostile tender offers are
complex transactions, and many strategic and tactical decisions must
be made on short notice. The atmosphere of a contested tender offer
is war-like, and the resources and the stamina of the contestants are
severely tested.

One expert writes that the most important member of the professional team, the acknowledged general, is usually the investment
banker who "organizes, structures, and evaluates, and coordinates
the deal." Troubh, Purchased Affection: A Primer on Cash Tender
Offers. 54 Harv.Bus.Rev. 79, 84 (July-Aug. 1976). While that is oft-
en the case, there are probably as many instances where the lawyer
is the field marshal, or at least he shares that role. In any event
lawyers and investment bankers are the two key professionals, and in
most takeovers the bidder has selected one of the well known specialists in this field. The professional in charge will usually select the
other members of the team who are necessary; the depositary banks,
soliciting agents, printers and advertising agents. The bidder can expect to be met with equally competent professionals on the other side,
and it is likely that the teams of lawyers and investment bankers
have each been mixed and matched with one another before.

Pre-offer Activity. The bidder will intensify its efforts as the
time approaches for making the offer. Of course, it must make the
final decision of whether to proceed, and to assist it in making that
decision it may decide to test the market. On occasion, the bidder
will accumulate a position in the target stock being careful to stay
below the 5% threshold that triggers the requirement of a filing under section 13(d) of the 1934 Act. This will permit the bidder to come
forward not as a total stranger to the company but as one with a
solid position that would otherwise have to be acquired at higher
prices than the tender offer. The pre-offer purchase also permits the
bidder to assess the likelihood of success by seeing how readily stock
can be purchased. There is another reason for the pre-tender offer
purchases that have nothing to do with facilitating the offer itself.
As we shall see, a tender offer can become an auction if another bidder decides to enter the fray. The first bidder may lose out to a
higher offer. At that point, the initial bidder will be consoled if it is
able to sell at a substantial profit the shares it acquired prior to the
announcement of the tender offer, as a result of the competitive tender offers. That is, the bidder is getting ready to be "topped" in the
contest. Knowing that it will at least be able to defray its costs may
encourage the bidder to begin the contest in the first place. However, more often bidders will not engage in open market purchases pri-
or to the tender offer to avoid driving up the price of the stock and

market speculation, and, more important, so as not to tip their hand to the target.

Setting The Price. The bidder will fix the price so that it offers an attractive premium over the market price, at least 20 to 25 percent. The bidder should probably be ready to raise its price if a competitive bidder enters the scene, or if it encounters resistance from management or shareholders at that price. Many bids are made wildly in excess of a 25% premium. In some very large tender offers, bidders have offered to double the market price to obtain the number of shares sought. In fact, evidence suggests that the average premium in recent years is about 90% over the price of the target's stock four weeks before the announcement.

In planning the bid, the bidder will also have to consider the terms on which the offer will be made. Apart from price, and whether the offer will be for cash or stock, or a combination of the two, the bidder will consider how many shares it seeks or is prepared to buy. The offer may be for any and all of the shares, which probably is most common because it is the most attractive to the target shareholders, or it may offer to purchase no less than a specified proportion, generally over half.

The bidder must arrange for financing of the tender offer before the offer is set in motion. Bidders have sometimes financed the tender offer through banks that have engaged in business with the target, and this has prompted accusations by the target company that the banks were breaching their fiduciary duty to the target. While of course confidences have to be observed, thus far the law has not prevented banks in this position from financing the tender offer. Washington Steel Corp. v. TW Corp., 602 F.2d 594 (3d Cir. 1979).

Proceeding with the Offer. In the primitive era of tender offers, the target company would be alerted to the commencement of the offer when the early edition of the New York Times hit the newsstands containing an offer to purchase the shares. A degree of civility gradually crept into the process so that the CEO of the bidder would telephone the CEO of the target to alert him to get to the newsstands early. The process was then further tamed. Before the tender offer is made, the bidder may write to the target company to express an interest in discussing an acquisition and inviting a friendly response. A price is frequently mentioned and some of the terms are spelled out. The bidder may indicate that it is desirous of retaining the management. Because such a letter is generally only a prelude to an unwanted bid should the target refuse negotiations, these invitations have come to be known as "bear hugs". However, because Rule 14d–2(b) may cause overture to trip the tender offer rules earlier than the bidder intends, the prior practice of a sudden strike may again become the norm.

In some situations, the target management's adverse reaction can be neutralized if the offer is preceded by an agreement that commits a large block to support of the offer. The bidder can "lock up" a large block to support the offer, which may convince target management that it has little chance for successful resistance or, indeed, of any alternative. The large block holder will receive the same price as all other holders, but may also receive certain additional benefits as compensation for its support.

One of the main reasons for a "lock up" agreement is to deter a competitive bid. The "lock up" may also take the form of acquiring an option from the target to purchase shares or valuable assets—an option that would be extended only to a friendly bidder—in order to provide a competitive edge or to clinch a deal. In the context of a competitive bidding situation "lock ups" present a possible preemption of the shareholders' choice and may conflict with management's legal duties.

The bidder's preference is to keep the tender offer open for a relatively short time because that maximizes pressure on the shareholders to accept before the market recedes to its lower levels, and also allows scant opportunity to the target management to defend itself. Ideally, the offer would be made on a Friday and remain open only until the next Friday giving the least amount of room to the target. Such offers came to be known as "Saturday night specials" probably because this device was used by Colt Manufacturing Company.

Changes in the law have now blunted the use of this practice. A tender offer cannot commence until certain documents have been filed, and thereafter the offer must remain open for a specified period. The 36 states that adopted tender offer legislation at one time all required filings with the state and the target at least 20 days prior to the time an offer commenced, but some of those statutes have been amended to avoid a conflict with federal law. Pre-commencement notification is no longer always required. The 1934 Act requires a filing to be made when the offer commences, and thereafter the offer must remain open for at least 20 business days.

In 1976, Congress adopted the Hart-Scott-Rodino Antitrust Improvements Act that requires a filing with the Federal Trade Commission and the Department of Justice of certain documents, and then requires the offering, if it is a cash offer, to remain open for at least 15 business days. If the FTC or the Justice Department requests additional information, the period of time in which the offering must remain open is extended. The statute contains detailed provisions governing its application and the exact nature of disclosure, which we need not detail here. In general, the Hart-Scott-Rodino Act applies if one party has sales or assets of one hundred million dollars or more and the other party has sales or assets of ten million dollars or more and bidder would own, as a result of the acquisition, 15% or more of the target's voting stock, or more than 15 million dollars of voting securities or assets.

After the bid is announced, the war begins in earnest. The target company will explore its defenses, assuming that its board of directors decides not to yield or remain neutral and let the shareholders make the decisions. Litigation will normally ensue with each side charging the other with violations of all Ten Commandments, and the securities laws as well. A common legal defense is that the acquisition would violate the antitrust laws, a defense which may be a "show stopper," if successful. While a violation consisting of inadequate or false disclosure, may be corrected; an antitrust impediment may be fatal.

Arbitrageurs. During the period of time in which the tender offer is open, perhaps the dominant person is the arbitrageur. Arbitrageurs are professional risk takers. They are brokers who purchase from the public at the current market price, which is always slightly below the tender offer price, with the expectation that they will tender to the bidder at the higher price and make a profit on the spread. The reason for the spread is because of the risk that the target will be able to prevent consummation of the tender offer by some means. If that happens, the price will recede to its pre-tender offer level. The arbitrageur assumes the risk of failure of the offer in return for the expected profit. For the shareholder who does not want to endure the risk or wait the period of time in which the tender offer is open, the recourse is to sell in the market. Virtually all of the buying activity in the market place that follows the announcement of the tender offer is by the arbitrageurs, and their bid for the stock effectively determines that market price until the completion of the tender offer. Offers are structured to appeal to the "arbs," as they are called.

The arbitrageurs will hold onto their shares they acquire in the market place until the last minute. They will be alert to the possibility that a competing bidder may enter the contest and offer a higher price. That, of course, means an especially large profit to the arbitrageurs. But arbs lose money, as well. Some tender offers are unsuccessful, and the price declines. In that case, the risk has been absorbed by the arbitrageurs, and the public shareholders who sold to them have received the benefits of a tender offer which did not succeed. The arbs will sell out promptly, and take their loss, looking for the next deal. This activity is not for the faint of heart, or nerve.

Ultimately, the tender offer will run its course. The bidder may succeed completely on the terms it originally determined, or it may have increased its price. Perhaps the target succeeded in litigation to prevent the offer or employed some other strategy to deny the bidder its prize. Perhaps a third party, maybe one solicited by the target (a "white knight"), acquired the company through merger or a competing tender offer. Or perhaps the bidder and the target compromised their differences, the bidder increased its price and offered security to the management, and the two marched off arm in arm to uncork the champagne at "21."

c.   What is a Tender Offer?

The prototype tender offer is a well advertised invitation to all the shareholders of the target to tender their shares to the bidder within a limited period of time for a price above the market price. Although the Williams Act does not define "tender offer," the Act's legislative history is abundantly clear that this transaction was the focus of Congress' attention.

There are two categories of transaction that test the scope of the statute: open market purchases and negotiated purchases. An aggressive program of open market purchases may amount to what is referred to as a "creeping tender offer." A purchaser may acquire shares through regular market facilities, at varying prices, without any disclosure of its activity so long as his purchase does not amount to 5% of the outstanding shares, which would trigger the filing requirements of § 13(d)(1). If the open market purchases were deemed to constitute a tender offer, they could not be made because it would be impossible to comply with the Williams Act. The pro rata, best price, and withdrawal provisions of the Act, not to mention the notice requirement, would be an effective barrier.

A negotiated purchase may consist of a purchase of a controlling block from a single holder, or it could mean a series of purchases from large holders, frequently institutions. The purpose may be to make a major investment, but more frequently it is a prelude to a tender offer. Negotiated purchases may also be made in conjunction with open market purchases. This activity may be barred by the Williams Act if the statute is construed to require that a tender must be made to all stockholders. The publicity resulting from a filing under the Act would also increase the cost.

The objective of the statute is to prevent the stampeding of investors into accepting an offer without adequate information. Investors may need the protection of the Act in situations other than the conventional tender offer, which explains the reluctance of Congress and the SEC to rigidify the definition. One commentator has suggested that the courts should "look at the shareholder impact of particular methods of a securities acquisition, classifying as tender offers those found capable of exerting the same sort of pressure on shareholders to make uninformed, ill-considered decisions to sell which Congress found the conventional tender offer was capable of exerting." Note, The Developing Meaning of "Tender Offer" Under the Securities Exchange Act of 1934, 86 Harv.L.Rev. 1250, 1275 (1973).

The SEC, in an *amicus* brief, in Brascan Limited v. Edper Equities Ltd., *infra*, has suggested that eight factors determined whether a tender offer is occurring:

1. Whether there is an active and widespread solicitation of public shareholders.

2. Whether the solicitation is for a substantial percentage of the stock.

3. Whether the offer is at premium over the market price.

4. Whether the terms of the offer are firm rather than negotiable.

5. Whether the offer is contingent on the tender of a fixed minimum (or perhaps subject to a ceiling) of shares.

6. Whether the offer is open for only a limited period of time.

7. Whether the offerees are subject to pressure to sell.

8. Whether public announcements of a purchasing program precede or accompany a rapid accumulation of large amounts of the target company's stock.

The Commission has since attempted codification of the definition. In 1979, it published a proposed definition that would cover many open market and privately negotiated acquisitions if they were for a large enough amount of stock and from a sufficiently large number of shareholders. Rel.No. 34–16385. Since that time the Commission staff has indicated that the proposal probably went too far. In February 1980 the Commission proposed far ranging statutory amendments to the Williams Act, which would include a legislative definition of tender offers. Like many definitions, it sacrifices flexibility for certainty, and when the enforcement officials propose the definition, it tends to include whatever *might* be included.

In Brascan Limited v. Edper Equities Limited, 477 F.Supp. 773 (S. D.N.Y.1979) the court concluded that a tender offer had not occurred by applying the SEC's eight part test. The buyer engaged in a program of open market purchases, carefully structured to minimize price impact, and solicited purchases from 30 to 50 institutions and 12 individuals with large holdings. The investors were all professionals. Although the court used the SEC tests, it expressed doubts as to the practicality of their application. *See also* Kennecott Copper Corp. v. Curtiss-Wright Corp., 584 F.2d 1195 (2d Cir. 1978).

So far, the "creeping tender offer," at least up to Williams Act's 5% limit, has been held not to come within the Act. The same is true of negotiated purchases from sophisticated investors, able to protect themselves in the bargaining process. (*See however* Cattlemen's Investment Co. v. Fears, 343 F.Supp. 1248 (W.D.Okl.1972) and S–G Securities, Inc. v. Fuqua Investment Co., 466 F.Supp. 1114 (D.C.Mass. 1978).

The furthest reach given to the meaning of tender offer was in Wellman v. Dickinson, 475 F.Supp. 783 (S.D.N.Y.1979). This complex case involved a purchase of 34% of the stock of Becton, Dickinson & Company by Sun Company, Inc., through its specially created subsidiary, L.H.I.W., Inc. (an acronym for Let's Hope It Works). Sun was interested in a quick acquisition of about one third of the stock. Through two investment bankers it contacted 30 institutions who were told that an unidentified large company was seeking at least 20% of the stock, would pay a top price of $45 (a substantial premium over the market), and that the goal was in reach. The institutions were given one hour to decide. The stock was paid for the next day. Practically all the institutions contacted accepted the deal, and the goal was exceeded.

The court found that this "lightning strike" was a tender offer. It applied the SEC's eight criteria and found that all but the publicity feature were present. Nevertheless, the court believed that the "basic evil which Congress sought to cure" infected the transaction. *Id.* at 822.

d. Tender Offer Litigation

Litigation is an important part of the defensive strategy in tender offers. Suits to prevent a takeover because it would violate the antitrust laws are common, but rarely successful. Even more common are suits charging a violation of the Williams Act, or some other provisions of the securities laws.

From a policy point of view, it is as true of tender offers as it is of proxy contests that the SEC cannot police the area without the assistance of private suits. No provision for private suits is found in the Williams Act, but § 14(e), using language suggestive of Rule 10b–5 (under which an implied private remedy was widely recognized at the time of the passage of the Williams Act), prohibits fraudulent, manipulative and deceptive acts in connection with a tender offer. Soon after the Act took effect, the Second Circuit recognized the availability of private right of action in a suit for an injunction brought by the target company. Electronic Specialty Co. v. International Controls Corp., 409 F.2d 937 (2d Cir. 1969).

The scope of private remedies under § 14(e) came before the Supreme Court in Piper v. Chris-Craft Industries, Inc., 430 U.S. 1, 97 S. Ct. 926, 51 L.Ed.2d 124 (1977). (See Part 5c of this section.) Piper Aircraft, the target of a takeover bid by Chris-Craft, found a "white knight" in Bangor Punta Corporation. Competing tender offers and buying programs ensued, and Bangor Punta ended up with control. Chris-Craft claimed that several securities laws violations occurred which were responsible for Chris-Craft's failing to gain control. The Second Circuit agreed, after seven years of complex litigation, and awarded damages of more than $25 million, plus interest, bringing the total award to almost $40 million.

The Supreme Court reversed. Noting that the statute makes no provision for a private cause of action, it concluded that no action by a defeated bidder for damages against the successful bidder was intended by Congress. "The legislative history * * * shows that the sole purpose of the Williams Act was the protection of investors who are confronted with a tender offer." 430 U.S. at 35.

Chief Justice BURGER then proceeded with the following analysis:

"Our conclusion as to the legislative history is confirmed by the analysis in Cort v. Ash, 422 U.S. 66 [95 S.Ct. 2080, 45 L.Ed.2d 26] (1975). There, the Court identified four factors as 'relevant' in determining whether a private remedy is implicit in a statute not expressly providing one. The first is whether the plaintiff is ' "one of the class for whose *especial* benefit the statute was enacted * * * " ' *Id.* at 78. (Emphasis in original.) As previously indicated, examination of the statute and its genesis shows that Chris-Craft is not an intended beneficiary of the Williams Act, and surely is not one 'for whose *especial* benefit the statute was enacted.' *Ibid.* To the contrary, Chris-Craft is a member of the class whose activities Congress intended to regulate for the protection and benefit of an entirely distinct class, shareholders-offerees. As a party whose previously unregulated conduct was purposefully brought under federal control by the statute, Chris-Craft can scarcely lay claim to the status of 'beneficiary' whom Congress considered in need of protection.

"Second, in Cort v. Ash we inquired whether there is 'any indication of legislative intent, explicit or implicit, either to create such a remedy or to deny one?' *Ibid.* Although the historical materials are barren of any express intent to deny a damages remedy to tender offerors as a class, there is, as we have noted, no indication that Congress intended to create a damages remedy in favor of the loser in a contest for control. * * *

"Chris-Craft argues, however, that Congress intended standing under § 14(e) to encompass tender offerors since the statute, unlike § 10(b), does not contain the limiting language, 'in connection with the purchase or sale' of securities. Instead, in § 14(e), Congress broadly proscribed fraudulent activities 'in connection with any tender offer * * * or any solicitation * * * in opposition to or in favor of any such offer * * * .'

"The omission of the purchaser-seller requirement does not mean, however, that Chris-Craft has standing to sue for damages under § 14(e) in its capacity as a takeover bidder. It may well be that Congress desired to protect, among others, shareholders-offerees who decided not to tender their stock due to fraudulent misrepresentations by persons opposed to a takeover attempt. * * * These shareholders, who might not enjoy the protection of § 10(b) under Blue Chip Stamps v. Manor Drugs Stores, could perhaps state a claim under § 14(e) even though they did not tender their securities. But increased protection, if any, conferred upon the class of shareholders-offerees by the elimination of the purchaser-seller restriction can scarcely be interpreted as giving protection to the entirely separate and unrelated class of persons whose conduct the statute is designed to regulate.

"Third, Cort v. Ash tells us that we must ascertain whether it is 'consistent with the underlying purposes of the legislative scheme to imply such a remedy for the plaintiff.' * * * We conclude that it is not. As a disclosure mechanism aimed especially at protecting shareholders of target corporations, the Williams Act cannot consistently be interpreted as conferring a monetary remedy upon regulated parties, particularly where the award would not redound to the direct benefit of the protected class. * * *

"Nor can we agree that an ever-present threat of damages against a successful contestant in a battle for control will provide a significant additional protection for shareholders in general. The deterrent value, if any, of such awards can never be ascertained with precision. More likely, however, is the prospect that shareholders may never be prejudiced because some tender offers may never be made if there is a possibility of massive damage claims for what courts subsequently hold to be an actionable violation of § 14(e). Even a contestant who 'wins the battle' for control may well wind up exposed to a costly 'war' in a later and successful defense of its victory. Or at worst—on Chris-Craft's damage theory—the victorious tender offeror or the target corporation might be subject to a large substantive judgment, plus high costs of litigation.

"In short, we conclude that shareholder protection, if enhanced at all by damages awards such as Chris-Craft contends for, can more directly be achieved with other, less drastic means more closely tailored to the precise congressional goal underlying the Williams Act.

"Fourth, under the Cort v. Ash analysis, we must decide whether 'the cause of action [is] one traditionally relegated to state law * * * .' * * * Despite the pervasiveness of federal securities regulation, the Court of Appeals concluded in this case that Chris-Craft's complaint would give rise to a cause of action under common-law principles of interference with a prospective commercial advantage. Although Congress is, of course, free to create a remedial scheme in favor of contestants in tender offers, we conclude, as we did in Cort v. Ash, that 'it is entirely appropriate in this instance to relegate [the offeror-bidder] and others in [that] situation to whatever remedy is created by state law,' (citation omitted) at least to the extent that the offeror seeks damages for having been wrongfully denied a 'fair opportunity' to compete for control of another corporation.

"What we have said thus far suggests that, unlike J. I. Case v. Borak, judicially creating a damages action in favor of Chris-Craft is unnecessary to ensure, the fulfillment of Congress' purposes in adopting the Williams Act. Even though the SEC operates in this context under the same practical restraints recognized by the Court in *Borak*, institutional limitations alone do not lead to the conclusion that any party interested in a tender offer should have a cause of action for damages against a competing bidder. First, as Judge Friendly observed in Electronic Specialty Co. v. International Controls Corp., 409 F.2d 937, 947 (C.A.2 1969), in corporate control contests the stage of preliminary injunctive relief, rather than post-contest lawsuits, 'is the time when relief can best be given.' Furthermore, awarding damages to parties other than the protected class of shareholders has only a remote, if any, bearing upon implementing the congressional policy of protecting shareholders who must decide whether to tender or retain their stock. Indeed, as we suggested earlier, a damages award of this nature may well be inconsistent with the interests of many members of the protected class and of only indirect value to shareholders who accepted the exchange offer of the defeated takeover contestant."

430 U.S. at 37–42.

In Electronic Specialty v. International Controls Corp., cited by the Court, Judge Friendly also commented upon the appropriate expectations that courts and litigants must have in the heat of a control battle. "The likeness of tender offers to proxy contests is not limited to the issue of standing. They are alike in the fundamental feature that they generally are contests. This means that the participants on both sides act, not 'in the peace of a quiet chamber' but under the stresses of the market place. They act quickly, sometimes impulsively, often in angry response to what they consider, whether rightly or wrongly, to be low blows by the other side. Probably there will no more be a perfect tender offer than a perfect trial. Congress intended to assure basic honesty and fair dealing, not to impose an unrealistic requirement of laboratory conditions that might make the new statute a potent tool for incumbent management to protect its own interests against the desires and welfare of the stockholders. These conditions bear on the kind of judgment to be applied in testing conduct—on both sides—and also on the issue of materality." 409 F.2d at 948.

If injunctive relief is the best remedy, will the plaintiff be entitled to an injunction merely upon showing that there has been a violation of the rules? The argument in favor of that approach is that rigid application of the rules will assure their compliance. Contestants should be discouraged from the temptation of engaging in improper conduct with the hope that they can argue to a judge that the injunction is too harsh. Moreover, the argument goes, the standard of care should be sufficiently high so that even negligent violations will be met with an injunction. However, the Supreme Court in Rondeau v. Mosinee Paper Corp., 422 U.S. 49, 95 S.Ct. 2069, 45 L.Ed.2d 12 (1975) held that it would not issue an injunction upon the mere showing of a failure to file a Schedule 13D when it was due. What was needed was a showing of irreparable harm.

The *Piper* Court noted that the issue of an implied cause of action under § 14(e) was not before it, and it intimated no view on the matter. 430 U.S. at 33, n. 22. Moreover, it observed that it was not ruling on whether the target corporation had standing to sue. Lower courts since that decision have upheld private rights, for all parties, in suits for injunctions.

e. State Regulation of Tender Offers

Thirty six states have adopted tender offer provisions, thirty five of which were enacted after the passage of the Williams Act. Nearly all of the statutes assert jurisdiction over offers for corporations that are incorporated in that state, although some also extend their laws to corporations whose principal place of business is in that state or who have "substantial" assets in that state. All of the statutes thus have extraterritorial effect if the requisite nexus is established, because they regulate the entire offer, and not just those made within the particular state.

All of the statutes require that a filing be made with the state and with the target corporation. The information required is usually the same as required by the Williams Act, although some states require substantially more. The key point of departure from the Williams Act is that under practically all the statutes the information must be filed anywhere from ten to sixty days *before* the offer can become effective, thus affording target management advance notice of the bid. No such pre-offer notification is required by the Williams Act; indeed, such a provision was contained in the bill when introduced and was eliminated from the final version.

Some state statutes provide for an administrative hearing, either automatically or upon the initiative of the state administrator or the target company. Most statutes limit the scope of the hearing to the question of whether full and fair disclosure has been made; others inquire into the substantive fairness of the offer. Unless these requirements have been met, the bidder may be enjoined from proceeding with the offer.

The state statutes usually contain provisions dealing with some substantive aspects of the tender offers, much in the manner of the Williams Act. Thus, there are requirements regarding pro rata acceptance of offers, withdrawal rights, and minimum offering periods, which are often longer than anything in the Williams Act.

There seems to be little doubt that the state laws were promoted by the managements of target companies who sought additional impediments to takeovers. Langvoort, State Tender-Offer Legislation: Interests, Effects and Political Competency, 62 Corn.L.Rev. 213 (1977). Since the Williams Act declared that it sought to avoid "tipping the balance" in favor or against tender offers, the issue is presented as to whether the state laws are preempted by the federal law. Section 28 of the Securities Exchange Act of 1934 provides, in pertinent part; "Nothing in this title shall affect the jurisdiction of the securities commission (or any agency or officer performing like functions) of any State over any security or any person insofar as it does not conflict with the provisions of this title or the rules and regulations thereunder."

Arguments against the validity of the state statutes are two-pronged. First, it is contended that the Williams Act preempts the state statutes, because the latter pursue an objective contradictory to the legislative purpose of evenhandedness of federal law. Preemption under this argument is not based on a specific conflict between mutually inconsistent requirements, but rather goes to the overall impact of the laws. However, since the SEC adopted Rule 14d–2 in 1979, a specific conflict has been created. That rule requires a tender offer to commence within five days of the announcement of certain information, and a filing with the state constitutes such an announcement. But the states generally prohibit the offer from commencing until a longer period has elapsed. Several courts have found the conflict to preempt the state statutes. Canadian Pacific Enterprises (U. S.) Inc. v. Krouse, 506 F.Supp. 1192 (S.D.Ohio 1981); Kennecott Corp. v. Smith, 507 F.Supp. 1206 (D.C.N.J.1981).

Second, the state statutes are said to constitute unlawful burdens on interstate commerce. This argument is more potent, because it cannot be cured by simple legislative tinkering. To counter it, the jurisdictional scope of the statutes would have to be so stringently curtailed that they would rarely serve as takeover deterrents.

In Edgar v. MITE Corp., 50 U.S.L.W. 4767 (June 23, 1982), the Supreme Court invalidated the Illinois statute. Justice White's opinion, in which only the Chief Justice joined entirely, said both that the Williams' Act's policy of neutrality preempted the state law and that the law constituted an impermissible burden on interstate commerce. Justice Blackmun joined in the preemption discussion but not in the Commerce Clause argument. Five justices joined in part, but not all of the Commerce Clause discussion. Justices Marshall, Brennan, and Rehnquist dissented on the grounds the case was moot (MITE Corp. having withdrawn its tender offer) and declined to discuss the merits. In sum, five of the justices opined that the Illinois statute was void because it imposed burdens on interstate commerce that were excessive in light of the state's interests; three opined that the state statute is preempted (two implicitly saying it is not) and three expressed no opinion at all.

Justice White's Commerce Clause argument had two branches. In the first (on which he was joined by only three other justices), he noted that the Illinois statute regulated interstate transactions taking place wholly outside the state (in this case purchases by a Delaware corporation of shares owned by non-Illinois residents). Indeed, as the statute was written, it could apply even where not a single shareholder of the target was an Illinois resident. The statute thus constituted a "direct" rather that an "incidental" restraint on interstate commerce and was therefore void even without an inquiry into the state interest involved.

The second branch of the argument was based on Pike v. Bruce Church, Inc., 397 U.S. 137, 90 S.Ct. 844, 25 L.Ed.2d 174 (1970), which held that a statute that has an incidental effect on interstate commerce is valid "unless the burden imposed on such commerce is clearly excessive in relation to the putative local benefits." U.S. at 142. Five justices agreed that the ability of the Illinois Secretary of State to block a tender offer on a finding that it was unfair to shareholders constituted a severe burden on interstate commerce not justified by any valid state interest.

It remains possible that the Court would uphold a state statute that imposes less severe burdens on commerce—such as, for example, Delaware's simple 20-day notice requirement—particularly if it were limited to cases involving a stronger state interest; but a close reading of the *MITE* opinions makes even that seem doubtful.

5. PROTECTION OF CONTROL

PROBLEM

GENERAL INDUSTRIES CORPORATION—PART II

A.

General Industries Corporation (GIC) operates diverse businesses. Its main facility is in a medium size town in Connecticut, where it employs 3,000 people. For many years, it has specialized in high technology products, including some recent work in biological research. GIC is one of the oldest research oriented companies, and it enjoys a high reputation for its innovation and high quality work. A large proportion of its employees are scientists, and substantial sums are spent on research and development. Those expenditures have grown in recent years, and in a number of instances it has been spent on activities that did not pan out commercially. As a result, the formerly upward trend of earnings has declined, accounting in large part for the adverse stock market reaction that has sent the stock from its one-time high of 90 to the 30's.

The 15 member board consists of seven management and eight non-management persons. The chairman of the board and chief executive officer is Roberta Samuels. Among the eight nonmanagement directors is William Post, the company's outside counsel.

The following events all occurred after the meeting Danton held with Tetley, as described in the Contest for Control Problem in Part B of this Chapter.

GIC recently announced that it has received a large contract from the National Institutes of Health to work on development of an immunization system against various types of cancer. The contract calls for a substantial commitment of GIC's resources, and the profit is small, partly in return for GIC's exclusive right to use any product that is developed. That ultimate payoff, however, is highly uncertain. Because of the size of the contract, and its adverse short term impact on growth, the matter was submitted to the board of directors for approval. The entire board heard a presentation from the scientists involved in the project and the chief financial officer and then voted unanimously to approve the project.

Following the public announcement, Danton decided to accelerate his effort to take control of GIC. He demonstrated to the board of Apex Petroleum Corporation, of which he is CEO, how profitable GIC could be under new management. He proposed to place an emphasis on consumer and industrial uses of GIC's expertise and eliminate some of the less profitable or riskier research, and relocate operations in Houston where Apex is headquartered. The board voted to commence a tender offer for GIC if he thought it was necessary, and to take all steps useful, including the accumulation of GIC stock.

Apex then purchased 60,000 shares, giving Apex and Danton a combined holding of 100,000 shares, representing 2% of the outstanding stock. Apex's average cost was $32 per share. Mrs. Samuels became concerned about the increased trading activity and discovered the source. Through financial intermediaries she was informed about Danton's views of what was needed for GIC. It was suggested to her that Danton and Apex would be willing to sell all their shares for $45 per share, or a total of $4.5 million. Funds would have to be borrowed, at slightly over the prime rate.

The board of GIC has scheduled a meeting for tomorrow to consider the situation. Mrs. Samuels has asked Post, the general counsel, who has asked you, to ponder and make recommendations, as to several possible courses of action that will be discussed at the meeting.

1. Should the company purchase the shares from Danton and Apex? If the purchase is made, should the company enter into any other agreement with Apex or Danton? Should the board be troubled by the costs involved? What business reasons support the transaction? Are any reasons needed apart from the desire to be rid of Danton and Apex? Can GIC attack Apex's and Danton's activities up to now as violations of the tender offer rules or requirements? What remedy is available?

2. The board will consider a proposed amendment to its charter that would require 80% stockholder approval, instead of 50%, for a merger with any person that directly or indirectly owns 5% or more of its stock, unless the board waives the requirement. What procedure is necessary to adopt the amendment? Do the procedures cre-

ate any legal or tactical problems for the board? Is there any impropriety in adopting the amendment?

3. The board will reconsider a merger offer it previously rejected with a large chemical company. Under the terms previously offered, shareholders would receive stock worth $40 per share, and the present management of GIC would continue to operate the GIC division. The chemical company has recently indicated its continued interest in the acquisition. Can the board now justify its renewed interest? What procedures do you recommend that the board follow?

Efforts to negotiate with Danton and Apex failed and Apex promptly announced the commencement of a tender offer for all shares of GIC at $42 per share. At the time of the announcement GIC shares were trading at $32. Apex made a filing on Schedule 14D–1. GIC's board subsequently convened a special meeting and determined to oppose the tender offer. GIC filed a Schedule 14D–9 and issued a press release characterizing the bidders as "corporate pirates" and describing the price as "grossly inadequate." Management urged the shareholders to stick with the present course, which it claims is in the best long term interest of the corporation and the shareholders.

A week later, the board approved the creation of an employee stock ownership trust which it has had under consideration for a long time. Under the plan, three million shares would be issued to a trust for the benefit of the employees. The trustees are Mrs. Samuels and two other employees of the company. No shareholder vote to approve the issuance is required under state law because the company has sufficient authorized but unissued shares available.

4. How do you advise the board about the likelihood of success of a shareholder suit challenging management's conduct in reacting to the tender offer? Does management's opposition to the tender offer create problems under either federal or state law? Can opposition to the offer justify the issuance of the shares? If the primary purpose was to oppose the offer, would that constitute a breach of fiduciary duty? Do the procedures followed create any problem? Are all directors in the same boat? Does the opposition to the tender offer, or the issuance of the shares violate §§ 14(d) or (e) of the '34 Act, Rule 14d–9, or Rule 14e–2? Is it a breach of a common law fiduciary duty?

a. An Overview of Defenses Against Takeovers

It is easy to be cynical about any reaction management has to a transaction affecting corporate control: they are doing it to protect their jobs. Such a reaction is not necessarily either discerning or helpful, however, and it may only be partially true.

Consider, for example, the following amendment to Control Data Corporation's certificate of incorporation adopted in 1978:

Tenth: The Board of Directors of the Corporation, when evaluating any offer of another party to (a) make a tender or exchange offer for any equity security of the Corporation, (b) merge or consolidate the Corporation with another corporation, or (c) purchase or otherwise acquire all or substantially all of the properties and assets of the Corporation, shall, in connection with the exercise of its judgment in determining what is in the interests of the Corporation and its stockholders, give due notice to all relevant factors, including without limitation the social and economic effects on the employees, customers, suppliers and other constituents of the Corporation and its subsidiaries and on the communities in which the Corporation and its subsidiaries operate or are located.

The cynical reaction is that Control Data's management is cleverly trying to give itself the broadest possible latitude to fend off a hostile tender offer, should one appear. Better still, by serving strong notice to any prospective bidder that it will face a fight to the finish if it puts its toes in CD's water, it will deter possible tender offers. On the other hand, isn't Control Data management doing precisely what many corporate critics, including the cynics, are demanding of modern management, which is a sensitivity to a large community of interests? Which view is correct? Does it make any difference why management proposed the amendment? Is it possible to plumb the "corporate" psychological depths once the stockholders have approved (which they did, but barely) for whatever many reasons *they* might have? One commentator has noted: "Thus, it is impossible to identify at the outset any path management might take which would eliminate the inherent conflict of interest; any action, whether rejection or approval, reflects the potential for diversion of benefit to management and away from shareholders." Gilson, A Structural Approach to Corporations: The Case Against Defensive Tactics in Tender Offers, 33 Stan.L.Rev. 819, 826 (1981).

The fact is, management has many resources and sufficient incentive to oppose a takeover attempt. The use of this power is often challenged, either as a breach of fiduciary duty under state law or as a violation of the various anti-fraud provisions of the '34 Act. Each provision presents problems, however. To establish a violation of Rule 10b–5 or Rule 14a–9 will require a showing of deception. Challenges are possible under § 14(e), the anti-fraud rule relating to tender offers, but that section will not apply unless a tender offer has been made. Allegedly fraudulent conduct to prevent a tender offer from being made is not covered. Lewis v. McGraw, 619 F.2d 192 (2d Cir. 1980), cert. denied 449 U.S. 951, 101 S.Ct. 354, 66 L.Ed.2d 214 (relating to the American Express-McGraw Hill contest described below).

Management can resist a takeover attempt fiercely. When Mc-Graw-Hill, Inc., opposed an offer from American Express Company, in early 1979, to buy McGraw-Hill shares at $40 per share (the pre-tender offer price was $26), its opposition was so bitter that it was described as a "scorched earth policy." (Institutional Investor, June 1979, p. 33.) The management questioned whether the bidder had violated various U. S. laws; it doubted whether American Express would continue to respect the editorial independence of Business Week, McGraw-Hill's leading publication, and it openly questioned the integrity of American Express' management. A number of hard hitting law suits were brought. (One of the outside directors of Mc-Graw-Hill was an officer of American Express.) Whatever merit these arguments might have, the fact remains that McGraw-Hill's management succeeded in preventing a transaction that would have been highly favorable for stockholders. Counsel to the board opined that they were within their rights to do so, that is, they need not feel compelled to facilitate the favorable opportunity for the stockholders. In counsel's view, "absent fraud or self-dealing, the controlling test is simply that directors use their reasonable business judgment." Directors are entitled to consider the interests of all stockholders including those who do not favor a sale and all relevant economic factors as to whether this is an appropriate time and opportunity to sell the company. Moreover, the board can weigh other considerations, such as questions of the legality of the offer and whether protracted litigation could follow the transaction. Opinion of Wachtell, Lipton, Rosen and Katz, January 30, 1979. Note that the legal opinion does not refer to the free press issue or other social conditions that management communicated to American Express.

Management resistance to a tender produces a varied response from shareholders. If it is partially successful, i.e., the bidder sweetens the offer or a higher bidder succeeds, the shareholders are gleeful. If it is completely successful, i.e., the bid is abandoned, the shareholders (or some of them) are glum and contentious. The management of Amax, Inc. so fiercely opposed an offer from Standard Oil of California of $78.50 per share when the market price of Amax was $38–a $4 billion offer—that the bid was withdrawn. Management called the bid "unimpressive" and not in the long term interests of the corporation. Some shareholders were, nonetheless, upset. See Wall Street Journal, May 8, 1981, p. 16.

The motives involved in any resistance to a takeover are more complex than mere self-protection or self-aggrandizement. For example, that explanation does not suffice with respect to outside directors who have little financial stake in management's survival. But even management, however unobjectively, is likely to have some thoughts about the welfare of the corporation, if only out of long conditioning by their lawyers. And doubtless there will be many instances where neutral observers would agree that a particular takeover would damage a company through mismanagement or ill considered policies. Under those circumstances, isn't management obliged to resist? Is the calculation of the corporation's best interest a simple arithmetic exercise as to whether the price offered for the stock exceeds its present market value? Is the long term interest of the corporation the same as the short term interest of the shareholders? One can argue that shareholders, as individuals have only short term interests. Do the company's traditions and its reputation count for anything? Would management of a company that has operated in the same community for generations be entitled to resist a takeover because it would move the company to sunnier climes, although at possibly higher profits? The response to a tender offer provides one of the most demanding tests of the fiduciary principle. For whom are the directors fiduciaries—the corporation or the shareholders? If the answer is "the corporation," does this then entitle the board to weigh factors not related to profits or stock prices? How far from profit maximization can the directors' interests stray? Is there any substance to the distinction between duties to the corporation and duties to the shareholders?

Are inquiries into motive and proper purpose the best approach to this dilemma? If so, then the legal issue of who has the burden of proof may prove the key to any lawsuit. Is there a better way to deal with the problem? Professor Gilson suggests that a better inquiry is into the proper allocation of responsibility between management and shareholders with respect to changes in control. Gilson, A Structural Approach to Corporations: The Case Against Defensive Tactics in Tender Offers, 33 Stan.L.Rev. 819, 831 (1981). In Switzerland, it might be noted, the answer is sure, and the defense is complete. Registered shares cannot be transferred without consent of the board of directors. Metz, Market Place, N.Y. Times, April 9, 1980, p. D6, col. 3.

In the ensuing pages we present some cases in which these issues have been raised. In this area of law and business, the questions seem to outnumber the answers, and policy analysis is of practical significance. We conclude the chapter on that note.

b. Corporate Repurchases

CHEFF v. MATHES

41 Del.Ch. 494, 199 A.2d 548 (1964).

CAREY, Justice.

This is an appeal from the decision of the Vice-Chancellor in a derivative suit holding certain directors of Holland Furnace Company liable for loss allegedly resulting from improper use of corporate funds to purchase shares of the company. Because a meaningful decision upon review turns upon a complete understanding of the factual background, a somewhat detailed summary of the evidence is required.

Holland Furnace Company, a corporation of the State of Delaware, manufactures warm air furnaces, air conditioning equipment, and other home heating equipment. At the time of the relevant transactions, the board of directors was composed of the seven individual defendants. Mr. Cheff had been Holland's Chief Executive Officer since 1933, received an annual salary of $77,400, and personally owned 6,000 shares of the company. He was also a director. Mrs. Cheff, the wife of Mr. Cheff, was a daughter of the founder of Holland and had served as a director since 1922. She personally owned 5,804 shares of Holland and owned 47.9 percent of Hazelbank United Interest, Inc. Hazelbank is an investment vehicle for Mrs. Cheff and members of the Cheff-Landwehr family group, which owned 164,950 shares of the 883,585 outstanding shares of Holland. As a director, Mrs. Cheff received a compensation of $200.00 for each monthly board meeting, whether or not she attended the meeting.

The third director, Edgar P. Landwehr, is the nephew of Mrs. Cheff and personally owned 24,010 shares of Holland and 8.6 percent of the outstanding shares of Hazelbank. He received no compensation from Holland other than the monthly director's fee.

Robert H. Trenkamp is an attorney who first represented Holland in 1946. In May 1953, he became a director of Holland and acted as general counsel for the company. During the period in question, he received no retainer from the company, but did receive substantial sums for legal services rendered the company. Apart from the above-described payments, he received no compensation from Holland other than the monthly director's fee. He owned 200 shares of Holland Furnace stock. Although he owned no shares of Hazelbank, at the time relevant to this controversy, he was serving as a director and counsel of Hazelbank.

John D. Ames was then a partner in the Chicago investment firm of Bacon, Whipple & Co. and joined the board at the request of Mr. Cheff. During the periods in question, his stock ownership varied between ownership of no shares to ownership of 300 shares. He was considered by the other members of the Holland board to be the financial advisor to the board. He received no compensation from Holland other than the normal director's fee.

Mr. Ralph G. Boalt was the Vice President of J. R. Watkins Company, a manufacturer and distributor of cosmetics. In 1953, at the request of Mr. Cheff, he became a member of the board of directors. Apart from the normal director's fee, he received no compensation from Holland for his services.

Mr. George Spatta was the President of Clark Equipment Company, a large manufacturer of earth moving equipment. In 1951, at the request of Mr. Cheff, he joined the board of directors of Holland.

Apart from the normal director's fee, he received no compensation from the company.

* * *

Prior to the events in question, Holland employed approximately 8500 persons and maintained 400 branch sales offices located in 43 states. The volume of sales had declined from over $41,000,000 in 1948 to less than $32,000,000 in 1956. Defendants contend that the decline in earnings is attributable to the artificial post-war demand generated in the 1946-1948 period. In order to stabilize the condition of the company, the sales department apparently was reorganized and certain unprofitable branch offices were closed. By 1957 this reorganization had been completed and the management was convinced that the changes were manifesting beneficial results. The practice of the company was to directly employ the retail salesman, and the management considered that practice—unique in the furnace business—to be a vital factor in the company's success.

During the first five months of 1957, the monthly trading volume of Holland's stock on the New York Stock Exchange ranged between 10,300 shares to 24,200 shares. In the last week of June 1957, however, the trading increased to 37,800 shares, with a corresponding increase in the market price. In June of 1957, Mr. Cheff met with Mr. Arnold H. Maremont, who was President of Maremont Automotive Products, Inc. and Chairman of the boards of Motor Products Corporation and Allied Paper Corporation. Mr. Cheff testified, on deposition, that Maremont generally inquired about the feasibility of merger between Motor Products and Holland. Mr. Cheff testified that, in view of the difference in sales practices between the two companies, he informed Mr. Maremont that a merger did not seem feasible. In reply, Mr. Maremont stated that, in the light of Mr. Cheff's decision, he had no further interest in Holland nor did he wish to buy any of the stock of Holland.

None of the members of the board apparently connected the interest of Mr. Maremont with the increased activity of Holland stock. However, Mr. Trenkamp and Mr. Staal, the Treasurer of Holland, unsuccessfully made an informal investigation in order to ascertain the identity of the purchaser or purchasers. The mystery was resolved, however, when Maremont called Ames in July of 1957 to inform the latter that Maremont then owned 55,000 shares of Holland stock. At this juncture, no requests for change in corporate policy were made, and Maremont made no demand to be made a member of the board of Holland.

Ames reported the above information to the board at its July 30, 1957 meeting. Because of the position now occupied by Maremont, the board elected to investigate the financial and business history of Maremont and corporations controlled by him. Apart from the documentary evidence produced by this investigation, which will be considered infra, Staal testified, on deposition, that "leading bank officials" had indicated that Maremont "had been a participant, or had attempted to be, in the liquidation of a number of companies." * * *

On August 23, 1957, at the request of Maremont, a meeting was held between Mr. Maremont and Cheff. At this meeting, Cheff was informed that Motor Products then owned approximately 100,000 shares of Holland stock. Maremont then made a demand that he be named to the board of directors, but Cheff refused to consider it. Since considerable controversy has been generated by Maremont's alleged threat to liquidate the company or substantially alter the sales force of Holland, we believe it desirable to set forth the testimony of Cheff on this point: "Now we have 8500 men, direct employees, so the problem is entirely different. He indicated immediately that he had no interest in that type of distribution, that he didn't think it was modern, that he felt furnaces could be sold as he sold mufflers, through half a dozen salesmen in a wholesale way."

Testimony was introduced by the defendants tending to show that substantial unrest was present among the employees of Holland as a result of the threat of Maremont to seek control of Holland. * * * Moreover, at approximately this time, the company was furnished with a Dun and Bradstreet report, which indicated the practice of Maremont to achieve quick profits by sales or liquidations of companies acquired by him. The defendants were also supplied with an income statement of Motor Products, Inc., showing a loss of $336,121.00 for the period in 1957.

On August 30, 1957, the board was informed by Cheff of Maremont's demand to be placed upon the board and of Maremont's belief that the retail sales organization of Holland was obsolete. The board was also informed of the results of the investigation by Cheff and Staal. Predicated upon this information, the board authorized the purchase of company stock on the market with corporate funds, ostensibly for use in a stock option plan.

Subsequent to this meeting, substantial numbers of shares were purchased and, in addition, Mrs. Cheff made alternate personal purchases of Holland stock. As a result of purchases by Maremont, Holland and Mrs. Cheff, the market price rose. * * * On September 4th, Maremont proposed to sell his current holdings of Holland to the corporation for $14.00 a share. However, because of delay in responding to this offer, Maremont withdrew the offer. At this time, Mrs. Cheff was obviously quite concerned over the prospect of a Maremont acquisition, and had stated her willingness to expend her personal resources to prevent it.

On September 30, 1957, Motor Products Corporation, by letter to Mrs. Bowles, made a buy-sell offer to Hazelbank. Although Mrs. Bowles and Mrs. Putnam were opposed to any acquisition of Holland stock by Hazelbank, Mr. Landwehr conceded that a majority of the board were in favor of the purchase. Despite this fact, the finance committee elected to refer the offer to the Holland board on the grounds that it was the primary concern of Holland.

Thereafter, Mr. Trenkamp arranged for a meeting with Maremont, which occurred on October 14–15, 1957, in Chicago. Prior to this meeting, Trenkamp was aware of the intentions of Hazelbank and Mrs. Cheff to purchase all or portions of the stock then owned by Motor Products if Holland did not so act. As a result of the meeting, there was a tentative agreement on the part of Motor Products to sell its 155,000 shares at $14.40 per share. On October 23, 1957, at a special meeting of the Holland board, the purchase was considered. All directors, except Spatta, were present. The dangers allegedly posed by Maremont were again reviewed by the board. Trenkamp and Mrs. Cheff agree that the latter informed the board that either she or Hazelbank would purchase part or all of the block of Holland stock owned by Motor Products if the Holland board did not so act. The board was also informed that in order for the corporation to finance the purchase, substantial sums would have to be borrowed from commercial lending institutions. A resolution authorizing the purchase of 155,000 shares from Motor Products was adopted by the board. The price paid was in excess of the market price prevailing at the time, and the book value of the stock was approximately $20.00 as compared to approximately $14.00 for the net quick asset value. The transaction was subsequently consummated. The stock option plan mentioned in the minutes has never been implemented. In 1959, Holland stock reached a high of $15.25 a share.

On February 6, 1958, plaintiffs, owners of 60 shares of Holland stock, filed a derivative suit in the court below naming all of the individual directors of Holland, Holland itself and Motor Products Corporation as defendants. The complaint alleged that all of the purchases of stock by Holland in 1957 were for the purpose of insuring the perpetuation of control by the incumbent directors. The complaint requested that the transaction between Motor Products and Holland be rescinded and, secondly, that the individual defendants account to Holland for the alleged damages. Since Motor Products was never served with process, the initial remedy became inapplicable. Ames was never served nor did he enter an appearance.

After trial, the Vice Chancellor found the following facts: (a) Holland directly sells to retail consumers by means of numerous branch offices. There were no intermediate dealers. (b) Immediately prior to the complained-of transactions, the sales and earnings of Holland had declined and its marketing practices were under investigation by the Federal Trade Commission. (c) Mr. Cheff and Trenkamp had received substantial sums as Chief Executive and attorney of the company, respectively. (d) Maremont, on August 23rd, 1957, demanded a place on the board. (e) At the October 14th meeting between Trenkamp, Staal and Maremont, Trenkamp and Staal were authorized to speak for Hazelbank and Mrs. Cheff as well as Holland. Only Mr.

Cheff, Mrs. Cheff, Mr. Landwehr, and Mr. Trenkamp clearly understood, prior to the October 23rd meeting, that either Hazelbank or Mrs. Cheff would have utilized their funds to purchase the Holland stock if Holland had not acted. (g) There was no real threat posed by Maremont and no substantial evidence of intention by Maremont to liquidate Holland. (h) Any employee unrest could have been caused by factors other than Maremont's intrusion and "only one important employee was shown to have left, and his motive for leaving is not clear." (i) The Court rejected the stock option plan as a meaningful rationale for the purchase from Maremont or the prior open market purchases.

The Court then found that the actual purpose behind the purchase was the desire to perpetuate control, but because of its finding that only the four above-named directors knew of the "alternative", the remaining directors were exonerated. No appeal was taken by plaintiffs from that decision.

* * *

Under the provisions of 8 Del.C. § 160, a corporation is granted statutory power to purchase and sell shares of its own stock. The charge here is not one of violation of statute, but the allegation is that the true motives behind such purchases were improperly centered upon perpetuation of control. In an analogous field, courts have sustained the use of proxy funds to inform stockholders of management's views upon the policy questions inherent in an election to a board of directors, but have not sanctioned the use of corporate funds to advance the selfish desires of directors to perpetuate themselves in office. Similarly, if the actions of the board were motivated by a sincere belief that the buying out of the dissident stockholder was necessary to maintain what the board believed to be proper business practices, the board will not be held liable for such decision, even though hindsight indicates the decision was not the wisest course. See Kors v. Carey, Del.Ch., 158 A.2d 136. On the other hand, if the board has acted solely or primarily because of the desire to perpetuate themselves in office, the use of corporate funds for such purposes is improper. See Bennett v. Propp, Del., 187 A.2d 405, and Yasik v. Wachtel, 25 Del.Ch. 247, 17 A.2d 309.

Our first problem is the allocation of the burden of proof to show the presence or lack of good faith on the part of the board in authorizing the purchase of shares. Initially, the decision of the board of directors in authorizing a purchase was presumed to be in good faith and could be overturned only by a conclusive showing by plaintiffs of fraud or other misconduct. In Kors, cited supra, the court merely indicated that the directors are presumed to act in good faith and the burden of proof to show to the contrary falls upon the plaintiff. However, in Bennett v. Propp, supra, we stated:

> We must bear in mind the inherent danger in the purchase of
> shares with corporate funds to remove a threat to corporate policy

when a threat to control is involved. The directors are of necessity confronted with a conflict of interest, and an objective decision is difficult. * * * Hence, in our opinion, the burden should be on the directors to justify such a purchase as one primarily in the corporate interest. (187 A.2d 409, at page 409).

* * *

To say that the burden of proof is upon the defendants is not to indicate, however, that the directors have the same "self-dealing interest" as is present, for example, when a director sells property to the corporation. The only clear pecuniary interest shown on the record was held by Mr. Cheff, as an executive of the corporation, and Trenkamp, as its attorney. The mere fact that some of the other directors were substantial shareholders does not create a personal pecuniary interest in the decisions made by the board of directors, since all shareholders would presumably share the benefit flowing to the substantial shareholder. Accordingly, these directors other than Trenkamp and Cheff, while called upon to justify their actions, will not be held to the same standard of proof required of those directors having personal and pecuniary interest in the transaction.

* * *

Plaintiffs urge that the sale price was unfair in view of the fact that the price was in excess of that prevailing on the open market. However, as conceded by all parties, a substantial block of stock will normally sell at a higher price than that prevailing on the open market, the increment being attributable to a "control premium". Plaintiffs argue that it is inappropriate to require the defendant corporation to pay a control premium, since control is meaningless to an acquisition by a corporation of its own shares. However, it is elementary that a holder of a substantial number of shares would expect to receive the control premium as part of his selling price, and if the corporation desired to obtain the stock, it is unreasonable to expect that the corporation could avoid paying what any other purchaser would be required to pay for the stock. In any event, the financial expert produced by defendant at trial indicated that the price paid was fair and there was no rebuttal.

The question then presented is whether or not defendants satisfied the burden of proof of showing reasonable grounds to believe a danger to corporate policy and effectiveness existed by the presence of the Maremont stock ownership. It is important to remember that the directors satisfy their burden by showing good faith and reasonable investigation; the directors will not be penalized for an honest mistake of judgment, if the judgment appeared reasonable at the time the decision was made.

* * *

[W]e are of the opinion that the evidence presented in the court below leads inevitably to the conclusion that the board of directors, based upon direct investigation, receipt of professional advice, and personal observations of the contradictory action of Maremont and his explanation of corporate purpose, believed, with justification, that there was a reasonable threat to the continued existence of Holland, or at least existence in its present form, by the plan of Maremont to continue building up his stock holdings. We find no evidence in the record sufficient to justify a contrary conclusion. The opinion of the Vice Chancellor that employee unrest may have been engendered by other factors or that the board had no grounds to suspect Maremont is not supported in any manner by the evidence.

As noted above, the Vice-Chancellor found that the purpose of the acquisition was the improper desire to maintain control, but, at the same time, he exonerated those individual directors whom he believed to be unaware of the possibility of using non-corporate funds to accomplish this purpose. Such a decision is inconsistent with his finding that the motive was improper, within the rule enunciated in Bennett. If the actions were in fact improper because of a desire to maintain control, then the presence or absence of a non-corporate alternative is irrelevant, as corporate funds may not be used to advance an improper purpose even if there is no non-corporate alternative available. Conversely, if the actions were proper because of a decision by the board made in good faith that the corporate interest was served thereby, they are not rendered improper by the fact that some individual directors were willing to advance personal funds if the corporation did not. It is conceivable that the Vice Chancellor considered this feature of the case to be of significance because of his apparent belief that any excess corporate funds should have been used to finance a subsidiary corporation. That action would not have solved the problem of Holland's over-capitalization. In any event, this question was a matter of business judgment, which furnishes no justification for holding the directors personally responsible in this case.

Accordingly, the judgment of the court below is reversed and remanded with instruction to enter judgment for the defendants.

NOTE—WHY CORPORATIONS PURCHASE
THEIR OWN SHARES

Corporations have various uses for their own stock, and these are often claimed to justify going into the market to purchase shares even when there is an impact on a control struggle. Thus, corporations need shares when stock options are exercised or when debentures or preferred stock are converted into common stock; corporations make acquisitions through different devices that require the issuance of securities; and companies acquire other property with their own stock. While the company can issue its authorized but unissued shares in these transactions, to do so would dilute the interests of the other shareholders, and produce lower earnings per share.

If the price of the stock is comparatively low, then it makes more sense for the company to buy its own shares in the market place and reissue those shares.

The potential profitability from stock repurchases is well recognized by economists and corporate financial officers. Suppose a corporation has excess funds and no internal investment opportunities that promise a high return on investment. It is possible, of course, to invest those funds by buying another business, but there is a high degree of risk in that, and perhaps antitrust impediments. It may then be best in these circumstances to distribute the cash to the stockholders. The soundest financial way to accomplish that distribution may be to repurchase some shares, because of the tax advantages to the recipients that sale to the corporation has over the payment of dividends.

Another advantage relates to the use of debt. Many economists believe that a corporate capital structure should include a fair amount of debt in order to maximize the value of the common stock. A company with very little debt may want to revise its capital structure by repurchasing some shares with borrowed funds.

When the stock price does not accurately reflect the company growth and earnings power, repurchase by a company of its own stock is said to be an excellent investment for the company. What is meant by that? If the profit margins of the company's operations exceed the cost of borrowed capital, then the value of a shareholder's investment will increase as shares are repurchased and the number of outstanding shares is reduced. One corporation that regularly engages in such a program of stock repurchase is Tandy Corporation, which explained to its stockholders in its 1977 annual report why it was doing so. In effect, the company said that stockholders could declare themselves a dividend, if they wanted cash, by selling their shares, and since the company was reducing the total number of shares, they could maintain their same relative position. At the same time, values per share have increased.

What effect does the repurchase have on control contest? In Cheff v. Mathes the answer at first seems obvious; the bidder has been removed from the scene. But what is to stop the bidder from starting over again, indeed, fueled by the cash generated by selling the shares in excess of the market price? With the funds now received, the bidder can buy more shares than he owned before. A naked repurchase of shares may thus aggravate the target's situation. What is necessary in this situation is a "standstill agreement" where the former bidder, when selling its shares to the corporation, agrees not to do certain things for a period of time. Thus, an agreement would prevent buying or bidding for shares of the target, directly or indirectly, (spelling out what that means in a contract) for, say, five years.

Repurchases from threatening bidders, at premium prices, have become a common occurrence. *See* "More Firms Paying Premium Prices to Wrest Shares from Antagonists," Wall Street Journal, January 8, 1981, p. 21. For example, Gulf & Western Industries, Inc., a frequent acquirer, bought a 10.4% of Robertshaw Controls Co. at an average price of $21.72 and resold it to the company for $24 and bought a 7.4% interest in Oxford Industries, Inc. for $11.79 and sold it for $17. These resales were at $4.25 and $3 respectively *above* the market prices. Gulf & Western made a $2.1 million profit, and both transactions occurred within a month.

If the target buys shares on the open market to fend off the bidder, there is a double impact. Suppose there are one million shares outstanding. The bidder needs 500,001 shares for control. If the target buys 100,000 shares, the bidder now needs 450,001 to win control. That is because treasury shares (as these shares are known except under the Model Act) cannot vote. But in truth the bidder's task may have been made more difficult. The price of the remaining shares may have been raised by the target's action. The added cost may be a bar to a successful takeover. The shares repurchased by the company were the ones that were for sale at the lowest price, and it will cost more to buy new shares, because the repurchases raised the price. Each situation has to be analyzed on its facts.

c. Defensive Mergers

The defensive merger is probably the most significant defense mounted against an unfriendly tender offer. While management might prefer to be left alone completely, unless some legal defense can totally thwart (as opposed to merely delay) a tender offer—a "show stopper" defense—it will be difficult to dissuade shareholders from accepting the lure of a higher price. As the old adage has it, "You can't beat sumthin' with nuthin'."

A more successful counter is a better price. Management seeks a bidder with whom it feels more compatible, who will top the initial bid. Such a rescuer is known in the business as a "white knight." Of course, the initial bidder can reply with an improved bid, and an auction of sorts takes place. United Technologies originally offered $40 for the shares of Babcock & Wilcox, in one of the early mammoth tender offers, and it soon found itself in competition with J. Ray Mc-Dermott Co. The latter finally won out at $65 per share. A few smiles at United Technologies might have been pardoned following the subsequent crisis at Three Mile Island, as the reactor had been built by B&W.

It has been said that "time is the enemy of the tender offer." That is because the more time management has, the more opportunity it has to mount various defenses, most particularly, to go in search of a "white knight." On the other hand, the bidder wants to allow as little time as possible, in order to shut off time for defenses and to put pressure on stockholders to accept the offer (or sell to arbitrageurs) while they have time.

One of the reasons why the bidder wants to shut off the opportunity for management to search for a white knight is the impact that this defense has on the bidder's costs. Even if the original bidder prevails, a bidding war will ensue in which the price will escalate. The market has seen 25% premiums become 100% premiums by the time the auction was over. From the shareholders' standpoint, one could argue that not only is such a defense permitted, it ought to be mandatory.*

The "white knight" defense has its dangers. Acquisitions require careful study, to determine whether they make sense and what is the correct price. The bidder is likely to have studied the target for months before it decided to make the bid. The target may have only days to identify a white knight and then conclude an extremely complex process. Investment bankers and lawyers have to assess a great deal of material and settle many difficult issues in a mercilessly short time. In this corporate war, it is the young lawyers and young analysts who prove to be the cannon fodder.

Of course the transaction may be criticized as having been undertaken for the wrong motivation—to preserve management's employment. It is true that ordinarily the management of the target will retain their positions in the white knight merger while they are far less certain to do so in a hostile takeover. It is unfair to generalize as to whether that is the reason for the transaction, however.

Apart from that legal question, management of both companies are vulnerable to attack that they did not meet the standard of due care, having decided without adequate study and professional counseling to enter into a type of transaction that prudence dictates should be subjected to further study.

d. Use of the Corporate Machinery

The structure of the corporate machinery provides a variety of opportunities to create devices, known as "shark repellent" provisions, that may be used by incumbent management to obstruct a takeover attempt. Some of these provisions are found in corporate by-laws, others in the certificate of incorporation and a few in contracts or resolutions of the board of directors.

The board has substantial influence in constructing the machinery. By-laws may be amended by action of the board alone. Contracts or resolutions of the board require only board action. The certificate of incorporation may be amended only with the approval of

* We do not necessarily endorse that view. Among other things, it overlooks the possible deterrence to initiating a tender offer if management is to be allowed too free a hand to combat tender offers. See Easterbrook and Fischel, The Proper Role of a Target's Management in Responding to a Tender Offer, 94 Harv.L.Rev. 1161 (1981).

the shareholders, but in practically all cases only after the board has acted. The board also controls the proxy machinery, as we have discussed earlier.

The various means by which the board can act upon the corporate machinery have a large potential impact on the outcome of a control contest. Many decisions affecting the corporate machinery *must* be made by the board; the concern is whether those decisions unfairly tilt the scales against a bidder. In other words, is there a good faith use of the corporate machinery, or has it become a management weapon to be used against a challenger?

In Schnell v. Chris-Craft Industries, Inc., 285 A.2d 437 (Del.Ch. 1971), the court found the board's decision to move up the date of an annual meeting to have been an unfair manipulation of the corporate machinery because it had been motivated by a desire to reduce the time available to an insurgent group to mount a proxy fight. In Lerman v. Diagnostic Data, Inc., 421 A.2d 906 (Del.Ch.1980), the board adopted a by-law amendment to allow the board to fix the date of the annual meeting and another amendment that required any candidate for election to the board, other than incumbents, to furnish detailed background information to the corporation not less than 70 days prior to the meeting. The board then fixed the date of the meeting 63 days thereafter, thus precluding any opposition candidate, even though it was aware of a planned challenge to management. The court found that the action of the board, in fixing the date at a point where no challenge could be made, was improper.

The decision in *Schnell* surprised the corporate community who had thought they possessed considerable freedom to tamper with such things as the date of the corporate annual meeting. An earlier decision in New York, Matter of Mansdorf v. Unexcelled, Inc., 28 A. D.2d 44, 281 N.Y.S.2d 173 (1st Dept. 1967), supported that view. There, the board advanced the meeting date by four months after it appeared that a proxy contest was looming, although this meant that only about 8 months would have elapsed since the previous meeting. The court held that this was in management's power and that the requirement of an annual meeting does not mean that meetings must be at 12 month intervals.

The conversion to staggered terms for directors, and possibly even the use of cumulative voting, can pose serious obstacles to a bidder. Cumulative voting is ordinarily not to management's liking, but if an outsider ends up with a majority interest, cumulative voting could favor management. Staggered directors' terms have the effect of diminishing the effectiveness of cumulative voting, and it may be that the conversion to staggered terms, in order to exclude a larger minority holder, violates management's fiduciary obligations. Hyer v. The Gibson-Homans Co., Fed.Sec.L.Rep. (CCH) ¶ 95,537 (E.D.N.Y. 1976).

The device perhaps best adapted to tender offer defense is the supermajority voting requirement. This charter provision requires certain types of transactions, most commonly mergers, to be approved by, say, 80 percent of the shares instead of the usual majority, if the other part of the transaction owns a substantial block, usually 5 percent of the shares. Thus, a bidder which acquires 51 percent of the stock would be unable to cause a merger in order to clean up the rest of the stock unless it won the vote of 80 percent of the shareholders. If management controlled 21 percent of the stock, it could veto a merger. Sometimes such a clause is drafted to apply only when the board (meaning the old board) so indicates. Another device is for the charter or by-laws to limit foreign ownership of the company's stock, perhaps ostensibly to protect the company from losing defense or national security business, but nonetheless deterring certain prospective bidders.

Obviously, careful planning is required to insert such a provision in the charter since it requires shareholder approval. Waiting until a tender offer is in the offing is usually too late.

As a matter of state law, such provisions have been upheld by the courts. Seibert v. Gulton Industries, Inc., 414 A.2d 822 (Del.Ch.1980). *See also* Seibert v. Milton Bradley Co., 380 Mass. 656, 405 N.E.2d 131 (1980). *But see* Young v. Valhi, Inc., 382 A.2d 1372 (Del.Ch.1978) where the court held a merger improper when it was used to eliminate certain provisions of the charter that could not be amended directly. *See* Black and Smith, AntiTakeover Charter Provisions: Defending Self-Help for Takeover Targets, 36 Wash. & Lee L.Rev. 699 (1979).

Since shareholder approval is required for an amendment to the charter, the SEC is concerned with the adequacy of the disclosure in the proxy statement seeking approval for the amendment. In Rel. No. 34–15230 (Oct. 13, 1978), the Commission announced its standards for adequate disclosure, revealing a more general concern about the propriety of defensive provisions.

The Commission described its policy of disclosure to shareholders whenever such a structural change was submitted to a vote involving proxy solicitation as follows:

Despite significant variations in the form and operation of antitakeover proposals, there are several areas in which certain basic disclosures are generally applicable. These include:

(a) The reason(s) for the proposal and the bases of such reason(s). The proxy or information statement should clearly indicate why management is proposing to amend the corporation's charter or by-laws. The term "bases" for the reasons means an explanation of the factors and/or principles supporting or serving as a foundation for the reason stated.

If the proposal is the result of management's knowledge of any specific effort to accumulate the issuer's securities or to obtain control of the issuer by means of a merger, tender offer, solicitation in opposition to management or otherwise, a description of any such effort should be included. If the measure is not the result of any specific effort, disclosure should be made to that effect and a statement included as to why, in the absence of such efforts, the measure is being proposed at this time.

* * *

(b) The over-all effects of the proposal, if adopted. The impact of the proposed amendments upon management's tenure and upon any proposal to alter the structure of the corporation should be disclosed. If appropriate, such disclosure should include statements that the over-all effects of the proposal, if adopted, may (would) be to render more difficult or to discourage a merger, tender offer or proxy contest, the assumption of control by a holder of a larger block of the corporation's securities and the removal of incumbent management. A statement that the proposal could make the accomplishment of a given transaction more difficult even if it is favorable to the interests of shareholders may be warranted. Thus, the disclosure should focus on the effects of making the removal of management more difficult even if such removal would be beneficial to shareholders generally, and the effects of limiting shareholder participation in certain transactions such as mergers or tender offers whether or not such transactions are favored by incumbent management.

(c) The advantages and disadvantages of the proposal. Although this item may overlap disclosure of the effects of the transaction, information should be included concerning the advantages and disadvantages of the proposal both to incumbent management and to shareholders generally. For example, if one of the effects of the proposal would be to render the accomplishment of a tender offer more difficult, the disclosure could include statements to the effect that such a provision may be beneficial to management in a hostile tender offer and may have an adverse impact on shareholders who may want to participate in such a tender offer. The favorable aspects of the proposal to either management or shareholders, should also be disclosed.

e. Corporate Issuances of Stock

One of the most decisive countermoves that management can make is to issue additional shares of the company's stock. In simple mathematical terms, the impact is obvious if the additional shares are issued to persons friendly to management. These issuances can take many forms, such as the acquisition of another company or its assets, or a particular property, in exchange for stock. The courts split on the propriety of this maneuver in the context of takeover bids.

Some courts have blocked the issuance of shares to prevent a change in corporate control. Condec Corp. v. Lunkenheimer Co., 43 Del.Ch. 353, 230 A.2d 769 (Del.Ch.1967), involved an attempt by Condec to buy control of Lunkenheimer Corp. Condec obtained slightly more than 50 percent of the outstanding common stock in two tender offers. Meanwhile, Lunkenheimer's management had negotiated an agreement for the sale of the company's assets to Textron, but Condec secured sufficient proxies to block the proposed sale, and the Textron offer was withdrawn.

Lunkenheimer management then turned to U.S.I., another interested suitor, and hastily concluded an agreement for the transfer of Lunkenheimer's entire business and assets to U.S.I. As part of the plan, a U.S.I. subsidiary subscribed for 75,000 authorized shares of Lunkenheimer in exchange for 75,000 shares of the same class of U.S.I. preference stock. This issuance of new Lunkenheimer shares overcame Condec's majority position.

Condec filed suit to enjoin the sale, alleging that the primary purpose of the sale of Lunkenheimer shares was to frustrate control by Condec, and thereby protect the personal interests of Lunkenheimer's officers and directors. The Delaware court agreed, and stated in addition, that it did not find

> that type of direct investigation, professional consultation or evidence of contradiction in the actions and explanations of corporate purpose on the part of Condec officials which would lead the management of Lunkenheimer to justifiably believe that Condec's aspirations represented a reasonable threat to the continued existence of Lunkenheimer, or at least its existence as now visualized by its management. Cheff v. Mathes, 230 A.2d at 776.

Although there was testimony to support the business soundness of the U.S.I. transaction, the court was particularly troubled by the haste of the U.S.I. agreement. It concluded that the primary purpose of the stock issuance was to prevent control from passing to Condec, and stated flatly, "Corporate machinery may not be manipulated to injure minority shareholders." *Id.*

If Lunkenheimer's board had a reasonable belief that an acquisition of control by Condec would be contrary to the best interests of the company, would the issuance have been valid? Does it matter why the board thought so? Should the court evaluate the board's reasons itself, or does the business judgment rule apply?

Other cases have gone the same way as Condec. In Chicago Stadium Corp. v. Scallen, 530 F.2d 204 (8th Cir. 1976), the Eighth Circuit affirmed the judgment of the district court in Minnesota enjoining a corporation from issuing voting stock to its president and enjoining the president from voting such stock at the shareholders' meeting. The president of Medical Investment Corp. (Medicor) maintained control with 16 percent of the stock, but plaintiff, with 52 percent, was threatening to remove him. Medicor's directors voted to issue 623,719 shares of voting common stock to the president in discharge of an alleged $311,859 debt to him, which would vest voting control in the president's hands.

The Eighth Circuit found a likelihood that the directors who caused the issuance of the shares would be considered to have breached their fiduciary duties to the stockholders. The defendants claimed that the stock issuance was a bona fide business transaction to extinguish a corporate debt, but the court found the issuance to be of "doubtful legality" and "doubtful adequacy." Not only had a majority of the board acted contrary to counsel's opinion of the probable invalidity of the action, but the board substantially undervalued the shares issued.

In Klaus v. Hi-Shear Corp., 528 F.2d 225 (9th Cir. 1975), shares were both purchased and sold while a tender offer was in progress. The critical transaction was the issuance of shares to a newly-formed Employee Stock Ownership Trust (ESOT). The Ninth Circuit denied relief under federal law because irreparable harm could not be shown. But an injunction against voting the shares held by the ESOT was held to be proper under state law because management had breached its fiduciary duty. Management failed to establish a compelling business reason why the ESOT had to be created at a time so clearly advantageous to incumbent management.

There are other significant cases, however, that have sustained the issuance of the shares in the face of a challenge that the transaction violated the fiduciary duties of management or some provisions of the federal securities laws.

Cummings v. United Artists Theatre Circuit, Inc., 237 Md. 1, 204 A.2d 795 (1964), involved a proxy contest for control of United Artists. Since 1949, United Artists and the Naify family, headed by Michael Naify, each owned a 50 percent interest in United Cal. When George Skouras became president of United Artists in 1950, the company was in a declining financial position, while United Cal remained in good financial condition. Because Skouras was dissatisfied with Naify's policy of plowing United Cal's earnings back into the corporation, he suggested to Naify that the two corporations enter into a merger or a buy-sell deal. Naify refused to consider these proposals until May 1963.

In 1962, the plaintiff, Maxwell Cummings, began acquiring large amounts of United Artists stock. He became a director in July 1962, but he did not inform Skouras until early 1963 that he wanted a change in management and Skouras' resignation. When Skouras disclosed to Michael Naify several of his discussions with Cummings, including Cummings' determination, if necessary to dissolve United Cal, the Naify family quickly entered into negotiations with Skouras.

Cummings then launched a proxy contest, demanding a shareholder's list and a special shareholder's meeting for the removal of all directors except himself. In short order, Skouras and the Naify family agreed upon an exchange of 725,000 shares of United Artists for the Naifys' 50 percent interest, which would give the Naifys firm control of United Artists. The board of United Artists approved the Naify deal at a regular meeting and at the same time rejected Cummings' requests for stockholder approval of the proposal and for postponement of the decision. Only Cummings dissented from the board action. The board also rejected Cummings' request for special stockholders meeting, taking into consideration counsel's opinion that the request did not conform with Maryland law or with the corporation's by-laws. (The court decided to the contrary.)

Cummings then petitioned for a writ of mandamus to compel the United Artists board to call a special stockholder meeting and requested injunctive relief to prevent the consummation of the exchange agreement. The lower court ordered the board to call the meeting but denied the injunction. The court found that "the exchange of stock with the Naifys was not only fair, but indeed critical to the United Artists Corporation, and that the principal motivation of the agreement was not to frustrate the attempt by Cummings and others to change the company's management, but rather a legitimate corporate purpose * * * ." Substantial tax savings, better management of United Artists' debt, a uniform purchasing organization, and more effective management of the theatres were cited as several reasons for the exchange.

The Maryland Court of Appeals agreed with the lower court. Although the agreement had been negotiated and approved with great speed and secrecy and without a prior valuation of United Artists' properties, the appellate court noted that the lower court had considered the board's familiarity with the negotiations and the financial standing of United Artists. "Where the lower court had before it sufficient evidence that the principal motive was not related to control, the effect on control caused by the board's action is not of compelling significance." 204 A.2d at 806.

See also Treadway Companies, Inc. v. Care Corp., 638 F.2d 357 (2d Cir. 1980), *infra* subsection (f), which permitted the issuance of stock to a white knight that thwarted a tender offer.

Are *Cummings* and *Condec* reconcilable? One practical rule that might be gleaned from the comparison is that the lawyer who can establish the strongest record at the trial level with respect to facts relevant to legitimate business transactions, will have the best chance of winning. But, this rule would seemingly apply whether or not the corporate action were *in fact* motivated by the reasons advanced at trial. Does this make sense in terms of policy considerations such as the scope of directors' fiduciary duties to shareholders and the corporation?　See Judge Cudahy's concurring and dissenting opinion in Panter v. Marshall Field Co., *infra*.

An interesting view is that of an English court in Bamford v. Bamford [Ch.1967] 3 W.L.R. 317, appeal dismissed [C.A.1968] 2 W.L. R. 1107, which held that a ratification of the stock issuance by the stockholders validated the transaction, even though it was the directors and not the stockholders who possessed the power to issue shares.

The courts are divided on how the matter is to be treated under federal law.　A claim under Rule 10b–5, that the issuance of stock was a breach of fiduciary duty because it served no legitimate corporate purpose and was intended only to frustrate a tender offer was denied because this was "precisely the kind of claim the Supreme Court in *Santa Fe* felt should be decided under state law."　Altman v. Knight, 431 F.Supp. 309 (S.D.N.Y.1977).　*See also* Oscar Gruss & Sons v. Natomas Co., Fed.Sec.L.Rept. (CCH) ¶ 96,258 (C.D.Cal.1976). However, in action under § 14(e), the issuance by Milgo Electronic Corporation of 18.4 percent of its stock to an English company, at a time when Applied Digital Data Systems, Inc., had announced its intent to make a tender offer, was found to be a breach of fiduciary duty.　The transaction was structured to barely avoid the stockholder voting requirements of the New York Stock Exchange (which require a shareholder vote if a listed company issues new stock equal to 20 percent or more of that already outstanding).　The court said that if it could be shown that no purpose other than to defeat the tender offer existed, the issuance of the new shares would violate § 14(e). Applied Digital Data Systems, Inc. v. Milgo Electronic Corp., 425 F. Supp. 1145 (S.D.N.Y.1977).　While the case arose under § 14(e) and not under Rule 10b–5, and there are statutory differences, it is important to note that the decision was prior to Santa Fe v. Green.

Of particular significance is the decision in Herald Co. v. Seawell, 472 F.2d 1081 (10th Cir. 1972), involving a struggle for control of a company that published the Denver Post newspaper.　The Denver Post is a large metropolitan newspaper with a long tradition of local ownership.　The Bonfils family had had a large ownership interest in the Post, and Helen Bonfils, the daughter of one of the Post's founders, was both an officer and director.　In May 1960, Samuel Newhouse, the owner of one of the nation's largest newspaper chains purchased 18 percent of the outstanding common stock of the Denver Post with the intent of acquiring the newspaper.　On July 7, 1960, the Post purchased 19,574 shares of its stock (about 21 percent of that outstanding) held by the U. S. National Bank as trustee for Children's Hospital at $260 per share.　The stock was not publicly traded, but this figure was probably below its investment value.　For several years prior to this purchase, the Post board of directors had contemplated establishing an employee stock ownership plan.　After the purchase, the board implemented an employee stock trust plan.　The

Post initially transferred approximately 3400 treasury shares to the trust. Helen Bonfils donated 1600 shares from her personal holdings. By December 1969, 415 of the eligible 1159 employees had purchased shares from the trust.

More than eight years after the purchase of the Children's Hospital stock, the Herald Company, which was owned by Newhouse, brought a derivative action on behalf of the Post against its officers and directors for misconduct, breach of trust and misuse of corporate assets. The plaintiff claimed that the board and the trustees of the employee stock trust had conspired to acquire sufficient shares of stock to vest control in Helen Bonfils. Among the numerous acts which the defendants allegedly committed was the creation of an "illusory stock trust" from which the defendants sold shares at prices which resulted in a decrease in the Post's surplus.

The district court determined that management's primary obligation was to earn profits for the company's shareholders, and ordered the public sale of several blocks of Post shares, including those remaining in the treasury from the Children's Hospital purchase and those transferred to the trust.

The Tenth Circuit reversed. On the question of the defendant's motive, the court found nothing bad or sinister in the purchase of stock to prevent the stock from being sold to Newhouse. The evidence established that the directors feared a Newhouse takeover would adversely affect the character and quality of the Post. The directors believed that local independent ownership was preferable and superior to chain ownership. They also knew that Newhouse had a reputation among his employees for having poor relations with labor. More importantly, the court noted that a newspaper had a larger duty than to increase profits. The Post had a threefold obligation: to the stockholders, to the employees, and to the public.

> Such a newspaper is endowed with an important public interest. It must adhere to the ethics of the great profession of journalism. The readers are entitled to a high quality of accurate news coverage of local, state, national and international events. The newspaper management has an obligation to assume leadership, when needed, for the betterment of the area served by the newspaper. Because of these relations with the public, a corporation publishing a great newspaper such as the Denver Post is, in effect, a quasi-public institution.

472 F.2d at 1095.

The court also believed that the defendants were sincerely concerned for their employees' welfare. Approximately 11 percent of the corporation's expenses were incurred on behalf of employee benefits such as medical insurance and retirement pensions. Moreover, within 35 years, the Post employees would probably own 85 to 90 percent of the paper.

Under Colorado law, the Post had the authority to adopt and to implement an employee stock trust plan. The court saw no reason why it should substitute its judgement for that of the board when the directors had acted honestly and with reason.

In 1978, the stockholders of the Hartford Courant, whose origins date back to 1764, rejected an extremely profitable offer to sell their shares to Capital Cities Communications, Inc., a newspaper chain. Most of the stock was employee owned. The prevailing feeling was that the present management was paternalistic towards its employees and that new management would have no interest in the community and in local news. Some stockholders felt strongly against being deprived of the greatly increased value for their shares. One employee observed, "we aren't a family; we're a business." Another noted, "Everyone has a price. There comes a point at which you can't refuse a good offer." Wall Street Journal, November 9, 1978, p. 48.

But are newspapers special? Could management justify resistance to a takeover by a company that promises new efficiencies, *i.e.*, a loss of jobs? The management of Towle Manufacturing Co., another company older than the Republic, which produces fine sterling silver flatware, opposed a takeover by a conglomerate with a modernistic name and no particular lineage. History, sentiment and perhaps elitism contributed to management's thinking. Can any of that stand up in court against the bottom line?

f.   Management's Response to a Tender Offer: Fight Fiercely, Fellows!

SEC rules under the Williams Act, as amended in 1979, require management to respond and inform the stockholders about management's view of the offer. Management, after all, is in a better position than the shareholders to assess the bidder's offer and comment on its fairness. Rule 14e–2 requires the target company to publish its views to the shareholders within 10 days after the tender offer commences, recommending acceptance or rejection, or stating that the target is unable to take a position and explaining why. Rule 14d–9, moreover, requires the target, its management and certain others to file a Schedule 14D–9 with the SEC and the bidder when a recommendation is made, and to provide certain information to the shareholders.

Among other things, the target company must describe any conflicts of interests between the target and its management, and the reasons for its recommendation. It is insufficient merely to state that the offer is, or is not, in the best interests of the shareholders. But how much analysis is required? Must the separate reasons of each of the directors be stated? This may be another example of how the disclosure requirements of the federal securities laws have a substantive impact. *See* Fleisher, SEC Rules Impose Obligations on Target Company's Managers, Legal Times (Wash.), April 27, 1981, p. 25.

Rules aside, management customarily is quick to attack the bidders and the adequacy of the bid. To what extent does a vigorous counterattack create a legal problem for management? The target company's management will be seen as having a conflict of interest when it examines an uninvited tender offer. While it is said that the outside directors are not "interested" because they have no financial stake in the outcome of a tender offer, is it accurate to conclude that they can therefore always be counted on to make an objective determination of the question: Can present management or the bidder provide better leadership for the corporation?

From another point of view, the decision whether to merge or to sell is just another business decision that management must make. It is necessary to evaluate the proposal, and if it is not in the best interests of the corporation to deal with the prospective suitor, then to reject the deal. Thus, the directors of the target must make some decision. It is rendered more difficult by the fact that the long term interests of the enterprise are not necessarily the same as the short term interests of the shareholders. For the latter, a sale at a high price is favorable, and it matters not to them once they have sold their shares that the buyer may not foster the long term growth of the corporation.

To a conscientious management and board, the lure to the stockholders of being able to sell out at a high price is a great worry. By strenuously opposing a tender offer, which management might feel is its duty, the management might, in effect, be making the decision that the bidder intends be made by the stockholders. Management's fear is that the stockholders are not capable of making an objective decision about the best interests of the corporation. It is comparable to the fear some have about the premiums offered to a controlling stockholder to sell his shares to a looter. In most situations, business decisions are entrusted to the management (or the board) and not left to the shareholders. The business judgment rule does not apply when the board has a conflict of interest. But do the stockholders not have a conflict of interests as well? How can this situation be resolved?

From a regulatory point of view the problem is one of the most perplexing in corporate law. Managerial accountability is heightened by a viable tender offer device. The possibility of displacing inefficient management is advanced. And yet there are no assurances this will be the ultimate result in any particular case. Some worry that billions are expended on takeovers instead of being used to create new capital facilities since it is easier to buy than to build, but not necessarily more productive. We will examine the public policy dimensions of this problem in the next section.

In practice, managements have rarely felt constrained by the law in using virtually all known combative methods to resist tender offers. They have employed talented counsel who are experienced on both sides to use all resources to thwart the challenge. Sometimes the result of all the resistance is to force the bidder to raise the price, perhaps assure management of continued employment, and for the fight to end. Another result is to provide time to management to discover a white knight who will top the first bid, and again the story ends happily for the stockholders. But other times the management is able to thwart the bid entirely, which finds the stockholders losing the opportunity to sell their stock at the higher price initially offered. That may lead to a further suit, one against the directors for having cost the loss of an opportunity.

The following materials explore these issues.

PANTER v. MARSHALL FIELD & CO.

646 F.2d 271 (7th Cir. 1981).

[This was the consolidation of several class actions brought by shareholders of Marshall Field & Co. ("Field") against the corporation and all ten directors, alleging that they had unlawfully deprived the shareholders of an opportunity to sell their shares to Carter Hawley Hale, Inc. ("CHH"), a national retail chain. CHH proposed to make an offer valued at $42 per share, in exchange for Field shares. Following an announcement by CHH that it would not proceed with the offer, the price of Field shares declined to $19. Damages calculated on the basis of the difference between the offering price and price after withdrawal, would exceed $200 million. Following a trial before a jury, the district court directed a verdict in favor of the defendants.

Field's has operated the major department store in Chicago since 1852. It also owns department stores in the Chicago suburbs, and in several other cities around the country. In 1977 it was the eighth largest department store chain in the United States.

In November and December 1977, CHH expressed an interest to Angelo Arena, Field's new president, in merging the two companies. Field's declined. Its outside counsel advised the board of directors that the proposed combination would violate the antitrust laws because of various contact points between Field and CHH subsidiaries. CHH had been advised by counsel that antitrust problems could be readily avoided. CHH then made a public announcement of its intention to offer shares of CHH worth $36 (later raised to $42) in exchange for Field shares then trading at $22. The board convened, joined by investment bankers and lawyers. It heard a report from management about the favorable prospects for the company, an opinion from its investment bankers that a share of Field stock was worth more than CHH's offer, and an opinion from counsel that the merger was illegal. The board then voted to reject the offer. Arena wrote to the shareholders, urging that independence was the best course for the company. Field's promptly commenced an antitrust suit against CHH. Shortly thereafter, Field's board voted to expand into a suddenly available opening in the Galleria shopping center in Houston, where CHH had a large store, and to acquire five stores in the Pacific Northwest, two of which were marginally profitable. Shortly thereafter, CHH announced that it would not proceed with the offer, in light of recent developments that made it doubt the wisdom of the merger.

Plaintiff argued that Field's resistance was based on a long term unannounced policy of independence that caused management to resist any tender offer or merger proposal, regardless of its merits, in order to protect management's jobs. The board had retained special counsel in 1969 for advice on how to respond to any tender offer, and was told that it should make acquisitions. Thereafter, several merger proposals to Field were turned down, usually closely followed by an acquisition by Field. Defendants said that these acquisitions were intended to build value within the company; plaintiffs said they were motivated by a desire to keep control at all costs. Plaintiffs also contended that the board gave no serious consideration to the CHH bid, but instead responded with classic anti-takeover maneuvers.

At this time the board consisted of ten members. Three were officers of the company. The other seven were outsiders, of whom one was a partner in the investment banking firm that had represented the company, and another was an officer of a bank where the company had substantial deposits.

Plaintiffs contended that management's response violated §§ 14 (e), 10(b) and Rule 10b–5 under the Securities Exchange Act of 1934, and common law fiduciary duty.]

PELL, Circuit Judge.

* * *

THE FEDERAL SECURITIES LAW CLAIMS

* * *

Because § 14(e) is intended to protect shareholders from making a tender offer decision on inaccurate or inadequate information, among the elements of § 14(e) plaintiff must establish is "that there was a misrepresentation upon which the target corporation shareholders relied * * *." Because the CHH tender offer was withdrawn before the plaintiffs had the opportunity to decide whether or not to tender their shares, it was impossible for the plaintiffs to rely on any alleged deception in making the decision to tender or not. Because the plaintiffs were never presented with that critical decision and therefore never relied on the defendants' alleged misrepresentations, they fail to establish a vital element of a § 14(e) claim as regards the CHH $42.00 offer.

* * *

The claim that the defendants are allowed to profit by their own wrong is irrelevant to this case. Such an argument would require proof of a causal link between the defendants' wrongful acts or omissions and the withdrawal of the tender offer. Here there is uncontroverted evidence that it was Field's recent acquisitions and plans for expansion that caused the withdrawal of the CHH tender offer. The decision to make acquisitions is one governed by the state law of directors' fiduciary duty. Therefore even if such conduct were a breach of the defendant directors' fiduciary duty, the plaintiffs would be relegated to their remedy at state law. This argument, therefore, cannot create a federal securities law claim when the alleged "wrong" the defendant committed is barred from federal scrutiny by the rule of Santa Fe Industries, 430 U.S. 462, 97 S.Ct. 1292, 51 L.Ed. 2d 480 (1977).

* * *

The gravamen of the plaintiffs' 10b–5 claim is that Field's directors acted pursuant to a long-standing undisclosed policy of independence and resistance to all takeover attempts, designed to perpetuate the defendant directors' control of the corporation. The plaintiffs assert that the defendants' failure to disclose this policy was an omission of a material fact which made other statements and conduct of the defendants misleading. They also claim that the policy motivated the defendant directors to make other misrepresentations or omissions of material facts in relation to Field's prospects and plans.

As the Supreme Court noted in Santa Fe Industries, Inc. v. Green, 430 U.S. 462, 477–78, 97 S.Ct. 1292, 1302–03, 51 L.Ed.2d 480 (1977), the rule is a manifestation of the "philosophy of full disclosure," embodied in the Securities Exchange Act of 1934; it therefore requires proof of the element of deception, and does not provide a remedy for the breach of fiduciary duty a director owes his corporation and its shareholders under state law. * * *

* * *

Even assuming that the plaintiffs were able to establish the existence of [an anti-takeover] policy, neither the policy nor a failure to disclose its existence can give rise to a federal securities law cause of action absent the element of manipulation or deception required by Rule 10b–5.

The critical issue in determining whether conduct meets the requirement of deception, the Court announced in *Santa Fe Industries*, is whether the conduct complained of includes the omission or misrepresentation of a material fact, or whether it merely states a claim for a breach of a state law duty. A board of directors' decision to oppose or welcome a takeover attempt involves the exercise of directorial judgment inherent in their role in corporate governance.

* * *

The plaintiffs' allegations that Field's directors rebuffed all acquisition attempts without regard to merit and failed to disclose the existence of an alleged policy so to act, are similarly insufficient to create a federal cause of action. Like the claims above, they simply state a claim for a breach of the fiduciary duty directors owe shareholders under state corporate law. This is precisely the type of claim the Supreme Court intended to bar from the federal forum when it announced the rule in *Santa Fe Industries.* * * *

* * *

THE STATE LAW CLAIMS

The plaintiffs here have also sought to establish that the defendants committed two violations of state law. First, they contend, the defendants breached their fiduciary duty as directors to the corporation and its shareholders by adopting a secret policy to resist acquisition regardless of benefit to the shareholders or the corporation; by failing to disclose the existence of such a policy; by making defensive acquisitions; and by filing an antitrust suit against CHH. Second, they argue that the defendants interfered with the plaintiffs' prospective economic advantage when that allegedly wrongful behavior caused CHH to withdraw its proposed tender offer before it became effective.

A. *The Business Judgment Rule*

Under applicable Delaware corporate law, claims such as those made by the plaintiffs are analyzed under the "business judgment" rule. The trial court described this rule as establishing that

> [d]irectors of corporations discharge their fiduciary duties when in good faith they exercise business judgment in making decisions regarding the corporation. When they act in good faith, they enjoy a presumption of sound business judgment, reposed in them as directors, which courts will not disturb if any rational business purpose can be attributed to their decisions. In the absence of fraud, bad faith gross overreaching or abuse of discretion courts will not interfere with the exercise of business judgment by corporate directors.

486 F.Supp. at 1194 (citations omitted). We find this an apt summary of appropriate Delaware law. In the recent case of Johnson v. Trueblood, 629 F.2d 287 (3d Cir. 1980), the U.S. Court of Appeals for the Third Circuit had occasion to analyze the purpose of the Delaware business judgment rule in the context of a takeover attempt. The plaintiffs contended that an allegation of a purpose to retain control was enough to shift the burden to incumbent directors to show the rational business purpose of the disputed transaction. In rejecting

that contention Chief Judge Seitz, formerly a Delaware Chancellor, stated:

> First, the purpose of the business judgment rule belies the plaintiffs' contention. It is frequently said that directors are fiduciaries. Although this statement is true in some senses, it is also obvious that if directors were held to the same standard as ordinary fiduciaries the corporation could not conduct business. For example, an ordinary fiduciary may not have the slightest conflict of interest in any transaction he undertakes on behalf of the trust. Yet by the very nature of corporate life a director has a certain amount of self-interest in everything he does. The very fact that the director wants to enhance corporate profits is in part attributable to his desire to keep shareholders satisfied so that they will not oust him.

> The business judgment rule seeks to alleviate this problem by validating certain situations that otherwise would involve a conflict of interest for the ordinary fiduciary. The rule achieves this purpose by postulating that if actions are arguably taken for the benefit of the corporation, then the directors are presumed to have been exercising their sound business judgment rather than responding to any personal motivations.

> Faced with the presumption raised by the rule, the question is what sort of showing the plaintiff must make to survive a motion for directed verdict. Because the rule presumes that business judgment was exercised, *the plaintiff must make a showing from which a factfinder might infer that impermissible motives predominated in the making of the decision in question.*

> The plaintiffs' theory that "a" motive to control is sufficient to rebut the rule is inconsistent with this purpose. Because the rule is designed to validate certain transactions despite conflicts of interest, the plaintiffs' rule would negate that purpose, at least in many cases. As already noted, control is always arguably "a" motive in any action taken by a director. Hence plaintiffs could always make this showing and thereby undercut the purpose of the rule.

Id. at 292–93 (emphasis added).

* * *

We also note that a majority of the directors of Field's were "independent": they derived no income from Field's other than normal directors' fees and the equivalent of an employee discount on merchandise. The presumption of good faith the business judgment rule affords is heightened when the majority of the board consists of independent outside directors.

The plaintiffs suggest that director Blair's independence was called into question by the fact that his investment banking firm did work for Field's. In Maldonado v. Flynn, 485 F.Supp. 274 (S.D.N.Y.

1980), the court dismissed such an implication as "a non sequitur and hardly worthy of comment." *Id.* at 283. We agree. Even less relevant was the plaintiffs' attempt to show that director Smith's independence was weakened because he owned a substantial share of a bank in which Field's deposited monies and had other accounts. That inference is so attenuated that the trial court properly excluded the evidence as irrelevant.

However, rather than proceeding under the business judgment rule, the plaintiffs here seek to apply a different test in the takeover context, and propose that the burden be placed upon the directors to establish the compelling business purpose of any transaction which would have the effect of consolidating or retaining the directors' control. In light of the overwhelming weight of authority to the contrary, we refuse to apply such a novel rule to this case.

B.   *The Breach of Fiduciary Duty*

1.   The Policy of Independence

The plaintiffs contend that they have presented sufficient evidence to go to the jury on the existence of the secret policy, both circumstantially, from the history of prior rebuffs, and directly, from the testimony of two Field's directors.

On the resistance to prior approaches, we have established above that evaluation and response to such approaches is within the scope of the directors' duties. The plaintiffs have presented no evidence of self-dealing, fraud, overreaching or other bad conduct sufficient to give rise to any reasonable inference that impermissible motives predominated in the board's consideration of the approaches. The desire to build value within the company, and the belief that such value might be diminished by a given offer is a rational business purpose. The record reveals that appropriate consideration was given to each individual approach made to Marshall Field & Company. The plaintiffs have failed to introduce evidence supporting a reasonable inference that any of the rejections of these approaches were made in bad faith. Therefore the presumption of good faith afforded by the business judgment rule applies, and the plaintiffs cannot survive the motion for directed verdict.

Having failed to establish the presence of an improper motive in any one of the defendants' responses to acquisition approaches, the plaintiffs seek to establish from the series of rejections the illogical inference that this reflects an invidious policy of independence regardless of benefit to the shareholders. All that the plaintiffs' evidence in this regard establishes is that Field's directors evaluated the merits of each approach made, and determined to implement their decisions as to each of the approaches by following the advice of counsel on how to respond to unwanted acquisition approaches.

* * *

2. The Defensive Acquisitions

The plaintiffs also contend that the "defensive" acquisitions of the five Liberty House stores and the Galleria were imprudent, and designed to make Field's less attractive as an acquisition, as well as to exacerbate any antitrust problems created by the CHH merger. It is precisely this sort of Monday-morning-quarterbacking that the business judgment rule was intended to prevent. Again, the plaintiffs have brought forth no evidence of bad faith, overreaching, self-dealing or any other fraud necessary to shift the burden of justifying the transactions to the defendants. On the contrary, there was uncontroverted evidence that such expansion was reasonable and natural. Thus even if the desire to fend off CHH was among the motives of the board in entering the transactions, because the plaintiffs have failed to establish that such a motive was the sole or primary purpose, as has been required by Delaware law since the leading case of Cheff v. Mathes, 41 Del.Ch. 494, 199 A.2d 548 (1964), the mere allegation, or even some proof, that a given transaction was made on "unfavorable" terms does not meet the fairly stringent burden the business judgment rules imposes on plaintiffs.

3. The Antitrust Suit

The plaintiffs also contend that the bringing of the antitrust suit against CHH was a breach of the directors' fiduciary duty. Because it is the duty of the directors to file an antitrust suit when in their business judgment a proposed combination would be illegal or otherwise detrimental to the corporation, their decision to file an antitrust suit is also within the scope of the business judgment rule. There was substantial evidence before the court that the defendants were fairly and reasonably exercising their business judgment to protect the corporation against the perceived damage an illegal merger could cause.

Not only were the directors acting in good faith reliance on the advice of experienced and knowledgeable antitrust counsel, which in itself satisfies the requirements of the business judgment rule, but one member of the board was an experienced antitrust lawyer with a background of experience to evaluate the soundness of the legal claims. * * * The plaintiffs have introduced no evidence that the suit was brought in bad faith, but merely cite it as an example of the defendants' desire to perpetuate their control. However, because the bringing of the suit clearly served the rational business purpose of protecting Field's from the damage forced divestiture would cause, it is protected by the business judgment rule. Field's decision to resolve the antitrust question through litigation in federal court rather than some other method or in some other forum is a matter for the discretion of the directors when it is exercised within the scope of the rule.

Because we find insufficient evidence on which a jury could base a rational verdict that the defendants breached any fiduciary duty, neither can any claim of concealment of bad faith activity give rise to a jury question. We therefore affirm the district court's ruling on the state law claims of breach of fiduciary duty.

* * *

V. CONCLUSION

We therefore conclude, as did the district court, that the plaintiffs have failed to provide a sufficient evidentiary basis on which reasonable jurors could find violations of either the federal securities laws, or state law. The judgment of the district court is affirmed.

CUDAHY, Circuit Judge, concurring in part and dissenting in part:

Unfortunately, the majority here has moved one giant step closer to shredding whatever constraints still remain upon the ability of corporate directors to place self-interest before shareholder interest in resisting a hostile tender offer for control of the corporation. There is abundant evidence in this case to go to the jury on the state claims for breach of fiduciary duty. I emphatically disagree that the business judgment rule should clothe directors, battling blindly to fend off a threat to their control, with an almost irrebuttable presumption of sound business judgment, prevailing over everything but the elusive hobgoblins of fraud, bad faith or abuse of discretion. I also disagree with the majority's view that misleading and deceptive representations about an offeror's proposal are immunized from the proscriptions of Section 14(e) if the offer is withdrawn before the shareholders have an opportunity to tender.

On the other hand, I agree with the majority that many of the Securities Act misrepresentation claims here represent impermissible transmutations of claims for breach of fiduciary duty into federal securities violations. This result is frequently obtained through allegations that the failure of directors to disclose the culpability of their activities or their improper motives are unlawful misrepresentations. There is, however, at least one clear exception. The jury should have been allowed to consider the company president's public letter of December 20, 1977, claiming a 13% increase in consolidated net income for the nine months ended October 31, when management expected a *decline* in earnings for the full year.

I.

Addressing first the state law claims of breach of fiduciary duty by the Board, the majority has adopted an approach which would virtually immunize a target company's board of directors against liability to shareholders, provided a sufficiently prestigious (and expensive) array of legal and financial talent were retained to furnish *post hoc* rationales for fixed and immutable policies of resistance to takeover. Relying on several recent decisions interpreting the Delaware business judgment rule, the majority fails to make the important distinction

> between the activity of a corporation in managing a business enterprise and its function as a vehicle for collecting and using capital and distributing profits and losses. The former involves corporate functioning in competitive business affairs in which judicial interference may be undesirable. *The latter involves only the corporation-shareholder relationship, in which the courts may more justifiably intervene to insist on equitable behavior.*

Note, Protection for Shareholder Interests in Recapitalizations of Publicly Held Companies, 58 Colum.L.Rev. 1030, 1066 (1958) (emphasis supplied).

The theoretical justification for the "hands off" precept of the business judgment rule is that courts should be reluctant to review the acts of directors in situations where the expertise of the directors is likely to be greater than that of the courts. But, where the directors are afflicted with a conflict of interest, relative expertise is no longer crucial. Instead, the great danger becomes the channeling of the directors' expertise along the lines of their personal advantage— sometimes at the expense of the corporation and its stockholders. Here courts have no rational choice but to subject challenged conduct of directors and questioned corporate transactions to their own disinterested scrutiny. Of course, the self-protective bias of interested directors may be entirely devoid of corrupt motivation, but it may nonetheless constitute a serious threat to stockholder welfare.

Despite this potential for abuse, the majority relies heavily on the business judgment rule's presumption of good faith in the exercise of corporate decision-making power and attaches special significance to the "independence" of Field's Board. The fact that Field's may have had a majority of non-management (independent) directors is hardly dispositive. The interaction between management and board may be very strong even where, as here, a relationship of symbiosis seems to prevail over the normal condition of "management domination." Whether the relationship is symbiotic or management "dominates," I do not think it necessary to rely primarily on such directly pecuniary relationships as one director's senior partnership in Field's investment banking firm (although this was admittedly a quite profitable arrangement) or another director's ownership of stock in a Field's depository bank (obviously a more attenuated interest) to establish a conflict of interest here. These factors deserve appropriate attention. But the very idea that, if we cannot trace with precision a mighty flow of dollars into the pockets of each of the outside directors, these directors are necessarily disinterested arbiters of the stockholders' destiny, is appallingly naive.

Directors of a New York Stock Exchange-listed company are, at the very least, "interested" in their own positions of power, prestige and prominence (and in their not inconsequential perquisites). They are "interested" in defending against outside attack the management which they have, in fact, installed or maintained in power—"their" management (to which, in many cases, they owe their directorships). And they are "interested" in maintaining the public reputation of their own leadership and stewardship against the claims of "raiders" who say that they can do better. Thus, regardless of their technical "independence," directors of a target corporation are in a very special position, where the slavish application of the majority's version of the good faith presumption is particularly disturbing.

* * *

II.

The basic error of the majority in the instant case is in holding as a matter of law that there was insufficient evidence to go to the jury on the state claims of breach of fiduciary duty. * * * There was abundant evidence from which a jury in this case could have concluded that Field's directors breached their fiduciary duties to the shareholders: 1) by pursuing a fixed, nondebatable and undisclosed policy of massive resistance to merger with, or acquisition by, a series of the nation's foremost retailers; 2) by making hasty and apparently imprudent defensive acquisitions to reduce Field's attractiveness as a takeover candidate and to force the withdrawal of the CHH offer; and 3) by hastily filing a major antitrust suit to further impair persistent acquisitive efforts of CHH.

[The judge then examined, in detail, the evidence in the case.]

III.

In addition, I disagree with the majority's conclusion that, because the CHH tender offer was withdrawn before plaintiffs had the opportunity to decide whether or not to tender their shares, any deception which Field's Board might have practiced cannot be a violation of Section 14(e) of the Williams Act. The type of rule which the majority advocates is simply an invitation to incumbent management to make whatever claims and assertions may be expedient to force withdrawal of an offer. Management could speak without restraint knowing that once withdrawal is forced there is no Securities Act liability for deception practiced before withdrawal took place. Such a rule provides a major loophole for escaping the provisions of Section 14(e) and obviously frustrates the remedial purpose of the Act.

* * *

To have taken this close case presenting a wide range of defensible inferences from the jury is a major disservice to stockholders everywhere. This case announces to stockholders (if they did not know it before) that they are on their own and may expect little consideration and less enlightenment from their board of directors when a tender offeror appears to challenge the directors for control. I believe that only the submission to jury verdict of cases like this one can restore confidence in our system of corporate governance. While I concur as to many of the Securities Act deception claims, I must respectfully dissent in the areas which I have indicated.

POST SCRIPT TO *MARSHALL FIELD'S*

Marshall Field's again faced a threat of takeover in the Spring of 1982 when Carl Icahn, a private investor, acquired approximately 30% of its stock. On a number of previous occasions, Icahn had purchased large positions in a company, and threatened to wage a proxy contest, but then disengaged, selling his shares back to the company at a large personal profit. That defensive strategy was not available to Field's because the company lacked the cash, having expended it for earlier acquisitions of companies that were strategically situated with respect to prospective unwanted bidders for Field's. See Nazem, *Marshall Field's Too Successful Strategy*, Fortune Mag., March 22, 1982, p. 81.

Field's found a rescuer in BATUS, Inc., the American subsidiary of British American Tobacco Company. BATUS made a friendly tender offer at $30 per share for 51% of Field's stock, declaring that it intended to cause a merger in which the remaining shares would receive $26.50 per share, a figure later raised to $30. Field's, it will be recalled, opposed the Carter Hawley Hale bid on anti-trust grounds, among other reasons, but management made no mention of the fact that BATUS owned a large Saks Fifth Avenue store three blocks from Field's Water Tower Place store in Chicago, or that Field's and Gimbels, another BATUS property, both operated in Milwaukee. While Field's again succeeded in warding off an unfriendly bid, the cost to its stockholders may have been considerable.

NOTE—THE BUSINESS JUDGMENT RULE

The majority and the dissent in *Marshall Field* divided most sharply over the application of the business judgment rule. Both opinions discussed at length two Second Circuit decisions (and the Third Circuit opinion in Johnson v. Trueblood) which applied the rule in a tender offer context.

Treadway Companies, Inc. v. Care Corp., 638 F.2d 357 (2d Cir. 1980) involved, among other things, Treadway's resistance to a takeover attempt by Care. To thwart Care's bid, Treadway found Fair Lanes, Inc. as a white knight to acquire 80 percent of Treadway stock. Toward that end, the board approved the sale of a large block of Treadway stock to Fair Lanes. The lower court enjoined the voting of those shares in a proxy contest between Treadway and Care over the election of directors because it found that the issuance was motivated principally by management's desire to perpetuate its own control.

In reversing the district court, Judge Kearse wrote as follows:

"On the face of things, there appears to be no inherent reason why the stock sale to Fair Lanes should not be analyzed under the foregoing business judgment rule. The possibility of a Care takeover was obviously a matter of great importance to Treadway and its shareholders. It was only reasonable that Treadway's board, which is charged with managing the corporation, should examine the situation to make a judgment as to where the best interests of Treadway lay. Once they determined that a Care takeover would be detrimental to Treadway, it was similarly reasonable that the directors should move to oppose it. * * * In thus acting on matters within the scope of their legitimate concern, the directors would seem to be protected by the business judgment rule. The district court, however, did not apply the standard business judgment analysis. Rather, it focused on the immediate step taken by Treadway's board to oppose the prospective Care takeover: the issuance and sale of a large block of stock. The unstated premise was that the business judgment rule does not apply to such transactions.

* * *

"The cases in this area demonstrate that the courts are sensitive to the risks of self-dealing and abuse which inhere in corporate stock transactions that are intended to affect control. But at the same time courts have recognized that in certain circumstances, it is proper for management to cause the corporation to enter into such transactions. The law in this area is something less than a seamless web; some of the cases are not easily reconciled. We have concluded, however, that far from constituting an area that is beyond the purview of the business judgment rule, these cases are best reconciled by reference to the analysis typically employed under that rule.

* * *

"In nearly all of the cases treating stock transactions intended to affect control, the directors who approved the transaction have had a real and obvious interest in it: their interest in retaining or strengthening their control of the corporation. It is this interest which causes the burden of proof to be shifted to the directors, to demonstrate the propriety of the transactions. * * *

"Turning to the record before us, we conclude that the evidence does not permit a finding that Care has carried that burden. The critical fact, in our view, is that the Treadway board was simply not acting to maintain its own control over the corporation. Rather, in approving the stock sale, they were moving Treadway toward a business combination with Fair Lanes. Fair Lanes had made the stock sale a precondition to further merger talks. From all that appears, Fair Lanes and Treadway had every intention of carrying through with that merger. Hall testified that Fair Lanes had been interested for some years in a possible merger with Treadway; and Care has not offered any evidence to suggest that the merger talks were a sham or a pretext, or that the Treadway directors did not seriously wish to pursue the merger. Moreover, Care made no showing that the directors other than Lieblich [Treadway's CEO] had any personal interest in having the merger consummated. Only Lieblich had reason to anticipate that he would be given any position, or have any role to play, in the new merged entity. The district court found that the other directors expected that they would lose their positions as Treadway directors and would not be offered new ones. This expectation seems reasonable in light of the facts that during the negotiations Fair Lanes had requested that it be allowed to name a majority of the Treadway directors immediately, and that after the proposed merger Fair Lanes would own more than 80% of Treadway's stock. Thus the consummation of the proposed business combination could not be expected to perpetuate control by these directors.

"On the basis of the foregoing, we can only conclude that Care has not demonstrated an interest on the part of Treadway's directors—other than Lieblich—such as would shift onto the directors the burden of proving fairness. The disinterested majority is therefore protected by the business judgment rule * * * and the transaction must be upheld unless Care has proven that it was entered into in bad faith."

638 F.2d at 381.

In Crouse-Hinds Co. v. InterNorth, Inc., 634 F.2d 690 (2d Cir. 1980), the target had negotiated a merger with another corporation before the bidder appeared. The target fiercely opposed the tender offer and proceeded with the merger, using a revised procedure that facilitated shareholder approval. The bidder sued to enjoin the merger on grounds that no valid business purpose was served. The district court interpreted *Treadway* to deny application of the business judgment rule since, under the merger, the directors would remain in office and therefore they were "interested." The Second Circuit, again in an opinion by Judge Kearse, reversed:

"We find no basis in the present case for the district court's conclusion that InterNorth [the bidder] carried its burden of demonstrating self-interest or bad faith on the part of the Crouse-Hinds [the target] directors. As his starting point, the district judge gave extended consideration to the decision in *Treadway*, in which we found that because the Treadway directors, other than the chairman, were not to remain in office after the merger, perpetuation of their control could hardly have been their motivation for actions in furtherance of the merger. * * * Unfortunately, the district judge inferred from this that a quite different proposition must also be true—*i.e.*, that if the directors are to remain on the board after the merger, perpetuation of their control must be presumed to be their motivation. This inference has no basis in either law or logic. *Treadway* did not disturb the normal requirement that a complaining shareholder present evidence of the directors' interest in order to shift the burden of proof to them."

634 F.2d at 702–03.

The federal district court in Delaware approached the business judgment issue from a different direction in Crane Co. v. Harsco Corp., 511 F.Supp. 294 (D.C.Del.1981). The board of Harsco authorized the purchase of the company's shares from the arbitrageurs, in order to defeat Crane's tender offer. The latter then sued, claiming a breach of fiduciary duty. The court found that the plaintiff had established a likelihood of success on this issue. Judge Wright explained:

"A corporation has a statutory right to purchase its own shares, and under the business judgment rule, the courts will not interfere with a stock purchase transaction provided the purchase is not for an improper purpose.

"It has long been established that, as a general rule, use of corporate funds to perpetuate control of the corporation is improper. Where the stock purchase occurs in the context of a tender offer, the directors have an inherent conflict of interest. In such situations, 'the burden should be on the directors to justify such a purchase as one primarily in the corporate interest.' [Bennett v. Propp, 41 Del. Ch. 14, 187 A.2d 405, 409 (1962).]

"Under this rule, Harsco can carry its burden in one of two ways. It can either show that some consideration other than the perceived threat to control was the primary reason for the stock purchase; or it can admit that the stock purchase was intended primarily as a defensive maneuver, and show that a change in control would constitute 'a clear threat to the future business or the existing, successful business policy' of the corporation.' Kaplan v. Goldsamt, 380 A.2d 556, 569 (Del.Ch.1977)."

511 F.Supp. at 305.

A failure to act with due care can betray management's attempt to rely on the business judgment rule. In Royal Industries Inc. v. Monogram Industries, Inc., Fed.Sec.L.Rept. (CCH) ¶ 95,863 (C.D.Cal. 1976), a tender offer for Royal was begun by Monogram on October 21, 1976. Royal's board promptly began its opposition, and on October 24, it reached agreement with Sar Industries, Inc. for the acquisition of that company for cash, evidently to create an antitrust defense. Royal had never heard of Sar until October 22. "Within the space of no more than three days, Royal claims it was able to conduct sufficient inquiry so as to determine the wisdom of spending well over a million dollars for a company with $0.00 in sales for the last reported period and a negative net worth." Id. at ¶ 91,135.

The court found that the transaction was improper because it was motivated "solely to thwart Monogram's proposed tender offer, it serves no proper corporate purpose, is a waste of Royal's corporate assets, is calculated to serve the interest of Royal's management to the exclusion or detriment of Royal shareholders, and should therefore be enjoined." *Id.* at ¶ 91,138.

Yet speed may be essential, given the dynamics of a tender offer. A decision delayed for study may be made by default. One cannot afford "paralysis by analysis." In *Crouse-Hinds*, the court noted "The fact that the initial decision to oppose the tender offer was made in four days does not prove that either that decision or the subsequent Exchange Agreement stemmed from a control motivation. Such decisions are required to be made promptly and are normally made quickly; and the district court recognized that this decision was not made without *Crouse-Hind's* having consulted its expert advisors in an effort to be objective." 634 F.2d 690, 704 (n. 24).

NOTE—LOCK–UPS AS A DEFENSE

Management of the target can facilitate the success of a white knight's bid, in preference to a hostile bidder, by agreeing to a lock-up. When Mobil Corporation made an unwelcome tender offer for Marathon Oil Company, Marathon's management went in search of a rescuer. They found United States Steel Corporation, but the latter insisted upon two conditions. First, they required an option to acquire 12 million shares, or 17% of the outstanding shares at $90 per share, when the tender offer U.S. Steel would make would be at $125 per share. Next, U.S. Steel obtained an option to acquire Marathon's 48% interest in oil and mineral rights in the Yates Field, an asset described as Marathon's crown jewel.

The Sixth Circuit reversed the District Court and granted Mobil's request for a preliminary injunction against the two options on grounds that they violated § 14(e) of the Williams Act. Mobil Corp. v. Marathon Oil Co., 669 F.2d 366 (6th Cir. 1981). The Court found that the options were "manipulative devices" because they did not allow other bidders to compete on equal terms with U.S. Steel and significantly discouraged competitive bidding for Marathon.

The Court found no need to answer the question of whether the lock up constituted a breach of fiduciary duty as a matter of state law. Would that question turn entirely on the fairness of the price of the option?

How are the options "manipulative"? Would it make any difference to Mobil whether it acquired Marathon with the Yates Field or its cash equivalent? How does one determine the cash equivalent? Who determines it? Is Mobil entitled to say that no one other than a purchaser of Marathon has a right to determine that question, and all prospective bidders should have an equal opportunity to make that determination?

Is there any justification for the issuance of the stock option? But is it manipulative if the shares are sold for fair value?

To what extent does the opinion cast a cloud on other types of "lock ups"? Will a sale or agreement to sell shares by a controlling person, or principal shareholder, to a bidder be viewed as manipulative? Is it any less so—than the company's grant of an option? What would prudent counsel advise? Two courts have since held other "crown jewel" dispositions not to be lock-ups, both expressing some doubts about the Sixth Circuit opinion. Whittaker Corp. v. Edgar, 535 F.Supp. 933 (N.D.Ill.1982), aff'd No. 32–1305 (7th Cir. 1982), and Marshall Field & Co. v. Icahn, Fed.Sec.L.Rept. (CCH) ¶ 98,616 (S. D.N.Y.1982).

C. PUBLIC POLICY CONSIDERATIONS

The Williams Act, adopted in 1968, expressed a public policy towards tender offers, as did the thirty-six state statutes. These laws do not answer all the questions; in fact they do not provide consistent answers to those questions they seek to answer.

The tender offer has become more commonplace since legislation began to regulate it, and experience has created new problems, new questions and the need to develop a public policy that will help shape answers. Public policy must include, and even start with, an empirical examination of the economic effects of control contests.

There is not a great abundance of economic studies of control contests. Most of the recent work by economists suggests that there are significant gains to the parties from successful tender offers. Kummer and Hoffmeister, Valuation Consequences of Cash Tender Offers 33 J.Finance 505 (1978) studied 88 cash tenders from 1956–1974 and concluded that "Take-overs lead to increased shareholder wealth for both the target and bidding firm." *Id.* at 516.

Dodd and Ruback, Tender Offers and Stockholder Returns, 5 J. Fin.Economics 351 (1977) used empirical data from a number of sources, and analyzed 386 offers. They found that there are abnormal gains to target company shareholders, including non-tendering shareholders, who saw improved values in the company's stock after the offer. Several different hypotheses could explain the gains. They found that the evidence supported the internal efficiency hypothesis which "contends that the assets of the target firm were not being utilized efficiently prior to the takeover attempt. The bidding firm is assumed to be motivated by information about the inefficiency." *Id.* at 354. Under this hypothesis, corporate takeovers are a means of disciplining inept management.

A study by Ronald W. Masulis, published by the SEC as Capital Market Working Papers No. 1, Acquisition of Technology-Based Firms by Tender Offer: An Economic and Financial Analysis, (Oct. 1980) examined forty-five offers for technology-based targets during the period 1968 to 1977. The gains found to have accrued to target company shareholders led the author to conclude, "As a result, capital formation by these firms is enhanced by the possibility that stockholders will eventually be able to sell their stock at a tender offer premium. The overall findings of this study consistently support the conclusion that tender offers for small technology-based firms are very similar in character and effect to other tender offers which have previously been studied. Consequently, even though there is a relatively small number of tender offers in the sample, the consistency of the results with the earlier findings based on much larger sample sizes suggests that these results are more robust than their sample size would indicate." *Id.* at 25.

A contrasting view is given by one of the leading tender offer lawyers. According to his evidence the price of the stock of the target companies in 36 defeated tender offers between December 1973 and January 1979, exceeded the tender offer price in more than 50 percent of the cases after a period of time ranging from six years to six months. His conclusion was that, contrary to popular belief, shareholders usually fare better by rejecting the tender offer than having it succeed. Lipton, Takeover Bids in the Target's Boardroom, 35 Bus. Law. 101 (1979). Later data apparently support that finding. Lipton, Takeover Bids in the Target's Boardroom: An Update After One Year, 36 Bus.Law. 1017 (1981).

Lipton's analysis contains serious flaws. As noted by Professor Gilson, he takes no account of general price movements nor does he discount future receipts to present values. Gilson, A Structural Approach to Corporations: The Case Against Defensive Tactics in Tender Offers, 33 Stan.L.Rev. 819, 857 (1981). Moreover, he fails to take into account the fact that the shareholder, upon receipt of the proceeds from the sale of his stock, would then reinvest the funds; they would not remain static. Yet he compares the price of the stock of the company that defeated a tender offer at some later date, while looking back at the earlier static tender offer price. For example, it is Lipton's contention that a stockholder who rejected a $15 bid for a stock formerly selling for $10 will eventually be better off because the stock will increase more than 50 percent, say, to 16. However, if that stockholder accepted the tender offer, and reinvested the proceeds in a stock that increased in value only 25 percent, his new investment would be worth $19.50 if we ignore all tax consequences. The problem is with comparing stock prices in different periods, which is not a meaningful exercise.

There is little persuasive data on what effect the tender offer has on the target company itself. The question, it would seem, is whether the successful tender results in efficiencies. Is the rate of return on the use of the assets formerly managed by the target management higher under the new management?

In addition to microeconomic issues, there are macroeconomic issues as well, but scant empirical data has been assembled on them. For example, how have hostile takeover bids affected concentration of assets in the economy? Have economic resources been inefficiently or efficiently used as compared to their alternative uses? Vast sums of credit have been utilized for takeover bids. Would these have been more efficiently deployed had loans gone elsewhere?

There are social consequences of tender offers, affecting the employees of the target company and the community where it is located. While there is little systematic empirical data, the Wall Street Journal reported the effects of Milwaukee, a city that has witnessed substantial losses of corporate headquarters. "And," noted the Journal, "the losses are affecting the local economy." Among the most affected are bankers, lawyers, accountants, public relations firms and suppliers. These functions tend to be moved out of town by the acquiring company. "Civic leaders worry about the effect on philanthropy, too," according to the Journal. In some cases there were reductions of as much as 25 percent to 50 percent in corporate giving. When companies are taken over, the executives frequently leave the community, and many of these people have been important in community affairs. "Executives sent in from the outside to run acquired companies often have less of a sense of community involvement and look on Milwaukee as just another career stepping stone." Wall Street Journal, September 15, 1981, p. 31.

Most of the studies and most of the views of scholars have focused on the target company and its shareholders. The effect on the bidder has been almost totally ignored. One commentator suggests that acquisitions that result in merely greater size and diversification, and do not create "synergistic" benefits cause a conflict of interest for the managers. Such an acquisition improves the compensation and the psychic rewards of managers, but merely exposes the shareholders to greater risk. Yet the law freely allows these transactions, the courts not having perceived any conflict of interest that would make the business judgment rule inapplicable. Note, The Conflict Between Managers and Shareholder in Diversifying Acquisitions: A Portfolio Theory Approach, 88 Yale L.J. 1238 (1979).

Yet another aspect of tender offer from the perspective of the bidding company was raised when United States Steel Corporation made an offer to acquire Marathon Oil Company, and the New York Times asked: "Does the United States Steel Corporation, the nation's largest steelmaker, have a special duty to concentrate its energies and its full financial resources on making steel? Or is it free to look for profits wherever opportunity beckons, even if this means borrowing several billion dollars to buy an oil company?" New York Times, December 2, 1981, p. D–1.

The issue is acutely raised in the case of U.S. Steel because, as noted by a lawyer who represented a group that opposed the closing of U.S. Steel's Youngstown works, "It's not as if the United States was able to do without steel."

The Times summarized the arguments in favor of diversification as follows: "Advocates of this position base their argument on classical free-market economics. The corporation, whatever it manufactures, is a private entity. The corporation is not only free but also obliged to make decisions that will bring its shareholders the greatest return on their invested capital. In vigorously pursuing profit, it helps the nation's economy operate most efficiently, pulling money out of unpromising ventures and shifting it to more profitable ones."

A spokesman for this view, Richard D. Utt, associate chief economist of the United States Chamber of Commerce, observed, "Preserving Youngstown and Akron and everyone's standard of living there would halt economic growth for the benefit of a few people."

The Times summarized the position against diversification as follows: "Advocates of the opposite view hold that corporations have social responsibilities to their employees, to their communities and to the economy as a whole. This is especially so if they have sought or accepted subsidies or other aid from the Government. When companies turn their back on a basic business, they can wreck local economies, uproot employees and leave the nation strapped. These social issues must be given equal weight with financial ones in corporate decision making."

Michael Harrington, chairman of the Democratic Socialist Organizing Committee observed, "You cannot for any length of time require a corporation to maintain an unprofitable operation, but the real question is the social cost of the transformation. Who pays for devastated communities and the unemployed workers? As long as a company pays the social costs of shutting down or moving into other areas, then—but only then—it has the right to move into other lines of business."

The duties of managers of the target company have come under the closest scrutiny. As we have seen, theirs' is the most sensitive role in the contest, and perhaps the most ambiguous. Two legal scholars who are well schooled in economics have analyzed the economic role of tender offers and related the implications to the legal rules governing target management. Easterbrook and Fischel, The Proper Role of Target's Management in Responding to a Tender Offer, 94 Harv.L.Rev. 1161 (1981).

They begin with the question of how bidders are able to identify undervalued stocks when market professionals cannot. They point to the synergistic gains that can result from combination, but then further question why expensive tender offers are used instead of negotiated mergers. This, they explain, shows the role unfriendly takeovers play in monitoring the performance of managers.

Corporate managers include persons who are working suboptimally because, being part of an organization, they are unable to capture all of the rewards of their efforts, but must share them with others in the organization. The costs of less than optimal management are described as "agency costs." They cause a firm's shares to trade for less than they would if these costs were zero.

Shareholders are generally unable to detect agency costs and, in any event, are in no position to do anything to reduce them. Managers may monitor each other's performance, and reduce agency costs, but their efforts are imperfect.

Easterbrook and Fischel contend that tender offers are a means of monitoring and comparing potential value with market value. Bidders pay a premium for the stock because the source of the premium is the reduction of the agency costs. The company is thus worth more in their hands than in the hands of present managers.

All parties benefit in the process, they say. The shareholders receive the premium; the bidder obtains the difference between new value and the amount paid to the shareholders and non-tendering shareholders receive part of the appreciation in the price of the shares. Most important, the realistic threat of a tender offer benefits all shareholders because it provides an incentive on the part of all managements to reduce agency costs by themselves so they will be less exposed to a takeover bid.

The conclusion they draw is far reaching: "It follows that any strategy designed to prevent tender offers reduces welfare. If the company adopts a policy of intransigent resistance and succeeds in maintaining its independence, the shareholders lose whatever premium over market value the bidder offered or would have offered but for the resistance or the prospect of resistance. This lost premium reflects a foregone social gain from the superior employment of the firm's assets." *Id.* at 1174.

Somewhat more surprising they say that "Even resistance that ultimately elicits a higher bid is socially wasteful. Although the target's shareholder may receive a higher price, these gains are exactly offset by the bidder's payment and thus by a loss to the bidder's shareholders. Shareholders as a group gain nothing; the increase in the price is simply a transfer payment from the bidder's shareholders to the target's shareholders." *Id.* Since there is a substantial cost to bidders imposed by management resistance, some offers are deterred by management's possession of the power to resist. Forebearance of a tender offer is a cost to the shareholders that they never realize. Easterbrook and Fischel argue that an efficient market for corporate control, operates as an effective substitute for the monitoring of management that shareholders are unable to perform. "With respect to tender offers, as elsewhere, the instructions to managers must be imposed from outside the corporation." *Id.* at 1182.

Finally, Easterbrook and Fischel contend that the business judgment rule is inappropriately applied to defensive tactics against tender offers because of "serious and unavoidable conflicts of interest that inheres in any decision on one's own ouster * * *." *Id.* at

1198. They call for managerial passivity, citing the activity of the Marshall Field directors as "a clear breach of fiduciary duty." *Id.* at 1202.

The Easterbrook-Fischel analysis places great faith in the workings of the market-place, but it may overlook several important considerations. Thus, while the notion of agency costs is a most useful insight, it may not be the only explanation for tender offers at premium prices. Another possible, if not more likely, reason for extremely high premiums is the fact that the market-place undervalues the *assets* of the target. Some of the richest tender offers have been for companies that own vast amounts of natural resources whose value has not been reflected in the stock price. The bargain may be due not to poor management but to the public's failure to perceive the size of the available resources. New management may have no different plans for the target than existing management. That may explain the tremendous interest in Conoco on the part of Seagrams, DuPont and Mobil. The same is true of Amax, the subject of a bid by Standard Oil of California; and Kennecott Copper Corp. by Standard Oil of Ohio.

Moreover, what about the bidder's agency costs? Most bidders are themselves large companies and there is no more reason to believe that they will be freer of suboptimal performance than was the target.

With these factors in mind, the tender offer does not appear *invariably* to be the socially useful mechanism for improving management, as Easterbrook-Fischel argue. Buying assets at a bargain could be socially disruptive. Of course, there are examples to support their thesis, but it does not explain every case.

Martin Lipton also sees the policy issue differently from Easterbrook-Fischel. He asks: "Whether the long-term interests of the nation's corporate system and economy should be jeopardized in order to benefit speculators interested not in the vitality and continued existence of the business enterprise in which they have bought shares, but only in a quicky profit on the sale of those shares? The overall health of the economy should not in the slightest degree be made subservient to interests of certain shareholders in realizing a profit on a takeover. Even if there were no empirical evidence that refuted the argument that shareholders almost always benefit from a takeover (as noted below, the empirical evidence is to the contrary) and even if there were no real evidence, but only a suspicion, that proscribing the ability of companies to defend against takeovers would adversely affect long-term planning and thereby jeopardize the economy, the policy considerations in favor of not jeopardizing the economy are so strong that not even a remote risk is acceptable." 35 Bus.Law. at 104–105 (emphasis omitted).

Lipton further observes, "After five decades of continuous efforts both to raise the consciousness of directors with respect to antitrust, disclosure and other issues of national policy, and to impose on corporations and their directors obligations to employees, customers and communities, it is impossible to contemplate a rule that would vitiate these concerns when the question is solely whether the shareholders may have an opportunity immediately to realize a premium over the current market price for their shares." *Id.* at 119.

Lipton then proposes the following procedure: Management should make a full presentation of all the relevant factors bearing on its own stewardship and the adequacy of the tender offer; investment bankers should opine as to the adequacy of the price; counsel should opine as to the legal issues and if a majority of the directors are personally interested in the outcome, they should then appoint a committee of independent directors. "Where the directors have made a reasonable good-faith decision to reject the takeover on one or more of the bases set forth above, the business judgment rule should apply equally to any and all defensive tactics." *Id.* at 124.

Harold Williams, then the chairman of the SEC, saw truth in the kaleidoscopic perceptions of tender offers both as regulators of management and as "a kind of unfair opportunity created by quirks in the market's valuation of a company or by overall market conditions." Tender Offers and the Corporate Director, Speech before the Seventh Annual Sec. Reg. Inst., San Diego, Calif., Fed.Sec.L.Rept. (CCH) ¶ 82,445 (Jan. 17, 1980).

The need to balance competing views led Williams to emphasize the role of independent directors.

> One wonders, as a matter of fundamental fairness, whether the interests of speculators and arbitrageurs, who move in and out of large positions with little regard to the strengths and weaknesses of the underlying enterprise, should be the decisive factor in determining a corporation's future * * * Although I recognize the essential value of marketplace discipline as a prophylactic against poor management, the benefits of that discipline are lost if management must behave as if the corporation is continuously on the block. For these reasons, the vehicle for balancing the competing concerns which must be weighed in evaluating a tender offer is to be found not in the marketplace but in the corporate boardroom. Directors should make the decision, as they do all other corporate policy decisions, and do so based on an assessment of the corporation as an institution with responsibilities to discharge, rather than simply seeking the best deal for their shareholders.

Williams emphasized the need for strong, independent directors to whom the job would be assigned.

*

INDEX

1164
INDEX
References are to Pages

1166   *INDEX*
References are to Pages

DERIVATIVE SUITS—Cont'd
Individual recovery, 636–637, 645–646.
Jurisdiction, 693–695.
Jury trial, 646–647.
Policy, 635–638, 640–642, 669–670.
Security for expenses, 687–693.
Legislation, 689–693.
Settlement, 704–708.
Direct action, 705–706.
Standing, 647–656.
Strike suit, 635, 636, 639.
Venue, 693–695.

DIRECTORS
In general, 26–27, 247–248.
Committees,
In general, 271–272.
Corporate governance, 782–785, 787–788, 789.
Derivative suits, role in, 671–686.
Power to approve transaction involving conflicts, 602.
Constituency, 775–782.
Corporate accountability,
In general, 770–772.
Delegation of authority, 343–346.
Derivative suits, role in, 656–665, 667–668, 670–686, 697–698.
Discretion, restriction of, 331–346.
Disinterested directors, approval of transactions, 599–602.
Duties, see Duty of Care; Duty of Loyalty.
Indemnification of, see Indemnification of Officers and Directors.
Informal action by, 266–270.
Insurance of, 722–724, 726–732.
Lawyers as, 121–122.
Liabilities, 210.
Meetings of, 266–271.
Notice, 270–271.
Quorum, 270–271, 342–343.
Outside, 772–774, 787–788.
Removal,
Cause, 289–293, 329–330.
Close corporation, 329–330.
Voting, greater-than-majority requirements, 342–343.

DISSENTERS' RIGHTS
See Appraisal Remedy.

DISSOLUTION
In general, 371–377.

DIVIDENDS
Business aspects, 202, 219–220.
Judicial control of, 211–219.
Legal capital and,
Reduction surplus, 206.
Restrictions, 204–206.
Revaluation surplus, 205–206.
Liability for unlawful dividends, 210.
Merger and, 978–985.
Model Business Corporation Act, 206–208.
Nimble dividends, 204.
Recapitalization and, 974–978.
Senior interest, protection of, 203–204.
Solvency, 203–204, 207–208.
Stock dividends, 208–209.
Surplus available for, 204–206.
Taxation of, 109–110.

DUTY OF CARE
In general, 31–34.
Business judgment rule, 32–34, 569–583, 818.
Causation of loss, 554–556.
Current trends, 559–560.
Duty to creditors, 553–554.
Illegal acts, 578–580.
Misfeasance, 577–580.
Nonfeasance, 551–554, 556, 561–568, 581–582.
Passive negligence, 551–554, 556, 561–568.
Reliance on others, 558–559.
Sale of control, 1053–1060.
Standard of care,
In general, 31–32, 550–551, 556, 564–565, 580–583.
Objective or subjective, 550–556, 557–558.
Tender offers, 1153–1154.
Waste of assets, 557–580, 740–749.

DUTY OF LOYALTY
In general, 31, 33–36, 585–594, 600–607.
Charter provisions, 602–603.
Corporate opportunity doctrine, 613–626, 1061–1065.
Disinterested director approval, 587–588, 601–604.
Executive compensation, 626–632.
Majority or controlling shareholders, 36–38, 608–613, 1061–1072.
Sale of control, 1061–1072.
Shareholder ratification, 594–600, 604–606.

†